The Corsini Encyclopedia of Psychology and Behavioral Science

Third Edition

The Corsini Encyclopedia of Psychology and Behavioral Science

Third Edition

VOLUME 1

Co-Editors

W. EDWARD CRAIGHEAD
University of Colorado
Boulder, CO

CHARLES B. NEMEROFF
Emory University School of Medicine
Atlanta, GA

Editorial Board

JOHN WILEY & SONS
New York • Chichester • Weinheim • Brisbane • Singapore • Toronto

ISBN 0-471-24096-6 (Volume 1)
ISBN 0-471-24097-4 (Volume 2)
ISBN 0-471-24098-2 (Volume 3)
ISBN 0-471-24099-0 (Volume 4)
ISBN 0-471-23949-6 (Four-volume set)

Printed in the United States of America
10 9 8 7 6 5 4 3 2 1

Preface

This revision of Raymond J. Corsini's successful *Encyclopedia of Psychology* is based on the need to update and expand the previous edition. Because of the advances in behavioral science and the relationship of those advances to psychology, this edition has been renamed to reflect the inclusion of those advances.

The major purpose of these volumes is to make the current knowledge in psychology and behavioral science available to the community at large. It is hoped that they will constitute a concise and handy reference for individuals interested in these topics. Each entry is designed to inform the reader on its particular topic; of necessity, however, an entry in an encyclopedia can be only a succinct summary of that topic. Cross-references are provided for the entries so that the reader can easily make his or her way to related topics for more detail.

In order to keep the encyclopedia to four volumes and still be inclusive of contemporary topics, several now-outdated topics were dropped from the prior edition. We updated about two-thirds of the prior edition, and replaced the remaining one-third with new topics. We have sought to keep the international flavor that Corsini had employed in the original encyclopedia; thus, we selected our contributors from an international list of scholars on the chosen topics.

Coordinating a publication of this magnitude is a formidable task, particularly when undertaken within the framework of one's regular job. Thus, we are extremely appreciative of those who have been so helpful in making this project possible. We are deeply grateful to the more than 1,000 authors who contributed to this encyclopedia; without them, these volumes would not have been. Our greatest appreciation is expressed to Alinne Barrera, Benjamin Page, and Fiona Vajk, who have served as managing editors for this project. We also express our gratitude to Nancy Grabowski (administrative assistant to W. Edward Craighead), who provided necessary support to the editors and managing editors. It is hard to imagine a better or more efficient working team than Kelly Franklin and Jennifer Simon at John Wiley & Sons. Even though many of us involved in this project have experienced numerous, and at times unbelievable, life events during the development and production of these volumes, the project has been brought to a successful and timely completion. We are happy and grateful to have been surrounded by such a fine group of wonderful and dedicated individuals.

In the final analysis, production of these volumes has allowed us to continue a warm friendship and professional collaboration begun about 15 years ago at Duke University Medical Center—a friendship and collaboration that have survived the selection, coordination, and editing of the contributions of well over 1,000 authors on more than 1,200 topics. We have treated patients together; we have conducted collaborative research; we have published together; we have presented together at professional meetings; and we have laughed and cried together in good times and bad. It has been a satisfying experience to edit these volumes together. We trust they will be useful to you, the reader.

W. Edward Craighead, PhD
Boulder, Colorado

Charles B. Nemeroff, MD, PhD
Atlanta, Georgia

Contributors List

NORMAN ABELES
Michigan State University

L. Y. ABRAMSON
University of Wisconsin

ROSEMARY C. ADAM-TEREM
Kapiolani Medical Center, Honolulu, HI

HOWARD S. ADELMAN
University of California, Los Angeles

BERNARD W. AGRANOFF
University of Michigan

LEWIS R. AIKEN
Pepperdine University

ICEK AJZEN
University of Massachusetts

GEORGE W. ALBEE
Florida Mental Health Institute

LYNN E. ALDEN
University of British Columbia

THERON ALEXANDER
Temple University

MARY J. ALLEN
California State College

LAUREN B. ALLOY
Temple University

G. HUGH ALLRED
Brigham Young University

NANCY S. ANDERSON
Emory School of Medicine

JOHN L. ADREASSI
City University of New York-Baruch College

J. E. ALCOCK
The Australian National University

L. B. AMES

RICHARD S. ANDRULIS
Andrulis Associates, West Chester, PA

HYMIE ANISMAN
Carleton University, Ottawa

H. L. ANSBACHER

RUBEN ARDILA
National University of Colombia

E. Ö. ARNARSON
University of Iceland

MARK ARONOFF
State University of New York, Albany

RICHARD M. ASHBROOK
Capital University

J. WILLIAM ASHER
Purdue University

J. A. ASTIN
University of Maryland School of Medicine

CAROL SHAW AUSTAD

ROBERT M. DAVISON AVILES
Bradley University

K. W. BACK

ALBERT BANDURA
Stanford University

DAVID H. BARLOW
Boston University

AUGUSTINE BARÓN, JR.
University of Texas, Austin

DANIEL BAR-TAL
Tel Aviv University

S. HOWARD BARTLEY
Memphis State University

VALENTINA BASSAREO
University of Cagliari, Italy

B. M. BAUGHAN
University of Colorado, Boulder

ANDREW SLATER BAUM
University of Pittsburgh Cancer Institute

ALAN A. BAUMEISTER
Louisiana State University

RAMÓN BAYÉS SOPENA
Universidad Autónoma de Barcelona

STEVEN BEACH
University of Georgia

AARON T. BECK
Beck Institute for Cognitive Therapy and Research

GARY S. BELKIN
Brown University

ALAN S. BELLACK
University of Maryland

JOEL B. BENNETT
Texas Christian University

THOMAS S. BENNETT
Brain Inquiry Recovery Program, Fort Collins, CO

HEATHER A. E. BENSON
University of Manitoba

P. G. BENSON
New Mexico State University

SHERI A. BERENBAUM
Southern Illinois University

S. BERENTSEN

LEONARD BERGER
Clemson University

JOANNE BERGER-SWEENEY
Wellesly College

GREGORY S. BERNS
Emory University

G. G. BERNTSON
Ohio State University

MICHAEL D. BERZONSKY
State University of New York, Cortland

SIDNEY W. BIJOU
University of Nevada

AIDA BILALBEGOVIC
Tufts University, Medford, MA

JEFFREY R. BINDER
Medical College Of Wisconsin

JERRY M. BINDER
Behavioral Health Consultant, Corona Del Mar

NIELS BIRMBAUER
University of Tübingen, Germany

D. W. BLACK
University of Iowa

THEODORE H. BLAU

BERNARD L. BLOOM
University of Colorado

MILTON S. BLOOMBAUM
Southern Oregon University

JODI L. BODDY
Simon Fraser University, British Columbia

C. ALAN BONEAU
George Mason University

EDWARD S. BORDIN
University of Michigan

EDGAR F. BORGATTA
University of Washington

P. BOSE
University of Florida

DALE E. BOWEN
Psychological Associates, Grand Junction, CO

A. D. BRANSTETTER

C. REGINALD BRASINGTON
University of South Carolina

MARGARET BRENMAN-GIBSON
Harvard Medical School

RONAL BRENNER
St. John's Episcopal Hospital, Far Rockaway, NY

WARRICK J. BREWER
The University of Melbourne & Mental Health Research Institute of Victoria

SARA K. BRIDGES
Humboldt State University

ARTHUR P. BRIEF
Tulane University

R. W. BRISLIN
University of Hawaii

GILBERTO N. O. BRITO
Instituto Fernendes Figueira, Brazil

DONALD E. BROADBENT
University of Oxford

J. D. BROOKE
Northwestern University

FREDERICK GRAMM BROWN
Iowa State University

ROBERT TINDALL BROWN
University of North Carolina, Wilmington

SHELDON S. BROWN
North Shore Community College

J. BROZEK

MARTIN BRÜNE
Ruhr University, Germany

B. R. BUGELSKI
State University of New York, Buffalo

GRAHAM D. BURROWS
University of Melbourne

JAMES M. BUTCHER
University of Minnesota, Minneaplois

ANN B. BUTLER
George Mason University

REBECCA M. BUTZ
Tulane University

J. T. CACIOPPO
University of Chicago

SHAWN P. CAHILL
University of Pennsylvania

JOHN B. CAMPBELL
Franklin & Marshall College

N. A. CAMPBELL
Brown University

TYRONE D. CANNON
University of California, Los Angeles

SAMUEL S. CARDONE
Illinois Department of Mental Health, Chicago

BERNARDO J. CARDUCCI
Shyness Research Institute, Indiana University Southeast

MARK CARICH
Adler School of Professional Psychology

PETER A. CARICH
University of Missouri

JOHN G. CARLSON
University of Hawaii, Honolulu

J. DOUGLAS CARROLL
Rutgers University

GIOVANNI CASINI
Tuscia University, Italy

T. CASOLI
I.N.R.C.A., Italy

LOUIS G. CASTONGUAY
Pennsylvania State University

CARL ANDREW CASTRO
Walter Reed Army Institute of Research

FAIRFID M. CAUDLE
College of Staten Island

JOSEPH R. CAUTELA

STEPHEN J. CECI
Cornell University

JAE-HO CHA
Seoul National University

PAUL F. CHAPMAN
University of Minnesota, Minneaplois

U. CHARPA
Cologne University, Germany

GORDON J. CHELUNE
The Cleveland Clinic Foundation

GLYN CHIDLOW
University of Oxford

IRVIN L. CHILD
Yale University

MARGARET M. CLIFFORD
University of Iowa

RICHARD WELTON COAN
Retired, University of Arizona

KIMBERLY PEELE COCKERHAM
Allegheny Ophthalmic and Orbital Associates, Pittsburgh

MARK S. COE
DePaul University

NORMAN J. COHEN
Baylor State University

P. COHEN-KETTENIS
Utrecht University, The Netherlands

RAYMOND J. COLELLO
Virginia Commonwealth University

GARY R. COLLINS
Trinity Evangelical Divinity School

MARY BETH CONNOLLY
University of Pennsylvania

M. J. CONSTANTINO
Pennsylvania State University

GERALD COOKE
Plymouth Meeting, PA

JEREMY D. COPLAND
Columbia University College of Physicians and Surgeons

STANLEY COREN
University of British Columbia

GERALD F. COREY
California State University, Fullerton

JOHN F. CORSO
State University of New York, Cortland

ERMINIO COSTA
University of Illinois, Chicago

JOSEPH T. COYLE
Harvard University

BENJAMIN H. CRAIGHEAD
Medical College of Virginia

W. EDWARD CRAIGHEAD
University of Colorado

PAUL CRITS-CHRISTOPH
University of Pennsylvania

ARNOLD E. DAHLKE
Los Angeles, CA

JOHN G. DARLEY
University of Minnesota, Minneaplois

WILLIAM S. DAVIDSON II
Michigan State University

EDWARD L. DECI
University of Rochester

CRISTINA MARTA DEL-BEN
Universidade de São Paulo, Brazil

H. A. DEMAREE
Kessler Medical Rehabilitation Research and Education Corporation

FLORENCE L. DENMARK
Pace University, New York

M. RAY DENNY
Michigan State University

DONALD R. DENVER
Quebec, Montreal, Canada

NORMAN K. DENZIN
University of Illinois, Urbana

SARAH E. DeROSSETT

FRANCINE DEUTSCH
San Diego State University

DAVID L. DEVRIES
Kaplan DeVries Institute

DONALD ALLEN DEWSBURY
University of Florida

ESTHER E. DIAMOND

MILTON DIAMOND
University of Hawaii, Honolulu

R. DIAZ-GUERRERO
University of Mexico

MANFRED DIEHL
University of Colorado

VOLKER DIETZ
University Hospital Balgrist, Zurich

R. DILLON

RAYMOND DINGLEDINE
Emory University School of Medicine

JOHN W. DONAHOE
University of Massachusetts

NICK DONNELLY
University of Southampton, UK

SYLVAIN DORÉ
Johns Hopkins University

MICHAEL G. DOW
University of South Florida

PETER W. DOWRICK
University of Hawaii, Manoa

JURIS G. DRAGUNS
Pennsylvania State University

CLIFFORD J. DREW
University of Utah

D. A. DROSSMAN
University of North Carolina

PHILIP H. DUBOIS

HUBERT C. J. DUIJKER
University of Amsterdam

BRUCE R. DUNN
The University of West Florida

M. O. A. DUROJAIYE
University of Lagos, Nigeria

TERRY M. DWYER
University of Mississippi School of Medicine

G. D'YDEWALLE
University of Leuven, Belgium

BARRY A. EDELSTEIN
West Virginia University

THOMAS E. EDGAR
Idaho State University

WILLIAM E. EDMONSTON, JR.
Colgate University

C. L. EHLERS
University of California, San Diego

HOWARD EICHENBAUM
Boston University

ROGER E. ENFIELD
West Central Georgia Regional Hospital, Columbus, GA

JOHN WILLIAM ENGEL
University of Hawaii, Honolulu

FRANZ R. EPTING
University of Florida

ANGELICA ESCALONA
Nova Southeastern University

DAVID RICHARD EVANS
University of Western Ontario

FREDERICK J. EVANS
Reading Hospital

ROBERT B. EWEN
Miami, FL

CORA E. EZZELL
Medical University of South Carolina

CLARA C. FAURA-GINER
Universidad Miguel Hernandez, Spain

HERMAN FEIFEL
Veterans Administration Outpatient Clinic, Los Angeles

LAURIE B. FELDMAN
State University of New York, Albany

EVA DREIKURS FERGUSON
Southern Illinois University

JOSEPH R. FERRARI
Depaul University

MICHAEL A. FIEDLER
University of Alabama, Birmingham

FRANK W. FINGER
University of Virginia

S. FINGER
Washington University

HAROLD KENNETH FINK
Honolulu, HI

NORMAN J. FINKEL
Georgetown University

CHET H. FISCHER
Radford University

DAVID A. FISHBAIN
University of Miami

DENNIS F. FISHER
U.S. Army Human Engineering Laboratory

DOUGLAS A. FITTS
University of Washington

REIKO MAKI FITZSIMONDS
Yale School of Medicine

DEBRA A. FLEISCHMAN
Rush-Presbyterian St. Luke's Medical Center

EDNA B. FOA
University of Pennsylvania

JAMES L. FOBES
Army Research Institute for the Behavioral Sciences

JOHN P. FOREYT
Baylor College of Medicine

BARBARA L. FORISHA-KOVACH
University of Michigan

GEORGE FOURIEZOS
University of Ottawa

MARCI GITTES FOX
Beck Institute for Cognitive Therapy and Research

NATHAN A. FOX
University of Maryland

J. FRANKENHEIM
National Institutes of Health

CALVIN J. FREDERICK
University of California, Los Angeles

MATS FREDERICKSON
Uppsala University, Sweden

C. R. FREEMAN
McGill University

W. O. FRIESEN
University of Virginia

ROBERT H. FRIIS
California State University, Long Beach

KARL J. FRISTON
Institute of Neurology, UK

BENJAMIN FRUCHTER
University of Texas, Austin

ISAO FUKUNISHI
Tokyo Institute of Psychiatry

TOMAS FURMARK
Uppsala University, Sweden

PAUL A. GADE
U. S. Army Research Institute

SOL L. GARFIELD
Washington University

G. GASKELL
University of York, UK

STEVEN J. GARLOW
Emory School of Medicine

TIMOTHY L. GASPERONI
University of California, Los Angeles

JEAN S. GEARON
University of Maryland

NORI GEARY
Weill Medical College of Cornell University

K. F. GEISINGER
Le Moyne College

MARK S. GEORGE
Medical University of South Carolina

T. D. GIARGIARI
University of Colorado, Boulder

KAREN M. GIL
University of North Carolina, Chapel Hill

RITA T. GIUBILATO
Thomas Jefferson University

THOMAS A. GLASS
Honolulu, HI

WILLIAM GLASSER
*The William Glasser Institute, Chatsworth,
CA*

J. M. GLOZMAN
Moscow University

CHARLES J. GOLDEN
Nova Southeastern University

ROBERT N. GOLDEN
*University of North Carolina School of
Medicine*

ARNOLD P. GOLDSTEIN
Syracuse University

JEFFREY L. GOODIE
West Virginia University

G. KEN GOODRICK
University of Houston

LEONARD D. GOODSTEIN
Washington, DC

BERNARD S. GORMAN
Nassau Community College

GILBERT GOTTLIEB
University of North Carolina, Chapel Hill

DONALD L. GRANT
Roswell, CTA

J. W. GRAU
Texas A & M University

MARTIN S. GREENBERG
University of Pittsburgh

W. A. GREENE
Eastern Washington University

SHELLY F. GREENFIELD
McLean Hospital, Belmont, MA

JAMES LYNN GREENSTONE
*Southwestern Academy of Crisis
Interveners, Dallas*

WILLIAM EDGAR GREGORY
University of the Pacific

SEBASTIAN P. GROSSMAN
University of Chicago

AMANDA J. GRUBER
McLean Hospital, Belmont, MA

ROBERT M. GUION
Bowling Green State University

LAURA GULI
University of Texas, Austin

G. GUTTMANN
University of Vienna

RUSSELL A. HABER
University of South Carolina

HAROLD V. HALL
Honolulu, HI

KATHERINE A. HALMI
Cornell University Medical Center

MARK B. HAMNER
Medical University of South Carolina

GREGORY R. HANCOCK
University of Maryland

FOREST W. HANSEN
Lake Forest College

J. M. HARPER
Brigham Young University

JOSEPH T. HART
University of Colorado

ALISHA B. HART
Kupat Holim Klalit, Tel Aviv

E. I. HARTLEY

SCOTT HARTMAN
*Center for Marital and Family Studies,
University of Denver*

DAVID B. HATFIELD
Eastern Washington University

ELAINE HATFIELD
University of Hawaii, Manoa

ROBERT P. HAWKINS
West Virginia University

STEPHEN N. HAYNES
University of Hawaii, Manoa

N. A. HAYNIE

DONALD A. HECK
Iowa State

S. R. HEIDEMANN
Michigan State University

J. HEIMAN
University of Washington

LYNNE M. HENDERSON
The Shyness Institute, Stanford

GREGG HENRIQUES
University of Pennsylvania

P. P. HEPPNER
University of Missouri, Columbia

GREGORY M. HEREK
University of California, Davis

EDWIN L. HERR
Pennsylvania State University

ALLEN K. HESS
Auburn University

ERNEST R. HILGARD
Stanford University

JEANNE SWICKARD HOFFMAN
Honolulu, HI

RALPH E. HOFFMAN
Yale School of Medicine

CHRISTINE HOHMANN
Morgan State University

P. Y. HONG
University of Kansas

B. HOPKINS
Seattle University

RONALD R. HOLDEN
Queen's University, Ontario

DAVID L. HOLMES
The Eden Institute, Princeton

DAVID SHERIDAN HOLMES
University of Kansas

WAYNE H. HOLTZMAN
University of Texas, Austin

BURT HOPKINS
Seattle University

J. HOSKOVEC

ARTHUR C. HOUTS
University of Memphis

ROBERT H. HOWLAND
University of Pittsburgh School of Medicine

C. H. HUBER
New Mexico State University

BRADLEY E. HUITEMA
Western Michigan University

LLOYD G. HUMPHRIES
University of Illinois, Champaign

MAX L. HUTT

G. W. HYNDE
University of Georgia

JAMES ROBERT IBERG
Chicago, IL

S. S. ILARDI
University of Kansas

DANIEL R. ILGEN
Michigan State University

Y. IWAMURA
Toho University, Japan

I. JACKSON
Brown University

L. JANOSI
Exponential Biotherapies, Inc.

ARTHUR R. JENSEN
University of California, Berkeley

QICHENG JING
Chinese Academy of Sciences, Beijing

DAVID W. JOHNSON
University of Minnesota, Minneaplois

JAMES H. JOHNSON
University of Florida

ORVAL G. JOHNSON
Centennial BOCES, La Salle, CO

ROGER T. JOHNSON
University of Minnesota, Minneaplois

EVE S. JONES
Los Angeles City College

LASZLO JANOSI
Exponential Biotherapies, Inc.

JON H. KAAS
Vanderbilt University

ROBERT B. KAISER
Kaplan DeVries Institute

AKIRA KAJI
Exponential Biotherapies, Inc.

JAMES W. KALAT
North Carolina State University

P. W. KALIVAS
Medical University of South Carolina

TOMOE KANAYA
Cornell

SAUL KANE
Queens College, City University of New York

BARRY H. KANTOWITZ
Battelle Institute, Seattle

RICHARD PAUL KAPPENBERG
Hawaii Professional Psychology Group, Honolulu

WERNER KARLE
Corona Del Mar, CA

NADINE KASLOW
Emory School of Medicine

A. J. KASTIN
University of New Orleans

BOJE KATZENELSON
University of Aarhus, Denmark

TERENCE M. KEANE
Boston University

A. J. KEARNEY
Behavior Therapy Institute

E. JAMES KEHOE
University of New South Wales

TIMOTHY KEITH-LUCAS
The University of the South

SALLY KELLER
Adelphi University

THOMAS M. KELLEY
Wayne State University

CAROLIN S. KEUTZER
University of Oregon

GREGORY A. KIMBLE
Duke University

JAMES E. KING
University of Arizona

BRENDA J. KING
University of Tennessee

DANIEL N. KLEIN
State University of New York

WALTER G. KLOPFER
Max J. Kobbert

MAX J. KOBBERT
Hochschule for Beildende Künste, Münster

ALBERT T. KONDO
University of Houston

S. J. KORCHIN

WILLIAM J. KOROTITSCH
University of North Carolina, Greensboro

SURESH KOTAGAL
Mayo Clinic

G. KOVACS
Dalhousie University

LEONARD KRASNER
Stanford University School of Medicine

DAVID R. KRATHWOHL
Syracuse University

ALAN G. KRAUT
American Psychological Society, Washington, DC

STEFAN KRUEGER
Yale School of Medicine

STANLEY KRIPPNER
Saybrook Graduate School, San Francisco

SAMUEL E. KRUG
MetriTech, Inc., Campaign, IL

CAROL LANDAU
Brown University Division of Medicine

PHILIPPE LANDREVILLE
Laval, Sainte-Foy, Quebec

TED LANDSMAN
University of Florida

CHRISTOPH J. G. LANG
University of Erlangen-Buremberg, Germany

GEORGE M. LANGFORD
Dartmouth College

KEITH LANGLEY
University of Strasbourg, France

E. K. LANPHIER
Pennsylvania State University

V. W. LARACH
Univerdidad de Chile

DAVID G. LAVOND
University of Southern California

ARNOLD A. LAZARUS
Center for Multimodal Psychological Services, Princeton

RICHARD S. LAZARUS
University of California, Berkeley

THOMAS H. LEAHEY
Virginia Commonwealth University

ROBERT A. LEARK
Pacific Christian College

ARTHUR LERNER
Los Angeles City College

RICHARD M. LERNER
Tufts University

L. S. LEUNG
University of Western Ontario

ALLAN LEVEY
Emory University

HARRY LEVINSON
The Levinson Institute

SHARON C. LEVITON
Southwestern Academy of Crisis Interveners, Dallas

EUGENE E. LEVITT
Indiana University School of Medicine

P. M. LEWINSOHN
Oregon Research Institute, Eugene

RONALD T. LEY
State University of New York, Albany

ANDRE L'HOURS
World Health Organization, Geneva

KAREN Z. H. LI
Max Planck Institute for Human Development

SHU-CHEN LI
Max Planck Institute for Human Development

P. E. LICHTENSTEIN

CAROL SCHNEIDER LIDZ
Touro College

SCOTT O. LILIENFELD
Emory University

G. LIN
National Institutes of Health

HENRY CLAY LINDGREN
San Francisco State University

RONALD LIPPITT

MARK W. LIPSEY
Vanderbilt University

A. LLOYD

JOHN E. LOCHMAN
University of Alabama, Tuscaloosa

JOHN C. LOEHLIN
University of Texas, Austin

JANE LOEVINGER
Washington University

DONALD N. LOMBARDI
Seton Hall University

WOLF-EKKEHARD LÖNNIG
*Max Planck Institut fur
    Züchtungsforschung, Köln, Germany*

JOSEPH LOPICCOLO
University of Missouri

JEFFREY P. LORBERBAUM
Medical University of South Carolina

O. IVAR LOVAAS
University of California, Los Angeles

ROBERT E. LUBOW
Tel Aviv University

J. O. LUGO
Fullerton, CA

K. LUKATELA
Brown University

ROBERT W. LUNDIN
Wheaton, IL

DAVID T. LYKKEN
University of Minnesota, Minneapolis

BRETT V. MACFARLANE
University of Queensland

ROBIN M. MACKAR
*National Institute on Drug Abuse, Bethesda,
    MD*

S. MADHUSOODANAN
*St. John's Episcopal Hospital, Far
    Rockaway, NY*

MICHAEL P. MALONEY
Pasadena, CA

HOWARD MARKMAN
*Center for Marital and Family Studies,
    University of Denver*

RONALD R. MARTIN
West Virginia University

C. MARTINDALE
University of Maine

P. MARUFF
La Trobe University, Australia

ROBERT C. MARVIT
Honolulu, HI

MELVIN H. MARX
N. Hutchinson Island, FL

JOSEPH D. MATARAZZO
Oregon Health Sciences University

BARBARA B. MATES
City College, NY

RYAN K. MAY
The University of Memphis

FAUZIA SIMJEE MCCLURE
University of California, San Diego

BARBARA S. MCCRADY
Rutgers University

JANET L. MCDONALD
Louis State University

JENNIFER J. MCGRATH
Bowling Green State University

JOHN PAUL MCKINNEY
Michigan State University

KATHLEEN MCKINNEY
University of Wisconsin

C. M. MCCLEOD
University of Toronto

JAMES H. MCMILLAN
Virginia Commonwealth University

PATRICK MCNAMARA
Boston University

NEIL MCNAUGHTON
University of Otago, New Zealand

JANICE MCPHEE
Florida Gulf Coast University

PAUL W. MCREYNOLDS
University of Nevada

HEATHER MEGGERS
University of Missouri

RICHARD MEILI
University of Bern, Switzerland

RONALD MELZACK
McGill University, Montreal

P. F. MERENDA
University of Rhode Island

STANLEY B. MESSER
Rutgers University

CINDY M. MESTON
University of Texas, Austin

JAMIE L. METSALA
University of Maryland

ANDREW W. MEYERS
The University of Memphis

K. D. MICHEVA
Stanford University

DAVID J. MIKLOWITZ
University of Colorado

STANLEY MILGRAM

MARK W. MILLER
Boston University

NEAL ELGAR MILLER
Yale University

RALPH R. MILLER
State University of New York, Binghamton

THEODORE MILLON
University of Miami

HENRYK MISIAK
Fordham University

AKIRA MIYAKE
University of Colorado

TAE-IM MOON

STEWART MOORE
University of Windsor, Ontario

JAMES A. MORONE
Brown University

DANIEL G. MORROW
University of New Hampshire

F. MUELLER
*Forschungszentrum Juelich GmbH,
    Germany*

K. L. MULLER
Rutgers University

R. MURISON
University of Bergen, Norway

FRANK B. MURRAY
University of Delaware

ANNE MYERS
St. Jerome Convent, Philadelphia

FRANCIS A. NEELON
Duke University

ROBERT A. NEIMEYER
University of Memphis

J. NEISEWANDER
Arizona State University

A. NELSON

ROSEMARY O. NELSON-GRAY
University of North Carolina, Greensboro

CORY F. NEWMAN

DAVID G. NICKINOVICH
University of Washington

PHILIP T. NINAN
Emory School of Medicine

J. T. NOGA
Emory University

TREVOR R. NORMAN
University of Melbourne

M. S. NYSTUL

WILLIAM H. O'BRIEN
Bowling Green State University

WALTER EDWARD O'CONNELL
Natural High Center, Bastrop, TX

W. O'DONOHUE

K. DANIEL O'LEARY
State University of New York, Stony Brook

G. A. OLSON
University of New Orleans

R. D. OLSON
University of New Orleans

MARLENE OSCAR-BERMAN
Boston University

THOMAS M. OSTROM
Ohio State University

J. BRUCE OVERMIER
University of Bergen, Norway

B. D. OZAKI
Honolulu Waldorf School

DANIEL J. OZER
University of California, Riverside

K. PACAK
National Institutes of Health

DAVID C. PALMER
Smith College

EDWARD L. PALMER
Davidson College

LOREN D. PANKRATZ
Oregon Health Sciences University

C. PANTELIS
University of Melbourne, Australia

WILLIAM M. PARDRIDGE
University of California School of Medicine, Los Angeles

ALAN J. PARKIN
University of Sussex, England

E. J. PARKINS
Nottingham University, England

H. MCILVANIE PARSONS
Human Resources Research Organization, Alexandria, VA

R. PATUZZI

PAUL PAULI
University of Tübingen, Germany

V. PEČJAK

PAUL PEDERSON
University of Alabama, Birmingham

T. M. PENIX

HAROLD BRENNER PEPINSKY
Ohio State University

KATHERINE L. PETERS
University of Alberta

C. PETERSON
University of Michigan

DONALD R. PETERSON
Rutgers University

CHARLES S. PEYSER
The University of the South

E. JERRY PHARES
Kansas State University

D. PHILIP
University of Florida

JESSICA M. PIERCE
Boston University

AARON L. PINCUS
Pennsylvania State University

LUIGI PIZZAMIGLIO
Universita Degli Studi di Roma, Italy

J. POIRIER
University of Washington

R. E. POLAND
University of California, Los Angeles

H. G. POPE, JR.
McLean Hospital, Belmont, MA

R. M. POST
National Institute of Mental Health

BRUNO POUCET
Centre National de la Recherche Scientifique, France

A. R. PRATKANIS
University of California, Santa Cruz

ANN B. PRATT
Capital University, Columbus, OH

ROBERT ALAN PRENTKY
Justice Resource Institute, Bridgewater, MA

AINA PUCE
Swinburne University of Technology, Australia

S. J. QUALLS
University of Colorado

MARK QUIGG
University of Virginia

KAREN S. QUIGLEY
Pennsylvania State University

RÉMI QUIRION
Douglas Hospital Research Center, Canada

ALBERT ISRAEL RABIN
Michigan State University

M. K. RAINA
Sri Aurobindo Marg, India

K. RAMAKRISHNA RAO
Duke University

U. RAO
University of California, Los Angeles

J. RAPPAPORT
University of Illinois, Chicago

MARK D. RAPPORT
University of Central Florida

RICHARD L. RAPSON
University of Hawaii, Manoa

NATHANIEL J. RASKIN
Northwestern University Medical School

R. L. RASMUSSON
Allegheny University of Health Sciences

A. RAVIV
Tel Aviv University

W. J. RAY
Pennsylvania State University

HERB REICH

ANTHONY H. REINHARDT-RUTLAND
University of Ulster

J. M. REINISCH
Indiana University

DANIEL REISBERG
Reed College

MAURICE REUCHLIN
Institute Nationale D'Orientation Professionale, Paris

MARY E. REUDER

G. R. REYES

CECIL R. REYNOLDS
Texas A&M University

GEORGE F. RHOADES, JR.
Ola Hou Clinic, Aiea, HI

ALEXANDER RICH
University of South Florida

DAVID C. S. RICHARD
Southwest Missouri State University

EDWARD J. RICKERT
University of Alabama, Birmingham

L. RIES

Y. RINGEL
University of North Carolina

ARTHUR J. RIOPELLE
Louisiana State University

CHRISTIE RIZZO
New York State Psychiatric Institute

DONALD ROBBINS
Fordham University

GARY JEROME ROBERTSON
Wide Range, Inc., Tampa

GEORGE H. ROBINSON
University of North Alabama

RONALD ROESCH
Simon Fraser University, British Columbia

MICHAEL J. ROHRBAUGH
University of Arizona

STEVEN PAUL ROOSE
Columbia University

R. ROSENBERG
Sleep Disorders Center, Evanston, IL

ROBERT ROSENTHAL
University of California, Riverside

SAUL ROSENZWEIG
Washington University

HELEN WARREN ROSS
San Diego State University

WILLIAM H. ROSS
University of Wisconsin

J. S. ROSSI
University of Rhode Island

B. O. ROTHBAUM
Emory University

DONALD K. ROUTH
University of Miami

PETER ROY-BYRNE
Harborview Medical Center, Seattle

MARK A. RUIZ
Pennsylvania State University

ROGER WOLCOTT RUSSELL
University of California, Irvine

J. J. RYAN
Central Missouri State University

DEBORAH SADOWSKI
Tufts University

W. S. SAHAKIAN

WILLIAM SAMUEL
University of California, San Diego

T. SAND
*Norwegian University of Science and
Technology*

WILLIAM C. SANDERSON
Rutgers University

JEROME SANES
Brown University

LAWRENCE J. SANNA
Washington State University

C. SANTERRE
University of Arizona

JOHN WYNNE SANTROCK
University of Texas-Dallas, Richardson

EDWARD P. SARAFINO
The College of New Jersey, Ewing

WILLIAM IRVIN SAUSER, JR.
Auburn University

ALICE D. SCHEUER
University of Hawaii, Honolulu

K. SCHMIDTKE
University of Frieberg, Germany

DAVID A SCHULDBERG
University of Montana

ALEXANDER JULIAN SCHUT
Pennsylvania State University

JULIE B. SCHWEITZER
Emory School of Medicine

D. L. SEGAL
University of Colorado

SAUL B. SELLS
Texas Christian University

J. SHANTEAU

D. H. SHAPIRO
University of California, Irvine

KENNETH JOEL SHAPIRO
*Psychologists for the Ethical Treatment of
Animals*

S. L. SHAPIRO
University of Arizona

J. A. SHARPE
University of Toronto

Y. SHAULY
Allegheny University of Health Sciences

ROBERT A. SHAW
Brown University

GLENN D. SHEAN
College of William and Mary

STEVEN D. SHERRETS
Maine Head Trauma Center, Bangor

EDWIN S. SHNEIDMAN
*University of California School of Medicine,
Los Angeles*

VARDA SHOHAM
University of Arizona, Tucson

BERNARD H. SHULMAN
Northwestern University Medical School

JULIE A. SHUMACHER
State University of New York, Stony Brook

M. SIGUAN
Barcelona, Spain

ELSA A. SIIPOLA
Smith College

ALCINO J. SILVA
University of California, Los Angeles

HIRSCH LAZAAR SILVERMAN

L. SILVERN
University of Colorado, Boulder

HERBERT A. SIMON
Carnegie Mellon University

ALAN SIMPKINS
University of Hawaii, Honolulu

M. BREWSTER SMITH
University of California, Santa Cruz

WILLIAM PAUL SMITH
Vanderbilt University

DAWN SOMMER
University of Texas, Austin

SUBHASH R. SONNAD
Western Michigan University

PETER W. SORRENSEN
University of Minnesota, St. Paul

JANET TAYLOR SPENCE
University of Texas, Austin

DANTE S. SPETTER
New England Medical Center, Boston

ROBERT P. SPRAFKIN
*Veterans Administration Medical Center,
Syracuse*

SCOTT STANLEY
*Center for Marital and Family Studies,
University of Denver*

KEVIN D. STARK
University of Texas, Austin

STEPHEN STARK
University of Illinois, Champaign

TIMOTHY STEENBERGH
The University of Memphis

ROBERT A. STEER
*University of Medicine and Dentistry of
New Jersey*

A. STEIGER
*Max Plank Institute of Psychiatry,
Germany*

ROBERT M. STELMACK
University of Ottawa

ROBERT H. STENSRUD
University of Northern Iowa

R. J. STERNBERG
Yale University

GERALD L. STONE
University of Iowa

WILLIAM S. STONE
Harvard University

HUGH A. STORROW
University of Kentucky

EZRA STOTLAND
University of Washington

GEORGE STRICKER
Adelphi University

RICHARD B. STUART
Weight Watchers International

D. I. SUCHMAN
University of Florida

ARTHUR SULLIVAN
Memorial University, Newfoundland

S. W. SUMERALL
William Jewell College

NORMAN D. SUNDBERG
University of Oregon

J. T. SUPER

ROBERT J. SUTHERLAND
University of New Mexico

H. A. SWADLOW
Brown University

SUSAN SWEARER
University of Texas, Austin

JULIAN I. TABER
Veterans Administration Medical Center, Reno

ANA TABOADA
University of Maryland

YASUMASA TANAKA
Gakushuin University, Tokyo

JAMES T. TEDESCHI
State University of New York

J. A. TESTA
University of Oklahoma

ALEXANDER THOMAS
New York University School of Medicine

S. M. THOMPSON
University of Maryland

BEVERLY E. THORN
University of Alabama, Tuscaloosa

B. MICHAEL THORNE
Mississippi State University

DAVID F. TOLIN
University of Pennsylvania

ELEANOR REARDON TOLSON
University of Washington

JOE TOMAKA
University of Texas, El Paso

LOUIS G. TORNATZKY
National Science Foundation, Washington, DC

DANIEL TRANEL
University of Iowa

FREDERICK TRAVIS
Maharishi University of Management, Fairfield, IA

WILLIAM T. TSUSHIMA
Straub Clinic and Hospital, Inc., Honolulu

LEONARD P. ULLMANN
Incline Valley, Nevada

E. ULVESTAD

RHODA KESLER UNGER
Montclair State College

SUSANA PATRICIA URBINA
University of Northern Florida

T. BEDIRHAN ÜSTÜN
World Health Organization, Geneva

A. L. VACARINO
University of New Orleans

P. VALDERRAMA-ITURBE
Mexico

P. VANDEL
Hospital Saint-Jacques, Bensancon, France

R. D. VANDERPLOEG
University of South Florida

KIRSTEN M. VANMEENAN
University of Maryland

ANTHONY J. VATTANO
University of Illinois, Champaign

FRANCES E. VAUGHAN
California Institute of Transpersonal Psychology, Menlo Park

P. E. VERNON

WILLIAM F. VITULLI
University of Southern Alabama

N. J. WADE
University of Dundee, Scotland

REX ALVON WADHAM
Brigham Young University

E. E. WAGNER
Forest Institute of Professional Psychology

RICHARD D. WALK
George Washington University

ARLENE S. WALKER-ANDREWS
Rutgers University

PATRICIA M. WALLACE
University of Maryland

ROGER N. WALSH
University of California, Irvine

ZHONG-MING WANG
Zhejiang University, China

WILSE B. WEBB
University of Florida

JOEL LEE WEINBERGER
Adelphi University

ARNOLD D. WELL
University of Massachusetts

W. W. WENRICH
University of North Texas

MICHAEL WERTHEIMER
University of Colorado

DONALD L. WERTLIEB
Tufts University

IAN Q. WHISHAW
University of Lethbridge, Alberta

M. A. WHISMAN
University of Colorado, Boulder

SARAH WHITTON
Center for Marital and Family Studies, University of Denver

ERIKA WICK
St. John's University

DELOS N. WICKENS
Ohio State University

RICHARD E. WILCOX
University of Texas, Austin

SABINE WILHELM
Massachusetts General Hospital, Charlestown

DOUGLAS A. WILLIAMS
University of Winnipeg

RICHARD H. WILLIS
University of Pittsburgh

J. WILSON
University of Minnesota, Duluth

MARGARET T. T. WONG-RILEY
Medical College of Wisconsin

MICHAEL L. WOODRUFF
East Tennessee State University

D. S. WOODRUFF-PAK
Temple University

MARGARET P. WOODS

T. E. WOODS
University of Wisconsin School of Medicine

ROBERT L. WOOLFOLK
Rutgers University

ANTHONY WRIGHT
University of Manitoba

TRISTAM D. WYATT
University of Minnesota, St. Paul

R. C. WYLIE

LARRY J. YOUNG
Emory University

L. M. YOUNGBLADE
University of Colorado

ZAHRA ZAKERI
Queens College, City University of New York

O. L. ZANGWILL
Cambridge, England

JOHANNES M. ZANKER
The Australian National University

PATRICIA A. ZAPF
University of Alabama

W. ZHANG
New York Medical College

DANIEL J. ZIEGLER
Villanova University

PHILIP G. ZIMBAROO
Stanford University

M. ZUCKERMAN
University of Delaware

FIONA VAJK: MANAGING EDITOR
BENJAMIN PAGE: MANAGING EDITOR
ALINNE BARRERA: MANAGER EDITOR

The Corsini Encyclopedia of Psychology and Behavioral Science

Third Edition

A

ABELES, NORMAN

Norman Abeles is professor of psychology and director of the Psychological Clinic at Michigan State University. He served as the 1997 president of the American Psychological Association (APA). The focus of his presidency was on aging, and he was instrumental in the establishment of an APA Committee on Aging. During his presidency, the Council of Representatives (the governing body of APA) established guidelines for the evaluation of dementia and age-related cognitive decline, and a work group developed a brochure titled *What the Practitioner Should Know About Working with Older Adults.* He established the Clinical Neuropsychological Laboratory at Michigan State University in 1982 and has coordinated the older adult track in the clinical psychology program at MSU, where he also served as the codirector of clinical psychology training from 1981 to 1996.

Born in Vienna, Austria, he received his BA from New York University and his MA and PhD from the University of Texas at Austin. He served as a senior Fulbright professor at the University of Utrecht in the Netherlands and later returned as a visiting professor there.

His programmatic research efforts include research on process and outcome in psychotherapy and the study of the interaction between mood and memory in older adults. During his tenure as director of the Psychological Clinic at Michigan State, he and his students developed what is considered to be the single largest psychotherapy tape library in any psychological clinic. Examples of published studies included, for example, such topics as early indicators of therapeutic alliance; symptom severity, psychotherapy and outcome; client satisfaction and meaningful change; and client expression of hostility in psychotherapy.

With regard to the study of the interaction between mood and memory in older adults, Abeles and his students have collected data on a number of older adult participants in mood and memory workshops. The research project includes both an assessment and an intervention component (cognitive behavioral workshops and relaxation workshops) and comparisons were made between control participants and experimental group members on memory functions, memory complaints, and social support variables. As the project developed, studies focused on the effects of targeted memory training on everyday memory and on memory complaints. A current study focuses on the comorbidity of anxiety and depression in older adults.

Abeles was the founding editor of the *Academic Psychology Bulletin* and served as the editor of *Professional Psychology: Research and Practice* from 1983 to 1988. He has also served as a member and chairperson of APA's Publications and Communications Board and as a member and chairperson of its Education and Training Board. He has also served as the secretary of the APA and as a member of its Board of Directors. He served several terms on the Council of Representatives (the governing body for the American Psychological Association). He is a past president of APA's Division of Clinical Psychology and Division of Psychotherapy, and a past president of the Michigan Psychological Association. He was vice-chairperson of the Council on the National Register of Health Service Providers in Psychology and is a former chairperson of the Michigan Psychology Board. He is a member of the US National Committee for the International Union of Psychological Sciences (1999–2005). He is also a member of the American Psychological Foundation and a member of the American Psychological Association's Insurance Trust.

Abeles continues to serve as a consultant to the Veteran Administration's Medical Center at Battle Creek, Michigan, and earlier he was a consultant and field selection officer for the Peace Corps. He has also been a vocational consultant and medical advisor to the Social Security Administration's Office of Hearings and Appeals. He was also elected a board member of the Council of Scientific Society Presidents. Abeles received the Distinguished Psychologist award from the Division of Psychotherapy of APA and was recognized by APA's Division of Adult Development and Aging for his contribution to the field of aging. He also received the Distinguished Contribution Award from the Clinical Geropsychology section of the Division of Clinical Psychology of APA. He also received the Distinguished Psychologist Award from the Michigan Psychological Association, of which he is a fellow and a life member. He is a diplomate of the American Board of Professional Psychology, a fellow of the American Psychological Association, and an elected member to the National Academies of Practice.

At Michigan State University, he served as an elected member of the Executive Committee of Academic Governance and as chairperson of that committee. The Executive Committee takes responsibility for determining the agenda of Academic Council, the faculty governance body at Michigan State. He also has served as an elected faculty liaison to the MSU Board of Trustees. Abeles is listed in *Who's Who in Health and Medicine,* the *International Dictionary of Biography, Who's Who in America,* and *Who's Who in the World.*

STAFF

ABNORMALITY

From time immemorial, individuals have consistently recognized a small group of people in their societies as psychologically "abnormal." Further, Murphy's research (1976) demonstrates that people in non-Western cultures, such as the Yorubas of Nigeria and the Yupic-speaking Eskimos of Alaska, readily recognize certain behaviors as abnormal. Many of these behaviors, such as talking to oneself, are similar to those regarded as abnormal in Western society. Murphy's findings suggest that the concept of abnormality is not entirely culturally relative, and that individuals in disparate cultures often label comparable behaviors as abnormal.

The preceding observations leave unanswered a critical question: What is abnormality? Put somewhat differently, what implicit criterion or criteria do individuals use to identify abnormality? Surprisingly, a conclusive answer to this question continues to elude thinkers in the field of psychopathology. In this entry, several conceptualizations of abnormality and their strengths and weaknesses are examined. All of these conceptualizations strive to provide a definition of abnormality that encompasses both physical and mental disorders, although most place primary emphasis on the latter.

The first and most radical conception examined here is that abnormality is entirely a function of subjective societal values. According to this *subjective values* model, which has been championed by Szasz (1960), abnormal conditions are those deemed by society to be undesirable in some way. Although this model touches on an important truth, namely that many or most abnormal conditions are perceived as undesirable, it does not explain why many socially undesirable behaviors, such as rudeness and laziness, are not perceived as pathological. A comprehensive definition of abnormality seems to involve more than subjective values.

Proponents of a *statistical* approach, such as Cohen (1981), posit that abnormality can be defined as statistical deviation from a norm. Thus, any behavior that is rare in the population is abnormal. Appealing in its simplicity as this conceptualization appears, it suffers from several weaknesses. First, the cutoff points for abnormality are scientifically arbitrary. Should abnormality be defined as the uppermost 1% of the population, the uppermost 3%, or some other figure? Second, a statistical approach provides no guidance regarding which dimensions are relevant to psychopathology. As a consequence, it erroneously classifies high levels of certain socially desirable dimensions, such as creativity and altruism, as abnormal. Third, a statistical approach erroneously classifies all common conditions as normal. For example, it implies that the bubonic plague ("Black Death"), which killed approximately one-third of Europe's population in the fourteenth century, was not abnormal because it was widespread.

Some theorists, such as Kraupl Taylor (1971), have embraced the pragmatic position that abnormality is nothing more than the set of conditions that professionals treat. According to this parsimonious "disorder as whatever professionals treat" view, psychologically abnormal conditions are those that elicit intervention from mental health professionals. Although this view avoids many of the conceptual pitfalls of other definitions, it fails to explain why many conditions treated by professionals, such as pregnancy, a misshapen nose corrected by plastic surgery, and marital conflict, are not by themselves regarded as pathological.

Advocates of a *subjective discomfort* model maintain that abnormal conditions are those that produce suffering in affected individuals. Although it is undeniable that many psychopathological conditions, such as major depressive disorder, produce considerable subjective distress, several other conditions, such as psychopathy (a condition characterized by guiltlessness, callousness, and dishonesty) and the manic phase of bipolar disorder (a condition characterized by extreme levels of elation, energy, and grandiosity), are often associated with little or no subjective distress. Moreover, like the statistical model, the subjective discomfort

model provides no guidance concerning what cutoffs should be used to define abnormality. How much discomfort is required for a condition to be pathological?

Most of the aforementioned definitions focus largely or entirely on subjective judgments concerning the presence of abnormality. In contrast, proponents of a *biological model,* such as Kendell (1975), contend that abnormality should be defined by strictly biological criteria, particularly those derived from evolutionary theory. For example, Kendell argued that abnormal conditions are characterized by a reduced life span, reduced biological fitness (the capacity of an organism to transmit its genes to future generations), or both. Despite its potentially greater scientific rigor relative to other models, a biological model is subject to numerous counterexamples. Being a soldier in a war tends to reduce one's longevity but is not a disorder; priesthood (which results in having no children) tends to reduce one's fitness but is similarly not a disorder. Moreover, a biological model falls victim to the same problem of arbitrary cutoffs that bedevils the statistical model: how much below average must life span or fitness be for the condition in question to be abnormal?

Whereas some of the preceding conceptualizations of abnormality primarily invoke social criteria, such as value judgments, others primarily invoke biological criteria. Wakefield (1992) suggests that the correct definition of abnormality requires both social and biological criteria. Specifically, he posits that all abnormal conditions are *harmful dysfunctions.* The *harm* component of Wakefield's conceptualization refers to social values regarding a condition's undesirability, whereas the "dysfunction" component refers to the failure of a system to function as "designed" by natural selection. Panic disorder is abnormal, according to Wakefield, because: (a) it is viewed by society as harmful; and (b) the fear system was not evolutionarily designed to respond with intense anxiety in the absence of objective danger. Wakefield's analysis is an important advance in the conceptualization of abnormality, because it distinguishes those features of abnormality that are socially constructed from those that are scientifically based. Nevertheless, his analysis assumes that all disorders involve failures of psychological or physiological systems. Yet, some disorders (e.g., anxiety disorders) probably represent evolved defensive reactions to subjectively perceived threats. Moreover, Wakefield's analysis presumes the existence of a clear-cut distinction between adaptive function and dysfunction. But the functioning of many systems, such as the anxiety system, may be distributed continuously, with no unambiguous dividing line between normality and abnormality.

In response to the problems with earlier efforts to provide an adequate definition of abnormality, some authors, such as Rosenhan and Seligman (1995) and Lilienfeld and Marino (1995), have proposed a *family resemblance* model of abnormality. According to this model, the concept of abnormality cannot be explicitly defined, because abnormality is an inherently fuzzy concept with indefinite boundaries. Instead, conditions perceived as abnormal share a loosely related set of characteristics, including statistical rarity, maladaptiveness, impairment, and the need for treatment. The family resemblance view implies that all efforts to construct a clear-cut definition of abnormality are doomed to failure. At the same time, this view implies that there will often be substantial consensus regarding which conditions are perceived as abnormal, because individuals rely on similar features when identifying abnormality.

REFERENCES

Cohen, H. (1981). The evolution of the concept of disease. In A. Caplan, H. Engelhardt, & J. McCarthy (Eds.), *Concepts of health and disease: Interdisciplinary perspectives* (pp. 209–220). Reading, MA: Addison-Wesley.

Kendell, R. E. (1975). The concept of disease and its implications for psychiatry. *British Journal of Psychiatry, 127,* 305–315.

Kraupl Taylor, F. (1971). A logical analysis of the medico-psychological concept of disease. *Psychological Medicine, 1,* 356–364.

Szasz, T. S. (1960). The myth of mental illness. *American Psychologist, 15,* 113–118.

Lilienfeld, S. O., & Marino, L. (1995). Mental disorder as a Roschian concept: A critique of Wakefield's "harmful dysfunction" analysis. *Journal of Abnormal Psychology, 104,* 411–420.

Murphy, J. M. (1976). Psychiatric labeling in cross-cultural perspective. *Science, 191,* 1019–1028.

Rosenhan, D., & Seligman, M. (1995). *Abnormal psychology* (3rd ed.). New York: Norton.

Wakefield, J. C. (1992). The concept of mental disorder: On the boundary between biological facts and social values. *American Psychologist, 47,* 373–388.

S. O. LILIENFELD
Emory University

CULTURE AND HEALTH
MENTAL ILLNESS
PSCHOPHYSIOLOGY

ACADEMIC APTITUDE TESTS

Although there is no universally accepted definition of academic aptitude, most psychologists would agree that academic aptitude tests assess cognitive capacity or potential that predicts how individuals will perform according to some criterion prior to receiving training or instruction. Academic aptitude tests predict degree of success in school learning tasks.

TYPES OF APTITUDE TESTS

There are many types of academic aptitude tests. One way to categorize the test is by the degree of specificity that is defined by the nature of the aptitude inherent in the development of the test. Figure 1 illustrates different kinds of academic aptitude tests on the basis of degree of specificity. Global tests, such as measures of intelligence, assess a wide variety of cognitive capabilities and predict, in a very general way, degree of success in most academic pursuits. Specific tests, on the other hand, predict degree of success in

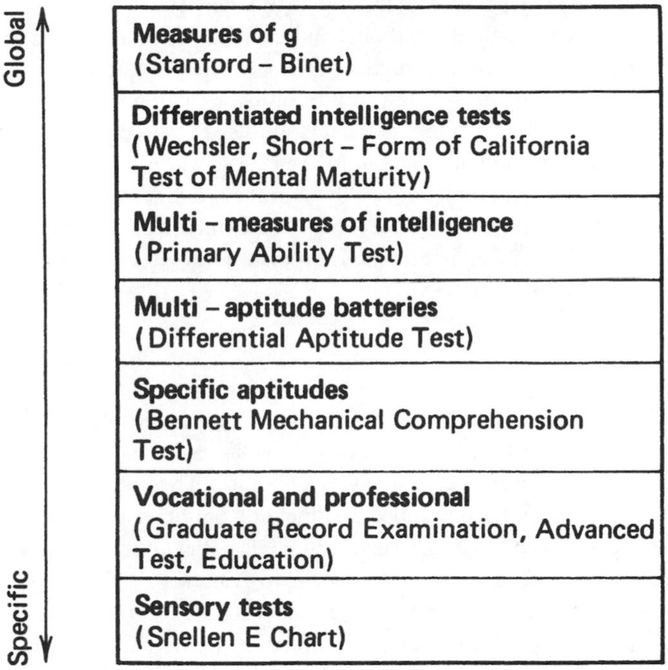

Figure 1. A continuum of degrees of specificity of content as measured by different kinds of tests. From *Principles of Educational and Psychological Measurement and Evaluation* (2nd ed.), by G. Sax, 1980 (Belmont, CA: Wadsworth). Reprinted by permission.

more limited areas such as mathematics, music, English, or art, and are appropriate for making placements in these specific areas.

While psychologists have distinguished aptitude from achievement tests, the differences are more in the purposes of the tests than the content. Aptitude tests frequently have broader coverage than achievement tests, but very often it is difficult to distinguish the tests on the basis of specific items. The primary difference is in purpose: Aptitude tests predict learning, whereas achievement tests assess past learning and present knowledge. Confusion is understandable since many achievement tests predict subsequent learning better than some aptitude tests, especially when the predicted achievement is in a narrowly defined area. According to Anastasi in *Psychological Testing* and Cronbach in *Essentials of Psychological Testing,* the difference between aptitude and achievement tests can be represented on a continuum from specific, school-focused achievements (e.g., teacher-made tests) to general capabilities such as intelligence. Aptitude tests such as the Scholastic Aptitude Test (SAT) and the Graduate Record Examination (GRE) would fall in the middle.

RELIABILITY AND VALIDITY OF APTITUDE TESTS

Aptitude tests should possess particular types of validity and reliability. It is essential that an aptitude test demonstrate predictive validity, that is, the extent to which test scores can predict a given criterion. Thus aptitude test scores are used not to determine performance on the items, but rather to predict a relevant criterion (e.g., the Miller Analogies Test might be used to predict graduate school success). Generally, correlation coefficients are used to describe the predictive relationship, and correlations of .40 to .50 are considered acceptable. For some aptitude tests, especially general tests of intelligence such as the Stanford–Binet, it is also desirable to have construct validity. Although more difficult to attain, construct validity establishes a theoretical basis for interpreting the scores.

For general aptitude tests it is desirable to have a stability estimate of reliability, since the results are used to predict behavior over a long period of time. For multiple tests within a general battery, it is also desirable to have data on the internal consistency of the subtests and the different scores. It is common to report correlations of .85 and higher for internal consistency estimates for standardized aptitude tests.

IQ TESTS

Historically, the most popular type of aptitude test lies at the global end of Figure 1: tests of intelligence. Volumes have been written both on intelligence and on intelligence tests. The first formal test of intelligence was developed by Binet and Simon in 1905 to identify retarded children in French schools. The Binet–Simon Test was translated into English and brought to America by Goddard in 1908, and in 1916 Terman adapted the translated test to create the Stanford–Binet Test (Terman worked at Stanford University). These tests were administered individually to children, one child at a time, and provided a single score of intelligence. The Stanford–Binet tests were revised in 1937, 1960, and 1972. Wechsler developed a set of individually administered intelligence tests that measured several factors. His tests are known as the Wechsler Preschool and Primary Scale of Intelligence, or WPPSI (1967); the Wechsler Adult Intelligence Scale, or WAIS (1968); and the Wechsler Intelligence Scale for Children–Revised, or WISC-R (1974). The Wechsler tests have subscales such as comprehension, similarities, vocabulary, block design, and object assembly, and provide a verbal, performance, and full scale score.

In 1917 the U.S. War Department, with the assistance of the American Psychological Association, developed and administered group intelligence tests called Army Alpha and Army Beta. These tests could be administered to a large number of individuals at one time and proved helpful in selecting commissioned and noncommissioned officers. Many other group intelligence tests were developed for school use following the same pattern as the Army Alpha. These tests are used far more extensively than individual tests, and include such tests as the California Test of Mental Maturity, the Cognitive Abilities Tests, the Herman–Nelson Test of Mental Ability, the Kuhlmann–Anderson Intelligence Tests, the Otis–Lennon Mental Ability Tests, and the SRA Tests of General Ability.

When intelligence test scores of a large group of children are graphed to show the frequency of each score, the result is a bell-shaped normal curve. The mean, or average score, is always 100, and the standard deviation is about 15. Children who score below 70 (lower 2% of population) may be diagnosed as mentally retarded, while scores above 130 (upper 2% of population) are sometimes placed in the gifted category. A single score is reported for an overall, general measure of intelligence. This score is referred to as IQ, or intelligence quotient, and should not be considered synonymous with intelligence. For many of the tests there are also scores reported for subscales and general factors that make up the single IQ score.

MULTIFACTOR APTITUDE TESTS

Multifactor aptitude tests contain a number of subtests that measure different aptitudes. The subtests assess a wider range of aptitudes than is found in the IQ test. The results can be very useful in vocational and educational counseling. The entire battery of tests is standardized on the same individuals, which permits comparisons across subtests and the identification of relatively strong and weak aptitudes.

One of the most widely used multiple aptitude batteries is the Differential Aptitude Test (DAT). The DAT has eight subtests: verbal reasoning, numerical ability, abstract reasoning, clerical speed and accuracy, mechanical reasoning, space relations, spelling, and language usage. The verbal reasoning and numerical ability subtests are combined to give a score comparable to a WISC-R or Stanford–Binet general IQ score. The DAT is used in grade 8 or 9 to provide relevant information to students as they plan for future education.

Other multifactor aptitude tests include the United States Employment Service General Aptitude Battery (GATB), which has twelve tests and reports nine scores; the Armed Services Vocational Aptitude Battery (ASVAB); the Nonreading Aptitude Test (NATB); the Comprehensive Ability Battery; the Guilford-Zimmerman Aptitude Battery; the International Primary Factors Test Battery; the Metropolitan Readiness Tests; and the Boehm Test of Basic Concepts (BTBC).

SPECIFIC APTITUDE TESTS

A large number of aptitude tests measure aptitudes in a specific area or for specific courses and professions. Specific aptitude tests are available to predict success in such areas as clerical and stenographic aptitude, vision and learning, vision and hearing, mechanical aptitude, musical and artistic aptitudes, and creativity. Aptitude tests that are used for selection into a course of study or profession include the Scholastic Aptitude Test (SAT), the American College Testing Program Test Battery (ACT), the Law School Admissions Test (LSAT), and the Medical College Admissions Test (MCAT).

USING APTITUDE TESTS

Aptitude tests are used pervasively at all levels of education to improve instruction, to provide feedback to students for counseling, and to determine selection. Knowledge of aptitude test scores may assist teachers in forming realistic expectations for students and in individualizing learning experiences. Comparing aptitude with achievement scores can identify discrepancies that suggest attention to either learner or instructional inadequacies. In vocational counseling, aptitude tests help point out differential aptitudes and compare relative strengths to skills required in different vocations. The results also help counselors to diagnose the reasons for student misbehavior. For example, an IQ test may indicate that a child is bored or frustrated in a class.

Perhaps the most important use of aptitude tests involves selection, classification, and placement. Aptitude tests are used to determine whether a child is mentally retarded. In situations where only a limited number of students may be admitted from a large group of applicants, aptitude tests provide a common basis of comparison for all students; in conjunction with other information, the scores are used to decide which students will be admitted. Thus aptitude tests can be used by teachers, counselors, administrators, and students to improve the quality of education and individual decision making. This assumes, however, that the results are not misinterpreted nor misused. Without a thorough understanding of such factors as cultural bias, error in testing, and score interpretation, there is a potential to overemphasize results.

SUGGESTED READING

Mehrens, W. A., & Lehmann, I. J. (1980). *Standardized test in education* (3rd ed.). New York: Holt, Rinehart & Winston.

Sax, G. (1980). Principles of educational and psychological measurement and evaluation (2nd ed.). Belmont, CA: Wadsworth.

J. H. McMILLAN
Virginia Commonwealth University

TEST STANDARDIZATION

ACADEMIC UNDERACHIEVEMENT

Underachievement is the attainment of a level of performance below an expected or predicted level; it implies a criterion and a predictor. Traditionally, IQ measures have been used to predict a level of achievement, and standardized achievement tests, to establish the criterion. A discrepancy of some stated magnitude expressed in standard scores frequently has served as the operational definition of underachievement for both research and field-classification activities.

The primary purpose of identifying underachievers is to enable instructors to tailor and target instruction to reduce or eliminate underachieving. The definition as well as the rationale associated with underachievement appears simple, sound, and practical. A more critical examination, however, reveals numerous problems. The classic critique by Thorndike includes a discussion of these problems. Thorndike suggested that underachievement can theoretically be viewed as a reflection of a system's inability to make accurate predictions; perfect predictions of achievement would, after all, preclude discrepancies and eliminate underachievement as well as overachievement. He put it this way: "As we are able to extend our understanding of the relevant factors, increase the accuracy of our forecasts, and so reduce overprediction, we will automatically reduce 'underachievement'" (1963, p. 5). This was Thorndike's way of emphasizing the responsibility educators and psychologists have for accurately explaining the discrepancies they label as underachievement. Aptitude-achievement discrepancies that serve as indices of under- and overachievement are explained by Thorndike in terms of four major factors:

1. *Errors of measurement.* A student's performance on both the criterion and predictor variable may produce two scores or composites on one day and two different scores or composites

the following day. His or her class ranking on these measures may also change from one day to the next, because of imperfections in the measures and measuring techniques.

2. *Heterogeneity of criterion.* Performance on teacher-made tests, grade-point average, course grades, and rank in class are all indicators of academic achievement and, as such, constitute potential criteria to be used in determining underachievement. However a grade of B, a GPA of 3.26, and a class ranking will have very different meanings, depending upon the group of students and the teacher involved. Furthermore, the relationship among these criteria will differ markedly across groups.

3. *Scope of predictors.* Preoccupation with IQ and other scholastic aptitude measures has handicapped educators in diagnosing and responding to underachievement problems. They must identify other stable factors related to aptitude-achievement discrepancies and thereby increase the validity of our predictors.

4. Manipulate variables. Some percentage of school underachievement can be eliminated by making changes in students' environments. Changes in texts, teachers, seating, or form of feedback may reduce underachievement.

Thorndike concluded his discussion of underachievement and overachievement with a plea for improved research. After identifying and discussing the deficiencies of experimental designs used to investigate this topic, he stated: "If these deficiencies are eliminated in future studies, it is to be hoped that we will have a richer yield of consistent and confirmed results" (1963, p. 67).

A year after Thorndike's treatise, Farquhar and Payne (1964) evaluated techniques commonly used to identify under- and overachievers. They concluded that there were four primary and distinctive categories into which these techniques could be classified:

1. *Central tendency splits.* These methods dichotomize a distribution of combined aptitude and achievement scores.

2. *Arbitrary partitioning.* This technique contrasts extreme groups and eliminates the central part of a distribution.

3. *Relative discrepancy splits.* Here a comparison is made of individuals' ranks on an aptitude measure and achievement measure (grade-point average).

4. *Regression.* This approach measures the discrepancy between actual and predicted achievement when the latter is determined from an aptitude measure.

Farquhar and Payne found marked differences in the proportion of under- and overachievers, depending upon the method of classification used. Annesley, Odhner, Madoff, and Chansky (1970) reported similar differences which they observed while investigating alternative classifications of first-graders.

Given the variety of classification methods used and the variety of predictor and criterion measures available, it is not surprising that the literature on underachievement is fraught with problems, including inconclusive results (Muller, 1969; Asbury, 1974), conflicting results (Shuey, 1966; Tyler, 1947/1965), misinterpretation of findings (Rainey, 1965), and methodological weaknesses (Thorndike, 1963). One might ask whether it is time to abandon this concept and its field of research. Krouse and Krouse (1981) argue against doing so, contending that this diagnostic classification is of potential usefulness to educators as well as clinicians. They propose that underachievement—admittedly a complex, multi-faceted phenomenon—be studied within the framework of a "multimodel theory" using skill deficits, self-control deficits, and affective factors to explain academic dysfunctions. While each of these three sets of factors has previously been individually recognized as a cause of underachievement (Brown, Wehe, & Hislam, 1971; Perri & Richards, 1977), Krouse and Krouse argue that what is needed is simultaneous study of these factors and their interactions.

Krouse and Krouse also recommend longitudinal studies and multitrait-multimethod data analyses for refining and validating the underachievement construct. Their reasoning, model, and recommendations are consistent with Thorndike's conclusions (1963). Although Thorndike facetiously suggested that we might even wish to relabel the phenomena of under- and overachievement as "over- and underintelligence," respectively, there was no intimation in his treatise that the concept of underachievement had outlived its usefulness.

REFERENCES

Annesley, F., Odhner, F., Madoff, E., & Chansky, N. (1970). Identifying the first grade underachiever. *Journal of Educational Research, 63,* 459–462.

Asbury, C. A. (1974). Selected factors influencing over- and underachievement in young school-age children. *Review of Educational Research, 44,* 409–428.

Brown, W. F., Wehe, N. O., & Hislam, W. L. (1971). Effectiveness of student-to-student counseling on the academic achievement of potential college dropouts. *Journal of Educational Psychology, 62,* 285–289.

Farquhar, W. W., & Payne, D. A. (1964). A classification and comparison of techniques used in selecting under- and overachievers. *Personnel and Guidance Journal, 42,* 874–884.

Krouse, J. H., & Krouse, H. J. (1981). Toward a multimodel theory of academic underachievement. *Educational Psychologist, 16,* 151–164.

Müller, P. (1969). *The tasks of childhood.* New York: McGraw-Hill.

Perri, M. G., & Richards, C. S. (1977). An investigation of naturally occurring episodes of self-controlled behaviors. *Journal of Counseling Psychology, 24,* 178–183.

Rainey, R. G. (1965). Study of four school-ability tests. *Journal of Experimental Education, 33,* 305–319.

Shuey, A. M. (1966). *The testing of Negro intelligence.* Lynchburg, VA: Bell.

Thorndike, R. L. (1963). *The concepts of over- and underachievement.* New York: Bureau of Publications, Teachers College, Columbia University.

Tyler, L. E. (1965). *The psychology of human differences* (3rd ed.). New York: Appleton-Century-Crofts. (Original work published 1947)

M. M. CLIFFORD
University of Iowa

HUMAN INTELLIGENCE
SCHOOL LEARNING

ACCOMMODATION

VISUAL ACCOMMODATION
Visual accommodation is the automatic adjustment process by which the lens of the eye adjusts to focus on objects at different distances. When the eye is at rest, the suspensory ligaments hold the lens firmly in a relatively flattened position. The resting eye is then in a far-point vision position and can focus on objects that are at least 20 ft. distant. Light rays passing through the cornea and aqueous humor then enter the pupil of the eye and pass through the lens, after which they pass through the vitreous humor and reach the retina in focus.

For near vision, closer than 20 ft., the ciliary muscles, located around and attached to the suspensory ligaments, contract. This causes relaxation of the suspensory ligaments, which then allow the flattened lens, which is elastic and soft, to thicken and bulge. The light rays are thus bent and fall, sharply focused, on the retina. Illumination level has been found to have an effect upon accommodation (Bartley, 1951). There have been various theories of the physiological mechanism for accommodation. Bartley notes as most likely the view that the sympathetic nervous system is responsible for a basic tonal background, through vascular innervation. The oculomotor nerve, through increased or decreased innervation, leads to positive and negative accommodation, or specific adjustment for focusing.

NERVE ACCOMMODATION
When a constant stimulus, such as an electric current, is applied to a nerve, the excitability of the nerve under the cathode, or negative electrode, increases quickly. With continued stimulation by current flow, there is a slow decrease in nerve excitability, known as accommodation, followed by a sudden drop when the current is stopped. Following cessation of the stimulating current, the nerve briefly becomes less sensitive to stimulation than it was before the current was turned on.

ACCOMMODATION IN INFANT DEVELOPMENT
The term "accommodation" was also used by Jean Piaget as part of his theoretical view of how infants develop cognitively. Accommodation refers to the infant's modification of concepts or notions of the world as a response to new experiences, or to experiences in-

consistent with a previously held notion. "Assimilation" refers to the incorporation into the child's cognitive structure of notions from elements of environmental experience. When an organized cognitive pattern develops through the processes of assimilation and accommodation, a schema or scheme (*pl. schemata*) is said to have developed. Schemata develop, according to Piaget, during the first two years, or the sensorimotor period, during which the infant develops mainly through sensorimotor activities. Piaget differentiated six stages of sensorimotor development.

REFERENCES

Bartley, S. H. (1951). The psychophysiology of vision. In S. S. Stevens (Ed.), *Handbook of experimental psychology.* New York: Wiley.

SUGGESTED READING

Anthony, C., & Thibodeau, G. (1983). *Textbook of anatomy and physiology* (11th ed.), New York: Mosby.

Davson, H. (1990). *Physiology of the eye* (5th ed.). New York: McGraw.

Gardner, E. (1975). *Fundamentals of neurology* (6th ed.). Philadelphia: Saunders.

Kandel, E. R., & Schwartz, J. J. (1985). *Principles of neural science* (2nd ed.). New York: Elsevier.

Piaget, J. (1952). *The origin of intelligence in children.* New York: International Universities Press.

Piaget, J. (1954). *The origins of intelligence.* New York: Basic Books.

Piaget, J. (1955). *The language and thought of the child.* New York: Meridian.

Piaget, J. (1963). *The psychology of intelligence.* New York: Littlefield, Adams.

Weiner, W. J., & Goetz, C. G. (Eds.). (1981). *Neurology for the nonneurologist.* Philadelphia: Harper & Row.

B. B. MATES
City College of New York, City University of New York

ADAPTATION
DEPTH PERCEPTION
EYE
PIAGET'S THEORY

ACCULTURATION

Acculturation is a process whereby individuals learn about the rules for behavior characteristic of a certain group of people. The term "culture" refers to the way of life of a people and includes the tools or methods with which they extract a livelihood from their environment. It also includes the web of social relations, understandings, and customs, and rules or attitudes about supernatural or supreme beings. These influences on a person's behavior determine ways of thinking, choices, and life goals. Customs and traditions for solving problems are passed from one generation to the next through pathways in the family and in the social institutions of the society.

Culture continues to influence people's lives over the entire life span. Some writers have maintained—as Mead did in *From the South Seas* (1939)—that individuals in the process of acculturation internalize the rules of the culture. Such internalization can have profound and lasting influence even on the physical functioning of people's bodies; it can even affect the traits passed on to the next generation through dictation of choices of mates.

Acculturation has broad meaning as an abstraction. With children, it means that they must conform to the patterns of behavior accepted and valued by the parents. Thus some freedom of choice must be forfeited by the child because of parental cajolery to internalize the prescribed codes of conduct.

Anthropologists see cultural patterns as fixed and as a part of the personality. Benedict in *Patterns of Culture* (1934) emphasized that human behavior comes to exemplify the culture in which the child grows up. To some degree, therefore, the culture lays out life's destiny and direction: Its ways become the child's ways. Eventually the child and adult see no other way or course of action save that dictated by the culture. An extreme emphasis on the concept allows little belief in individuality or freedom except within cultural rules.

REFERENCES

Benedict, R. F. (1960). *Patterns of culture.* New York: Mentor. (Original work published 1946)

Mead, M. (1939). *From the South Seas (studies of adolescence and sex in primitive societies).* New York: Morrow.

SUGGESTED READING

Adler, L. L. (1982). Cross-cultural research and theory. In B. B. Wolman (Ed.), *Handbook of developmental psychology.* Englewood Cliffs, NJ: Prentice-Hall.

Weisfeld, G. E. (1982). The nature-nurture issue and the integrating concept of function. In B. B. Wolman (Ed.), *Handbook of developmental psychology.* Englewood Cliffs, NJ: Prentice-Hall.

T. ALEXANDER
Temple University

ENVIRONMENTAL PSYCHOLOGY
ETHNOCENTRISM
RITES OF PASSAGE
SOCIAL PSYCHOLOGY

ACETYLCHOLINE

Acetylcholine (ACh) is a neurotransmitter that is widely distributed in the nervous system, where it is released from neurons that are referred to as "cholinergic." Acetylcholine was the first neurotransmitter to be identified, largely through the efforts Otto Loewi and Henry Dale in the first quarter of the 20th century. In the peripheral nervous system, ACh is released by axon terminals of the spinal and cranial motor neurons and causes contraction of the skeletal muscles. In the peripheral autonomic nervous system, ACh is released by the preganglionic sympathetic neurons, and by both the preganglionic and postganglionic parasympathetic neurons. It has prominent autonomic functions, including the regulation of cardiac contraction, the regulation of vascular constriction, the regulation of smooth muscle contraction in the intestines, bladder, urogenital tract, iris, and bronchioles, the regulation of the adrenal medulla, and the regulation of the salivatory, tear, and sweat glands.

The axons of cholinergic neurons are very dense throughout the gray matter of the central nervous system. These axons originate from cholinergic neurons that are clustered in nuclei in the brainstem and basal forebrain. These nuclei were named Ch1 through Ch8 ("Ch" for cholinergic) by Marsel Mesulam and colleagues. The Ch1 and Ch2 nuclei are located in the region of the medial septal area, and their axons mainly innervate the hippocampus. The Ch3 nucleus is located just ventral to Ch2 and Ch4. It projects to olfactory areas of the brain, and is more prominent in rodents than in primates. The large Ch4 nucleus is located in the nucleus basalis of Meynert, which is at the ventral surface of the brain just anterior to the hypothalamus. The Ch4 nucleus projects massively to the entire cerebral cortex, and also has projections to some subcortical regions. The cholinergic neurons of the pedunculopontine tegmental (Ch5) and lateral dorsal tegmental (Ch6) nuclei are located in the rostral brainstem. They provide an especially dense innervation to the thalamus, and they also project to the spinal cord, brainstem, cerebellum, and regions of the subcortical forebrain. Smaller nuclei include the medial habenular nucleus (Ch7), which projects to the ventral brainstem, and the parabigeminal nucleus (Ch8), which mainly innervates the superior colliculus. An additional source of ACh is the cholinergic interneurons that are distributed throughout the striatum, and that are the major source of ACh in that structure.

Consistent with its widespread distribution in the nervous system, ACh has been implicated in numerous behavioral and physiological processes, including sensory processing, motor control, ingestive behavior, thermoregulation, aggression, sexual behavior, arousal, wakefulness, attention, and memory. The identification of massive ascending projections from the Ch5 and Ch6 nuclei led to the idea that they are a component of the ascending reticular activating system (ARAS). The ARAS was proposed in the 1940s as a brainstem center that controls the behavioral states of wakefulness and arousal. Subsequent work demonstrated that the cells in Ch5 and Ch6 increase their activity during the transition from sleep to either wakefulness or rapid eye movement (REM) sleep. Stimulation of Ch5 and Ch6 induces features of wakefulness and arousal, including a desynchronized cortical EEG and enhanced transfer of sensory information to the cerebral cortex. The cholinergic nuclei of the basal forebrain (Ch1–4) appear to have parallel functions. Their activity also increases during behavioral arousal, especially in response to novel and rewarding stimuli, and stimulation of the region of Ch4 causes an ACh-mediated desynchronization of the cortical EEG and enhanced sensory responses in cortical neurons.

Additional brainstem centers, including the monoaminergic nuclei, are also considered to be components of the ARAS.

The role of ACh in attention and memory has been documented in many studies. Administration of cholinergic antagonists to human subjects impairs their performance on sustained attention tests and in perceptual intrusion paradigms such as the Stroop test; Human subjects also exhibit deficits in declarative memory similar to those of Alzheimer's disease. Animals show deficits in a variety of memory tasks after the administration of cholinergic antagonist or after lesions to the cholinergic nuclei of the basal forebrain. In the early 1980s, it was realized that the cholinergic cells of the basal forebrain are substantially depleted (up to 85% in Ch4) in Alzheimer's disease. The cholinergic hypothesis suggested that the loss of ACh might be the primary causal factor in Alzheimer's disease. However, the loss of cholinergic cells now is thought to be secondary to other pathological processes. Nevertheless, the loss of ACh is likely to contribute substantially to the memory deficits in Alzheimer's disease. Acetylcholinesterase inhibitors that increase the concentration of ACh in the brain are commonly prescribed for Alzheimer's disease.

Numerous drugs are known to affect cholinergic neurotransmission by altering the processes of synthesis, storage, release, metabolism, and receptor binding of ACh. Acetylcholine is synthesized from choline and acetyl coenzyme A by the enzyme choline acetyl transferase. Once synthesized, ACh is transported into synaptic vesicles by the vesicular ACh transporter protein, which can be selectively inhibited by the drug vesamicol. The release of ACh can be inhibited by a number of toxins, such as the highly toxic botulinum and tetanus toxins. After ACh is released, it affects the activity of nearby cells by binding to neurotransmitter receptor proteins, and a variety of drugs are known to activate or inhibit ACh receptors. Acetylcholine is cleared from the extracellular space by acetylcholinesterase, which is a highly efficient metabolic enzyme. A variety of acetylcholinesterase inhibitors are known, including reversible inhibitors (e.g., physostigmine, tacrine) and irreversible inhibitors (e.g., the organophosphorous compounds developed as nerve gases).

The effects of ACh are mediated by the muscarinic and nicotinic families of neurotransmitter receptors, both of which have multiple subtypes that are in many cases pharmacologically distinct. Nicotinic receptors can be formed by different combinations of the alpha, beta, gamma, delta, and epsilon subunits, and their complexity is further increased by expression of multiple isoforms of some subunits. In general, nicotinic receptors mediate fast excitatory effects by forming ligand gated ion channels in the cell membrane. At neuromuscular synapses, the postsynaptic nicotinic receptors cause muscle contraction. In the autonomic nervous system, nicotinic receptors mediate many of the effects of the preganglionic axon terminals, and are also found at some postganglionic parasympathetic axon terminals along with muscarinic receptors. In the central nervous system, nicotinic receptors are also widely distributed.

Five types of muscarinic receptors, designated m1 through m5, have been identified by molecular biological techniques. Their pharmacology corresponds approximately to the pharmacologically characterized M1 to M4 muscarinic receptor types. Unlike the nicotinic receptors, muscarinic effects are slow and are mediated by G-protein–linked second messenger systems. The muscarinic receptors mediate many of the effects of ACh in the central nervous system, and at the terminals of the postganglionic autonomic neurons.

SUGGESTED READING

Everitt, B. J., & Robbins, T. W. (1997). Central cholinergic systems and cognition. *Annual Review of Psychology, 48,* 649–684.

Feldman, R. S., Meyer, J. S., & Quenzer, L. F. (1997). Acetylcholine. *Principles of neuropsychopharmacology* (pp. 235–276). Sunderland, MA: Sinauer.

Geula, C., & Mesulam, M.-M. (1994). Cholinergic systems and related neuropathological predilection patterns in Alzheimer disease. In R. D. Terry, R. Katzman, & K. L. Bick (Eds.), *Alzheimer disease* (pp. 263–291). New York: Raven.

Steriade, M., McCormick, D. A., & Sejnowski, T. J. (1993). Thalamocortical oscillations in the sleeping and aroused brains. *Science, 262,* 679–685.

J. F. SMILEY
Northwestern University Medical School

CENTRAL NERVOUS SYSTEM NEUROCHEMISTRY

ACTION POTENTIAL

The action potential is a self-propagating change in membrane voltage conducted sequentially along the axon of a neuron that transmits information from the neuron cell body or sensory ending to the axon terminal. The action potential is initiated either as the consequence of summation of local electronic potentials in the region where the axon arises from the neuron cell body (axon hillock), or as a result of a sufficiently large generator potential in the sensory ending. Once initiated, the action potential is conducted without change in magnitude along the axon until it invades the axon terminal and causes release of quanta of neurotransmitter molecules.

To understand the action potential it is necessary to understand the resting membrane potential. To record the resting membrane potential and the action potential one electrode is inserted into the cell while a second electrode remains outside the cell. The voltage potential between the two electrodes is amplified and measured. For most neurons the measured resting membrane potential is from -60 to -70 millivolts (mV); the inside of the cell is negative relative to the outside of the cell.

The resting membrane potential is determined by the relative distribution of positively or negatively charged ions near the extracellular and intracellular surfaces of the cell membrane. Positive sodium (Na^+) and potassium (K^+) ions and negative chloride (Cl^-) and organic (A^-) ions are important for both the resting membrane potential and the action potential. The positively charged ions are called *cations* and the negatively charged ions are called *anions.* The organic anions are mostly proteins and organic acids.

During the resting state Na^+ and Cl^- have higher extracellular than intracellular concentrations, and K^+ and A^- are more highly concentrated within the cell. The organic ions never leave the intracellular compartment, and in most neurons Cl^- is relatively free to pass through the membrane. Three factors contribute to determining the ionic distribution across the membrane. The first factor is the relative permeability of the membrane to each ion species. The second factor is the concentration gradient of each ion species. The third factor is the electromotive force created by the separation of charges across the semipermeable membrane.

Because the inside of the cell is negative relative to the outside, and there is a lower intracellular concentration of Na^+, the sodium cations would flood into the cell if the membrane were freely permeable to Na^+. At rest, however, the cell membrane is not freely permeable to Na^+. Permeability of a membrane to any given ion species is controlled by the number of membrane channels available for that particular species. Membrane channels are made of proteins that extend from the extracellular to the intracellular surface of the membrane (i.e., they are membrane-spanning). The membrane channels may be always open, or nongated, or open only under certain conditions. Channels that open or close depending on conditions are called gated channels. Whether gated channels are open or closed depends on the conformation of the proteins that form the walls of the channel. When the neuron membrane is at rest the gated channels for Na^+ are closed. The Na^+ that does enter flows through the nongated, nonspecific channels in the membrane, but is actively extruded from the cell by the sodium-potassium pump. This pump is made of carrier proteins and uses metabolic energy supplied by adenosine triphosphate (ATP). Na^+ and K^+ are linked in transmembrane transportation such that three Na^+ ions are transported out of the cell for every two K^+ ions that are transported into the cell. The Na^+–K^+ pump maintains the intracellular and extracellular concentrations of these ions, which is necessary for homeostatic osmotic equilibrium across the cell membrane as well as creation of the resting membrane potential.

During the resting state the membrane channels do not allow movement of Na^+ into the cell. However, some Na^+ does enter the cell through non-specific membrane channels. Na^+ does this because it has a higher concentration outside than inside and, therefore, flows down its concentration gradient. Additionally, the electromotive force created by the relative intracellular negativity propels Na^+ inward. The sodium-potassium ATP-coupled pump counteracts the influx of Na^+ ions in the resting state.

The membrane is also not fully permeable to K^+ in the resting state, but K^+ ions are, compared to Na^+ ions, freer to move through the cell membrane. That is, the neuron membrane is more permeable to K^+ than to Na^+. For this reason K^+ moves more readily down its concentration gradient than Na^+, and the resting membrane potential is, therefore, closer to the K^+ equilibrium potential than the Na^+ equilibrium potential.

To summarize, in the resting state the paucity of open membrane channels for Na^+ and K^+ and the Na^+–K^+ pump serve to maintain an excess of extracellular Na^+ and intracellular K^+. The magnitude of the resting membrane potential is the result of the degree of separation of these cations and the presence of the organic anions within the cell. Because the membrane is more permeable to K^+ than Na^+, the resting membrane potential more closely approximates the equilibrium potential for K^+ than for Na^+.

The Na^+ and K^+ channels are voltage-gated. This means that a change in voltage across the membrane changes the conformation of the channel protein to either open or close the channel. If the membrane depolarizes and the membrane potential becomes more positive, the Na^+ channels begin to open. On dendrites and cell bodies, channels are opened by neurotransmitters released at the synapse from other cells. The neurotransmitters bind to receptors on the target neuron and open chemically gated ion channels. If the neurotransmitter is excitatory the postsynaptic membrane is slightly depolarized in the area of the synapse. This depolarization is less than required for generation of an action potential. However, depolarizing excitatory postsynaptic potentials (EPSPs) sum at the axon hillock with hyperpolarizing inhibitory postsynaptic potentials (IPSPs). If the resulting change in membrane polarity at the hillock is a depolarization that exceeds about 10 mV an action potential is initiated.

Depolarization at the axon hillock causes voltage-gated Na^+ channels to open. The number of Na^+ channels opened by the depolarization is proportional to the amount of positive change in membrane potential until threshold for action potential initiation is exceeded, at which time essentially all of the Na^+ channels in the area of threshold depolarization open and Na^+ rushes into the axon. The membrane potential then moves rapidly (about 0.5 ms) toward Na^+ equilibrium potential until it becomes about +55 mV. This is the rising phase of the action potential; when it reaches its peak, Na^+ channels close and voltage-gated K^+ channels open. K^+ leaves the cell and, in combination with decreased Na^+ conductance, reverses the depolarization. The K^+ channels stay open long enough not only to return the membrane potential to its resting level, but to cause a brief (about 2 ms) overshoot hyperpolarization. During the early part of the hyperpolarizing phase of the action potential Na^+ channels can not reopen and another action potential can not be generated. This is known as the absolute refractory period. This prevents action potentials from summating. As the membrane continues to repolarize an action potential can be generated if a stronger than normal stimulus is applied to the axon. This is known as the relative refractory period. Within 2.5 ms after peak depolarization of the action potential, the resting Na^+–K^+ concentrations are restored and the system is ready for reactivation.

The action potential propagates because the ionic current flow at one point of the membrane causes changes in current flow in the adjacent membrane toward the axon terminal. The current flow changes the transmembrane voltage potential and opens Na^+ channels. The entire sequence just described is then repeated. In myelinated axons, the current flow occurs only at the nodes of Ranvier. In addition to lacking the electrical insulation provided by myelin, the nodes of Ranvier also have a far greater concentration of Na^+ channels than do the parts of the axon covered by myelin. The result of the presence of myelin is that the action potential jumps from one node to the next (saltatory conduction). This produces more rapid conduction of the action potential than is possible in nonmyelinated axons.

REFERENCES

Koester, J. (1991). Membrane potential. In E. R. Kandel, J. H. Schwartz, & T. M. Jessell (Eds.), *Principles of neural science* (3rd ed., pp. 81–94). New York: Elsevier.

Koester, J. (1991). Voltage-gated ion channels and the generation of the action potential. In E. R. Kandel, J. H. Schwartz, & T. M. Jessell (Eds.), *Principles of neural science* (3rd ed., pp. 104–118). New York: Elsevier.

Siegelbaum, S. S., & Koester, J. (1991). Ion channels. In E. R. Kandel, J. H. Schwartz, & T. M. Jessell (Eds.), *Principles of neural science* (3rd ed., pp. 66–79). New York: Elsevier.

Shepherd, G. M. (1994). The membrane potential, Ch. 5; The action potential, Ch. 6. *Neurobiology* (3rd ed., pp. 87–121). New York: Oxford.

Smock, T. K. (1999). Communication among neurons: The membrane potential, Ch. 3. *Physiological psychology: A neuroscience approach* (pp. 47–87). Upper Saddle River, NJ: Prentice Hall.

M. L. WOODRUFF
East Tennessee State University

CENTRAL NERVOUS SYSTEM
NEUROCHEMISTRY
PSYCHOPHYSIOLOGY
SODIUM-POTASSIUM PUMP

ADAPTATION

Like many other words in psychology, "adaptation" has multiple meanings. At the basis of all the meanings, however, is the concept carried by its Latin root, *adaptare,* to fit.

Among ethologists, who think that characteristic species-typical behaviors are distillations of evolutionary processes, each physical and behavioral characteristic of a species is the product of and contributes to its adaptive radiation, the multiplication of individuals that can survive in the changing environment, and the diversification of the species in a diverse environment. Such adaptation is genetically based and requires numerous generations to be accomplished.

In contrast to this genetic adaptation are phenotypic adaptations, often only seconds in duration, which occur within the life span of an individual. The results of these adaptations are not transmitted to the offspring, although the capacity for such adaptation is. Implicit in the concept is the alteration of an individual by the presence of a persistent, nontoxic or nontraumatic, nonfatiguing stimulus, or by the prolonged cessation and absence of a customary, persistent stimulus, as for example weightlessness. Further examples of such adaptation include the gradual diminution in the coldness of water after we immerse our hand in it; the reduction in loudness of a tone after a few seconds; and the return of sight (though colorless) after a period in a darkened room following exposure to bright lights, and the return of comfortable color vision after reexposure to a brightly lighted environment. The mechanisms involved in these examples are all different: stimulus (receptor) failure in the cold; activation of an acoustic reflex (plus receptor change); and bleaching and regeneration of photo-pigments plus neural change in the retina. In general, scientists tend to think of this kind of adaptation as occurring in or affecting the receptor, whereas the term for a similar phenomenon—"habituation"—is reserved for those situations in which more central events are at least involved if not prominent.

A so-called "General Adaptation Syndrome" was proposed by Selye (1950) as part of our typical response to dangerous environmental challenge. This syndrome is an extension of Cannon's Emergency Syndrome (1932/1960), the "flee, fright, or fight" syndrome, consisting of a rapid total body response to the challenge. This response is mediated by the sympathetic nervous system. Selye's General Adaptation Syndrome develops after prolonged exposure to environmental (e.g., cold), physiological (e.g., poison), or psychological (e.g., maternal separation) perturbation. The adrenal glands increase in size and they lose and regain lipids because of activation by anterior pituitary release of adrenocorticotropic hormone (ACTH). Corticosteroids are then released into the blood stream to prepare the body for physical emergencies. A stage of resistance develops if the first alarm reaction does not satisfactorily remove the threat. A consequence of the second stage is that the individual becomes susceptible to additional, unrelated stresses. If the danger is prolonged, the reactions progress to the stage of exhaustion and, perhaps, death. Many manifestations of the adaptation syndrome have been observed in lower animals, but they often are difficult to detect in humans. Other concepts (e.g., acclimatization) have been proposed to account for many of the data.

REFERENCES

Cannon, W. B. (1960) *The wisdom of the body.* New York: Norton. (Original work published 1932)

Selye, H. (1950). *Stress.* Montreal, Canada: Acta.

A. J. RIOPELLE
Louisiana State University

ACCOMMODATION
GENERAL ADAPTATION SYNDROME
HABITUATION

ADDICTION

"Addiction" is a term widely used to indicate any type of excessive repetitive involvement with an activity or substance, and is applied as readily to exercise, reading, and television viewing as to alcohol, cocaine, or heroin use. Such broad use of the term detracts from its technical value, and in this entry the term will be used to refer only to substance use. When considering problematic patterns of use,

two distinct patterns, abuse and dependence, are described (American Psychiatric Association, 1994). Substance abuse refers to life problems from substance use—use in situations in which it is physically dangerous, use interfering with occupational role or with family and other social relationships, or use resulting in legal difficulties. In contrast, substance dependence is more syndromal. Physiological components of dependence may include tolerance—the need for increasing amounts of the substance to attain the same behavioral and subjective effects, or withdrawal—a physical syndrome activated by cessation of use of the substance. Behavioral components include using larger amounts of the substance over longer periods of times than intended, spending excessive amounts of time obtaining, using, and recovering from use of the substance, or using instead of engaging in other recreational and social pursuits. Psychological components include continued use despite knowledge of medical or psychological conditions caused or worsened by substance use, and desire or actual attempts to cut down or stop using the substance. Use of a range of substances, including alcohol, other sedative/hypnotic/anxiolytic drugs, cocaine, other stimulants, heroin, cannabis, hallucinogens, inhalants, and nicotine, can lead to substance abuse or dependence. A withdrawal syndrome is associated only with alcohol, sedative/hypnotic/anxiolytic drugs, heroin, and nicotine.

EPIDEMIOLOGY

Use of alcohol is common; regular use or abuse of other drugs is less common (Grant & Dawson, 1999). At some time in their adult lives two-thirds of Americans have been regular drinkers (consumed at least 12 drinks in a year). In contrast, just under 16% of Americans are regular drug users (illicit use of a drug at least 12 times in a year) at some point in their lives. The lifetime prevalence of substance abuse and dependence varies by substance, with different prevalence rates for men and women. Alcohol abuse or dependence is most common, with a lifetime prevalence for men of 25.5% and for women of 11.4%. In contrast, 8.1% of men and 4.2% of women have had any form of drug abuse or dependence at some time in their lives. The most common drug of abuse/dependence is cannabis, followed by prescription drugs, cocaine, amphetamines, hallucinogens, opiates, and sedatives.

ETIOLOGY

The causes of addiction are complex and involve an interplay among three dimensions—the biological, the psychological, and the social. The relative importance of each dimension varies with the specific substance of abuse and with the individual user. Considerable research has attempted to identify the causes of dependence at the cellular or molecular level. A number of different neuronal changes have been suggested as causing alcohol dependence, including changes in neuronal membranes, changes in the excitability and function of nerve cells mediated through the calcium and GABA receptor/chloride channels, changes in the activity of excitatory neurotransmitter systems, and changes in second messenger systems (Moak & Anton, 1999). Research on opiate dependence has failed to find changes in opiate receptors associated with addiction. However, at the subcellular level, chronic exposure to opiates has been demonstrated to lead to long-term change changes in specific G protein subunits (Stine & Kosten, 1999).

Substance use disorders run in families, and research has attempted to distinguish genetic from familial aspects of etiology. Both twin and adoption studies suggest a heritable component to alcohol dependence. With other drugs, some studies are suggestive of genetic elements, such as evidence of common drug preferences in monozygotic twins, and increased risk for drug dependence in families (Hesselbrock, Hesselbrock, & Epstein, 1999). The relationship between family history and the development of alcohol or other substance dependence, however, is not absolute—the majority of offspring from families with alcohol abuse/dependence do not develop problems; and the majority of those with alcohol abuse/dependence do not have a clear family history (Fingarette, 1988).

Among those with familial alcohol or drug problems, the mechanisms by which inherited risk is expressed are not clear. The most common mechanism appears to be through specific temperament or personality—persons high in sensation-seeking, low in harm-avoidance, and low in reward-dependence. Consequently, those with inherited risk for alcohol or drug dependence are at greater risk for conduct disorder or antisocial personality.

Psychological research has demonstrated the importance of interactions between the individual and environment. Repeated exposure to drug-use situations can lead to conditioned physiological responses to the situations that are similar to physiological responses to the actual drug (Rohsenow et al., 1994). The development of strong positive expectancies about the effects of certain drugs can also contribute to continued use (Brown, Christiansen, & Goldman, 1987). Individuals may use substances to enhance positive moods as well as to cope with negative emotions, and those with other psychological problems are at particularly high risk for the development of substance-use disorders as well.

Alcohol and drug use occurs in a social context. Introduction to alcohol and drug use most commonly occurs with either peers or family members. Individuals who are at high risk for using drugs and for other problem behaviors often join with peers of similarly high risk level, and these peer groups then may influence those within the group to continue to use or experiment with other substances and other high risk behaviors.

PREVENTION

Prevention of addiction has taken many forms, including broad-brush prevention programs in schools; prevention targeted at specific populations, such as pregnant women; and environmentally focused interventions that change laws and policies, decrease access to the substance, and increase penalties. Individually and environmentally focused interventions have been successful in preventing or delaying the onset of use, decreasing use among those already using, and decreasing harmful consequences to the individual or to others.

TREATMENT

Treatment efforts include both psychological and pharmacological approaches. A number of psychological therapies are effective in

the treatment of substance abuse/dependence. Brief, motivationally focused interventions are effective for individuals with milder problems, and also may enhance treatment outcomes when combined with ongoing treatments (Bien, Miller, & Tonigan, 1993). Cognitive-behavioral therapies, including community reinforcement treatment, relapse prevention, social skills training, and behavioral couples therapy, have good support for their effectiveness in treating alcohol dependence (McCrady & Langenbucher, 1996). Community reinforcement combined with the use of vouchers (Higgins et al., 1994), and family therapy (Liddle, 1995) are effective in treating drug dependence. Outcomes for those who complete long-term treatment in therapeutic communities are good, but dropout rates are high (Simpson & Curry, 1997). Treatments to facilitate involvement with self-help groups such as Alcoholics Anonymous or Narcotics Anonymous also are effective (Project MATCH Research Group, 1997), and continued active participation in self-help groups is correlated with better outcomes.

Separate from medications for withdrawal, effective pharmacotherapies to treat substance use disorders are somewhat limited in number. Naltrexone, acamprosate, and disulfiram have evidence supporting their use in the treatment of alcohol dependence. Methadone, LAAM (1-α-acetylmethadol), and buprenorphine have strong evidence of effectiveness in the treatment of opioid dependence. Nicotine replacement products are effective in the initial phases of treatment for nicotine dependence, and bupropion appears to be effective for longer-term pharmacotherapy (Barber & O'Brien, 1999).

CONCLUSIONS

The term "addiction" is over-used, but is useful in referring to a range of substance use problems. Etiology of these problems is complex, with multiple biological, psychological, and social factors contributing. Prevention is possible, and a number of effective treatments are available.

REFERENCES

American Psychiatric Association (1994). *Diagnostic and statistical manual of mental disorders* (4th edition). Washington, DC: Author.

Barber, W. S., & O'Brien, C. P. (1999). Pharmacotherapies. In B. S. McCrady & E. E. Epstein (Eds.), *Addictions: A comprehensive guidebook* (pp. 347–369). New York: Oxford University Press.

Bien, T. H., Miller, W. R., & Tonigan, J. S. (1993). Brief interventions for alcohol problems. A review. *Addiction, 88,* 315–336.

Brown, S. A., Christiansen, B. A., & Goldman, M. S. (1987). The Alcohol Expectancy Questionnaire. An instrument for the assessment of adolescent and adult expectancies. *Journal of Studies on Alcohol, 48,* 483–491.

Fingarette, H. (1988). *The myth of heavy drinking as a disease.* Berkeley: University of California Press.

Grant, B. F., & Dawson, D. A. (1999). Alcohol and drug use, abuse, and dependence: Classification, prevalence, and comorbidity. In B. S. McCrady and E. E. Epstein (Eds.), *Addictions: A comprehensive guidebook* (pp. 9–29). New York: Oxford University Press.

Hesselbrock, M., Hesselbrock, V., & Epstein, E. (1999). Theories of etiology of alcohol and other drug use disorders. In B. S. McCrady & E. E. Epstein (Eds.), *Addictions: A comprehensive guidebook* (pp. 50–74). New York: Oxford University Press.

Higgins, S. T., Budney, A. J., Bickel, W. K., Foerg, F. E., Donham, R., & Badger, G. J. (1994). Incentives improve outcome in outpatient behavioral treatment of cocaine dependence *Archives of General Psychiatry, 51,* 568–576.

Liddle, H., & Dakof, G. A. (1995). Family-based treatment for adolescent drug use: State of the science [Monograph]. In E. Rahdert & D. Czechowicz (Eds.), *Adolescent drug abuse: Clinical assessment and therapeutic interventions* (pp. 218–254). Rockville, MD: National Institute on Drug Abuse Research.

McCrady, B. S., & Langenbucher, J. W. (1996). Alcoholism treatment and health care reform. *Archives of General Psychiatry, 53,* 737–746.

Moak, D., & Anton, R. (1999). Alcohol. In B. S. McCrady & E. E. Epstein (Eds.), *Addictions: A comprehensive guidebook* (pp. 75–94). New York: Oxford University Press.

Project MATCH Research Group (1997). Matching alcoholism treatments to client heterogeneity: Project MATCH posttreatment drinking outcomes. *Journal of Studies on Alcohol, 58,* 7–29.

Rohsenow, D. J., Monti, P. M., Rubonis, A. V., Sirota, A. D., Niaura, R. S., Colby, S. M., Wunschel, S. M., & Abrams, D. B. (1994). Cue reactivity as a predictor of drinking among male alcoholics. *Journal of Consulting and Clinical Psychology, 62,* 620–626.

Simpson, D. D., & Curry, S. J. (Eds.). (1997). Drug abuse treatment outcome study [Special issue]. *Psychology of Addictive Behaviors, 11*(4), 211–337.

Stine, S. M., & Kosten, T. R. (1999). Opioids. In B. S. McCrady & E. E. Epstein (Eds.), *Addictions: A comprehensive guidebook* (pp. 141–161). New York: Oxford University Press.

B. S. McCRADY
Rutgers—The State University of New Jersey

DRUG REHABILITATION
SUBSTANCE ABUSE
ALCOHOLISM TREATMENT

ADLER, ALFRED (1870–1937)

Alfred Adler founded the school of Individual Psychology, a theory of personality and psychopathology, and a method of psychotherapy. Based on the concepts of the unity, goal striving, and active participation of the individual, it is a humanistic value psychology rather than a mechanistic drive psychology. It stresses cognitive rather than unconscious processes. Adler accepted being called "father of the inferiority complex."

Adler graduated from the Vienna medical school in 1895 and became a general practitioner. He soon wrote some articles on public health issues, in line with his early interest in the social democratic movement. In 1902 he was invited by Freud with three others for weekly discussions of problems of neurosis. From these meetings the Vienna Psychoanalytic Society developed, of which Adler became president in 1910.

In 1911 Adler resigned from the society to form the Society for Free Psychoanalytic Research, soon afterward renamed the Society of Individual Psychology. He objected primarily to what became known as Freud's metapsychology, then essentially limited to the mechanistic concepts of libido and repression. Adler sought a conception of neurosis "only in psychological terms, or terms of cultural psychology." In this quest he had published in 1907 his *Study of Organ Inferiority and Its Psychical Compensation,* broadening the biological foundation from sex to the entire organism; in 1908 a paper on the aggression drive, a drive to prevail, replacing sex as the primary drive; and in 1910 a paper on inferiority feeling and masculine protest as overcompensation, replacing the concept of drive altogether with one of value. Masculine protest in its original sense was shortly afterward replaced by striving for power, for superiority. Adler saw the individual in its unity and goal orientation operating as if according to a self-created life plan, later called lifestyle. Drives, feelings, emotions, memory, the unconscious, all processes are subordinated to the life style.

In 1912 Adler presented his new psychology in *The Neurotic Constitution.* It contained most of his main concepts, except that of social interest. He introduced this last concept in 1918. It became, with striving for overcoming and inferiority feelings, Adler's most important concept—the criterion for mental health. In cases of psychopathology, which Adler called failures in life, the aptitude for social interest has not been adequately developed. Such persons are striving on the socially useless side for personal power over others, as against the healthy, socially useful striving for overcoming general difficulties. The psychotherapist raises the patient's self-esteem through encouragement, demonstrates the patient's mistakes to the patient, and strengthens his or her social interest. The therapist works for a cognitive reorganization and more socially useful behavior. Particularly, early recollections and birth-order position, but also dreams, are used to give the patient an understanding of his life style.

During the 1920s Adler became largely interested in prevention. This included child-guidance training of teachers at the Vienna Pedagogical Institute, where Adler had his first academic appointment; the establishment of numerous child-guidance centers in public schools; and adult education courses that resulted in his popular book, *Understanding Human Nature.*

From 1926 on Adler visited the United States regularly, lecturing to a wide range of audiences. He was a successful speaker, attracting up to 2,000 listeners. In 1932 he became professor of medical psychology at Long Island Medical College. In 1934 he settled permanently in New York City.

In 1897 he had married Raissa Timofejevna Epstein, a radical student from a highly privileged Jewish family in Moscow, who later worked at times with her husband. They had four children, three girls and a boy, of whom the second child, Alexandra, and the third, Kurt, became Adlerian psychiatrists. Alfred Adler died of a heart attack on May 28, 1937, in Aberdeen, Scotland.

Regarding Adler's work there is a paradox: His concepts have been generally validated and have entered most personality theories, including psychoanalysis in particular, yet this has remained largely unrecognized. However, the Adlerian tradition is being continued by the North American Society of Adlerian Psychology, which publishes both a newsletter and the quarterly *Individual Psychology*, holds regular meetings, and sponsors workshops. There are Adlerian training institutes as well as scores of local organizations, family education centers, and study groups, for which the groundwork was done largely by Rudolf Dreikurs (1897–1972). Abroad, Adlerian societies exist in numerous countries, the largest being in West Germany, which publishes the quarterly *Zeitschrift für Individualpsychologie*. An International Association of Individual Psychology holds congresses every 3 years. Affiliated with it is the International Committee for Adlerian Summer Schools and Institutes, which conducts a yearly 2-week institute in various countries.

H. L. ANSBACHER

ADLERIAN PSYCHOTHERAPY

Adlerian psychotherapy was originally developed by Alfred Adler (1912, 1917, 1927, 1933, 1939) while a member of Sigmund Freud's group. After their separation in 1911, Adler rapidly expanded the outline of his theory and continued to elaborate it until his death in 1937. Since then, his followers have further developed the theory and procedures.

Adler's theory shared some of psychoanalysis's tenets: psychic determinism, the purposive nature of behavior, the existence of many motives outside conscious awareness, and the notions that dreams could be understood as a mental product, and that insight into one's own unconscious motives and assumptions had curative power. Adler, however, rejected the energy model of libido and replaced it with a future-oriented model of striving toward a subjectively determined position of significance, which was much more teleological. He rejected the tripartite structure of personality (id–ego–superego), replacing it with a holistic personality-as-unity model. This resulted in much more emphasis on what psychoanalysis called ego functions and far less emphasis on id drives. Adler's human was an active striver trying to cope with the tasks of life but hampered by mistaken apperceptions and faulty values.

Adlerian psychotherapy uses a flexible approach. Thus what the Adlerian therapist does may at times resemble psychoanalysis, existential analysis, Sullivan's interpersonal analysis, Rogers' client-centered approach, Berne's transactional analysis, the rational-emotive approach of Ellis, the cognitive therapy of Kelly or Beck, or even the social learning approach of Rotter and Bandura.

THE MODEL OF MAN

Adlerians visualize the organism as an open system striving for fulfillment and completeness with continuous development. The manner of striving is determined by the interaction between innate programs and early life experiences. Feedback from early life experiences leads to various perceptual discriminations that become an organized perceptual system with core constructs guiding further perceptual processing of incoming information. The perceptual system, a subsystem of the organism, has the task of organizing stimuli into a meaningful Gestalt in order to facilitate organismic striving. This subsystem functions as a creative self, a self-directing principle which creates a set of subjective assumptions that begin as a rule of thumb for coping with the world and grow into a set of rules for perceiving and acting in the world. These rules are consistent over time and become more fixed and generally function outside conscious awareness. Adler called these rules the lifestyle—the overall master program the perceptual system has created. The presence of a master plan makes the personality a unity. The elucidation of the lifestyle becomes an important part of psychotherapy.

While some maladaptive behavior may be a consequence of stress, far more important are those maladaptations which result from faults in the master plan—faulty strivings based upon faulty learning, inappropriate imitation of models, unfortunate reinforcements by significant others, and mistaken values. When the person has given the wrong meaning to life he finds coping more difficult, goal attainment out of reach, life situations more stressful, and self-satisfaction more elusive. The person with a skewed lifestyle is more vulnerable to insecurity, disturbed human relations, pessimistic discouragement, feelings of inferiority (low self-esteem), and fear of facing the tasks of life.

The right meaning of life, according to Adler, is the recognition that humans need each other, must respect each other and learn to bond and cooperate in common tasks, rather than engage in destructive competition or narcissistic vanities. Appropriate values, appropriate aspirations, open-mindedness toward life, self-understanding, reasonable interpersonal skills, and *Gemeinschaftsgefühl* (social interest) all help to give the right meaning to life.

THE THEORY OF THERAPY

In spite of its flexible approach, Adlerian therapy is as systematic as psychoanalysis. The therapist has specific goals and specific diagnostic methods for understanding the patient. The goals of the therapist are to reveal the person to himself or herself and to encourage the person to make useful changes in coping with life. To do this, the therapist has four tasks: (a) to establish a therapeutic relationship, (b) to understand the person's assumptive universe, (c) to reveal these assumptions to the person in such a way that (d) they become subject to self-correction and facilitate change.

Psychotherapy takes place as a dialogue. The therapist is both spectator and participant, engaging with the person and constantly assessing the latter's movements or coping strategies. Into the dialogue, the person brings current concerns as well as the long-range goals of his or her lifestyle. Thus the appropriate personality material is always more or less available for the therapist to see. The therapist is not neutral, but displays active concern and uses dialogue, clarification, and interpretation in a systematic way. Dreikurs' *Psychodynamics, Psychotherapy and Counseling* (1967) describes some of the assumptions the Adlerian therapist uses: (a) Everyone can change; (b) one never knows oneself, therefore psychotherapy is a process of learning about oneself; (c) the main relationship task of the therapist is to preserve cooperation; (d) the most effective interpretations are those revealing the purpose of symptoms and other behavior; (e) the statements of the therapist should convey a sense of worth and faith in the person's inner strength; (f) the therapist should promote the person's feeling of belonging; (g) much of psychotherapy is a correction of faulty social values; and (h) by his or her own behavior, the therapist offers a model for good human behavior and effective coping strategies.

THE PRACTICE OF THERAPY

Assessment

Because the goal of therapy includes changing crucial mistakes in the person's assumptive universe, most Adlerians try to understand this aspect of the person at or near the beginning of the therapeutic relationship. This can be done in a systematized set of formal interviews, if the person is capable of and ready for such cooperation, or it can be done in a more casual way with the less ready person, to allow the relationship to grow while relief is provided for immediate distress, symptoms, and life situation stresses. The two main areas of investigation that lead to an understanding of these basic assumptions (the lifestyle) are the family constellation and early childhood recollections. The investigation requires that the person have reached that point in relating to the therapist where he or she willingly talks about early family life.

In line with his holistic view of the mental life, Adler considered memories of early life to be retrospectively constructed under the influence of the lifestyle. The purpose of memory is to aid adaptation to the tasks of life. Therefore examination of the childhood situation reveals how the person reconstructed the past to be an aid in the present. The story of the patient's childhood provides the keys to understanding the lifestyle. The family constellation is the story of early experiences with parents and siblings, and shows the adaptive movements the person made in responding to the challenges of these early interpersonal relationships. In effect, it shows how the person found a niche in the family ecological system: who the models were, which behaviors were reinforced by the environment, and the directions in which the person as child began to train for future adaptive movements. Early difficulties, loss of or rejection by a parent, areas of successful striving, and areas of life in which the person met early discouragement, all shed light on future adaptive behavior.

The earliest childhood recollections are of special significance, since they constitute a projective technique for direct assessment of the meaning that the person has given to life. They reveal the child's interpretation and response to the early challenges of life, its ability or lack of it to overcome difficulties, and the master plan for coping with the contingencies of existence.

From this material the therapist tries to understand the person's master plan and specifically to recognize where this plan leads to maladaptive behaviors. If the therapist has understood well, he or she can relate the person's present difficulties to these errors of perception—the mistaken conclusions about life as portrayed in the lifestyle. In essence, the therapist should now know the personality factors that contribute to the current difficulty. Having understood

these factors and their effects, the therapist is ready to impart understanding to the person. Assessment, however, remains a continuing process all through therapy, both in continually refining the therapist's understanding, and in continually applying the understanding to the patient's behavior in life and productions in therapy.

This continuous assessment requires the therapist to be sensitive to all the patient's behavior, both verbal and nonverbal. Adler specifically recommended that the therapist learn to use empathy and intuition in order to become an expert guesser—to try to see events from the person's point of view, and look for future evidence to test the accuracy of his or her own assumptions about the person. The technique of guessing consists of finding parts that fit together into a comprehensible whole that reveals the person as engaging in consistent movement toward a subjective chosen goal of significance. In this sense, Adlerians are holistic and teleological. All behavior, even symptoms, is considered adaptive in intent.

Adler's term for nonconsensual assumptions is "private logic." These assumptions are usually outside immediate awareness. What one experiences consciously is ideas, emotions, interests, urges, and impulses which one explains by various rationalizations, or denies or ignores. What the therapist sees are hidden motives, safeguarding tendencies, and movements to preserve the more or less fictional values of the lifestyle.

Promoting Insight

The person is largely unaware of his or her private logic, of the master plan and many underlying motives for thoughts, feelings, and actions. While it is possible for personality change to take place without insight into one's own dynamics, insight is usually a requirement for change, and interpretation is the chief tool for promoting insight. The therapist operates from the assumption that the patient does not know what is wrong; it is the therapist's job to reveal it. Adlerians interpret very specific items: the hidden motives behind behavior, the direction of movement, and the self-defeating and unrealistic assumptions.

Hidden Motives

Motives are interpreted in terms of purpose. The purpose of a symptom may be to safeguard against a defeat of one's plans, to neutralize expected antagonism from another, to gain a spurious victory, or otherwise to safeguard self-esteem. The purpose of an intense emotion is to facilitate an action, sometimes against one's better judgment.

Direction of Movement

The underlying movements are either advances toward appropriate solutions to the challenges of life, retreats from these tasks, or attempts to detour around them. Thus the symptom of depression can be understood as a backward movement, mania as an impulsive plunge forward. Compulsions are sidetracking movements; fearfulness and indecision are hesitating movements.

Self-Defeating and Unrealistic Assumptions

The basic mistakes found in the lifestyle can all be understood as mistakes in common-sense thinking. These include misfocusing, closed-mindedness, constricted categories of thought, overabstract rather than denotative thinking, reification of idiosyncratic ideas, failure to validate premises, excessively high expectations or aspirations, and inaccurate characterization of events, all the result of failure to make appropriate perceptual discriminations.

Technique of Interpretation

Insight, while not always leading to change, provides information about what ought to be changed. Some interpretations are readily accepted by the person because they provide a welcome clarification of what has been happening to him or her and a gratifying self-understanding. Other interpretations are resisted because they confront the person with aspects of the self which threaten self-esteem or the sense of self-control. Adlerians often couch interpretations in tentative language such as "Perhaps . . ." or "Could it be that . . . ?" and so allow the person to disagree. Where appropriate, dramatic illustrations, metaphors, or aphorisms may be used to help the person toward self-discovery.

Real insight arouses affect. Recognizing one's real intentions often makes it impossible for the person to continue to feel like a victim or to demand special privilege. Recognizing one's own mistaken assumptions helps the person to stop misconstruing life and devise more effective coping strategies.

Relationship

Therapy is a dialogue that requires cooperation. The first task of the therapist is to win the patient to a meaningful cooperation. Using the patient's own desire to be helped, the therapist behaves like an interested friend who shows that he or she understands the patient and accepts the patient as worthwhile. The therapist does this by making no pejorative judgments concerning the patient's behavior, by making remarks which show understanding and respect for the patient's feelings, and by finding something positive in the patient on which to comment. By sympathetic attitude and carefully constructed questions, the therapist inquires further and further into the patient's life, thoughts, feelings, dreams, fantasies, and problems. The good relationship is one of open discussion, with the patient being attentive to interpretations and open to self-examination.

Transference

The therapist will expect that, when therapy goes well, the patient will have fond feelings for him or her. These fond feelings are treated as the natural tendency for human beings to bond to each other when cooperating in a common task. In addition, however, the patient will bring into the therapy situation his or her characteristic ways of coping with tasks and relationships, as well as distorted assumptions and unconscious expectations. These are treated as lifestyle phenomena and are interpreted as such, especially where they interfere with learning new, improved adaptive behavior. Although a full-blown transference neurosis may occur, it is not encouraged and seldom considered necessary for successful therapy. While the transference neurosis may provide opportunity for additional self-learning, the Adlerian considers it an artificial product of therapy itself, and a private agreement between patient and therapist for the patient to behave in an infantile way.

To deliberately encourage it would in most cases make therapy unnecessarily long.

Resistance

There are many reasons for the phenomenon of resistance; of these, four are major. A common cause of resistance is failure of the therapist and patient to share common goals. If the patient is not in the market to buy what the therapist has for sale, no sale will take place. A second reason for resistance is the patient's use of the *depreciation tendency* (devaluing what others have to offer) as a major safeguarding tendency to preserve his or her positive self-esteem. A third cause is the natural resistance of the patient to any intervention which threatens to invalidate his or her constructs, and a fourth, the ingrained perceptual set of some people which rigidly resists discrepant information (cf. Kelly's "impermeable constructs"). Handling resistance requires continued sensitivity by the therapist to the current frame of mind of the patient, and the ability to track the patient's movement back and forth between openness and defensiveness.

Facilitating Change

Change is made possible by the creative power of the patient to reconstruct his or her own perceptual system through increased understanding. The desired direction of change is toward increased awareness of unconscious motives and self-defeating behaviors; increased sense of personal competence; increased ability to understand others and relate to them effectively; realistic self-identification and self-acceptance; replacement of inappropriate self-aggrandizing values with prosocial values (social interest); recognizing one's real needs in place of the fantasied goals of personal superiority; and active courageous engagement with the tasks of life.

The insight into the mistaken assumptive universe and its consequences is only the first step toward change. Overcoming the reluctance to confront life directly is just as important. Active engagement includes the willingness to try alternative behaviors, to give up special safeguards and special demands for entitlement, and the willingness to accept setbacks in the process of learning new coping strategies. The therapist acts as guide, counselor, supporter, and encourager of these new behaviors. Some of these straightforward behaviors are modeled by the therapist. The therapist's unqualified support of courageous movement provides the patient with some security even in the face of difficulties (the therapist shows faith in the patient). In addition, the therapist judiciously suggests tasks which will provide an experience of success and warns against tasks for which the patient does not seem ready.

THERAPEUTIC PROCESS

So long as new learning continues and behavior change ensues, the therapist is satisfied to continue the same way. As different problems come into focus, the understanding of the lifestyle is applied again to their resolution. Dreams are important signals of pending movements and often foreshadow the emergence into awareness of new insights or new difficulties. The increase or diminution of symptomatic complaints shows the back-and-forth movements of the patient in therapeutic progress. Plateaus are respites between tasks. New behavior takes a certain amount of time to learn. As the patient proceeds, he or she eventually learns to understand symptoms, emotions, behavior, and dreams and so becomes much more knowledgeable about himself or herself. At these times, intervals between therapy sessions become longer and eventually the patient is ready to terminate.

Termination does not mean the end of personal growth. In therapy the patient has learned a method for self-understanding and continues to use this method. Years after therapy has ended the patient may continue to discover new insights and continue the process of personal growth. By the same token, therapy never has an absolute end. The patient may return to the therapist in the future to cope better with a life stress or to take up some previously unfinished business.

THERAPEUTIC MODALITIES

The flexibility of Adlerian psychotherapy allows for many combinations of techniques. Group psychotherapy is considered a very useful tool and is often combined with individual therapy. Family therapy and psychodrama have been extensively used by Adlerians, as have special interest groups such as groups of adolescents, groups of parents coping with the problems of raising children, and groups of teachers trying to cope with children. Many of these groups are more educational than therapeutic in intent and are an attempt to apply Adlerian insights to everyday living problems.

Adlerian therapists work in all settings including schools, drug and alcohol programs, and correctional institutions. Adlerian techniques of child rearing and child education have become especially widespread, and Adlerian insights have been used in personnel counseling, management programs, and resolution of disputes between conflicting groups.

REFERENCES

Adler, A. (1917). *Study of organ inferiority and its psychical compensation.* New York: Nervous and Mental Diseases.

Adler, A. (1939). *Social interest: A challenge to mankind.* New York: Putnam.

Dreikurs, R. (1967). *Psychodynamics, psychotherapy, and counseling: Collected papers.* Chicago: Alfred Adler Institute.

SUGGESTED READING

Ansbacher, H. L., & Ansbacher, R. R. (Eds.). *The individual psychology of Alfred Adler.*

Dinkmeyer, D. C., Pew, W. L., & Dinkmeyer, D. C., Jr. (1979). *Adlerian counseling and psychotherapy.* Monterey, CA: Brooks/Cole.

B. H. SHULMAN
Northwestern University

PSYCHOANALYSIS
PSYCHOTHERAPY

ADOLESCENT DEVELOPMENT

Adolescence spans the second decade of life, a phase described as beginning in biology and ending in society (Petersen, 1988). Adolescence may be defined as the life span period in which most of a person's biological, cognitive, psychological, and social characteristics are changing in an interrelated manner from what is considered childlike to what is considered adult-like. When most of one's characteristics are in this state of change one is an adolescent.

Adolescence requires adjustments to changes in the self, family, and peer group, and often to institutional changes as well. Not all young people undergo these transitions in the same way, with the same speed, or with comparable outcomes. Individual differences are thus a key part of adolescent development, and are caused by differences in the timing of connections among biological, psychological, and societal factors—with no one of these influences (e.g., biology) acting either alone or as the "prime mover" of change (Petersen, 1988; Lerner & Galambos, 1998). In other words, a major source of diversity in developmental trajectories are the systematic relations that adolescents have with key people and institutions in their social context; that is, their family, peer group, school, workplace, neighborhood, community, society, culture, and niche in history (Lerner, 1995). These person-context relations result in multiple pathways through adolescence (e.g., Offer, 1969).

In short, inter-individual differences and intra-individual changes in development typify this period of life. Both dimensions of diversity must be considered in relation to the general changes of adolescence. The following examples of such general changes illustrate the nature and importance of diversity in adolescence.

MULTIPLE LEVELS OF CONTEXT ARE INFLUENTIAL DURING ADOLESCENCE

Adolescence is a period of extremely rapid transitions in physical characteristics. Indeed, except for infancy, no other period of the life cycle involves such rapid changes. While hormonal changes are part of the development of early adolescence (Petersen, 1988), they are not primarily responsible for the psychological or social developments during this period. Instead, the quality and timing of hormonal or other biological changes influence, and are influenced by, psychological, social, cultural, and historical factors (Lerner & Galambos, 1998, Stattin & Magnusson, 1990).

Good examples of the integrated, multilevel changes in adolescence arise in the area of cognitive development during this period (Graber & Petersen, 1991). Global and pervasive effects of puberty on cognitive development do not seem to exist. When biological effects are found they interact with contextual and experiential factors (e.g., the transition to junior high school) to influence academic achievement (Simmons & Blyth, 1987). Perspectives on adolescence that claim that behavioral disruptions or disturbances are a universal part of this period of life (e.g., Hall, 1904) might lead to the assumption that there are general cognitive disruptions inherent in adolescence. However, evidence does not support this assumption. Rather, cognitive abilities are enhanced in early adolescence as individuals become faster and more efficient at processing information—at least in settings in which they feel comfortable in performing cognitive tasks (Ceci & Bronfenbrenner, 1985). In turn, pubertal timing is not predictive of gender differences on such tasks as spatial cognition. Girls' earlier maturation does not result in general sex differences in cognition (Graber & Petersen, 1991).

Thus, relations among biology, problem behaviors associated with personality, and the social context of youth illustrate the multiple levels of human life that are integrated throughout adolescent development. For example, the biological changes of early pubertal maturation have been linked to delinquency in adolescent girls, but only among girls who attend mixed-sex schools (Caspi, Lynam, Moffitt, & Silva, 1993) or among those who socialize with older friends instead of same-age friends (Stattin & Magnusson, 1990). Early maturation among girls in single-sex schools or in sex-age peer groups was not linked with higher delinquency.

CHANGING RELATIONS BETWEEN ADOLESCENTS AND THEIR CONTEXTS PRODUCE DEVELOPMENT IN ADOLESCENCE

The period of adolescence is one of continual change and transition between individuals and their contexts. These varying relations constitute the basic process of development in adolescence and underlie both positive and negative outcomes that occur (Lerner & Galambos, 1998). When biological, psychological, cognitive, and social changes of adolescence occur simultaneously (e.g., when menarche occurs at the same time as a school transition), the risk of problems occurring in a youth's development is greater (Simmons & Blyth, 1987).

However, most developmental trajectories across adolescence involve positive adjustment on the part of the adolescent. For instance, for most youth there is a continuation of warm and accepting relations with parents (Grotevant, 1998). Accordingly, when major conflicts occur often in a family, parents should be concerned. The most optimal adjustment occurs among youth who are encouraged by their parents to engage in age-appropriate autonomy while maintaining strong ties to their family (Galambos & Ehrenberg, 1997).

CONCLUSIONS

The theoretically interesting and socially important changes of adolescence constitute one reason why this age period has attracted increasing scientific attention (e.g., Petersen, 1988; Lerner & Galambos, 1998). To advance basic knowledge and the quality of the applications aimed at enhancing youth development, scholarship should be directed increasingly to elucidating the developmental course of diverse adolescents.

In turn, policies and programs related to interventions must be tailored to the specific target population, and in particular, to a group's specific developmental and environmental circumstances (Lerner & Galambos, 1998). Because adolescents are so different from each other, one cannot expect any single policy or intervention to reach *all* of a given target population or to influence everyone in the same way.

Therefore, the stereotype that there is a single pathway through the adolescent years—for instance, one characterized by inevitable "storm and stress" (Hall, 1904)—cannot be expected to stand up in the face of current knowledge about diversity in adolescence. In future research and applications pertinent to adolescence, scholars and practitioners must extend their conception of this period to focus on changing relations between the individual characteristics of a youth and his or her complex and distinct ecology.

REFERENCES

Caspi, A., Lynam, D., Moffitt, T. E., & Silva, P. A. (1993). Unraveling girls' delinquency: Biological, dispositional, and contextual contributions to adolescent misbehavior. *Developmental Psychology, 29,* 19–30.

Ceci, S. J., & Bronfenbrenner, U. (1985). Don't forget to take the cupcakes out of the oven. *Child Development, 56,* 152–164.

Galambos, N. L., & Ehrenberg, M. F. (1997). The family as health risk and opportunity: A focus on divorce and working families. In J. Schulenberg, J. L. Maggs, & K. Hurrelmann (Eds.), *Health risks and developmental transitions during adolescence* (pp. 139–160). Cambridge: Cambridge University Press.

Graber, J. A., & Petersen, A. C. (1991). Cognitive changes at adolescence: Biological perspectives. In K. R. Gibson & A. C. Petersen (Eds.), *Brain maturation and cognitive development. Comparative and cross-cultural perspectives* (pp. 253–279). New York: Aldine de Gruyter.

Grotevant, H. D. (1998). Adolescent development in family contexts. In N. Eisenberg (Ed.), *Handbook of Child Psychology: Vol. 3* (pp. 1097–1149) W. Damon, Editor-in-chief. New York: Wiley.

Hall, G. S. (1904). *Adolescence: Its psychology and its relations to psychology, anthropology, sociology, sex, crime, religion, and education.* New York: Appleton.

Lerner, R. M., & Galambos, N. L. (1998). Adolescent development: Challenges and opportunities for research, programs, and policies. In J. T. Spence (Ed.), *Annual review of psychology* (Vol. 49, pp 413–446). Palo Alto, CA: Annual Reviews.

Offer, D. (1969). *The psychological world of the teen-ager.* New York: Basic Books.

Petersen, A. C. (1988). Adolescent development. In M. R. Rosenzweig (Ed.), *Annual review of psychology* (Vol. 39, pp. 583–607). Palo Alto, CA. Annual Reviews.

Simmons, R. G., & Blyth, D. A. (1987). *Moving into adolescence: The impact of pubertal change and school context.* Hawthorne, NJ: Aldine.

Stattin, H., & Magnusson, D. (1990). *Pubertal maturation in female development.* Hillsdale, NJ: Erlbaum.

R. M. LERNER, A. BILALBEGOVIC, & D. SADOWSKI
Tufts University

ADOLESCENT DEVELOPMENT
HUMAN DEVELOPMENT
IDENTITY FORMATION
MORAL DEVELOPMENT

ADOPTED CHILDREN

INTRA- AND EXTRAFAMILIAL ADOPTION

A distinction is made between intrafamilially and extrafamilially adopted children. In intrafamilial or kinship adoption, children are adopted either by blood relatives or by family members by marriage, frequently a stepparent of the adopted child. In such cases a genuine desire to adopt is less likely to be the primary motivating force than in extrafamilial adoption, except when childless family members wish to build their own nuclear family. The classical intrafamilial adoption occurs as a consequence of a perceived duty to adopt a child or children left unprotected by their biological parent/s due to adverse circumstances. Members of the extended family may be motivated by love for the child they already know, a sense of family obligation, pity, or to prevent the return of custodial rights to parents who have abandoned or otherwise endangered the child. One benefit of intrafamilial adoption is that a child grows up within a familial environment, where family history is available. If good family relationships prevail, the transition to and integration into the new family are less traumatic than in adoption by strangers. However, intrafamilial adoptees are not always genuinely welcome. Not having freely chosen to add a new member to the family, a family can turn on an adoptee as an intruder. The extra knowledge from family history can be used as a tool for psychological abuse. Among the most welcome intrafamilial adoptees are children freely sought and wanted, preferably as infants, by child-loving relatives, such as a childless couple. These children generally fare well, especially in regard to parental attention and education. They are most likely given up because of poverty of single parenthood. Intrafamilial ties, albeit altered, are usually maintained, classifying it as "open adoption." The Adoption Assistance and Child Welfare Act (1980) brought about an increase in kinship adoptions (Phillips, 1999).

The majority of adoptions are extrafamilial ones. Adoption motivation can be varied. Infertile couples may wish to create a family, while other couples seek out children of a specific gender to balance a single-gender sibling constellation, or to prevent a stranger from having an abortion. Foster children may already have become de facto family members which de jure still has to get confirmed. Altruism plays a role in many adoptions, as parents are moved by a child's need for a permanent family. However, adoptions are also pursued for other reasons. Despite scrutiny by authorities, selfish purposes normally surface only after the fact, when evidence emerges that a child was adopted to provide cheap labor, fill the role of baby sitter for younger siblings, or, in the worst-case scenario, to be used as a sex object. Sometimes people are touched by television reports portraying severely neglected children, for example orphans in Romania and Russia, or by political and religious leaders who promote adoptions. A pastor inspired the 200 residents of a small Texas town to adopt 40 children (ABC News, 1999). Governmental adoption appeals combined with a tax incentive (higher for children with special needs) have increased the number of annual adoptions in the U.S. The 1996 presidential Memorandum on adoption and alternate permanent placement for waiting children in the public child welfare system revealed that there were 450,000 children in the national foster care system of which 100,000 were adoptable or in need of a permanent home under an enduring guardianship. Waiting time for a permanent placement was "typically over 3 years" or "much longer." 1998 presidential remarks during National Adoption Month referred to 100,000 children "still waiting for permanent adoptive homes."

Adoption following the (re)marriage of a child's parent will provide, at least formally, equal status to children coming from two single-parent households when forming one new family. However, psychodynamically, the situation of the child adopted by a stepparent is often more comparable to that of a regular stepchild, especially when the adoptee resents the family merger, or the adopting stepparent fears serious financial consequences as a result of the adoption. Not all stepchildren welcome being adopted. Older children should not be adopted without their consent. However, giving stepchildren a choice to be adopted can also put a burden on them if they are ambivalent about it. In order to become fully integrated into the new family legally, the child is forced to renounce the biological parent, at least symbolically, as demonstrated by the name change. If the child is firmly attached to this parent who was removed by, for example, divorce or death, the child may face a serious loyalty conflict. Declining the adoption offer made by the stepparent may have negative consequences if it is taken as a rejection. Siblings split over differing decisions regarding adoption can strain sibling relationships at a time when their bond seems to be the safest and most enduring family bond. This is particularly crucial when the biological parent's interest in remarriage was experienced as shifting attention from the children to the new spouse. Stepparents are likely motivated to adopt by the goal of balancing status discrepancies among stepsiblings in order to meld the family factions into one single family unit. In view of the different psychological issues facing the intrafamilial, extrafamilial, and stepparent adoptee, statistics and research should clearly distinguish between adoption positions.

In the United States adopting special needs children was, in the 1990s, rewarded with a special tax break for the year of the adoption. However, many parents are unable to sense what is involved in including a special needs child as a family member. Ideally, parents willing to adopt a child with special needs should first take care of the child as foster parents, in order to find out how well they can endure the stress created by either the child's own distress, which they may not be able to alleviate, or by their own inability to cope with the disruption the child's problems cause the family.

According to Lang (1997), 25% of domestic adopted children in the U.S. are special needs children. Special needs may be related to physical or emotional/behavioral/delinquency problems. The fact that many adoptees with medical problems fare better than adoptees with psychological problems may be related to the fact that parents' expectations with regard to children's medical needs match reality outcomes more closely than parental expectations of how a child's emotional problems will affect the family and themselves as caregivers. Among children with special needs are those with histories of various types of mental illness, emotional disorders, and acting-out behaviors, such as fire setting. One issue parents may not be aware of is that many of the special needs children may already have been through various placement attempts and may therefore be discouraged by 10 to 20% failed attempts to bond with caregivers who ultimately rejected them (Lang, 1997). They may be unable to muster any positive feelings, but will watch developments with a sense of detachment. One major problem is that parents have great difficulty finding substitutes, much less a placement, for special needs children during vacation periods, leaving parents on duty without a break. Family break-ups have been reported due to the relentless stress created by special needs children, which can seriously affect the relationship between spouses as well as with biological children (e.g., resentment of parental attention, embarrassment about an adoptee's appearance). Successful outcomes are related to parent/family qualities including flexible expectations, coping and listening skills, resourcefulness, rejection tolerance, sense of humor, generous forgiving, applause readiness, patience, and love (Lang, 1997).

TELLING CHILDREN ABOUT ADOPTION: HOW AND WHEN
Informing children about their adoption status is of major importance (Wrobel et al., 1998), especially if they were adopted as infants or young children. There are many ways of sharing the adoption issue with children, including by drawing a picture book telling the actual adoption story (Burki, 1963). Adoption should remain a topic of open communication within the family. New questions may emerge over time as older children seek further clarification. The fact that some children will not initiate such conversations does not mean that they are indifferent; they will, however, express themselves when the conversation is started by others (Wrobel et al., 1998). Making adoption a familiar household subject even before the child grasps the meaning of the word makes it unnecessary to break difficult news to the child later. The concept grows naturally with the child's cognitive development and comes embedded in a positive emotional framework. A majority of opinions suggest that children should learn about their adoption as early as they can comprehend what it means. A concept such as "birth mother" reportedly can be understood by children as young as age 2 1/2 (Silber & Dorner, 1990). Psychoanalytically-oriented professionals may oppose this, suggesting that a latency period disclosure is less disruptive, since earlier information about adoption might interfere with a successful Oedipus complex resolution (Brinich, 1980). However, taking the chance that the adoption information may reach the child from a source other than the parents may place the trust between parents and child at risk. How the child is told is extremely important. Children should keep dealing with their adoption on a continuous basis and learn to understand it flexibly, commensurate with their cognitive development (Brodzinsky & Brodzinsky, 1997; Brodzinsky et al., 1984). Even when adoptees are not told until adulthood, prudent timing of the adoption disclosure is of major psychological importance. Such a disclosure can, for example, overthrow a person's career or marriage plans, particularly if they were made to please the parents presumed to be the biological ones.

Infertile couples with unresolved issues about having had to resort to adoption to have a family need to work out their personal problems before sharing information about adoptions with they children. This will prevent them from contaminating their message on an emotional level, inadvertently portraying adoption as an inferior way of building a family.

ACCEPTANCE, REJECTION, IDENTIFICATION
The child adopted into an extra-marital familial setting is confronted with specific problems in terms of acceptance, rejection, identification, and separation. Adoptees have to deal with the reasons for the rejection by their biological parents and at times also with the reasons—not always entirely altruistic—for being wanted by their new parents. Identifying with the adopting parents may be a complex task, if truth and fantasy about the lost parents interfere. The identification issue may be complicated by parental counter-identification problems, especially if the child is of much different appearance (ethnically or racially) or of a different intellectual level, or if the parents ever imply or state that the child's unacceptable behavior is attributable to biological heritage. Not convinced that family bonds are forever, adoptees appear especially vulnerable to even a semblance of rejection. Even normal parental limit setting can be interpreted as a rejection. Being sensitive to weak, unstable, or conditional parent-child bonding, adopted children can act out and seriously test parental love. While actually seeking confirmation of the unconditional acceptance they had hoped for, they sometimes precipitate the very rejection they feared. Unlike most infant adoptees, children traumatized by separation and parental deprivation are more likely to cling to their adoptive parents initially, but then they go through a more turbulent time when seeking to separate from their parents in adolescence. The implied rejection in having been given up for adoption renders adopted children extremely sensitive to real or perceived rejection. If children are passed through homes of relatives or foster parents or placed in other care facilities, each change is likely to be counted as one more rejection. Moreover, the experience of being publicly classified as a non-biological child can be traumatic. Parents who introduce a child as "our adopted son/daughter" are perceived as distancing themselves from the child, assigning second-class family membership to the "outsider," which translates into one more intensely felt rejection.

In contrast, statements by adoptive parents such as, "We had a choice and we picked you" are a powerful defense against the perceived rejection by the biological parents. Although being unwanted and rejected can lead to low self-esteem, a comparison of normal children—both adopted and non-adopted—revealed no difference in self-concept between the two groups (Norvell & Guy, 1977). Other studies concur with the finding that adoption becomes a negligible factor in individuals who are able to make a positive adjustment.

SEARCH FOR BIOLOGICAL PARENTS
Despite the presumed rejection by their birth parents, many adopted children—especially while feeling misunderstood by their parents during adolescence—begin to search for their biological parents. Many believe that birth parents could better understand them and might be ideal to identify with. Among goals motivating

the search are the wishes to meet the parent/s as person/s, find additional family members, increase self-understanding and clarify identity issues, obtain information on genetic endowment including illness predisposition, and erase the birth parents' presumed rejection and replace it with an acceptable scenario. Some searches yield positive results. Others lead to parents either in negative life circumstances or unwilling to enter a personal relationship so as not to disrupt their current situation. Understanding parents assist their adopted children in finding their birth parents and refuse to interpret the urge to search as a rejection. Initiation of and persistence at searching vary tremendously. For example, in Brenner's 1993 study of transracially adopted children, all the Black but only some of the Asian and Caucasian children initiated a search for their birth parents. Kim's (1995) data revealed that among Korean children adopted in Denmark, two-thirds had no interest in finding out about their families of origin. Searches can be hindered by adoption laws governing the disclosure of information on birth parents. Laws vary considerably among states and countries; some laws were passed to protect not only adoptees but also the rights of biological parents and their families (Sorosky, Baran, & Pannor, 1978).

OPEN, CLOSED, AND MEDIATED ADOPTION

Closed or confidential adoption was standard practice in the past. In response to the psychological problems and genetic information gap caused by this practice, new avenues have been explored. Open adoption is increasingly becoming the mode of choice (Berry et al., 1998). Open adoption refers to information sharing and/or actual contacts between biological and adoptive parents. Communication may be limited to the time before the child is placed with the new parents or it may continue as long as the parties involved remain interested. Ideally, open adoption gives the adoptee a chance not only to obtain information but also, by mutual consent, to get to know biological relatives, or to maintain established ties if the child had lived with biological family members prior to adoption. Contacts may be in person, by phone, or by mail. Approximately three-quarters of adoptive parents remained comfortable with the openness even several years after the adoption, as long as they had some control over the contacts. Changes made in the number of contacts were mostly decreases, down to no contact within two years in about 15% of the cases studied. Changes to reduce or discontinue contact were more often initiated by birth parents than by adoptive families (Berry et al., 1998). Adopted children's adjustment (positive behavior) was better in children from open adoption families. Perceptions of birth parents were more positive when there was contact between the families, and most crucially, the adoptees felt less rejected (Berry, 1991; Pannor & Baran, 1984). Even contact decreases over time may not be interpreted by the child as a sign of rejection, but as a chance to spend more time with peers. Many dynamics in these relationships are similar to those governing relationships between children and a divorced parent.

Concern that contact with the birth family may confuse the child and create identity problems generally appears to be unfounded. On the contrary, unanswered questions arising in confidential adoption contribute more to an adoptee's identity problems, while open adoption helps children understand adoption without negatively affecting their self-esteem. Having been given up for adoption can be understood positively rather than being interpreted as a rejection (Wrobel et al., 1996). Another concern about open adoption is whether it jeopardizes a strong attachment to the adoptive parents (Kraft et al., 1985) and/or increases fears in the child about adoption permanence (Rosenberg, 1992). It appears that parents willing to enter open adoption arrangements are available for communication and feel capable of handling both issues successfully. Of greater concern are birth parents who, after a change in circumstances such as a significant economic improvement, desire to undo the adoption. Aware of the fact that it cannot be accomplished legally, they may resort to other means. Among them might be attempts at alienation of affection, stressing the importance of biological ties, demanding more time with the child or even offering a teen the option to move in with the biological parent/s, creating an opportunity adolescents—when temporarily in conflict with the adoptive parents—find hard to resist.

There is no consensus as to when children who either never knew their birth parents, or have no memories of them, might best be introduced to biological relatives. It may be wise to let them make the connection as early as possible. Very young children take facts as they are and need no explanation. Having one mother who gave birth to the baby and another to live with is perfectly acceptable, particularly if, in the child's mind, it has always been that way.

Proponents of open adoption insist that adopted children have a right to obtain all information available about their birth parents and about the circumstances rendering them adoptable (Melina & Roszia, 1993). As attitudes about adoption are changing, change in adoption laws follow. A psychologically challenging fact was reported by the National Center for State Courts (Flango & Flango, 1995): While in 1992 the adoption rate nationally was 31.2 per thousand live births, adoption rates in open record law states were higher (AK 53.5, KS 48.4). This may indicate that birth parents and adoptive parents are more comfortable with open records and confirm adoption as a celebrated family event instead of a secretive transaction subject to authority control.

Mediated adoption offers an intermediate solution between open and closed adoption. A third party shares information between biological and adoptive families without disclosing identities (McRoy et al., 1988). It is a more comfortable option for families uncomfortable with open adoption, as when a baby is adopted from an incarcerated mother. The family does not wish to reveal name or whereabouts, but is willing to allow information to be exchanged so as not to deprive the adoptee. Later, the child will be able to choose whether to meet the birth mother or not. Critics of this type of adoption point out that information passed on by intermediaries might cause adoptees to misunderstand or misinterpret data related to their birth parents and/or circumstances leading to the adoption (Bevan & Pierce, 1994). Intra-familial communications in cases of mediated adoption were found to be easier with mothers, while fathers preferred to become involved after the children already had some understanding about their birth parents (Wrobel et al., 1998).

INTERRACIAL ADOPTION

In the United States there is a disparity between the number of Caucasians willing to adopt and the number of Caucasian candidates available for adoption. As a consequence, there has been an increase in international, interethnic, and interracial adoptions. While the numbers of available parents are such that intraracial matches cannot be achieved for all children, categorical opposition to interracial adoptions is unrealistic and works against the well-being of children in need of loving parents. Although objections to interracial adoptions have been raised (e.g., Hermann, 1993), research has shown that no psychological harm came to African American children due to their adoption into White families (Alexander & Curtis, 1996). They developed a positive racial identity and their adjustment was excellent (Shireman & Johnson, 1986). When Black adoptees were found to have more problems than Whites, the cause was unrelated to race: the African American children had been older when adopted and had come from more unstable and abusive backgrounds (Rosenthal, Croze, & Curiel, 1990).

In interviews with interracial adoptees, however, the degree of diversity in schools and community emerged as a factor related to child comfort. Racially and ethnically integrated communities offer a better backdrop for interracial adoption. The Multiethnic Placement Act of 1994 prohibits racial ethnic bias in making selections of adoption and foster care placements (Alexander, 1996). If foster parents bond with a child of a different race and wish to adopt the child, they can no longer be prevented from adopting on racial grounds. While opponents of interracial adoption are quick to point out that intraracial adoption is preferable, they fail to provide data comparing outcomes of cases of interracially adopted children raised in stable homes to outcomes of cases of children remaining un-adopted, being farmed out to foster homes and child care facilities.

INTERNATIONAL ADOPTION

Legalized abortion, a decrease in the number of adoptable Caucasian children, acceptance of single parenthood, and financial support from the government have caused the number of adoptable children in the U.S. to drop significantly. While there were about 80,000 non-relative adoptions annually in the late 1960s, only about 50,000 children were adopted per year in the late 1980s (Kim, 1995). Many couples unable to find Caucasian children for adoption in the United States turned either to adopting U.S. children of other racial backgrounds or to adopting children from abroad. International adoptions can be a taxing experience for parents. Unforeseen issues, like demands for bribes, delays, and legal problems, can impact the emotional child readiness of would-be parents (Gorning, 1993). Notably, when both parents are not equally committed to adopting, there can be a negative spillover to the relationship with the adoptee and to the marital relationship. This situation may be exacerbated when, contrary to unrealistic parent expectations, the child who finally arrives in the U.S. manifests regressive, anxious, or rejecting behavior instead of joy and gratefulness. In situations of adoption from a U.S. foster home or a children's home, visits and weekend trips can allow the child to get acquainted with the prospective parents. In contrast, most international adoptees are transplanted into the homes of strangers in one finalizing move.

For about 30 years Korean children were the most sought-after foreign adoptees. Later, Romanian and more recently Russian children became favorite U.S. adoptees. Ever since the Korean War, Korean children have been brought to the U.S. Initially, there were war orphans and Amerasian children, many fathered by U.S. soldiers. Later, adoptable children came from poverty stricken homes or were children, especially girls, who had been abandoned. Korean children, as a group, have made excellent adjustments, living up to expectations that they would be quiet, high achieving, responsible, socially mature, and without emotional problems. Even those who displayed some regressive features during the initial post-adoption period adjusted well over time. Similarly, positive results were obtained in studies of Korean adoptees in Scandinavian countries, Holland, and Germany. Korean children adopted into the United States were on average older than U.S. adopted Caucasian children. Some Koreans adopted as older children created some difficulty for their parents during adolescence, but on follow-up into adulthood showed no differences in adjustment when compared with their untroubled adolescent counterparts. They were also more interested in their racial/ethnic identity than the children adopted at a younger age. Korean adoptees have good self-esteem and identify themselves primarily as American, not as Korean or Korean American. However, compared to Caucasian adoptees, some would prefer to have a less identifying appearance. On average, Korean adoptees did better than U.S.-born Caucasian adoptees. Kim (1995) also suggests that adjustment advantages may be related to overrepresentation of girls among Korean adoptees. The adoptee flow from Korea was curtailed after the 1988 Olympic games in Seoul. Following a *New York Times* report on "Babies for Export," the Korean government curbed the children's exit. In 1991, 2,552 Romanian adoptees put the Koreans, with 1,817, in second place for foreign adoptions.

After news reports on neglected and abused children in Romania, many U.S. families adopted Romanian children. In contrast to the Korean children, most Romanian adoptees had endured serious hardships. Studies dealing with Romanians adopted into the United Kingdom and Canada offered information and insights (O'Conner et al., 1999; Rutter and the English and Romanian adoptees study team, 1998; Chisholm et al., 1995). Most children had been institutionalized, some since birth. All had experienced some degree of neglect, physical and psychological deprivation, serious malnutrition at developmentally critical times, and in some cases, abuse. Social deprivation included lack of a specific caretaker to bond with; the child/caretaker ratio reached 20 to 1, resulting in attachment disorders. Many of the adoptees suffered from disinhibited attachment disorder, displaying indiscriminate friendliness with strangers. The time span from 5 to 13 months turned out to be a highly sensitive period for the development of healthy or disturbed attachment behavior. Cognitive skills of Romanian children adopted into the United Kingdom before the age of six months were nearly equal to those of children adopted from within the United Kingdom, while those adopted later, up to age two, showed distinct cognitive impairment. One factor remained puzzling. Some children who were equally deprived during critical developmental phases were able to overcome their problems and make good adjustments. Similar reports came from families with children adopted from Russian orphanages.

MENTAL HEALTH AND RELATED ISSUES

Adoptees have been reported to be more maladjusted than their peers and are overrepresented in clinical populations (Offord et al., 1969; Wierzbicki, 1993; Bohman & von Knorring, 1979; Schecter et al., 1964). Although this may imply that adopted children, as a group, have more mental health problems than their non-adopted peers, there is no evidence that being adopted is a major factor affecting mental health, as attested to by the fact that Korean children did not match this profile (Kim, 1995). Overrepresentation may merely indicate that adopted children are more readily referred to mental health clinics because parents find it easier to admit problems, lacking biological ties that might reflect negatively on themselves. Another issue Berry (1992) points out is that adoptive parents often have misconceptions about what is normal behavior in children, and when adoptees do not meet their unrealistic expectations, maladjustment is reported. This may also explain why only and first-adopted children have been considered to be at greater risk for behavioral problems (Brodzinsky & Brodzinsky, 1992).

The research with non-clinical samples of adopted and non-adopted children showing the adopted children with more severe symptomatology have to be considered flawed, as the research was based on ratings by mothers, knowing the adoption status of the children. Only results obtained by "blind" raters can be considered valid. The study further revealed a gender difference in complaints, portraying boys as less communicative and more hyperactive, while girls, though sharing hyperactivity, were more depressed and aggressive (Brodzinsky et al., 1987). A Canadian study found more adoptees diagnosed with Attention Deficit Disorder (Deutsch et al., 1982). Huth's report (1978) compiling the results of major studies on adopted children concluded that the number of psychological problems, as well as the degree of psychopathology, in adopted and non-adopted children is about the same. A 1993 Canadian follow-up study (Lipman et al., 1993) found that adoptees did not fare significantly worse than non-adopted children in psychiatric and "educational morbidity" or addiction, but that the risk for substance abuse was greater in adopted girls while poor school performance, but not adoption alone, in adopted boys was a risk marker for psychiatric disorder.

Natural children may more often develop internalizing problems that do not attract social attention, while in adopted children problems like lying, stealing, and aggressive (including sexual) acting out predominate, inviting public attention and sometimes mandatory agency referral. A correlation was found between a child's age at the time of permanent placement with the adopting family and acting out behavior. Based on the age at placement the probability of an adoptee acting out was found to be as follows: up to 3 months: none; 3 to 12 months: possible; 12 months on: expected (Offord et al., 1969). However, this information does not apply to Korean adoptees. It was also found that sex difference is no predictor of antisocial behavior in adoptees, although boys are more likely to exhibit antisocial behavior if the family is hurt (e.g., through divorce). Regardless of gender, having a biological relative with a personality disorder or alcoholism serves as a predictor of antisocial behavior in the adoptee (Cadoret & Cain, 1980).

Kety and colleagues (1978) studied adoptees and both their adoptive and biological families. In the biological but not the adoptive families of adoptees who became schizophrenic, they found a high rate of accidental death and potential and actual suicides, as well as a "significant concentration of schizophrenic spectrum disorders," thus, the adoptees' psychopathology seems to be related primarily to biological lineage—compounded by environmental, possibly alimentary factors—but not to adoption of the adopting family. To the contrary, research done in Finland (Tienari et al., 1987) suggests that being raised in a healthy adoptive home presents a protective factor in safeguarding children with a genetic vulnerability to schizophrenia. In this context, the question arises whether social acting-out behavior is related to living with adoptive families, or whether adopted children are more likely to come from an undesirable genetic background, given that many adoptees are conceived and born outside of socially responsible circumstances.

No information could be found on whether or not there is an increased genetic vulnerability to mental illness in adoptees compared with the general population. While biological lineage is unrelated to adoption, early childhood experiences are not. Of major significance is whether the child reaches the adoptive family soon after birth or later after major negative experiences, be these related to the biological family, foster homes, or institutional settings. Exposure to depersonalizing institutions, multiple rejections or abusive foster care placements, or the experience of being given up for adoption only after becoming unmanageable tend to intensify any propensity for maladjustment or delinquency and may trigger a mental illness for which biological prerequisites are met. On the positive side, children who, at an early age, are adopted away from a destabilizing setting and transferred to a nurturing environment are likely to make a good adjustment, keeping their genetic propensity for mental illness dormant (Tienari et al., 1987). Here, adoption is highly beneficial compared to the lot of unadopted children with a biological predisposition for mental illness, who must grow up in their biological family's environment, which is often characterized by mental illness, addiction, absent parents, abuse, neglect, or homelessness, thus putting them at greater risk for mental illness or at best exposing them to negative adult models.

Even depression could not be tied to adoption. Eley and colleagues (1998), evaluating data from the Colorado Adoption Project, found no evidence of genetic heritability in adoptees suffering from depressive symptoms in middle childhood. Instead, depression was related to unshared environmental factors, such as serious illness before age five, death of a significant person, friendship problems, and so forth. However, the authors predict that stronger genetic influence will likely be uncovered as the subjects under study pass through adolescence into adulthood.

Two prominent effects found in Romanian adoptees are Attachment Disorder (AD) and cognitive impairment. Children suffering from the disinhibited type of AD displayed affection and indiscriminate friendliness towards strangers (O'Conner et al., 1999). As with the outcome of cognitive impairment, AD was correlated with serious deprivation during critical developmental periods. The etiologically relevant social, emotional, and nutritional deprivation took place before adoption. Although the abnormal developments had evolved in Romanian adoptees, the conditions were unrelated to adoption.

Overall, mental health problems are not readily tied to adoption. Heredity and environmental circumstances are factors with adoptees as with other children. Even an established factor, like age at adoption, is not the correct indicator for the link to maladjustment. Factors likely to play an etiological role in maladjustment and mental illness, although equally applicable to all children, may be somewhat more prevalent in the adoptable and adopted population. Specific data on this prevalence—not magnified by biased clinic referrals—appear to be unavailable.

Identity confusion may be the one condition that can be related directly to adoption. It is difficult to construct a cohesive sense of identity when the building blocks consist of negative messages (birth family, abandonment, neglectful institutions, rejecting or abusive foster settings), contradicting positive messages from adoptive family, teachers, and social environments, and speculation based on an information gap in cases of closed adoption. If the child is, in addition, an interracial adoptee, rejected by White peers and by peers of color as a "coconut" for being dark on the outside but white at the core, due to the White family's influence, it can be difficult to attain a firm sense of identity that is congruent with the inner self. Working through the contradictions and establishing a healthy sense of identity can be a major therapeutic task (Nadelman 1997; Brodzinsky, 1997b). However, similar issues have been reported among non-adopted children, most eminently by Erik Erikson (1968), whose identity confusion resulted from the conflicting identity constellation created when this blond Danish boy became the stepson of a German Jewish pediatrician. For adoptees, having identity issues to work on seems to be the norm.

IQ

Older research on adopted children's IQs favored genetic theories, showing that the adopted children's IQs were affected only moderately by the adopting family's home environment (Munsinger, 1975; Scarr & Weinberg, 1976). Newer research found that both Black and White adoptees perform better on IQ tests if they are being raised in a White family, presumably because IQ tests are White-culture based (Weinberg et al., 1992). On the other hand, as the Toronto Adoption Study showed, the effects on IQ and language in children born to cocaine addicts were only mild to moderate if the child was adopted by middle- to upper-class parents, as opposed to being reared by their addicted, biological mothers of low economic means and limited education (Koren et al., 1998). Intellectually ambitious parents, especially without children of their own to compare, may have unrealistic expectations about academic achievement. Even children with a normal IQ may not be able to live up to parental aspirations, which engenders friction and sometimes reports of maladjustment (Berry, 1992).

GOVERNMENT INTEREST IN ADOPTION

In recent years, the federal government's awareness of problems associated with children's welfare has risen considerably. Adoption of eligible children has emerged as the favorite ameliorating action. A number of press releases from the White House highlight recent adoption related efforts: (a) 1996 Memorandum on adoption and alternate permanent placement for waiting children in the public child welfare system; (b) 1996 Health and Human Services initiative to promote adoption of children from foster care to 54,000 by 2002; (c) 1997 Adoption and Safe Families Act to shorten waiting time for adoption and provide health insurance coverage in subsidized adoptions; (d) 1998 announcement of plan to expand Internet usage informing about children available for adoption; (e) 1998 Presidential Remarks at a National Adoption Month Reception referring to 100,000 children "still waiting for permanent adoptive homes"; (f) 1999 various support services, including health insurance, are provided for foster and homeless children who remain unadopted; extension of services to age 21; and (g) 1999 raising public awareness in National Adoption Month and raising adoption goal for 2002 to 56,000.

While laws expediting adoption are being written and other efforts are made on behalf of adoptable and adopted children, *de lege ferenda* it needs to be noted that it must become illegal for authorities to disrupt strong psychological bonds between young children and their caregivers, no matter what the legal status of the family unit is.

REFERENCES

ABC News Report, *Good Morning America,* 11/08/1999.

Adoption Assistance and Child Welfare Act. (1980). P.L. 96–272, 94 Stat. 500.

Alexander, R., Jr. & Curtis, C. M. (1996). A review of empirical research involving the transracial adoption of African American children. *Journal of Black Psychology, 22,* [2], 223–235.

Berry, M. (1991). Adoptive parents' perceptions of, and comfort with, open adoption. *Child Welfare, 72,* 231–253.

Berry, M. (1992). Contributors to adjustment problems of adoptees: A review of the longitudinal research. *Child and Adolescent Social Work Journal, 9,* 525–540.

Berry, M., Cavazos Dylla, D. J., Barth, R. P., & Needell, B. (1998). The role of open adoption in the adjustment of adopted children and their families. *Children and Youth Services Review, 20,* 151–171.

Bevan, C. S., & Pierce, W. (1994). *Secrecy, privacy and confidentiality in adoption.* Paper presented at Conference on Building Families: Ethical and Policy Issues in Adoption, Minneapolis, MN.

Bohman, M., von Knorring, A. L. (1979). Psychiatric illness among adults adopted as infants. *Acta Psychiatrica Scandinavica, 60,* 106–112.

Brenner, E. M., (1993). Identity formation in the trans-racially adopted adolescent. (Doctoral dissertation, California School of Professional Psychology, 1993). *Dissertation Abstracts International, 15,* 3871.

Brinich, P. (1980). Some potential effects of adoption on self and object representations. *The Psychoanalytic Study of the Child, 35,* 107–133.

Brodzinsky, A., & Brodzinsky, D. M. (1997). Clinical assessment issues in the treatment of adopted children. *New Jersey Psychologist, 47,* 16–19.

Brodzinsky, D. M. (Ed.). (1997a). Clinical issues in adoption. *New Jersey Psychologist, 47,* 16.

Brodzinsky, D. (1997b). Clinical issues and interventions in adoption. *New Jersey Psychologist, 47,* 23–26.

Brodzinsky, D. M., & Brodzinsky, A. B. (1992). The impact of family structure on the adjustment of adopted children. *Child Welfare, 71,* 69–76.

Brodzinsky, D. M., Singer, L. M., & Braff, A. M. (1984). Children's understanding of adoption. *Child Development, 55,* 869–878.

Brodzinsky, D. M., Radice, C., Huffman, L., & Merkler, K. (1987). Prevalence of clinically significant symptomatology in a nonclinical sample of adopted and nonadopted children. *Journal of Clinical Child Psychology, 16,* 350–356.

Burki, V. (1963). *Of all the children, we wanted you. The illustrated story of Tommy's adoption.* Unpublished manuscript.

Cadoret, R. J., & Cain, C. (1980). Sex differences in predictors of anti-social behavior in adoptees. *Archives of General Psychiatry, 37,* 1171–1175.

Chisholm, K., Carter, M. C., Ames, E. W., & Morison, S. J. (1995). Attachment security and indiscriminately friendly behavior in children adopted from Romanian orphanages. *Development and Psychopathology, 7,* 283–294.

Deutsch, C. K., Swanson, J. M., Bruell, J. H., Cantwell, D. P., Weinberg, F., & Baren, M. (1982). Overrepresentation of adoptees in children with the attention deficit disorder. *Behavior Genetics, 12,* 231–238.

Eley, T. C., Deater-Deckard, K., Fombonne, E., Fulker, D. W., & Plomin, R. (1998). An adoptive study of depressive symptoms in middle childhood. *Journal of Child Psychology and Psychiatry, 39,* 337–345.

Erikson, E. H. (1968). *Identity: Youth and crisis.* New York: Norton.

Flango, V. E., & Flango, C. R. (1995). National Center for Court Statistics, How many children were adopted in 1992? *Child Welfare 74,* 1012–22.

Gorning (1993). International adoptions. *Michigan Family Law Journal. Special Edition.* 41–43.

Hermann, V. P. (1993). Transracial adoption: "Child-saving" or "child-snatching". *National Black Law Journal, 13,* 147–164.

Huth, W. (1978). Psychische Störungen bei Adoptivkindern – Eine Uebersicht über den Stand der klinischen Forschung. *Zeitschrift für klinische Psychologie und Psychotherapie, 26,* 256–270.

Kety, S., Rosenthal, D., Wender, P., Schulsinger, F., & Jacobsen, B. (1978). The biologic and adoptive families of adopted individuals who became schizophrenic: Prevalence of mental illness and other characteristics. In L. C. Wynne, R. L. Cromwell, & S. Matthysse (Eds.). *The nature of schizophrenia: New approaches to research and treatment,* 25–37. New York: Wiley.

Kim, W. J. (1995). International adoption: A case review of Korean children. *Child Psychiatry and Human Development, 25,* 141–154.

Koren, G., Nulman, I., Rovet, J., Greenbaum, R., Loebstein, M., & Einarson, T. (1998). Long-term neurodevelopmental risks in children exposed in utero to cocaine. The Toronto Adoption Study. In J. A. Harvey, B. E. Kosofsky (Eds.). Cocaine: Effects on the developing brain. *Annals of the New York Academy of Sciences, 846,* 306–313. New York: New York Academy of Sciences.

Kraft, A., Palombo, J., Woods, P., Mitchell, D., Schmidt, A., & Tucker, N. (1985). Some theoretical considerations on confidential adoption. Part III: The adopted child. *Child and Adolescent Social Work Journal, 2,* 135–153.

Lang, R. (1997). Working with special needs adoptive families. *New Jersey Psychologist, 47,* 20–22.

Lipman, E. L., Offord, D. R., Boyle, M. H., Racine, Y. A. (1993). Follow-up of psychiatric and educational morbidity among adopted children. *Journal of the American Academy of Child and Adolescent Psychiatry, 32,* 1007–1012.

McRoy, R. G., Grotevant, H. D., & White, K. L. (1988). *Openness in adoption: New practices, new issues.* New York: Praeger.

Melina, L. R., & Roszia, S. K. (1993). *The open adoption experience.* New York: Harper Collins.

Munsinger, H. (1975). The adopted child's IQ. *Psychological Bulletin, 82,* 623–654.

Multiethnic Placement Act. (1994). P.L. 103–382. §551–553, 108 stat. 3518.

Nadelman, A. (1997). Assessment and treatment of attachment-impaired adopted children. *New Jersey Psychologist, 47,* 4, 27–29.

Norvell, M. & Guy, R. F. (1977). A comparison of self-concept in adopted and non-adopted adolescents. *Adolescence, 12,* 443–448.

O'Conner, T. G., Breedenkamp, D., Rutter, D., & The English and Romanian (ERA) Study Team. (1999). Attachment disturbances and disorders in children exposed to early and severe deprivation. *Infant Mental Health Journal, 20,* 10–29.

Offord, D. R., Hershey, M. D., Aponte, J. F., & Cross, L. A. (1969). Presenting symptomatology of adopted children. *Archives of General Psychiatry, 20,* 110–116.

Pannor, R., & Baran, A. (1984). Open adoption as standard practice. *Child Welfare, 63,* 245–250.

Phillips, N. K. (1999). Adoption of a sibling: Reactions of biological children at different stages of development. *American Journal of Orthopsychiatry, 69,* 122–126.

Rosenberg, E. B. (1992). *The adoption life cycle.* New York: Free Press.

Rosenthal, J. A., Croze, V. & Curiel, H. (1990). Race, social class and special needs adoption. *Social Work, 35,* 532–539.

Rutter, M., & the English and Romanian adoptees (ERA) study team. (1998). Developmental catch-up, and deficit, following adoption after severe global early privation. *Journal of Child Psychology and Psychiatry, 39,* 465–476.

Scarr, S., & Weinberg, R. R. (1976). IQ test performance of black children adopted by white parents. *American Psychologist, 31,* 726–739.

Schechter, M., Carlson, P., Simmons, J. Q., III, & Work, H. (1964). Emotional problems in the adoptee. *Archives of General Psychiatry, 10,* 109–118.

Shireman, J. F., & Johnson, P. R. (1986). A longitudinal study of black adoptions: Single parent, transracial, and traditional. *Social Work, 31,* 172–176.

Silber, K., & Dorner, P. M. (1990). *Children of open adoptions.* San Antonio, TX: Corona.

Sorosky, A., Baran, A., & Pannor, R. (1978). *The adoption triangle.* Garden City, NY: Anchor.

Tienari, P., Lahti, I., Sorri, A., Naarala, M., Moring, J., & Wahlberg, K-E. (1987). The Finnish adoptive family study of schizophrenia. *Journal of Psychiatric Research, 21,* 437–445.

Weinberg, R. A., Scarr, S., & Waldman, I. D. (1992). The Minnesota transracial adoption study: A follow-up IQ test performance at adolescence. *Intelligence, 16,* 117–135.

White House Press Release. (12/14/1996). *Steps to increase adoptions and alternate permanent placements for waiting children, in the public child welfare system.* Washington, D.C.: U.S. Government Printing Office.

White House Press Release. (11/19/1997). *President Clinton signs the Adoption and Safe Families Act of 1997.* Washington, D.C.: U.S. Government Printing Office.

White House Press Release. (11/19/1997). *Remarks by the President and First Lady at adoption bill signing.* Washington, D.C.: U.S. Government Printing Office.

White House Press Release. (11/24/1998). *Expansion of the Internet to increase adoptions.* Washington, D.C.: U.S. Government Printing Office.

White House Press Release. (1/29/1999). *Hillary Rodham Clinton announces new efforts to support transitioning foster care youth.* Washington, D.C.: U.S. Government Printing Office.

White House Press Release. (11/1/1999). *Raising public awareness: National Adoption Month.* Washington, D.C.: U.S. Government Printing Office.

Wierzbicki, M. (1993). Psychological adjustment of adoptees: A meta-analysis. *Journal of Clinical Child Psychology, 22,* 447–454.

Wrobel, G. M., Ayers-Lopez, S., Grotevant, H. D., McRoy, R. G., & Friedrick, M. (1996). Openness in adoption and the level of child participation. *Child Development, 67,* 2358–2374.

Wrobel, G. M., Kohler, J. K., Grotevant, H. D., & McRoy, R. G. (1998). Factors related to patterns of information exchange between adoptive parents and children in mediated adoptions. *Journal of Applied Developmental Psychology, 19,* 641–657.

E. WICK
St. John's University

HERITABILITY OF PERSONALITY

IDENTITY FORMATION

ADRENAL CORTEX

The adrenal glands are located superior to the kidneys at the level of the 11th or 12th thoracic vertebra, and consist of two anatomically and chemically distinct structures: an outer cortical region in which steroid hormones are synthesized, and an inner medullary area in which catecholamines are produced. The cortex is divided into three zones: the *zona fasciculata* secretes glucocorticoids; the *zona reticularis* is responsible for adrenal androgen production;and the *zona glomerulosa* releases mineralocorticoids.

The glucocorticoids represent the end product of the hypothalamic-pituitary-adrenal (HPA) axis, and are involved in a myriad of functional responses in the organism. These hormones serve as major regulators of carbohydrate and lipid metabolism; adaptation to stress; in linking sleep and waking states; food-seeking and cognitive behaviors; controlling emotional states; mediating anaphylactic and immune responses; modulating the responses to neurochemicals, hormones, and growth factors; and in the differentiation and development of cells (Munck, Guyre, & Holbrook, 1984; Tsigos & Chrousos, 1994). In humans, cortisol is the principal natural glucocorticoid, whereas in many animals, corticosterone is the primary glucocorticoid.

REGULATION OF GLUCOCORTICOID SECRETION

The main driving force behind glucocorticoid secretion is corticotropin-releasing-hormone (CRH) acting in synergy with arginine-vasopressin (AVP), both of which are primarily released from the paraventricular nucleus (PVN) of the hypothalamus. CRH stimulates the coticotroph cells in the anterior pituitary to secrete corticotropin (ACTH) which, in turn, influences the adrenal cortex. Three separate regulatory forces are involved in the secretion of glucocorticoids under physiological conditions and during times of stress. A circadian rhythm of basal activity is under the influence of the suprachiasmatic nucleus. Stress-induced responses are more complex and involve afferent inputs from numerous brain regions, including the locus ceruleus and autonomic systems in the brain stem, the amygdala-hippocampus complex, and the cerebral cortex. Finally, a feedback inhibitory input is provided by glucocorticoids.

Circadian Rhythm of Cortisol

In general, changes in plasma cortisol occur in parallel with those of ACTH. The rhythm of ACTH secretion results, in turn, from periodic changes in CRF. Cortisol levels peak in the early morning just prior to awakening, marking the onset of circadian activation.

There is a gradual decline throughout the day until it reaches a nadir during the early hours of nocturnal sleep, then rises abruptly during the later part of sleep (Van Cauter & Turek, 1995). There is an endogenous nature to this periodicity, with minimal influence from factors other than the circadian oscillator. The ontogeny of the circadian periodicity of the HPA system is closely associated with the development and maturation of the central nervous system. Once the circadian rhythm has developed, it persists throughout life.

Under many physiological conditions and in a wide variety of pathological states, the overall pattern of circadian rhythm is unchanged, although changes in the timing and/or the amplitude of the HPA periodicity might occur. Some exceptions include Cushing's syndrome, disorders involving abnormalities in the binding and/or metabolism of cortisol (e.g., hyperthyroidism, alcoholic cirrhosis), and certain diseases of the central nervous system (specifically, localized hypothalamic lesions).

Glucocorticoid Secretion under Stressful Conditions

Living organisms survive by maintaining a complex dynamic equilibrium that is constantly challenged by intrinsic or extrinsic disturbing forces or stressors. In response to a stressor exceeding a threshold magnitude, the organism changes its behavior and physiology to maintain homeostasis. Behavioral adaptation includes increased arousal and alertness, heightened attention, and suppression of feeding and sexual behavior. Concomitantly, physical adaptation occurs and includes functions that redirect energy sources to the stressed body site, where they are needed most. In this adaptive process, glucocorticoids, along with catecholamines, form the frontline of defense. Under stressful conditions, adrenalectomized animals are unable to sustain the necessary cardiovascular tone and blood glucose levels, and thus perish.

Similar to baseline conditions, glucocorticoid secretion during stress is dependent upon the release of CRH and AVP, although the magnitude of PVN activity is influenced by the nature and intensity of the stressor. Simultaneously, the locus ceruleus/norepinephrine-sympathetic system (autonomic-arousal system) becomes activated during stress, facilitating the release of epinephrine and norepinephrine from the adrenal medulla and the peripheral sympathetic nervous system. The PVN and the autonomic-arousal system are anatomically and functionally connected to each other, as well as to the mesocortical/mesolimbic systems and the hippocampal formation. During stress, a number of complex interactions are involved in the regulation of glucocorticoid and catecholamine secretion. For example, glucocorticoids regulate catecholamine biosynthesis in the adrenal medulla, and catecholamines stimulate ACTH release from the anterior pituitary. In addition, several other neuropeptides and neurotransmitter systems can influence the regulation of these hormones.

Glucocorticoids and the Pathophysiology of Stress Response

Generally, the stress response, with the resultant elevation of glucocorticoid levels, is meant to last only for a limited duration. The time-limited nature of this process renders its accompanying catabolic and immunosuppressive effects beneficial, with no adverse consequences. Chronic activation of the stress system, however, threatens the health of the organism. For example, prolonged exposure to elevated glucocorticoid levels results in suppression of anabolic processes; muscle atrophy; reduced sensitivity to insulin; a risk for diabetes, hypertension, hyperlipedemia, arterial disease, peptic ulcers, amenorrhea, impotency, and immunosuppression; and the impairment of growth and tissue repair (Munck et al., 1984). In addition, elevated glucocorticoid levels are associated with psychopathology, neuronal damage, and impaired cognitive function (McEwen, 1994; Tsigos & Chrousos, 1994). Hence, an efficient endocrine response to stress is one that is rapidly mobilized in the presence of a threat and then effectively terminated once the threatening condition is no longer present.

Regulation of Glucocorticoid Secretion through Negative Feedback

Inhibition of glucocorticoid secretion is achieved primarily through the action of glucocorticoids themselves. This negative feedback inhibition is partly achieved by glucocorticoid binding to specific corticoid receptors in the pituitary and in limbic structures. Based on biochemical and functional characteristics, two types of corticoid receptors have been described (McEwen, 1994). Type I or mineralocorticoid receptor (MR) has stringent specificity, binding selectively to corticosterone in many animals. The type II or glucocorticoid receptor (GR) has a lower affinity for corticosterone than the MR, and its highest affinity is for potent synthetic glucocorticoids, such as dexamethasone. In the brain, MR is densely localized in hippocampal and septal neurons, whereas GR is widely distributed, including hippocampus, hypothalamus, and pituitary cells. The receptor characteristics and distribution complement each other, thus providing the organism with the ability to modulate HPA responses. The MR, because of its limited distribution in the brain, has only a low capacity to bind corticosterone, despite its high affinity. The MR appears to be operative at low corticosterone concentrations and may offer tonic inhibition at the nadir of the circadian rhythm. When high glucocorticoid levels are present, the MR become saturated and the corticosteroids then bind to GR thereby ensuring a return to homeostasis.

ASSOCIATION BETWEEN GLUCOCORTICOID REGULATION AND PSYCHOPATHOLOGY

Several lines of research support the association between glucocorticoid regulation and psychiatric disorders (Holsboer, 1989; Tsigos & Chrousos, 1994). Both physical and psychological stressors have been shown to be temporally related to psychiatric illness. Because glucocorticoids are intricately linked to the neurobiology of stress, alterations in glucocorticoid levels and/or activity are expected in association with psychiatric conditions. Indeed, altered function of the HPA axis has been shown in a variety of psychiatric disorders, including depression, anxiety disorder, alcoholism, anorexia nervosa, and schizophrenia. Also, pharmacological studies indicate that glucocorticoids directly modulate neurotransmitter function and behavioral systems, as well as the activity of psychotropic agents. Furthermore, there is evidence that glucocorticoids have genomic effects in the brain and regulate transcription of many genes, including those that code for behaviorally active neuropeptides. Therefore, a greater understanding of the effects of glucocorticoids at the molecular level, and their interactions with different neurotransmitter systems, should provide important clues to the pathophysiology and treatment of these disorders.

SUMMARY

In summary, because glucocorticoids target almost all organ systems of the body to regulate a myriad of functional responses, alterations in their level and/or activity can lead to diverse functional consequences in the organism.

REFERENCES

Holsboer, F. (1989). Psychiatric implications of altered limbic-hypothalamic-pituitary-adrenocortical activity. *Psychiatry and Neurological Sciences, 238,* 302–322.

McEwen, B. S. (1994). Corticosteroids and hippocampal plasticity. *Annals of the New York Academy of Sciences, 746,* 134–142.

Munck, A., Guyre, P. M., & Holbrook, N. J. (1984). Physiological functions of glucocorticoids in stress and their relation to pharmacological actions. *Endocrine Reviews, 5,* 25–44.

Tsigos, C., & Chrousos, G. P. (1994). Physiology of the hypothalamic-pituitary-adrenal axis in health and dysregulation in psychiatric and autoimmune disorders. *Endocrinology and Metabolism Clinics of North America, 23,* 451–466.

Van Cauter, E., & Turek, F. W. (1995). Endocrine and other biological rhythms. In L. J. DeGroot (Ed.), *Endocrinology, vol. 3* (pp. 2487–2548). Philadelphia: W. B. Saunders Company.

U. RAO & R. E. POLAND
University of California, Los Angeles

ADRENAL GLANDS
PITUITARY
CIRCADIAN RHYTHM

ADRENAL GLANDS

The adrenal glands (often called suprarenal glands in humans) are paired structures located just above the kidneys. Each adrenal is comprised of an outer cortex and an inner medulla. Secretions of the cortex are controlled by circulatory hormones produced in the anterior pituitary gland (adenohypophysis), while medullary output is under direct control of the sympathetic nervous system. The adrenal cortex has three layers: the outer zona glomerulosa, the intermediate zona fasciculata, and the inner zona reticularis.

Several steroid hormones, synthesized from cholesterol, are secreted by the adrenal cortex and are important in the maintenance of blood volume, blood pressure, and blood glucose levels, as well as the response of the organism to stress. These hormones are so crucial to the organism that death quickly follows removal of the adrenal cortices. Cortisol is the primary glucocorticoid secreted by the adrenal in humans. Corticosterone is secreted in small quantities in humans but is the primary glucocorticoid secreted in the rat.

These substances are classified as glucocorticoids because of their effect on glucose metabolism and because they are secreted by the zonae fasciculata and reticularis. The glucocorticoids also suppress inflammatory responses.

Aldosterone is secreted by the zona glomerulosa and is categorized as a mineralcorticoid because of its ability to alter electrolyte balance in the body. Aldosterone stimulates the distal tubule of the kidney to resorb sodium ions and causes a decrease in sodium concentration in sweat.

Adrenocorticotropic hormone (ACTH), released by the adenohypophysis, maintains the structural integrity of the outer two layers of the adrenal cortex and stimulates secretion of the glucocorticoids. Synthesis and release of ACTH are controlled by corticotropin-releasing factor (CRF). CRF is produced in the hypothalamus. Levels of glucocorticoid in the circulation provide negative feedback for secretion rate of CRF and, therefore, ultimately of the glucocorticoids themselves. The reninangiotension system produces complex feedback regulation between the adrenal and the kidney to control the secretion of aldosterone.

Chromaffin cells in the adrenal medulla synthesize and release the catecholamines epinephrine (adrenaline) and norepinephrine (noradrenaline). Secretion of norepinephrine and epinephrine is under control of sympathetic preganglionic fibers from the 8th through the 11th thoracic vertebral segments. The chromaffin cells act as postganglionic neurons. Secretion of the catecholamines depends upon the behavioral state of the organism. Secretion is very low during sleep, increases during emission of routine, nonstressful activities, and surges markedly during physical or psychological stress.

SUGGESTED READING

Christy, N. P. (Ed.). (1971). *The human adrenal cortex.* New York: Harper & Row.

Frankenhaeuser, M. (1975). Experimental approaches to the study of catecholamines and emotion. In L. Levi (Ed.), *Emotions: Their parameters and measurement.* New York: Raven Press.

Yates, F. E., Marsh, D. J., & Maran, J. W. (1980). The adrenal cortex. In V. B. Mountcastle (Ed.), *Medical physiology.* St. Louis, MO: Mosby.(Original work published 1918)

M. L. WOODRUFF
East Tennessee State University

ENDORPHINS/ENKEPHALINS
NEUROCHEMISTRY

ADULT DEVELOPMENT

The life-span approach to adult development includes the study of: (a) the phase of life from the end of formal education to the beginning of retirement; (b) the effects of preadulthood life on adult development and the subsequent effect of adult development on old age and dying; (c) adulthood development as such; (d) the interdisciplinary approach to development across different cultural settings and over historical time; and (e) the search for goals and

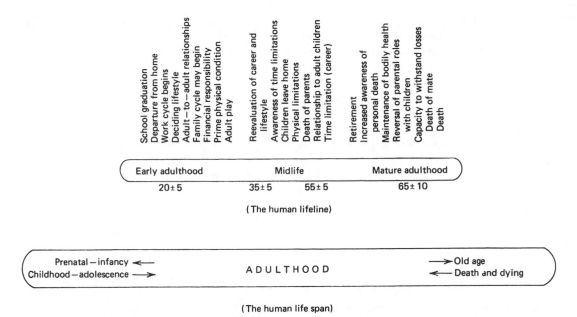

Figure 1.   The human lifeline of life events during adulthood from the perspective of the entire human life span.

means for optimizing both adult development and its childhood precursors and its subsequent effect on later life.

DEFINITION OF ADULT DEVELOPMENT

In technologically advanced societies there are no clear guideposts for entering adulthood such as the initiation rites among primitive societies. Historically, there has been no clear demarcation among the various age-related stages of human development. According to Aries (1962), infants, children, and adults were for centuries considered to be only quantitatively or physically different; infants were viewed as scaled-down adults who merely needed to get bigger before joining the mainstream of adult society. Early paintings portrayed infants with adult facial features and clothing; toys were first used by adults and later passed on to children. There was no children's literature. During the sixteenth century youngsters aged 13–15 were already full participants in the adult community. Boys as young as 11 were soldiers in European armies. It was not until the seventeenth and eighteenth centuries, with the emergence of modern concepts of childhood, family care, and education, that the distinction between childhood and adulthood began.

Adulthood is usually divided into three segments—early, middle, and mature—with increasing awareness of a new "substage" to characterize those on the threshold of full adulthood (usually college students) based on the analysis of White (1975/1966) and Keniston (1975). The criteria for deciding on the age limits of each substage depend on whether one is interested in chronological or legal age (years since birth), functional age (measures of skills and competencies), existential age (how old one feels), or other measures such as skeletal age, hormonal age, emotional age, social age, moral age, and so forth. The most appropriate age would be a composite of these measures of maturity, as well as others.

The age range for youth is typically from 16 through 21 years, although the upper limits often reach into the mid-20s. Characteristics of the special subculture of youth include:

1. *Deepening of interests.* From a large pool of interests, hobbies, and explorations, youth must now focus on occupational and lifestyle choices and begin to develop required competencies, sustained interests, and long-term commitments to choices.

2. *Humanizing of values.* There is a gradual realization that to connect with the adult society one must begin to break away from sole participation in youth's culture, and to realize the unity of all humanity regardless of age, background, and geographic location. Young people sense the need to care for others as an extension of caring for self. Concern for improving world conditions is part of the idealism and romanticism of youth.

3. *Stabilizing of self-concept.* Young people need to test out their "real selves" in the arena of intimate and relatively stable human relationships. The more assured youths are about their values, the less risk they run of being overwhelmed during the give-and-take of social interactions. Eventually youth must see themselves as separate individuals who are capable of union with others while still maintaining their own individualities.

The age when important life events occur is a significant means for defining adult development. Hultsch and Plemons (1979) define a life event as a noteworthy occurrence that produces a significant change in the course of a person's life. A chronological listing of life events may be referred to as a human lifeline and may serve as a "social and biological clock." Neugarten and Datan (1973) believe that, with these measures of human time, adults within similar cultures and historical time span can estimate if their life course is on time, before time, or after time. Figure 1 illustrates a human lifeline for the three major phases of early, middle, and mature adulthood within the broader framework of the entire human life span.

LIFE-SPAN ADULT DEVELOPMENT

Adulthood is the least explored age span, even though it extends over two-thirds of the human life span. There are an increasing number of adulthood publications with a non-life-span perspective, such as academic texts on early adulthood by Bocknek (1980), on the growth of personality by White (1972), on life after college graduation by Cox (1970), and on the search for identity by Erikson (1968). Summarizing development from early to middle adulthood are books by Gould (1978), Levinson et al. (1978), Lowenthal, Thurnher, & Chiriboga (1975), and Neugarten (1964); and in popular books by McGill (1980), Feinberg, Feinberg, & Tarrant (1978), and Ellison (1978). In essence, over time adults are still part of what they were before they became different.

Early Adulthood

Search for stability of identity in terms of occupation and lifestyles: exploration of and increasing commitments to adult roles. Search for greater independence from parents and teachers: making one's own decisions even when it is precarious to establish self-reliance. Search for intimacy with a partner: learning that intimacy requires mutual trust, support, and sharing of both positive and negative feelings; possible beginning of family or single-life cycle.

Middle Adulthood

Taking stock of life and deciding on rededication or a search for new identity. Extending qualities of caring and responsibility to the community at large and directing and assisting younger people not in the family. Becoming more of one's own person on the job, within the family, and in fulfilling one's talents and dreams. Becoming more capable of reasoning and managing one's affairs, guiding teenage children, and meeting the needs of aging parents.

Mature Adulthood

Change of life signaled by menopause in women and climacteric in men. Increased awareness of life's mortality and that one's dreams must be achieved now or become a "never never." General physical decline with corresponding bodily concerns; decline in speed of movements and rate of learning and thinking and short-term memory (about 30 seconds). Reasoning and thinking continue to improve.

The life-span adult development viewpoint is based on the observation that there are both stability and change throughout the course of human life. The non-life-span view is that significant development is over by about age 20 as measured by "increments," that adulthood is a long plateau, and that development in terms of "decrements" typifies life until death. Figure 2 contrasts these two views of human development.

CHARACTERISTICS OF ADULT DEVELOPMENT

The long stretch of adulthood is more influenced by a diversity of "social clocks" than the fairly "universal biological clocks" that gave the major impetus to early development. In general, although adult developmental changes are more gradual and less sequential and predictable than those at the extreme ends of the human life span, they are just as essential for continual growth, whether they

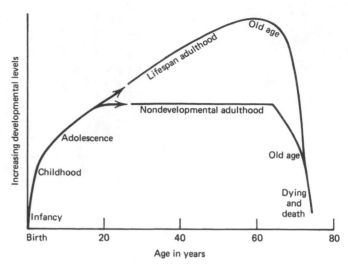

Figure 2.   A comparison of life span adulthood with nondevelopmental adulthood.

be happy or unhappy experiences. Change seems to be the natural state of affairs of the mind, body, and self.

It seems that the search for life-span theories and for those developmental processes which form essential linkages among age-related stages and events could begin only after developmentalists had first accepted the concept of life-span human development. Current research can be analyzed in terms of biological, social, and psychological developments.

Biological Development

The muscles, skeleton, and inner organs reach their maximum potentials during the mid-20s, except for the thymus and brain (Tanner, *Fetus Into Man,* 1978). The thymus gland and other lympnoid-type tissues, essential components of the body's disease- and stress-fighting system, reach maximum growth before adolescence and continue declining throughout the course of life. It seems that there is an urgent need for developing the immune system's ability to withstand stress early in life. Other vital organs begin their decline about age 40. Brain cell formation, 90–95% complete by year one, seems to be all over by age three, along with myelinization, which influences the speed of nerve impulses (Chase, 1976). Continued development for another 10 to 15 years occurs among the interconnections of brain cells, the dendrites, and the supporting glial cells. Although there is a commonly reported gradual brain weight loss of about 7% between ages 20 and 80 (Brody, 1980), Tomlinson (1972) found no such significant brain weight loss with age among intellectually healthy persons ranging in age from 65 to 92. Research with animals reveals that the number of interconnections can be either increased or decreased through corresponding amounts of environmental stimulation (Rosenzweig et al., 1968), raising the exciting possibility that the human brain is also dynamic and open to change throughout the course of life.

Beginning with early adulthood there are slow, almost imperceptible changes with age. These gradual declines become more apparent after age 30 in such functions as reaction time, body strength, and cardiovascular work performance, whereas other body declines such as vision and audition do not become disturbing until about age 50. There is a nearly linear decline in most body functions occurring at the rate of about 1% per year during adulthood and old age (Bierman & Hazzard, 1973). Nevertheless, regular exercise and proper nutrition seem to extend longevity, happiness, and sexual activities, as observed in the Vilcabamba people of Ecuador (Halsell, 1976) and the Abkhazians in Russia's Caucasus (Wolf, 1977).

SOCIAL DEVELOPMENT

The concept of adult socialization emerged gradually during the 1950s as research demonstrated that the socialization process continued beyond adolescence. Adult socialization may be viewed as a sequence of learned social roles in terms of major life events, as illustrated in Figure 1. When such social age expectations are combined with other developmental schedules such as those proposed by Havighurst in *Developmental Tasks and Education* (1950/1979), and those proposed by Erikson in *Childhood and Society* (1963) and *Adulthood* (1978) on life-span psychosocial development and cross-cultural adulthood development, an orientation toward a life-span human development of socialization begins to emerge.

Thus far, adult socialization has revealed two major life span characteristics. Neugarten (1964) suggests that there is a predictable progression from an outward-directed orientation to life heavily influenced by external controls, toward *interiority,* a more passive, introverted, self-directed existence in which the maturing adult depends more and more on a developing inner system of beliefs. Thus, over time, human beings tend to become more unique and self-actualizing. The second trend, reported both by Neugarten and by Jung in "The Stages of Life" (1969), is a gradual reversal of sex roles after middle age. Men tend to become more passive and nurturant, whereas women tend to become more domineering and outgoing.

PSYCHOLOGICAL DEVELOPMENT

Research reveals significant personality improvements toward higher levels of competencies as evidenced in *The Growth of Logical Thinking* (Inhelder & Piaget, 1958), in moral development (Kohlberg, 1973), in higher-order motivational drives as described by Kuhlen (1964), and even in the kinds of defense mechanisms employed when under pressure, as proposed by Vaillant (1977). When under stress, mature adults tend to use humor, provide assistance to others, plan for the future, and postpone reacting to current unavoidable conflicts. Brim & Kagan (1980) provide evidence for positive developments throughout the life span for such measures as inner control, general competencies, and self-esteem. Toward the end of mature life and with old age looming, there is an increased movement toward inner life, self-reflection, and detachment from external affairs. On the other hand, there are also stable adulthood characteristics such as assertiveness, gregariousness, and emotionality, as tabulated by Neugarten (1964) and Costa and McCrae (1980).

TRANSITIONS

From birth until death, transitions are universal experiences. Each stage, phase, or life event has its beginning, development, and end. Then it is time to part, to grieve, to begin again, to celebrate, and to grow again. Bridges (1980) believes that every transition begins with an *ending* which marks the beginning of renewal in life, a *neutral zone* which is a time of confusion and reorientation, and a *new beginning* which is the launching of new experiences. The following three stages are suggested for successful transitions between major phases of human development.

1. *Separation mourning.* Separation mourning refers to the process, first of realizing that the time for a change or for parting is pending, and second, of grieving because one must let go of a way of life, parents, friends, children, or a job, and "letting go" is like dying a little. Emotional withdrawal has to take place so that the developing person can be freed from the "old love" in order to experience a "new love." Finally, separation mourning means accepting that it is all right to feel depressed about leaving behind what was often so dear, so both the departing and those left behind may grow again.

2. *Journey turmoils.* The journey between phases of development may last for months or years. Growth or individuation proceeds as a person resolves the doubt, disorientation, and gnawing pain or guilt while forming a stronger sense of what he or she wants and how to get it. If it is the person's first solo journey into self-development, the turmoils may be terrifying; the young person may need some support from new friends or a mentor.

3. *Renewal peaks.* These are those "magic" moments when one knows that one has created a new way of living, feeling, relating, and caring. Each successful transition represents a "rebirth" and another opportunity for looking at oneself and others with continued freshness of appreciation.

REFERENCES

Aries, P. (1962). *Centuries of childhood: A social history of family life.* New York: Knopf.

Bierman, E. L., & Hazzard, W. R. (1973). Biology of aging. In D. Smith & E. Bierman (Eds.), *The biologic ages of man.* Philadelphia, PA: Saunders.

Bocknek, G. (1980). *The young adult.* Monterey, CA: Brooks/Cole.

Bridges, W. (1980). *Transitions: Making sense of life's changes.* Reading, MA: Addison-Wesley.

Brody, H. (1980). *Neuroanatomy and neuropathology of aging.* In E. W. Busse & D. G. Blazer (Eds.), *Handbook of geriatric psychiatry.* New York: Van Nostrand Reinhold.

Chase, H. P. (1976). Undernutrition and growth and development of the human brain. In J. D. Lloyd-Still (Ed.), *Malnutrition and intellectual development.* Littleton, MA: Publishing Sciences Group.

Costa, P. T., Jr., & McCrae, R. R. (1980). Still stable after all these years: Personality as a key issue in adulthood and old age. In P. B. Baites & O. G. Brim, Jr. (Eds.), *Life-span development and behavior* (Vol. 3). New York: Academic Press.

Cox, R. D. (1970). *Youth into maturity.* New York: Mental Health Materials Center.

Ellison, J. (1978). *Life's second half: The pleasures of aging.* Old Greenwich, CT: Devin-Adair.

Erikson, E. H. (1963). Psychosocial crises in the life-cycle. Adapted from *Childhood and society.* New York: Norton.

Erikson, E. H. (1968). *Identity: Youth and crisis.* New York: Norton.

Erikson, E. H. (1978/1958). *Young man Luther.* New York: Norton.

Feinberg, M. R., Feinberg, G., & Tarrant, J. J. (1978). *Leavetaking.* New York: Simon & Schuster.

Gould, R. L. (1978). *Transformations: Growth and change in adult life.* New York: Simon & Schuster.

Halsell, G. (1976). *Los viejos—Secrets of long life from the Sacred Valley.* Emmaus, PA: Rodale Press.

Havighurst, R. J. (1950/1979). *Developmental tasks and education* (3d ed.). New York: Longman.

Hultsch, D. F., & Plemons, J. K. (1979). Life events and life-span development. In P. B. Baltes & O. G. Brim, Jr. (Eds.), *Life-span development and behavior* (Vol. 2). New York: Academic Press.

Inhelder, B., & Piaget, J. (1958). *The growth of logical thinking: From childhood to adolescence.* New York: Basic Books.

Jung, C. G. (1969). The stages of life. In *The collected works: Structure and dynamics of the psyche* (Vol. 8). New York: Pantheon.

Keniston, K. (1975). Prologue: Youth as a stage of life. In R. J. Havighurst, P. H. Dreyer, & K. J. Rehage (Eds.), *Youth: The 1974 yearbook of the National Society for the Study of Education.* Chicago: University of Chicago Press.

Kohlberg, L. (1973). Continuities in childhood and adult moral development revisited. In P. B. Baites & K. Warner Schaie (Eds.), *Life-span developmental psychology: Personality and socialization.* New York: Academic Press.

Kuhlen, R. G. (1964). Developmental changes in motivation during the adult years. In J. E. Birren (Ed.), *Relations of development and aging.* Springfield, IL: Thomas.

Levinson, D. J., Darrow, C. N., Klein, E. B., Levinson, M. H., & McKee, B. (1978). *The seasons of a man's life.* New York: Knopf.

Lowenthal, M. F., Thurnher, M., & Chiriboga, D. (1975). *Four stages of life: A comparative study of women and men facing transitions.* San Francisco: Jossey-Bass.

McGill, M. E. (1980). *The 40 to 60 year old male.* New York: Simon & Schuster.

Neugarten, B. L., et al. (Eds.). (1964). *Personality in middle and later life.* Chicago: University of Chicago Press.

Neugarten, B. L., & Datan, N. (1973). Sociological perspectives on the life cycle. In P. B. Baites & K. Warner Schaie (Eds.), *Lifespan development psychology and socialization.* New York: Academic Press.

Tanner, J. M. (1978). *Education and physical growth* (2nd ed.). New York: International Universities Press.

Tomlinson, B. E. (1972). Morphological brain changes in nondemental people. In A. M. Van Praag & S. F. Kalverboer (Eds.), *Aging of the central nervous system: Biological and psychological aspects.* Haarlem, Netherlands: De Erven F. Bohn N. V.

Vaillant, G. D. (1977). *Adaptation to life.* Boston: Little, Brown.

White, R. W. (1972). *The enterprise of living: Growth and organization in personality.* New York: Holt, Rinehart & Winston.

White, R. W. (1975/1966). *Lives in progress.* New York: Holt.

Wolf, S. (1977). Presidential address: Social anthropology in medicine. The climate you and I create. *Trans-American Clinical and Climatological Association, 88,* 1–17.

SUGGESTED READING

Colarusso, C. A., & Nemroff, R. A. (1981). *Adult development: A new dimension in psychodynamic theory.* New York: Plenum.

Duvall, E. M. (1971). *Family development.* Philadelphia: Lippincott.

Egan, G., & Cowan, M. A. (1980). *Moving into adulthood.* Monterey, CA: Brooks/Cole.

Eurich, A. C. (Ed.). (1981). *Major transitions in the human cycle.* Lexington, MA: Lexington.

Knox, A. B. (1977). *Adult development and learning.* San Francisco: Jossey-Bass.

Mayer, N. (1978). *The male mid-life crisis.* New York: Signet.

J. O. Lugo
Fullerton, CA

BONDING AND ATTACHMENT
LIFE SPAN DEVELOPMENT
MIDDLE AGE

AFFERENT

Axons that are presynaptic to a neuron are commonly called afferents. In their terminal knobs is stored the neurotransmitter which will be released into the synaptic cleft and which will bind to receptors on the postsynaptic dendrites and soma. Thus, the topic of afferents is extremely broad. Much information about afferent function has been obtained from the study of primary afferents.

PRIMARY AFFERENTS

Primary afferents refer to the cells whose axons serve somatosensory receptors and which proceed to the central nervous system (CNS) through the dorsal roots of sensory nerve input to the spinal cord. The cell bodies of primary afferents are dorsal root ganglion cells located in the peripheral nervous system. The central axonal terminations are in the CNS. The terminations may occur on synapses to postsynaptic cells at that segmental level, at close segments, or at some distance from the entry point, even to the first synapse being in the brain stem at the dorsal column nuclei.

Primary afferents serve receptors for touch, thermal sensations, proprioceptive sensations from displacement of muscles and joints, and pain. Their sensory nerve classification is into groups I, II, III, and IV, on the basis of decreasing axonal diameter and decreasing conduction velocity. Most human physiology texts have a table showing these parameters and most currently are incorrect (Peters & Brooke, 1998). This is because the data were obtained using feline nerves, which conduct much faster than human ones. A very rough rule of thumb is to halve the velocity and diameter to translate from cat to human. Human sensory classification group Ia fibres conduct in the approximate range of 40 to 60 minutes per second.

COMPLEXITY OF PRIMARY AFFERENT EFFECTS

Human physiology texts describe some of the common connections between primary afferents and motoneurons, serving the stretch reflex, the flexor withdrawal reflex, the inverse myotatic reflex, and so forth. What is not usually addressed is that these are simple paths surrounded by extremely complex additional projections of those afferents to other motoneurons and interneurons of the spinal cord, and powerful modulating inputs onto those paths from spinal interneuronal pools. Regarding the former, Eccles (the Nobel prize winner in neurophysiology) and colleagues in the 1960s described many of these complexities in the cat (see the diagrams in Baldissera et al., 1981), with significant additional understanding reported in that chapter and also more recently (Jankowska, 1992; for humans, Pierrot-Deseilligny et al., 1981). The latter effects were recognized by Sherrington at the start of the twentieth century and have recently been shown to be important for human performance of tasks (Brooke et al., 1997). When these two sources of complexity—projection complexity and modulation complexity—are taken into account, it becomes clear that specific somatosensory receptor discharge can have widespread effects over neuronal pools of the spinal cord and brain and that the strength of the effect can be modulated from profound to minimal.

REGULATORY EFFECTS OF PRIMARY AFFERENTS IN MOTOR CONTROL

Primary afferents play a significant role in motor control (Pearson, 1993). In locomotion, primary afferents transmit sensory information on load bearing, muscle stretch, joint position, and cutaneous sensations and are involved in such matters as the transition from stance to swing or from static to dynamic balance in the initiation of stepping. Their reflex effects, ipsi- and contralaterally through Ia and cutaneous afferent activation, in the human are substantially modulated over cycles of activities such as walking (Brooke et al., 1997). In addition to spinal paths from sensory receptors to motoneurons and motor interneurons, it is clear that primary afferent activity regulates the activity of other primary afferents in complex and organized ways (Rudomin et al., 1998). Often, this involves presynaptic inhibition (Stein, 1995). One afferent is inhibited as a consequence of activity in another afferent, activity which leads, via a spinal route, to activation of presynaptic inhibitory interneurons that bear on the first afferent and reduce the size of transmitted action potentials. As a result, there is reduction in the amount of neurotransmitter released and in the size of postsynaptic EPSPs. Such sensori-sensory conditioning is seen across much of the animal kingdom (Watson, 1992).

GAIN CONTROL IN HUMAN PRIMARY AFFERENT TRANSMISSION OVER SPINAL PATHS

In humans, Ia transmission monosynaptically to leg motoneurons—for example, the H (Hoffmann) reflex—is attenuated by muscle spindle activation of Ia afferents serving uniarticular extensor muscles of the hip or knee or, probably, ankle. The inhibitory pathway is, at least in part, spinal through presynaptic inhibitory interneurons (Brooke et al., 1997). Such centripetal sensori-sensory conditioning is complemented by centrifugal conditioning arising from the brain and from central pattern-generating networks of the spinal cord and brain stem (Rudomin et al., 1998). For example, immediately before voluntary plantar flexion movement, H reflex magnitudes in the plantar flexor muscle soleus increase considerably.

There seems to be clear separation of the control of Ia afferents and cutaneous afferents during locomotion. Locomotor-induced modulation of cutaneous afferent affects on motoneurons appears to arise from centrifugal conditioning but, unlike the Ia pathways described above, not as attenuation from centripetal conditioning from somatosensory afferents activated as a consequence of the movement per se (Brooke et al., 1999). The meaning of this fundamental separation of afferent control in locomotion remains to be established.

Primary afferent activation can also reveal novel membrane characteristics of motoneurons. A brief burst of Ia afferent firing can reset membrane currents so that plateau potentials occur in mammals, a rapid series of action potentials from a depolarized plateau (Kiehn, 1991). Such repetitive motoneuronal firing, continuing well beyond the duration of the Ia afferent burst, then can be terminated by a brief burst of firing of high threshold primary afferents. Involvement of such plateau potentials has been demonstrated in stance (Kiehn, 1991).

GAIN CONTROL IN HUMAN PRIMARY AFFERENT TRANSMISSION OVER ASCENDING PATHS

Excitation of primary afferents in peripheral nerves at low stimulus intensities rapidly results (from arms, 15+ ms, legs 25+ ms) in somatosensory evoked potentials (SEPs) measured from scalp electrodes recording from the somatosensory reception areas of the cerebral cortex. As described above for spinal Ia reflexes, the ascending path from fast-conducting afferents to the brain can be attenuated at spinal levels by activation of other Ia afferents (Staines et al., 1997). The effect is observed as reduced magnitudes of SEPs, despite constant stimulation. Further, just as the brain can centrifugally control primary afferent transmission in Ia spinal reflexes, so it can also control the transmission through the ascending path (Rudomin et al., 1998). The centrifugal control alters transmission initiated by primary afferents as a function of the subject's motor "set" (Prochazka, 1989). For example, SEPs are attenuated following learning that involves those pathways online, and are further attenuated when the involvement becomes predictable to the subject (Nelson et al., 1998). The attenuation reduces SEP magnitudes by as much as 50% of initial control values. Accompanying behavioral evidence of failure to use the pathways in predictable conditions suggests that the brain control of transmission from the primary afferents is linked to a switch from reactive to predictive control. Such a switch likely reflects a difference in brain sites involved in the motor control for the tasks. Thus, stimulation of primary afferents and observation of subsequent neural response shed light on the neural organization for skilled behavior.

SUMMARY

Primary afferent complexity involves connectivity, specific gain modulation, and postsynaptic membrane modifiability. Key understandings are:

1. There are mechanisms for both centripetal and centrifugal control of primary afferent transmission, and the two can exist in combination.

2. Both pre- and postsynaptic modulation occur, as well as some specialized receptor modulation (e.g., modulated gamma drive onto muscle spindle intrafusal fibres).

3. Motoneuronal membrane ion channels can change action potential state in response to afferent discharge.

The functional significance emerging is that this complexity represents opportunities to tune the weighting of the contribution of somatosensory receptor sensing of the environment, thus altering the CNS neural nets determining the motoneuronal activation that leads to differences in behaviors.

REFERENCES

Baldissera, F., Hultborn, H., & Illert, M. (1981). Integration in spinal neuronal systems. In *Handbook of Physiology; Section 1, The Nervous System, Vol. II, Motor Control* (pp. 509–595). Ed. V. B. Brooks. Bethesda, MD: American Physiological Society.

Brooke, J. D., Cheng, J., Collins, D. F., McIlroy, W. E., Misiaszek, J. E., & Staines, W. R. (1997). Sensori-sensory afferent conditioning with leg movement: Gain control in spinal reflex and ascending paths. *Progress in Neurobiology, 51,* 393–421.

Brooke, J. D., McIlroy, W. E., Staines, W. R., Angerilli, P. A., & Peritore, G. F. (1999). Cutaneous reflexes of the human leg during passive movement. *Journal of Physiology, 15,* 619–628.

Jankowska, E. (1992). Interneuronal relay in spinal pathways from proprioceptors. *Progress in Neurobiology, 38,* 335–378.

Kiehn, O. (1991). Plateau potentials and active integration in the "final common pathway" for motor behaviour. *Trends in Neuroscience, 14,* 68–73.

Nelson, A. J., Brooke, J. D., McIlroy, W. E., Bishop, D. C., Norrie, R. G., & Matthew, A. (1998). Increased gain of human somatosensory evoked potentials (SEPs) when a variable cue to target location must be acquired. *Soc. Neurosci. Abs., 24,* 1662.

Pearson, K. G. (1993). Common principles of motor control in vertebrates and invertebrates. *Annual Reviews of Neuroscience, 16,* 265–297.

Peters, M. H., & Brooke, J. D. (1998). Teaching students erroneous information in neuroscience. *Journal of Motor Behavior, 30,* 285–287.

Pierrot-Deseilligny, E., Morin, C., Bergego, C., & Tankov, N. (1981). Pattern of group I fibre projections from ankle flexor and extensor muscles in man. *Experimental Brain Research, 42,* 337–350.

Prochazka, A. (1989). Sensorimotor gain control: A basic strategy of motor systems? *Progress in Neurobiology, 33,* 281–307.

Rudomin, P., Romo, R., & Mendell, L. M. (Eds.). (1998). *Presynaptic inhibition and neural control.* Oxford: Oxford University Press.

Staines, W. R., Brooke, J. D., Misiaszek, J. E., & McIlroy, W. E. (1997). Movement-induced gain modulation of somatosensory potentials and soleus H reflexes evoked from the leg. II. Correlation with rate of stretch of knee extensor muscles. *Experimental Brain Research, 115,* 156–164.

Stein, R. B. (1995). Presynaptic inhibition in humans. *Progress in Neurobiology, 47,* 533–544.

Watson, D. H. D. (1992). Presynaptic modulation of sensory afferents in the invertebrate and vertebrate nervous system. *Comparative Biochemistry and Physiology, 103 A,* 227–239.

J. D. Brooke
Northwestern University Medical School

AFRICA, PSYCHOLOGY IN

In Africa, the scientific study of psychology began during the early years of the 20th century. Mallory Wober (1975) has provided a detailed review of published articles and some of the unpublished reports of scientific investigations of psychological issues in Africa. Since 1900, some 1,500 published scientific papers reporting research on various aspects of psychology in Africa have been produced. Robert Levine (1961) has reviewed the available works from the point of view of anthropology and psychology. The bibliography of Irvine and colleagues (1969) included related writings as well. Leonard Doob (1965) presented a critical review of the major questions for African psychological studies to which investigators have directed their attention. Jan Hoorweg (1974) wrote a short summary showing the direction of research investigations of various topics in psychology in Africa. Apart from these brief summaries, surveys, and annotated bibliographies, Frederick Wickert (1967) and Wober (1975) are major sources of information on psychology in Africa. Wickert provided an extensive account of over 50 studies hitherto available only in French. Wober provided an account of psychological research available up to 1974.

Analysis of psychology publications in Africa shows that the largest number of articles appeared during 1950 to 1965. There had been a steady growth from 1920 to 1950, and an increase in the number of African psychologists who published their investigations during 1965 and 1970. The quality of such publications also has improved tremendously. As the number of African psychologists grows, as more of them gain experience in research activities and are spared administrative chores, as funds become more available for research, as avenues of publication become more available, as opportunities for the application of research results from African psychological studies increase—in short, as psychology grows as a discipline and as an applied science in Africa—all these factors will be reflected in increasing reports of African psychological studies. However, a great deal of such published material is already available, characterized by its broad coverage and degree of specialization, so that careful selection is necessary in describing questions to which psychological investigations have been directed.

BLACK AFRICA AS A TARGET AREA

Psychological research in Africa has dealt primarily with black Africans, as they alone, of all the peoples of Africa, cannot trace their cultural base to another continent. Yet black Africa is not a homogeneous cultural area. Early psychological investigations were carried out by foreign psychologists in French- or English-speaking areas of Africa and the literature on African psychology reflects the differing research interests of these psychologists. Within any given African country, there are groups that are heterogeneous not only in language, but also in political structure and ethnic culture: Nomadic societies coexist with pastoral societies. Religious affiliation varies from Christianity to Islam to traditional. Traditional societies coexist with modern societies and with societies in transition.

The diversity of African societies in close geographical proximity presents numerous opportunities for cross-cultural research, which has been reflected in published studies. This same diversity, however, may prevent any generalization about the psychology of the African. At present, numerous conflicting and very different findings are reported from investigations on the same topic. Often, perfect replications of investigations are impossible in two African groups because of the different languages needed in research situations, or other necessary modifications in the research tools which may be dictated by the subjects' cultural differences. Many of the results are tentative at best. Often they are inadvertently misleading, perhaps because most of the investigators are not African. No human being can divorce his or her own personality from the topic being investigated. Each investigator's interests, prejudices, cultural background, qualifications, and abilities are interwoven with the topics chosen for investigation. What we now have in psychology in Africa is substantially a European or American view.

THE TRAINING OF AFRICAN PSYCHOLOGISTS

Before 1960, the only training opportunity in psychology for African scholars was through a postgraduate degree in education earned in English-speaking countries or through the école normal superior programs in French-speaking countries. By 1965, a handful of African scholars trained in the United Kingdom, France,

Belgium, or the United States had returned to their countries, mainly to assume academic positions on the faculties of education in African universities. Teaching and research activities in psychology as a subject in its own right began as offshoots of teaching and research in education, social anthropology, or sociology in East, West, and Central Africa, with staff and financial support from the British and the French governments through their overseas development offices, and also from foundations (in particular, the Ford and Carnegie Foundations in the United States). The work of Gustav Jahoda in Ghana since 1954, André Ombredane in Zaire (1951–1958), and Marshall Segall in Uganda since 1959 are examples of efforts that set the pattern of psychological research in black Africa. The activities of social science research institutes led to the establishment of departments of psychology in many African universities. An example is the University of Zambia, which established a Department of Psychology in 1968 as a result of the activities of the Rhodes–Livingstone Institute of Social Research. Alistair Heron, a psychologist, became the director of that institute in 1963, and established the Human Development Research Unit in 1965. Among the aims of the unit were:

1. Sponsorship of research programs to ascertain the extent to which psychological knowledge obtained through scientific research in Europe and the United States could be generalized to Central Africa.

2. Provision of locally derived data for use in dealing with social, educational, and planning problems of a rapidly developing country.

3. Provision of research bases for the teaching of psychology at the university.

These objectives apply with equal force to the beginnings of psychology departments in all African universities, even though such clear statements of aims and such careful planning as at Zambia, are difficult to find elsewhere. Today there are 14 departments of psychology in 10 African countries, with five in Nigeria alone. Many of the staff members of these departments of psychology are Africans. A great deal of effort is being expended to implement research and publication programs but very few of these have actually been executed. In addition to a chronic shortage of research facilities, there are inadequate library facilities, insufficient financial grants for research, inadequate equipment, and an overburdened staff with little time for research and the production of publications on psychology in Africa.

PROFESSIONAL PRACTICE OF PSYCHOLOGY

In the past 10 years, with the increasing number of students who have completed psychology courses in the universities, the status of psychology has been improving. Far too little postgraduate work is done, however, to enable African psychologists to address themselves to interesting research and professional questions. Africans who graduate from departments of psychology often are not fully qualified to practice psychology or to engage in research. Without postgraduate training, psychology as a degree program is, in

Africa, as in most universities worldwide, a part of nonspecialist programs of basic university education. Graduates of departments of psychology, therefore, often find themselves in the civil service or in commerce and industry in administrative positions. Only in rare cases are they employed in areas demanding skills in psychology, which is as it should be because further professional training is necessary for such work. A few universities offer postgraduate courses in guidance and counseling, clinical psychology, and industrial psychology. Nigeria, Zambia, and Zimbabwe have created posts for clinical psychologists, educational psychologists, and industrial psychologists. Psychologists also work, in these and other countries, in schools and centers created by Ministries of Education for the purpose of giving guidance and counseling to school-age children. Psychologists are also employed in testing for purposes of selection for educational and industrial training in many African countries. Education ministries and examination bodies are the largest employers of psychology graduates. Graduates of other disciplines who have had postgraduate training in educational or other aspects of psychology are employed, together with psychology graduates, to carry out aptitude and ability testing for selection and training purposes, as well as in the assessment of achievement at the end of specific training programs.

Few clinical psychologists are employed in African countries, because there are as yet few qualified clinical psychologists who can make their need felt in local health services. In Zimbabwe and Nigeria, a handful of clinical psychologists are working in hospitals, but under adverse conditions. The growth of psychology departments and professional training facilities for psychology graduates may provide an increasing demand for the utilization of psychologists' skills in industry, health services, education, and social services.

PSYCHOLOGICAL ASSOCIATIONS

There are few psychological associations in Africa, which is one reason why psychology is underdeveloped there—there are no strong professional groups to advance its cause. Nigeria, Zambia, and Zimbabwe have national associations of psychology, and there is an Association of African Psychologists for French-speaking African psychologists. In many African countries, there are not enough psychologists to form national associations. Discussion is in progress concerning an expansion of the membership of the Association of African Psychologists to include psychologists from all African countries.

Africans are usually ill-informed about psychology. One function for any conference held must be the dissemination of information to various agencies concerning the uses of psychology as a science and as a profession. The attention of governments, industries, and businesses is often called to the value of psychology in contributing toward the solution of societal problems. The fact remains, however, that the number of psychologists in any particular African country is too small to make the desired impact on the public. At present, no African psychological association is a member of the International Union of Psychological Sciences—a reflection of the difficulties African associations have in establishing sizable membership, a strong constitution, firm criteria for membership, and a source of income through membership subscription. There is a definite awareness of the need to strengthen the association at home before venturing into the international arena. Also, few African psychologists participate in international conferences. For example, at the Biennial Conference of the International Association for Cross-Cultural Psychology (IACCP), which took place in Aberdeen, Scotland, in July 1982, there were 21 psychologists from the entire African continent, only seven of whom were black. And at the 20th Congress of Applied Psychology (International Association for Applied Psychology) in Edinburgh later in the same month, only 10 black African psychologists were present at the important conference, which meets every four years; there were only nine at Leipzig at the 22nd International Congress of Psychology (International Union of Psychological Sciences' Congress), which marked 100 years of psychology. This pattern of poor attendance is partly attributable to the cost of travel. When IACCP held meetings of its African chapter in 1973 in Ibadan, Nigeria, and in 1975 in Nairobi, Kenya, African psychologists attended in large numbers.

Michael Durojaiye of Nigeria was president of IACCP from 1974 to 1976, and since 1978 has been a member of the executive committee of the International Union of Psychological Sciences. The late Michael Ogbolu Okonji was a member of the executive committee of the IACCP and the International Society for Behavioral Development. Tape Goze of the Ivory Coast has joined the executive committee of the International Association for Applied Psychology.

PUBLICATION

The *Nigerian Journal of Psychology,* published once a year, is principally comprised of proceedings of annual conferences. This is the only journal outside South Africa devoted to scientific papers in psychology. Other articles are found in nonpsychological journals.

PSYCHOLOGICAL STUDIES IN AFRICA

A selection of studies is briefly described in the following with a view to highlighting the main topics in the areas of physical and psychomotor development, child rearing, cognitive development, ability testing, perception, motivation, attitudes, vocational aspiration, personality, and mental health.

It is important to emphasize that Africa is a huge continent and that no study can cover all African peoples. The diversity of African social organization and cultures prevents findings carried out in any part of Africa from being generalized in any meaningful way to other parts of Africa.

Physical and Psychomotor Development

Physical development. Longitudinal studies of physical development are rare in Africa. In Nigeria, Uganda, Tanzania, Zambia, and Gambia, physical growth shows the influence of climatic conditions, disease-carrying insects, and the availability of food. Kwoshiorkor affects a large number of children in Sierra Leone (from whence it took its name) and in other parts of black Africa. This disease of malnutrition is known to cause the death of many African babies.

Psychomotor development. Marcel Geber, writing with R. F. A. Dean, observed that the Moro reflex was weak in Ugandan newborns and was absent in infants over 4 days old (Geber & Dean, 1957). Examination of 107 babies not older than 8 days led the authors to conclude that these African babies were precocious in psychomotor ability as compared with babies in Europe. The climate and altitude of Kampala did not account for the precocity as European and Asian babies born in the same hospital did not show the same motor ability. Numerous investigations from different parts of Africa have tested different African infants and their findings support Geber and Dean. Mallory Wober (1975) reviewed these studies. His conclusions were that: (a) African infants show high psychomotor development in the first year of life; and (b) the achievements decline in the second and third years of life.

Not all investigators agree with Geber and Dean. Neil Warren (1972) provided a criticism of Geber's work on grounds of technicalities: the test used, the sketchy statistics, the inappropriateness of Gesell's norms, the inadequate sampling, improper comparison with European observations, and lack of precision in estimating ages of infants. Research evidence that does not support Geber and Dean's thesis was also reviewed. The conclusion was that there were no indisputable differences between the patterns of psychomotor development of African babies and those of babies elsewhere.

Child-Rearing Practices

Certain practices have been reported to characterize the way African parents rear their children. Children are highly valued in African societies. An African woman feels truly fulfilled by becoming a mother (Kaye, 1962; Salamone, 1969; Biesheuvel, 1959). For many Africans, to be childless is a serious misfortune. These statements are found to be true in East, Central, West, and South Africa.

After the child is born, breast-feeding, personal contact, a great deal of physical handling, and steady and cheerful emotional relationship between mother and child are the rule in the first year of life. Infants are invariably carried in their mothers' arms or on their mothers' backs. Other relatives, especially other women in the extended family circle, and friends and acquaintances readily participate in play relationships with the infant. These attitudes are shared by both traditional and modern African families, all of whom attend with great patience to the needs of the child. Some mothers in urban settings who work are often able to maintain this pattern of infant care through maids engaged for the sole purpose of looking after the baby in the first year of life.

Another important child-rearing practice is weaning. Traditionally weaning is done at the outset of another pregnancy. It is also common for an infant to be weaned from the breast by the age of 18 months whether or not the mother is pregnant again. One method of dealing with weaning has been to separate the child from the mother, with the grandmother assuming the child's care. The attendant emotional problems that separation brings to the child have been described elsewhere (Durojaiye, 1976). In many urban and rural settings today, separation from the mother is of short daily duration, and distress at the mother's departure is short lived. Regularity of separation brings about adaptability in the child, thus minimizing distress and sensitizing the child to the routine of daily separation.

Surveys of child-rearing practices in various countries of Africa indicate wide differences between urban, educated, high-socioeconomic-status families and rural, traditional, low socioeconomic status families. For the majority of African families of low socioeconomic status, the following are some characteristics of child-rearing practice: limited verbal interaction between mother and child (Munroe et al., 1981; Super & Harkness, 1982), infrequent father-child play situations, authoritarian tendency in the relationship between the adult and the child, emphasis on obedience and respect as primary and desirable outcomes, training of children to participate in household chores and in the economic activities of the parents at an early age, strict and nonpermissive discipline schedules, early segregation of sex roles, and a carefree attitude toward privacy.

Cognitive Development

The course and level of cognitive development in African children has been investigated by Abiola (1965). He tested children from two social groups at each age from 1 to 5 years using items from the Gesell test and the Merrill Palmer test. He reported that the scores of the two groups were similar at the age of 1 year, diverged at ages 2 and 3 years, and converged at the age of 5 years. In her own study of the same group of children, Barbara Lloyd (1971, 1977) used a longitudinal design and found gaps between the ability levels of the two social groups up to the age of 8 years on the Stanford–Binet intelligence scale.

The work of Charles Super (1972) in Zambia shows what may be an indication of the true state of affairs with regard to the intellectual development of African children. Super's subjects were urban and rural children aged 4 to 9 years. He found that achievements in visual analysis and integration improved with age, for both schooled and unschooled groups. "Cognitive maturity and logical thought," as indicated by the absence of contradictions and consistent sorting of the color forms, appeared to be established by the age of 7 years. Delayed auditory feedback was reacted to after the age of 5 years, indicating changes that stem from physiological developments of brain organization. Schooling was reported as accounting for the increase in cognitive and verbal scores of 7- and 8-year-old children. Similarly, urban children were generally better in test situations.

Good nutrition, positive adult-child interaction, opportunities in the environment for constructive play and exploration, schooling, and the challenges posed by urban complex life are some important factors in permitting African children to demonstrate and apply the abilities that studies show they have.

Ability Testing

Measurement of the ability of African subjects was of interest to early investigators, who wanted to know how African blacks compared with whites in Africa and elsewhere. One of the earliest investigations in this area was carried out by Loram (1917) in South Africa. The results obtained for Africans reflected the inferior educational opportunities open to them at that time. Loram showed that while an equivalent of $15 (U.S.) was being spent yearly on the education of a white child in South Africa, only 30 cents was spent each year to educate a black child. Loram proposed educational reforms that have been largely ignored for the past 80 years. There is a yawning gap between the expenditures on education for blacks and for whites in South Africa. And the gap in the environmental and social conditions of the two races is even wider, and continues to widen.

Other investigations that followed Loram (Loades & Rich, 1917; Porteus, 1937) concluded that the development of the intelligence of Africans was inferior to that of the whites. Porteus attributed this to genetic differences. His conclusion was presaged by Fick (1929) and echoed by Jansen van Rensburg (1938). Simeon Biesheuvel (1943) criticized Fick's work that compared abilities along racial lines (1982). For the past 40 years, Biesheuvel's main point has been that the test results are questionable because it is impossible to find black and white groups in South Africa who have experienced equivalent social conditions or opportunities.

The idea that "intelligence and intellectual behavior are culturally specific" has been put forth by Crijns (1962). Many investigations of intellectual abilities of Africans have failed to take this simple principle into consideration. One characteristic of African subjects in test situations that has been supported consistently by various investigators is the tendency of Africans to take their time in solving a problem. Ombredane and colleagues (1958) found that the Congolese were slower than the Belgians, not because of slower thought processes, but because of a general lack of interest in speedy performance.

A different approach to testing ability was employed by Robaye and co-workers (1960), who found that when their Congolese apprentices memorized instructions for carrying out a mechanical task, they performed as well as did the white pupils.

Testing selection. Selective recruitment for educational and industrial training purposes is unavoidable in many African countries where there are scarce resources to spend on the education or training of a small number of individuals from a large population of eligible citizens. Thus the need to determine who will make the best use of available resources in the time required has been served by selection testing.

Industrial selection. One of the first selection criteria was provided by MacDonald (1944–1945), who found a correlation of 0.43 between his tests and the criterion for military performance. Actual testing for jobs all over Southern and Central Africa was carried out by Biesheuvel (1952) of South Africa. Mine workers of all grades were selected by the General Adaptability Battery. Verhaegen (1962) later found a correlation between tests and performance in the first year of a technical school for the Union Minière in Katanga.

The problem of obtaining quantitative assessments of performance has been difficult for investigators in Africa, where employing authorities had few records of employee performance, where no supervisors' ratings existed, and where, as in most cases, selection was for employment in new areas of works. Often too, the fact that workers were satisfactory was not related to their own satisfaction in the job. Thus Taylor (1967) described how he had helped in the selection of noncommissioned officers, tradesmen, and students for technical education in Ghana as early as 1953. The army

and commercial firms reported satisfaction with their selections. From these beginnings grew an accepted part of selection procedure for employment and for admission to top training programs in technical and professional institutions other than universities and related educational establishments.

Educational selection. By far the most interesting aspect of selection for investigators was educational selection. Scott (1950) adapted a form of the Gabbani–Ballard Test in Sudan and obtained correlations that improved with increases in education, suggesting that the process of education produced qualitative changes in manifested abilities. Cooper (1961) reported that correlations of –0.24 to 0.74 were found between test results and success on various subjects at a technical school in Nigeria. Meanwhile, Price-Williams (1961) found a correlation of 0.69 to 0.79 between test results and teachers' ratings of observed ability in rural Nigerian school children. The same pattern was reported by Fontaine (1963) after administering the progressive matrices to 2000 pupils in Mali. He obtained a correlation of 0.93 for higher grades. Predictive validity was confirmed by Taylor and Bradshaw (1965), who reported Nigerian primary school pupils who had high scores on six subtests were later found to have gained admission to secondary schools. Schwarz (1963) devised ways of administering tests to ensure fairness to candidates with limited schooling.

In East Africa, work by Silvey (1963, 1972) and Somerset (1968) has helped to underscore the value of good schools and the limitations of the junior schools, thus leaving examinations to serve as predictors of success at the secondary school. Irvine (1965, 1966, 1969) evolved tests to predict later performance in schools.

In general, practical experience has convinced many observers that little reliance should be placed on test scores as the sole criteria for selection purposes. Health, family background, school quality, and age influence the extent to which a good estimate of a pupil's potential can be obtained. Improved living conditions and education change the patterns of test prediction for many African children. Flexibility, a liberal attitude, and sensitivity are required in responding to the emerging needs and performance of the individual child, pupil, or apprentice. Sociopolitical considerations mandate that educational and industrial training opportunities be made available to applicants from backward areas. As education improves for school-age children, testing will become more reliable.

Patterns of abilities. Factor analytic studies designed to map structures of abilities in Africans have been reported. African subjects did accomplish tests that yielded factors familiar in Western tests, although the ordering differed. The usual labeling of factors such as mechanical, numerical, and verbal was obtained, as well as unusual ones such as "male educational aptitude," "acculturation," and "cognitive westernization" to describe the subjects. Existing evidence indicates that the structure of ability in African and Western males is similar. More appropriately, when more educated Africans are tested with Western tests, more factors are obtained that resemble European or North American structures.

Perception

Pictorial perception. Three-dimensional perception is usually regarded as difficult for Africans. Anecdotal reports of explorers and missionaries and writings of anthropologists abound that indicate this view. Jahoda and his coauthors (1977) demonstrated that 3-year-old children in Ghana and Zimbabwe who had had little experience with pictures recognized the subject matter of pictures they were shown. As far as recognition of objects in line drawing is concerned, evidence shows that African school children learn effectively from line drawings in textbooks.

Hudson (1960, 1967) concluded that African subjects are less efficient in perceiving pictorial depth than white subjects. Black adults did worse than white and black school children, and black children more poorly than whites. These findings have been largely confirmed by numerous investigations (Mundy-Castle, 1966; Kilbride et al., 1968; Deregowski, 1968).

Visual illusion. The view that African subjects tended to make inferences about things they see, interpreting them as they know them rather than as they see them, was first suggested in studies of picture perception. When Allport and Pettigrew (1957) tested for illusion with the rotating trapezoidal window, the results for urban Africans and Europeans were identical. However, rural Africans mostly did not see the illusion, whereas other subjects mostly did. Two illusions—Muller–Lyer (M–L) and Horizontal–Vertical (H–V)—have received the attention of psychologists in Africa. The explanation given by Segall and his associates (1966) for the Muller–Lyer illusion was that people living in a "carpentered world" have specific associations with ingoing and outgoing fins. People in a carpentered environment would be more susceptible to illusion.

Rotation was frequently noted when African subjects reproduced a diamond or a square. Work by Deregowski (1972a, 1971) showed that whereas education reduced errors, culture influenced the ways in which diagrams are copied. Another factor, proposed by Berry (1966), is context dependence, which made some Africans see shapes in terms of objects familiar to them. However, Serpell found that when Zambian children were asked to bend wire to copy various shapes, they did better, thus suggesting that they possess an efficient proprioceptive perceptual skill.

Perception of time. The term "African time" is commonly heard, implying that Africans tend not to keep strictly to an appointed time. No doubt it is generally appreciated that Africans relate to time as they cope with seasonal changes, sowing and harvesting, hunting, and the milestones of human life, all of which are time-structured events.

It is important to emphasize that an essential function of education in Africa is to teach Western conventions of perceptual skills so as to enable African people to function adequately in societies that make increasing use of Western-style technology. Education, it is hoped, will reduce whatever physical, ecological, or cultural factors negatively affect correct perception.

Other perceptions. Some perceptual skills, however, are strong in many Africans. Perception of signs and symbols of natural events, of weather, of the sky and the stars, and of paths of animals are important in traditional life, visual skills displayed in playing complex African games have not been researched. Auditory skills of Africans have been mentioned by many writers. Ombredane (1956) has said that African intellectual organization is a musicochoreographic structure. Maistriaux (1960) described it as musicorhythmic.

Motivation

The study of motivation in Africans has been limited. Popular opinion holds that Africans have tended to be motivated by group feelings. The traditional African behaved in a way socially approved by the extended family. Economic achievement was principally important not for the satisfaction of the individual, but for the benefit of the family. The context of child rearing emphasized group feeling. The dependence of the individual on the family and the responsibility to it were carefully fostered in many African cultures (Munroe et al., 1972). Anthropological studies of African peoples support those views. Psychological studies of dreams, first carried out by Lee (1958) among the Zulus, have provided information on motivation. Zulu women reported dreams that showed the influence of ancestral spirits and childbirth. A similar study in Uganda revealed that the Baganda dreams were about kinsmen, indicating the importance of social relationships.

The concept of achievement motivation advanced by McClelland implies that people have a need to achieve or to perform well according to a recognized standard of excellence. Traditional African expression of this phenomenon was commonly believed to be social rather than individualistic, and related to community needs. Examination of "need achievement (n Ach)" among Nigerian subjects was carried out by Levine (1966) through analysis of dreams and essays of secondary-school boys. The topic for the essay was "success." Levine found that dreams reported by Ibo people most often contained achievement imagery. The Ibos also mentioned self-development as a principal ambition more often than did the two remaining groups studied—the Yoruba and the Hausa people. Child-rearing practices were seen as responsible for levels of need achievement. Following this, a study by Okorodudu (1967) showed that the father's absence and the mother's marital status together related to self-development and individualistic determination to succeed. This was not related to scholastic success, however. But need achievement as revealed through thematic apperception testing was found to be associated with the prosperity of the Chagga of Tanzania (Ostheimer, 1969). The role of child-rearing practices in fostering achievement motivation has also been studied by Durojaiye (1976), who reported that permissiveness and encouragement of adventure by Yoruba parents were associated with good scholastic progress and ambition for self-development in children.

Attitudes

Research interest that led to investigations of patterns of attitudes of Africans had been aroused by the social change going on in Africa. It was important to identify those attitudes that corresponded to traditional forms of society and those that resulted from colonialism and other Western influences. Another concern was to see if new attitudes emerged from the experience of social change.

Biesheuvel (1955) and Jahoda (1961) are the leaders in attitude studies in Africa. After studying the attitudes of Zulu and Ghanaian subjects, respectively, these investigators independently reached the conclusion that in traditional matters—belief, family, values—traditional attitudes persisted. In other areas, school children tested agreed with Western statements of opinion. Dawson

(1967) set out to examine the attitudes of Creoles, Mende, Temne, and Fulbe workers in Sierra Leone with a new questionnaire that permitted a measure of agreement or disagreement with traditional or with Western statements separately; also with semi-Western or semi-traditional statements. Thus, on each attitudinal topic, there were four statements. Dawson found differences among the subject groups. The traditionally aggressive Creoles supported more Western statements than did the pastoralist Fulbe, who showed a slight support overall for traditional statements.

Gilbertson (1971) in Ghana found that support for Western ideas by children was associated with ownership of a television set by the family. Also, children who agreed with both traditional and Western ideas also agreed with compromise items. Bormans (1968) found a coexistence of traditional and Western attitudes. Klineberg and Zavalloni (1969) found compromise statements among students who described themselves as innovators. In daily life in Africa today, educated and professional Africans exhibit attitudes that represent a synthesis of Western and traditional patterns.

Several other studies of attitudes have been done with other ethnic and tribal groups. Studies of stereotypes toward tribal feeling have shown that while the notion of the tribe is now rejected by many African intellectuals, it remains a psychological reality. Attitudes toward women and marriage remain largely traditional. Western education and training improve progressive ideas but do not remove superstitious beliefs (Jahoda, 1970). A study of attitude toward birth control (Molnos, 1970) showed that childlessness is generally unwelcome in East Africa. The present attitudes of Africans reflect the interaction of traditional attitudes with colonialism, technology, education, and travel.

Personality

Jahoda (1961) pointed out that despite numerous attempts to generalize about African personality, "the chastening fact is that our ignorance in this sphere remains almost complete." This statement remains true today. Scientific studies of personality in Africa began with Ritchie (1943), who linked harsh weaning with a feeling of dependence on parents, and ultimately on any external authority. As Crijns (1966) pointed out, this suggestion of "insecure self" or "weak superego" personality development in Africans was echoed by many French and Belgian psychologists. Jahoda (1961) found that the higher the educational level of Ghanaians, the more integrated was their value system and the more autonomous their orientation to whites. He found little evidence of feelings of inferiority or dependence.

Witkin (1967) proposed a concept of field dependence that linked child-rearing practices to cognitive style and general personality. He designed the Rod and Frame Test and the Embedded Figures Test to detect cognitive performance associated with field dependence. Berry (1967) related field independence to child-rearing styles and forms of economy, and found that the field-dependent Temne farmers in Sierra Leone were conscientious, compliant, and conservative. Other psychologists who have applied the field-independence theory have not always obtained a confirmation of Berry's results. Edgerton (1971) undertook a study

of the Pokol and the Kamba of Kenya, the Seber of Uganda, and the Hehe of Tanzania, and administered personality questions, Rorschach tests, and pictures designed to explore values. He found that the most acculturated group, the Kamba, was "less affectionate, less concerned with cattle, less independent, less fearful and less depressed." Two personality dimensions emerged from Edgerton's massive data. The first dimension he called emotionality: farmers showed "closed" and pastoralists showed "open" emotionality. His second dimension was action—pastoralists tended toward more "direct" action and farmers toward more "indirect" action.

Vocational Aspiration

In many African countries, aspiration greatly outstrips opportunities. Frustration follows unemployment, and increased misery and poverty have been the experience of many who leave school. Such people continue to turn to urban areas for jobs and thus the effort to provide rural orientation does not arrest the flight from the land (Foster 1968). In West Africa, studies by Clignet (1964), Foster (1965), Abiri (1966), and McQueen (1965) showed how education was regarded in relation to making a living. In some studies, the expectations of students were considered unrealistic in terms of available opportunities. Education was perceived as a means of social mobility in East and West Africa (Silvey, 1969; Koff, 1967; King, 1971). Durojaiye (1970), however, showed that educational and occupational choices, when there is no pressure of the uncertainty of earning a living, can be related to the pupils' genuine interests. African subjects rated familiar jobs, male-oriented jobs, and essential services higher than other types. Perceived levels of income correlated with perceived prestige (Foster 1965). Prestige hierarchy was found to be similar (Hicks, 1966; Irvine, 1969). Job aspirations of African pupils are directed toward the professions, well-paid jobs, and jobs in cities (Clignet, 1964). More education brings higher aspirations, but realism is reflected in lowered aspirations after a period of unemployment (Wallace & Weeks, 1972).

Mental Health

The fear in many African countries is that unrealistic vocational aspirations and the ensuing frustration caused by unemployment or dissatisfaction with the work obtained may lead not only to political difficulties, but also to crime and mental ill health. Industrialization and urbanization bring with them changes. The mental health of many Africans today depends on their ability to adjust to social change.

The performance of African workers in industry is another potential source of maladjustment. The values of various incentives have been studied. Proper behavior on the part of management and supervisors, good work situations, satisfactory wages, and promotion were some of the common incentives preferred. Hauser (1963) found that strict supervision and lack of satisfaction at work related to high absenteeism in workers in Dakar. Psychological adjustment to urban life and to industrialization constitutes a major concern in many African countries today.

Mental health problems have other sources in the African environment. Malnutrition, disease, or disorders of body chemistry may affect psychological functioning. Thus Carothers (1972) described how, throughout Africa, many endemic infections have caused brain damage and damage to normal psychological functioning. Malaria is a common example. A biochemical source of mental ill health was indicated in the work of Leighton (1969), who found that 81% of villagers and 95% of urban dwellers in his Nigeria sample had symptom patterns psycho-physiological in nature. Also, electroencephalographic studies by Mundy-Castle (1970) point to the possibility of malnutrition causing mild brain injury in Ghanaian subjects. On the other hand, there are some social-psychological and psychocultural explanations for mental illness that are strongly held by many Africans, literate and illiterate alike. Belief in witchcraft is widespread, and is regarded as a major cause of mental illness.

A report by the World Health Organization (1960) asserted that "most African societies recognized and considered abnormal what in Western terms are called epilepsy, mania, florid schizophrenia, acute confusion, marked dementia, agitation and severe mental defect." In 1968, Ellenberger reported a broad conclusion of a Pan-African psychiatrists' conference that the biological predisposition to health or ill health is probably distributed similarly among all people, but that cultural factors determine symptom patterns and reactive conditions.

Cultural factors also have been reported to account for mental ill health in Nigeria, in Ghana (Fortes & Mayer, 1966), and in both rural and urban areas of Ethiopia (Giel & Van Luijk, 1969–70). Leighton (1969) pointed out that it is social cultural disintegration that causes mental illness, not social change. Different cultures have different accounts of the origins of mental illness, and some types of illness are either tolerated or unclassified by traditional healers in some cultures. Also, Western psychiatrists have recorded different incidences for depression in different African countries.

The therapeutic approach to mental illness is another point on which psychiatrists do not agree. Orley (1970) was rather cautious about integrating traditional healers' work into psychiatric treatment. The position, however, in many African communities is that the traditional healers understand the cultural background and the family context of the patient. They are believed to be competent and capable of procuring remedies. Their results may be no more than a "placebo effect," but unless such healers fail, many patients will not be brought to a psychiatrist. The social and collective approach to the treatment of mental ill health is recognized by many religious sects in Africa also. It is not uncommon for a patient to receive help from a psychiatrist, a traditional healer, and the church simultaneously—all with the support of relatives and friends.

CONCLUSIONS

Present and future efforts in psychology in Africa will be seen in work directed to improvements in conditions and processes of learning, achievement of personal and social adjustment through guidance and counseling, and promotion of mental health through psychological services in industry, in the community, and in hospitals. Psychological research in Africa will reflect activities in these areas as well.

REFERENCES

Abiola, E. T. (1965). The nature of intellectual development of Nigerian children. *Teacher Education, 6*, 37–57.

Abiri, J. O. O. (1966). The educational attitudes of some Nigerian adolescent grammar school pupils. *West African Journal of Education, 10*, 118–121.

Berry, J. W. (1967). Independence and conformity in subsistence-level societies. *Journal of Personality and Social Psychology, 7*, 415–418.

Biesheuvel, S. (1943). *African intelligence.* Johannesburg: South African Institute of Race Relations.

Biesheuvel, S. (1952). Personnel selection tests for Africans. *South African Journal of Science, 49*, 3–12.

Biesheuvel, S. (1952). The occupational abilities of Africans. *Optima, 2*, 18–22.

Biesheuvel, S. (1955). Incentives and human relations in industry. *Industrial Review of Africa, 2*, 1–7.

Biesheuvel, S. (1959). Further studies on the measurement of attitudes towards western ethical concepts. *Journal of the National Institute of Personnel Research, 7*, 141–155.

Biesheuvel, S. (1959). *Race, culture and personality.* Johannesburg: South African Institute of Race Relations.

Biesheuvel, S. (1959). *The development of personality in African cultures.* Lagos: Commission for Technical Cooperation in Africa, South of the Sahara.

Bormans, M. (1968). Contribution à l'étude des mentalités sur la famille: Ce qu'en pensent les jeunes Sahariens. *Revue Occident Musulman, 5*, 15–39.

Carothers, J. C. (1972). *The mind of man in Africa.* London: Stacey.

Clignet, M. R. (1964). Education et aspirations professionelles. *Tiers Monde, 5*, 61–82.

Crijns, A. G. J. (1962). African intelligence: A critical survey of cross cultural research in Africa south of the Sahara. *Journal of Social Psychology, 57*, 283–301.

Crijns, A. G. J. (1966). African basic personality structure: A critical review of bibliographical sources and of principal findings. *Gawein, 14*, 239–248.

Dawson, J. L. M. (1967). Traditional versus western attitudes in West Africa: The construction, validation and application of a measuring device. *British Journal of Social and Clinical Psychology, 6*, 81–96.

Doob, L. W. (1965). Psychology. In R. Lystad (Ed.), *The African World.* London: Pall Mall Press.

Durojaiye, M. O. A. (1970). *Psycho-cultural constraints on formal education of the African child.* Presented at Universities of East Africa Social Sciences Conference, Dar es Salaam.

Durojaiye, M. O. A. (1976). *A new introduction to educational psychology.* London: Evans.

Edgerton, R. B. (1971). *The individual in cultural adaptation.* Berkeley, CA: University of California Press.

Fick, M. L. (1929). Intelligence test results of poor white, native (Zulu), coloured and Indian schoolchildren and the educational and social implications. *South African Journal of Science, 26,* 904–920.

Fontaine, C. (1963). Notes sur une expérience d'application de tests au Mali (1962–1963). *Revue de Psychologie Appliquée, 13,* 235–246.

Fortes, M., & Mayer, D. Y. (1966). Psychosis and social change among the Tallensi of northern Ghana. *Cahiers d'Etudes Africaines, 6,* 5–40.

Foster, P. J. (1965). *Education and social change in Ghana.* London: Routledge & Kegan Paul.

Foster, P. J. (1968). Some remarks on education and unemployment in Africa. *Manpower and Unemployment Research in Africa, 1,* 19–20.

Geber, M., & Dean, R. F. A. (1957). The state of development of newborn African children. *Lancet, 272,* 1216–1219.

Giel, R., & Van Luijk, J. M. (1969–1970). Psychiatric morbidity in a rural village in South-Western Ethiopia. *International Journal of Social Psychiatry, 16,* 63–71.

Gilbertson, S. (1971). *Television attitudes and cognitive dissonance phenomena in Ghana.* M. Sc. thesis, University of Bristol.

Hauser, A. (1963). *Facteurs humaines affectant la productivité des travailleurs industriels du Cap-Vert.* Dakar: Institut de Science Economique Appliquée.

Hicks, R. E. (1966). Occupational prestige and its factors. *African Social Research, 1,* 41–58.

Hoorweg, J. C. (1974). Africa (south of the Sahara): Review of psychological literature. In V. S. Sexton & H. Misiak (Eds.), *Psychology around the world today.* Monterey, CA: Brooks/Cole.

Hudson, W. (1960). Pictorial depth perception in sub-cultural groups in Africa. *Journal of Social Psychology, 52,* 183–208.

Hudson, W. (1967). The study of the problem of pictorial perception among unacculturated groups. *International Journal of Psychology, 2,* 90–107.

Irvine, S. H. (1965). Adapting tests to the cultural setting: A comment. *Occupational Psychology, 39,* 13–23.

Irvine, S. H. (1966). Towards a rationale for testing attainments and abilities in Africa. *British Journal of Educational Psychology, 36,* 24–32.

Irvine, S. H. (1969). Factor analysis of African abilities and attainments: Constructs across cultures. *Psychological Bulletin, 71,* 20–32.

Jahoda, G. (1961/1962). Aspects of Westernisation: A study of adult-class attitudes in Ghana: I. *British Journal of Sociology, 12,* 375–386; II, *13,* 43–56.

Jahoda, G. (1970). Supernatural beliefs and changing cognitive structures among Ghanaian university students. *Journal of Cross-Cultural Psychology, 1,* 115–130.

Jahoda, G. (1971). Retinal pigmentation, illusion susceptibility and space perception. *International Journal of Psychology, 6,* 159–208.

Kaye, B. (1962). *Bringing up children in Ghana.* London: Allen & Unwin.

King, K. J. (1971). *Education and ethnicity in the Rift Valley: Maasai, Kipsigis and Kikuyu in the school system.* Institute for Development Studies, Staff Paper no 113, Nairobi.

Klineberg, O., & Zavalloni, M. (1969). *Nationalism and tribalism among African students. A study of social identity.* Paris: Mouton.

Koff, D. R. (1967). Education and employment perspective of Kenya primary pupils. In J. R. Sheffield (Ed.), *Education, employment and rural development.* Nairobi: East African Publishing House.

Lee, S. G. (1958). Social influences in Zulu dreaming. *Journal of Social Psychology, 47,* 265–283.

Leighton, A. H. (1969). A comparative study of psychiatric disorder in Nigeria and rural North America. In S. C. Plog, & R. B. Edgerton (Eds.), *Changing perspectives in mental illness.* New York: Holt, Rinehart & Winston.

Levine, R. A. (1961). Africa. In F. L. K. Hsu (Ed.), *Psychological anthropology.* Homewood, IL: Dorsey Press.

Levine, R. A. (1966). *Dreams and deeds: Achievement motivation in Nigeria.* Chicago: University of Chicago Press.

Lloyd, B. B. (1971). The intellectual development of Yoruba children: A re-examination. *Journal of Cross-Cultural Psychology, 2,* 29–38.

Lloyd, B. B. (1977). The intellectual development of Yoruba children. Additional evidence and a serendipitous finding. *Journal of Cross-Cultural Psychology, 8,* 3–16.

Loades, H. R., & Rich, S. G. (1917). Binet tests on South African natives—Zulus. *Journal of Genetic Psychology, 24,* 373–383.

Loram, C. J. (1917). *The education of the South African native.* London: Longman Green.

Maistriaux, R. (1960). Les methodes actives en terre d'Afrique. *Problèmes Sociaux Congolais, 49,* 7–56.

McQueen, A. J. (1965). Aspirations and problems of Nigerian school leavers. *Inter-African Labour Research Bulletin, 12,* 35–42.

Molnos, A. (1970). *Attitudes towards family planning in East Africa.* Munich: Weltforum Verlag.

Mundy-Castle, A. C. (1970). Epilepsy and the electroencephalogram in Ghana. *African Journal of Medical Science, 1,* 221–236.

Munroe, R. L., Munro, R. H., & Whiting, B. B. (Eds.) (1981). *Handbook of cross-cultural human development.* New York: Garland.

Okorodudu, C. (1967). Achievement training and achievement motivation among the Kpelle in Liberia: A study of household structure antecedents. *Dissertation Abstracts, 29,* 1527–1529.

Ombredane, A. (1956). Etude psychologique des noirs Asalampasu. I. Le comportement intéllectuel dans l'épreuve du matrix-couleur. *Memoires de l'Academie Royale des Sciences Coloniales. Ire Classe, 6,* fasc. 3.

Ombredane, A., Bertelson, P., & Beniest-Noirot, E. (1958). Speed and accuracy of performance of an African native population and of Belgian children on a paper and pencil perceptual test. *Journal of Social Psychology, 47,* 327–337.

Orley, J. (1970). *Culture and mental illness.* Nairobi: East African Publishing House.

Ostheimer, J. M. (1969). Measuring achievement motivation among the Chagga of Tanzania. *Journal of Social Psychology, 78,* 17–30.

Porteus, S. D. (1937). *Intelligence and environment.* New York: Macmillan.

Price-Williams, D. R. (1961). A study concerning concepts of conservation of quantities among primitive children. *Acta Psychologica, 18,* 297–305.

Ritchie, J. F. (1943). *The African as suckling and as adult. A psychological study.* Rhodes-Livingstone Institute paper no 9.

Robaye, E., Robaye, F., & Falmagne, J. C. (1960). Le testing de l'éducabilité dans un groupe de noirs congolais. *Bulletin de l'Academie Royale des Sciences d'Outre-Mer, Nouvelle Série, 6,* 295–321.

Salamone, F. A. (1969). Further notes on Hausa culture and personality. *International Journal of Social Psychiatry, 16,* 39–44.

Schwarz, P. A. (1963). Adapting tests to the cultural setting. *Educational and Psychological Measurement, 23,* 673–686.

Scott, G. C. (1950). Measuring Sudanese intelligence. *British Journal of Educational Psychology, 20,* 43–54.

Silvey, J. (1963). *Testing ability tests: The measurement of ability among African schoolboys.* East African Institute for Social Research Conference, Dar es Salaam.

Silvey, J. (1969). The occupational attitudes of secondary school leavers in Uganda. In R. Jolly (Ed.), *Education in Africa.* Nairobi: East African Publishing House.

Silvey, J. (1972). A longitudinal study of ability and attainment from the end of primary to the end of secondary school in Uganda. In L. J. Cronbach & P. J. D. Drenth (Eds.), *Mental tests and cultural adaptations.* The Hague: Mouton.

Somerset, H. C. A. (1968). *Predicting success in school certificate.* Nairobi: East African Publishing House.

Super, C. M. (1972). *Cognitive changes in Zambian children during the late preschool years.* Report no 22. Human Development Research Unit, University of Zambia.

Super, C. M., & Harkness, S. (1982). The infant's niche in rural Kenya and metropolitan America. In L. L. Adler (Ed.), *Issues in cross-cultural research.* New York: Academic Press.

Taylor, A., & Bradshaw, G. D. (1965). Secondary school selection: The development of an intelligence test for use in Nigeria. *West African Journal of Education, 9,* 6–11.

Taylor, A. (Ed.) (1967). *Educational and occupational selection in West Africa.* London: Oxford University Press.

Van Rensburg, J. A. (1938). The learning ability of the South African native compared with that of the European. *Research series no. 5.* Pretoria: South African Council for Educational and Sociological Research.

Verhaegen, P. (1962). Possibilité d'une orientation scolaire basée sur les épreuves psychologiques chez des enfants africains. *Revue de Psychologie Appliquée, 12,* 123–133.

Wallace, T., & Weeks, S. G. (1972). Youth in Uganda: Some theoretical perspectives. *International Social Science Journal, 24,* 354–361.

Warren, N. (1972). African infant precocity. *Psychological Bulletin, 78,* 353–367.

Wickert, F. R. (1967). *Readings in African psychology from French language sources.* East Lansing, MI: African Studies Center, Michigan State University.

Witkin, H. A. (1967). A cognitive style approach to cross cultural research. *International Journal of Psychology, 2,* 233–250.

Wober, M. (1975). *Psychology in Africa.* London: International African Institute.

World Health Organization. (1960). *Expert Committee on Mental Health* (8th Report). Geneva: Author.

M. O. A. DUROJAIYE
University of Lagos, Nigeria

AGGRESSION

Aggression is complex and multiply determined in its causes, difficult to predict, and in many instances hard to control.

THEORIES OF AGGRESSION

Aggression as Instinct

The belief that aggression is instinctive is popular among the general American public. In the 1960s, three books championing the instinctive basis of aggression were widely received in the United States: Lorenz's *On Aggression,* Ardrey's *The Territorial Imperative,* and Morris' *The Naked Ape.* Each espoused the view that aggression springs primarily from an innate fighting instinct. According to this view, aggressive energy growing from this instinct is spontaneously generated within the person continuously and at a constant rate. As time passes, aggressive energy is said to build up. The more that has accumulated, the weaker the stimulus necessary to set it off or release it into overt aggressive behavior. If enough time has passed since its last expression, overt aggression may occur spontaneously, with no apparent releasing stimuli. In this view, aggressive energy inexorably accumulates and inexorably must be expressed. The best one can hope for is its displaced expression into channels which are not antisocial, the usual example suggested being competitive athletics.

Instinct theory, a blend of anecdote, analogical leaps, unsystematic journalism, and undefined concepts, is seductively appealing. It is irresponsible, in the sense that, according to the theory, aggressive urges accumulate and must be expressed independently of the individual's choice. The theory is comprehensive, in that it can sweepingly explain diverse forms and rates of aggression when no other single cause, by itself, can do so. Most contemporary scientific views of aggression in America agree that one contributing factor is a genetic-physiological capacity to aggress. But to accept an unknown and unknowable accumulation of unseeable and unmeasurable energy as the basis for aggressive behavior is to use a mythology almost totally unsupported, and in fact largely refuted, by scientific evidence. For example, the so-called cathartic expression of purported aggressive instinctual energy characteristically does not lead to reduced levels of overt aggression, as a "draining-off" phenomenon would predict. In fact, the opposite is more likely to occur. Overt aggression usually leads to more, not less, overt aggression. The catharsis effect is one of many instances in which the instinct theory fails to accord with much-replicated scientific findings.

Instinct theorists have probably done a major disservice to efforts at advancing society's understanding and control of aggression. Their popularity may be viewed as a major diversion from the scientific study of aggression.

Aggression as Drive

As scientific interest in the purported instinctual basis of aggressive behavior waned, it was replaced by the concept of drive. For over two decades, American scientific efforts relative to aggression focused upon drive concepts. As Baron (1977) observes:

... the notion of spontaneously generated aggressive energy has been largely dismissed by the great majority of researchers in this field. The more general suggestion that aggression stems from an aggressive motive or drive (i.e., a heightened state of arousal that can be reduced through overt acts of aggression) has enjoyed a much more favorable reception. (p. 21)

The major work responsible for initiating this viewpoint, and for shaping much of the relevant research on aggression, was *Frustration and Aggression,* by Dollard, Doob, Miller, Mowrer, and Sears (1939). Their frustration-aggression hypothesis held that: (a) frustration always leads to some form of aggression; and (b) aggression always stems from frustration. Early research, however, revealed that frustration at times had nonaggressive consequences, and that aggression could have nonfrustrating antecedents. The underlying drive notion was then broadened to reflect such findings (Miller, 1941). For example, the basic hypothesis was altered to read, "Frustration produces instigations to a number of different types of responses, one of which is an instigation to aggression" (Miller, 1941, p. 338). It was in response to the same broadened perspective on the consequences of frustration that such notions as the frustration-regression hypothesis (Barker, Dembo, & Lewin, 1941) and the frustration-fixation hypothesis (Maier, 1949) also appeared.

Other aspects of the drive theory sought to describe events likely to affect frustration-induced aggression. The strength of the instigation, it was proposed, is a function of the importance of the frustrated goal response, the degree of frustration, and the number of frustrated response sequences. As part of their effort to explain occasions in which frustration failed to instigate aggression, Dollard and his colleagues examined the role of inhibitory forces, especially punishment. In their view, the likelihood that aggression would be inhibited varied directly with the amount of punishment anticipated.

Subsequent research on drive-related phenomena—punishment as inhibition, displacement, catharsis—proved far more complex than the aggression-as-drive perspective put forth. The drive theory construct of displacement and its research reflection in studies of scapegoating behavior reveal the construct to be an interesting and provocative initial formulation, but of limited predictive utility.

As Bandura notes, in addition to knowing about the level of instigation to aggression and blocks to its direct expression, accurate prediction of displaced aggression requires knowledge "about the individual's learned response of thwarting; about the types of reactions modeled by influential figures to potential victims; about the social sanctions for aggressing toward different classes of people; about the likelihood of counteraggression by different victims; and about the self-evaluative reactions the aggressor experiences upon hurting people possessing certain characteristics" (1973, p. 36).

The course of much of the research on the frustration-aggression hypothesis and its derivative propositions often proved not to be smooth. While much was learned about frustration and aggression, definitional problems persisted and the relationship of these two variables suffered from a largely insoluble circularity. As Johnson (1972) notes, "The presence of frustration was taken to mean that subsequent behavior was likely to be aggressive, and the presence of aggression was used as evidence that the preceding experience had been frustrating" (p. 133). Berkowitz and Feshbach focused largely on drive theory, and both were active in efforts to revise and extend frustration-aggression thinking. Berkowitz (1962) suggested that stimuli regularly associated with aggression may gradually acquire the capacity to elicit aggressive actions from individuals previously provoked. Frustration, he proposed, induces anger which by itself leads not to overt aggression but instead to a readiness or set to respond aggressively. Actual overt aggression, Berkowitz suggested, will not occur unless suitable aggression-relevant cues are present. These cues are usually stimuli (people, places, objects, etc.) associated with current or previous anger instigators.

Feshbach's contribution (1970) may be seen as transitional between the drive and social learning views of aggression. He proposed that the likelihood that a given act of aggression would follow a given instance of frustration is importantly influenced by learning events, for example, modeling and reinforcement. Feshbach has taken drive theory in two additional directions. First, he suggests that infliction of injury is not really the major goal of most overt aggression; rather, it is the pain caused in the other person which serves to restore or bolster the aggressor's self-esteem or sense of power. It follows from such thinking that nonaggressive means for enhancing self-esteem should reduce the aggressive

Table 1. Social Learning Theory of Aggression

Acquisition	Instigation	Maintenance
I. *Neurophysiological* Genetic Hormonal CNS (e.g., hypothalamus, limbic system) Physical characteristics	I. *Aversive* Frustration Adverse reductions in reinforcement 　Relative deprivation 　Unjustified hardships Verbal threats and insults Physical assaults	I. *Direct External Reinforcement* Tangible (material) Social (status, approval) Alleviation of aversiveness Expression of injury
II. *Observational Learning* Family influences (e.g., abuse) Subcultural influences (e.g., delinquency) Symbolic modeling (e.g., television)	II. *Modeling Influences* Disinhibitory-reduced restraints Facilitative Emotional arousal Stimulus-enhancing (attentional)	II. *Vicarious Reinforcement* Observed reward (Receipt-facilitation effect) Observed punishment (Escape-disinhibitory effect)
III. *Direct Experience* Combat Reinforced practice	III. *Incentives Inducements* Instrumental aggression Anticipated consequences IV. *Instructional Control* V. *Delusional Control* VI. *Environmental Control* Crowding Ambient temperature Noise Physical environment	III. *Neutralization of Self-Punishment* Moral justification Palliative comparison Euphemistic labeling Displacement of responsibility Diffusion of responsibility Dehumanization of victims Attribution of blame to victims Misrepresentation of consequences Graduated desensitization

drive, a process difficult to conceptualize in usual drive theory terms. Feshbach's second innovation suggests that aggression may be reduced when the individual can redefine or reinterpret the stimuli to which he or she has begun to respond aggressively, thus truncating the likelihood of actual, overt aggressive behavior. The seminal works of Berkowitz and Feshbach are examples of the theorizing and broad empirical effort that drive theory has engendered. The writings of Buss (1961) and Zillmann (1979) are also to be noted.

Aggression as Social Learning

Much of American psychology after the 1950s shifted its concern away from unobservable, purported inner determinants of behavior toward external influences on overt responses. Human behavior has been studied extensively in terms of eliciting stimuli and reinforcing consequences. As Bandura (1973) comments:

Researchers repeatedly demonstrated that response patterns generally attributed to underlying forces could be induced, eliminated, and reinstated simply by varying external sources of influence. These impressive findings led many psychologists to the view that the causes of behavior are found not in the organism, but in environmental forces. (p. 8)

With specific regard to aggression, this extreme situational determinism perspective tended to reject inner determinants. But, it appears, the pendulum swung too far.

It is apparent that overt aggression can be predicted with much greater accuracy from knowledge of such stimulus considerations as social contexts, potential targets, the person's role, and the quality of reward available for behaving aggressively, than from in-depth assessments of the inner state of the individual. Stimulus-

response considerations assume a highly significant role in social learning theory. But so, too, do inner cognitive determinants of overt behavior.

Social learning theory is a cognitive/stimulus-response view not only of aggression, but also of a wide variety of other behaviors. The processes responsible for aggression are, according to this view, essentially identical to the processes relevant to the learning, performance, and maintenance of most forms of overt behavior (Bandura, 1969, 1973). Table 1 is a summary statement of the processes which, according to social learning theory, are responsible for the individual's *acquisition* or original learning of aggressive behaviors, the *instigation* of overt acts of aggression at any given point in time, and the *maintenance* of such behavior (Bandura, 1973, 1978; Feldman, 1977; Neitzel, 1979).

Social learning theory acknowledges that a given individual's potential to behave aggressively probably stems from neurophysiological characteristics. Genetic, hormonal, central-nervous system, and resultant physical characteristics of the individual, it is held, all influence one's capacity or potential to aggress, as well as the likelihood that specific forms of aggression will, in fact, be learned.

Given the neurophysiological capacity to acquire and retain aggression in one's behavioral repertoire, Bandura suggests that such acquisition proceeds by means of direct or vicarious experiences. In both instances, the role of reinforcement looms large. Overtly aggressive acts, occurring in the context of trial-and-error behavior or under instructional control of others, are likely, when reinforced, to increase the probability that aggression will be learned or acquired by the individual. Bandura views reinforced practice as a particularly consequential event in the learning of aggression via direct experiences, be it childhood pushing and shoving, adolescent fighting, or adult military combat.

But heaviest emphasis for the acquisition of aggression is placed upon vicarious processes. Such observational learning is held to emanate from three types of modeling influences: familial, subcultural, and symbolic. The physically abused child who strikes out at peers and, as an adult, batters his or her own child, may have acquired such behaviors via observation of his or her own parents. Subcultural modeling influences on the acquisition of aggression are exemplified by the behavior of adolescents in response to their observation of peer aggression. Vicarious symbolic modeling on television, in the papers, and in comic books is apparently also a major source for learning aggression. Crucial is the fact that such aggression usually works. The aggressive model, be it parent, peer, or television character, is often reinforced for behaving aggressively. Individuals tend to acquire those behaviors for which they observe others being rewarded. The likelihood of such acquisition is enhanced by certain characteristics of the model (e.g., perceived expertness; high status; same sex, age, and race as the observer), of the behavior being modeled (e.g., clarity, repetition, difficulty, detail, enactment by several models), and of the observer—that is, the person viewing and learning from the model (e.g., similarity to the model, friendliness toward the model, instructions to imitate, and—most important, as noted above—reward for imitating).

In summary, of the three diverse American approaches to understanding the origins and nature of aggressive behavior, the instinct view was, and remains, largely a detour away from an empirically based and societally useful comprehension of aggression and its control. Drive theory was also inadequate in many particulars, but served, and continues to serve, a major heuristic function via the research and theoretical efforts to which it has given rise. Social learning theory, in our view, represents the most theoretically sound, empirically supported, and pragmatically useful view of aggression available. As a good scientific stance should be, it is a testable, logically consistent set of constructs of increasingly demonstrable validity.

INSTIGATION

Once having learned how to aggress—and when, where, with whom, and so forth—what determines whether the individual will in fact do so? According to social learning theory, the actual performance of aggressive behaviors is multiply determined.

Aversive Events

Aversive events may serve as an evocation of aggression. Frustration is seen as one such aversive instigator, as in drive theory. But, unlike in drive theory, frustration is at the same time but one instigator among several, and also a phenomenon recognized to have several generally equipotential possible consequences in addition to aggression, such as regression, withdrawal, dependency, psychosomatization, self-anesthetization with drugs and alcohol, and constructive problem solving. Adverse reductions in reinforcement are a second purported type of aversive instigation to aggression. Commentators on collective aggression have pointed to this instigation, especially in the form of a perceived sense of deprivation relative to others or hardship perceived as unjustified—rather than

deprivation or hardship in an absolute sense—as a major source of mob violence, riots, and the like. Verbal insults and physical assaults are additional, and particularly potent, aversive instigators to aggression. Toch (1969), has shown that insults most likely to evoke physical assault include threats to reputation and manly status, and public humiliation. Physical assault as an aversive instigation to reciprocal behavior is most likely to occur when avoidance is difficult and the level of instigating assaultiveness is both high and frequent.

Modeling Influences

Just as modeling influences are a major means by which new patterns of aggression are acquired, so they can also function as significant instigators to overt aggressive behavior. If we observe another person (the model) behaving aggressively and not being punished for it, this observation can have a disinhibitory effect. Through a process akin to vicarious extinction of fear, such disinhibition can result in overt aggression by the observer. Should the model be rewarded for the displayed aggression, a response facilitation effect may occur. The model's behavior now functions as an inducement to engage in matching behavior. The sight of others behaving aggressively often engenders emotional arousal in the observer, and considerable empirical evidence exists that arousal facilitates the occurrence of aggressive behavior, especially in persons for whom such a response is well-practiced and readily available. Bandura (1978) also notes that modeling may influence the likelihood of aggression through its stimulus-enhancing effects. The observer's attention, for example, may be directed by the model's behavior to particular implements and how they may be aggressively utilized.

Incentive Inducements

Feshbach (1970) and others have drawn the distinction between angry aggression and instrumental aggression. The goal of the former is to hurt another individual; the latter is an effort to obtain rewards. Incentive inducements to aggression relate to this second definition. Bandura (1978) comments: "A great deal of human aggression . . . is prompted by anticipated positive consequences. Here the instigator is the pull of expected reward rather than the push of painful treatment" (p. 46). Incentive inducements are clearly a major factor in many instances of individual and collective aggression.

It is appropriate to point out here that aggression very often pays, that incentive-induced aggression often lets the aggressor obtain the sought-after incentive, and that therein lies one of the obstacles—perhaps the most fundamental one—to successful, widespread aggression control.

Instructional Control

Individuals may aggress against others because they are told to do so. Obedience is taught and differentially rewarded by family and school during childhood and adolescence, and by many social institutions during adulthood (at work, in military service, etc.). To quote Bandura (1973): ". . . as Snow (1961) has perceptively observed, 'When you think of the long and gloomy history of man, you will find more hideous crimes committed in the name of obedience than have been committed in the name of rebellion'" (p. 175).

Delusional Control

Bizarre beliefs, inner voices, paranoid suspiciousness, perceptions of divine messages, delusions of grandeur—may all function as apparent instigators to aggression. The aggression may be justified in self-defensive terms, in messianic terms, as an expression of heroic responsibility, or on similar bases. While delusional control is not to be minimized, it is probable that the frequency of this form of instigation is greatly overestimated. The publicity associated with the relatively few instances of this type, the frequency with which it is used as a defense of insanity in murder trials, and its appeal as an absolver of personal responsibility, all contribute to its overestimated frequency.

Environmental Control

As psychologists in recent years have become increasingly interested in the effects on behavior of external events, even founding the subfield of environmental psychology, there has been an increased examination of external events as instigators to aggression. Crowding, temperature, noise, and other characteristics of the environment have been studied. Evidence reveals that each may instigate aggression. Whether aggressive behavior does in fact grow from crowded conditions, hot days and nights, high noise levels, or the like, appears to be a somewhat complicated function of the physical intensity of these environmental qualities, their personalogical perception, the levels of emotional arousal they engender, and their interaction, external constraints, and other considerations.

MAINTENANCE

Social learning theory is both a cognitive and a traditional S-R theory. This same dual focus is apparent in what sustains aggressive behavior once acquired. Bandura comments: "As has been amply documented in psychological research, behavior is extensively controlled by its consequences. The principle applies equally to aggression. Aggressive modes of response, like other forms of social behavior, can be induced, eliminated, and reinstated when the effects they produce are altered" (1978, p. 47).

Thus, whether aggressive behavior persists, disappears, or reappears is largely a matter of reinforcement. When aggression pays, it tends to persist; when unrewarded, it tends to be extinguished. This S-R notion applied to aggression becomes more complex in social learning theory, as the number and types of reinforcements which maintain aggression become elaborated.

Direct External Reinforcement

Aggressive behavior is influenced by the extrinsic rewards it elicits. Such rewards may be tangible or social, or may consist of the alleviation of aversive treatment, or possibly the inducing of expressions of pain by the person against whom one is aggressing.

Vicarious Reinforcement

Vicarious processes are important for the maintenance of aggression. The aggression-maintaining effects of observing others receive reward for aggressing comes about, Bandura (1978) suggests, via: (a) its informational function; (b) its motivational function; and (c) its disinhibitory effect, as when the observer sees others escaping punishment for their aggressive behaviors.

Self-Reinforcement

Social learning theory proposes that there are also self-produced consequences by which individuals regulate their own behavior. With regard to aggression, most persons learn that aggressive behavior should be negatively sanctioned, and they do so by what they say, do, or feel about themselves following their own aggressive behavior. There also exist persons whose self-reinforcement is such that overt aggression is a rewardable source of pride. They are prone to combativeness and derive enhanced feelings of self-worth from its success.

A number of other self-originated processes are suggested in social learning theory as factors which maintain aggressive behavior. These are primarily neutralizations of self-punishment. They may take the several forms listed in Table 1, each of which is a cognitive effort on the part of the aggressor to justify, excuse, ignore, or otherwise avoid self-condemnation for aggression and its consequences.

PREDICTION OF AGGRESSION

The timing and target of aggression prevention efforts may be optimally guided when one knows who is going to be aggressive and where and when such behavior will occur. High levels of accurate prediction have proven difficult to obtain. On a broad level of inquiry, it has been established that aggressive criminal behavior consistently correlates with such demographic and related variables as past criminal behavior, age, sex, race, socioeconomic status, and opiate or alcohol abuse. But such actuarial probabilities are of modest value in predicting the overt behavior of any given individual or individuals.

Some have posited that successful prediction might follow from the accurate identification and use of childhood characteristics of adult aggressors. Many such possible predictors have been suggested; few have been empirically examined. Hellman and Blackman (1966) suggest that enuresis, pyromania, and cruelty to animals be used for such predictive purposes. Based on surveys conducted with mental health professionals, Goldstein (1974) concluded that a largely agreed-upon constellation of childhood predictors of adult violence were maternal deprivation, poor identification with the father, enuresis, pyromania, cruelty to animals, and abuse by one or both parents. Empirical predictive studies are not totally lacking, however; Lefkowitz, Eron, Walder, and Heusmann, in *Growing Up to be Violent* (1977), report statistically significant childhood predictors of aggression at age 19 as: (a) aggression at age 8 (the best predictor); (b) the father's upward social mobility; (c) low identification of the child with parents; and (d) a preference for violent television programs. McCord (1979) reported as statistically significant predictors: (a) lack of supervision during childhood; (b) a mother lacking in self-confidence; and (c) chronic parental aggressiveness. Wolfgang, Figlio, and Sellin (1972) found a number of residential moves, lower IQ men-

Table 2.   Validity Studies of the Clinical Prediction of Violent Behavior

Study	Percent True Positive	Percent False Positive	Percent True Negative	Percent False Negative	Number Predicted Violent	Number Predicted Nonviolent	Follow-up Years
Kozol et al. (1972)	34.7	65.3	92.0	8.0	49	386	5
Steadman & Cocozza (1974)	20.0	80.0	—	—	967	—	4
Cocozza & Steadman (1976)	14.0	86.0	84.0	16.0	154	103	3
Steadman (1977)	41.3	58.7	68.8	31.2	46	106	3
Thornberry & Jacoby (1979)	14.0	86.0	—	—	438	—	4

tal retardation, and fewer school grades completed to be reliable childhood predictors of adult aggression. Thus the potential array of useful childhood predictors of aggression is rather modest. Findings reported are partly untested speculation, partly untested consensus, and partly empirically identified predictors of potential interest and usefulness that await replication and continued examination.

Efforts to predict the overt aggression of any given adult or specific groups of adults by means of other characteristics have generally yielded unsatisfactory outcomes. In *The Clinical Prediction of Violent Behavior* (1981), Monahan critically reviewed the five major investigations which have sought to examine the utility of psychological test and interview data for predicting aggression. The outcomes of these predictive efforts are summarized in Table 2.

It is clear from Table 2 that clinical prediction of adult aggression yields a dismaying number of mispredictions. False positives, in particular—predicted to be aggressive, but with no actual aggression ensuing—are very high across all five studies. Monahan (1981) notes that "the 'best' clinical research currently in existence indicates that psychiatrists and psychologists are accurate in no more than one out of three predictions of violent behavior over a several-year period" (p. 47).

AGGRESSION CONTROL

Individual Interventions

Relaxation training, rooted historically in decades-old techniques originated by Jacobson (1964), is popular in contemporary therapeutic usage—especially as a component of systematic desensitization procedures (Wolpe, 1969)—and is empirically demonstrated to be effective in an extended series of investigations (King, 1980). It is an effective means for reducing the tension and arousal states so often viewed as precursors to overt aggression.

Self-control training as an approach to anger and aggression control has taken several forms, chief among them being to teach the target person to engage in a process variously termed rational restructuring (Goldfried, Decenteceo, & Weinberg, 1974), cognitive self-instruction (Meichenbaum, 1975), and stress inoculation (Novaco, 1977), the central feature of which is learning to make verbal self-statements that effectively self-instruct the person to respond to feelings of anger and arousal with more reflective and less aggressive behavior. It is an aggression-control intervention of demonstrated efficacy and growing utilization (Hamberger & Lohr, 1980; Snyder & White, 1979).

Communication skills training utilizes didactic techniques to literally teach constructive communication behaviors (Bornstein et al., 1981; Gottman et al., 1976; Jacobson & Martin, 1976). Targeted focus on an especially useful approach to conflict resolution by means of *negotiation training* (Kifer et al., 1974; Patterson, Hops, & Weiss, 1975; Weiss, Birchler, & Vincent, 1974) follows the more general communication skills training. Finally, to maximize the likelihood that conflict-resolving, negotiated agreements are in fact lived up to, the parties to the conflict are taught to draw up and execute written agreements known as *behavioral contracts* (Jacobson, 1978; Stuart, 1971; Weiss, 1975). This commonly grouped-together triad of interventions appears to be an especially promising approach to aggression control and the consequent reduction of interpersonal conflict.

Contingency management, the use of rewards and nonphysical punishment, has the longest investigative history of the interventions considered here. Contingency management is an especially potent aggression-control intervention, particularly in those applications which combine rewards to increase constructive or prosocial behaviors (Pinkston et al., 1973; Sewell, McCoy, & Sewell, 1973), with the application of such nonphysical punishments as extinction (Brown & Elliott, 1965; Williams, 1959), time out (Bostow & Bailey, 1969; Calhoun & Matherne, 1975), and response cost (Iwata & Bailey, 1974; Kaufman & O'Leary, 1972) to decrease aggressive or antisocial behavior.

Psychotherapy has not proven especially effective (Adams, 1962; Redl & Wineman, 1957). Psychotherapeutic applications responsive to salient patient characteristics—such as peer group responsiveness among aggressive adolescents—proved more effective in reducing aggression (Vorrath & Bendtro, 1974; Richardson & Meyer, 1972). Instructional therapies, which usually derive their specific procedures from social learning theory, have quite consistently demonstrated their behavior-change effectiveness (Bornstein, Bellack, & Hersen, 1980; Goldstein et al., 1980; Spence & Marzillier, 1981).

Small-Group Interventions

Psychological skill training uses a series of psychoeducational procedures to teach aggression-management skills. Teaching procedures often include modeling, behavioral rehearsal, and performance feedback. The skill-enhancement effectiveness of this intervention has been broadly and reliably demonstrated (Bellack & Hersen, 1979; Elder, Edelstein, & Narick, 1979; Goldstein, 1981; Michelson & Wood, 1980).

Character education—in the form of its major, contemporary expression, the Character Education Curriculum (Mulkey, 1977 a, b)—is a comprehensive series of lessons in prosocial character traits designed especially for elementary school utilization.

Values clarification, seeking to enhance prosocial values without resorting to indoctrination, rests on rather different assumptions and techniques. The goals are to help students develop, clarify, and apply their own values by freely and thoughtfully choosing among alternative values (Raths, Harmin, & Simon, 1966; Simon, Howe, & Kirschenbaum, 1972). Empirical research has provided some tentative and partial support for the effectiveness of values clarification in decreasing destructive attitudes and behavior and in increasing constructive alternatives (Raths et al., 1966; Kirschenbaum, 1975).

Moral education, reflected especially in the work of Kohlberg (1968), is a particularly prominent small-group intervention designed to teach prosocial alternatives to aggression.

Other small-group interventions have also been reported. These include Ultimate Life Goals (Beck, 1971), Learning to Care (McPhail, Ungoed-Thomas, & Chapman, 1975), Public Issues (Newman & Oliver, 1970), Moral Components (Wilson, 1971), Psychological Education (Mosher & Sprinthall, 1970), Classroom Meetings (Glasser, 1969), and Identity Education (Weinstein & Fantini, 1970).

REFERENCES

Adams, S. (1962). The PICO project. In N. Johnston, L. Savitz, & M. E. Wolfgang (Eds.), *The sociology of punishment and correction.* New York: Wiley.

Ardrey, R. (1980). *The territorial imperative.* New York: Atheneum. (Original work published in 1966)

Bandura, A. (1969). *Principles of behavior modification.* New York: Holt, Rinehart & Winston.

Bandura, A. (1969). Social-learning theory of identificatory processes. In A. D. Goslin (Ed.), *Handbook of socialization theory and research.* Chicago: Rand McNally.

Bandura, A. (1971). Psychotherapy based upon modeling principles. In A. E. Bergin & S. L. Garfield (Eds.), *Handbook of psychotherapy and behavior change: An empirical analysis.* New York: Wiley.

Bandura, A. (1973). *Aggression: A social learning analysis.* Englewood Cliffs, NJ: Prentice-Hall.

Bandura, A. (1978). Learning and behavioral theories of aggression. In I. L. Kutash, S. B. Kutash, & L. B. Schlesinger (Eds.), *Violence: Perspectives on murder and aggression.* San Francisco: Jossey-Bass.

Bandura, A. (1978). The self-system in reciprocal determinism. *American Psychologist, 33,* 344–358.

Barker, R., Dembo, T., & Lewin, K. (1941). Frustration and regression. In R. G. Barker, J. S. Kounin, & H. F. Wright (Eds.), *Child behavior and development.* New York: McGraw-Hill.

Baron, R. A. (1977). *Human aggression.* New York: Plenum.

Beck, C. (1971). *Moral education in the schools: Some practical suggestions.* Toronto, Canada: Institute for Studies in Education.

Bellack, A. S., & Hersen, M. (Eds.). (1979). *Research and practice in social skills training.* New York: Plenum.

Berkowitz, L. (1962). *Aggression: A social psychological analysis.* New York: McGraw-Hill.

Bornstein, M., Bellack, A. S., & Hersen, M. (1980). Social skills training for highly aggressive children. *Behavior Modification, 4,* 173–186.

Bornstein, P. H., Anton, B., Harowski, K. J., Weltzein, R. T., McIntyre, T. J., & Hocker-Wilmot, J. (1981). Behavioral-communications treatment of marital discord: Positive behaviors. *Behavior Counseling Quarterly, 1,* 189–199.

Bostow, D. E., & Bailey, J. B. (1969). Modification of severe disruptive and aggressive behavior using brief time out and reinforcement procedures. *Journal of Applied Behavior Analysis, 2,* 31–37.

Brown, P., & Elliott, R. (1965). Control of aggression in a nursery school class. *Journal of Experimental Child Psychology, 2,* 103–107.

Buss, A. H. (1961). *The psychology of aggression.* New York: Wiley.

Calhoun, K. S., & Matherne, P. (1975). The effects of varying schedules of timeout on aggressive behavior of a retarded girl. *Journal of Behavior Therapy and Experimental Psychiatry, 6,* 139–143.

Dollard, J., Doob, L. W., Miller, N. E., Mowrer, O. H., & Sears, R. R. (1939). *Frustration and aggression.* New Haven, CT: Yale University Press.

Elder, J. P., Edelstein, B. A., & Narick M. M. (1979). Modifying aggressive behavior with social skills training. *Behavior Modification, 3,* 161–178.

Feldman, M. P. (1977). *Criminal behavior: A psychological analysis.* New York: Wiley.

Feshbach, S. (1970). Aggression. In P. H. Mussen (Ed.), *Carmichael's manual of child psychology* (Vol. 2). New York: Wiley.

Glasser, W. (1969). *Schools without failure.* New York: Harper & Row.

Goldfried, M. R., Decentecio, E. T., & Weinberg, L. (1974). Systematic rational restructuring as a self-control technique. *Behavior Therapy, 5,* 247–254.

Goldstein, A. P. (1981). *Psychological skills training.* New York: Pergamon Press.

Goldstein, A. P., Sprafkin, R. P., Gershaw, N. J., & Klein, P. (1980). *Skillstreaming the adolescent.* Champaign, IL: Research Press.

Goldstein, R. (1974). Brain research and violent behavior. *Archives of Neurology, 30,* 1–18.

Gottman, J., Notarius, C., Markman, H., Bank, S., Yoppi, B., & Rubin, M. E. (1976). Behavior exchange theory and marital decision making. *Journal of Personality and Social Psychology, 34,* 14–23.

Hamberger, K. L., & Lohr, J. M. (1984). *Stress and stress management: Research and applications.* New York: Springer.

Hellman, D., & Blackman, N. (1966). Enuresis, fire-setting, and cruelty to animals: A triad predictive of adult crime. *American Journal of Psychiatry, 122,* 1431–1435.

Iwata, B. A., & Bailey, J. S. (1974). Reward versus cost token systems: An analysis of the effects on students and teacher. *Journal of Applied Behaviors Analysis, 7,* 567–576.

Jacobson, E. (1964). *Anxiety and tension control.* Philadelphia, PA: Lippincott.

Jacobson, N. S. (1978). Problem solving and contingency contracting in the treatment of marital discord. *Journal of Consulting and Clinical Psychology, 45,* 92–100.

Jacobson, N. S., & Martin, B. (1976). Behavioral marriage therapy: Current status. *Psychological Bulletin, 83,* 540–556.

Johnson, R. N. (1972). *Aggression in man and animals.* Philadelphia, PA: Saunders.

Kaufman, K. F., & O'Leary, K. D. (1972). Reward, cost, and self-evaluation procedures for disruptive adolescents in a psychiatric hospital school. *Journal of Applied Behavior Analysis, 5,* 293–310.

Kifer, R. E., Lewis, M. A., Green, D. R., & Phillips, E. L. (1974). Training predelinquent youths and their parents to negotiate conflict situations. *Journal of Applied Behavior Analysis, 7,* 357–364.

King, N. J. (1980). The therapeutic utility of abbreviated progressive relaxation: A critical review with implications for clinical progress. In M. Hersen & A. Bellack (Eds.), *Progress in behavior modification.* New York: Academic Press.

Kirschenbaum, H. (1975). Recent research in values education. In J. Cholvat (Ed.), *Values education: Theory/practice/problems/prospects.* Waterloo, Canada: Wilfrid Laurier University Press.

Kozol, H., Boucher, R., & Garofalo, R. (1972). The diagnosis and treatment of dangerousness. *Crime and Delinquency, 18,* 371–392.

Lefkowitz, M., Eron, L., Walder, L., & Heusmann, L. (1977). *Growing up to be violent.* New York: Pergamon.

Lorenz, K. Z. (1966). *On aggression.* New York: Harcourt Brace Jovanovich.

Maier, N. R. F. (1949). *Frustration: The study of behavior without a goal.* New York: McGraw-Hill.

McCord, J. (1979). Some child rearing antecedents to criminal behavior in adult men. *Journal of Personality and Social Psychology, 37,* 1477–1486.

McPhail, P., Ungoed-Thomas, J. R., & Chapman, H. (1975). *Learning to care: Rationale and method of the lifeline program.* Niles, IL: Argus Communications.

Meichenbaum, D. (1975). A self-instructional approach to stress management: A proposal for stress inoculation training. In I. Sarason & C. Spielberger (Eds.), *Stress and anxiety* (Vol. 2). New York: Wiley.

Michelson, L., & Wood, R. (1980). Behavioral assessment and training of children's social skills. In M. Hersen & A. Bellack (Eds.), *Progress in behavior modification.* New York: Academic Press.

Miller, N. E. (1941). The frustration-aggression hypothesis. *Psychological Review, 48,* 337–342.

Monahan, J. (Ed.). (1981). *The clinical prediction of violent behavior.* Washington, DC: National Institute of Mental Health.

Morris, D. (1967). *The naked ape.* New York: McGraw-Hill.

Mosher, R., & Sprinthall, N. Psychological education in the secondary schools. *American Psychologist, 25,* 911–916.

Mulkey, Y. J. (1977a). *Character education and the teacher.* San Antonio, TX: American Institute for Character Education.

Mulkey, Y. J. (1977b). *Teacher training for character education.* San Antonio, TX: American Institute for Character Education.

Neitzel, M. T. (1979). *Crime and its modification.* New York: Pergamon Press.

Newman, F., & Oliver, D. (1970). *Clarifying public issues: An approach to teaching social studies.* Boston: Little, Brown.

Novaco, R. W. (1977). Stress inoculation: A cognitive therapy for anger and its application to a case of depression. *Journal of Consulting and Clinical Psychology, 45,* 600–608.

Patterson, G. R., Hops, H., & Weiss, R. L. (1975). Interpersonal skills training for couples in early stages of conflict. *Journal of Marriage and the Family, 1,* 295–303.

Pinkston, E. M., Reese, N. M., LeBlanc, J. M., & Baer, D. M. (1973). Independent control of a preschool child's aggression and peer interaction by contingent teacher attention. *Journal of Applied Behavior Analysis, 6,* 115–124.

Raths, L. E., Harmin, M., & Simon, S. B. (1966). *Values and teaching: Working with values in the classroom.* Columbus, OH: Merrill.

Redl, F., & Wineman, D. (1957). *The aggressive child.* New York: Free Press.

Richardson, C., & Meyer, R. C. (1972). Techniques in guided group interaction programs. *Child Welfare, 51,* 519–527.

Sewell, E., McCoy, J. F., & Sewell, W. R. (1973). Modification of an antagonistic social behavior using positive reinforcement for other behavior. *The Psychological Record, 23,* 499–504.

Simon, S. B., Howe, L. W., & Kirschenbaum, H. (1972). *Values clarification: A handbook of practical strategies for teachers and students.* New York: Hart.

Snyder, J. J., & White, M. J. (1979). The use of cognitive self-instruction in the treatment of behaviorally disturbed adolescents. *Behavior Therapy, 10,* 227–235.

Spence, S. H., & Marzillier, J. S. (1981). Social skills training with adolescent male offenders: II. Short term, long term and generalized effects. *Behavior Research and Therapy, 19,* 349–368.

Steadman, H. J. (1977). A new look at recidivism among Patuxent inmates. *Bulletin of the American Academy of Psychiatry and the Law, 5,* 200–209.

Steadman, H. J., & Cocozza, J. J. (1974). *Careers of the criminally insane.* Lexington, MA: Lexington Books.

Stuart, R. B. (1971). Behavioral contracting within the families of delinquents. *Journal of Behavior, Therapy and Experimental Psychiatry, 2,* 1–11.

Thornberry, T., & Jacoby, J. (1979). *The criminally insane: A community followup of mentally ill offenders.* Chicago: University of Chicago Press.

Toch, H. (1969). *Violent men.* Chicago: Aldine.

Vorrath, H. H., & Bendtro, L. K. (1974). *Positive peer culture.* Chicago: Aldine.

Weinstein, G., & Fantini, M. (1970). *Toward humanistic education: A curriculum of affect.* New York: Praeger.

Weiss, R. L. (1975). Contracts, cognition, and change: A behavioral approach to marriage therapy. *The Counseling Psychologist, 5,* 15–26.

Weiss, R. L., Birchler, G. R., & Vincent, J. P. (May, 1974). Contractual models for negotiation training in marital dyads. *Journal of Marriage and the Family,* 321–330.

Williams, C. D. (1959). The elimination of tantrum behavior by extinction procedures. *Journal of Abnormal and Social Psychology, 59,* 269.

Wilson, J. (1971). *Practical methods of moral education.* London: Heinemann.

Wolfgang, M. E., Figlio, R. M., & Sellin, T. (1972). *Delinquency in a birth cohort.* Chicago: University of Chicago Press.

Wolpe, J. (1982). *The practice of behavior therapy.* New York: Pergamon Press. (Original work published 1969)

Zillman, D. (1979). *Hostility and aggression.* Hillsdale, NJ: Erlbaum.

A. P. GOLDSTEIN
Syracuse University

CHILD ABUSE
PERSONALITY DISORDERS
SADOMASOCHISM
SPOUSE ABUSE
TANTRUMS
VIOLENCE

AGING AND INTELLIGENCE

Phenomena of intellectual aging are investigated at various levels. Principal findings of age effects on cognition during normal aging are reviewed with respect to research approaches at the behavioral, information-processing, and biological levels. The psychometric approach has the longest tradition (dating back to Galton, 1883; Binet, 1890; Spearman, 1904), and focuses on the measurement of "cognitive products" (e.g., Newell & Simon, 1972; Rybash, Hoyer, & Roodin, 1986). The information-processing approach emerged from the rise of information theory and computers in the 1940s, and attempts to identify information-processing mechanisms as explanations for age differences in psychometric intelligence (e.g.,

Carrol, 1974; Jensen, 1987; Hunt, 1980; Salthouse, 1991). The cognitive neuroscience approach emerged in the 1980s, and focuses on understanding the neurobiological implementations of cognition (e.g., Gazzaniga, 1995; Goldman-Rakic, 1997). These approaches complement each other and should be considered conjointly for a comprehensive overview of aging and intelligence.

THE PSYCHOMETRIC APPROACH

The existing psychometric data on aging and intelligence indicate four major phenomena. First, intellectual aging is multifaceted. Second, cross-sectional age differences are generally more pronounced than longitudinal age changes; however, after accounting for cohort effects, practice effects, and selective attrition, the two methods in general show converging patterns. Third, aging contracts the factor space of intellectual abilities. Fourth, the relationship between sensory and cognitive functioning strengthens in old age.

Intellectual Aging Is Multifaceted

While some abilities show gradual age-related declines in most individuals, other abilities remain relatively stable or even show positive age changes up until the 60s (Baltes & Lindenberger, 1997; Hertzog & Schaie, 1986; Hollingworth, 1927; Jones & Conrad, 1933; Matarazzo, 1972; Schaie, 1989, 1990, 1994, 1996). Different theoretical frameworks have been offered to distinguish vulnerable and maintained abilities. Multifactorial models of intelligence (e.g., the *Gf-Gc* theory, Cattell, 1971; Horn, 1982) suggest that abilities in the fluid (*Gf*) domain, reflecting an individual's capacity in problem solving, information organization, and concentration, are more biology-based. In contrast, abilities in the crystallized (*Gc*) domain reflect the acquisition and use of culture-based information. In a similar vein, the two-component model of lifespan cognition (Baltes, 1987, 1993) distinguishes between abilities reflecting basic mechanisms of information processing that are relatively universal and more biologically driven (the cognitive mechanics) and abilities reflecting the abilities that are more experience-based and culture-dependent (the cognitive pragmatics). Figure 1 shows that cross-sectional age gradients of primary mental abilities (Schaie, 1985; Thurstone & Thurstone, 1949) in the fluid-mechanic domain (verbal memory, reasoning, spatial orientation, and perceptual speed) decline linearly beginning in the 40s. However, abilities in the crystallized-pragmatic domain (verbal and numeric abilities) remain stable until the 60s or 70s (Schaie & Willis, 1993; Baltes, Staudinger, Maercker, & Smith, 1995). However, individuals differ in the onset and rate of these age gradients. In summary, abilities that are more biology-based decline earlier and faster than the more culture-based abilities (Baltes, Lindenberger, & Staudinger, 1998).

Age Differences and Age Changes

Cross-sectional and longitudinal sampling schemes are both utilized in cognitive aging research (see Collins & Horn, 1991; Magnusson & Casaer, 1993, for methodological reviews). In cross-sectional studies, age differences are based on average performance across age groups (or cohorts), assessed at a single oc-

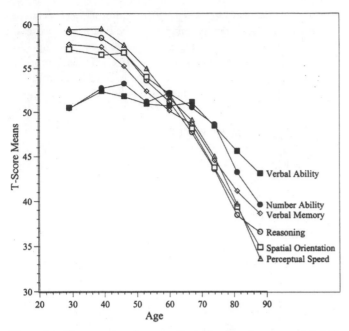

Figure 1. Cross-sectional age gradients for six primary mental abilities (N = 1628). Abilities were assessed with 3 to 4 different tests, and are scaled in a T-score metric (Data source based on Schaie & Willis, 1993; Figure adapted from Lindenberger & Baltes, 1994).

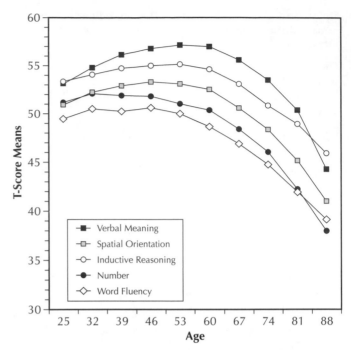

Figure 2. Estimated longitudinal age changes in five primary mental abilities. The change trajectories are based on 3,524 test records that were available for two occasions of measurement 7 years apart (Data source based on Table 5.1, Schaie, 1996).

casion. In longitudinal studies, within-individual age changes are repeatedly assessed across multiple occasions. While modest cross-sectional negative age differences are found in the early 50s for some (for example, spatial orientation, perceptual speed, and verbal memory) and by the 60s for most abilities, moderate longitudinal negative age changes in most abilities (with the exception of numeric ability and perceptual speed) are usually not evident until the mid-70s or early 80s (Hayslip, 1994; Schaie, 1983, 1996). Discrepancies between cross-sectional and longitudinal age gradients (Figure 1 and Figure 2) are due to cohort effects in cross-sectional studies (Schaie, 1965) and practice effects and selective attrition in longitudinal studies (Lindenberger & Baltes, 1994). Inferences about age gradients of intellectual functioning should therefore integrate cross-sectional and longitudinal findings. Cohort-sequential designs, such as those used in the Seattle Longitudinal Study (SLS; Schaie, 1983, 1996), and recent developments of multivariate latent growth models (McArdle, Hamagami, Elisa, & Robbins, 1991), allow such joint considerations. After controlling for cohort and historical time effects, discrepancies between cross-sectional age differences and longitudinal age changes are reduced (Salthouse, 1991; Schaie, 1994, 1996). In addition, studies extending to very old age have provided opportunities for observing age differences and age changes in the 90s and beyond (e.g., the Berlin Aging Study, Baltes & Meyer, 1998; the Georgia Centenarian Study, Poon, Sweaney, Clayton, & Merriam, 1992, the Kungsholmen Project, Small & Bäckman, 1997; Perls et al., 1993). In studies involving the very old, the effect of selective mortality on sample composition should be considered (Maier & Smith, 1999).

Dedifferentiation of Ability Structure

Recent investigations show that the psychometric structure of intellectual functioning no longer follows the *Gf-Gc* distinction in very old age (Lindenberger & Baltes, 1994). Much cross-sectional data also show that correlations among subscales are generally larger in older samples, indicating an increasing degree of ability dedifferentiation (Balinsky, 1941, Lienert & Crott, 1964; Baltes, Cornelius, Spiro, Nesselroade, & Willis, 1980; Hayslip & Sterns, 1979; Cunningham, 1980; Baltes & Lindenbeger, 1997; Babcock, Laguna, & Roesch, 1997). Similar patterns have also been found in longitudinal studies, although the trends of dedifferentiation are not as strong as in the cross-sectional findings (McHugh & Owens, 1954; Schaie et al., 1998).

Strong Sensory-Cognitive Connection in Old Age

Ability dedifferentiation generalizes beyond the intellectual domain. Specifically, a series of recent studies using simple measures of sensory acuity (Baltes & Lindenberger, 1997; Lindenberger & Baltes, 1994; Salthouse, Hancock, Meinz, & Hambrick, 1996), contrast sensitivity, and muscle strength (Anstey, Lord, & Williams, 1997), report an increase in the sensory-cognitive correlation with advancing age in age-heterogeneous samples. In line with the fluid-mechanic and crystallized-pragmatic distinction, Figure 3 shows that measures of sensory acuity are more closely related to *Gf* abilities than to *Gc* abilities in old age. Conversely, socio-biographical predictors correlated more with abilities in the *Gc* than in the *Gf* domain. Some have interpreted the strengthening of the sensory-cognitive link in old age as an indication of general neurological decline affecting both domains of functioning (Baltes

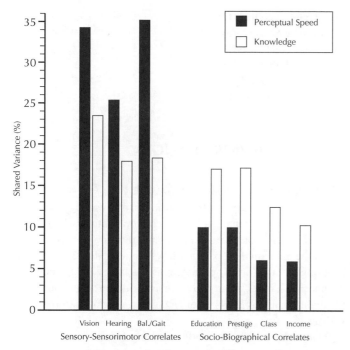

Figure 3. Differential Correlational links of perceptual speed, a marker of the fluid mechanics, and verbal knowledge, a marker of the crystallized pragmatics, to biological and socio-biographical indicators (Figure adapted from Lindenberger & Baltes, 1997).

& Lindenberger, 1997). The nature of the sensory-cognitive link is, however, currently still under debate.

THE INFORMATION-PROCESSING APPROACH

In formulating theories of intelligence, researchers have explored potential information-processing mechanisms (or components) that may mediate age-related differences in intelligence. A common hypothesis of cognitive aging is that aging constrains general cognitive resources (GCRs). Relationships between the following three aspects of GCRs, working memory, processing speed, and inhibitory mechanisms, and abilities in the *Gf* domain have been investigated most extensively in recent years.

Working Memory

Working memory (WM) refers to the ability to simultaneously hold information in immediate memory while transforming the same or other information (Baddeley, 1986). Working memory, associated with higher-level cognition, seems a plausible candidate processing mechanism for negative age differences in *Gf*. Age-related declines in WM performance have been well-documented (Craik & Jennings, 1992). Furthermore, large-scale studies on the relationships between problem solving, integrative reasoning, and WM show that a large portion of age-related variance in *Gf* is shared with age-related differences in WM (Salthouse, 1991).

Processing Speed

The speed hypothesis posits that intellectual declines have biological underpinnings, such as age-related neuronal slowing, which lead to the slowing of basic cognitive operations, with exacerbated effects in more complex tasks (Birren, 1964; Cerella, 1990; Jensen, 1993). Besides clear age-related declines in various behavioral measures of processing speed (Salthouse, 1996), many correlational analyses show that the observed age-associated variance in *Gf* is greatly reduced or eliminated after controlling for individual differences in processing speed (Hertzog, 1989; Lindenberger, Mayr, & Kliegl, 1993; Salthouse, 1991, 1996). The speed hypothesis continues to develop with the use of more direct measures of conduction speed (Vernon & Mori, 1992), with the decomposition of processing speed into distinctive types (Mayr & Kliegl, 1993; Salthouse, 1996), and with comparisons between time-limited versus time-unlimited tasks.

Inhibitory Mechanisms

It has also been proposed that aging impairs inhibitory processes and leads to cluttering within WM, greater distractibility, and difficulty in suppressing previously relevant information or responses (Hasher & Zacks, 1988). Negative age differences on Stroop color naming, negative priming, and proactive interference provide evidence for this view (Zacks & Hasher, 1994). In correlational studies, measures of interference proneness have accounted for significant proportions of age-related variance in cognitive performance (Salthouse & Meinz, 1995). The link between inhibitory decline and age-related changes in *Gf* awaits more empirical support, and improved measurement tools. Moreover, the original conception of inhibition has evolved into a multi-component framework (Hasher, Zacks, & May, in press), which continues to be elaborated. It should be noted that the abovementioned three aspects of GCRs, though mostly considered independently, may be interrelated (Baltes, Staudinger, & Lindenberger, 1999).

THE COGNITIVE NEUROSCIENCE APPROACH

Recent developments in cognitive neuroscience have motivated researchers to investigate functional relationships between aging deficits in basic cognitive mechanisms and the biological underpinnings of those deficits. The biological correlates of age effects on intelligence examined so far involve molecular and neuronal mechanisms, and brain electrical responses.

Molecular Correlates

ApoE is a plasma protein involved in cholesterol transportation. There is recent consensus that the ϵ_4 variant of ApoE is a risk factor for developing Alzheimer's disease and may also be related to mild forms of cognitive impairment (indexed by Mini-Mental State Examination and the Digit-Symbol subtest of the Wechsler Adult Intelligence Scale) occurring in normal aging (see Maclullich, Seckl, Starr, & Deary, 1997; Small, Basun, & Bäckman, 1998, for reviews).

Neural Correlates

There is consensus that during the course of normal aging, the concentration of dopamine in the striatum and basal ganglia decreases by 5–10% in each decade of life (Gabrieli, 1998; Schneider, Rowe, Johnson, Holbrook, & Morrison, 1996). Functional relationships between age-related deficits in the dopaminergic system and age-related decrements in aspects of the GCRs have also been documented. For instance, it was found that the density of dopamine receptors in the nigrostriatum was negatively associated with reaction time (RT) and positively associated with RT variance (Spirduso, Mayfield, Grant, & Schallert, 1989). In addition, many studies have demonstrated that working-memory function is reduced in aged monkeys due to attenuated dopaminergic function (for reviews, see Arnsten, 1998; Goldman-Rakic, 1997).

ERP Correlates

There is evidence for age-related increases in the latency and variability of event-related P300 potentials (ERPs; see Kuegler, Taghavy, & Platt, 1993, for a review). Furthermore, ERP latency correlated with IQ negatively in general (see Deary & Caryl, 1997, for a review).

CONCLUSIONS

Psychometric studies conducted since the 1920s have documented that intellectual aging is not a unitary process. Culture-based intelligence is maintained into the 70s; whereas biology-based intellectual abilities begin declining in the 40s. There has also been increasing interest in understanding cognitive and neurobiological mechanisms that may underlie age-related declines in fluid-mechanic abilities. At the information-processing level, cognitive factors, such as working memory, processing speed, and inhibitory mechanisms, are correlated with age differences in intelligence. Furthermore, there is emerging consensus that the prefrontal cortex and its supporting neuromodulation mechanisms underlie such cognitive functions. At present, the cross-level link from brain aging to intellectual aging continues to be refined.

REFERENCES

Baltes, P. B., & Mayer, U. (1998). *The Berlin Aging Study.* Cambridge, UK: Cambridge University Press.

Collins, L. M., & Horn, J. L. (Eds.). (1991). *Best methods for the analysis of change.* Washington, DC: American Psychological Association.

Gazzaniga, M. S. (Ed). (1995). *The cognitive neurosciences.* Cambridge, MA: MIT Press.

Lindenberger, U., & Baltes, P. B. (1994). Aging and intelligence. In R. J. Sternberg (Ed.), *Encyclopedia of Human Intelligence* (Vol. 1, pp. 52–66). New York: MacMillan.

Salthouse, T. A. (1991). *Theoretical perspectives on cognitive aging.* Hillsdale, NJ: Erlbaum.

Schaie, K. W. (1996). *Intellectual development in adulthood: The Seattle Longitudinal Study.* Cambridge, UK: Cambridge University Press.

Schneider, E. L., Rowe, J. W., Johnson, T. E., Holbrook, N. J., & Morrison, J. H. (Eds.). (1996). *Handbook of the biology of aging* (4th ed). New York: Academic Press.

S. C. Li
K. Z. H. Li
Max Planck Institute for Human Development,
Berlin, Germany

AGING: BEHAVIOR CHANGES

THE PATTERNING OF HUMAN BEHAVIOR

Until the 20th century, relatively little was known about the patterning of human behavior. Strong environmentalists had maintained that behavior was a result of environmental forces impinging on the individual. In past centuries even hereditarians, though believing that the way people behave is to a large extent dependent on inherited factors, did not go so far as to outline or emphasize the possibility that human behavior changes in a highly patterned way with age.

That older people behaved differently from when they were young was, of course, generally accepted. But the notion that behavior changed in so patterned a way that this patterning could be objectively measured and charted seems not to have been considered.

Arnold Gesell was perhaps the first scientist to attempt to chart in detail the minute progressions of age development; to a large extent, it became his life's work. Though some believed that Gesell did not pay proper respect to the environment or to the interaction of the individual with the environment, he in fact respected both of these factors. He stated specifically: "Environmental factors support, inflect and modify but they do not generate the progressions of development" (Gesell, 1942, p. 281). He also stated: "The organism always participates in the creation of its environment, and the growth characteristics of the child are really the end-product expressions of an interaction between intrinsic and extrinsic determiners. Because the interaction is the crux, the distinction between these two sets of determiners should not be drawn too heavily" (Gesell, 1940, p. 159).

Nevertheless, Gesell's work and that of his staff always focused primarily on the changes in behavior expected to occur as the organism ages. Through some 300 publications, Gesell outlined the specific behavior changes which might be expected from infancy through the first 16 years of life, and developed behavior tests which he and his staff perfected.

Evaluation of the age level of any given individual's behavior was arrived at by subjecting the person (infant or child) to a series of graded behavior tests such as reaction to one-inch cubes, the copying of geometric forms, the completion of the incompleted figure of a man, and other similar tasks. After many years of research, graded norms were published to cover behavior from 4 weeks of age through 10 years (Ames et al., 1979; Ilg et al., 1964/1978; Knobloch & Pasamanick, 1974).

Even though, as students of human behavior have made quite clear, every human being is an individual and differs in many ways from every other—even from an identical twin—developing be-

Table 1.   Stages of Equilibrium and Disequilibrium

	Even	Breakup	Calm	Withdrawal	Expansion	Transition	Equilibrium
Ages							
	2	2½	3	3½	4	4½	5
	5	5½–6	6½	7	8	9	10
	10	11	12	13	14	15	16

Source: L. B. Ames, C. Gillespie, J. Haines, & F. L. Ilg, *The Gesell Institute's child from one to six: Evaluating the behavior of the preschool child* (New York: Harper & Row, 1979). Copyright © 1979 by the Gesell Institute of Human Development. Reprinted by permission of Harper & Row, Publishers, Inc.

havior nevertheless appears to be highly similar from person to person so far as any group is concerned. Certainly it seems similar enough to justify our describing expected behavior characteristic at any age level. The Gesell studies suggest that behavior characteristic of any age amounts to more than just the sum of specific abilities which the individual can master or express at that age. Each advancing age appears also to have its own individuality. There are ages of equilibrium and ages of disequilibrium, ages of inward and ages of expansive behavior. These follow each other in an apparently systematic and predictable order. For the period 2 to 16 years the following sequence has been identified, as shown in Table 1 (Ames et al., 1979, p. 10).

AFTER SIXTEEN

Needless to say, it does not seem probable that patterned, predictable age-related changes in behavior should stop at 16 years. It has always been the Gesell presumption that such changes continue throughout the entire life span. The possibility that this may well be so has been followed up by investigators such as Levinson et al. (1978) and popularizers such as Sheehy (1976).

The major reason for not pursuing the matter at the Gesell Institute past 16 and into the middle ages was that age changes appear to slow down as the organism matures. In fetal life, major and conspicuous changes occur more or less on a weekly basis. During the first year of life it has been possible to categorize changes on a monthly basis. This slows down to six-monthly intervals from two through six years of age and to yearly intervals from six to sixteen years of age. After that the intervals become much greater and thus increasingly difficult to define.

In addition, the relative contributions of heredity and environment to any person's behavior might be different at different times of life. Observations suggested that in the earliest years and again in old age, hereditary factors might play a major role. In mid-life and even as early as the early 20s, environmental factors seem to play a relatively larger role. For all these reasons, age changes in the years following 16 seem difficult to determine.

SEVENTY AND OVER

The Gesell Institute, however, clung to the possibility that specific age-related changes in behavior could be discovered and charted in later life, and that such changes might once again become somewhat clear-cut in very old age. So the Institute undertook an analysis of such behavior changes as might be identifiable in the human organism from approximately age 70 on.

In the expectation that one might be able to identify 70-, 80-, or 90-year-old behavior, a substantial number of elderly men and women were examined. The tool used was the Rorschach Inkblot Test. In earlier publications (Ames et al., 1971; Ames et al., 1974), these investigators had proposed and substantiated the notion that response to a projective technique such as the Rorschach would change in a patterned way with age. Since the Rorschach seemed suitable for individuals of any age, this technique was employed.

Expecting reasonably clear-cut patterns of response to show themselves as being characteristic of people in the several decades of old age, the experimenters were surprised to discover that chronological age did not, as in childhood, appear to determine the kind of response given. Though behavior in children appears to *develop* in a rather consistent manner—as a rule, 10-year-olds are more capable in nearly all respects than 5-year-olds—behavior in the elderly appears to *deteriorate* in a highly individual manner almost unrelated to chronological age.

Thus, though behavior of 70-year-old individuals may on the average be somewhat more intact than that of 80- or 90-year-olds, exceptions to this rule are so many and so marked that any given age designation is not a very accurate indication as to what one may expect of an individual. In place of the usual age designations, then, elderly subjects were identified on the basis of their Rorschach responses as *normal adult, intact presenile, medium presenile,* or *deteriorated presenile.* These stages precede the totally deteriorated condition commonly known as senile psychosis.

The *normal adult* elderly person, regardless of chronological age, responds both on behavior tests and in everyday life as does the hypothetically "normal" younger adult. The *intact presenile* individual shows some slippage but still in most instances can maintain daily routines, including the handling of finances, and is quite capable of living alone. The modest onset of presenility can be observed in small ways. The elderly person tends to be mildly forgetful, somewhat egocentric, and set in his or her ways.

The *medium presenile* individual shows a good deal of slippage and will do best if living in a protected atmosphere, even though such an individual may superficially appear quite alert and even moderately capable. People falling in this category are often greatly misunderstood by those around them. Superficially they may be able to behave in a quite "normal" way, make a reasonably good appearance, and carry on usual conversations. They then confound and disturb relatives, friends, and those caring for them by behaving in a childish or irrational way. Others are then apt to become impatient, feeling that these individuals could do better if they would only try. On the other hand, the *deteriorated presenile*

Table 2. Summary Table Showing Mean Age of Performance of Different Groups on All Tests

| | Age in Years | | | | | | | | | |
| | Mean Age | | Incomplete Man | | Bender Gestalt | | Visual Three | | Tree Test | |
Rorschach Classification	F	M	F	M	F	M	F	M	F	M
Normal (4)	79	75	8.7	8.0	9.3	10.0	8.0	9.0	9.7	10.0
Intact Presenile (27)	78	77	6.8	6.3	7.5	7.7	6.0	7.0	6.9	7.7
Medium presenile (51)	82	84	5.3	5.4	5.8	6.2	5.5	5.5	5.2	5.7
Deteriorated (10)	78	85	4.9	3.8	4.7	4.8	5.0	—	4.5	4.8
Scores for Tests Which Yield Objective Scores										
Normal (4)					.7[a]	.0[a]	9.0[b]	10.5[b]		
Intact (27)					3.2	2.8	6.1	7.4		
Medium (51)					5.7	5.0	4.2	4.7		
Deteriorated (10)					8.0	8.0	3.3	—		

Source: From L. B. Ames, Calibration of Aging. *Journal of Personality Assessment,* 1974, *38*(6), p. 509. Reprinted by permission.
[a] Bender scores are in terms of error; thus a low score is better than a high one.
[b] Visual Three scores are in terms of successful performance; thus a high score is better than a low one.

person obviously needs protection, though even here the person falls short of sheer senile dementia.

Since it became apparent that age designations were not appropriate for describing the successive stages which occur as the individual grows older, the goal of the Gesell Institute researchers shifted. Instead of attempting to describe behavior at the specific older ages (70, 80, 90), they sought instead to describe the descending stages of behavior integrity in terms of categories.

TESTING LEVELS OF FUNCTION IN THE AGING

Though the administration in the Masonic Home in Wallingford, Connecticut, where much of the preliminary research was carried out, considered that the classification of integrity (or lack of integrity) of function made possible by the Rorschach test was helpful in understanding and dealing with patients, it was felt that the Rorschach was too technical to be of general usefulness.

Thus what was needed was a supplementary battery of tests to make the desired distinctions between levels of function in the elderly. The Gesell Cubes, Copy Forms, and other Gesell tests were tried, but these proved too easy for all but the most deteriorated subjects and thus did not effectively differentiate the other levels of function. A new battery was assembled. This included, as well as the Rorschach, the Gesell Incomplete Man, the Bender Gestalt, Monroe's Visual Three Memory for Designs, and Ilg's Color Tree Test, in which the subject is given crayons and asked to draw a tree (Ames, 1974).

As Table 2 shows, individuals who can be rated as normal adult on the Rorschach score in the eight- to ten-year-old age level on other tests in the battery. Intact preseniles range from six to seven years; medium preseniles from five to six years; and deteriorated individuals for the most part around four years. Differences between average scores of individuals at the four levels of intactness turned out to be statistically significant.

The differences shown in this table may seem small to the uninitiated, but to those informed about developing child behavior they are large indeed. For example, if those dealing with the medium

presenile adult should think in terms of what one can and cannot expect of a 5½-year-old, they will be more effective than if they think of him or her as an adult who is merely not quite clear in the head.

Placing the supposedly "normal adult" person at the 9- to 10-year-old level, however, is somewhat deceptive and could lead to error in dealing with the person. That this adult is so rated does not actually mean that he or she is necessarily behaving merely like a child of this age. Most of the tests (other than the Rorschach) used in the investigation described here have their ceiling at or near 10 years of age. Thus it is assumed that the 10-year-old child will respond to the Incomplete Man Test by giving a practically "perfect" performance. Except for the Bender Gestalt, for which—rather arbitrarily—an age level of 11 years is given for a response without error, it is not possible on other present tests to obtain a rating of over 10 years of age. With tests whose ceiling might be higher, it is assumed that "normal adult" elderly individuals could rate considerably higher than the present test battery permits.

CONSISTENCY OF RANK ORDER FROM TEST TO TEST

If the battery of tests chosen is to be useful, and if behavior is assumed to have enough shape and consistency to be measured effectively, one would need to establish that in a group of aging individuals there is relative consistency of performance from one test to another.

If a group of elderly individuals is examined on a battery of tests, the usual finding is that, as with people of any age, any one individual may function somewhat better on some tasks than on others. In general, though, the more intact will perform rather consistently well on all tests, the less intact less well.

To demonstrate the extent to which it is possible to show consistency of excellence (or maturity) of function on the several tests used in the present battery, six individuals were selected who showed clear differences in maturity on the Rorschach, the test which seems best to evaluate intactness of intellectual and emo-

Table 3.   Relative Consistency of Rank Order of Ss from Different Rorschach Categories Examined on a Battery of Four Other Psychological Tests

Rorschach Rating	Inc. Man Age	Bender Errors[a]	Visual Three Scores[b]	Tree, Age
Dr. A., normal	8½ years	0	10½ years	10 years
Mr. G., intact	8 years	2	7½ years	8 years
Mr. J., intact	6½ years	3	5½ years	7 years
Mr. P., medium	5½ years	3	5 years	5½ years
Mrs. B1, medium	4 years	6	2 years	4 years
Mrs. B2, deteriorated	3 years	16	0	4½ years

Composite Compared with Rorschach Rank Order

Including Rorschach		Without Rorschach	
Dr. A.:	1,1,1,1,1 = 5	Dr. A.:	1,1,1,1 = 4
Mr. G.:	2,2,2,2,2 = 10	Mr. G.:	2,2,2,2 = 8
Mr. J.:	3,3,3,3,3 = 15	Mr. J.:	3,3,3,3 = 12
Mr. P.:	4,4,4,4,4 = 20	Mr. P.:	4,4,4,4 = 16
Mrs. B1.:	5,5,5,5,6 = 26	Mrs. B1.:	5,5,5,6 = 21
Mrs. B2.:	6,6,6,6,5 = 29	Mrs. B2.:	6,6,6,5 = 23

Source: From L. B. Ames, Calibration of aging. *Journal of Personality Assessment,* 1974, *38*(6), p. 517 Reprinted with permission.

[a] Bender scores are in terms of error; thus a low score is better than a high score.

[b] Visual Three scores are in terms of successful performance; thus a high score is better than a low score.

tional functioning (or its lack). Table 3 indicates the consistency with which that individual who functioned most effectively on the Rorschach also functioned most effectively on each of the other four tests involved, and so on for five other individuals selected on the basis of the Rorschach performance.

BEHAVIOR CHANGES IN THE ENTIRE LIFE SPAN

Gesell studies of aging led to the diagrammatic expression of the course of intellectual function during the human life span as an elongated diamond (see Figure 1). Schematically, one may say that cognitive and other functions increase and improve through perhaps the first 20 years or so of life, and then may be assumed to hold their own for the next 40–60 years. Finally, there appears to be in most a gradual closing and narrowing down, with behavior reverting systematically to ways characteristic of ever earlier age levels.

The effectiveness of those caring for elderly individuals can be increased if the latter's level of intactness or deterioration is respected. A well-chosen psychological test, or preferably a battery of such tests, can determine the level of functioning of the elderly. Since performance ratings from test to test remain fairly consistent, we can assume that the individual who performs relatively

well (as compared to others in any group) on one test will perform relatively well on others.

Gesell researchers have long maintained that young children should start school and be subsequently promoted on the basis of their behavior age rather than their chronological age. The same principle seems to hold for old age. In old age as in childhood, the behavior age rather than the chronological age should guide our expectations of function—a consideration that could change retirement practices in this country. Such practices might, effectively, be based on the way the person functions rather than on the chronological age as such.

REFERENCES

Ames, L. B. (1974). Calibration of aging. *Journal of Personality Assessment, 38*(6), 505–529.

Ames, L. B., Gillespie, C., Haines, J., & Ilg, F. L. (1979). *The Gesell Institute's child from one to six.* New York: Harper & Row.

Ames, L. B., Métraux, R. W., Rodeil, J. L., & Walker, R. N. (1974). *Child Rorschach responses.* New York: Brunner/Mazel.

Ames, L. B., Métraux, R. W., & Walker, R. N. (1971). *Adolescent Rorschach responses.* New York: Brunner/Mazel.

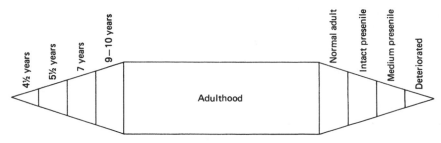

Figure 1.   Human life span as a diamond.

Gesell, A. (1940). The stability of mental-growth careers. In *Intelligence: its nature and nurture.* Bloomington, IL: Public School Publishing.

Gesell, A. (1942). The documentation of infant behavior in relation to cultural anthropology. In *Proceedings of the 8th American Scientific Congress, Anthropological sciences* (Vol. 2). Washington, DC: Department of State.

Ilg, F. L., Ames, L. B., Haines, J., & Gillespie, C. (1978/1964). *School readiness.* New York: Harper & Row.

Knobloch, H. & Pasamanick, B. (Eds.). (1974). *Gesell and Amatruda's developmental diagnosis: The evaluation and management of normal and abnormal neuropsychologic development in infancy and early childhood* (3rd ed.). New York: Harper & Row.

Levinson, D. J., Darrow, C. N., Klein, E. B., Levinson, M. H., & McKee, B. (1978). *The seasons of a man's life.* New York: Knopf.

Sheehy, G. (1976). *Passages: Predictable crises of adult life.* New York: Dutton.

L. B. AMES

ALZHEIMER'S DISEASE
HYPERTENSION
RESIDENTIAL ALTERNATIVES

AGING: PHYSIOLOGICAL AND BEHAVIORAL CONCOMITANTS

Numerous age-related changes can occur in our bodies, leading to a wide range of behavioral and psychological changes. To illustrate, we have described some of the age-related physiological changes in two of the sensory systems (hearing and vision), the cardiovascular system, and the musculo-skeletal system, and their behavioral and psychological effects. It is very important to appreciate that many of these changes are not inevitable consequences of aging.

HEARING

Various types of hearing losses occur with increasing age (Heckheimer, 1989) *Conductive hearing loss* involves an interference with the transmission of sound through the auditory canal, tympanic membrane, or middle ear. This type of hearing loss may be due to presbycusis (a stiffening of the bones in the middle ear along with thickening and decreased flexibility of the ear drum); wax accumulation; tympanic membrane perforation; otitis media; and otosclerosis (a fixation of the middle ear ossicles). *Sensorineural hearing loss* involves damage to the inner ear, the hair cells in the inner ear, or the eighth cranial nerve. Other types of hearing loss include *mixed hearing loss* (a conductive loss is concomitant with a sensorineural loss), and *central hearing loss* (damage to the nerves or nuclei of the central nervous system that are involved in audition).

These types of hearing loss may lead to specific hearing impairments in older adults. First, older adults may experience difficulty in hearing high-frequency sounds, including high-pitched voices (e.g., children) and high-frequency sounds associated with mechanical defects (e.g., squeaking brakes).

Second, older adults may have trouble hearing relevant information in the presence of background noise, such as conversations in noisy environments. Consequently, older adults may frequently request that information be repeated, or they may rely on other contextual cues, such as lipreading.

Third, older adults may have more difficulty recognizing consonant sounds of shorter durations at lower decibel levels. Therefore, when in conversation, older adults may be likely to ask speakers to talk more loudly. Similarly, older adults may be likely to adjust the volume levels upward on radios or television sets.

Fourth, older adults may experience more difficulty hearing rapidly presented speech with a low degree of context. Therefore, whenever novel information is spoken rapidly (e.g., messages over public announcement systems), older adults may miss important details, and solicit the information from others.

Fifth, older adults may experience difficulty hearing and understanding speech that lacks normal fluctuations in tone and rhythm. This difficulty may arise when speaking to another person with an unwavering speech style; it may also occur when interacting with various media that feature undifferentiated, computer-generated speech.

These age-related declines in hearing may have additional behavioral consequences (e.g., social isolation or depression). Individuals may become irritated with their hearing difficulties and with the speech characteristics of others that interfere with auditory perception. Older adults may even become paranoid about what others may be saying about them, given the perception that others are mumbling or speaking softly to purposefully exclude the older listener.

VISION

Several age-related changes that occur in the visual system may influence the behavior of older adults. First, older adults require greater amounts of light to see, because of the increased density and opacity of their lenses and the decreased number of photoreceptors (Whitbourne, 1998). Second, this increased density may cause older adults to experience glare when viewing bright objects due to the scattering of light within the lens. Third, due to the increased lens density and the loss in flexibility of the eye capsule, older adults are more likely to experience difficulty with accommodation. The increased density causes yet a fourth problem, a decrease in depth perception with age. An increased yellowing of the lens and pigmentation of the vitreous humor may cause age-related problems with color discrimination. Finally, macular degeneration, which is experienced by most individuals in their 70s and 80s, causes an age-related decrease in the visual field.

The behavioral consequences of the foregoing problems can be quite significant. The increased difficulty in seeing objects in reduced light and greater susceptibility to glare can lead individuals to increasingly restrict their evening driving and walking. These changes in vision can also lead to increased accidents and falls resulting from failure to see hazardous objects: this, in turn, may lead to diminished self-esteem. Changes in color perception may create difficulties in correctly matching clothing and facial makeup, and sometimes may cause others to question the individual's aesthetic sensibilities (Whitbourne, 1998). These changes can also affect one's understanding of color-coded information and diminish one's appreciation of artwork, movies, and scenery. Diminished visual acuity can lead to difficulty reading, watching television, recognizing friends, and learning and remembering the distinctive features of the faces of new acquaintances. Finally, the embarrassment associated with these problems can lead to increased social isolation and decreased social activities.

CARDIOVASCULAR AND RESPIRATORY SYSTEM

Changes associated with the cardiovascular and respiratory systems may have significant effects on behavior, not to mention their relationship to mortality among older adults. However, not all older adults experience the same levels of decline of the cardiovascular and respiratory systems. Exercise, disease, and genetic predisposition are important factors, in addition to the effects of aging, in the determination of cardiorespiratory fitness.

Increased age is often associated with reduced cardiopulmonary fitness of the older adult. The amount of blood ejected from the heart and the sensitivity of the heart to neural stimulation, which controls the timing and rate of heart contractions, decrease with age.

Aging also results in structural changes of the lungs (e.g., decreased elastic recoil and increased rigidity of the chest wall) that limit lung capacity and the efficiency of the gas exchange. The consequences of cardiovascular and respiratory changes may include a decreased ability to cope with physical stress. The older adult may become more easily fatigued and experience shortness of breath more quickly than will younger adults. Consequently, the older adult may become fearful of activities associated with physical exertion and frustrated with the associated limitations, and therefore may pursue activities that are more sedentary. All of these limitations can also lead to lowered self-esteem.

MUSCULOSKELETAL SYSTEM

Musculoskeletal changes also have important implications for the daily behavior of the older adult. Muscle mass decreases 10 to 20% from ages 60 to 70, and 30 to 40% from ages 70 to 80, and can lead to increased weakness. Muscle endurance also diminishes with age. Bone mass decreases as bones become more porous, therefore making the bones more susceptible to fractures. The cartilage in the joints also degenerates with age, resulting in increased joint pain and stiffening of the joints. It should be noted, however, that musculoskeletal changes can be reduced (e.g., by increasing muscle strength and endurance) in both younger and older adults via exercises of sufficient intensity, duration, and frequency.

As with the cardiorespiratory changes, age-related musculoskeletal changes may result in older adults' being less willing to undertake physically demanding tasks. These changes may also contribute to older adults' becoming more easily fatigued and moving more cautiously, particularly on slippery surfaces. The restricted range of movement often associated with age-related musculoskeletal changes may further contribute to the problem. Individuals may demonstrate difficulty climbing stairs or getting up from a sitting position. The older adult may develop a fear of falling because of weakness in the legs or a fear of breaking bones when ambulating. Ultimately, older individuals may restrict participation in enjoyable and leisure activities and experience diminishing self-esteem. Furthermore, the chronic pain sometimes associated with musculoskeletal changes has been related to an increased incidence of depression. In summary, numerous changes occur in the aging body that can have substantial behavioral and psychological effects. Fortunately, the human body exhibits amazing resilience, accommodation, and adaptation to the aging process.

REFERENCES

Heckheimer, E. (1989). *Health promotion and the elderly in the community.* Philadelphia: W. B. Saunders Company.

Whitbourne, S. (1998). Physiological aspects of aging: Relation to identity and clinical implications. In B. Edelstein (Ed.), *Clinical Geropsychology* (Vol. 7, pp. 1–24). Oxford, UK: Elsevier.

B. A. EDELSTEIN
J. L. GOODIE
R. R. MARTIN
West Virginia University

AGING: BEHAVIOR CHANGES
ALZHEIMER'S DISEASE
GERIATRIC PSYCHOLOGY

AGRANOFF, BERNARD W. (1926–   )

Bernard W. Agranoff was born in 1926 of Russian immigrants in Detroit, MI, and received his early education in the Detroit public schools. He enrolled in Cass Technical High School as an art student, and then transferred into the science curriculum. In 1944, he was recruited into a Navy accelerated premedical training program at the University of Michigan, and then attended the Wayne State Medical School in Detroit, where he received his medical degree. Following internship in Sayre, PA, he was awarded a postdoctoral fellowship by the National Foundation for Infantile Paralysis to train under the guidance of F. O. Schmidt in the biology department of the Massachusetts Institute of Technology. There he was exposed to and stimulated by the exciting research environment and acquired many physical and chemical techniques that were later to prove useful to him. After fulfilling a two-year military service requirement as a medical officer in the clinical chemistry facility at the US Naval Medical Center Hospital in Bethesda, MD, he joined the Section on Lipid Chemistry of the Laboratory of Neurochemistry of the National Institute of Neurological Diseases and Blindness of the NIH. This marked the beginning of his biochemical and neurochemical career.

Working in the laboratory of R. O. Brady, he studied the biosynthesis of phosphatidylinositol. Taking a cue from the then-recent findings of E. Kennedy that CDP-choline and CDP-ethanolamine were biosynthetic precursors of phospholipids, he searched for an analogous inositol-containing nucleotide. In 1957, he discovered instead a novel liponucleotide, cytidinediphosphodiacylglycerol (CDP-DAG; also CMP-phosphatidate) that reacted enzymatically with free inositol to form phosphatidylinositol. This important finding was made more than 25 years before the central role of phosphoinositides in signal transduction was fully appreciated. CDP-DAG was later shown to be the obligatory metabolic progenitor of the phosphatidylglycerols and all of the bacterial glycerophospholipids. Agranoff next worked with F. Lynen at the Max Planck Institute of Cellular Chemistry in Munich. There he participated in studies that led to the discovery of the enzymatic conversion of isopentenyl pyrophosphate to dimethylallyl pyrophosphate, a crucial step in the biosynthesis of terpenes, including cholesterol. On returning to the United States, he became increasingly interested in the biochemical basis of learning and memory. Colleagues at the NIH still recall imprinted mallard ducklings following him down the corridors of Building 10.

In 1960, he accepted a joint appointment in the Mental Health Research Institute and in the department of biological chemistry at the University of Michigan. The director of laboratories of the newly established Institute was R. W. Gerard, an early leader in neuroscience and an eloquent spokesman for the role of neurochemistry in understanding behavior and mental disease. Gerard's influence catalyzed Agranoff's decision to enter further into investigating the underlying biochemical mechanisms of learning and memory.

In 1964, he initiated his well-known studies of learning and memory in goldfish and demonstrated that while inhibition of protein synthesis in the brain did not block acquisition of a new behavior, it did prevent consolidation into long-term storage of a shock avoidance task. These studies, primarily employing the protein synthesis inhibitor puromycin, thus distinguished the mechanisms for the formation of short-term and long-term memory. He and his colleagues also showed that blockers of RNA (but not of DNA) synthesis blocked memory formation and, further, that the environment of fish during the consolidation period also played a vital role in triggering the onset of the memory fixation process. His 1967 *Scientific American* article on memory in goldfish is considered a landmark in the establishment and recognition of neuroscience as a discipline. It was widely reprinted and is remembered by many present-day neuroscientists as influential in making their early career choices.

To leap from these interventive pharmacological experiments to biochemical approaches proved challenging. On the assumption that long-term memory formation required the synthesis of new proteins, particularly those inferred to be involved in synaptic remodeling or growth, he directed further efforts to the study of optic nerve regeneration in the goldfish, a useful model that emerged from the research of R. Sperry. Agranoff and A. Heacock discovered a protein doublet, termed P68/70, which was synthesized in the retinal ganglion cells at a greatly accelerated rate during optic nerve regeneration and which was eventually cloned and shown to have homology with CNPase, a glial marker in mammalian brain. This and other regeneration-related proteins remain of great interest in the eventual understanding of the biochemical basis of learning and memory.

Through the years, Agranoff also continued his interest in the biochemistry of lipids. His laboratory discovered acyldihydroxyacetone phosphate, which was subsequently shown by his postdoctoral fellow A. Hajra to be the obligatory precursor of long-chain ether lipids. A by-product of Agranoff's continued interest in the phosphoinositides was the famous "turtle" model, which facilitates recognition of the stereoisomers of inositol phosphates for the novice. Its use is recommended by the Nomenclature Committee of the International Union of Biochemistry.

A further interest for Agranoff has been functional imaging in the brain, primarily with his former student and later collaborator K. Frey, dealing with quantitative imaging of receptors in vivo using positron emission tomography.

From 1985 to 1995, he served as director of the Mental Health Research Institute, narrowing its focus in the direction of cellular neurobiology and biological psychiatry. He has been co-editor through six editions (1972–1999) of the reference textbook *Basic Neurochemistry,* published under the imprimatur of the American Society for Neurochemistry (ASN). He is past president of the ASN and past chairman of the International Society for Neurochemistry, and has also served on the Council of the Society for Neuroscience. Among his honors are election to the Institute of Medicine of the National Academy of Sciences, Michigan Scientist of the Year Award, and the Wayne State University Medical School Distinguished Alumnus Award. He has given many honor lectures, including the prestigious Henry Russel Lecture at the University of Michigan. He is a fellow of the American Psychological Society, the American College of Neuropsychopharmacology, and the American Association for the Advancement of Science.

Among his avocations are matters relating to food and wine, shared with his wife, Raquel. Neurochemistry and gourmandise are in the tradition of J. L. W. Thudichum, a nineteenth-century scientist-physician often cited as the founder of modern neurochemistry, who wrote chemical treatises on the brain, on food, and on wine. In that tradition, Agranoff coined the term "molecular gastronomy" and convened two well-remembered tongue-in-cheek symposia mixing chemical sensing, brain metabolism, and gastronomy for neurochemists in connection with meetings of the Society for Neuroscience in Atlanta in 1979 and in Cincinnati in 1980.

In recognition of his critical role in establishing the field of neuroscience as a discipline, he was named the first Ralph Waldo Gerard Professor of Neurosciences in the department of psychiatry at the University of Michigan.

STAFF

AGRAPHIA

DEFINITION

Agraphia (or dysgraphia) is a systematic disorder of written language due to cerebral disease (Benson & Cummings, 1985; Bub & Chertkow, 1988; Hinkin & Cummings, 1996). Sensu stricto, it denotes a disturbance of a form of writing, be it handwriting, typing,

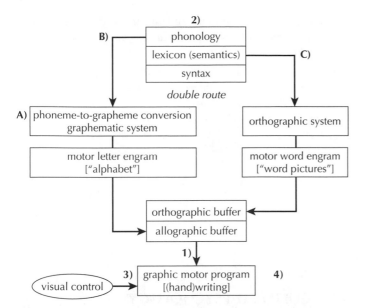

Figure 1. Proposed neurolinguistic model of writing. The letters and numbers indicate the presumed sites of disruption (cf. text).

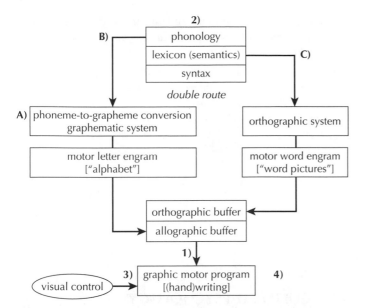

Figure 2. Handwriting of a 66-year-old right-handed man who had suffered a left temporal cerebral hematoma one month previously. He developed transcortical-sensory aphasia. On dictation ("Wohin wird sie es mir bringen?" [Where is she going to take it for me?]) he wrote "wi nin gricht es sich," producing literal and verbal paragraphias. Similar phonemic and verbal paraphasias were also present in his spontaneous speech. On an aphasia test he scored 7/30 points for letter/word synthesis (severely impaired) and 16/30 points for writing to dictation (markedly impaired). He also had mild alexia (20/30 points).

synthesis of letter or word cards, Braille, or shorthand writing. However, other than with oral speech, spatial or apraxic disorders may also contribute to agraphia. It is not contingent on motor or sensory impairment, although combinations may occur. If the dominant arm is paralyzed, writing may be attempted with the nondominant arm. In rare instances callosal lesions may cause unilateral agraphia (Roeltgen, 1993, 1997). Merely dysarthric or anarthric patients experience no difficulties in writing. As a companion of aphasia, agraphia usually reflects its pattern and severity, thus, combined with aphasia it is considered part of the supramodal language deficit (Kaplan, Gallagher, & Glosser, 1998; Ulatowska, Baker, & Stern, 1979).

OCCURRENCE
Agraphia rarely either coexists with alexia or exists in isolation. Its hallmark is paragraphias (see Figure 1), either on a letter (literal paragraphias) or word (verbal or semantic paragraphias) level. Additionally, automatisms, perseverations, and syntactic or word-finding difficulties may occur as with spoken language.

MODEL OF WRITING
The model of a central language system requires at least three components: phonology (rules for speech sound production), lexicon (vocabulary arranged for semantic content), and syntax (rules for sentence construction). Within the secondary language system of writing, the same components are tapped, augmented by a phoneme-to-grapheme conversion system triggering the motor patterns for letters (see Figure 2) and an orthographic system. Graphemes are the smallest written units that may alter the meaning of a word and are not necessarily letters.

While strings of letters are generated via the phonological route, entire words are produced via the semantic route. Though some readers might use only one of these two modes, they usually work simultaneously, in parallel fashion (dual-route hypothesis). They

may, however, be impaired selectively, producing different types of agraphia.

Clinical Examination
Examination for agraphia includes spontaneous writing, writing to dictation, and written naming. A distinction between linguistic and spatial components of agraphia is best made using copying. To compensate for impaired motor abilities, letter or word synthesis using printed material may be used. Testing for kinesthetic reading, letter synthesis using sticks (matches), oral spelling, and reading may also be useful.

Clinical Varieties
From a clinical point of view several types of agraphia are distinguished:

1. *Pure agraphia* is a severe inability to write in the absence of gross aphasia or alexia, leading to scribbling or misspelling. In some cases production of single, barely legible words may be possible. Lesions are found in the left parieto-occipital region or second frontal gyrus (Exner's center). The distinction between pure and apraxic agraphia is questioned by some authors (Kaplan et al., 1998).

2. *Aphasic agraphia* is associated with and part of aphasia, whose type and severity it reflects. For example, in Wernicke's aphasia, verbal paragraphias may be frequent, whereas in Broca's aphasia they rarely occur. Generally speaking, the writing impairment is at least as severe as the oral language deficit. Therefore, screening for agraphia may be used in testing for aphasia. Lesions are located in the classical language zones in the distribution of the middle cerebral artery.

    Neurolinguistically, three subtypes of aphasic agraphia may be defined:
    a. *Lexical agraphia* is a disability to convert phonemes to graphemes, especially with irregular spelling, resulting in phonetic writing without lexical control. Lesion sites are the posterior superior parietal lobule and the angular gyrus.
    b. *Phonologic agraphia* is the holistic writing of words with occasional failure to produce entire words, which cannot be written in a letter-by-letter fashion. The patient fails in dictated pronounceable nonsense words, while succeeding in well-known imageable words. Lesion site is the anterior inferior supramarginal gyrus or the adjoining insula.

c. *Semantic agraphia* patients may successfully write real and nonsense words to dictation, but they have difficulties in written confrontation naming or description. Deep and surface agraphia analogous to deep and surface alexia (dyslexia) have been distinguished. *Deep agraphia* is characterized by semantic paragraphias (substitutions, omissions or additions, e.g., "airplane" for "propeller" [Roeltgen, 1997]), while in *surface agraphia* mostly literal paragraphias are produced (e.g., "propettle" for "propeller"). In languages such as English with irregular orthography, surface agraphia seems to be more frequent than in languages with regular orthography. A particular finding in Japanese is that the regular, phonologic, and syllabic kana characters may be preserved, whereas the irregular, semantic, and ideographic kanji characters may be misproduced.

3. *Spatial agraphia* causes letters or words to be incorrectly placed, closed-in, omitted, of quite unequal shape and size, or augmented by superfluous strokes. In *neglect agraphia* words or letters at the right or left margin of a page are omitted, or the margin of the written-on area shows a marked slope towards one side. Patients often suffer from right parietal brain injury and although are not aphasic, do present with spatial deficits in non-language tasks, too.

4. *Apraxic agraphia* causes single letters to be malformed or confused according to their graphic (e.g., the letters "M" and "W") rather than their phonetic similarity. Orally, words can be spelled properly. This variety is consequent to the loss of graphic motor programs necessary for writing. Apraxic agraphia, which resembles pure agraphia, has been described in terms of a modality-specific apraxia, but (ideomotor) apraxia is usually present in non-language tasks. In the agraphia of Gerstmann's syndrome, elements of aphasic, spatial, and apraxic agraphia mingle. Usually, lesions are found in the left parietal lobe, especially near the angular and supramarginal gyri.

REFERENCES

Benson, D. F., & Cummings, J. L. (1985). Agraphia. In Frederiks, J. A. M. (Ed.), *Handbook of clinical neurology: Vol. 1 (45). Clinical neuropsychology* (pp. 457–472). Amsterdam: Elsevier.

Bub, D., & Chertkow, D. (1988). Agraphia. In Boller, F., & Grafman, J. (Eds.), *Handbook of neuropsychology: Vol. 1* (pp. 393–414). Amsterdam: Elsevier.

Hinkin, C. H., & Cummings, J. L. (1996). Agraphia. In Beaumont, J. G., Kenealy, P. M., & Rogers, M. J. C. (Eds.), *The Blackwell dictionary of neuropsychology* (pp. 21–31). Cambridge: Blackwell.

Kaplan, E., Gallagher, R. E., & Glosser, G. (1998). Aphasia-related disorders. In Sarno, M. T. (Ed.), *Acquired aphasia* (3rd ed., pp. 309–339). San Diego: Academic Press.

Roeltgen, D. (1993). Agraphia. In Heilman, K. M., & Valenstein, E. (Eds.), *Clinical neuropsychology* (3rd ed., pp. 63–89). New York: Oxford University Press.

Roeltgen, D. (1997). Agraphia. In Feinberg, T. E., & Farah, M. J. (Eds.), *Behavioral neurology and neuropsychology* (pp. 209–217). New York: McGraw-Hill.

Ulatowska, H. K., Baker, T., & Stern, R. F. (1979). Disruption of written language in aphasia. In Whitaker, H., & Whitaker, H. A. (Eds.), *Studies in neurolinguistics: Vol. 4* (pp. 241–268). New York: Academic Press.

C. J. G. LANG
University of Erlangen
Nuremberg, Germany

APHASIA
BRAIN INJURIES

AGRICULTURAL PSYCHOLOGY

In contrast to other social sciences that have developed specialized subdisciplines and/or application interests in agriculture, psychology historically has not been known for its concern with rural issues. For instance, there has not been any psychological counterpart to such social science specialties as agricultural economics, rural sociology, agricultural marketing, or rural geography. Nonetheless, psychological perspectives have interacted with agricultural issues in several domains: (a) assessment of the therapeutic needs of rural populations, (b) investigation of farming tasks and skills, (c) analysis of expert agricultural judges, (d) evaluation of farm management decisions, and (e) statistics and experimental design.

THERAPEUTIC NEEDS

Rural life is often portrayed in an idyllic, down-to-earth fashion. Rural communities are assumed to be less stressful and more humane than urban life. However, epidemiological studies have shown that serious mental health problems exist in rural communities (Henggeler, 1983). In fact, Husaini, Neff, and Stone (1979) found that many interpersonal problems have higher rates of incidence in rural areas. Despite the need, rural communities often lack many of the mental health services taken for granted in cities. Hoagland (1978) reported that only 17.5% of rural poverty areas had adequate mental health services (compared to 49% of urban poverty areas).

One major reason for this lack of mental health services is that most clinicians and counselors are trained in large urban universities. Faculty (and students) are thus unfamiliar with the values, concerns, and even the language of rural living. Consequently, specialized programs have evolved to prepare mental healthcare providers with the skills and abilities to cope with problems encountered in rural communities. For example, Heyman (1983) described a model for preparing community psychologists to work in rural regions of the country. Similarly, Edgerton (1983) considered some ingenious methods that mental health professionals have used to cope with the limitations of providing services in rural contexts, for example, traveling clinics and in-school centers.

One issue that has received much attention in studies of rural communities has been child abuse. Such abuse involves a pathological interaction between the child, the caregiver, and the situation. Rural environments are different in many respects from the more widely understood urban environment. It should not be surprising, therefore, to find that rural child abuse is perceived in a different light and frequently goes unreported. Nonetheless, home-based early intervention programs are successful in helping at-risk children in rural areas (Rosenberg & Reppucci, 1983).

FARMING TASKS AND SKILLS

Traditionally, farmers and ranchers were expected to be proficient in many manual and physical tasks. Work psychologists have been involved in examining these skills. For example, Tomlinson (1970) found that dairy workers must be proficient in nine separate tasks, ranging from operating milking machines to evaluating the health of cows. Thus, a traditional farmer or rancher needed to be a jack-of-all-trades, with general skills in many areas.

However, with the increased mechanization and computerization in agriculture, there has been a shift in the skills needed. Instead of many general abilities, more specialized skills are now necessary. Moreover, instead of emphasizing manual skills, modern agribusiness places greater demand on cognitive abilities. For example, Matthews (1978) reported that handling a modern combine harvester involves simultaneous monitoring and control of at least seven tasks. Given the complexity of the cognitive demands, there has been considerable concern over the human factors component in increasingly high rates of farm accidents (Mainzer, 1966).

With the trend away from small family farms to large corporate farming, there is a greater need for farmers with problem solving and management skills (Stevens, 1970). This has produced changes in both the education and the practice of today's farmers. As a result, behavioral investigators have turned their interests toward analysis of higher thought processes (Shanteau, 1992).

AGRICULTURAL EXPERTISE

Many early insights into the psychology of expertise arose from studies of agricultural workers. For instance, one of the earliest known studies of experts in any domain was conducted in 1917 by Hughes. His data revealed that corn rated highest by expert corn judges did not produce the highest yield. In 1923, Wallace (later Vice President under Franklin Roosevelt) reanalyzed Hughes' data using path analysis. He showed that corn judges largely agreed with each other, but that their ratings correlated only slightly with crop yields.

Trumbo, Adams, Milner, and Schipper (1962) asked licensed grain inspectors to judge samples of wheat. Nearly one third of the samples were misgraded and, when graded a second time, over one third were given a different grade. Also, increased experience made judges more confident, but not necessarily more accurate. Finally, more experienced judges tended to overgrade the wheat samples (perhaps the original form of grade inflation). One source of errors in agricultural judgment is the presence of irrelevant factors. Gaeth and Shanteau (1984) noted that nondiagnostic material (e.g., excessive moisture) significantly impacted the decisions of soil judges. They also found that cognitive training was successful in compensating for the presence of these irrelevant materials. Another approach to improving expert judgment was observed in weather forecasting. Murphy and Winkler (1977) found that precipitation forecasts could be improved using a feedback system based on Brier scores (a quadratic scoring system). Since then, the accuracy of weather forecasts has increased dramatically (Stewart, Roebber, & Bosart, 1997).

FARM MANAGEMENT DECISIONS

There have been frequent analyses of the choices needed to manage a farm. Most of this work has been concerned with how economic decisions should be made. There has been concern recently about helping farmers cope with cognitive limitations when they make choices. Rajala and Sage (1979) considered various methods intended to help farmers think more effectively about their decisions. For instance, farmers consistently make suboptimal allocations when buying crop or drought insurance (Anderson, 1974). However, Kunreuther (1979) found that farmers could be persuaded to think more effectively about buying insurance, for example, by taking a longer time perspective.

Insights into marketing and consumer behavior have come from studies in agriculture. For instance, the pioneering analysis of new product diffusion by Rogers (1962) was based on farmers' willingness to adopt new agricultural equipment. Rogers' classification of individuals into innovators, early adopters, early majority, late majority, and laggard is now widely accepted.

STATISTICS AND EXPERIMENTAL DESIGN

One area where there has been a longstanding interface between psychology and agriculture has been in the development of statistical analysis and research design. A century ago, psychologists such as Galton were instrumental in building the basis of modern statistical thinking (Gigerenzer et al., 1989). Through such seminal efforts, later psychologists (for example, Cattell and Thurstone) built the foundation for the application of statistics to behavioral research.

Parallel to this effort, statisticians working in agricultural settings (such as Fisher) developed much of what is now considered standard experimental design and analysis. According to Brown (1972), concepts of random assignment and factorial designs initially were proposed to advance agricultural science. Indeed, many terms commonly used today in statistics, for example, split plot designs, reflect an agricultural background.

In summary, although agricultural psychology is not normally recognized as a subfield of psychology, there have been many applications of behavioral ideas in agricultural settings. Moreover, agricultural issues have impacted psychology in a variety of often unappreciated ways.

REFERENCES

Anderson, D. R. (1974). The national flood insurance program: Problems and potentials. *Journal of Risk and Insurance, 41,* 579–599.

Brown, B. W. (1972). Statistics, scientific method, and smoking. In J. M. Tanur (Ed.), *Statistics: A guide to the unknown.* San Francisco: Holden-Day, Inc.

Edgerton, J. W. (1983). Models of service delivery. In A. W. Childs & G. B. Melton (Eds.), *Rural psychology.* New York: Plenum Press.

Gaeth, G. J., & Shanteau, J. (1984). Reducing the influence of irrelevant information on experienced decision makers. *Organizational Behavior and Human Performance, 33,* 263–282.

Gigerenzer, G., Switjink, Z., Porter, T., Daston, L. J., Beatty, J., & Kruger, L. (1989). *The empire of chance: How probability changed science and everyday life.* London: Cambridge Univ. Press.

Henggeler, S. W. (1983). Needs assessments in rural areas: Issues and problems. In A. W. Childs & G. B. Melton (Eds.), *Rural psychology.* New York: Plenum Press.

Heyman, S. R. (1983). Problems in program development and the development of alternatives. In A. W. Childs & G. B. Melton (Eds.), *Rural psychology.* New York: Plenum Press.

Hoagland, M. (1978). A new day in rural mental services. In *New dimensions in mental health: Report from the Director,* National Institute of Mental Health. Washington, D.C.: U.S. Government Printing Office.

Hughes, H. D. (1917). An interesting corn seed experiment. *The Iowa Agriculturalist, 17,* 424–425.

Husaini, B. A., Neff, J. A., & Stone, R. H. (1979). Psychiatric impairment in rural communities. *Journal of Community Psychology, 7,* 137–146.

Kunreuther, H. (1979). Why aren't they insured? *The Journal of Insurance, No. 5.*

Mainzer, W. (1966). Accident prevention in the cowshed. *British Journal of Industrial Medicine, 23,* 24.

Matthews, J. (1978). The farm worker. In W. T. Singleton (Ed.), *The analysis of practical skills.* Baltimore: University Park Press.

Murphy, A. H., & Winkler, R. L. (1977). Can weather forecasters formulate reliable probability forecasts of precipitation and temperature? *National Weather Digest, 2,* 2–9.

Rajala, D. W., & Sage, A. P. (1979). On information structuring in choice making: A study of systems engineering decision making in beef cattle production. *IEEE Transactions on Systems, Man, and Cybernetics, SMC-9,* 525–533.

Rogers, E. M. (1962). *Diffusion of innovations.* New York: The Free Press.

Rosenberg, M. S. & Reppucci, N. D. (1983). In A. W. Childs & G. B. Melton (Eds.), *Rural psychology.* New York: Plenum Press.

Shanteau, J. (1989). Psychological characteristics of agricultural experts: Applications to expert systems. In A. Weiss (Ed.), *Climate and agriculture: Systems approaches to decision making.* Lincoln, NE: University of Nebraska Press.

Stevens, G. N. (1970). The human operator and quality inspection of horticultural produce. *Journal of the Institute of Agricultural Engineering, 25,* 1.

Stewart, T. R., Roebber, P. J., & Bosart, L. F. (1997). The importance of the task in analyzing expert judgment. *Organizational Behavior and Human Decision Processes, 69,* 205–219.

Tomlinson, R. W. (1970). The assessment of workload in agricultural tasks. *Journal of the Proceedings of the Institute of Agricultural Engineering, 25,* 18.

Trumbo, D., Adams, C., Milner, M., & Schipper, L. (1962). Reliability and accuracy in the inspection of hard red winter wheat. *Cereal Science Today, 7,* 62–71.

Wallace, H. A. (1923). What is in the corn judge's mind? *Journal of the American Society of Agronomy, 15,* 300–304.

SUGGESTED READING

Childs, A. W., & Melton, G. B. (1983). *Rural psychology.* New York: Plenum Press.

Dillon, J. L., & Scandizzo, P. L. (1978). Risk attitudes of subsistence farmers in northeast Brazil: A sampling approach. *American Journal of Agricultural Economics, 60,* 425–435.

Kohler, W. (1929). Simple structural functions in the chimpanzee and the chicken. In W. D. Ellis (Ed.), *A source book of gestalt psychology.* New York: Harcourt Brace.

Lorenz, K. (1937). *The companion in the bird's world, 54,* 245–273.

Meadows, A. W., Lovibond, S. H., & John, R. D. (1959). The establishment of psychophysical standards in the sorting of fruit. *Occupational Psychology, 33,* 217.

Phelps, R. H., & Shanteau, J. (1978). Livestock judges: How much information can an expert use? *Organizational Behavior and Human Performance, 21,* 209–219.

Seabrook, M. F. (1972). A study of the influence of cowman's personality and job satisfaction on yield of dairy cows. *Journal of Agricultural Laboratory Science, 1.*

J. SHANTEAU

APPLIED RESEARCH
EXPERIMENTAL DESIGNS
MANAGEMENT DECISION MAKING

AINSWORTH, MARY D. SALTER (1913–1999)

Ainsworth received the BA, MA, and PhD (1939) from the University of Toronto. She was appointed assistant professor at University of Toronto (1946), professor at Johns Hopkins University (1963), commonwealth professor at University of Virginia (1975), and professor emeritus from 1984. Ainsworth devoted a lifetime to researching infant-mother relationships and introduced a 20-minute controlled laboratory technique called the "strange situation."

At London's Tavistock Clinic, under John Bowlby's direction, she investigated the effects on personality of infant-mother separation (1950). This was the beginning of a 40-year productive scholarly association with Bowlby, establishing a new field of scientific study by means of Bowlby's ethological theories of attachment, separation, and loss and by Ainsworth's empirical longitudinal studies from home visits and the strange situation technique.

Ainsworth wrote numerous scientific articles and books. She also extended her research into attachment beyond infancy by examining other affectional bonds throughout the life cycle. Ainsworth was cited as one of the outstanding *Models of achievement . . . of eminent women in psychology* (O'Connell & Russo, 1983) and received the APA's award for Distinguished Scientific Contribution (1989), its award for Distinguished Professional Contributions to Knowledge (1987), and was elected a fellow of the American Academy of Arts and Sciences (1992).

S. S. BROWN
Northshore Community College

AKATHISIA

Akathisia is a complex psychomotor syndrome, consisting of a subjective (emotional) and an objective (motor) component (Brüne & Bräunig, 1997; Sachdev, 1995b) (see Figures 1 and 2). Subjectively distressing inner restlessness and repetitive movements of the legs are the most frequent symptoms, predominantly emerging when the patient is in a standing or sitting position with some relief when lying. However, none of the symptoms is pathognomonic, making it difficult to distinguish akathisia from other forms of restlessness as well as from other movement disorders (Sachdev, 1994b, 1995b) (see Figure 3).

- Inner restlessness
- Urge to move (tasikinesia)
- Inability to remain still
- General unease
- Discomfort
- Inability to relax
- Poor concentration
- Dysphoria
- Anxiety
- Fear
- Terror, rage
- Suicidal ideation
- Aggressive thoughts

Figure 1. Subjective symptoms of akathisia

Sitting position
- Fidgetiness of arms and hands
- Face rubbing
- Rubbing, caressing, or shaking of arms or hands
- Rubbing or massaging of legs
- Tapping, picking on clothes
- Crossing and uncrossing of arms
- Crossing and uncrossing of legs
- Swinging or kicking crossed legs
- Toe tapping
- Frequently squirming in chair, straightening motions
- Rocking and twisting of the body

Standing position
- Marching on the spot
- Changing stance
- Flexing and extending knees
- Rocking from foot to foot
- Pacing, repetitive walking

Figure 2. Objective symptoms of akathisia

The term "akathisia" (from the Greek for "not to sit") was introduced by Haskovec in 1901. Haskovec considered akathisia to be of functional origin in "hysteria" and "neurasthenia" (1901). Between the 1920s and 1940s, Bing, Sicard, and Wilson observed akathisia in patients suffering from postencephalitic parkinsonism and in idiopathic parkinson syndromes (Sachdev, 1995a).

Although first mentioned long before neuroleptics became available, akathisia is nowadays mostly associated with the administration of neuroleptic drugs. Classical neuroleptics are much more likely to produce akathisia than atypical neuroleptics. Other agents, such as serotonin reuptake inhibitors, are suspected of causing an akathisia-like syndrome, but to date this remains a matter of controversy (see Figure 4).

Akathisia is of specific clinical relevance since it may complicate the treatment by noncompliant and impulsive behaviors, possibly including assaultive and suicidal actions (Van Putten, 1975). Moreover, akathisia is sometimes mistaken as psychotic agitation or even overlooked, which may lead to genuine worsening of the psychosis (Van Putten, 1975; Weiden, Mann, Haas, Mattson, & Frances, 1987).

Akathisia generally has an acute beginning within hours or days after initiation of neuroleptic treatment. High dosages and rapid dose increment are especially predisposing factors to produce acute akathisia (Sachdev & Kruk, 1994). However, several subtypes of akathisia have been described according to onset during neuroleptic treatment with more ambiguous risk factors (see Figure 5). When taking a chronic course, subjective distress may decrease and the movement patterns may become more "stereotyped." Whether there is an overlap with tardive dyskinesia remains unclear (Barnes & Braude, 1985).

Subjective component prominent
- Psychotic agitation
- Anxiety
- Agitation due to affective disorder
- Drug withdrawal syndromes
- Neuroleptic dysphoria
- Agitation due to organic disorder (e.g., dementia, hypoglycemia)

Objective component prominent
- Restless-legs syndrome
- Tardive dyskinesia
- Stereotypies
- Tremor
- Myoclonus
- Restless, repetitive movements due to organic disorder (e.g., pacing in dementia, hyperactivity in Tourette's syndrome)

Figure 3. Differential diagnosis of akathisia

- Classical neuroleptics (e.g., phenothiazines, butyrophenones)
- Atypical neuroleptics (e.g., clozapine, risperidone, olanzapine)
- Serotonin reuptake inhibitors[1]
- Tricyclic antidepressants combined with oestrogen[2]
- Serotonin antagonists[2]
- Anticonvulsants[2]
- Lithium[2]
- Calcium channel antagonists[2]

[1] questionable, few systematic studies
[2] case reports

Figure 4. Drugs causing akathisia

Acute akathisia: Onset within six weeks after initiation of treatment, dose increment, or change of drug-type; concurrent medication not decreased or discontinued.

Chronic akathisia: Symptoms persist for over three months; specify acute, tardive, or withdrawal onset.

Tardive akathisia: Onset at least three months after initiation of treatment, dose increment, or change of drug-type; no dose increment or change of drug within six weeks prior to onset; concurrent medication not decreased or discontinued.

Withdrawal akathisia: Onset within six weeks after discontinuing or marked reduction of dose; prior to onset, duration of treatment at least three months; concurrent medication not decreased or discontinued.

Pseudoakathisia: Typical objective symptoms without subjective distress.

Figure 5.   Subtypes of drug-induced akathisia (modified after Sachdev, 1994b)

Prevalence and incidence rates vary widely, depending on the applied diagnostic threshold, clinical ratings, subtyping, and clinical samples (Brüne & Braünig, 1997; Sachdev, 1995b; Van Putten, May, & Marder, 1984). Conservative ratings reveal mean prevalence rates of 30 to 40% in patients on neuroleptics (Sachdev, 1995b). Since the 1980s, several clinically useful rating scales for akathisia have been published (Barnes, 1989; Chouinard, Ross-Chouinard, Annable, & Jones, 1980; Fleischhacker et al., 1989; Sachdev, 1994a).

The pathophysiology of akathisia is far from being fully understood. This is complicated further by the absence of an overall sufficient animal model available for both the subjective and the objective components of akathisia. Dopamine depletion is considered to be crucial for developing akathisia, but compared to other neuroleptic-induced extrapyramidal side effects, the pathways involved and relations to other neurotransmitter circuits are dubious. Akathisia may best be viewed as resulting from the interaction of dopaminergic neurones with noradrenergic, serotonergic, cholinergic, GABAergic, glutamatergic, and opioid systems (Sachdev, 1995b).

Early diagnosis is critical, due not only to the possible complications associated with akathisia but also to the impending dilemma of insufficient or delayed treatment response. Thus, preventive measures, such as choosing the lowest effective dose and the stepwise increment of dose, are indispensable (Sachdev, 1995b). Moreover, routine clinical check for extrapyramidal side effects and behavioral observation (e.g., during occupational therapy or other group therapies) is emphasized (Brüne & Braünig, 1997). If akathisia is present, stopping the offending drug or at least reducing the dose is considered to be the best option (Sachdev, 1995b). However, in highly agitated patients, waiting for a spontaneous wearing-off may be impracticable. Anticholinergic drugs, beta-adrenergic drugs, and benzodiazepines are effective for acute treatment, yet response rates are variable. If onset of akathisia is less acute, change of neuroleptic class or administration of atypical agents is proposed. Treating chronic or tardive akathisia is less promising, but systematic studies are lacking (Brüne & Braünig, 1997; Sachdev, 1995b).

REFERENCES

Barnes, T. R. E. (1989). A rating scale for drug-induced akathisia. *British Journal of Psychiatry, 154,* 672–676.

Barnes, T. R. E., & Braude, W. M. (1985). Akathisia variants and tardive dyskinesia. *Archives of General Psychiatry, 42,* 874–878.

Brüne, M., & Bräunig, P. (1997a). Akathisie. *Fortschritte der Neurologie und Psychiatrie, 65,* 396–406.

Chouinard, G., Ross-Chouinard, A., Annable, L., & Jones, B. D. (1980). Extrapyramidal Symptom Rating Scale. *Canadian Journal of Neurological Sciences, 7,* 233.

Fleischhacker, W. W., Bergmann, U. J., Perovich, R., Pestreich, L. U., Borenstein, M., Lieberman, J. A., & Kane, J. M. (1989). The Hillside Akathisia Scale: A new rating instrument for neuroleptic induced akathisia. *Psychopharmacology Bulletin, 25,* 222–226.

Haskovec, L. (1901). L'Akathisie. *Revue Neurologique, 9,* 1107–1109.

Sachdev, P. (1994a). A rating scale for acute drug-induced akathisia: Development, reliability, and validity. *Biological Psychiatry, 35,* 263–271.

Sachdev, P. (1994b). Research diagnostic criteria for drug-induced akathisia: Conceptualization, rationale and proposal. *Psychopharmacology, 114,* 181–186.

Sachdev, P. (1995a). The development of the concept of akathisia: A historical overview. *Schizophrenia Research, 16,* 33–45.

Sachdev, P. (1995b). *Akathisia and restless legs.* New York: Cambridge University Press.

Sachdev, P., & Kruk, J. (1994). Clinical characteristics and predisposing factors in acute drug-induced akathisia. *Archives of General Psychiatry, 51,* 963–974.

Van Putten, T. (1975). The many faces of akathisia. *Comprehensive Psychiatry, 16,* 43–47.

Van Putten, T., May, P. R. A., & Marder, S. R. (1984). Akathisia with haloperidol and thiothixene. *Archives of General Psychiatry, 41,* 1036–1039.

Weiden, P. J., Mann, J., Haas, G., Mattson, M., & Frances, A. (1987). Clinical nonrecognition of neuroleptic-induced movement disorders: A cautionary study *American Journal of Psychiatry, 144,* 1148–1153.

M. BRÜNE
Ruhr-University, Bochum

ANTIDEPRESSANT MEDICATIONS
ANTIPSYCHOTIC DRUGS

AKIL, HUDA

After receiving her undergraduate degree at the American University of Beirut, Huda Akil obtained a PhD in psychobiology from UCLA, where she gained experience in behavioral techniques. Together with J. Liebeskind, she described the phenomenon of stimulation-produced analgesia, and explored its neurochemical nature. This work, suggesting the existence of an endogenous opioid system, presaged the discovery of the endorphins. She pursued her postdoctoral training at Stanford University, under J. D. Barchas, where she learned biochemical and immunological techniques for the study of neurotransmitters, receptors, and neuropeptides. With her colleagues she first characterized the phenomenon of stress-induced analgesia and its mediation by endogenous opioids. While at Stanford, she also initiated a long-standing collaboration with S. J. Watson on the anatomical distribution of opioid systems in the brain.

In 1978, Akil was recruited to the University of Michigan as an assistant professor in the department of psychiatry and an assistant research scientist in the Mental Health Research Institute. Between 1993 and 1996, Akil became the director of the Neuroscience Graduate Program at the University of Michigan. She currently holds the Gardner Quarton Distinguished Chair of Neuroscience in Psychiatry and is a senior scientist and codirector of the Mental Health Research Institute.

At Michigan she focused on two research areas: the brain biology of stress and depression, and the biology of endorphins and other molecules related to substance abuse. In each of these areas, she takes a broad-based approach, examining the system at a cellular, molecular, and integrative level.

In studying stress and mood disorders, her laboratory and that of Watson have described the brain circuits which underlie responses to stress and the termination of the stress response, as well as on the specific molecules expressed within these circuits. This work has included the cloning of the brain mineralocorticoid receptor and studies of its alternative splicing and differential regulation. Related studies have focused on the association of the glucocorticoid and mineralocorticoid receptors with heatshock proteins, and the role of these chaperone proteins in the function of the steroid receptors. At the neuroanatomical level, research described specific pathways that are activated by unique stressors, with special emphasis on psychological stress such as social defeat. Her group has recently focused on differences in brain responses as a function of the animal's ability to control the stressful situation. In human studies, the endocrine dysregulation seen in depressed subjects has been the subject of intensive investigation. More recently, the differential impact of a social stressor on depressed subjects versus controls is being investigated.

In the arena of endorphins, the Akil-Watson group has cloned two of the opioid receptors and a related orphan receptor (the Orphanin FQ receptor) and is actively involved in studying their unique pharmacology, their expression, their molecular structure, and their involvement in specific circuits which contribute to the development and maintenance of addictive behavior. In addition, the Akil laboratory has had a long-standing interest in the processing of endogenous opioid peptides and the regulation of that processing. Work from the Akil laboratory has demonstrated that during a number of physiological processes, including chronic stress and chronic exposure to morphine, there is an alteration not only in the absolute level of opioid peptides in brain, but in the nature of the mixture of peptides being secreted. Thus, an animal on chronic morphine secretes more of the form of beta-endorphin

which acts as a physiological antagonist rather than a full agonist at the opioid receptors. This notion that endogenous ligands may have different degrees of efficacy and that altering their mix can change the overall tone of the system was novel but is now becoming widely accepted. The Akil laboratory has also been interested in interactions between the opioids and other neurotransmitter systems, including dopaminergic and glutamatergic systems. This group was the first to describe the role of the NMDA receptor in opiate tolerance and dependence. More recent work has been focusing on the effects of stress on the acquisition of drug-taking behavior and on the neurobiological basis of individual differences in this interaction. The feature that most clearly characterizes this research approach is the integration of numerous tools and research strategies in an effort to understand the biological bases of emotional behavior and to use this understanding to approach the study of human emotions, in both health and disease.

Akil has an extensive and often-cited bibliography. Among other honors, she has given a number of named lectures, including the Yale Flynn Lecture in 1997, and several Grass lectures. She was secretary of the International Narcotics Research Conference (INRC), has served on the Mental Health Board of the Institute of Medicine, and on the Organizing Committee for the Decade of the Brain Symposia, as well as serving on a number of NIH study sections, study groups, and advisory committees. She received the NIDA Pacesetter Award in 1993, and was the corecipient (with Watson) of the Pasarow Award for 1994. In 1998, she received the Sachar Award from Columbia University and was also the recipient of the Bristol Myers Squibb Unrestricted Research Funds Award. She is the past president (1998) of the American College of Neuropsychopharmacology (ACNP) and the treasurer-elect of the Society for Neuroscience. In 1994, she was elected to the membership of the Institute of Medicine, National Academy of Science.

STAFF

ALBEE, GEORGE W. (1921–   )

George W. Albee was born in 1921 and grew up in Saint Mary's, PA. He graduated from Bethany College, WV, in 1943, spent three years in the Air Force, and in 1946 entered graduate school at the University of Pittsburgh. That fall he was among the first trainees in the nation appointed to the new Veterans Administration Clinical Psychology program. He received his PhD in August 1949 and spent the next two years in a research appointment at Western Psychiatric Institute of the University of Pittsburg School of Medicine.

In 1951, Albee went to Washington to work for the American Psychological Association (APA) as assistant executive secretary. Albee, F. Sanford, J. Hildreth, and M. Harlow comprised the entire APA professional staff at a time when APA occupied seven rooms in the old American Association for the Advancement of Science building. Albee was in charge of the placement office, public information, and public relations. He started the *Employment Bulletin* and hired M. Amrine, an experienced science writer, to run the press room at the 1952 convention. Albee and Amrine, who stayed on for 17 years, collaborated in numerous public information projects.

In the fall of 1953, Albee went to Finland for a year on a Fulbright professorship at Helsinki University. He returned to be an associate professor at Western Reserve University (WRU) in Cleveland, Ohio. He was named professor in 1956 and in 1958 became the George Trumbull Ladd Distinguished Professor of Psychology.

During his 16 years at WRU, Albee chaired the department on three occasions and was director of the clinical program. Albee, E. Lane, and their students published a lengthy series of studies on childhood intellectual development in adult schizophrenics. Albee and M. Dickey published the first study of human resources in the mental health professions.

On leave in 1957, Albee served as director of the Task Force on Manpower of the Joint Commission on Mental Illness and Health. The book he wrote as a report on the nation's mental health human resources shortages was a major factor in redirecting national strategy in intervention.

In 1963, for his Ohio Psychological Association Presidential Address, he produced his "Declaration of Independence for Psychology." He called for the establishment of psychological centers for training and for service delivery by psychologists, and he attacked the medical model imposed on psychology students. He was recalled to service by President Carter and served as coordinator of the Task Panel on Prevention of the President's Commission on Mental Health (1977–1978).

By the mid-1960s, Albee was in continuing, often acrimonious debate with psychiatry over the inappropriateness of the illness model of mental and emotional disorder and over medical hegemony. Albee's involvement in this debate continues, with clinical psychology also becoming a target of his wrath for devoting so much of its resources to one-to-one intervention in mental disorder rather than to prevention.

Albee has been active in the affairs of APA for more than four decades; he received APA's Distinguished Professional Contribution Award in 1975. He was a participant in the Miami, Chicago, Vail, and Utah clinical training conferences. He has been a member of the Board of Professional Affairs and the Ethics Committee; and (on numerous occasions) a member of the Council of Representatives. He was president of Division 12 (Clinical) in 1966–1967, and president of APA in 1969–1970. He was a founding fellow of the American Psychological Society (1988) and an organizer and first president (1989) of the American Association for Applied and Preventive Psychology.

When Albee moved to the University of Vermont, he established, in 1975, the Vermont Conference on the Primary Prevention of Psychopathology (VCPPP). Through 1993, VCPPP has held 17 conferences bringing together researchers, policymakers, and implementers of prevention programs throughout the world. VCPPP became one of the world's leading forums for stimulating discussion and disseminating information on all aspects of the prevention of psychopathology. The books resulting from the conferences, many of which Albee has coedited, have helped shape the field and define its agenda. The World Federation for Mental Health (WFMH) has established the Albee Lecture on Prevention delivered at each WFMH meeting by a world leader in prevention and mental health promotion.

In 1991 Albee retired as professor emeritus at the University of Vermont. He is courtesy professor at the Florida Mental Health Institute. He continues to write extensively about the social origins of mental disorders and about social justice as prevention.

In 1993 The American Psychological Foundation awarded Albee its Gold Medal Award for Lifetime Contributions to Public Service. Their citation says:

For a distinguished career of extraordinary range and depth—writing, teaching, and professional activity—that has fundamentally influenced public policy and approaches to the prevention of mental emotional disorder. He has focused his sharp intellect and boundless energy on critically questioning conventional wisdom. He then acted as its conscience, often and courageously incurring its wrath (and that of psychiatry) in the process. George Albee has communicated his views clearly, consistently, and convincingly in lectures, articles, and government and professional committees for more than 40 years, particularly his beliefs that eliminating social evils will be far more effective in increasing the sum of human happiness and decreasing misery than one-to-one therapeutic interventions. A founder of the Vermont Conference on the Primary Prevention of Psychopathology, Albee has been a prime mover of this now internationally influential forum for the latest thinking and research in prevention of mental and emotional disorder. The American Psychological Foundation Gold Medal Award is appropriate recognition of George Albee's contributions to the public good—with a sharp mind, a compassionate heart, humor, and an ability to convey to others (and thus enlist their enthusiastic support) the joy of fighting the good fight.

STAFF

ALCOHOLISM TREATMENT

Recovery from alcoholism would best be facilitated by the continuum of treatment that a service delivery system provides (Annis, 1979; Pattison, 1979). There are many variables to examine when designing this type of system. An initial concern should be the scope of the geographic area to be serviced, which can range from a worldwide perspective down to a specific neighborhood. Upon determining the geographic area, an assessment of alcoholism service needs is called for. This includes identifying the population in need of services, identifying existing services, recognizing service gaps, and examining the resources needed to complete the service delivery system.

The largest percentage of available alcoholism services is for adult males. There has been some recognition of the need for increased services for women, adolescents, families of alcohol abusers and alcoholics, and other groups. The economic situation may dictate more accountability of existing services and an examination of possible duplication of programming in any designated geographic area. Finally, the need for new services such as day care and vocational training for women, has become apparent. When an alcoholism program is being planned for a particular community, stereotyped attitudes toward alcohol abuse or alcoholism often appear. Reduced property values, dangerous "drunks," violence, bums roaming the streets, and screeching police cars and ambulances invading the neighborhood—such are the concerns verbalized. A great deal of community preparation and involvement is necessary to introduce a program for the alcoholic clientele.

TREATMENT SYSTEM COMPONENTS

Emergency Services

Emergency services is the first level of care for the person who is acutely ill or in crisis. The services can include medical evaluation, treatment and supervision, diagnostic evaluation, treatment planning, and triage to the appropriate level of care, if necessary. There are three types of emergency services generally available for the individual with an alcohol abuse or alcoholism problem.

1. *Medical.* Medical services are usually provided in a hospital emergency room. Generally, there is variation in the methods used in hospital emergency rooms to provide some level of detoxification. An alternative setting is a community-based medical detoxification facility not within a hospital.

2. *Nonmedical.* Community-based, social-setting detoxification agencies are examples of an emergency care model. There is an emphasis on supportive counseling, medical stabilization, and preparation for the next level of care within the network of services. Staffing is usually by a combination of alcoholism counselors, paramedics, and individuals identified with a specific health care discipline. The usual length of stay is a maximum of 5 days.

3. *Psychological.* Often individuals who are abusing alcohol experience a high level of stress and anxiety and, therefore, seek out a crisis intervention program to alleviate these feelings. Alcoholism issues often emerge as a person begins treatment for an initial psychiatric disorder. In this kind of setting, it is important to arrive at a differential diagnosis to effect an appropriate referral and treatment plan.

Inpatient Care

Inpatient care provides for 24-h supervised care under the direction of a physician in a hospital or a comparable medical setting. In a hospital setting, this service is usually provided on the general medical floor. The three primary referral categories are: (a) individuals who are in need of medical detoxification; (b) medical conditions associated with alcoholism, such as ulcers, hepatitis, pancreatitis, and so on; and (c) psychiatric emergencies due to alcoholism.

Intermediate Care

Intermediate care is usually referred to as residential care. It is designed for people who cannot reside in an independent living situation while attempting to deal with their alcohol abuse or alcoholism problem. Examples of residential care for alcohol abuse or alcoholism are the following:

1. *Residential Rehabilitation.* Residential rehabilitation is intensive treatment, usually using an array of treatment modalities such as individual, group, and family therapy; Alcoholics Anonymous (AA); vocational and recreation therapy; and a variety of treatment techniques. Lengths of stay generally vary from 21 to 30 days. Some residential rehabilitation programs are designed for special populations such as chronic recidivists. The issue of a client's motivation or readiness for treatment usually arises when there is an intake assessment. Controversy continues regarding the criteria for determining motivation, and whether applicants for admission can deal with this issue relative to their current state of recovery.

2. *Halfway Houses.* A halfway house is a residential facility that is viewed as a step between an intensive inpatient program and independent living. There is usually a minimum amount of treatment offered within the halfway house, with an emphasis on linking into community-based agencies and support systems. Generally, there is a resident manager who often lives within the facility. There are house rules, and a structured environment is provided for the residents. A halfway house is often an alternative to returning to a stressful home situation before developing the skills and confidence to cope with those stresses. The average length of stay is usually 3 to 12 months, with a range of treatment approaches. The 12 steps of AA are an integral, and sometimes focal, treatment modality.

3. *Partial Hospitalization.* Partial hospitalization is viewed as serving the client who needs more intensive treatment but may be maintained in an independent living situation for a portion of the day. *Day treatment* is designed for the client who has a living situation and is not in need of this level of intensive treatment in a residential setting. The number of hours range from 2 to 8 a day. Some programs are time limited. The treatment modalities include individual, group, and family therapy; AA; and vocational and occupational therapy. The *evening hospital* is designed for individuals who have their days planned, with employment or structured activities, but who have difficulty dealing with leisure time in the evenings. This program can be helpful to those who feel isolated and lonely when they return to their living arrangements. Supportive counseling is generally available. A *drop-in center* provides a resource for socialization, supportive counseling, information, and education for the alcohol abuser or alcoholic and concerned parties. Ideally, it is available 7 days a week and has evening hours. Such centers are usually community based and have volunteers as well as staff. Members of Alcoholics Anonymous are typically generous in volunteering their time to this endeavor. *Intensive outpatient rehabilitation* is similar to day treatment but can be offered in the evening as well, for those who are employed or otherwise occupied during the daytime hours. The number of hours varies from 2 to 8 a day, for 1 to 7 days a week. The traditional modalities of psychotherapy are used as part of the treatment plan. Partial hospitalization programs recognize the need for assessing the clients' ability to manage their lives and sobriety during the hours that they are not in treatment. Backup and supportive services are considered vital in developing a treatment plan for individuals in these programs.

Outpatient Care

Outpatient care is a nonresidential service that may be located in a community-based setting or a hospital. The recipient is a person with an alcohol abuse or alcoholism problem who can be sustained in an independent living situation while participating in a treatment plan for recovery. This is one of the most widely used treatment categories in the alcoholism field. Individual, group, family, and couples therapy is generally used as well as AA groups, medication, Antabuse, relaxation, and the treatment of sexual dysfunctions.

Outreach

Outreach services facilitate the identification of individuals with alcoholism problems, advocate early intervention, and assist in providing access to the service delivery system. Many individuals are reluctant to discuss or admit to alcohol abuse. Therefore, the sensitivity with which an outreach person approaches the task is a key variable. This also is when one attempts to clarify the myths and realities related to alcohol abuse and alcoholism.

Aftercare

Aftercare is designed to ensure a continuum of care in the aftercare plan development. This may include contacts by telephone, letter, questionnaire, or contact with other significant individuals in the client's life. Individuals with an alcohol abuse or alcoholism problem are often described as prone to fall through the cracks when progressing from one level of treatment to another. There is a high rate of unsuccessful follow-through of an aftercare plan. The most common source of information is the grapevine within the alcoholism community.

Other Services

There is an array of other services not offered directly but that may significantly influence the delivery of services to the client. Prevention provides the correct information in a meaningful fashion, so that an individual will not begin to abuse alcohol. A secondary goal would be to identify issues and problems that a person might be experiencing, so they would not lead to alcohol abuse. Information can be disseminated through written materials, discussions with various groups, and media presentations. Training is an ongoing delivery of basic information in all aspects of alcohol abuse or alcoholism. Many alcoholism and related programs have continuous training for their staff, identified as in-service training. Of course, basic training in the alcohol abuse and alcoholism area is offered to many groups, individuals, agencies, and organizations.

TREATMENT METHODS

The choice of treatment system usually depends on the population, resources, and program philosophy.

Alcoholics Anonymous

Alcoholics Anonymous is based on 12 steps and 12 traditions offered as guide for recovery from the disease of alcoholism (Anonymous, *Alcoholics Anonymous,* 1976). Each individual is encouraged to develop and work on his or her own program for recovery. Usually, a person is coupled with a sponsor, a recovering AA alcoholic who has sustained sobriety over a long period of time.

Alanon

Alanon is designed for spouses of recovering or practicing alcoholics and for significant others in the alcoholic's life. It is based on the 12 steps and 12 traditions of AA, and the format is a regular group meeting.

Alateen

Alateen is offered to the children of alcoholic parents, the age level usually being adolescence. The 12 steps and 12 traditions are used as a base for these group meetings.

Alatot

Alatot focuses on younger children of recovering or practicing alcoholics or significant others in the alcoholic's life. Like Alateen, it is based on the 12 steps and 12 traditions of AA. The format is a group setting.

Adult Children of Alcoholics (ACOA)

Adults who acknowledged that one or both parents or caregivers were abusing or addicted to alcohol have become active members of Adult Children of Alcoholics (ACOA) self-help groups, which are based on the AA 12-step philosophy. In addition to the self-help model, individual, group, and family therapy have been used by this population.

Psychotherapy

Psychotherapy provides a therapist-counselor to assist the patient-client in understanding his or her feelings and thoughts in individual or group psychotherapy. The psychodynamic approach to the treatment of alcohol abuse and alcoholism assumes that the drinking behavior is but a symptom of an underlying pathology that must be specifically treated. An alternative model assumes that alcoholism is a disease or illness and that, even though sobriety is achieved, basic issues that may impede one from being comfortable and happy as a sober person are in need of exploration and resolution.

Family therapy is designed to examine the relationships and communication patterns within a family structure (Steinglass, 1977). There is a basic assumption that dynamics are present in the family system that let each family member assume an integral role in maintaining a balance within the family unit. The goal of family therapy is to identify this system of relationships and agreements and then use interventions that will lead to well-functioning, productive interactions.

A primary concept within the framework of family therapy is co-dependence. Co-dependence has been defined as a primary disease and a disease within every member of an alcoholic family. It can be viewed as a dysfunctional pattern of living and problem solving that is nurtured by an unreasonable set of rules within the family system. A co-dependent person can be one who is human-relationship dependent and focuses his or her life around an addictive agent. Some characteristics of co-dependents are: (a) not trusting one's own perceptions; (b) care taking; (c) lacking boundaries; (d) becoming indispensable; and (e) becoming a martyr.

Children's therapeutic play groups are intended to provide an educational and supportive environment for children of alcoholic parents or caretakers. The age range is typically 2 to 11 years. Activities are introduced to engage the children, some of which are specifically related to alcohol use and abuse. Materials are sensitive to the child's development.

Therapeutic workshops are typically a short-term, time-limited approach, focusing on specific problem areas. They are often weekend experiences, career-planning workshops, or problem-solving meetings. Terms such as "sensitivity groups" and "marathon" are used in this treatment method (Zimberg, Wallace, & Blume, 1978).

Recreational and occupational therapy is an activity-oriented process designed to reduce tensions through exercise, athletics, and other endeavors. Occupational therapy typically involves a work-related project, with the construction of a specific item.

Behavior therapy emphasizes two goals regarding alcohol abuse and alcoholism: (a) to eliminate excessive alcohol consumption as a dominant response to stress and other aversive situations; and (b) to establish alternative adaptive models of coping behavior (Miller, 1976). Behavior therapists often view alcohol abuse and alcoholism within a social learning framework. Behavioral approaches include: (a) aversion conditioning to shift the perception of drinking-related stimuli from positive to negative, by associating drinking with uncomfortable or aversive events; (b) operant conditioning to change the drinking response as well as those variables that have influenced the drinking behavior; (c) cognitive behavior therapy to assist individuals cognitively to restructure their maladaptive thoughts in an effort to eliminate dysfunctional behavior such as excessive drinking; and (d) multidimensional behavioral approaches to focus on the antecedents and consequences of drinking patterns.

Drug therapy can provide drugs specific to alcohol abuse and alcoholism—namely, disulfiram (Antabuse) and cyanamide (Temposil). The ingestion of alcohol while one of these drugs is present in the body will cause an adverse reaction such as facial flushing, nausea, heart palpitations, and vertigo (Kitson, 1977)—reactions that are not usually life-threatening. There are various ways to distribute these drugs, such as having a helping person—usually a counselor—administer the drug at a specified meeting time, so as to provide a personal interchange. The most destructive use of these drugs would be as a punitive measure, under the guise of setting limits. An individual with poor impulse control or bad judgment would not be a good candidate for this therapeutic intervention. Psychoactive drugs such as Valium, Librium, Lithium, and Thorazine have also been used in the treatment of alcohol abuse and alcoholism. These drugs are viewed either as a primary therapeutic intervention or, more commonly, as one component of a total treatment plan. Medications are used with this population as a means of stabilizing their physical being. This is especially true during the detoxification phase of treatment.

REFERENCES

Annis, H. M. (1979). The detoxication alternative to the handling of public inebriates: The Ontario experience. *Journal of Studies on Alcohol, 40,* 196–210.

Kitson, T. M. (1977). The disulfiram-ethanol reaction: A review. *Journal of Studies on Alcohol, 38,* 96–113.

Miller, P. M. (1976). *Behavioral treatment of alcoholism.* New York: Pergamon Press.

Pattison, E. M. (1979). The selection of treatment modalities for the alcoholic patient. In J. H. Mendelson & N. K. Mello (Eds.), *The diagnosis and treatment of alcoholism.* New York: McGraw-Hill.

Steinglass, P. (1977). Family therapy in alcoholism. In B. Kissin & H. Begleiter, (Eds.), *Treatment and rehabilitation of the chronic alcoholic: The biology of alcoholism* (Vol. 5). New York: Plenum.

Zimberg, S., Wallace, J., & Blume, S. B. (Eds.). (1978). *Practical approaches to alcoholism psychotherapy.* New York: Plenum.

S. S. CARDONE
Illinois Department of Mental Health

BEHAVIOR THERAPY
PROGRAM EVALUATION

ALL-OR-NONE LAW

Applied to the axon (a single, relatively lengthy process) of a nerve cell or neuron, the all-or-none law states simply that transmission of a nerve impulse occurs either all the way or not at all. That is, if the changes—movement of charged particles or ions—that produce the nerve impulse reach a certain threshold level, then the impulse (also called the action potential or spike potential) is conducted nondecrementally from its origin to the end of the axon.

Another way the law is sometimes expressed is that axonal transmission is independent of the stimulus that produces it. As long as the stimulus causes enough ionic movement to exceed a threshold, the nerve impulse occurs all the way, without decreasing as it travels the length of the axon. A mild stimulus that surpasses the threshold produces the same nerve impulse as an intense stimulus. The nervous system codes intensity by the rate of generation of action potentials, not by whether they occur. A neuron's action potentials are analogous to signals from a telegraph key; a neuron cannot send bigger or faster action potentials any more than a telegraph operator can send bigger or faster signals with the telegraph key.

The all-or-none concept applies to other tissue as well; the principle was first demonstrated in 1871 in heart muscle by American physiologist Henry P. Bowditch. In 1902, English physiologist F. Gotch discovered evidence for an all-or-none effect in nerves, but the effect was not convincingly proven until Edgar Douglas Adrian's work, for which he received a Nobel prize in physiology in 1932. Adrian's work was preceded by studies performed by K. Lucas, who actually named the law in an article published in 1909.

Like most of the nervous system's so-called laws, the all-or-none law has been found to have exceptions. For example, some neurons can produce a series of action potentials that grow successively smaller, thus disobeying the law.

B. M. Thorne
Mississippi State University

ACTION POTENTIAL
ELECTROENCEPHALOGRAPHY
NEUROCHEMISTRY

ALLPORT, GORDON WILLARD (1897–1967)

Gordan WillardAllport gained the bachelor's and doctoral degrees at Harvard University. His PhD thesis foreshadowed his life's work, since it dealt with the psychology of personality, and its assessment. For two years he traveled and studied in Turkey, Germany, and England. Returning as an instructor at Harvard, he was appointed assistant professor of psychology at Dartmouth College in 1937. He came back to Harvard in 1930 and stayed there till his retirement, serving for several years as chairman of the psychology department. He was president of the American Psychological Association in 1939 and received numerous honorary doctorates. His outstanding position in the psychology of personality attracted many students to Harvard, who now hold posts of distinction in American and other universities.

He regarded personality as the natural subject matter of psychology and believed that other standard topics, such as human learning, could not be studied adequately without taking into account the self or ego who wanted to learn. His approach was eclectic, drawing on a wide variety of sources: McDougall's theory of motives, experimental and social psychology, psychometric studies of personality traits, German *verstehende* psychology, and psychodynamic theories. However, he was strongly opposed to Freudian views of the unconscious; his position was much closer to that of Adler. He rejected any reductionist theory that attributed human behavior to innate instincts, childhood conditioning, or repressed complexes. Personality is an organized whole, not a bundle of habits and fixations. It is present now, and it looks to the future rather than the past. Thus in his book *Becoming* (1955) he argued that the self can make choices and to some extent influence the development of its own personality. A fundamental part in personality growth is played by what Allport called the functional autonomy of motives—that is, the emergence of new motivational systems. For example, a son may take up medicine because his father is a doctor; but gradually his interests develop, and medicine becomes a goal in its own right, independent of the initial drive.

Allport was not given to extreme views. He avoided writing dogmatically or provocatively and preferred courtesy to controversy. He could aptly be called one of the first humanists in psychology, but he did not allow his humanitarian sentiments to interfere with scientific integrity and logical thinking in his writings. He realized, however, that there is a fundamental contradiction between the scientific and intuitive views of man. These he referred to as the nomothetic and idiographic standpoints. The nomothetist tries to arrive at general laws that apply to all human kind, and his procedures are based on accurate measurements of behavior. Inevitably this involves fragmentation of the individual into measurable variables. But the idiographic view sees each particular individual as a unique whole and relies largely on intuitive understanding. Allport believed that the two should be combined. Nomothetic characteristics can be measured, for example, by personality questionnaires which measure extraversion, dominance, anxiety, etc. But idiographic description must be based on case study data, or inferred from personal documents such as diaries or imaginative writing. But he rejected the usefulness of projective techniques for understanding normal people, as distinct from neurotics. He himself did devise certain tests of personality traits, atti-

tudes, and values, but saw little point in factorial studies of personality.

Allport's personality theory put him at odds with the vast majority of American psychologists, who had been indoctrinated by behaviorist empiricism. Nevertheless, they did respect his viewpoint. He dealt with the bewildering complexity of personality by positing personality traits as the basic units or components. A trait is a generalized type of behavior which characterizes each individual and distinguishes that person from others. It is a real and causal neuropsychic structure, not merely biosocial—that is, deriving from the impressions of people who observe the individual. This concept has been attacked by later writers who point out the frequent inconsistency, rather than the generality, of people's behavior in different situations. Unfortunately, Allport did not live long enough to answer such critics as Mischel, who regard personal behavior as determined more by the situation than by internal traits. But he did allow for the uniqueness of each individual personality by distinguishing common traits—variables that occur in different strengths in all persons—from unique traits or personal dispositions peculiar to the particular person.

While Allport's main work was the development of a comprehensive theory of personality, he had wide-ranging interests, including eidetic imagery, religion, social attitudes, rumor, and radio. The book that probably has the greatest practical and social value is his analysis of *The Nature of Prejudice* (1954). His major book is *Pattern and Growth in Personality*.

It is appropriate to close with the citation he received when awarded the Gold Medal of the American Psychological Foundation in 1963: "To Gordon Willard Allport, outstanding teacher and scholar. He has brought warmth, wit, humanistic knowledge, and rigorous enquiry to the study of human individuality and social process."

P. E. VERNON

ALPHA RHYTHMS

Ensembles of synchronously active cortical neurons generate electromagnetic field potentials, which can be measured by scalp electrodes in electroencephalography (EEG) or by helmet-mounted detectors in magnetoencephalography (MEG). The alpha frequency band is defined to be between 8 and 13 Hz (Berger, 1929). It should be emphasized that an EEG rhythm is defined by its frequency, by its distribution on the scalp, and by its reactivity. The classical alpha rhythm is prominent at electrodes overlying the occipital (visual) cortex, and, to a lesser extent, over the posterior temporal and parietal areas. Alpha rhythm occurs in a condition of relaxed wakefulness with eyes closed (or in total darkness) and it disappears (or is depressed) upon eye opening (object fixation). Less severe (and inconsistent) depression occurs during task solving, for example, mental arithmetic, and the alpha rhythm disappears gradually during drowsiness.

A slower rhythm (5–6 Hz) with alpha reactivity and distribution is evident in 4- to 6-month-old infants. Visually deprived and congenitally blind children do not develop the alpha rhythm. The alpha frequency matures and reaches the approximate average values of 8 Hz at age 3 years, 9 Hz at age 9 years, and 10 Hz at age 15 years. The interindividual variability among healthy children is quite large, and it is difficult to make statements about delayed maturation unless the deviation from the normal average value is quite large.

About 6 to 10 % of healthy subjects have low voltage alpha activity, below 20 µV, but brief runs of well-defined alpha rhythm may be induced by eye closure or hyperventilation in these subjects. In general, alpha amplitude is higher in children than in adults. Skull thickness is on the average greater on the left side, probably explaining why the occipital alpha amplitude is higher on the right than on the left side in most healthy subjects. Consistent amplitude asymmetries exceeding 2:1 are usually considered abnormal. Alpha variant rhythms with a frequency of half (around 5 Hz) or two times (around 20 Hz) the normal alpha rhythm frequency may be recorded in some healthy subjects (Markand, 1990).

Alpha rhythm peak frequency correlates with cerebral blood flow and metabolism (Sulg, 1984), and low frequencies are encountered in a number of metabolic, infectious, and degenerative disorders, which affects cortical gray matter diffusely—dementia of Alzheimer's type. Unilateral slowing or loss of alpha rhythm occurs in the presence of traumatic, neoplastic, infectious, or vascular lesions of one occipital lobe.

Other physiological rhythms within the alpha frequency band are the mu rhythm (9–11 Hz activity recorded over the sensorimotor cortex, blocked by movements of the contralateral extremity) and the tau rhythm. Tau is recordable with invasive electrocorticography or by MEG over the temporal regions (Hari, 1993). Mu rhythm is found in about 10% of routine EEGs of healthy subjects, and it may represent a sub-harmonic of the 20 Hz sensorimotor cortical rhythm (Niedermeyer, 1993). It should be noted that mu often is the only routinely recorded alpha-band rhythm in the EEG of infants and small children. In order to see the proper alpha rhythm, passive eye closure or recording in darkness should be attempted. Abnormal alpha coma pattern occur in some comatose patients. The outcome is variable, depending on the underlying condition, but it is most often poor.

Subdural and intracortical recordings, as well as source localization EEG and MEG studies, have shown that the alpha rhythm has multiple generators within the cerebral cortex (Williamson, Kauffman, Lu, Wang, & Karron, 1997). The rapidly changing activation and inactivation of these generators can be viewed (or hypothesized) as concatenated global microstates, in which the individual microstate may be considered an atom of thought (Lehmann & Koenig, 1997). In dogs, the generator has been pinpointed to cortical layer V. Although early studies of barbiturate spindles in the cat suggested that the alpha rhythm was driven by feedback inhibition of thalamic relé cells (Andersen & Andersson, 1968), more recent studies in dogs suggest that both corticocortical and thalamo-cortical connections are of importance. The alpha activity in two thalamic nuclei (pulvinar and the lateral geniculate nucleus) shows significant correlation with cortical alpha activity, but intracortical coherence is of greater magnitude. It has been suggested that both intrinsic membrane ion channel properties and local neuron network properties determine rhyth-

mic behavior, possibly as an efficient way to reset the membrane potential (and hence reactivity) simultaneously in a large number of neurons (Lopes da Silva, 1991).

Using spectral analysis and coherence methods on EEG and MEG data from closely spaced electrodes or detectors, it has been possible to draw conclusions about, for example, maturation of cortico-cortical connections. The coherence-function has become a particularly popular tool because it measures how well the activity from two electrodes follows the same basic rhythm (are in phase), and the method may accordingly reveal information about functional connectivity between different parts of the brain during various tasks and states (Gevins, Leong, Smith, Le, & Ju, 1995). It should be emphasized that the so-called smearing effects of volume conduction and the effects of different types of EEG-reference electrodes may influence the results and make interpretations difficult.

Event-related desynchronization (ERD) of central and occipital alpha rhythms represents activation of those cortical areas that are active in vision, motor preparation, or selective attention (Pfurtscheller, Stancák, & Neuper, 1996). Desynchronization of the lower part of the alpha band may be related to attention, but intention should also be considered. It should be emphasized that desynchronization may be a reflection of preserved synchrony within a larger number of smaller ensembles of cortical neurons, ensembles that may be too small to be detected individually by EEG or MEG. Indeed, event-related alpha-oscillations in the visual and auditory cortex following visual and auditory stimuli respectively have been described (Basar, Basar-Eroglu, Karakas, & Schürmann, 1999). If the source location of ERD and ERS activity can be identified, it is possible to infer which cortical areas are involved in various tasks.

The classical notion (which has been questioned recently) is that alpha rhythmicity and event-related synchronization (ERS) represent a state of inactivity (idling). Examples include enhanced mu activity during visual processing and the enhanced hand-area mu activity during foot movement. Alpha and mu rhythms have been linked to a state of expectancy in awake cats (Rogeul-Buser & Buser, 1997).

Can alpha rhythm frequency predict cognitive performance? Conflicting results have been published in the EEG literature (Markand, 1990). Recent results suggest that subjects with relatively good memory performance have higher alpha frequency than subjects with bad performance. This has been found within both healthy subjects and patients with Alzheimer's type dementia. ERD in the upper part of the alpha band may reflect semantic memory performance, while ERS in the slower 4 to 7 Hz theta band may reflect episodic memory and encoding of new information (Klimesch, 1999). Dyslectic children have also been reported to have reduced alpha power.

Considerable progress has been made toward a better understanding of the basic mechanisms behind alpha rhythms and brain function during recent years, but these efforts have not yet improved the clinical utility of EEG. High-resolution EEG and MEG equipment combined with mathematical tools can reduce the effects of volume conduction and take individual magnetic resonance image–based head and brain shape into account. This will hopefully increase the possibility of investigating brain oscillations and EEG rhythms further. The important general methodological questions related to standardization, reliability, and blinding will need increasing attention in future studies. Carefully planned studies with well formulated hypotheses about the relationship between EEG or MEG rhythms and sensation, cognition, and performance are needed.

REFERENCES

Andersen, P., & Andersson, S. (1968). *Physiological basis of the alpha rhythm.* New York: Appleton-Century-Croft.

Basar, E., Basar-Eroglu, C., Karakas, S., & Schürmann, M. (1999). Are cognitive processes manifested in event-related gamma, alpha, theta and delta oscillations in the EEG? *Neuroscience Letters, 259,* 165–168.

Berger, H. (1929). Über das Elektroenkephalogramm des Menschen. Archiv für Psychiatrie, *87,* 527–570.

Gevins, A., Leong, H., Smith, M. E., Le Jian, D.R. (1995). Mapping cognitive brain function with modern high-resolution electroencephalography. *Trends in Neuroscience, 18,* 429–436.

Klimesch, W. (1999). EEG alpha and theta oscillations reflect cognitive and memory performance: A review and analysis. *Brain Research Reviews, 29,* 169–195.

Lehmann, D., Koenig, T. (1997). Spatio-temporal dynamics of alpha band electric fields, and cognitive modes. *International Journal of Psychophysiology, 26,* 99–112.

Lopes da Silva, F. (1991). Neural mechanisms underlying brain waves: From neural membranes to networks. *Electroencephalography and Clinical Neurophysiology, 7,* 81–93.

Markand, O. N. (1990). Alpha rhythms. *Journal of Clinical Neurophysiology, 7,* 163–189.

Niedermeyer, E. (1993). The normal EEG in the waking adult. In E. Niedermeyer & F. H. da Silva (Eds.), *Electroencephalography: Basic principles, clinical applications and related fields* (pp. 131–152). Baltimore: Williams & Wilkins.

Hari, R. (1993). Magnetoencephalography as a tool of clinical neurophysiology. In E. Niedermeyer & F. H. da Silva (Eds.), *Electroencephalography: Basic principles, clinical applications and related fields* (pp. 1035–1061). Baltimore: Williams and Wilkins.

Pfurtscheller, G., Stancák, A., Jr., & Neuper, C. (1996). Event-related synchronization (ERS) in the alpha band—an electrophysiological correlate of cortical idling: A review. *International Journal of Psychophysiology, 24,* 39–46.

Rogeul-Buser, A., & Buser, P. (1997). Rhythms in the alpha band in cats and their behavioral correlates. *International Journal of Psychophysiology, 26,* 191–203.

Sulg, I. (1984). Quantitative EEG as a measure of brain dysfunction. In G. Pfurtscheller, E. H. Jonkman, & F. H. Lopes da Silva (Eds.), *Progress in neurobiology: Vol. 62. Brain ischemia: Quantitative EEG and imaging techniques* (pp. 65–84). Amsterdam: Elsevier.

Williamson, S. J., Kaufmann, L., Lu, Z. L., Wang, J. Z., Karron, D. (1997). Study of human occipital alpha rhythm: The alphon hypothesis and alpha suppression. *International Journal of Psychophysiology,* 26, 63–76.

T. SAND
Norwegian University of Science and Technology

BRAIN WAVES
ELECTROENCEPHALOGRAPHY

ALTRUISM

In the technical language of evolutionary biologists, altruistic behavior is behavior by one organism such that the chances of its own survival—or the survival of its offspring—are diminished in favor of that of other members of the species. The standard interpretation of this behavior is that it is advantageous for the whole genetic pool protected by adaptive behavior, but not for the individual. Thus altruistic behavior will be more frequent, the higher the common heredity; close relations show higher altruism than more distant relations, family higher than nonfamily, etc. Altruism in this way is connected with group selection, the theory that evolution proceeds at the group, not the individual level; groups which include altruistic behavior would have improved survival chances.

Doubts have been expressed about whether true altruism can be proven, or whether behavior which looks altruistic to an observer can really be accounted for by self-directed motives; this argument is tied up with the general controversy on the extent of group selection. The argument for group selection and corresponding altruistic behavior was made by Wynne-Edwards in *Animal Dispersion in Relation to Social Behavior.* By the nature of the question no direct proof can be given, only plausibility of interpretation of any observation, but no disproof can be made either. In the same way, this concept has been applied to human behavior, but its validity remains tentative.

The term itself, altruism, was coined by Auguste Comte as part of his accounting for social units; altruism in this sense means selfless concern for the welfare of others, and may occur without any risk to the altruist. Altruism—like imitation, suggestion, and sympathy—was used in early sociology as a general explanation of social behavior. Like these other terms, altruism fell into disuse when the unitary explanation of society was abandoned; in the meantime the term had entered the common language from its sociological origin.

More recently, altruism has become a topic in experimental social psychology under the general heading of prosocial behavior. Research interest in the field arose after much work had been done on antisocial behavior, especially aggression. As an applied problem, the reduction of aggression was important, but so was the promotion of prosocial behavior. Two types of action which have been studied extensively are helping behavior and bystander intervention. In both these fields the conditions of this behavior have to be specified: we know that both of them occur and do not occur, so that the question of a universal does not arise. Altruistic behavior can thus be seen as exchange behavior, as a function of the relationship—that is, as dependent on relative status, familiarity with the environment, and the availability of alternate actors who could do the appropriate act.

In a larger sense, altruistic behavior is a function of social norms. Children are socialized into acceptance of these norms. The capacity to accept certain norms seems to be determined by developmental stages. How these norms arose in the first place is little considered by social psychologists, and their biological or social value is not discussed. Thus in social psychological discussions it remains open whether altruistic behavior is necessary for the existence of societies or whether pure individualistic, competitive behavior could form a stable social base.

SUGGESTED READING

Latané, B., & Darley, J. M. (1970). *The unresponsive bystander: Why doesn't he help?* New York: Appleton-Century-Crofts.

Macaulay, L., & Berkowitz, L. (Eds.). (1970). *Altruism and helping behavior.* New York: Academic Press.

K. W. BACK

BYSTANDER INVOLVEMENT
LOVE
TERRITORIALITY

ALZHEIMER'S DISEASE

Alzheimer's disease (AD) is a progressive neurodegenerative disease that primarily affects cortical function. It was first characterized by Alois Alzheimer in 1906, during a lecture given at the 37th Conference of South-West German Psychiatrists (Maurer, Volk, & Gerbaldo, 1997). Alzheimer described a woman with progressive cognitive decline, hallucinations, delusions, and impaired social functioning. An autopsy later performed on that patient revealed the pathologic hallmarks of plaques and neurofibrillary tangles (Alzheimer, 1906).

The functional definition of the disorder has evolved over time and is now generally accepted to include an acquired, persistent, progressive impairment of intellectual capabilities in at least three of the following areas of cognition: language; visuospatial skills; emotion or personality; and higher cognitive function (abstraction, calculation, judgment, and executive function: Cummings & Benson). Some diagnostic criteria, such as those established in the *DSM-IV,* require that memory impairment be present and that it be accompanied by dysfunction in at least one of the other domains listed above (see Table 1; American Psychiatric Association, 1994). These deficits should be severe enough that usual activities or relationships are adversely affected.

The prevalence of Alzheimer's disease has been steadily increasing over the past decade along with the rise in the percentage of the population over age 65. It has been reported that 15% of individuals over age 65, and up to 50% of individuals over age 80, meet diagnostic criteria for AD (Evans et al., 1989; Pfeffer, Afifi, & Chance, 1987). Approximately 7 million persons are predicted to be affected by the early 21st century (U.S. Congress, 1987; Evans, et al., 1990).

The scientific basis of the degenerative changes seen in AD has been an area of intense study, and in the last two decades researchers have accumulated many new insights into the disease process. The cholinergic hypothesis of AD proposes that the functional deficits are, at least in part, a result of the loss of cholinergic neurons in the nucleus basalis of Meynert and the diagonal band of Broca, which have widespread projections to all cortical areas. This hypothesis is supported by extensive preclinical and clinical studies. Currently approved therapies for AD (e.g., donepezil and other cholinesterase inhibitors) also target central cholinergic systems, and have been partially effective in enhancing cognitive function in affected persons.

Advances have also been made in understanding the genetic predisposition to the development of AD. Early-onset familial AD has been linked to mutations of genes coded on chromosomes 14 and 1, which have been named presenilin 1 and presenilin 2, respectively (Schellenberg et al., 1992; Levy-Lahad et al., 1995; Campion et al., 1995), as well as to the chromosome 21 locus of the β amyloid precursor protein. The amyloid precursor protein has also been implicated in late-onset sporadic forms and in the AD that invariably occurs in middle-aged persons with trisomy 21 or Down syndrome (Goldgaber, Lerman, McBride, Saffiotti, & Gajdusek, 1988; Tanzi et al., 1987). Abnormal processing of this protein leads to the deposition of an increased proportion of Aβ peptides containing 42 rather than 40 residues (Suzuki et al., 1994). This appears to enhance aggregation of Aβ, resulting in accelerated development of plaque formation (Jarrett, Berger, & Hansbury, 1993; Selkoe et al., 1994). Finally, the Apo E genotype, coded-for by chromosome 19, has been shown to be a significant contributor to AD susceptibility (Pericak-Vance et al., 1991). There are three common alleles (ε_2, ε_3, and ε_4) the combinations of which allow for six different genotypes. The presence of each ε_4 allele increases the risk of developing AD by a factor ranging 2.84, with as many as 90% from individuals who have two copies of the allele being affected. (Corder et al., 1993; Farrer et al., 1997).The clinical presentation of Alzheimer's disease varies widely, and is dependent on the stage of the disease at which the patient is brought for evaluation. The clinical signs and symptoms associated with the early stage of the disease include frequent repetition of stories or questions, misplacing belongings, becoming lost while driving, difficulty managing finances, and subtle language disturbance. The term "anomic aphasia" has been used to describe the language dysfunction seen in this stage of the disease. This aphasia is characterized by difficulty finding the correct word, both when speaking or writing, and difficulty with confrontational naming (Mesulam, 1985). Delusions may accompany this stage of the disease, and often include ideas of infidelity or theft of money and possessions (Rubin, Drevets, & Burke, 1988).

Symptoms of the moderate stage of the disease include difficulty with independent performance of the activities of daily living, such as dressing and bathing; becoming lost in familiar surroundings; difficulty recognizing familiar faces; and a transcortical sensory aphasia (Mesulam, 1985). Behavioral disturbances are common, and include agitation and aggression (Jost & Grossberg, 1996). Hallucinations may also manifest at this stage, and are most often described as complex visual phenomena. Other types of hal-

Table 1.   Comparison of NINDS-ARDA and *DSM-IV* Criteria for the Diagnosis of Alzheimer's Disease.

NINDS-ARDA Criteria for Probable Alzheimer's Disease	DSM-IV Criteria for Dementia of the Alzheimer's Type

A. Include the following:
  1. Dementia established by clinical examination and documented by the Mini-Mental Test, Blessed Dementia Scale, or some similar examination, and confirmed by neuropsychological tests.
  2. Deficits in two or more areas of cognition.
  3. Progressive worsening of memory and other cognitive functions.
  4. No disturbance of consciousness.
  5. Onset between ages 40 and 90, most often after age 65.
  6. Absence of systemic disorders or other brain diseases that in and of themselves could account for the progressive deficits in memory and cognition.
B. The diagnosis is supported by the following:
  1. Progressive deterioration of specific cognitive functions, such as language (aphasia), motor skills (apraxia), and perception (agnosia).
  2. Impaired activities of daily living and altered patterns of behavior.
  3. Family history of similar disorders, especially if confirmed neuro-histopathologically.
	A. The development of multiple cognitive deficits manifested by both:
	  1. Memory impairment (impaired ability to learn new information or to recall previously learned information) and
	  2. One (or more) of the following cognitive disturbances:
	    a. aphasia (language disturbance)
	    b. apraxia (impaired ability to carry out motor activities despite intact motor function)
	    c. agnosia (failure to recognize or identify objects despite intact sensory function)
	    d. disturbance in executive functioning (i.e., planning, organizing, sequencing).
	B. The cognitive deficits in Criteria A1 and A2 each cause significant impairment in social or occupational functioning and represent a decline from a previous level of functioning.
	C. The course is characterized by gradual onset and continuing cognitive decline.
	D. The cognitive deficits in Criteria A1 and A2 are not due to any of the following:
	  1. Other central nervous system conditions that cause progressive deficits in memory and cognition (e.g., cerebrovascular disease, Parkinson's disease, Huntington's disease, subdural hematoma, normal pressure hydrocephalus, brain tumor).
	  2. systemic conditions that are known to cause dementia (e.g., hypothyroidism, vitamin B12 or folic acid deficiency, hypercalcemia, neurosyphilis, HIV infection).
	  3. substance induced conditions.
	E. The deficits do not occur exclusively during the course of a delirium.
	F. The disturbance is not better accounted for by another Axis I disorder (e.g., Major Depressive Disorder, Schizophrenia).

lucinations, such as auditory hallucinations and formication, are unusual, and suggest the presence of another metabolic, toxic, or psychiatric condition.

The late stage of AD is characterized by profound impairment in even simple activities such as eating, swallowing, and walking. Patients are often bed-bound, and use only a very few words or become globally aphasic. The cumulative result is an increased risk of decubitus ulcers, aspiration pneumonia, and urosepsis from indwelling catheters.

Diagnosis of Alzheimer's disease is based on the presence of the features delineated previously and the exclusion of other etiologies. Common screening tools for dementia include the Mini-Mental State Exam, which provides normative data for healthy elderly subjects and patients with dementia based on age and educational status, and the lengthier Mattis Dementia Rating Scale (Folstein, Folstein, & McHugh, 1975; Green, Woodard and Green, 1995). The clock test has also been described as a screening measure for multiple cognitive domains. Performance of the test includes presenting the patient with a drawing of a large circle and asking him or her to imagine that it is a clock, writing the numbers in the appropriate positions and placing the hands at 10 minutes after 11 (Sunderland et al., 1989).

An appropriate serologic evaluation for the patient identified as cognitively impaired is intended to rule out treatable or reversible causes of dementia, such as those listed in Table 2. This should include a blood count with differential, a chemistry panel (with sodium, calcium, blood urea nitrogen, and liver function en-

zymes), vitamin B-12 and folate levels, thyroid stimulating hormone assay, and a fluorescent treponemal antibody assay or equivalent test (Corey-Bloom et al., 1995). An Rapid Plasma Reagin (RPR) is not an acceptable screening tool for syphilis, since it may become negative late in the course of disease, when cognitive sequelae most commonly occur. A recent advance in the diagnosis of AD is the commercial availability of a cerebrospinal fluid (CSF) analysis of tau and Aβ proteins. This test has a sensitivity of 59% and a specificity of 96% for ruling in AD, and a sensitivity of 62% and a specificity of 100% for ruling out AD (Motter et al., 1995). It is not useful as a screening tool, but may aid in the confirmation of AD in the case of an individual older than 60 years who has cognitive impairment. However, the limited sensitivity and invasive nature of the test have diminished its utility.

Neuroimaging investigations for Alzheimer's disease are also indicated to rule out conditions such as subdural hematomas, hydrocephalus, and space occupying lesions. CT-scanning and magnetic resonance imaging (MRI) are both acceptable studies, with the MRI being more sensitive for vascular lesions and transependymal flow of CSF (as is seen in normal pressure hydrocephalus). Abnormalities such as cortical atrophy, especially in the perisylvian and medial temporal regions, and compensatory dilatation of the lateral ventricles may occur in AD, but are nonspecific (Mann, Neary, & Testa, 1994). Positron emission tomography (PET) and Single-photon emission computed tomography (SPECT) scanning of patients with AD characteristically reveal hypometabolism in the posterior temporal and parietal lobes, even

Table 2.   Disease Processes That Should Be Considered in the Differential Diagnosis of Dementia and Their Principle Methods of Evaluation

Treatable causes of dementia that must be excluded primarily by serologic studies:

Neurosyphilis
Hypothyroidism
Vitamin B12 deficiency
Folate deficiency
Hypercalcemia
Hypo- or hypernatremia
Renal dysfunction
Liver dysfunction
Chronic drug intoxication
HIV infection

Treatable causes of dementia that must be excluded primarily by neuroimaging studies:

Normal pressure hydrocephalus
Subdural hematoma
Multi-infarct dementia
Subcortical arteriosclerotic encephalopathy (Binswanger's disease)
Space-occupying lesions (tumor, abscess, etc.)
Demyelinating diseases (multiple sclerosis, PML)

Other causes of dementia that may be excluded by EEG:

Subclinical seizures
Creutzfeld-Jakob disease

Other causes of dementia that must be excluded primarily by clinical features:

Pseudodemetia (depression)
Pick's disease
Parkinson's disease
Progressive Supranuclear Palsy
Diffuse Lewy Body disease
Cortical-basal-ganglionic degeneration
Huntington's disease

early in the disease (Chawluk, Grossman, & Calcano-Perez, 1990). While these studies are more specific for AD, they are not commonly employed in the evaluation of individuals with cognitive impairment, and are most useful when attempting to discriminate AD from other cortical dementias such as Pick's disease, which characteristically shows fronto-temporal hypometabolism.

Current therapies for AD are based primarily on augmenting the central cholinergic system, as mentioned previously. The three commercially available acetylcholinesterase inhibitor drugs; tacrine, donepezil, and rivastigmine, have similar efficacy, but differ in side effect profiles. Tacrine has been associated with significant hepatotoxicity in more than 25% of patients, and is no longer commonly used. Donepezil has been shown to be effective in delaying the process of deterioration in patients with AD. In clinical trials, donepezil therapy, at a dose of 10 mg/day, resulted in cognitive improvement in 53% of patients, versus improvement in 26% of patients treated with placebo (Rogers et al., 1998). Rivastigmine, at a dose of 12 mg/day, resulted in improvement in 55% of patients vs improvement in 45% patients treated with placebo. This dose was, however, associated with discontinuation of the drug secondary to adverse side effects (mainly gastro-intestinal) in 23% of patients. (Rosler et al., 1999). Other anti-cholinesterase drugs, such as ep-

tastigmine, and metrifonate, are also available in some countries, and may be approved for AD in the United States.

Other therapies employed in the treatment of AD include vitamin E, an antioxidant that appears to delay progression of the disease (Sano et al., 1997). Several epidemiologic studies suggest that estrogen may delay the onset and reduce the risk of AD in postmenopausal women; however, clinical trials are still necessary (Tang et al., 1996). Ginkgo biloba has been touted as a natural remedy for AD, but a minority of clinical trials have been positive and then with only a mild beneficial effect over placebo (p = .04; Le Bars et al., 1997). Other evidence suggests that nonsteroidal anti-inflammatory drugs (NSAIDs) may provide neuroprotection in AD, possibly delaying onset and slowing progression (McGeer, Schulzer, & McGeer, 1996). Studies to further evaluate these benefits are currently underway. Until safety and efficacy issues are addressed with prospective studies, precautions against use of NSAIDs for AD should be heeded because of the risk of serious adverse effects, such as peptic ulcer and renal impairment.

Finally, psychotherapeutic interventions such as family counseling are often needed to help families come to terms with a patient's changing abilities and and as they experience the grief associated with perceived loss (Kaplan & Saddock, 1989). While the diagnosis may be perceived by some as catastrophic news, education and contact with community support (e.g., the Alzheimer's Association) and others may help lessen the anxiety and fear of the unknown, and enable individuals to function better and for longer periods within their families and in their own homes.

REFERENCES

Alzheimer, A. (1906). Uber einen eigenartigen schweren Erkrankungsprozeff der Hirnrinde. *Neurologisches Centralblatt, 23,* 1129–1136.

American Psychiatric Association. (1994). *Diagnostic and Statistical Manual of Mental Disorders* (4th ed.). Washington, DC: Author.

Campion, C., Fiaman, J., Brice, A., Hannequin, D., Dubois, B., Martin, C., Moreau, V., Charbonnier, F., Didierjean, O., & Tardieu, S. (1995). Mutations of the presenilin 1 gene in families with early onset Alzheimer's disease. *Human Molecular Genetics, 4,* 2373–2377.

Chawluk, J., Grossman, M., & Calcano-Perez, J. (1990). Positron emission tomographic studies of cerebral metabolism in Alzheimer's disease. In *Modular deficits in Alzheimer type dementia.* Cambridge, MA: The MIT Press.

Corder, E., Saunders, A., Strittmatter, W., Schmechel, D., Gaskell, P., Small, G., Roses, A., Haines, J., & Pericak-Vance, M. (1993). Gene dose of apolipoprotein E type 4 allele and the risk of Alzheimer's disease in late onset families. *Science, 261,* 921–923.

Corey-Bloom, J., Thal, L., Galasko, D., Folstern, M., Drachman, D., Raskind, M., & Lanska, D. (1995). Diagnosis and evaluation of dementia. *Neurology, 45,* 211–218.

Cummings, J., & Benson, D. *Dementia: A clinical approach.* Boston: Butterworth-Heinneman.

Evans, D. A., Funkenstein, H. H., Albert, M. S., Scherr, P., Cook, N., Chown, M., Hebert, L., Hennekens, C., & Taylor, J. (1989). Prevalence of Alzheimer's disease in a community population of older persons. *Journal of the American Medical Association, 262*, 2551–2556.

Evans, D. A., Scherr, P. A., Cook, N. R., Albert, M., Funkenstein, N., Smith, L., Hebert, L., Wetle, T., Branch, L., Chown, M., Hennekens, C., & Taylor, J. (1990). Estimated prevalence of Alzheimer's disease in the United States. *Milbank Quarterly, 68*, 267–287.

Farrer, L. A., Cupples, L. A., Haines, J. L., Hyman, B., Kukull, W., Mayeux, R., Myers, R., Pericak-Vance, M., Risch, N., & van Duijn, C. (1997). Effects of age, sex, and ethnicity on the association between apolipoprotein E genotype and Alzheimer's disease. *Journal of the American Medical Association, 278*, 1349–1356.

Folstein, M. F., Folstein, S. E., & McHugh, P. R. (1975). "Minimental state." A practical method for grading the cognitive state of patients for the clinician. *Journal of Psychiatric Research, 12*, 189.

Goldgaber, D., Lerman, M. I., McBride, O. W., Saffiotti, U., & Gajdusek, D. C. (1988). Characterization and chromosomal location of a cDNA encoding brain amyloid of Alzheimer's disease. *Science, 241*, 1507–1510.

Green, R., Woodard, J., & Green, J. (1995). Validity of the Mattis Dementia Rating Scale for detection of cognitive impairment in the elderly. *Journal of Neuropsychiatry and Clinical Neurosciences, 7:*357–60.

Jarrett, J. T., Berger, E. P., & Lansbury, P. T., Jr. (1993). The carboxy terminus of the beta amyloid protein is critical for the seeding of amyloid formation: Implications for the pathogenesis of Alzheimer's disease. *Biochemistry, 32*, 4693–4697.

Jost, B. C., & Grossberg, G. T. (1996). The evolution of psychiatric symptoms in Alzheimer's disease: A natural history study. *Journal of the American Geriatric Society, 44*, 1078–1081.

Kaplan, H., & Saddock, B. (1989). *Comprehensive textbook of psychiatry* (5th ed.). Baltimore: Williams and Wilkins.

LeBars, P., Katz, M., Berman, N., Itil, T., Freedman, A., & Schatzberg, A. (1997). A placebo controlled, double blind, randomized trial of an extract of ginko biloba for dementia. *Journal of the American Medical Association, 278*, 1327–1332.

Levy-Lahad, E., Wijsman, E. M., Nemens, E., Anderson, L., Goddard, K. A. B., Weber, J. L., Bird, T., & Schellenberg, G. (1995). A familial Alzheimer's disease locus on Chromosome 1. *Science, 269*, 970–973.

Mann, D., Neary, D., & Testa, H. (1994). *Color atlas and text of adult dementias.* London: Mosby-Wolfe.

Maurer, K., Volk, S., & Gerbaldo, H. (1997). Auguste D and Alzheimer's disease. *Lancet, 349*, 1546–1549.

McGeer, P., Schulzer, M., & McGeer, E. (1996). Arthritis and anti-inflammatory agents as possible protective factors for Alzheimer's disease: A review of 17 epidemiologic studies. *Neurology, 47*, 425–432.

Mesulam, M. (1985). *Principles of behavioral neurology.* Philadelphia: F. A. Davis.

Mesulam, M., & Geula, C. (1994). *Alzheimer disease.* New York: Raven.

Motter, R., Vigo-Pelfrey, C., Kholodenko, D., Barbour, R., Johnson-Wood, K., Galasko, D., Chang, L., Miller, B., Clark, C., & Green, R. (1995). Reduction of β-amyloid peptide$_{42}$ in the cerebrospinal fluid of patients with Alzheimer's disease. *Annals of Neurology, 38*, 643–648.

Pericak-Vance, M. A., Bebout, J. L., Gaskell, P. C., Yamaoka, L., Hung, W., Alberts, M., Walker, A., Bartlett, R., Haynes, C., Welsh, K., Earl, N., Heyman, A., Clark, C., & Roses, A. (1991). Linkage studies in familial Alzheimer's disease: Evidence for chromosome 19 linkage. *American Journal of Human Genetics, 48*, 1034–1050.

Pfeffer, R. I., Afifi, A. A., & Chance, J. M. (1987). Prevalence of Alzheimer's disease in a retirement community. *American Journal of Epidemiology, 125*, 420–436.

Rogers, S., Farlow, M., Doody, R., Mohs, R., Friedhoff, L., & Donepezil Study Group (1998). A 24 week, double blind, placebo controlled trial of donepezil in patients with Alzheimer's disease. *Neurology, 50*, 136–145.

Rosler, M., Anand, R., Ciein-Sain, A., Gauthier, S., Agid, Y., Dal-Bianco, P., Stahelin, H., Hartman, R., & Gharabawi, M. (1999). Efficacy and Safety of rivastigmine in patients with Alzheimer's disease: international randomised controlled trial. *British Medical Journal, 318*, 633–640.

Rubin, E. H., Drevets, W. C., & Burke, W. J. (1988). *Behavioral complications in Alzheimer's disease.* Washington, DC: American Psychiatric Press.

Sano, M., Ernesto, C., Thomas, R., Klauber, M., Schafer, K., Grundman, M., Woodbury, P., Growdon, J., Cotman, C., Pfeiffer, E., Schneider, L., & Thal, L. (1997). A controlled trial of selegeline, alpha tocopherol, or both as treatment for Alzheimer's disease. *New England Journal of Medicine, 336*, 1216–1222.

Schellenberg, G. D., Bird, T. D., Wijsman, E. M., Orr, H. T., Anderson, L., Nemens, E., White, J., Bonnycastle, L., Weber, J., Alonso, M., Potter, H., Heston, L., & Martin, C. (1992). Genetic linkage evidence for a familial Alzheimer's disease locus on Chromosome 14. *Science, 258*, 668–671.

Selkoe, D. J. (1994). Alzheimer's disease: A central role for amyloid. *Journal of Neuropathology and Experimental Neurology, 53*, 438–447.

Sunderland, T., Hill, J. L., Mellow, A. M., Lawlor, B., Gundersheimer, J., Newhouse, P., & Grafman, J. (1989). Clock drawing in Alzheimer's disease: A novel measure of dementia severity. *Journal of American Geriatrics, 37*, 725–729.

Suzuki, N., Cheung, T. T., Cai, X.-D., Odaka, A., Otvos, L., Jr., Eckman, C., Golde, T., & Younkin, S. (1994). An increased percentage of long amyloid b protein precursor (bAPP717) mutants. *Science, 264*, 1336–1340.

Tang, M., Jacobs, D., Stern, Y., Marder, K., Schofield, P., Gurland, B., Andrews, H., & Mayeux, R. (1996). Effect of oestrogen during menopause on risk and age at onset of Alzheimer's disease. *Lancet, 348,* 429–432.

Tanzi, R. E., Gusella, J. F., Watkins, P. C., Bruns, G. A. P., St. George-Hyslop, P. H., Van Keuren, M. L., Patterson, D., Pagan, S., Kurnit, D., & Neve, R. (1987). Amyloid beta protein gene: cDNA, mDNA distribution and genetic linkage near the Alzheimer locus. *Science, 235,* 880–884.

United States Congress, Office of Technology Assessment. (1987). *Losing a million minds: Confronting the tragedy of Alzheimer's and other dementias.* Washington, DC.

ANGELA V. ASHLEY
A. LEVEY
Emory University School of Medicine

CENTRAL NERVOUS SYSTEM DISORDERS

AMERICAN PSYCHIATRIC ASSOCIATION

The American Psychiatric Association, founded in 1844, is the oldest national medical society in the United States. For the first 50 years it remained a small organization of medical superintendents of American institutions for the insane. In 1892 the name was changed to the American Medico-Psychological Association, and the present name was adopted in 1921. Membership has grown from 900 in 1918 to over 26,000 in 1981. This represents 70% of the estimated 31,000 psychiatrists in the United States. More than 400 members are from other countries. All members other than honorary must be physicians with some specialized training and experience in psychiatry.

The objectives of the Association are to improve the treatment, rehabilitation, and care of the mentally retarded and emotionally disturbed; to promote research, professional education in psychiatry and allied fields, and the prevention of psychiatric disabilities; to advance the standards of all psychiatric services and facilities; to foster the cooperation of all who are concerned with the medical, psychological, social, and legal aspects of mental health and illness; to make psychiatric knowledge available to other practitioners of medicine, to scientists in other fields, and to the public; and to promote the best interests of patients and those actually or potentially making use of mental health services.

The Association is governed by an elected board of trustees, and by an assembly composed of representatives from each of 25 district branches. Almost all states have a district branch of the Association the purpose of which is to represent the profession and further the objectives of the Association in the communities they serve.

Programs and policies originate in studies and recommendations of nine councils. These councils have many task forces, committees, and commissions which function under their sponsorship. The association has special components to facilitate action in areas of high priority. A division of government relations aids in guiding Congress and federal agencies in the development of legislation. The Commission on Judicial Action represents psychiatry

in court cases throughout the county. The Division of Public Affairs provides the public with information and education. The employed staff of the Association work at the central office in Washington, DC, and number about 150. The medical director is the senior staff officer.

R. C. MARVIT
Honolulu, Hawaii

AMERICAN PSYCHOLOGICAL ASSOCIATION: STRUCTURE

AMERICAN PSYCHOLOGICAL ASSOCIATION (APA)

The American Psychological Association (APA) is a scientific and professional membership association incorporated in the District of Columbia. Founded in 1892, APA was the world's first national psychological association, and it remains the largest. In 1945, APA was reorganized to encompass several smaller psychological groups, becoming, in effect, a new organization with a broader mission, but retaining the APA name.

The mission of the new APA was expanded to include professional as well as scientific issues, and a concern for psychology's contributions to the public interest. A new, multifaceted structure that included divisions (substantive interest groups) and affiliated state and provincial psychological associations was developed to reflect the diversity of APA's membership and its expanded size and mission.

The reorganization, the broadened mission, and the rapidly increasing size and complexity of the association led to a decision to establish, in 1946, a central office with an executive officer and a staff to provide services to the membership.

MEMBERSHIP

In 1998, the membership of APA reached a total of 155,000 full members and affiliates. The members of APA exercise their authority over the affairs of the association by voting directly for by-law changes and for the APA president, and through the election of members to serve on the Council of Representatives. The membership consists of several classes: Members, Fellows, Associate Members, and Affiliates. Affiliates, who are not members of the association, include International Affiliates, Student Affiliates, and High School Teacher Affiliates.

COUNCIL OF REPRESENTATIVES

The Council of Representatives has full authority over the affairs and funds of the association. The members of the council are elected by the members of the two primary constituencies: the divisions, which are an integral part of the association's structure, and the state and provincial psychological associations (SPPA), which are affiliates of APA. The council elects the members of all standing boards and committees created by the by-laws. Council also elects the recording secretary and the treasurer, and confirms the appointment of the chief staff officer (chief executive officer).

BOARD OF DIRECTORS

The council elects six of its members to serve, along with the elected officers (president, past-president, president-elect, treasurer, recording secretary, and chief executive officer, ex officio), as members-at-large of the 12-person Board of Directors, which manages the affairs of the association, subject to the final authority of the council. In its corporate role, the board oversees the business of the association. With the advice and assistance of the Finance Committee, which is elected by council, the board presents an annual budget for the approval of council and monitors any deviations from the budget during the year. The board acts for council between the council's twice-yearly meetings. The president, who is elected by the membership at large, chairs both the council and the board of directors.

BOARDS AND COMMITTEES

Much of the work of the association is done on a volunteer basis by the members serving on boards, committees, and other work groups, which carry out a wide variety of tasks as indicated by some of their titles: ethics, membership, accreditation, scientific affairs, continuing education, and so on. In the course of their work, committees often generate proposals for new policies or new activities for the association. Ordinarily, these proposals are submitted for review by the Board of Directors and referred by the board to the council for final determination.

DIVISIONS

In its first half-century, APA had a relatively homogeneous membership consisting mostly of college and university faculty members, but with its reorganization to include a more diverse membership, 19 divisions were established to reflect the special interests of the members. By 1997, APA had 50 divisions, representing areas of specialization (e.g., clinical, counseling, developmental), areas of special interest (e.g., international affairs, women's issues, psychology and the law), and areas of employment (e.g., public service, independent practice, military). Divisions range in size from 300 to 7500. Even the smallest divisions have officers, by-laws, a newsletter, and an annual business meeting. Some divisions have, in addition, divisional journals and other publications, staff, administrative offices, and other characteristics of independent professional organizations.

STATE AND PROVINCIAL ASSOCIATIONS (SPPA)

Each state, two U.S. territories, and six Canadian provinces have psychological associations that are affiliated with APA and are entitled to seek representation on the Council of Representatives. State and provincial psychological associations (SPPAs) range in size from 25 to 6,000 and in complexity from small groups that meet only occasionally, to large organizations with substantial personnel and operations. Most SPPAs have offices, a paid executive director, newsletters, annual meetings, and officers.

CENTRAL OFFICE

The American Psychological Association's (APA) central office, which houses virtually all of APA's employees and operations, is located a few blocks from the U.S. capitol in Washington, D.C. With nearly 500 employees, the central office provides staff for all of the boards and committees, operates a large publishing house, invests in stocks, manages real estate, and interacts with private, state, and federal agencies and organizations. In addition to annual revenues of $12 million in member dues and fees plus $11 million from publications, the central office generates additional income of almost $15 million to support the activities and services of APA. General dues represent only 18% of the revenues needed to run APA.

The executive vice president and chief executive officer (CEO), as the chief administrative officer of the association, is responsible for the management and staffing of the central office and for running the business aspects of APA. The Board of Directors oversees the work of the CEO and evaluates the CEO's performance on an annual basis.

Directorates

The activities of the central office are organized into seven units, referred to as directorates and offices. The professional concerns of the membership are reflected in the four directorates: Science, Practice, Education, and Public Interest. Each directorate is headed by an executive director who is responsible for staff and programs and a budget of several million dollars. Each directorate has a standing board or committee, which provides general oversight for the activities of the directorate. The executive directors, and, through them, the staff, report to the CEO.

Those activities that do not fit easily into one of the four directorates are managed by one of four major offices: Central Programs, Financial Affairs, Publications and Communications, and the Executive Office.

The Executive Office provides coordination among the APA offices and directorates; oversees all central office operations; maintains contact with other national and international organizations; provides support to the officers, Board of Directors, Council of Representatives, and APA governance; and conducts all association elections.

APA GRADUATE STUDENTS

The APA Graduate Student organization (APAGS) is a student affiliate category that provides psychology students with the *Monitor* and the *American Psychologist* as well as access to APA publications and services. This organization permits psychology graduate students to participate more actively in APA, to elect their own officers, and to carry out projects of interest to them. In 1998, there were approximately 61,237 student affiliates, of whom 35,744 were APAGS members.

ANNUAL CONVENTION

The annual convention has always been a major APA activity. The convention is held in different parts of the country, usually in August, and regularly attracts 12,000 to 20,000 participants. The program is primarily organized by the divisions, each of which has an assigned number of hours depending upon the size of the division and the participation of its members in prior conventions.

FEDERAL ADVOCACY

Because of the importance of congressional actions and the activities of many federal agencies to psychology, APA employs a number of staff members who specialize in advocacy and are trained to provide information and assistance in policy development. These staff members review proposed legislation, identify areas relevant to psychology's agenda, and advocate on behalf of psychologists. They also work actively with federal agencies to assure that psychology participates in programs that are appropriate.

INTERORGANIZATIONAL ACTIVITIES

The American Psychological Association maintains contact and communication with a large number of psychology and psychology-related organizations throughout the world. Each of the directorates maintains contact with U.S. psychological organizations that relate to their domain, and APA participates in many interdisciplinary coalitions for advocacy and information exchange. The Office of International Affairs publishes a newsletter for several thousand APA international affiliates, maintains contact with virtually all other national psychological societies, and participates actively in international congresses, including sponsoring and organizing the 1998 International Congress of Applied Psychology.

R. D. FOWLER, CEO
American Psychological Association

B. J. PEET
American Psychological Association

AMERICAN PSYCHOLOGICAL ASSOC.: CODE OF ETHICS

An expanded version of this article appeared in the *Encyclopedia of Psychology,* "American Psychological Association: Structure." Copyright 2000 American Psychological Association and Oxford University Press.

AMERICAN PSYCHOLOGICAL ASSOCIATION *CODE OF ETHICS*

The American Psychological Association (APA) promulgated the first *Code of Ethics* for psychologists in 1953. Based on the work of a committee organized in 1947 (Canter, Bennett, Jones, & Nagy, 1994), this publication had further basis in the work of another committee, this one formed in 1938 and devoted to ethical concerns. The formalization and codification of ethical standards was ultimately a response to the increasing professionalization of psychology, a development that began during World War II.

The first *Code of Ethics* (APA, 1953) was developed using an empirical, critical-incident methodology (Hobbs, 1948), which had been unprecedented among associations. Rather than using an a priori method to determine ethical principles, the authors surveyed the membership of the association for descriptions of past incidents in which decisions with ethical implications had been made, and requested a discussion of the ethical issues involved. This material then formed the basis for many drafts of the first *Code of Ethics,* each of which was distributed to the membership for commentary before the final version was adopted.

Since the introduction of the original *Code of Ethics,* numerous revisions, either minor or major, have been adopted. These changes, regardless of scope, serve to keep the *Code* current and responsive to new issues, to changing views on traditional issues, and to legal imperatives that influence ethical behavior. It would be accurate to describe the *Code of Ethics* as a living document whose approach to ethics is influenced by current events rather than being based on universal ethical principles. Each revision of the *Code of Ethics* contains a set of ethical principles (or standards) without the inclusion of illustrative incidents.

The *Code of Ethics* presently in force was published in 1992 (APA, 1992), although a committee currently is working on a new revision. Although the critical-incident methodology was not employed for the 1992 edition, the revision was informed by the history of ethical complaints that had been filed, so that an empirical basis was built into the revision process. The alterations to the *Code* took six years and involved many iterations of the APA membership, the Ethics Committee, the Revision Comments Subcommittee, and the Council of Representatives of APA. The resulting document was intended to be accessible both to psychologists and to consumers of psychological services, and to provide guidelines that would increase the quality of psychological services and also reduce the risk of harm to the consumers.

The code of ethics of any professional association is enforceable only with regard to members of the association yet such a code also informs the basis of many state boards' conceptions of ethics. Board members, in turn, are asked to make judgments on the professional conduct of licensed professionals. In psychology, the *Code* is the foundation of the ethical instruction mandated by accreditation for its students. Thus, the influence of the *Code* is far broader than its scope of enforceability. Similarly, although the maximum penalty that can be exacted for a serious violation of the *Code* is simply expulsion from the organization, this expulsion is publically noted, other groups with relevant jurisdiction are informed (and may take independent action), and matters such as insurability are affected, so that the penalty is much more severe than expulsion by itself.

The 1992 *Code of Ethics* has two major sections, as well as introductory material. The first section of the *Code* consists of six General Principles, which, although aspirational rather than enforceable, can be used to interpret the enforceable standards that follow. These principles are concerned with the areas of Competence, Integrity, Professional and Scientific Responsibility, Respect for People's Rights and Dignity, Concern for Others' Welfare, and Social Responsibility. Their approach informs the rest of the document, particularly the more specific principles that make up the largest portion of the document.

The General Principles' specific, directly-enforceable translation is the Ethical Standards. The 102 standards are contained in eight sections; the first, General Standards, is potentially applicable to the professional and scientific activities of all psychologists, and is amplified in many of the subsequent standards. This section indicates, among other things, that the *Code* applies only to the professional, and not the personal, activities of psychologists, and that, when the *Code* conflicts with the law, the psychologist may choose to conform with the law, but *must* attempt to resolve the conflict in a manner consistent with the *Code.*

The second standard concerns Evaluation, Assessment, or Intervention. It is predominantly, but not exclusively, applicable to clinical activities. The standard concerning Advertising and Other Public Standards is much more permissive than previous Codes had been, and was heavily influenced by rulings of the Federal Trade Commission. The fourth standard concerns Therapy and may be the area of major concern to most practitioners. It is complemented by the next standard, which concerns Privacy and Confidentiality, although the latter standard goes beyond the clinical activities of psychologists. The sixth standard concerns Teaching, Training Supervision, Research, and Publishing. Its presence makes clear that the *Code of Ethics* is not restricted in its scope to professional practice, but is intended to be applicable to the activities of all psychologists. The seventh standard, Forensic Activities, is new, and reflects the increasing involvement of psychologists in forensic activities. It applies to all forensic activities, and not just the activities of forensic psychologists. This section has been an area of disproportionate action, perhaps because of the adversarial nature of the arena in which this activity takes place. The last standard addresses Resolving Ethical Issues, and indicates the responsibility of psychologists to be familiar with and to help uphold the ethical standards of the discipline.

Although the *Code* itself consists only of bare statements, an excellent commentary has been developed (Canter et al., 1994) for those who wish further information about the meaning of the principles. It is only through the commitment of the individual psychologist to the Code of Ethics that psychology can progress toward a firm foundation in ethical and responsible conduct.

REFERENCES

American Psychological Association. (1953). *Ethical standards of psychologists.* Washington, DC: Author.

American Psychological Association. (1992). Ethical principles of psychologists and code of conduct. *American Psychologist, 47,* 1597–1611.

Canter, M. B., Bennett, B. E., Jones, S. E., & Nagy, T. F. (1994). Ethics for psychologists: A commentary on the APA Ethics Code. Washington, DC: American Psychological Association.

Hobbs, N. (1948). The development of a code of ethical standards for psychology. *American Psychologist, 3,* 80–84.

G. STRICKER
Adelphi University

AMERICAN PSYCHOLOGICAL ASSOCIATION

AMERICAN PSYCHOLOGICAL SOCIETY (APS)

The American Psychological Society is the national organization devoted to scientific psychology. Established in 1988, APS's membership exceeded 15,000 in 5 years, making it probably the fastest growing scientific society in the world. The society's mission is to promote, protect, and advance the interests of scientifically oriented psychology in research, application, and improvement of human welfare.

APS members include psychologists engaged in scientific research or the application of scientifically grounded research findings without regard for specialties. APS represents members—including nearly 500 outside the United States—whose interests span the entire gamut of psychological science subdisciplines. Requirements of membership are a doctoral degree or evidence of sustained and significant contributions to scientific psychology; student affiliates are also accepted. Distinguished contributions are recognized by Fellow status or, in cases of superior achievement, by specific awards.

APS serves its members and pursues its mission through a variety of activities administered or overseen by its Washington, DC, office, consisting as of 1992 of an executive director and nine staff members, exemplifying its informal motto of "lean and nice."

PUBLICATIONS

APS publishes two bimonthly scholarly journals, *Psychological Science* and *Current Directions in Psychological Science. Psychological Science* presents the latest developments in psychological science for the purposes of promoting interdisciplinary knowledge among psychologists as well as presenting scientific psychology to nonpsychologists. *Current Directions in Psychological Science* publishes minireview articles, spanning the range of cutting-edge psychological research. The society also publishes *The APS Observer,* a newsletter that features the current activities of the society, national and international events that affect the society or psychology, noteworthy psychological research, and employment listings.

ANNUAL CONVENTION

A 3-day annual meeting, featuring the latest in scientific research and theory, is held each June (the meeting site varies from year to year). Addresses and symposia explore major issues in psychological science from a variety of perspectives. Poster presentations highlight specific research questions and findings, and exhibits offer the latest in published research and technological developments.

STUDENT CAUCUS

APS offers its student affiliates the opportunity to serve in a leadership role within the society. The APS Student Caucus (APSSC) elects its own officers and advocates who advise the board of directors on issues of student membership recruitment, retention, and conversion as well as accreditation and employment concerns. The APSSC also oversees the formation of student chapters and administers a mentorship program, guest lecture program, and a student travel award fund.

ACHIEVEMENT AWARDS

APS recognizes exceptional contributions to scientific psychology with its William James Fellow Award, two of which are awarded each year. Two new awards—the James McKeen Cattell Award in applied psychology and a still unnamed award for significant contributions to the discipline during the early stages of one's career—are scheduled to be awarded beginning in 1993.

FORMATION

The impetus for creating APS came from the recognition that: (a) The needs and interests of scientific and academic psychologists were distinct from those of members of the professional community primarily engaged in clinical practice; and (b) that there was a strong need for a society that would advance the interests of the discipline in ways that specialized organizations were not intended to do. An interim group, the Assembly for Scientific and Applied Psychology (ASAP), had sought repeatedly to reform the American Psychological Association (APA) from within, but efforts to increase the autonomy of academically oriented psychologists within the APA framework were rejected by a membershipwide vote of that organization. Following the failure of these reorganization efforts, the APS became the official embodiment of the ASAP reform effort, and the new organization was launched August 12, 1988, when a mail ballot of the membership was approved 419 to 13.

One indication that APS was an organization waiting to happen has been its membership growth, surpassing 5,000 members in 6 months. Other indications are the strides APS has made in unifying and strengthening the science of psychology.

SUMMITS

One of APS's first activities was to convene the Summit of Scientific Psychological Societies in January 1989. Attendees representing more than 40 different psychological organizations addressed the role of science advocacy, how to enhance the identity of psychology as a coherent scientific discipline, the protection of scientific values in education and training, the use of science in the public interest, and scientific values in psychological practice. Subsequent summit meetings, involving representatives of 70 organizations, produced the *Human Capital Initiative* (*HCI*), a national behavioral science research agenda. The document targets six critical contemporary problems facing the nation, communities, and families that can be helped by psychological science: worker productivity, schooling and literacy, the aging society, drug and alcohol abuse, mental and physical health, and violence in American society. The *HCI* is intended as guidance for Congress and federal research agencies in planning behavioral science research activities. Future summits will formulate specific research initiatives, addressing other cross-cutting concerns.

The APS-sponsored summit of 1992 addressed accreditation criteria and procedures for graduate psychology education programs. Although the suggested accreditation system applies only to doctoral programs aimed at training clinical, counseling, or school psychologists, accreditation affects graduate education in psychology in numerous ways and, therefore, is an issue of concern to all psychologists. The most direct influence is on the content and curriculum of the programs themselves, but accreditation requirements also affect the distribution of resources across different programs, the use of faculty time, and the priorities of graduate students within those departments.

ADVOCACY

A primary reason APS was founded was to provide a distinct Washington presence for scientific psychology. APS is widely recognized as an active leader in advancing the interests of basic and applied psychological, behavioral, and social science research in the legislative arena and in the federal agencies that support these areas of research. Through APS's efforts, Congress has directed several federal research agencies to give greater priority to behavioral science research funding, resulting in an increase of millions of dollars for psychology investigators. APS was a primary force behind the creation of a separate directorate for behavioral and social sciences at the National Science Foundation (NSF). At the National Institutes of Health (NIH), APS's efforts resulted in improved visibility for health and behavior research and a more prominent place for psychological research within NIH's mission and long-term strategic plan. As one of the core constituent groups of the National Institute of Mental Health (NIMH), APS has shaped the funding policies and programs of the agency to be more responsive to the training and research needs of psychological and behavioral science. APS also helped ensure that the behavioral science mission of NIMH would be preserved during the transfer of NIMH to NIH, effective October 1992.

Despite its relative youth, APS already has established itself as the preeminent society of scientific psychologists.

A. G. KRAUT
American Psychological Society

AMINO ACID NEUROTRANSMITTERS

In the past, amino acids were considered to be unlikely neurotransmitters because of their high concentration and virtually ubiquitous distribution in the brain; this was inconsistent with the characteristics of established neurotransmitters such as norepinephrine, which have uneven brain distribution and neuron-specific biosynthetic pathways. However, it is now apparent that certain amino acids play a major role in chemical neurotransmission in the nervous system. Specifically, L-glutamic acid and the structurally close L-aspartic acid serve as the major excitatory neurotransmitters in brain, occupying up to 40% of all synapses. Gamma amino butyric acid (GABA) is the major inhibitory neurotransmitter in the brain, occupying another 40% of all synapses. In addition, glycine is a significant inhibitory neurotransmitter in the brainstem and spinal cord. Thus, in aggregate, up to 80% of all synapses in the central nervous system utilize these four amino acids as their neurotransmitters. Most, if not all, of these amino acid–releasing neuronal systems also have co-localized neuropeptides such as somatostatin, substance P, or N-acetyl-apartyl-glutamate, each of which modulates the postsynaptic effects of the amino acid neurotransmitter.

Amino acid neurotransmitters exert their electrophysiologic effects primarily through receptors that are ligand-gated ion channels intercalated in the neuronal membrane. Typically, these receptors are heteromeric pentamers of polypeptides that form the receptor channel complex. In the case of the excitatory neurotransmitters, the channel transduces cations, primarily Na^+ but also Ca^{2+}, resulting in membrane depolarization. Conversely, GABA and glycine receptors reside on channels that transduce Cl^-, thereby hyperpolarizing the neuronal membrane. The inhibitory GABAergic synapses tend to be concentrated on the proximal dendrites and around the neuronal cell body, whereas the glutamatergic inputs are localized primarily at the distal ends of dendrites. The neuron is constantly summating the simultaneous effects of localized depolarization by glutamatergic afferents and hyperpolarization by GABAergic afferents so that when depolarization reaches the threshold of approximately –30 mV, an action potential is generated.

In addition to the ligand-gated channels, there are families of amino acid receptors whose intraneuronal effects are mediated by G proteins and have been designated glutamate metabotropic receptors (mGluR) and GABA-B receptors. The activation of these G-protein mediated receptors results in much more prolonged alterations in neuronal metabolic states than does the rapid onset/offset of the ligand-gated ion channels and appears to play an important role in modulating amino acid neurotransmission.

GABAERGIC NEURONS

GABA is synthesized from L-glutamic acid by glutamic acid decarboxylase, a pyridoxine-dependent enzyme that removes the α carboxyl group. Aside from expressing glutamate decarboxylase, GABAergic neurons also express a sodium-dependent high-affinity transporter for GABA that effectively removes it from the synaptic cleft and terminates its activity. GABA can also be enzymatically degraded by GABA-transaminase, an enzyme localized to the mitochondria.

In cortico-limbic structures, GABA is utilized primarily by inhibitory interneurons, whereas in subcortical structures GABA is also localized to projecting neuronal systems such as the striato-palatal pathway and the cerebellar Purkinje cells. In the spinal cord, glycine is located in interneurons such as the Renshaw cells of the ventral horn. Glycine is also inactivated at these synapses by a Na^+-dependent high-affinity transporter for glycine.

The GABAergic neuronal system is the target of several classes of neuropsychotropic medications, including anticonvulsants, anxiolytics, and sedative-hyponotics. Barbiturates such as pentobarbital and phenobarbital have anticonvulsant properties, with phenobarbital used clinically because of its long half-life. The barbiturates exert direct effects on the GABA channel by prolonging its open time, thereby enhancing inhibition. These direct effects result in a rather narrow therapeutic window, with doses as little as three-fold above those causing sedation resulting in respiratory suppression. Also, the generalized effects on GABA receptors results in cognitive dulling with phenobarbital at doses associated with anticonvulsant efficacy.

The GABA receptor has a second site to which benzodiazepines bind, thereby enhancing its responsiveness to GABA. Thus, benzodiazepines do not act directly but rather indirectly at subpopulations of GABA receptors. This indirect mechanism of action provides a large therapeutic-to-toxic interval so that benzodiazepines, when taken alone in overdose, rarely cause respiratory depression and death. Long-acting benzodiazepines such as diazepam, clonazepam, and chlordiazepoxide have been proven effective in reducing situational anxiety. However, prolonged use of benzodiazepines can be associated with desensitization and the development of dependence, especially with short-acting benzodiazepines such as alprazolam. Abrupt withdrawal of benzodiazepines in tolerant individuals can result in life threatening seizures. Conversely, the acute intravenous administration of diazepam is an effective treatment for status epilepticus.

Valproic acid is a short organic acid that has been proven to be an effective anticonvulsant with negligible sedating effects in the therapeutic range. The mechanism of action of valproic acid is complex and may involve inhibition of GABA-transaminase, thereby potentiating the synaptic action of GABA in the brain. Recent studies have demonstrated the efficacy of valproic acid in preventing the recurrence of manic episodes in individuals suffering from Bipolar Disorder. As it has a better side-effect profile, valproic acid is replacing lithium salts as the drug of choice in prophylaxis of Bipolar Disorder. Gabapentin, a recently introduced and effective anticonvulsant, enhances GABA's synaptic action by inhibiting its reuptake by the transporter.

GLUTAMATERGIC NEURONS

Glutamatergic neuronal systems in the brain are primarily projecting neurons and include the pyramidal neurons of the cortico-limbic system, the excitatory thalamo-cortical afferents, the climbing fibers of the cerebellum, the ascending and descending excitatory pathways in the spinal cord, and the primary sensory afferents. However, local circuit glutamatergic systems do exist, including the granular cells of the hippocampus and of the cerebellum. The neurotransmitter pool of glutamate is synthesized from glutamine provided by the surrounding astrocytes. The synaptic action of glutamate is terminated by sodium-dependent high-affinity transporters. While glutamatergic neurons express a transporter, there are glutamate transporter on the astroglia (GLT-1 and GLAST) that play the primary role in maintaining low concentrations of glutamate in the extracellular space. The effectiveness of these transport mechanisms for preventing nonspecific activation of glutamate receptors is demonstrated by the fact that the tissue concentration of glutamate in the brain is several μ whereas the concentration of glutamate in the extracellular space under normal circumstances is low μM. However, in situations of energy failure such as anoxia, the loss of the ATP-dependent sodium gradient causes a massive efflux of glutamate.

The excitatory effects of glutamate both at the synapses and at extrasynaptic sites are mediated by a family of glutamate-gated ion channels, components of which are designated by their most potent synthetic or conformationally restricted agonists and include the AMPA receptor, the kainic acid (KA) receptor, and the NMDA receptor. Four genes have been demonstrated to encode for polypeptides (GLUR 1–4) that individually or in combination form the various subtypes of AMPA receptors. Both post-translational editing and GLUR subtype affect the biophysics and calcium conductance of AMPA receptors. Five additional genes (GLUR 5–7, KA-1, KA-2) encode peptides that form the KA class of receptors. The GLUR (5–7) polypeptide encodes for the channel, where a KA-1 and-2 are peptides that alter the biophysical characteristics of the KA channel complex. The AMPA/KA receptors mediate excitatory postsynaptic currents (EPSCs) that result from stimulation by glutamatergic afferents.

The NMDA receptor consists of a complex of both the NR-1 subunit, which forms the channel, and one of four NR-2 subunits (NR-2 A–D) which define biophysical and pharmacologic characteristics of the NMDA receptor. The NMDA receptors do not play a direct role in excitatory neurotransmission but, through their recruitment, can markedly alter the consequences of excitatory neurotransmission. The NMDA receptor is a voltage-gated ion channel that is silent at resting membrane potential because the channel is occluded by Mg^{2+}. Upon depolarization, the Mg^{2+} is extruded, permitting the channel to transduce not only Na^+ but also Ca^{2+}, an important intracellular signaling ion. The receptor also possesses a modulatory site to which glycine and D-serine bind; this site must be occupied in order for glutamate to trigger the opening of the ion channel. Within the channel is a site to which the dissociative anesthetics such as ketamine and phencyclidine (PCP, or "angel dust") bind. The occupancy of this site by dissociative anesthetics blocks the ion channel, providing a noncompetitive antagonism of NMDA receptors. It is this mechanism of action that accounts for the psychotomimetic effects of the dissociative anesthetics, and has served as a basis for the NMDA receptor hypofunction hypothesis of schizophrenia. Kynurenic acid is an endogenous antagonist at NMDA receptors. Astroglial cells that envelop the excitatory synapse regulate the availability of glycine and D-serine, required for NMDA receptor function as well as the concentrations of kynurenic and N-acetyl-aspartyl glutamate, which inhibit NMDA receptor function.

NEUROPLASTICITY

Glutamate plays a major role in modifying the synaptic connectivity and efficacy during development and in adulthood. NMDA receptor activation on immature neurons is associated with survival in vitro and with increased response to endogenous trophic factors. Glutamate acting via NMDA receptors is one of the factors controlling the migration of immature neurons to their final resting place; and both glutamate and GABA regulate neurite extension during CNS differentiation. Ethanol inhibits NMDA receptors and potentiates GABA receptors, and these effects in utero appear to account for the central nervous system effects of fetal alcohol syndrome.

Glutamate plays a major role in use-dependent alterations in synaptic efficacy—the so-called Hebbian synapse—which has been linked to learning and memory. As characterized in the hippocampal formation, long-term potentiation (LTP) is evoked by a brief period of tetanic stimulation of glutamatergic afferents resulting in a persistent increase in postsynaptic responses with subsequent lower levels of stimulation of afferants. In many glutamatergic synapses studied, LTP requires both the activation of AMPA/KA and NMDA receptors, although LTP has been demonstrated to occur in the absence of NMDA receptor involvement. A converse phenomenon, long-term depression (LTD), significantly attenuates synaptic efficacy. These activity-dependent modifications of synaptic efficacy have been linked to learning in spatial memory paradigms in the hippocampus. Finally, persistent utilization of glutamatergic projection can result not only in enhancement of synaptic efficacy, but also in actual growth of new spines in synaptic terminals in the mature brain.

EXCITOTOXICITY

Persistent activation of NMDA and AMPA/KA receptors can cause neuronal degeneration, a process that has been designated "excitotoxicity." Given the number of glutamate receptor subtypes and their variation in biophysical characteristics, it is not surprising that excitotoxic neuronal degeneration is a complex phenomenon. Two forms of neuronal death have been described. First, massive activation of glutamate receptors causes an osmotic disruption of neuronal integrity secondary to the influx of Na^+ and Ca^{2+}, resulting in necrosis. Persistent low levels of glutamate receptor activation, especially in compromised neurons, or brief periods of high levels of glutamate receptor activation can result in a delayed form of neuronal degeneration, which has all of the characteristics of programmed cell death or apoptosis. Under these circumstances, cellular involution, nuclear clumping, activation of endonucleases, and activation of cell death programs involving caspases have been shown to occur. Neuronal degeneration resulting from energy failure such as hypoxia is mediated predominantly by NMDA receptors, with necrosis occurring at the core and apoptosis in the surrounding penumbra. However, AMPA receptor–mediated neuronal degeneration has been shown after ischemia wherein a down-regulation of the Ca^{2+} impermeable GLUR-2 permits Ca^{2+} influx through the remaining AMPA receptors.

Excitotoxicity has been implicated in the pathophysiology of a number of neurodegenerative disorders. Injection of NMDA receptor antagonists into the striatum of experimental animals can faithfully reproduce the neuropathology of the hereditary neurodegenerative disorder Huntington's disease. Recent studies in mice transgenic for the mutant human Huntington's gene suggest that it sensitizes neurons to their glutamatergic activity via NMDA receptors. In amyotrophic lateral sclerosis, postmortem findings suggest impairments in astroglial glutamate transport in the ventral horn, resulting in motor neuron degeneration via AMPA/KA receptors. The pathogenic amyloid that accumulates in Alzheimer's disease sensitizes neurons to the excitotoxic action of glutamate. As noted previously, energy failure caused by localized ischemia in stroke, hypoxemia in drowning, or profound hypoglycemia results in massive release of brain glutamate, causing widespread excitotoxic neuronal death. Pharmaceutical research is now directed at developing drugs that attenuate excitotoxicity by blocking either the glutamate receptor responses or the downstream consequences of the activation of glutamate receptors, such as oxidative stress and induction of programmed cell death pathways or apoptosis.

In summary, glutamic acid and GABA are the two dominant neurotransmitters in the brain that mediate rapid neurotransmission via ligand-gated ion channels. Dysfunction of these neuronal systems has been implicated in a variety of neuropsychiatric disorders, including epilepsy, anxiety disorders, schizophrenia, and neurodegenerative disorders. The remarkable heterogeneity of the family of receptors that mediate the effects of amino acid neurotransmitters, which represent 80% of brain synapses, permits targeted pharmacologic interventions to treat these devastating disorders.

J. T. COYLE
Harvard Medical School

GABA RECEPTORS
NEUROCHEMISTRY
NEUROTRANSMITTERS

AMPA RECEPTORS

AMPA ([RS]-alpha-amino-3-hydroxy-5-methyl-4-isoxazole propionic acid) receptors belong to the subclass of glutamate receptors known as ionotropic or ion channel receptors (iGluRs), which also include the kainic acid (KA) and *N*-methyl-D-aspartate (NMDA) families. AMPA receptors were originally called "quisqualate receptors" because of their affinity for quisqualic acid, derived from the Cambodian quisquala tree. However, the seaweed toxin kainic acid (KA) was also found to activate these receptors to a lesser degree. Further studies revealed that [³H]AMPA (AMPA labeled with radioisotope tritium) distinguished this group of receptors more clearly from [³H]KA binding sites in brain tissue. Glutamic acid is the major endogenous ligand for the iGluRs, though additional so-called EAAs (excitatory amino acids), named for their generation of excitatory postsynaptic potentials (EPSPs), are also present in the brain, including L-aspartate, quinolinate, and homocysteate. The other major subclass of receptors activated by glutamate, the metabotropic type (mGluRs), are guanine nucleotide binding protein (G-protein)-coupled and are voltage-gated as opposed to iongated. The AMPA receptor/channel complex, along with the KA and NMDA iGluR channel types, are the main mediators of excitatory neurotransmission in the brain. They also have many roles outside the central nervous system.

MOLECULAR DIVERSITY OF STRUCTURE

AMPA-type glutamate ion channels are synthesized in vivo from four subunits (GluR1–4 or GluRA-D). The GluR1–4 subunits are assembled in various combinations to form the protein structure of a channel, which is either homomeric (all the same subunit) or heteromeric (more than one type of subunit). The types of subunits assembled determine the functional characteristics of the channel, as noted later. The AMPA-type channels function in the neuronal or glial cell membrane to conduct the influx of ions (particularly Na⁺·

K⁺· Ca⁺⁺) and rapidly desensitize in the ongoing presence of ligands.

The GluR1–4 subunit proteins belong to a single family of genes (based on sequence homology), yet each subunit is coded by a different gene, namely GRIA1 (GluR1) at chromosome 5q32–33, GRIA2 (GluR2) at 4q32–33, GRIA3 (GluR3) at Xq25–26, and GRIA4 (GluR4) at 11q22–33 (Dingledine, Borges, Bowie, & Traynelis, 1999).

The AMPA receptor subunits are structurally similar and have a similar transmembrane topology, possessing three transmembrane (M1, M3, and M4) domains and one reentrant membrane (M2) domain facing the cytoplasm. The N-terminus is extracellular and the C-terminus is intracellular (Figure 1). The binding domain for a ligand such as glutamate is in the pocket formed by S1 and S2. S1 is before M1, and S2 is after M3 in the transmembrane topology (Figure 2). Subunit stoichiometry within a functional AMPA receptor is uncertain at this time, with evidence supporting either a tetrameric or pentameric structure. The four subunits, GluR1–4, are each diverse in their molecular variation via posttranscriptional and posttranslational mechanisms, which result in significant functional variations depending on brain region, developmental stage, and states of health or disease. These variations are determined by the regulatory elements of the genes, the mechanisms of which are under intensive study.

Posttranscriptional (RNA) Modifications

Each GluR subunit undergoes posttranscriptional modifications involving at least two mechanisms. One of these is the alternative splicing of mRNA. The resulting splice variants, called flip (i) and flop (o), result from the splicing-out of one of two possible modules within the mRNA. Flip and flop variants effect significant structural and functional channel variation on the extracellular side of the membrane preceding TM4. They are of vital importance in determining the desensitization properties of the receptor/channel complex. Another source of variation results from RNA editing at the Q/R and R/G sites in the mRNA. In domain TM2 of GluR1–4, a particular glutamine (Q; codon CAG) can be edited enzymatically to an arginine (R; codon CIG). This editing is nearly complete in GluR2 (>99%), resulting in near impermeability to calcium, low single-channel conductance, and a nearly linear current-voltage relation. Calcium impermeability in most brain regions is essential for survival; a single edited GluR2 subunit in a multimeric AMPA channel is sufficient to confer this protection. GluR2–4 are also edited at an additional site called the R/G site, which is located just before the flip/flop coding region and which diminishes and hastens desensitization.

Posttranslational (protein) Modifications

AMPA ion channels undergo phosphorylation, which may play a role in synaptic plasticity and are tightly regulated by phosphokinases such as PKA, PKC, CaMKII, and others. Phosphorylation generally potentiates AMPA receptor activation, with evidence that it occurs by keeping the channel open longer or more often. AMPA receptors also contain four to six *N*-glycosylation sites which influence binding of ligands to the receptor pocket, with effects that depend on the type of ligand and the subunit's flip/flop

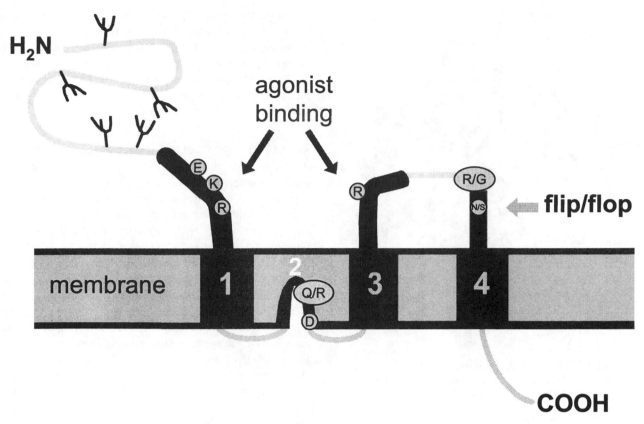

Figure 1. AMPA receptor topology.

Q/R (glutamine/arginine), R/G (arginine/glycine) are editing sites; N/S are asparagine (N) and serine (S) residues that confer specific desensitization properties (via cyclothiazide sensitivity) to the flip and flop modules; E (glutamate), K (lysine), and R (arginine) are amino acid residues that determine the binding site for glutamate and other EAAs (Reprinted with permission of author K. Borges, 1998).

specification. The calcium-dependent protease calpain is believed to act at the GluR1 C-terminus to alter its signaling capacity via a proteolytic mechanism.

Protein-Protein Interactions Involving AMPA Receptor Proteins

Recent experimental findings have begun to outline a rich complex of protein interactions involved in the trafficking, assembly, clustering, and membrane anchoring of AMPA subunits, presumably crucial to maintenance of the appropriate number and functional types of AMPA channels. Involved proteins include the PDZ-domain bearing proteins GRIP1 (glutamate receptor interacting protein), GRIP2, PICK1 (protein interacting with C kinase), ABP (AMPA binding protein), and EphrinB1; the secreted lectin and immediate early gene *Narp* (neuronal activity-regulated pentraxin); and NSF (N-ethylmaleamide-sensitive factor). The protein-protein interactions carried out by these entities in the AMPA family are analogous to those in other glutamate receptor subclasses (e.g., PSD-95 and NMDA channels) and in other receptor families (e.g., agrin at acetylcholine sites).

DEVELOPMENTAL ASPECTS OF DIVERSITY

The GluR1–4 subunits and their molecular variants appear to follow specific ontogenetic, regional, and disease-specific patterns, presumably to meet the current needs of the organism. For example,

the edited form of GluR2 becomes increasingly prevalent with maturity, as required to restrict calcium ion flux through the AMPA-type channels. The GluR2 subunit is also present in the AMPA-type channels throughout the brain except for a few select regions (e.g., Bergmann glia in the cerebellum), but appears to be downregulated during ischemic events, thereby increasing the vulnerability of normally protected regions. The flip and flop isoforms are also observed to follow developmental lines. Flip forms are more prevalent before birth and continue their expression into adulthood in rodents, while flop forms begin at low levels of expression until postnatal day 8, then upregulate to a level similar to the flip variants. The flip forms tend to desensitize more slowly and to a lesser degree than flop forms. It is highly possible then that disturbance of ontogenetic expression patterns in GluR subunits may eventually explain some developmental disorders and other pathogenetic mechanisms.

AMPA RECEPTORS IN HEALTH

Glutamate receptors contribute to processes of normal development, synaptic plasticity, learning, and excitatory neurotransmission of humans, nonhuman primates, rodents, *Drosophila* species (fruit fly), and *C. elegans* (roundworm). They also participate with NMDA receptors in the coordination of LTP (long-term potentiation) and related synaptic mechanisms subserving memory functions. Glutamate neurons project from most cerebral cortical re-

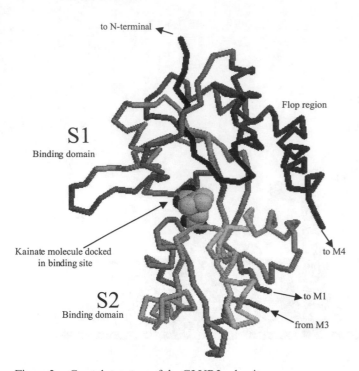

to N-terminal

S1
Binding domain

Flop region

Kainate molecule docked
in binding site

to M4

S2
Binding domain

to M1

from M3

Figure 2.   Crystal structure of the GLUR2 subunit.

Labels adapted with permission from R. Dingledine, 1999; protein structure 1GR2 from Protein Data Bank, Brookhaven, CT, using Chime 2.2.

http://www.rcsb.org/pdb/cig/explore.cgi?job=graphics&pdbId=1GR2&page= &pid=20804932397729&opt=chime

gions to other areas of cortex, the basal ganglia, the brainstem ventral tegmental area, and other sites. This strongly suggests powerful local and global organizational and regulatory functions for the AMPA and other glutamate receptor subtypes in the brain.

There are also nonneural AMPA receptors such as those in the skin which participate in pain sensation and those in cardiac ganglia of currently unknown function.

AMPA RECEPTORS IN DISEASE

A recently proposed model of glutamate excitotoxicity highlights the importance of molecular diversity of AMPA subunit expression. It hypothesizes that cells are vulnerable to injury from excessive Ca^{++} influx after any of a number primary insults affecting the expression of edited GluR2 subunits (such as ischemia, hypoxia, hypoglycemia, epilepsy). AMPA receptor expression is also altered under conditions of stress in the hippocampus. Perhaps a peak in the expression of AMPA receptors at 20 to 22 weeks of gestation in the human may increase vulnerability to excitoxicity at that time, since AMPA receptors have been shown to increase during the prenatal period in rats, when there is also observed a greater vulnerability to excitotoxic injury.

In Rassmussen's encephalitis, a severe childhood form of epilepsy often requiring cerebral hemispherectomy because of its poor response to available anticonvulsant regimens, recent evidence supports an autoimmune mechanism involving the GluR3 subunit as an autoantigen.

Thus, current evidence supports roles for AMPA receptor involvement in excitotoxic injury through various pathophysiologic

mechanisms such as epilepsy, stroke, ischemia, hypoxia, trauma, extreme stress, hypoglycemia, or hypercortisolemia, as well as in neurodegenerative diseases (e.g., Huntington's disease, Alzheimer's disease, Parkinson's disease). Pathophysiological roles for AMPA receptors have been suggested, and are under continuing study, in other neuropsychiatric disorders such as mood disorders, schizophrenia, and anxiety disorders.

AMPA RECEPTORS AS PHARMACOTHERAPEUTIC SITES

AMPA receptors are widespread in the brain, including most regions of the cerebral cortex, hippocampus, amygdala, thalamus, hypothalamus, brainstem, and spinal cord. The regional variations in expression of the subunits, splice variants, and editing efficiency are apparent and are likely involved in local and global network function. AMPA receptors are being studied as potential therapeutic targets in diseases such as Alzheimer's disease, cerebrovascular disease (preventive and poststroke), epilepsy, schizophrenia, neural trauma, and other conditions involving cognitive impairments. Such promise has been raised by the successes reported for AMPA agonists (AMPAmimetics or AMPAkines) to enhance maze-learning in age-associated memory impairment in mice and for antagonists (blockers) to prevent the spread of necrosis in ischemic events. Agonists and antagonists of varying specificity for AMPA receptor variants are being studied, with goals of safer and more effective treatments for neuroprotection from toxins, ischemia, hypoxia, physical and emotional trauma, hypoglycemia, hypercortisolemia, neurodegenerative mechanisms, neurodevelopmental disorders, cognitive disorders, and epilepsy.

CONCLUSION

It should be apparent that there is tremendous molecular complexity of glutamate receptors. This appears to be true for all receptors studied thus far. Additional details regarding the complexity of expression, anatomical location, and functions in disease and health may be found in the literature, with the reference by Dingledine cited as a very recent and comprehensive review article on glutamate AMPA receptors.

In this brief description of the AMPA receptor family of the glutamate class of receptors, we see a burgeoning of basic biomedical knowledge. The future promises much more detail, not only of the AMPA family of receptors/channels, but also of their interactions with other neural systems in health and in disease. With this new knowledge of molecular and neural mechanisms and tools to manipulate them should come a wealth of possibilities for the explanation and treatment of significant clinical conditions such as stroke, epilepsy, dementia, and other neuropsychiatric disorders.

REFERENCE

Dingledine, R., Borges, K., Bowie, D., & Traynelis, S. F. (1999). The glutamate receptor ion channels. *Pharmacological Reviews, 51*(1), 7–61.

J. T. NOGA
Emory University

AMPHETAMINE EFFECTS

Amphetamine, a potent sympathomimetic amine, has pronounced stimulant effects on the central and peripheral nervous systems. This compound produces a variety of physiological effects, including alterations in systolic and diastolic blood pressures, contraction of smooth muscles, and, in high doses, increased oxygen consumption. Behaviorally, the drug is known to produce appetite suppression, hyperthermia, wakefulness, alertness, decreased sense of fatigue, improved concentration, elevations of mood, elation, euphoria, and increased speech and motor activity (Innes & Nickerson, 1971). In infrahuman animals the most prominent effects of the drug are increased locomotor activity, the induction of stereotypy consisting mainly of repeated grooming, licking, gnawing, and sniffing, as well as the induction of stimulus perseveration in which animals repeatedly visit places or objects previously explored (Kokkinidis & Anisman, 1980).

Prolonged use of amphetamine, or high doses of the drug, may result in fatigue and depression, and some individuals may experience headache, dizziness, vasomotor disturbances, agitation, confusion, dysphoria, apprehension, or delirium (Innes & Nickerson, 1971). Moreover, it has been reported that the behavioral consequences of repeated amphetamine consumption may be virtually indistinguishable from the symptom profile that characterizes paranoid schizophrenia. This latter effect, it seems, has been largely responsible for the attention devoted to the analysis of amphetamine actions, and repeated attempts have been made to develop animal models of schizophrenia using acute and repeated treatments of amphetamines and other catecholamine stimulants (Kokkinidis & Anisman, 1980).

A considerable body of evidence has indicated that the behavioral consequences of amphetamine are due to the drug's propensity to induce the release and block the reuptake of the catecholamines, dopamine and norepinephrine (Costa & Garattini, 1970). Experiments in which synthesis of catecholamines are inhibited suggest that the action of amphetamine depends on the presence of newly synthesized catecholamines. Moreover such experiments, together with studies involving neurotoxic lesions of catecholamine nerve terminals, indicate that some of the more prominent behavioral consequences of amphetamine (e.g., locomotor excitation and stereotyped motor patterns) are related to dopamine changes induced by the drug, whereas other behavioral consequences of amphetamine (e.g., stimulus perseveration and possibly exploration and attentional changes) appear to be subserved by norepinephrine neurons (Iversen, 1977; Kelly, 1977; Kokkinidis & Anisman, 1980). It has also been suggested that the behavioral consequences of amphetamine involve dopamine neurons in different brain sites. For instance, activity of dopamine neurons in the nucleus accumbens have been posited to subserve locomotor excitation, whereas the stereotyped responses are thought to involve the caudate (Kelly, 1977). Moreover, it appears that low doses of amphetamine inhibit firing rates of neurons in the caudate and nucleus accumbens, whereas higher doses result in increased striatal neuron firing, but unit activity in the nucleus accumbens remains inhibited (Rebec & Zimmerman, 1980).

Prolonged exposure to amphetamine was reported to result in apparent tolerance to the mood-altering, anorexigenic, and hyperthermic effects of the drug (Kosman & Unna, 1968). In contrast, the motor consequences and altered cognitive patterns associated with amphetamine intoxication are exacerbated with repeated drug intake (Ellinwood, 1974; Griffith, Cavanaugh, Held, & Oates, 1970). Various propositions have been advanced to account for the response enhancements seen after chronic amphetamine treatment, including conditioned drug effects, alterations in catecholamine synthesis, and hypersensitivity of dopamine receptors. In addition, it is possible that chronic amphetamine produces receptor proliferation that ultimately results in receptor supersensitivity (see the review in Kokkinidis & Anisman, 1980). A similar view has been forwarded to account for mechanisms subserving the schizophrenic symptomatology (Lee & Seeman, 1980). It is also possible that chronic treatment with amphetamine alters activity in the striatal-nigral pathway (Aghajanian & Bunney, 1973) or reduces the sensitivity of autoreceptors (self-inhibitory) present on presynaptic dopamine neurons (Muller & Seeman, 1979).

Inasmuch as amphetamine modifies both norepinephrine and dopamine neuronal activity, both these transmitters may influence the behavioral disturbances associated with chronic use of the drug. Kokkinidis and Anisman (1980) suggested that the increased dopamine activity may be responsible for heightened arousal and motor excitation, while reduction of norepinephrine may induce deficits in filtering relevant environmental information. The conjoint consequences of these two (and possibly other) neurochemical alterations leads ultimately to a behavioral syndrome reminiscent of schizophrenia.

REFERENCES

Aghajanian, G. K., & Bunney, B. S. (1973). Central dopaminergic neurons: Neurophysiological identification and responses to drugs. In E. Usdin & S. H. Snyder (Eds.), *Frontiers in catecholamine research.* New York: Pergamon.

Costa, E., & Garattini, S. (1970). *Amphetamine and related compounds.* New York: Raven.

Ellinwood, E. H. (1974). Behavioral and EEG changes in the amphetamine model of psychosis. In E. Usdin (Ed.), *Neuropsychopharmacology of monoamines and their regulatory enzymes.* New York: Raven.

Griffith, J. D., Cavanaugh, J. H., Held, J., & Oates, J. A. (1970). Experimental psychosis induced by the administration of d-amphetamine. In E. Costa & S. Garattini (Eds.), *Amphetamines and related compounds.* New York: Raven.

Innes, I. R., & Nickerson, M. (1971). Drugs acting on postganglionic nerve endings and structures innervated by them (sympathomimetic drugs). In L. S. Goodman & A. Gilman (Eds.), *The pharmacological basis of therapeutics.* New York: Macmillan.

Iversen, S. D. (1977). Brain dopamine systems and behavior. In L. L. Iversen, S. D. Iversen, & S. H. Snyder (Eds.), *Handbook of psychopharmacology* (Vol. 8). New York: Plenum.

Kelly, P. H. (1977). Drug-induced motor behavior. In L. L. Iversen, S. D. Iversen, & S. H. Snyder (Eds.), *Handbook of psychopharmacology* (Vol. 8). New York: Plenum.

Kokkinidis, L., & Anisman, H. (1980). Amphetamine models of paranoid schizophrenia: An overview and elaboration of animal experimentation. *Psychological Bulletin, 88,* 551–579.

Kosman, M. E., & Unna, K. R. (1968). Effects of chronic administration of amphetamine and other stimulants on behavior. *Clinical and Pharmacological Therapeutics, 9,* 246–254.

Lee, T., & Seeman, P. (1980). Elevation of brain neuroleptic/dopamine receptors in schizophrenia. *American Journal of Psychiatry, 137,* 191–197.

Muller, P., & Seeman, P. (1979). Presynaptic subsensitivity as a possible basis for sensitization by long-term dopamine mimetics. *European Journal of Pharmacology, 55,* 149–157.

Rebec, G. V., & Zimmerman, K. S. (1980). Opposite effects of d-amphetamine on spontaneous neuronal activity in the neostriatum and nucleus accumbens. *Brain Research, 201,* 485–491.

H. ANISMAN
Carleton University

NEUROCHEMISTRY
OBESITY
PSYCHOPHARMACOLOGY

AMPUTEES AND PHANTOM LIMB PAIN

The existence of unusual or painful sensations in an amputated limb has been recognized for centuries. The phenomenon was first documented by the French military physician Ambrois Pare in 1551. However, the term "phantom limb pain" was not used until Mitchell discussed phantom limbs in 1871. The International Association for the Study of Pain Task Force on Taxonomy defines phantom pain as "Pain referred to a surgically removed limb or portion thereof" (Merskey & Bogduk, 1994). Other terms used include "phantom sensation" and "stump pain," which are taxonomically different from phantom pain.

Phantom pain is characterized by continuous cramping, aching, burning sensations, and may be associated with shocklike paroxysms. Pain may progressively resolve with time; however, it often becomes a pervading feature of the sufferer's life, and in 5 to 10% of patients the pain may actually worsen (Melzack, 1971). Frequency of attacks may range from a few per year, to hourly recurrences. Episodes of pain may last from seconds to days. Description of the pain by patients usually involves a stabbing component associated with a painful loss of sensation or so-called pins and needles. Patients experience difficulty performing activities of daily living and may not be able to maintain gainful employment.

The recorded prevalence of phantom pain in amputee patients varies greatly. While it is estimated that almost 100% of amputees experience some kind of phantom, the proportion of those who experience phantom pain may be up to 80% or more (Wartan, Hamann, Wedley, McColl, 1997). While amputees who experience phantom pain may also experience stump pain, there are conflicting reports as to the correlation between the intensity of stump pain and the presence of phantom pain (Sherman, Sherman, & Parker, 1984). There are, however, data to suggest a correlation between the presence and intensity of phantom sensations and phantom pain (Montoya, Larbig, Grulke, Flor, Taub & Birbaumer, 1997).

PAIN MEMORIES

Although the mechanism for the development of phantom pain is still fervently debated by researchers, there does appear to be some agreement as to the influence of preamputation pain on the development and severity of phantom pain (Nikolajsen, Ilkajaer, Kroner, Christensen, & Jensen, 1997). This phenomenon is often referred to as "pain memory." Several case reports exist stating that the nature and intensity of phantom pain mimics that experienced by the patient immediately before the amputation event. There are also reports stating that the pain may be similar to that experienced several years before the amputation.

Data from the Nikolajsen study indicate an increased incidence of phantom pain in the first six months following amputation in patients who experienced preoperative pain, compared to those who did not. Two years following amputation there was no longer a correlation. While there may be a relationship between the intensity of preamputation pain and the presence of phantom pain, there may not be a correlation between the presence of preamputation pain and the duration or nature of phantom pain.

THE NEUROMATRIX

While painful conditions of a neurogenic nature often present with similar symptoms, the diversity of etiology of the conditions is so great as to render it difficult to describe them globally. In an attempt to describe the development of phantom phenomena in this manner, Melzack published the concept of a neuromatrix (Melzack, 1990). Briefly, this involves a network of neurons that links different areas of the brain, including the somatosensory cortex, the thalamocortical area, and the limbic system. Input from the periphery and the cortex itself is coprocessed by these areas and shared to other regions of the brain to develop an overall picture of the intact body. These connections may be strengthened or weakened by the experience of the patient. Hence the concept brings into play the phenomenon of pain memory and the notion that our emotional experiences can influence pain development in our physical body. Melzack has suggested that the neuromatrix may maintain a long-term representation of the amputated limb.

The observation that people with congenitally deficient limbs (aplasia) and those who undergo amputation early in childhood experience phantom sensations and phantom pain suggests a degree of genetic hard-wiring of the neuromatrix (Melzack, Israel, Lacroix, & Schultz, 1997). Melzack reported that 20% of congenitally limb-deficient patients and 42% of early childhood amputees experienced phantom pain. Subjects in the early childhood amputee group experienced onset of the phantom earlier than did the congenitally limb-deficient group, whose phantoms were more likely to be rigid, motionless, and painful. Several subjects in the congenitally limb-deficient group only experienced their phantom limb following stimulation of the stump. In most cases the phantom resolved when the prosthesis was in place or the subject was physically active. The phantom limb could be perceived during times of stress or simply as a result of someone's referring to it.

CORTICAL REORGANIZATION FOLLOWING AMPUTATION

So why are some phantom limbs painful while others are not? Evidence implicates cortical reorganization in the etiology of phantom pain (Birbaumer et al., 1997). For many years case reports have demonstrated an ability to ilicit sensations in the phantom limb by stimulating anatomically-unrelated areas. By touching an area on the face one may cause the patient to experience sensation in the phantom finger. This suggests the cortex is receiving stimuli that it perceives to originate in the phantom via neuronal reorganization. Advanced neural imaging techniques have been able to demonstrate cortical reorganization in patients experiencing phantom pain. There is no corresponding cortical reorganization demonstrable in amputees not experiencing phantom pain.

Birbaumer et al. (1997) were able to reverse cortical reorganization measured via neuroelectrical source imaging in phantom pain patients using a regional anesthetic block. Reorganization remained unchanged in patients whose phantom pain was not resolved by the block. The concept of cortical reorganization, occurring over time, may explain the phenomenon of telescoping of the phantom. Telescoping is the term used to describe the gradual shrinking and eventual disappearance of a phantom limb. This phenomenon may reflect ongoing cortical reorganization.

Whatever causes this most-unexplainable of human afflictions, it is clear that a deeper understanding of the causes of phantom pain is required before effective treatments can be determined. At present, the mainstays of therapy involve various surgical procedures to the stump, transcutaneous electrical nerve stimulation, and regional anesthetic blockade. Oral maintenance therapy includes tricyclic antidepressants, anticonvulsants, and sodium channel blockers. At best these drugs can cause a remittance of pain in 50% of patients (MacFarlane, Wright, O'Callaghan, & Benson, 1997). Management is limited by the lack of data from high quality, randomized clinical trials of various therapeutic procedures.

REFERENCES

Birbaumer, N., Lutzenberger, W., Montoya, P., Larbig, W., Unertl, K., Topfner, S., Grodd, W., Taub, E., & Flor, H. (1997). Effects of regional anaesthesia on phantom limb pain are mirrored in changes in cortical reorganisation. *Journal of Neuroscience, 17*(14) 5503–5508.

MacFarlane, B. V., Wright, A., O'Callaghan, J., & Benson, H. A. E. (1997). Chronic neuropathic pain and its control by drugs. *Pharmacology and Therapeutics, 75,* 1–19.

Melzack, R. (1971). Phantom limb pain: Implications for treatment of pathological pain. *Anaesthesiology, 35,* 409–419.

Melzack, R. (1990). Phantom limbs and the concept of a neuromatrix. *Trends in Neuroscience, 13*(3), 88–92.

Melzack, R., Israel, R., Lacroix, R., & Schultz, G. (1997). Phantom limbs in people with congenital limb deficiency or amputation in early childhood. *Brain, 120,* 1603–1620.

Merskey, H., & Bogduk, N. (1994). *Classification of chronic pain: Descriptions of chronic pain syndromes and definitions of pain terms* (2 ed.). Seattle: IASP.

Montoya, P., Larbig, W., Grulke, N., Flor, H., Taub, E., & Birbaumer, N. (1997). The relationship of phantom limb pain to other phantom limb phenomena in upper extremity amputees. *Pain, 72,* 87–93.

Nikolajsen, L., Ilkajaer, S., Kroner, K., Christensen, J. H., & Jensen, T. S. (1997). The influence of preamputation pain on postamputation stump and phantom pain. *Pain, 72,* 393–405.

Sherman, R. A., Sherman, C. J., & Parker, L. (1984). Chronic phantom and stump pain among American verterans: Results of a survey. *Pain, 18,* 83–95.

Wartan, S. W., Hamann, W., Wedley, J. R., & McColl, I. (1997). Phantom pain and sensations among British verteran amputees. *British Journal of Anaesthesiology, 78,* 652–659.

H. A. E. BENSON
University of Manitoba, Winnipeg

B. V. MACFARLANE
University of Queensland, Australia

A. WRIGHT
University of Manitoba, Winnipeg

PAIN

AMYGDALA

The amygdala is a collection of nuclei located along the medial wall of the temporal lobe. Amygdaloid nuclei are classified as either cortex-like or noncortex-like, based on neuronal morphology. The cortex-like nuclei, which include the lateral, basal, accessory basal, periamygdaloid, amygdalohippocampal area, and cortical nuclei, possess pyramidal-like neurons similar to the pyramidal neurons of the cortex. The noncortex-like nuclei, which include the central and medial nuclei, possess neurons similar to the medium spiny neurons of the striatum and do not possess pyramidal-like neurons. Each of the amygdaloid nuclei has distinct inputs and outputs, suggesting that they serve distinct functional roles. However, the amygdaloid nuclei are also interconnected, suggesting that circuitry within the amygdaloid nuclei allows the amygdala to function as a unit in processing information. In regard to information processing within the amygdala, sensory input is received primarily through the cortex-like nuclei and output is relayed primarily through the noncortex-like nuclei.

The amygdala is a component of the limbic system, which is thought to be involved in learning, memory, emotion, and motivation. The amygdala receives highly-integrated unimodal and polymodal sensory information and sends information to cortical, limbic, endocrine, autonomic, and motor areas. These anatomical connections suggest that the amygdala is ideally located for monitoring the environment and modifying physiological and behavioral responses accordingly. Indeed, the amygdala has been implicated in processing emotional stimuli, associative learning, memory, attention, arousal, and social behavior.

One of the first clues regarding the function of the amygdala was that symptoms of the Klüver-Bucy syndrome, including a loss of reactivity to emotional stimuli, were produced by amygdala lesions in monkeys. These monkeys willingly approached fear-inducing stimuli. This finding suggested that the amygdala is involved in processing the emotional significance of environmental stimuli. Several additional lines of evidence support this idea. Unilateral lesions of the amygdala along with cuts through the optic chiasm and forebrain commissures produce a disconnection of visual input from one eye to the amygdala. Monkeys restricted to viewing threatening stimuli through the eye disconnected from the amygdala remain calm and fail to show defensive reactions to the stimuli. When these same monkeys are allowed to view the fearful stimuli through the other eye, however, they exhibit appropriate defensive reactions, suggesting that the intact amygdala processes the emotional significance of the stimuli. The amygdala also plays a role in processing reward, as animals will perform an operant response to obtain mild stimulation of the amygdala, and lesions of the amygdala disrupt appropriate responses to changes in reward magnitude. Electrophysiological studies indicate that amygdala neurons are more responsive to complex emotional stimuli than to simple neutral stimuli. In humans, imaging studies have demonstrated that the amygdala is activated by photographs of facial expressions, and is more strongly activated by fearful faces than by angry or happy faces. Furthermore, patients with amygdala damage have difficulty comprehending the emotional category and intensity of facial expressions. Moreover, stimulation of the amygdala in humans and animals evokes emotional responses and species-specific defense reactions, respectively.

The amygdala is also involved in associative learning through which initially neutral stimuli gain biological significance (i.e., survival value). The most well-documented example of this associative learning is fear conditioning, in which a fearful event or stimulus (unconditioned stimulus) is paired with an initially neutral stimulus (conditioned stimulus). Subsequently, the conditioned stimulus comes to elicit conditioned fear responses in the absence of the unconditioned stimulus. These responses include conditioned freezing behavior, startle reactivity, and autonomic responses. There are strong and converging lines of evidence that the amygdala is involved in fear conditioning.

Although the amygdala may play a prepotent role in information processing and associative learning involving aversive fearful stimuli, its function is not limited to aversively-motivated learning, as it also plays a role in stimulus-reward associations. For instance, monkeys exhibit emotional reactions when presented with familiar palatable foods; however, they exhibit relatively little interest when presented with novel palatable foods. Upon tasting the novel foods, the monkeys learn to associate other sensory aspects of the foods with the taste of the foods. Subsequently, exposure to the foods elicits learned emotional responses and preferences for certain foods over others. Amygdala lesions disrupt acquisition of emotional responses and preferences for the novel palatable foods, suggesting that the animals are unable to associate the appearance of a new food with its palatability. Through stimulus-reward associations, initially neutral environmental stimuli gain incentive salience via

their ability to predict reward. Consequently, these stimuli come to produce both incentive motivation (reflected by approach behaviors) and secondary reinforcing effects. These behavioral effects are also disrupted in animals with amygdala lesions, particularly lesions of the basolateral amygdaloid nuclei. For instance, animals with basolateral amygdala lesions fail to acquire operant responding reinforced by presentation of a stimulus light (secondary reinforcer) that had been paired previously with delivery of a water reinforcer (primary reinforcer).

Memory for emotional events is superior to memory of nonemotional events. This phenomenon may be due, at least in part, to hormones that are released in response to stress that modulate effects on memory by binding to receptors in the amygdala. Stress hormones, such as epinephrine and corticosterone, produce a dose-dependent enhancement of memory when given post-training. Post-training administration corresponds to the time at which these hormones are naturally released in response to a stressful event and at which consolidation of the memory for the event occurs. Amygdala lesions abolish the memory-enhancing effects of these hormones, and direct injection of the hormones into the amygdala produces memory-enhancing effects. Psychomotor stimulants, such as amphetamine, may also modulate learning and memory evident as enhancement of responding for secondary reinforcers. Lesions of the central amygdala disrupt psychomotor stimulant-induced enhancement of responding for secondary reinforcers.

The amygdala, particularly the central nucleus, is involved in modulating attention and arousal. The central nucleus of the amygdala projects to several brain regions that are thought to be involved in attention and arousal, including cholinergic basal forebrain neurons, autonomic regulatory nuclei in the medulla, and the lateral tegmental area of the brainstem. In rabbits, a conditioned stimulus predictive of an aversive shock produces an increase in spontaneous firing of amygdala neurons that correlates with excitability of cortical neurons as measured by cortical electroencephalogram (EEG) activity. The cortical EEG activity is thought to reflect an increase in attention. Evidence from functional magnetic resonance imaging studies in humans suggests that the amygdala responds to stimuli processed at a subconscious level. Specifically, subjects given very brief presentations of happy or fearful faces followed immediately by longer presentations of neutral faces report seeing only the neutral faces, yet the amygdala is more strongly activated when the neutral faces are preceded by fearful faces, rather than by happy faces. These findings suggest that the amygdala constantly monitors the environment for biologically relevant stimuli and may modulate moment-to-moment levels of attention. Many conditioned responses mediated by the amygdala, including conditioned autonomic responses and an arrest of ongoing activity, may serve to enhance attention to environmental stimuli. Furthermore, lesion and brain stimulation studies across species suggest that the amygdala is involved in orienting responses to environmental stimuli.

The amygdala plays an important role in social behavior. In general, stimulation of the amygdala elicits rage and attack behaviors, whereas lesions of the amygdala decrease aggressive behaviors across species. Stimulation and lesion studies also suggest that the amygdala is involved in social rank and affiliation, as well as sexual and maternal behaviors. Radiotelemetry data from a social group suggest that electrical activity of the amygdala is strongest when animals are being chased or aggressed upon, or given ambiguous social information.

Amygdala dysfunction has been implicated in the pathophysiology of a number of neurological and psychiatric disorders. The amygdala is among several structures in the temporal lobe that are involved in epileptic (seizure) disorders. Repeated electrical or pharmacological stimulation with subthreshold stimuli of the amygdala eventually induces the development of seizures. This experimentally-induced seizure activity is referred to as kindling, and is used as an animal model of epilepsy. The amygdala has also been implicated in other disorders known to involve temporal lobe pathology, including schizophrenia and Alzheimer's disease. Imaging studies have indicated that amygdala volume is reduced in patients presenting these disorders. The amygdala may also play a role in depression, anxiety, and Posttraumatic Stress Disorder. Most antidepressant and anxiolytic medications produce effects via either benzodiazepine, norepinephrine, or serotonin receptors, the amygdala has a large population of these receptors. Furthermore, direct injection of benzodiazepine anxiolytic drugs reduces behavioral reactions that are thought to reflect fear and anxiety. Moreover, imaging studies have found that depressed patients exhibit an increase in metabolic activity in the amygdala that correlates with measures of depressive symptoms and that is reduced by antidepressant treatments. The amygdala has also been implicated in the reinforcing effects of drugs of abuse. Furthermore, imaging studies suggest that the amygdala likely plays a role in the ability of drug-associated stimuli (e.g., drug paraphernalia) to elicit drug craving.

SUGGESTED READING

Aggleton, J. P. (Ed.). (1992). *The amygdala: Neurobiological aspects of emotion, memory, and mental dysfunction.* New York: Wiley-Liss.

McGinty, J. F. (Ed.). (1999). Advancing from the ventral striatum to the extended amygdala. *Annals of the New York Academy of Sciences, 877,*

J. NEISEWANDER
Arizona State University

EMOTION
LEARNING
LIMBIC SYSTEM
MEMORY
MOTIVATION

ANALYSIS OF COVARIANCE (ANCOVA)

The analysis of covariance (ANCOVA) has goals similar to those of analysis of variance; that is, it uses estimates of variability to test hypotheses about group means. However, ANCOVA differs from the standard analysis of variance (ANOVA) because it uses information about not only the dependent variable, Y, but also about an additional variable, X, called the covariate, which is correlated with the dependent variable. The ANCOVA procedure can be thought of as a hybrid of standard ANOVA and regression procedures. It attempts to control statistically for differences in the covariate that would result in error variability, and hence would reduce the efficiency of an analysis of variance. The potentially greater efficiency of ANCOVA, however, is obtained at the cost of additional complexity and stronger assumptions that must be made about the data. ANCOVA results are also frequently misunderstood.

ANCOVA is perhaps best understood with the help of an example. Suppose we wish to test the effectiveness of, say, four different software packages designed to develop problem-solving skills in fourth-graders. Children are assigned randomly to work with each of the software packages; their scores on a problem-solving test given after working with the package for three months are the values of Y, the dependent variable. We also have available scores, X, on a pretest of problem-solving skills given before the children started working with the packages. Suppose we use ANOVA to test the null hypothesis that the software packages are equally effective. The means of the instructional groups will reflect not only the effects of the software packages, but also other sources of variability, including individual differences in problem-solving ability. The ANOVA can be thought of as a test of whether a model in which there is a treatment effect, that is, a component corresponding to the effect of working with one of the packages,

$$Y_{ij} = \mu + \alpha_j + \varepsilon_{ij}$$

accounts for the data better than does a restricted model in which there are no treatment effects,

$$Y_{ij} = \mu + \varepsilon_{ij}$$

where Y_{ij} is the test score of the ith subject in the jth treatment (here, software package) group, μ is a common component, α_j is the effect of the jth treatment, and ε_{ij} is the error variability associated with the score. The larger the error variability, the more the treatment effects will be obscured. Because the children were *randomly* assigned to treatment groups, preexisting individual differences in problem-solving ability will not differ systematically across groups; however, they will contribute to the error variability, and thus to the between-group variability. If all children had equal problem-solving ability (as indicated by equal scores on the covariate) before working with the software packages, we would have a much better chance of assessing how effective the packages were. ANCOVA attempts to remove the component of the dependent variable predictable on the basis of the pretest by adding a regression component to each of the above models. It tests the model

$$Y_{ij} = \mu + a_j + \beta(X_{ij} - \overline{X}) + \epsilon_{ij}$$

against the restricted model

$$Y_{ij} = \mu + \beta(X_{ij} - \overline{X}) + \epsilon_{ij}$$

where β is the regression coefficient or slope. An increase of power may be achieved because, if the treatment and error components are adjusted by removing the variability accounted for by the regression on X, the test statistic may be much larger. In effect, the ANCOVA is trying to assess whether there would be a treatment effect if all of the children had equal scores on the covariate.

ASSUMPTIONS AND INTERPRETATION

In ANCOVA, there are assumptions of normality and homogeneity of variance similar to those in ANOVA. However, additional assumptions follow from the attempt to statistically control for differences in the covariate.

Linearity and Homogeneity of Regression Slopes

ANCOVA adjusts for differences in the covariate by removing variability accounted for by a linear regression on the covariate. If there is a nonlinear component to the relationship between X and Y, the ANCOVA significance tests will be biased. Moreover, it is assumed that the same regression adjustment is appropriate for each treatment group. This means that unless the slopes of the regression equations of Y on X are the same for each treatment group, ANCOVA should not be used. If there are different slopes, the interesting question is not what would happen if all the subjects had the same score on the covariate, but rather, what would the situation be at different values of the covariate. Therefore, a test for homogeneity of regression slopes should be conducted before an ANCOVA is performed.

Assumption of the Independence of Treatment and Covariate

It is not possible to interpret the results of an ANCOVA in which the covariate varies systematically with the treatment effect. Using X as a covariate removes any part of Y predictable by a linear regression on X. However, if the value of X depends on the treatment condition, performing an ANCOVA will not only remove error variability, but may remove part of the effect of the treatment itself.

Suppose, in the example of the software packages, that students could choose to spend extra time working with the packages, and we desired to control for the amount of time they spent. In other words, we would like to know what performance would have been like if each student spent an equal amount of time working with the package he or she was assigned. However, because the amount of time a student chose to spend working with a package might reflect how understandable, interesting, and helpful the package is, the time spent would be related to the effectiveness of the package. Therefore, any adjustment based on the covariate would tend to remove part of the treatment effect. If one is concerned about time spent, there is no substitute for conducting a true experiment in which both software package and time spent are independent variables.

Random Assignment to Treatment Conditions as Opposed to Using Intact Nonequivalent Groups

In ANCOVA, the distinction between randomized and nonequivalent group designs is important. When subjects are randomly assigned to groups, the groups should not vary systematically on the covariate, and interpretation is straightforward. However, when intact groups that differ on the covariate are assigned to different treatments, the treatment is confounded with characteristics of the group and the results of an adjustment may be not be interpretable. Any adjustment based on the covariate will result in adjustments of any correlated characteristics as well, and will result in the kinds of difficulties of interpretation that occur in correlational research.

SUGGESTED READING

Huitema, B. E. (1980). *The analysis of covariance and alternatives.* New York: Wiley.

Myers, J. L., & Well, A. D. (1995). *Research design and statistical analysis.* Hillsdale, NJ: Erlbaum.

A. D. WELL
University of Massachusetts

ANALYSIS OF VARIANCE (ANOVA)
STATISTICS IN PSYCHOLOGY

ANALYSIS OF VARIANCE (ANOVA)

Analysis of variance (ANOVA) is one of the most commonly used statistical techniques in psychological research. The basic approach (and the reason for the name of the procedure) is to use estimates of variability to test hypotheses about group means.

As a more specific example, consider an experimental design with a single factor (independent variable) that has, say, four levels. Suppose that the scores at each level are the numbers of items correctly recalled by participants in a memory experiment and the factor is learning strategy; that is, the levels of the factor correspond to different learning strategies. Each learning strategy can be thought of as associated with a hypothetical population of scores: all the scores that have been or could be obtained using the strategy if the experiment were conducted over and over again. If the participants in the current experiment are appropriately chosen and assigned to the learning groups, the scores actually obtained in the four groups can be thought of as random samples from the populations associated with the different strategies. ANOVA can be used to test the "null hypothesis" that the means of the populations corresponding to the different strategies are all the same. That is, ANOVA provides a procedure for deciding whether the data collected in the experiment provide sufficient evidence to reject the null hypothesis, so that the strategy factor can be considered to be statistically significant.

Even if the null hypothesis were true, we would not expect all the sample means in our experiment to be equal. Any true differences among the different strategies will be obscured by random error variability in the obtained scores. That is, scores may differ from one another, not only because they are associated with different learning strategies, but also because of a possible host of additional variables. For example, some participants might be better learners than others or be more motivated to perform well in the experiment. Perhaps for some participants background noise or other factors interfered with learning during the experiment. Because of this uncontrolled error variability, even if participants were assigned randomly to groups so that the groups would not differ systematically, the more talented or motivated participants would not be distributed exactly evenly across the groups, and so the group means would be expected to differ from one another. The ANOVA procedure attempts to determine whether the group means associated with the different levels of an independent variable or factor differ from one another by more than would be expected on the basis of the error variability.

The mean of the variances of the scores *within* each group provides one estimate of the error variability. If the null hypothesis is true, the variability *among* the group means can be used to generate another estimate of the error variability. Under certain assumptions, the ratio of these two estimates is distributed as the F distribution if the null hypothesis is true. If the null hypothesis is not true, the estimate based on the group means should be larger than that based on the within-group variability, because it includes not only random variability, but all systematic variability due to the difference in the population means, and the ratio of the estimates should be larger than would be expected from the F distribution. In standard usage, if the value obtained for the ratio of the two estimates would place it in the extreme upper tail (the usual criterion is the upper 5%) of the F distribution, the null hypothesis is rejected.

Analysis of variance can deal with the effects of several factors in the same analysis. If we apply analysis of variance to a design with two factors, we can test whether each is significant. Moreover, we can test whether there is a significant interaction between the factors; that is, whether there is a joint effect of the two factors that cannot be determined by considering each factor separately (see the entry dealing with factorial designs).

The null hypotheses tested by an ANOVA are very general. For tests of a *main effect,* the null hypothesis is that the population means of a factor are all equal. For tests of the interactions of two or more factors, the null hypothesis is that the joint effects—that is, the effects that cannot be obtained by adding up the main effects of the factors in question—are all 0.

There are many different kinds of ANOVA designs. When each subject provides a single score at only one combination of levels of the factors in the design, we have what is called a pure *between-subjects design.* When each subject provides a score at every combination of levels of the factors in the design, we have a pure *within-subjects* or *repeated-measures design.* It is common to encounter *mixed designs* in which a given subject provides scores at all levels of one or more within-subjects factors, but at only one level of one or more between-subjects factors.

ANOVA is commonly employed to analyze the data from experiments. It is less appropriate for data obtained from correlational research, because ANOVA treats all factors as categorical and uncorrelated.

SUGGESTED READING

Keppel, G. (1991). *Design and analysis: A researcher's handbook.* Englewood Cliffs, NJ: Prentice Hall.

Moore, D. S. (1995). *The basic practice of statistics.* New York: Freeman.

Myers, J. L., & Well, A. D. (1995). *Research design and statistical analysis.* Hillsdale, NJ: Erlbaum.

A. D. WELL
University of Massachusetts

ANALYSIS OF COVARIANCE
STATISTICS IN PSYCHOLOGY

ANALYTICAL PSYCHOLOGY

"Analytical psychology" is the name Swiss psychologist Carl Gustav Jung (1875–1961) gave to his theoretical and methodological approach to the psychology of the unconscious following his break with Freud and psychoanalysis in 1913. Unlike psychoanalysis, analytical psychology does not hold the structure of the unconscious to be limited to contents that were initially a part of consciousness. While it does not deny the psychoanalytic view that the unconscious includes contents that were once conscious, it does hold that the unconscious also includes contents not yet capable of becoming conscious (i.e., symptoms) and contents incapable of ever becoming fully conscious (i.e., the symbolic manifestation of the archetypes of the collective unconscious). Moreover, analytical psychology maintains that the dynamics at issue in the formation of the unconscious are not exhausted by repression. Analytical psychology contests neither the psychoanalytic account of the *felt* incompatibility between conscious and preconscious (as well as unconscious) contents, nor the consequent mechanism of repression resulting in the dissociation of the latter contents from consciousness. However, it maintains that an additional dynamic, rooted in the inability of consciousness to apperceive psychic contents, also results in psychic contents' having a subliminal and therefore an unconscious status. Apperception is defined by analytical psychology as the psychic process whereby new contents are assimilated into consciousness on the basis of their similarity to the contents already existing in consciousness.

FORMATION OF THE UNCONSCIOUS

Analytical psychology's theory of an apperceptive dynamic resulting in psychic unconsciousness has its basis in the same observation that underlies the psychoanalytic theory of repression: that certain psychic contents possessing sufficient energy to enter consciousness nevertheless are incapable of becoming conscious. Controlled word association experiments, along with psychotherapeutic encounters in the clinic and consulting room, provide the data that support the hypothesis common to psychoanalysis and analytical psychology of a quantitative threshold between consciousness and unconsciousness. In addition, psychoanalysis and analytical psychology agree that there is also a qualitative factor operative in the threshold between consciousness and unconsciousness. Finally, they share the view that this qualitative factor indicates that much of what goes on in the mind or psyche has a psychogenic origin that cannot be directly reduced to biophysical causes.

ATTITUDE TYPES AND THE FOUR FUNCTIONS OF CONSCIOUSNESS

Analytical psychology diverges from psychoanalysis in its theory of the qualitative factors at issue in the blocking of psychic contents—whose energy is sufficient for conscious entrance—from entering consciousness. According to analytical psychology, in addition to psychoanalysis's theoretical formulation of this qualitative factor in terms of conflicts between the so-called ego instincts and sexually charged libido, there are also qualitative factors that involve: (a) the apperceptive conflict between the two basic attitudes that govern the flow of psychic energy (introversion and extroversion); and (b) the apperceptive conflict among the four basic functions of consciousness (thinking, feeling, sensation, and intuition).

Analytical psychology holds that two different basic attitudes characterize an individual's orientation to subjective and objective reality. The extroverted attitude values objective reality over subjective reality, such that there is a stronger tendency for psychic energy to flow toward objects and objective processes than toward the ego and subjective processes. The habitual and therefore superior development of this attitude yields individuals of the extroverted type. The introverted attitude values subjective reality over objective reality, such that there is a stronger tendency for psychic energy to flow toward the ego and subjective processes rather than toward objects and objective processes. The habitual and therefore superior development of this attitude yields individuals of the introverted type.

According to analytical psychology, successful adaptation to reality eventually demands of the individual the apperception of both the objective and subjective dimensions of reality. The typical dominance of one attitude, however, hinders the apperception of the aspects of reality connected with the non-dominant, and therefore inferior, attitude. This typical situation precludes a balanced adaptation to reality and results in a one-sided psychological orientation. As a consequence, when either the subjective or objective aspect of reality presents demands upon the individual for adaptation that are best met by the individual's less-developed, inferior attitude, these demands will frustrate the ability of the individual's more-developed, superior attitude to apperceive the aspects of reality connected to the inferior attitude. The individual's experience of the maladaptation of its superior attitude to apperceive the aspects of reality connected with its inferior attitude manifests what analytical psychology terms "symptoms." These symptoms function to disrupt the habitual flow of psychic energy to the dimension of reality that comprises the goal of choice for the individual's superior attitude. As a result, such symptoms function to compensate for the one-sidedness of this choice by calling attention to the need for further psychological development of the individual's inferior attitude.

As with introversion and extroversion, analytical psychology theorizes that there are conflicts involved in the apperceptive dynamism of the four basic functions of consciousness: thinking, feeling, sensation, and intuition. This theory of functions holds that the dominance of any of these basic functions results in an individual whose apperceptive adaptation to reality is typologically oriented. The theory further maintains that the functions group themselves into pairs of opposites, such that the superior function-

ing of thinking will yield an inferior functioning of feeling; and the superior functioning of intuition will yield an inferior functioning of sensation. This dynamic is reversible, so that superior feeling yields inferior thinking, and superior sensation yields inferior intuition. Finally, the theory of functions maintains that individuals typically adapt to reality in a manner that favors the most developed function, resulting in a one-sidedness that is analogous, mutatis mutandis, to the one-sidedness manifested by the attitude types. Likewise the conflict between superior and inferior function(s) emerges when reality makes demands upon the individual that require its apperception by the less developed function(s). To the extent that the greater share of the flow of psychic energy is taken up by the favored function, analytical psychology maintains that the less developed functions will remain beyond the conscious threshold, despite the demands made by reality for its apperception via these latter functions. As a result, the dominant function will experience the inferior function(s) that are demanded for the apperception of reality in terms of symptoms that disturb its apperception of the aspect of reality to which it is directed. The dynamic of these symptoms is held to compensate such one-sidedness by calling to attention the need for further psychological development of the inferior functions by the individual.

THEORY OF COMPLEXES

Analytical psychology's theory of complexes is rooted in its understanding of apperception as the psychic process by which a new content is articulated with similar, already existing contents in such a way that it becomes understood, apprehended, clear. As such, apperception is the bridge that connects the already existing constellated contents with the new one. According to analytical psychology, apperception is either active or passive. When apperception is active, the bridge between the already existing and new contents is fashioned by the association of similar contents. When the apperception is passive, the conditions are lacking for an associative bridge based upon the similarity of the already existing contents and new contents. This has as its result the dissociation between the former and latter contents, which, paradoxically, functions apperceptively to link the two. The paradoxically apperceptive apprehension of new contents that occurs in dissociation manifests these contents as symptoms.

The absence of an associative link between ego-consciousness and unconscious contents (i.e., the symptoms) in passive apperception does not preclude for analytical psychology the existence of associations with respect to the latter contents. Rather, the theory of complexes maintains that the existence of associations that refer psychic contents to other such dissociated contents and therefore *not* to the ego, can be both observed and investigated. By the term "complex," analytical psychology understands the loose association of passively apperceived contents, which lack an associative link to ego-consciousness. The complex is manifest in terms of fantasy images that constellate themselves around the symptomatic manifestation of the compensatory affect of the inferior attitude and inferior functions upon consciousness. Because the images at issue here for analytical psychology lack an active apperceptive link with ego-consciousness, they should not be confused with the familiar and perhaps most readily accessible meaning of the term "image": that is, image in the sense of representative, yet diminished picture of a known original. Precisely because the imaginal qualities of passively apperceived contents do not manifest an active apperceptive bridge to ego-consciousness, they lack the relation to the known original that determines this familiar, representational meaning of image. This is not to suggest, however, that for analytical psychology the images at issue in passive apperception do not point or refer beyond themselves. They do, and indeed, it is in none other than this reference beyond themselves that comprises their very status as an image. Nonetheless, since that to which they refer does not manifest an active apperceptive connection with ego-consciousness, the very crux of their imaginal status involves an aspect of the unknown insofar as—from the vantage of that which is intelligible with respect to active apperception—the referent of these images remains concealed. Analytical psychology calls such images "symbols."

The problem of establishing a link between ego-consciousness and the unknown referents of the images associatively constellated by the complex is a major methodological issue in analytical psychology's theory of the unconscious. At issue in establishing this link is the transformation of symptoms into psychic contents capable of establishing an active connection with a likewise transformed ego-consciousness. The consciousness of these symptomatic manifestations is termed the "feeling-toned" element of the complex. The initial establishment of the existence of the complex occurs on the basis of the method of free association established by psychoanalysis. According to analytical psychology, however, this method is limited—by its focus on personal associations—in its ability to account for the full scope of the associative connections that are yielded by the passively apperceived psychic contents (i.e., by the fantasy images whose reference is to other images and not ego-consciousness). To overcome this limitation, analytical psychology developed an interpretive method to explore the transpersonal and therefore collective context of the associative connections disclosed by complexes.

PERSONAL AND COLLECTIVE UNCONSCIOUS

Analytical psychology understands the personal character of the associations yielded by the symptomatic (i.e., dissociated) images of the complex to provide evidence for a personal unconscious, and it understands the transpersonal character of those associations yielded by the symptomatic images that refer not to ego consciousness but to other images to provide evidence for a collective unconscious. The methodical unfolding of the transpersonal context of the associations at issue in the collective unconscious involves what analytical psychology calls the "amplification" of the associations of images that refer not to ego consciousness but to other images. Speaking of this method, Jung writes that "I adopt the method of the philologist, which is far from being free association, and apply a logical principle which is called *amplification*. It is simply the seeking of parallels" (Jung, 1935/1970, p. 92). Proceeding in this manner, the initial appearance of associated images is guided by parallel material drawn from dreams, literature, myth, religion, and art. The point of departure for the amplification of as-

sociations is always the question: "How does the thing appear?" The guidance provided by the parallel material with respect to the initially appearing associated images functions to facilitate a conscious propensity to assimilate, and therefore to actively apperceive, hints or fragments of lightly-toned unconscious complexes and, by associating them with parallel elements, to elaborate them in a clearly visual form.

ARCHETYPES AND INDIVIDUATION

The employment of the interpretive method of amplification results in analytical psychology's becoming a depth psychology that unfolds a topology of the collective associative designs—termed "archetypes"—that surround the nucleus of the complex. The most basic archetypes identified by analytical psychology include: the persona (the socially accepted mask assumed by the ego); the shadow (the undeveloped and therefore infantile aspects of the ego); the anima and animus (counter-sexual images in men and women, respectively, which apperceptively link their personal unconsciouses to the collective unconscious); and the self (the transpersonal basis of the ego and therefore of the conscious personality). The therapeutic goal of analytical psychology is the self-conscious differentiation of ego-consciousness from the various archetypes that become constellated in the course of the life of an individual. The process of striving to realize this goal is termed "individuation." The crucial role of the analytical distinction between ego-consciousness and the archetypal contents of the collective unconscious in the process of individuation is signaled in the name Jung gave to his psychology in order to distinguish it from psychoanalysis: analytical psychology.

REFERENCE

Jung, C. G. (1970). Analytic psychology: Its theory and practice. New York: Vintage Books. (Original work published 1935)

SUGGESTED READING

Jung, C. G. (1918). *Studies in Word Association.* London: Routledge & Kegan Paul.

Jung, C. G. (1969). On psychic energy. In *The structures and dynamics of the psyche.* Princeton: Princeton University Press. (Original work published 1928)

Jung, C. G. (1969). On the nature of the psyche. In *The structures and dynamics of the psyche.* Princeton: Princeton University Press. (Original work published 1947)

Jung, C. G. (1970). *Two essays on analytical psychology.* Princeton: Princeton University Press. (Original work published 1917)

Jung, C. G. (1973). *Aion: Researches into the phenomenology of the self.* Princeton: Princeton University Press. (Original work published 1951)

Jung, C. G. (1976). *Psychological types.* Princeton: Princeton University Press. (Original work published 1920)

B. HOPKINS
Seattle University

ARCHETYPES
PSYCHOANALYSIS
PSYCHOLOGY AND PHILOSOPHY
TRANSPERSONAL PSYCHOLOGY

ANASTASI, ANNE (1908–   )

Anastasi is most closely associated with the development of differential psychology. She received the BA from Barnard and the PhD from Columbia, the latter at age 21. Although her long-standing plan had been to specialize in mathematics, a course using Pillsbury's *Essentials of Psychology* as the text aroused her interest in this field. Then a course with Harry L. Hollingworth and an article by Charles Spearman clinched matters, the latter convincing her that psychology and mathematics could be combined. Her Columbia professors included Henry E. Garrett (her dissertation adviser), Albert T. Poffenberger, Carl J. Warden, and Robert S. Woodworth as well as visiting professors Richard M. Elliott and Clark L. Hull. Through her husband, John P. Foley, Jr., who had majored in psychology at Indiana University, she was exposed to the ideas of J. Robert Kantor. To all these influences she attributes her generalist orientation and her firm commitment to psychology as an objective science.

Anastasi taught at Barnard, Queens College (CUNY), and Fordham University. Her major books include *Differential Psychology, Fields of Applied Psychology,* and *Psychological Testing.* Her research centered chiefly on factor analysis and traits, problems of test construction, and the interpretation of test scores with special reference to the role of cultural factors in individual and group differences. Active in association affairs throughout her professional life, Anastasi was president of the American Psychological Association in 1972, the first woman to be elected to this office in 50 years. The holder of several honorary degrees, she received many awards including the APA Distinguished Scientific Award for the Application of Psychology (1981), the American Psychological Foundation Gold Medal (1984), and the National Medal of Science from the president of the United States (1987).

STAFF

ANDROGENS, ESTROGENS, AND BEHAVIOR

Androgens and estrogens are the primary sex hormones. Although both males and females produce and respond to both androgens and estrogens, there are sex differences in the levels of these hormones, especially during prenatal life, again at puberty, and in adulthood. On average, males have higher levels of androgens than do females, and females have higher levels of estrogens than do males. Androgens and estrogens produce physical sex differences—for example, in reproductive function and body proportions. Androgens and estrogens also contribute to (but do not determine) sex differences in psychological characteristics.

STUDIES IN NONHUMAN MAMMALIAN SPECIES

Experimental studies in mammals have convincingly demonstrated that androgens and estrogens affect a wide range of behaviors that ordinarily show sex differences. Hormones affect behavior in two ways, depending on when they are present.

Studies in Nonhuman Mammals: Behavioral Effects of Early Androgens and Estrogens

In early life, when the brain is developing, hormones produce permanent changes in the structure of the brain; these are called organizational effects. These structural changes make a difference in behavior. In both genetic males and females, high levels of androgen present during critical periods of development are associated with high levels of male-typical behavior (behavior that is higher in level or frequency in males than in females) and low levels of female-typical behavior (behavior that is higher in level or frequency in females than in males). Administering high levels of androgens to female rodents and primates during the prenatal and neonatal periods, when the brain is developing, causes them to show sexual behavior that is more typical of males than of other females. Compared to typical females, they also engage in more rough play, are more aggressive, and perform better in mazes on which males usually do better than females. Conversely, depriving male animals of androgen during these sensitive periods causes them to behave in ways that are more typical of females than of other males. Further, certain regions of the rat brain show sex differences and changes with excess or reduced levels of androgens and metabolites; such regions include the hypothalamus, which is involved in sexual behavior, and the hippocampus, which is involved in spatial learning.

It appears that some of these masculinizing effects actually result from the conversion of androgen to estrogen in the brain. Although females have high levels of estrogen, they are not masculinized because their estrogen is inactivated and therefore is unavailable in the brain.

Androgens have long been considered to be both necessary and sufficient for sexual differentiation, with male-typical development resulting from high levels of androgens and female-typical development resulting from low or absent androgens. Thus, female-typical development has been seen to be a passive process. However, estrogens from the ovaries may also be important in producing sex differences. For example, depriving female rats of ovarian estrogens results in reduced sexual behavior and decreased activity. (Note that these estrogens have different effects than do estrogens that are converted from androgens in the brain.)

Studies in Nonhuman Mammals: Behavioral Effects of Later Androgens and Estrogens

Many behavioral variations due to sex hormones are caused by variations that occur during early sensitive periods when the brain is developing. But, the hormones that circulate in the body throughout adolescence and adulthood may continue to affect behaviors later in life; these later effects are called activational effects. The hormones alter some types of neural activity, and thus behaviors that are affected by that activity. Studies in animals show that sexual behaviors are the ones most dramatically affected by circulating hormones, but nonsexual behaviors may also be affected by circulating hormones. For example, changes in estrogen across the estrous cycle in female rats are associated with variations in motor function, sensory perception, and learning and memory. These behavioral changes are mediated by estrogen effects on underlying brain regions, including the striatum, cerebellum, and hippocampus.

HUMAN STUDIES OF BEHAVIORAL EFFECTS OF ANDROGEN AND ESTROGENS

In people, as in other species, behavior is affected by hormones in two ways: organizational changes to the brain during early development and activation of brain systems later in life.

Behavioral Effects of Prenatal Androgens and Estrogens in People

The organizational effects of sex hormones occur during prenatal development. This reflects the fact that the sexual differentiation of the genitalia occurs early in gestation, and sex differences in hormone concentrations are greatest during weeks 8 through 24 of gestation. It is not possible or ethical to manipulate hormones during prenatal life, so our knowledge about the human behavioral effects of hormones comes from special situations, including so-called experiments of nature, in which prenatal hormones have been altered because of a genetic disease or because pregnant women took drugs with masculinizing effects. Recent studies have also involved normal individuals with typical variations in prenatal hormones determined through amniocentesis. These studies of hormone effects on human behavior are largely consistent with studies in other species in suggesting that many aspects of behavior are affected by the levels of androgens present early in development.

The best-studied experiment of nature is congenital adrenal hyperplasia (CAH), a genetic disease in which the fetus is exposed to high levels of androgens beginning early in gestation. If sexual differentiation of human behavior is affected by the levels of androgens that are present during critical periods of development (as occurs for human physical sexual differentiation and for both physical and behavioral sexual differentiation in other mammals), then females with CAH should be behaviorally more masculine and less feminine than a comparison group of females without CAH—and they are, in many, but not all, ways. Compared to their unaffected sisters or to other same-sex controls, females with CAH are more interested in boys' toys and activities and less interested in girls' toys and activities in childhood and in adolescence, are more likely to report the use of physical aggression in conflict situations, have higher spatial ability, are less interested in infants and feminine appearance, and are less likely to engage in heterosexual activity and more likely to fantasize about and be sexually aroused by other women. On the other hand, most females with CAH have female-typical gender identity.

Findings from females with CAH have been confirmed from other experiments of nature. For example, girls who were exposed to masculinizing hormones because their mothers took medication (androgenizing progestins) during pregnancy are more likely than their unexposed sisters to report using aggression in conflict situations. Converging evidence for these special cases has come from

normal individuals with typical variations in prenatal hormones. For example, 7-year-old girls who had high levels of testosterone in utero (determined from amniotic fluid at 14–16 weeks of gestation) had better spatial ability than girls who had low levels of prenatal testosterone.

It is interesting that much more is known about the behavioral effects of prenatal androgens than the effects of prenatal estrogens in human beings. This may reflect the fact that there are few experiments of nature in which only estrogen production is disrupted and the possibility that most of the behavioral effects of estrogen occur later in development.

Although prenatal sex hormones clearly affect some aspects of later behavior, the neural mechanisms for these effects are currently not known. There are reports of sex differences in brain structure, but these have not yet been related to sex differences in behavior, nor to prenatal hormone exposure.

Behavioral Effects of Circulating Androgens and Estrogens in People

Sex hormones continue to affect behavior later in life, probably by activating neural circuits organized early in development. Androgens seem to have some effect on aggression, but the effect is small and is bidirectional; that is, aggression itself can increase androgen levels. There is also some evidence that androgens facilitate spatial ability in a curvilinear fashion. High spatial ability is associated with relatively high androgens in females, but relatively low androgens in males, but keep in mind that even males on the low end of normal have higher levels of androgen than do females on the high end of normal.

Estrogens also affect behavior later in life, especially some aspects of cognition. This information comes from studies examining how cognitive abilities vary in relation to fluctuating estrogen levels across the menstrual cycle, with the use of oral contraceptives, at menopause, and in people receiving estrogen treatment. Estrogen facilitates aspects of motor function, perhaps by modulating left-hemisphere regions involved in praxis. Estrogen also facilitates memory, so that postmenopausal women receiving estrogen supplementation have better memory than women not taking estrogen. Brain imaging studies suggest that these acute cognitive effects of estrogen work directly through changes in brain activity, especially in regions involved in memory, including the frontal lobes and hippocampus.

CONCLUSIONS

Androgens and estrogens have powerful effects on human behavior, as they do on human physical characteristics and on behavioral and physical characteristics in nonhuman mammals. Androgens and estrogens exert some of their effects directly on the brain, by changing its structure early in life and its activity throughout life. However, sex hormones may also affect behavior indirectly. For example, hormones might alter sensory thresholds, facilitating performance on tasks through improved sensation or perception, or increasing sensitivity to environmental input. Exposure to high levels of prenatal androgen may affect not only the behavior of the individual, but social responses to the individual. For example, a predisposition to play with car and trucks produced by exposure to high levels of prenatal androgens may be increased over time by gifts received from adults. It is important to remember that hormones affect behavior in complex ways, as one of a set of influences, and not as determinants.

SUGGESTED READING

Becker, J. B., Breedlove, S. M., & Crews, D. (Eds.). (1992). *Behavioral endocrinology.* Cambridge: MIT Press.

Berenbaum, S. A. (Ed.). (1998). Gonadal hormones and sex differences in behavior [Special issue]. *Developmental Neuropsychology, 14.*

Collaer, M. L., & Hines, M. (1995). Human behavioral sex differences: A role for gonadal hormones during early development? *Psychological Bulletin, 118,* 55–107.

Goy, R. W. (Ed.). (1996). Sexual differences in behavior [Special issue]. *Hormones and Behavior, 30.*

Kimura, D. (1999). *Sex and cognition.* Cambridge: MIT Press.

Wallen, K. (1996). Nature needs nurture: The interaction of hormonal and social influences on the development of behavioral sex differences in rhesus monkeys. *Hormones and Behavior, 30,* 364–378.

Williams, C. L. (Ed.). (1998). Estrogen effects on cognition across the lifespan [Special issue]. *Hormones and Behavior, 14.*

S. A. BERENBAUM
Southern Illinois University School of Medicine, Carbondale

HORMONES & BEHAVIOR
SEX DIFFERENCES

ANDROGYNY

Although the idea that a single individual can embody components of both masculinity and femininity was introduced to psychology by Carl Jung in his essay on "Anima and animus," modern psychology paid little attention to this idea until the concept of androgyny was introduced by Sandra Bem (1974), who argued that masculinity and femininity constitute complementary domains of positive traits and behaviors and that, in principle, it is possible for a person to be both masculine and feminine, agentic and communal, instrumental and expressive, depending on the situational appropriateness of these various modalities. The concept of agency and communion, as associated with maleness and femaleness respectively, was drawn from the earlier work of Bakan (1966), while the concept of instrumentality and expressiveness came from Parsons and Bales (1955).

Bem constructed an operational measure of androgyny in her instrument, the Bem Sex Role Inventory (BSRI). Almost simultaneously Spence, Helmreich, and Stapp (1974) also produced an instrument designed to measure androgyny.

Although researchers have abandoned the original concept of androgyny as a prescription for mental health, the concept of androgyny has been useful to psychology. In particular, dialogues in the area have sensitized psychologists to the multidimensional aspects of sex and gender. Future research in the area may suggest ways that social definitions about sex roles are incorporated into personal identity, into the self, and into the way people process their perceptions about social reality.

REFERENCES

Bakan, D. (1966). *The duality of human existence.* Boston: Beacon.

Bem, S. L. (1974). The measurement of psychological androgyny. *Journal of Consulting and Clinical Psychology, 42,* 155–162.

Jung, C. G. (1953). Anima and animus. In *Two essays on analytical psychology: Collected works of C. G. Jung* (Vol. 7). New York: Bollinger Foundation.

Spence, J. T., Helmreich, R. L., & Stapp, J. (1974). The Personal Attributes Questionnaire: A measure of sex-role stereotypes and masculinity-femininity. *JSAS Catalog of Selected Documents in Psychology, 4,* 127.

SUGGESTED READING

Bem, S. L. (1975). Sex role adaptability: One consequence of psychological androgyny. *Journal of Personality and Social Psychology, 31,* 634–643.

Bem, S. L., & Lenney, E. (1976). Sex typing and the avoidance of cross-sex behavior. *Journal of Personality and Social Psychology, 33,* 48–54.

Bem, S. L., Martyna, W., & Watson, C. (1976). Sex typing and androgyny: Further explorations of the expressive domain. *Journal of Personality and Social Psychology, 34,* 1016–1023.

Deaux, K., & Major, B. (1977). Sex-related patterns in the unit of perception. *Personality and Social Psychology Bulletin, 3,* 297–300.

Massad, C. M. (1981). Sex role identity and adjustment during adolescence. *Child Development, 52,* 1290–1298.

Spence, J. T., & Helmreich, R. L. (1978). *Masculinity and femininity: Their psychological dimensions, correlates, and antecedents.* Austin, TX: University of Texas Press.

R. K. UNGER
Montclair State College

SEX ROLES

ANESTHESIA

The use of general anesthesia to prevent pain during surgery began in the United States in the 1800s. Surgeons soon began using anesthesia for all their cases and turned to the nurses with whom they worked to administer the anesthetic while they operated. Few, if any, physicians initially focused their practice on the daily administration of anesthetics. As anesthesia matured into a unique specialty, more nurses and physicians devoted themselves to the field, and anesthesia is now a recognized specialty of both disciplines. Registered Nurses with a baccalaureate degree become Certified Registered Nurse Anesthetists (CRNAs) after one or more years of acute-care work experience and at least two years of master's education in anesthesia. Physicians now most commonly become anesthesiologists after completing medical school and a 4-yr residency, but the law allows any physician to administer anesthetics.

In general, there are three different types of anesthesia provided for surgical and diagnostic procedures: sedation, regional anesthesia, and general anesthesia.

SEDATION

Sedative drugs depress the central nervous system, causing a decrease in a person's awareness and a reduction in anxiety. Some sedative drugs also cause amnesia lasting from minutes to hours, depending on the drug and dose administered. Sedation is most often administered prior to surgery to relieve anxiety, during unpleasant diagnostic procedures, or during regional anesthesia and surgery. This last use is a most important one. Regional anesthesia has significant advantages over general anesthesia in some circumstances but most people do not easily accept the idea of being awake during their surgery. Sedation allows patients to feel asleep during a regional anesthetic and often prevents any memory of the surgical experience.

The type and amount of sedation administered is based on a patient's physical condition, weight, the procedure being performed, and his or her level of anxiety. Sedation necessitates close observation of the patient, because sedation and general anesthesia exist on a continuum. At some point (which is different for each individual), as more and more medication is administered sedation gives way and general anesthesia is produced. Oversedation can result in problems with breathing and other anesthetic complications. All but the lightest sedation should be administered by an anesthetist or other health-care provider skilled and experienced in airway management and the assessment of oxygenation and breathing. In most cases this individual should have no responsibilities other than sedating and monitoring the patient.

REGIONAL ANESTHESIA

Local anesthetic drugs temporarily disable the function of nerves, including those that carry pain sensation. Injecting a local anesthetic renders part of the body insensible to pain and is called "regional anesthesia." How long the anesthesia will last depends on the drug, how much is injected, and where it is injected. Regional anesthesia can be used to numb a small area of skin, a single nerve, or a large region of the body—as much as from the upper chest down to the feet. Regional anesthesia can be used both for minor superficial procedures and for some types of major surgery. Local anesthesia is commonly used around a wound edge before stitches are sewn in. A common type of nerve block is used by dentists to numb a large area of the mouth with a single injection. Epidural blocks are commonly used to anesthetize a large area of the body during labor pains or prior to a cesarean section. In some cases regional anesthesia is the preferred anesthetic, while in others it is an alternative to general anesthesia.

Regional blocks wear off gradually and sensations such as touch, pressure, pain, and the ability to use voluntary muscles in the anesthetized area all return to normal at different speeds. The individual will usually experience a so-called pins and needles feeling before normal sensation completely returns.

GENERAL ANESTHESIA

General anesthetics are powerful drugs that temporarily depress brain function and result in a loss of consciousness. But general anesthetics do more than just make a person unconscious. They also produce insensibility to pain, prevent memory, and relax or paralyze voluntary muscles. During a general anesthetic the brain's ability to regulate essential functions such as breathing and body temperature is diminished. In addition to administering an anesthetic, the anesthetist monitors, supports, and (when necessary) controls, these vital functions.

While the initiation of general anesthesia is quick, it is a time when many critical tasks are performed. In adults, anesthetic drugs are usually injected into an intravenous line to put the patient to sleep, and then anesthetic vapor is inhaled through a breathing circuit. For infants and young children the anesthetic vapor is often inhaled first and an intravenous line started for additional drugs after the child is asleep.

Many surgeries benefit from relaxation of skeletal muscles. In these cases, drugs are administered that completely paralyze voluntary muscles. Such drugs make it impossible for patients to breathe on their own, but anesthetists are very skilled at ventilating patients during surgery. Paralysis is eliminated prior to the end of anesthesia either by allowing the drugs to wear off or by administering other drugs to counter their effects so that patients can breathe on their own. Awaking from general anesthesia occurs when anesthetic drugs are allowed to wear off. Anesthetists carefully control the anesthetic drugs given in order for the patient to emerge from general anesthesia at, but not before, the desired time. This takes experience and a detailed understanding of the drugs used and the patient's response to those drugs. Initially, awakening is quite quick, allowing the patient to respond to commands and to breathe without assistance. If, for reasons of health or type of surgical procedure, the patient must be left on a ventilator with a breathing tube in place, the anesthetist may take the patient to an intensive care unit asleep rather than awaking him or her from the anesthetic.

Recovering from General Anesthesia

Complete recovery from general anesthesia continues for some time after the patient wakes up. Patients commonly remain amnestic for minutes and sometimes hours after awaking from anesthesia. It often takes even longer for normal mental acuity to return, with some difficulty at complex mental tasks lasting several days. Inhaled anesthetics are primarily eliminated through the lungs. Small amounts of anesthetic gases are exhaled for hours to days.

OTHER SERVICES FURNISHED BY ANESTHESIA PROVIDERS

Life Support

In addition to giving anesthesia, anesthetists often provide emergency airway management throughout the hospital and establish circulatory access with arterial and intravenous lines. Anesthetists are very skilled at placing and using artificial airway devices and ventilating patients manually or with mechanical ventilators, as these tasks are performed during general anesthesia. When patients outside the operating suite experience breathing problems anesthesia is often called to establish an airway, especially if others have difficulty doing so.

Pain Management

Pain management is provided by physicians, surgeons, and anesthetists; many different ways of relieving pain exist. Most people are familiar with pills and injections that reduce pain, but for some, these methods are insufficient or are contraindicated by the patient's condition. Anesthetists have special skills in some areas of pain relief that are useful after surgery or in non-surgical patients; as a result, some physician anesthesiologists and nurse anesthetists specialize in pain management.

Patient controlled analgesia (PCA) allows patients to push a button that injects pain medicine into their intravenous line whenever they need it. The PCA pump is programmed to deliver a set dose when the patient pushes the button. A preset time interval must pass between each dose. Once the total dose given reaches the programmed limit the PCA pump will not give any more medicine until the next hour. Properly programmed, PCA allows the patient control over when pain medicine is received, which helps reduce the anxiety associated with pain. Patient controlled analgesia also results in better pain relief than intermittent intramuscular injections.

When a regional block is produced, whether it completely eliminates sensation and muscle tone from an area (anesthetic) or simply reduces pain sensation in that area (analgesia) depends upon the drug or combination of drugs used, dose, and strength. For this reason, regional blocks not only can be used for surgical anesthesia but also are ideal for some types of pain relief. One advantage of a regional anesthetic for surgery is that it need not end when the surgery ends; it can be used for pain relief afterwards in many cases. For example, the duration of pain relief following an epidural anesthetic can be extended by continuing to infuse pain medicine through the epidural catheter after surgery. Local anesthetics, either alone or combined with opioids, are commonly used for pain relief. When regional pain blocks affect the legs patients are usually confined to bed. Even dilute concentrations of local anesthetic affect leg muscle strength enough to increase the risk of falling.

When opioids are added to a spinal or epidural anesthetic they provide pain relief that persists after the anesthetic block has stopped working. Some opioids provide hours of postoperative pain relief when used in this way, often enough that patients can go straight to oral pain medications once the regional analgesia has worn off. Regional analgesia often provides better pain relief than either injections or PCA.

M. A. FIEDLER
University of Alabama

ANGELL, JAMES ROLAND (1867–1949)

James RolandAngell is best known as one of the founders of the functionalist school of psychology at the University of Chicago in the first quarter of the 20th century. He had studied with John Dewey at the University of Michigan, before Dewey came to Chicago as an early participant in the functionalist movement. Angell received the MA under William James at Harvard. He never received the PhD degree, although in the course of his career he was granted 23 honorary doctorates.

By the time Angell came to the University of Chicago, the grains of functionalism had been sown. He was appointed chairman of the psychology department, a position he held for 25 years until he left to become president of Yale. By the time Angell left Chicago, functionalism had become an extremely popular school of psychology.

In 1903 Angell published his first views on functional psychology in an article in the *Philosophical Review* attacking structuralism. The following year he published *Psychology: An Introductory Study of the Structure and Functions of Human Consciousness.* Extremely popular, the book went into a fourth edition by 1908. The book was somewhat eclectic, bringing together what was known about psychology at the time, but it did have a strong functionalist flavor. The introduction stated, "Mind seems to be the master device by means of which the adaptive operations of organic life may be made most perfect."

Angell's clearest exposition of the functionalist position was in his presidential address to the American Psychological Association in 1906, in which he stated the following points characterizing what functional psychology was all about.

1. Functional psychology is the study of mental operations as opposed to contents. The task of the functional psychologist is to discover how a mental process worked.

2. Functional psychology should be considered a study of the functional utilities of consciousness. The adaptation of mental functions to environmental demands enables an organism to survive.

3. Functional psychology is concerned with the entire psychophysical relationship between the organs of the body and the environment. There is a constant interaction between mind and body.

R. W. LUNDIN
Wheaton, Illinois

ANHEDONIA

The term "anhedonia," as its Greek roots indicate, refers to the absence of hedonism, or a lack of desire to experience pleasure and avoid pain. Coined in 1896 by Theodule Ribot to refer to the absence of emotion in patients with hepatic disease, anhedonia was equated with a type of pathological depression or melancholy by William James (1902), who believed that it was on a continuum with anguish but was less serious. Nevertheless, the concept of anhedonia was given little further attention in the medical or psychological literature.

Bleuler (1911/1950) observed that the disappearance of affect signaled the onset of dementia praecox or schizophrenia, and Rado (1957) specified that the affect in question was a diminished capacity for pleasure. Meehl (1962) provided a name for the phenomenon by resurrecting the term "anhedonia" and proposed that measures for it be developed to identify persons at risk for schizophrenia.

In line with Meehl's proposal, Chapman, Chapman, and Rawlin (1976) published three true-false scales to measure physical and social anhedonia and to indicate psychosis-proneness: the Physical Anhedonia Scale, the Perceptual Aberration Scale, and the Nonconformity Scale. Items in the scales had been selected from a large pool of rationally developed statements, according to how well they discriminated between hospitalized schizophrenic and nonschizophrenic patients in regard to levels of anhedonia. Norms were obtained for gender, age, and social groups among university undergraduates; persons whose scores were 2 standard deviations (SD) above the mean were considered to be at higher than normal risk for the development of psychosis.

Scores on the physical and social anhedonia scales have been found to be positively correlated with each other and negatively correlated with scores for social competence (Haberman, 1979), social desirability, sensation seeking (McCann, Mueller, Hayes, Sheeuer. & Marsala, 1990), and effective coping behaviors (Scheuer et al., in progress), among others. They have also been significantly correlated with several patterns of MMPI subscale scores (Penck, Carpenter, & Rylee, 1979). However, some studies have not found a relationship between anhedonia levels and responses to specific emotion-provoking stimuli (Berenbaum & Thornton, 1986) and have suggested that anhedonia is not a consistent sign of schizophrenia, but a consequence of mental disturbance, poor status, and low educational levels (Schuck, Leventhal, Rothstein, & Izizarry, 1984).

Longitudinal studies to address the basic question of whether high anhedonia scores reliably predict psychosis remain to be done. Ethical as well as practical questions about obtaining and using such scores, and particularly any potentially harmful effects of such use, also remain to be asked and answered. Norms for anhedonia levels in various ethnocultural groups also need to be obtained; in fact, normal differences already have been observed among Caucasian and Asian-American groups.

Overall, the relationship of anhedonia and psychosis appears to be clinically significant but insufficiently researched; it has diagnostic value but, at present, uncertain predictive value, and unexplored preventive or therapeutic value.

Although anhedonia has been of interest mainly as a possible predictor of schizophrenia, it was early observed in other disorders, both physical and psychological, and deficits in the ability to experience pleasure are recognized as parts of syndromes ranging from dementia to posttraumatic stress disorder. Anhedonia is not considered to be a disorder in itself but only a symptom of disorder, and, in fact, the term has not yet appeared in either most professional manuals or standard dictionaries. Its usefulness as a concept, however, has become apparent.

REFERENCES

Bleuler, E. (1950). *Dementia praecox: Or the group of schizophrenias* (J. Zinkin, Trans.). New York: International Universities Press. (Original work published 1911)

Chapman, L. J., Chapman, J. P., & Rawlin, M. L. (1976). Scales for physical and social anhedonia. *Journal of Abnormal Psychology, 85,* 374–382.

McCann, S. C., Mueller, C. W., Hays, P. A., Shceuer, A. D., & Marsella, A. J. (1990). Scales for physical and social anhedonia. *Journal of Abnormal Psychology, 85,* 374–382.

Meehl, P. E. (1962). Schizotaxia, schizotypy, schizophrenia. *American Psychologist, 17,* 827–838.

Penck, W. E., Carpenter, J. C., & Rylee, K. E. (1979). MMPI correlates of social and physical anhedonia. *Journal of Counseling Psychology, 47,* 1046–1052.

Rado, S. (1957). *Psychoanalysis of behavior: Collected papers.* New York: Grune & Stratton.

Ribot, T. (1896). *La psychologie des sentiments.* Paris: Alcan.

Schuck, J. R., Leventhal, D., Rothstein, H., & Izizarry, V. (1984). Physical anhedonia and schizophrenia. *Journal of Abnormal Psychology, 93(3),* 342–344.

A. D. Scheuer
University of Hawaii

DEPRESSION
EMOTIONS
HOPELESSNESS
PERSONALITY ASSESSMENT
PERSONALITY TYPES
SCHIZOPHRENIA

ANIMAL COMMUNICATION

Animal communication has occurred when one animal has been shown to influence the behavior of another. The kinds of influence generally subsumed under the category of communication are those mediated via the sense organs of the animal receiving the signal. A situation wherein one animal responds to another's call is an instance of communication, whereas an animal altering another's behavior by injuring it would not be regarded as having communicated.

COMMUNICATION SYSTEMS

A communication system entails the interaction of several elements. There must first be a *signal*—generally some behavioral pattern emitted by an organism that is the *sender.* Signals are emitted in varying *contexts,* and the significance of the signal can vary with the context in which it is emitted. Signals travel in various *channels,* such as a vocal-auditory channel, and must be discriminated from the other *noise,* or irrelevant background activity, in that channel. The signal must reach another animal, the *receiver,* whose behavior is altered. The sender and receiver can be said to share a *code,* which includes the complete set of all possible signals.

Sensory Modalities

Communication can occur in any sensory modality to which the organisms are responsive. Fireflies provide an excellent example of communication in a visual channel. They are active at night, with females generally remaining on the ground and males flying about. Flying males emit flashes of a color, intensity, frequency of occurrence, and duration that are characteristic of the species. Females answer in a similarly specific manner after a latency dependent on the species and temperature. Gradually, the male hones in on the female's signal and pairing takes place (Lloyd, 1966). Many of the courtship and aggressive displays of birds, which have been much studied by ethologists, function primarily in the visual modality.

Perhaps the best-known signals in the auditory modality are the songs of birds and the calls of such animals as frogs and crickets. Perhaps the most dramatic signals are those of humpback whales (Payne & McVay, 1971). The elements constituting these songs last between 7 and 30 minutes before they are repeated. These signals can be transmitted for many miles in the oceanic sound channel.

Tactile signals require close proximity but are common in social species such as many primates. Chimpanzees, for example, convey relatively subtle messages via their sense of touch. Many other species utilize tactile signals during courtship and copulation to achieve appropriate timing and orientation of the events surrounding reproduction.

Chemical signals are quite important in many species, especially mammals and insects, but are less generally recognized. *Pheromones* are chemical signals that function within species and *allomones* communicate among species, as between prey and predator. *Hormones* mediate chemical communication within an organism. There are many examples of important mammalian social odors (Brown, 1979). The rate at which mice reach puberty is affected by the presence of pheromones; in general, pheromones from animals of the same sex retard, and those from the opposite sex accelerate, the appearance of puberty. A female mouse that has mated with one male will display a blockage of pregnancy, or Bruce effect, if exposed to a strange male or the odor of a strange male a couple of days later. Female rats emit a maternal pheromone that aids young pups in finding them (Leon, 1974). The estrous cycles of female rats housed near each other tend to become synchronized; a similar menstrual synchrony has been found in humans (Graham & McGrew, 1980).

Other communication channels are used by specialized species. The ultrasonic systems of bats and dolphins are well-known. Some species of fishes use an electrical system both to locate objects and to communicate (Hopkins, 1980).

Different modalities have particular advantages for communicative signals. Chemical signals, for example, are slow to fade, move around corners, can be used at night, and are useful at long range. However, their rates of transmission are slow and they are difficult to localize. Auditory and visual signals travel much faster and are more easily localizable. Auditory signals are much more effective at night and in the presence of barriers, such as trees, than are visual signals.

Significant Examples

Perhaps the most famous example of naturally occurring animal communication is the so-called dance language of honeybees (von Frisch, 1950) Foraging bees that have located a rich food source return to the hive and communicate the location of the food sources to their hive mates. If the food is less than 100 meters away a simple round dance is used. To communicate longer distances, a waggle dance is utilized. The waggle is performed on a vertical surface and assumes a pattern that approximates a figure 8. Between the two loops of the 8 is a straight run that communicates much. The duration of the straight run correlates with the distance of the food source. The direction of the straight run, relative to gravity, indicates the direction to the food source, relative to the sun. Thus the forager performs a straight run oriented straight up when the receiver is to fly directly toward the sun, and straight down when the food source is in the opposite direction. Like many communication systems, the honeybee language is multimodal, with visual, tactile, auditory, and chemical aspects. Although the communication value of the dance aspect has been questioned, it does appear to be highly specific under many circumstances (Gould, 1976).

Perhaps the most publicized examples of animal communication in psychology are studies of language in chimpanzees. Early researchers met with limited success when attempting to condition chimps to vocalize. More recently, however, several researchers have trained animals to use rather complicated communication systems by relying on gestures and operant responses. Gardner and Gardner (1969) employed American Sign Language, the system used by many deaf humans, and succeeded in establishing a complex signal repertoire. The chimp, Washoe, could both send and receive an impressive catalogue of such signals. Premack and Premack (1972) taught their chimp, Sarah, to position plastic symbols in particular order so as to convey messages. Rumbaugh and Gill (1976) used a computerized system with Lana, who had to depress a set of operant response keys in the appropriate order as part of her language system. The extent to which these systems represent true language, and especially the use of grammatical rules, remains quite controversial (Marx, 1980; Terrace, 1979).

EVOLUTION

The evolution of communicative systems has been elaborated through comparative research. Evolutionarily, signals can originate in any of a variety of behavioral patterns, such as the incipient movements an animal makes when about to attack, or displacement activities, the out-of-context behaviors often occurring in situations of conflict. Over many generations, signals tend to become ritualized in ways that permit the signal to function in a relatively clear and unambiguous manner. The motivational context of the signal may change over evolutionary time; often, conspicuous structures such as color patches evolve along with the behavioral aspects of a signal.

Classically, communication has been interpreted as a mutual sharing of information that functions for the good of the species.

In more recent theorizing, however, it is proposed that each individual is selected to maximize a personal level of inclusive fitness. Communication, then, may be viewed as an effort on the part of the sender to manipulate the behavior of the receiver for the sender's own advantage. Receivers, for their part, will be selected to disregard signals whose influence would be harmful to them (Dawkins & Krebs, 1978). In this context, one might expect senders to be favored if they can avoid transmitting certain kinds of information about their probable behavior in conflict situations. Indeed, it might even be advantageous to transmit false information in an effort to manipulate the behavior of the other organism to one's own advantage. Rather than viewing communication as a system evolved through cooperation, many workers now believe that it reflects a compromise between selective pressures acting on both sender and receiver, and that both engage in a game through which the system can be used to their own advantages.

REFERENCES

Brown, R. E. (1979). Mammalian social odors: A critical review. *Advances in the Study of Behavior, 10,* 103–162.

Dawkins, R., & Krebs, J. R. (1978). Animal signals: Information or manipulation? In J. R. Krebs & N. B. Davies (Eds.), *Behavioral ecology: An evolutionary approach.* Sunderland, MA: Sinauer.

Gardner, R. A., & Gardner, B. T. (1969). Teaching sign language to a chimpanzee. *Science, 165,* 664–672.

Gould, J. L. (1976). The honey bee dance—Language controversy. *Quarterly Review of Biology, 51,* 211–244.

Graham, C. A., & McGrew, W. C. (1980). Menstrual synchrony in female undergraduates living on a coeducational campus. *Psychoneuroendocrinology, 5,* 245–252.

Hopkins, C. D. (1980). Evolution of electric communication channels of mormyrids. *Behavioral Ecology and Sociobiology, 7,* 1–13.

Leon, M. (1974). Maternal pheromone. *Physiology and Behavior, 13,* 441–453.

Lloyd, J. E. (1966). Studies on the flash communication system in *Photinus* fireflies. *Publications of the Museum of Zoology, University of Michigan, 130,* 1–95.

Marx, J. L. (1980). Ape-language controversy flares up. *Science, 207,* 1330–1333.

Payne, R. S., & McVay, S. (1971). Songs of humpback whales. *Science, 173,* 587–597.

Premack, A. J., & Premack, D. (1972). Teaching language to an ape. *Scientific American, 227*(4), 92–99.

Rumbaugh, D. M., & Gill, T. V. (1976). Language and the acquisition of language-type skills by a chimpanzee (Pan). *Annals of the New York Academy of Sciences, 270,* 90–123.

Terrace, H. S. (1979). *Nim: A chimpanzee who learned sign language.* New York: Knopf.

von Frisch, K. (1950). *Bees: Their vision, chemical senses, and language.* Ithaca, NY: Cornell University Press.

SUGGESTED READING

Sebeok, T. A. (Ed.). (1977). *How animals communicate.* Bloomington, IN: Indiana University Press.

Smith, W. J. (1977). *The behavior of communicating.* Cambridge, MA: Harvard University Press.

D. A. Dewsbury
University of Florida

COMMUNICATION PROCESSES
ETHOLOGY

ANIMAL MODELS

When one studies animals as analogues to humans, one is said to be using an "animal model." Models are basic and powerful tools in biological and behavioral sciences, which explains in part why so much research aimed at understanding human physiology, brain, and behavior is actually done with animals. The key word for understanding models is "analogy." Use of a model is not a claim of identity with that being modeled. Rather, a model is a convergent set of analogies between the real world phenomenon and the system that is being studied as a model for that phenomenon. Animal models are widely used in psychology: (a) as a conceptual framework to recognize new relationships and interactions among the environment, central nervous system, and behavior; (b) to generate and test hypotheses for understanding environment, brain, and behavior interrelations; and (c) to study these interrelations under simpler and more controlled conditions than can be achieved in research with humans. Animal models often allow for the discovery of causal relations not possible in research on humans.

Animal models have a long and distinguished history in studies of both normal and abnormal behavior. However, while other life sciences (e.g., anatomy, physiology, and pharmacology) broadly accept both the homological and analogical bases for the use of animal models, some critics—often with little grounding in biological science—occasionally deride animal models in psychology as tools for understanding human behavior. This schism parallels the divide between the mechanistic and humanistic traditions, and between the theory of evolution of Charles Darwin and the theory of psychophysical dualism between body and mind of René Descartes. Evolutionary theory projects a continuity of morphology, physiology, and the emergent emotions and "mind" from animals to humans.

At the more biological end of the continuum of behavioral neuroscience and psychological research and application, the use of animal models finds general acceptance and is largely non-controversial. This research includes that on neural mechanisms of motivation, emotion, learning, perception, and even memory and its dysfunction in aging, drug dependency, and addiction, as well as psychopharmacology. Animal models are an established, integral component of the process of understanding in these areas. Animal models (and evolutionary analyses) more controversially have been and continue to be extended with some success into the behavioral neuroscience of problem solving and thinking, social interactions and cultural structures, and even psychiatry (Stevens & Price, 1996).

Animal models exist at many levels: some do not even involve the whole organism, and those that do range from simple invertebrates to closely related mammalian species. Yet each has yielded lasting and important understanding of basic processes common to all animals, including humans. Studies of neuron transmission in the giant squid axon form a cornerstone of our knowledge of the central nervous system in higher organisms. At the neural network level, studies of multicellular interactive increases in sensitivity, called "long-term potentiation," in a slice of tissue from the hippocampus of rats has led to new insights into the molecular and neurophysiological bases of learning. At the level of whole non-mammalian organisms, experiments on learning and memory in mollusks have yielded some understanding at the molecular, neurochemical, and neural network interaction levels of the differences between non-associative and associative learning (Madden, 1991).

Animal modeling continues to reveal biological bases of complex behavioral traits through genetic analyses of behavior. For example, the use of mice in selective breeding, the molecular transfer of genes, or the "knockout" of genes, has demonstrated that different complex behavioral and social traits—for example, aggression or coping with challenges—reflect inheritable differences in biobehavioral strategies for adapting to environmental demands. These kinds of behavioral differences are paralleled by differences among the animals' brains (e.g., sensitivity to the dopamine agonist apomorphine) and physiology (e.g., adrenal gland output) (Koolhaas et al., 1999). Such animal models indicate likely biological bases for complex human behaviors and help us to make educated guesses as to which traits in humans we should analyze from a behavior-genetic perspective. The Minnesota Twin Studies have confirmed in identical twins reared apart that genetic factors even contribute significantly to global factors and traits, such as personality (Waller, Kojetin, Bouchard, Lykken, & Tellegen, 1990).

Animal models have also provided understanding of psychosomatic disorders and disease vulnerability. For example, animal studies definitely established the associations among genetics, psychological stress, behavioral coping, long-term physiological changes, and gastrointestinal pathology that are analogues to the suspected causal mechanisms for ulcer diseases in humans (Weiner, 1991). More recently, the use of animal models has provided a solid scientific basis for the whole new field of psychoneuroimmunology—the study of the interplay among psychological state, immunity, and illness. For example, despite a significant number of anecdotes, genuine links between psychological state, immunity, and cancer were fiercely opposed by the medical establishment until the publication of numerous controlled studies that used animal models in which behavioral stress was directly observed to modulate immunocompetence and the progress of the tumor (Newberry, Gordon, & Meehan, 1991).

Animal modeling becomes more difficult and more controversial as it attempts to address behavioral issues in psychopathology (Mineka & Zinbarg, 1991). Animal models promise an understanding of psychopathology not as bizarre distortions of behavior, but rather, as the consequence of lawful psychological processes whose principles and mechanisms may be elucidated scientifically. Ivan Pavlov was the first to argue that experimentally-induced behavioral dysfunction in animals might teach us about human dysfunction. In appetitive classical conditioning experiments with dogs, he observed that requiring a dog to learn a series of increasingly difficult discriminations between a circle and an ellipse resulted in its behavior's finally becoming so agitated and erratic that the dysfunction was designated *experimental neurosis.* In subsequent research with children challenged in an analogous auditory discrimination task, the children too became erratic and distressed. More importantly, Pavlov and his associates found bromide salts to be an effective therapy, modeled first in the dogs and then applied in the children. Two of Pavlov's American students, Horsley Gantt and Howard Liddell, continued this line of research with animals in an attempt to define the potential for the emotional hazards to animals and humans that might arise "accidentally" in the course of normal learning experiences, and the principles that underlie this potential.

These observations by Pavlov and his students that maladaptive behavior patterns in animals could be conditioned (i.e., learned) and that they were analogous to human neuroses inspired others to explore new forms of psychopathology based in animal research; for example rats faced with unsolvable problems developed behavioral fixations that model compulsivity, while punishment of cats' consummatory behavior resulted in persistent fears analogous to phobic neuroses that were treatable by a forced extinction procedure. This second result proved particularly seminal for contemporary clinical psychologists, because it prompted Joseph Wolpe (1958) to perform experiments with cats from which were derived the principles for *reciprocal inhibition* therapy for phobias so widely used today with human patients. This example clearly demonstrates the heuristic, hypothesis-generating, and applied value of animal models in contemporary psychopathology research. Furthermore, Wolpe's work encouraged others to pursue the study of animal models that have proved useful in understanding the dynamics of other kinds of applied issues.

Some scientists have proposed the essential features that animal models of human psychopathology should strive toward: There should be a similarity of symptoms, essential causes and cures, and underlying physiology, as well as a specificity to the particular disorder. However, it should be clear that these criteria are impossible to fulfill; they reflect an ideal, rather than a prerequisite.

Numerous models of human psychopathologies, some more complete and useful than others, have been developed. Perhaps well-known to the general reader is Harry Harlow's modeling of the effects of maternal separation, using non-human primates, and the resulting recognition of important differences between the nutritional and the stress-buffering/comforting functions fulfilled by a mother—the latter being most critical. The dramatic consequences of maternal separation for the young primate (loss of appetite, social withdrawal, and later on, impaired social and parental behavior) were likened to the psychopathological effects of neglect in institutionalized human infants (i.e., anaclitic depression; Spitz & Wolf, 1946). This model of depression (Suomi, Mineka, & Harlow, 1983) is critical to our understanding, from a behavioral neuroscience perspective, of the psychological problems of orphans or neglected children raised in unstimulating environments. Later studies discovered that the mechanisms of this changed behavior lie in changed neuroendocrine system (hypothalamic-pituitary-adrenal axis and ornithine decarboxylase-pituitary axis) responsivity of young non-human primates and even of young rats separated from their mothers (Kuhn & Schanberg, 1998). In addition to obvious social interventions that are suggested by this research on animal models, behavioral therapeutic interventions with premature babies to provide extra tactile comforting has been applied and proved effective in speeding the discharge of the infants from the hospital.

The influential learned helplessness model of depression (Miller, Rosellini, & Seligman, 1977), based on behavioral research with dogs, has been seminal both in understanding the etiology of some forms of depression and to the development of therapeutic strategies. The model has stimulated: (a) active hypothesis testing about depression; (b) studies of the neurochemistry of depression; and (c) behavioral screening for therapeutic drugs. Study of animal models of depression has demonstrated that behavioral manipulation of the organism changes the brain's neurochemistry. It is a common misunderstanding that psychobiologists focus their work on animal models because they believe that the root of human psychopathology is biological. As exemplified by the learned helplessness model, the comparative psychologist might start with a non-physiological, environmental-behavioral manipulation that induces a set of behavioral and physiological symptoms with similarities to the human condition to be modeled; these same symptoms also will have behavioral (and mental) consequences, which in turn have additional neurochemical consequences (Weiss, 1991). That is, contemporary animal models make clear that neuroscience and behavior are not in a linear chain from one to the other but are in a continuously interdependent, interacting circle.

Other areas of human psychopathology have not been so readily modeled in animals—for example, schizophrenia. Part of the problem in this case is the plethora of human symptoms, each imperfectly associated with schizophrenia, and a lack of agreement about what should be focused upon in the initial analogy. Moreover, in schizophrenia, some of the most important diagnostic criteria relate to verbal behaviors—something for which there is no easy analogue in animal behavior.

An area of special promise for employing animal models is the understanding of aging and its commonly associated dementias, in which neurophysiological changes have far-reaching and devastating psychological effects. At present, the nature of senile dementias is not understood from the behavioral, physiological, neuroscience, or cognitive perspectives. Animal models can contribute to knowledge in all these, including the determination (and reduction) of the risk factors, and the fundamental nature of expressed disability. Certainly there have been imminent breakthroughs in selected aging-related dysfunctions, such as Korsakoff's disease, in the neurological, cognitive, and behavior therapeutic analyses and their interplay (Overmier, Savage, & Sweeney, 1999).

Biobehavioral dysfunctions, psychiatric disorders, and neurological diseases must continue to be studied to bring relief to literally tens of millions of sufferers; and until some significant grasp is made on the processes involved, scientists are deterred from certain classes of research with human subjects and patient populations, such as experimenting with etiologies or with therapies that involve not-yet-understood physiological changes. Animal research can help, because such a grasp is to be gained only through the use of living organisms. It is particularly surprising that animal models should today be the focus of intellectual hostility in a society for which psychological problems and mental disorders pose such a large threat to human well-being, and for which history provides so much evidence of the scientific power and success through the use of animal models.

There are, of course, ethical considerations in the use of animals for research. The species employed must be chosen with care and knowledge of its basic physiology; the numbers of animals necessary for a successful experimental test should be carefully determined; and the research should be performed strictly within the guidelines laid down by legal authorities and prior peer review. Scientists are obligated to demonstrate that the modeling processes are understood and that the analogies in the model developed are sound. Such models may necessarily involve the induction of distress; after all, physical and/or emotional distress are involved in the etiology of many common forms of human dysfunction.

Despite the conceptual, scientific, and societal challenges associated with the use of animal models, the demand for advances in physiology, neuroscience, and psychology necessitate that animal models continue to be used.

REFERENCES

Bond, N. W. (Ed.). (1984). *Animal models in psychopathology.* Sydney, Australia: Academic Press.

Davey, G. (Ed.). (1983). *Applications of conditioning theory.* London: Methuen.

Kuhn, C. M., & Schanberg, S. M. (1998). Responses to maternal separation: Mechanisms and mediators. *International Journal of Developmental Neuroscience, 16,* 261–270.

Miller, W. R., Rosellini, R. A., & Seligman, M. E. P. (1977). Learned helplessness and depression. In J. D. Maser & M. E. P. Seligman (Eds.), *Psychopathology: Experimental models* (pp. 104–139). San Francisco: W. H. Freeman and Company.

Newberry, B. H., Gordon, T. L., & Meehan, S. M. (1991). Animal studies of stress and cancer. In C. L. Cooper & M. Watson (Eds.), *Cancer and stress* (pp. 27–43). Chichester, England: Wiley.

Overmier, J. B., Savage, L. M., & Sweeney, W. A. (1999). Behavioral and pharmacological analyses of memory offer new behavioral options for remediation. In M. Haug & R. Whalen (Eds.), *Animal models of human emotion and cognition.* (pp. 231–245). Washington, DC: American Psychological Association.

Panksepp, J. (1998). *Affective neuroscience: The foundations of human and animal emotions.* New York: Oxford University Press.

Spitz, R. A., & Wolf, K. M. (1946). Anaclitic depression: An enquiry into the genesis of psychiatric conditions in early childhood, II. *Psychoanalytic Study of the Child, 2,* 313–342.

Suomi, S. J., Mineka, S., & Harlow, H. F. (1983). Social separation in monkeys as viewed by several motivational perspectives. In

E. Satinoff & P. Teitelbaum (Eds.), *Handbook of behavioral neurobiology: Vol. 6. Motivation* (pp. 543–584). New York: Plenum Press.

Waller, N. G., Kojetin, B. A., Bouchard, T. J., Lykken, D., & Tellegen, A. (1990). Genetic and environmental influences on religious interests, attitudes, and values: A study of twins reared apart and together. *Psychological Science, 1,* 138–142.

Weiner, H. (1991). From simplicity to complexity (1950–1990): The case of peptic ulceration: I. Human studies. *Psychosomatic Medicine, 53,* 467–490.

Weiss, J. M. (1991). Stress-induced depression: Critical neurochemical and electrophysiological changes. In J. Madden IV (Ed.), *Neurobiology of learning, emotion and affect* (pp. 123–154). New York: Raven Press.

Wolpe, J. (1958). *Psychotherapy by reciprocal inhibition.* Stanford, CA: Stanford University Press.

SUGGESTED READING

Bond, N. W. (Ed.). (1984). *Animal models in psychopathology.* Sydney, Australia: Academic Press.

Davey, G. (Ed.). (1983). *Applications of conditioning theory.* London: Methuen.

Hanin, I., & Usdin, E. (Eds.). (1977). *Animal models in psychiatry and neurology* (pp. 17–26). Oxford, England: Pergamon.

Haug, M., & Whalen, R. E. (Eds.). (1999). *Animal models of human emotion and cognition.* Washington, DC: American Psychological Association.

Koolhaas, J. M., Korte, S. M., De Boer, S. F., Van Der Vegt, B. J., Van Reenen, C. G., Hopster, H., De Jong, I. C., Ruis, M. A., & Blokhuis, H. J. (1999). Coping styles in animals: Current status in behavior and stress-physiology. *Neuroscience & Biobehavioral Reviews, 23,* 925–35.

Madden, J., IV. (Ed.). (1991). *Neurobiology of learning, emotion and affect* (pp. 3–28). New York: Raven Press.

Mineka, S., & Zinbarg, R. (1991). Animal models of psychopathology. In C. E. Walker (Ed.), *Clinical psychology: Historical and research foundations* (pp. 51–86). New York: Plenum Press.

Panksepp, J. (1998). *Affective neuroscience: The foundations of human and animal emotions.* New York: Oxford University Press.

Stevens, A., & Price, J. (1996). *Evolutionary psychiatry: A new beginning.* London: Routledge.

J. B. OVERMIER
R. MURISON
*Deptartment of Biological & Medical Psychology,
University of Bergen, Norway*

NEURAL NETWORK MODELS
PERCEPTUAL ORGANIZATIONS
PSYCHOPHARMACOLOGY
RESEARCH METHODOLOGY

ANOMIC APHASIA

The inability to retrieve particular words denoting things such as concrete entities (named by nouns), actions (named by verbs), or spatial relationships (named by prepositions) is termed "anomia." Anomia is a frequent part of the symptom complex that characterizes patients with aphasia (Goodglass & Wingfield, 1997; Tranel & Anderson, 1999), the latter referring to disturbances of the comprehension and formulation of verbal messages caused by acquired damage to language-related brain structures (typically in the left hemisphere). In some patients, however, anomia occurs as an isolated manifestation of acquired brain dysfunction, and in this situation, the designation of "anomic aphasia" applies.

It is important to clarify that the ability to retrieve a particular word to designate an entity or event is different from the ability to retrieve conceptual knowledge regarding that entity or event (Pulvermuller, 1999; Tranel & Damasio, 1999). That is, there is a distinction between knowing what something is (recognition) and knowing its name (naming). In anomic aphasia, patients have lost the ability to retrieve names of things, but they do not have problems recognizing things. The patients can generate descriptions that indicate that they have normal knowledge of what things are (sometimes referred to as semantics), even if the patients cannot name those items. For example, when shown a picture of a camel, a patient may say, "That is an animal that has humps on its back, lives in the desert, and can go for a long time without water." Or when shown a picture of Bill Clinton, the patient may say, "That guy was a president, had an affair, had a southern accent." Such descriptions indicate that retrieval of conceptual knowledge is intact in the patient, even if naming is severely impaired. Incidentally, this phenomenon also occurs in the realm of normal experience, particularly under conditions of fatigue, distraction, or in connection with normal aging; that is, normal individuals may experience the inability to retrieve a particular name (especially proper names) even though they know perfectly well what it is that they are attempting to name.

In principle, anomia can occur in connection with any sensory modality—for example, when attempting to name a picture of something, to name a sound, to name a smell, or to name something that is felt by the hand. Also, anomia can occur in the course of verbal discourse, as when one is speaking and suddenly cannot retrieve the name for a particular concept that is part of the intended sentential expression. The overwhelming majority of scientific inquiries into the phenomenon of anomia, however, have focused on the visual modality, and have used paradigms in which subjects are presented pictures (or actual objects) and asked to name them (cf. Goodglass & Wingfield, 1997). This format, known as visual confrontation naming, is also the standard paradigm for assessing naming in patients with aphasia. As a consequence, most of our current knowledge regarding the neural correlates of word retrieval, and most extant theoretical accounts of this process, are heavily tied to the visual modality.

Most of the classic aphasia syndromes, including Broca's (nonfluent) and Wernicke's (fluent) aphasia, are associated with brain damage in the vicinity of the sylvian fissure in the left hemisphere (the left hemisphere being dominant for language in the vast majority [about 98%] of right-handed individuals and in the majority [about 70%] of left-handed individuals). Anomic aphasia, by contrast, is associated primarily with damage to structures outside the classic language regions, although still in the left hemisphere (Tranel & Anderson, 1999). Specifically, anomic aphasia is most often caused by damage to the left anterior temporal lobe, to the inferior and lateral aspect of the left temporal lobe, or to the left occipitotemporal junction. Careful studies of patients with anomic aphasia, using modern neuroanatomical and neuropsychological techniques, have revealed a number of intriguing associations between specific brain structures and specific types of naming impairment (Damasio & Tranel, 1993; Damasio, Grabowski, Tranel, Hichwa, & Damasio, 1996; Tranel, Damasio, & Damasio, 1997). Recently, studies using functional neuroimaging procedures (positron emission tomography, functional magnetic resonance imaging) have corroborated several of these findings (Damasio et al., 1996; Martin, Wiggs, Ungerleider, & Haxby, 1996).

The neuropsychological evidence from the studies adduced above has indicated that retrieval of proper nouns—that is, names denoting unique entities such as persons and places—is associated with the anterior left temporal lobe, the region known as the temporal pole. Immediately behind the temporal pole, in the inferior and lateral aspect of the temporal lobe, is a region that has been associated with the retrieval of names for animals. And further back, in the vicinity of the temporal-occipital junction, is a region that has been associated with the retrieval of names for tools and utensils. These associations may appear arbitrary or even bizarre, but there are principled accounts of why the human brain may be organized in such a fashion (Damasio & Damasio, 1994; Damasio et al., 1996; Gordon, 1997; Humphreys, Riddoch, & Price, 1997; Pulvermuller, 1999; Tranel, Damasio, & Damasio, 1997). For example, it has been suggested that factors such as whether an entity is unique (e.g., Tom Hanks) or non-unique (e.g., a screwdriver), whether it is living (e.g., a pig) or nonliving (e.g., a hammer), whether it is manipulable (e.g., a wrench) or non-manipulable (e.g., a giraffe), or whether it makes a distinctive sound (e.g., a rooster) or not (e.g., a thimble), are important in determining which neural structures will be used in the mapping and retrieval of knowledge for entities, including their names (Tranel, Logan, Frank, & Damasio, 1997).

Another intriguing dissociation involves the distinction between words for concrete entities (nouns) versus words for actions (verbs). There is consistent evidence, from both the lesion and functional imaging studies adduced previously, indicating that different brain regions are important for these different grammatical categories of words. Specifically, the retrieval of nouns has been related to structures in the left inferior temporal lobe and the left occipitotemporal junction, whereas the retrieval of verbs has been related to structures in the left premotor/prefrontal region (in front of the Rolandic sulcus). Again, this dissociation may appear rather curious on the surface, but there are compelling explanations of why the brain has organized knowledge in different regions to subserve words from different grammatical categories (Damasio & Tranel, 1993; Kemmerer & Tranel, in press).

Pure forms of anomic aphasia—that is, severe naming impairments unaccompanied by other speech or linguistic deficits—are relatively rare, occurring far less frequently than most of the classic aphasia syndromes (Tranel & Anderson, 1999). Nonetheless, patients with anomic aphasia have afforded a unique opportunity to learn how the brain subserves the process of word retrieval, and how different brain structures are specialized for retrieval of different classes of words. Thus, while anomic aphasia remains important as a clinical disorder, its prepotent interest lies in the realm of scientific study of the way the human brain operates language processes. This, in turn, can help inform rehabilitation efforts aimed at patients with acquired disturbances of naming.

REFERENCES

Damasio, A. R., & Damasio, H. (1994). Cortical systems for retrieval of concrete knowledge: The convergence zone framework. In C. Koch (Ed.), *Large-scale neuronal theories of the brain* (pp. 61–74). Cambridge, MA: MIT Press.

Damasio, A. R., & Tranel, D. (1993). Nouns and verbs are retrieved with differently distributed neural systems. *Proceedings of the National Academy of Sciences, 90,* 4957–4960.

Damasio, H., Grabowski, T. J., Tranel, D., Hichwa, R., & Damasio, A. (1996). A neural basis for lexical retrieval. *Nature, 380,* 499–505.

Goodglass, H., & Wingfield, A. (Eds.). (1997). *Anomia: Neuroanatomical and cognitive correlates.* New York: Academic Press.

Gordon, B. (1997). Models of naming. In H. Goodglass & A. Wingfield (Eds.), *Anomia: Neuroanatomical and cognitive correlates* (pp. 31–64). New York: Academic Press.

Humphreys, G. W., Riddoch, M. J., & Price, C. J. (1997). Top-down processes in object identification: Evidence from experimental psychology, neuropsychology and functional anatomy. *Philosophical Transactions of the Royal Society of London B, 352,* 1275–1282.

Kemmerer, D., & Tranel, D. (in press). Verb retrieval in brain-damaged subjects: I. Analysis of stimulus, lexical, and conceptual factors. *Brain and Language.*

Martin, A., Wiggs, C. L., Ungerleider, L. G., & Haxby, J. V. (1996). Neural correlates of category-specific knowledge. *Nature, 379,* 649–652.

Pulvermuller, F. (1999). Words in the brain's language. *Behavioral and Brain Sciences, 22,* 253–336.

Tranel, D., & Anderson, S. (1999). Syndromes of aphasia. In F. Fabbro (Ed.), *Concise encyclopedia of language pathology* (pp. 305–319). Oxford, England: Elsevier Science Limited.

Tranel, D., & Damasio, A. R. (1999). The neurobiology of knowledge retrieval. *Behavioral and Brain Sciences, 22,* 303.

Tranel, D., Damasio, H., & Damasio, A. R. (1997). On the neurology of naming. In H. Goodglass & A. Wingfield (Eds.), *Anomia: Neuroanatomical and cognitive correlates* (pp. 65–90). New York: Academic Press.

Tranel, D., Logan, C. G., Frank, R. J., & Damasio, A. R. (1997). Explaining category-related effects in the retrieval of conceptual and lexical knowledge for concrete entities: Operationalization and analysis of factors. *Neuropsychologia, 35,* 1329–1339.

D. Tranel
University of Iowa

APHASIA
BRAIN INJURIES

ANOREXIA NERVOSA

DEFINITION AND CLINICAL DESCRIPTIONS

The disorder of anorexia nervosa (AN) is defined by four major criteria:

1. Refusal to maintain body weight at a normal minimum for age and height.
2. An intense fear of gaining weight. This fear, present even when the patient is in an emaciated condition, may be denied, but it is demonstrated by an intense preoccupation with thoughts of food, irrational worries about gaining weight, and rigorous exercising programs with severe restriction of total food intake in order to prevent weight gain.
3. A disturbance of body conceptualization. Parts of the body such as the thighs and abdomen are experienced as being excessively large, and the evaluation of the self is mainly in terms of body weight and shape. Finally, the denial of illness and the underweight condition are hallmark symptoms of this disorder.
4. Amenorrhea or cessation of menstrual cycles.

There are two subtypes of AN: the restrictor type (AN-R) and the binge-purge type (AN-BP). The restrictors lose weight by restricting food intake and exercising; the binge-purge type engage in binge eating and in purging behavior, such as self-induced vomiting, laxative abuse, and diuretic abuse.

Impulsive behaviors, including stealing, drug abuse, suicide attempts, self-mutilations, and mood lability, are more prevalent in AN-BP than in AN-R. The AN-BP type also have a higher prevalence of premorbid obesity, familial obesity, and debilitating personality traits (Halmi, 1999).

Most of the physiological and metabolic changes in AN are secondary to the starvation state or purging behavior. These changes revert to normal with nutritional rehabilitation and the cessation of purging behavior. Hypokalemic alkalosis occurs with purging; affected patients may have hypokalemia and physical symptoms of weakness, lethargy, and at times, cardiac arrhythmias, which may result in sudden cardiac arrest. Persistent vomiting causes severe erosion of the enamel of teeth with loss of teeth and parotid gland enlargement (Halmi, 1999). Chronic food restriction produces osteoporosis and fractures.

EPIDEMIOLOGY

Industrialized countries experienced a consistent increase in the incidence of AN over a period from 1931 to 1986 (Hoek, 1993). A study conducted in northeastern Scotland (Halmi, 1999) found an almost six-fold increase in the incidence of anorexia (from 3 per 100,000 to 17 per 100,000 cases) between 1965 and 1961. The male to female ratio for eating disorders consistently lies between 1 to 10 and 1 to 20 (Hoek, 1993).

Anorexia nervosa is rare in non-western, poorly industrialized countries (Lee, Leung, & Lee, 1996). Individuals and groups who are exposed to the ideal of a slender body type seem to be at risk for developing an eating disorder (Crago, Schisslak, & Estes, 1996). A review of eight studies in the 1980s (Gard & Freeman, 1996) failed to support a higher socioeconomic class–prevalence in AN.

ETIOLOGY AND RISK FACTORS

Anorexia nervosa is best conceptualized by a multidimensional model, which emphasizes the interaction of biological, psychological, and cultural factors. Within each of these areas, research has identified factors that predispose, precipitate, and maintain the eating disorder.

Genetic Factors

In a series of 67 twin probands, the concordance for restricting AN (66%) was markedly higher for monozygotic twins than for dizygotic (0%). A familial aggregation of AN and BN (bulimia nervosa) is present in AN probands.

A vulnerability to destabilization of the endocrine and metabolic mechanisms affecting eating behavior may cause the full-blown eating disorder the stress of severe dieting. Neurotransmitter serotonin pathways modulate feeding and inhibitory behaviors. There is evidence of aberrations in this neurotransmitter system in anorectic patients.

Because AN predominately starts during puberty (there is a bimodal peak for onset at ages 14 to 15 and age 18), Crisp (1984) developed the hypothesis that AN reflects an attempt to cope with maturational problems through the mechanism of avoidance of biological maturity.

A genetic predisposition to develop AN could be a particular personality type. There is evidence that a rigid, inhibited, and perfectionistic personality may be at risk for developing AN of the restricting type (Halmi, 1999).

Family Functioning

Studies of families of anorectics find more rigidity in the family organization, less clear interpersonal boundaries, and a tendency to avoid open discussions of disagreements among themselves, as compared with control families (Halmi, 1999).

Stressful Events

Stressful life events may be a risk factor for developing AN. Studies investigating the relationship between sexual abuse and eating disorders have produced highly discrepant results. A low rate of sexual abuse has been reported among anorectic restrictors relative to either bulimic anorectics or to normal weight bulimics (Waller, Halek, & Crisp, 1993).

Normative developmental events, such as the onset of puberty, leaving home, or beginning a new school, can precipitate an eating disorder. Adverse life events, such as the death of a close relative, the breakup of a relationship, or an illness, may also precipitate an eating disorder.

Course of Illness

Long-term follow-up research indicates that about one-fourth of anorectics recover from the disorder, one-fourth stay chronically ill with no improvement, and about half have partial improvement. Most of the partially improved have bulimic behaviors. Mortality rates at 10 years after presentation for treatment are 6.6%, and at 30 years are 18 to 20% (Eckert et al., 1995).

Patients with an earlier age of onset (i.e., between 13 and 18) recover from the disorder more quickly. Most studies have found purging behavior to be a predictor of poor outcome.

TREATMENT

There are few outpatient controlled treatment studies of AN. Open studies have indicated that the most effective is a multifaceted treatment approach, which includes medical management, psycho-education, and individual therapy under both cognitive and behavior therapy principles. Controlled studies have shown that children under the age of 18 respond better if they have family therapy (Halmi, 1999). Nutritional counseling and pharmacological intervention can also be useful components of the treatment plan.

Treatment levels range from a specialized eating disorder inpatient unit to a partial hospitalization or day program to outpatient care, depending on the weight, medical status, and psychiatric comorbidity of the patient. Medical management usually requires weight restoration, nutritional rehabilitation, rehydration, and correction of serum electrolytes for hospitalized patients. Cyproheptadine in high doses can facilitate weight gain in AN-R patients, and serotonin reuptake inhibitors may be effective in preventing relapse (Halmi, 1999).

Cognitive and behavioral therapy principles can be applied with both inpatients and outpatients. Behavior therapy is effective for inducing weight gain. Cognitive therapy techniques for AN have been extensively described (Kleifield, Wagner, & Halmi, 1996). These include monitoring food intake, feelings and emotions, binge/purge behaviors, and problems in interpersonal relationships. Cognitive therapy also uses the techniques of cognitive restructuring and problem solving.

Family Therapy

A family analysis should be done on all AN patients who are living with their families, and a decision made as to what type of family therapy or counseling is advisable. Most clinicians find it necessary to combine individual therapy with some method of family counseling.

At the present time, no treatment modality can predict recovery in a specific AN patient.

REFERENCES

American Psychiatric Association. (1994). *Diagnostic and statistical manual of mental disorders* (4th ed.). Washington, DC: Author.

Crago M., Schisslak, C. M., & Estes, L. S. (1996). Eating disturbances among American minority groups: A review. *International Journal of Eating Disorders, 19,* 239–248.

Crisp, A. H. (1984). Premorbid factors in adult disorders of weight, with particular reference to primary AN (weight phobia). *Journal of Psychosomatic Research, 14,* 1–22.

Eckert, E. D., Halmi, K. A., Marchi, E. P., et al. (1995). Ten-year follow-up of AN: Clinical course and outcome. *Psychological Medicine, 25,* 143–156.

Gard, M. C., & Freeman, C. P. (1996). The dismantling of a myth: A review of eating disorders and social economic status. *International Journal Eating Disorders, 20,* 1–12.

Halmi, K. A. (1999). Eating disorders: AN, bulimia nervosa and obesity. In K. E. Hales, S. C. Yudofsky, & J. Talbot (Eds.), *American psychiatric textbook of psychiatry* (3rd ed., pp. 983–1002). Washington, DC: American Psychiatry Association Press, Inc.

Hoek, H. (1993). Review of the epidemiological studies of eating disorders. *International Reviews of Psychiatry, 5,* 61–64.

Kleifield, E. I., Wagner, S., & Halmi, K. A. (1996). Cognitive-behavioral treatment of AN. *Psychiatric Clinics of North America, 19,* 715–737.

Lee, S., Leung, T., & Lee, A. M. (1996). Body dissatisfaction among Chinese undergraduates and its implication for eating disorders in Hong Kong. *International Eating Disorders Journal, 20,* 77–84.

Waller, G., Halek, C., & Crisp, A. H. (1993). Sexual abuse as a factor in AN: Evidence from two separate case series. *Journal of Psychosomatic Research, 37,* 873–879.

SUGGESTED READING

Treasure, J., and Holland, A. J. (1989). Genetic vulnerability to eating disorders: Evidence from twin and family studies. In M. H. Remschmidt and M. Schmidt (Eds.), *Child and youth psychiatry: European perspectives* (pp. 59–68). New York: Hogrefe and Hubert.

K. A. HALMI
Cornell University, Weill Medical College

APPETITE DISORDERS
BODY IMAGE
EATING DISORDERS
OBESITY

ANTABUSE

Antabuse (disulfiram), a drug used as a supplementary therapy for alcoholism, was originally used in the manufacture of rubber. When the chemical settled on workers' skin, many developed dermatitis (Schwartz & Tulipan, 1933). If they inhaled it, they discovered that they could no longer tolerate alcohol. Later, beginning in the 1940s, therapists tried giving the drug as a therapy, on the theory that alcoholics would avoid alcohol to avoid the severe psychological consequences.

Antabuse alters the metabolism of alcohol. Ethanol (ethyl alcohol) is metabolized in the liver by the enzyme alcohol dehydrogenase into aidehyde (a toxic chemical). Aldehyde is then metabolized by the enzyme aldehyde dehydrogenase (also known as aldehyde NAD-oxidoreductase) into acetate, which is a source of energy. Antabuse and a similar drug, Temposil (calcium carbimide), bind to the the copper ion of aidehyde dehydrogenase and thereby inactivate it. Consequently, after someone drinks ethanol, it is converted to aldehyde, which accumulates instead of being converted to acetate. Symptoms of aidehyde accumulation include flushing of the face, increased heart rate, nausea and vomiting, headache, abdominal pain, and labored breathing.

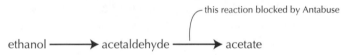

Many sources note that Antabuse is not significantly more effective than a placebo, citing a study by Fuller and Roth (1979). That criticism is somewhat misleading, however. The study included two placebo groups, one that was told their pill was Antabuse and one that was told it was not. The Antabuse group abstained no better than did the placebo group who believed they were taking Antabuse; both groups abstained better than those who knew they were taking a placebo. In other words, the drug was effective as a deterrent; people who believed they were taking Antabuse had an increased probability of abstention. Those who at some point tried drinking alcohol either became ill (Antabuse group) and quit taking the pill, or failed to get sick (placebo group) and discovered that the pill did not cause the threatened effects.

Results of other controlled experiments have been inconsistent, however. A review of 24 studies concluded that Antabuse has little effect on the probability of complete abstinence, but does on the average decrease the number of drinking days and the total consumption of alcohol (Hughes & Cook, 1997). A major problem in all studies has been compliance; many alcoholics are not compliant with the drug or take it sporadically. When therapists have taken measures to increase compliance, such as having someone's friend or relative supervise the daily pill-taking, the results have been more encouraging (Azrin, Sisson, Meyers, & Godley, 1982). One promising idea is to develop an implant that would provide sustained release in appropriate quantities; however, that strategy has not yet been adequately tested (Hughes & Cook, 1997).

REFERENCES

Azrin, N. H., Sisson, R. W., Meyers, R., & Godley, M. (1982). Alcoholism treatment by disulfiram and community reinforcement therapy. *Journal of Behavior Therapy and Experimental Psychiatry, 13*, 105–112.

Fuller, R. K., & Roth, H. P. (1979). Disulfiram for the treatment of alcoholism: An evaluation in 128 men. *Annals of Internal Medicine, 90*, 901–904.

Hughes, I. C., & Cook, C. C. H. (1997). The efficacy of disulfiram: A review of outcome studies. *Addiction, 92*, 381–395.

Schwartz, L., & Tulipan, L. (1933). An outbreak of dermatitis among workers in a rubber manufacturing plant. *Public Health Reports, 48*, 908–814.

J. W. KALAT
North Carolina State University

ALCOHOLISM TREATMENT
PSYCHOPHARMACOLOGY

ANTERIOR PITUITARY GLAND

The anterior pituitary gland, also referred to as the adenohypophysis, is a small, bean-shaped organ located in the area of the sella turcica of the brain below the level of the hypothalamus. It comprises one of the many hormone-secreting tissues that make up the endocrine system, which consists of a number of different hormonally-responsive and secretory tissues that function to regulate the normal physiology of life. The hypothalamus, long thought to be the so-called concertmaster of the endocrine orchestra, and the anterior pituitary gland, which may be thought of as the conductor of the endocrine orchestra, serve in a unique fashion to link important electrochemical signals from the brain and nervous system with the chemical (or hormonal) signals of the endocrine system. Furthermore, the anterior pituitary gland regulates a number of important metabolic processes by integrated control of the activity of other endocrine glands (e.g., thyroid, adrenal, gonads) through the secretion of one of at least six different target hormones. These clinically important hormones include growth hormone (GH), prolactin (PRL), adrenocorticotropin hormone (ACTH), thyroid-stimulating hormone (TSH), follicle-stimulating hormone (FSH), and luteinizing hormone (LH).

ANATOMY OF THE ANTERIOR PITUITARY GLAND

The hypothalamus and the pituitary gland are generally considered together as the hypothalamic-pituitary unit, emphasizing the unique and integrated relationship of the two. The description of the hypophysial portal system in the 1930s provided the first glimpse into the anatomical link by which the hypothalamus exerts control over the pituitary gland. Subsequent studies—which demonstrated that hypothalamic lesions resulted in a block in the release of pituitary hormones, whereas stimulation of the hypothalamus resulted in hormonal secretion—have served to highlight a humoral and not a neuronal connection. However, proof of the portal vessel chemotransmitter hypothesis proposed by Geoffrey Harris in the 1940s was not established until 1969 by the isolation from the hypothalamus of thy-

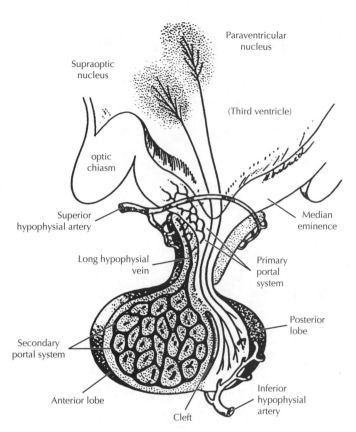

Figure 1.   Neuroanatomy and vascular supply of the anterior pituitary gland. A sagittal view of the human pituitary gland demonstrating the anatomical relationship to the hypothalamus and superimposed diagrammatic representation of the portal hypophysial vasculature. (Adapted from Becker's *Principle and Practice of Endocrinology and Metabolism,* Becker, K. L. ed. 2nd Edition, 1995).

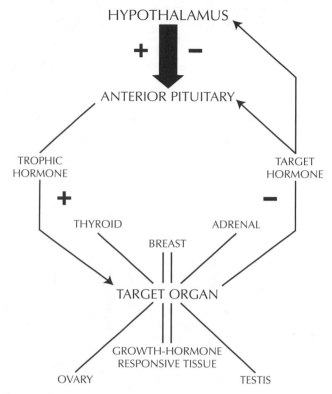

Figure 2.   Regulation of hypothalamic-pituitary-target organ activity—feedback loops. Hypothalamic stimulatory and inhibitory hormones regulate anterior pituitary gland "trophic hormone" release which then functions to modify target organ activity. Stimulation of target organs generate "target hormones" which provide negative and under certain circumstances positive feedback to both the hypothalamus and the anterior pituitary gland.

rotropin-releasing hormone (TRH), which was shown to regulate the pituitary-thyroid axis. Further investigations of the effects of hypothalamic extracts on pituitary function have led to the firm establishment of the concept of hypothalamic releasing and inhibitory hormones as coordinating the overall secretory function and activity of the adenohypophysis. Subsequently, the releasing factors regulating the pituitary-gonadal axis (gonadotropin-releasing hormone [GnRH]), pituitary-adrenal axis (corticotropin-releasing hormone [CRH]), and the pituitary–growth hormone axis (growth hormone–releasing hormone [GHRH], stimulatory, and somatostatin [SRIH], inhibitory) were all isolated and characterized.

The pituitary gland is composed of two parts: the neurohypophysis and the adenohypophysis (~80% of the whole gland), each of which has a separate embryologic origin. The adenohypophysis, except for the neurovascular elements, receives no functional innervation by way of the posterior pituitary or the hypothalamus. An humoral pathway is established via the hypophysial portal system of veins that take origin in the capillary loops in the median eminence of the tuber cinereum and subsequently drains into sinusoids of the anterior lobe terminating in the cavernous sinus. This system of rich vascular support to the anterior pituitary has major implications for the regulation of adenohypophysial hormone secretion. Uptake and delivery of these specialized hor-

mones are favored by the presence of fenestrated capillaries within the pituitary gland (Figure 1).

REGULATION

The anterior pituitary gland is under the regulation of (a) releasing (stimulatory) factors produced by the hypothalamus; and (b) long-loop negative (inhibitory) feedback from the target organ products (e.g., thyroxine, cortisol, estradiol). The hypothalamic releasing factors are also regulated by long-loop (predominantly negative) feedback from the peripheral endocrine organs. Additionally, the neurons secreting the releasing factors are activated or inhibited by neuronal input from the central nervous system (e.g., circadian rhythm, stress). Of note is the fact that the development of the capacity for expression of pituitary hormone secretion depends upon a variety of transcription factors, the best known of which is Pit-1 (Figure 2).

The hypothalamic releasing factors are GHRH, SRIH (somatostatin), TRH, GnRH, and CRH, which are all peptides with the exception of dopamine, which is a monoamine. Hypothalamic growth hormone–releasing hormone (GHRH) stimulates GH gene transcription, synthesis, and secretion. SRIH inhibits GH and TSH secretion. Thyrotropin-releasing hormone (TRH) stimulates TSH and PRL secretion. Hypothalamic dopamine inhibits

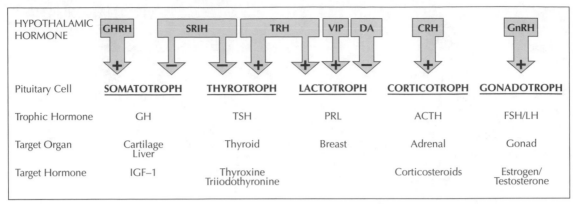

HYPOTHALAMIC HORMONE	GHRH	SRIH	TRH	VIP	DA	CRH	GnRH
	+	−	−	+	+	−	+	+
Pituitary Cell	**SOMATOTROPH**	**THYROTROPH**	**LACTOTROPH**	**CORTICOTROPH**	**GONADOTROPH**
Trophic Hormone	GH	TSH	PRL	ACTH	FSH/LH
Target Organ	Cartilage Liver	Thyroid	Breast	Adrenal	Gonad
Target Hormone	IGF–1	Thyroxine Triiodothyronine		Corticosteroids	Estrogen/ Testosterone

ACTH = adrenocorticotrophic hormone
CRH = corticotropin-releasing hormone
DA = dopamine
FSH = follicular-stimulating hormone
GHRH = growth hormone-releasing hormone
GnRH = gonadotropin-releasing hormone
IGF–1 = insulin-like growth factor 1

LH = lutenizing hormone
PRL = prolactin
SRIH = somatostatin
TRH = thyrotropin-releasing hormone
TSH = thyroid-stimulating hormone
VIP = vasoactive intestinal polypeptide

Figure 3.   The various hypothalamic-pituitary-target organ hormones and their actions. Regulation of anterior pituitary axis by the hypothalamic releasing factors. ACTH = adrenocorticotropic hormone; CRH = corticotropin-releasing hormone; DA = dopamine; FSH = follicular-stimulating hormone; GHRH = growth hormone-releasing hormone; GnRH = gonadotropin-releasing hormone; IGF-1 = insulin-like growth factor 1; LH = luteinizing hormone; PRL = prolactin; SRIH = somatostatin; TRH = thyrotropin-releasing hormone; TSH = thyroid-stimulating hormone; VIP = vasoactive intestinal polypeptide. (Adapted from *The Pituitary,* Melmed, S. ed., 1995).

both prolactin and TSH synthesis and release. Gonadotropin-releasing hormone (GnRH) stimulates FSH and LH secretion, and corticotropin-releasing hormone (CRH) stimulates proopiomelanocortin (POMC) synthesis and secretion for eventual enzymatic processing to ACTH and other peptides (including melanocyte-stimulating hormone [MSH] related sequences and B-endorphin).

The hypophysiotrophic hormones produced in various hypothalamic neurons terminate in the infundibulum and enter the hypophysial portal circulation for transport to capillaries surrounding the secretory cells of the anterior pituitary, where they bind to specific high-affinity membrane receptors. This receptor interaction, which occurs through various second messenger systems (including cyclic AMP and the phosphoinositol pathway), results in gene expression with consequent hormone synthesis and secretion. The pituitary hormones then regulate peripheral hormone release after binding to specific receptors on target organs (Figure 3).

FUNCTION
As the master endocrine gland, the pituitary functions to maintain normal physiology and plays a major role in lipid, protein, carbohydrate, water, and electrolyte metabolism. It regulates and coordinates function of the thyroid gland, adrenocortical tissues, and gonadal organs, thereby influencing growth; neurologic and sexual development; maintenance of hemodynamic stability (in addition to promoting normal physiological mechanisms involved in pregnancy and lactation); memory and sleep; and water and food intake. Another important aspect is the integration of the endocrine system and the nervous system with consequent impact of the pituitary on neurocognition and behavior. Further-

more, disruption of the hypothalamic-pituitary-target organ axis (e.g., pituitary hormone deficiency [destructive lesions] or pituitary hormone excess [functional tumor]) can result in profound changes in neuropsychiatric well-being. The anterior pituitary gland exerts its influence by directly controlling the activities of these other endocrine glands through the release of its trophic hormones.

The various pituitary cells that elaborate these hormones from the adenohypophysis have been characterized by their distribution, histology, ultrastructure, and immunocytochemistry. Older methods of characterizing the anterior pituitary utilized the tinctorial response to hematoxylin and eosin, which stained the cells as acidophils, basophils, and chromophobes. Of the acidophilic subgroup, the somatotrophs, which produce growth hormone (GH, important for general somatic growth), are found in the lateral portions of the anterior lobe and comprise approximately 50% of the total adenohypophysial cells. The lactotrophs, randomly distributed throughout the adenohypophysis, generate prolactin, which stimulates the mammary gland in pregnancy or in pathological states to produce milk (galactorrhea), and which account for 10 to 25% of all anterior pituitary cells.

The corticotrophs are basophilic cells accounting for 15 to 20% of the adenohypophysial cell population, and are found anteromedially. They predominantly secrete ACTH, which acts to influence the steroidogenic tissues (in the cortex of the adrenal gland) that mediate carbohydrate, androgen, and mineral metabolism. Other basophilic cells include the thyrotrophs and gonadotrophs, which produce TSH and FSH/LH, respectively. Composed of a single identical α subunit, these glycoproteins are identified by their

Table 1.   Hormones of the Hypothalamic-Pituitary-Target Organ Axis. Normal physiologic effects and function of trophic and target hormones of the hypothalamic-pituitary-target organ axis. Disruption of this integrated system by way of pituitary hormone deficiency or excess results in clinically significant pathological states. (Adapted from *Endocrine Pathophysiology*, (1st ed.), edited by C. B. Niewoehner.)

	Hypothalamic Hormones				
	Growth hormone-releasing hormone and somatostatin (inhibitory)	Thyrotropin-releasing hormone	Corticotropin-releasing hormone	Gonadotropin-releasing hormone	Dopamine (inhibitory)
Pituitary cell type	Somatotroph	Thyrotroph	Corticotroph	Gonadotroph	Lactotroph
Pituitary hormones	Growth hormone	Thyroid-stimulating hormone	Adrenocorticotropic hormone	Luteinizing hormone and follicle-stimulating hormone	Prolactin
Target organs	Liver, cartilage, and other tissues	Thyroid gland	Adrenal cortex	Ovaries and testes	Breast
Target organ hormones	Insulin-like growth factor-1 (somatomedin-C)	Thyroxine (T_4) and trilodothyronine (T_3)	Glucocorticoids (cortisol), mineralocorticoids, and androgens	Estrogen, progesterone, and testosterone	
Target organ hormones—major actions	Linear growth[a] and cell proliferation	Thermogenesis, growth,[a] and CNS maturation[a]	Stress response and sodium retention	Sexual maturation, menstrual cycle, gamete production, libido, and fertility	Milk production
Pituitary hyperfunction	Acromegaly and gigantism[a]	Hyperthyroidism (rare)	Hypercortisolism (Cushing's disease)		Galactorrhea, amenorrhea, infertility, and impotence
Pituitary hypofunction	Dwarfism[a]	Hypothyroidism	Adrenal insufficiency	Amenorrhea, infertility, decreased libido, and impotence	No lactation postpartum

Note. CNS = central nervous system.
[a]Seen only in children.

structurally distinct β subunit. Thyrotrophs, the least common anterior pituitary cell type (<10%), are found in both the anterolateral and anteromedial portions of the gland. The most important role of TSH is regulation of thyroid gland function. Finally, the gonadotrophs, which constitute 10 to 15% of adenohypophysial cells, are distributed throughout the entire anterior lobe. These cells synthesize and release FSH and LH, both of which function in conjunction to coordinate the growth and development of gonadal tissue (the ovary and testis), to facilitate puberty and sexual maturation, and in addition, to support the physiology of pregnancy and lactation.

As can be appreciated, disruption of this integrated hypothalamic-pituitary unit leads to pathological states that can have major clinical consequences, including abnormal phenotype, infertility, and death, in addition to a wide spectrum of neurologic sequelae such as emotional lability, depression, obtundation, and coma (Table 1). It is clear, then, that both the concertmaster and the conductor of the endocrine system are vital to sustaining life.

N. A. CAMPBELL
I. JACKSON
Brown University

HORMONES AND BEHAVIOR
HYPOTHALAMUS
PITUITARY

ANTEROGRADE AMNESIA

Anterograde Amnesia is defined as an inability to remember new information following brain injury or disease and is a defining feature of the amnesic syndrome. Behaviorally, patients with anterograde amnesia have profound problems remembering day-to-day events or names of new people. At a clinical level, this deficit is manifest in extremely poor performance on tests of free recall, paired associate learning, and forced choice recognition. Using the Wechsler Memory Scale–Revised, on the presumption that the patient's IQ was about average, a significant anterograde amnesia would be diagnosed if the patient's delayed memory index fell below 80. In high IQ patients, a higher delayed memory index would still indicate significant anterograde loss if the discrepancy with IQ was greater than 20 points. In patients of low IQ, the delayed memory index would have to be correspondingly lower for a significant anterograde deficit to be identified.

An important feature of anterograde amnesia is that it is not normally associated with any extensive impairment of language or intellect, unless the diagnosis under consideration is that of dementing illness such as Alzheimer's disease. Information about personal identity and ongoing close relationships is also preserved. Furthermore, patients with anterograde amnesia show normal performance on tests of immediate apprehension such as digit span and block span. Patients presenting anterograde amnesia will normally show good levels of previously acquired skill performance (e.g., typing, musical ability) and some ability to acquire new skills. Impaired immediate memory and/or the apparent loss of everyday living skills in a case of anterograde amnesia should be regarded with suspicion, and the alternative diagnosis of malingering or psychogenic disturbance should be considered.

Patients with anterograde amnesia will also present varying degrees of retrograde amnesia—loss of memory for the time period prior to the brain injury. The extent of retrograde amnesia present in a case of anterograde amnesia can be extremely variable, ranging from a few minutes to many years, depending on the nature of the underlying brain damage. There is no good evidence that the extent of anterograde and retrograde amnesia are correlated.

Anterograde amnesia is associated with a wide range of etiologies which lead to its appearance as either a permanent or transient symptom. Permanent anterograde amnesia is a characteristic feature of Wernicke-Korsakoff Syndrome, closed head injury, carbon monoxide poisoning, encephalitic illnesses (most notably herpes simplex and varicella zoster encephalitis), temporal lobectomy, tumor, ischaemic attack (both cortical and subcortical), ruptured aneurysms, and anoxic episodes induced by cardiac failure or specific interruption of the cerebro-vascular system (e.g., failed hanging attempts). In addition, most dementing illnesses have anterograde amnesia as a prominent and early feature. Transient causes of anterograde amnesia include transient global amnesia, transient epileptic amnesia, and memory loss induced by electroconvulsive therapy. Marked anterograde amnesia is a principal feature of post-traumatic amnesia—this is the transient confusional state following a closed head injury. Various drugs, notably the benzodiazepine group, can also induce temporary states of anterograde impairment. This property of these drugs has proved clinically useful in procedures such as endoscopy and dentistry but has also been exploited criminally. Profound intoxication with alcohol or other recreational drugs such as marijuana can also induce an anterograde memory impairment.

As one might expect from its diverse etiology, the neuroanatomical basis of anterograde amnesia is complex. Damage to the temporal lobe has long been associated with anterograde memory impairment, but the crucial structures involved have only recently been identified. Specifically, it appears that the hippocampal formation is essential for normal anterograde function. Damage to the hippocampus is relatively easy to sustain because parts of this structure, notably the fields of the hippocampus proper (CA1-CA4), seem particularly vulnerable to a range of brain insults such as head injury and anoxia. The structure also appears to be targeted by various viral infections such as that caused by herpes simplex.

A second brain region associated with anterograde amnesia is the midline of the diencephalon. Within this region the mamillary bodies, mamillo-thalamic tract, and dorso-medial nucleus of the thalamus have been particularly associated with profound anterograde amnesia, most notably in cases of Wernicke-Korsakoff Syndrome but also in certain forms of thalamic stroke. In addition, there is evidence that damage to the fornix—a efferent structure from the hippocampus to the mamillary bodies—is also implicated in cases of anterograde memory loss.

The various structures implicated in anterograde amnesia are all parts of the limbic system, and this has led to the view that these structures form some kind of "memory circuit" in which interruption at any point can result in anterograde memory loss. However, an alternative theory is that the various brain structures implicated in anterograde amnesia perform different mnemonic processes. This problem has clouded the debate over the underlying cause of amnesia. A failure in consolidation—those processes required to transform a temporary memory trace into a permanent reconfiguration of synaptic connections representing that memory—has long been a favored explanation for anterograde memory impairment following hippocampal damage. In contrast, the deficit associated with diencephalic lesions seems less straightforward and may reflect a specific inability to remember certain aspects of information such as spatial and temporal cues.

Finally, it must be noted that anterograde amnesia can also be found in association with damage to the frontal cortex, most commonly following ruptured aneurysms of the anterior communicating artery and associated vasospasm of the anterior cerebral artery. The form of anterograde impairment here is often milder and may be associated with the phenomenon of confabulation—the generation of implausible memories which the patient nonetheless believes to be true. Anterograde amnesia following frontal lobe damage is also the only form of memory impairment in which one would expect to observe illusory memory phenomena. Anterograde amnesia caused by frontal lobe damage is thought to be attributable to higher-level deficits in the regulation of memory activity, such as the allocation of attention, the determination of encoding strategies, and the organization and retrieval of memories.

REFERENCE

Parkin, A. J. *Memory and amnesia: An introduction.* Hove, UK: Psychology Press.

A. J. PARKIN, DECEASED
University of Sussex, England

BRAIN INJURIES
MEMORY
RETROGRADE AMNESIA

ANTIANXIETY DRUGS

Anxiety, a subjective emotional state, is characterized by pervasive feelings such as apprehension and dread, and often accompanied by physical symptoms such as muscle tension, tremors, palpitations, chest pain, headache, dizziness, and gastrointestinal distress. Anxiety may or may not be connected to stressful or fearful stimuli. Most antianxiety agents (called anxiolytics, day-time sedatives, minor tranquilizers) belong to a larger class of psychoactive substances, the sedative-hypnotics. While differing in chemical structure and potency, all sedative-hypnotics are capable of producing a continuum of depressive states, including relief of anxiety, disinhibition, sedation, sleep, anesthesia, coma, and death (the result of depression of respiratory centers in the brain). All sedative-hypnotics function as antianxiety agents, but historical, marketing, and safety considerations, and slight differences in mechanism of action, led to the use of certain substances over others.

The oldest anxiolytic drug, ethyl alcohol, is similar in many respects to other sedative-hypnotics, but is used primarily for social and recreational, rather than medical, purposes. Three other substances with a long history are the alcohols chloral hydrate and paraldehyde, and a nonalcohol, bromide. Barbiturates, first synthesized in the late 1800s, are prescribed to produce drowsiness or sedation. Because barbiturates produces rapid tolerance (larger doses are needed to maintain the effect) and physical dependence (evidenced by withdrawal syndrome upon cessation of drug taking), and because they are potent respiratory depressants, synthesis of nonbarbiturate sedative-hypnotics in the 1950s was welcomed. In fact, nonbarbiturate sedative-hypnotics—a prototype of which is Meprobamate (Miltown, Equanil)—are equally dangerous in terms of tolerance, dependence, and respiratory depression. These drugs were marketed as minor tranquilizers, falsely implying a safer and more specific treatment of anxiety. In addition, use of the term "minor tranquilizer" implies that these drugs are on a spectrum with antipsychotic medications (known as major tranquilizers), whereas they are very different in mechanism and behavioral action.

In the 1960s benzodiazepines (Valium, Librium) were synthesized, and soon became the most widely prescribed drugs in the United States. Benzodiazepines are more selective than other sedative-hypnotics in suppressing anxiety, probably due to a selective affinity for specific receptors in the limbic system (known as benzodiazepine receptors). Although tolerance is a problem with all sedative-hypnotics, benzodiazepines, stimulating less production of metabolic enzymes in the liver than do other sedative-hypnotics, are less likely to produce tolerance. Physical dependence upon benzodiazepines does occur, but only with high doses over a long period of time. Duration of action of the benzodiazepines, being longer than that of other sedative-hypnotics, enables fewer doses to be taken, but increases the risk of buildup if frequent doses are taken. The most important advantage of the benzodiazepines is the large dose, much greater than anxiolytic doses, required to produce respiratory depression; this wide safety margin makes the drug almost nonlethal. However, behavioral depressant effects of the benzodiazepines, if combined with effects of other sedative-hypnotics (e.g., alcohol), may depress respiration in a supraadditive or synergistic manner (i.e., more than the sum of the respiratory depression of the single drugs added together).

Representative benzodiazepines chlordiazeproxide [Librium], diazepam [Valium], oxazepam [Serax], flurazepam [Dalmane], clonazepam [Clonopin], chlorazepate [Tranxene], lorazepam [Ativan], and prazepam [Vestran]—differ from each other primarily in the way they are marketed: Dalmane is promoted for sleep-inducing action; Clonopin, for seizure disorders; others, for anxiety, tension, hyperexcitability, insomnia, and muscle tension. There are differences in duration of action; Serax is often prescribed when short duration is desired.

A few substances not included in the sedative-hypnotic class are sometimes used as antianxiety agents. Antihistamines such as hydroxyzine (Vistaril) are particularly useful in anxiety-related skin conditions; anticholinergic side effects of dry mouth and blurred vision reduce potential for abuse. Tricyclic antidepressants such as doxepin (Sinequan) are used when anxiety accompanies depression. Beta-adrenergic blockers like propranolol (Inderal) are usually prescribed when anxiety accompanies a medical condition such as hypertension or tachycardia, and reduce the sympathetic discharge associated with anxiety.

SUGGESTED READING

Goodman, L. S., & Gilman, A. (1974). *The pharmacological basis of therapeutics* (4th ed.). New York: Macmillan. (Original work published 1941)

Julien, R. M. (1981). *A primer of drug action* (3rd ed.). San Francisco: Freeman. (Original work published 1975)

B. E. THORN
University of Alabama

ANTIDEPRESSANT MEDICATIONS
ANTIPSYCHOTIC DRUGS
ANXIETY
NEUROPSYCHOLOGY
PSYCHOPHARMACOLOGY

ANTIDEPRESSANT MEDICATIONS

Medications effective in reducing the symptoms of major depression are called antidepressants. The Food and Drug Administration requires controlled, double-blind studies showing safety and efficacy before approving an antidepressant medication to be available in the United States.

Major Depressive Disorder is characterized by sadness and an inability to experience pleasure. Associated symptoms include decreased self-esteem; feelings of hopelessness and worthlessness; excessive guilt; and difficulty with concentration, memory, and making decisions. Anxiety manifested as fear, nervousness, or excessive worry are also common in depression. A greater focus on bodily sensations can result in somatic symptoms. Sleep difficulties marked by reduced or excessive sleep and a change in appetite with weight loss or gain are also present. Suicidal ideas can lead to suicide attempts with the potential to succeed. The diagnosis of major depression requires these symptoms to be present fairly continuously for a minimum of two weeks and to be associated with significant distress and/or impairment in role function.

There are different forms of major depression, including those seen in bipolar disorder, in which individuals have not only episodes of depression but also forms of mania; melancholia, characterized by symptoms such as a distinct quality of sadness, inability to experience pleasure, and early morning awakening; and atypical depression, in which the depression is more responsive to environmental events and associated with an increase in appetite and need for sleep. Depressive symptoms that fall below the threshold to be called major depression are called Dysthymia (which is a chronic, lower grade depression, though still impairing), or "minor" depressions.

Depression is believed to arise from a combination of genetic vulnerabilities and environmental factors. Traumatic experiences, particularly if they occur in childhood, are a potential environmental risk factor for the development of depression.

Medications to treat depression are classified based on their chemical structure and pharmacological effect. Three major classes of antidepressants are available in the United States. These are the tricyclic antidepressants (TCAs), monoamine oxidase inhibitors (MAOIs), and selective serotonin reuptake inhibitors (SSRIs). The initial effects of these medications in the brain are primarily on two chemical messengers called neurotransmitters: norepinephrine and serotonin. The TCAs have a prominent effect in blocking the recycling of norepinephrine. Commonly used TCAs included imipramine (trade name Tofranil), amitryptaline (Elavil), doxepin (Sinequan), desipramine (Norpramin), and nortriptyline (Pamelor, Aventyl). One TCA, clomipramine (Anafranil), also powerfully blocks the recycling of serotonin. The MAOIs inhibit an enzyme, monoamine oxidase, important in the physiological breakdown of norepinephrine and serotonin. Commonly used MAOIs include phenelzine (Nardil) and tranylcypramine (Parnate). The SSRIs selectively block the recycling of serotonin. These include fluoxetine (Prozac), sertraline (Zoloft), paroxetine (Paxil), fluvoxamine (Luvox), and citalopram (Celexa).

Some antidepressant medications do not fall easily into the above groups. Buproprion (Wellbutrin) is believed to block the recycling of norepinephrine as well as another neurotransmitter, dopamine. Venlafaxine (Effexor) blocks the recycling of both serotonin and norepinephrine. Nefazodone (Serzone) blocks the recycling of serotonin and additionally a specific serotonin receptor. Mirtazapine (Remeron) impacts a specific norepinephrine receptor on the serotonin cell, increasing its firing rate while simultaneously blocking some serotonin receptors.

The benefits of antidepressant medications are rarely immediate but accrue gradually over several weeks. The maximum benefit may not plateau for several months. The initial effect of antidepressants begins a cascade of effects in the neurons that is ultimately believed to alter their activity at the level of genes; this accounts for the delay in obtaining the full benefits of antidepressant medications.

Antidepressant medications, in addition to their therapeutic benefits, may also have unwanted effects. These side effects can be explained by their pharmacological effects in areas other than the sites involved in their beneficial effects, or because of effects on other receptors. The TCAs appear to have the largest number of such unwanted effects, including potential effects on the electrical conduction system in the heart. This effect makes them particularly dangerous if taken in overdose. The TCAs' effects on the cholinergic, histaminergic, and alpha-1 adrenergic receptors mediate the majority of their adverse effects. MAOIs indiscriminately inhibit the monoamine oxidase enzyme, and as a result have the potential to interact with other medications or with food substances such as cheese. Such an interaction may increase blood pressure, which, if high enough, can potentially cause strokes and even death. The newer antidepressants, such as the SSRIs, are less likely to cause serious side effects because of the greater selectivity in their pharmacological actions. However, with the exceptions of Serzone, Wellbutrin, and Remeron, their potential for causing sexual side effects seems to be greater.

Antidepressants have been increasingly recognized as being effective for treating a variety of conditions other than major depression. These include Dysthymia and all of the anxiety disorders, such as Generalized Anxiety Disorder, Panic Disorder, Obsessive Compulsive Disorder, Post-traumatic Stress Disorder, and Social Anxiety Disorder.

In a general group of patients with major depression, roughly 10–20% are intolerant to the first antidepressant tried. Of those remaining, roughly half are able to tolerate the medications without any significant side effects. Side effects, when they occur, may fade as the individual gets used to the medication. Occasionally, side effects develop gradually over time.

An adequate trial of an antidepressant requires a minimum of a month or two on an adequate dose. Roughly two-thirds of the individuals will obtain at least a 50% reduction in the severity of their depressive symptoms. A quarter to a third may achieve remission, considered a full or close to a full level of response. Partial responders or those who fail to respond might choose to either switch the medication to another class of antidepressants or augment the first antidepressant with one of several choices. Individuals who fail to respond to antidepressant medications may respond to electroconvulsive therapy, believed to be the most powerful treatment available for major depression.

REFERENCES

Tollefson, G. D., & Rosenbaum, G. F. (1998). Selective serotonin reuptake inhibitors. In A. F. Schatzberg & C. B. Nemeroff (Eds.), *American Psychiatric Press textbook of psychopharmacology* (2nd ed.) (pp. 219–238). Washington, D.C.: American Psychiatric Press.

Robinson, R. G., & Travella, G. I. (1996). Neuropsychiatry of mood disorders. In B. S. Fogel, R. B. Schiffer, and S. M. Rao (Eds.), *Neuropsychiatry*. Baltimore, MD: Williams and Wilkens.

P. T. NINAN
Emory School of Medicine

DEPRESSION
PSYCHOPHARMACOLOGY
PSYCHOPHYSIOLOGY
NEUROCHEMISTRY

ANTIPSYCHOTIC DRUGS

Antipsychotic drugs were introduced in the United States in about 1956. For centuries there was anecdotal information concerning *rauwolfia serpentia,* a root used in India for a whole range of psychological problems. Reserpine, a rauwolfia alkaloid, was reported in the treatment of schizophrenia in India as early as 1943.

As more effective classes of antipsychotic drugs were developed, they were used on a large scale in psychiatric institutions to treat schizophrenia. Accompanied by changes in public policy, these medications were partially responsible for the reduction in the number of people in veteran and state hospitals. The control of psychotic symptoms made ambulatory care, as well as individual, group, family, and milieu therapy, more accessible to people with schizophrenia. Greenblatt and his colleagues, in *Drug and Social Therapy in Chronic Schizophrenia,* found that patients treated with antipsychotic medication showed more improvement than those treated without medication. However, the highest rate of improvement was reported by patients who received a combination of chemotherapy and intensive social therapy. Many studies have replicated these results, and most authorities recommend that antipsychotic medication be prescribed as only one part of an overall treatment plan.

The major classes of antipsychotic drugs and some trade names are listed in Table 1. Reserpine, a rauwolfia alkaloid, is rarely used. The phenothiazines are by far the most widely researched of the antipsychotic medications, but Davis (1980) concluded that there is little evidence to support the use of one specific type of antipsychotic drug over another. Effective daily doses range considerably, based on individual differences.

Although antipsychotic drugs can be used to treat certain organic psychoses such as amphetamine intoxication, their primary use has been in treating the symptoms of schizophrenia. The antipsychotic drugs usually control agitation and combative behavior within days, but changes in cognition such as psychotic thinking, hallucinations, and delusions may require four to six weeks. Greater therapeutic results have been reported in people who have been ill less than two years.

Side effects vary with the class of medication, but most of the antipsychotic drugs can produce extrapyramidal effects. The parkinsonian syndrome includes muscular rigidity, tremor, changes in posture, shuffling gait, and psychomotor retardation. Bizarre movements of the tongue, facial movements, and restlessness are also commonly reported, in addition to these extrapyramidal reactions. A rare but very serious side effect is agranulocytosis. A dramatic side effect of long-term use of antipsychotic medication is tardive dyskinesia, characterized by grimacing, jerky arm movements, and lip smacking.

Many side effects can be controlled by the administration of antiparkinsonian drugs, careful monitoring, and sensitive dosage scheduling by the physician. In a volume of *Schizophrenia Bulletin,* several psychiatrists (Mosher & Meltzer, 1980; Schutz, 1980) recommended the use of brief drug-free periods, the lowest possible dosage, and greater emphasis on psychosocial treatment of schizophrenia in order to prevent and reduce the tardive dyskinesia.

Given the side effects, it is clear that although antipsychotic drugs can benefit schizophrenics greatly, they must be used conservatively and with attention to the individual's response.

Table 1.   Antipsychotic Drugs

Class		Name		Manufacturer
		Generic	Trade	
I	Butyrophenones	Haloperidol	Haldol	McNeil
II	Dibenzoxapines	Loxapine	Loxitane	Lederle
III	Dihyroindolones	Molindone	Moban	Endo
IV	Rawolfia alkaloid	Reserpine	Serpasial	Ciba
			Rau-sed	Squibb
			Sandril	Lilly
			Raurine	Westerfield
			Vio-serpine	Rowell
			Reserpoid	Upjohn
V	Thioxanthenes	Chlorprothixene	Taractan	Roche
		Thiothizene	Navane	Roerig
VI	Phenothiazines			
	A. Aliphatic	Chlorpromazine	Thorazine	Smith, Kline & French
		Triflupromazine	Vesprin	Squibb
		Promazine	Sparine	Wyeth
	B. Piperazine	Prochlorperazine	Compazine	Smith, Kline & French
		Perphenazine	Trilafon	Schering
		Trifluoperazine	Stelazine	Smith, Kline & French
		Fluphenazine	Prolixin	Squibb
			Permitil	Schering
		Acetophenazine	Tindal	Schering
		Butaperazine	Repoise	Robins
		Carphenazine	Proketazine	Wyeth
	C. Piperidine	Thioridazine	Mellaril	Sandoz
		Mesoridazine	Serentil	Boehringer
		Piperacetazine	Quide	Dow

REFERENCES

Davis, J. M. (1980). Antipsychotic drugs. In H. I. Kaplan, A. M. Freedman, & B. J. Sadock (Eds.), *Comprehensive textbook of psychiatry III.* Baltimore: Williams & Wilkins.

Mosher, L. B., & Meltzer, H. Y. (1980). Drugs and psychosocial treatment: Editors' introduction. *Schizophrenia Bulletin, 6*(1), 8–9.

Schutz, C. G. (1980). Discussion of neuroleptics and psychosocial treatment. *Schizophrenia Bulletin, 6*(1), 135–138.

SUGGESTED READING

Honigfeld, G., & Howard, A. (1973). *Psychiatric drugs: A desk reference.* New York: Academic Press.

C. LANDAU
Brown University

NEUROCHEMISTRY
PSYCHOPHARMACOLOGY

ANTISOCIAL PERSONALITY DISORDER

Antisocial Personality Disorder (ASP) is characterized by a pattern of socially irresponsible, exploitative, and guiltless behavior that begins in childhood or early adolescence and is manifested by disturbances in many areas of life, including family relations, schooling, work, military service, and marriage. Typical behaviors include criminality and failure to conform to the law, failure to sustain consistent employment, manipulation of others for personal gain, frequent deception of others, and failure to develop stable interpersonal relationships. Other attributes of ASP include lacking empathy for others, rarely experiencing remorse, and failing to learn from the negative results of one's experiences.

Antisocial behavior has been described throughout recorded history, yet formal descriptions date only to the early 19th century. Philippe Pinel, a leader in the French Revolution and founding father of modern psychiatry, used the term *manie sans delire* to describe persons who were not insane but had irrational outbursts of rage and violence. Scottish physician James Pritchard wrote about moral insanity, which he identified as a condition in which otherwise normal people willfully engaged in antisocial behavior. In the late 19th century, German psychiatrists coined the term *psychopathy* to describe a broad range of deviant behaviors and eccentricities, and implied that psychopathic personality resulted from constitutional factors. The term was later popularized by the American psychiatrist Hervey Cleckley, who furnished the first coherent description of antisocial personality disorder in *The Mask of Sanity,* originally published in 1941.

The term *Sociopathic Personality Disturbance* was introduced in the first edition of the *Diagnostic and Statistical Manual of Mental Disorders* (*DSM-I*), a compendium of recognized mental disorders published in 1952, and was replaced by *Antisocial Personality Disorder* in 1968 in *DSM-II.* Like sociopath, the term antisocial implies that the disturbance is directed against society and its rules and regulations.

Antisocial Personality Disorder has been found in persons from all nations, racial and ethnic groups, and societies. Research shows that in the United States from 2% to 4% of men and 0.5% to 1% of women exhibit ASP. The percentages are much higher in psychiatric hospitals and clinics, prisons, among the homeless, and among alcohol and drug addicted persons.

CLINICAL MANIFESTATIONS

Antisocials typically report a history of childhood behavioral problems such as fights with peers, conflicts with adults, lying, cheating, stealing, vandalism, fire-setting, running away from home, and cruelty to animals or other children. As the antisocial youth reaches adulthood, other problems develop reflecting age-appropriate responsibilities such as uneven job performance, unreliability, irresponsibility, reckless behavior, and inappropriate aggression. Criminal behavior, pathological lying, and the use of the aliases are also characteristic of the disorder. Marriages are often marked by instability or emotional and physical abuse of the spouse; separation and divorce are common.

NATURAL HISTORY

The disorder is chronic, though tends to be worse early in its course, and patients tend to improve with increasing age. At a 30-year follow-up study, sociologist Lee Robins found that of 82 subjects, 12% were in remission and another 20% were deemed improved; the remaining antisocials were considered as disturbed as, or more disturbed than, at the onset of the study. The median age for improvement in her study was 35 years. The most dangerous and destructive behaviors may improve or remit, but other troubling symptoms of ASP continue. Thus, while the aging antisocial may become less troublesome to the community, many remain personally troubled, and some fail to improve at all.

Nearly two-thirds of antisocial persons suffer an alcohol or drug use disorder. Mood disorders, anxiety disorders, sexual dysfunction, paraphilias, other personality disorders (e.g., borderline personality), and pathological gambling are also frequent. Antisocial persons sometimes attempt suicide, and mortality studies show elevated rates of death from natural causes as well as accidents, suicides, and homicides.

ETIOLOGY

The cause of ASP is unknown, but a growing body of evidence suggests that its cause is multifactorial. ASP has long been known to run in families, and may be genetically transmitted to some extent. Family studies have shown that nearly one-fifth of first-degree relatives of antisocials are themselves antisocial. ASP is more commonly found in both identical twins than among non-identical twins, and offspring of antisocial parents adopted in childhood are more likely to develop ASP than adoptees without an antisocial parent.

Chronic nervous system underarousal is thought by some researchers to underlie ASP. This theory is supported by evidence that antisocials have low resting pulse rates, low skin conductance, and show an increased amplitude on event-related potentials. Possibly, individuals with chronically low arousal seek out potentially dangerous or risky situations to raise their arousal to more optimal levels, in order to satisfy their craving for excitement.

The central nervous system (CNS) neurotransmitter serotonin has been linked with impulsive and aggressive behavior. Low levels of cerebrospinal fluid 5-hydroxyindolacetic acid (5-HIAA)—a metabolite of serotonin—have been found in men who killed with unusual cruelty and/or committed arson. It is thought that serotonin may help dampen impulsive and violent behavior, and for this reason may play a role in ASP.

Other evidence points towards abnormal CNS functioning in ASP. Adrian Raine and his colleagues found abnormal function in the prefrontal cortex in a group of criminals who had either attempted or committed murder, using positron emission tomography. More recently, these investigators showed that antisocial men had a measurable reduction in prefrontal gray matter volume using structural magnetic resonance imaging. It has been hypothesized that impulsive or poorly controlled behavior stems from a functional abnormality in these brain regions.

The social and home environments also contribute to the development of antisocial behavior. Parents of troubled children typically show a high level of antisocial behavior themselves, and their homes are frequently broken by domestic abuse, divorce, separation, or the absence of a parent. Good supervision is less likely in broken homes because parents may not be available, and antisocial parents often lack the motivation to keep an eye on their children. Another factor that may influence the development of antisocial behavior is the presence of deviant peers. Antisocial children tend to choose similar children as playmates. These relationships can encourage and reward aggression and other antisocial behaviors.

ASSESSMENT OF THE ANTISOCIAL

The patient's history forms the most important basis for diagnosing ASP. In assessing the antisocial patient, family members and friends can become helpful informants, able to fill in the gaps. Records of previous clinic or hospital visits can provide additional diagnostic clues. A review of the medical history is important, particularly because ASP increases the risk of acquiring HIV and other sexually transmitted diseases and predisposes individuals to traumatic injuries and drug and alcohol use.

Psychological testing is not generally necessary, but tests may be helpful when patients refuse to permit interviews with relatives or have no other informants. The Minnesota Multiphasic Personality Inventory (MMPI) yields a broad profile of personality functioning, and a particular pattern of results indicates ASP. The Psychopathy Checklist has been used to measure the severity of the disorder in criminal populations, and appears to predict both criminal recidivism and parole violations. Tests of intelligence and educational achievement may provide useful information about the patient. Antisocial patients generally score about ten points lower than non-antisocials on traditional IQ tests, and are also more likely to show evidence of learning disabilities.

MANAGING ASP

Antisocial patients who seek help can be evaluated and treated on an outpatient basis where an array of services is available, including neuropsychological assessment, individual psychotherapy, medication management, and family or marital counseling. Cognitive therapy has recently been used to treat ASP and involves evaluating situations in which distorted beliefs and attitudes (e.g., "my actions have no consequences") interfere with the patient's functioning or success at achieving goals. The major goal of therapy is to help patients understand how they create their own problems, and how their distorted perceptions prevent them from seeing themselves as others do. Working with antisocial patients can be very difficult, because antisocial persons tend to blame others, have a low tolerance for frustration, are impulsive, and rarely form trusting relationships.

MEDICATIONS

While no medications are routinely used or specifically approved for the treatment of ASP, several drugs have been shown to reduce aggression, the chief problem of many antisocials. The best documented is lithium carbonate, found to reduce anger, threatening behavior, and assaultiveness among prisoners. More recently, the drug was shown to reduce behaviors like bullying, fighting, and temper outbursts in aggressive children. Phenytoin (Dilantin), an anticonvulsant, has also been shown to reduce impulsive aggression in prison settings. Other drugs have been used to treat aggression primarily in brain-injured or mentally retarded patients, with varying degrees of success. These include carbamazepine, valproate, propranolol, buspirone, trazodone, and the antipsychotics. Tranquilizers from the benzodiazepine class should not be used to treat antisocials as they are potentially addictive and may lead to behavioral dyscontrol. Medication targeted at comorbid major depression, anxiety disorders, or Attention-Deficit/Hyperactivity Disorder may help to reduce antisocial behavior. Similarly, antisocial substance abusers who stop abusing are less likely to engage in antisocial or criminal behaviors, and have fewer family conflicts and emotional problems.

Antisocials with spouses and families may benefit from marriage and family counseling. Bringing family members into the process may help antisocial patients understand the impact of their disorder has others. Therapists who specialize in family counseling may be helpful in addressing such problems as maintaining an enduring attachment to one's spouse or partner, the inability to be an effective parent, problems with honesty and responsibility, and the anger and hostility that can lead to domestic violence. Antisocials who were poorly parented themselves may need special help to learn appropriate parenting skills.

PREVENTION OF ASP

Prevention efforts should target those at greatest risk for ASP—namely, children with conduct disorder. Preventive measures should focus on teaching children how to recognize and reject bad behavior, how to make acceptable judgments between right and wrong, and how to connect actions with consequences. Parents may need special training that shows them how to identify and correct misbehavior as it occurs, and how to steer their children away from negative influences like delinquent peers. Antiviolence programs such as those offered in some in public schools may help children find alternatives to lashing out.

SUGGESTED READING

Black, D. W. (1999). *Bad boys, bad men—Confronting Antisocial Personality Disorder.* New York: Oxford University Press.

Cleckley, H. (1976). *The mask of sanity: An attempt to clarify some issues about the so-called psychopathic personality,* 5th edition. St. Louis: CV Mosby.

Hare, R. D. (1993). *Without conscience: The disturbing world of the psychopaths among us.* New York: Pocketbooks.

Raine, A. (1993). *The psychopathology of crime: Criminal behavior as a clinical disorder.* New York: Academic Press.

Raine, A., Lencz, T., Bihrle, S., LaCasse, L., Colletti, P.: Reduced prefrontal gray matter volume and reduced autonomic activity in antisocial personality disorder. Arch. Gen. Psychiatry 2000; 57: 119–127.

Robins, L. N. (1966). *Deviant children grown up.* Baltimore: Williams and Wilkins.

D. W. BLACK
University of Iowa

PERSONALITY DISORDERS
PSYCHOPATHIC DISORDERS

ANXIETY

One of the best definitions of anxiety, put forth over fifteen years ago by Kandel (1983), remains highly apt and appropriate today:

Anxiety is a normal inborn response either to threat—to one's person, attitudes, or self-esteem—or to the absence of people or objects that assure and signify safety.

Anxiety is an emotion and state of mind characterized by aversive cognitive (apprehensive expectation of negative experience or consequences), physiologic (autonomic hyperarousal with multiple somatic symptoms such as palpitations, sweating, chest pain, dizziness, diarrhea), and behavioral (hypervigilance, scanning versus avoidance, paralysis of action, inability to perform) components. Its relationship to fear states in animals remains ambiguous. Fear is usually defined as an adaptive and appropriate response to clear-cut, external threat; anxiety is often thought to be excessive or inappropriate in relation to the stimulus and often extends well beyond the provoking situation (i.e., the cognitive aspect of anxious anticipation and uncertainty about the future). This distinction may simply reflect the more highly complex and developed human brain, whose frontal lobes allow for a degree of planning and rehearsal of future events and outcomes not possible in animals, along with a capacity for symbolism that facilitates multiple higher-order contextual associations with negative affect. While a certain amount of anxiety, analogous to fear, is adaptive in helping the organism prepare a response to a demanding situation, excess anxiety is maladaptive, characterizes a number of the clinical anxiety disorders, and also occurs as a significant symptom complex in other psychiatric disorders, most notably depression.

PSYCHOLOGICAL APPROACHES

Until recently, virtually all conceptualizations of anxiety were purely psychological and heavily focused on the role of the environment (Craig, Brown, & Baum, 1995). Freud and subsequent psychoanalysts emphasized the importance of early childhood experience as it was stored in the brain/mind. Internal conflicts based on these memories and recollections served as a cognitive stimulus for anxiety. While the potential threat of societal punishment and/or guilt over unacceptable impulses and wishes was the source of anxiety for Freud, later self-psychology theorists such as Kohut focused on anxiety as it related to developmental experiences that had damaged and threatened the individual's self-esteem.

Learning and behavior theorists conceptualized anxiety as due to more proximate causes in the individual's current environment. By seeing anxiety as a response to a specific stimulus that could be maintained by reinforcing consequences, behaviorists employed an understanding of the immediate triggers and consequences of the anxiety response to design specific treatment interventions for anxious patients. This strictly behavioral approach was most helpful in understanding the acquisition of and difficulty in extinguishing phobias (i.e., excessively fearful responses to concrete environmental situations and cues). Later theorists added a more cognitive element to these behavioral concepts in order to better understand the role of internal cognitive stimuli as potential triggers or reinforcing factors in the development of anxiety responses. This most recent development moved the discussion back in line with the psychoanalysts and, at the same time, this cognitive focus allowed learning theorists to bridge the gap between the more behaviorally-concrete, animal fear and the more human (i.e., cognitive) element of anxiety.

NEUROSCIENCE PERSPECTIVES

Recent developments in understanding the basic neurobiology of anxiety have allowed theorists to combine a neuroscience and behavioral/learning perspective to understand the role of both nature and nurture in determining the anxiety response. In this conceptualization, both external and internal (i.e., cognitive) environments play important roles in modulating activity in key brain areas that control the processing of environmental signals and the propensity for an anxiety response. This dual contribution is consistent with the equal and important role of both medication and psychotherapeutic approaches to the treatment of the various anxiety disorders.

The amygdala is an almond-shaped brain structure below the cerebral cortex and deep inside the temporal lobes. It serves as a central integrative brain center that coordinates both stimulus processing and anxiety response generation (Ledoux, 1996). This coordination is made possible by a rich set of reciprocal connections to higher cortical centers that process and compare multiple sensory and cognitive signals and to lower brainstem centers that regulate blood pressure, pulse, respiration, digestion, and other arousal-related functions. In animals, lesioning the amygdala prevents acquisition of a conditioned emotional response (i.e., animals cannot learn the association between, for example, an electric shock and a light signal). In other words, the amygdala is a key brain structure underlying the organism's ability to learn an association between various environmental contexts and danger/anxiety/apprehension.

Many studies of the anxiety and stress response have implicated key hormones and neurotransmitters. Prominent among these are CRH, which modulates adrenal cortisol response; norepinephrine, which controls the signal-to-noise ratio, thereby alerting the organism to the relevance of certain stimuli; and serotonin, which plays a key role in controlling sensory input to the amygdala as well as modulating anxiety responsivity. Brain norepinephrine synergizes with CRH in activating arousal of the peripheral sympathetic nervous system and the central nervous system; the amygdala plays a key role in orchestrating this response, and these hormones may provide feedback to the amygdala that potentiates the anxiety response.

It is of some interest that the responsivity of a number of these stress hormones has been linked to developmental experience by an elegant series of studies. These studies show that early adverse life experiences appear to set thresholds for the activity of these various stress response systems. Separation, loss, hardship, and abuse serve to increase the individual's tendency for hormone/neurotransmitter-related hyperarousal (Coplan et al., 1998). These findings are consistent with studies showing an increased rate of early adverse life experiences, especially separation and loss, in patients with various pathologic anxiety disorders.

It is clear that there are significant genetic contributions to anxiety (Plomin, DeFries, McClearn, & Rutter, 1997). Twin studies have examined a dimension of fearfulness called "behavioral inhibition" as well as shyness, observed in both the home and laboratory setting, and found genetic influences. There is also significant heritability for the personality characteristics of "neuroticism," which overlaps significantly with anxiety. Studies of infants of anxious patients have also shown early temperamental findings of behavioral inhibition before one year of age associated with an increased cortisol and heart rate response (Kagan, 1997) consistent with the setting of lower thresholds for stress response system activation noted above. However, twin studies also show a significant role for the environment. This is consistent with the same studies' findings that a proportion of behaviorally inhibited infants no longer meet behavioral inhibition criteria at age seven, while some older children acquire this response at age seven, but were not seen as behaviorally-inhibited as infants.

In the context of this neurobiologic system that modulates anxiety response, the dual roles of both medication and psychotherapy can be readily appreciated. Many commonly used antidepressant medications (which all have potent anti-anxiety effects) work on neurotransmitter systems in lower brainstem centers that control input and outflow from the amygdala. The more purely anti-anxiety medications (i.e., benzodiazepine tranquilizers) work in the amygdala itself, directly dampening certain inputs and perhaps affecting output. In contrast, the role of psychotherapy is probably to work at higher cortical centers, which will affect sensory input to the amygdala as well as modify amygdala processing itself via the reciprocal connections, thereby affecting proclivity to generate an anxiety response and the likelihood that this response can be extinguished with new experience and learning. The greater effectiveness of combined treatment with both modalities, often observed in studies of anxious patients, can be readily appreciated from this point of view.

REFERENCES

Craig, K. J., Brown, K. J., & Baum, A. (1995). Environmental factors in the etiology of anxiety. In F. E. Bloom & D. J. Kupfer (Eds.), *Psychopharmacology: The fourth generation of progress* (pp. 1325–1337). New York: Raven.

Coplan, J. D., Trost, R., Owens, M. J., Cooper, T., Gorman, J. M., Nemeroff, C. B., & Rosenblum, L. A. (1998). Cerebrospinal fluid concentrations of somatostatin and biogenic amines in grown primates reared by mothers exposed to manipulated foraging conditions. *Archives of General Psychiatry, 55,* 473–477.

Kagan, J. (1997). Temperament and the reactions to unfamiliarity. *Child Development, 68,* 139–143.

Kandel, E. R. (1983). From metapsychology to molecular biology: Explorations into the nature of anxiety. *American Journal of Psychiatry, 140*(10), 1277–1293.

LeDoux, J. E. (1996). *The emotional brain.* New York: Simon and Schuster.

Plomin, R. DeFries, J. C., McClearn, G. E., & Rutter, M. (1997). *Behavioral genetics.* New York: Freeman.

P. Roy-Byrne
Harborview Medical Center

ANTIANXIETY DRUGS
EMOTIONS
FEAR
STRESS
STRESS RESPONSE

APHASIA

A language disturbance produced by lesion or disease in the brain is called aphasia. These disorders are distinguished from those produced by other causes such as mental retardation, paralysis of the vocal apparatus, or sense organ disorders. Several different systems have been proposed to categorize various types of language disturbances, based on symptomatology. Most of these proposals make at least a general distinction between disturbances that primarily affect the ability to speak (expressive, or Broca's aphasia), and the ability to understand language (receptive, or Wernicke's aphasia). Aphasias that affect a very limited speech ability (such as the ability to read written language) are rarely seen, but their existence has provided information about the relationship between different brain areas and specific language functions.

Paul Broca (1824–1880) was the first to link types of aphasia with specifically located lesions in the brain. He demonstrated an association between damage in the left hemisphere and aphasia. Of the 20 cases of severe aphasia that he and his colleagues studied, all had damage primarily on the left side, and 19 had damage in the third frontal convolution, an area now called Broca's area, adjacent to the parts of the motor cortex that control the muscles of the face, throat, mouth, and tongue. Patients who suffer brain damage in this part of the brain usually show characteristic disturbances in the ability to produce written and spoken language. Symptoms include little speech, spoken slowly and arduously; poor articulation; improper sentence structure; and omission of small grammatical words and word endings. They may understand both spoken and written language well, however, and often their ability to sing familiar songs remains unaffected.

Carl Wernicke (1848–1905) identified another kind of aphasia that produces disturbances in the ability to understand language (receptive aphasia) as well as in speaking. Patients typically have fluent and rapid speech, but their utterances are devoid of content or meaning. They choose inappropriate words and add nonsensical syllables. This kind of aphasia is also usually associated with brain damage on the left side, but the damage is posterior to Broca's area. It usually includes an area in the temporal lobe, now called Wernicke's area, which lies between the primary auditory cortex and the angular gyrus. The region probably provides a connection between visual and auditory centers of the brain.

More specific types of aphasia have also been observed. Word deafness, for example, refers to an individual who can hear normally, read, and write, but cannot understand spoken language. This disorder occurred in a patient who suffered damage in the auditory pathway to the auditory cortex on the left side, and also in the callosal fibers that connect the auditory areas on the right side of the brain to the left side. Thus the patient's language areas were intact, but they were disconnected from his auditory areas, and he could not understand spoken language.

Based on observations of patients with different kinds of aphasia, and on his study of the sites of brain damage, Wernicke proposed a theory of language production that is still valid. The underlying utterance originates in Wernicke's area and then is transferred to Broca's area, where a coordinated program for the utterance is produced. This program is then passed to the motor cortex, which activates the appropriate motor sequences required for the specific utterance. The fiber pathways between the two language areas, and the cortical areas for vision and audition, play critical roles. Damage to them can produce unusual types of aphasia, such as word deafness.

SUGGESTED READING

Geschwind, N. (1965). Disconnexion syndromes in animals and man. *Brain, 88,* 23–194.

Geschwind, N. (1970). The organization of language and the brain. *Science, 27,* 940–945.

P. M. WALLACE
University of Maryland

COMMUNICATION PROCESSES

APPETITE DISORDERS

Appetite disorders are characterized by gross disturbances in eating behaviors; they include anorexia nervosa and bulimia. The essential feature of anorexia nervosa is reduction of total food intake followed by life-threatening weight loss. Initially, anorectics restrict food intake for fear of becoming obese, but in later stages of the illness there is loss of appetite. Clinical symptoms include intense fear of gaining weight, preoccupation with food, amenorrhea in females, distorted body image, and bizarre eating habits. Anorexia nervosa usually occurs between ages 10 and 30 and is more prevalent among females. Adequate studies have not been conducted to establish definite predisposing factors in anorexia nervosa.

Bulimia is characterized by recurrent episodes of binge eating. The term "bulimia" means "voracious appetite"; during the binge these individuals rapidly consume large quantities of high caloric foods. Bulimics are preoccupied with their weight and make repeated attempts to control it through dieting, vomiting, and laxatives. They are aware of their abnormal eating behaviors and often experience remorse and depression following a binge. Though some anorexic individuals engage in binge eating, bulimia is not considered a subcategory of anorexia nervosa. Onset of illness occurs usually in adolescence and is more prevalent among females. The predisposing factors in bulimia are unknown.

T. I. MOON

OBESITY

APPLIED RESEARCH

DEFINITION AND BACKGROUND

Applied research brings the scientific method to bear on problems and issues of direct relevance to a given societal need or question. Because it is focused toward problem solving within society, it is distinct from basic research, which is the pursuit of scientific knowledge for the sole purpose of extending scientific understanding and the knowledge base.

Applied psychologists are PhD graduates of universities, where they are extensively trained in the scientific method. Within this experimental method, the scientist develops an hypothesis based on existing knowledge and observations, then formulates an experiment to test the hypothesis, conducting systematic empirical observation and data gathering under carefully controlled conditions. Data are analyzed using appropriate, established statistical methods, and the outcome of the analysis determines whether the hypothesis is supported or rejected.

The distinction between applied and basic research forms a continuum rather than a dichotomy. A neuroscientist, for example, may seek to determine whether neuronal lesions in the hippocampus accelerate neuronal sprouting. As the scientist applies drug treatments to these lesions, she or he may discover a drug that effectively accelerates the sprouting process. This discovery, in turn, may prove to have long-range applications for patients who have suffered some form of spinal injury and resulting paralysis. Though at first the point was not to address a societal problem, the findings may prove to have direct societal applicability. On this basic/applied continuum, many outcomes of basic research have proved relevant in addressing given societal problems. The distinction lies in the starting point—whether the societal problem was directly addressed within the research or whether the research sought solely to extend the existing scientific knowledge base.

HISTORY

As early as 1908, Hugo Munsterberg stated, "The time for . . . Applied Psychology is surely near, and work has been started from most various sides. Those fields of practical life which come first in question may be said to be education, medicine, art, economics, and law." Hailed as "the first all-around applied psychologist in America," Munsterberg shaped the field, brought definition to it, and outlined its potential uses in business and industry. Equally significant was the pioneering influence of Walter Dill Scott. In the same year that Munsterberg predicted the era of applied psychology, Scott was bringing that era closer to fruition with his book *The Psychology of Advertising.* Seven years later he became the first psychologist to receive an appointment as professor of applied psychology at an American university (Carnegie Institute of Technology).

The early branches of applied research closely reflected the industrial orientations of their pioneers. Three of the basic research disciplines gave early birth to applied research offspring. Psychological testing produced personnel selection and classification; experimental psychology parented human factors engineering; and personality/social psychology provided the background setting for work in employee relations. The early history of applied research is, in effect, the history of industrial psychology as well.

WORLD WAR II LANDMARK

Prior to the 1940s, most psychologists were associated with universities and were conducting basic research. World War II brought with it an unprecedented range of problems requiring rapid scientific attention. Not all aviator recruits were created equal in their ability to fly planes, and selection methods were needed to determine those best suited for piloting. A highly sophisticated Nazi propaganda network challenged the United States' ability to counter-respond effectively. American citizens' attitudes toward food and product consumption needed to be changed in support of the war effort. And not least of all, returning war veterans brought with them psychological and emotional problems in numbers unprecedented within the U.S. mental health community. The pressure of such severe mental and emotional distress in such great proportions confronted a formerly basic research discipline with a "real world" clinical problem of incredible magnitude. In these areas and others, applied research was brought to the front line and needed to respond scientifically, effectively, and rapidly.

RANGE OF APPLIED RESEARCH SETTINGS

The range of applied research settings spans the broad range of society itself. Problems are scientifically addressed in settings ranging from hospitals, clinics, and other human service facilities to business and industry, courts and correctional institutions, law enforcement and community policing, government and military services, consulting and research organizations, clinical and counseling practice, and community planning.

The problems and questions are as wide-ranging as the settings themselves. Hospitals and clinics may need help in addressing problems related to preparing patients and their families for major surgery or working with those who have experienced a specific type of trauma. Business and industry may need assistance in personnel selection for given positions "on the line" or in upper-level management. A given industry may need to determine how to most effectively design a workspace within a factory or the controls within an airplane cockpit to minimize fatigue and maximize performance efficiency. Community planners may need to know what elements to build into their communities and architectural designs to create living spaces and communities conducive to positive social interaction and emotional health. Schools may need to effectively test student strengths and counsel these students on compatible career matches. All of these and related matters require the knowledge, expertise, and training of applied psychology and applied research.

BASIC/APPLIED TENSION

The formally stated goal of the American Psychological Association (APA) gives testimony to the tension and growth that applied research has brought to the discipline. The American Psychological Association's goal is "to advance psychology as a science, a profession, and as a means of promoting human welfare."

No members of the profession felt this implication more prominently than did clinical psychologists. Unable to meet their applied research and psychotherapy oriented needs within the APA, they formed state and national splinter groups (e.g., the American Association of Applied Psychology, Psychologists Interested in the Advancement of Psychotherapy) in which their applied research interests and activities could be effectively and meaningfully shared. The fact that splinter groups and their members now live under the APA roof is prominent evidence of the professional growth which has occurred within the Association. It is also a tribute to the efforts of pioneers such as Carl Rogers who devoted extensive time and personal energy to the task of unifying. The threefold goal—science, profession, human welfare—has now attained a visible balance within the professional activities and commitments of the APA.

The thoughts of basic researchers within colleges, universities, and research centers were a mirror image of those of the clinical psychologists involved in the earlier splintering. Convinced that the APA had now become a predominantly applied professional organization, they founded the American Psychological Society (APS). The organization's stated purpose, reminiscent of that of the APA, is "To promote, protect, and advance the interests of scientifically oriented psychology in research, application, and the improvement of human welfare." Many psychologists hold membership in both organizations, and only the future can determine whether APA and APS will continue as separate identities.

RAPID GROWTH AND SOCIETAL NEED

The growth and complexity of societal questions and needs have spawned a corresponding growth in applied research. Whereas only a few applied research divisions existed in the APA fifty years ago, several applied research divisions exist today. Among them are such divisions as The Society for the Psychological Study of Social Issues (9), Consulting Psychology (13), The Society for Industrial and Organizational Psychology (14), and Education/School/Counseling Psychology (15, 16, and 17, respectively). Other divisions relate to such areas as Public Service (18), Military Psychology (19), Adult Development and Aging (20), Rehabilitation (22), Consumer Psychology (23), Psychopharmacology and Substance Abuse (28), Mental Retardation and Developmental Disabilities (33), and Population and Environmental (34). The divisions are as vast and wide-ranging as societal needs themselves.

As one views the vast range of areas and divisions it becomes readily apparent that applied research will continue its rapid growth. Within this growth is the ever-present danger that psychologists may fractionate into their respective avenues of applied issues and problems. At the same time, it is good to remember that all are united in scientific training and in commitment to the scientific method, empirical observation, and systematic data gathering and analysis.

REFERENCES

Anastasi, A. (1979). *Fields of applied psychology.* New York: McGraw-Hill.

Braithwaite, A. (1989). *Applied psychologist.* New York: Open University Press/Taylor & Francis.

Davidson, M. A. (1977). The scientific/applied debate in psychology: A contribution. *Bulletin of the British Psychological Society, 30,* 273–278.

Schultz, D. P., & Schultz, S. E. (1997). *Psychology and work today.* New York: Prentice-Hall.

E. L. PALMER
Davidson College, Davidson, North Carolina

CONSUMER RESEARCH
FIELD RESEARCH

APPROACH-AVOIDANCE CONFLICT

Approach-avoidance conflict occurs when approach and avoidance tendencies of similar strength are opposed to each other. More generally, "conflict occurs when two or more incompatible reaction tendencies are instigated simultaneously" (Kimble, 1961). Conflict can involve approach-approach, avoidance-avoidance, approach-avoidance, or multiple combinations of these. "Approach-avoidance conflict is by far the most important and the most common form of conflict in animal behaviour" (McFarland, 1987). The approach-avoidance reaction tendencies can be elicited by stimuli that generally produce the reactions in a particular species, or by stimuli that are normally neutral but have acquired the ability to elicit the reactions through learning. Study of the former has illuminated the function of the behaviors involved; study of the latter has illuminated control of them. Approach-avoidance conflict is currently important as an assay for anti-anxiety drug action and for the consequent insight it provides into the neural basis of human anxiety disorders.

Analysis of conflict in the wild (ethology) has shown that when, for example, a source of food is close to a source of threat (as when it is being held by a human), animals will approach while they are far from the held food but will move away again when too close to the human holding the food, and, usually, will ultimately adopt an ambivalent posture at some intermediate distance (see McFarland, 1987). Here, the animal needs to obtain lunch without becoming lunch for someone else. The functional importance of correct resolution of this kind of conflict has led to ritualization of behavior associated with many conflicts. "Conflict behaviour is [also] often replaced by other seemingly irrelevant, behaviour . . . termed displacement activity" (McFarland, 1987). Thus, conflict results not only in a mixture of approach and avoidance behavior (which in a simple robot would result in unending oscillation at an intermediate distance) but a variety of complicated and sometimes apparently bizarre behaviors that may resolve the conflict by replacing the conflicting tendencies with some completely different behavior.

Analysis of approach-avoidance conflict in the laboratory provides some explanation of the ethological observations. Miller in 1944 (Kimble, 1961; Gray, 1987) proposed a model, the details of which have since been essentially confirmed. Both the tendency to approach a desired object and the tendency to avoid a feared object increase as the object gets closer to the animal (as measured by the strength with which the animal will pull toward or away from the object; see Gray, 1987). The avoidance gradient is steeper than the approach gradient; thus, at large distances, the animal approaches, while at short distances it avoids, and at equilibrium conflict behavior is observed (see Gray, 1987, for cases in which the avoidance gradient may be reduced).

Recently, ethoexperimental analysis (Blanchard & Blanchard, 1989) has extended this picture to temporal as well as spatial distance. (Ethoexperimental analysis involves the use of ethological measures and experimental manipulations within an ecologically consistent laboratory setting). When a cat is present, rats avoid an arena containing food. When there is no sign of a cat, rats enter the arena and eat the food. When a cat has recently been present or when the smell of a cat is present, the rats engage in an approach-avoidance oscillation accompanied by "risk analysis" behavior. Here, extensive assessment of the environment and the use of a "stretch-attend" posture may be seen not as ritualization or displacement activity but as behavior that will actively resolve the conflict (in favor of approach or avoidance) by gathering new information.

Blanchard and Blanchard (1989) ascribe pure avoidance to fear and distinguish it from risk analysis in the presence of threat, which they ascribe to anxiety. The implied relation between these behaviors and equivalent human clinical dysfunction is supported by the fact that the former are sensitive to anti-panic agents and the latter to anti-anxiety agents (Blanchard, Griebel, Henrie, & Blanchard, 1997). A mass of data from conventional experimental analysis suggest that avoidance within an approach-avoidance conflict (resulting from fear or frustration) is sensitive to anti-anxiety drug action, but pure avoidance (resulting from fear or frustration) is not (Gray, 1977). As with the ethological analysis, this suggests that approach-avoidance conflict involves more than a simple balance between approach and avoidance, and that it involves special mechanisms that produce ritualized behavior, displacement activity, and (given the drug data) an increase in avoidance tendencies that would, in ecological circumstances, result in more conservative behavior than if approach and avoidance were simply allowed to sum arithmetically.

A shift toward risk-proneness in approach-avoidance conflict with little change in pure approach or pure avoidance is characteristic not only of anti-anxiety drug action, but also of septal and hippocampal lesions. This fact has led to the proposal that anti-anxiety drugs produce their behavioral effects by impairing the control of hippocampal theta activity (Gray, 1982). In its most recent form (Gray & McNaughton, in press), this theory explicitly proposes that the septo-hippocampal system receives information about approach and avoidance tendencies, detects conflict, and (particularly with approach-avoidance conflict) increases avoidance tendencies. Given the previous distinction made by the Blanchards between fear and anxiety, the theory holds that generalized anxiety disorder (but not simple phobia or panic) involves hyperactivity of the septo-hippocampal system (McNaughton, 1997). This hyperactivity can be viewed as increasing the level of fear (or anticipation of loss of reward), and hence, as moving the point of intersection of approach and avoidance gradients further from sources of threat.

Approach-avoidance conflict, then, has been under detailed investigation for many decades with a clear picture now emerging of its structure, function, and psychological properties. Dysfunction of the mechanisms controlling approach-avoidance conflict appears fundamental to anxiety disorders. Detailed neural mechanisms and sites of action of therapeutic drugs on those neural mechanisms are now being discovered as substrates of the psychological processes involved (e.g., Crestani, et al., 1999). Of particular cause for optimism is that in this topic, ethology, behavior analysis, cognitive psychology, psychopharmacology, and behavioral neuroscience appear to be producing a single, coherent, integrated story.

REFERENCES

Blanchard, R. J., & Blanchard, D. C. (1989). Antipredator defensive behaviors in a visible burrow system. *Journal of Comparative Psychology, 103*(1), 70–82.

Blanchard, R. J., Griebel, G., Henrie, J. A., & Blanchard, D. C. (1997). Differentiation of anxiolytic and panicolytic drugs by effects on rat and mouse defense test batteries. *Neuroscience and Biobehavioral Reviews, 21,* 783–789.

Crestani, F., Lorez, M., Baer, K., Essrich, C., Benke, D., Laurent, J. P., Belzung, C., Fritschy, J.-M., Lüscher, B., and Mohler, H. (1999). Decreased GABA$_A$-receptor clustering results in enhanced anxiety and a bias for threat cues. *Nature Neuroscience, 2,* 833–839.

Gray, J. A. (1977). Drug effects on fear and frustration: Possible limbic site of action of minor tranquilizers. In L. L. Iversen, S. D. Iversen, & S. H. Snyder (Eds.), *Handbook of psychopharmacology: Vol. 8. Drugs, neurotransmitters and behaviour* (pp. 433–529). New York: Plenum Press.

Gray, J. A. (1982). *The neuropsychology of anxiety: An enquiry in to the functions of the septo-hippocampal system.* Oxford, England: Oxford University Press.

Gray, J. A. (1987). *The psychology of fear and stress.* London: Cambridge University Press.

Gray, J. A., & McNaughton, N. (in press). *The neuropsychology of anxiety: An enquiry in to the functions of the septo-hippocampal system.* Oxford, England: Oxford University Press.

Kimble, G. A. (1961). *Hilgard and Marquis' conditioning and learning.* New York: Appleton-Century-Crofts.

McFarland, D. (1987). *The Oxford companion to animal behaviour.* Oxford, England: Oxford University Press.

McNaughton, N. (1997). Cognitive dysfunction resulting from hippocampal hyperactivity—A possible cause of anxiety disorder. *Pharmacology Biochemistry and Behavior, 56,* 603–611.

Miller, N. E. (1944). Experimental studies of conflict. In J. M. Hunt (Ed.), *Personality and the behavioural disorders.* New York: Ronald.

N. McNaughton
University of Otago
New Zealand

FEAR
PHOBIAS

APTITUDE TESTING, IMPORTANCE OF

Aptitude testing involves estimating an individual's potential to perform a criterion of interest on the basis of measures of that individual's knowledge, skills, abilities, or other attributes. Such testing is important for selection efforts, such as determining who has the greatest likelihood of excelling in a school or technical training program. Aptitude testing is also central to personnel classification; that is, matching individuals to jobs or job tasks on the basis of aptitudes. Since many aptitudes exhibit developmental change, aptitude testing also is important for validating theories of the nature and course of such change (English, 1998).

Assessment can be *concurrent,* in which case the aptitude test, or *predictor,* and the outside criterion against which the predictor is being validated occur at the same point in time. The assessment can be *predictive,* where the predictor occurs in the present and the criterion will occur in the future. Alternatively, the assessment can be *postdictive,* as when the predictor occurs in the present and the criterion has occurred in the past.

The results of aptitude assessment can fruitfully be linked to intervention in educational, occupational, and clinical settings (Sternberg, Torff, & Grigorenko, 1998). In addition to measuring learning, tests can be *agents* of learning. Such *learning tests* are designed to foster learning during assessment (Dempster, 1996).

ISSUES IN APTITUDE TEST DESIGN AND DEVELOPMENT
Researchers are interested in elucidating (a) relationships between aptitudes and the criterion measures that the aptitudes predict, (b) types of aptitudes being measured and interrelationships between the aptitudes, (c) the manner in which the aptitudes are measured, and (d) the psychometric properties of tests in given testing sessions. Psychometric issues include standardizability, reliability, validity, and adverse impact.

Test administration issues include the time available for testing, resources and technology needed for administration and scoring of aptitude tests, and adaptability of tests and testing equipment for different test sites. *Test utility* issues include ease of administration, costs associated with training test administrators, maintaining test sites and equipment, and preparing test materials. *Implementation* of testing programs that have broad applicability in a timely manner remains an important challenge. Furthermore, tests should be designed to minimize attrition.

CONCEPTIONS OF APTITUDE
Theoretical notions regarding the origins of aptitude guide approaches to aptitude testing and directly address the above issues (Dillon, 1996; Flanagan & Genshaft, 1997). Performance on aptitude measures may result from a range of biological, cognitive, and social factors including (a) activation of competence, (b) trainability, (c) changes in learning and development resulting from mediated learning experiences, (d) guided experience, and (e) direct experience (Gottfredson, 1997).

APTITUDE TESTING FRAMEWORK
Testing paradigms can be considered along four dimensions: aptitudes, methods, measures, and timing.

Aptitude Dimensions
The level of specificity of predictors, domains tapped, and the prior knowledge demands of aptitude tests are all important factors in aptitude testing. Aptitude dimensions range from neurophysiolog-

ical, electrophysiological, and perceptual processes to information processing components (Dillon, 1996) and metacomponents (Sternberg, 1998; Sternberg, Torff, & Grigorenko, 1998); knowledge and reasoning aptitudes (Dillon & Vineyard, 1999); school subject aptitudes (Greene, 1996; Jacobs, 1998; Skehan, 1998; Sparks & Ganschow, 1996); sociocultural attributes (Lopez, 1997); personality, temperament, attitude, and motivational attributes; and interpersonal attributes such as social problem solving aptitudes including environmental adaptation aptitudes (Sternberg, 1997).

Information processing theory and methodologies have enabled researchers to decompose reasoning and other IQ test-type tasks into their distinct information processing components, such as encoding, rule inference, rule application, and confirmation. Researchers have studied the functioning of these component processes during complex thinking and problem solving (e.g., Dillon, 1996). Considerable attention has been paid to issues in special education testing (Carver & Clark, 1998; Forness, Keogh, & MacMillan, 1998; Greenspan & McGrew, 1996; Grigorenko & Sternberg, 1997) and aptitude testing in gifted education programs (Sternberg, 1998b).

A great deal of interest has been displayed in robust ability and aptitude models that include attributes that occur in everyday life, in addition to or in place of traditional academically oriented attributes. Two such robust and practically oriented programs are *Practical Intelligence for School* (Williams, Blythe, White, Li, Sternberg, & Gardner, 1996) and Howard Gardner's *Theory of Multiple Intelligences* (Gardner, 1993, 1995; 1997; Reid & Romanoff, 1997). These programs are based on the assumption that traditional approaches to both aptitude measurement and instruction focus on a narrow range of abilities and skills, ignoring other attributes. Aptitude testing programs have been linked to Sternberg's (1998) and Gardner's aptitude frameworks (e.g., Gardner, 1993; 1995, 1997; Sternberg, Ferrari, & Clinkenbeard, 1996).

Research in *tacit knowledge;* that is, knowledge that is not specifically taught but is learned during the course of daily living or learned by oneself on the job, has been fruitful in accounting for variation in performance in a variety of settings (e.g., John & Mashna, 1997). In addition to one's possession of various abilities, research in cognitive flexibility has helped researchers to understand the manner in which individuals select and deploy tactics as the demands of a task or situation warrant (Dillon & Vineyard, 1999; Fox, 1997). Aptitude models may include measures of personality, temperament, and intellectual style. In addition, researchers may productively examine relationships between measures of cognition and affect as well as relationships between the two constructs and measures of academic and occupational success.

Beyond specification of the origins and nature of aptitudes, it is useful to attempt to understand the relationships between aptitudes. Crawford, Deary, Allan, and Gustafsson (1998) and Gustafsson and Snow (1996) discuss research in the hierarchical model of ability organization and the possible use of ability profiles to advance the theoretical and applied study of aptitude. The intended purpose of aptitude or ability testing determines the necessary degree of specificity in the measurement of ability dimensions. In instances where precise specification of general and specific ability constructs is necessary, ability profiles may yield important information about the organization of abilities and aptitudes.

Methods of Test Administration and Measures Taken from Tests

Methods of test administration and data collection include computerized adaptive testing, dynamic testing, paper-and-pencil testing, observational data collection, document analysis, portfolio assessment, and job sample measures. Conceptions of aptitude differ in the nature of the databases on which the different models rest. Some researchers use complex and extensive statistical methods to uncover mental structures and processes, while other researchers base their conceptions of aptitude on interpretations of psychological observations and experimental findings. Still other researchers employ psychophysiological, neurophysiological, electrophysiological, or information-processing paradigms, sometimes coupled with experimental manipulations. Finally, some researchers use *curriculum-based assessment* (CBA) or *performance assessment* (PA) paradigms, which boast connections between assessment, curriculum, and instruction (Cantor, 1997; Elliott & Fuchs, 1997; Swisher & Green, 1998).

Timing

Aptitude tests can be given to determine who has the highest probability of succeeding in a particular education or training program. Aptitude tests also can be given prior to initial job selection. Subsequent to job selection, testing is used for the purpose of classification to particular jobs. Testing also is undertaken for job enhancement, such as for retention, promotion, or selection to advanced training programs.

CRITERION MEASURES: VALIDATING APTITUDE MODELS

Criterion measures, against which aptitude models are validated, are derived from a variety of school and occupational arenas. Common criterion measures include performance in (a) high school and college, (b) military training, (c) medical school preparation courses and medical school, and (d) complex workplace activities.

TESTING IN THE 21ST CENTURY

Kyllonen (1996), Schulz and Nicewander (1997), and Wang and Vispoel (1998) offer the following goals of testing in the 21st century: to develop testing systems that are broad-based, precise, quick, and implemented in a short time frame. In addition, important technology associated with aptitudes and abilities measurement should be used, including computer delivery, item-generation technology, multidimensional adaptive technology, comprehensive cognitive aptitudes and abilities measurement, time-parameterized testing, and latent factor-centered design.

REFERENCES

Carver, R. P., & Clark, S. W. (1998). Investigating reading disabilities using the rauding diagnostic system. *Journal of Learning Disabilities, 31,* 453–471.

Crawford, J. R., Deary, A., & Gustafsson, J.-E. (1998). Evaluating competing models of the relationship between inspection time and intelligence. *Intelligence, 26*(1), 27–42.

Cantor, A. S. (1997). The future of intelligence testing in the schools. *The School Psychology Review, 26,* 255–261.

Dempster, F. N. (1996). Using tests to promote classroom learning. In R. F. Dillon (Ed.), *Handbook on testing.* Westport, CT: Greenwood.

Dillon, R. F. (1996). *Handbook on testing.* Westport, CT: Greenwood.

Dillon, R. F., & Vineyard, G. M. (in press). Convergent and discriminant validation of flexible combination ability. *Resources in education.*

Elliott, S. N., & Fuchs, L. S. (1997). The utility of curriculum-based measurement and performance assessment as alternatives to traditional intelligence and achievement tests. *The School Psychology Review, 26*(2), 224–233.

English, A. (1998). Uncovering students' analytic, practical and creative intelligences: One school's application of Sternberg's triarchic theory. *School Administrator, 55,* 28–29.

Flanagan, D. P., & Genshaft, J. (1997). Issues in use and interpretation of intelligence tests in the schools: Guest editors' comments. *The School Psychology Review, 26,* 146–149.

Forness, S. R., Keogh, B. K., & MacMillan, D. L. (1998). What is so special about IQ? The limited explanatory power of cognitive abilities in the real world of special education. *Remedial and Special Education, 19,* 315–322.

Fox, C. M. (1997). A confirmatory factor analysis of the structure of tacit knowledge in nursing. *Journal of Nursing Education, 36,* 459–466.

Gardner, H. (1993). *Multiple intelligences: The theory in practice.* New York: Basic Books.

Gardner, H. (1995). Reflections on multiple intelligences: Myths and messages. *Kappan, 77,* 202–209.

Gardner, H. (1997). Multiple intelligences as a partner in school improvement. *Educational Leadership, 55,* 20–21.

Greenspan, S., & McGrew, K. S. (1996). Response to Mathias and Nettelbeck on the structure of competence: Need for theory-based methods to test theory-based questions. *Research in Developmental Disabilities, 17,* 145–160.

Grigorenko, E., & Sternberg, R. J. (1997). Styles of thinking, abilities, and academic performance. *Exceptional Children, 63,* 295–312.

Gustafsson, J.-E., & Snow, R. E. (1996). Ability profiles. In R. F. Dillon (Ed.), *Handbook on testing.* Westport, CT: Greenwood.

Jacobs, E. L. (1998). KIDTALK: A computerized language screening test. *Journal of Computing in Childhood Education, 9,* 113–131.

John, B. E., & Mashna, M. M. (1997). Evaluating a multimedia authoring tool. *Journal of the American Society for Information Science, 48,* 1005–1022.

Kyllonen, P. (1996). Smart testing. In R. F. Dillon (Ed.), *Handbook on testing.* Westport, CT: Greenwood.

Lopez, R. (1997). The practical impact of current research and issues in intelligence test interpretation and use for multicultural populations. *The School Psychology Review, 26,* 249–254.

Reid, C., & Romanoff, B. (1997). Using multiple intelligence theory to identify gifted children. *Educational Leadership, 55,* 71–74.

Schulz, E. M., & Nicewander, W. A. (1997). Grade equivalent and IRT representations of growth. *Journal of Educational Measurement, 34,* 315–331.

Skehan, P. (1998). *A cognitive approach to language learning.* Oxford, England: Oxford University Press.

Sparks, R. L., & Ganschow, L. (1996). Teachers' perceptions of students' foreign language academic skills and affective characteristics. *The Journal of Educational Research, 89,* 172–185.

Sternberg, R. J. (1997). Successful intelligence: A broader view of who's smart in school and in life. *International Schools Journal, 17,* 19–31.

Sternberg, R. J. (1998a). Metacognition, abilities, and developing expertise: What makes an expert student? *Instructional Science, 26*(1–2), 127–140.

Sternberg, R. J. (1998b). Ability testing, instruction, and assessment of achievement: Breaking out of the vicious circle. *NASSP Bulletin, 82,* 4–10.

Sternberg, R. J. (1998c). Teaching and assessing for successful intelligence. *School Administrator, 55,* 26–27, 30–31.

Sternberg, R. J., Ferrari, M., & Clinkenbeard, P. R. (1996). Identification, instruction, and assessment of gifted children: A construct validation of a triarchic model. *Gifted Child Quarterly, 40,* 129–137.

Sternberg, R. J., Torff, B., & Grigorenko, E. L. (1998). Teaching triarchically improves school achievement. *Journal of Educational Psychology, 90,* 374–384.

Swisher, J. D., & Green, S. B. (1998). An empirical study comparing curriculum-embedded assessment and traditional aptitude measures for predicting job-related outcomes for students with disabilities. *Educational Assessment, 5,* 57–70.

Wang, T., & Vispoel, W. P. (1998). Properties of ability estimation methods in computerized adaptive testing. *Journal of Educational Measurement, 35,* 109–135.

Williams, W. M., Blythe, T., White, N., Li, J., Sternberg, R. J., & Gardner, H. (1996). *Practical intelligence for school.* New York: HarperCollins.

R. DILLON

INDUSTRIAL PSYCHOLOGY

ARCHETYPES

Carl Jung introduced the term *archetype* into psychological theory, and he is primarily responsible for the development of the concept to which it refers. Jung recognized two basic layers in the unconscious—the personal unconscious, whose contents are derived from present lifetime experience, and the collective unconscious, whose contents are inherited and essentially universal within the species. The collective unconscious consists of archetypes. Jung described these as primordial images that have existed from the remotest times, but images that lack clear content. Their specific content as realized images is supplied by the material of conscious experience. Thus, the archetype as such is an empty form that must be inferred, or derived by abstraction, from a class of experienced images or symbols.

Jung (1969) noted that the term was first used by Philo Judaeus and later appeared in the writings of Irenaeus and Dionysius the Areopagite. In such ancient uses, it had a meaning close to that of Plato's *ideas.* A similar concept recurs over the centuries in idealistic philosophy and was emphasized by Romantic philosophers of the 19th century.

Jung acknowledged an intellectual lineage that can be traced to Plato, but he contended that his use of the term *archetype* is more empirical and less metaphysical than the use of the same or corresponding terms by idealistic philosophers. He arrived at the concept initially through a study of psychotic patients and augmented his understanding through a more comprehensive study of symbol systems. To the extent that he used experience as a springboard for theory, Jung can be regarded as more Aristotelian than Platonic. Yet, to the extent that Jung's theory of archetypes is valid, it leads to the paradoxical conclusion that only a limited empiricism is possible. For Jung, the archetypes are the most fundamental ingredients of the whole psyche. They are the forms that underlie everything we perceive, imagine, and think. Through progressive accumulation and elaboration of specific contents, the archetype becomes manifest in the image and then in the conscious idea, and even the basic concepts of philosophy and science can be regarded as ultimately rooted in archetypal forms. Thus, while Jung's concept of the archetype may be partly empirical, it necessarily rests on its own archetypal base.

Jung noted that this concept is akin to that of the instinct. Each term refers to an inborn predisposition, and in each case it is a predisposition that must be inferred from a certain class of effects. The term *instinct* refers to a predisposition to act in a certain way, while *archetype* refers to a predisposition toward a certain kind of "psychic apprehension." One might surmise that in both cases we are dealing with a tendency that has evolved and become universal within a species because it has survival value. Jung, however, did not provide a biological rationale for the archetype, and he considered it rather futile to speculate on its origin. He merely suggested that if the archetype ever "originated," its origin must have coincided with that of the species.

Jung began to develop the archetype concept during his early work at the Burghölzli Hospital, where he observed that some of his relatively uneducated psychotic patients experienced universal religious and mythological symbols. In many instances it was clear that the patient could not have learned of the symbol through formal study, and the appearance of the symbol in the patient's ideation or imagery had to represent a spontaneous eruption of unconscious material not derived from experience during the present lifetime. Jung subsequently explored the archetypal realm through an intensive examination of his own dreams and waking fantasies. He developed a method of "active imagination," by which he was able to secure a spontaneous flow of dream-like material in a waking state. He studied religious symbolism, mythology, tribal lore, and such occult disciplines as alchemy in quest of evidence of universal motifs. Thus, his conclusions can be said to rest on an extremely broad base of observational data.

The archetypes to which Jung devoted the greatest amount of attention in his writings include the shadow, the anima and animus, the wise old man, the magna mater (or great earth mother), the child, and the self (Jung, 1968). Each of these archetypes collects a great deal of associated content, which varies according to the experience of the individual and colors a large portion of our total experience. The behavioral, intellectual, and perceptual qualities over which we fail to develop much conscious control remain with us as a kind of unexamined dark side and become associated with the shadow. The feminine qualities that a man fails to realize consciously in himself become associated with his anima, while the unrealized masculine qualities of the woman become associated with her animus. Thus, each archetype becomes the core of a system of content that varies a bit from one individual to another.

The archetypes noted above tend to be experienced in personified form. They may appear as figures in our dreams, and they provide the source of such cultural symbols as gods and goddesses. They also enter extensively into our interpersonal experience, for we frequently project them onto other people. Each of these archetypes can be expressed in a great variety of personifications. A given anima image, for example, may be positive or negative, and may emphasize any of a number of possible qualities—sexuality, beauty, wisdom, spirituality, moral virtue, destructiveness, and so forth. There are other archetypes, which Jung (1969) called archetypes of transformation, that do not appear in a personal form. They are expressed in many of the situations, places, implements, and events of our dreams, and they govern corresponding motifs in folklore. Jung believed he had identified the most important archetypes. Yet, if his basic assumptions are valid, it may be assumed that the total number of archetypes is indefinitely large and that an exhaustive inventory is not feasible.

REFERENCES

Jung, C. G. (1968). *Aion: Researches into the phenomenology of the self. The collected works of C. G. Jung, Vol. 9, Pt. II.* Princeton, NJ: Princeton University Press.

Jung, C. G. (1969). *The archetypes and the collective unconscious. The collected works of C. G. Jung, Vol. 9, Pt. I.* Princeton, NJ: Princeton University Press.

R. W. Coan
University of Arizona

ANALYTICAL PSYCHOLOGY

ARISTOTLE (384–322 B.C.)

Aristotle was a student in Plato's Academy in Athens. Later, he tutored Alexander the Great at Philip of Macedonia's court. Aristotle's early writings reflected his schooling in the theory of ideas at the Academy, whereas his later works are a chronicle of the gradual development of his own philosophical position.

Aristotle created a new science of logic, the art and method of correct thinking. His methods made two important contributions. First, his thinking was more analytical than Plato's, although there was no dominant insight such as the theory of ideas. Instead, Aristotle used his concepts—form, matter, substance, cause, potentiality, actuality, substratum—as *tools* for problem solving. Second, he evolved a technique for surveying all previous and possible answers to a question. By classifying an infinite number of solutions to the problem, it is possible to formulate an efficient method that reveals the characteristics of any good answer to the problem. The incorrect solutions can then be eliminated by comparing them to an equivalent answer that can be shown to be unacceptable. The *self-evident principles* are those universal truths that no properly disciplined mind can deny.

In Aristotelian thought, knowledge is expanded to include two classifications: theoretical science and practical science. Theoretical science, as in Plato's definition, represents what is necessarily and always true; practical science represents what is merely true in many cases and of value for practical action, but need not be true if human beings desire to make some change. Informed opinion is, therefore, a kind of practical knowledge.

As a teacher and philosopher, Aristotle's subject matter and writings were voluminous. The library of his titles is often divided into works of logic, science, aesthetics, and philosophy.

N. A. Haynie

ARTIFICIAL INTELLIGENCE

Artificial intelligence (AI) is a domain of research, application, and instruction concerned with programming computers to perform in ways that, if observed in human beings, would be regarded as intelligent. Intelligence is attributed to human beings when they play chess or solve the Tower of Hanoi puzzle, or learn to do such things; computer programs that can perform any of these tasks even moderately well, or can learn to do so, are examples of artificial intelligence. Today, sophisticated and powerful programs are able to steer automobiles on highways and discover chemical reaction paths from data about the inputs and outputs of multi-stage chemical reactions; they can simulate the processes that humans use to read problem instructions and form a mental representation of the problem structure; they diagnose diseases; they simulate the behavior of human participants in experiments on verbal learning, concept formation, and recovery of information from long-term memory; and they perform many other tasks of comparable complexity.

COMPUTERS AND INTELLIGENCE

When modern electronic digital computers emerged from their security wraps after World War II, they were employed mainly to carry out numerical computations efficiently. But it was soon observed (perhaps first by the English logician, A. M. Turing; Luger, 1995) that computers were not limited to numbers but could process all kinds of symbols or patterns, literal and diagrammatic as well as numerical. Appropriately programmed, a computer can read a bit of text describing a simple situation (e.g., "the cat is chasing the dog,"), and then examine an associated diagram or picture and decide whether the text describes the visual situation. Artificial intelligence programs exploit capabilities like these, although often in much more complex situations, as the examples cited earlier indicate.

A digital computer may be called a physical symbol system, for it is capable of inputting (reading), outputting (writing), organizing (associating), storing, copying, and comparing symbols. It is also capable of branching, or following different courses of action depending on whether two symbol structures are observed to be the same or different. The fundamental hypothesis of AI is that just these capabilities are required (and sufficient) for intelligent behavior. Two corollaries follow: First, because computers demonstrably have these capabilities, they can be programmed to behave intelligently. Second, because people can behave intelligently, their brains are (at least) physical symbol systems (Newell & Simon, in Luger, 1995).

THE TWO BRANCHES OF AI

This fundamental hypothesis of AI and its corollaries are empirical hypotheses, the validity of which can only be determined by experiment and empirical test. Research in AI consists of building computer programs and testing both the range of tasks the computers can perform and the processes they use to perform them. The research is aimed at two distinct goals, one of them pursued mainly by computer scientists and engineers, and the other mainly by psychologists and cognitive scientists.

AI as an engineering science aims to broaden the capabilities of computers for intelligent behavior in order to augment and assist human intelligence in real-world tasks. This kind of AI makes no claims to imitate the processes of human intelligence—only to produce intelligent responses to the demands of a given task. AI programs in this category may use arithmetic processes far beyond human capabilities. Thus Deep Blue, the grand master–level chess program that defeated the world's champion, Garry Kasparov, in 1997, may explore millions of branches of the game tree before choosing a move; while we know that a human grand master seldom explores more than a hundred. Of course, AI programs are not barred from borrowing human processes when these are known and can enhance program effectiveness. (Deep Blue, for example, is not a pure brute force program, but incorporates a vast amount of chess knowledge of the kind used by human grand masters), but the choice and mix of methods for these applications is based on efficiency, not on resemblance to human processing.

AI as cognitive science aims to simulate the actual processes that human beings use in their intelligent behavior. Computer simulation programs are intended as theories that describe and explain human performance. Technically, a computer program is a system of difference equations, closely analogous to the differential equations used to express physical theories. A program predicts the next action of a system as a function of its present state.

AI programs designed for human simulation are tested by comparing the computer output, second by second when possible, with human behavior to determine the similarity of both the outcome and the behavior paths of computer and person. Thus, in an experiment, people may be asked to speak aloud while they are solving problems in algebra or geometry. A computer program is then written to solve problems of the same kind, using only processes known (or thought) to be available to people (e.g., with appropriate limits on available knowledge, computational speed, and short-term memory capacity).

HISTORY OF AI AS COGNITIVE SCIENCE

This article examines AI of this second kind, used as a tool for psychology. Its antecedents in precomputer times were goal-seeking artificial organisms, like Grey Walter's "turtle," a small robot on wheels, which navigated about a room and sought out an electric outlet to recharge its batteries when they were low. (For an account of the history to 1979, see McCorduck, 1979.) Computer-based AI had its beginnings in the middle 1950s. Early research studied well-structured, puzzle-like tasks and games like chess and checkers, where human behavior could be compared experimentally with the computer output, and there was much commingling of research with the applied branch of AI, described above. The AI research produced a basic understanding of human problem solving as (nonrandom) search guided by heuristics or rules of thumb, and confirmed Selz's and Duncker's early emphasis on means-ends analysis as a central human tool for solving problems (Newell & Simon, 1972).

The Tower of Hanoi problem requires moving a pyramid of disks, one at a time, from one to another of three posts without ever placing a large disk atop a smaller one. People (and the computer simulation) ultimately set the goal of moving the largest disk to the final goal post, noticing what smaller disks block that move as illegal, setting the goal of moving the largest of these smaller disks out of the way, and then repeating this pattern until the problem is solved. The computer program may be designed either to carry out this kind of means-ends analysis (a performance program) or to start with a more primitive search and gradually acquire the efficient strategy (a learning program).

As research expanded into domains like chess playing, medical diagnosis, and chemical analysis, it became clear that successful performance by human professionals depends on rapidly accessing large bodies of knowledge stored in memory by recognizing cues (a process often called *intuition*). Experiments showed that human experts can recognize 100,000 or more familiar patterns to access this information in long-term memory. For example, physicians recognize disease symptoms and thereby recall their knowledge of the disease, the treatment of the disease, and further diagnostic tests. In the 1980s, research in the cognitive science branch of AI began to emphasize the organization of long-term memory (semantic memory) and its acquisition through learning processes.

Early cognitive simulations handled only a narrow range of tasks. The General Problem Solver (GPS) began to separate problem-solving processes that apply to many tasks from the special knowledge needed for each particular task (Luger, 1995). GPS was followed by C. S. Novak's ISAAC System ("ISAAC," from "Isaac Newton"; Simon, 1996), which accepts natural-language instructions for problems in mechanics, and Hayes and Simon's UNDERSTAND (Simon, 1996), which can build representations of new tasks from descriptions in natural language. Further generality is achieved by the unified theories of cognition, including SOAR (State, Operator, and Result), a program that attempts generality in learning and problem solving (Newell, 1990); the ACT (Adaptive Control Theory) systems of J. R. Anderson, which focus on both learning in semantic memory and on problem solving (Anderson, 1999); and EPAM (Elementary Perceiver and Memorizer), which focuses on verbal learning, perception, and categorization (Luger & Stubblefield, 1998).

PROGRAMMING LANGUAGES FOR AI

From the beginning, AI required new programming languages especially adapted to its needs. List-processing languages (initially developed in 1956 by Newell, Shaw, and Simon, and succeeded by Lisp, developed by J. McCarthy about 1960) allowed for flexible organization of memory by associations and by representations of such psychological concepts as directed associations and schemas. Associations (e.g., "What is a correlative of dog?;" "cat" would be an answer) had been introduced into psychology by the Würzburg School and the Gestaltists, and representations (structures or "pictures" of objects) had been introduced by Bartlett (1932). In this way, basic components of psychological theory like these are built into the programming language itself. A list-processing language represents memory as a network of tests for discriminating among objects by their features (the "index"), with symbol structures at each leaf node of the net that hold the information about the objects or concepts sorted to that node (the "encyclopedia").

Around 1970, production system languages, derived from ideas of logician E. L. Post, were adapted to psychology (Newell & Simon, 1972). Their basic instruction format is a sophisticated elaboration of classical stimulus-response connections. Each production consists of an "if" clause followed by a "then" clause. When the "if," or condition, matches information held in short-term memory, then an associated action (the "then") is taken. Matching the conditions achieves recognition; the action may manipulate information in memory or it may produce an external motor response. Thus, in the Tower of Hanoi, the following instructions might be used: "If the movement of disk Y from stake p to stake r is blocked by disk W, and by no larger disk, then set the goal of moving disk W to stake q [internal action]," or "If the goal is to move disk Y to stake q and the move is legal, then make the move [external action]."

Production systems also provide a powerful model of learning, for they can create and annex new productions that employ new skills. For example, production systems have learned to solve equations in algebra by examining worked-out examples of solutions and then manufacturing new productions containing the solution processes observed in the examples. These ideas have been used to create curricula for teaching algebra and geometry by the study of worked-out examples.

CONNECTIONIST SYSTEMS AND THEIR LANGUAGE

The AI systems described to this point operate at the symbolic, or functional, level. They do not simulate the detailed workings of the neurons that implement them. They are concerned with the brain's "software," not its "hardware." It is precisely because they deal with information processes, not neurons, that they can be simulated by computers that employ entirely different physical devices, like chips, to carry out the same symbolic processes. The first explanations of how physical switching circuits can perform all the functions of logical reasoning and of all-or-none nerve action predate computers (McCorduck, 1979).

Another branch of AI employs "connectionist" or Parallel Distributed Processing (PDP) structures, also called "nerve nets," the components of which are nodes and links that can be regarded as very abstract representations of nerves or groups of neurons (Rumelhart & McClelland, 1986). These systems are also capable of learning, and they have been mainly used to simulate lower-level sensory, perceptual, and categorizing processes. They are organized into linked interacting nodes that operate as an input ("sensory") layer, connected to additional nodes ("hidden layers") that connect with output nodes ("response" layer). Signals input to the net activate various nodes in the hidden layers, which in turn activate particular output nodes. The response corresponds to the most strongly activated output node. Feedback about the correctness of the response then causes changes in the levels of activation of the various nodes in the system and their links, and these changes alter the responses to signals, gradually improving the responses. The degree of resemblance of these structures to real nerve structures and their processes is still a matter of investigation and debate.

There is also still great uncertainty about the spheres of mental functioning in which symbolic systems or connectionist systems provide the better modeling tools. Up to the century's end, far more experience has been gained with symbolic systems than with connectionist models of complex cognitive behavior.

CONTRIBUTIONS OF AI MODELING TO COGNITIVE PSYCHOLOGY

AI has thus far been most successful with so-called higher mental processes, including language. Until rather recently, progress has been slower in imitating the sophisticated sensory and pattern-extraction processes of the human eye and ear, and in linking these with motor processes (robotics). Research progress continues, however, on all fronts, with some specialization of groups concerned with problem solving and memory, with sensory pattern recognition, and with robotics. AI research with cognitive science goals is to be found primarily in psychology departments, but to some extent also in linguistics and neurobiology. AI research aimed at expert systems for practical application is pursued in computer science and, increasingly, in science and engineering departments that find applications in their domains (for example, architectural design, discovery of reaction paths for chemical synthesis, aids to expository writing, drawing, musical composition, and so on).

AI methods and techniques were important in bringing about the "cognitive revolution" in psychology in the 1960s and 1970s, and computer simulation and analysis of verbal protocols are now standard research tools in experimental psychology. To illustrate the kinds of insights gained into human psychology with these and other AI methods, I will describe some examples of such research.

ARTIFICIAL INTELLIGENCE AND MATHEMATICAL THEOREM PROVING

Finding proofs for theorems in mathematics and logic was an early task for AI. With few exceptions, including several of the very first theorem provers (the Logic Theorist, the Geometry Theorist, and a program to solve algebra word problems), this effort has been directed at providing intelligent assistance to human logicians and mathematics, and not at understanding human cognitive performance. Rarely has there been much borrowing of selective heuristic search and recognition methods from psychology. Nevertheless, some lessons have been learned that are quite relevant for psychology.

In a few cases, new theorems have been found and proved, and in the case (Appel & Haken, 1979) of the celebrated Four Color Theorem ("four colors are sufficient to color every map so that countries sharing a common border have different colors"), the computer played an indispensable role in exploring exhaustively the several hundred special cases into which the problem could be divided. Appel and Haken present a dramatic account of the sophistication of the computer program and its mathematical ideas, which sometimes exceeded their own in quality.

At this point. . . the program. . . began to surprise us. At the beginning, we would check its arguments by hand so we could always predict the course it would follow. . . but now it suddenly started to act like a chess-playing machine. It would work out compound strategies based on all the tricks it had been "taught" and often these approaches were far more clever than those we would have tried. Thus it began to teach us things about how to proceed that we never expected. In a sense it had surpassed its creators in some aspects of the "intellectual" as well as the mechanical parts of the task (p. 175).

Most automated theorem provers use methods (e.g., the resolution method) that mainly exploit computer speed and size, and perform systematic searches far beyond human capabilities. In spite of this, or perhaps because of it, little new logic or mathematics has emerged from these efforts. A tempting conclusion is that effective theorem provers, even those not aimed at human simulation, will need to draw extensively on the "tricks" that human mathematicians use to avoid intolerable complexity and computation. A price paid for following this alternative route is that human heuristic methods trade off between certainty of success and efficiency of search, and will sometimes fail to find proofs even when these exist.

ARTIFICIAL INTELLIGENCE IN PHYSICS PROBLEM SOLVING

Problem solving in physics has been an active research topic in AI. Novak's ISAAC program (Simon, 1996) is an excellent example. Using verbal textbook statements of problems about static forces, ISAAC represents the problems diagrammatically, uses the diagram to construct appropriate equations, and solves them. Although no detailed comparison was made with human solution methods, other research on human problem solving in similar do-

mains strongly suggests that ISAAC simulates such methods rather well. Of course, to extend it to other topics, it would have to acquire a larger vocabulary and collection of mental representations, as well as more knowledge of laws of physics and methods of solution. But as these extensions do not raise basic questions of principle, ISAAC is an impressive demonstration of concept.

Another system, FERMI ("flexible expert reasoner with multidomain inference"), combines scientific principles, general methods, and domain-specific knowledge to solve problems in particular areas of physical science. FERMI contains mutually accessible hierarchical structures of knowledge and method schemas which are general across domains. A principle of decomposition allows FERMI to solve difficult problems by decomposing them into simpler ones: For example, FERMI can decompose a complex mathematical function into a series of simple integrable functions. Knowledge in FERMI is organized hierarchically, so that knowledge at both lower and more specific levels can be inherited from higher and more general levels (for example, vector fields and scalar fields can inherit all the properties that have been assigned to fields).

SIMULATION OF SCIENTIFIC DISCOVERY PROCESSES

Programs like ISAAC and FERMI solve problems by applying existing scientific theory. Scientists and engineers also modify and extend their theories; that is, they make scientific discoveries. How they do this is important to the psychology of human intuition, ingenuity, and creativity, and these are important to the processes of learning.

The automatic mathematician, AM (Luger & Stubblefield, 1998), did not prove new theorems, but invented new concepts by modifying and recombining old ones. AM was not given specific problems to solve, but had to find concepts that fit its own criteria of "interestingness." A concept was interesting if it was related to other interesting concepts, if examples of it could be found but were reasonably rare, if it represented one extreme of another concept, and so on. Starting with knowledge of a few simple mathematical concepts, like sets and positive integers, AM discovered rational numbers (fractions), prime numbers, imaginary numbers (numbers involving the square roots of negative numbers), and many other concepts. It also hypothesized that every even number can be represented as the sum of two prime numbers (the Goldbach Conjecture, which has never been proved or disproved).

A different exploration, examining bodies of data searching for new laws (patterns) in them, produced computer programs, including BACON and several others, which rediscovered Galileo's laws of acceleration, Ohm's law of electrical current, and Kepler's third law of planetary motion, among others, using no prior theory and only the data available to the original discoverers (Simon, 1996). Laboratory experiments later showed that human subjects could make the same discoveries without prior knowledge of them, using methods very similar to those incorporated in BACON.

Experimental procedures for generating data from which theories may be extracted were simulated by the KEKADA program (Luger, 1995), modeling the way in which German biochemist H. Krebs discovered the chemical pathway for urea synthesis, and M. Faraday discovered the generation of electric currents by moving magnetic fields. (The name KEKADA is a joke—the Hindi word for "crab," it is a word play on the name "Krebs.") The programs matched, in considerable detail, the events recorded in the laboratory notebooks of Krebs and Faraday. The program contains operators that propose experiments, and use the outcomes of experiments to propose new hypotheses and strategies. For example, when an experiment produces surprises (results conflicting with beliefs derived from previous knowledge), the program designs new experiments to delimit the scope of the surprising phenomena and to search for its causes.

The programs described above are largely driven by data, with new theory as their product. Less research has been done in the reverse direction, which is equally important: using existing theory to develop new theory. However, the BACON system ("BACON" from "Sir Francis Bacon"), supplemented by general principles, has modest discovery capabilities of this kind. Given empirical data about the temperatures of liquids before and after they are mixed, it can derive Black's law of temperature equilibrium for the mixture by purely data-driven means. But given, instead, the principles of conservation of mass and of heat, BACON can discover the equilibrium law without examining any empirical data, for these principles alone are strong enough to entail the law. Similarly, whereas BACON derives Kepler's third law retroductively from the data, the law can also be inferred deductively from Newton's laws of motion and the inverse square law of gravitation. Other programs, including FERMI, use analogy to infer new theories from existing ones—for example, analogies from water pressure lead to theories of magnetic force.

Of course, human discovery activities include not only cognitive processes but also motivational and affective processes that are not represented in these programs. The present programs operate without any need for monetary reward, esteem, fame, concern for the social value (or potential harm) of their discoveries, intellectual excitement, or any of the other motives that may drive human curiosity.

COGNITIVE THEORIES OF LANGUAGE

In an important sense, our species is defined by its ability to communicate in natural language. Consequently, there has been considerable interest in natural language processing by computers, either to understand human capabilities or to complement and interact with them. Computer programs for encoding grammars, recognizing speech sounds, understanding spoken language, and translating from one language to another date from the earliest years of AI, although they are still far from reaching the level and generality of normal human competence.

In 1972, a simulation called ZBIE (the name has no special meaning) was built. ZBIE simulated a child learning language by observing simple scenes that contain objects and their relations (e.g., "The cat chases the dog") at the same time that it hears sentences describing the scenes (Simon, 1996). It learns the words for the objects, the relations, and the ways of forming them into sentences, so that when presented later with other scenes, containing objects and relations seen previously but not together, it can form new sentences describing them. In this way, ZBIE successfully learned vocabulary and grammar (and the associated meanings) of elementary French, German, and Russian. Working with the slower and smaller computers of 25 years ago, it reached only an elementary level, but provided an impressive demonstration of concept, and a potential general theory of language learning.

COGNITIVE THEORIES IN THE ARTS

The basic strategy of building cognitive theory by computer modeling has been to select tasks that appear feasible and, when their performance has been simulated, to move on to tasks exercising new facets of human thought. In this way, AI has moved, in less than a half century, from simple puzzles and laboratory tests to tasks at a professional level, including a number that require human performers to use insight and creativity. If there are limits to this progress, they have not yet slowed it. Fields beyond those already mentioned that are still at the frontier of this exploration include activities where motivation and emotion are important, and activities in the fine arts.

The use of simulation in the study of emotions has not gone very far, although one serious model of paranoid behavior has been constructed and shown to produce behavior with considerable verisimilitude to the symptoms of paranoia. Another model has some modest capabilities for behaving as a nondirective psychotherapist in interaction with patients (McCorduck, 1979).

In the fine arts, there has been more substantial activity and progress. The first programs for composing credible music (exercises in counterpoint, and music somewhat akin to J. Cage's stochastic compositions) appeared as early as 1958, and these capabilities have now been extended much further, but without much attention to simulating the processes of human composers. In the graphic arts, the Aaron program, developed over more than a quarter century by H. Cohen, has capabilities for producing drawings and paintings of considerable artistic interest (McCorduck, 1990). Cohen has not undertaken to simulate human painting processes closely, but to investigate the ways in which drawings and paintings evoke cognitive and emotive reactions from human viewers: the ways in which meanings can be invested in them.

CONCLUSION

AI continues to grow in importance as a tool of research in psychology, providing a language in which theories of human thinking can be stated, and methods of simulation and comparison with human data for testing theories empirically. It has yielded enormous gains in our understanding of human thought processes at the level of information processing. Much work lies ahead to extend these gains to the social and emotional domains, and to connect symbolic theories with our growing understanding of the neural system that implements the symbolic processes. As we now know a great deal about the "software" of the brain, it is time to link this knowledge with the "hardware."

REFERENCES

Anderson, J. R. (1999). *Cognitive psychology and its implications* (4th ed.). New York: Freeman.

Appel, K., & Haken, W. (1979). The four-color problem. In L. A. Steen (Ed.), *Mathematics today: Twelve informal essays* (pp. 153–180). New York: Springer-Verlag.

Bartlett, F. C. (1932). *Remembering: A study in experimental and social psychology.* London: Cambridge University Press.

Feigenbaum, E. A., & Feldman, J. (Eds.). (1963). *Computers and thought.* New York: McGraw-Hill.

Luger, G. F. (Ed.). (1995). *Computers and intelligence: Collected readings.* Cambridge, MA: MIT Press.

Luger, G. F., & Stubblefield, W. A. (1998). *Artificial intelligence* (3rd ed.). Reading, MA: Addison-Wesley Longman.

McCorduck, P. (1979). *Machines who think.* San Francisco: Freeman.

McCorduck, P. (1990). *Aaron's Code.* New York: Freeman.

Newell, A. (1990). *Unified theories of cognition.* Cambridge, MA: Harvard University Press.

Newell, A., & Simon, H. A. (1972). *Human problem solving.* Englewood Cliffs, NJ: Prentice-Hall.

Newell, A., & Simon, H. A. (1995). Computer science as empirical inquiry: Symbols and search. In G. F. Luger (Ed.), *Computers and intelligence: Collected readings* (pp. 91–119). Cambridge, MA: MIT Press.

Rumelhart, D. E., & McClelland, J. L. (Eds.). (1986). *Parallel distributed processing: Explorations in the microstructure of cognition* (2 vols.). Cambridge, MA: MIT Press.

Simon, H. A. (1996). *The sciences of the artificial* (3rd ed.). Cambridge, MA: MIT Press.

SUGGESTED READING

Barr, A., Cohen, P. R., & Feigenbaum, E. A. (Eds.). (1981–1989). *The handbook of artificial intelligence* (4 vols.). Reading, MA: Addison-Wesley.

Ericsson, K. A., & Simon, H. A. (1984). *Protocol analysis: Verbal reports as data.* Cambridge, MA: MIT Press.

Van Lehn, K. (Ed.). (1990). *Architectures for intelligence.* Hillsdale, NJ: Erlbaum.

H. A. SIMON
Carnegie Mellon University

COGNITIVE PSYCHOLOGY
PROBLEM SOLVING

ARTS, PSYCHOLOGY OF

Psychology of the arts deals with four main topics: how art is created; why the arts have changed across time in the way they have rather than in some other way; how art is perceived; and what factors are involved in the appreciation of art. Except for the question of art history, all of these topics overlap with other topics that are not focally concerned with the psychology of art. The question of the nature of creativity deals with both scientific and artistic creativity; photographs in a family album are perceived in much the same way that a painting is perceived; and appreciation of beauty or ugliness in nature is closely related to appreciation of beauty or ugliness in art.

Until the 20th century, there was little disagreement as to the definition of art. It was held to be an imitation of reality that, except in rare cases, should be beautiful. It may not be apparent that music is mimetic, but the ancient Greeks held that it is the most imitative of the arts in that it imitates human emotions. In the 20th century, however, opinions changed rapidly. Abstract painting does not represent anything and is often quite ugly. Marcel Duchamps's *Fountain* (a urinal) and Andy Warhol's *Brillo Box* (which he bought at a grocery store) were exhibited and accepted as works of art. Several theorists have argued that works of art must be novel or else be useless in the practical sense of that term. However, many novel and useless things are not what we would want to call art. The current consensus is that anything that the art world says is art, *is* art (Davies, 1991).

CREATIVITY

It is generally agreed that genius-level creativity is an emergenetic trait; that is, the creative genius must have a number of traits (e.g., ability to think in a particular manner, high self-confidence, specific talent, fairly high intelligence). If any of these traits is lacking, the individual will not be creative. None of these traits is especially rare, but it is extremely rare to find them all present in the same person. Kris (1952) proposed that creative inspiration occurs in a state of primary process cognition (the quasi-random type of thought found in reveries). This type of thinking facilitates the discovery of a creative idea. When analyzed, creative ideas are found to have brought together ideas or images previously thought to be unrelated to one another. Primary process cognition is usually associated with mental illness. There is now very solid evidence that creativity is genetically related to psychosis as well as to criminality and alcoholism (Eysenck, 1995). Creative artists are seldom schizophrenic, but they do show a very high rate of bipolar or manic-depressive illness and, especially among writers, of alcoholism.

ART HISTORY

To be considered a work of art, an artifact must be novel. Martindale (1990) proposed an evolutionary theory of art history based upon this simple fact. The pressure for novelty has been present since art was first produced, whereas other pressures have come and gone. Though need for novelty may be a weak force, it is a consistent one. Thus, it in large part ends up determining the course of art history. To produce a novel idea, Kris argues that one must regress toward primary process cognition. To produce an even more novel idea, one must regress even further. However, such regression will work for only so long. For example, a simplified definition of a poetic style is that it is a lexicon of permissible words and the rules for combining these words. The first poets using the style think of the obvious combinations. As time passes, poets must engage in more and more primary process cognition to think of creative poems, and this leaves its mark on their work. Eventually, all usable word combinations will be used, so that a new style is needed that allows poets to keep increasing novelty but with less primary process cognition. Thus, we should expect novelty or unpredictability to increase monotonically, and content indicative of primary process cognition to oscillate exactly out of phase with degree of stylistic change. This is exactly what is found in studies of the history of poetry, music, and a number of the visual arts.

There is very little evidence that art reflects society in any direct way, but serious scholars, including mainstream Marxist theorists, have never argued that it does. If art reflected society or the spirit of the times, we would expect people to like it (anyone who has ever studied the preference for modern art knows that virtually everyone hates it). In the 1950s, abstract expressionist painting was chaotic, whereas architecture was severe and simple. This could not have been the case if art reflected the spirit of the times. However, Simonton (1994) and others have shown that social factors do have an influence on the arts. For example, international wars have an adverse effect upon creativity. On the other hand, political fragmentation enhances creativity.

PERCEPTION OF ART

Now that anything an artist or the art world says is art *is,* by definition, art, one wonders if we perceive art in a different way than we perceive non-art. A pile of bricks at a construction site is not art. The very same pile of bricks in a museum is art. Are the bricks perceived in a different way in each of the two locations? There is no research on this topic, but one imagines that there might well be differences due to attention. People tend to pay little attention to their sensations and perceptions. At the construction site, we would just glance at the bricks. In the museum, we would focus our attention on them and perhaps find something pleasing—or displeasing—in their arrangement or coloring. A beautiful painting does not have to be in a museum to grasp our attention, as there is something in the painting that makes us attend to it. Several psychologists, most notably Rudolf Arnheim (1966), have dealt with the perception and the creation of art from the perspective of Gestalt psychology.

APPRECIATION OF ART

Gustav Theodor Fechner (1876) founded the scientific psychological study of art. Fechner argued that aesthetics should be approached from an empirical angle rather than from philosophical speculations. By aesthetics, Fechner meant the study of beauty. In those simpler times, psychology of art was a subset of aesthetics, because an artifact was not considered to be art unless it was beautiful. Fechner and other early scientific psychologists such as Wundt and Külpe held that aesthetics was an important area of psychology. They tended to work with simple stimuli, such as rectangles and color chips, as they did not have the techniques to analyze whole works of art.

In the epoch during which behaviorism was the dominant paradigm in psychology, very little work was done on psychology of the arts. Berlyne (1971) brought about renewed interest in the field with a theory emphasizing the importance of novelty, complexity, and surprise in the arts, and introduced powerful new techniques,

such as multidimensional scaling, that allowed the study of actual works of art rather than of simple forms only (1974). It appears that Berlyne overemphasized the importance of novelty and underemphasized the importance of meaning in determining preference for art works (Martindale, 1988), but we would not know this if he had not revivified the field.

REFERENCES

Arnheim, R. (1966). *Toward a psychology of art.* Berkeley: University of California Press.

Berlyne, D. E. (1971). *Aesthetics and psychobiology.* New York: Appleton-Century-Crofts.

Berlyne, D. E. (Ed.). (1974). *Studies in the new experimental aesthetics: Steps toward an objective psychology of aesthetic appreciation.* Washington, DC: Hemisphere.

Davies, S. (1991). *Definitions of art.* Ithaca, NY: Cornell University Press.

Eysenck, H. J. (1995). *Genius: The natural history of creativity.* Cambridge: Cambridge University Press.

Fechner, G. T. (1876). *Vorschule der Aesthetik.* Leipzig: Breitkopf und Härtel.

Kris, E. (1952). *Psychoanalytic explorations in art.* New York: International Universities Press.

Martindale, C. (1988). Cognition, psychobiology, and aesthetics. In F. Farley & R. Neperud (Eds.), *The foundations of aesthetics, art, and art education* (pp. 7–42). New York: Praeger.

Martindale, C. (1990). *The clockwork muse: The predictability of artistic change.* New York: Basic Books.

Simonton, D. K. (1994). *Greatness: Who makes history and why.* New York: Guilford.

C. MARTINDALE
University of Maine

AESTHETICS
BEAUTY
CREATIVITY
HISTORY OF ART

ASCH, SOLOMON (1907–1996)

Asch received the PhD from Columbia University in 1932. He taught at the New School for Social Research in New York City and at Rutgers University. He was a close friend and colleague of Max Wertheimer, one of the founders of the Gestalt school of psychology. In 1952 he wrote a text, *Social Psychology,* much in keeping with the tenets of Gestalt psychology.

He is best known for a series of experiments (1956) on the effects of group pressure on a single individual. In these experiments the situation was so contrived that all members of a group were in collusion except one. For example, subjects were asked to compare the length of lines as longer or shorter. Those in collusion purposely made incorrect judgments, so the single naive subject was caught between what he or she wanted to report and what was reported by the other members of the group. The general tendency was for the single subject to go along with the reports of his peers, despite the fact that his or her own sensory discriminations indicated otherwise. With an increase in the size of the majority group, the pressure toward conformity was strengthened. Conformity did not occur for all subjects. Some maintained their independence in what they judged to be correct, going against the consensus of the majority.

STAFF

ASIA, PSYCHOLOGY IN

Within the new global context of our lives, Western psychology will need to be repositioned as one of many psychologies worldwide, rather than as the only or dominant psychology.

Marsella, 1998, p. 1286

OVERVIEW

For far too long, Western psychologists assumed that their own psychologies were the only ones worthy of serious consideration and that those of other cultures amounted to little more than primitive superstitions. This unfortunate attitude is changing rapidly and many non-Western psychologies, especially those of Asia, are now recognized as sophisticated and valuable.

Studying Asian psychologies and conducting their therapeutic practices—such as meditation and yoga—confer major benefits, both theoretical and practical. These theoretical benefits include greater appreciation of other cultures; exposure to alternative and often complementary views of human nature, potential, health, and pathology; the demonstration that psychological development can proceed beyond conventional levels; and evidence that cognitive capacities (such as concentration and insight) and emotional capacities (such as compassion and joy) can be developed to remarkable degrees. Practical benefits include the use of Asian techniques, such as meditation and yoga, which considerable research show to be simple, inexpensive, and effective therapies for a wide variety of psychological and psychosomatic issues.

There are, of course, many Asian psychologies, and they vary widely in sophistication. For the sake of simplicity we will limit discussion here to four—the yogic and Buddhist psychologies of India and the Taoist and neo-Confucian systems of China. These are among the most venerable, sophisticated, and influential. While they display inconsistencies and contradictions—what psychology does not?—they also display significant commonalities and have therefore been referred to as aspects of the "perennial wisdom," "perennial psychology," or "consciousness disciplines" (Wilber, 1996).

A developmental framework will allow a better understanding of the natures and goals of various Asian psychologies and their relationships to Western systems. Researchers increasingly describe development as progressing through three major stages: preconventional, conventional, and postconventional, which are also called prepersonal, personal, and transpersonal. We are born without a coherent sense of self or social conventions; that is, we are at first prepersonal and preconventional. Most people eventually mature to the personal, conventional level and remain there. However, increasing evidence suggests that the usual personal, conventional level does not represent the limit of human possibilities and that further development to transpersonal, postconventional levels is possible (Alexander & Langer, 1990; Wilber, 1996). Psychotherapies address three correlative levels of health—pathology reduction, existential issues, and transpersonal concerns.

Western psychologies have developed sophisticated maps of prepersonal and personal stages of development and techniques for alleviating the stages' corresponding pathologies. More recently, Western psychologies have focused on existential issues and most recently have begun to explore the transpersonal level. By contrast, Asian psychologies and therapies focus almost exclusively on existential and transpersonal concerns. They contain detailed descriptions of transpersonal capacities and stages and claim that their therapeutic techniques, such as meditation and yoga, foster development of these capacities and stages. On the other hand, Asian psychologies offer little insight on early development or for the treatment of severe psychopathology (Walsh, 2000).

The primary emphases of Asian traditions are on phenomenology and direct, personal experience. Practitioners claim that the disciplines are highly experimental. Another major emphasis is on testing their claims via direct experience, and Asian psychologies create instructions through which anyone can test for himself or herself the validity of the psychologies' techniques, claims, and results.

PERSONALITY

Asian psychologies both originate from and lead to ideas about human nature, health, pathology, and potential that differ significantly from traditional Western views. We can summarize the Asian studies under the headings of consciousness, identity, motivation, psychopathology, and psychological health.

Consciousness

In *The Varieties of Religious Experience* William James remarked (1958, p. 298):

Our normal waking consciousness . . . is but one special type of consciousness, whilst all about it, parted from it by the filmiest of screens, there lie potential forms of consciousness entirely different. We may go through life without suspecting their existence; but apply the requisite stimulus, and at a touch they are there in all their completeness. . . . No account of the universe in its totality can be final which leaves these other forms of consciousness quite disregarded. How to regard them is the question. . . . At any rate, they forbid a premature closing of our accounts with reality.

Asian psychologies agree completely. They recognize multiple states of consciousness and that some states may be associated with specific functions and abilities not available in our usual states. Perceptual sensitivity, attention, the sense of identity, and affective, cognitive, and perceptual processes may all vary with the state of consciousness in precise and predictable ways.

Some states are termed functionally specific and a few are true higher states. Functionally specific states are those in which specific functions can be performed better than in the usual state. True higher states possess the effective functions of the usual conditions, plus heightened perceptions, insights, or affects outside the realm of day-to-day experience (Walsh & Vaughan, 1993).

If higher states do exist, then our usual state must be suboptimal. This is exactly the claim of Asian psychologies. They argue that our usual state of consciousness is dreamlike and illusory. They assert that to a significant extent we are prisoners of our minds, trapped by a continuous inner fantasy-dialogue that creates an all-consuming illusory distortion (*maya*) of perception and reality. Thus the "normal" person is seen as "dreaming." When the dream is especially painful or disruptive, it becomes a nightmare and is recognized as psychopathology. Since the vast majority of the population dreams, the true state of affairs goes unrecognized. When individuals permanently disidentify from dreams, they are able to recognize the true nature of both their former state and that of the population. This awakening, known variously as *wu, moksha* liberation, or enlightenment, is the aim of Asian psychologies (Goldstein, 1983).

To some extent this is an extension, rather than a denial, of traditional Western psychology and psychiatry, which have long recognized that a broad range of perceptual distortions exist which are unrecognized by naive subjects (Langer, 1989). But Asian psychologies assert these distortions are more pervasive and harmful than is generally recognized; that the consensual reality we share is largely illusory; that these distortions can be recognized and reduced by specific mental training; and that doing so fosters psychological development to transconventional, transpersonal levels.

Identity

Western psychologists usually assume that our normal, natural, and optimal identity is egoic. The term *ego* is used here in the Asian usage, implying a sense of self as inextricably linked to the body and separate from other people and things: "skin encapsulated" as Alan Watts put it. Asian psychologies hold a different perspective, one in line with their claims about the dreamlike nature of our usual state of consciousness. They suggest that our egoic identity is illusory and constricted, and that this claim is directly testable by anyone willing to cultivate perceptual sensitivity via meditative-yogic practices.

What has been reported by meditators across millennia, and more recently by Westerners trained in these practices, is that under microscopic meditative examination what was formerly thought to be a solid, unchanging ego is recognized as a continuously changing flux of thoughts, images, and emotions (Goldstein, 1983). The usual egoic self-sense is thus deconstructed and revealed to be an illusory product of imprecise awareness. With this recognition, there begins a corresponding dissolution of the experience of oneself as a separate, isolated ego. With continued practice, the gradual refinement of perception results in a "peeling away" of awareness from successively subtler layers of identification. Finally, awareness is said to no longer identify itself exclusively with anything; and without identification of any one thing to

the exclusion of another thing, the me–not me, self–not self dichotomy is transcended. In the words of the Zen master Yasutani Roshi (Kapleau, 1980), this is "the direct awareness that you are more than this puny body or limited mind. Stated negatively, it is the realization that the universe is not external to you. Positively, it is experiencing the universe as yourself" (p. 143).

Asian psychologies suggest that existential and psychoanalytic claims about the impossibility of resolving psychodynamic conflicts and existential givens such as finitude, meaning, and suffering are indeed correct at the egoic level. From this perspective, existentialists might be said to have rediscovered part of the Buddha's First Noble Truth: that unsatisfactoriness is part of life and (for the untrained mind) is accompanied by angst. However, the Buddha went further, and in the remaining three Noble Truths pointed to a crucial cause of suffering (addiction/craving) and the means for escaping it. Asian psychologies therefore suggest that existential and psychodynamic conflicts are specific to the egoic identity and can be at least partly transcended by developing nonegoic, or more specifically transegoic, states of consciousness (Wilber, 1996; Feuerstein, 1998).

Motivation

Asian psychologies, especially yogic psychology, tend to see motives as hierarchically organized in a manner analogous to that suggested by Maslow (1968) and Wilber (1996). Motives with a clear physiological and survival basis such as hunger and thirst are seen as most powerful. When these are fulfilled, then less powerful needs (such as sexual and power strivings, for example) may emerge as effective motivators in their turn. However, Eastern psychologies emphasize the importance of "higher motives," such as self-transcendence and selfless service, which are rarely recognized in Western psychology (Feuerstein, 1998).

One motivational factor that is given great emphasis and is viewed as a major determinant of pathology and suffering is attachment, which closely corresponds to our Western concept of addiction. Indeed, in his Second Noble Truth, the Buddha stated that the cause of suffering is ultimately craving or attachment. His Third and Fourth Truths state that suffering can be escaped by extinguishing attachment (Goldstein, 1983). Attachment is said to reduce flexibility and choices; to fuel greed, possessiveness, jealousy, and frustration; and to underlie defenses. From this perspective, psychological suffering is a feedback signal, indicating the existence of attachments and the need to let them go.

Attachment invariably gives rise to its mirror image—aversion, which is the dislike of, and the desire to withdraw from, an experience. Whereas attachment says "I must have something in order to be happy," aversion says "I must avoid something in order to be happy." Aversion is said to underlie anger and aggression.

Psychopathology

The Asian view of psychopathology centers around three ideas: immaturity, unhealthy mental qualities, and the "three poisons" of greed, hatred, and delusion.

Asian psychologies regard our usual adult state as a form of arrested development and would agree with Maslow (1968, p. 16) that "it seems more and more clear that what we call 'normal' in psychology is really a psychopathology of the average, so undramatic and so widely spread that we don't even notice it ordinarily." From this perspective, development has proceeded from preconventional to conventional, but has then faltered and come to a premature halt.

At this stage the mind operates suboptimally, many potentials and capacities remain unrealized, and various unhealthy mental qualities flourish. These unhealthy qualities are said to include, for example, attentional difficulties such as distractability and agitation, cognitive deficits such as mindlessness, disruptive emotions such as anger and jealousy, and problematic motives such as sloth and selfishness (Goldstein, 1983; Feuerstein, 1998).

Three mental qualities are regarded as especially destructive and as the roots of psychopathology. These are the "three poisons" of delusion, attachment, and aversion. Delusion is a mental dullness or mindlessness that misperceives and misunderstands the nature of the mind and reality and thereby spawns pathology-inducing beliefs, motives, and behaviors. As a famous Zen teacher summarized it, "When the deep meaning of things is not understood, the mind's essential peace is disturbed to no avail" (Sengstan, 1975).

Psychological Health

The Asian ideal of health extends beyond pathology reduction to encompass existential and transpersonal concerns. Health is defined primarily in terms of the following three changes: (a) the reduction of unhealthy qualities, especially the three poisons; (b) cultivation of healthy qualities; and (c) maturation to transpersonal stages of development.

Asian psychologies emphasize that specific healthy mental qualities must be deliberately cultivated to ensure psychological health and maturity. Examples of such qualities include the Confucian sage Mencius' "four constant virtues" of ethicality, propriety, compassion, and wisdom and the Buddhists' "seven factors of enlightenment." These seven qualities or capacities of mind include three energizing factors, three calming factors, and one balancing factor. The three energizing factors are effort, rapture (intense joy), and investigation of one's experience; the three calming factors are calm, concentration, and equanimity; the balancing factor is mindfulness. The factor of mindfulness—precise awareness of the nature of the stimuli being observed—might be regarded as a highly developed form of the Freudian "observing ego." It heightens awareness and balances the arousing and calming factors (Goldstein, 1983).

This seven-factor model of well-being allows interesting comparisons with Western psychotherapies, which have emphasized the energizing factors of effort and investigation. However, Western therapies have largely overlooked the potentiating effects of the calming factors. Concentration provides a laser-like penetrating power to awareness, while calm and equanimity create mental stability. Together they make it possible for awareness to penetrate into the depths of the psyche and to explore and heal it more effectively. Buddhist psychology, therefore, emphasizes that cultivating and balancing *both* arousing and calming factors results in optimal insight and growth.

Such growth includes maturation to transpersonal stages and capacities. These include, for example, postformal operational

cognition and wisdom, postconventional morality, transpersonal emotions such as encompassing love and compassion, and meta-motives such as self-transcendence and selfless service (Wilber, 1996; Feuerstein, 1998). The natural expressions of this transformation are said to include reduced egocentricity; less preoccupation with "the physical foursome" of money, power, prestige, and sensuality; and greater concern with the welfare of others. In an enlightened individual it is said that "all self-centered striving ceases" (Sengstan, 1975).

ASIAN DISCIPLINES AND THERAPIES

The applied side of Asian psychologies focuses on disciplines and therapies designed to foster psychological and spiritual development and well-being. While Asia has devised many such disciplines, and continues to create new ones such as the Japanese Morita and Naikan therapies, the best known are the classical techniques of meditation and yoga (Feuerstein, 1998).

Meditation refers to a family of techniques that train awareness and attention in order to bring mental processes under greater voluntary control. This control is used to reduce destructive mental qualities; to cultivate beneficial qualities such as concentration, compassion, and insight; and to enhance psychological and spiritual growth and well-being.

Yoga refers to a family of disciplines with similar aims as those of meditation. However, yogas are more inclusive disciplines that encompass meditation, ethics, lifestyle modification, body postures, breath control, and intellectual study. In the West the best known of yoga disciplines are the body postures, which are sometimes mistaken for the totality of yoga. In fact, postures constitute only one part of a far larger discipline.

In addition to specific meditative and yogic techniques, Asian systems, like contemplative traditions around the world, emphasize seven central practices and goals (Walsh, 1999):

1. Redirecting motivation and moving up the hierarchy of needs, especially by reducing attachment and aversion

2. Transforming emotions, especially reducing problematic ones such as anger and fear, and cultivating beneficial emotions such as love and compassion

3. Living ethically to reduce destructive mental qualities such as greed and to foster helpful qualities such as empathy and generosity

4. Developing concentration

5. Enhancing awareness

6. Fostering wisdom

7. Increasing generosity and altruism

To give just two examples of Asian techniques and resultant skills—which until recently Western psychologists considered impossible—consider the cultivation of love and lucid dreaming. Several meditations are specifically designed to cultivate the encompassing, unconditional love known as *bhakti* in the East and *agape* in the West. Dream yoga is a 2,000-year-old discipline for developing lucid dreaming, or the ability to know one is dreaming while still asleep. Advanced practitioners claim to maintain awareness and continue their meditation and exploration of the mind throughout the night, a claim now supported by electroencephalographic studies (Mason et al., 1997). These capacities hint at the remarkable abilities, developmental possibilities, and powers of mind—some as yet unrecognized by Western psychologists—that Asian psychologies have discovered in their 3,000-year-long exploration of our inner universe.

Anyone may benefit from modest amounts of practice of Asian techniques. However, mastering these disciplines and fostering the full range of mental capacities and developmental possibilities that they entail, can be very demanding. The intensity and duration of training required may be quite extraordinary by Western standards and is often reckoned in decades. In the words of the yogic sage Ramana Maharshi, "No one succeeds without effort. Mind control is not your birthright. Those who succeed owe their liberation to perseverance" (Kornfield, 1977, p. 9). Likewise, the Swiss existential psychiatrist Medard Boss, one of the first Westerners to examine Asian practices, suggested that compared with the extent of yogic self-exploration "even the best Western training analysis is not much more than an introductory course" (Boss, 1963, p. 188).

Even modest amounts of practice can, however, produce significant psychological, physiological, and biochemical changes, as several hundred experimental studies have shown (Murphy & Donovan, 1997). In the psychological arena, meditation can enhance perceptual sensitivity, empathy, creativity, intelligence, academic achievement, sense of self-control, and marital satisfaction. Several studies suggest that it may foster maturation as measured by scales of ego, moral and cognitive development, and self-actualization (Alexander & Langer, 1990).

Clinically, meditation may ameliorate psychological disorders such as anxiety, phobias, insomnia, and posttraumatic stress, and is associated with reduced use of both legal and illegal drug use. Psychosomatic benefits include reduction of blood pressure, cholesterol, and the severity of angina, asthma, migraine, and chronic pain (Murphy & Donovan, 1997). Meditation and yoga are also components of lifestyle change programs demonstrated to reverse coronary artery disease.

General health may also improve. Meditators use less than normal amounts of medical and psychiatric care and a geriatric population of meditators showed greater longevity than controls. How much of this general health enhancement is actually due to meditation and how much is due to associated factors (such as healthy lifestyle) remains unclear. It is also unclear whether meditation is more effective in treating some clinical disorders than other self-regulation strategies such as relaxation training, biofeedback, and self-hypnosis (Shapiro & Walsh, 1984).

THE MEETING OF EAST AND WEST: EXPERIMENTAL STUDIES AND INTEGRAL THEORIES

Findings have emerged from several areas that lend preliminary support to several Asian claims. One area of research concerns states of consciousness. For example, research on altered states reveals a far broader spectrum of states than previously recognized. Studies of what Maslow termed peak experiences suggest that these experiences are more likely to occur in the psychologically healthy, may result in psychologically beneficial effects, and appear to parallel certain transcendent states described in Eastern psychologies (Walsh & Vaughan, 1993).

Research has also demonstrated the potency of several Asian techniques. Studies of meditation have revealed a range of psychological, physiological, and biochemical effects; biofeedback has transformed the voluntary control of the internal states from an unlikely yogic boast to an everyday practice; and electroencephalography has demonstrated that lucid dreaming, a capacity long dismissed as impossible, is potentially available to us all. Most importantly, research has revealed that adult psychological development can proceed to transconventional, transpersonal stages, stages similar to some of those described for centuries by Asian psychologies (Wilber, 1996).

Because they focus on different aspects of health and development, Asian and Western psychologies may be partly complementary. One of the major challenges for the 21st century will be to synthesize Asian and Western systems into an overarching integral psychology that honors and includes both. The writings of Wilber (1996) provide the best example to date of this possibility.

REFERENCES

Alexander, C., & Langer, E. (Eds.). (1990). *Higher stages of human development.* New York: Oxford University Press.

Boss, M. (1963). *A psychiatrist discovers India.* New York: Basic Books.

Feuerstein, G. (1998). *The Shambhala guide to yoga.* Boston, MA: Shambhala.

Goldstein, J. (1983). *The experience of insight.* Boston, MA: Shambhala.

James, W. (1958). *The varieties of religious experience.* New York: New American Library.

Kapleau, P. (1980). *The three pillars of Zen.* Garden City, NY: Anchor/Doubleday.

Kornfield, J. (1977). *Living Buddhist masters.* Boston: Shambhala.

Marsella, A. (1998). Toward a "global community psychology": Meeting the needs of a changing world. *American Psychologist, 43,* 1282–1291.

Maslow, A. H. (1968). *Toward a psychology of being* (2nd ed.) Princeton, NJ: Van Nostrand.

Mason, L., Alexander, C., Travis, F., et al. (1997). Electrophysiological correlates of higher states of consciousness during sleep in long-term practitioners of the transcendental meditation program. *Sleep, 20,* 102–110.

Murphy, M., & Donovan, S. (1997). *The physical and psychological effects of meditation* (2nd ed.). Sausalito, CA: Institute of Noetic Sciences.

Sengstan. (1975). *Verses on the faith mind* (R. Clarke, Trans.). Sharon Springs, NY: Zen Center.

Walsh, R. (1999). *Essential spirituality: The seven central practices for awakening heart and mind.* New York: Wiley.

Walsh, R., & Vaughan, F. (Eds.). (1993). *Paths beyond ego: The transpersonal vision.* Los Angeles: J. Tarcher.

Wilber, K. (1996). *A brief history of everything.* Boston, MA: Shambhala.

R. N. WALSH
University of California, Irvine

ASSERTIVENESS TRAINING

Assertiveness training (AT) was introduced by Andrew Salter (1961) and popularized by Joseph Wolpe (1958) and by Wolpe and Lazarus (1966). Rarely used alone, AT is most frequently one aspect of a broader therapeutic program. The goals of AT include: (a) increased awareness of personal rights; (b) differentiation among non-assertiveness, assertiveness, aggressiveness, and passive-aggressiveness; and (c) learning both verbal and nonverbal assertiveness skills. Assertiveness skills involve saying "no"; asking for favors or making requests; expressing both positive and negative feelings; and initiating, continuing, and terminating conversations (Lazarus, 1971).

Assertiveness training, as generally practiced, requires determining the specific situations in which the client characteristically behaves maladaptively, that is, either unassertively, aggressively, or passive-aggressively. While self-report inventories are available for assessing the client's general responses to situations that require assertiveness (Alberti & Emmons, 1995; Wolpe & Lazarus, 1966), most contemporary assertiveness inventories are constructed to be situation-specific. Behaviorally, while it is desirable to observe the client in the actual problematic situation, it is routine to role-play the unproductive interaction with the therapist.

If assessment demonstrates that the client is always unassertive, aggressive, or passive-aggressive, then more traditional therapies are recommended (Alberti & Emmons, 1995). However, if there are specific troublesome situations in which the client could perform with increased assertiveness, AT is indicated. Clients are often resistant to AT because of cultural, familial, or religious proscriptions against being assertive. These reservations require careful consideration and discussion, if AT is to proceed efficiently.

There is no universally formulated program called "assertiveness training." However, the following five methods are commonly used to increase assertiveness in specific situations. First, response acquisition learning involves increasing assertiveness through modeling and behavioral instruction. The focus is on the verbal, nonverbal, cognitive, and affective components of assertiveness. Second, response reproduction includes performing the new responses using role playing, behavior rehearsal, or response practice. Third, response refining shapes and strengthens the new behavior with appropriate feedback and coaching. Fourth, cognitive restructuring challenges irrational beliefs that interfere with assertiveness and generates cognitions that promote assertiveness. Finally, generalization instruction involves attempting new behav-ior in vivo and encourages transfer to new situations. The above procedures are continued until the client demonstrates appropriate assertiveness.

Early formulations about the theoretical basis for AT assumed either an anxiety-produced response inhibition (Wolpe & Lazarus, 1966) or a skills deficit (Lazarus, 1971). Current research has established the importance of cognitive and information-processing factors in generating assertive behavior. Cognitions that limit assertion include unassertive irrational beliefs, inappropriately stringent self-evaluative standards, and faulty expectations concerning the consequences of behaving assertively.

Recent AT research has focused on reducing anxiety in psychiatric patients (Aschen, 1997), stress management training (Kiselica, Baker, Thomas, & Reedy, 1994), use of AT in school settings to reduce aggressive behavior (Studer, 1996), enhancing social skills training and increasing self-confidence in college students (Thompson, Bundy, & Wolfe, 1996), Assertiveness training is also being used in behavioral health and behavioral medicine programs, such as lowering blood pressure, smoking cessation, and anger control (Larkin & Zayfert, 1996).

REFERENCES

Alberti, R., & Emmons, M. (1995). *Your perfect right: A guide to assertive behavior* (7th ed.). San Luis Obispo, CA: Impact.

Aschen, S. (1997). Assertion training therapy in psychiatric milieus. *Archives of Psychiatric Nursing, 11,* 46–51.

Kiselica, M., Baker, S., Thomas, R., & Reedy, S. (1994). Effects of stress inoculation training on anxiety, stress, and academic performance among adolescents. *Journal of Counseling Psychology, 41,* 335–342.

Larkin, K., & Zayfert, C. (1996). Anger management training with mild essential hypertensive patients. *Journal of Behavioral Medicine, 19,* 415–433.

Lazarus, A. (1971). *Behavior therapy and beyond.* New York: Mc-Graw-Hill.

Salter, A. (1961). *Conditioned reflex therapy: The direct approach to reconstruction of personality.* New York: Farr, Straus.

Studer, J. (1966). Understanding and preventing aggressive responses in youth. *Elementary School Guidance and Counseling, 30,* 194–203.

Thompson, K., Bundy, K., & Wolfe, W. (1996). Social skill training for young adolescents: Cognitive and performance components. *Adolescence, 31,* 505–521.

Wolpe, J. (1958). *Psychotherapy by reciprocal inhibition.* Stanford, CA: Stanford University Press.

Wolpe, J., & Lazarus, A. (1966). *Behavior therapy techniques.* London: Pergamon Press.

C. H. FISCHER
Radford University

BEHAVIOR THERAPY
COUNSELING
PSYCHOTHERAPY
SOCIAL SKILLS TRAINING

ATKINSON, RICHARD C.

An internationally respected scholar in cognitive science and psychology, Richard C. Atkinson received his undergraduate degree from the University of Chicago and went on to study mathematics and psychology at Indiana University, where he received his PhD in 1955. He began his academic career at Stanford University and was a member of the Stanford faculty from 1956 to 1980, except for a 3-year period at the University of California, Los Angeles. In addition to serving as professor of psychology at Stanford, he held appointments in the School of Engineering, School of Education, Applied Mathematics and Statistics Laboratories, and Institute for Mathematical Studies in the Social Sciences.

From 1975 to 1980 he served as deputy director and then as director of the National Science Foundation. At NSF he had a wide range of responsibilities for science policy at a national and international level, including negotiating the first memorandum of understanding in history between the People's Republic of China and the United States, an agreement for the exchange of scientists and engineers.

Atkinson left NSF to become chancellor of the San Diego campus of the University of California, where he served for 15 years before his appointment as president of the University of California System in 1995, a position he currently holds.

Atkinson's research has dealt with problems of memory and cognition. He is best known for the Atkinson-Shiffrin model, a theory of memory that has helped in clarifying the relationship between brain structures and psychological phenomena, in explaining the effects of drugs on memory, and in formulating techniques that optimize the learning process. His 1968 paper (written with Richard M. Shiffrin), "Human Memory: A Proposed System and its Control Processes," postulates two dimensions of memory: structures for storing memories, including sensory register, short-term store, and long-term store; and strategies used by the individual to operate and control memory, among them such processes as rehearsal, coding, and search. The model—which has come to be known as the modal model of memory—was supported by a rich body of empirical research. It has become one of the most cited references in empirical psychology and has had a shaping influence on the field of memory over the last three decades.

His work reflects a long-standing interest in enhancing the learning process, both in a practical sense and in the development of mathematical models for optimization. He developed one of the first computer-controlled systems for instruction, which served as a prototype for the commercial development of computer-assisted instruction. Reading instruction under computer control for young school children has been an important application of his research.

Atkinson is the author of many books and articles. His scientific contributions have resulted in election to the National Academy of Sciences, the Institute of Medicine, the National Academy of Education, and the American Philosophical Society. He is past president of the American Association for the Advancement of Science, former chair of the Association of American Universities, and the recipient of numerous honorary degrees. A mountain in Antarctica has been named in his honor.

STAFF

ATTACHMENT STYLES

Unraveling the nature of the bonds that form between people and identifying the sources of variation in relational characteristics among people are prominent topics in the social sciences. One approach to explaining and predicting the variations in close personal relationships is to classify individuals based on consistent patterns of interpersonal behavior and emotional reactions to relational partners. A variety of typologies based on Bowlby's (1969) attachment theory have been proposed for classifying interpersonal tendencies according to prototypical categories known as attachment styles.

ATTACHMENT THEORY

From the perspective of attachment theory, many aspects of human relatedness evolved to support the survival of infants, who are born helpless and are thus highly vulnerable to predation and to fatal accidents. Because human infants must maintain close physical proximity to a responsive and protective caregiver, an attachment-maintaining behavioral system is thought to have developed as an adaptation to constrain infant mortality rates. Without such consistent protection and nurturance, children are unlikely to attain puberty and produce progeny of their own. Thus, children of nurturing and protective parents are endowed with an adaptational advantage that results in a greater likelihood of their familial genetic legacy enduring and influencing the characteristics of their species.

Given the propositions outlined above, attachment theory is clearly rooted in theories of evolutionary biology and child development. However, attachment-maintaining traits are not understood to be purely heritable and are instead attributed to experiential learning transmitted from parent to child in a manner consistent with social learning theory (Bandura, 1977). Indeed, when Bowlby first presented the ideas that led him to formulate attachment theory he was characterized by his detractors in the British psychoanalytic community as a behaviorist (Bretherton, 1997).

Recently, attachment theory has been extended beyond its more circumscribed beginnings in child development and romantic bonding to explain the interpersonal regulation of affect (Fuendeling, 1998) and the cognitive representation of relational experiences and expectations (Baldwin, Keelan, Fehr, Enns, & Koh-Rangarajoo, 1996). Furthermore, what was once understood as a theory pertaining mainly to developmental psychology has been adopted by researchers in the domains of clinical and social psychology, as well as primatology and behavioral neuroscience. As attachment theory is applied across diverse cultures in manifold domains by researchers trained in disparate disciplines, there is some danger that its principles will be distorted to fit so many aims that a corresponding loss of coherency will result. For instance, Main (1999) raised the objection that attachment has been applied in such an overly general manner to pertain to all affectionate relationships that its unique relevance to enhancing children's safety under conditions of perceived threat is often lost.

TYPOLOGY OF ATTACHMENT STYLES

Individual relational patterns, known as *attachment styles,* have been observed to emerge during infancy and are linked to the sensitivity, responsiveness, and consistency of children's caregivers (Ainsworth, Blehar, Waters, & Wall, 1978). These patterns are held to provide evidence of flexible but enduring cognitive structures termed *internal working models* (Bowlby, 1969), which in turn guide interpersonal expectations and relational behaviors while influencing the meanings attributed to interpersonal experiences throughout the lifespan (Shaver, Collins, & Clark, 1995).

Infants whose cries and other signals of distress consistently receive warm, sensitive, and nurturing care tend to develop a style of responding well to soothing behavior from others. Such children appear to expect nurturance and to thrive on it. These children demonstrate a balance of exploratory interest in their environment and reliance upon the caregiver as a secure base in times of insecurity or distress. The attachment style of children fitting this description is deemed to be a *secure* one. Adults who are comfortable with depending on others and having relational partners depend on them are considered to exhibit a secure *adult attachment pattern.* Patterns of attachment behavior at any age that deviate substantially from this model are characterized as *anxious* or *insecure.*

Anxious attachment styles have been defined by various terms, including ambivalent, avoidant, and disorganized/disoriented among children and preoccupied, dismissive, and fearful among adults. Children who seem reticent to seek parental care and who may even show somewhat more interest in the attention of adult strangers may be classified as *avoidant.* The corresponding style of adults who adopt an extremely self-reliant attitude and who express little desire for relationships with others is termed *dismissive.* If, however, an adult's pattern of devaluing relationships contains evidence of chronic interpersonal anxiety and concerns about how well they themselves can function in close relationships, the classification of a *fearful* attachment style is more fitting.

Some children heartily protest the absence of their caregivers, but are difficult to soothe when their signals of distress are responded to. This pattern has been attributed to inconsistencies in the sensitivity and responsiveness of the child's caregivers. Such inconsistent care undermines the child's ability to reliably predict the caregiver's behavior, thus raising the child's anxiety in anticipating that the caregiver's response may be delayed, inadequate, or unpleasant. This style of anxious attachment may be classified as *ambivalent,* because the child appears to relate to the parent as alternately desirable and aversive. When adults perceive relationships as highly desirable, but seem prone to anxious concerns about rejection and to require excessive reassurance from their partners, they are likely to be classified as exhibiting a *preoccupied* attachment style.

The most recent classification of attachment in children, termed *disorganized* (Main & Solomon, 1986), was created to capture the behavior patterns of children who fit poorly in the other attachment categories. These children display idiosyncratic and contradictory sequences of attachment responses that may reflect the insensitive and erratic characteristics of their caregivers. Parent-child relationships in this group have sometimes been characterized as highly conflictual or hostile, and these children have been shown to be at elevated risk for disorders of conduct and defiance (Lyons-Ruth, 1996). The corresponding category on Main's Adult Attachment Interview (AAI; George, Kaplan, & Main, 1985) is termed *unresolved,* in reference to the frequent association between unresolved issues of loss and trauma in childhood and this attachment style. Members of this attachment category tend to experience fear in close personal relationships. When methods of attachment assessment other than the AAI are employed, such individuals may be more likely to be classified with the previously noted *fearful* attachment style.

METHODS OF ASSESSING ATTACHMENT STYLES

Although attachment classification was pioneered by means of observing infants in the *strange situation test* (Ainsworth, Blehar, Waters, & Wall, 1978), later studies examined attachment styles in adults by employing either interviews or self-report measures. The previously mentioned Adult Attachment Interview (George, Kaplan, & Main, 1985) is the most prominent example of the interview approach.

Researchers desiring measures that lend themselves to use with larger population samples have developed paper and pencil measures yielding various indices of self-reported attachment tendencies. Early examples of this method included the three-category approach of Hazan and Shaver (1987) and the four-category approach of Bartholomew and Horowitz (1991). Later developments of these measures have departed from categorical assignment and allowed individuals to rate the degree of correspondence between themselves and each of the attachment style prototypes. These scores can then be combined to develop a more complex picture of individual differences in adult attachment styles. An alternative method has been to disassemble the attachment prototypes into their constituent statements, which can be rated on a Likert-type scale. The scores can then be combined to provide indices of various theoretical dimensions or subscales.

One such method (Bartholomew & Horowitz, 1991) yields scores along dimensions of anxiety about oneself in relationships (model of self) and one's appraisal of the reliability and desirability of others as attachment partners (model of other). These dimensions within attachment styles can then be used to make finer distinctions regarding linkages between attachment styles and other personal and interpersonal characteristics. This approach is congruent with the conceptualization of internal working models of the self and of the attachment figure described earlier as components of attachment theory.

REFERENCES

Ainsworth, M. D. S., Blehar, M. C., Waters, E., & Wall, S. (1978). *Patterns of attachment: Assessed in the strange situation and at home.* Hillsdale, NJ: Lawrence Erlbaum Associates.

Baldwin, M. W., Keelan, J. P. R., Fehr, B., Enns, V., & Koh-Rangarajoo, E. (1996). Social cognitive conceptualization of attachment styles: Availability and accessibility effects. *Journal of Personality and Social Psychology, 71,* 94–109.

Bandura, A. (1977). *Social learning theory.* Englewood Cliffs, NJ: Prentice Hall.

Bartholomew, K., & Horowitz, L. M. (1991). Attachment styles among young adults: A test of a four-category model. *Journal of Personality and Social Psychology, 61,* 226–244.

Bowlby, J. (1969). *Attachment and loss: Vol. I. Attachment.* Middlesex, England: Penguin Books.

Bretherton, I. (1997). The origins of attachment theory: John Bowlby and Mary Ainsworth. In S. Goldberg, R. Muir, & J. Kerr (Eds.), *Attachment theory: Social, developmental, and clinical perspectives* (pp. 45–84). Hillsdale, NJ: Analytic Press.

Fuendeling, J. M. (1998). Affect regulation as a stylistic process within adult attachment. *Journal of Social and Personal Relationships, 15,* 291–322.

George, C., Kaplan, N., & Main, M. (1985). *The Adult Attachment Interview.* Unpublished manuscript, Department of Psychology, University of California, Berkeley.

Hazan, C., & Shaver, P. R. (1987). Romantic love conceptualized as an attachment process. *Journal of Personality and Social Psychology, 52,* 511–524.

Lyons-Ruth, K. (1996). Attachment relationships among children with aggressive behavior problems: The role of disorganized early attachment patterns. *Journal of Consulting and Clinical Psychology, 64,* 64–73.

Main, M. (1999). Attachment theory: Eighteen points with suggestions for future studies. In J. Cassidy & P. R. Shaver (Eds.), *Handbook of attachment: Theory, research, and applications.* New York: Guilford Press.

Main, M., & Solomon, J. (1986). Discovery of a new, insecure-disorganized/disoriented attachment pattern. In M. Yogman & T. B. Brazelton (Eds.), *Affective development in infancy* (pp. 95–124). Norwood, NJ: Ablex.

Shaver, P. R., Collins, N., & Clark, C. L. (1995). Attachment styles and internal working models of self and relational partners. In G. J. O. Fletcher & J. Fitness (Eds.), *Knowledge structures in close relationships.* Hillsdale, NJ: Lawrence Erlbaum Associates.

G. R. REYES

ATTENTION

Attention can be defined as a readiness on the part of the organism to perceive stimuli that surround it. Historically, the concept of attention has occupied a central position in the field of psychology. In the late 19th and early 20th centuries the functionalist and structuralist schools of psychology regarded attention as a core problem in the field, while emphasizing different aspects of it. The functionalists centered on the selective nature of attention as an active function of the organism based on its motivational state. Thus, while recognizing that attention can sometimes be passive or reflexive, they concentrated on its volitional aspects and on the fact that attention determines that which the organism experiences. The structuralists, on the other hand, saw attention as a state of consciousness which consists of increased concentration and results in sensory clearness. They, therefore, chose to study the conditions which tend to maximize the prominence or clearness of a sensation.

A great deal of experimental work during the early years of the 20th century was devoted to determining the impact of the intensity of a stimulus, such as the loudness of sounds, the brightness of lights, and the strength of pressure, on attentional processes. The duration of a stimulus and the concomitant phenomena of adaptation and fatigue were also studied exhaustively. In addition, comparisons were made of the attentional value of stimuli in different sensory modalities, at different locations vis-à-vis the subject, and of different degrees of novelty. The temporal relations of stimuli, especially repetition and suddenness, as well as the value of movement, color, and size as determiners of attention, were also investigated.

Gestalt psychologists, associationists, behaviorists, and psychoanalytic theorists tended to neglect attention in their postulations, or to relegate it to a relatively unimportant role. Thus, little significant progress was made in the field of attention through the years when these various schools were vying for preeminence in psychology. Since the mid-1950s, however, there has been a resurgence of interest in cognitive psychology in general and in attention in particular, as the various subdisciplines of psychology, such as psychopathology and learning, have come to recognize its centrality once again.

Modern Russian psychologists pioneered the study of the orienting reflex or orienting response, which consists of a cluster of physiological changes that occur in an organism as a response to changes in its surroundings and which are conceived as physiological correlates of attention. These correlates include changes in electrical brain activity, and in the electrical activity of the skin, pupillary dilation, tightening of the skeletal muscles, increased cerebral blood volume, and postural shifts. The orienting reflex results in improved reception of stimulation and increased learning. In the United States, the work initiated by the Russians has been pursued through intense study of individual differences in the strength of the orienting reflex and the concomitants of those differences.

Another broad area of research in attention has evolved from efforts to explain the fact that organisms attend to only a small portion of all the stimuli that impinge on them. Broadbent (1958) dealt extensively with this selectivity of attention and postulated a filtering mechanism which selects stimuli on the basis of their physical characteristics. Subsequently, Treisman (1960) posited a two-channel model of selective attention, whereby one primary channel is attended to, while a second, nonattended channel processes semantic information from other sources in an attenuated fashion. This mechanism allows for further processing of incoming information relevant to the subject. Deutsch and Deutsch (1963) modified the model of selective attention still further by postulating that the selection occurs only after all incoming stimuli have been processed to some extent and meaning has been derived from them. Still more recently, theorists have begun to stress that the limits of attention depend on the processing capacity of the organism, in relation to the demands of tasks in which they are involved.

The work of neurophysiologists and neuroanatomists such as Hernández-Péon (1961) and others has resulted in the identification of a diffuse structure in the brain stem, called the reticular formation, which appears to mediate the processes of arousal, attention, and stimulus selection. The study of the reticular formation, also known as the reticular activating system, and its connections to other important brain regulatory systems has provided a basis for physiological explanations of the influence of motivation, sleep, sensory input, learning, and endogenous as well as exogenous chemical substances on the process of attention. Currently, work on the neurological as well as the psychological basis of attention continues unabated. Much of the recent work on attention points to its critical relevance in the eventual explanation of a host of psychopathological phenomena such as schizophrenic disorders, hyperactivity, and mental retardation.

REFERENCES

Broadbent, D. E. (1958). *Perception and communication.* London: Pergamon.

Deutsch, J. A., & Deutsch, D. (1963). Attention: Some theoretical considerations. *Psychological Review, 70,* 80–90.

Hernández-Péon, R. (1961). Reticular mechanisms of sensory control. In W. A. Rosenblith (Ed.), *Sensory communication.* Cambridge, MA: Massachusetts Institute of Technology.

Treisman, A. M. (1960). Contextual cues in selective listening. *Quarterly Journal of Experimental Psychology, 12,* 242–248.

SUGGESTED READING

Norman, D. A. (1977). *Memory and attention: An introduction to human information processing* (2nd ed.). New York: Wiley.

S. P. URBINA
University of Northern Florida

INFORMATION PROCESSING
SELECTIVE ATTENTION
SOCIAL COGNITION

ATTENTION DEFICIT/HYPERACTIVITY DISORDER (ADHD)

DESCRIPTION

Attention-deficit/hyperactivity disorder (ADHD) is most commonly characterized by persistent inattention and/or excessive motor restlessness and impulsive behavior. Earlier names for ADHD included Minimal Brain Dysfunction, Hyperkinetic Impulse Disorder, Attention Deficit Disorder with or without Hyperactivity, and Attention Deficit Disorder, Residual Type. Since the 1994 publication of the fourth edition of the *Diagnostic and Statistical Manual of Mental Disorders* (*DSM-IV*), ADHD has been reorganized into three subtypes: predominantly inattentive (ADHD-I), predominantly hyperactive-impulsive (ADHD-HI), and combined (ADHD-C). The inattentive subtype requires six or more symptoms of inattention and five or fewer hyperactive/impulsive symptoms. The hyperactive/impulsive subtype consists of six or more symptoms of hyperactivity/impulsivity and five or fewer inattentive symptoms. The combined subtype requires six or more out of nine symptoms from both the inattentive and hyperactive/impulsive categories. Symptoms on the inattentive list are related to poor attention and organizational skills, forgetfulness, and distractibility. Symptoms on the hyperactive/impulsive list refer to restlessness, excessive talking, and interrupting.

According to *DSM-IV,* the symptoms must be present for at least six months and observable by seven years of age. The minimum age of observability has been a subject of recent debate, with some professionals proposing that the "age of onset" requirement be broadened to include symptoms at any time during the childhood years. For the purpose of diagnosis, symptom manifestation should be developmentally inappropriate and exhibited in two or more settings (e.g., home and school). Rates of persistence of ADHD into adulthood vary from 11% to 70% depending on the methods used to assess symptomatology (Barkley, 1998). Adults with ADHD tend to have lower academic attainment, lower socioeconomic status, poorer social functioning, higher automobile driving risks, and comorbid diagnosis of antisocial personality disorder.

PREVALENCE

Prevalence rates of ADHD in the childhood population vary, with expert opinion most often citing an incidence of approximately 3 to 5% (American Psychiatric Association, 1994). The variance appears to be related to the source of the informants completing rating scales (e.g., parents, teachers, or both), the geographic location of the sample, and the criteria used to establish a diagnosis of ADHD. Prevalence rates in adults are even more speculative, but are estimated to be about 4.7% (Barkley, 1998). The disorder is more common in males, with Barkley (1998) citing 3 males to 1 female for non-referred samples. However, again, the sex ratio varies according to the sample and the referral source.

DIAGNOSIS

The diagnosis of ADHD remains difficult, with no single test to assess it and a heavy reliance on subjective measures. The variability in the training of the professionals who attempt to diagnosis children and adults with ADHD adds to questions about the reliability of the diagnosis. A comprehensive evaluation of ADHD in adults or children should assess the presence or absence of symptomatology, differential diagnosis from other disorders that mimic ADHD, and the possibility of comorbid psychiatric disorders. At a minimum, the evaluation should include a clinical interview, a medical evaluation that has been conducted within the past year, standardized behavior rating scales from parents and teachers, and direct observation of the patient. The evaluation for both children and adults includes a family history, as well as documentation regarding developmental, social, and academic functioning. An adult evaluation incorporates a review of employment history, including supervisory feedback if available; alcohol/substance use history; legal history; and input from a spouse or friend, as well as parents, when possible. In addition, adults are asked to provide information regarding their childhood via academic records and transcripts, retrospective-childhood self rating scales, and rating scales completed by a parent or another individual (e.g., an older sibling) who knew the patient as a child. The interview should also screen for depression, anxiety, stress, mania, bipolar disorder, thought disorders, and Tourette or tic disorder. Common conditions that may coexist with ADHD and that warrant careful screening include Oppositional Defiant Disorder, Conduct Disorder, Antisocial Personality Disorder (for adults), and learning disorders. An assessment of intellectual, academic, neuropsychological, attentional, and memory functioning is desirable for purposes of differential diagnosis, as well as for pointing out individual strengths and weaknesses. Psychoeducational testing can also be useful when a low level of intellectual functioning or a learning disability mimics or coexists with ADHD. Neuroimaging techniques (e.g., MRI, PET, SPECT) are not yet considered valid for diagnostic purposes at this time and are warranted only if there are concerns regarding gross neurological impairment.

TREATMENT

Treatment of ADHD should be individualized depending upon the presenting concerns. Clinicians, parents, and patients should remember that the most problematic symptoms fluctuate with age and circumstances. Treatment approaches typically include behavioral interventions combined with medication. Interventions begin by educating the patient as well as his or her family (e.g., parents or spouse) about ADHD, its etiology, and its treatment. Behavioral interventions for children include parent training in contingency management, social skills training, and school interventions. The intensity and sophistication of the behavioral treatment can vary dramatically from program to program, based on the child's needs, as well as on the ability of parents and school personnel to follow through with prescribed recommendations. Behavioral interventions are particularly important when addressing comorbid symptoms, such as conduct problems, anxiety, social skill deficits, or problems related to academic performance. Behavioral treatments for adults often focus on developmentally-appropriate self-monitoring techniques (e.g., a self-prescribed reward for completing a project at work on time), time management skills, organizational skills, social skills in interpersonal and occupational settings, and vocational counseling. Adults may also choose to have an individual therapist or "coach" to monitor daily progress. Marital therapy is often indicated for couples when a spouse has been struggling with symptoms of ADHD.

The use of pharmacological interventions is warranted if the symptoms are interfering significantly with functioning at home, school, or work. Psychostimulant medications (e.g., methylphenidate, dextroamphetamine) are considered safe and effective treatments for ADHD and are used to treat children as well as adults whose diagnoses have been confirmed through extensive psychological evaluation. Stimulants, typically considered the first line of defense, can produce improvements in impulse control, attention, on-task behavior, and social behavior. Other medications, including bupropion and tricyclic antidepressants, are considered when there are additional concerns regarding a history of substance abuse, coexisting depression, or when the stimulants produce significant side effects. All medication therapy requires ongoing monitoring for efficacy and side effects, particularly because symptoms of the patient may change over time.

NEUROBIOLOGIC BASES OF ADHD

The etiology of ADHD is unknown, although the disorder is now considered a disorder of the brain and development. A wave of recent genetic studies has suggested that a substantial genetic component contributes to the disorder. Most of the genetic research has focused on candidate genes involved in dopaminergic transmission. Neuroimaging research into the brain structure and function of children and adults with ADHD has shown significant differences between controls and subjects with ADHD in frontal and basal ganglia anatomy and function. The long term goal of many of these neurobiologic studies is to help investigators develop new medications that will be more specific in symptom reduction and produce fewer side effects.

REFERENCES

Barkley, R. A. (1998). *Attention deficit hyperactivity disorder* (2nd ed.). New York: Guilford Press.

American Academy of Child and Adolescent Psychiatry (1997). Practice parameters for the assessment and treatment of children, adolescents, and adults with attention-deficit/hyperactivity disorder *Journal of the American Academy of Child and Adolescent Psychiatry, 36* (Suppl.), 85–121.

J. B. SCHWEITZER
Emory University

ACADEMIC UNDERACHIEVEMENT
BEHAVIOR THERAPY
CONDUCT DISORDER
EARLY CHILDHOOD DEVELOPMENT
PSYCHOSTIMULANT TREATMENT FOR CHILDREN

ATTITUDE THEORY

Positive and negative attitudes are shown by people of all ages and from all cultures. This ubiquity of attitudes has long been a source of fascination to social theorists.

HISTORY

From its beginnings in the early years of this century, social psychology was concerned with studying attitudes. The term has encompassed a variety of psychological and behavioral dispositions. People can have an expectant attitude (such as that of a foot racer waiting for the starting gun), a disgruntled attitude (as when our request for a salary raise is denied), a cooperative attitude (as when we are asked for help), or an authoritarian attitude (in relation to outgroups and interpersonal relations). The pervasiveness of attitudes in our social world is well established. At the same time, their ubiquity created serious problems for the development of a theoretical understanding of attitudes. Too many different kinds of dispositions have been bunched together under the "attitude" heading.

The earliest theoretical efforts were directed toward devising sets of categories into which different attitudes could be classified. A number of dichotomies were proposed for distinguishing between fundamental types of attitudes, including mental/physical, voluntary/nonvoluntary, and conscious/unconscious. Discussions of the attitude concept during the 1930s were dominated by such distinctions.

This diversity in usage of the term "attitude" and these categorical distinctions are still found in nontechnical discussions of attitudes. Since the 1930s, however, the technical usage has employed a much more restricted definition. The attitude concept is distinguished from other dispositions such as situation-specific expectancies (e.g., set), personality characteristics (e.g., authoritarianism), traits (e.g., cooperativeness), or moods (e.g., happiness).

CONCEPTUAL PROPERTIES OF AN ATTITUDE

The most prominent feature of an attitude is its evaluative character, the disposition to respond toward an object in a positive or negative manner. Attitudes thus can range from very favorable to very unfavorable on an evaluative continuum.

Attitude is a hypothetical construct, since it is not directly observable; its existence must be inferred from stimulus-response patterns. Several properties help distinguish it from allied dispositions such as personality dimensions and moods. There must be a specific attitude object, that is, an identifiable concept, action, or entity toward which evaluative responses can be directed. It is an enduring disposition, relatively stable over time and over situations.

Theory attempts to relate this hypothetical construct to observables. Attitude theorists assume that attitudes are acquired through experience. One important enterprise is to establish antecedents of attitude formation and change. All theorists assume that attitudes exert a directive influence on overt responses. Thus, a second descriptive enterprise now is to determine the consequences of attitude; a fully comprehensive theory of attitudes would provide an understanding of both antecedents and consequences.

Approaches to the development of attitude theory focus on the processes through which attitudes develop and affect our lives. These theories draw upon the various psychological processes that have been studied in the areas of reinforcement and learning, cognition and memory, and needs and motivation. To a lesser extent, attitude theories may also draw upon work by perceptual, physiological, and genetic researchers. The aim of this process approach is to develop a theory transportable across all attitude objects and across all settings in which attitudes are affected or expressed. Consequently, one does not find theories specific to racial attitudes, peer group influences, or television advertisements. A single theory anchored in basic psychological processes should accommodate all such specific concerns.

ANTECEDENTS

Attitude researchers have invested far more effort in studying the antecedents of attitudes than the consequences. Perhaps the widespread belief in the relevance of attitudes to social behavior has inspired greater interest in how attitudes can be changed (and therefore manipulated) to improve society. An extensive array of antecedent variables have been explored, most of which relate to the effects of persuasive communications. The communication process can be divided into five components: source (e.g., communicator credibility); message (e.g., use of fear appeals); channel (e.g., direct experience vs. mass media) receiver (e.g., intelligence of the audience); and destination (e.g., temporal decay of induced change).

A comprehensive attitude theory should be able to explain findings in all these areas. Unfortunately, no single, unifying theory of attitude is accepted by all researchers in the field. Textbooks on attitude theory describe well over 30 distinct theoretical formulations. Four separate classes of attitude theory can be identified. They have in common the view that attitudes can be represented as an evaluative disposition falling somewhere on a pro-to-anti continuum. They differ, however, in the extent to which supplementary features are integral to the hypothetical construct.

The undifferentiated view defines attitude as being nothing more nor less than an evaluative disposition. Attitude is an unelaborated concept referring only to a location on the evaluative continuum. Past experiences, informational influences, reinforcements, and motivational pressures all contribute to the attitude at the time they occur. The resulting attitude is the cumulative accretion of those past events. Each life experience makes its contribution at the time of occurrence and thereafter remains irrelevant to the status of the attitude. Theories that draw heavily on principles of classical conditioning and reinforcement often adopt this undifferentiated approach. So, too, do theories that view attitudes as the result of sequential information integration processes or concept formation processes.

The second category of theory views attitude as the set of beliefs the person holds about the attitude object. In this case, the basic elements of an attitude are the individual beliefs or cognitions. The overall evaluative disposition is but one of several attributes that characterize the attitude. The evaluative disposition is the resultant of all those beliefs that are salient at the time the observed response is initiated. In this view of attitude, there is no single true evaluative disposition, only an average that emerges over a variety of responses. Each response derives from a different sample of the belief set; evaluative consistency emerges because all samples are taken from the same population of beliefs.

A variety of other properties of the attitude or belief set are of potential interest. For example, one may study the dimensionality of the beliefs, or the extent to which logical and affective consistency exists among the beliefs. Little theoretical work has been done on the antecedents of belief dimensionality. However, a number of theories have taken up the problem of logical, psychological, and affective consistency. This approach allows for the possibility that existing beliefs can affect the interpretation of new information.

A third point of view refers to the set of motivational forces operating on the person that are relevant to the attitude object. The basic elements of an attitude consist of the values, needs, drives, motives, and personality dispositions of the person. Typically, this set contains only the more enduring (rather than situationally determined) motivational dispositions. This view is sometimes referred to as the functional approach, since attitudes (their formation and change) are seen as functionally satisfying the person's more basic motivational needs.

A wide variety of these attitude-relevant functions have been identified. Attitudes can serve an *instrumentality* function, in which they are used to obtain rewards and avoid punishments in our social world. People often espouse attitudes as a way of managing the impressions others form of them. Attitudes can serve a *value-maintenance* function, in which they are viewed as deriving from (and providing sustenance to) more basic values like equality and financial security. Attitudes can serve a *knowledge* function, helping us deal effectively with the complex and overwhelming flow of information encountered in life. Attitudes allow us to simplify this information by reducing it to categories specific to each attitude object and then attaching a positive or negative response disposition to the category.

Attitudes can serve a *consistency* function, since people need to view themselves as reasonable and consistent in their attitudes and beliefs; awareness of inconsistencies is uncomfortable and motivates the person to restore cognitive equilibrium. Attitudes can serve a *uniqueness* function, letting people develop attitudes that distinguish them from others in their social group. Attitudes can serve an *ego-defensive* function, defending the person against unflattering self-truths deriving from antisocial impulses and inner conflicts, and from sources of information external to the self. Attitudes can serve a *reactance* function: Since people resist threats to their freedom to think and feel as they choose, they adopt attitudes directly opposite to those advocated by a coercive source.

The evaluative characteristic of attitudes operates in the service of these motives: Positive attitudes emerge only if basic motivational needs are satisfied by positive responses toward the attitude object. The observed attitudinal response will be determined by whatever set of motives is dominant at the time of the response. And so, like the set of beliefs conception, the set of motives view assumes there is no single true attitude; consistency over responses derives from the stability of the person's underlying motive structure.

The fourth category of attitude theory takes the position that attitudes are nonexistent. Whereas other theorists agree that attitudes are unobservable, this category of theorist believes them to be social fictions. Being nonexistent, attitudes should not be given the scientific status of a hypothetical construct. These theorists readily acknowledge that people can and do describe themselves as possessing attitudes. However, they maintain that this does not mean that a concept of attitude must be invoked to explain these responses. Instead, it is argued that self-reports of attitudes are the result of self-perception processes in which people review their own past behaviors relevant to the attitude object and induce what their attitude must be.

If attitudes do not exist, it is meaningless to speak of their causal antecedents and consequences. However, these theorists have found it useful to study the perceived antecedents of the observable attitude response. This has led to an analysis of the environmental cues used when people attribute attitudes to themselves and to others.

CONSEQUENCES

The ideal attitude theory should encompass both antecedents and consequences, but most theoretical efforts have focused on the antecedents. Regarding consequences, theories would need to show how an attitude combines with other theoretical variables to affect the particular response system being observed. Instead, most theories are content with the unelaborated assertion that an attitude will have a directive influence (in a positive or negative direction) on the observed response. Rarely does a theory designate what categories of overt response should and should not be affected, nor do they usually indicate the circumstances under which attitudes exert their influence.

Most of the empirical work on the consequences problem has been done by researchers interested in attitude measurement. Attitudes have been shown to correlate with distortions in logical thinking, memory, social judgments, perceptions of factual accuracy, information seeking, nonverbal communication, and a wide variety of social behaviors.

Two kinds of consequences have received special attention. Most researchers who have developed theories of antecedents have used verbal measures of attitude. They have accepted the premise that people can accurately describe their own beliefs and attitudes. Some researchers, however, have examined the circumstances under which such verbal reports do and do not accurately reflect the underlying attitude. The results of this response bias research have been used primarily to improve the research methods used in testing predictions regarding the antecedents of attitudes.

A great deal of work has been done on how attitudes affect behaviors. Some important factors are whether the attitude was formed on the basis of direct experience with the attitude object, and how salient the attitude is at the time of the behavior. Some authorities have argued that overall attitude is only marginally relevant to specific actions. More important is the attitude toward the act itself, since that attitude incorporates feelings about the attitude object, the type of behavior, and the temporal-social context in which the behavior is elicited.

When the hypothetical construct includes more than just an evaluative disposition (as with the set of beliefs and set of motives approaches), other properties of attitudes also provide a conceptual basis for studying consequences. For example, internally consistent attitudes have a stronger effect on behavior than do inconsistent ones. Organized belief sets should have the same effects as cognitive schemas. Ego-involved attitudes (i.e., those closely linked to central values) are viewed as affecting responses more strongly than less personally relevant attitudes.

UNRESOLVED ISSUES

Several attitudinal phenomena are not yet well understood by attitude theorists. Little is known about the sudden and intense emotional arousal that attitudes sometimes produce. Little is known about how attitudes lead people to make enormous personal sacrifices in behalf of their loved ones and ideals. Little is known about the massively dramatic reversals in attitude that sometimes occur (as in the case of emotional trauma, religious conversion, and love at first sight). Although enormous strides in understanding attitudes have been made since the early years of this century, these and other unresolved issues indicate that fundamental questions are still unanswered.

SUGGESTED READING

Fleming, D. (1967). Attitude: The history of a concept. *Perspectives in American History, 1,* 287–365.

Greenwald, A. G., Brock, T. C., & Ostrom, T. M. (Eds.). (1968). *Psychological foundations of attitudes.* New York: Academic Press.

Ostrom, T. M. (1968). The emergence of attitude theory: 1930–1950. In A. Greenwald, T. Brock, & T. Ostrom (Eds.), *Psychological foundations of attitudes.* New York: Academic Press.

Petty, R. E., & Cacioppo, J. T. (1981). *Attitudes and persuasion: Classic and contemporary approaches.* Dubuque, IA: Brown.

Petty, R. E., Ostrom, T. M., & Brock, T. C. (Eds.). (1981). *Cognitive responses in persuasion.* Hillsdale, NJ: Erlbaum.

Smith, M. B., Bruner, J. S., & White, R. W. (1956). *Opinions and personality.* New York: Wiley.

T. M. Ostrom
Ohio State University

AGGRESSION
ATTITUDES
EMOTIONS
MOTIVATION
SELECTIVE ATTENTION
SOCIAL COGNITION

ATTITUDES

Throughout the history of social psychology, the attitude construct has played a central role in the explanation of social behavior. Attitude is usually defined as a disposition to respond favorably or unfavorably to an object, person, institution, or event. People can hold attitudes of varying degrees of favorability toward themselves and toward any discriminable aspect of their environment. Positive, widely shared attitudes toward relatively abstract goals (freedom, honesty, security) are known as values.

As an unobservable, hypothetical construct, attitude must be inferred from measurable responses that reflect positive or negative evaluations of the attitude object. People can be asked to express their attitudes directly, by judging the object of the attitude as good or bad or by rating their degree of liking for it. Alternatively, attitudes can be inferred more indirectly from other responses to the object. Three categories of responses are distinguished, following a classification that goes back at least to Plato: Attitudes can be inferred from *cognitive responses* or beliefs (reflecting the individual's perception of, and information about, the attitude object), *affective responses* (feelings toward the object), and *conative responses* (behavioral intentions, tendencies, and actions with respect to the object). For example, attitudes toward an ethnic group can be inferred from stereotyped beliefs (whether valid or biased) that attribute certain traits, abilities, manners, and lifestyles to members of the group in question; from such affective or emotional responses as expressions of admiration or contempt for the ethnic group; and from intentions or overt actions that reflect tendencies to approach or avoid members of the group under consideration.

Although attitudes are sometimes viewed as containing all three response classes or components, most social psychologists identify and define attitudes in terms of overall evaluation. Beliefs, feelings, intentions, and behaviors are viewed as related to, but conceptually distinct from, attitudes. In the 1950s, social psychologists posited a basic need for people to maintain consistency among their beliefs, attitudes, and actions. Inconsistency (dissonance, imbalance, incongruity) was said to be psychologically aversive, motivating the individual to change beliefs, attitudes, or behavior in such a way as to establish consistency (or at least reduce the degree of inconsistency) among these forces.

ATTITUDE FORMATION

Functional Approach

Early attempts to identify the origins of attitudes focused on the needs or functions that attitudes may serve. Thus, attitudes were assumed to have instrumental or utilitarian functions (helping people attain rewards and avoid punishments), knowledge functions (organizing and simplifying people's experiences), expressive functions (enabling emotional release), and ego-defensive functions (protecting and enhancing the self). Although it generated considerable interest, the functional approach to attitudes has produced only a modest amount of research and has been of limited practical value.

Behavioral Approach

By defining attitude as an implicit, evaluative response to a stimulus, behaviorally oriented social psychologists have used principles of classical conditioning to explain attitude formation. Repeated, systematic association between the attitude object (conditioned stimulus) and a positively or negatively valued event (unconditioned stimulus) is assumed to produce a favorable or unfavorable reaction (attitude) to the object. Controversy revolves around the question of awareness, or the extent to which awareness of the object-event contingencies is a necessary requirement for conditioning of attitude. Although the issue has not been completely resolved, few studies have clearly demonstrated automatic conditioning of attitude without contingency awareness.

Cognitive Approach

A general trend toward cognitive or information-processing explanations of social behavior has brought a concomitant decline in the importance accorded to needs and automatic conditioning processes. Instead, stress is now placed on the role of information as a basis of attitude formation. According to this view, beliefs—representing people's subjective knowledge about themselves and their world—are the primary determinants of attitudes. Each belief links the attitude object to a positively or negatively valued attribute: thus smoking (the object) causes lung cancer (the attribute). Generally speaking, the greater the number of beliefs that associate the object with positive attributes, and the smaller the number of beliefs that associate it with negative attributes, the more favorable is the resultant attitude toward the object. More precise formulations are provided by expectancy–value models of attitude. According to these models, the value or utility of each attribute contributes to the attitude in direct proportion to the person's subjective probability (strength of belief) that the object has the attribute in question. The sum or average of these weighted attribute evaluations is said to determine the overall attitude toward the object.

According to the expectancy–value model, attitudes toward an object are formed automatically and inevitably as we acquire new information (and form new beliefs) about the object's attributes and as the subjective values of these attributes become linked to the object. People can, of course, form many different beliefs about an object, but only a relatively small number influence attitude at any given moment. It is these accessible beliefs that are considered to be the prevailing determinants of a person's attitude. Consistent with other dual-mode processing models, when people are confronted with an important decision or issue, attitudes can be based on considerable reflection, taking into account all available information, while in other instances such attitudes may be expressed with little contemplation, drawing on only a small number of immediately accessible beliefs.

Causal relations between beliefs and attitudes can also operate in the reverse direction. Attraction or hostility toward another person may be justified or rationalized by attributing positive or negative characteristics to the person. Ethnic, religious, national, and sex-role stereotypes are often the results, rather than the causes, of prejudicial attitudes.

ORIGINS OF BELIEFS

The assumption that attitudes have an informational foundation ties the question of attitude formation to the origins of our beliefs about ourselves and about our social environment.

Direct Experience

One important source of information about objects, people, and events is direct experience. Thus one may learn that cigarette smoking produces unpleasant odors, that a certain television program portrayed a great deal of violence, or that overweight reduces physical stamina. Based on personal experience, beliefs of this kind tend to be held with great confidence and to resist change. Often, they reflect reality quite accurately. Over time, however, many factors tend to distort memory for events and thus reduce the accuracy of beliefs based on direct experience. As a general rule, these distortions serve to increase the internal consistency and coherence of remembered events.

Secondhand Information

There are limits to the number and kinds of beliefs that can be formed by way of direct experience. Much of our information is acquired through conversation with other people or communicated to us by a variety of sources such as television, radio, newspapers, and books. Many factors are found to influence acceptance of such secondhand information and its incorporation into the receiver's belief system. Foremost are the coherence and persuasive powers of the information provided in the communication. Additional factors include credibility of the source, type of appeal (e.g., appeals based on fear or humor), and personality characteristics of the receiver.

Inferences

Information obtained by means of direct experience or verbal communication can provide the basis for a variety of inferences. Many of our beliefs are the result of such inference processes. For example, people form far-ranging impressions of another person on the basis of one or two items of information about that person. An individual described as responsible tends also to be viewed as persevering, honest, tidy, careful, and so on. These inferences are said to follow from intuitive or implicit theories of personality.

Much research in social psychology has focused on the processes whereby people form inferences about their own and other people's behavior. Early analyses likened individuals to naive scientists who, for the most part, make systematic use of available information in their attempts to explain their own or another person's actions. Research soon revealed, however, that social judgments, like other human inferences, are subject to systematic biases and errors that can be classified as either motivational or cognitive in origin.

Motivational biases are characterized by a tendency to draw inferences that serve the individual's needs and desires. Among these motivations are the needs to enhance and protect the ego and to control one's fate. Research evidence has been interpreted as showing that people readily accept credit for success but are reluctant to accept blame for failure, and that they tend to believe that people deserve their accidental misfortunes and fortuitous achievements.

Cognitive biases originate in the limitations of otherwise reasonable inference processes. They arise because of people's limited ability to attend to and properly process all the information available to them. Among the cognitive biases that have been identified are tendencies to overemphasize or underemphasize situational as opposed to internal determinants of behavior; to rely heavily on individual cases at the expense of statistical summary information; to base one's judgments on preconceived ideas and theories while disregarding relevant information that has no clear place in these ideas or theories; and to persevere in such judgments despite discrediting evidence.

ATTITUDES AND BEHAVIOR

From its inception, the attitude concept has been invoked to explain social behavior. Because attitudes are considered to be behavioral dispositions, it is natural to assume that they direct, and in some sense determine, social action. Racial prejudice (negative attitudes toward racial or ethnic groups) is blamed for discriminatory behavior, political actions are traced to liberal or conservative attitudes, and many behaviors related to sex and the family are explained by reference to religion. As a general rule, positive attitudes are expected to produce favorable behaviors toward the attitude object, while negative attitudes are expected to produce unfavorable behaviors.

Casual observation appears to support the idea of a close association between attitudes and behavior. In fact, the assumption that attitudes can be used to predict and explain social actions went largely unchallenged until the late 1960s. By that time, however, there was growing evidence that a strong relation between verbal expressions of attitude and overt behavior could not be taken for granted. Controlled studies failed to find relations between racial attitudes and such actions as accepting members of the racial group in a hotel or restaurant, conforming with their views or behaviors, or extending an invitation to members of that group. Among many other negative findings it was reported that attitudes toward cheating failed to predict actual cheating behavior, that attitudes toward another person were unrelated to cooperation or competition with that person, and that work-related attitudes had little to do with absenteeism, tardiness, or turnover.

Under the weight of this negative evidence, social psychologists were forced to reexamine the nature of attitude and its relation to social behavior. Increased understanding resulted from renewed recognition that attitude is an unobservable, hypothetical construct that must be inferred from measurable responses to the attitude object. Verbal responses (usually classified as "attitude") and overt actions (termed "behavior") are both observable expressions of an underlying disposition. However, a strong empirical relation between verbal responses and overt actions can be expected only if the two types of reactions reflect exactly the same underlying disposition (i.e., the same attitude). Thus, although unrelated to any single action, verbal expressions of attitude toward an ethnic group are found to be strongly related to aggregate measures of discriminatory behavior that involve different actions toward various members of that group, observed in different contexts and on different occasions. Such aggregate measures of behavior reflect a general disposition to respond favorably or unfavorably to the group, just as does the verbal measure of attitude toward the group in question. By the same token, a person's degree of religiosity often fails to predict single church-related activities, but it is strongly related to religious behavior that aggregates across different types of religious activities, contexts, and occasions.

Single behaviors, on the other hand, can be predicted from attitudes toward the behaviors themselves—for example, attitudes toward smoking marijuana (rather than global attitudes toward the counterculture), attitudes toward attending church services (as opposed to attitudes toward the church), or attitudes toward donating blood (instead of global attitudes concerning altruism). However, response tendencies reflected in attitudes toward specified

actions can change as a result of situational demands or unanticipated events. Individuals also vary in their susceptibility to the influence of such external factors. While attitudes toward behaviors tend to produce corresponding behavioral intentions, the extent to which these intentions are actually carried out is moderated by situational factors and individual difference variables. Nevertheless, barring unforeseen events, behavioral attitudes and intentions are usually found to be quite accurate predictors of subsequent actions.

SUGGESTED READING

Ajzen, I. *Attitudes, personality, and behavior.*

Allport, G. W. *The nature of prejudice.*

Eagly, A. H., & Chaiken, S. *The psychology of attitudes.*

Campbell, D. T. Social attitudes and other acquired behavioral dispositions.

Fishbein, M., & Ajzen, I. *Belief attitude, intention, and behavior.*

McGuire, W. J. The nature of attitudes and attitude change.

Pratkanis, A. R., Breckler, S. J., & Greenwald, A. G. *Attitude structure and function.*

I. AJZEN
University of Massachusetts, Amherst

INTERPERSONAL PERCEPTION
STEREOTYPING

AUDITORY DISORDERS

Auditory disorders may consist of hearing loss, otorrhea, pain, and tinnitus.

HEARING LOSS

Conductive Hearing Loss

This type occurs when there is a disease or obstruction in the auditory conductive mechanism: the external auditory canal, the tympanic membrane, or the middle ear space and structures. A conductive loss is evidenced in an ear which shows a greater than 10 dB difference in pure tone air and bone conduction audiograms averaged over frequencies in the speech range; however, speech discrimination is normal. Factors producing conductive hearing losses include occlusion by cerumen or foreign objects, tumor, or congenital atresia of the external auditory canal; disease or perforation of the tympanic membrane; otosclerosis; or impairment of free air flow to the middle ear space via the Eustachian tube.

Sensorineural Hearing Loss

The designation "sensorineural" represents two different sites of lesions in the auditory system. A sensory loss is produced by damage, degeneration, or developmental failure of hair cells in the organ of Corti or any structure within the cochlear duct. A neural loss is produced by similar deficiencies central to the cochlear duct, including the spiral ganglion, the cochlear nucleus, and the acoustic portion of the VIIIth cranial nerve. Unless a definite site of lesion is determined by specific diagnostic tests for a given hearing loss, the term sensorineural is used to cover both possibilities.

Sudden sensorineural hearing loss may occur because of a variety of etiological factors. These include viral infection, ischemia of the cochlea due to occlusion of the labyrinthine vessels, rupture of the oval or round window, a fracture line of the head through trauma, acoustic tumor, Ménière's disease, and mumps.

Progressive hearing loss occurs primarily with aging and is termed presbycusis. As shown by Corso in *Aging Sensory Systems and Perception,* presbycusis may begin in the early 30s and affects both ears similarly. For frequencies above approximately 1000 Hz, men have poorer hearing for pure tones than women, age held constant; below approximately 500 Hz, women have poorer hearing. Four subclasses of presbycusis have been identified by Gacek and Schuknecht (1969); these involve degeneration or disorders in the sensory or neural structures of the cochlea, or in its associated mechanical and metabolic processes.

A second etiological factor in progressive hearing loss is exposure to excessive noise over long time periods, as in a work environment. Noise-induced hearing loss affects mostly the frequencies in the region of 4000 Hz. However, continued noise exposure gradually deepens and widens the audiogram notch, so that hearing sensitivity becomes progressively worse and extends to frequencies in the speech range—below 4000 Hz. Thus speech discrimination is impaired, with poor speech understanding especially in noisy environments.

Ototoxicity due to certain antibiotic drugs may lead to progressively reduced hearing or total bilateral deafness. These drugs include various members of the mycin group such as streptomycin, neomycin, and kanamycin.

Ménière's disease, syphilis, tumors of the VIIIth cranial nerve, and hereditary factors may produce progressive sensorineural hearing losses of the unilateral or bilateral type. The degree of impairment in speech discrimination depends upon the severity of the prevalent disorder.

Nonprogressive hearing loss of the sensorineural type may be associated with congenital factors including maternal rubella, family history of early deafness, parental blood incompatability, prematurity, and ear infections. Audiological tests usually show bilateral hearing loss and reduced speech discrimination.

Mixed Hearing Loss

A mixed hearing loss has a conductive and a sensorineural component. Thus, both air and bone conduction thresholds are depressed. Ordinarily this type of loss is associated with chronic otis media or otosclerosis. In either case, speech discrimination may be reduced and hearing loss is progressive.

OTORRHEA

Otorrhea is defined as the drainage of fluid from the external auditory canal and may be the presenting symptom of ear disease. Diseases can occur in the external auditory canal or the middle ear and may be acute or chronic. The hearing loss related to acute otitis media is usually mild to moderate, and conductive in type. When chronic otis media establishes itself, the hearing loss is typically conductive and progressive, and may be quite severe. If complications occur involving the labyrinth, an associated sensorineural hearing loss may occur.

PAIN

The ear is served by three nonauditory cranial nerves (V, IX, X) and two cervical nerves (C2 and C3) that also supply other areas of the head and neck. Ear pain is a prominent symptom in acute or serous otitis media and mastoiditis, in which infection of the middle ear or mastoid space produces fluids that create excessive pressure behind the tympanic membrane. The hearing loss in acute or serous otitis media may vary from mild to severe; in mastoiditis, hearing is usually normal or only slightly impaired.

TINNITUS

Tinnitus is the hearing of sounds within a person's head. In objective tinnitus the sound originates within the individual and may be heard by an examiner; in subjective tinnitus the sound is heard only by the individual. Tinnitus may develop suddenly or slowly, over several hours or days; it may be present constantly or intermittently; it may be unilateral, bilateral, or central in localization. The sound may be heard as loud or soft, and may be high or low in pitch. The temporal pattern of the auditory experience may be pulsatile with the heart beat, steady, clicking, or blowing with respiration. Tinnitus is a typical concomitant of sensorineural hearing loss; however, it may be associated with a vast number of other etiological factors, such as external otitis, otitis media, Eustachian tube dysfunction, vascular anomolies, hypertension, and muscular spasms.

REFERENCES

Corso, J. F. (1981). *Aging sensory systems and perception.* New York: Praeger.

Gacek, R. R., & Schukaecht, H. F. (1969). Pathology of presbycusis. *International Audiology, 8,* 199–209.

SUGGESTED READING

Jerger, S., & Jerger, J. (1981). *Auditory disorders: A manual for clinical evaluation.* Boston: Little, Brown.

Martin, F. N. (Ed.). (1981). *Medical audiology: Disorders of hearing.* Englewood Cliffs, NJ: Prentice-Hall.

Newby, H. A. (1979). *Audiology* (4th ed.). Englewood Cliffs, NJ: Prentice-Hall.

J. F. CORSO
State University of New York

AUSTRALIA, PSYCHOLOGY IN

A truly insightful understanding of the development of psychology in any nation demands an appreciation of the cultural setting in which it was born and nurtured. Jonathan Rinehart's volume *The Australians* (1966) begins: "It [Australia] was never really intended as a place for people . . . the great land slept on in its southern seas, while on all other continents the human race developed and spread and made its artifacts and began its ceremonies." A lasting human habitation in Australia began about 10,000 years ago. Originating in islands to the north, aborigines arrived with their own cultures: small, nomadic tribes speaking many different tongues and bringing with them their few primitive Stone Age implements. Later, traders from Asia knew the continent's northern coasts and seamen from several European nations, sailing too long during the "roaring forties," came to grief on the western coasts. In 1988, Australia celebrated its bicentennial, first as a colony and then as a nation; it was only some 200 years ago that Europeans first established a permanent settlement there. The successful American revolution ended the first British empire; Australia was chosen to play a part in the development of a second empire—a place for the transportation of undesirable persons who could no longer be sent to America.

As would be expected, British culture was also transported to Australia, including models for intellectual and professional life. Taft (1982) has commented: "Thus, it should not be surprising that Australia reproduced the prevailing patterns of British and German Psychology, and later American, with little added that was characteristically Australian." Be that as it may, Australian psychology has its own characteristics, its own places in the context of world psychology (Russell, 1977).

ROOTS OF AUSTRALIAN PSYCHOLOGY

More specifically, from what in British and German psychology did the Australian version arise? Clearly it was influenced significantly by British empirical philosophy. The "earliest possible date" (O'Neil, 1977) for the establishment of higher education in Australia is 1850. The first universities were staffed to a great extent by scholars from Britain, who brought prevailing British orientations with them. In British universities, the psychology of the times was mainly in the hands of the academic staff, many of whom held appointments in "moral philosophy," such as James Ward and G. F. Stout. Henry Laurie, appointed to a "Chair of Mental and Moral Philosophy" at Melbourne University in 1886; Francis Anderson, to a "Chair of Logic and Mental Philosophy" at Sydney University in 1890; and William Mitchell, as professor of "Mental and Moral Philosophy" at Adelaide University, were all educated in philosophy in Scotland. The influence of such senior scholars showed itself in an emphasis upon human experience observed empirically as the basis for the knowledge that would constitute a systematic discipline of psychology. Systematic structure for them had come from John Stuart Mill and Alexander Bain and their British predecessors. As Edwin Boring (1950) has observed, Wilhelm Wundt and German experimental psychology had taken their systematics from the same sources—and their experimental method from physiology.

The biological sciences were also features in Australian psychology, its second major root arising from the quantal steps taken by such intellectual giants as Charles Darwin, Herbert Spencer, and Francis Galton. O'Neil (1977) has pointed out that: "The first

Lecturer in Psychology appointed, *circa* 1890, in the University of Sydney . . . gave lectures to medical students . . . and in the University of Melbourne a fairly early anatomist interested himself in the relation of brain size and intelligence." As its counterparts elsewhere, Australian psychology had a leg in the camps of both the biological and social sciences. It continues to struggle to keep a rational position between a naive behaviorism, which appears to view behavior as somehow independent of the other properties of living organisms (i.e., biochemical, electrophysiological, morphological), and a naive reductionism, which seemingly accepts the premise that when all facts are known about every cell, it will be possible to add them all together to describe the total organism.

THE AUSTRALIAN PSYCHOLOGICAL COMMUNITY

The Australian psychological community is relatively small compared with those in Europe and North America. Exact data are not available as to the total number of persons engaged in scientific and professional activities that might be called "psychological." Seeking an institutional identity, Australian psychologists first came together in 1945 as a branch of the British Psychological Society, showing once again the characteristic tie to "the old country." Twenty years later, the branch budded itself off as the Australian Psychological Society (APS).

Membership in the society has increased progressively since its founding (Over, 1981b): 1970, 1,176; 1,975, 1,840; 1,980, 2,688. Results of a 1970 APS-sponsored study of university graduates employed full-time in settings across Australia involving psychological knowledge and skills reported a total of 2154, a number roughly twice that of APS membership at that time. Circumstances have changed since then, and the proportion has become much more favorable to APS membership (Taylor, 1982). Not all qualified persons in any country are motivated to join their national societies. And not all those who hold positions requiring psychological knowledge and skills meet the standards of qualification established by the national society.

With the exception of Honorary Fellows (never more than 10 at any one time), all classes of APS membership are based upon qualifications approved by the society's council. Minimum qualifications involve successful completion of four years of academic training, of which no less than 50% shall have been devoted to psychology as a main subject in a degree-granting institution or institutions (APS bylaws). Advancement from Associate Member to Member to Fellow requires evidence of further training, experience, and/or "substantial and original contribution to the advancement of psychological knowledge or practice. . . ." Analysis of the APS 1980 membership directory (Over, 1981b) showed the percentages of members with their highest academic qualifications: bachelor's degree, 31.3%; postgraduate diploma, 13.3%; master's degree, 29.7%; and the doctorate, 25.7%.

The reasons why APS plays a central institutional role in the Australian psychological community can be summarized as follows (Taylor, 1982):

1. APS is the largest psychological society in Australia.
2. APS is the nation's senior psychological society.

3. APS members are found in all Australian states and territories, and in other countries as well.

4. APS membership includes psychologists in every area of psychological teaching, research, and practice.

5. The society has no restrictions on membership other than qualifications in psychology.

6. A substantial majority of Australian psychologists belong to APS.

7. APS views on a wide variety of issues are sought by commonwealth and state governments and by nongovernmental organizations.

8. APS membership is a qualification for professional registration in many states and is required by many employers.

9. APS is recognized internationally, being the sole organization representing Australian psychology with membership in the International Union of Psychological Science.

10. As a responsible organization, APS has established a *Code of Professional Conduct,* which serves as a guide to members and plays a significant part in protecting the general public against incompetence and malpractice wherever psychological services are so offered.

The nature of their discipline has also encouraged the establishment of a number of organizations oriented toward the interests of specialized groups within the Australian psychological community.

Achievements by individual psychologists have been recognized by the award of fellowship in such national organizations as the Academy of Social Sciences in Australia (FASSA) and the Australian College of Education (FACE). These trends are indicative of the fact that development of the discipline has resulted in increasing specialization of knowledge, skills, and interests within psychology, while, at the same time, strengthening the position of psychology in relation to a wide variety of other disciplines.

The relative growth in numbers of qualified psychologists is one index of the acceptance by society generally of the contributions they can make in meeting society's needs. Using data for the 1970–1973 period, Taylor and Taft (1977) have provided rough comparisons between the index, "population per psychologist," for Australia and for the two nations that have had the greatest influence on psychology in Australia: Australia, 7,765; Britain, 11, 817; United States, 5,733.

EDUCATION AND TRAINING OF PSYCHOLOGISTS

The practice of psychology in any of its specialties, academic or applied, demands advanced education and training at the tertiary or postgraduate level. Such opportunities were not available until higher education was introduced to the Australian scene—"1850 is the earliest possible date . . ." (O'Neil, 1977). Over half a century passed before the first psychology laboratory was established at the Melbourne Teachers' College by John Smyth in 1903. As stated earlier, psychology was being taught well before that date, usually by academic staff themselves educated in philosophy. In a sense, it was "smuggled" in under the guise of mental or moral philosophy.

Appointment of the first associate professor of psychology was made in 1921, and of the first professor in 1928. The distinction of taking this bold step went to the University of Sydney. Both titles were awarded to H. Tasman Lovell, "perhaps the most comprehensively synoptic . . ." (O'Neil, 1977) of the pioneers of Australian psychology.

Under Lovell's guidance, a full Department of Psychology developed at Sydney, the first in Australia. Until the close of World War II, only two other university psychology departments had been established: at the University of Western Australia in 1930 and the New England University College in 1939. The three other pre-1945 universities continued to relegate psychology to be a constituent of mental philosophy, education, or medicine. Contributions by psychologists during World War II changed the situation very significantly during the following peacetime years, with a marked expansion in programs occurring especially during the 1970s.

The newly discovered interest in psychology was soon reflected in increased student enrollment. Reports by the Australian Bureau of Statistics (university statistics), which provide evidence of this expansion, have been analyzed by Over (1981b) for 1974, 1976, and 1978. In terms of the total numbers of undergraduate plus postgraduate degrees awarded, there was an increase in 1976 of 20% over 1974 and in 1978 of 40% over 1974. There also was an increase of 70.5% in graduates qualified at the honors degree level or beyond, persons who should have been able to satisfy requirements for APS membership.

In Australia, two groups of institutions have been given responsibilities for teaching psychology. Innovations by a Labor Government during the 1970s added the second group to the already established university sector by combining institutes of technology and teacher training colleges to form colleges of advanced education, or CAEs. By tradition, as well as by legal statutes and state acts under which they operate, the universities have the dual responsibilities for research and scholarship and for education and training. The CAEs have a stronger emphasis on vocational training, although research is carried out, especially by the older establishments. Research in psychology and the advanced education and training of psychologists remain activities associated mainly with the universities. In rank order of seniority, the degrees they offer are bachelor of arts (or science) pass, bachelor of arts (or science) honors, master of arts (or sciences), doctor of philosophy. Pass degrees usually involve three years of study; honors, four. Masters' degrees may be acquired either through research or by course work (a recent innovation); the PhD only by research. Universities may also provide postgraduate programs leading to diplomas in such specialties as applied psychology, clinical psychology, and educational psychology. University statistics prepared by the Australian Bureau of Statistics show the distribution of graduates at these various levels. Data for 1978 have been analyzed by Over (1981b): Among a total of 1,609 graduates, 1,193 were pass degrees, 242 were honors, 43 were diplomas, 101 were masters, and 30 were PhDs.

Although much attention has been given in the preceding to the key roles played by educational institutions in the development of Australian psychology, it must be kept clearly in mind that, as a "frontier" country, Australia has always focused particular attention on the solution of practical problems. Applications of psychology in education, in medicine, in mental retardation, and in clinical problems with children began to occur in the 1910s, with what has been described as "spectacular developments" (Taft, 1982) during the 1920s and 1930s. All but two of the first 20 chairmen of the Australian Branch of the British Psychological Society were persons with full-time professional experience outside universities. "Education" in psychology was strongly supported in institutions of higher education, but much "training" by way of practical experience occurred within Australian government departments, state education systems, hospitals, homes for the mentally retarded, and such privately sponsored organizations as the Australian Council for Educational Research, whose foundation was made possible by a grant from the Carnegie Corporation, and the Australian Institute of Industrial Psychology, a nonprofit organization.

EMPLOYMENT OF PSYCHOLOGISTS

Earlier it was suggested that psychology was smuggled onto the Australian scene under the guise of "mental" or "moral philosophy." J. McKeen Cattell, as president of the 1929 International Congress of Psychology held at Yale University, commented on the presence of psychologists in the United States during the same period: "A history of psychology in America prior to the last fifty years would be as short as a book on snakes in Ireland since the time of St. Patrick. In so far as psychologists are concerned, America was then like Heaven, for there was not a damned soul there." Employment for psychologists was equally scarce in Australia.

There is ample evidence among the various specialties within psychology—and, indeed, within other areas of human knowledge—that, when a new frontier is recognized and its potential applications perceived, opportunities for employment begin to appear. Progress is often slow at first, increasing as qualified members of the profession prove their worth. A survey conducted at the request of the Australian Psychological Society (Kidd, 1971) provides an overall view of the general areas of employment available to graduates in psychology half a century after the founding of the nation's first department of psychology. From a small handfull of staff and students in 1921, the survey identified 2,154 graduates in psychology in 1970 who were employed in the following areas: teaching and research at tertiary institutions (32.7%), counseling services and educational psychology (28.4%), clinical psychology (15.8%), personnel psychology (9.0%), vocational guidance (7.9%), market research and marketing (5.0%), mass media (1.1%), and social psychology (0.6%). Classification of the workplaces of a sample of APS membership 10 years later (Over, 1981b) showed that 26.7% were in universities, 25.3% in government and semigovernment agencies, 17.7% in the private sector, 16.0% in other tertiary institutions, and 14.3% in state education departments. Both the numbers of qualified persons and the breadth of opportunities for employment had expanded to meet the Australian society's demands.

Employment of psychologists is not inherently exempt from the vicissitudes of a nation's economy. As in many other nations in the 1980s, psychologists were feeling the effects of financial pressures in a period of inflationary economic trends. Analysis of the situation in Australia led Over (1981a) to conclude: "Psychology Departments will face many problems over the next 20 years following the abrupt end to expansion within the university system after two decades of rapid growth." He predicted that the career paths of recent and future graduates would be affected, innovation limited, and problems of obsolescence in knowledge and skills. Such changes in the university sector, which involves so significant a percentage of qualified personnel, cannot but create ripples—even waves—in other sectors of employment of psychologists. Although these comments introduced a discordant note into what has been a generally optimistic discussion, it is realistic to do so if the story of psychology in Australia is to be up to date.

Recently the history of twentieth-century Australian psychology has been especially attractive to a number of writers, 25 of whom have contributed to *Psychology in Australia: Achievements and Prospects* (Nixon & Taft, 1977). Because any human enterprise reflects the personalities of those who initiate and engage in it, there is frustration at having to leave so brief an account of Australian psychology at this point. O'Neil (1977) has written more fully about what kinds of people the "pioneers" really were: H. Tasman Lovell and A. H. Martin, Sydney University; John Smyth, Melbourne University; Gilbert Phillips, Sydney Teachers' College; H. L. Fowler, University of Western Australia; K. S. Cunningham, Australian Council for Educational Research; Bernard Muscio, Sydney University (Philosophy); and Stanley Porteus, Melbourne. Readers interested in becoming acquainted with Australian psychology in greater depth should consult the Further References, or, better still, visit Australia to see for themselves how the development of psychology has been and is now influenced by the pluses and minuses of growth in a country lucky in its wealth of natural resources and its standard of living, no longer so isolated by the "tyranny of distance" (Blainey, 1966), but perhaps still overly inhibited by the "critical harshness" of its cultural environment (Hearnshaw, 1978).

REFERENCES

Blainey, G. N. (1966). *The tyranny of distance.* Melbourne, Australia: Sun Books.

Boring, E. G. (1957/1950/1929). *A history of experimental psychology* (2nd ed.). New York: Appleton-Century-Crofts.

Hearnshaw, L. S. (1978). Review of Nixon and Taft, 1977. *Australian Journal of Psychology, 30,* 104–105.

Kidd, G. A. (1971). *The employment of psychologists in Australia.* Sydney, Australia: Sydney University Appointments Board.

Nixon, M., & Taft, R. (Eds.) (1977). *Psychology in Australia: Achievements and prospects.* Rushcutters Bay, Australia: Pergamon Press (Australia).

Over, R. (1981b). Employment prospects for psychology graduates in Australia. *Australian Psychologist, 16,* 335–345.

Over, R. (1981a). Impending crises for psychology departments in Australian universities. *Australian Psychologist, 16,* 221–233.

Rinehart, J. (1966). *The Australians.* Adelaide, Australia: Rigby.

Russell, R. W. (1977). Australian psychologists in the world context. In M. Nixon, & R. Taft, (Eds.), *Psychology in Australia: Achievements and prospects.* Rushcutters Bay, Australia: Pergamon Press.

Taft, R. (1982). Psychology and its history in Australia. *Australian Psychologist, 17,* 31–39.

Taylor, K. (1982). "Standing up" for this APS. *Bulletin of the Australian Psychological Society,* 8–10.

Taylor, K. F., & Taft, R. (1977). Psychology in the Australian Zeitgeist. In M. Nixon & R. Taft (Eds.), *Psychology in Australia: Achievement and prospects.* Rushcutters Bay, Australia: Pergamon Press (Australia).

R. W. RUSSELL
University of California, Irvine

AUSTRIA, PSYCHOLOGY IN

Whenever Austrian psychologists travel abroad, they are usually greeted with the observation that they come from the cradle of psychoanalysis, the home of Sigmund Freud. However, what these psychologists often do not know is that Austrian psychology has a long-standing empirical and experimental tradition; that it has placed great emphasis on quantification and mathematical formularization, and that, in general, it has regarded the biological basis of psychic phenomena as the necessary starting point for any psychological research.

For this reason, Freud was not accorded proper recognition by professional psychologists during his lifetime: From their point of view, his work simply lay outside the realm of psychology proper and belonged instead to medical science. Thus Charlotte Bühler, the wife of Karl Bühler, the head of the first Department of Psychology at the University of Vienna (created for him in 1923), said in her autobiography that her husband's relationship with psychoanalysis "was unfortunately mostly negative. The reasons for this were manifold. Karl's main reason was that his interests were in the first instance in experimental psychology. . . ." And this explains a fact that later was often remarked upon with surprise—namely, that Freud never had any contact with Bühler, although he lived only a few hundred yards away from the latter's Department of Psychology. Bühler's successor, Hubert Rohracher, has the following to say about Freud in his autobiography: "I never heard his name mentioned in psychologist circles; he was considered purely a physician with whose ideas one did not need to deal."

This attitude has changed, of course, and today there are close contacts between the Department of Psychology and the Institute of Depth Psychology at the University of Vienna, which still is a part of the School of Medicine, and is now headed by Hans Strotzka. One result of these contacts has been that psychology in Austria now also deals with psychoanalytical questions, but in the experimental and empirical way typical of the Vienna school—to the mutual advantage of both disciplines.

Even Viktor Frankl's Logotherapy, although not primarily empirical, is not outside the range of experimental-psychological investigations. The first empirical control studies of his work were carried out at the Psychology Department in Vienna, and the department maintains harmonious personal and professional contacts with him, in a way characteristic of the Vienna school: upholding a clearly defined theoretical position while at the same time viewing other schools with open mindedness and tolerance. There are not many places where such a peaceful coexistence of the most heterogeneous approaches can be witnessed.

Looking back in history, we do not, at first, find anyone among the philosophical ancestors of psychology who could have provided the basis for this scientific orientation.

The University of Vienna was founded in 1365 by the Hapsburg Rudolf IV and was thus the second German-speaking university after Prague. Its original faculties were law, medicine, and liberal arts. In 1384, Pope Urban VI established the faculty of Roman Catholic theology, in those days the most important of all the faculties. Thus the role of philosophy within the university was defined: For about 400 years it was to be the handmaiden of theology (*ancilla theologiae*). The faculty of liberal arts was at that time preparatory, and had to be attended by all students aspiring to continue their studies at one of the three higher faculties—medicine, law, or theology. Moreover, the state intervened again and again, for example, in 1554 with the *nova reformatio* and in 1623 with the *sanctio pragmatica,* which called upon the Jesuits to head the faculty of liberal arts as well.

In 1773, the Jesuit order was suppressed by Pope Clement XIV, but this did not mean the end of restrictions on philosophy in Austria; indeed the faculty was now granted only a single chair and subsequently came under the complete control of the state. Finally, the professors were permitted to read nothing but prescribed and censored texts; and philosophy as a field of teaching became totally insignificant.

In 1848, the university reforms of Count Thun-Hohenstein put an end to this state of affairs and opened the door to a spirit of enthusiasm, which—perhaps because it had been suppressed for so long—now developed with great liveliness.

Franz Brentano (1838–1917), who taught at the University of Vienna from 1874 to 1895, was the founder of the Act Psychology (Vienna school). Starting from the traditional Aristotelian-scholastic philosophy, he developed a psychology based on "immanent objectivity." Research was to be fused with strictly empirical methods—that is, the most precise observation and description of all psychic phenomena. His basic attitude was expressed in one of the tenets of Brentano's early work that won him his professorship: "The method of philosophy is no different from that of the natural sciences."

These ideas were taken up by Alexius Meinong (1853–1920), who developed the philosophy of the Theory of Objects. As a psychologist, he applied his greatest efforts to a critical examination of Gestalt psychology, which had been founded by Christian von Ehrenfels (1859–1932), who taught first in Graz and later in Vienna and Prague (Graz school). Although this was not necessarily to be expected from his basic ideas, Meinong, too, was greatly interested in experiments. He used his private means to set up a laboratory and in 1886/1887 he taught the first practical course in experimental psychology in Austria.

The next step leads us to a group of expressly science-oriented researchers: Ernst Mach (1838–1916), Ludwig Boltzmann (1844–1906), and Moritz Schlick (1882–1936). All three of these men came from physics; even Schlick had written his dissertation for Max Planck and had been the first to philosophically evaluate the theory of relativity. Schlick became the center of a circle that proposed to reform philosophy and later became famous as the Vienna Circle: Hans Hahn, Victor Kraft, Herbert Feigl, Otto Neurath, Rudolf Carnap. Thus logical empiricism had been explicitly founded! Karl Popper and Ludwig Wittgenstein, although they never actually attended the meetings of the Vienna Circle, were also in close contact with it through some of its members.

The ideas of Alfred Adler (1870–1937), too, are more alive today in the field of medicine than in psychology, and not without some justification, if one considers the origin of Individual Psychology: Adler had first practiced medicine in Vienna as a general practitioner and only his keen sense of the relationship between environment and illness had kindled his interest in psychiatry—after extensive studies in psychology and philosophy.

How quickly his ideas were applied outside the area of medicine itself, and especially in pedagogy, is shown by the fact that one of his most important disciples was the educator Oskar Spiel, who, beginning in the 1930s and continuing on after World War II (from 1946 as the principal of an experimental school in Vienna), applied Individual Psychology to school pedagogy.

While maintaining a definitely empirical-scientific attitude, the Department of Psychology at the University of Vienna is in close personal and professional contact with Oskar's son, Professor Walter Spiel, the head of the Clinic of Child and Adolescent Psychiatry, as well as with Professor Erwin Ringel, both important contemporary representatives of Individual Psychology.

This was the background for the work of Karl Bühler (1879–1963), who, rather than carrying out research in psychology within the framework of philosophy, as had been the case before, headed the first Department of Psychology in Vienna. Born near Heidelberg, he had studied medicine and philosophy and had obtained his M.D. degree at Freiburg im Breisgau in 1903 and his Ph.D. degree at Strasbourg the following year. In 1905, he became an assistant at the University of Würzburg, and two years later was teaching there. Next he went to Bonn, and from 1916 on he was professor in Munich. At the beginning of World War I, he became the head of the psychological testing center for army automobile drivers in Munich. After the war, he served as a professor, first in Dresden, and from 1922 on in Vienna.

Under his leadership, psychology in Vienna began to flourish. Lectures that previously had been attended by some 20 students attracted more than 1,000 and had to be held in the largest lecture hall of the university, the Auditorium Maximum. (Even now, more than half a century later, introductory courses in psychology are still taught in that same auditorium, since for many years psychology has ranked as the most popular of the "fashionable" fields of study in Vienna.)

Bühler established intensive foreign contacts: He was a guest lecturer in the United States and was asked to prepare the World Congress of Psychology, to take place in Vienna in 1940. However, more than 20 years were to pass before Bühler would return to Europe as president of an international congress (1960 in Bonn).

In May 1938, as a consequence of the national socialist takeover of Austria, he was forced to retire. Barely a year later, his pension was discontinued. His wife Charlotte happened to be in London at the time of Hitler's invasion, and she succeeded in arranging his escape via Norway. Eventually he accepted an offer to teach at St. Thomas College in St. Paul, Minnesota. After World War II ended, he was invited to return to the chair of psychology at the University of Vienna, but he refused. He died on October 24, 1963, and is buried in Los Angeles.

Bühler's main interest was the investigation of thought processes, whose underlying principles he attempted to establish by means of sophisticated experiments.

Closely connected with his fate was that of his wife Charlotte Bühler. Born in Berlin-Charlottenburg in 1893, she came from a family that was predominantly Jewish, but she had been christened and raised as a Protestant. At an early age, she was particularly interested in thought experiments, and without realizing it, she began to duplicate Karl Bühler's experiments with paired thoughts. She met him later in the course of her studies with H. Rickert, Carl Stumpf, Kurt Lewin, and Oswald Külpe. In 1916, she married Bühler in Berlin and followed her husband to Dresden, where she started teaching at the university in 1920. After Karl Bühler was offered the chair of psychology at the University of Vienna, she founded the school of developmental psychology there, which was subsequently developed further by Hildegard Hetzer, Lotte Schenk-Danzinger, and Sylvia Bayr-Klimpfinger. She, too, formed many contacts abroad, above all with Arnold Gesell and Edward Thorndike, both of whom she had met while studying in the United States for a year.

In 1943, Hubert Rohracher (1903–1972) was appointed to the chair of psychology in Vienna that had become vacant due to the political troubles of the time. He was to have a profound influence on psychology not only in Austria, but in the entire German-speaking area. His maxim of basing the study of psychology as much as possible on biology became the guiding principle of the Vienna school.

Born at Lienz in Tyrol, Rohracher also studied two fields: law at Innsbruck; and philosophy and psychology in Munich with Erich Becher and Richard Pauli. (In those days, one was not permitted to study at two different faculties or universities simultaneously, but he decided to take the risk.) After graduating in psychology in 1926 and in law in 1927, he went to Innsbruck and worked with Theodor Erismann, a researcher with a philosophic bent who nevertheless experimented most skillfully: He designed the experiments with "reversal eyeglasses" to study learning processes in optical perception. Erismann's pupil and eventual successor, Ivo Kohler, later developed these ideas further—another example of how Austrian research was oriented toward the psychology of learning even in such borderline areas.

From 1930 on, Rohracher worked as assistant to Erismann, and in 1932, began to teach psychology at Innsbruck. In 1934, his interests led him to enroll at the school of medicine, where he became acquainted with the publications of Hans Berger, who had just begun to study the electrical phenomena of the brain. Rohracher immediately recognized the tremendous importance of these newly discovered phenomena for psychology and was very creative with regard to methodology. He tried to measure the electric currents of the brain capacitively and inductively, although it was not until 1968 that the first successful inductive recordings of brain currents were made in the United States. In 1935, he went to work with Agostino Gemelli in Milan and began the systematic study of the psychological significance of the electroencephalogram (EEG).

After the national socialist invasion of Austria in 1938, Rohracher lost his position at the university. One year later he was drafted into the army. Despite his "political untrustworthiness," which caused him serious difficulties with the ruling powers, he was quite unexpectedly called to the University of Vienna as professor of psychology in 1943. His studies on the EEG had obviously aroused the interest of those in power, making them turn a blind eye to his political views.

This may have been one of the reasons why Rohracher did not continue his EEG studies at that time, but turned to the investigation of microvibration, a fine tremor of the skeletal musculature that had been discovered by him and was to be a subject of his research for the rest of his life. Of particular importance, however, were his investigations of the electrical activity of the brain, which were zealously continued by his pupil and eventual successor, Giselher Guttmann.

Many of Rohracher's disciples still teach at universities outside of Austria. Among them: Walter Toman, who now teaches at the University of Erlangen, West Germany, after spending many years at Brandeis University, Waltham, Massachusetts; Kurt Pawlik at Hamburg, who is well known for his work on factor analysis and EEG studies; Klaus Foppa at Berne, Switzerland, an expert on learning theory; and Gustav Lienert, who has done fundamental work in the fields of biostatistics and pharmacopsychology at various West German universities (Marburg, Düsseldorf, Nürnberg).

To give an overview of psychology in Austria in the early 1980s, let us look at those universities where psychology can be studied as a major field.

In Graz, Ferdinand Wienhandl continued the tradition of Gestalt psychology developed by Meinong, Vittorio Benussi, and Stephen Witasek. His successor is Erich Mittenecker, a disciple of Rohracher, and since 1968 full professor at the University of Graz. He is a representative of the empirical-scientific approach and is especially interested in the significance of learning processes in many different areas of psychological study. One of the issues he has investigated is the possibility of explaining psychophysiological laws by means of learning theory. Large-scale studies on statistics and information theory are characteristic of his basic approach.

Helmuth Huber is particularly interested in psychophysiology and specializes in psychophysiological activation diagnostics and therapy (biofeedback techniques). The application of learning theory in clinical psychology is the main interest of Lilian Blöschl, whose work is an important factor inspiring the further development of behavior therapy. Social psychology is represented by Gerold Mikula and methodology by Erich Raab, who also works on experimental esthetics. The Department of Neuropsychology and Memory Research, headed by Günter Schulter, concentrates on problems of dominance as well as electrical correlates of attention.

At the University of Innsbruck, Kohler continued the tradition of Erismann. As his minor subject, he had studied physics, a fact that shows his science-oriented approach. His experiments in perceptual psychology were very sophisticated and he saw and investigated connections to cybernetics and neuropsychology. He retired in 1981. Dieter Klebelsberg is primarily interested in questions of applied psychology: One of his specialties is traffic psychology and he does both field work and work in the laboratory using simulation. In addition, questions of pharmacopsychology such as the interindividual range of reactions and coping processes are investigated.

At Salzburg University's Department of Psychology, Wilhelm Joseph Revers specializes in clinical psychology, and has carried out numerous studies in the field of music psychology in cooperation with the Herbert von Karajan Foundation. Erwin Roth works in differential psychology, especially with theories of intelligence and personality, but he is also greatly interested in the electrical phenomena of the brain.

The Department of Psychology at the University of Vienna has grown considerably since the days of Rohracher. One branch, methodology and differential psychology, is headed by Gerhard Fischer. His main interest is mathematical psychology, especially the development of probabilistic measurement models and attempts to develop procedures for optimal parameter estimation and to test techniques that permit the probabilistic measurement of changes such as learning effects. The departments of Developmental Psychology and Applied Psychology, now headed by Brigitta Rollett and Paolo Innerhofer, respectively, are oriented toward learning theory and therapeutic applications. Werner Herkner, who specializes in social psychology, is working on balancing and attribution theories, also with a view toward practical application.

The Department of General Psychology, headed by Guttmann, is mostly concerned with the electrical activity of the brain, whereby emphasis is placed on practical applications such as psychodiagnostics by means of event-related potentials; the relationship between DC potentials and learning ability (Brain Trigger Design—triggering v.z., a learning process, by the brain of the person being tested); activation control by means of biofeedback; and self-control techniques.

The historical retrospect and the present state of psychology in Austria point up the particular problems of a small country, where for centuries science and scholarship have had to hold their own against the pressure of forces outside the university. In the twentieth century, this pressure assumed catastrophic dimensions, albeit with the positive side effect that the ideas of a comparatively small group became known worldwide.

This was true of psychoanalysis: After most of his disciples had fled from Vienna, Freud himself left for London in 1938, at the age of 82, and he died there on September 23, 1939, the very month in which World War II began. It was also true of the early Vienna school. At the same time as the Bühlers, many other important personalities left Austria, for example, Egon Brunswik, Else Frenkel, Rudolf Dreikurs, and Paul Lazarsfeld. Their tragic fate has helped their ideas to spread with particular forcefulness and has led to international contacts that have outlasted all political troubles. The cultivation of international contacts is considered to be of particular importance for scholarship in this neutral country on the border between East and West.

The year 1991 ushered in a new era in the history of applied psychology in Austria. Two new laws regarding psychologists' position in society came into effect as of January 1, 1991. As of this date, psychologist and psychotherapist are legally protected, academic professions in their own right. Before this legislation, any "Tom, Dick or Harry" could, with legal impunity, prefix his or her occupational definition with the term *psychological* (counselor, adviser, expert, etc.). These vocations (and their analogous professional-identification prefixes) have been given equal footing with other professions, in particular with those in the field of health care such as pharmacists, physicians, dentists, and so on. By force of these laws, the personal competence and responsibility of the psychologist and psychotherapist in the execution of his or her profession has been juridically buttressed, and the status of these professions clarified. The laws further provide special reference to the occupations within the framework of public health service.

The law limiting use of the title psychologist to those who have completed the academic study program aims at protecting and unambiguously defining the title in the interests of the consumer. Should the psychologist in question have completed an additional 2 years of postgraduate training in public health, he or she is then legally permitted to carry the title clinical psychologist. Should this postgraduate training be primarily focused on prevention and prophylaxis, he or she may then acquire the title health psychologist. Thus the practice of the profession within the framework of public health has, for the first time, been legally defined and allowances made for an optimization of the general state of Austrian public health. The exact criteria for granting either of these professional titles are still in the preparation stage and not yet in the form of legal paragraphs.

The legislation defining the scope of the psychologist's activities in public health has, however, taken effect:

On the basis of the competence gained through completion of the course of study and training as stipulated by this federal law, [the psychologist's field of activity includes] the examination, interpretation, modification and prediction of human experience and behavior by means of scientific-psychological insights and methods. . . . It is to include, in particular, clinical-psychological diagnoses as well as counselling, and the preparation of prognoses, attests, and expert opinions as to also the application of psychological methods of treatment as prophylactic, therapeutic and rehabilitative measures for individuals as well as groups.

An academic degree (*magister,* or doctor of philosophy) in psychology qualifies one for independent practice in the psychosocial field of the profession, insofar as the person in question is engaged in theoretical and practical supervision. Completion of such supervision foresees 160 hours of participation in advanced theoretical instruction and 1,480 hours of practical experience at an accredited public health or social welfare institution. Of these, at least 150 hours of practice must be completed at an institution of public health within the time span of 1 year. Furthermore, the candidate is to participate in 120 hours (minimum) of supervised therapeutic or counseling activity, whereby the purpose of the supervision is to provide support in concrete cases that are to be discussed with the supervisor and to offer the opportunity for self-reflection. The supervisor must be a psychologist who has many years of experience in the particular field.

It must be emphasized that the legal definition of the professional category itself is solely that of psychologist. A psychologist can belong to a professional group which calls itself psychotherapists, but membership in such a group is not in any way prerequisite to practice as a psychologist. In contrast to the right to call oneself health psychologist or clinical psychologist, the paths leading to admittance to practice as psychotherapist are varied, in keeping with the philosophy behind the specifications that this practice has interdisciplinary roots. Thus a diploma from many secondary-level institutions of education satisfy the entrance requirements for the various courses leading to qualification as psychotherapist. Institutions at the secondary level of education are those offering college-preparatory curricula or those preparatory to specific professions requiring special (e.g., medical-technical, pedagogical, and nursing) skills.

In accordance with the modern realities of the media society, the new laws allow for limited public solicitation, insofar as its message is verfied and factual. Analogous to the priest's and physician's oath to secrecy, the psychologist also is obliged to guarantee silence in regard to his or her professional practice. The official instance for professional questions is the Federal Council of Psychologists. This council decides, among other things, on issues such as licensing and accreditation of therapeutic approaches. The list of bona fide psychologists and psychotherapists as well as the approved therapeutic approaches are public and available in the federal chancellor's office of the Austrian government.

The fledgling psychotherapists seeking instruction and certification can choose from a broad sample of approaches available in Austria. Within the category of psychoanalytically oriented approaches, for example, instruction is offered in classic psychoanalysis (although access is limited for nonphysicians), individual psychology (Adlerian), analytical psychology (Jungian) and guided affective imagery. The category of behavioral therapy offers classical Skinnerian operant conditioning therapeutic methods as well as newer cognitive forms (e.g., Bandura, Beck, Homma, Mahoney, and Meichenbaum). Those preferring the humanistic approach can choose from client-centered psychotherapy (Rogers), Gestalt therapy (Lewin), psychodrama (Moreno), and different types of group therapy (e.g., Berne, Bion, Bateson-Jackson-Watzlawick, and Haley).

The distinction between humanistic and systemic gets fuzzy, as evident, along the lines of group therapy. Some of these protagonists consider themselves humanistic and others stress the systemic. But the Austrian ambiente allows the novice ample choices. Logotherapy (Frankl) is by far the best represented existentially oriented procedure in Austria, perhaps because Frankl is a native son. Suggestive procedures certifiable in Austria are, e.g., hypnosis, autogenic training, and neurolinguistic programming (Bandler, Grinder). These represent the mainstreams in Austrian psychotherapy, and they are, on the whole, traditional. Nonetheless, techniques of more exotic forms of therapy also can be learned and licensed (in deference to their practitioners, no examples provided, to avoid the accusation of labeling).

The laws securing the legal definition of psychologist in Austria are considered, at least by their proponents, to be unique in the world. They have been in the making for more than 20 years and opposition to psychologists' official intrusion into the field of public health has not met with a warm welcome by all members and groups of related professions.

All institutions of higher learning presently offering psychology as a major are public (federal) and tuition free. By federal law, anyone having earned his or her baccalaureat diploma from an academically oriented secondary school (*matura* or *abitur*) or the equivalent is eligible for enrollment at any Austrian university. The situation of psychology as an academic pursuit is heterogeneous. The institute at the university of Vienna was struggling during most of the 1980s to cope with the extreme popularity of the subject among the students. The capacity, whether in regard to the physical properties, faculty/student ratio, or support in the form of nonscientific personnel, is at best strained. At the same time, the small academic representation of psychology within the Institute for Pedagogical Sciences in Klagenfurt, Carenthia, is fighting for survival against governmental proposals for its dissolution. The institutes at the universities in Grax, Salzburg, and Innsbruck enjoy conditions more conducive to uninhibited academic pursuits. The youngest institute of psychology is at the University of Linz. Here our colleagues enjoy a more intimate atmosphere and students are actually courted. Research in Linz emphasizes the fields of social, forensic, and industrial-organizational psychology. The lopsided distribution of students among the (human and material) resources in Austria has led to an inevitable semiisolation of the mammoth in Vienna (ca. 5,000 students in the master's program in psychology) from its counterparts in its various provincial capitals.

Fortunately, one of the most recent developments regarding psychology in Austria is the business and industrial community's awareness that academic psychologists are not just a part of their tax burden (federally supported universities), but concrete assets on the managerial staff. Work-setting analysis, an understanding of the components and dynamics of social interaction, ecopsychological considerations, etc. have gained parity with technical know-how and programming expertise. Private industry is realizing that technocratic skills do not suffice as a key to success and is recruiting young talent whose curricula have included psychology.

Finally graced with the mantle of legal identity and recognized by the business community as a vital asset, psychology in Austria has every reason to look into the future with confidence.

G. GUTTMANN
University of Vienna

AUTHORITARIAN PERSONALITY

The "authoritarian personality" is a term applied to a particular personality pattern studied by a team of researchers at the University of California, Berkeley, during the 1940s (Adorno, 1950), originally sponsored by the Jewish Welfare Board in an effort to determine if there were personality factors in anti-Semitic attitudes. Adorno, a German-Jewish émigré social scientist, represented the Board throughout and participated in all the planning of the research, while R. N. Sanford was the on-the-scene director of the research.

The researchers at first sought to identify an anti-Semitic personality, but found themselves broadening the concept to ethnocentric personality. This, in turn, was broadened to fascist personality. The scale became known as the F scale, even when the concept was relabeled "antidemocratic" personality and "authoritarian" personality. (The ethnocentric scale was retained in the final battery as the E scale.) The first results were published as "the antidemocratic" personality (Frenkel-Brunswik, Levinson, & Sanford, 1947). But by the time the full report, *The Authoritarian Personality,* was published in 1950, the configuration had become "authoritarian."

In the years since, Rokeach has successively moved on to "rigid," "dogmatic," and "closed" personality (1960). Gregory (1957) has come to call it "the authority-dependent personality," and found seven different characteristics in this pattern: rigidity, compulsiveness, conformity, dogmatism, concreteness, literalness, and pedantry.

While the Berkeley researchers found a high correlation between ethnocentrism and authoritarianism, Christie (Christie & Garcia, 1951) discovered that the correlations found in California did not hold in Texas, where ethnocentrism was more deeply ingrained culturally. With Jahoda, Christie later (1954) edited a critique of the authoritarian personality research. Frenkel-Brunswik (1949) found "intolerance of ambiguity" to be a characteristic of this personality type.

The Authoritarian Personality is undoubtedly one of the most comprehensive studies of personality yet made. There can be little doubt that the research pointed to personality configurations of a complex nature related to social rigidity and lack of adaptation. When defined in such terms as "rigidity," "dogmatism," "two-valuedness," "intolerance of ambiguity," and "authority-dependence," the concept obviously touches on one of the major problems of personality and functioning.

REFERENCES

Adorno, T. W. (1950). *The authoritarian personality.* New York: Harper.

Christie, R., & Garcia, J. (1951). Subcultural variation in authoritarian personality. *Journal of Abnormal Social Psychology, 46,* 457.

Christie, R., & Jahoda, M. (Eds.). (1954). *Studies in the scope and method of "The authoritarian personality."* New York: Free Press.

Frenkel-Brunswik, E. (1949). Intolerance of ambiguity as an emotional and perceptual personality variable. *Journal of Personality, 18,* 108–143.

Frenkel-Brunswik, E., Levinson, D. J., & Sanford, R. N. (1947). The antidemocratic personality. In T. M. Newcomb & E. L. Hartley (Eds.), *Readings in social psychology.* New York: Holt.

Gregory, W. E. (1957). The orthodoxy of the authoritarian personality. *Journal of Social Psychology, 45,* 229.

Rokeach, M. (1960). *The open and closed mind.* New York: Basic Books.

W. E. GREGORY
University of the Pacific

ETHNOCENTRISM

AUTISM

Of all the diagnostic categories in *DSM-IV* (American Psychiatric Association [APA], 1994), Autistic Disorder is considered the most severe impairment in functioning. Autism is characterized by early onset and severe developmental delays evident in the following behaviors: (a) little or no expressive or receptive language, the child being mute or echolalic; (b) limited or no social interaction with adults and peers; (c) failure to form emotional attachments, as shown by resistance to being cuddled and indifference to parents' coming and leaving; (d) restricted attention, as when behaving as if blind and deaf; (e) failure to imitate the behaviors of others; (f) limited or no toy play; (g) limited self-help skills, such as dressing, eating with utensils, and using a potty chair or toilet; and (h) IQ scores falling in the retarded range of intellectual functioning. The child appears unaware of common dangers and needs to be watched closely to prevent accidental death, as in drowning or being run over by a car. Ritualistic and repetitive behaviors such as rocking, twirling, and lining of objects are excessive, as are tantrums including self-injurious behaviors. Motor behaviors, such as sitting and walking, fall within the typical range, and most autistic individuals show adequate development of fine motor skills. Special skills may be noted, such as superior memory for visual stimuli (e.g., birthdates, license plates), as evidenced in the child's insisting on sameness (e.g., insisting on using the same route to school or other familiar destinations).

The incidence of autism is estimated to fall between 1 in 500 to 1 in 1,000 births, it is the third most common childhood disorder after cerebral palsy and mental retardation, and occurs at a higher rate than childhood cancer, cystic fibrosis, multiple sclerosis, and Down syndrome. The ratio of boys to girls is 4:1. Autism is almost always chronic, less than 5% recover, and the remaining require life-long protective and institutional care. The estimated average cost per individual is $40,000 per year or $2,400,000 for the 60 or more years that such services need to be rendered.

TREATMENT

A large number of interventions have been proposed, including special education, speech therapy, auditory integration, sensory motor training, holding therapy, facilitated communication, psychodynamic therapy, floor time, and the option method. None have been supported by empirical data in peer-reviewed journals. Psychopharmacological interventions are likely to help reduce disruptive behaviors such as injury of self and others. The passage of PL94-142 (The Education for all Handicapped Children Act) has helped reduce the detrimental effects of institutionalization and has brought the problems of disabled individuals to public attention, allowing parents a more active role in determining their child's future.

Behavioral intervention based on empirical laws of learning is considered the treatment of choice, and numerous experimentally sound studies over the last 40 years attest to its effectiveness. Major progress has been made in reducing harmful behaviors such as self-injury, and in building complex behaviors such as language. Intensive behavioral intervention has reported significant increase in IQ scores and educational functioning and is particularly effective if: (a) it is started before the child is four years of age; (b) it is intensive—40 hours a week of one-on-one intervention, lasting for an average of two years; (c) it addresses each behavioral delay and teaches learning strategies, such as imitation; (d) it is conducted in the child's home and community, involving family members as cotherapists to help generalize treatment gains across persons and environments; and (e) it helps the child develop relationships with typical peers so as to optimize development.

Treatment follow-up data reflect significant increases in intellectual, educational, social, and emotional development for 47% of children, with evidence of relapse for the non–best outcome children. No pivotal behavior has been identified that, once altered, would have significant therapeutic effect on behaviors not targeted for intervention. Similarly, there is ample evidence for situation specificity in treatment effects. Both limitations necessitate that most or all behaviors be targeted for intervention in most or all environments.

The effectiveness of early intervention may be attributed to alterations in neurological structures. Laboratory studies on animals have shown that alterations in neurological structures are quite possible as a result of changes in the environment in the first years of life. Furthermore, children under the age of three years overproduce neurons, dendrites, axons, and synapses that may allow infants and preschoolers to compensate for neurological anomalies more completely than do older children.

ETIOLOGY

Earlier clinical impressions of parental neglect as the cause of autism have been rejected in scientific research and replaced by theories of multiple causes of biological origin (genetic, pharmacological, infectious, etc.). Behavioral genetic studies yield a heritability estimate as high as .9, but precise chromosomal abnormalities have not been identified. There is evidence of functional and structural abnormalities in several brain regions in autism. High-resolution structural imaging techniques and postmortem studies have demonstrated differences in several regions, including the amygdala, hippocampus, septum, mammillary bodies, frontal lobes, corpus callosum, and cerebellum. Postmortem studies have also shown that the brains of individuals with autism tend to be slightly larger and heavier than normal. Such studies have also suggested that certain cells in the central nervous system of autistic persons exhibit differences in size and number when compared to those of typically developing individuals. Functional imaging techniques (like ERP, PET, SPECT, and fMRI) emphasize imbalance in inter-regional and inter-hemispheric brain metabolism and blood flow, abnormalities in the cingulate gyrus, and altered patterns of activation and conduction time. To date, neuroimaging data are inconclusive. While studies propose various abnormalities of brain structure and function, no focal defect has been discovered. Despite the dearth of conclusive information currently available on the structural and/or physiological variables underlying autism, findings to date have opened the door to a very active field of scientific inquiry.

SUGGESTED READING

Bailey, A., Phillips, W., & Rutter, M. (1996). Autism: Towards an integration of clinical, genetic, neuropsychological, and neurobiological perspectives. *Journal of Child Psychology and Psychiatry, 37,* 89–126.

Rapin, I. (1997). Autism. *New England Journal of Medicine, 337,* 97–104.

Smith, T. (1999). Outcome of early intervention for children with autism. *Clinical Psychology: Research and Practice, 6,* 33–49.

O. I. LOVAAS
University of California, Los Angeles

BEHAVIOR THERAPY
MENTAL RETARDATION

AUTOMATIC THOUGHTS

Automatic thoughts are spontaneous ideas—ideations or thought typically indicated by internal self-statements or self-talk. Cognitive theories emphasize the roles of belief systems, cognitive schematas, intellectual processes, and automatic thoughts in behavioral operations. Each individual has a frame of reference, variously called personality, lifestyle, worldview, etc., within which one copes with life. One's inner belief structure depends on past experiences, learnings, goals, purposes, and core belief structures. Automatic thoughts differ from belief structures. Merluzzi and Boltwood (1989) state, "an important distinction between automatic thoughts or self statements and underlying schemata or belief systems [is] automatic thoughts are spontaneous self statements or ruminations. . . . In contrast cognitive schematas are seen as relatively stable, enduring traits like cognitive patterns" (p. 256). Similarly, Beck and Weishaar (1989b) distinguish between automatic and voluntary thoughts. Voluntary thoughts are fully conscious self-determined decisions. Automatic thoughts "are more stable and less accessible than voluntary thoughts [and] are generally quite powerful" (Beck & Weishaar, 1989a, p. 28). Both voluntary thoughts and automatic thoughts are consistent with one's core beliefs or schematas.

Beck and Weishaar (1989b) point out that a variety of situations, events, or circumstances may trigger underlying core beliefs and generate automatic thoughts. More specifically, automatic thoughts "intercede between a stimulus event and one's emotional and behavioral reactions to it" (Beck & Weishaar, 1989a, p. 28).

UNCONSCIOUS PROCESSES

Automatic thoughts are considered to be unconscious or lying below the surface of immediate conscious awareness. They are spontaneous self-statements, stemming from core beliefs out of conscious awareness.

APPLICATIONS

Use of automatic thoughts in psychology center around changing belief systems through psychotherapy. In cognitive and cognitive–behavioral therapies, the primary focus is on changing the clients' "distorted" or dysfunctional belief systems. Client's belief systems are explored and accessed. Albert Ellis outlines 12 irrational beliefs (Criddle, 1975), and Beck outlines primarily six cognitive distortions or distorted thoughts—belief processes (Beck & Weishaar, 1989a, 1989b). Others have added to and modified irrational beliefs and cognitive distortions (McMullin, 1986).

Core beliefs can be accessed by having people monitor their own spontaneous self-statements or automatic thoughts. These are then challenged and changed. Therapy problems can be resolved by changing one's views of the problems via automatic thoughts, a kind or paradigmatic shift in thinking, known in psychotherapy jargon as *reframing*.

REFERENCES

Beck, A., & Weishaar, M. (1989a). Cognitive therapy. In A. Freeman, K. J. Simon, L. E. Beutler, & H. Arkowitz (Eds.), *Comprehension handbook of cognitive therapy*. New York: Plenum.

Beck, A., & Weishaar, M. (1989b). Cognitive therapy. In R. Corsini & D. Wedding (Eds.), *Current psychotherapies*. Itasca, NY: Peacock.

Criddle, W. (1975). Guidelines for challenging irrational beliefs. *Rational Living, 9*(1), 8–13.

McMullin, R. E. (1986). *Handbook of cognitive therapy techniques.* New York: Norton.

Merluzzi, T. V., & Boltwood, M. D. (1989). Cognitive assessment. In A. Freeman, K. M. Simon, L. E. Beutler, & H. Arkowitz (Eds.), *Comprehensive handbook of cognitive therapy*. New York: Plenum.

M. S. CARICH
Adler School of Professional Psychology

CONSCIOUSNESS
DEFENSE MECHANISMS
IDIODYNAMICS, SUPERSEDING PERSONALITY THEORY
PERCEPTUAL ORGANIZATION
UNCONSCIOUS, THE

AUTONOMIC NERVOUS SYSTEM

The autonomic nervous system supplies motor fibers to the heart, the stomach, the pancreas, the small and large intestines, the sweat glands, peripheral blood vessels, and other internal organs, tissues, and glands. Its main functions are to regulate physiological processes involving these internal organs, such as blood pressure and body temperature, and to prepare the body for emergencies by initiating appropriate physiological adjustments.

ANATOMY

The pathways of the autonomic nervous system include neurons in both the central and peripheral nervous systems. They begin with nerve cells in the brain stem and spinal cord. The axons of these cells, called preganglionic fibers, leave the central nervous system through cranial nerves (in the brain) or ventral roots (in the spinal cord) and travel to autonomic ganglia. These neurons then synapse with postganglionic fibers, which are distributed to various organs and glands.

The autonomic nervous system has two divisions, based on the anatomical distribution of the autonomic fibers: the sympathetic division and the parasympathetic division. These two components also have different functions. The preganglionic fibers of the sympathetic division begin in the spinal cord, leave through the ventral roots, and travel to the ganglia in the sympathetic trunks, located along either side of the vertebral column. These two elongated trunks extend from the base of the skull to the end of the vertebral column. The preganglionic fibers synapse in the ganglia of these sympathetic trunks. Then the postganglionic fibers leave the trunks and travel to the various organs and glands innervated by the sympathetic division. Some of these include the heart, the stomach, the small intestine, the pancreas, the large intestine, the salivary glands, the eye, and numerous blood vessels throughout the body.

The parasympathetic division of the autonomic nervous system is also called the craniosacral system because of its anatomical distribution. The preganglionic fibers leave the central nervous system through certain cranial nerves (oculomotor, facial, glossopharyngeal, vagus, and accessory), and also through the sacral (lower) part of the spinal cord. They travel to their visceral destinations, and synapse in ganglia located in or near their target organs. Parasympathetic fibers reach many of the same organs and glands as sympathetic fibers, including the heart, the stomach, the small intestine, and the pancreas. However, there are several exceptions. For example, the parasympathetic fibers do not innervate peripheral blood vessels.

The autonomic nervous system is primarily under the control of nuclei in the hypothalamus. This area of the brain is involved in many activities, including the control of body temperature, eating, drinking, sexual behavior, and many emotional behaviors. The autonomic nervous system participates in some of these activities under the direction of the hypothalamus.

BIOCHEMISTRY

The two main neurotransmitters used in the autonomic nervous system are acetylcholine and norepinephrine. Acetylcholine appears at both sympathetic and parasympathetic preganglionic synapses, and also in postganglionic parasympathetic neurons. Drugs that mimic postganglionic parasympathetic stimulation are called parasympathomimetic, and include acetylcholine and

several anticholinesterases. Most postganglionic sympathetic synapses use norepinephrine, but other neurotransmitters are used as well. Drugs that have similar effects as postganglionic sympathetic stimulation are called sympathomimetic, and include catecholamines, amphetamine, and cocaine. These drugs also usually have profound effects on the central nervous system as well.

FUNCTIONS

The two primary functions of the autonomic nervous system are: (a) to maintain homeostasis in the body, and (b) to prepare the body for emergencies. The sympathetic and parasympathetic divisions play important roles in these functions. In general, activation of the sympathetic division produces more widespread effects throughout the body, and its activation is important in the body's response to stress. Parasympathetic fibers, however, usually have more localized effects on individual target organs and glands. When both sympathetic and parasympathetic fibers innervate the same organ, they usually have opposite effects. For example, parasympathetic activation causes a slowing of cardiac contractions, whereas sympathetic activation causes heart rate to increase.

The homeostatic function of the autonomic nervous system is illustrated by its role in several physiological processes, including the control of blood pressure, thermoregulation, and pupil dilation. For example, a decrease in room temperature stimulates the sensory neurons in the skin that are sensitive to temperature. These neurons send impulses to the spinal cord and brain. The hypothalamus, which also contains cells sensitive to blood temperature, triggers activities designed to conserve heat, such as constriction of peripheral blood vessels and shivering. As body temperature rises, these processes are reversed.

The autonomic nervous system's response to stress is primarily due to widespread sympathetic activation and the accompanying changes in many body organs. In the presence of a stressor, sympathetic activation produces an increase in heart rate, increase in blood pressure, pupil dilation, inhibition of peristalsis, increase in sweat gland activity in the palms, release of hormones from the adrenal glands, and other changes. These physiological adjustments concentrate the body's resources in functions that are important during a physical threat, particularly the muscles. Blood supply to the skin and to the internal organs is reduced, while blood supply to the heart and muscles is increased. Physiological processes that are less important during an emergency, such as digestion, are inhibited. Sympathetic activation, and the changes in the endocrine system that accompany it, prepare the organism to fight or flee by mobilizing energy resources and temporarily increasing physical strength. Chronic sympathetic activation, however, is known to be associated with health problems.

The term "autonomic" implies that this component of the nervous system is automatic and not under voluntary control. However, many autonomic functions can be regulated by conscious activity, using appropriate procedures. Biofeedback, for example, enables many hypertensive patients to reduce their blood pressure.

SUGGESTED READING

Brown, T. S., & Wallace, P. M. (1980). *Physiological psychology.* New York: Academic Press.

Gardner, E. (1975). *Fundamentals of neurology.* Philadelphia & London: Saunders. (Original work published 1963)

P. M. WALLACE
University of Maryland

CENTRAL NERVOUS SYSTEM
NEUROPSYCHOLOGY
SYMPATHETIC NERVOUS SYSTEM

AUTOSHAPING

Autoshaping typically occurs when biologically primed stimulus-response relations interact with and occasionally override operantly learned, potentially incompatible response-reinforcer relations. It may also be referred to as "misbehavior of organisms." The name is derived from quick operant shaping that occurred without apparent reinforcement of successive approximations. Typically, the behavior observed depends upon the object or goal received; for example, food appears to release eating behavior and water to release drinking behavior. Although initially thought to manifest only among simpler mammals, autoshaping may occur in a variety of animals, including humans (Siegel, 1978). Consensus regarding etiology is lacking, though this is not a result of irregularities in data; the phenomenon of autoshaping is valid and reliable.

EXAMPLE

Pigeons quickly learn key pecking responses when a key is illuminated and provides a reliable and salient cue for the delivery of food (Brown & Jenkins, 1968). However, attempts to operantly extinguish or negatively punish pecking generally fail, leading one to question whether the behavior was acquired through operant training or some other modality.

THEORIES OF AUTOSHAPING

As with much behavior, autoshaping resides in the gap between nature and nurture. It represents an interaction between organism and environment, phylogeny and ontogeny, and respondent and instrumental processes. Each of these explanations represents a different level of analysis related to the puzzle of autoshaping.

Though the formal study of autoshaping largely began in the late 1960s, the existence of the phenomenon may have been foreshadowed by Darwin's theory of evolution (1859), which posited natural selection as the mechanism whereby species-specific morphogenesis and behavior would need to show environmental adaptation (i.e., functionality) with regard to subsistence and reproduction. At worst, the new structure or behavior could not impair the animal's relative ability to compete for basic resources. Influenced by Darwin's work, William James (1890) implied the existence of autoshaping in discussions of instinct. According to James, an instinct was defined as "the faculty of acting in a such a way as to produce certain ends, without foresight of the ends, and without previous education in the performance" (p. 383). But instincts were not to be considered immutable stimulus-response relations; they were to be considered "blind" to the resultant consequences of the action only on the first occurrence of the behavior, after which they could be "disguised or modified." Hence, fixed action patterns, a term used interchangeably with instinct by ethologists, may be more or less fixed depending upon the effect of the behavior, as well as the species under consideration. James implicated the existence of a process whereby innate, hard-wired behavior might interact with and be modified by resultant environmental stimuli.

Lorenz (1957), an early ethologist, posited the more widely held view that due to the simplicity of the nervous system of lower animals, constraints on stimulus perception and response are more likely than in humans, and that those responses would be adaptive to the survival of the animal. This view of instinct proposed a mechanism whereby the animal perceived a stimulus that *released* a species-specific response (e.g., pecking) designed to provide a specific consequence (e.g., food). This paradigm also adhered to the assumption that instinctive responses were unlearned, yet were modifiable, although the modification would only be found in the offspring. Lorenz postulated that the fixed action pattern released by a specific stimulus should be referred to as an instinct; all supporting, orienting, or learned behaviors maintaining or modifying an instinct are to be considered appetitive responses. In practice, however, the line between instinctive and appetitive behaviors remained blurred, perhaps because the etiology of instincts, or phylogenically predisposed fixed action patterns, was not well understood.

Better understood are ontogenic models for acquiring behavior within the life of the animal. Two specific forms of learning, classical and operant conditioning, appear relevant to autoshaping. In the above example of autoshaped pecking in pigeons, it was originally thought that innate aspects of the bird provided for, or predisposed the bird for, rapid shaping via reinforcement of successive approximations of pecking. However, introducing terms like "innate aspect" or "predisposition" weakened the scientific explanation, as those terms were not operationally defined, did little to advance the understanding of the data, and were usually tautological (i.e., based in circular reasoning). Brown and Jenkins (1968) were the first to report that noncontingent food presentation temporally contiguous with key illumination resulted in pigeon pecking. Furthermore, Williams and Williams (1969) conducted the first example of omission training with pigeons, whereby the presentation of food was contingent upon the non-occurrence of pecking. Under an omission training model, behavior under operant control would cease or become greatly reduced. However, the pigeons continued to exhibit pecking over many trials without food. This study underscored the implausibility that autoshaping was maintained by contingent reinforcement with food, even if intermittently or superstitiously. This prompted researchers to investigate the possibility that key pecking was classically conditioned.

The rationale for considering classical conditioning as the mechanism of action for autoshaping stems from the fact that within each operant there resides the potential for simultaneous classical conditioning (for in depth discussion, refer to texts by Davis & Hurwitz, 1977; Honig & Staddon, 1977; Rachlin, 1976; and Schwartz, 1989). Due to the stimulus properties of consequences, particularly primary consequences, neutral stimuli that reliably precede and predict delivery may become conditioned. In other words, reinforcers and punishers may also serve as unconditioned stimuli-unconditioned response (US-UR) pairs, inadvertently creating conditioned stimuli (CS) and and responses (CR). In the example with pigeons, the food pellet was contingently delivered upon pecking at the key when illuminated. This food pellet, both a potential reinforcer and paired US-UR, might allow the light inside the key to become a CS that elicits a key pecking response (CR) that closely approximates a normal unconditioned eating response (UR). This model fits the data well, as autoshaped behaviors closely approximate the normal phylogenic response released by the "goal" stimulus. In a further testing of this model, noncontingent delivery of the food maintained key pecking as long as the illumination preceded and was temporally contiguous to the food delivery; that is, CS continued to evoke the CR when it reliably predicted the US—>UR delivery (Brown & Jenkins, 1968). Later, Jenkins (1977) altered the predictability of the CS so that it no longer preceded the food delivery. Classical conditioning extinction curves were noted, as were spontaneous remission curves when contiguity was re-established. Jenkins also noted that maintenance of the pecking response was best when both contiguity and contingency were in place; that is, classical and operant conditioning may be additive processes.

In summary, autoshaping appears to be primarily a function of classical conditioning in that underlying US-UR relations are a requisite condition. However, operant consequences may also serve as US-UR pairs, allowing the occurrence of classical conditioning. Autoshaping per se only manifests when operant training appears to be "overriding" US-UR patterns, or, in the terms of James and Lorenz, attempting to modify instinctive fixed action patterns for obtaining goals. Hence, behaviors exhibited during autoshaping continue to defy simple categorization and precise etiologic explanation.

REFERENCES

Brown, P., & Jenkins, H. (1968). Auto-shaping of the pigeon's key peck. *Journal of the Experimental Analysis of Behavior, 11,* 1–8.

Darwin, C. A. (1859). *The origin of species by means of natural selection.* London: J. Murray.

Davis, H., & Hurwitz, H. M. B. (1977). *Operant-Pavlovian interactions.* New York: Wiley.

Hergenhahn, B. R., & Olson, M. H. (1997). *An introduction to theories of learning* (5th edition). Upper Saddle River, NJ: Prentice-Hall, Inc.

Honig, W. K., & Staddon, J. E. R. (1977). *Handbook of operant behavior.* Englewood Cliffs, NJ: Prentice-Hall.

James, W. (1890). *Principles of psychology.* New York: H. Holt.

Jenkins, H. (1977). Sensitivity of different response systems to stimulus-reinforcer and response-reinforcer relations. In H.

Davis & H. M. B. Hurwitz (Eds.), *Operant-Pavlovian interactions* (pp. 47–66). New York: Wiley.

Lorenz, K. (1957). Companions in the life of birds, reprint. In C. Schiller (Ed.), *Instinctive behavior.* New York: International Universities Press.

Rachlin, H. (1976). *Behavior and learning.* San Francisco: W. H. Freeman & Company.

Schwartz, B. (1989). *Psychology of learning and behavior* (3rd edition). New York: W. W. Norton & Company.

Siegel, R. K. (1978). Stimulus selection and tracking during urination: Autoshaping directed behavior with toilet targets. *Journal of Applied Behavior Analysis, 10* (2), 255–265.

Williams, D., & Williams, H. (1969). Auto-maintenance in the pigeon: Sustained pecking despite contingent non-reinforcement. *Journal of the Experimental Analysis of Behavior, 12,* 511–520.

D. B. Hatfield
Eastern Washington University

**CLASSICAL CONDITIONING
OPERANT CONDITIONING**

AVOIDANT PERSONALITY

The diagnostic label "avoidant personality," or "avoidant personality disorder" (APD), was first included in the third edition of the *Diagnostic and Statistical Manual of Mental Disorders* (American Psychiatric Association [APA], 1980) to describe individuals who desire friends but whose concerns about criticism and rejection lead to social inhibition and avoidance. Although the initial diagnostic criteria were modified in the *DSM-IV,* the general conceptualization of this condition remained much the same. According to current criteria, the avoidant person:

1. avoids occupational activities that involve significant interpersonal contact because of fears of criticism, disapproval, or rejection.

2. is unwilling to get involved with people unless certain of being liked.

3. shows restraint within intimate relationships because of the fear of being shamed or ridiculed.

4. is preoccupied with being criticized or rejected in social situations.

5. is inhibited in new interpersonal situations because of feelings of inadequacy.

6. views self as socially inept, personally unappealing, or inferior to others.

7. is unusually reluctant to take personal risks or to engage in any new activities because of potential embarrassment (APA, 1994).

Avoidant personality disorder is estimated to occur in .5% to 1% of the general population and in 10% of individuals seeking outpatient treatment from mental health clinics. This personality pattern occurs equally in men and women. According to the *DSM-IV,* APD is present by early adulthood, although many avoidant individuals report that they have been socially anxious as long as they can remember. Individuals with APD commonly display a variety of Axis I disorders, in particular the anxiety disorders, affective disorders, and schizophrenic spectrum disorders. Empirical studies also indicate that between 15% and 30% of alcohol abusers meet the criteria for APD, which suggests that longstanding social avoidance may increase vulnerability to substance dependence.

Personality types characterized by social sensitivity and withdrawal appear in earlier clinical descriptions of personality disorders, most notably in depictions of the schizoid and phobic character styles. For example, Fenichel's (1945) descriptions of the phobic character include features, such as the phobic avoidance of desired objects, that parallel current descriptions of the avoidant individual. However, contemporary conceptualizations of avoidant personality disorder have their origins in Theodore Millon's biosocial learning theory. Millon proposed that the avoidant pattern develops when a child with a fearful or anxious temperament is exposed to early social experiences characterized by persistent deprecation, rejection, and humiliation (e.g., Millon, 1981). Avoidant individuals learn what Millon labeled an "active-detached" coping pattern. This consists of behavioral strategies designed to protect the person from the painful emotions he or she expects to result from interpersonal encounters Millon's writings gave life to and continue to guide contemporary views of the avoidant individual.

More recently, cognitive and interpersonal theories of APD have been proposed. Aaron Beck and Arthur Freeman, in their book *Cognitive Therapy of Personality Disorders* (1990), emphasized the mediating role of the cognitive schemas that develop in response to traumatic early social experiences and/or biological sensitivities. According to these writers, schemas—the cognitive structures that organize experience—include beliefs and rules of conduct, which for the avoidant person take such forms as "If people get close to me they will reject me" and "Don't stick your neck out." Although accurate in an historical sense, these schemas are hypothesized to lead to distortions in processing current social information and to the adoption of maladaptive interpersonal strategies. Interpersonal theories are quite similar; however, interpersonal writers emphasize the contribution of self-perpetuating transactional cycles to the onset and maintenance of APD (Barber, Morse, Krakauer, Chittams, & Crits-Christoph, 1997). According to these writers, early social experiences lead avoidant individuals to develop core relational schemas, or focal interpersonal conflicts, that color their interpretations of current interactions. As a result, they adopt behaviors that provoke negative reactions from others, thereby confirming their original beliefs. Thus, people with APD are caught in a cyclical process of unwittingly reenacting the early significant relationships that led to the development of their underlying fears.

Avoidant personality disorder shares features with several other clinical syndromes, notably the Axis I category of generalized social phobia (GSP) and the Axis II categories of schizoid and dependent personality disorders. The overwhelming majority of individuals with APD also meet diagnostic criteria for GSP, and as many as 60% of patients with GSP meet criteria for APD (e.g., Fahlen, 1995). Comparative studies indicate that patients with APD report greater social anxiety and depression and lower self-esteem, and display more comorbid diagnoses than do patients with GSP alone, but few other differences emerge. The high rate of comorbidity, similarity in diagnostic criteria, and absence of qualitative differences between APD and GSP suggest that the two conditions may represent different points along a continuum of symptom severity. Although some early writers argued that APD was largely indistinguishable from schizoid personality disorder, empirical studies indicate that all of the symptoms of APD except social withdrawal correlate negatively with schizoid symptoms and that differential diagnosis is not difficult (Trull, Widiger, & Frances, 1987). Of greater diagnostic concern is overlap with dependent personality disorder (DPD). Research suggests that only the symptom of social withdrawal reliably discriminates the two conditions, and in practice, diagnoses of APD and DPD often co-occur (Trull et al., 1987). Overall, distinctions between avoidant personality and GSP and DPD require further study.

There are also similarities between the features of APD and personality traits such as shyness and social timidity. The primary distinction is that APD is characterized by greater distress and impairment. Shyness and social timidity stem in part from innate differences in physiological reactivity to environmental change (e.g., Kagan, Reznick, & Snidman, 1988). This raises the possibility that individuals with APD either have stronger dispositional tendencies than do shy people or that they have experienced more negative social events that exacerbate this biological vulnerability.

A variety of treatment strategies for APD have been evaluated, including cognitive-behavioral, interpersonal, and pharmacological regimens. Empirical studies show that behavioral and cognitive-behavioral treatment programs produce significant improvement in social comfort and activity in avoidant individuals (Alden, 1989; Renneberg, Goldstein, Phillips, & Chambless, 1990; Stravynski, Belisle, Marcouiller, Lavallee, & Elie, 1989). Although interpersonal dynamic psychotherapy has also been found to be beneficial (Barber et al., 1997), research indicates that dynamic treatment may be less effective than cognitive-behavioral regimens. Overall, psychological treatments produce significant gains in avoidant patients and these gains are maintained, at least over the year following treatment termination. On a less positive note, a substantial number of APD individuals remain at the low end or below normative levels of social functioning even after treatment. This suggests that avoidant individuals may require a longer course of treatment or that biological factors or early trauma may limit change. Pharmacological regimens have also been examined, primarily in the context of treating patients with social phobia. The monoamine oxidase inhibitors (MAOIs), particularly phenelzine, and the selective serotonin-reuptake inhibitors (SSRIs) are considered the most effective pharmacological interventions presently available (e.g., Liebowitz et al., 1992). Even here, however, a substantial number of medication-responsive patients continue to meet criteria for APD. Further work on the treatment of this longstanding condition is required.

REFERENCES

Alden, L. E. (1989). Short-term structured treatment for avoidant personality disorder. *Journal of Consulting & Clinical Psychology, 57,* 756–764.

American Psychiatric Association. (1980). *Diagnostic and statistical manual of mental disorders* (3rd ed.). Washington, DC: Author.

American Psychiatric Association. (1994). *Diagnostic and statistical manual of mental disorders* (4th ed.). Washington, DC: Author.

Barber, J. P., Morse, J. Q., Krakauer, I. D., Chittams, J., & Crits-Christoph, K. (1997). Change in obsessive-compulsive and avoidant personality disorders following time-limited supportive-expressive therapy. *Psychotherapy, 34,* 133–143.

Beck, A. T., & Freeman, A. (1990). *Cognitive therapy of personality disorders* (pp. 257–282). New York: Guilford.

Fahlen, T. (1995). Personality traits in social phobia, I. Comparisons with healthy controls. *Journal of Clinical Psychiatry, 56,* 560–568.

Fenichel, O. (1945). *The psychoanalytic theory of the neurosis.* New York: Norton.

Kagan, J., Reznick, S., & Snidman, N. (1988). Biological bases of childhood shyness. *Science, 240,* 167–171.

Liebowitz, M. R., Schneier, F., Campeas, R., Hollander, E., Hatterer, J., Fyer, A., Gorman, J., Papp, L., Davies, S., Gully, R., & Klein, D. F. (1992). Phenelzine versus atenolol in social phobia: A placebo-controlled comparison. *Archives of General Psychiatry, 49,* 290–300.

Millon, T. (1981). *Disorders of personality DSM-III: Axis II.* New York: Wiley-Interscience.

Renneberg, B., Goldstein, A. J., Phillips, D., & Chambless, D. L. (1990). Intensive behavioral group treatment of avoidant personality disorder. *Behavior Therapy, 21,* 363–377.

Stravynski, A., Belisle, M., Marcouiller, M., Lavallee, Y., & Elie, R. (1994). The treatment of avoidant personality disorder by social skills training in the clinic or in real-life setting. *Canadian Journal of Psychiatry, 39,* 377–383.

Trull, T. J., Widiger, T. A., & Frances, A. (1987). Covariation of criteria sets for avoidant, schizoid, and dependent personality disorders. *American Journal of Psychiatry, 144,* 767–771.

SUGGESTED READING

Brown, E. J., Heimberg, R. O., & Juster, H. R. (1995). Social phobia subtype and avoidant personality disorder: Effect on severity of social phobia, impairment, and outcome of cognitive behavioral treatment. *Behavior Therapy, 26,* 467–486.

Herbert, J. D., Hope, D. A., & Bellack, A. S. (1992). Validity of the distinction between generalized social phobia and avoidant personality disorder. *Journal of Abnormal Psychology, 101,* 332–339.

L. E. ALDEN
University of British Columbia

COGNITIVE BEHAVIOR THERAPY
PERSONALITY DISORDERS
SHORT-TERM THERAPY
SOCIAL PHOBIA

B

THE BABINSKI SIGN

In 1896, Joseph François Félix Babinski (1857–1932) published a brief report regarding the clinical sign that now bears his name. Babinski noted, as had others before him, that stimulation of the soles of the feet of some patients with unilateral paralysis induced extension of the great toe on the paralyzed side rather than the expected flexion response (Babinski, 1896). Unlike his predecessors, Babinski recognized and called attention to the diagnostic importance of this reflex response (for example, in differentiating structural from hysterical paralysis). Babinski later expanded his understanding of the diagnostic significance of the "toe phenomenon" (Babinski, 1898), and described the fanning of the lateral toes that may accompany extension of the great toe (Babinski, 1903).

The sign is best elicited by having the patient lie supine with the leg uncovered for observation and supported by the examiner. The patient is warned about what is about to happen; then a stimulus (ranging from light touch to moderately firm and slightly noxious pressure from a dull-pointed object, such as a wooden applicator stick or a key) is applied to the lateral plantar surface of the foot in a gently sweeping motion from heel to ball (van Gijn, 1995). An extensor response may at times be evoked by stimuli applied to a number of other loci on the foot and leg, but the interpretation of the response is the same no matter the stimulus used to evoke it. A positive (extensor) response is mediated by contraction of the long extensor muscle of the great toe (extensor hallucis longus), and it is this muscular response that is the hallmark of the sign. At times, careful observation for tightening of the extensor hallucis longus tendon may resolve doubts about whether the sign is present.

Extension of the toe (lifting it away from the perceived noxious stimulus on the sole) is part of a generalized flexion response of the muscles in the stimulated limb, so the Babinski response may be accompanied by visible flexion of thigh on hip, leg on knee, and foot on ankle brought about by contraction of the tibialis anterior, hamstrings, tensor fasciae latae, and iliopsoas muscles (Bassetti, 1995).

The clinical significance of the Babinski sign can be seen by a review of its developmental course. A positive (that is, extensor) response can be seen in otherwise normal infants, although the reported prevalence varies widely from less than 10% to more than 90% of newborns (Hogan & Milligan, 1971; Jaynes, Gingold, Hupp, Mullett, & Bodensteiner, 1997). The pyramidal tracts of the central nervous system, carrying neurons from the motor cortex into the spinal cord, subserve voluntary muscle function throughout the body. As these tracts mature during the first 6 months of life, the toe response of infants changes from extensor to flexor and is virtually extinguished by the age of 9 to 12 months (Katiyar, Sen, & Agarwal, 1976); the entire flexion response of the lower extremity diminishes along with the extinction of the Babinski response (van Gijn, 1995).

Because maturation of the pyramidal tracts is thought to underlie the developmental disappearance of the Babinski response, it is not surprising that reappearance of this response later in life (or persistence after the first year of life), especially lateral asymmetry of response, should be indicative of disease affecting the pyramidal tract. As noted by Babinski, the sign is often found in patients with destructive lesions of the motor fibers innervating the foot itself; in these patients careful testing often reveals motor weakness of the affected limb or at least disturbances of fine motor function (Bassetti, 1995).

Now, more than 100 years after its initial description, the extensor response of the great toe remains one of the best known and clinically useful of the eponymic signs in clinical medicine. Its unilateral presence almost always indicates serious structural abnormalities of the upper motor neurons serving the affected limb. The finding of a positive Babinski response after the first year of life should be considered abnormal and appropriate neurological investigation undertaken to identify the nature and location of the abnormal process.

REFERENCES

Babinski, J. (1896). Sur le réflexe cutané plantaire dans certains affections organiques du système nerveux central. *Comptes Rendus de la Société de Biologie, 48,* 207–208.

Babinski, J. (1898). Du phénomène des orteils et de sa valeur sémiologique. *Semaine Médicale, 18,* 321–322.

Babinski, J. (1903). De l'abduction des ortreils. *Revue Neurologique (Paris), 11,* 728–729.

Bassetti, C. (1995). Babinski and Babinski's sign. *SPINE, 20,* 2591–2594.

Hogan, G. R., & Milligan, J. E. (1971). The plantar reflex of the newborn. *New England Journal of Medicine, 285,* 502–593.

Jaynes, M. E., Gingold, M. K., Hupp, A., Mullett, M. D., & Bodensteiner, J. B. (1997). The plantar response in normal newborn infants. *Clinical Pediatrics, 36,* 649–651.

Katiyar, G. P., Sen, S., & Agarwal, K. N. (1976). Plantar response during infancy. *Acta Neurologica Scandinavica, 53,* 390–394.

van Gijn, J. (1995). The Babinski reflex. *Postgraduate Medical Journal, 71,* 645–648.

F. A. NEELON
Duke University

DEVELOPMENTAL PSYCHOLOGY
REFLEXES

BACON, FRANCIS (SIR) (1561–1636)

Sir Francis Bacon's lineage was that of a ranking family. He was an attorney, a Member of Parliament and Lord Keeper of the Great

Seal. He studied at Trinity College, Cambridge. In 1620 he published his most celebrated book, *Novum Organism.*

His writings fall into three classes: professional, literary, and philosophical. It is in his psychology (then considered philosophy) that his influence has been most marked. His writings preceded John Lock's *Essay Concerning Human Understanding* but had a strong influence on it. In Bacon's *Novum Organism* he wrote, "Man who is the server and interpreter of nature can act and understand no further than he can observe either in the operation or contemplation of the method and order of nature." It is suggested by scholars that through the practical tendency of his philosophy and through John Locke, Bacon was the father of British empiricism. Bacon proposed that the value of understanding is assessed in terms of the potential benefit to the human race. If a project can do an individual little or no good in his or her daily affairs of life, then the presumption is that it is worthless.

In an earlier work, *The Advancement of Learning,* Bacon's empiricism is more limited. In it he stated that what we today would call human psychology bears the stamp of heriditary influences. Bacon stated that in science there were two kinds of experiments: (a) those that shed light, and (b) those that would bear fruit. Both were necessary for scientific inquiry.

He was the first of a series of philosophers (mostly British) to call a halt to medieval speculation and superstition. He can be paraphrased as saying, "Open your eyes and look at the world as it is."

R. W. LUNDIN
Wheaton, Illinois

BAIN, ALEXANDER (1818–1903)

Alexander Bain was a Scotsman and spent his entire life in Aberdeen. Although he devoted most of his efforts to psychology, the chair he held at the University of Aberdeen beginning in 1860 was actually in logic. His two most important works were *The Senses and the Intellect* (1855) and *The Emotions and the Will* (1859). These books have been considered by many to be the first real books on psychology.

Along with Herbert Spencer, Bain was the last in the line of British associationists which began with John Locke over a century earlier and continued into the nineteenth century with David Hartley, James Mill, and John Stuart Mill. Like a number of his predecessors, Bain stressed two basic laws of association, similarity and contiguity. In the latter instance, for example, sensations and feelings come together in close succession in such a way that, when one of them is brought to mind, the other will most likely occur.

Like no other psychologist before him, Bain brought together in his works all that was known about psychology up to his time. He was interested in every mode of experience and analysis of its contents. He also wrote on learning (habit), memory, and retention.

He has been considered the first modern physiological psychologist. He drew on the vast literature of 19th-century physiology of the nervous system. He discussed the sense organs and how they worked. He wrote on the reflex and recounted what was known about the brain and how it worked. In all of this he attempted to relate the mental events of experience and their physiological correlates.

In 1876 Bain founded *Mind,* the first psychological journal in any country, though it had more of a philosophical bent than subsequent journals to be founded in Germany and America. He appointed one of his pupils, Croom Robertson, to be its first editor. In this journal Bain published many of his most important papers.

Bain brought associationism to a point where it was not merely a verbal description, but could be demonstrated in the experimental studies of Pavlov, Wundt, and Thorndike.

R. W. LUNDIN
Wheaton, Illinois

BALTES, PAUL B.

Paul B. Baltes, born in 1939 in Saarlouis, Germany, is director of the Center of Lifespan Psychology at the Max Planck Institute for Human Development, Berlin, and professor of psychology at the Free University of Berlin. He received his doctorate from the University of Saarbrücken (Saarland, Germany) in 1967 under the mentorship of E. Boesch, who himself was a doctoral student of J. Piaget and A. Rey.

Before returning to Germany in 1980, Baltes spent 12 years as professor of psychology and human development at several American institutions, including West Virginia University, Pennsylvania State University (where he directed the Division of Individual and Family Studies), and as a fellow at the Center for Advanced Study in the Behavioral Sciences (1977–78, 1990–91, 1997–98).

Baltes is best known for his contributions to (a) creating the field of lifespan psychology, (b) the psychological study of wisdom, and (c) the articulation and testing of models of successful development and aging. In the latter field, together with his late wife, Margret Baltes, he proposed a systemic metatheory of ontogeny which characterizes lifespan development as the orchestration of three processes: selection, optimization, and compensation.

Another signature of Baltes' career are his many roles in interdisciplinary organizations and science policy. For instance, he is active in the US Social Science Research Council (from 1996 until 2000 he has served as chair of its Board of Directors), the Berlin-Brandenburg Academy of Sciences, and the European Academy of Science. Regarding interdisciplinary work, Baltes is engaged primarily in two projects: he chairs (together with K. U. Mayer) the Berlin Aging Study and, together with the sociologist N. Smelser, he is coeditor-in-chief of the 26-volume *International Encyclopedia of the Social and Behavioral Sciences* (Elsevier) which is scheduled to appear in 2001.

Baltes is author or editor of 15 books and more than 250 scholarly articles and chapters. For his work, he has been honored with numerous awards, including honorary doctorates and election as foreign member to the American Academy of Arts and Sciences and the Royal Swedish Academy of Sciences. Among the awards are the International Psychology Award of the American Psychological Association (1995), the Kleemeier Award of the Gerontological Society of America (1991), the German Psychology Award

(1994), the Aristotle Prize of the European Federation of Psychological Associations (1997), the Novartis Prize of the International Association of Gerontology (1999), and jointly with M. Baltes the Longevity Prize of the IPSEN Foundation (2000).

STAFF

BANDURA, ALBERT

Albert Bandura is David Starr Jordan Professor of Social Sciences in Psychology at Stanford University. He received his bachelor's degree from the University of British Columbia in 1949 and his PhD degree in 1952 from the University of Iowa. After completing his doctorate, Bandura joined the faculty at Stanford University, where he has remained to pursue his career. He served as chairman of the department of psychology and was honored by Stanford by being awarded an endowed chair.

Bandura is a proponent of social cognitive theory. This theory accords a central role to cognitive, vicarious, self-regulatory, and self-reflective processes in human adaptation and change. Social cognitive theory is rooted in an agentic perspective. In this view, people are self-organizing, proactive, self-reflecting, and self-regulating, not just reactive organisms shaped and shepherded by environmental forces or driven by concealed inner impulses. Human functioning is the product of a dynamic interplay of personal, behavioral, and environmental influences. In this model of triadic reciprocal causation, people are producers as well as products of their environment. His book, *Social Foundations of Thought and Action: A Social Cognitive Theory,* provides the conceptual framework and analyzes the large body of knowledge bearing on this theory.

Bandura's initial program of research centered on the prominent role of social modeling in human motivation, thought, and action. At the time, psychologists focused almost exclusively on learning through the consequences of one's actions. Bandura showed that the tedious and hazardous process of trial and error learning can be shortcut through social modeling of knowledge and competencies exhibited by the rich variety of models. He rightfully pointed out that modeling was not simply response mimicry. By extracting the rules underlying the modeled styles of behavior, people generate new behavior patterns in a similar style but go beyond what they have seen or heard. He further showed that, in addition to cultivating new competencies, modeling influences alter motivation by instilling behavioral outcome expectations, and create emotional proclivities and value systems through the emotional expressions of others toward given persons, places, or things. Bandura also notes that a lot of modeling goes on in creativity. By novel synthesis of existing innovations or adding new elements to them, something new is created. Modeling influences can promote creativeness by exemplifying diversity for novel syntheses and fresh perspectives that weaken conventional mind sets.

The revolutionary advances in the technology of telecommunications have made symbolic modeling a key vehicle in the social diffusion of ideas, values, and styles of behavior worldwide. Recognizing the growing power of the symbolic environment in people's lives, Bandura extended his theorizing and research to the mechanisms through which symbolic modes of modeling produce their widespread social effects.

Another major focus of Bandura's theorizing addressed the extraordinary symbolizing capacity of humans. By drawing on their symbolic capabilities, people can comprehend their environment, construct guides for action, solve problems cognitively, support forethoughtful courses of action, gain new knowledge by reflective thought, and communicate with others at any distance in time and space. By symbolizing their experiences, people give structure, meaning, and continuity to their lives.

A further distinctive feature of social cognitive theory that Bandura singles out for special attention is the capacity for self-directedness. People plan courses of action, anticipate their likely consequences, and set goals and challenges for themselves to motivate, guide, and regulate their activities. After adopting personal standards, people regulate their own motivation and behavior by the positive and negative consequences they produce for themselves. They do things that give them satisfaction and a sense of self-worth, and refrain from actions that evoke self-devaluative reactions. The human capacity for self-management is an aspect of the theory that makes it particularly apt to the changing times. The accelerated pace of informational, social, and technological changes has placed a premium on people's capabilities to exert a strong hand in their own self-renewal and functioning through the course of life.

The capability for self-reflection concerning one's functioning and personal efficacy to produce effects is another human attribute that is featured prominently in social cognitive theory. Bandura regards the self-efficacy belief system as the foundation of human motivation, well-being, and personal accomplishments. Unless people believe that they can bring about desired outcomes by their actions, they have little incentive to act or to persevere in the face of difficulties. A wealth of empirical evidence documents that beliefs of personal efficacy touch virtually every aspect of people's lives—whether they think productively, self-debilitatingly, pessimistically, or optimistically; how well they motivate themselves and persevere in the face of adversities; their vulnerability to stress and depression; and the life choices they make.

Human lives are not lived in isolation. Bandura, therefore, expanded the conception of human agency to include collective agency. People work together on shared beliefs about their capabilities and common aspirations to better their lives. This conceptual extension makes the theory applicable to human adaptation and change in collectivistically-oriented societies as well as individualistically-oriented ones. In his book, *Self-Efficacy: The Exercise of Control,* Bandura sets forth at length the basic tenets of his theory of self-efficacy and its fruitful applications to the fields of life-course development, education, health, psychopathology, athletics, business, and international affairs.

Viewed from the social cognitive perspective, the major distinguishing mark of humans is their endowed plasticity and learnability. Their specialized neurophysiological structures and systems provide a vast potentiality that can be fashioned by direct and vicarious experience into diverse forms within biological constraints. Bandura cites the remarkable cultural diversity of behavior patterns and the rapid pace of social change as testimony that biology permits a wide range of possibilities.

Bandura's contributions to psychology have been recognized in the many honors and awards he has received. He was elected to the presidencies of the American Psychological Association and Western Psychological Association, and was appointed Honorary President of the Canadian Psychological Association. Some of the awards he has received include the Distinguished Scientific Contributions Award of the American Psychological Association; The Distinguished Scientist Award, Division 12 of the APA; the William James Award of the American Psychological Society for outstanding achievements in psychological science; the Distinguished Contribution Award from the International Society for Research in Aggression; a Guggenheim fellowship; the Distinguished Scientist Award of the Society of Behavioral Medicine, and the Robert Thorndike Award for Distinguished Contribution of Psychology to Education, American Psychological Association. He has been elected to the American Academy of Arts and Sciences and the Institute of Medicine of the National Academy of Sciences. He is the recipient of many honorary degrees.

STAFF

BARBER, THEODORE X. (1927–   )

Theodore Xenophon Barber, distinguished hypnosis researcher and theoretician, was born in 1927 and grew up partly in his native Greece and partly in Ohio. He received a PhD in psychology from American University in 1956 and, during the subsequent three years, was a National Institutes of Health (NIH) research fellow at Harvard University. Barber's career henceforth consisted of virtually full-time (experimental and clinical) hypnosis research (conducted primarily at the Medfield Foundation in Massachusetts), which was supported continuously by long-term research grants from NIH.

Barber's extensive research, spanning from about 1960 to the present, was critically evaluated by distinguished historian of hypnosis Alan Gauld in the final chapter (entitled "Barber and Beyond") of his authoritative *A History of Hypnotism* (Cambridge University Press, 1992) and in *Contemporary Hypnosis* (1999, Vol. 16[3]). Gauld divided Barber's research into three phases. In the first phase, during the 1960s, Barber presented incisive critiques of virtually all important earlier hypnosis research; a new methodology for the conduct of rigorous work in the area; reevaluations and reconceptualizations of exotic hypnotic phenomena; and the important discovery that, with or without a traditional ("drowsy . . . sleepy") hypnotic induction, experimental subjects obtain high scores on hypnotic susceptibility or suggestibility scales (manifesting age-regression, analgesia, hallucinations, post-hypnotic behavior, amnesia, etc.) when they have strong positive sets (composed of positive attitudes toward the hypnotic or suggestive test situation, positive motivations to experience hypnosis and/or the suggested effects, and positive expectancies that they can experience what is suggested), which lead to a readiness to think and imagine along with the suggestions while letting go of interfering thoughts. Gauld judged this first phase of Barber's research as constituting a revolution in hypnosis research and theory, since it "had a stronger influence on both conceptual and methodological aspects of con-

temporary hypnotism than any other [research]" (1992, p. 583), and "strikingly influenced academic thinking about hypnosis . . . and led to a widespread sweeping away of older assumptions, and a clearing of the decks" (1999, p. 146).

Gauld judged Barber's postrevolutionary "work in the 1970s and 1980s on hypnosis, suggestibility, and creative imagination, and on gifted fantasizers" (1999, p. 146) as resulting in "what may prove to be the most interesting of all the lines of inquiry in which Barber has been involved" (1992, p. 584); namely, the discovery that a subset of dramatically responsive hypnotic subjects are fantasy-prone individuals. Barber and Sheryl C. Wilson discovered (and others later confirmed) that 2 to 4% of (student) subjects are exceptionally responsive to hypnotic suggestions (given with or without a hypnotic induction), primarily because they have a hypnosis-conducive fantasy talent derived from a unique life history. During childhood, each spent an incredibly large proportion of his or her time in fantasy-based activities such as pretend-play, make-believe, vivid daydreaming, imaginative reliving of pleasurable sexual experiences, and interactions with such entities as imaginary companions and guardian angels. As adults, they secretly continue to spend much of their time fantasizing, and they insist they see, hear, feel, smell, and experience what they fantasize. In hypnosis experiments they use their well-developed talent for vivid, realistic fantasy to see, hear, and interact with the suggested (hallucinatory) object, to experience age-regression as they supplement their early memories with their fantasies of the suggested earlier time, to experience hypnotic analgesia by deliberately fantasizing they are in a different situation (without the pain stimulus), and so on.

The third phase of Barber's hypnosis research, in the 1990s, culminated in a new, multidimensional paradigm of hypnosis, a new way of thinking about the topic with new research proposals that, according to Gauld (1999), "could lead to a rather welcome clearing of cluttered decks, much as did [Barber's] earlier [revolutionary] proposals of thirty years ago and more" (p. 148).

In addition to the two types of very good hypnotic subjects (the positively-set and the fantasy-prone) that Barber had delineated previously, his new paradigm included a third type, which he labeled the "amnesia-prone hypnotic virtuoso." These amnesia-prone individuals, comprising about 1% of (student) subjects, have three interrelated characteristics. First, in hypnotic situations they typically respond in such a way that many earlier and recent investigators (from Puységur and Pierre Janet to Eugene Bliss and Deidre Barrett) called them "somnambules" or "deep trance subjects"; that is, after a traditional hypnotic induction, they appear to enter a trance state associated with a sleep-like appearance, passivity, and automatic-like responsiveness to suggestions, plus post-hypnotic amnesia. They manifest various kinds of amnesias in their lives, typically including amnesia for virtually all of their childhoods, amnesia for other scattered periods in their lives, lapses or micro-amnesias in their daily lives, and amnesia for their night dreams and for their few, if any, daydreams. Both their trance-like hypnotic behavior and their various amnesias are typically related to childhood physical, psychological, and/or sexual abuse during which they learned to blank out or enter a so-called away state, and to block out or mentally compartmentalize (repress, dissociate, or forget) particular stimuli or events.

In Barber's new paradigm, the characteristics of subjects interact with powerful variables present in the hypnotic situation to determine their precise behaviors. That is, all individuals exposed to hypnotic procedures—the highly responsive positively-set, fantasy-prone, and amnesia-prone subjects and the less talented or less motivated (and thus less responsive) subjects—are affected, albeit differently for the different kinds of subjects, by four situational factors: (a) social factors, including social rules, roles, and expectations that obligate the socialized individual to cooperate and to meet the social demands of the hypnotic situation; (b) the hypnotist's characteristics and unique skills, including communicative ability, creative ideas, and ability to form a positive interpersonal relationship with the subject; (c) the effectiveness of the induction procedure in guiding the subject to think along with the suggestions; and (e) the depth of meaning, creativity, and power of the suggested ideas.

Barber's new hypnosis paradigm unified the two long-combative schools of hypnosis: the trance school (which pivoted on such concepts as somnambulism, automatism, amnesia, and dissociation) versus the non-trance (or suggestion) school (which focused on attitudinal, motivational, expectancy, and social psychological variables). Barber showed that the conflicting schools each touched on part of the truth, since they were referring to different kinds of responsive hypnotic subjects (the former to the amnesia-prone, the latter primarily to the positively-set and secondarily to the fantasy-prone). The new paradigm was presented by Barber in a series of publications: *Clinical Hypnosis and Self Regulation,* APA, 1999; *Contemporary Hypnosis,* 1999, Vol. 16(3); and *American Journal of Clinical Hypnosis,* 2000, Vol. 42(3). He summarized his prior research in two books that he authored: *Hypnosis: A Scientific Approach,* 1969, and *LSD, Marihuana, Yoga, and Hypnosis,* 1970; and in a series of books he co-authored or co-edited: *Hypnosis, Imagination, and Human Potentialities,* 1974; *Advances in Altered States of Consciousness and Human Potentialities,* 1976; *Biofeedback and Self-Control,* 1970–1978; and *Biofeedback and Behavioral Medicine,* 1979–1980. Barber also wrote a critique of research in psychology (*Pitfalls in Human Research: Ten Pivotal Points,* 1976) and a critique of comparative psychology that documented intelligent awareness in animals (*The Human Nature of Birds: A Scientific Discovery with Startling Implications,* 1993).

STAFF

BARLOW, DAVID H.

David H. Barlow received his BA from the University of Notre Dame, his MA from Boston College, and his PhD from the University of Vermont in 1969. Barlow has published over 400 articles and chapters and over 20 books, mostly in the areas of anxiety disorders, sexual problems, and clinical research methodology. He has served on the editorial boards of 19 different journals.

He is formerly professor of psychiatry at the University of Mississippi Medical Center and professor of psychiatry and psychology at Brown University, and founded clinical psychology internships in both settings. He was also distinguished professor in the department of psychology at the University at Albany, State University of New York, and director of the Phobia and Anxiety Disorders Clinic. Currently, he is professor of psychology, research professor of psychiatry, director of clinical training programs, and director of the Center for Anxiety and Related Disorders at Boston University, one of the largest teaching and research clinics of its kind in the world. Research ongoing at the Center includes basic explorations of the nature of anxiety and negative affect using methods of experimental psychopathology, as well as the development and evaluation of new approaches to nosology in preparation for the run up to *DSM-V.* Treatment outcome research most usually takes the form of large multicenter clinical trials looking at the separate and combined effects of drugs and psychosocial treatments. Research in the Child and Adolescent Fear and Anxiety Treatment Program focuses on developing new treatments for childhood anxiety disorders and exploring early psychological and social factors that create vulnerabilities for the development of anxiety disorders in later childhood. An additional research emphasis focuses on the effective dissemination of proven psychosocial interventions to frontline clinical settings and methods to facilitate this dissemination. This latter focus is accomplished in collaboration with Mental Health and Substance Abuse Corporations of Massachusetts, a network of over 90 frontline mental health clinics delivering services in all corners of the state.

A fellow of every major psychological association, Barlow has received many awards in honor of his excellence in scholarship. Barlow is the recipient of the 2000 American Psychological Association (APA) Distinguished Scientific Award for the Applications of Psychology. He is also the recipient of the Science Dissemination Award from the Society for a Science of Clinical Psychology of the APA. During the 1997–1998 academic year he was Fritz Redlich Fellow at the Center for Advanced Study in the Behavioral Sciences at Stanford, California. Other awards include the First Graduate Alumni Scholar Award from the Graduate College, The University of Vermont; the Distinguished Scientist Award from the Society for a Science of Clinical Psychology of the APA; the Excellence in Research award from the State University of New York at Albany; and a MERIT award from the National Institute of Mental Health for long-term contributions to the clinical research effort. He is past president of the Society of Clinical Psychology (Division 12) of the American Psychological Association, past president of the Association for the Advancement of Behavior Therapy, past associate editor of the *Journal of Consulting and Clinical Psychology,* and past editor of the journals *Behavior Therapy* and *Journal of Applied Behavior Analysis.* Currently, he is editor of the journal *Clinical Psychology: Science and Practice.* He was also chair of the American Psychological Association Task Force of Psychological Intervention Guidelines, was a member of the *DSM-IV* Task Force of the American Psychiatric Association and was cochair of the Work Group for revising the anxiety disorder categories. He is also a diplomate in Clinical Psychology of the American Board of Professional Psychology and maintains a private practice.

At leisure he plays golf, skis, and retreats to his home in Nantucket, where he writes, walks on the beach, and visits with his island friends.

STAFF

BARTLETT, FREDERIC C. (1886–1979)

Frederic C. Bartlett, the leading British psychologist of his time, did much to further experimental psychology in the United Kingdom. After graduating in philosophy in the University of London, he moved to Cambridge with the initial intention of studying anthropology under W. H. R. Rivers. However, World War I intervened and, on the advice of Charles S. Myers, Bartlett turned to experimental psychology and virtually took charge of the Cambridge Psychological Laboratory when Myers left Cambridge for war service. After the war, Bartlett succeeded Myers as director of the laboratory and in 1931 was appointed the first professor of experimental psychology in the university. He held this post until his retirement in 1952, but remained active for some years thereafter as an honorary consultant to the Applied Psychology Unit which he himself had built up during and after World War II.

Bartlett's psychological standpoint was strongly empirical, with a distinct bias toward applied interests. His intellectual approach was greatly influenced by three Cambridge teachers: James Ward, a philosopher with a background in physiology; Rivers, who began in physiology and medicine but is best known for his later works in ethnology; and Myers, who likewise qualified in medicine but whose subsequent career was devoted wholly to psychology. Myers provided Bartlett with his first real introduction to experimental psychology and invited him to assist in the revision of his *Textbook of Experimental Psychology* (Myers, 1909/1925), which was for many years the standard British source.

Although an accomplished teacher, Bartlett is best remembered for his outstanding achievement in directing research. His own early work fell largely within the traditional sphere of human experimental psychology and is best represented by his celebrated book, *Remembering,* based upon a successful fellowship dissertation submitted many years earlier to St. John's College, Cambridge. This book represented both a clean break with the Ebbinghaus tradition and an attempt to study memory in circumstances akin to those of everyday life.

Bartlett's studies led him to stress the constructive rather than reproductive aspects of recall and to repudiate the classical trace theory, which he considered wholly inappropriate to the realities of memory. In its place, he proposed an admittedly vague theory of schemata adapted from Henry Head's 1920 work on sensation and the cerebral cortex. Unfortunately, this theory proved too speculative to gain wide acceptance, though it led many people to think rather differently about the nature and dynamics of memory (Oldfield & Zangwill, 1943; Zangwill, 1972).

During and after World War II, Bartlett turned his department almost exclusively to wartime activities. A wide variety of practical problems, for the most part relating to training methods, fatigue, and human performance, were referred to the department, and its considerable success depended on Bartlett's exceptional psychological acumen together with the ingenuity and skill of his research workers, in particular a young man of outstanding originality, Kenneth Craik.

As a result of his wartime experience, Bartlett became increasingly preoccupied with the need to base experimental psychology upon the solution of practical problems, being convinced that advances in basic psychological theory would come only through such an approach (Bartlett, 1948). Although this standpoint had its critics, Bartlett's good sense and authority did much to narrow the gap between fundamental and applied psychology and to endow psychological experiments with more realistic flavor.

Bartlett was a fellow of the Royal Society of London and a foreign associate of the U.S. National Academy of Sciences. He was the recipient of many honors, including honorary degrees from the universities of Athens, Edinburgh, London, Louvain, Oxford, Princeton, and Padua.

O. L. ZANGWILL
Cambridge, England

BATESON, GREGORY (1904–1980)

Gregory Bateson studied at the University of Geneva, and received the BA and MA from Cambridge. He conducted anthropological research with the Baining and the Sulka of the Gazelle Peninsula and with the Iatmul of New Guinea. He served at various times with the American Museum of Natural History, the Museum of Modern Art, and the O.S.S. He also was a visiting professor or lecturer at Harvard University, the New School for Social Research, the University of Hawaii, and the Langley Porter Clinic. In 1950 he joined the Veterans Administration Hospital in Palo Alto, California, as ethnologist.

Bateson was at one time married to Margaret Mead, with whom he coauthored Naven (1928), a picture of the culture of a New Guinea tribe. He is also the author of Steps to an Ecology of Mind (1972) and Mind and Nature: A Necessary Unity (1979).

P. E. LICHTENSTEIN

BATTERED PEOPLE

Battered people are victims of intentional physical abuse among family members. This includes child abuse, spouse abuse, abuse of older family members, and abuse among siblings. Child abuse is the only area universally singled out for special legal consideration, with laws requiring the reporting of suspected cases. Abuse between spouses or other adults has received less attention, possibly because society feels adults can advocate for themselves whereas children cannot. Many people also believe that, if abused adults tolerate mistreatment, they either deserve it or would reject help anyway.

It is impossible to estimate accurately the rates of various types of abuse. Within the United States the sanctity of the family and the rights of family members—particularly parents and especially fathers—to guide the family without outside interference or intrusion is valued. This concern for the privacy and independence of the family has placed a barrier between it and the outside world.

Protection of this position has at times insulated families from the police, the courts, and the probing eye of the researcher. However, the American family experiences a considerable amount of internal violence. The severity of the problem is at least partially reflected in known statistics presented in a review of violence in the American family by Straus, Gelles, and Steinmetz (1980). These statistics indicate that violence within the family is one of the leading causes of death, injury, and emotional pathology.

While individuals from lower socioeconomic levels and minorities are overrepresented in the statistics, the problem appears to cut across all races and levels of socioeconomic status. All forms of violence within the family are less detectable at the higher levels of social and economic positions.

The first organized efforts to address the problems of family violence in the United States were undertaken by the American Society for the Prevention of Cruelty to Animals in 1874. This organization was asked to intervene on behalf of a foster child named Mary Ellen who had been beaten daily by her stepmother.

The 1960s saw a rapid growth in concern and legislation to address the problem of child abuse. By 1968 protective services for children, and laws requiring the reporting of suspected cases, were provided universally in all 50 states. While some states also provided for protective services for adults who cannot adequately advocate for themselves, general attention to other forms of family violence was—and in many ways still is—lacking. Abuse of older parents and grandparents by family members and abuse among siblings have still received almost no attention in our laws and our research, and not enough in our social concern.

The situation is somewhat brighter in the area of spouse abuse. In 1971 a woman named Erin Pizzey started a refuge for abused women in England and later wrote *Scream Quietly or the Neighbors Will Hear* (1974). The first organized efforts in this country relative to spouse abuse came in 1972, when a group called Women's Advocates began a telephone information and referral service for battered women in St. Paul, Minnesota. Two years later this group set up the first known refuge in the United States for battered wives and their children.

Despite the growing focus on violence within the family, little good research across the spectrum is available. Yet some general facts are known. First and maybe foremost, violence begets violence. Regardless of the type of battering or the target, individuals who were or are themselves abused are more likely than nonbattered people to resort to violence in the future. This appears to be especially true for males, and not surprisingly, males are more likely to commit the abuse.

Where the abuse is exclusively between adults, nearly 50% of the time there is mutual violence. It is impossible to completely understand the role of such violence. It may involve self-defense or a jointly escalating pattern. Males tend to inflict graver injuries and use more dangerous instruments of violence such as a gun or knife.

In most cases, the injuries inflicted are not premeditated. Frequently, they are, however, the result of exaggerated efforts to gain or maintain control over the other person. Violence in these households tends to be taken for granted; the abuser is often impulsive and unable to control emotions. Emotions rapidly build to an extreme, although sufficient control is generally maintained to avoid inflicting serious permanent injury or death.

This controlled lack of control is also seen in the fact that the abuse is most likely to take place at home, and that the individuals involved are not necessarily violent people generally. Each type of abuse can and does exist independent of the other forms, although they do seem to be frequently related. Some authorities on family violence believe these findings indicate that abuse—in some forms and to some degree—is sanctioned within the context of the family home, and that the loss of control is learned or of lesser importance.

All forms of abuse are much more likely with the presence of alcohol. Abuse also appears to become more likely when the family is under stress, or when the abuser has a poor history of dealing with stress, though the majority of abusive individuals are not so emotionally disturbed as to be diagnosed as psychotic. The environment is also a factor: Abuse is more likely in homes where there are more than two children, where there is considerable stress, and where decision making is largely in the hands of one person.

All these factors describe households where abuse is likely, and characteristics of the abuser, but do little to explain the specific causes. Implicit in these descriptions is the notion that social factors are of prime importance in understanding causes and interventions. Clearly, much more research into psychological and even biological factors needs to be pursued, as well as additional investigation of prevention programs, interventions, and long-range consequences.

Interventions currently focus primarily upon the social issues. It is of prime importance to first stop what is often an escalating pattern of abuse. Both shelters and foster placements serve these needs, but neither is a satisfactory solution for elderly victims. Some form of outside supervision of what is going on within the home may be necessary. Day care and baby-sitting services for children may provide a break in the routine, as well as additional protection and supervision of the child.

Recourse to the police and courts may well be necessary in the more extreme cases, to provide the required motivation for treatment or to stop the abusive patterns. Additional laws recognizing the various forms of abuse and providing for more ready legal access and reporting, should be of assistance as well. Individual, family, and marital counseling will be necessary in many cases. Group therapy and supporting groups such as Parents Anonymous are important in preventing further violence within the family.

A more global focus on the role of violence in our culture and the socioeconomic pressures will be required to address the problem within the larger society. Reducing the social isolation of families and the sexist attitudes within the society should help set the stage for more general intervention and prevention.

REFERENCES

Pizzey, E. (1974). *Scream quietly or the neighbors will hear.* London: Penguin.

Straus, M., Gelles, R., & Steinmetz, S. (1980). *Behind closed doors: Violence in the American family.* Garden City, NY: Anchor.

SUGGESTED READINGS

Cook, J., & Bowles, R. (Eds.). (1980). *Child abuse: Commission and omission.* Scarborough, Ont.: Butterworth.

Davidson, T. (1978). *Conjugal crime: Understanding and changing the wifebeating problem.* New York: Hawthorn.

Finkelhor, D. (1979). *Sexually victimized children.* New York: Free Press.

Kadushin, A., & Martin, J. (1981). *Child abuse: An interactional event.* New York: Columbia University Press.

S. D. SHERRETS
Maine Head Trauma Center

AGGRESSION
BYSTANDER INVOLVEMENT
CHILD ABUSE
DISPLACEMENT (SOCIAL)
STRESS
VIOLENCE

BAYLEY, NANCY (1899–   )

A pioneer in longitudinal multidisciplinary research, Bayley was born to a family that homesteaded in the Northwest in the mid-1800s. Trained as a psychologist at the University of Washington (BS, MS) and the State University of Iowa (PhD, 1926), she also acquired expertise on physical growth at Iowa and through later study and collaboration with outstanding anatomists and physicians.

Among Bayley's seminal studies are longitudinal research on much of the life span; techniques for measuring behavioral, motor, and physical development; and assessment of interactions between behavioral and biological development. She was one of the first to consider the life span as a frame of reference for research; to report change as well as stability in IQ, and the maintenance of IQ in adulthood; to study the influence of maternal behavior on offspring; and to examine associations of behavior with body build and with rate of physical maturing.

Bayley began her career at the University of Wyoming. In 1928 she joined the Institute of Child Welfare at the University of California, Berkeley. There she founded the Berkeley Growth Study and developed scales for assessing early mental and motor development. The revised Bayley Scales of Infant Development are used worldwide by scientists and professionals from a number of disciplines; they are the most carefully standardized instruments available for this age range.

From 1954 to 1964 Bayley was chief of the Section on Early Development, Laboratory of Psychology, National Institute of Mental Health. She returned to Berkeley in 1964 and retired in 1968. Among her many honors are presidencies of the Society for Research in Child Development, the Western Psychological Association, and the Division on Developmental Psychology and the Division on Adult Development and Aging of the American Psychological Association; the Gold Medal Award of the American Psychological Foundation; the APA Distinguished Scientific Contribution Award; the G. Stanley Hall Award for Distinguished

Contributions to Developmental Psychology; and the American Education Research Association Award.

STAFF

BAYLEY SCALES OF INFANT DEVELOPMENT (Bayley Scales)

The Bayley Scales are carefully constructed measures for assessing the development of infants and young children, ages 1 to 30 months. Test content is organized into two separate scales: the Mental Scale and the Motor Scale. The Mental Scale, which contains 163 items, assesses the precursors of cognitive development, including perceptual acuity, discrimination, acquisition of object constancy, memory, rudimentary problem solving, early verbal communication, classification, and generalization. The Motor Scale, which contains 81 items, assesses body control, large muscle coordination, and manipulation of the hands and fingers. A third component, the Infant Behavior Record (IBR), is a rating scale completed after administration of the Mental and Motor Scales and provides the clinician a means of evaluating the child's environmental interaction and response. Administration of the Mental and Motor Scales requires a minimum of 45 minutes (Bayley, 1969).

Standardization of the Bayley Scales used a stratified quota sampling procedure designed to represent the U.S. population. The sample consisted of 1262 children distributed nearly equally among the 14 age groups from 2 through 30 months. Performance of this sample was used to obtain the Mental Development Index (MDI) and the Psychomotor Development Index (PDI). Both the MDI and PDI are age-based normalized standard scores with a mean of 100, and a standard deviation of 15. Interpretation of the IBR is based largely on clinical judgment, although the percentage of the standardization sample rated at each scale level is given (Bayley, 1969).

Intercorrelations between the Mental and Motor Scales range from 0.24 to 0.78, with a median of 0.46, for the 14 standardization age groups. Split-half reliabilities for the Mental Scale range from 0.81 to 0.93, with a median of 0.88; for the Motor Scale, 0.68 to 0.92, with a median of 0.84.

REFERENCES

Bayley, N. (1969). *Manual for the Bayley scales of infant development.* New York: Psychological Corp.

G. J. ROBERTSON
Wide Range, Inc.

INFANT DEVELOPMENT
INTELLIGENCE MEASURES

BECK, AARON T.

A native of Providence, RI, Aaron T. Beck had an interest in psychiatry and psychology as far back as he can remember. At Brown University, he was associate editor of the Brown *Daily Herald* and received a number of honors and awards, including Phi Beta Kappa, the Francis Wayland Scholarship, the Bennett Essay Award, and the Gaston Prize for Oratory. After graduating magna cum laude in 1942, he embarked on a career in medicine at Yale Medical School. He served a rotating internship, followed by a residency in pathology at the Rhode Island Hospital.

Although initially interested in psychiatry, he found the then-current approaches to be nihilistic and unrewarding, and decided on a career in neurology, attracted by the high degree of precision that characterized this discipline. During his residency in neurology at the Cushing Veterans Administration (VA) Hospital, he rotated through psychiatry and was intrigued by the dynamic psychoanalysts, F. Deutsch and E. Semrad. When he complained to his colleagues that psychoanalytic theories seemed very farfetched, they explained that they had once felt the same but had discovered that this attitude was simply an indication of their resistance. He concluded that the only way he could validly evaluate the psychoanalytic concepts was to follow their advice and undergo a personal analysis.

Beck spent two years as a fellow at the Austen Riggs Center at Stockbridge, where he became impressed with modified psychoanalytic approaches as powerful tools for treating sicker patients. He was particularly influenced by the clinical approaches of R. Knight, M. Brenman, E. Erickson, D. Rapaport, and R. Schafer. His interest in cognition, derived from Rapaport's ego psychology, was stimulated at this time.

The Korean War shifted Beck's area of work to the Valley Forge Army Hospital, where he was assistant chief of neuropsychiatry. Following his graduation from the Philadelphia Psychoanalytic Institute in 1956, he was most influenced by his contacts with L. J. Saul, a progressive and empirically oriented psychoanalyst in the tradition of Alexander and French. Convinced that psychoanalysis offered important insights into psychological disorders, Beck decided to use accepted research methodology to "validate" psychoanalytic hypotheses and, thus, to convince the skeptical that psychoanalysis is a valid theory and therapy.

Beck's first research study involved the testing of the psychoanalytic hypothesis that depression was caused by hostility turned against the self. The findings from his experimental work on dreams and other ideational data, combined with his clinical observations, led Beck to discard psychoanalytic theory and to formulate his cognitive theory and therapy of depression and other psychiatric disorders. To his surprise, he found that by teaching depressed patients to examine and test their negative ideas, they were able to correct their dichotomous thinking, overgeneralizations, arbitrary inferences, and so on, and their depression would start to improve. (Beck later learned that A. Ellis had made similar observations several years earlier.) The important concepts that he developed were cognitive specificity (i.e., each disorder has a specific cognitive content), cognitive bias, and cognitive vulnerability, the idea that patients with a particular cognitive constellation were predisposed to develop a disorder when their experiences impinged on this vulnerability (which consisted, to a large extent, of a cluster of dysfunctional beliefs).

Beck joined the University of Pennsylvania in 1954 and is currently the University's professor emeritus of psychiatry. Faculty appointments have included visiting professorships at Harvard University (1982) and Oxford University (1985). Since 1994, he has been president of the Beck Foundation for Cognitive Therapy and Research.

From his early research in the late 1950s, Beck developed his cognitive theory and therapy of psychopathology. In his work he pursued a specific strategy for classifying and treating psychological problems. First, he evolved formulations for the specific type of psychopathology, and then developed measures and inventories for measuring these constructs. He then conducted research to test the specific cognitive formulations. He finally developed treatment manuals and conducted clinical trials. The various treatment manuals crystallized into volumes on the cognitive therapy of depression, anxiety, panic and phobias, couples' problems, substance abuse, personality disorders, and suicidal behavior.

In order to implement his successive research projects, Beck developed a number of instruments, including, among others, the Beck Depression Inventory, the Beck Hopelessness Scale, the Beck Anxiety Inventory, the Self-Concept Test, the Sociotropy-Autonomy Scale, the Suicide Intent Scale, and the Scale for Suicide Ideation. His various inventories are among the most widely used psychological instruments. In a long-term study, Beck found that hopelessness, as measured by the Beck Hopelessness Scale at the time of the patient's index admission to a hospital, predicted ultimate suicide within 10 years. This finding was later confirmed with psychiatric outpatients.

Since 1959 Beck has directed funded research investigations of the psychopathology of depression, suicide, anxiety disorders, panic disorders, alcoholism, drug abuse, and personality disorders and of cognitive therapy of these disorders. His work has been consistently supported by the National Institute of Mental Health and the Center for Disease Control and Prevention.

Beck has received numerous awards and honorary degrees including a Doctor of Medical Science honorary degree from Brown University and a Doctor of Humane Letters degree from Assumption College. He is the only psychiatrist to receive research awards from the American Psychological Association and the American Psychiatric Association. He has also received the PSYCHE Award and awards from the Society for Psychopathology Research, Society for Psychotherapy Research, the New York Academy of Medicine, American Suicide Foundation, Albert Einstein College of Medicine, Brown University, and the California Psychological Association. He is also a senior member of the Institute of Medicine of the National Academy of Sciences. He has authored and coauthored over 400 publications, including 14 books.

Since completing his recent volume, *Prisoners of Hate: The Cognitive Basis of Anger, Hostility and Violence,* Beck has begun work on the cognitive therapy of schizophrenia. His research and clinical work has stimulated a vast amount of research by other investigators. Cognitive therapy has been recognized as the fastest growing psychotherapy in the world.

STAFF

THE BECK DEPRESSION INVENTORY–II

The Beck Depression Inventory–II (BDI–II; Beck, Steer, & Brown, 1996) is a 21-item self-report instrument for measuring the severity of depression in adolescents and adults according to symptoms corresponding to the criteria for diagnosing major depressive disorders listed in the American Psychiatric Association's (1994) *Diagnostic and Statistical Manual of Mental Disorders, Fourth Edition (DSM-IV)*. It is the upgraded version of the amended Beck Depression Inventory (BDI–IA; Beck & Steer, 1993), which, in turn, replaced the original instrument developed by Beck, Ward, Mendelson, Mock, and Erbaugh (1961).

The BDI–II is scored by summing the highest rating for each of the 21 symptoms, and a four-point scale ranging from zero to three is employed for each item. Respondents are asked to rate each symptom for the past two weeks including today. The instrument generally requires between five and ten minutes to complete. Beck, Steer, and Brown (1996) suggested the following cut-off score guidelines for evaluating the severity of self-reported depression in patients diagnosed with major depressive disorders: Total scores from 0 to 13 are "minimal," and those from 14 to 19 are "mild." Scores from 20 to 28 are "moderate," and scores from 29 to 63 are "severe."

Research indicates that the overall psychometric characteristics of the BDI–II are similar to those for BDI–IA, which is one of the most widely used measures for assessing the severity of depression in psychiatric patients and screening for possible depression in normal populations (Archer, Maruish, Imhof, & Piotrowski, 1991; Piotrowski & Keller, 1992). For example, Beck, Steer and Brown, (1996) reported that the internal consistencies (Cronbach coefficient alphas) of the BDI–II and the BDI–IA were, respectively, .91 and .89 in 140 outpatients who were diagnosed with various *DSM–IV* psychiatric disorders. Furthermore, the Pearson product-moment correlations of both instruments' total scores for these outpatients with sex, ethnicity, age, and the diagnosis of a mood disorder were within a hundredth of one point of each other for the same variables.

However, the mean BDI–II total score was approximately 2 points higher than it was for the BDI–IA, and approximately one more symptom on average was endorsed on the BDI–II than on the BDI–IA. The mean BDI–II total scores of women have consistently been found to be higher than those of men. In studying the psychometric characteristics of the BDI–II in 105 adolescent (12 to 17 years old) female and 105 adolescent male psychiatric outpatients, Steer, Kumar, Ranieri, and Beck (1998) reported the girls' mean BDI–II score was approximately five points higher than that of the boys.

Reliability. The internal consistency of the BDI–II has repeatedly been described as high, with a coefficient alpha of approximately .90 in adolescent (Steer, Kumar, Ranieri, & Beck, 1998) and

adult psychiatric patients (Steer, Ball, Ranieri, & Beck, 1997), as well as in college students (Dozois, Dobson, & Ahnberg, 1998; Osman, Downs, Barrios, Kopper, Gutierrez, & Chiros, 1997; Steer & Clark, 1997). In addition Beck, Steer, and Brown (1996) reported that for 26 outpatients who completed the BDI–II before their first and second cognitive therapy sessions, the one-week test-retest reliability was high ($r = .93$).

Validity. For their normative samples of 500 outpatients who were diagnosed with various psychiatric disorders and 120 college students, Beck, Steer, and Brown (1996) described a number of analyses that pertained to the convergent and discriminant validities of the BDI–II. For example, the BDI–II was more positively correlated with the revised Hamilton Psychiatric Rating Scale for Depression (Riskind, Beck, Brown, & Steer, 1987) ($r = .71$) than it was with the revised Hamilton Rating Scale for Anxiety (Riskind et al., 1987) ($r = .47$) in 87 outpatients. Steer, Ball, Ranieri, and Beck (1997) later administered the BDI–II to 210 psychiatric outpatients along with the SCL–90–R (Derogatis, 1983) and found that the BDI–II was more positively correlated with scores on the Depression subscale ($r = .89$) than it was with scores on the Anxiety subscale of the SCL–90–R ($r = .71$).

Factor Structure. Beck, Steer, and Brown (1996) concluded that the BDI–II was composed of two positively correlated *cognitive* and *noncognitive (somatic-affective)* dimensions for both psychiatric outpatients and college students. The noncognitive factor is represented by somatic symptoms, such as loss of energy, and affective symptoms, such as irritability, whereas the cognitive factor is composed of psychological symptoms such as self-dislike and worthlessness. Steer, Ball, Ranieri, and Beck (1999) also identified these two factors in 210 adult (≥18 years old) outpatients who were diagnosed with *DSM-IV* depressive disorders, as did Steer, Kumar, Ranieri, and Beck (1998) in 210 adolescent psychiatric outpatients. These two dimensions were also found by Steer and Clark (1997) in 160 college students and by Dozois, Dobson, and Ahnberg (1998) in 1,022 college students. However, after analyzing the BDI–II responses of 230 college students, Osman and colleagues (1997) concluded that a three-factor model representing *negative attitudes, performance difficulty,* and *somatic elements* might be more appropriate for describing the factor structure of the BDI–II than is a two-factor model.

REFERENCES

American Psychiatric Association. (1994) *Diagnostic and statistical manual of mental disorders* (4th ed.). Washington, DC: Author.

Archer, R. P., Maruish, M., Imhof, E. A., & Piotrowski, C. (1991). Psychological test usage with adolescent clients: 1990 survey findings. *Professional Psychology: Research and Practice, 22,* 247–252.

Beck, A. T., Steer, R. A., & Brown, G. K. (1996). *Manual for the Beck Depression Inventory–II.* San Antonio, TX: Psychological Corporation.

Beck, A. T., & Steer, R. A. (1993). *Manual for the Beck Depression Inventory.* San Antonio, TX: Psychological Corporation.

Beck, A. T., Ward, C. H., Mendelson, M., Mock, J., & Erbaugh, J. (1961). An inventory for measuring depression. *Archives of General Psychiatry, 4,* 561–571.

Derogatis, L. R. (1983). *SCL–90–R administration, scoring, and procedures manual–II.* Townson, MD: Clinical Psychometric Research.

Dozois, D. J. A., Dobson, K. S., & Ahnberg, J. L. (1998). A psychometric evaluation of the Beck Depression Inventory–II. *Psychological Assessment, 10,* 83–89.

Osman, A., Downs, W. R., Barrios, F. X., Kopper, B. A., Gutierrez, P. M., & Chiros, C. E. (1997). Factor structure and psychometric characteristics of the Beck Depression Inventory–II. *Journal of Psychopathology and Behavioral Assessment, 19,* 359–375.

Piotrowski, C., & Keller, J. W. (1992). Psychological testing in applied settings: A literature review from 1982–1992. *Journal of Training in the Practice of Professional Psychology, 6,* 74–82.

Riskind, J. H., Beck, A. T., Brown, G., & Steer, R. A. (1987). Taking the measure of anxiety and depression: Validity of the reconstructed Hamilton scales. *Journal of Nervous and Mental Disease, 175,* 474–479.

Steer, R. A., Ball, R., Ranieri, W. F., & Beck, A. T. (1997). Further evidence for the construct validity of the Beck Depression Inventory–II with psychiatric outpatients. *Psychological Reports, 80,* 443–446.

Steer, R. A., Ball, R., Ranieri, W. F., & Beck, A. T. (1999). Dimensions of the Beck Depression Inventory–II in clinically depressed outpatients. *Journal of Clinical Psychology, 55,* 117–128.

Steer, R. A., & Clark, D. A. (1997). Psychometric characteristics of the Beck Depression Inventory–II with college students. *Measurement and Evaluation in Counseling and Development, 30,* 128–136.

Steer, R. A., Kumar, G., Ranieri, W. F., & Beck, A. T. (1998). Use of the Beck Depression Inventory–II with adolescent psychiatric outpatients. *Journal of Psychopathology and Behavioral Assessment, 20,* 127–137.

R. A. STEER
University of Medicine and Dentistry of New Jersey School of Osteopathic Medicine

A. T. BECK
Beck Institute for Cognitive Therapy and Research

DEPRESSION
MEASUREMENT

BEERS, CLIFFORD W. (1876–1943)

Clifford W. Beers graduated from Yale University. While still a young man he developed a manic-depressive psychosis and for 3 years was a patient in several state and private mental hospitals. Following his recovery he wrote a popular and influential book, *A Mind That Found Itself,* which described the inadequate and often inhumane treatment of patients in our mental hospitals. The book evoked a positive response on the part of many leading citizens, which led Beers to organize the first Society for Mental Hygiene in Connecticut in 1908. In 1909 he assisted in the formation of the National Committee for Mental Hygiene and became the acknowledged leader of the mental hygiene movement. His work was instrumental in educating the public and promoting the establishment of clinics aimed at prevention as well as treatment of mental illness.

In 1930 Beers promoted the First International Congress of Mental Hygiene. He also founded the International Committee for Mental Hygiene. Beers's lifelong efforts were rewarded by the existence at the time of his death of a powerful mental hygiene movement that he had brought into being, sustained, and strengthened.

P. E. LICHTENSTEIN

BEHAVIOR MODIFICATION

Behavior modification is the field of study that focuses on using principles of learning and cognition to understand and change people's behavior (Sarafino, 1996). Although not all experts in this field would include cognitive processes in the definition (see Lee, 1992; Sweet & Loizeaux, 1991; Wolpe, 1993), these processes have been widely adopted and applied by behavior modification professionals since the early 1970s (Dobson, 1988; Kazdin, 1978; Mahoney, 1993; Williams, Watts, MacLeod, & Mathews, 1988).

DEFINING CHARACTERISTICS OF BEHAVIOR MODIFICATION

The field of behavior modification has several characteristics that make its approach unique (Kazdin, 1978; Wixted, Bellack, & Hersen, 1990). First, professionals in this field focus on people's behavior, which can be *overt,* such as motor or verbal acts, or *covert,* such as feelings, thoughts, or physiological changes. As a result, their approach typically involves: (a) defining current status and progress in terms of behavior rather than of traits or other broad features; (b) measuring the behavior in some way; and (c) whenever possible, assessing covert behaviors, such as fear, in terms of overt actions. Efforts to improve behavior can be directed at a behavioral *deficit*—that is, the behavior occurs with insufficient frequency, strength, or quality—or a behavioral *excess*—that is, it occurs too frequently or strongly. The behavior to be changed is called the *target behavior.*

Second, although behavior modification professionals recognize that injury and heredity can limit the abilities of an individual, they assume that human behavior is, for the most part, learned and influenced by the environment. The most basic types of learning are *respondent (classical) conditioning,* in which a stimulus gains the ability to elicit a particular response by being paired with an unconditioned stimulus that already elicits that response, and *operant conditioning,* in which behavior is changed by its consequences.

The methods applied in behavior modification generally involve altering the antecedents and consequences of the target behavior.

Third, behavior modification has a strong scientific orientation. As a result, there is a major focus on carefully gathering empirical data, analyzing and interpreting the data, and specifying the precise methods used to gather and analyze the data. The field is also quite pragmatic, emphasizing the need to find and use techniques that work, as indicated by carefully conducted research.

Fourth, behavior modification techniques for changing behavior often have clients or subjects become active participants, such as by performing "homework" and "self-management" activities, in the process of modifying their behavior.

HISTORY OF BEHAVIOR MODIFICATION

Behavior modification developed from the perspective called *behaviorism,* which emerged with the work of John B. Watson (1913, 1930) and B. F. Skinner (1938, 1953). This perspective emphasizes the study of observable and measurable behavior and proposes that nearly all behavior is the product of learning, particularly operant and respondent conditioning.

Three lines of research laid the foundation for behaviorism. Pavlov (1927) demonstrated the process of respondent conditioning. Watson and Rayner (1920) showed that an infant, "Little Albert," learned to fear a white rat through respondent conditioning. And Thorndike (1898, 1931) studied how "satisfying" and "annoying" consequences—which we now call reinforcement and punishment—affect learning. Other studies formed the basis for applying the ideas of behaviorism by showing that conditioning techniques could effectively reduce fears (Jones, 1924) and improve problem behaviors of psychiatric patients (Ayllon & Michael, 1959; Lindsley, 1956).

The field of behavior modification now includes the areas of the experimental analysis of behavior, which examines basic theoretical processes in learning; applied behavior analysis, which emphasizes application to socially important problems in various settings; and behavior therapy, which focuses on application in psychotherapy settings.

APPLICATION AND TECHNIQUES OF BEHAVIOR MODIFICATION

Behavior modification techniques have been applied successfully in a wide variety of settings and with many types of behaviors and populations (Sarafino, 1996). They have been used to improve general parenting skills, help parents correct children's problem behaviors, enhance instructional methods in schools, improve classroom conduct, train developmentally disabled children in self-help skills, reduce substance abuse, reduce depression and anxiety, promote health and prevent illness, and improve worker productivity and safety.

The techniques used in modifying behavior are quite varied. Operant techniques include some that deal with the consequences of behavior. In *reinforcement,* consequences strengthen the target behavior Positive reinforcement involves introducing a pleasant event after the target behavior, and negative reinforcement involves removing or reducing an aversive circumstance if the target behavior occurs. *Extinction* is a procedure whereby eliminating the rein-

forcers of a target behavior weaken that behavior. When *punishment* is used as a consequence, it suppresses the target behavior. Operant techniques also address the antecedents of the target behavior. For instance, *prompting* involves using a stimulus to remind individuals to perform a behavior they know how to do or help them perform a behavior they do not do well. Other operant methods concentrate on the behavior itself. *Shaping* improves a target behavior by requiring better and better performance to receive reinforcement, and *chaining* is used to develop complex motor behaviors by organizing simple responses into a sequence.

Respondent techniques are usually applied to reduce conditioned emotional responses, such as fear or anger. One technique is extinction, in which a conditioned response is weakened by repeatedly presenting the conditioned stimulus without the unconditioned stimulus. Another method is *systematic desensitization,* whereby a conditioned emotional response is reduced by having the person experience increasingly strong conditioned stimuli while maintaining a relaxation response. The conditioned stimuli are arranged in a hierarchy from a very weak stimulus to a very intense one.

Other behavior modification techniques include *modeling,* a vicarious process in which individuals learn a behavior by watching someone else perform it (biofeedback), and various cognitive methods, such as relaxation training, thought-stopping, and covert sensitization. *Biofeedback* is a technique that teaches people to regulate physiological functioning by presenting moment-by-moment information about the status of the body system. The form of relaxation that is most commonly applied in behavior modification is progressive muscle relaxation, which has the person alternately tense and relax separate muscle groups. Once the relaxation response is mastered, the procedure can be used by itself or as part of systematic desensitization. *Thought stopping* is a technique in which individuals interrupt distressing thoughts by saying "Stop" emphatically, either aloud or covertly. *Covert sensitization* is a method that is used to teach a person to dislike a liked event, such as drinking alcohol, by pairing it repeatedly with an aversive event in an imagined situation.

Applying behavior modification is a creative enterprise that organizes techniques into programs that are tailored to meet the needs of specific clients in particular circumstances.

REFERENCES

Ayllon, T., & Michael, J. (1959). The psychiatric nurse as a behavioral engineer. *Journal of the Experimental Analysis of Behavior, 2,* 323–334.

Dobson, K. S. (Ed.). (1988). *Handbook of cognitive-behavioral therapies.* New York: Guilford.

Jones, M. C. (1924). The elimination of children's fears. *Journal of Experimental Psychology, 7,* 382–390.

Kazdin, A. E. (1978). *History of behavior modification: Experimental foundations of contemporary research.* Baltimore: University Park Press.

Lee, C. (1992). On cognitive theories and causation in human behavior. *Journal of Behavior Therapy and Experimental Psychiatry, 23,* 257–268.

Lindsley, O. R. (1956). Operant conditioning methods applied to research in chronic schizophrenia. *Psychiatric Research Reports, 5,* 118–139.

Mahoney, M. J. (1993). Introduction to special section: Theoretical developments in the cognitive psychotherapies. *Journal of Consulting and Clinical Psychology, 61,* 187–193.

Pavlov, I. P. (1927). *Conditioned reflexes.* (G. V. Anrep, Trans.). New York: Oxford University Press.

Sarafino, E. P. (1996). *Principles of behavior change: Understanding behavior modification techniques.* New York: Wiley.

Skinner, B. F. (1938). *The behavior of organisms.* New York: Appleton-Century-Crofts.

Skinner, B. F. (1953). *Science and human behavior.* New York: Macmillan.

Sweet, A. A., & Loizeaux, A. L. (1991). Behavioral and cognitive treatment methods: A critical comparative review. *Journal of Behavior Therapy and Experimental Psychiatry, 22,* 159–185.

Thorndike, E. L. (1898). Animal intelligence: An experimental study of the associative processes in animals. *Psychological Review Monograph Supplements, 2* (No. 8).

Thorndike, E. L. (1931). *Human learning.* New York: Century.

Watson, J. B. (1913). Psychology as the behaviorist views it. *Psychological Review, 20,* 158–177.

Watson, J. B. (1930). *Behaviorism.* New York: Norton.

Watson, J. B., & Rayner, R. (1920). Conditioned emotional reactions. *Journal of Experimental Psychology, 3,* 1–14.

Williams, J. M. G., Watts, F. N., MacLeod, C., & Mathews, A. (1988). *Cognitive psychology and emotional disorders.* New York: Wiley.

Wixted, J. T., Bellack, A. S., & Hersen, M. (1990). Behavior therapy. In A. S. Bellack & M. Hersen (Eds.), *Handbook of comparative treatments for adult disorders.* New York: Wiley.

Wolpe, J. (1993). Commentary: The cognitivist oversell and comments on symposium contributions. *Journal of Behavior Therapy and Experimental Psychiatry, 24,* 141–147.

E. P. SARAFINO
The College of New Jersey

BEHAVIOR THERAPY
BEHAVIORISM
COVERT CONDITIONING
PSCHOTHERAPY
TOKEN ECONOMIES

BEHAVIOR THERAPY

A series of terms often used interchangeably in psychology with somewhat different origins and meanings are: behavior therapy, behavior modification, behavioral engineering, behavior influence, applied behavior analysis, behaviorism, cognitive behavior modification, conditioning, operant conditioning, S-R approach, social learning, vicarious learning, reinforcement, contingency management, stimulus control, and multimodal therapy.

The first known use of the term *behavior therapy* in the literature was in a 1953 status report by Lindsley, Skinner, and Solomon, referring to their application of operant conditioning research (on a plunger-pulling response) with psychotic patients. Lindsley had suggested the term to Skinner, based on the simplicity of "behavior" and the linkage, via "therapy," to other treatment procedures.

Independently of this early usage and of each other, Arnold Lazarus (1958) used the term to refer to Joseph Wolpe's application of the "reciprocal inhibition" technique to neurotic patients, and Hans Eysenck (1959) used it to refer to the application of "modern learning theory" to the behavior of neurotic patients. Eysenck based his observations on the procedures of a group of investigators then working at the Maudsley Hospital in London. These early investigators consistently defined behavior therapy in terms of "learning theory." In *The Practice of Behavior Therapy,* for example, Wolpe (1973) states that "behavior therapy, or conditioning therapy, is the use of experimentally established principles of learning for the purpose of changing unadaptive behavior. Unadaptive habits are weakened and eliminated; adaptive habits are initiated and strengthened" (p. xi).

In the first article devoted to "behavior therapy" published in the *Annual Review of Psychology,* Krasner (1971) argued that 15 streams of development within the science of psychology came together during the 1950s and 1960s to form this new approach to behavior change. These streams may be briefly summarized as follows:

1. The concept of behaviorism in experimental psychology (e.g., Kantor, 1969).

2. The research in instrumental (operant) conditioning of Thorndike (1931) and Skinner (1938).

3. The development of the technique of reciprocal inhibition as a "treatment" procedure (Wolpe, 1958).

4. The experimental studies of a group of investigators at Maudsley Hospital in London under the direction of Eysenck (Eysenck, 1964).

5. The application of conditioning and learning concepts to human behavior problems in the United States, from the 1920s through the 1950s, by such investigators as John B. Watson, Mary Cover Jones, William H. Burnham, Knight Dunlap, Edwin R. Guthrie, Harry L. Hollingworth, O. Hobart and Willie Mowrer, Gerald R. Pascal, E. Lakin Phillips, Kenneth W. Spence, and Edward Tolman.

6. Interpretations of psychoanalysis in terms of learning theory (e.g., Dollard & Miller, 1950), enhancing learning theory as a respectable base for clinical work.

7. The concept of classical conditioning derived from Ivan Pavlov as the basis for explaining and changing both normal and deviant behavior.

8. Theoretical concepts and research studies of social role learning and interactionism in social psychology and sociology

(e.g., George Homans, George H. Mead, Talcott Parsons, and Theodore Sarbin).

9. Research in developmental and child psychology emphasizing vicarious learning and modeling (e.g., Albert Bandura, Sidney W. Bijou, Donald N. Baer, Jacob L. Gewirtz, Neal E. Miller, and John Dollard).

10. Social influence studies of demand characteristics, experimenter bias, hypnosis, and placebo.

11. An environmentally based social learning model as an alternative to the "disease" model of human behavior (Bandura, 1969; Ullmann & Krasner, 1965).

12. Dissatisfaction with psychotherapy and the psychoanalytic model, as evidenced by strong critiques (e.g., Eysenck, 1952).

13. The development of the idea of the clinical psychologist within the scientist–practitioner model.

14. A movement within psychiatry away from the then orthodox focus on internal dynamics and pathology, toward concepts of human interaction and environmental influence (e.g., Adolph Meyer and Harry Stack Sullivan).

15. A utopian emphasis on the planning of social environments to elicit and maintain the best of human behavior (e.g., Skinner, 1948).

These streams of development were not independent of each other and were continually in a process of interacting, changing, and developing. The elements of the belief system common to behavior therapy adherents include a statement of concepts, so they could be tested experimentally; the notion of the "laboratory" as ranging from animal mazes through the basic human learning studies to hospitals, schools, homes, and the community; research as treatment and treatment as research; and an explicit strategy of therapy or change.

The unifying factor in behavior therapy is its derivation from experimentally established procedures and principles. The specific experimentation varies widely but has in common all the attributes of scientific investigation, including control of variables, presentation of data, replicability, and a probabilistic view of behavior.

It is useful to seek the commonalities and general principles that characterized the work of early investigators identified with "behavior therapy." Perhaps the most important of these commonalities was the role identification of the investigators themselves. Those interested in basic research saw socially important applications for their work. Those involved in applications viewed their work as derived from more basic laboratory research. They conceived of themselves as behavioral scientists investigating and applying to the basic processes of change in human behavior. Thus clinical phenomena were investigated through operationally defined and experimentally tested research studies.

The approach to "maladaptive" behavior, as to all behavior, was through a psychological rather than a medical model. Hence the behavior therapist dealt directly with behavior rather than indirectly with underlying or "disease" factors that "cause" symptoms. The psychological model may have been labeled *social learning* or *social reinforcement*—terms used to emphasize the observation

that other human beings are a source of meaningful stimuli that alter, direct, or maintain an individual's behavior. The major commonality in these investigations was "the insistence that the basis of treatment stems from learning theory, which deals with the effect of experience on behavior. . . . The basis of behavior modification is a body of experimental work dealing with the relationship between changes in the environment and changes in the subject's responses" (Ullmann & Krasner, 1965, p. 1).

In effect, the term *behavior therapy* was used to denote the modification of clinical or maladaptive behavior. Because the focus was on the behavior that was observable and definable, the concern of the therapist started with the question: "What do we wish to accomplish through our application of learning theory?" (Ullmann & Krasner, 1965, p. 2).

Bandura, in an influential and widely cited book, placed *the principles of behavior modification* (using that term as synonomous with behavior therapy) within the conceptual framework of social learning. "By requiring clear specification of treatment conditions and objective assessment of outcomes, the social learning approach . . . contains a self-corrective feature that distinguishes it from change enterprises in which interventions remain ill-defined and their psychological effects are seldom objectively evaluated" (Bandura, 1969, p. v). Bandura integrated the by then greatly expanded investigations derived from the influence of Skinner, Wolpe, and the British group, and placed particular emphasis on research on vicarious, symbolic, and self-regulatory processes.

A broader framework comes from those who view behavior therapy in the wider context of social learning or behavior influence. Ullmann and Krasner (1965) described behavior therapy as "treatment deductible from the sociopsychological model that aims to alter a person's behavior directly through the application of general psychological principles." This was contrasted with *evocative psychotherapy* which is "treatment deductible from a medical or psychoanalytic model that aims to alter a person's behavior indirectly by first altering intrapsychic organizations" (p. 37).

Kanfer and Phillips (1970) classified four types of behavior therapy, a categorization still in use: interactive therapy, requiring extended series of personal interviews using the therapists' verbal behavior to catalyze changes in the patient; instigation therapy, using suggestions and tasks to teach the patient to become his or her own therapist; replication therapy, changing behavior by replicating a critical segment of the patient's life within the therapy setting; and intervention therapy, disruption by the therapist of narrow response classes as they appear in the patient's interactions with his or her natural environment.

The behavior therapy movement has developed to the point at which there are growing numbers of excellent histories as to the broad developments and specific issues involved in terminology, theory, research, and technology (e.g., Franks, 1969; Kazdin, 1978; Krasner, 1982, 1990; Krasner & Ullmann, 1973; Rachlin, 1980; Wilson, 1978).

Related to the increase in formal and informal histories is an increase in autobiographical materials in the form of books, chapters, and recordings (Keller, 1968, 1977; Mowrer, 1976; Skinner, 1976, 1979; and many others).

Illustrations of the growth of the behavior therapy movement are the development of professional organizations, journals, annual reviews, and handbooks, for example, the Association for Advancement of Behavior Therapy (AABT) in 1966; the Association for Behavior Analysis (ABA) 1974; *Journal of Behavior Therapy and Experimental Psychiatry* (1969); *Behavior Therapy* (1969); *The Behavior Analyst* (1977); *International Handbook of Behavior Modification and Therapy* (2nd ed.), edited by Bellack, Hersen, and Kazdin (1990); *Handbook of Behavior Therapy and Psychological Science,* edited by Martin (1991); *Annual Review of Behavior Therapy: Theory and Practice* (Vol. 1), edited by Franks and Wilson (1974); and many others in all categories. The organizations, journals, and annual reviews have all continued on into the 1990s.

A later categorization of behavior therapy comes from Kazdin and Wilson (1978). They describe the different approaches in "contemporary" behavior therapy as: applied behavior analysis; neobehavioristic mediational S-R model; cognitive-behavior modification; social learning theory; and multimodal behavior therapy.

Applied behavior analysts is used to describe those investigators whose application of operant principles derives from the Skinnerian influence in a wide range of clinical and social institutions. These are the "radical behaviorists" whose basic assumption is that behavior is a function of its consequences. Intervention procedures are evaluated in terms of single-case experimental design, in which the subject serves as his or her own control.

Applied behavior analysts use environmental variables to effect behavioral changes. A wide range of intervention techniques have been developed on the basis of principles generally derived from laboratory research, such as reinforcement, stimulus control, punishment, and extinction (Kazdin, 1975). Many, if not most, of the techniques used in community applications illustrate applied behavior analysis.

A second approach labeled by Kazdin and Wilson as the *neobehavioristic mediational S-R model* applies the principles of classical conditioning derived from the earlier works of Pavlov, Hull, Guthrie, Mowrer, and Miller. Wolpe (1958, 1990) has been most responsible for integrating this material into a systematic treatment approach. Concepts of intervening variables and hypothetical constructs (e.g., Hull and Mowrer) warrant the use of a mediational terminology. This is further exemplified by the use of unobservable processes, such as the imagined representation of anxiety-eliciting stimuli in systematic desensitization.

The newest group of behavior therapists use the term *cognitive-behavior modification* and the concept of cognition to denote their approach to intervention procedures (e.g., Beck, 1976; Dryden & Scott, 1990; Ellis, 1986; Mahoney, 1974, 1977; Meichenbaum, 1977). These investigators emphasize the importance of, and focus on, cognitive processes and private events as mediators of behavior change. Key concepts of this group include assumptive models of reality, attributions of one's own behavior and that of others, thoughts, images, self-statements, self-instruction, sets, response strategies, and other constructs to account for "cognitive processes." There is considerable ongoing controversy between the "traditional" behavior therapists and the "cognitive" behavior therapists.

The *social learning approach* to behavior therapy has been conceptualized by Bandura. Behavioral response patterns are influenced by external stimulus events (primarily through classical conditioning), by external reinforcement, and most important, by cognitive mediational processes. Behavior change is effected primarily through a symbolic modeling process in which learning occurs through the observation and coding of representational processes based on these observations or even on imagined material.

Social learning theory emphasizes the reciprocal interaction between the individual's behavior and the environment. The individual is considered capable of self-directed behavior change. Bandura (1977a, 1977b, 1986) has integrated the social learning approach in the concept of "self-efficacy," which emphasizes individuals' expectations about their own behavior as they are influenced by performance-based feedback, vicarious information, and psychological changes.

Lazrus's concept (1971) of *multimodal behavior* therapy remains highly controversial. Investigators are uncertain whether it really belongs within the fold of behavior therapy or goes "beyond."

Krasner (1980) and his collaborators use the concept of *environmental design* in an approach to behavior change that links applied behavior analysis and social learning concepts with elements of environmental psychology, "open education," architecture, and social planning.

Of the many areas in which behavior therapy has affected human behavior one of the most important has been in the field of "health." In the mid-1970s and early 1980s, the term *behavioral* combined itself with the label *medicine* (Agras, 1982; Brownell, 1984). In the introduction to a special issue of the *Journal of Consulting and Clinical Psychology* devoted completely to behavioral medicine, Blanchard (1982) noted that he first became aware of the term *behavioral medicine* in the title of Birk's edited book, *Biofeedback: Behavioral Medicine* (1973).

In the early 1970s the self-identified behaviorists emerged from the laboratory, the clinic, and the mental hospital into the "natural" social environment. They were guided by earlier applications of behavioral principles in schoolrooms and hospitals and were also influenced by the national concern about and debates on the social issues of the 1960s. A new generation of behaviorists began to take on the total natural and synthetic environment as the focus for investigation and social change, so as to create a "better environment" for members of society. For example, Nietzel, Winett, MacDonald, and Davidson, in a chapter on "environmental problems" in a book appropriately entitled *Behavioral Approaches to Community Psychology* (1977), cover the topics of litter control, recycling, energy conservation, transportation, architectural design, and population change.

The behaviorists are stressing a new-old theme: the urgency of finding solutions to the environmental problems of our society and the belief that the behaviorists can contribute to those solutions. The postwar theme of a "better society" as the goal of the behaviorists thus returns, although it has really been part of the behavioral stream throughout its history.

Virtually all the early investigators in this field believed that there was a very close linkage between their research and the social and ethical applications and implications of this research (Kanfer, 1965; Krasner, 1965, 1969; Stolz, 1978; Ullmann, 1969; Ulrich, 1967). The controversy as to whether science is value-free or value-laden has been an integral part of the behavior therapy history (Krasner & Houts, 1984). The view of an integral research/societal linkage was most clearly influenced and led by Skinner's writings, particularly *Walden Two* (1948). This novel, written by a scientist whose basic research itself had not yet had very much impact on the field of psychology, raised issues pertaining to social systems, ethics, and morality; it anticipated the social and ethical issues arising from behavior therapy that became concerns in the 1970s and 1980s. Throughout, the growing concern on the part of both professionals and public has been "behavior therapy for what?" What is desirable behavior on the part of a human being in a given set of circumstances and who is to decide?

Recent developments in the history of behavior therapy have evoked the concerns and criticisms of two of the most influential of the creators of behavior therapy: Skinner and Wolpe. In an 1987 *American Psychologist* paper Skinner raised a question in the title of his article: "Whatever happened to psychology as the science of behavior?" He argued that psychology has remained "primarily a search of internal determiners" and blamed the growth of "cognitive psychology" as a major reason for this development. His disenchantment with the current scene of behavior therapy was also expressed in the title of his 1982 APA invited address: "Why are we not acting to save the world?" Wolpe's feelings were expressed in a 1986 paper titled "Misrepresentation and underemployment of behavior therapy." He reviewed the current literature in the field and concluded that despite its well-documented record of success in the treatment of many human problems "behavioral therapy is little taught in departments of psychiatry because of an inaccurate image based on misinformation" (p. 192).

In conclusion, here is a cautiously optimistic view expressed by Franks and Rosenbaum in their introduction to the book *Perspectives on Behavior Therapy in the Eighties* (1983) in which they contend,

Behavior therapy as it now stands, then, is healthy despite, or perhaps because of, its variations and complexity. But it does present certain problems for the practitioner as well as the researcher. How the behavior therapist practices, what techniques to use, the approach to problems of strategy, and even the matter of patient/therapist relationships will inevitably depend upon the explicit theoretical orientation of the clinician concerned and the implicit philosophical and cultural milieu prevailing at the time. (p. 8)

REFERENCES

Agras, W. S. (1982). Behavioral medicine in the 1980s: Nonrandom connections. *Journal of Consulting Clinical Psychology, 50,* 797–803.

Bandura, A. (1969). *Principles of behavior modification.* New York: Holt, Rinehart & Winston.

Bandura, A. (1977a). Self-efficacy: Toward a unifying theory of behavioral change. *Psychological Review, 84,* 191–215.

Bandura, A. (1977b). *Social learning theory.* Englewood Cliffs, NJ: Prentice-Hall.

Bandura, A. (1986). *Social foundations of thought and action: A social cognitive theory.* Englewood Cliffs, NJ: Prentice-Hall.

Beck, A. T. (1976). *Cognitive therapy and the emotional disorders.* New York: International Universities Press.

Bellack, A. S., Hersen, M., & Kazdin, A. E. (Eds.). (1990). *International handbook of behavior modification and behavior therapy* (2nd ed.). New York: Plenum Press.

Birk, L. (Ed.). (1973). *Biofeedback: Behavioral medicine.* New York: Grune & Stratton.

Blanchard, E. G. (1982). Behavioral medicine: Past, present and future. *Journal of Consulting and Clinical Psychology, 50,* 795–796.

Brownell, K. D. (1984). Behaviorial medicine. In G. T. Wilson, C. M. Franks, K. D. Brownell, & P. C. Kendall (Eds.), *Annual review of behavior therapy* (Vol. 9.) (pp. 180–210). New York: Guilford Press.

Dollard, J., & Miller, N. E. (1950). *Personality and psychotherapy: An analysis in terms of learning, thinking, and culture.* New York: McGraw-Hill.

Dryden, W., & Scott, M. (Eds.). (1990). *An introduction to cognitive-behaviour therapy: Theory and applications.* Loughton, UK: Gale Centre.

Ellis, A. (1986). *Handbook of rational-emotive therapy.* New York: Springer.

Eysenck, H. J. (1952). *The scientific study of personality.* London: Routledge & Kegan Paul.

Eysenck, H. J. (1959). Learning theory and behaviour therapy. *Journal of Mental Science, 195,* 61–75.

Eysenck, H. J. (1964). The nature of behaviour therapy. In H. J. Eysenck (Ed.), *Experiments in behaviour therapy.* Oxford: Pergamon.

Franks, C. M. (Ed.). (1969). *Behavior therapy.* New York: McGraw-Hill.

Franks, C. M., & Rosenbaum, M. (1983). Behavior therapy: Overview and personal reflections. In M. Rosenbaum, C. M. Franks, & Y. Jaffe (Eds.), *Perspectives on behavior therapy in the eighties* (pp. 3–16). New York: Springer.

Franks, C. M., & Wilson, G. T. (Eds.). (1973). *Annual review of behavior therapy: Theory and practice* (Vol. 1). New York: Brunner/Mazel.

Kanfer, F. H. (1965). Issues and ethics in behavior manipulation. *Psychological Reports, 16,* 187–196.

Kanfer, F. H., & Phillips, J. S. (1970). *Learning foundations of behavior therapy.* New York: Wiley.

Kantor, J. R. (1969). *The scientific evolution of psychology* (Vol. 2) Chicago: Principia Press.

Kazdin, A. (1978). Behavior therapy: Evolution and expansion. *The Counseling Psychologist, 7,* 34–37.

Kazdin, A. E. (1975). Characteristics and trends in applied behavior analysis. *Journal of Applied Behavior Analysis, 8,* 332.

Kazdin, A. E., & Wilson, G. T. (1978). *Evaluation of behavior therapy.* Cambridge, MA: Ballinger.

Keller, F. S. (1968). "Good-bye, teacher . . ." *Journal of Applied Behavior Analysis, 1,* 79–89.

Keller, F. S. (1977). *Summers and sabbaticals.* Champaign, IL: Research Press.

Krasner, L. (1965). The behavioral scientists and social responsibility: No place to hide. *Journal of Social Issues, 21,* 9–30.

Krasner, L. (1969). Behavior modification—Values and training: The perspective of a psychologist. In C. M. Franks (Ed.), *Behavior therapy: Appraisal and status.* New York: McGraw-Hill.

Krasner, L. (1971). Behavior therapy. *Annual Review of Psychology, 22,* 483–532.

Krasner, L. (1982). Behavior therapy: On roots, contexts, and growth. In G. T. Wilson & C. M. Franks (Eds.), *Contemporary behavior therapy* (pp. 11–62). New York: Guilford.

Krasner, L. (1990). History and behavior modification. In A. S. Bellack, M. S. Hersen, & A. E. Kazdin (Eds.), *International handbook of behavior modification and therapy* (2nd ed.) (pp. 3–25). New York: Plenum.

Krasner, L., & Houts, A. (1984). A study of the "value" systems of behavioral scientists. *American Psychologist, 39,* 850.

Krasner, L., & Ullmann, L. P. (1973). *Behavior influence and personality: The social matrix of human action.* New York: Holt, Rinehart & Winston.

Lazarus, A. A. (1958). New methods in psychotherapy: A case study. *South African Medical Journal 33,* 660–664.

Lazarus, A. A. (1971). *Behavior therapy and beyond.* New York: McGraw-Hill.

Lindsley, O. R., Skinner, B. F., & Solomon, H. C. (1953). *Studies in behavior therapy* (Status Report 1). Waltham, MA: Metropolitan State Hospital.

Mahoney, M. J. (1974). *Cognition and behavior modification.* Cambridge, MA: Ballinger.

Mahoney, M. J. (1977). Reflections on the cognitive-learning trend in psychotherapy. *American Psychologist, 32,* 5–13.

Martin, P. R. (Ed.). (1991). *Handbook of behavior therapy and psychological science: An integrative approach.* Elmsford, NY: Pergamon.

Meichenbaum, D. (1977). *Cognitive behavior modification: An integrative approach.* New York: Plenum.

Mowrer, O. H. (1976). The present state of behaviorism. *Education, 97,* 4–23.

Nietzel, M. T., Winett, R. A., McDonald, M. L., & Davidson, W. S. (1977). *Behavioral approaches to community psychology.* Elmsford, NY: Pergamon.

Rachlin, H. (1980). *Behaviorism in everyday life.* Englewood Cliffs, NJ: Prentice-Hall.

Skinner, B. F. (1938). *The behavior of organisms: An experimental analysis.* New York: Appleton-Century.

Skinner, B. F. (1948). *Walden two.* New York: Macmillan.

Skinner, B. F. (1976). *Particulars of my life.* New York: Knopf.

Skinner, B. F. (1979). *The shaping of a behaviorist: Part two of an autobiography.* New York: Knopf.

Skinner, B. F. (1987). Whatever happened to psychology as the science of behavior? *American Psychologist, 42,* 780–786.

Stolz, S. B. et al. (1978). *Ethical issues in behavior modification.* San Francisco: Jossey-Bass.

Thorndike, E. L. (1931). *Human learning.* New York: Appleton.

Ullmann, L. P. (1969). Behavior therapy as a social movement. In C. M. Wagman (Ed.), *Cognitive science and concepts of mind: Toward a general theory of human and artificial intelligence.* New York: Praeger. M. Franks (Ed.), *Behavior therapy: Appraisal and status* (pp. 495–523). New York, McGraw-Hill.

Ullmann, L. P., & Krasner, L. (1965). What is behavior modification? In L. P. Ullmann & L. Krasner (Eds.), *Case studies in behavior modification.* New York: Holt, Rinehart & Winston.

Ulrich, R. (1967). Behavior control and public concern. *Psychological Record,* 229–234.

Wilson, G. T. (1978). On the much discussed nature of the term "behavior therapy." *Behavior Therapy, 9,* 89–98.

Wolpe, J. (1958). *Psychotherapy by reciprocal inhibition.* Stanford, CA: Stanford University Press.

Wolpe, J. (1990). *The practice of behavior therapy* (4th ed.). Elmsford, NY: Pergamon.

L. KRASNER
Stanford University

BEHAVIOR MODIFICATION
COGNITIVE BEHAVIOR THERAPY
COVERT CONDITIONING
MULTIMODAL THERAPY
PSYCHOTHERAPY

BEHAVIORAL INHIBITION

Inhibitory conditioning is said to occur if the conditioned stimulus (CS) signals a reduction in the probability of the unconditioned stimulus (US). Introduced into learning theory from physiology, where it had been discussed for more than one hundred years, the term arises from the seminal work of Pavlov (1927) in his studies of conditioned reflexes in hungry dogs. Pavlov found that a neutral CS, such as the sound of a metronome, could acquire significance to the animal if it were reliably paired (or reinforced) with the delivery of a biologically potent US, such as meat powder. After a number of CS–US pairings, the CS would come to evoke a conditioned response (CR), such as salivation. This learning, known as excitatory conditioning, allowed the animal to prepare for the US in advance of its arrival. Inhibitory conditioning is the counterpart of excitatory conditioning. A CS signaling a reduction in the probability of the US acquires inhibitory properties, and suppresses any CR that might otherwise occur.

In *Conditioned Reflexes* (1927), Pavlov describes four experimental procedures that he believed would produce inhibition: (1)

reduced responding to an excitatory CS when it is joined by an inhibitory CS and the compound is unreinforced; (2) extinction of a previously reinforced CS; (3) a reduction in responding to an unreinforced CS, while another CS is concurrently reinforced; and (4) diminution of the amplitude of the CR during the early portion of a lengthy CS paired with a US. The first procedure is now the paradigmatic instance of what is called inhibitory conditioning.

Although Pavlov emphasized the importance of inhibitory conditioning, the idea was not well received initially. A revival of interest in inhibitory conditioning occurred in the late 1960s. Factors important in this reawakening included the incorporation of inhibitory conditioning into correlative accounts of conditioning (e.g., Rescorla, 1967). The concept of inhibition had also proven to be a powerful vehicle for understanding a wide range of behavioral phenomena. Of special interest were clinically relevant phenomena such as the persistence of phobic avoidance in the absence of further traumatic events. But the key development was Rescorla's (1969) introduction of the summation and retardation tests. These special tests could be applied to detect the presence of inhibition independently of the conditions under which it was observed. Since Pavlov's time, the idea that a CS may possess inhibitory properties has stirred a great deal of controversy. How can a CS be declared inhibitory merely on the basis of a reduction in CR probability?

To resolve such a controversy, it is necessary to rule out alternative accounts. Three general types of alternatives have been offered. One invokes competition between incompatible reactions, although the competing behavior is often never identified. The second possibility is that an inhibitory CS draws attention away from other excitatory stimuli and is merely an attentional distractor. The third is that reduced responding is not a matter of inhibition but rather of less excitation.

Rescorla (1969) noted that if inhibition involved learning that a particular CS and US were negatively correlated, an inhibitory CS should have properties opposite to those of an excitatory CS. One test designed to show the oppositional properties of an inhibitory CS was called summation. If a CS were truly inhibitory, it should reduce the probability that an excitatory CS would evoke its usual CR when the two stimuli were presented in compound for the first time. To rule out attentional distraction, the reductions obtained should be greater than those produced by a control CS that was uncorrelated with the US. Further evidence of inhibition is shown by retardation of acquisition in which the inhibitory CS is transformed into an excitatory CS. The required finding is that conditioning should proceed more slowly than transformation of a neutral CS into an excitor. These two tests, taken together, are still accepted by most in the field as firm evidence of inhibitory conditioning.

Although Rescorla's definition provides a set of operations for producing a conditioned inhibitor and for verifying its status as one, the psychological basis for the learning is not clear. On the basis of Pavlov's work, one might speculate that an inhibitory CS signals a period during which the US is absent. This can be shown to be false. If two distinctive CSs are paired on separate trials with the same US, and both CSs together are then combined with a third CS and the triplet is reinforced, it turns out that the third CS acquires

the properties of a conditioned inhibitor, even though it did not signal a period in which the US would not occur (Kremer, 1978). However, this procedure also suggests an answer. When two excitatory CSs are combined, unusually high levels of excitation are elicited—higher than can be sustained by the US. Hence, although the third CS does not predict the nonoccurrence of the US, it does predict a US that is less than predicted by the two excitatory CSs. A conditioned inhibitor, therefore, seems to result when a CS is *underreinforced* in the presence of other excitatory stimuli or contexts. This is currently the most accepted psychological account. The principles of this account are captured in a well-corroborated conditioning model proposed by Wagner and Rescorla (1972).

Acceptance of Rescorla's tests for inhibitory conditioning eventually led to the discovery that excitation and inhibition are not opposites in the sense that one prohibits the other (Williams, Overmier, & LoLordo, 1992). For example, a first CS can signal that a later CS will not be reinforced even if the first CS is itself excitatory. This special type of inhibition controlled by the first CS is called *negative occasion setting* (Holland, 1984). Additional evidence that CSs can simultaneously act in an excitatory and inhibitory manner is found in experiments on extinction. When an excitatory CS is extinguished, it does not actually lose its excitatory power as the term "extinction" suggests. Instead, the excitatory CS acquires a new inhibitory association, which joins the already present excitatory association. That extinction does not erase the original excitatory association is abundantly clear if one reminds the animal of the earlier association. For example, if acquisition takes place in a different experimental context than extinction, a return to the context of acquisition causes renewal of the original CR (Bouton, 1993). Renewal is of obvious importance for our understanding of anxiety disorders. It suggests that conditioned fears are never truly lost (extinguished) but are only inhibited. It should be apparent from this last example that inhibitory conditioning is a rich area for both application and research.

REFERENCES

Bouton, M. E. (1993). Context, time, and memory retrieval in interference paradigms in Pavlovian learning. *Psychological Bulletin, 114*, 80–99.

Holland, P. C. (1984). Differential effects of reinforcement of an inhibitory feature after serial and simultaneous feature negative discrimination training. *Journal of Experimental Psychology: Animal Behavior Processes, 10*, 461–475.

Kremer, E. F. (1978). The Rescorla-Wagner model: Losses in associative strength in compound conditioned stimuli. *Journal of Experimental Psychology: Animal Behavior Processes, 4*, 22–36.

Pavlov, I. P. (1927). *Conditioned reflexes.* Oxford, UK: Oxford University Press.

Rescorla, R. A. (1967). Pavlovian conditioning and its proper control procedures. *Psychological Review, 74*, 71–80.

Rescorla, R. A. (1969). Pavlovian conditioned inhibition. *Psychological Bulletin, 72*, 77–94.

Wagner, A. R., & Rescorla, R. A. (1972). Inhibition in Pavlovian conditioning: Application of a theory. In R. A. Boakes & M. S.

Halliday (Eds.), *Inhibition and learning.* London: Academic Press.

Williams, D. A., Overmier, J. B., & LoLordo, V. M. (1992). A reevaluation of Rescorla's early dictums about Pavlovian conditioning, *Psychological Bulletin, 111,* 275–290.

D. A. Williams
University of Winnipeg

CLASSICAL CONDITIONING
INHIBITORY CONDITIONING
REINFORCEMENT
STIMULUS GENERALIZATION

BEHAVIORAL MEDICINE

Behavioral medicine integrates behavioral with biomedical knowledge relevant to physical health and disease. It brings together the relevant parts of the behavioral sciences of psychology, epidemiology, sociology, and anthropology with the biomedical sciences of physiology, endocrinology, immunology, pharmacology, anatomy, nutrition, and the branches of medicine and public health, along with the related professions of dentistry, nursing, social work, and health education. It involves basic and applied research, the application of its knowledge and techniques to prevention, diagnosis, therapy, and rehabilitation, and the evaluation of these applications.

The Surgeon General's Report, *Healthy People* (1979), presented the following key challenge to behavioral medicine. At the beginning of this century the leading causes of death were influenza, pneumonia, diphtheria, tuberculosis, and gastrointestinal infections. Since then, the yearly death rate from these diseases per 100,000 people has been reduced from 580 to 30.* As a result of these and other advances, the burden of illness has changed to deaths and disabilities in which behavior plays an important role, as for example heart attacks, cancer, cirrhosis of the liver, and injuries from accidents, violence, or poisons. The report quoted an estimate that 50% of mortality from the 10 leading causes of death in the United States can be traced to lifestyles, and concluded that the major opportunity for further improvements in health is in the area of changing unhealthy behaviors. The foregoing conclusion and specific problems and opportunities were further documented in detail by a series of Institute of Medicine studies edited by Hamburg and others in the report *Health and Behavior.*

IMPORTANT BUT RECALCITRANT TYPES OF UNHEALTHY BEHAVIOR

Smoking is one of the important lifestyle factors harmful to health and is clearly a form of voluntary behavior. Converging lines of evidence show that cigarettes are causal factors in producing cardiovascular disease; cancer of the mouth, lungs, and esophagus; and respiratory conditions such as emphysema, bronchitis, and chronic obstructive lung disease. The effects depend on the dose, and the risk is reduced by quitting. Experiments on several different species of animals prove that cigarette smoke causes cancer in the lungs and other organs. Nicotine has been found to be a primary reinforcer for smoking, because most people report little satisfaction from smoke that lacks nicotine, even if it contains all the other constituents of tobacco smoke. When the nicotine content of smoke is reduced, most people change their smoking behavior, inhaling more, smoking each cigarette nearer to the end, and/or consuming more cigarettes in ways that tend to maintain the previous dose of nicotine. Thus low-nicotine cigarettes may be more harmful than helpful. The withdrawal symptoms and difficulties that many people encounter in trying to quit smoking indicate that nicotine can be addictive.

Sixty percent of the regular smokers in the United States have tried to quit at some time, and 30% more would like to quit. But only 1 in 10 who try to quit succeed for more than a short time. While various Quit Clinics may achieve up to 70% short-term success, the long-term success rate in this possibly different population is no better than that of those who go it alone. Smokers in quit-smoking programs, and alcoholic and heroin addicts after abstinence-oriented treatments, all show similar curves of relapse over time. In each of these three types of addiction, emotions such as anger or frustration count for many first instances of backsliding, and one slip, or at the most two, cause continued resumption of the addictive behavior. More research is needed on the bases of these addictions and how to avoid the first slip that leads to relapse. Nevertheless, reports by the Surgeon General, and a moderate amount of media campaigns to which psychologists have contributed, have effected significant reductions in smoking, especially among better-educated adult males.

The extreme difficulty of permanently breaking the smoking habit has caused investigators to concentrate on trying to understand the factors that cause children to start smoking, and on using this understanding to design programs to prevent them from starting. Such programs have actively involved young people in developing strategies to counteract pressures from peers, adults, and the media. For example, after viewing films of adolescents using various techniques to resist different inducements to smoke, students participate in role-playing situations in which they resist pressure to try a cigarette. Successful programs also emphasize the immediate consequences of smoking such as increased heart rate, messiness, and odors, rather than remote dangers such as lung cancer. After two years, follow-up studies indicate that the incidence of

---

*The progress in applications of microbiology, surgery, vaccines, antidepressants, and drugs such as insulin and antibiotics that have produced enormous reductions in human misery could not have been produced without causing some experimental animals to suffer. The success of animal activists in establishing ever more encumbering and expensive regulations restricting the use of the relatively few animals in the behavioral and other biomedical research that benefits humanity, contrasts ironically with the lack of similar regulations for the vastly larger number of animals exploited as pets confined to unnatural conditions in city apartments or suffering in hunting and fishing for no nobler cause than pure sport. If the goals of the current crop of radical animal activists had been achieved before the time of Pasteur, hundreds of millions of people would have suffered needless misery and premature death. Some of the research in behavioral medicine has been a special target of radical animal activists who would eliminate all biomedical research.

smoking among students exposed to such programs is approximately half that of controls.

Alcohol abuse contributes to cirrhosis of the liver, pancreatitis, several types of cancer, accidents, violence, fires, and lost production. In 1975 the direct and indirect costs of alcohol abuse in the United States were estimated at $45 billion. In some developing countries the problem of alcoholism is even greater than in industrialized ones; it is estimated that intoxication produces a 50% reduction in the effectiveness of the badly needed, too-small corps of educated people in key positions in these countries. Studies have shown that genetic and cultural and other psychosocial factors contribute to alcoholism, though we need to learn far more about the specific details. While a number of different treatment programs are successful for some people, the average rate of long-term success is discouragingly low, a fact that suggests emphasis on prevention. On the other hand, the amount of high-grade research devoted to alcoholism has been relatively small in relation to the social and economic importance of the problem.

Diet can also affect health. Anorexia nervosa, an extreme form of self-starvation occurring mostly in young girls, can be extremely damaging to health and causes death in a significant number of cases. Unbalanced diets deficient in proteins, vitamins, or essential elements are also harmful. A larger national problem, however, is obesity. Compared with those of average weight, men and women 20 to 30% overweight have a mortality 20 to 40% greater, and those 50 to 60% overweight have a mortality 150 to 250% greater. Obesity increases the risk of hypertension, diabetes, and heart disease, and complicates surgery; reduction in overweight can be a significant factor in treating certain cases of hypertension and diabetes.

The fact that the incidence of obesity in people born into the upper social classes is lower than in those born into the lower ones suggests that obesity is subject to control by some sort of influence in the social environment; there is also evidence for hereditary factors. Treatments as different as psychoanalysis and behavior therapy can cause some obese people to return permanently to normal weight. But, as in the case of smoking and alcoholism, relapse rates for many patients are discouragingly high. Because the goal of loss of weight can be measured objectively, the problem of obesity provides a challenging opportunity to test the effectiveness of different forms of intervention. At the level of basic research, many advances have been made in understanding parts of the mechanism of weight regulation, but an overall understanding has not yet been achieved.

Type A behavior has been defined as hard-driving, competitive, impatient, and hostile. Studies (one of them on 3,500 people) following up those with this kind of behavior have shown that they are approximately 2½ times as likely to have heart attacks as those with less evidence of such traits, who are designated as Type B. Even when the additional risk factors of smoking, obesity, and hypertension were partialed out, the Type As were still twice as likely to have heart attacks as the Type Bs. While this difference shows that some significant phenomenon must be involved, many Type As do not get heart attacks and some Type Bs do. Active areas of research involve trying to find a better classification, to investigate the pathophysiological mechanisms involved, to discover factors that may protect Type As, and to try to change Type A behavior—hopefully in ways that do not interfere with high

productivity—so as to find out whether such changes will reduce the risk of heart attacks.

Noncompliance is another problem. If everyone followed their doctor's recommendations, it would be easy to get rid of those behaviors known to be unhealthy. But in many cases, following the doctor's orders involves giving up some immediate gratification or encountering some immediate inconvenience or extra effort to achieve a greater but remote satisfaction, or to avoid a severe but remote consequence. Thus the fact that immediate outcomes are more effective than delayed ones works strongly against compliance. For example, studies have estimated that approximately one-third to one-half of patients do not take the drugs that are prescribed. Psychologists who study such problems have found that having the reason for the prescribed procedure adequately explained does help some, but often this is not enough. A book edited by Irving Janis, *Counseling on Personal Decisions,* summarizes field studies on specific types of behavior that can increase the ability of health-care professionals to influence patients. To achieve compliance and other health-restoring effects, he concludes that it is important for patients to have a relationship with the therapist that is warm and affectionate and that bolsters their self-confidence.

EFFECTS OF EMOTIONAL STRESS AND OTHER PSYCHOSOCIAL FACTORS

Epidemiological, clinical, and life-change studies have shown that conditions that loosely may be described as stressful increase the likelihood of a wide range of medically undesirable consequences. Among the many conditions studied are rapid social change, social disorganization, migration to a radically different environment, bombing raids and disasters, loss of a spouse, overstimulation, monotony, and lack of control over important aspects of work or the environment. Instead of any specific psychosomatic effect to be predicted from any specific type of stressor, typical results have been increased risks for a wide variety of disorders such as sudden cardiac death, myocardial infarction, hypertension, stroke, diabetes, gastrointestinal problems, multiple sclerosis, tuberculosis, influenza, pneumonia, headaches, and insomnia.

Often, stressful conditions that have a disastrous effect on some people may have little or no effect on others. Some of these individual differences probably are innate, but others depend on psychosocial factors such as how a threat is perceived and the coping responses performed to deal with it. Coping responses and their consequences have been studied in patients subjected to drastic stresses such as paralysis from a spinal lesion, severe burns, open-heart surgery, or cancer.

Social support accounts for the ability of certain people to resist strong stressors. Epidemiological and clinical evidence has shown that those with extensive supporting social contacts are less likely to die prematurely than those who lack both social and community ties. Unfortunately, the healing effect of unusually good social support, of gratification, and of positive emotions such as hope, love, joy, and mirth have received much less study than the negative effects of stresses such as fear and suppressed anger.

Experimental Confirmation

While the evidence in the foregoing studies is impressive, much of it is subject to alternative interpretation. For example, at least 20 studies show that people living in certain stable, relatively simple societies have blood pressure that is unusually low and does not increase with age. But when people of the same genetic stock migrate to the radically different conditions of cities, they have higher blood pressure that does increase with age. While these results show that some environmental factor must be involved—and increased stress is a probable one—other explanations such as decreased exercise or increased salt and fat in the diet are difficult to rule out.

Controlled experiments, however, can rule out alternative interpretations. For example, an experiment has shown that if mice raised in isolation are put into a colony composed of narrow passageways designed to produce repeated conflicts, they develop high blood pressure through a series of stages apparently analogous to those in human essential hypertension, and die prematurely of strokes, kidney damage, and other types of cardiovascular pathology associated with high blood pressure. When mice that have not been reared in isolation are placed in this same colony, they develop a stable social organization with far fewer conflicts and do not develop hypertension or die prematurely.

Other experimental studies show that psychological stress can produce stomach lesions, that when the strength of physical stress from electric shock is strictly controlled, purely psychological variables, such as the ability to learn the discrimination of when it is dangerous and when it is safe, or the ability to perform a simple coping response, can reduce the extensiveness of these lesions by as much as a factor of 5, while the necessity to perform a conflict-inducing coping response can produce a large increase in the extensiveness of stomach lesions.

Many other experiments have shown that conditions that may be described as stressful can reduce the effectiveness of the immune system as measured directly, and also as measured by resistance to experimental infections and implanted tumors. The latter effects are especially complex and not yet well understood; in some cases, stress can have the opposite effect of increasing the effectiveness of the immune system.

Mechanisms for the Effect of the Brain on the Body
It has long been known that the brain and its neurohumoral systems control vital functions such as breathing, heart rate, blood pressure, blood flow, temperature, digestion, intestinal motility, and fluid and electrolyte balance.

Evidence has increasingly shown the degree to which functions of lower centers of the brain can be modified by functions of higher ones. For example, when blood pressure goes up in the emotionally calm animal, stimulation of the baroreceptors in the carotid artery elicits reflexes which cause the heart to slow down and the arterioles to dilate, so that blood pressure returns to normal. But under conditions of fear or rage, impulses from higher centers inhibit these reflexes, so that blood pressure is free to continue to increase. In addition to their implications for behavioral medicine, results such as these mean that reflex pathways in the nervous system cannot be understood without taking account of the behavioral state of the organism.

It has long been known that psychological factors can have a strong effect on pain. With susceptible patients, deep hypnosis has been used as a substitute for a general anesthetic in major surgery. The readily observable behavioral and physiological responses that a very hungry dog makes to a painful stimulus can be eliminated, if that stimulus is made a signal for food. This phenomenon has been called counterconditioning. When, after lengthy exposure to deadly combat, a soldier is severely wounded and being evacuated to the rear as the first step in being sent home, he may show little signs of pain and not request morphine, in contrast with a similarly injured civilian for whom the injury means serious problems instead of merciful escape. These phenomena may be explained by pathways that have been discovered in which nerve impulses inhibit pain. These pathways involve the release of opiate-like peptides the action of which is intermediate between the brief ones of neurotransmitters and the longer-lasting ones of hormones.

Massive discharges from the sympathetic nervous system, occurring for example during fear, have been shown to cause damaged hearts to fibrillate and thus produce sudden death. A number of the different cells in the immune system have been found to have receptors for, and be affected by, a number of different hormones and peptides that are under the control of the brain and are released during emotional stresses. Studies of mechanisms such as these have increased our understanding of how the brain controls the health of the body.

Effects of Stress via Behavior
Another of the effects of stressful situations, especially when they cannot be controlled, is depression. Mild discouragement or depression can cause neglect of personal hygiene, diet, and other ways of taking good care of oneself. Severe depression can cause catastrophic neglect or positively harmful behaviors, including suicide. In addition to these behavioral factors, it is possible that there are as yet poorly understood physiologically adverse effects of depression and giving up, and conversely, positive effects of a strong will to live.

PSYCHOLOGICAL PROBLEMS PRODUCED BY INJURY, DISEASE, AND AGING
Another aspect of behavioral medicine is taking care of the psychological problems induced by injury or illness. Some patients may be stressed and depressed by their injury or their illness, and thus add to their condition adverse physiological and behavioral effects which can make their condition worse, leading to further stresses and discouragement in a continuing downward spiral. This is especially likely to occur with an injury or chronic illness, the initial effects of which are not rapidly counteracted by a natural healing process. Conversely, if patients who have slid downhill in this way can be mobilized to cope with stresses and take better care of themselves, they can be started on an upward spiral toward making the most of what is left of their potentialities. Some of the conditions creating strong emotional and behavioral problems for the patient are paralysis from high lesions of the spinal cord, crippling injuries, severe burns, diagnosis of cancer, anticipation of major surgery, a heart attack, dialysis for kidney failure, epilepsy, hemophilia, and diabetes. Such conditions, especially in childhood, can pose severe problems of anxiety, of feeling stigmatized, and

of compliance with inconvenient or aversive medical regimes. Old age can produce manifold problems of adjustment to radically changed circumstances of life. In the elderly, feelings of weakness may cause depression, or symptoms of depression may be mistaken for senility. Behavioral medicine is making increasing contributions to such problems.

DIAGNOSIS

Behavioral studies have shown that if conditions such as severe astigmatism are not corrected early enough, defects in acuity will remain even after appropriate corrective lenses are fitted. These findings created the need for an early way of refracting the eyes of infants before they could report on which lenses enabled them to see a chart best. One method has been to use the average evoked potential elicited by a black-and-white checkerboard pattern. The potentials are reduced when the image is fuzzy from being out of focus. A simpler test evolved from research showing that infants have a strong tendency to look at a pattern rather than at an unstructured part of a visual field. Similarly, averaged auditory-evoked potentials have been used as a means of testing the hearing of infants and hence detecting early types of deafness that can interfere with the all-important acquisition of human speech.

Behavioral research on sleep has led to a test that is useful in diagnosing the basis of male impotence. Spontaneous erections that occur during REM sleep indicate that the impotence is psychological rather than organic, while failure to secure such erections indicates an organic cause. An interview probing for rewards that are contingent on symptoms of back pain has been found useful in predicting which patients with histories of severe chronic pain are likely not to benefit from spinal surgery.

THERAPY AND REHABILITATION

In applications to physical medicine, an important advance has been the development of behavioral techniques useful in therapy and rehabilitation. An attractive feature of many of these techniques is that, instead of the patients having something done to them, they teach the patients to do something for themselves.

Given the effects of stressful conditions on health and the fact that illness can be a strong stressor, it is understandable that providing comfort and support has always been an important part of the art of medicine. But, with the development of effective technologies, this time-consuming function has tended to be neglected by specialists in physical medicine, creating a need for the services of specialists in behavioral medicine. For a considerable number of cases that come into a health care facility, social and emotional problems lie behind the somatic complaint. Thus it has been found that providing suitable forms of brief psychotherapy can reduce the total load on the clinic, even though the time spent on the psychotherapy is included as a part of that load.

Many different forms of psychological therapy have been found useful in medical settings. A general eclectic understanding of learning theory, cognitive processes, psychodynamics, social factors, and the specific medical details of the condition being treated, is a useful and often essential background for applying any specific behavioral technique. Three general approaches—behavior therapy, relaxation training, and biofeedback—will be described, but they by no means exhaust the possibilities.

Behavior Therapy

Behavior therapy applies a variety of experimentally derived principles of learning, and also clinically derived techniques, to the modification of behavior. A central idea in applications to physical medicine is that when sickness behavior is reinforced more strongly than health behavior, it will persist after the organic cause has disappeared. Powerful reinforcers for such behaviors are the sympathy and attention of family members and care-facility staff, relief from aversive responsibilities and duties, disability payments, and pain-killing or sleep-inducing medications. A sample of the type of sickness behaviors commonly reinforced in this way includes signs of pain such as wincing, limiting physical activity, asking for pain-killing drugs, extreme dependence, fatigue, weakness, headaches, dizziness, and various other complaints that are either without an organic cause or are disproportionate, so that the patient is not making full use of his or her potential capabilities. It is profitable to try behavior therapy when adequate organic causes are absent, strong reinforcement for sickness behavior is evident, and it is practicable to withhold these reinforcements and to provide reinforcements for health behavior first in the health-care situation and then in the patient's normal environment.

A first step in behavior therapy is a functional analysis of the patient's problems; the specific items of behavior, including verbal and emotional responses, that need to be reduced; the stimulus situations that elicit them; and the outcomes that reinforce them. For this purpose, interviews are often supplemented by having the patient record the circumstances of a critical item of behavior, such as lighting a cigarette or having a headache. In many cases it may be necessary specifically to train the patient in health behavior as a way of reaching the goals that previously were achieved by sickness behavior. For example, patients who use headaches as a way of escaping incessant and unreasonable demands may have to be given assertiveness training in standing up for their legitimate rights and being able to say "no."

Behavior therapists try to devise some quantitative measure of the undesirable behavior to be reduced and the desirable behavior to be learned. A base line of performance is secured before the therapy and treatment is designed, so that the therapist can determine whether the procedures are successful and, if not, can reanalyze the situation and try something else. An objective record of improvement also motivates the patient.

One of the successful techniques of training is to shape the desired response by rewarding any responses that bias the behavior in the desired direction and then, before administering reward, gradually requiring closer approximations to the correct responses. Similarly, a difficult task is divided into small components each of which can be mastered with reasonable time and effort. For example, at one medical center sophisticated prosthetic devices lay collecting dust in closets because the task of learning to use them was too difficult. By breaking the task up into units and rewarding success for each step, the psychologist was able to train the patients up to the level where successful use rewarded continuing performance. Behavior therapists have invented many ingenious techniques for breaking bad habits and teaching good ones.

Behavior therapy has been useful in many medical settings. One of the earliest and best-evaluated uses has been in treating pain that has no discoverable organic basis. It also has been used to teach patients to control symptoms as diverse as vomiting and enuresis, to minimize the deficit of patients whose ability to perform activities of daily living has been reduced by physical illness or injury, and to help the elderly achieve greater independence. It has helped patients to comply with medical regimens—for example, to take prescribed medications, to improve the use of atrophied muscles by conscientiously exercising, and to participate in other forms of physical therapy. Phobias of medical procedures such as having blood drawn, injections, dialysis, and dental work have been eliminated by training patients to relax and then introducing them gradually to progressively more fear-inducing steps of the procedure, in combination with demonstrations by the therapist or other calm models. But the foregoing examples do not begin to exhaust the diverse applications.

Relaxation Training

Relaxation training was developed by Jacobson in the 1930s. He taught patients to go systematically through the body from the fingers to the toes, tensing muscle groups and then relaxing them, concentrating on the sensations produced by relaxation, and then learning to become progressively more and more relaxed. To this procedure have been added concentration on relaxing imagery, monotonous repetition of a word, regular deep breathing, and passive concentration on producing sensations of warmth and heaviness. Patients are instructed to practice at home, often with the help of tape recordings, so as to canvass life situations (waiting for a red light, hearing the telephone ring) that elicit tension, and to make these become cues for eliciting rapid relaxation. For many patients, such procedures appear to reduce stress and have been found to reduce hormonal and other physiological indices of stress. But in some patients deep relaxation produces feelings of disorientation, of being out of control, or it arouses frightening images—effects that must be handled by more traditional psychotherapeutic procedures. It is possible to be completely relaxed but panic-stricken.

Conscientious practice of relaxation has been found to be helpful in treating patients with a variety of conditions such as headaches, Raynaud's disease (a painful and eventually injurious vasoconstriction of the fingers in response to stress or cold), asthma, and cardiac arrhythmias. It is a helpful component of natural childbirth.

Biofeedback

Biofeedback uses measuring instruments to give patients and their therapists better information (i.e., feedback) about what is happening in their bodies. It is useful when: (a) The medically desirable direction of change is clear; (b) a response that can produce such a change is potentially learnable; (c) the response that can produce that change has been prevented by the patient's poor or mistaken perception of what is being done; and (d) moment-to-moment measurements can provide better information. For example, some patients with neuromuscular disorders produced by strokes or injuries

may be unable to produce perceptible relaxation of a muscle that should be relaxed or contraction of one that should be contracted. But if the electrical activity of a muscle (EMG) is recorded and displayed as a dot moving on a television screen, its motion informs them of small changes in the desired direction and enables them to practice increasing these until they have made the correct response. This display also gives therapists better information than they can secure from their own sense organs and thus helps them to teach the correct response. More sophisticated displays can deal with the correct coordination and timing of the responses. After initial training, patients can use the information on the television screen to guide their own practice, so that the therapist is relieved from constant vigilance. As the patients learn to make larger correct responses during such practice, they can be taught to discriminate the sensations indicating the correctness of their responses, so that eventually they no longer need the help of the measuring instrument.

Many patients who apparently had reached the limit of improvement by traditional physical therapy methods (themselves a type of behavioral treatment) have been helped by biofeedback to make further significant improvement. When the training aided by biofeedback enables reasonably young patients or birth-injured children, who previously had been unable to do so, to feed and dress themselves or to work and support themselves, the accumulative financial savings in health-care costs over the years of expected life make the treatment enormously cost-effective.

While many patients without neuromuscular disorders can learn to relax, as effectively or more so, without having to pay attention to the instruments, their use is a definite advantage in other cases. For example, the therapist may observe that a patient who has been progressively relaxing suddenly starts to tense up. Then it may be useful to find out what thoughts or images are producing the disturbance. Other patients may simply not know whether they are relaxing or not. For example, certain patients with bruxism—an excessive grinding of the teeth that can wear them down and also produce facial pain—report a tenseness in a region of the head that is relieved when they clench their teeth. Moment-to-moment measurements of the EMG can convince them that they are inducing distracting tension in this area instead of relaxing—an important step toward teaching them to correct their bad habit. With other patients, using feedback from a variety of responses—muscular relaxation, warming of the hands, increasing skin resistance—that indicate a lowering of the arousal of their sympathetic nervous system associated with the fight-or-flight response, may be useful in teaching them to be calmer.

Most people are unable to detect moderate changes in blood pressure. Patients with high spinal lesions who were unable to tolerate upright postures during more than 2 years because their blood pressure always fell so low that they fainted, have been rewarded first for small and then for larger increases in blood pressure, until they learned to produce large increases that enabled them to tolerate upright positions and participate in a more normal range of activities. Special tests showed that they very probably had learned direct voluntary control over the visceral function of blood pressure, rather than influencing it indirectly via responses of the skeletal musculature. In certain studies a combination of training in relaxation, warming the hands, and increasing skin resistance has produced reductions in blood pressure that are reasonably large. If further research shows that they transfer from the clinic to life, they should be useful in treating a considerable number of cases of high blood pressure. But this remains to be seen.

Biofeedback has been found useful in treating a variety of other conditions such as fecal incontinence, drug-resistant epilepsy, and painfully poor circulation in the legs. Advances in miniaturized electronic technology are providing portable measuring devices that allow more extensive therapeutic training in normal life, as well as the identification of situations especially stressful to the patients as a first step toward teaching them to cope better.

As psychologists and other behavioral scientists have extended their activities from mental to other aspects of health, they have found many new problems to investigate and useful applications to develop.

REFERENCES

Hamburg, D. A., Elliott, G. R., & Parron, D. L. (1982). *Health and behavior. Frontiers of research in the biobehavioral sciences.* Washington, DC: National Academy Press.

Janis, I. L. (Ed.). (1982). *Counseling on personal decisions.* New Haven, CT: Yale University Press.

Surgeon General. (1979). *Healthy people.* Washington, DC. U.S. Government Printing Office.

SUGGESTED READING

Basmajian, J. V. (Ed.). (1979). *Biofeedback: Principles and practice for clinicians.* Baltimore: Williams & Wilkins.

Dembroski, T. M., Weiss, S. M., Shields, J. L., Haynes, S. G., & Feinleib, M. (Eds.). (1978). *Coronary-prone behavior.* New York: Springer-Verlag.

Fordyce, W. E., Fowler, R. S., Lehmann, J. F., DeLateur, B., Sand, P. L., & Trieschmann, R. B. (1973). Operant conditioning in the treatment of chronic pain. *Archives of Physical Medicine and Rehabilitation, 54,* 399–408.

Frankenhaeuser, M. (1976). The role of peripheral catecholamines in adaptation to understimulation and overstimulation. In G. Serban (Ed.), *Psychopathology of human adaptation.* New York: Plenum.

Levy, S. M. (Ed.). (1982). *Biological mediators of behavior and disease: Neoplasia.* New York: Elsevier Biomedical.

Lindeman, J. E. (1981). *Psychological and behavioral aspects of physical disability.* New York: Plenum.

Melamed, B. G., & Siegel, L. J. (1980). *Behavioral medicine. Practical applications in health care.* New York: Springer.

Miller, N. E. (1978). Biofeedback and visceral learning. *Annual Review of Psychology, 29,* 373–404.

Miller, N. E. (1983). Behavioral medicine: Symbiosis between laboratory and clinic. *Annual Review of Psychology, 34,* 1–31.

Pomerleau, O. F., & Brady, J. P. (Eds.). (1979). *Behavioral medicine: Theory and practice.* Baltimore: Williams & Wilkins.

Selye, H. (Ed.). (1980). *Selye's guide to stress research.* New York: Van Nostrand Reinhold.

Smith, D. A., Galosy, R., & Weiss, S. M. (Eds.). (1982). *Circulation, neurobiology, and behavior.* New York: Elsevier/North Holland.

Weiss, S. M., Herd, J. A., & Fox, B. H. (1981). *Perspectives on behavioral medicine.* New York: Academic Press.

N. E. MILLER
Yale University

BEHAVIOR MODIFICATION
BIOFEEDBACK
ENDORPHINS/ENKEPHALINS
HEALTH PSYCHOLOGY
HYPNOSYS AS A THERAPEUTIC TECHNIQUE
PSYCHOPHYSIOLOGY
PSYCHOSOMATIC DISORDERS

BEHAVIORAL MODELING

Much human learning takes place vicariously. Indeed, more *social learning* occurs from observing others than from personally interacting and experiencing the outcomes. Observation provides information about what may be learned (alternative behaviors, potential consequences, etc.). When it occurs under the right circumstances, the observation results in immediate personal change.

Modeling is defined as the process in which an individual (the model) illustrates behavior that can be imitated or adapted in the thoughts, attitudes, or overt behaviors of another individual (the observer). The model may be live, filmed, described in any other medium such as print—or even imagined. The term "behavioral modeling" is distinguished from mathematical modeling and so on. Otherwise, the simpler term "modeling" is used. When intended observers are used as their own models, the process is called "self-modeling." These applications are quite different procedurally and in theoretical basis (Dowrick, 1999).

APPLICATIONS

Modeling has been widely applied and evaluated in a variety of areas. Representative examples are described below under headings in six broad categories.

Professional Training

Modeling is often used in the training of human service personnel. For example, videotaped modeling has been used as the major component in training health care personnel to handle psychiatric emergencies, and as a key component in the training of job coaches. Other popular areas include the training of teachers and counselors, where it accounts for larger gains in skill acquisition than role playing or feedback.

Social Skills and Daily Living

Modeling by *invivo* demonstration is widely used as part of social skills training. Video modeling is the staple of many packaged programs and is underused in other situations. It has been the primary component in training programs ranging from teaching young, isolated children to overcome their shyness, to providing alternatives to social behavior related to drug abuse, aggression, and other illicit or unhealthy activity. For example, films of age-appropriate students coping with social pressure to smoke cigarettes have been effective in programs at junior high schools. It may be noted that the programs with greatest effectiveness are those that illustrate adaptive coping (resisting coercion without destroying friendships), not negative consequences (early, gruesome death by cancer).

Parent and Child Issues

Different forms of modeling have been widely used in programs for parent training. While there is clearly no substitute for realistic practice in acquiring skills for child care and management, it is equally clear that observing effective models is almost essential even to begin such practice. Most parent training is predicated by conduct problems of children. Therefore, children must be taught communication and self-control skills as well. Modeling proves effective for this purpose, using either peers or adults.

Preparing for Medically-Related Treatments

The need to prepare people, especially children, for potentially invasive or scary treatment procedures has been extensively served by modeling strategies. Information (e.g., what steps are involved in the procedure) is important to emotional and long-term attitudes, but modeling is more essential to immediate behavioral change.

Motor Performance

Sports and other body coordination skills are widely taught using some form of demonstration by peers, coaches, or experts. Physical therapists also use modeling as the major component in rehabilitation through therapeutic exercises. The commercial video market is replete with examples, usually by experts, for the development of individual skills (golf, tennis, aerobics, skiing, etc.). Participants in team sports often watch videotapes of opponents, not just to find weaknesses, but to seek out and imitate superior team playing strategies. Motor performance applications are situations in which special technical effects of video modeling are most useful (e.g., slow motion, still frames).

Diverse Populations

Appropriately designed modeling has obvious application to individuals with disabilities and other forms of diversity, who by definition may lack suitable models in their natural environment. Well-documented examples exist in the teaching of daily living skills, such as shopping for young adults with autism. Other types of skills for which modeling-based training has been developed include social skills, recreation, communication (e.g., sign language), vocational skills, and academics. Whereas it would seem most appropriate to use peers as models, often the models are experts or adults from the dominant culture who perform demonstrations, carefully constructed to match the individuality or developmental level of the intended trainees.

GENERAL PRINCIPLES

A modeling procedure focuses on the skill to be learned, its context, and its consequences. The modeled event is effective if the observer (a) absorbs the skill information, and later (b) has the opportunity, motive, and self-belief to use it (cf. Bandura, 1997). Much research in the last 40 years has contributed to an understanding of these components.

The characteristics of the model contribute to the effectiveness of the procedure. The use of similar models, multiple models, and coping (as opposed to "mastery") performances have been shown to assist effectiveness. These factors contribute to the ability of the viewer to absorb the skill information. They help to ensure that some of the skills demonstrated are attainable at an appropriate level of use by the observer.

When the model is similar, the observer will pay more attention and is more likely to be motivated to replicate the demonstrated behavior. Because the *activity* is important, behavioral similarity counts more than looks, social background, and so forth, and unusual models, such as clowns, can gain attention without effective absorption of the skill information. The use of multiple models can improve the magnitude of effect and its generalization to other settings.

Coping (better called struggling) models are sometimes, but not always, more effective than mastery models, who demonstrate only expert performance. High status models can also be effective. These potentially contrary results are understood by considering how the individually demonstrated skills are applicable at the observer's ability level, and how the specific model may support later motivation and sense of self-efficacy.

The characteristics of the observer and the setting also affect the efficacy of modeling. Sometimes observational learning must first be taught as a skill in itself—for example, young children with autism may not have learned to imitate others. Emphasizing a positive outcome or reward for the target behavior can enhance the effectiveness of a model. But it is important to note the frequent failure of "negative outcome modeling" to act as a deterrent. The reverse is often the case, sometimes tragically. More than once, for example, televised dramatizations of teenage suicides, intended to be a deterrent, have been followed by increases in suicides of young people.

Modeling is well documented as a powerful intervention in its own right, but it is mostly used along with other procedures, such as supplementary information and opportunity to practice. It will normally take its place early in the learning sequence: basic information, modeling, practice, feedback, and feedforward. It can also be used as a sophisticated component in advanced learning applications.

REFERENCES

Bandura, A. (1997). *Self-efficacy: The exercise of control.* New York: Freeman.

Dowrick, P. W. (1999). A review of self modeling and related interventions. *Applied and Preventive Psychology, 8,* 23–39.

P. W. DOWRICK
University of Hawaii, Manoa

BEHAVIORISM

Behaviorism was the most significant movement in experimental psychology for the first three quarters of the 20th century. It was launched by Watson in 1913, but had already begun in the work of psychologists such as Thorndike and Pavlov, and remains influential today despite an increasing chorus of criticism after about 1960.

The history of behaviorism is told elsewhere in this encyclopedia; this article is a rational reconstruction of the movement, focusing on psychological rather than philosophical behaviorism. The name "behaviorism" implies that there is only one kind of behaviorism, but this is far from the case. There have been many behaviorisms, and they can be classified and defined in several ways. Several rational reconstructions of behaviorism are therefore possible, and some are listed at the end of this article.

MENTALISM: WHAT BEHAVIORISM REJECTS

Prior to behaviorism, experimental psychologists studied the mind, which they defined as conscious experience, and their research tool was one or another form of introspection. Among themselves they disagreed over what counted as scientific introspection: Wundt insisted on a highly controlled form of self-report, whereas Titchener and the Würzburg group allowed retrospective analyses of mental processes, and William James advocated ordinary armchair introspection. They also disagreed about how to explain conscious experience. Some advocated a reductionist approach, in which experience was to be explained by reference to underlying physiological processes. Others preferred to cite unconscious mental processes as the cause of experience. Still others advocated pure phenomenology, in which experience was described but not causally explained. In any case, all were mentalists in taking mind as the subject matter of psychology to be investigated by introspection. Behaviorism rejects the mentalistic definition of psychology and therefore mentalism's research method of introspection. Behaviorists define psychology as the science of behavior, and they study behavior, eschewing attempts to enter their subjects' minds.

VARIETIES OF BEHAVIORISM

Classical Behaviorism

Historically, the most important distinction among versions of behaviorisms is that between Watson's original classical behaviorism—boldly stated but imprecisely worked out—and a variety of more sophisticated systems inspired by him, known collectively as neobehaviorism. In his paper "Psychology as the Behaviorist Views It", Watson (1913, p. 158) spelled out the fundamental faith of all behaviorists:

Psychology as the behaviorist views it is a purely objective experimental branch of natural science. Its theoretical goal is the prediction and control of behavior. Introspection forms no essential part of its methods, nor is the scientific value of its data dependent upon the readiness with which they lend themselves to interpretation in terms of consciousness. The behaviorist, in his efforts to get a unitary scheme of animal response, recognizes no dividing line between man and brute. The behavior of man, with all of its refinement and complexity, forms only a part of the behaviorist's total scheme of investigation.

Watson sets out the essential contrasts with mentalism: the subject matter of psychology is to be behavior, not mind or consciousness; its methods are objective, and introspection is to be rejected; and behavior is not to be interpreted or explained by reference to mental processes. Watson laid down the behaviorist's creed, but although he continued to expound his own version of behaviorism (see his *Behaviorism*), the movement was taken in different directions by his successors, the neobehaviorists.

Methodological Versus Metaphysical Behaviorism

Philosophically, one must distinguish two main justifications for rejecting mentalism and choosing behaviorism. A methodological behaviorist concedes that mental events and processes are real, but maintains that they cannot be studied scientifically. The data of science, says the methodological behaviorist, must be public events, such as the motions of the planets or chemical reactions that all researchers can observe. Conscious experience, however, is necessarily private; introspection may describe it (often inaccurately), but does not make it public for all to see. Therefore, to be scientific, psychology must study only overt behavior and reject introspection. However real and however fascinating, consciousness, methodologically speaking, cannot be scientific psychology's subject matter. The exploration of subjective experience is left to the arts.

The metaphysical behaviorist makes a more sweeping assertion: Just as the physical sciences have rejected demons, spirits, and gods, showing them to be myths, so the psychologist must reject mental events and mental processes as mythical. This is not to say that mental concepts such as "idea" are necessarily meaningless (though they may be), any more than the concept "Zeus" is meaningless. We can describe Zeus and account for why people believed in him, while nevertheless asserting that the word "Zeus" never referred to anything that ever existed. Similarly, says the radical behaviorist, we can describe the conditions under which people use "idea" or any other mental concept, and account for why they believe they have minds, and still assert that "idea" or "mind" and so on do not refer to anything that really exists, except perhaps certain behaviors and certain stimuli. Therefore, psychology must be behavioristic, because there is no mind to investigate: Behavior is all there is.

Watson's own position is unclear. He typically defended behaviorism on methodological grounds but, especially in his later writings, asserted the metaphysical claim, too. The various neobehaviorists came down on different sides.

Varieties of Neobehaviorism

Once begun by Watson, the movement of behaviorism—like all movements—was changed by its later adherents. The major varieties of neobehaviorism are formal behaviorism, including logical behaviorism and purposive (or cognitive) behaviorism; informal behaviorism; and radical behaviorism. All but the last are forms of methodological behaviorism; radical behaviorists uphold metaphysical behaviorism.

Formal Behaviorism.   While the behaviorist takes the subject matter of psychology to be behavior, he does not necessarily rule out talking about unobserved processes that may be used to explain observed behavior. Indeed, under the influence of logical positivism and operationalism the formal behaviorist made it his job to explain observed behavior in terms of a theory consisting of just such unobserved entities. However, these entities were not conceived as mental processes actually taking place in a person (or animal) and perhaps accessible to introspection, but were defined *behavior-theoretically;* that is, a given unobserved theoretical construct was operationally defined in terms of either manipulations performed on the animal or some aspect of its stimulus environment, or a measurable aspect of its behavior. In this way formal behaviorists hoped to gain scientific status by accepting methodological behaviorism, while aspiring to the same kind of explanatory theory found in physics or chemistry, where unobserved theoretical terms are commonplace.

The logical behaviorism of Hull and his associates was the most completely developed program of formal behaviorism. Following the lead of Newton and physics generally, Hull set out a hypothetico-deductive learning theory proposed to be valid for all mammals. The theory was stated as a set of axioms from which, via operational definition, predictions about behavior were derived that could then be put to the test.

To exemplify the method, consider the following (simplified) axiom from Hull's *Principles of Behavior* (1943):

$$_sE_R = {_sH_R} \times D$$

or in words; *reaction potential* ($_sE_R$) is equal to *habit strength* ($_sH_R$) times *drive* (D).

Reaction potential refers to the momentary tendency of an organism (e.g., a rat) to make a particular response (e.g., run down an alley). It may be measured, or operationally defined, in several ways, including latency (how long after we let him go does he get started), speed, strength (how much weight will be pull to get to the other end), or resistance to extinction of the response. The concept of habit strength claims that, when an organism learns something, it is learning something we cannot see except for when it happens to occur—namely, as a habit—and that the strength of the habit may be great or small. Operationally, habit strength was defined in terms of the number of times the organism has been reinforced for making a response such as running down an alley and finding food at the other end. Finally, drive refers to the motivational state of the organism, and may be operationally defined in terms of number of hours without food or water. In doing an experiment, we can manipulate the values of $_sH_R$ and D, predict the value of $_sE_R$, measure its actual value, and check the prediction with the result.

$_sE_R$, $_sH_R$, and D are theoretical constructs or intervening variables. We do not observe reaction potential, habit strength, or drive

directly; rather, we define them on the basis of what we do to the organism or on the basis of our measurement of its behavior. The theoretical strategy of formal behaviorism, then, is to permit theorizing about unobservable entities as long as one does not conceive of them mentalistically as something the organism has inside. Instead, theoretical constructs should be conceived of as intervening variables defined over stimuli and responses.

Tolman's purposive or cognitive behaviorism, when contrasted with Hull's logical behaviorism, shows how different two behaviorisms can be in detail while retaining allegiance to Watson's broad creed. Tolman rejected the mechanistic "muscle-twitchism" of Watson and Hull. For them, learning consisted in associating certain stimuli with specific motor responses, thus eliminating reference to purpose or cognition, which they regarded as mysterious and mentalistic. Tolman, on the other hand, conceived of behavior as ineluctably purposive (in that animals are always acting to move toward or away from some goal) and of learning as ineluctably cognitive (its purpose being not to respond to stimuli, but to learn about one's environment).

Nevertheless Tolman, like all behaviorists, shunned introspection and the study of consciousness. He constructed a theory that was much less fully elaborated than Hull's, despite the fact that it was he who introduced intervening variables to psychology. Tolman claimed that purpose, cognition, and expectancies could be defined theoretically through behavior. Tolman maintained that purposiveness was a property of behavior itself, or could be treated as an operationally defined intervening variable.

Therefore, although Hull's and Tolman's learning theories were ever at odds, both are different theoretical and research strategies carried out within methodological, formal behaviorism. Following Watson, they abandoned mentalism for the objective study of behavior and, following the logical positivists, constructed theories of learning containing unobserved but nonmental, operationally defined theoretical constructs.

It needs to be said, however, that while Hull and Tolman theoretically followed operationalist and logical positivist guidelines, each one deviated sharply from them. Hull had a secret agenda to create a learning machine, and his theory was a description of that machine dressed in postulate form. Although Tolman, too, talked like a logical positivist, he thought of cognitive maps and expectancies as real things inside organisms' heads, not just as operationally defined constructs having no reality beyond theoretical convenience. In a narrow sense, then, neither Hull nor Tolman was a practicing formal behaviorist, because their theories were about something other than behavior: for Hull, the processes inside his learning machine, and for Tolman, cognitive processes inside living organisms. Their followers were truer to the behaviorist creed.

Informal Behaviorism.   In any case, after the golden age of theory in the 1930s and 1940s, behaviorism went through further evolution. This was more true of Hull's logical behaviorism than of Tolman's purposive behaviorism, because Hull had more followers and left behind a more fully developed theory. The neo-Hullian behaviorism of the post-World War II era is sometimes called neobehaviorism, but a more descriptive phrase would be informal behaviorism or "liberalized S-R theory." The major hallmark of the movement was lessened concern with axiomatic grand theory and increased willingness to talk about the higher mental processes in human beings, if done in S-R mediational terms. Formal behaviorism thus became less rigidly formal and more flexible in handling important human phenomena such as language and problem solving.

The informal behaviorists developed one of Hull's notions into a central cognitive process. Hull had explained some learning phenomena by postulating that organisms sometimes make fractional, unobservable responses (r) which have stimulus consequences (S), so that part of a learned S-R behavior chain is covert: $S \rightarrow r \rightarrow s \rightarrow R$. Hull conceived mediating r-s pairs as covert peripheral responses (e.g., a rat might slightly salivate at even the beginning of a well-learned maze). The informal behaviorist, including Miller, Berlyne, Kendler, and Kendler, conceived r-s pairs as central brain processes that nevertheless followed the usual laws of S-R learning, and so could be incorporated into operational S-R theories of learning with no abandonment of behaviorism.

The informal behaviorists were thus able to talk about thinking, memory, problem solving, and language in S-R behavior theory terms, treating them as covert parts of learned S-R connections. In this way the range of behavior explicable in S-R terms was increased. A notable result was social learning theory, a marriage of neo-Hullian behaviorism and psychoanalysis, with some of Freud's postulated mental mechanisms being treated as covert mediating behaviors.

Historically, informal behaviorism has proven less a substantive position than a bridge from formal behaviorism to more cognitive, information-processing viewpoints. Once permitted to step inside the organism, as the central mediating response allowed behaviorists to do, there is little reason to think of the brain as an S-R device beyond mere prejudice in favor of S-R language. Once the prejudice is overcome, the attraction of the increased flexibility of information-processing language, accompanied by no loss of theoretical vigor, becomes irresistible. Whether one ceases to be a behaviorist upon giving in is an open question.

Radical Behaviorism.   The purest form of behaviorism is Skinner's radical behaviorism—essentially the same as the less-well-known interbehaviorism of Kantor. Skinner rejected methodological behaviorism for the more radical assertion of metaphysical behaviorism: Mind and mental talk are cultural myths to be exploded and discarded.

Methodological behaviorists identified the mental with the private, and made the latter off-limits for science. Skinner rejected the identification, recognizing that private events must figure in scientific psychology. A toothache is a private event, or stimulus, that powerfully controls one's behavior, leading one to take aspirin and visit the dentist. Radical behaviorism does not therefore reject an organism's private world, but studies it scientifically. However, it is a behaviorism because it rejects the mind and aims at the prediction and control of behavior.

Ordinary, everyday mentalistic talk is explained in three ways. First, some alleged mental events like toothaches are really just physical processes in the body that we have learned to label. There is no difference in principle between a public stimulus like a pinprick and a private one like toothache except that one person alone has access to the latter event. Second, some mental events, especially feelings, are just collateral by-products of environmental influence and resulting behavior, but play no role in determining behavior. So one may "feel satisfied" if praised by one's boss, but what controls the behavior is the praise itself—the reinforcer—and not the collateral feeling. Unlike private stimuli, which may exert control over behavior, collateral feelings do not, and they may be ignored by scientific psychology, however much they fascinate the phenomenologist. Finally, many mentalistic terms are simply rejected outright as myths, being regarded as verbal operants taught by our culture and entirely devoid of reference. So, for example, free will is regarded as a myth (since all behavior is determined) invented largely in the Enlightenment as a reaction to the pain control used by oppressive authoritarian governments. Such myths Skinner and his followers regard as dangerous, since they stand in the way of effective application of behavioral technology and a scientific pursuit of happiness.

In its essence though not at all in its details, radical behaviorism is the closest of all the neobehaviorisms to Watson's classical behaviorism. For the radical behaviorists, as for Watson, talk of mind is something to be exorcised by all, not just by scientists, as a relic of our superstitious, prescientific past. With positivism, radical behaviorists assert that whatever cannot be observed does not exist, and that the world and its people would be better off abandoning comforting illusions to face bravely the material facts of life. Mind, they hold, should go the way of Zeus, Odin, and the imaginary friends of our childhood.

Behaviorism Today

Radical behaviorism is the only behaviorism exerting serious influence today. It has its own division within the American Psychological Association and its own journals, *The Experimental Analysis of Behavior* and *Applied Behavior Analysis.* The other behaviorisms have passed into history, their founders' intellectual descendents having altered them beyond recognition.

But behaviorism as a philosophy and a historical movement remains an object of interest to psychologists, philosophers, and historians. An important unresolved question is the current status of behaviorism. Although formal and informal behaviorism are clearly gone, and radical behaviorism's importance is waning, it is clear that there has been no return to prebehavioristic mentalism. Cognitive psychologists still aim for the prediction and control of behavior, reject introspection for objective methods, have relatively little to say about consciousness, and study both humans and animals (as well as computers). In other words, they still could subscribe to Watson's basic creed, while rejecting his "muscle-twitchism" as did Tolman and the informal behaviorists. It is possible, then, that cognitive psychology is a new form of behaviorism with historical roots in Tolman's purposive behaviorism and Hull's fascination with learning machines. Or, if one insists that cognitive science's willingness to postulate real inner processes sets it off sharply from behaviorism, perhaps a new term is needed which encompasses both behaviorism and cognitive science, distinguishing both from traditional mentalism. Edmund Ions has coined a possible name: *behavioralism.*

SUGGESTED READING

Hull, C. L. (1943). *Principles of behavior.* New York: Appleton-Century-Crofts.

Leahey, T. H. (2000). *A history of psychology.* Upper Saddle River, NJ: Prentice-Hall.

O'Donohue, W., & Kitchener, R. (Eds.). (1998). *Handbook of behaviorism.* Orlando, FL: Academic Press.

Skinner, B. F. (1974). *About behaviorism.* New York: Knopf.

Watson, J. B. (1913). Psychology as the behaviorist views it. *Psychological Review, 20,* 158–77.

T. H. LEAHEY
Virginia Commonwealth University

FUNCTIONALISM
LOGICAL POSITIVISM
MIND/BODY PROBLEM
OPERATIONALISM
RELIGION AND PSYCHOLOGY
STRUCTURALISM

BÉKHTEREV, VLADIMIR MIKHAÏLOVÏCH (1857–1927)

Vladimir Mikhaïlovïch Békhterev received the MD from St. Petersburg in 1881, studied with Charcot and duBois-Reymond, spent a year with Wundt, and then returned to found the first two experimental psychology laboratories in Russia—in 1886 at Kazan, and in 1895 at St. Petersburg, where he spent most of his career.

He also founded the first journal anywhere with "experimental psychology" in the title—the *Review of Psychiatry, Neuropathology, and Experimental Psychology,* 1896—and, in 1907, a psychoneurological institute with special departments for mental cases, alcoholics, epileptics, and neurosurgery.

Békhterev is best known for his work on associated reflexes (usually referred to by Ivan Pavlov's term "conditioned reflexes"). Working about the same time as Pavlov, Békhterev gave breadth to the area. Whereas Pavlov dealt primarily with glandular secretions, Békhterev conditioned motor withdrawal responses: the paw of a dog, the hand of a man. He also used such reflexes as the sudden application of cold to the skin, which produces a breath-catching reflex. Békhterev conceived of the associated reflex as the basis for all behavior, and worked with speech as a complex reflex. John B. Watson drew on the 1913 German/French translation of Békhterev's book for the 1915 American Psychological Association presidential address, at a time when he had only a few translated articles of Pavlov. Despite Békhterev's more extensive methodology, Pavlov was more comprehensive and had a more stimulating conceptualization, so that today we have Pavlovian conditioning. Also, for political reasons, Lenin supported Pavlov over Békhterev.

Whereas Pavlov was primarily a neurologist who disdained psychology, Békhterev was far more behavioral and interested in pedagogical problems, including child rearing. For example, he emphasized that music should be present from the child's first days for aesthetic training to occur. He studied reaction time, the span of attention, and the point in development when the vestibular reflexes first appear (on the 15th day in humans). In neuroanatomy and medicine, labels bearing his name are still used, as for instance Békhterev's disease.

C. S. PEYSER
The University of the South

BELGIUM, PSYCHOLOGY IN

The growth of psychology in Belgium into a full-fledged discipline and recognized profession is probably more intimately linked to the historically important research work of some individuals than may be the case in other countries. The first steps were taken by Joseph Plateau (1801–1883) with his work on color perception at the University of Ghent. The psychophysical methods of the German Gustav Fechner were elaborated by Delboeuf (1831–1896) at the University of Liège. Delboeuf introduced the concept of sense distance, i.e., sensations can be arranged in a continuum so that there are observable degrees of distance between them even though they cannot be measured directly. Although Delboeuf's studies had almost no impact on further research in the field, he is considered by Boring (1950) as having played the most important role in psychophysics next to Fechner and Müller. At the Royal Observatory and the Belgian Military Academy, Adolphe Quetelet (1796–1874) introduced quantitative methods in various social sciences, including psychology. He was the first to apply the laws of normal distribution (Gaussian curve) to the measurement of moral qualities, mental disorders, and criminal behavior. This application enabled Francis Galton and other English psychologists to develop a whole range of statistical methods for studying individual differences.

The first laboratory of experimental psychology was established at the University of Ghent in 1891. However, the first research activities came from Louvain/Leuven with the establishment of a laboratory of experimental psychology at the University of Louvain/Leuven by initiatives taken by Désiré Mercier (1851–1926) when he erected the new Institute of Philosophy there. Although the first director of the laboratory was Thiéry, who had studied in Leipzig under Wilhelm Wundt, the major impetus came from his successor Albert Michotte (1881–1965). His principal work evolved from studies on voluntary choice to the perception of causality. Michotte's impact, through his extensive personal contacts and research work and the initiatives he took to improve psychology in Belgium, has been lasting and profound.

Although the research in psychology was of high quality at the different universities, it took a long time before regular programs of psychology were made available. Moreover, in almost all universities, psychology grew up within the programs in education. In Ghent, Van Biervliet (1859–1945) worked out an educational psychology based on experimental methods, and Decroly (1871–1932) in Brussels was mainly concerned with developing new educational methods. Before World War II, most psychology programs were given at the four universities (Brussels, Ghent, Louvian/Leuven, and Liège) in the Institute of Educational Sciences. Gradually, psychology emerged as a more important field that provided more career opportunities. Therefore, the institutes of educational science (belonging generally to the faculty of letters) became more and more institutes of (sometimes applied) psychology and educational science. The number of students enrolling in psychology increased rapidly from 1965 until the mid-1970s. Because of its unique position (although a social science, psychology has laboratories) and the large number of students, all the universities, except Liège, transformed the institutes into independent faculties.

There are now six main universities in Belgium. The Catholic University of Louvain/Leuven was divided in 1968 into two new universities: one Flemish speaking, which stayed in Louvain/Leuven, and the other French speaking, which moved to a new campus, Louvain-la-Neuve. They account for the largest number of students from the Flemish and French parts of the country, respectively. The same language split occurred at the Free University of Brussels, although in this case both universities remained in the same vicinity, near the center of Brussels. The two remaining universities, Ghent (Flemish speaking) and Liège (French speaking), are state universities, although all of them are supported by the state at about the same level. In response to the large increase of students at the end of the 1960s, local universities were established, except for a few programs at the University of Mons. This decentralization, however, was not carried out for psychology. A typical psychology program begins with 2 years that lead to the title of candidate in psychology. This diploma is of no immediate career value. It is followed by 3 years during which the student specializes in one or another field of psychology and must write a master's thesis to earn the diploma of licentiate. Only a few continue on to a doctoral degree. It takes 4 to 7 years to finish a doctoral dissertation, and some universities require that it be published before the degree is conferred.

With the licentiate degree, most students try to find work as industrial-organizational psychologists or as clinical or vocational psychologists. Although finding jobs is not easy, the situation is no worse in psychology than in other academic fields.

Outside the universities, some schools have created courses that prepare the student for the position of assistant psychologist. The function of an assistant psychologist consists mainly of testing subjects under the supervision of a university-trained psychologist or medical personnel.

To give a complete survey of the research activities in the six universities would take too much space. The main research activities and centers before 1970 are described by Joseph Nuttin in *Psychology in Belgium* (1961), in a special issue of *Psychologica Belgica* published in 1971, and in a chapter on psychology in Belgium to appear in the *Annual Review of Psychology* at the occasion of the 25th International Congress of Psychology to be held in Brussels. Today, all the main orientations of North American psychology can be found in Belgium. Although some emphases on particular research issues are discernible at the different universities, almost all domains of psychological research can be found in each of them. It is probably also fair to say that someone trained at one particular university is not significantly better qualified than someone from any other university. There are almost no research centers outside the universities. The story of the efforts to obtain legal recognition of psychology as a profession is long and complex. It is closely related to the existence and activities of psychological associations. The Belgian Psychological Society was created in 1947, and all of its members are university trained. The goal of the society, according to its first constitution rules, was "to sustain the exchange of views among its members, to coordinate their work, and to see to the safeguarding of their professional interests as well as their social and legal working conditions." The Belgian Psychological Society is a member society of the International Union of Psychological Science. Moreover, some members have played an active role in the international union, and two members (Michotte and Nuttin) have been presidents of the union and one is currently the deputy secretary-general, which is remarkable considering the small size of the country. The 15th International Congress of Psychology was organized in Brussels in 1957, and the next (25th) congress will again be held in Brussels in 1992, at both times organized by the Belgian Psychological Society, which also publishes the scientific journal *Psychologica Belgica.*

In the early 1960s, two other associations, whose main concern was the regulation of psychological practice, together with the Belgian Psychological Society, evolved a code of ethics and a working paper on legal prescriptions for regulating the work of the psychologist. But as a result of disagreements among the psychologists as well as difficulty in obtaining a parliamentary approval, legal recognition had not been reached by the end of the 1960s. This had a major effect on the activities of the Belgian Psychological Society, which almost collapsed. In 1974, a new executive committee of the society was elected and new negotiations began. Meanwhile, new associations had been formed that became active in the field of clinical and industrial psychology. At some universities, alumni in psychology (and educational sciences) joined together and began to hold regular meetings. It became clear that the Belgian Psychological Society no longer could act alone in the campaign to obtain legal recognition, and so the executive committee began a long series of negotiations with the other associations to form a federation of psychological associations. Almost all the associations finally agreed, and the Belgian Federation of Psychologists was formally established on December 1, 1979. To become a member of the group, one must belong to at least one of the cooperating associations, and this membership automatically makes one a member of the federation. The major short-term purpose of the federation is to obtain legal protection of the title and profession of psychologist. Within the federation, the Belgian Psychological Society now has a more clearly defined goal: to facilitate communication among research scholars from the different universities and to keep all Belgian psychologists abreast of the latest advances in psychological research and application. Both the Federation of Belgian Psychologists and the Belgian Psychological Society have organizational structures that reflect the politicolinguistic situation of

Belgium. For example, the Belgian Psychological Society has two secretaries general and two deputy secretaries, one of each for the Flemish-speaking and French-speaking parts of the country.

REFERENCES

Boring, E. G. (1957/1950/1929). *A history of experimental psychology* (2nd ed.). New York: Appleton-Century-Crofts.

Nuttin, J. (1961). *Psychology in Belgium.* Louvain, Belgium: Leuven University Press.

G. D'YDEWALLE
University of Leuven, Belgium

BELIEF IN A JUST WORLD

DEFINITION, HISTORY, AND CONCEPTUALIZATION

The belief in a just world refers to a set of beliefs and processes that convey and maintain faith in the idea that the world is a fair and just place where people get what they deserve and deserve what they get. In psychology, the concept originated largely with the writings of Melvin J. Lerner, who first described the concept in the 1960s and who continues to write on the subject today. Lerner's interest in the belief in a just world arose from his efforts to explain why highly educated university students consistently condemned victims of poverty as "lazy and no good," while denying evidence showing them to be victims of socioeconomic changes beyond their control. According to Lerner, in order to maintain psychological equanimity, engage in goal-directed behavior, and plan for the future, people need to believe that they live in a just world, a place where they can get what they deserve, at least in the long run.

The belief in a just world is a functional delusion. First, belief in a just world helps reduce existential terror (i.e., concerns that result from the combination of a random world with our ability to comprehend both its meaninglessness and our own insignificance and mortality). Specifically, without the assurance that victims of negative events or circumstances deserve their fates, or that they will ultimately be compensated, people would be overcome by the continued suffering that surrounds them and fear that similar, seemingly random fates could befall them. The belief in a just world reduces existential terror by allowing one to avoid the thought that bad things happen to good people, and more generally, the implication that the world is a valueless and unfair place.

Second, the belief in a just world encourages people to commit to long-range goals and facilitates the socially regulated behavior of day-to-day life. The belief in a just world encourages goal-directed, instrumental behavior by providing the rationalization or justification necessary for such behaviors. Specifically, without the knowledge that hard work and good deeds will be rewarded, either now or in the future, there is little reason to persist in these endeavors. Finally, the belief that violators of societal regulations will be punished not only helps us feel safe, but actually helps to keep society orderly by discouraging misconduct.

MAINTENANCE PROCESS AND REACTIONS TO INJUSTICE

In reality, the world is inundated with instances of potential injustice; such instances arouse strong emotional reactions typically ranging from empathic pain, concern, or pity, to revulsion, fear, or even panic (Lerner, 1980). In order to reduce negative emotion and maintain belief in a just world, people have developed sophisticated ways to defend themselves against reality and its potential injustices.

Lerner outlines both rational and "nonrational" strategies that function to eliminate or neutralize threats to the belief in a just world. Rational strategies include prevention or restitution when social devices (e.g., social agencies) or one's own efforts may prevent injustice, restore justice, or at least compensate the victims of injustice. Acceptance of one's limitations occurs when one recognizes that despite occurrences of injustice, there is only so much that one person can do to maintain justice. Here, the individual convinces him- or herself that if given infinite time and resources, justice could be achieved or maintained.

Nonrational strategies are more varied and include denial of and withdrawal from the unjust situation, and multiple ways of reinterpreting the event, including reinterpretation of the outcome, reinterpretation of the cause, and reinterpretation of the character of the victim. Denial involves selective perception of the environment so as to avoid evidence of injustice, whereas withdrawal involves physically removing oneself from areas of potential injustice, or as a preventive measure, structuring one's life so as to avoid situations likely to reveal injustice. Overall, reinterpretation refers to reevaluating unjust situations in such a way as to remove the injustice (i.e., so that it no longer seems to exist). Reinterpretation of the outcome involves maintaining that people benefit in the long run from their suffering, that suffering makes one a better person, or that some people are happy in their suffering. Reinterpretation of the cause, or behavioral blame, refers to attributing the victim's fate to something he or she did or failed to do. Thus, justice would have prevailed if only the victim had done the right thing. Finally, reinterpretation of the character of the victim, or characterological blame, refers to denigrating the personal qualities of the victim such that the victim becomes the type of person who deserves his or her unjust fate.

Because rational and nonrational strategies provide only temporary relief for acute regulation of injustice, Lerner contends that people also develop long-term strategies to maintain belief in a just world. Such strategies include developing a sense of ultimate justice, where, despite short-term setbacks, justice wins out in the long run, or where victims are compensated (or punished) in the afterlife. People may also compartmentalize differing cultures or subcultures into just and unjust ones. Therefore, not all cultures need be just, and injustices are acceptable (i.e., not personally threatening) as long as they occur in cultures other than our own.

RESEARCH ON BELIEF IN A JUST WORLD

Although research on many psychological constructs wanes with time, research on the belief in a just world has remained strong throughout the 1990s, and is poised to continue into the coming decades. Furthermore, and as a testimony to his original insight, Lerner's articulation of the theoretical basis of the just-world hypothesis remains little changed to this day, nearly 35 years after his initial formulation. Theoretical advancements have been mostly at the margins: What are the boundary conditions for belief in a just world? Are there multiple just and unjust worlds? What is the nature of the person who believes in a just world?

Current and past research on the belief in a just world falls into one of several categories. For example, a large number of studies have examined how people cope with injustice, in particular, their reactions to the victims of injustice. Such studies include many traditional investigations of behavioral and characterological blame, with victimized groups including victims of rape or incest, the homeless, victims of spousal abuse, members of stereotyped groups, and people with diseases such as cancer or AIDS. Another extensive area of research has examined the role of the belief in a just world in social processes other than reactions to victimization. Included here are studies examining how the belief in a just world relates to perceived risk assessment, facilitates coping with acute stress, is associated with life and marital satisfaction, contributes to practice of health behaviors, and relates to religiosity and recovery from illness. By and large, these studies have highlighted the adaptive function of believing in a just world. Smaller but no less important areas of just-world research include studies of the nature of the belief (e.g., is there a just world for self vs. for others?), development and revision of individual difference measures, studies of the relation of belief in a just world to political beliefs and ideologies, and cross-cultural studies of the belief in a just world.

REFERENCES

Lerner, M. J. (1980). *The belief in a just world: A fundamental delusion.* New York: Plenum Press.

SUGGESTED READING

Montada, L., & Lerner, M. J. (Eds.). (1998). *Responses to victimizations and belief in a just world.* New York: Plenum Press.

J. TOMAKA
University of Texas at El Paso

FUNDAMENTAL ATTRIBUTION ERROR
SOCIAL PSYCHOLOGY

BELL, SIR CHARLES (1774–1842)

Sir Charles Bell became one of the most eminent physiologists, surgeons, and lecturers of his time. He was widely known not only in Great Britain but in France as well. He held chairs as professor of physiology, anatomy, and surgery in the College of Surgeons at the University of London, and in 1835 accepted a chair as professor of surgery at the University of Edinburgh.

In his own time his discoveries in physiology were considered by many to be the most important since Harvey's discovery of the circulation of the blood. He is best known for his discovery that the sensory fibers of a mixed nerve enter the spinal cord at the dorsal root, whereas the motor fibers of the same nerve leave the cord by a ventral root. The differentiation of the sensory and motor nerve functions had been known by Galen, but subsequently this knowledge had been lost sight of by later physiologists, who held that the nerves function indiscriminately in carrying both sensory and motor impulses. Bell's work, *Idea of a New Anatomy of the Brain,* was published privately as a monograph of only 100 copies around 1811. It later appeared in a larger work.

Working quite independently in France, François Magendie came to the same discovery and published his work 7 years later. A controversy arose as to the priority of the discovery. The discovery is now known as the Bell-Magendie law.

R. W. LUNDIN
Wheaton, Illinois

THE BELL-MAGENDIE LAW

The Bell-Magendie Law refers to the discovery, in the early 1800s, that sensory nerves enter the spinal cord by way of the dorsal roots of the spinal nerves and motor nerves exit the spinal cord by way of the ventral roots. Recognition for making the discovery was attributed jointly to Charles Bell and François Magendie for their independent work. Prior to their observations, it was held that nerves were tubular conduits that served both sense and motor functions. The discovery of functionally distinct sensory and motor nerves revealed, for the first time, clear evidence of the basic structure of the nervous system. Articulation of the physiology of the spinal reflex arc and the architecture of the nervous system in terms of the specific function of sensory and motor nerves developed directly and swiftly from this first fact of neural localization.

Charles Bell (1774–1842) was an accomplished Scottish anatomist and surgeon. In 1811, he wrote a pamphlet titled *Idea of a New Anatomy of the Brain: Submitted for the Observation of his Friends.* The pamphlet was privately printed and distributed to one hundred friends and colleagues. In this pamphlet, he outlined a rationale for the study of brain function and speculated about the location of higher mental functions in the brain. He considered that the function of specific nerves are determined from their origin in different parts of the brain. During this discourse, he noted that spinal roots emerging from the vertebra fused together to form larger nerves. His opinion that these spinal nerve roots were functionally distinct was put to the test in a simple experiment. When he severed the posterior (dorsal) root the muscles of the back did not convulse, but he observed a convulsion of the muscle when he touched the anterior (ventral) root.

In 1822 François Magendie (1783–1855), a French physician and physiologist, published his findings from experiments in which he cut unilaterally some of the posterior spinal roots, anterior spinal roots, or both posterior and anterior roots. Magendie had devised a clever procedure that enabled him to cut anterior roots without damaging the posterior roots. He noted that sensation (pain) was not elicited when the severed posterior root was touched, whereas the limb moved spontaneously when the anterior root was intact. Severing the anterior roots, however, caused the limb to go flaccid, while sensitivity remained when the posterior root was intact. Magendie concluded that the anterior and posterior roots of the nerves emanating from the spinal cord have different functions, with the posterior root pertaining to sensibility, while the anterior root was linked to movement.

Following the publication of Magendie's article in 1822, a challenge to the priority of the discovery was issued by Charles Bell, and subsequently by his brothers-in-law John Shaw and Alexander Shaw in various texts and journals. Bell's unpublished 1811 pamphlet was cited as the basis for his claim to be the first to establish that sensory and motor nerves were distinct entities. This campaign to assign priority for the discovery to Bell was quite successful. Bell was lauded for the discovery by many eminent physiologists and scholars throughout the nineteenth century, such as Sherrington, who made seminal contributions to the physiology of spinal reflex arcs; Neuberger, a respected medical historian; and even by some of Magendie's contemporary French physicians such as Flourens. Scholars who have more recently examined documents relevant to the discovery, however, dispute Bell's claim for priority.

An analysis of the controversy was thoroughly documented by Cranefield (1974), in a text that includes a facsimile of Bell's annotated letter to his friends, as well as facsimiles of all of the material by Bell, John Shaw, and Magendie on which the claim for priority can be based. Clearly, there is no challenge to Magendie's experiment which is precise, elegant, and unambiguous in demonstrating, and correctly interpreting, the sensory function of the posterior spinal root and the motor function of the anterior spinal root. Several issues were raised that cast doubts on Bell's claim. That Bell's pamphlet was privately printed and circulated, rather than published in a scientific journal that was open to public scrutiny, certainly detracts from the authority of discovery. Second, during the period 1816 to 1823, Bell and John Shaw published numerous articles on the anatomy of the brain and nerves, but in none of these was there a specific statement about the functions of the spinal nerve roots. This indifference is in marked contrast to the importance of the discovery claimed by Bell after Magendie's publication in 1822. Finally, following the procedure described in *Idea of a New Anatomy of the Brain,* there was no basis for suggesting the sensory function for the anterior spinal roots.

REFERENCES

Bell, C. (1811). Idea of a new anatomy of the brain: Submitted for the observations of his friends. Reprinted in: Cranefield, P. F. (1974), *The way in and the way out: François Magendie, Charles Bell and the roots of the spinal nerves.* New York: Futura.

Cranefield, P. F. (1974). *The way in and the way out: François Magendie, Charles Bell and the roots of the spinal nerves.* New York: Futura.

Magendie, F. (1822). Expériences sur les fonctions des racines des nerfs rachidiens. *Journal de Physiologie Expérimentale et Pathologique, 2,* 276–279.

Magendie, F. (1822). Expériences sur les fonctions des racines des nerfs qui naissent de la moelle épinière. *Journal de Physiologie Expérimentale et Pathologique, 2,* 366–371.

SUGGESTED READING

Brazier, M. A. B. (1988). *A history of neurophysiology in the 19th century.* New York: Raven.

R. M. STELMACK
G. FOURIEZOS
University of Ottawa

NERVOUS SYSTEM
NEUROPHYSIOLOGY

BENDER GESTALT

The Visual Motor Gestalt Test was developed by Lauretta Bender in 1938. Both conceptually and methodologically, the test relied heavily on concepts and materials derived from the founders of Gestalt Psychology: Max Wertheimer, Kurt Koffka, and Wolfgang Köhler. The gestalt function may be defined as that function of the integrated organism whereby it responds to a given constellation of stimuli as a whole; the response itself being a constellation, or pattern, or gestalt (Bender, 1938, p. 3). For Bender and the Gestalt psychologists, pathological integrative dysfunctions would be revealed by ruptures or modifications in the final products of the visual motor reproductions of the original visual configurations as perceived by organisms.

STIMULI

Bender (1938) carefully chose nine of Wertheimer's (1923) original designs for the Visual Motor Gestalt Test on the basis of principles ("laws") put forward by the founders of Gestalt psychology.

ADMINISTRATION

The ease of administration of the Bender Test certainly contributes to its popularity among psychologists. Variations in administration procedures, however, are not uncommon even for the standard administration (Lezak, 1995). Some examiners request that patients copy all the designs on a single sheet of paper to verify the patients' capacity for organization in a limited space, while other examiners provide their patients with a stack of sheets and leave them free to copy the designs on as many sheets as they see fit. Likewise, there are variations in the extent of structure and information about the test material that the examiner offers to the patient. In addition to variations in the standard administration, there are other modalities for the administration of the test. One such variant is the stress administration, which involves the repetition of the test under the stress of time pressure, as described by Lezak (1995) and standardized by Brito and Santos (1996). McCann and Plunkett (1984, cit. in Lezak, 1995) added a 10-second recall administration, copying with the nonpreferred hand, and the "perfect" administration: the patient is allowed to copy the designs a second time, correcting any errors that might have been committed initially. Furthermore, Brito and colleagues (1998) reported an extensive normative study on two other modalities of administration: immediate and delayed recall of all designs collectively.

SCORING PROCEDURES

Bender (1938) used her test mostly as a clinical tool to observe the performance of her patients. Apparently, she never intended to score the test either qualitatively or quantitatively. Nevertheless, several scoring procedures were developed over the years to tap into the potential of the test to assess visuoperceptive cortical functions or as a projective technique for the study of personality. Standardized and validated objective scoring systems have several advantages, especially for research purposes (Koppitz, 1975).

The best-known scoring procedure seems to be the one devised by Pascal and Suttell (1951), who identified over 100 scorable characteristics of the Bender Test in adolescents and adults. Keogh and Smith (1961, cit. in Koppitz, 1975) and Koppitz (1975), among others, devised scoring systems for kindergarten and elementary school children. Furthermore, Koppitz (1975) included emotional indicators in the analysis of test protocols. Other researchers have developed scoring procedures centered on whole performance rather than on the analysis of individual reproductions. A prototypical example of such a scoring system would be the Psychopathology Scale devised by Hutt (1985, cit. in Lezak, 1995). Hutt, in addition, developed another scale which taps into the projective potential of the Bender Test: the Adience-Abience Scale.

TEST PROPERTIES

Developmental studies on the Bender Test have shown that age, social class, cultural factors, ethnic group, and academic standing impact significantly on test performance (Koppitz, 1975; Brito et al., 1998). Additionally, developmental Bender and IQ test scores are significantly correlated, but only within the average and below average IQ range (Koppitz, 1975). Furthermore, Brito and Santos (1996) reported that the number of emotional indicators, according to criteria devised by Koppitz (1975), is higher in boys and decreases significantly with age. The additional finding of Brito and Santos (1996) that the number of emotional indicators significantly correlates with factor scores derived from the Composite Teacher Rating Scale (Brito & Pinto, 1991) suggests that the number of emotional indicators is a valid measure.

BENDER TEST AND CHILD NEUROPSYCHOPATHOLOGY

Bender (1938) reported on the abnormal test productions of Francine, a schizophrenic child. Additionally, the Bender Test has been used in the identification of children with learning difficulties (Koppitz, 1975). It has also been used to determine the neuropsychological correlates of hyperactivity and inattention in school children (Brito, Pereira, & Santos-Morales, 1999), neuropsychological assessment of the effects of stimulant medication (Brown & Borden, 1989), and biofeedback training of children with Attention Deficit Hyperactivity Disorder (Hodes, 1989).

BENDER TEST AND ADULT AND GERIATRIC NEUROPSYCHOPATHOLOGY

Bender and the Gestalt psychologists considered that pathological integrative dysfunctions would be revealed by ruptures or modifications in the final products of the visual motor reproductions of the original stimuli. Bender (1938) presented a significant amount of information on the abnormal test results of patients with schizophrenia and manic depressive psychoses. Furthermore, Bender (1938) showed that patients with organic brain disease (e.g., aphasia and Korsakoff syndrome) also produced abnormal reproductions of the test stimuli. As reviewed by Lezak (1995), performance on the Bender Test has been shown to distinguish healthy control subjects from schizophrenic and Korsakoff patients, but not to distinguish between the two patient groups. The test has also been shown to detect mental status changes in Alzheimer disease and Korsakoff patients. Although Lezak (1995) considers that poor performance on the test is most likely in patients with right parietal lesions, a normal performance cannot be construed to rule out organic brain pathology.

Flexible and creative adaptations of the administration of the Bender Test will guarantee its continued use as a valuable tool in the clinical behavioral neurosciences.

REFERENCES

Bender, L. (1938). *A visual motor gestalt test and its clinical use.* New York: The American Orthopsychiatric Association. Research Monographs No. 3.

Brito, G. N. O., Alfradique, G. M. N., Pereira, C. C. S., Porto, C. M. B., & Santos, T. R. (1998). Developmental norms for eight instruments used in the neuropsychological assessment of children: Studies in Brazil. *Brazilian Journal of Medical and Biological Research, 31,* 399–412.

Brito, G. N. O., Pereira, C. C. S., & Santos-Morales, T. R. (1999). Behavioral and neuropsychological correlates of hyperactivity and inattention in Brazilian school children. *Developmental Medicine and Child Neurology, 41,* 732–739.

Brito, G. N. O., & Pinto, R. C. A. (1991). A Composite Teacher Rating Scale: Analysis in a sample of Brazilian children. *Journal of Clinical and Experimental Neuropsychology, 13,* 417–418.

Brito, G. N. O., & Santos, T. R. (1996). The Bender Gestalt Test for 5- to 15-year old Brazilian children: Norms and validity. *Brazilian Journal of Medical and Biological Research, 29,* 1513–1518.

Brown, R. T., & Borden, K. A. (1989). Neuropsychological effects of stimulant medication on children's learning and behavior. In C. R. Reynolds & E. Fletcher-Janzen (Eds.), *Handbook of clinical child neuropsychology.* New York: Plenum.

Hodes, R. L. (1989). The biofeedback treatment of neuropsychological disorders of childhood and adolescence. In C. R. Reynolds & E. Fletcher-Janzen (Eds.), *Handbook of clinical child neuropsychology.* New York: Plenum.

Koppitz, E. M. (1975). *The Bender Gestalt Test for young children. Vol. II. Research and application.* New York: Grune & Stratton.

Lezak, M. D. (1995). *Neuropsychological assessment* (3rd ed.). New York: Oxford University Press.

Pascal, G., & Suttell, B. (1951). *The Bender Gestalt Test.* New York: Grune & Stratton.

G. N. O. BRITO
Instituto Fernandes Figueira, Niteroi, Brazil

CLINICAL ASSESSMENT
GESTALT PSYCHOLOGY
PROJECTIVE TECHNIQUES

BENTON, ARTHUR (1909–   )

Arthur Benton was born in New York City in 1909 and educated at Oberlin College (BA, 1931; MA, 1933) and Columbia University (PhD, 1935). His early training was in general experimental psychology, but a research assistantship in the laboratory of Carney Landis at the New York State Psychiatric Institute (1934–1936) directed his interest toward psychopathology and clinical psychology. From 1936 to 1941 he was a clinical psychologist at the New York Hospital–Cornell University Medical Center and the New York Hospital–Westchester Division. Commissioned an officer in the U.S. Navy in 1941, he was first an instructor in the School of Aviation Medicine at the U.S. Naval Air Station in Pensacola, Florida, and subsequently senior psychologist at the U.S. Naval Hospital in San Diego, California. It was at the latter clinical facility that his evaluations of patients with penetrating brain wounds led him to focus his interest on clinical neuropsychology. After World War II he became associate professor of psychology at the University of Louisville School of Medicine (1946–1948), then professor of psychology and director of the graduate training program in clinical psychology at the University of Iowa (1948–1958). In 1958 he became professor of neurology and psychology at Iowa and established a neuropsychological laboratory in the Department of Neurology of the University of Iowa Hospitals and Clinics. He became professor emeritus in 1978, at which time the laboratory he had established in the Department of Neurology was designated the Benton Neuropsychological Laboratory.

Benton's teaching and research covered a variety of aspects of clinical neuropsychology, including hemispheric cerebral dominance, brain injury in childhood, aphasia, perceptual disabilities, and the development of neuropsychological assessment procedures. His laboratory attracted many students and became internationally known for its contributions, which included over 300 research papers and a number of monographs authored by Benton and his coworkers.

Benton served as president of the American Orthopsychiatric Association (1964–1965), president of the International Neuropsychological Society (1970–1972), and secretary general of the Research Group on Aphasia of the World Federation of Neurology (1972–1978). In his role as an educator in the rapidly developing field of clinical neuropsychology he gave courses at the Universities of Milan (1964), Amsterdam (1971), Helsinki (1974), Tokyo (1975), Melbourne (1977), Paris (1979), and Victoria, British Columbia (1980). During the spring semester of 1968 he was a visiting

scientist in the Neurosurgical Clinic of the Hôpital Saint-Anne in Paris. Similarly, he held an appointment as Directeur d'Etudes Associé at the Ecole des Haute Etudes (Paris) during the spring semester of 1979.

Among the honors Benton received during the course of his career were the Distinguished Contribution Award of the American Psychological Association (1978), the Outstanding Scientific Achievement Award of the International Neuropsychological Society (1981), the Samuel Torrey Orton Award of the International Dyslexia Society (1982), the Distinguished Service Award of the American Board of Professional Psychology (1985), the Distinguished Clinical Neuropsychologist Award of the National Academy of Neuropsychology (1989), and the Gold Medal Award of the American Psychological Foundation (1992). He received honorary degrees from Cornell College (DSc, 1978) and the University of Rome (PsyD, 1990).

In 1985, Louis Costa and Otfried Spreen edited a collection of Benton's papers under the title *Studies in Neuropsychology.* A selection of Benton's historical essays, *Exploring the History of Neuropsychology,* is scheduled for publication by Oxford University Press in August, 2000.

STAFF

BERNE, ERIC L. (1910–1970)

Eric L. Berne received the MD from McGill University in 1935. After a psychiatric residency at Yale, he was on the staff of Mount Zion Hospital in New York and undertook training at the New York Psychoanalytic Institute. After almost 10 years of affiliation with the San Francisco Psychoanalytic Institute, he parted company "on friendly terms" with the Freudian movement and 5 years later published his *Transactional Analysis in Psychotherapy* (1961). Most of his time was devoted to private clinical practice. Although intended for a professional audience, his book *Games People Play* (1964) became a best seller.

Transactional analysis (TA) is a system of group therapy that takes its name from analyzing interactions between individuals in terms of three ego states in each of us: the child (feelings and desires up to age 6), the parent (parental values and rules), and the adult (an approach to the world based upon previous observations of what occurs). Transactions that are parallel (my child to your parent and vice versa) can last almost indefinitely, but a response that is not parallel usually ends the conversation (my child to your parent, answered by your adult to my adult). Berne denied the obvious parallel with Freud's id, superego, and ego, claiming that his triad were all ego functions.

Underlying everything is the script theory (similar to Adler's lifestyle): Early in life each person fashions a life script that he carries out, usually unknowingly. One of four life positions is assumed, combinations of I'm (not) O.K. and you're (not) O.K. To play out the life script and also obtain stroking (time and attention of others), one engages in games. A maladaptive individual might play "kick me" with the payoff of depression and confirmation that "I'm not O.K., you're O.K."

Group therapy, for Berne, should be maintained on the adult-to-adult level. He was known for having one group observe a second group session and then join them to make comments and observations; the positions were then reversed. The tone of Berne's approach is perhaps best summed up in the conditions required of an alcoholic before being accepted for therapy: The alcoholic must give up alcohol and take Antabuse regularly as proof of sincerity. The elimination of alcohol consumption, however, is *not* the cure: Cure occurs only when the individual has restructured sufficiently so as to resume social drinking without the alcoholic life script.

The *Transactional Analysis Journal* founded by Berne continues, as does the International Transactional Analysis Association, which certifies expertise in TA.

C. S. PEYSER
The University of the South

BERNHEIM, HIPPOLYTE (1840–1919)

Hippolyte Bernheim was a well-known neurologist who practiced medicine in Nancy, France. He was converted to the use of hypnosis by A. A. Liébeault when the latter apparently cured a patient suffering from sciatica after Bernheim had failed (1882). Eventually, both Bernheim and Liébeault followed Braid's theory that hypnosis was really nothing more than suggestion. He published several papers on the subject in 1884. Together, Bernheim and Liébeault founded a clinic which became known as the Nancy School. This developed in opposition to a school founded in Paris by Jean M. Charcot, who held that hypnosis was really a hysterical symptom which had its foundation in a weak nervous system.

Bernheim and Liébeault were convinced that hypnosis as a therapeutic device could be used on persons who were not hysterical. However, the fact that hypnosis was successful gave Bernheim some qualms, since he realized that the will of man was not always free. This meant that when a person was put under hypnosis, new attitudes and beliefs, when suggested, could be accepted uncritically by the patient, who would behave accordingly.

The clinic at Nancy became a rival with Charcot's in Paris. Although the two schools seemed theoretically far apart, both used hypnosis primarily to treat neurotic patients.

R. W. LUNDIN
Wheaton, Illinois

BETA AND GAMMA RHYTHMS

Beta and gamma rhythms were first studied in the human electroencephalogram (EEG) recorded from the scalp. Beta rhythm is defined in general as "any EEG rhythm over 13 Hz" (IFSECN, 1974). Typically, it is a rhythm from 13 to 35 Hz. Gamma rhythm is commonly used by neuroscience researchers to designate neural activity of a frequency of about 30 to 100 Hz, including the 40-Hz oscillations. Beta and gamma EEGs are of relatively low amplitude (< 30 μV) in the EEG, and their quantification normally requires computer analysis, with careful separation of muscle artifacts (Niedermeyer, 1999).

Three main types of beta rhythms are commonly observed in the scalp EEG of human adult subjects: (a) a fronto-central beta rhythm that can be blocked by contralateral movement or tactile stimulation; (b) a diffused beta rhythm without specific reactivity; and (c) a posterior beta rhythm that can be blocked by visual activity, similar to the occipital alpha rhythm (Kuhlo, 1976). An increase in beta rhythm has been reported in neuropsychiatric patients, but Kuhlo (1976) concluded that "no adequate evidence exists at present of any relationship between normal or excessive beta activity and psychiatric disorders." A pronounced increase in beta-frequency EEG was found with drugs that enhance gamma-amino-butyric acid-A (GABA{-}A) receptor functions, including sedative doses of barbiturates and benzodiazepam (Kozelka & Pedley, 1990) and the anesthetic propofol. Neural circuitry that involves GABAergic interneurons in the cortex is likely responsible for the generation of the drug-induced beta and gamma rhythms (Leung, 1985; Jefferys, Traub, & Whittington, 1996). The regional loss of the spontaneous or barbiturate-induced beta rhythm is a sign of local cortical dysfunction.

After Jasper and Andrews (1938), the term "gamma rhythm" has not been adopted for use in clinical EEG (IFSECN, 1974). The recent interest in gamma rhythm stems from animal experiments that have shown the importance of gamma rhythm in sensory information processing in the brain (Freeman, 1991; Singer & Gray, 1995). In the visual cortex, microelectrode recordings reveal that single neurons may code for various features of a visual object, like size, form, and orientation. These features must be combined to yield an unambiguous representation of the object; this is commonly referred to as the binding problem. It is proposed that the spatially dispersed neurons that code for different features may synchronize through gamma oscillations, thus forming a dynamic assembly of neurons that represents an object uniquely (Singer & Gray, 1995). Similar processes may exist in the auditory, somatosensory, and motor cortices. In the olfactory bulb and cortex, the spatial distribution of gamma amplitudes is suggested to underlie representation of an olfactory event (Freeman, 1991). In the hippocampus, gamma waves may mediate neural processing and enhance interactions among the entorhinal cortex and various subfields of the hippocampus (Leung, 1998; Bragin et al., 1995). The pathological synchronization of hippocampal gamma waves after seizure or phencyclidine induces behavioral hyperactivity resembling psychosis in animals (Leung, 1985; Ma & Leung, in press). Gamma rhythms have also been found in subcortical structures using magnetoencephalogram or depth electrodes. In particular, structures that strongly connect with the cerebral cortex, including the thalamus (Ribary et al., 1991; Steriade, Contreras, Amzica, & Timofeev, 1996) and basal forebrain nuclei, also manifest gamma rhythms.

Multiple mechanisms underlie the high-frequency oscillations in the brain. Freeman (1991) advocated synaptic interactions among populations of excitatory and inhibitory neurons as the basis of the gamma oscillations. Llinas and others (Llinas, Grace, & Yarom, 1991) discovered that single neurons may oscillate at various frequencies, including beta and gamma frequencies. In the brain, local neural circuits generate beta or gamma activity that may readily synchronize with other local and distant circuits. Many parts of the brain respond preferentially to gamma rather than other frequencies, and thus temporal synchronization across spatially distributed domains may be achieved dynamically.

REFERENCES

Bragin, A., Jando, G., Nadasdy, Z., Hetke, J., Wise, K., & Buzsaki, G. (1995). Gamma (40–100 Hz) oscillation in the hippocampus of the behaving rat. *Journal of Neuroscience, 15,* 47–60.

Freeman, W. J. (1991). The physiology of perception. *Scientific American, 264,* 78–85.

IFSECN. (1974). A glossary of terms commonly used by clinical electroencephalographers. *Electroencephalography and Clinical Neurophysiology, 37,* 538–548.

Jasper, H. H., & Andrews, H. L. (1938). Electroencephalography: III. Normal differentiation of occipital and precentral regions in man. *Archives of Neurology & Psychiatry, 39,* 96–115.

Jefferys, J. G. R., Traub, R. D., & Whittington, M. A. (1996). Neuronal networks for induced '40 Hz' rhythms. *Trends in Neuroscience, 19,* 202–208.

Kozelka, J. W., & Pedley, T. A. (1990). Beta and mu rhythms. *Journal of Clinical Neurophysiology, 7,* 191–207.

Kuhlo, W. (1976). Typical normal rhythms and significant variants: C. The beta rhythms. In G. E. Chatrian & G. C. Lairy (Eds.), *Handbook of electroencephalography and clinical neurophysiology* (Vol. 6a, pp. 29–46). Amsterdam: Elsevier.

Leung, L. S. (1985). Spectral analysis of hippocampal EEG in the freely moving rat: Effects of centrally active drugs and relations to evoked potentials. *Electroencephalography & Clinical Neurophysiology, 60,* 65–77.

Leung, L. S. (1998). Generation of theta and gamma rhythms in the hippocampus. *Neuroscience & Biobehavior Review, 22,* 275–290.

Llinas, R. R., Grace, A. A., & Yarom, Y. (1991). In vitro neurons in mammalian cortical layer 4 exhibit intrinsic oscillatory activity in the 10- to 50-Hz frequency range. *Proceedings of the National Academy of Sciences, USA, 88,* 897–901.

Ma, J., & Leung, L. S. (1999). Medial septum mediates the increase in postictal behaviors and hippocampal gamma waves after an electrically induced seizure. *Brain Research, 833,* 51–57.

Niedermeyer, E. (1999). The normal EEG of the waking adult. In E. Niedermeyer & F. H. Lopes da Silva (Eds.), *Electroencephalography* (4th Ed.). Baltimore: Williams & Wilkins.

Ribary, U., Ioannides, A. A., Singh, K. D., Hasson, R., Bolton, J. P., Lado, F., Mogilner, A., & Llinas, R. (1991). Magnetic field tomography of coherent thalamocortical 40-Hz oscillations in humans. *Proceedings of the National Academy of Sciences, USA, 88,* 11037–11041.

Singer, W., & Gray, C. (1995). Visual feature integration and the temporal correlation hypothesis. *Annual Review of Neuroscience, 18,* 555–586.

Steriade, M., Contreras, D., Amzica, F., & Timofeev, I. (1996). Synchronization of fast (30–40 Hz) spontaneous oscillations in intrathalamic and thalamocortical networks. *Journal of Neuroscience, 16,* 2788–2808.

L. S. Leung
University of Western Ontario

BRAIN WAVES
ELECTROENCEPHALOGRAPHY

BETTELHEIM, BRUNO (1903–1990)

Bruno Bettelheim received the PhD at the University of Vienna, the same year the Nazis invaded Austria. He was not able to escape from Austria and was sent to prison and then the concentration camps of Buchenwald and Dachau. He eventually came to the United States and began a long association with the University of Chicago. For 34 years he directed the university's Orthogenic School, a residential treatment center for children with emotional problems. He was particularly concerned with autistic and psychotic children. Here he was able to gather data for his theories, which tended to be psychoanalytic in opposition to the more biological approaches to childhood psychoses. He is well known for the case of "Joey, the Mechanical Boy." In it he proposed that the boy's autistic behavior was the result of parental aloofness and neglect.

He authored many books, including *Dialogues with Mothers, Children of the Dream, The Uses of Enchantment: The Meaning and Importance of Fairy Tales,* and *Love Is Not Enough.* His last book, *Good Enough Parents,* was published in 1982. From these titles one can discern his interest in children and parenting.

R. W. Lundin
Wheaton, Illinois

BIBLIOTHERAPY

The term bibliotherapy is derived from two Greek words—*biblion* (book) and *therapeia* (healing)—and designates a form of supportive psychotherapy. Bibliotherapy has come to mean the application of all literary genres to the therapeutic process, including printed and nonprinted matter and audio-visual aids.

Bibliotherapy is sometimes practiced on a one-to-one basis. Usually, however, it is practiced on a group basis in hospitals, in clinics, and in educational, gerontological, mental health, and correctional centers. As an ancillary tool in the psychotherapeutic experience, bibliotherapy is used with individuals who are involved in counseling as an informational experience, as well as with the more serious types of disturbed personalities.

Bibliotherapy materials can be powerful and dynamic tools for tapping large vistas of unknown feelings and for clarifying unresolved conflicts. The reading matter selected may be for purposes of sharing information or of addressing emotional needs, and is particularly effective when geared to the level of feeling and understanding of the individual.

The dynamics at work in a bibliotherapy session are as varied as in any therapeutic experience. All the usual defense mechanisms operate. Thus, a therapist may find a person identifying with a character in a story or play, while at the same time the person feels guilty and anxious over a similar relationship in a real-life experience. Or a person may discover a character or circumstance in a story or play reminiscent of father, mother, siblings, authority figures, and others in the person's immediate life or the past.

In general, benefits of bibliography can be found in the relief of stress and frustration and in the gaining of insight into a person's characteristic ways of behaving, which may lead to appropriate changes and better communication.

The Hospital Division of the American Library Association established the first committee on bibliotherapy in 1939. This committee has conducted surveys, provided bibliographies, and proposed research projects. In recent years librarians have become more involved in the bibliotherapy movement because of their affinity to literature. Instrumental in this direction has been the Association of Mental Health Librarians and the Bibliotherapy Roundtable. A recent development in the library profession has been the emergence of a federal position of bibliotherapist. Appropriate therapy training and supervision, in addition to one year of experience as a bibliotherapist, are needed to qualify for this position.

The field of bibliotherapy is an expanding one, and in addressing itself to standards, ethics, and training, it appears to be gaining wider acceptance as a therapeutic tool.

SUGGESTED READING

Griffin, J. (1978). Practical considerations of bibliotherapy. In A. Lerner (Ed.), *Poetry in the therapeutic experience.* Elmsford, NY: Pergamon.

Hynes, A. M. (1981). Some observations on process in bibliopoetry therapy. *The Arts in Psychotherapy, 8,* 237–241.

Menninger, K. (1961). Reading as therapy. *American Library Association Bulletin, 55,* 316–319.

Rubin, R. J. (1978). *Using bibliotherapy: A guide to theory and practice.* Phoenix, AZ: Oryx.

A. LERNER
Los Angeles City College

BIJOU, SIDNEY W.

Sidney W. Bijou, currently Distinguished Professor Emeritus of psychology at the University of Nevada-Reno, received the BS degree in 1933 from the University of Florida, the MA degree in 1937 from Columbia University, and the PhD degree in 1941 from the University of Iowa in experimental psychology. He pursued a post-graduate year of study at Harvard with B. F. Skinner in 1961 on a senior fellowship from the U.S. National Institutes of Mental Health. His first academic position was at Indiana University, where he was assistant professor of psychology and founding director of the Clinical program. After a brief tenure, he accepted an appointment at the University of Washington, where he was professor of psychology and director of the Institute of Child Development. After 18 years, he was lured to the University of Illinois, where he was professor of psychology, director of the Child Behavior Laboratory, a member of the Institute of Research on Exceptional Children, and an associate in the Center for Advanced Study. Later, he was professor of psychology and special education at the University of Arizona.

He served as president of both the Association for Behavior Analysis and the Division of Child Psychology of the American Psychological Association. He served on 12 editorial journal boards and was the founding editor of the *Journal of Experimental Child Psychology.* Among his honors are a Fulbright fellowship to lecture and study at the National University of Venezuela and a fellowship from the Japan Society for the Promotion of Science. He received the G. Stanley Hall Award in Child Psychology, the Edgar A. Doll Award in Mental Retardation, and the Don Hake Award in Basic and Applied Psychology, from the American Psychological Association. He also received the Award for International Contribution to Behavior Analysis and the Award for Distinguished Service to Behavior Analysis from the Association for Behavior Analysis, and the Distinguished Scientific Award from the National Association for Retarded Citizens.

The main thrust of his work was on research and conceptual analysis of normal and deviantly developing children, which was generously supported by grants from the National Science Foundation, the National Institute of Mental Health of the US Public Health Service, and the US Office of Education. He and his colleagues showed through research that empirical behavior principles could be applied to the study of young children. They followed this advance with the development of an experimental method to study young children in natural settings, such as the home and the school. Their work was then applied to the treatment of children with developmental problems such as retardation, autism, and incorrigibility; and also applied to the individualized classroom teaching of young handicapped children. Research was also directed at training parents to engage in positive parenting practices. Bijou's paper on parent training and his ones on methodology for research in natural settings were noted for the outstanding number of citations they received in professional journals by the Institute of Scientific Information.

Bijou's writings included books on the behavioral principles of child development and the application of these principles to development in infancy and early childhood. These volumes were used widely in both child development and behavior analysis college courses. He also published books and articles on the education and treatment of children with behavior problems. Bijou has often been referred to as "the father of child behavior therapy."

STAFF

BILINGUALISM

We call bilingual the individual who knows two languages to the same extent and depth and is able to use them on any occasion with the same effectiveness. Besides commanding two languages, what characterizes a bilingual person is the capacity to keep the two linguistic systems separate, so as to switch easily from one to the other.

This definition refers to the perfect or ideal bilingual. What we encounter in real life are individuals who approach this definition in varying degrees. Any study on bilingualism must start by determining the degree of bilingualism of the subjects under study, the knowledge they have of each language, and the way they use them. Language tests specially designed for academic or clinical examinations and questionnaires can be used for that purpose. The subject's familiarity with each language can also be measured by laboratory techniques.

EARLY BILINGUALISM

The oldest and to a certain extent most interesting studies on bilingualism by Ronjat (1913) and Leopold (1939–1949) refer to children learning to speak in two languages at the same time. The data show that a child who grows up in a bilingual context learns to speak the two languages without difficulty, although with some slowness. These children very soon present the characteristics typical of bilinguals: they keep the two linguistic systems separate and switch from one to the other easily. Bilingual children internalize both languages very early, but normally adopt one of them as their first language.

BILINGUALISM AND MENTAL DEVELOPMENT

For many years studies on bilingualism have sought to determine whether bilingualism favors or impairs intellectual development. Saers's research (1923) with Welsh children seemed to prove that it was harmful. Similar results were inferred from studies carried out in the United States with immigrant children. But in the 1960s Peal and Lambert (1962) presented results which showed a favorable influence, and other research (Balkan, 1970) confirms them. On the whole today it is thought that in well-balanced social circumstances and with correct teaching, bilingualism is not detrimental and may even help develop certain intellectual aspects such as flexibility and creativity. However, very often these social and pedagogical conditions are not fulfilled, because bilinguals are often members of underprivileged social groups.

BILINGUALISM AND PERSONALITY

If language were only an instrument for communication, knowing and using several languages would not present any special problem. But at the same time every language expresses the culture of a given society or a specific group, and is also the way the members of the group communicate among themselves, so that speaking the language becomes a token of belonging to the group and even a proof of group loyalty.

When the group or the cultures corresponding to the languages spoken by the bilingual appear to the latter as confronted or incompatible—as is often the case with immigrants or members of a linguistic minority—then bilingualism can produce very serious personal problems. On the other hand, if the two groups or cultures represented by the two languages seem compatible or even complementary, then bilingualism can be an enriching personal experience.

REFERENCES

Balkan, L. (1970). *Les effets du bilinguisme français anglais sur les aptitudes intellectuelles.* Brussels: AIMAV.

Leopold, W. F. (1939–1949). *Speech development of a bilingual child.* Evanston, IL: Northwestern University Press.

Peal, E., & Lambert, W. E. (1962). The relation of bilingualism to intelligence. *Psychological Monographs, 76.*

Ronjat, J. (1913). *Le developement du langage chez un enfant bilingue.* Paris: Champion.

Saers, D. J. (1923). The effects of bilingualism on intelligence. *British Journal of Psychology, 14.*

SUGGESTED READING

Appel, R., & Muysken, P. (1987/1993). *Language Contact and Bilingualism.* London: Arnold.

Baker, C., & Prys Jones, S. *Encyclopedia of Bilingualism and Bilingual Education.* Multilingual Matters: Clevedon, England.

Homby, P. (Ed.). (1927). *Bilingualism: Psychological, social and educational implications.* New York: Academic Press.

Kelly, L. G. (1968). *Description and measurement of bilingualism.* Presented at International Seminar on Bilingualism. Toronto: Moncton.

Lambert, W. E., & Tucker, G. R. (1972). *Bilingual education of children. The Saint Lambert experiment.* Neubury: Rowley.

McLaughlin, B. (1978). *Second-language acquisition in childhood.* Hillsdale, NJ: Erlbaum.

Romaine, S. (1995). *Bilingualism.* Oxford: Blackwell.

M. SIGUAN
Barcelona, Spain

BINET, ALFRED (1857–1911)

Alfred Binet took his first degree in law at Paris. While in Paris he became acquainted with Jean Charcot and studied hypnosis under him. His interests changed to the natural sciences, in which he received his second degree. He became particularly interested in the higher mental processes of humans.

Binet also became interested in abnormal psychology and wrote The Alterations of Personality and Suggestability. In addition, he became concerned about the thinking processes in children and drew much of his data by studying his daughters. He gave them problems to solve and asked them to report to him the steps they went through in the process. All this led to his concept of intelligence. He became aware that considerable individual differences existed in children. He realized that there were those who were slow, whom he identified as "feebleminded." He was sharply critical of the medical profession for considering mental deficiency a disease.

He was aware of the work of Ebbinghaus on memory and forgetting, as well as the research on sensory, perceptual, and motor measures which included reaction time, sensory acuity, and the span of attention. In association with Victor Henri he discovered that there were different kinds of memory: visual memory, memory for numbers, musical memory, and memory for sentences. Together they developed tests to measure these different types of memory.

All these studies set the stage for the development of a scale of intelligence. In 1904 the Minister of Public Instruction appointed a committee to recommend what should be done about the education of subnormal children in the schools of Paris. The decision to place them in special schools depended on the development of some means of identifying them. Binet was called upon to develop a test which became the first scale for the measurement of intelligence. In 1905 this test appeared as a result of the collaboration of Binet and Theodore Simon. The scale consisted of a series of tasks of increasing difficulty. In 1908 the test was revised and the individual tasks were arranged, not only according to difficulty, but also according to the age at which the average child could complete them.

In the tryouts of the tests these tasks were arranged and rearranged so as to be appropriate for various age levels. If a test was too easy at the 8-year level, for example, then it was placed at an earlier level, say, at 7 years. The general rule was that if 60 to 90% of the children passed it at a given level, that level was appropriate for the test. Thus the mentally retarded child who performed appreciably below the norm for his or her age was considered a deviant from the norm and could be identified. In this way the mental age of a child could be computed, regardless of his or her actual chronological age. Three degrees of mental retardation were identified: idiot (lowest), imbecile, and moron.

The last of Binet's revisions appeared in 1911, the year of his death. He added new tests, and discarded old ones that he thought depended too much on school information. He also designated a given number of tests for a particular year, so mental age could be expressed in months. If there were six tests at a particular age level, each test passed could be given a score of 2 months at that level. Thus all the tests passed, regardless of the years at which they were passed, could be added together to give a total mental age.

Binet never developed the concept of the IQ or intelligence quotient. This was developed by a German psychologist, William Stern. Mental age (MA) divided by the actual chronological age (CA) times 100 equaled the IQ.

$$\frac{MA}{CA} \times 100 = IQ$$

R. W. LUNDIN
Wheaton, Illinois

BIOFEEDBACK

Biofeedback is best understood as a closed feedback loop consisting of a person or other animal, a response, a means to detect the response, and a mechanism for displaying the response to the person or animal emitting the response—the response is thus fed back. As an example, a person can be instructed to increase his or her heart rate; the heart rate is then detected by a monitor and fed back to the person. A feedback loop is thereby established, so that changes in heart rate can be displayed. Biological systems are filled with such feedback loops to maintain homeostatic integrity—for example, body temperature, blood sugar, blood pressure, and endocrine levels. Fluctuations are kept within very narrow limits by such feedback loops. However, biofeedback is probably not so reflexive in nature, but is more closely associated with the central nervous system and learning processes.

One impetus for the development of biofeedback was therapeutic: to develop voluntary control over processes considered automatic and self-regulatory in nature. Processes such as heart rate, blood pressure, and gastric secretion change along their respective dimensions, depending upon metabolic needs and emotional states. But when such processes move beyond certain limits, then the health and proper functioning of the organism become compromised. Biofeedback–self-regulation, as a therapy, can be viewed as a learning technique to help keep systems within those limits, with little of the side effects of more traditional therapies. A second stimulus for the development of biofeedback came from theorists concerned with disproving the hypothesis that responses innervated by the autonomic nervous system were not modifiable by reward learning. This position held that such responses were capable of being modified only through the conditional response techniques developed by I. P. Pavlov. A third impetus came from the interest in self-control of conscious states. The fact that electroencephalographic (EEG) rhythms might be modifiable by providing information to a person regarding EEG activity led to increased biofeedback research. Finally, the notion that self-regulation of neuromuscular function might help alleviate certain types of pain, such as headache, or lead to recovery of muscular function following trauma or disease, further helped the development of biofeedback.

Early experimental reports indicated that human subjects might be able to control voluntarily vasomotor responses, electrodermal activity, and heart rate. In the first of these studies a Russian investigator, Lisina, claimed that when individuals were allowed to view a polygraph displaying their vasomotor responses to electric shock, they learned to produce vasodilation to escape the shock (the usual response to cutaneous electrical stimulation is vasoconstriction). Following these early studies, a number of laboratories began publishing data claiming to have effected instrumental learning in a variety of autonomically mediated responses with both human and animal subjects. Besides the usual methodological objections, criticism centered on the mechanism underlying such changes. The mediation issue was formulated, which held that true instrumental learning was not occurring. Instead, it was argued, the subjects were somehow mediating the autonomic response either through cognition (i.e., thinking calming or emotional thoughts) or covert striate muscular activity (either intended, with no movement, or actual, with movement). Although this issue remains unresolved, studies on subjects paralyzed by spinal lesions and plagued by hypotension indicated that neither cognitions, small muscular twitches, nor actual movements could account entirely for the biofeedback-produced changes. Autonomic instrumental learning is also influenced by such variables as type of feedback, awareness, instructions, homeostatic restraints, and links between somatic and autonomic response systems. Biofeedback has been applied to Raynaud's disease, cardiac abnormalities, migraine headache, hypertension, functional diarrhea, and asthma, as well as to other problems with autonomic involvement such as anxiety, eczema, and sexual arousal. Although the mechanism of action for the changes produced with the biofeedback procedures remains controversial, the application of the technique continues to expand. Biofeedback is, in fact, the method of choice in treating Raynaud's disease.

The application of biofeedback techniques to problems resulting from neuromuscular dysfunction has shown considerable promise. A number of reports are available on a wide array of disorders, ranging from headache to foot drop. Neuromuscular feedback has shown impressive specificity of control by successfully training subjects to either activate or inhibit the activity of single motor muscle units. A proliferating medical use of biofeedback is in the control of fecal incontinence.

Attempts have been made to modulate EEG activity either through biofeedback or manipulation of cognitive states thought to underlie a specific range of EEG frequencies. Results of such studies showed that biofeedback for alpha (8–12 Hz) did change and was accompanied by changes in psychological state. Increased alpha was related to feelings of relaxed attention and absence of anxiety. Whether increases in alpha produced psychological changes or the psychological states produced the EEG changes became part of the mediation issue. Evidence available strongly implicates the role of eye movement in the production or suppression of alpha, and this oculomotor hypothesis is the most salient explanation regarding alpha control. Convergence, divergence, and focusing of the eyes are related to the amount of alpha produced. Correlated psychological states with such changes are at least partly due to expectations. Attempts have also been made to relate theta EEG, 4 to 7 Hz, to the psychological states of dreamlike imagery and creative insight. Finally, attempts have been made to modify sensorimotor rhythm (12–14 Hz) to reduce epileptic seizures. Results showed that modification occurred in the 6- to 8-Hz band with a concomitant reduction of seizures.

Evaluation of the biofeedback research and its clinical applications reveals problems that closely parallel other areas of scientific psychology and their applications. Theory development, mechanism of action, experimenter bias, placebo, and long-term benefits have all received some attention, and merit more.

SUGGESTED READING

Basmajian, J. V. (Ed.). (1979). *Biofeedback—Principles and practice for clinicians.* Baltimore: Williams & Wilkins.

Hatch, J. P., Fisher, J. G., & Ruch, J. D. (Eds.). (1987). *Biofeedback: Studies in clinical efficacy.* New York: Plenum.

Gatchel, R. J., & Blanchard, E. B. (Eds.). (1993). *Psychophysiological disorders: Research and clinical applications.* Washington, DC: American Psychological Association.

W. A. GREENE
Eastern Washington University

ADAPTATION
BEHAVIORAL MEDICINE
THORNDIKE'S LAWS OF LEARNING

BIOGRAPHICAL DATA

Biography—the writing of a life (from Greek *graphein* and *bio*)—is an ancient interest of humankind. The *Odyssey,* the *Bible,* and Plutarch's *Lives* are examples. In everyday life even a short conversation upon meeting a person is likely to include questions about background. Professionals working with people obtain histories of health events, employment, and education. In psychological lore, it is often said that the best predictor of future behavior is past behavior—especially under similar circumstances. Despite this widespread and age-old interest, there is no widely accepted test or inventory and little psychological research using systematic scoring of personal histories over the lifespan.

Five major sources for constructing possible scores or indexes from life history data are the following: (a) interviews with the target person and acquaintances; (b) written biographies and autobiographies; (c) personal documents and products, such as diaries or works of artists; (d) institutional records such as school reports, application blanks, and hospital charts; and (e) specially constructed biographical inventories and checklists. The first four are usually used impressionistically and informally, but they may be quantified by counting frequencies of specified events or by rating or coding the nature of the material. An interesting example is *Letters from Jenny,* Gordon Allport (1965), coded for emotions and thoughts 301 letters written when Jenny was aged 58 to 70; many letters were critical of her son's women friends.

Organizational and industrial psychologists have taken the lead in biodata research, often using standardized application blanks quantified by attaching weights to items. As early as 1894 an insurance company was using standard forms for selecting salespeople (Owens, 1976). Later, military and industrial psychologists developed forms. In World War II psychologists demonstrated good validity, with coefficients ranging from .25 to .45, in predicting success in training US pilots, navigators, and army officers (Owens, 1976). Weights of items on the biodata form, sometimes called a biographical information blank (BIB) can be validated against outcome criteria such as supervisors' ratings or productivity. Such a biodata score may have a variety of items, such as marital status, previous job tenure, health conditions, or hobbies. Care must be taken to specify the relevance of items to the position and to avoid misleading or illegal bias from background factors such as minority status, sex, age, or disability (Sharf, 1994). Dean, Rusell and Muchinsky (1999) summarize biodata selection technology and argue for its value, both practical and theoretical, for performance prediction.

A biographical inventory or checklist is a set of items representative of life history events or experiences, which aim to be pertinent to the purpose of assessment. Psychometric techniques, using such indicators as health status, social adjustment, and job success, will select and weight items. Items on inventories emphasize factual events or conditions, but some items may verge on the attitudes and subjective impressions found in personality inventories. All of these self-report procedures are subject to the usual criticisms of life history reporting, such as poor recall, intentional or unintentional distortion, and various test-taking attitudes. Especially if biographical items are transparently related to the situation of assessment, subjects may slant responses to get a job, or avoid incarceration, for instance. These problems are similar to those found on all self-report inventories. Kessler (1997) argues for intensive interviewing rather than checklists and inventories to improve accuracy of reports.

Personality inventories often include life history items, but there are few published inventories specific to biography. One is the M-B History Record, with seven scales titled, for example, "Social Misfit" and "Introversion." There is also a verbal projective technique, Bruhn's Early Memories Procedure, which, however, produces no scores. Reviews of these can be found in volumes of the Mental Measurements Yearbooks. Another more limited approach is that of checklists and inventories of life changes on which subjects indicate whether they have had various stressful events, but these refer only to the last few weeks or months and are not life histories. As lifespan theory (e.g., Baltes, Staudinger, & Lindenberger, 1999) develops, it seems likely that inventories and other procedures will be produced to measure important variables over a long period of time.

REFERENCES

Allport, G. W. (1965). *Letters from Jenny.* New York: Harcourt Brace.

Baltes, P. B., Staudinger, U. M., & Lindenberger, U. (1999). Lifespan psychology: Theory and application to intellectual functioning. *Annual Review of Psychology, 50,* 471–507.

Dean, M. A., Russell, C. J., & Muchinsky, P. M. (1999). Life experiences and performance prediction: Toward a theory of biodata. In G. R. Ferris (Ed.), *Research in human resources management* (Vol. 17, pp. 245–281). Stamford, CT: JAI Press.

Kessler, R. C. (1997). The effects of stressful life events on depression. *Annual Review of Psychology, 48,* 191–214.

Owens, W. A. (1976). Background data. In M. D. Dunnette (Ed.), *Handbook of industrial and organizational behavior.* Chicago: Rand-McNally.

Sharf, J. C. (1994). The impact of legal and equal employment opportunity issues on personal history inquiries. In G. S. Stokes, M. D. Mumford, & W. A. Owens (Eds.), *Biodata handbook: Theory, research, and use of biographical information in selection and performance prediction* (pp. 351–390). Palo Alto, CA: CPP Books.

SUGGESTED READING

Mumford, M. D., Stokes, G. S., & Owens, W. A. (1990). *Patterns of life history: The ecology of human individuality.* Hillsdale, NJ: Erlbaum.

Stokes, G. S., Mumford, M. D., & Owens, W. A. (Eds.). (1994). *Biodata handbook: Theory, research, and use of biographical information in selection and performance prediction.* Palo Alto, CA: CPP Books.

N. D. SUNDBERG
University of Oregon

BIOLOGICAL CLOCKS AND SEASONAL BEHAVIOR

The biological rhythms, detectable at all levels of organization, constitute a temporal structure in all animal species. These rhythms concern many biological parameters and have clinical implications, mainly in psychiatry.

Human rhythms are determined by endogenous pacemakers, which are located in the hypothalamus. The hypothalamus is in interrelation with other elements of complex human biology such as the endocrine system, which is affected, via the cortex cerebri, by environmental factors such as light, darkness, seasons, noise, food, and stress. Thus, endogenous pacemakers adapt their impulses to other environmental rhythms. These complex interferences regulate our biological clocks. A dysfunction of one factor may induce a rhythm modification, which alters another rhythm, and so on, and may result in a clinical disorder, often a psychiatric illness. In this manner, our living patterns are controlled by the interrelation between endogenous pacemakers and exogenous rhythms.

The biological rhythms of different functions become apparent at different times after the birth. In the infant, the development of rhythmicity must represent a combination of the genetic potential of the maturation process in the brain, and of the varying influences of environment. The alternation of light and darkness is perhaps the most obvious of external rhythms; but similar alternations of noise and silence and the attention that the infant receives from adults may also be of importance. In the adult, the biological rhythms are represented by the periodic regular cyclic variations of the biological processes, describing a sinusoidal function with individual characteristics of periodicity and amplitude.

The human rhythms are represented mainly by circadian and circannual rhythms, characterized, respectively, by a period of 21 to 27 hours and a longer period of more than 27 hours, such as a month or season. The human circadian system is composed of at least two oscillators, which are self-sustained and coupled to each other. One of these oscillators is strong and controls body temperature, REM-sleep propensity, and cortisol secretion; the other is weak and controls the sleep-wake cycle and sleep related neuroendocrine activity. These oscillator systems may be affected by many factors such as organic diseases, drugs, and environmental factors, which may lead to psychological disorders.

Studies of seasonal patterns of incidence of psychiatric disorders have highlighted the role of seasonally-regulated environmental factors on internal biological processes. Since ancient times the relationship between seasons and mood has been noted, and numerous investigations have indicated a seasonal variation in the incidence of affective illness.

Depression has been described as most common in spring and autumn, and the influence of climatological factors (mainly photoperiod) on seasonal affective disorders (SADs) have been shown. One study reported cases of SAD with summer depression and winter hypomania, and Lemoine described summer SAD (or SAD reverse) in which the temperature factor was more implicated than the daylight factor. One biological explanation has been a seasonal variation in human brain serotonin concentrations, which has been implicated in the biochemistry of affective disorders.

But if seasonal rhythms influence depressive illness, a dysregulation of circadian rhythms was found as well. There is evidence that the sleep and neuroendocrine dysfunctions observed in depressive patients are correlated with a phase advance of the circadian strong oscillator with respect to the weak oscillator. Clinical studies suggest that antidepressants can slow or delay circadian rhythms. Other therapies modifying biological rhythms may improve depressive mood. Sleep deprivation, for example, has been found to lead to rapid improvement of depressive symptomatology, and reports have shown that artificial lengthening of the photoperiod (phototherapy) may have therapeutic effects in depressive illness. The biological parameter implicated in the mechanism of action of this therapy is melatonin, for which rhythm appears to be an endocrine code of the environmental light-dark cycle conveying photic information that is used by an organism for both circadian and seasonal temporal organization.

Some authors have suggested a relationship between the season of one's birth and the occurrence of affective disorders. Season of birth/conception has also been examined as a possible factor in the depression of women who have given birth. However, although a significant seasonal variation in the occurrence of postnatal depression has been found with the largest peak occurring in autumn, there are discrepancies in the data concerning the influence of the season of conception on the frequency of postpartum mental illness.

The seasonal variation in suicides has been studied in several countries. Suicides were found to be most frequent in spring and summer in Finland, and in May and September in France. Seasonal variations of other psychiatric illnesses have been less studied, although a possible link between season of birth and schizophrenia (winter and spring peaks) has been described. Biological reasons may exist, as dopamine has been implicated in the biochemistry of schizophrenia, and there is a seasonal variation in human brain dopamine concentrations.

The number of hospitalizations for alcoholism seems to peak in the spring, and there seem to be peaks in spring and summer births among alcoholics.

Human performance efficiency also has circadian rhythms in healthy individuals. One study determined that a simple manual dexterity task is almost entirely under the control of the temperature rhythm oscillator, whereas a more complex cognitive task demonstrates a periodicity that appears to be influenced by those oscillators controlling temperature and the sleep/wake cycle.

Even for human sexuality seasonal variations exists, as they do in other mammals, with a peak in autumn, probably linked to the seasonal variation of testosterone activity.

A better knowledge of all these rhythm interferences and their clinical implications brings to mind the possibility that by modify-ing these influences we may be able to alleviate the patient's symptoms. New approaches to the treatment of all these disorders involve direct manipulation of the biological rhythms.

SUGGESTED READING

Ballard, C. G., & Mohan, R. N. C. (1993). Seasonal variation in the prevalence of postnatal depression. *European Journal of Psychiatry, 7,* 73–76s.

Castrogiovanni, P., Iapichino, S., Pacchierotti, C., & Pieraccini, F. (1998). Season of birth in psychiatry: A review. *Neuropsychobiology, 37*(4), 175–181.

Fossey, E., & Shapiro, C. M. (1992). Seasonality in psychiatry: A review. *Canadian Journal of Psychiatry, 37* (5), 299–308.

Lemoine, P. (1995). Chronobiology and chronotherapy. In J. L. Senon, D. Sechter, & D. Richard (Eds.), *Thérapeutique psychiatrique* (pp. 471–492). Paris: Hermann.

Mills, J. N. (1975). Development of circadian rhythms in infancy. *Chronobiologia, 2,* 363–371.

Modestin, J., Ammann, R., & Wurmle, O. (1995). Season of birth: Comparison of patients with schizophrenia, affective disorders and alcoholism. *Acta Psychiatrica Scandinavia, 91*(2), 140–143.

Pevet, P. (1998). Mélatonine et rythmes biologiques. *Thérapie, 53,* 411–420.

Rosenthal, N. E., Sack, D. A., Gillin, J. C., Lewy, A. J., Goodwin, F. K., Davenport, Y., Mueller, P. S., Newsome, D. A., & Wehr, T. A. (1984). Seasonal affective disorder: A description of the syndrome and preliminary findings with light therapy. *Archives of General Psychiatry, 41,* 72–80.

Sechter, D., Bonin, B., & Bizouard, P. (1996). Phototherapy: A treatment for mood disorders? In H. Greppin, R. Degli Agosti, & M. Bozon (Eds.), *Vistas on biorhythmicity* (pp. 295–301). Geneva, Switzerland: University of Geneva.

Souêtre, E., Salvati, E., Belugou, J. L., Douillet, P., Braccini, T., & Darcourt G. (1987). Seasonality of suicides: Environmental, sociological and biological covariations. *Journal of Affective Disorders, 13,* 215–225.

Wehr, T. A., & Goodwin, F. K. (1981). Biological rhythms and psychiatry. In Arieti, Brodie, *American handbook of psychiatry* (Vol. 7, pp. 46–74). New York: Basic Books.

Wirz-Justice, A., Graw, P., Krauchi, K., Sarrafzadeh, A., English, J., & Sand, L. (1996). "Natural" light treatment of seasonal affective disorder. *Journal of Affective Disorders, 37,* 109–120.

Wirz-Justice, A., & Wehr, T. A. (1983). Neuropsychopharmacology and biological rhythms. *Advances in Biological Psychiatry, 11,* 20–34.

P. VANDEL
Hospital Saint-Jacques, Bensancon, France

BIOLOGICAL RHYTHMS
CIRCADIAN RHYTHMS

BIOLOGICAL RHYTHMS

Biological rhythms are cyclic processes taking place within organisms. They have to do with much of the activity of life on earth. Their cycles may be circadian (lasting about a day) or may last longer, such as the monthly menstrual cycle. This rhythmic activity is determined by processes and forces both inside and outside the body. An example of a biological rhythm is that of the change from sleep to a wakened state. Such a change between sleep and wakeful behavior comes from biological clocks in the cells and organs of the body. Accordingly, the cells of our bodies contain timers, or individual clocks, which in association with RNA (ribonucleic acid) process proteins in a cyclic 24-hr period.

But not all the biological clocks' dynamics come from in-processes. Some influences come from the environment, as for example the effects of the rotation of the earth and moon. Most human activity is affected by the revolutions of the earth around the sun and the moon's orbit around the earth.

The effect of the sun and moon in producing rhythms on the biology of the earth is much more widespread than is apparent at first glance. The growing of crops, for example, depends on the seasons and the earth's position in relation to the sun. The moon affects the waterways and oceans and thereby creates rhythms for wildlife dependent on the receding of water in order to find food. Wildlife activity in turn can affect the food chain.

In human beings, circadian rhythms are often changed by physical processes taking place internally. Variation, for example, in body temperature follows a circadian rhythm with the low parts of the cycle occurring in the early morning and late at night. At the highest point, midday, one finds the best performance on complex tasks.

When we change our activity from our normal rhythm we cause confusion in our bodies, as when we experience jet lag. The change from east to west or west to east interrupts the usual pattern of sleep and activity our bodies are accustomed to. We do not feel well until our body functioning adapts to a new cycle of sleep and wakefulness.

Biological rhythms are just beginning to be understood in their importance in our lives since, as in other areas of human behavior, we have difficulty in separating biological from environmental influences, as Chumlea pointed out in "Physical growth in adolescence." Perhaps our future activity will be regulated to take advantage not only of the high point in our daily cycle, but also of the individual differences in rhythm.

SUGGESTED READING

Alexander, T. (1972). *Children and adolescents: A biocultural approach to psychological development.* New York: Aldine-Atherton. (Original work published 1969)

Carlson, N. R. (1977). *Physiology of behavior.* Boston: Allyn & Bacon.

Shepherd-Look, D. L. (1982). Sex differentiation and the development of sex roles. In B. B. Wolman (Ed.), *Handbook of developmental psychology.* Englewood Cliffs, NJ: Prentice-Hall.

T. ALEXANDER
Temple University

BIPOLAR AFFECTIVE DISORDER (MANIC-DEPRESSIVE ILLNESS)

CLINICAL DESCRIPTION AND COURSE

Bipolar Affective Disorder, formerly known as manic-depressive illness, is a psychiatric disorder involving wide-ranging fluctuations in mood, activity, and cognition. It affects between 0.8% and 1.4% of the population. When depressed, bipolar persons experience a sad mood, loss of interests, fatigue, psychomotor retardation or agitation, loss of concentration, insomnia, feelings of worthlessness, and suicidality. During mania, patients experience euphoric, elevated, or irritable mood states; racing of thoughts (or the verbal concomitant, flight of ideas); increased activity and energy; impulsive and high-risk behaviors; an inflated sense of self-worth, or grandiose delusions; distractibility; and a decreased need for sleep (American Psychiatric Association, 1994). Manic episodes are generally more damaging to the bipolar person and those around him or her than are depressive episodes.

Bipolar I patients usually alternate between the two extremes of mania and depression, or they experience mania and depression simultaneously in mixed affective episodes. A small proportion of bipolar I patients have only manic episodes without major depressions. Bipolar II patients experience debilitating depressions that alternate with hypomanic episodes. Hypomania is a mild form of mania with many of the same symptoms but in attenuated form. Hypomania is not associated with significant functional impairment, psychosis, or the need for hospitalization.

Bipolar I patients are equally often men and women, but Bipolar II patients are more frequently women. Women appear to have a preponderance of depressive over manic or hypomanic episodes, whereas the reverse appears true of men. In parallel, the first onset of Bipolar Disorder is usually a depressive episode in a woman and a manic episode in a man.

The course of the disorder varies considerably from person to person. Some bipolar persons return to a euthymic, normal mood state between episodes. However, by some estimates (e.g., Harrow, Goldberg, Grossman, & Meltzer, 1990), more than half of the patients have significant symptoms during the intervals between major episodes. The average duration of episodes varies from 4 to 13 months, with longer durations reported in studies from the pre-pharmacological era (Goodwin & Jamison, 1990). Episode duration has decreased significantly since the advent of mood-stabilizing agents such as lithium carbonate or the anticonvulsants (discussed later). But even with active medication, about 40% of bipolar patients experience a recurrence of the illness in a one-year period, and 73% in a 5-year period (Gitlin, Swendsen, Heller, & Hammen, 1995). Between 13 and 20% of patients are rapid cyclers (Calabrese, Fatemi, Kujawa, & Woyshville, 1996), who experience four or more episodes of depression, mania, hypomania, or mixed affective disorder in a single year; these patients are disproportionately women. There are several known predictors of increased cycling of the disorder, including medication nonadherence, presence of psychosis, alcohol and drug abuse, sleep deprivation, and in some patients, the use of antidepressant medications.

Bipolar Disorder is associated with high personal, social, and economic costs. About 33% of Bipolar I patients cannot maintain employment in the 6 months after a manic episode; over 50% show declines in occupational functioning over the 5 years after an episode. The suicide rate is believed to be about 30 times greater than that of the normal population (Guze & Robins, 1970). Bipolar disorder is also associated with marital dysfunction and high rates of divorce, general health complications, legal problems, and problems in the adjustment of children (e.g., Coryell, Andreasen, Endicott, & Keller, 1987; Coryell et al., 1993; Dion, Tohen, Anthony, & Waternaux, 1989; Goldberg, Harrow, & Grossman, 1995; Hammen, Burge, Burney, & Adrian, 1990; Silverstone & Romans-Clarkson, 1989). In 1991, the economic costs of bipolar disorder were $45 billion in the United States alone (Wyatt & Henter, 1995).

Most bipolar patients develop the illness between the ages of 19 and 23. However, prepubertal and adolescent onsets of the disorder are being increasingly recognized. Between 20 and 40% of bipolar patients have their first onsets in childhood or adolescence, and about 20% of depressed adolescents eventually switch into mania. The early-onset forms of the disease are associated with a stronger genetic liability (greater familial aggregation) than the later-onset forms. There is also evidence that the age at onset of the disorder is becoming younger in successive generations. If bipolar teenagers are not treated early, they can fall behind, sometimes irreparably, in social, school, and work functioning (Geller & Luby, 1997; McClellan & Werry, 1997).

ETIOLOGY

Genetic and Biological Predispositions

Bipolar Disorder unquestionably runs in families. In one study, concordance rates between identical twins were 79%, and between fraternal twins, 24% (Bertelsen, Harvald, & Hauge, 1977). The family pedigrees of bipolar probands are characterized by increased rates of Bipolar Disorder, Major Depressive disorder, and alcoholism. By some estimates, about 20% of the first-degree relatives of bipolar patients have major affective disorders (Gershon, 1990). Although several gene loci have been identified, there is a particularly promising set of findings linking Bipolar Disorder to loci on the long arm of chromosome 18. This linkage is strongest among families of bipolar patients who are comorbid for Panic Disorder (MacKinnon et al., 1998).

Bipolar Disorder is presumed to involve imbalances in the activity of catecholamine, serotonergic, cholinergic, or dopamine systems. However, it is unclear whether these imbalances are specific to Bipolar Disorder or which neural pathways are involved. A recent theory of dysfunction in the activity of signal-transducing guanine nucleotide-binding proteins (G-proteins) is gaining credibility. Bipolar patients have higher platelet levels of stimulatory G-protein subunits than do normal comparison subjects, even when patients are examined in the remitted state (Mitchell et al., 1997). In parallel, lithium carbonate—the primary medication used in treating bipolar disorder—has been found to reduce G-protein

function in animals (Avissar, Schreiber, Danon, & Belmaker, 1988) and in normal humans (Risby et al., 1991).

Psychosocial Factors

There is increasing evidence that Bipolar Disorder is affected by psychosocial stress. Two domains have been studied: negative affective relationships within the patient's family, and stressful life events. Regarding the former, prospective studies indicate that bipolar patients who, following an acute illness episode, return to family or marital environments that are high in expressed emotion (i.e., those containing relatives who are highly critical, hostile, or emotionally overinvolved) are more likely to relapse at 9-month or one-year follow-up than those who return to low-key family environments (for a review, see Miklowitz, Wendel, & Simoneau, 1998). It is not clear whether stress within the family is a primary eliciting factor for symptoms, whether bipolar symptoms in patients evoke family conflicts, or whether patients' symptoms and family conflicts are both traceable to third variables, such as a shared genetic vulnerability to mood disorder.

Episodes of Bipolar Disorder often follow major life events (Johnson & Roberts, 1995). Various theories have been advanced for explaining this association. One model views the core dysfunction in Bipolar Disorder as one of instability, and postulates that mood disorders are strongly affected by changes in the circadian clock (Ehlers, Frank, & Kupfer, 1988; Ehlers, Kupfer, Frank, & Monk, 1993). Life events that affect sleep/wake rhythms and other daily routines (e.g., the birth of a baby) do appear potent in eliciting manic, but not depressive, episodes (Malkoff-Schwartz et al., 1998). Another model postulates that life events interact with a faulty behavioral activation system that is sensitive to reward cues. Life events that involve goal striving (e.g., a job promotion) may stimulate this system, which then produces an aroused state associated with greater motivation for rewards, heightened affect, and increased sociability or risk taking (Depue & Iacono, 1989; Johnson & Roberts, 1995; Meyer, Johnson, & Carver, in press). Both models help explain why mood disorder episodes often follow both positive and negative life events.

A third model, the kindling hypothesis (Post, 1992), postulates that bipolar episodes are often precipitated by an external agent (i.e., life stress) at the beginning phases of the illness, but that patients become increasingly sensitized to stress over time. In later stages of the disorder, episodes occur spontaneously, without external stressors; eventually, the illness takes on an autonomous, self-perpetuating course. Evidence for the kindling hypothesis is inconsistent, however. Hammen and Gitlin (1997) found that among bipolar patients who'd had recurrences, those with a greater number of prior episodes were more likely to have experienced a major stressor in the 6 months prior to their recurrence, and to relapse more quickly after the stressor, than were patients with fewer prior episodes.

TREATMENT

Biological Approaches

The primary treatments for Bipolar Disorder are pharmacological. Lithium carbonate was the first mood stabilizer to come into wide use. It appears to be effective for about 50 to 60% of patients in controlling the acute symptoms of the disorder and preventing future episodes. More recently, anticonvulsant medications such as divalproex sodium (Depakote) and carbamazepine (Tegretol) have been used as substitutes for or in conjunction with lithium, usually for lithium-refractory patients, patients who complain of lithium's side effects, or patients with atypical presentations (i.e., mixed episodes or rapid cycling).

Most mood stabilizers appear to be more effective in controlling and preventing manic symptoms than depressive symptoms. For this reason, they are often combined with antidepressants from the selective serotonin reuptake inhibitor class (e.g., paroxetine, or Paxil), the monoamine oxidase inhibitor class (e.g., tranylcypromine, or Parnate), or the novel antidepressant class (e.g., bupropion, or Wellbutrin). Although often effective in controlling depressive symptoms, antidepressants pose risks to bipolar patients, because they can elicit hypomanic or manic episodes or lead to an acceleration of mood cycling.

Antipsychotic agents and anxiolytic compounds are often added to the patient's lithium or anticonvulsant regimen, depending on the patient's clinical presentation. Electroconvulsive therapy (shock treatment) is recommended for treatment-refractory patients, particularly when they are in severe depressive states. Other recent treatment approaches that require more investigation include new anticonvulsants such as lamotrigine (Lamictal), bright light treatment, and omega-3 fatty acids (fish oil).

Medications for Bipolar Disorder have side effects. For example, lithium and divalproex sodium are associated with weight gain, nausea, and trembling. Goodwin and Jamison (1990) reported that between 18 and 53% of patients discontinued their medications at some point during their lives. In addition to the troublesome side effects, patients report disliking the idea of having their moods controlled by a medication, and often miss their high, euphoric periods (Jamison, Gerner, & Goodwin, 1979). Some complain of a loss of creativity due to medications. Indeed, there is evidence of a linkage between Bipolar Disorder and artistic creativity, as evidenced by the number of writers, artists, and musicians who have had the disorder or a mild form of it (Jamison, 1993).

Psychosocial Approaches

Psychosocial therapy is used as an adjunct to drug treatment, and is viewed as a way to mollify the symptomatic course of the disorder, enhance patients' compliance with medications, and increase patients' abilities to manage stressors that may evoke symptoms. Psychosocial treatment has been recommended for bipolar patients for many years, but only recently has research begun to support its utility. Three treatments have received some, albeit limited, empirical support. One is family or marital therapy, particularly psychoeducational approaches that focus on teaching patients and their family members about Bipolar Disorder and how to manage it, and effective ways to communicate and solve family problems (e.g., Miklowitz & Goldstein, 1997). A second treatment is interpersonal and social rhythm therapy, an individual therapy that focuses on helping the patient understand and renegotiate the interpersonal context associated with mood disorder symptoms (Frank, 1995; Frank et al., 1997). The patient learns to master conflicts associated with inter-

personal loss experiences, disputes, skill deficits, and role transitions. Patients also learn to stabilize sleep/wake rhythms and other daily routines, particularly in the face of environmental triggers for disruption. A third model is individual cognitive-behavioral therapy, in which patients learn to identify, evaluate, and restructure cognitive distortions, and develop illness management strategies such as behavioral activation, drug compliance monitoring, and the appropriate use of support systems (e.g., Basco & Rush, 1996).

CONCLUSION

Bipolar Disorder is a genetically- and biologically-based illness of mood states. It takes a tremendous economic, social, and personal toll on sufferers and their family members. Recent advances in biological and psychosocial research have clarified some of the predisposing factors for the disorder and have identified triggers for the disorder's cycling. In parallel, advances in its pharmacological and psychological management are being translated into treatment algorithms that have the potential to improve community-based care for this often debilitating disorder.

REFERENCES

American Psychiatric Association. (1994). *Diagnostic and statistical manual of mental disorders (4th ed.)*. Washington, DC: Author.

Avissar, S., Schreiber, G., Danon, A., & Belmaker, R. H. (1988). Lithium inhibits adrenergic and cholinergic increases in GTP binding in rat cortex. *Nature, 331,* 440–442.

Basco, M. R., & Rush, A. J. (1996). *Cognitive-behavioral therapy for bipolar disorder.* New York: Guilford.

Bertelsen, A., Harvald, B., & Hauge, M. (1977). A Danish twin study of manic-depressive disorders. *British Journal of Psychiatry, 130,* 330–351.

Calabrese, J. R., Fatemi, S. H., Kujawa, M., & Woyshville, M. J. (1996). Predictors of response to mood stabilizers. *Journal of Clinical Psychopharmacology, 16*(Suppl. 1), 24–31.

Coryell, W., Andreasen, N. C., Endicott, J., Keller, M. (1987). The significance of past mania or hypomania in the course and outcome of major depression. *American Journal of Psychiatry, 144,* 309–315.

Coryell, W., Scheftner, W., Keller, M., Endicott, J., Maser, J., Klerman, G. L., & Coryell, W. (1993). The enduring psychosocial consequences of mania and depression. *American Journal of Psychiatry, 150,* 720–727.

Depue, R. A., & Iacono, W. G. (1989). Neurobehavioral aspects of affective disorders. *Annual Review of Psychiatry, 40,* 457–492.

Dion, G., Tohen, M., Anthony, W., & Waternaux, C. (1989). Symptoms and functioning of patients with bipolar disorder six months after hospitalization. *Hospital and Community Psychiatry, 39,* 652–656.

Ehlers, C. L., Frank, E., & Kupfer, D. J. (1988). Social zeitgebers and biological rhythms: A unified approach to understanding the etiology of depression. *Archives of General Psychiatry, 45,* 948–952.

Ehlers, C. L., Kupfer, D. J., Frank, E., & Monk, T. H. (1993). Biological rhythms and depression: The role of zeitgebers and zeitstorers. *Depression, 1,* 285–293.

Frank, E. (1995). *Regularizing social routines in patients with bipolar I disorder.* Paper presented at the 34th Annual Meeting of the American College of Neuropsychopharmacology, San Juan, Puerto Rico.

Frank, E., Hlastala, S., Ritenour, A., Houck, P., Tu, X. M., Monk, T. H., Mallinger, A. G., & Kupfer, D. J. (1997). Inducing lifestyle regularity in recovering bipolar disorder patients: Results from the Maintenance Therapies in Bipolar Disorder protocol. *Biological Psychiatry, 41,* 1165–1173.

Geller, B., & Luby, J. (1997). Child and adolescent bipolar disorder: A review of the past 10 years. *Journal of the American Academy of Child and Adolescent Psychiatry, 36,* 1168–1176.

Gershon, E. S. (1990). Genetics. In F. K. Goodwin & K. R. Jamison, *Manic-depressive illness* (pp. 373–401). New York: Oxford University Press.

Gitlin, M. J., Swendsen, J., Heller, T. L., & Hammen, C. (1995). Relapse and impairment in bipolar disorder. *American Journal of Psychiatry, 152,* 1635–1640.

Goldberg, J. F., Harrow, M., & Grossman, L. S. (1995). Course and outcome in bipolar affective disorder: A longitudinal follow-up study. *American Journal of Psychiatry, 152,* 379–385.

Goodwin, F. K., & K. R. Jamison (1990). *Manic-depressive illness.* New York, Oxford University Press.

Guze, S. B., & Robins, E. (1970). Suicide and primary affective disorders. *British Journal of Psychiatry, 117,* 437–438.

Hammen, C., Burge, D., Burney, E., & Adrian, C. (1990). Longitudinal study of diagnoses in children of women with unipolar and bipolar affective disorder. *Archives of General Psychiatry, 47,* 1112–1117.

Hammen, C., & Gitlin, M. J. (1997). Stress reactivity in bipolar patients and its relation to prior history of the disorder. *American Journal of Psychiatry, 154,* 856–857.

Harrow, M., Goldberg, J. F., Grossman, L. S., & Meltzer, H. Y. (1990). Outcome in manic disorders: A naturalistic follow-up study. *Archives of General Psychiatry, 47,* 665–671.

Jamison, K. R. (1993). *Touched with fire: Manic-depressive illness and the artistic temperament.* New York: Maxwell Macmillan International.

Jamison, K. R., Gerner, R. H., & Goodwin, F. K. (1979). Patient and physician attitudes toward lithium: Relationship to compliance. *Archives of General Psychiatry, 36,* 866–869.

Johnson, S. L., & Roberts, J. E. (1995). Life events and bipolar disorder: Implications from biological theories. *Psychology Bulletin, 117,* 434–449.

MacKinnon, D. F., Xu, J., McMahon, F. J., Simpson, S. G., Stine, O. C., McInnis, M. G., & DePaulo, J. R. (1998). Bipolar disorder and panic disorder in families: An analysis of chromosome 18 data. *American Journal of Psychiatry, 155,* 829–831.

Malkoff-Schwartz, S., Frank, E., Anderson, B., Sherrill, J. T., Siegel, L., Patterson, D., & Kupfer, D. J. (1998). Stressful life events and social rhythm disruption in the onset of manic and depressive bipolar episodes: A preliminary investigation. *Archives of General Psychiatry, 55,* 702–707.

McClellan, J., & Werry, J. S. (1997). Practice parameters for the assessment and treatment of children and adolescents with bipolar disorder. *Journal of the American Academy of Child and Adolescent Psychiatry, 36* (Suppl. 10), 157–176.

Meyer, B., Johnson, S. L., & Carver, C. (in press). Exploring behavioral activation and inhibition sensitivities among college students at-risk for mood disorders. *Journal of Psychopathology and Behavioral Assessment.*

Miklowitz, D. J., & Goldstein, M. J. (1997). *Bipolar disorder: A family-focused treatment approach.* New York: Guilford.

Miklowitz, D. J., Wendel, J. S., & Simoneau, T. L. (1998). Targeting dysfunctional family interactions and high expressed emotion in the psychosocial treatment of bipolar disorder. *In Session: Psychotherapy in Practice, 4,* 25–38.

Mitchell, P. B., Manji, H. K., Chen, G., Jolkovsky, L., Smith-Jackson, E., Denicoff, K., Schmidt, M., & Potter, W. Z. (1997). High levels of Gs in platelets of euthymic patients with bipolar affective disorder. *American Journal of Psychiatry, 154,* 18–223.

Post, R. M. (1992). Transduction of psychosocial stress into neurobiology of recurrent affective disorder. *American Journal of Psychiatry, 149,* 999–1010.

Risby, E. D., Hsiao, J. K., Manji, H. K., Bitran, J., Moses, F., Zhou, D. F., & Potter, W. Z. (1991). The mechanisms of action of lithium: II. Effects on adenylate cyclase activity and beta-adrenergic receptor binding in normal subjects. *Archives of General Psychiatry, 48,* 513–524.

Silverstone, T., & Romans-Clarkson, S. (1989). Bipolar affective disorder: Causes and prevention of relapse. *British Journal of Psychiatry, 154,* 321–335.

Wyatt, R. J., & Henter, I. (1995). An economic evaluation of manic-depressive illness. *Social Psychiatry and Psychiatric Epidemiology, 30,* 213–219.

D. J. MIKLOWITZ
University of Colorado

DEPRESSION

BIRTH ORDER

Birth order refers to the ordinal sequence of birth for each child in a family. Some researchers identify five positions: only, first, second, middle, and last-born. Others use only, first, middle, and last-born. Alfred Adler was the first theorist in modern psychology to note the significance of psychological birth order position in the development and dynamics of personality. Adler recognized that the addition of each child to the family would have a profound effect on the family system—the birth of each child would alter the interactions, roles, and responsibilities of each family member. Adler is credited with creating the term "birth order," and he described characteristics that are expected with the sequence of birth (the ordinal position). While birth order is important, Adler suggested that the "psychological order" of the child might be more important than the order itself. In Adlerian psychology, the psychological birth order position is distinguished from the ordinal position. The psychological birth order position is a vantage point from which a child will perceive and evaluate the self, others, and the world, and from which the child will form convictions about what is required to belong in society.

FAMILY CONSTELLATION

The term *family constellation* is used to describe the family environment—the parents, siblings, and others living in the family of origin. The family constellation represents a group of "bodies," each of which has a place in relation to the places of the other members. The family constellation is a term suggested by Adler to describe the psychological birth order. Sulloway (1996) uses the term *functional birth order* to describe the kind of environment into which children are born.

VARIABLES

Adler suggested a number of family variables that might influence the child's perception of the order and create a different psychological order from the ordinal position. These variables influence how the child will evaluate the birth order position and decide whether that particular birth order is the best or the worst position in the family. A firstborn may evaluate the heavy responsibilities expected of the oldest child and decide that it is easier to be lazy than to assume a leadership role. A middle child may determine that the leadership demonstrated by the oldest child is inferior and decide to assume the leadership role. All children evaluate their birth order positions in relation to the other siblings and decide on a pattern of behavior that enables each child to be unique in that family structure. Corsini and Manaster (1982) maintain that the most important factors relative to birth order and personality development are the child's perception of the role to be played, its demands, and its expectations. Age spacing and the other variables listed later may influence such perceptions, but the child will create and be responsible for these perceptions.

In the study of birth order, the sex of the child is an important variable because each child will establish sex-role identity by finding a role model within the family. Parents have different sex-role expectations for each child and will reinforce or reward the child's behaviors in accord with those expectations.

The age separation between siblings is another critical consideration in the development of personality. Children who are born closely spaced will have a strong influence on each other because they are likely to play together extensively. Children who are born several years apart are likely to have less influence on each other than those who are closely spaced. When children are born a minimum of five years apart, the family is considered to have a complete second generation of children within the same family.

The family structure is important to consider when examining the various influences on the child. The family structure includes the sex and the birth order of each child. A family of four children could have a birth order and sequence combination to form sixteen different family structures. A family of four boys is very different from a family of four girls. Another family of four children (girl, boy, girl, boy) will be quite different from a family of four mixed-sex children (girl, girl, boy, boy). Birth order will influence how siblings are likely to group and interact together.

Parents hold different expectations for each child based on sex and age. The firstborn daughter is often required to assume responsibilities and act as the "Junior Mom" by supervising younger siblings. Similarly, the firstborn son is often expected to be the "Junior Dad." The lastborn child is usually recognized as the "baby" and may utilize learned helplessness to occupy other people with its problems. Parents may pamper the youngest child, and give him or her many privileges that older siblings did not receive.

Parents may be influenced to choose a favorite child based on their own birth order. A parent who was the lastborn in his or her own birth order may identify with the lastborn child. When a parent and child establish a strong bond, the other children seek another role model.

How parents interact with each child is often influenced by the parents' ages. Teenage parents are very energetic and are more likely to play with the child; parents in their late thirties are more likely to be academic and read to the child. Parents who are in their thirties are likely to provide a different socioeconomic environment for a firstborn child than teenage parents. Parents in their thirties are more likely to own their own home and live in a neighborhood with other children, whereas teen parents may find that they have to live with one of their parents. Because the family culture of parents in their thirties is quite different from the family culture of teenage parents, children reared within these cultures will be likely to hold values that reflect these unique family situations.

A family with multiple births (twins, triplets, quads, and quints) will have special circumstances because of their "shared environment." Often, multiple-birth siblings will bond closely and develop a private language or symbols for communication. Twins (especially identical) that experience similar family environments will often develop common traits. A child who requires special care (for example, a handicapped child) will alter the expectations for each member of the family. Each member will have some role in the care of the handicapped child. Any conditions that may lead the parents to give special consideration or protection to a child may have an influence on the family environment. A parent who has several miscarriages before the successful birth of a child may become an overprotective parent. The death of a sibling during childhood will have a profound effect on each of the surviving family members.

Significant progress in the ability to estimate birth order proportions in the U.S. population was made by Borowick, Moore, and Trower (1996). Drawing from data from Vital Statistics of the United States, they demonstrated a method of utilizing birth certificate information to more accurately estimate U.S. birth order population proportions. The method used data on live births by cohorts of women during specified five-year periods and the percentage of their births in each birth order position. The study estimated the birth order proportions for working-age adults based on all cohorts of women whose children were born between 1896 and 1950. Borowick, Moore and Trower (1996) found that 6.4% of the population sample were only children, 26.6% were firstborns, 40.4% were middleborns, and 26.6% were lastborn children.

FIRSTBORN

According to Corsini and Manaster (1982), the first child is an only child for the period of time until there are other children. When a second child is born, this only child becomes a firstborn with a secondborn sibling. For a period of time, the firstborn child has the undivided attention of the parents, and as such may establish a "throne." Later, when a second child arrives, the firstborn child may be "dethroned." Firstborn children often feel entitled to the honor of the first position and strive to maintain a position of superiority over the siblings. Corsini and Manaster suggest that firstborn children are conservative and hold a positive attitude toward the past by stressing tradition (holding to the community values and laws) because such traditions will enable them to remain in power. According to Ernst and Angst (1983), firstborn children identify more with the parental values, tend to support the status quo, and follow the parent's wishes. "The tendency for first borns to excel in school and in other forms of intellectual achievement is consistent with their strong motivation to satisfy parental expectations" (p. 240).

Firstborn children are consistently found to have higher academic achievement scores and higher grade point averages, make up a larger proportion of the college population, and score higher on standardized tests of verbal aptitude. The relationship between birth order and academic achievement appears consistently in the research findings.

Sulloway (1996) identified five global dimensions for firstborns that consistently emerge in the literature: extraversion, agreeableness, conscientiousness, neuroticism, and openness to experience. According to Sulloway, "firstborns enjoy the advantages of being bigger, stronger, and smarter than the younger siblings" and finds that they are overrepresented among political leaders (p. 68). Sulloway (1996) suggests that firstborns should be more antagonistic than laterborns, and finds that they are rated higher in the physical uses of power. Sulloway's study (1996) finds that firstborns are more anxious about their status, more emotionally intense than laterborn children, slower to recover from upsets, and more likely to exhibit anger and vengefulness.

SECONDBORN

For a period of time, the firstborn has no rivals and is able to rule over a small kingdom. Adler developed the term "dethronement" to describe the feelings of the firstborn child at the time of arrival of the secondborn child. According to Dreikurs (1967), the firstborn child is in the unique position of having the undivided attention of the parents; however, with the arrival of the second child, the firstborn becomes "dethroned." Sometimes a child who has lost this power will be captivated by the importance of power and authority. As the child grows up, that firstborn child may seek to ex-

ercise authority and may exaggerate the importance of rules and laws.

Corsini and Manaster (1982) suggest that the secondborn child has a "standard bearer" ahead. The secondborn child has the benefit of examining the strengths and weaknesses of the older child and will usually make special efforts to excel in those areas where the oldest child is weak. Secondborn children tend to be highly verbal; the firstborns listen to the parents, but the secondborns have the benefit of sibling conversation. Overheard conversations are important resources for secondborn children who are learning the language of adults and children.

Hanna and Harper (1992) utilized the Systems Theory of Ordinal Position to examine the interactions between secondborn and fourthborn children. Hanna and Harper found that secondborns made more responses coded as assertions and fourthborns made more responses coded as questions. The findings of Hanna and Harper give support to the concept of nonshared environments among siblings. In a study of parental influence and birth order, Holmes and Tiefenthaler (1997) found that mothers spend considerably more time with their firstborn children than the secondborn child, and that the secondborn child would receive more time with the mother than a thirdborn child.

Messer (1997) analyzed household food allocation in India, Nepal, Madagascar, Mexico, and Peru. A review of the ethnographic studies on the five countries indicated relative values attributed to females, males, and children of different ages. Household-level cultural, economic, and biological factors contributed to intentional and benign nutritional neglect by male decision makers, favoring males as better investments and preferring child feeding based on sex (males) and birth order (firstborn).

MIDDLEBORN

Parents and other adults have clear expectations of firstborn, lastborn and only children. The expectations for the middle child are not as clearly defined and consequently the middle child may be required to define the role of the middle child in the family. According to Corsini and Manaster (1982), the middle child may perceive the position of middleborn to be an untenable position. The oldest child has the privileges and power of greater age, while the lastborn is not pressed to perform as responsibly or as well. The middle child may feel squeezed from both sides and feel particularly neglected and without a place; conversely, the middle child may feel less pressure from role expectations and be able to excel by establishing his or her own definition of success.

Honda (1996) performed an analysis of historical data on youths in Japan and found that while members of the same household tended to be similarly educated, they held diverse occupations. This resulted in little social mobility through education and a system that perpetuated itself. While the status of one's household in the community influenced educational attainment, the birth order within the household had a stronger relationship to the choice of occupation. Honda further suggested that birth order and occupation may have influenced the physical well-being. Firstborn sons tended to enjoy good health and tall stature relative to their laterborn counterparts. Short stature was associated with trades with low socioeconomic status. Youth with poor health (hindering their employment in crafts) tended to become Buddhist priests.

Lieberman, Shaffer, and Reynolds (1985) found that males are more likely to support prevailing cultural beliefs, while those in the middle child position (particularly females) are more likely to reject these and support more humanitarian, revolutionary scientific trends. In a study of intelligence, Ram and Montsion (1998) found that the math skills of children in larger families are lower than the skills of those children with one sibling (or only children).

Evidence continues to suggest that the family environment contributes to the development of the personality. Malkus (1994) found four structural factors (relationship status of biological parents, birth order, family size, and the number of parents in the household) that correlated with adolescent substance abuse. Abusers were more likely to be members of large families, to have parents who were divorced, and to live in single-parent homes.

Salmon (1998) found that females place a higher value on kinship roles and relationships. Salmon also found that middleborn children tend to be less close to parents, less inclined to turn to them in need, and less likely than firstborns and lastborns to engage in genealogical research.

LASTBORN

According to Corsini and Manaster (1982) the lastborn child has no challenge from behind—all competitors are ahead. Older siblings may treat the lastborn child as a baby, not as a competitor. The lastborn child has the possibility of being pampered and being faced with fewer demands. He or she may come to expect that others will (and should) take care of the "baby." The lastborn may utilize charm and a helpless manner to keep the other siblings busy with his or her problems, or a lastborn child may perceive this position as one with the greatest challenge, and that child may become determined to step ahead of all others, surpassing the older siblings in achievements. Sulloway (1996) found that laterborn children were more inclined to question authority and to resist pressure to conform. He reported that laterborn children were more risk-oriented and more likely to engage in dangerous physical activities.

According to Russell (1997), the birth order of the baby boomer generation may have a significant effect on society because firstborn children tend to support the status quo, while laterborn children tend to rebel. Only 32% of children born during the 1950s were firstborns, compared to 41% in the 1930s and a record 43% in 1994. This first baby boomer generation of children are entering positions of power and supporting conservative social issues. Sutton-Smith and Rosenberg (1970) found that laterborns are reported to be more altruistic, empathetic, and peer-oriented.

ONLY CHILD

Because the only child does not have the experience of living with siblings, only children tend to have exaggerated senses of importance. The only child may become spoiled and expect to be the center of attention, or he or she may be reluctant to share attention or materials with others because the child has never been required to share.

Many positive aspects of the only child include the lack of sibling rivalry, an enjoyment of spending time alone, an appreciation of being the only recipient of parents' emotional and financial resources, and the development of a close relationship with parents. Challenges for only children include not having a sibling confidant, feeling pressure to succeed, seeking undivided attention from others, and experiencing difficulty in connecting and negotiating with peers. Some only children mature earlier and have a strong identification with adults. Only children become the sole caretaker of aging parents. According to Falbo (1977), there is no evidence to support the belief that only children are selfish, lonely, or maladjusted.

RESEARCH

Ernst and Angst (1983) conducted a landmark study of birth order by analyzing more than a thousand research studies. Ernst and Angst concluded that birth order effects are artifacts of poor research design. Sulloway (1996) performed a meta-analysis of the studies conducted by Ernst and Angst (1983), and pooled the studies to gain statistical power. According to Sulloway, "the literature on birth order exhibits consistent trends that overwhelmingly exceed chance expectations" (p. 74).

Stewart and Stewart (1995) reviewed more than 1,000 birth order research studies and found a pattern of changes in topics chosen by researchers. Topics such as achievement, intelligence, personality, and psychopathology received heavy attention in the 1970s and 1980s. In the 1990s the research emphasis shifted to cross-cultural factors, parent-child interactions, development, and family relations. Stewart and Stewart (1995) found that little of the existing body of research has addressed how birth order information could be used to change the lives of individuals through psychotherapy.

Zajonc and Markus formulated the confluence model to explain the impact of birth order on cognitive achievement as a function of the confluence of two factors—family intellectual environment and the teaching function. According to this theory, the average mental age of children is thought to decline with each successive birth, and the teaching function effect assumes that older children are intellectually stimulated by the opportunity to mentor younger siblings—an opportunity that is denied to lastborn and only children. Zajonc and Mullally (1997) propose that the confluence model offers several solutions that genetic and developmental theories cannot explain.

Shulman and Mosak (1977) suggest that birth order assessment and research is often faulty because it fails to recognize that it is the psychological position of the child within the family which is crucial. They suggest that the psychological order can be understood for each subject idiographically and not through nomothetic laws. Shulman and Mosak suggest that the criteria of birth order characteristics provide helpful clues toward the understanding of the uniqueness of an individual rather than understanding the typicality of an individual.

REFERENCES

Adler, A. (1931). *What life should mean to you.* Boston. Little, Brown.

Borowick, K. S., Moore, K. K., & Trower, J. (1996). Estimating birth order proportions in the U.S. population. *Individual Psychology, 52*(3), 217–233.

Brasington, C. R. (1994). Birth order. In *Encyclopedia of psychology* (Vol. 1, pp. 152–154). New York: Wiley.

Cherry, C. M. (1990). *The relationship between birth order and academic achievement.* (ERIC Document Reproduction Service No. ED 344 668)

Corsini, R., & Manaster, G. (1982). *Individual psychology.* . Austin, TX: Peacock.

Dreikurs, R. (1967). *Psychodynamics, psychotherapy, and counseling.* Chicago: Adler Institute.

Ernst, C., & Angst, J. (1983). *Birth order: Its influence on personality.* New York: Springer-Verlag.

Falbo, T. (1977). The only child: A review. *Journal of Individual Psychology, 33,* 47–61.

Griffith, J., & Powers, R. (1984). *An Adlerian lexicon.* Chicago: Americas Institute of Adlerian Studies.

Hanna, S., & Harper, J. M. (1992). Interactional differences in second- and fourthborns: Applications of a theory. *American Journal of Family Therapy, 20*(4), 310.

Honda, G. (1996). Short tailors and sickly Buddhist priests: Birth order and household effects on class and health in Japan. *Continuity and Change, 11*(2), 273–294.

Holmes, J., & Tiefenthaler, J. (1997). Cheaper by the dozen? The marginal time costs of children in the Philippines. *Population Research and Policy Review, 16*(6), 561–578.

Lieberman, L., Shaffer, T. G., & Reynolds, L. T. (1985). Scientific revolution and birth order. *Individual Psychology, 41*(3), 328–335.

Malkus, B. M. (1994). Family dynamic and structural correlates of adolescent substance abuse: A comparison of families of nonsubstance abusers and substance abusers. *Journal of Child and Adolescent Substance Abuse, 3*(4), 39–52.

Messer, E. (1997). Intra-household allocation of food and health care: Current findings and understandings. *Social Science and Medicine, 44*(11), 1675–1684.

Ram, B., & Montsion, N. (1998). *Does sibling "size matter"? Canadian evidence.* Paper presented at the International Sociological Association, Demography Division Statistics, Ottawa, Ontario, Canada.

Roberts-Lisen, L. C. (1998). "I always knew that mom and dad loved me best": The experience of being an only child. *Dissertation Abstracts International* 59–01A, 337 AAI9823121.

Russell, C. (1997). Birth order and the baby boom birth order of baby boomers and how it affects society. *American Demographics 19*(3), 10.

Salmon, C. A. (1998). Sex, birth order, and the nature of kin relations: An evolutionary analysis. *Dissertation Abstracts International* 59–08B, 4542: AAINQ30111.

Shulman, B. H., & Mosak, H. H. (1977). Birth order and ordinal position: Two Adlerian views. *Journal of Individual Psychology, 33,* 114–121.

Stewart, A., & Stewart, E. (1995). Birth order bibliography and index. *Individual Psychology, 51*(1), 21–36.

Sulloway, F. (1996). *Born to rebel.* New York: Random House.

Sutton-Smith, B., & Rosenberg, B. G. (1970). *The sibling.* New York: Holt, Rinehart, and Winston.

Takan-Yuriko, O. (1996). Birth order effects on early language development: Do second-born children learn from overheard speech? *Child Development, 67*(2), 621–634.

Vurdien-Rajen, R. (1992). *A study of the relationship between birth order and reading achievement among seventh and eighth graders.* (ERIC Document Reproduction Service No. ED 380 774)

White, J., Campbell, L., & Stewart, A. (1995). Associations of scores on the White-Campbell Psychological Birth Order Inventory and the Kern Lifestyle Scale. *Psychological Reports, 77*(3), 1187.

Zajonc, R. B., & Mullally, P. R. (1997). Birth order: Reconciling conflicting affects. *The American Psychologist, 52*(7), 685.

C. R. Brasington
University of South Carolina

ALDERIAN PSYCHOLOGY
DEVELOPMENT
SIBLING RELATIONSHIPS

BLEULER, EUGEN (1857–1939)

Paul Eugen Bleuler spent most of his career in Zurich at the psychiatric hospital of the university. He received his MD from Bern and studied briefly with Charcot at Salpêtrière. He encouraged his assistant Jung to apply Freud's theories to the hospital patients. Piaget was another colleague. Some consider his writings to anticipate the existential movement, with a direct link through his student Binswanger.

Bleuler's classic 1908 paper "Dementia praecox" was based on 647 cases observed over an eight-year period. He proposed the name schizophrenia because the dementia was not uniform but occurred only at certain times in relation to certain types of questions. His 1911 *Dementia Praecox: Or the Group of Schizophrenias* continued his careful analysis, emphasizing that the disorder was not due to brain damage with its inevitable deterioration, but rather that the prognosis was related to the extent of the symptoms. Carefully distinguishing between primary and adjunctive symptoms, he introduced concepts such as neologism, word salad, and negative speech into the descriptive vocabulary. Bleuler added the category of simple schizophrenia to Kraepelin's three (hebephrenic, paranoid, catatonic). His 1916 *Textbook of Psychiatry* had added two additional fundamental concepts to the analysis of schizophrenia: autism, meaning loss of contact with reality, and ambivalence, designating the concurrent existence, at the intellectual, emotional, or volitional level, of mutually exclusive contradictions.

An excellent practicing psychiatrist, Bleuler postulated that underlying schizophrenia was a loosening of association. He also identified neurasthenia as a preschizophrenic symptom rather than a disorder in its own right, and similarly identified hypochondriasis as a mask for severe mental illness—usually schizophrenia, some types of depression, or early organic psychosis.

C. S. PEYSER
The University of the South

BLOCK DESIGN TEST

The block design test, developed by Samuel C. Kohs, was based upon an extensive 1921 study and published in 1923. It was intended as a nonverbal test of intelligence which presumably tapped analytic and synthetic aspects of cognitive functions. Kohs's findings demonstrated that the test correlated reasonably well with results obtained on the Stanford–Binet Test of Intelligence (r = 0.81) in a wide age range from 2 years 7 months to adulthood (although applicable norms are not reliable below 5 years of age). Revision of both the directions for the test and the norms continued by other workers for a number of years. Principal revisions were by Hutt (1930, 1932), who demonstrated that scoring based on the number of successful trials/plus time taken for completion, excluding the counting of moves made by the subject in manipulating the colored blocks, yielded higher correlations with other measures of intelligence. The test consists of colored designs which S is asked to reproduce by utilizing multicolored cubes.

This test is still used extensively as part of intelligence test batteries, as by Wechsler in his WAIS (Wechsler Adult Intelligence Test). The test has also been found to be highly useful in analyzing aspects of constructive intelligence involving the conversion of perceptual impressions into planned constructive behavior. Such conversions require unimpaired functioning of the parieto-occipital regions of the left hemisphere of the cortex; impairment in such functions is indicative of organic brain syndrome, as Luria demonstrated in *The Working Brain*. Moreover, observations of Ss behavior during the test can provide valuable information about some personality characteristics.

REFERENCES

Hutt, M. L. (1930). A simplified scoring method for the Kohs block-designs test. *American Journal of Psychology, 42,* 450–452.

Hutt, M. L. (1932). The Kohs block-designs test: A revision for clinical practice. *Journal of Applied Psychology, 16,* 298–307.

Kohs, S. C. (1920). The block-design tests. *Journal of Experimental Psychology, 3,* 357–376.

M. L. HUTT

INTELLIGENCE MEASURES
WECHSLER INTELLIGNECE TESTS

BLOOD-BRAIN BARRIER

The blood-brain barrier (BBB) is the interface between blood and the brain and therefore plays a significant role in many disciplines including psychology, psychiatry, nutrition, general metabolism, as well as pharmacology, neurology, and neurosurgery (Pardridge, 1998a). The blood-brain barrier is present in the brain of all vertebrates, is formed within the first trimester of human fetal life, and is illustrated in Figure 1A. The anatomical localization of the blood-brain barrier is the capillary endothelium of brain (Figure 1B). Unlike capillary endothelial cells in peripheral tissues, the endothelial cells of capillaries perfusing the brain and spinal cord are joined together by epithelial-like, high resistance tight junctions that eliminate the normal paracellular pathway of solute flux from blood to the organ interstitium (Brightman, Reese, & Feder, 1970). There is also a 99% reduction in the pinocytosis in endothelia of the central nervous system (CNS), and this eliminates the normal transcellular pathway of free solute exchange between blood and the organ interstitum. Since the normal paracellular and transcellular pathways for free solute exchange are absent in the capillaries perfusing the brain and spinal cord, circulating molecules gain access to brain or spinal cord by only one of two processes: (a) free diffusion based on the lipid solubility and molecular weight of the molecule; and (b) catalyzed transport (Pardridge, 1998b). The latter involves either carrier-mediated transport (CMT) for low molecular weight nutrients such as glucose and amino acids (Figure 1C), or receptor-mediated transcytosis (RMT) for certain circulating peptides such as insulin, leptin, and transferrin (Figure 1D). The CMT and RMT systems are individual proteins expressed by specific genes within the capillary endothelium, and they mediate the transport of these molecules across both the luminal plasma membrane of the capillary endothelium at the blood surface and the abluminal membrane of the capillary endothelium at the side of the brain interstitial fluid. The two luminal and abluminal membranes are separated by approximately 300 nm of endothelial cytoplasm. Therefore, transport across the blood-brain barrier is a process of molecular transfer through two membranes in series.

If a molecule does not have access to one of the specialized CMT or RMT systems within the BBB membranes, then there is no significant uptake of the molecule by brain. This is exemplified in Figure 1A, which is a film autoradiogram of a sagittal section of a mouse sacrificed 15 minutes after the intravenous injection of radiolabeled histamine, a small molecule of molecular weight of approximately 100 Daltons. Small molecules readily penetrate the porous capillaries perfusing all organs except for the brain or spinal cord (Figure 1A). The small molecule cannot cross the capillary barrier in the brain because there are no paracellular or transcellular pathways for free solute exchange in the CNS microvasculature and there is no histamine transport system at the luminal membrane of the BBB.

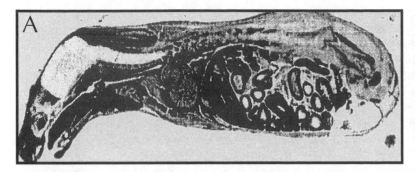

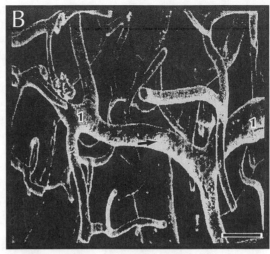

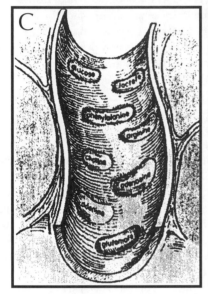

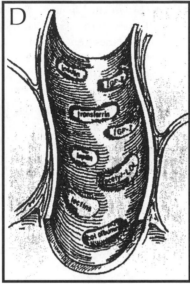

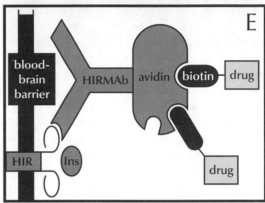

Figure 1.   (A) Autoradiogram of the mouse sacrificed 15 minutes after the intravenous injection of [14C] histamine, a small molecule that readily crosses the capillary wall in peripheral tissues, but does not cross the capillary endothelial wall, which makes up the blood-barrier (BBB), in brain or spinal cord. (B) Scanning electron micrograph of a vascular cast of the human cerebellar cortex. The magnification is 40 microns. From (4). (C) Carrier-mediated transport systems for nutrients. A representative nutrient for 8 different transport systems is shown. Any given transport system may mediate the BBB transport of a group of substrates of common molecular structure. (D) Receptor-mediated transcytosis (RMT) systems for insulin, insulin-like growth factor (IGF)-I, transferrin, IGF-II, and leptin. The receptor-mediated endocytosis system is shown for acetylated-low density lipoprotein (LDL). Absorptive-mediated transcytosis systems are shown for lectins and cationized (cat.) albumin. (E) Chimeric peptide technology for BBB delivery of drugs that normally do not cross the BBB. The drug is monobiotinylated and bound to a conjugate of avidin and a brain transport vector. The most active BBB transport vector is a monoclonal antibody (MAb) against the human insulin receptor (HIR). The HIRMAb binds an exofacial epitope on the HIR which is distinct from the binding site for insulin (Ins), and this binding catalyzes the RMT of the HIRMAb, and any attached drug, through the BBB in vivo.

The anatomical locus of the BBB is the vascular endothelium in the brain which is depicted in a scanning electron micrograph of a vascular cast of the human cerebellar cortex (Figure 1B). The capillaries are approximately 40 microns apart and it takes a small molecule (such as glucose) around 1 second to diffuse 40 microns. The capillary transit time in the brain is approximately 1 second. Therefore, the angioarchitecture of the brain has evolved to allow for instantaneous solute equilibration throughout the brain interstitium, once the molecule crosses the limiting membrane which is the BBB. The BBB is comprised of the luminal and abluminal membranes of the capillary endothelium. The endothelial cell shares a capillary basement membrane with the pericyte, which sits on the brain side of the endothelium. The pericyte has an antigen presentation role in the CNS (Duvernoy, Delon, & Vannson, 1993). More than 99% of the brain surface of the capillary basement membrane is invested by astrocyte foot processes. The distance between the astrocyte foot process and the capillary endothelium is only 20 nm or 200 Angstroms,

and this distance is equal to the thickness of the capillary basement membrane. There are no tight junctions between astrocyte foot processes, and the astrocyte foot process constitutes no permeability barrier in the brain. Because the astrocyte does not comprise any component of the permeability barrier per se, BBB function is often asserted to be derived solely from the endothelial cell. In fact, there are paracrine interactions between the capillary endothelium, the pericyte, and the astrocyte foot process. These two other cells of the microcirculation, the astrocyte and the pericyte, play significant roles in solute and cellular trafficking between blood and brain.

BIOLOGICAL TRANSPORT AT THE BLOOD-BRAIN BARRIER

Lipid Mediated Transport

Molecules that are lipid soluble and have a molecular weight under a 500 Dalton threshold are able to cross the BBB in pharmacologically significant amounts (Pardridge, 1998b). All present-day CNS drugs in clinical practice fulfill these dual criteria of lipid solubility and molecular weight under a 500 Dalton threshold. If a molecule lacks both of these criteria, it is unlikely the molecule will cross the BBB in pharmacologically significant amounts, unless the molecule has affinity for one of the CMT or RMT systems in the BBB. In the absence of this, the molecule will need a brain drug delivery system if the drug is to be used as a neuropharmaceutical. Since more than 98% of the drugs that emanate from high throughput receptor-based CNS drug discovery programs will not cross the BBB, and will give an autoradiogram picture comparable to that of histamine (Figure 1A), the presence of the BBB poses a significant problem for future CNS drug development. On this basis, it is important that there be parallel progress in both CNS drug discovery *and* CNS drug delivery so that these two pathways can be merged in the overall CNS drug development process. Unfortunately, less than 1% of present day CNS drug development is devoted to CNS drug delivery, and over 99% is applied to CNS drug discovery.

Carrier-Mediated Transport

Different classes of circulating nutrients gain access to brain via different carrier-mediated transport systems localized within the BBB. The hexose carrier transports glucose, 2-deoxyglucose, 2-fluorodeoxyglucose, 3-O-methylglucose, galactose, and manose, but not fructose. The large neutral amino acid transporter transports approximately 14 neutral amino acids in the circulation with a higher affinity for the large neutrals (which are dietary essential amino acids) relative to the small nonessential neutral amino acids. The Km of the BBB neutral amino acid transport system is low and approximates the plasma concentration of circulating amino acids (Pardridge, 1977). Conversely, the Km of neutral amino acid transporters in peripheral tissues is in the 1–10 mM range; that is, 10–100-fold higher than the plasma concentrations of amino acids. Accordingly, the brain is uniquely sensitive to the effects of competition at BBB transport sites. Therefore, a selective increase in the plasma concentration of a single large neutral amino acid such as phenylalanine will have an inhibitory effect on the brain uptake of other circulating neutral amino acids that share this common transport system. This explains how the brain concentration of tryptophan, and its derivatives such as serotonin, are decreased when the plasma concentration of a particular amino acid (e.g., phenylalanine) is increased above the normal level. This situation arises with the dietary ingestion of excessive amounts of aspartame, a dietary sweetener which is aspartyl phenylalanine methyl ester. Aspartame consumption in high doses gives rise to high blood phenylalanine levels, following hydrolysis of the dipeptide in the gut. The monocarboxylic acid carrier transports lactate, pyruvate, and the ketone bodies, β-hydroxybutyrate and aceto-acetate. These are principal carbon sources for brain energy metabolism in states of ketosis such as prolonged fasting, a high-fat diet, or the postnatal period. In addition to the nutrients shown in Figure 1C, there are carrier-mediated transport systems for thyroid hormones and water-soluble vitamins such as folic acid and biotin.

Receptor-Mediated Transcytosis

Certain circulating peptides (such as insulin, insulin-like growth factor [IGF]-1, IGF-2, transferrin, or leptin) gain access to the brain via receptor-mediated transcytosis systems localized within the brain capillary endothelium (Figure 1D). These processes explain how insulin is found in the brain although it is not synthesized there. Leptin is secreted by fat cells in response to a meal and crosses the BBB on the leptin receptor to induce satiety. In animals given a high-fat diet, there is a significant upregulation of the BBB leptin receptor protein which is derived from the short-form transcript, which is one of the differentially processed mRNA molecules produced by the leptin gene.

The receptor-mediated transport systems for the peptides shown in Figure 1D have been identified for the human BBB using isolated human brain capillaries as an in vitro model system of BBB transport (Pardridge, 1991). It is convenient to isolate capillaries from human brain. Therefore, it is now possible to perform biochemical studies of human BBB transport systems, and this has been done for both the RMT and the CMT systems.

DRUG DELIVERY USING THE ENDOGENOUS CMT AND RMT SYSTEMS

Present day CNS drug delivery strategies are often aimed at increasing the lipid solubility of the drug. While this may increase the BBB permeability coefficient, this "lipidization" also increases the permeability coefficient of the drug in all peripheral tissues, which results in a parallel decrease in the plasma area under the concentration curve (AUC) for the drug (Pardridge, 1998b). The brain uptake of a drug, expressed as percent of injected dose delivered per gram of brain, is an equal function of the BBB permeability-surface area (PS) product, and the plasma AUC of the drug. Since these two factors (BBB PS product, plasma AUC) are inversely affected by lipidization, there tends to be minimal increases in brain uptake of a drug following lipidization. An alternative approach to solving the CNS drug delivery problem is to structure drugs in such a way that they will have access to one of the endogenous CMT transport systems. A classical example of this is the use of L-DOPA for the treatment of Parkinson's disease. L-DOPA is a large neutral amino acid that gains access to brain via transport on the BBB neutral amino acid transport system (Pardridge, 1977). Once inside the brain, L-DOPA is converted by aromatic amino acid decarboxylase to dopamine, which then enhances dopaminergic function in patients with Parkinson's disease. Dopamine, like histamine (Figure 1A), does not cross the BBB, but its precursor, L-DOPA, does cross the BBB via CMT on the neutral amino acid transporter (Figure 1C).

There are over 200 neuropeptide neuromodulator systems in the CNS, and each of these receptors has an affinity for more than 200 neuropeptides produced in the brain. In contrast, there are only about a dozen receptor systems for the monamine or amino acid neurotransmitter systems. Therefore, the remarkable diversity of brain function apparently arises from the diversity of neuropeptide expression in the brain. On this basis, it would be advantageous to image the regional expression of different receptor systems within the brain using endogenous peptides as peptide radiopharmaceuticals for CNS imaging. The problem here is that the peptide radiopharmaceutical does not cross the BBB. This problem can be solved by the use of chimeric peptide technology (Pardridge, 1991). Chimeric peptides are formed by conjugating a nontransportable peptide to a BBB transport vector. The latter is comprised of an endogenous peptide or peptidomimetic monoclonal antibody (MAb) that undergoes transcytosis through the BBB on one of the RMT systems (Figure 1E). For example, anti-transferrin receptor (TfR) or antihuman insulin receptor (HIR) MAbs bind exofacial epitopes on the BBB TfR or HIR to mediate the transcytosis of these peptidomimetic MAbs through the BBB.

A model peptide radiopharmaceutical is epidermal growth factor (EGF), and the epidermal growth factor receptor (EGFR) is overexpressed in brain tumors. After intravenous injection of the EGF peptide radiopharmaceutical conjugated to the BBB drug delivery system (Figure 1E), there was neuroimaging of the tumor in vivo. In the absence of conjugation of the EGF peptide radiopharmaceutical to a BBB drug delivery system, there was no uptake of the EGF by either normal brain or the brain tumor, due to the lack of transport of this peptide across the BBB in either normal brain or brain tumor (Pardridge, 1999). These studies demonstrate that it is possible to use a peptide radiopharmaceutical that does not normally cross the BBB to image regional neuropeptide receptor systems within the CNS. The use of peptide radiopharmaceuticals that are capable of transport through the BBB could also be used to image the upregulation or downregulation of neuropeptide receptor systems localized within the CNS using the cognate peptide as a peptide radiopharmaceutical to image the respective receptor system.

BLOOD-BRAIN BARRIER FUNCTION IN PSYCHOLOGIC STRESS

BBB disruption occurs when the blood-brain barrier breaks down in pathologic states. BBB disruption can also be achieved through a variety of toxicologic interventions. For example, the intra-carotid arterial infusion of noxious agents such as 2-M-manitol, alkylating agents, acidosis, or heavy metals will cause BBB disruption. Severe pathologic states such as ischemia, head trauma, or advanced brain tumors will also cause BBB disruption.

The disruption of the BBB is not normally associated with physiologic CNS function in nondisease states. However, there is evidence that the BBB is transiently disrupted in states of severe emotionality. When rats are subjected to a conditioned fear response, there is focal BBB disruption in the hippocampus and somatosensory cortex (Hayes, Pechura, Povlishock, & Becker, 1985). Soldiers serving in the Gulf War were administered nerve gas antidotes that do not normally cross the BBB and do not normally have CNS side effects (Friedman, Kaufer, Shermer, Hendler, Soreq, & Tur-Kaspa, 1996). However, there was an incidence of side effects from these drugs of almost 50% in soldiers subjected to the severe emotionality of combat situations and fear of imminent death. There is evidence that the BBB is disrupted in such severe states of emotionality in humans, which caused the nerve gas antidote to enter the brain because of a porous BBB in certain regions of the brain. A similar phenomena may also occur in elderly patients who are acutely admitted to a hospital. This is a state of severe stress for these elderly patients and the BBB may be disrupted in the first 24 hours of hospitalization, which may underlie the high incidence of CNS neurotoxicity of drugs that do not normally cross the BBB. The biochemical basis of BBB disruption is poorly understood and is an area in need of additional research. Once the biochemical basis of this process is elucidated, new drugs may be developed to prevent BBB disruption in states of severe emotionality.

CONCLUSION

Since the blood-brain barrier forms the interface between blood and brain, this important membrane has been given only marginal attention within the neurosciences. Neuroscientists have historically neglected this important membrane and have failed to incorporate BBB biology within the overall neuroscience paradigm. This is a serious mistake at both the levels of pure and applied science. At the level of applied science, the failure to incorporate BBB cellular and molecular biology within the molecular neurosciences explains why less than 1% of current CNS drug development is devoted to CNS drug delivery and more than 99% is devoted to CNS drug discovery. This imbalance is imprudent since more than 98% of all new CNS drugs do not cross the BBB and will require BBB drug delivery strategies. In the absence of BBB drug delivery technologies, the new CNS drugs will be useless as neuropharmaceuticals for humans. This problem can be rectified by incorporating brain capillary endothelial transport biology into the molecular neurosciences. This will ensure that growth in CNS drug delivery is fostered in parallel with the growth in CNS drug discovery. At the level of pure science, it is likely that the capillary endothelial cell sends signals to both astrocytes and neurons which regulate brain function and learning. In the myocardium, the endothelial cells secrete factors which regulate myocardial fiber contractility (Ramaciotti, Sharkey, McClellan, & Winegrad, 1992). In the brain, there is paracrine signaling between astrocytes and neurons and between astrocytes and endothelial cells. It is likely that there is also paracrine signaling from endothelial cells to astrocytes and from endothelial cells to neurons, apart from the transport of nutrients across the endothelial barrier to brain cells.

REFERENCES

Brightman, M. W., Reese, T. S., & Feder, N. (1970). Assessment with the electron-microscope of the permeability to peroxidase of cerebral endothelium and epithelium in mice and sharks. In C. Crone and N. A. Lassen, (Eds.), *Capillary permeability* (p. 463).

Duvernoy, H., Delon, S., and Vannson, J. L. (1983). The vascularization of the human cerebellar cortex. *Brain Research, 11,* 419–480.

Friedman, A., Kaufer, D., Shemer, J., Hendler, I., Soreq, H., and Tur-Kaspa, I. (1996). Pyridostigmine brain penetration under stress enhances neuronal excitability and induces early immediate transcriptional response. *Nature Medicine, 2,* 1382–1385.

Hayes, R. L., Pechura, C. M., Povlishock, J. T., and Becker, D. P. (1985). Changes in blood-brain barrier function associated with conditioned fear in rats. In *Procedures of the Sixth International Symposium on Brain Edema* (pp. 224–227). New York: Springer-Verlag.

Pardridge, W. M. (1977). Regulation of amino acid availability to the brain. In R. J. Wurtman and J. J. Wurtman (Eds.), *Nutrition and the brain* (Vol. 1, pp. 141–204). New York: Raven.

Pardridge, W. M. (1991). *Peptide drug delivery to the brain.* New York: Raven.

Pardridge, W. M. (1998a). Blood-brain barrier methodology and biology. In W. M. Pardridge (Ed.), *Introduction to the blood-brain barrier: Methodology, biology, and pathology* (pp. 1–8). Cambridge, UK: Cambridge University Press.

Pardridge, W. M. (1998b). CNS drug design based on principles of blood-barrier transport. *Journal of Neurochemistry, 70,* 1781–1792.

Pardridge, W. M. (1999). Non-invasive drug delivery to the human brain using endogenous blood-brain barrier transport systems. *Pharmaceutical Science and Technology Today, 2,* 49–59.

Ramaciotti, C., Sharkey, A., McClellan, G., and Winegrad, S. (1992). Endothelial cells regulate cardiac contractility. *Procedures of the National Academy of the Sciences of the United States of America, 89,* 4033–4036.

W. M. PARDRIDGE
University of California, Los Angeles

BRAIN INJURIES
CENTRAL NERVOUS SYSTEM
IGF

BODY IMAGE

People are affected in a very fundamental way by how they perceive their bodies and how they think others perceive them. This perception is related to societal standards and cultural concepts. Thus in certain cultures a hefty body is considered attractive, while in other cultures the ideal is a slim and trim figure. Persons are not simply affected by the social and cultural standards of physical beauty; rather, their attitudes and evaluations of certain body traits determine how they feel about themselves.

If persons feel basically unattractive, unappealing, or in some way physically inferior, these self-perceptions are likely to have a powerful effect on other areas of their lives. For example, a man may think that his ears are too big and his nose ill-shaped, that he has an ugly complexion, and that he is too short and not muscular enough. Perhaps he believes that others will not want to approach him because of his appearance, in which case he may well send messages telling others that he is basically unattractive, that they will not like him, and should keep away.

Consider also the example of an overweight woman. She may not like her excessive weight and may even be ashamed to look in the mirror. It may give her great discomfort to talk about her body and how she feels about it, and she may avoid people because of it. In reality, this person is probably getting certain payoffs for keeping herself overweight, even if they are negative. By convincing herself that she is rejected because of her fat, she does not have to look at other dimensions of herself. Or she may keep weight on as a way of getting constant parental attention, even if that attention consists of nagging her to watch what she eats. Whatever her reasons for being overweight, this situation has an impact on how she views herself, her level of self-esteem, and the choices she makes in other areas of her life.

It is useful to consider the sources of one's decisions as related to body image. Individuals might ask themselves questions such as the following: As children or adolescents, did they feel embarrassed about certain physical characteristics? As they matured and these characteristics changed, did their perceptions of these characteristics also change? Where did they pick up certain attitudes about their bodies? It is important that individuals challenge themselves with respect to the evidence that justifies their current self-perception.

In discussing the relationship between body image and the healthy personality, Jourard commented that a healthy body ideal is one that is not too discrepant from the cultural concept of an ideal body, but that is revised by the person to make allowances for uniqueness and individuality. His and Landsman's *Healthy Personality* (1974/1980) points out that people modify their views of the ideal body to make allowances for increasing age, so they can continue to regard themselves as reasonably attractive at each stage of life. This adjustment is important, since otherwise one may aspire to unrealistic and unattainable goals. In Jourard's view, an accurate body concept is essential for achieving a healthy personality. Unfortunately, many people have been taught erroneous beliefs about their bodies. They may become alienated from their bodies, and lose the capacity to pay attention to the messages their bodies are sending to themselves and to others.

One's body image—the picture and evaluation of one's body—is a basic part of one's self-concept. While cultural standards of beauty are critical in forming this self-evaluation, one's attitudes are even more influential in determining one's self-concept. One of the problems with uncritically accepting cultural norms of the ideal body is that few people really attain them. For those who fall drastically short of these cultural ideals, the result can be devastating in terms of self-worth as it relates to body image. It is thus essential for individuals to make an honest assessment of how they see their bodies and how they feel about them. This subjective evaluation of their bodies is at least as powerful as their objective physical traits and fortunately is open to change. Once persons make an evaluation of their bodies, they have the capacity to challenge certain cultural standards and their degree of conformity with these standards. If they do not like certain characteristics, they are in a position to change some of these traits. At the very least, they can change their attitudes about some bodily characteristics, which can have a significant effect on changing other areas of their lives.

REFERENCES

Jourard, S. M., & Landsman, T. (1980). Healthy personality: *An approach from the viewpoint of humanistic psychology.* New York: Macmillan. (Original work published 1974)

SUGGESTED READING

Atwater, E. (1979). *Psychology of adjustment: Personal growth in a changing world.* Englewood Cliffs, NJ: Prentice-Hall.

Corey, G. (1983). *I never knew I had a choice.* Monterey, CA: Brooks/Cole.

Kleinke, C. L. (1975). *First impressions: The psychology of encountering others.* Englewood Cliffs, NJ: Prentice-Hall (Spectrum).

Lowen, A. (1958). *The language of the body.* New York: Collier.

G. F. COREY
California State University

BOGARDUS SOCIAL DISTANCE SCALE

The Bogardus Social Distance Scale was one of the first techniques for measuring attitudes toward racial and ethnic groups. The basic concept behind the Bogardus scale is that the more prejudiced an individual is against a particular group, the less that person will wish to interact with members of that group (Dawes, 1972). Thus, the items that comprise a Bogardus scale describe relationships into which a respondent might be willing to enter with a member of the specified cultural group (e.g., spouse, friend, neighbor, co-worker, citizen, visitor from another country, etc.). Items are worded in terms of either inclusion or exclusion. "Would you accept an 'X' as a spouse?" is an example of an inclusion question; "Would you keep all 'Ys' out of America?" is an example of an exclusion question. The attitude or esteem in which the respondent holds the specified group is defined as the closeness of relationship that the respondent reports as being willing to accept with a member of that group. In Bogardus' early work (1928), he found that white Americans maintained relatively small social distances from groups such as the British, Canadians, and Northern Europeans, but greater social distances to Southern Europeans. Groups that differed racially (e.g., Blacks and Asians) were subject to even larger social distances.

Extending the typical use of Bogardus scales, Triandis and Triandis (1960) used multi-factor experimental designs to separate the independent effects of varying aspects of group membership (e.g., race, religion, and occupation). They later showed that various aspects of group membership of the respondents correlate with the social distances the group members assign to various other groups (1962). Thus, Americans were found to consider race an important variable while Greeks considered religion to be more critical. Personality factors, such as dogmatism, have also been shown to be related to one's proclivity to desire relatively large social distances from groups other than one's own.

The Bogardus scale is a type of Guttman scale. Thus, someone willing to accept members of a certain group as friends would also be willing to accept them as neighbors, co-workers, fellow citizens, and all other relationships more distant than friendship. While the responses of some individuals do occasionally reverse the rank-ordered nature of the items, average responses of groups (e.g., cultural or racial groups) tend to maintain the order in a well-constructed Bogardus scale (Triandis & Triandis, 1965). Hence, the Bogardus approach to attitude measurement is an effective means of estimating the esteem in which one group of individuals is held by other distinct groups.

While the Bogardus approach to measuring attitudes between and among groups is primarily of historical importance, it continued to be used in recent years. It has generally been employed to assess attitudes in the sense of social distances among both ethnic and racial groups (e.g., Adler, 1985; Kleg & Yamamoto, 1998; Kunz & Yaw, 1989; Law & Lane, 1987) and among various psychologically defined groups (Maddux, Scheiber, & Bass, 1982) and groups representing those with various disabilities (Eisenman, 1986; Tolor & Geller, 1987).

REFERENCES

Adler, L. L. (1985). Projected social distances as an indicator of attitudes. In P. Pedersen (Ed.), *Handbook of cross-cultural counseling and therapy* (pp. 247–255). Westport, CT: Greenwood.

Bogardus, E. S. (1928). *Immigration and race attitudes.* Boston: Heath.

Dawes, R. M. (1972). *Fundamentals of attitude measurement.* New York: Wiley.

Eisenman, R. (1986). Social distances toward Blacks and the physically disabled. *College Student Journal, 20,* 189–190.

Kidder, L. H. (1981). *Research methods in social relations.* New York: Holt, Rinehart and Winston.

Kleg, M., & Yamamoto, K. (1998). As the world turns: Ethno-racial distances after 70 years. *Social Science Journal, 35,* 183–190.

Kunz, P. R., & Yaw, O. S. (1989). Social distance: A study of changing views of young Mormons toward Black individuals. *Psychological Reports, 65,* 195–200.

Law, S. G., & Lane, D. S. (1987). Multicultural acceptance by teacher education students: A survey of attitudes toward 12 ethnic and national groups and a comparison with 60 years of data. *Journal of Instructional Psychology, 14,* 3–9.

Maddux, C. D., Scheiber, L. M., & Bass, J. E. (1982). Self-concept and social distance in gifted children. *Gifted Child Quarterly, 26,* 77–81.

Tolor, A., & Geller, D. (1987). Psychologists' attitudes toward children having various disabilities. *Psychological Reports, 60,* 1177–1178.

Triandis, H. C., & Triandis, L. M. (1960). Race, social class, religion and nationality as determinants of social distance. *Journal of Abnormal and Social Psychology, 61,* 110–118.

Triandis, H. C., & Triandis, L. M. (1962). A cross-cultural study of social distance. *Psychological Monographs, 76*(540).

Triandis, H. C., & Triandis, L. M. (1965). Some studies of social distance. In I. D. Steiner & M. Fishbein (Eds.), *Current studies in social psychology.* New York: Holt, Rinehart & Winston.

K. F. GEISINGER
Le Moyne College

CULTURAL BIAS IN TESTS
PREJUDICE AND DISCRIMINATION
STEREOTYPING

BORDERLINE PERSONALITY

Prior to the fashionable status it achieved in the 1970s, the label "borderline" was most often assigned when a clinician was uncertain about the diagnosis of a patient. Recognizing that many patients do exhibit mixed symptoms of indeterminant seriousness and changing character, certain theorists, notably Otto Kernberg in *Borderline Conditions and Pathological Narcissism,* and Theodore Millon in *Modern Psychopathology,* proposed that the borderline concept be formally employed to represent a mid-range level of personality cohesion or prognostic severity. Although their view was that the borderline designation is best construed as a moderately decompensated level of functioning observable among different personality types and symptom constellations, the 1980 *Diagnostic and Statistical Manual of Mental Disorders* (*3rd ed.*) characterized the syndrome as a discrete entity, a specific and identifiable disorder that possesses its own distinctive clinical features.

The most salient symptom ascribed to these personalities is the depth and variability of their moods. Borderlines typically experience extended periods of dejection and disillusionment, interspersed on occasion with brief excursions of euphoria and significantly more frequent episodes of irritability, self-destructive acts, and impulsive anger. Most individuals with this personality will have had checkered histories in either personal relationships or in school or work performance. Few persevere to attain mature goals and many exhibit an extreme unevenness in fulfilling normal social functions and responsibilities. Their histories show repeated setbacks, a lack of judgment and foresight, tendencies to digress from earlier aspirations, and failures to utilize their natural aptitudes. Most appear not to learn from their troubled experiences and involve themselves in the same imbroglios and quandaries as before. Disturbances in identity and goals are extremely common, evident in uncertainties regarding self-esteem, gender, and vocational aims. Their periodic moody contrariness often alternates with subjective feelings and complaints of isolation, emptiness, or boredom.

Because of its newness as a formal diagnostic designation, the label "borderline" has no historical tradition or clinical literature. Nevertheless, there are precursors that refer to essentially the same constellation of traits. Thus, in the eighth edition of his *Lehrbuch,* Kraepelin described what he termed the "excitable personality" in the following manner: "the coloring of mood is subject to frequent change . . . periods are interpolated in which they are irritable and ill-humored, also perhaps sad, spiritless, anxious; they shed tears without cause . . . they are mostly very distractible and unsteady in their endeavors" (1921). Schneider referred to a "labile personality" in *Psychopathic Personalities,* depicting such individuals as "characterized by the abrupt and rapid changes of mood . . . and [exhibiting] sporadic reactions of a morose and irritable character" (1923/1950, pp. 116–120). Stern was the first among those of a psychoanalytic persuasion to apply the designation "borderline" in 1938 to a group of treatment-resistant neuroses. Schmideberg in 1947, Wolberg in 1952, and Knight in 1953 also presented thoughtful papers on borderline functioning from an analytic perspective. More recent is the work of Kernberg, who portrayed the syndrome in the following manner in *Borderline Conditions and Pathological Narcissism:* "Such patients . . . present . . . a lack of clear identity and lack of understanding in depth of other people . . . a lack of impulse control, lack of anxiety tolerance, [and a] lack of sublimatory capacity" (1975, pp. 161–162). Drawing upon a biosocial-learning approach to personality, Millon formulated the following diagnostic criteria for the borderline individual in *Disorders of Personality:*

1. Intense endogenous moods (e.g., continually fails to accord mood with external events; is either depressed or excited or has recurring periods of dejection and apathy interspersed with spells of anger, anxiety, or euphoria).

2. Dysregulated activation (e.g., experiences desultory energy level and irregular sleep-wake cycle; describes time periods which suggest that affective-activation equilibrium is constantly in jeopardy).

3. Self-condemnatory conscience (e.g., reveals recurring self-mutilating and suicidal thoughts; periodically redeems moody behavior through contrition and self-derogation).

4. Dependency anxiety (e.g., is preoccupied with securing affection and maintaining emotional support; reacts intensely to separation and reports haunting fear of isolation and loss).

5. Cognitive-affective ambivalence (e.g., repeatedly struggles to express attitudes contrary to inner feelings; simultaneously experiences conflicting emotions and thoughts toward self and others, notably love, rage, and guilt).

REFERENCES

Kernberg, O. F. (1975). *Borderline conditions and pathological narcissism.* New York: Aronson.

Knight, R. P. (1953). Borderline states. *Bulletin of the Menninger Clinic, 17,* 1–12.

Millon, T. (1969). *Modern psychopathology: A biosocial approach to maladaptive learning and functioning.* Philadelphia: Saunders.

Millon, T. (1981). *Disorders of personality: DSM-III, Axis II.* New York: Wiley-Interscience.

Schmideberg, M. (1947). The treatment of psychopaths and borderline patients. *American Journal of Psychotherapy, 1,* 45–55.

Schneider, K. (1950). *Psychopathic personalities.* London: Cassell. (Original work published 1923)

Wolberg, A. (1952). The "borderline patient." *American Journal of Psychotherapy, 6,* 694–701.

T. MILLON
University of Miami

DIAGNOSTIC AND STATISTICAL MANUAL OF MENTAL DISORDERS
PERSONALITY DISORDERS

BOREDOM

Boredom is an emotional state ranging from mild to severe unpleasantness, which people describe as a feeling of tedium, monotony, ennui, apathy, meaninglessness, emptiness, wearisomeness, and lack of interest or connection with the current environment. Plutchik's structural model of eight basic emotions (1980) places boredom as being close to, but milder than, loathing and disgust and bordering the other mild emotions, annoyance and pensiveness. Boredom is the state, and boredom proneness is the trait—a tendency to experience tedium and lack of personal involvement and enthusiasm, to have a general or frequent lack of sufficient interest in one's life surroundings and future. The most commonly used measure of boredom and boredom proneness, as with many internal emotional conditions, such as depression and anxiety, is some form of self-report. Behavioral indicators (seldom used in research) could include yawning, "glazed eyes," slumped posture, restlessness, and such signs of inattention as looking around the room. Emotions or states opposite to boredom include interest, enthusiasm, involvement, engagement, "flow", and optimal stimulation.

Paradoxically, boredom is interesting—for both practical and theoretical reasons. Boredom is of practical importance because of its alleged relationships to many social problems, such as delinquency, dropping out of school, drug abuse, depression, low morale, poor industrial production, job turnover, and institutionalization within prisons, mental hospitals, military settings, and nursing homes. Being boring is a condition that all lecturers, entertainers, and advertisers try to avoid. Although boredom is an emotion that probably everyone has experienced, it has received much less research attention than emotions such as depression and anger. In a review covering 1926 to 1980, Smith (1981) found less than one article per year on boredom. However, in the 20 years after 1980, the pace of research and theoretical activity increased, and PsycINFO citations occurred at the rate of 8 or 9 a year.

In addition to practical reasons, there are important theoretical reasons to understand boredom as a motivational concept connecting inner feelings and motives with environmental conditions. A variety of theories relate boredom to attention, arousal, information-processing, and stimulus underload. Berlyne (1960, p. 187) stated that boredom is "a drive that is reduced through divertive exploration and aroused when external stimuli are excessively scarce or excessively monotonous." The most common theoretical approach construes boredom as occurring in situations with less than the optimal level of stimulation. Theorists tend to emphasize either external conditions or internal predispositions or characteristics. Industrial research is mainly concerned with external conditions as they affect productivity. In contrast, Zuckerman (1979) emphasized internal elements and saw boredom susceptibility as a part of a stimulus-seeking model. For existentialists, a distinction may be made between existential boredom (the realization of the lack of intrinsic meaning in life and the need to create that meaning) and neurotic boredom (an anxious lack of interest or purpose in life). Psychoanalytic thought brings in another research-generating element—sense of control; for instance, Fenichel (1951, p. 359) stated that boredom occurs "when we must not do what we want to do, or must do what we do not want to do."

Boredom involves ongoing person-environment relationships—the fit of the individual's characteristics to the situation's characteristics. Csikszentmihalyi (1975, 1990) explored the balance of boredom with anxiety, both being mismatches between environmental challenge and personal competence. Boredom occurs in situations in which a person's capabilities are greater than situational opportunities for expression, while anxiety comes when the environment demands more of the person that he or she is able to perform or give at the time. The achievement of balance occurs in "flow," a condition of pleasurable absorbed interest in an activity. Cross-cultural issues also offer possible theoretical challenges for exploring boredom as an important relation between person and environment.

Research on boredom falls into three general kinds. One kind consists of experiments in which conditions are manipulated using a stimulus situation assumed to be boring, such as the monotonous task of crossing out a given letter on pages of random letters, or tasks requiring vigilance. Another research approach involves studying the experience of daily life; this has been mainly done by Csikszentmihalyi and his associates (1988, 1990) who ask for responses to beeper calls. A third approach is to correlate ratings or questionnaires about boredom with other measures or conditions.

In devising his Stimulus Seeking Scale, Zuckerman (1979) included a Boredom Susceptibility subscale which has been used in many studies. Another of the few relevant measures is the Boredom Proneness scale, or BP (Farmer & Sundberg, 1986), a 28-item self-report scale, which shows good reliability and some evidence of validity, but does not correlate significantly with the Zuckerman subscale. Vodanovich and Kass (1990a) identified five factors in the BP scale conceptually very similar to those discussed in the literature: external stimulation, internal stimulation, affective responses to boredom, perception of time (slowness), and constraints (on self-initiated actions). Males appear to be more boredom-prone than females (Vodanovich & Kass, 1990b). Boredom may be highest in adolescence and seems to decrease with age (Shaw, Caldwell, & Kleiber, 1996; Birdi, Warr, & Oswald, 1995), and cultural and ethnic differences have been observed (Sundberg, Latkin, Farmer, & Sauod, 1991; Watt & Vodanovich, 1992). Among other things, studies suggest that BP may relate to disinclination to vote, narcissism, forms of self-absorption, pathological gambling, health status, lack of creativity, and depression. Interpersonal elements, such as loneliness and lack of purpose in life, seem to be related to boredom.

Zuckerman (1979, 1986) has been a proponent of physiological factors in boredom and sensation-seeking in line with Eysenck's theory. Eysenck postulated that the arousal systems of extroverted people require more stimulation that those of introverts; therefore, in seeking optimal levels of stimulation, extroverts are more outgoing, carefree, and impulsive. In his review, Smith (1981) noted that the most consistent finding was that extroverts were especially vulnerable to boredom. Hamilton (1983a) found increases in capacity for sustained attention in relation to biological indicators during development in later childhood and adolescence.

Coping with boredom is another area of study. Hamilton (1983a, 1983b) has been particularly interested in this topic and has developed a brief self-report measure of intrinsic enjoyment and boredom coping. She and her colleagues have found these measures to be related to ability to attend to a performance task for long periods—an important element in many industrial and military situations requiring continuous vigilance. Hamilton (1983b) argued for training attentional habits to prevent psychopathology. Fantasy is one way of coping with monotonous situations, and a paucity of fantasy may be related to boredom proneness. A number of clinicians have been concerned about coping with boredom during psychotherapy either on the part of the patient or the therapist; boredom is seen as an indicator of problems in transference or countertransference. The positive function of boredom may be to alert a person to do something different.

In conclusion, boredom seems to be generating more and more research attention. At this point, the findings suggest hypotheses for many kinds of studies. There is a strong need for theoretical development relating the variety of empirical results to a larger theory of emotions.

REFERENCES

Berlyne, D. E. (1960). *Conflict, arousal and curiosity.* New York: McGraw-Hill.

Birdi, K., Warr, P., & Oswald, A. (1995). Age differences in three components of employee well-being. *Applied Psychology: An International Review, 44,* 345–373.

Csikszentmihalyi, M. (1975). *Beyond boredom and anxiety.* San Francisco: Jossey-Bass.

Csikszentmihalyi, M., & Csikszentmihalyi, I. S. (1988). *Optimal experience: Psychological studies of flow in consciousness.* Cambridge, UK: Cambridge University Press.

Fenichel, O. (1951). On the psychology of boredom. In D. Rappaport (Ed.), *Organization and pathology of thought.* (pp. 349–361). New York: Columbia University Press.

Hamilton, J. A. (1983a). Development of interest and enjoyment in adolescence: I. Attentional capacities. *Journal of Youth and Adolescence, 12,* 355–362.

Hamilton, J. A. (1983b). Development of interest and enjoyment in adolescence: II. Boredom and psychopathology. *Journal of Youth and Adolescence, 12,* 363–372.

Plutchik, R. (1980). *Emotion: A psychoevolutionary synthesis.* New York: Harper & Row.

Shaw, S. M., Caldwell, L. L., & Kleiber, D. A. (1996). Boredom, stress and social control in the daily activities of adolescents. *Journal of Leisure Research, 28,* 274–292.

Smith, R. P. (1981). Boredom: A review. *Human Factors, 23,* 329–340.

Sundberg, N. D., Latkin, C. A., Farmer, R. F., & Saoud, J. (1991). Boredom in young adults: Gender and cultural comparisons. *Journal of Cross-Cultural Psychology, 22,* 209–223.

Vodanovich, S. J., & Kass, S. J. (1990a). A factor analytic study of the Boredom Proneness Scale. *Journal of Personality Assessment, 55,* 115–123.

Vodanovich, S. J., & Kass, S. J., (1990b). Age and gender differences in boredom proneness. In J. W. Neuliep (Ed.), *Handbook of replication research in the behavioral and social sciences* [Special Issue]. *Journal of Social Behavior and Personality, 5,* 297–307.

Watt, J. D., & Vodanovich, S. J. (1992). An examination of race and gender differences in boredom. *Journal of Social Behavior and Personality, 7,* 169–175.

Zuckerman, M. (1979). *Sensation seeking: Beyond the optimal level of arousal.* Hillsdale, NJ: Erlbaum.

Zuckerman, M. (1986). Sensation seeking and the endogenous deficit theory of drug abuse. *National Institute of Drug Abuse Research Monograph Series, 74,* 59–70.

SUGGESTED READING

Csikszentmihalyi, M. (1990). *Flow: The psychology of optimal experience.* New York: Harper & Row.

Farmer, R., & Sundberg, N. D. (1986). Boredom proneness—The development and correlates of a new scale. *Journal of Personality Assessment, 50,* 4–17.

Mikulas, W. L., & Vodanovich, S. J. (1993). The essence of boredom. *Psychological Record, 43,* 3–12.

N. D. SUNDBERG
University of Oregon

ACADEMIC UNDERACHIEVEMENT
ATTENTION
EMOTIONS
MOTIVATION
SENSATION SEEKING

BORING, EDWARD G. (1886–1968)

Edward G. Boring studied psychology at Cornell University under E. B. Titchener, and received the doctorate in 1914. He went to Clark University in 1919, but moved to Harvard in 1922 and remained there for the rest of his career as a general experimental psychologist. He influenced many generations of students through his teaching of the introductory course in psychology at Harvard.

Although Boring accomplished some classical research on his own, most of his publications were theoretical. He served as editor of *American Journal of Psychology* from 1920 until his death, writing many papers and editorials. Boring is most famous for his histories of psychology. His *History of Experimental Psychology* was first published in 1929; the 1950 edition, a widely accepted classic, is still considered by many to be the outstanding history. The book's theme brought together the individual creative scientist and the *Zeitgeist,* or spirit of the times, and explained how the interaction of the two influenced the direction of psychology.

One of Boring's early books, *The Physical Dimensions of Consciousness,* defined the basic terms of psychology such as sensation, consciousness, and body-mind dualism. He theorized that the body-mind split was not necessary for psychology. In effect, Boring began to move away from Titchener's dualism toward monism, the belief that there is basically only one kind of reality.

Because of his long and distinguished career at Harvard, and his service to psychology in general through its organizations and institutions, Boring was popularly referred to as "Mr. Psychology."

N. A. HAYNIE

BOUCHARD, THOMAS J., JR.

Thomas J. Bouchard grew up in Manchester, New Hampshire. After service in the U.S. Air Force, which provided him with training as an in-flight aircraft and engine mechanic on C-124s, he went on to receive his undergraduate training at the University of New Hampshire and the University of California at Berkeley, graduating Phi Beta Kappa in 1963. In 1966 he received a PhD from Berkeley, under the tutelage of Harrison Gough and Donald MacKinnon at the Institute of Personality Assessment and Research in the Department of Psychology. Bouchard taught and conducted research at the University of California at Santa Barbara from 1966 to 1969. He joined the University of Minnesota Department of Psychology in 1969 and has been there since then, serving as chair of the department from 1985 to 1991. He has been director of the Minnesota Center for Twin and Adoption Research since 1983, and served on the executive committee of the Institute of Human Genetics at the University of Minnesota from 1985 to 1998.

Bouchard's career, while always focusing on human individual differences, has been varied. His initial research work was in social psychology (small group performance) and personality. He moved on to work and teach in industrial/organizational psychology, serving as associate editor of the *Journal of Applied Psychology* from 1977 to 1980. He began work in behavior genetics in 1972 and launched the Minnesota Study of Twins Reared Apart (MISTRA) in 1979. In 1983, with colleagues in the psychology department, he helped launch the large and ongoing Minnesota Twin Family Registry (MTFR). He served as an associate editor of the journal *Behavior Genetics* from 1982 to 1986.

Bouchard is a fellow of the American Association for the Advancement of Science, the American Psychological Association (APA), the American Psychological Society, and the American Association for Applied and Preventative Psychology. He has served as president of the Behavior Genetics Association (1993–1994) and vice president of the International Society for Twin Studies (1989–1992). He was a founding member of the International Genetic Epidemiology Society and served on the board of directors of the Society for the Study of Social Biology from 1995 to 1997. He was the 1995 distinguished scientific speaker for APA and received the 1995 Galton Award from the Galton Institute for the Study of Biology and Society (U.K.).

His major research contribution in recent years has been estimating the various types of environmental and genetic influence on human psychological and medical/physical characteristics. Data from MISTRA and MTFR have replicated findings of other researchers that highlight the importance of both environmental and genetic factors as sources of influence on the variance in such psychological traits as mental abilities and personality, when individuals are reared in the normal (non-traumatic) range of environments. The minimal influence of common family environment on most personality traits is now one of the most replicated yet still controversial findings in psychology. More interestingly, data from MISTRA strongly suggest that genetic factors also influence, at a moderate level, a number of human traits that have seldom been studied by behavior geneticists and that have been widely believed to be influenced by environmental factors alone. Examples include such traits as job satisfaction, work values, psychological interests, religiousness, social attitudes, and psychomotor learning. The findings are controversial and require constructive replication. If they are confirmed, however, they seriously challenge a large number of prevailing theories in the social sciences.

This broad array of findings (moderate heritability of most reliably-measured psychological characteristics) has led Bouchard and his colleagues to formulate a theory to explain them, namely the theory of Experience Producing Drives. This theory (based on an earlier formulation by K. Hayes) proposes that the genome (a distal cause) impresses itself on the psyche largely by influencing the nature, selection, and impact of experiences during development. Environmental factors constitute the apparent proximal cause of psychological trait variance, and environments are necessary for trait development, but the mechanism at work is the steady pressure of the genome on environmental selection. When exposed to sufficiently supportive and varied environmental choices, human beings create their own unique psychological environments; the impact of the continuing experience of these environments is counted as genetic influence. This view implies that even high heritabilities for psychological traits do not imply genetic determinism, nor do they preclude effective interventions in the shaping of behavior. It does imply that rich environmental choice will maximize the equally rich diversity of the human genome.

STAFF

BOWER, GORDON H. (1932–   )

Gordon H. Bower was born December 30, 1932 and grew up in rural Scio, Ohio. An accomplished baseball player and jazz trumpet player in high school, Bower's intellectual interests were fanned by his parents (former schoolteachers) and some inspiring high school teachers. In high school he acquired an abiding interest in Freudian psychoanalysis and decided to become a psychiatrist alongside his career as a baseball pitcher. After high school (from which he graduated valedictorian of his small class of 36 pupils) he turned down offers to play professional baseball in order to accept a baseball scholarship to (Case) Western Reserve University in Cleveland. Although he had success pitching in college and in semipro leagues, he eventually decided to pursue a career in professional psychology. While in college, he worked during one summer as a ward attendant at the Cleveland State Mental Hospital, and the next year as a research assistant to the psychology staff there. He became disenchanted with the prospect of working with psychotically ill patients, and turned his attention more toward experimental psychology. He was especially influenced by CWRU psychology professor Charles Porter, a freshly-minted Yale PhD who persuaded Bower that the future of psychology lay in more rigorous quantitative approaches based on Hull's learning theory. Accordingly, upon graduation from CWRU and before jumping into psychology, Bower received a Woodrow Wilson Fellowship to study mathematics and philosophy of science for one year at the University of Minnesota, where he was influenced by Herbert Feigl, Michael Scriven, and Paul Meehl. It was there also that he acquired a deep interest in mathematical learning theory, and in fact initiated and led a graduate seminar on that topic.

The following year (1955) Bower returned to his primary interest in learning theory and was admitted to Yale's psychology graduate program and given a research assistantship with Professor Neal E. Miller, a major figure in the history of American learning theory. Bower did collaborative research with Miller for the next 4 years. In Miller, Bower found a perfect role model for a research scientist. Bower's early research with Miller was on the newly discovered reward effect from brain stimulation, and his first publication with Miller reported discovery of dual reward-punishment sites in the rat brain. In his later years at Yale, Bower also worked collaboratively with Frank Logan on his micromolar theory of learning, and carried out his dissertation jointly with Logan and Miller.

Midway through graduate school, in 1957, Bower married Sharon Anthony, a professor of theater and acting at Louisiana State University. They spent the following summer at Stanford University while he attended a Social Science Research Council workshop on mathematical learning theory. There, Bower met and worked with many psychologists who were to become key innovators in the mathematical psychology movement of the 1960s—Norman Anderson, Dick Atkinson, Bob Bush, William Estes, Eugene Galanter, Frank Restle, George Miller, Saul Sternberg, and Patrick Suppes. He contributed two chapters to the conference volume, *Studies in Mathematical Learning Theory* (1959).

After receiving his PhD in June, 1959, Bower was hired by the Stanford psychology department, where he has remained throughout his career. He has benefitted from working with many able colleagues and from collaboration with a succession of brilliant graduate students and postdoctoral students, many of whom have become leaders in cognitive psychology.

Bower's research at Stanford began in 1959 with studies of operant conditioning and animal learning, with an early interest in incentive motivation, frustration theory, reinforcement scheduling, and discrimination learning. He gradually became more interested in human learning, mathematical models, and computer-simulation models of human learning. In the early 1960s he developed the one-element model of all-or-none learning and successfully applied it to many examples of associative learning. This model was in certain respects the most elegant and powerful theoretical model of that era. Bower and Tom Trabasso extended the model to describe hypothesis-testing behavior of subjects who are learning concept; their research and theorizing was summarized in their book *Attention in Learning* (1968). In 1963, Bower began developing mathematical models that considered short-term memory to be a capacity-limited storage medium for material being entered into and retrieved from long-term memory. This early work described both time-decay queueing models and fixed-space displacement models of how information in short-term memory might be processed and forgotten. This class of models became popular in the Atkinson-Shiffrin buffer model that guided research over the next decade. During the mid-1960s Bower also became a collaborator with E. R. Hilgard on the third edition of the widely-used and cited text *Theories of Learning,* which Bower revised through several later editions.

In late 1960s Bower began investigating organizational factors for improving memory, examining the value of ancient mnemonic devices, mental imagery, and grouping factors. This led to his increasing concern with how adults learn by relating new material to things they already know; this led in turn to viewing linguistic propositions as new relational combinations of semantic concepts from long-term memory. These ideas on propositional learning and retrieval were developed with John Anderson and were set forth in their influential book *Human Associative Memory* (1973), which soon became a citation classic in modern cognitive psychology. The book set forth a novel associative theory of how people learn and interrelate facts and answer questions about them, and these ideas were applied widely both to verbal learning paradigms and to people's learning from language inputs. Bower's next research extended those ideas to deal with the way people learn coherent clusters of information, such as the event sequences described in simple narratives. His research on narrative understanding and on the mental models people construct from that understanding has occupied a good part of his later professional life. His research has been supported continuously since 1960 by the National Institute of Mental Health (NIMH) and has resulted in over 235 publications.

Along with his primary interest in memory, Bower has maintained two other important strands of work: One concerns the role of emotion in learning and memory; the other concerns behavior modification techniques applied to neurotic problems. He found that induced emotional states serve as powerful attentional filters, as distinctive contexts for compartmentalizing learning, and as potent triggers for stimulating recall of memories acquired while in the same mood. These ideas led him into areas of social-personality psychology, where he has investigated the influence of various emotions (e.g., happiness and sadness) on people's biases in thinking, judging themselves and others, evaluating their lives and careers, explaining their successes and failures, and predicting their futures. Regarding the second strand of work, Bower has taught classes on behavior modification techniques, has lectured at behavior therapy conferences, and has co-authored a popular self-help book, *Asserting Yourself,* with his wife, Sharon Bower, based on her work in assertive communication.

Bower has performed many professional services. He has served as consulting editor of numerous professional journals; has edited an annual volume of research papers, *The Psychology of Learning and Motivation,* through 25 volumes; and has served on research grant review panels for governmental agencies. His many professional honors include: election to the Society of Experimental Psychologists (SEP, 1965), the National Academy of Sciences (1973), and the American Academy of Arts and Sciences (1975); presidencies of the American Psychological Society (APS 1991–1993), the Western Psychological Association (1990), the

Cognitive Science Society (1987), Division 3 (Experimental) of the American Psychological Association (1975), and the Psychonomic Society (1975). He was the first recipient in 1975 of the A. R. Lang Endowed Professorship Chair at Stanford University, where he has also served 3-year stints as chair of the psychology department and associate dean. He has received honorary doctorates from the University of Chicago and Indiana State University, and has been honored by the Distinguished Scientific Contributions Award of APA (1979), the Warren Medal from SEP (1986), the William James Fellow Award from APS (1989), and the Wilbur Cross Medal from Yale University for a Distinguished Scientific Career (1995). He has served as senior science advisor to the Science Directorate of APA since 1993 and also advisor to the director of NIMH, where he coordinated a comprehensive review for Congress of the contributions of basic behavioral research to the mission of NIMH. Bower and his wife have three grown children.

STAFF

BOWLBY, JOHN (1907–1990)

Bowlby is known for work on the ill effects of maternal deprivation on personality development, and for formulating attachment theory as a way of conceptualizing a child's tie to the mother. The son of a London surgeon, he studied medicine and psychology at Cambridge, completed his medical training in London (1933), and specialized in child psychiatry and psychoanalysis. After five years as an Army psychiatrist, he joined the Tavistock Clinic and Tavistock Institute of Human Relations, where he worked full time (1946–1972) as a clinician, teacher, and researcher in child and family psychiatry.

Believing that the influence of children's real experiences with their parents had been greatly underestimated in accounting for personality disorders and neuroses, he selected the responses of very young children to brief or long separations from parents as a focus for research. His early publications include "Forty-four juvenile thieves" and *Maternal Care and Mental Health,* the latter contributing to radical changes in the care of children in hospitals and institutions.

In 1951, dissatisfied with existing psychological and psychoanalytic theorizing as a way of understanding children's social and emotional development, he began developing a new conceptual framework drawing on ethology, control theory and, later, cognitive psychology, as well as psychoanalysis. Preliminary papers appeared in 1958–1963, followed by the trilogy, *Attachment and Loss* (1973, 1980). Influential colleagues have been Robert A. Hinde and Mary D. S. Ainsworth.

STAFF

BRAID, JAMES (1795–1860)

James Braid is generally credited to be the discoverer of hypnosis, although the phenomenon had been known and practiced earlier by Mesmer, Elliotson, and Esdale. Following the denunciation of Anton Mesmer's practice of animal magnetism as a fraud in the late 18th century in Paris, this technique was considered disreputable by the medical profession.

Braid was a British surgeon who witnessed demonstrations of mesmerism (animal magnetism) in 1841. At first he was skeptical of what he observed, but eventually he became convinced that this was a genuine phenomenon which needed to be explained. He described the mesmeric trance as a "nervous sleep" and invented the term "neuryponology." In time, the first part of the term was dropped and the word "hypnotism" remained. Mesmer had contended that his powers to cure resided in magnetic powers which came from outer planetary forces. Braid obviously did not accept this notion, and as a member of the medical profession felt that there had to be some physiological cause residing in the subject. He found that he could induce this nervous sleep by having a subject fixate on some visual object placed above the line of vision. He thus concluded that the mesmeric phenomenon was caused by paralyzing the levator muscles of the eyelids through their continued action in the protracted state.

Braid later realized that the factor of suggestion was of primary importance. His real significance for psychology is that he took the phenomenon out of the realm of mystical explanation and put it on a physical basis.

R. W. LUNDIN
Wheaton, Illinois

BRAIN-DERIVED NEUROTROPHIC FACTOR

Brain-derived neurotrophic factor (BDNF) is one of a series of peptide growth factors secreted from neurons and having its own specific receptor. Nerve growth factor (NGF) has TRKA as its receptor, BDNF has TRKB, and neurotrophic factor 3 (NT-3) acts at the TRKC receptor. These neurotrophic factors appear to have different functions at different stages of neurogenesis and development.

It appears that they are crucial for the initial neuronal and synaptic connectivity of the central nervous system (CNS), during which cells that "fire together, wire together." At this stage of development, many of the neurotrophic factors are secreted by the cell bodies of the stimulated (postsynaptic) neurons, picked up by axon terminals, and retrogradely transported back to the nucleus of the innervating neuron; in this manner they alter the patterns of gene expression for maintenance of synaptic efficacy and even neuronal survival. In addition to a role in the basic wiring diagram of the CNS, it would appear that they are also involved in a more subtle sculpting and resculpting of the CNS based on experience-dependent neural plasticity.

In the adult animal, BDNF appears to be integrally involved in long-term potentiation and other models of learning and memory. For example, in genetically modified mice in which BDNF is knocked out, long-term potentiation fails. This failure appears to be physiologically and functionally relevant to the animal because it is unable to navigate based on spatial cues to find a previously discovered submerged platform in the Morris water maze test.

Although it has not been definitively demonstrated, considerable new evidence suggests that BDNF and related neurotrophic factors may be released in a feed-forward fashion with neuronal firing, rather than simply having uptake and retrograde transfer back to the innervating neuron. This is potentially of considerable interest in the dentate granule cells of the hippocampus, which not only are involved in the trisynaptic glutamate-based excitatory circuitry important for learning and memory, but also, are capable of producing (and likely releasing) BDNF from their presynaptic terminals.

In the amygdala kindling paradigm wherein repeated subthreshold stimulations of the amygdala eventually come to evoke full-blown tonic-clonic seizures, the dentate granule cells show dendritic sprouting, as well as axonal sprouting onto the ca3 pyramidal cells. While kindling induces increases in BDNF mRNA expression, stresses decrease in the same area of the dentate granule cells of the hippocampus.

There is some specificity of the effects on BDNF as a function of both anatomical area involved and specific type of neurotrophic factor. Thus, although stress decreases BDNF in the hippocampus, it increases NT-3, and the effects on BDNF are in the opposite direction in the hypothalamic-pituitary-adrenal axis, which hypothetically could contribute to the increased size of the pituitary and adrenal glands in patients with major depression.

In neonatal rat pups, 24 hours of maternal deprivation results in substantial decrements in BDNF in the hippocampus and a doubling in the rate of the diffuse neuronal apoptosis that occurs in the 12-day-old animal. Repeated experiences of maternal deprivation for three hours in the first 10 days of life result in an animal that is permanently hyperactive and hypercortisolemic, as well as prone to alcohol and cocaine self-administration as compared with its nondeprived litter mates. These biochemical and behavioral defects are reversed by chronic treatment with serotonin-selective antidepressants but return when these treatments are discontinued. While alterations in BDNF or other neurotrophic factors have not been definitively linked to these long-term biochemical and behavioral changes in this psychosocial stressor paradigm, they provide a plausible mechanism.

The potential bidirectionality of such experiential effects is further emphasized by the work of Meaney and colleagues, who observed that 15 minutes of maternal deprivation resulted in increased maternal attention and licking upon reunion and subsequently thereafter, and thus engendered protective effects against stress-related hypercortisolemia and even age-related decline in hippocampal structure and memory loss. Parallel effects were observed in the offspring of mothers who were high natural lickers of their infants compared with those who naturally engaged in lesser degrees of this grooming and contact behavior.

Many of the currently utilized psychotropic agents have effects on neurotrophic factor gene expression, including that of BDNF. Smith and colleagues were the first to demonstrate the opposite effects of stress and antidepressants on BDNF mRNA in the hippocampus; these data were replicated and extended by Duman and colleagues at Yale. They found that antidepressants as a class, including electroconvulsive therapy, increase BDNF gene expression following chronic administration. Moreover, there is partial amelioration of some of the stress-induced decrements in BDNF gene expression if antidepressants are used prior to or concurrently with the stress induction.

From the clinical perspective this raises the potential of different types of benefit from long-term antidepressant prophylaxis in individuals with recurrent unipolar depression. They prevent recurrent depression, and to the extent that the preclinical data in animals are relevant to the human condition—and some preliminary autopsy data from the Stanley Foundation brain collection are at least consistent with this perspective—it is possible that antidepressants could be partially protective to the effects of stressors on BDNF gene expression. This might be useful and neuroprotective in its own right, but to the extent that some types of stressors are involved in the triggering of affective episodes, this could be involved in depression prophylaxis.

Preliminary evidence also suggests that BDNF is positive in some animal paradigms predictive of the efficacy of antidepressants, further raising the speculation that more direct targeting of BDNF specifically for therapeutic purposes, either by increasing BDNF itself or increasing activity at its TRKB receptor, may ultimately provide a new approach to the therapeutics of depression, possibly at a level of primary as well as secondary prevention.

SUGGESTED READING

Alter, C. A., Cai, N., Bliven, T., Juhasz, M., Conner, J. M., Acheson, A. L., Lindsay, R. M., & Wiegand, S. J. (1997). Anterograde transport of brain-derived neurotrophic factor and its role in the brain. *Nature, 389,* 856–860.

Duman, R. S., Heninger, G. R., & Nestler, E. J. (1997). A molecular and cellular theory of depression. *Archives of General Psychiatry, 54,* 597–606.

Gaiddon, C., Loeffler, J. P., & Larmet, Y. (1996). Brain-derived neurotrophic factor stimulates AP-1 and cyclic AMP-responsive element dependent transcriptional activity in central nervous system neurons. *Journal of Neurochemistry, 66,* 2279–2286.

Korte, M., Staiger, V., Griesbeck, O., Thoenen, H., & Bonhoeffer, T. (1996). The involvement of brain-derived neurotrophic factor in hippocampal long-term potentiation revealed by gene targeting experiments. *Journal of Physiology, 90,* 157–164.

Korte, M., Kang, H., Bonhoeffer, T., & Schuman, E. (1998). A role for BDNF in the late-phase of hippocampal long-term potentiation. *Neuropharmacology, 37,* 553–559.

Nibuya, M., Morinobu, S., & Duman, R. S. (1995). Regulation of BDNF and TRKB mRNA in rat brain by chronic electroconvulsive seizure and antidepressant drug treatments. *Journal of Neuroscience, 15,* 7539–7547.

Nowak, R. (1992). Cells that fire together, wire together. *Journal of the National Institutes of Health Research, 4,* 60–64.

Siuciak, J. A., Lewis, D. R., Wiegand, S. J., & Lindsay, R. M. (1997). Antidepressant-like effect of brain-derived neurotrophic factor (BDNF). *Pharmacology, Biochemistry and Behavior, 56,* 131–137.

Smith, M. A., Makino, S., Kvetnansky, R., & Post, R. M. (1995). Effects of stress on neurotrophic factor expression in the rat brain. *Annals of the New York Academy of Sciences, 771,* 234–239.

Smith, M. A., Makino, S., Kvetnansky, R., & Post, R. M. (1995). Stress and glucocorticoids affect the expression of brain-derived neurotrophic factor and neurotrophin-3 mRNAs in the hippocampus. *Journal of Neuroscience, 15,* 1768–1777.

R. M. POST
National Institute of Mental Health

CENTRAL NERVOUS SYSTEM

BRAIN EVOLUTION

Neurons evolved shortly after multicellular animals evolved themselves. The fundamental design of a generalized neuron is a cell with long processes that allow rapid cell-to-cell communication over long distances within an organism. Much of the receptive and intracellular biochemical apparatus of ion channels, protein-messenger cascade systems, and molecular extracellular release mechanisms had evolved previously. The breakthrough of gaining cells with the combination of release mechanisms and long processes allowed an explosive new radiation of multicellular animals, most of which are characterized by bilateral symmetry and a centralized nervous system. Centralized nervous systems are composed either of a localized collection of ganglia or a unitary brain; the term "brain" will be used here loosely to refer to both conditions.

BRAIN ELABORATION: A REPEATING THEME

Brain evolution is a story of brain diversity. Brains have independently evolved multiple times in the many separate lines of invertebrate and vertebrate groups. In some groups, brains have retained simple organization or have become secondarily simplified; within their particular niches, animals with relatively simple brain organization have been evolutionarily successful. In many other instances, brains have become enlarged and elaborated with more distinct neuronal cell groups (nuclei), more extensive interconnections of these cell groups, lamination of the neurons and fiber (axonal) systems in some regions, and a greater variety of neuronal cell types.

Among invertebrates, brain enlargement and elaboration have occurred independently multiple times (e.g., within mollusks such as *Nautilus,* squid, and octopus and arthropods such as insects). The higher brain center of a cockroach, for example, has a neuronal density that is one and a half times greater than that in the cerebellum, the most neuronally dense part of the primate brain (Strausfeld, Buschbeck, & Gomez, 1995). Often, anatomical complexity is presumed to correlate with behavioral complexity, but neural-behavioral assessment of various cognitive functions remains to be adequately explored. Among vertebrates, brain enlargement and elaboration have occurred independently for some members within each major group—jawless fishes, cartilaginous fishes, ray-finned (including bony) fishes, and tetrapods (see Butler & Hodos, 1996).

SEMINAL EVENTS IN VERTEBRATE HISTORY

With the transition from invertebrates to vertebrates, several major evolutionary events occurred that established the basis for most parts of our nervous systems, including major gains in sensory system structure and the motor neuron-musculature system (see Butler & Hodos, 1996; Nieuwenhuys, ten Donkelaar, & Nicholson, 1998). The brain and spinal cord were greatly enlarged, and the paired vertebrate sensory systems—including the olfactory, visual, somatosensory, auditory, vestibular, gustatory, and lateral line (mechanosensory and electrosensory) senses—all were gained. Motor neuronal pools for the muscles of the face and throat (pharynx) regions and, subsequently, for eye muscles and then jaw and neck muscles were gained. In the ancestral line leading to tetrapods, sets of paired appendages and a muscular tongue were gained along with their respective motor nuclei, while the lateral line system was lost.

BRAIN EVOLUTION IN VERTEBRATES

In those groups with enlarged and elaborated brains, the more dorsal parts of the brain (embryologically derived from the dorsal, alar plate part of the neural tube) tend to show more variation than the more ventral (basal plate-derived) parts. Structural elaboration is often correlated with a major exploitation of a particular sensory aspect of the world or with the gain of complex behaviors (see Butler & Hodos, 1996). For example, catfishes have a highly elaborate gustatory receptor system and large, laminated gustatory lobes in the dorsal part of the brainstem, and mormyrid fishes, which are electrosensory, have greatly expanded parts of the cerebellum and lateral line lobe, which are alar-plate derived. Mormyrids have complex electrosensory communication systems, including the exchange of individual recognition signals, and they build nests and care for their young. Many tropical reef fish have greatly enlarged forebrains and complex territorial, courtship, and parental behaviors.

Within the brainstem across amniotes (reptiles, birds, and mammals), similarities exist for many of the core nuclei concerned with maintenance of internal body functions, arousal and alertness, postural control, and related functions, as well as in the nuclei for the sensory and motor cranial nerves. Variation is marked for the alar plate-derived, sensory part of the trigeminal nerve, which in most amniotes supplies touch, pain, and related sensations for the face. The trigeminal nerve supplies the receptors for the independently re-evolved mechanosensory and electrosensory senses in platypuses, for infrared stimuli in some snakes, and for a magnetic-sensitive system in birds.

Similarly, some of the other alar plate-derived brainstem structures are quite variable across amniotes. Within the hindbrain, the cerebellum varies markedly in its degree of development, with the neocerebellar hemispheres being greatly expanded in primates, including humans, for control of limb movements as well as some aspects of sensory processing. Within the midbrain, the tectum, which is its dorsal part, is also highly variable. The rostral part of the tectum, the superior colliculus, is involved in visual localization functions. It is of modest size in mammals but reaches its apogee in birds. The caudal part of the tectum, the inferior colliculus, processes auditory stimuli and is elaborately developed in bats as part of their echolocation sonar system and in birds, such as owls, which hunt in darkness and localize their prey by sound.

A major difference in forebrain structure occurred at the split of ancestral amniotes into the line leading to mammals on the one hand and the line leading to nonmammalian amniotes—reptiles and birds—on the other. Although the nuclei of the dorsal thalamus that relay sensory inputs to the pallial (dorsal) part of the telencephalon are remarkably similar across amniotes (Karten, 1991; Butler & Hodos, 1996), major differences occur in the anatomical arrangement of the neuronal populations of their projection targets. In mammals, the elaborately layered neocortex (isocortex) of the telencephalon receives the thalamic input and is one of the defining features of mammals. Reptiles and birds may have cell populations that are homologous to those present in neocortex but that are organized as nuclei rather than in layers (Karten, 1991); alternatively, similar sensory projections may have evolved independently to either similarly or differently derived sets of neurons (Northcutt & Kaas, 1995).

All modern mammals are derived from an ancestral stock with somatomotor, auditory, and visual cortical regions occupying similar relative positions on the cerebral hemispheres (Krubitzer, 1998). Within various orders of mammals, the number of cortical sensory areas has independently increased, and each area has become dedicated to the analysis of specific aspects of the sensory input (Kaas, 1994). Many primates, for example, have over twenty visual cortical areas, each of which analyze different aspects and combinations of the visual input. Some mammals with prominent whiskers, such as rodents, have specialized, cylindrically-shaped regions in the somatosensory cortex called barrels that each receive the input from a single whisker.

Neocortex in humans has few truly unique features compared to other primate brains. The volume of neocortex relative to the total volume of the brain is only what one would expect for a generalized primate (Passingham, 1979). Language was arguably the most important evolutionary gain for our species (Deacon, 1997), but even here, the parts of the brain used for language comprehension and motor speech have precedent areas in other primates (Preuss, 1995). Current research work is resulting in new insights being gleaned from comparative embryological studies indicating that small changes in the genome and in the complex developmental program can have profound effects on the phenotype. Some of the most difficult persistent questions concern the complex relationships between cytoarchitecture and function.

REFERENCES

Butler, A. B., & Hodos, W. (1996). *Comparative vertebrate neuroanatomy: Evolution and adaptation.* New York: Wiley-Liss.

Deacon, T. W. (1997). *The symbolic species: The co-evolution of language and the brain.* New York: Norton.

Kaas, J. H. (1994). The evolution of isocortex. *Brain, Behavior and Evolution, 46,* 187–196.

Karten, H. J. (1991). Homology and evolutionary origins of the "neocortex." *Brain, Behavior and Evolution, 38,* 264–272.

Krubitzer, L. (1998). What can monotremes tell us about brain evolution? *Philosophical Transactions of the Royal Society of London - Series B: Biological Sciences, 353,* 1127–1146.

Nieuwenhuys, R., ten Donkelaar, H., & Nicholson, C. (1998). *The central nervous system of vertebrates.* Berlin: Springer-Verlag.

Northcutt, R. G., & Kaas, J. (1995). The emergence and evolution of mammalian neocortex. *Trends in Neurosciences, 18,* 373–379.

Passingham, R. E. (1979). Brain size and intelligence in man. *Brain, Behavior and Evolution, 16,* 253–270.

Preuss, T. M. (1995). The argument from animals to humans in cognitive neuroscience. In M. S. Gazzaniga (Ed.), *The cognitive neurosciences.* Cambridge, MA: The MIT Press.

Strausfeld, N. J., Buschbeck, E. K., & Gomez, R. S. (1995). The arthropod mushroom body: Its functional roles, evolutionary enigmas and mistaken identities. In O. Breidbach & W. Kutsch (Eds.), *The nervous system of invertebrates: An evolutionary and comparative approach.* Basel: Birkhàuser Verlag.

A. B. BUTLER
*Krasnow Institute for Advanced Study
and George Mason University*

EVOLUTION
NEOCORTEX, THE
NEURONAL EVOLUTION
SENSORY AND MOTOR SYSTEMS

BRAIN IMAGING IN AFFECTIVE NEUROSCIENCE

Emotions are conceptualized as action-related feelings associated with neurophysiological changes. Emotional reactions may be (a) positive or negative of varying intensity, (b) learned, innate, or a combination of the two, (c) transient states such as fear, anger, or happiness or enduring moods such as depression, and (d) manifested as approach, avoidance, or neither type of behavior. Basic knowledge about the neural underpinnings of emotion stems from several decades of animal research utilizing lesion, electrical stimulation, pharmacological, and single cell recording techniques. During recent years functional neuroimaging has been applied to study normal and pathological emotions in humans. These streams of research have been of profound importance in the development of *affective neuroscience* (Davidson & Sutton, 1995).

NEUROIMAGING

Brain imaging techniques include electroencephalography (EEG), magnetoencephalography (MEG), positron emission tomography (PET), single photon emission computed tomography (SPECT), computerized axial tomography (CT), functional magnetic spectroscopy (MRS), and structural (MRI) and functional magnetic resonance imaging (fMRI). Imaging tools may reveal both structure and function and permit measures of electrical, magnetic, metabolic, and neuroreceptor/neurotransmittor characteristics. The first wave of neuroimaging studies concerned research on cognitive processes and psychopathology, for example, imaging of dopamine receptors in schizophrenics or regional cerebral blood flow in anxiety disordered patients. A lesson from the early imaging literature is that the concept of cognitive or emotional centers is simplified because even simple tasks may require widespread activation in neural networks.

AFFECTIVE STYLE

Although imaging studies typically report data that are averaged over groups of people, individuals vary in quality and intensity of their reactions to similar emotional stimuli. This is often referred to as *affective style* (Davidson & Irwin, 1999), presumably reflecting differences in variables such as temperament, personality, and psychopathological vulnerability. Electrocortical studies of affective style have suggested that left frontal activation is associated with positive emotions and approach behavior, while right frontal activity predicts negative emotions and avoidance. Affective style has also been related to emotionally determined individual differences in amygdala activity. The neural response in the amygdala correlates with aversive emotional reactions in general and fear in particular (Davidson & Irwin, 1999).

EMOTIONAL EXPERIENCE AND PERCEPTION

Emotions may be induced internally in imaginary or self-generated emotional states, or externally in perceptually-driven emotions, although the former maneuver has been used less frequently in neuroimaging. One exception is a study by Kosslyn and colleagues (1996) in which the negative emotional content of stimuli was observed to increase activity in the occipital cortex during both perception and imagery conditions. It is possible that the neural circuits underlying self-generated and perceptually-driven emotions overlap. Although self-generated emotions invariably involve feelings, perceiving emotion in others may tax cognitive processes rather than generating an emotional experience. Hence, it is important to distinguish the perception from the experience of emotion. Emotional perception studies have imaged the neural networks involved in perceiving facial expressions of primary emotions, such as fear and disgust, presented both consciously and unconsciously (Morris et al., 1996; Phillips et al., 1997; Whalen et al., 1998). Activity in the amygdala seems to undergo rapid habituation both during emotional perception and induction. Recently, it has been argued that the amygdala responds to biologically significant stimuli, but predominantly in ambiguous situations (Whalen, 1998).

Mainly unpleasant emotions have been studied in induction studies, often involving pharmacological probes (e.g., yohimbine, procaine, or cholecystokinin tetrapetide administration) or sensory stimulation using visual (e.g., films/pictures) or auditory (e.g.,

scripts/tapes) stimuli. Only a small number of studies have extended into the olfactory, gustatory, and somatosensory modalities. In an examination of 25 neuroimaging publications on brain and emotion in healthy individuals, Maddock (1999) noted that the inferior frontal and posterior cingulate cortices, and in particular the right retrosplenial cortex, were the regions most frequently activated by emotional conditions.

EMOTIONAL LEARNING AND MEMORY

Fear conditioning processes might be of importance in the etiology of anxiety disorders. In experimental fear conditioning the emotional impact of a stimulus is altered; that is, it is transformed into a conditioned stimulus capable of eliciting fear reactions after repeated pairings with aversive unconditioned stimuli such as electric shocks. Numerous animal studies support the finding that the amygdala has a crucial role in the expression and acquisition of such associative fear memories (LeDoux, 1996). Moreover, in humans, lesion and neuroimaging studies suggest that the amygdala is involved in fear conditioning (Whalen, 1998) and in the formation of long-term memories of emotional events (Cahill et al., 1996).

NEUROPSYCHIATRIC APPLICATIONS

Emotional dysregulation, although part of many psychiatric conditions, is especially prominent in anxiety and mood disorders. A number of symptom provocation studies of patients with Panic, Phobic, General Anxiety, Post-traumatic Stress, and Obsessive-Compulsive Disorders have been performed to elucidate the pathophysiology of anxiety. Metabolic abnormalities in the orbitofrontal cortex, the cingulate, and the caudate nucleus have been noted in studies of Obsessive-Compulsive Disorder. In other anxiety states, the anterior paralimbic cortex and sometimes the amygdala region have been activated, although findings are mixed (Rauch & Shin, 1997).

In major depression, metabolic abnormalities have been consistently reported in the prefrontal, cingulate, amygdala, and thalamic regions. Functional imaging data suggest that depression is associated both with mood-dependent and trait-like neurophysiological abnormalities in brain regions that are at least partly related to anatomical abnormalities revealed by structural imaging (Drevets, 1998).

FUTURE DIRECTIONS

The past decade has witnessed a large increase in neuroimaging studies of emotion. Measures of oxygen consumption, glucose metabolism, and regional cerebral blood flow have successfully revealed neural correlates of thoughts and feelings. The next decade might involve dynamic receptor imaging that could enhance our understanding of the associated neurochemistry. Comparisons of behavioral and pharmacological treatment effects on receptor or transmittor characteristics could reveal whether separate or common neurochemical mechanisms operate. By studying receptor characteristics during emotional activation, the dynamics of neural transmission could be described.

REFERENCES

Cahill, L., Haier, R. J., Fallon, J., Alkire, M. T., Tang, C., Keator, D., Wu, J., & McGaugh, J. L. (1996). Amygdala activity at encoding correlated with long-term free recall of emotional information. *Proceedings of the National Academy of Sciences of the USA, 93,* 8016–8021.

Davidson, R. J., & Irwin, W. (1999). The functional neuroanatomy of emotion and affective style. *Trends in Cognitive Sciences, 3,* 11–21.

Davidson, R. J., & Sutton, S. K. (1995). Affective neuroscience: The emergence of a discipline. *Current Opinion in Neurobiology, 5,* 217–224.

Drevets, W. C. (1998). Functional neuroimaging studies of depression: The anatomy of melancholia. *Annual Review in Medicine, 49,* 341–361.

Kosslyn, S. M., Shin, L. M., Thompson, W. L., McNally, R. J., Rauch, S. L., Pitman, R. K., & Alpert, N. M. (1996). Neural effects of visualizing and perceiving aversive stimuli: A PET investigation. *Neuroreport, 7,* 1569–1576.

LeDoux, J. E. (1996). *The emotional brain: The mysterious underpinnings of emotional life.* New York: Simon & Schuster.

Maddock, R. J. (1999). The retrosplenial cortex and emotion: New insights from functional neuroimaging of the human brain. *Trends in Neuroscience, 22,* 310–316.

Morris, J. S., Frith, C. D., Perrett, D. I., Rowland, D., Young, A. W., Calder, A. J., & Dolan, R. J. (1996). A differential neural response in the human amygdala to fearful and happy facial expressions. *Nature, 383,* 812–815.

Phillips, M. L., Young, A. W., Senior, C., Brammer, M., Andrew, C., Calder, A. J., Bullmore, E. T., Perrett, D. I., Rowland, D., Williams, S. C. R., Gray, J. A., & David, A. S. (1997). A specific neural substrate for perceiving facial expressions of disgust. *Nature, 389,* 495–498.

Rauch, S. L., & Shin, L. M. (1997). Functional neuroimaging studies in posttraumatic stress disorder. *Annals New York Academy of Sciences, 821,* 83–98.

Whalen, P. J. (1998). Fear, vigilance, and ambiguity: Initial neuroimaging studies of the human amygdala. *Current Directions in Psychological Science, 7,* 177–188.

Whalen, P. J., Rauch, S. L., Etcoff, N. L., Mcinerey, S. C., Lee, M. B., & Jenike, M. A. (1998). Masked presentations of emotional facial expressions modulate amygdala activity without explicit knowledge. *Journal of Neuroscience, 18,* 411–418.

M. Fredrikson
T. Furmark
Uppsala University, Sweden

EMOTIONS
NEUROIMAGING

BRAIN INJURIES

The brain can suffer injury in diverse ways: metabolic or structural abnormalities that are genetically inherited or perinatally induced; trauma from civilian accidents or military combat; toxicity from drugs, heavy metals, or poisonous gases; malnutrition; infections or diseases; tumors; cerebrovascular accidents (stroke); surgical removal of brain tissue for relief of epilepsy, intractable pain, or serious psychiatric symptomatology; or aging-related disorders (e.g., Alzheimer's disease).

Early perinatal brain lesions tend to be more extensive and diffuse than those incurred later in life. Early lesions are often detected by abnormalities in behavior observed during later development, and the time of onset of the damage can only be approximated in relation to presumed prenatal events. By contrast, lesions incurred beyond infancy often can be linked to a specific event or to an approximate onset in the symptomatology, and premorbid behavior can be compared with post-injury behavior. Some injuries in adulthood can produce clearer abnormalities than others. For example, destruction of an area of the cerebral cortex in the anterior region of the right frontal lobe may produce subtle changes in emotional functions and personality, while a lesion in the analogous area in the left frontal lobe may cause a noticeable disruption in normal speech. Similarly, a lesion in the left frontal lobe near the junction with the parietal lobe can result in loss of language comprehension, but no such problem occurs after an analogous lesion on the right side of the brain.

Brain damage may have divergent effects, depending upon the locus and extent of the damage. For example, clinically, it has been noted that lesions in distinctly different areas of the brain will disrupt visual perception at different levels of processing. Damage in the optic nerve, superior colliculi, certain thalamic way stations, and cortex of the occipital lobes will interfere with visual functioning at the level of stimulus input, or processing of stimulus features. Damage in the temporal lobes adjacent to the occipital lobes will disrupt visual perception at a higher level of analysis, such as evaluating the importance or meaningfulness of stimuli, or remembering what the stimuli are. If the damage is on the left side, verbal comprehension of written material (e.g., reading) is impaired. Finally, damage in the frontal lobes may interfere with the level of expression of responses to the stimulus. Not surprisingly, left frontal damage can interfere with language expression (e.g., writing words).

Because brain damage does not always result in immediately apparent symptoms, localization of the site and assessment of the extent of damage may be difficult. For example, while an analysis of a specific sensory function, such as the integrity of the visual fields, can reveal basic sensory defects, more subtle cognitive and intellectual defects may require careful scrutiny. Functions involved in attention, motivation, emotion, and language often must be measured through the skillful administration and interpretation of tests specifically designed to elucidate organically based impairments. Descriptions of many of these tests may be found in books by Lezak (1995) and Spreen and Strauss (1998), as well as in a chapter by Oscar-Berman and Bardenhagen (1998).

Accidental head trauma, generally called traumatic brain injury or TBI, is a common yet severely disabling disorder. Because of the shape of the skull and the way the brain rests inside this bony case, violent blows to the head often seriously impact the prefrontal cortex and its connections with other brain regions. Severe frontal dysfunction leads to relaxed inhibitory control over appetitive and sexual drives and thus to inappropriate social behaviors that can prevent the TBI patient from returning to full functional independence.

Neurologists, neuropsychiatrists, and neuropsychologists rely on a variety of imaging and recording techniques for visualizing brain abnormalities in their patients. The techniques are used to measure parameters such as cerebral blood-flow patterns and obstructions, ventricular size, regional glucose utilization, the presence of abnormal tissue masses, and seizure activity. Such techniques include angiography, X-ray computerized tomography (CT scans), structural and functional magnetic resonance imaging (MRI and fMRI scans), magnetic resonance spectroscopy (MRS), positron emission tomography (PET scans), single photon emission computed tomography (SPECT scans), electroencephalography (EEG), evoked potentials (EP), and magnetoencephalography (MEG). Each technique provides the neurologist and neuroscientist with a particular type of information about the structure or function of the brain.

Some techniques use X-rays to reveal images of abnormal blood flow through cerebral arteries (carotid angiography), or lesions produced by stroke or brain tumors (CT scans). MRI scans provide images of the brain without X-rays, and because of the nature of the signal that produces MRI images, the scans can easily visualize small tumors, multiple sclerosis plaques, and infarctions. Another group of imaging techniques such as PET, SPECT, and fMRI provide images of regional cerebral blood flow, blood volume, or glucose metabolism, all of which are closely coupled under normal conditions and correlate with neuronal activity, and are thus indirect measures of brain functioning. Electrical changes in the brain can be measured with another set of techniques, which includes EEG, EP, and MEG. These procedures generally entail the attachment of electrodes to the scalp at standard locations in order to pick up electrical signals reflecting brain functioning. The signals are amplified and interpreted for the presence of abnormalities. For a summary of various neuroimaging techniques, see Kertesz (1994) and Thatcher (1995).

REFERENCES

Kertesz, A. (Ed.). (1994). *Localization and neuroimaging in neuropsychology.* San Diego: Academic Press.

Lezak, M. D. (1995). *Neuropsychological assessment* (3rd ed.). Oxford: Blackwell Scientific Publications.

Oscar-Berman, M., & Bardenhagen, F. (1998). Nonhuman primate models of memory dysfunction in neurodegenerative disease: Contributions from Comparative Neuropsychology. In A. Tröster (Ed.), *Memory in neurodegenerative disease* (pp. 3–20). New York: Cambridge University Press.

Spreen, O., & Strauss, E. (1998). *A compendium of neuropsychological tests.* (2nd ed.). New York: Oxford University Press.

Thatcher, R. (Ed.). (1995). *Functional neuroimaging.* New York: Plenum.

M. Oscar-Berman
P. McNamara
*Boston University School of Medicine, and
Boston VA Medical Center*

NEUROPSYCHOLOGY
PSYCHOSURGERY

BRAIN LATERALITY

Laterality refers to the functional asymmetry of the two cerebral hemispheres of the brain. That is, though the two halves of the brain work as a coordinated whole, many functions are subserved more by one hemisphere than by the other.

Wide interest in the functional lateralization of the human cerebrum dates from the 1860s, when the French physician Paul Broca made public his findings that several patients with speech dysfunctions were found on autopsy to have lesions in the left frontal lobe. While early theory held that the left hemisphere was the dominant hemisphere, it has gradually become apparent that each hemisphere has functions in which it plays a more dominant role than the other.

The most obvious asymmetry related to the human brain is handedness, which is often related to the lateralization of other functions. In right-handers, it is almost always true that speech functions are found primarily in the left hemisphere. While this is also true in the majority of left-handers, the latter are more likely than right-handers to have speech functions either primarily in the right hemisphere or distributed between both hemispheres. Left-handers apparently are likely to have less functional asymmetry than right-handers (Bryden, 1965; Lake & Bryden, 1976).

Structural asymmetries have been found in the human brain (Galaburda, LeMay, Kemper, & Geschwind, 1978; Wada, Clarke, & Hamm, 1975), with some areas being larger on one side than on the other, particularly in the areas associated with speech. While there is often speculation about the functional effects of these structural asymmetries, the exact connections have not yet been demonstrated.

There are a variety of methods for studying hemisphere asymmetries. One is by autopsy, which reveals lesions associated with behavioral dysfunction observed prior to the subject's death. Another is by observation of functional deficits present in people with identifiable lesions. Lesions can be identified by neurosurgery, X-ray, or computerized tomography (CT) scan, a technique that involves rotating an X-ray source around the head and using a computer to reconstruct a picture of a selected brain slice. Yet another involves direct electrical stimulation of various sites on the exposed brain (the brain has no pain receptors), to observe the affected functions (Penfield & Roberts, 1959). Measures of brain activity associated with sensory perception during performance of various tasks have included: recording electrical activity with an electroencephalogram (Molfese, Freeman, & Palermo, 1975; Wood, Goff, & Day, 1971); measuring blood flow in the brain by tracing radioactive isotopes (Lassen, Ingvar, & Skinhoj, 1978); and measuring the metabolic rate in the brain (Plum, Gjedde, & Samson, 1976).

Two other techniques have yielded a great deal of information about laterality, by allowing observation of the function of one hemisphere independent of the other. The first is the split-brain technique, classic studies of which have been done by Roger Sperry and his colleagues (Myers & Sperry, 1958; Sperry, 1968) and by Gazzaniga and his colleagues (Gazzaniga, 1970). The procedure involves surgically severing the corpus callosum, the mass of nerve fibers connecting the two hemispheres. This technique, used to halt the interhemispheric spread of seizures, yields an opportunity to observe asymmetry by allowing researchers to present sensory material received by only one hemisphere and observe the person's response. For example, information about an object placed in one hand, out of the split-brain subject's sight, or a stimulus presented to only one side of the field of view, would be relayed only to the opposite cerebral hemisphere.

The other technique that allows observation of lateralized functions is injection of sodium amytal into the carotid artery on one side of the neck, which anesthetizes the cerebral hemisphere on that side only (Wada & Rasmussen, 1960). Tasks that cannot be performed under the anesthesia are assumed to be under some control of that hemisphere.

Exceptions exist for every rule pertaining to asymmetrically represented functions. However, there are functions that are more commonly lateralized. The most obvious of these is language, which in most right-handed people is represented predominantly in the left hemisphere. For this reason, the left hemisphere has long been called the dominant one, while the right has been called the minor or silent hemisphere. Damage to the left hemisphere, or unilateral presentation of information to the right hemisphere, often causes difficulty in speaking, reading, naming, or understanding spoken language. Functions that are most often under primarily right-hemisphere control include visual-spatial reasoning and memory, tactile and visual recognition of form, musical ability, and copying and drawing geometric figures (Gazzaniga, 1970; Lezak, 1976-1983).

Nebes (1974) described differences in the ways the two hemispheres process information. Left-hemisphere processing involves analysis of information in a logical sequential manner, whereas right-hemisphere processing involves more synthesis of information in a simultaneous manner. Lezak's review (1976) of the findings of several studies indicates that there may be some differences in emotional functioning involving the two hemispheres as well, as reflected in different patterns of emotional response to unilateral brain damage.

Even in split-brain subjects, the functions usually represented in one hemisphere can be accessed by the other through use of peripheral nervous system mechanisms. Gazzaniga and his colleagues labeled this process "cross-cuing" (Gazzaniga, 1970; Gazzaniga & Hillyard, 1971). One example is when a stimulus presented to the right hemisphere results in some emotional response which is interpreted by the left hemisphere in such a way that the person can make a verbal response. Information may therefore pass from one hemisphere through peripheral nerve fibers to the other hemisphere, even when direct interhemispheric transfer across the corpus callosum is impossible.

Despite the evidence for laterality in the human cerebrum, the normal brain operates in a coordinated, unified manner. Kinsbourne (1982) emphasizes that lateralized functioning of one hemisphere is complementary to that of the other. The laterality of the brain provides a means of processing different components of information, rather than performance of separate types of activity.

REFERENCES

Bryden, M. P. (1965). Tachistoscopic recognition, handedness, and cerebral dominance. *Neuropsychologia, 3,* 1–8.

Galaburda, A. M., LeMay, M., Kemper, T. L., & Geschwind, N. (1978). Right-left asymmetries in the brain. *Science, 199,* 852–856.

Gazzaniga, M. S. (1970). *The bisected brain.* New York: Appleton-Century-Crofts.

Gazzaniga, M. S., & Hillyard, S. A. (1971). Language and speech capacity of the right hemisphere. *Neuropsychologia, 9,* 273–280.

Kinsbourne, M. (1982). Hemispheric specialization and the growth of human understanding. *American Psychologist, 37,* 411–420.

Lake, D. A., & Bryden, M. P. (1976). Handedness and sex differences in hemispheric asymmetry. *Brain and Language, 3,* 266–282.

Lassen, N. A., Ingvar, D. H., & Skinhoj, E. (1978). Brain function and blood flow. *Scientific American, 239,* 62–71.

Lezak, M. D. (1983). *Neuropsychological assessment.* New York: Oxford University Press. (Original work published 1976)

Molfese, D. L., Freeman, R. B., Jr., & Palermo, D. S. (1975). The ontogeny of the brain lateralization for speech and nonspeech stimuli. *Brain and Language, 2,* 356–368.

Myers, R. E., & Sperry, R. W. (1958). Interhemispheric communication through the corpus callosum. Mnemonic carry-over between the hemispheres. *Archives of Neurology and Psychiatry, 80,* 298–303.

Nebes, R. D. (1974). Hemispheric specialization in commisurotomized man. *Psychological Bulletin, 81,* 1–14.

Penfield, W., & Roberts, L. (1959). *Speech and brain mechanisms.* Princeton, NJ: Princeton University Press.

Plum, F., Gjedde, A., & Samson, F. E. (1976). Neuroanatomical functional mapping by the radioactive 2-dioxy-d-glucose method. *Neurosciences Research Program Bulletin, 14,* 457–518.

Sperry, R. W. (1968). Hemisphere deconnection and unity in conscious awareness. *American Psychologist, 23,* 723–733.

Wada, J. A., Clarke, R., & Harem, G. (1975). Cerebral hemispheric asymmetry in humans. *Archives of Neurology, 32,* 239–246.

Wada, J. A., & Rasmussen, T. (1960). Intracarotid injection of sodium-amytal for the lateralization of cerebral speech dominance: Experimental and clinical observations. *Journal of Neurosurgery, 17,* 266–282.

Wood, C. C., Goff, W. R., & Day, R. S. (1971). Auditory evoked potentials during speech perception. *Science, 173,* 1248–1251.

T. S. Bennett
Brain Inquiry Recovery Program

BRAIN INJURIES
NEUROPSYCHOLOGY
SPLIT-BRAIN RESEARCH

BRAIN SPECIALIZATION

SPECIALIZATION AND INTEGRATION

The brain adheres to two fundamental principles of organization; functional integration and functional specialization were the integration among specialized cortical areas depends upon cortico-[sub]cortical connections and the neuronal interactions they mediate. The characterization of functional specialization is important in many areas of neuroscience and provides an infrastructure within which normal brain function can be understood (e.g., cognitive neuroscience) and how things might go wrong (e.g., neuropsychology and clinical neuroscience).

The distinction between specialization and integration relates to the distinction between localizationism and [dis]connectionism that dominated thinking about brain function in the 19th century. Since the early anatomic theories of Gall, the identification of a particular brain region with a specific function has become a central theme in neuroscience. However, functional localization per se was not easy to demonstrate. For example, a meeting entitled "Localisation of function in the cortex cerebri" in 1881 addressed the difficulties of attributing function to a cortical area, given the dependence of cerebral activity on underlying connections (Phillips, Zeki, & Barlow, 1984). Goltz (1881), although accepting of the results of electrical stimulation in the dog and monkey cortices, considered the excitation method inconclusive in that the movements elicited might have originated in related pathways or that the current could have spread to distant areas. In short, the excitation method could not be used to infer functional localization because localizationism discounted interactions among different areas. It was concluded that lesion studies should supplement excitation experiments. Ironically, it was observations of patients with brain lesions (Absher & Benson, 1993) some years later that led to the concept of disconnection syndromes and the refutation of localizationism as a sufficient account of cortical organization.

Functional localization implies that a function is localized in an area, whereas specialization suggests that a cortical area is specialized for some aspects of cognitive, perceptual, or sensorimotor processing. The cortical infrastructure supporting a single function may involve many specialized areas, the union of which is mediated by functional integration. In this view, functional specialization is meaningful only in the context of functional integration and vice versa.

THE NATURE OF FUNCTIONAL SPECIALIZATION

The functional role played by any component (e.g., cortical area, subarea, or neuronal population) of the brain is defined by its connections. Certain patterns of cortical projections are so common that they could amount to rules of connectivity. "These rules revolve around one, apparently, overriding strategy that the cerebral cortex uses—that of functional specialization" (Zeki, 1990). Functional specialization demands that cells with common functional properties be grouped together. This architectural constraint necessitates both convergence and divergence of cortical connections. Extrinsic connections between cortical regions are not continuous but occur in patches or clusters. This patchiness has, in some instances, a clear relationship to functional specialization. For example, V2 (a visual area at the back of the brain) has a distinctive cytochrome oxidase staining pattern consisting of thick stripes, thin stripes, and inter-stripes. When recordings are made in V2, directionally selective (but not wavelength- or color-selective) neurons are found exclusively in the thick stripes. Retrograde (i.e., backward) labelling of cells in V5 is limited to these thick stripes. V5 is a functionally homogeneous area that is specialized for visual motion. Evidence of this nature supports the notion that patchy connectivity is the anatomical substrate of functional specialization. If neurons in a given area share a common responsiveness (by virtue of their connections) to some sensorimotor or cognitive attribute, then this functional specialization is also an anatomical one.

The search for specialized cortical areas still rests upon the axis established in the 19th century, namely the lesion-deficit model and brain excitation methods. Current approaches rely on the functional deficits following circumscribed brain injury and on functional neuroimaging. Although important, the inferences about neuronal architectures, based solely on the lesion-deficit model, remain fundamentally limited. Neuroimaging, on the other hand, has revolutionized our view of the brain, literally and conceptually. Challenging subjects with the appropriate sensorimotor attribute or cognitive process should lead to activity changes in, and only in, the relevant specialized areas. This is the model upon which functional imaging is based.

SPECIALIZATION AND FUNCTIONAL IMAGING

The tenet of functional neuroimaging is that the difference between two tasks can be formulated as a separable cognitive or sensorimotor component and that the regionally-specific differences in brain activity identify the corresponding specialized area. The first applications addressed the functional anatomy of word processing (Petersen, Fox, Posner, Mintun, & Raichle, 1989) and functional specialization in extrastriate cortex (Lueck et al., 1989). The latter studies involved presenting visual stimuli with and without some sensory attribute (e.g., color, motion, etc.). The areas highlighted, by comparing the ensuing scans, were identified with homologous areas in monkeys that showed selective electrophysiological responses to equivalent stimuli. Most studies of functional specialization employ statistical parametric mapping to provide what can be thought of as X-rays of significant brain responses (see Figure 1, the cortical area indicated on the lower right is visual area V5, re-

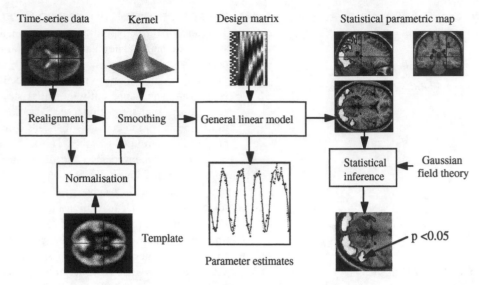

Figure 1.

ferred to previously, and shows significant motion-sensitive responses elicited by alternate presentations of stationary and moving dots).

Over the past years an enormous amount has been learned about functional brain architectures, with an exponential growth in human brain mapping. The current endeavour aims to combine this neo-phrenology with other disciplines such as cognitive neuroscience, neuropsychology, neuroanatomy and electrophysiology, clinical neuroscience, and theoretical neurobiology.

REFERENCES

Absher, J. R., & Benson, D. F. (1993). Disconnection Syndrome: An overview of Geschwind's contributions. *Neurology, 43,* 862–867.

Goltz, F. (1881). In W. MacCormack (Ed.), *Transactions of the 7th international medical congress* (Vol. 1, pp. 218–228). London: JW Kolkmann.

Lueck, C. J., Zeki, S., Friston, K. J., Deiber, N. O., Cope, P., Cunningham, V. J., Lammertsma, C., Kennard, R. S. J., & Frackowiak, (1989). The colour centre in the cerebral cortex of man. *Nature, 340,* 386–389.

Petersen, S. E., Fox, P. T., Posner, M. I., Mintun, M., & Raichle, M. E. (1989). Positron emission tomographic studies of the processing of single words. *Journal of Cognition and Neuroscience, 1,* 153–170.

Phillips, C. G., Zeki, S., & Barlow, H. B. (1984). Localization of function in the cerebral cortex: Past, present and future. *Brain, 107,* 327–361.

Zeki, S. (1990). The motion pathways of the visual cortex. In C. Blakemore (Ed.), *Vision: Coding and efficiency* (pp. 321–345). Cambridge, U.K.: Cambridge University Press.

K. J. Friston
Institute of Neurology, U.K.

BRAIN STEM

The brain stem, which consists of the midbrain, pons, and medulla oblongata, connects the cerebrum above to the spinal cord below. It is a highly organized structure which, in addition to conveying ascending and descending tracts, contains the nuclei of the cranial nerves III to XII and is responsible for a number of complex functions, including control of respiratory and cardiovascular activity and regulation of the level of consciousness.

The *midbrain* is the shortest segment of the brain stem. It consists of a ventral and a dorsal portion separated by the ventricular space. The dorsal or posterior portion is called the tectum and consists of four rounded swellings, the superior and inferior colliculi. The ventral or anterior portion is called the tegmentum and contains the reticular formation, the nuclei of cranial nerves III and IV, and ascending and descending pathways.

The *pons* is readily identified from the midbrain above and from the medulla oblongata below as a large bulge on the ventral surface of the brain stem lying on the dorsum sellae of the sphenoid bone. The dorsal or posterior surface of the pons is taken up superiorly by the superior cerebellar peduncles, while inferiorly it forms the upper part of the floor of the fourth ventricle. The pons contains ascending and descending tracts and connections with the cerebellum, as well as the nuclei of cranial nerves V to VIII.

The *medulla oblongata* extends from the lower limit of the pons to a level just above the first pair of cervical nerves, where it is continuous with the spinal cord. It is somewhat pyriform in shape, larger superiorly than inferiorly. The dorsal surface of the medulla oblongata forms the lower part of the floor of the fourth ventricle in the cephalad half. The ventral surface is made up of the pyramids containing the corticospinal tracts. The medulla oblongata contains the nuclei of cranial nerves IX through XII, which exit along its lateral aspects. The caudal half of the medulla oblongata represents a transition to the spinal cord, with cross-sectional organization and a central canal similar to the cord.

Given the complexity of the structure of the brain stem and the proximity of the motor and sensory tracts and cranial nerve nuclei, it is not surprising that disturbances in brain stem function can be seen with very small lesions. Until the advent of computerized tomography (CT) in the late 1970s, the brain stem could be imaged only by indirect means. Even CT is not ideal, primarily because of distortions of the image caused by the surrounding bone. Magnetic resonance imaging (MRI) is now the imaging modality of choice for patients in whom a lesion in the brain stem is suspected.

Lesions that may affect the brain stem include vascular malformations such as angiomas, which may be a cause of spontaneous hemorrhage, infectious diseases such as tuberculosis (although this is rare in developed countries), demyelinating diseases such as multiple sclerosis, and tumors.

Classically occurring in children at a median age of between five and 10 years, brain stem tumors account for as many as 15% of all brain tumors in this age group. Evidence suggests that the incidence of brain stem tumors has been increasing, although this is likely due in large part to better detection using MRI of lesions that in the past may have gone undiagnosed.

There are several types of brain stem tumors, each characterized by a distinct clinical presentation and MRI appearance. These include focal tumors, most often seen in the midbrain; dorsal exophytic tumors that grow from the dorsal aspect of the medulla into the forth ventricle; and cervicomedullary tumors that originate in the upper cervical cord or medulla and grow posteriorly to project into the fourth ventricle. These types account for approximately 20% of all brain stem tumors. Some, notably focal tumors arising in the tectum, may do well without any therapeutic intervention. Others may do well after surgery alone or, if this is not possible, after treatment with radiotherapy. In contrast, approximately 80% of all brain stem tumors are of the so-called diffuse intrinsic kind. These are high grade astrocytomas that grow very rapidly and cause multiple neurological deficits. Surgery is not indicated and these patients are treated with radiotherapy alone. In spite of a satisfactory early response to treatment, outcome is very poor. The median time to progression after treatment with radiotherapy is only of the order of six months, and the median survival time is less than one year. Less than 10% of patients will be alive two years or more after treatment. Several groups are actively undertaking research studies using various types and combinations of chemotherapy with radiotherapy in the hope of achieving an improved outcome for children with these tumors, as yet without success.

REFERENCE

Freeman, C. R., & Farmer, J-P. (1998). Pediatric brain stem gliomas: A review. *Int. J. Radiat. Oncol. Biol. Phys., 40,* 265–271.

C. R. FREEMAN
McGill University, Montreal

BRAIN INJURIES

BRAIN WAVES

Neuronal activity, partly electrical in nature, can be recorded by using an electroencephalograph (EEG). The record of the changes in electrical activity in the brain across time is the electroencephalogram, commonly called brain waves. Berger (1873–1941), a German psychiatrist, first developed the technique.

In the normal person, brain waves vary dramatically. The frequency of brain waves ranges between 1 and 100 cycles/second. The magnitude of voltage changes within the waveforms is usually about 50 microvolts, although some waves as high as 1 millivolt have been found in normal individuals. The pattern of a person's brain waves is a global and rather crude measure of brain function, but it has been related loosely to states of consciousness and also to abnormalities in the brain.

In human beings, brain waves are recorded from electrodes placed in several locations on the scalp. The potential differences between the electrodes are amplified and recorded on moving chart paper as a function of time. These potential differences originate from neurons in the cerebral cortex, and are almost certainly due to synaptic field potentials. These are the excitatory and inhibitory postsynaptic potentials produced in response to the release of neurotransmitter substances by the presynaptic neuron. Neurons oriented at right angles to the surface of the cortex probably play the major role in the production of brain wave patterns.

Brain waves have been grouped according to their frequencies and labeled with Greek letters. The most common frequencies include alpha (8–12 cps), beta (13 cps and faster), theta (4–7 cps), and delta (3 cps and slower).

Certain rhythmical brain waves are present in different areas of the brain. The alpha rhythm, for example, can be recorded from electrodes placed on the posterior quadrants of the head.

BRAIN WAVES AND SLEEP

Brain wave records have proven useful in investigations of sleep. During sleep the pattern of brain wave activity reflects the person's state of consciousness fairly accurately. The waking state is usually characterized by a high degree of beta activity. As the person falls asleep, the brain waves begin to show higher amplitude and lower frequency, passing through several stages. These stages merge into one another and are not entirely distinct. Stage 0 is a waking state just preceding sleep, characterized by the presence of the alpha rhythm. Stage 1 shows similar wave patterns, but somewhat lower voltage activity, and loss of alpha rhythm. Stage 2 is identified by the appearance of "sleep spindles": very brief (½–2 second) bursts of 13 to 16-cycle-per-second brain wave activity. This stage also shows "K complexes," or sharp rises and falls in the waveform. Stage 3 is a transition stage, containing both spindles and K complexes of Stage 2, and some of the slower waves predominant in Stage 4—the final and deepest stage, which contains mainly delta waves ranging from ½ to 3 cycles/second.

Another waveform that appears during sleep is called REM. The pattern is similar to Stage 1, but the individual is clearly asleep. This stage is associated with rapid eye movements (REMs) of one or two per second which occur in short bursts. It is also accompanied by complete loss of muscle tonus in the antigravity muscles, penile erections in males, and rapid spiking activity in the pons, geniculate bodies, and occipital cortex. REM sleep probably represents periods of dreaming, since most subjects report a dream if they are awakened during this stage of sleep. In contrast, only about 20% of subjects awakened during other stages of sleep report dreaming.

BRAIN WAVES AND CLINICAL DIAGNOSIS

Despite their limitations, brain waves have also been valuable in clinical diagnosis of brain abnormalities. There are no waveforms or frequencies that are clearly abnormal, and brain waves are interpreted in the entire context of behavior and other neurological tests. The site and extent of brain damage after a stroke, for example, can often be determined by recording brain waves from several locations on the scalp. Brain waves are particularly useful in the diagnosis and evaluation of disorders such as epilepsy, brain tumors, cerebral infections, coma, and brain death. Serial brain wave recordings are used to follow the course of recovery after traumatic head injuries, strokes, or other brain injuries.

Computerization has contributed enormously to the usefulness of brain wave records. The computer can filter particular frequencies, analyze lengthy records, and average records. One important advance in the computerization of brain wave records is the evoked potential. The presentation of an abrupt environmental stimulus produces no visible change in an EEG record, because the electrodes are recording from a huge neuron population and the neuronal response to the stimulus might only affect a small fraction of that population. The spontaneous activity in all the other neurons whose electrical activity is contributing to the brain wave pattern masks the activity in the neurons of interest. However, if the stimulus is presented repeatedly, the brain wave records can be averaged by computer. The spontaneous and random activity in the records will eventually average to zero and "wash out." The consistent response of the neuron population to the repeated presentation of the stimulus will remain. This residual waveform pattern is the evoked potential. It is widely used in research on the auditory and visual systems.

SUGGESTED READING

Chusid, J. G. (1979/1970). *Correlative neuroanatomy and functional neurology.* Los Altos, CA: Lange.

P. M. WALLACE
University of Maryland

CENTRAL NERVOUS SYSTEM
NEUROPSYCHOLOGY
PSYCHOPHYSIOLOGY

BREUER, JOSEPH (1842–1905)

As a successful physician in Vienna, Joseph Breuer is best known for his association with Sigmund Freud in the early years of the psychoanalytic movement. Prior to his first encounters with Freud, Breuer had been treating a young woman known as Anna O. (Her real name was Bertha Poppenheim.) She manifested a variety of hysterical symptoms including paralyses, anesthesias, and a phobia. Along with hypnosis, Breuer had been using the talking out method in treating her symptoms. He discovered that, if placed under hypnosis and encouraged to talk out her feelings and recall her past experiences, she felt better after being removed from the hypnotic state.

In 1886 Freud and Breuer became acquainted. It was a difficult time for Freud as he had recently married and was in dire financial straits. The elder Breuer was helpful to Freud and lent him money. They discussed some of his cases and in particular, Anna O. Freud became increasingly interested in Breuer's methods and began using them on his own patients. In 1895 they collaborated on *Studies in Hysteria,* with Breuer as the senior author.

Their association cooled and Freud abandoned the use of hypnosis in favor of free association or the talking out method. Freud had found that hypnosis often did not work and the patients' symptoms returned. Freud and Breuer also differed in their attitude toward transference, the strong emotional attachment that the patient developed toward the analyst. Sometimes there was a countertransference as well in which the analyst developed attachments for patients. All this disturbed Breuer greatly, but Freud found that transference was a necessary aspect of successful analysis. On the basis of these differences the two men ended their association and Freud continued to develop his own psychoanalytic theory and therapy.

R. W. LUNDIN
Wheaton, Illinois

BROADBENT, DONALD E. (1926–1993)

Primarily an occupational or "human factors" psychologist, Donald E. Broadbent was probably best known for an early advocacy of information-processing models for human beings. His first book, *Perception and Communication,* was described in an APA citation as "the first systematic treatment of the organism as an information-processing system, with a specific structure that could be investigated by experiment."

Broadbent was schooled at Winchester College and at Pembroke College, Cambridge, with the original aim of working in physical science. While in the Royal Air Force, however, he decided that the problems of human interaction with technical systems were of greater interest and importance than those systems alone, so he took up psychology on returning to Cambridge. He was a pupil of Sir Frederic Bartlett, and upon graduation joined the staff of the Applied Psychology Unit in Cambridge, where he worked for twenty-five years.

As director of the unit, Broadbent worked with his staff on a wide variety of problems, from the design of postal zip codes to the difficulties of shift work. Prevailing academic theories in psychology proved little suited to the handling of the data which emerged from these studies, because it was clear that human work involved internal processes mediating between stimulus and response. Hence Broadbent's espousal of theorizing in terms of information, and the need to consider the selective functions that cause some stimuli to have much larger effects than others ("attention"). This approach is now widely approved in human experimental psychology, and indeed in other specializations as well.

His later work led to *Decision and Stress*. His more general and philosophical works are *Behaviour* and *In Defence of Empirical Psychology*. In the 1970s Broadbent moved to Oxford to concentrate on his research.

STAFF

BROCA, PAUL (1824–1880)

Paul Broca became one of the most eminent physicians and surgeons of his time. He is best known to us today for a specific discovery regarding the localization of the speech area in the brain. Prior to Broca's discovery, the doctrine of Pierre Florens had maintained that the brain functioned in a unitary manner.

Broca's discovery came about in a rather unique way. In a hospital for mentally disturbed patients outside Paris known as Bicêtre, there resided a man whose only defect was an inability to speak. He could communicate by signs and otherwise appeared to be mentally normal. In 1861 the patient was put under Broca's care; Broca examined him but found no defects in his vocal apparatus. Five days later the patient died, and Broca immediately performed an autopsy. He found a lesion in the third frontal convolution of the left cerebral hemisphere. He presented his finding to the French Society of Anthropology.

This area of the brain became known as "Broca's area" and for some time was specified as the speech area of the brain. This was the first real challenge to Florens's doctrine of the unity of brain function. Later research indicated that speech is too complicated a mechanism to be confined to one specific area of the brain.

Broca's name is also closely associated with the modern development of physical anthropology. His research involved the study of craniology, for which he developed techniques and methods. He also studied the comparative morphology of the brain, as well as the topology of the brain and skull.

R. W. LUNDIN
Wheaton, Illinois

BRODMANN'S CYTOARCHITECTURAL MAPS

Even though Korbinian Brodmann published the major summary of his earlier work, "Localization in the Cerebral Cortex," nearly 100 years ago in 1909, there is hardly a current textbook in the neurosciences that does not contain one or more of his illustrations of how the cortex of the brain is subdivided into areas. The areas, for Brodmann, were the "organs" of the brain. They were recognized histologically by regional differences in the appearance of thin sections of brain tissue stained for cell bodies by the Nissl method. Because the stained neurons systematically vary in size, shape, and packing density across the thickness of the cortical sheet, Brodmann and others distinguished layers of cells within the cortex by differences in cell types and density. Brodmann played a major role in standardizing the classification of these layers by recognizing six main layers and several sublayers. More importantly, Brodmann and others at that time used regional differences in the thickness and cell characteristics of layers to distinguish different regions of the cortex, the cortical areas. Brodmann named areas both by location or some feature (e.g., the caudal postcentral area or area 1 and the giant pyramidal cell area or area 4) and by number in the arbitrary order in which areas were studied, from area 1 near the center of the human brain to more posterior areas such as 2, 5, and 7 or more anterior areas such as 3, 4, and 6. Current investigators generally refer to the areas by their numbers rather than their German names or English equivalents.

Brodmann assumed, as did others at that time, that the structural differences between areas reflected functional differences. Thus, each area was thought to be anatomically specialized for certain functions, although Brodmann concluded that each area probably did not mediate a single function, and more than one area likely contributed to each function. In brief, Brodmann's maps were intended to illustrate the functionally significant divisions of the cortex.

While the cortical maps of Brodmann continue to have impact, those of his contemporaries are rarely seen. Brodmann had greater success because he published complete maps, naming all parts of the cortex, and he published maps for a number of mammalian species. Thus, his maps can be used to show the subdivisions of the human brain, as well as animal brains within the taxonomic groups commonly used in research. His maps of the cortex of different mammals allow the results of animal research to be related to the human brain. Area 4 (motor cortex), for example, might be studied in a monkey or a cat, and the results considered relevant to area 4 of humans. The comparative aspects of Brodmann's studies were very important to the widespread use of his maps.

Brodmann's maps were not only theories of how the cortices of humans and other mammals are functionally organized; they also reflect Brodmann's views of how brain differences evolved. He proposed that some brain areas existed in early mammals and have been widely retained. Thus, most mammals have an area 17, or primary visual cortex, and an area 4, or primary motor cortex. Other areas were retained in some mammals, but differentiated into additional areas in mammals with larger, more advanced brains. For example, some mammals, such as rabbits, have a single somatosensory field, termed 1–3, while others, such as monkeys, have areas 1, 2, and 3 as separate fields. The assumption was that over the course of evolution, some areas would differentiate into two or more areas so that larger, more advanced brains would end up with more subdivisions than smaller, more primitive brains.

Brodmann's views were not remarkably different from those held today. He wrote at a time when some investigators still held that all parts of the cortex had the same functions, and the "localizationists," those who believed that different parts of the cortex

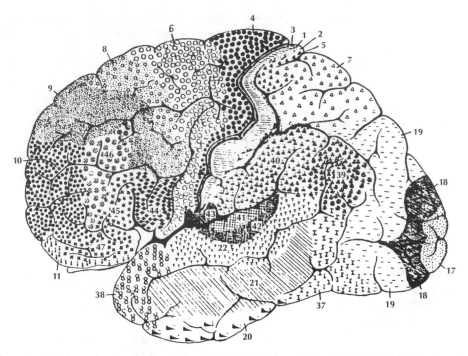

Figure 1.   Brodmann's map of a human brain. The lateral view with anterior to the left. Numbers denote many of Brodmann's forty-four proposed areas. Other areas appear on a medial view of the cerebral hemisphere (not shown).

have different functions, had not yet completely won the day. Now the concept of the cortex as a mosaic of areas, each with specialized functional roles, has been fully accepted. Brodmann's proposal that the human brain (Fig. 1) has a large number of areas of functional significance, while various other mammals, such as hedgehogs (Fig. 2), have fewer, is also part of current thinking. What is different is that current investigators also recognize that it is very difficult to identify most cortical areas, and that this is best done by considering regional differences in connections and types of neuronal activity in addition to histological distinctions. Although cytoarchitectonic specializations can be pronounced, so that area 17 (visual cortex) can be quite easy to recognize within and across species, most cortical areas are not so distinct. Thus, even current proposals, based on several different sources of information, vary considerably in how they subdivide the cortex. Present evidence indicates that Brodmann correctly identified some subdivisions of the cortex in some species, and correctly identified some areas as the same or homologous across some species. Nevertheless, many of his proposed areas do not correspond to areas defined in modern studies, and Brodmann clearly misidentified some areas across species. Thus, primary somatosensory cortex, area 3b, of monkeys and humans (Fig. 1) is incorrectly identified as area 1 in a prosimian primate and as the combined areas 5 and 7 of posterior parietal cortex in an insectivore (Fig. 2). Modern brain maps tend to incorporate Brodmann's terms for some areas even if they have been redefined, and use newer terms for regions of the cortex now divided quite differently.

While modern maps of the cortex are now emerging for humans, monkeys, and other mammals, Brodmann's maps, as well as his terms, remain in use. This is partly because Brodmann's maps are so well known that they remain an effective way to communi-

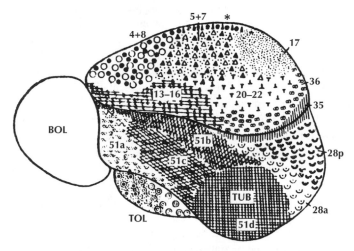

Figure 2.   Brodmann's map of a hedgehog, a small insectivore. A small cap of neocortex over the olfactory bulb and olfactory cortex (areas 51 and 28) corresponds to all of the cortex shown in the lateral view of the human brain (Fig. 1). The region of primary somatosensory cortex (area 3) is misidentified as areas 5 plus 7. Brodmann proposed fewer cortical areas in hedgehogs than humans.

cate information about the general region of the brain under study. Although "area 7" does not correspond to a single functional subdivision of the cortex in humans and monkeys, and the relationship of this area 7 to the area 7 of rats or cats is uncertain, we do know that someone studying "area 7" is investigating the cortex in the parietal region that is posterior to the primary somatosensory cortex. Thus, the terms usefully indicate general location in regions of the brain where the functional organization remains uncertain.

Modern maps will improve and add certainty in regions of the cortex now poorly understood, and the areas proposed in these maps will increasingly replace those of Brodmann. Nevertheless, some of Brodmann's terms and subdivisions will likely remain in modern maps because they do correspond to functional subdivisions. Brodmann distinguished 44 cortical areas in the human brain, but even this large number is probably too small. Current evidence indicates that monkeys have over 30 visual areas alone, and some of Brodmann's larger visual areas, such as area 19, clearly contain several recently proposed visual areas.

Brodmann raised another issue that has not yet been fully resolved. He recognized that some of his areas had sharp borders, while the cytoarchitectonic features of other areas gradually changed from one area to another. We now have evidence for more areas with sharp borders, and it is possible that all areas have functionally sharp borders. Yet, as Brodmann surmised, regions of the cortex might exist where localization is not precise, and areas gradually merge from one to the next.

Given his great impact, Brodmann's career was unfortunately short. He was born in 1866 and received a medical degree in 1895. Most of Brodmann's research took place in Oskar Vogt's neurobiological laboratory in Berlin between 1901 and 1910. Brodmann died unexpectedly after a short illness in 1918, at a time when it appeared he would start to make further contributions to the understanding of cortical organization.

REFERENCE

Gary, L. J. (Trans. and Ed.). (1994). *Brodmann's "Localisation in the Cerebral Cortex."* London: Smith-Gordon.

J. KAAS
Vanderbilt University

BRUCH, HILDE (1904–1984)

Hilde Bruch graduated from the University of Freiburg in Germany in 1928 with an MD degree. She trained in physiology at the University of Kiel and in pediatrics at Leipzig. She left Germany in 1933 and after one year in London came to the United States. She began her studies of childhood obesity while working at the Babies Hospital in New York. This work led her to seek psychiatric training at the Phipps Clinic of Johns Hopkins Hospital, and psychoanalytic training at the Washington-Baltimore Institute. Returning to New York, she practiced psychoanalysis until 1964 and worked as psychotherapeutic supervisor at the New York State Psychiatric Institute. Continuing to be interested in obesity, she became involved in the study of anorexia nervosa and the relationship of eating disorders to schizophrenic development. In 1964 she went to Houston as professor of psychiatry at Baylor College of Medicine.

Bruch published more than 250 papers in scientific and professional journals, and six books, including *Eating Disorders, Learning Psychotherapy* and *The Golden Cage: The Enigma of Anorexia Nervosa.* In 1981 Bruch was given the American Psychiatric Association's Founders Award as well as the Agnes Purcell McGavin Award. The American Medical Association honored her with the Joseph B. Goldberger Award in Clinical Nutrition.

STAFF

BUFFERING HYPOTHESIS

The buffering hypothesis asserts that social support provides protection against the stress which produces psychological or physiological disorder or disease. The stress-buffering function of social support has been of considerable interest to behavioral and medical scientists, especially since a 1979 study in Alameda County, California, showed that social conditions, such as marriage and group membership, were related to mortality (S. Cohen, 1991).

There are several issues in research on the buffering hypothesis. Of particular importance is the definition and measurement of three variables: stress, social support, and outcome (disorder or health). Psychological stress is usually measured on a checklist or inventory by self-report of major life events of the last few months, such as death in the family, divorce, and changes in work, weighted by experts' ratings of stress to give a total score. This method originated with Holmes & Rahe in 1967, and was elaborated by Sarason, Johnson, and Siegel in 1978. A less-used kind of measure is called "daily hassles," such as burdensome household chores and waiting in traffic (Lazarus, DeLongis, Folkman, & Gruen, 1985). Social support is measured in three ways: (a) Social network membership (sometimes called social integration), such as living with a family, belonging to a club, or attending a church; (b) perceived social support, such as self-report of availability of people to discuss problems or provide material aid; and (c) support behaviors, such as reported or observed actions of helping from specified persons. The first two methods have received the most research attention. The outcome or dependent variables are physical or psychological disorders (or health), such as depression, recovery from surgery, smoking cessation, and development of cancer or AIDS symptoms in infected people. Sheldon Cohen, Kessler, and Gordon (1997) provide a review of measures of stress, and Lawrence Cohen, Hettler, and Park (1997) cover social support and personality studies.

In general, the findings across many studies with the first two social support measures have been positive. In a review chapter, Sheldon Cohen (1991, p. 231) concluded, "The epidemiological data on the role of social integration in morbidity and mortality have clearly established that the social environment plays an important role in health and well being . . . (and) when a perceived availability of social support measure is used, these effects reliably occur in the prediction of psychological and physical symptoms." It appears that the body's immune system is affected by social support. People who get colds readily are likely to have poor social support (S. Cohen, 1996). A quick overview of abstracts of articles since Cohen's conclusions demonstrate that a majority of studies show positive results. A few studies of animals (e.g., Smith, Mc-

Greer-Whitworth, & French, 1998) also support the buffering hypothesis.

Beyond these generally positive findings, many theoretical and research questions remain. One issue is whether the results are due to main effects or buffering effects. Is social support a true buffering effect, having no influence of its own but being entirely conditional upon the presence of stress? A related issue is the place of social support in the chain of multiple cause and effect, as represented in the diathesis-stress theories of psychopathology (Monroe & Simons, 1991). Diathesis refers to predispositions to disorder from biological or early experiential causes. Social "support" and "nonsupport" interact with other variables throughout the life cycle.

An important theoretical task in clarifying the buffering hypothesis is the integration of the many possible variables into a model explaining why social support works. S. Cohen (1992) presented a transactional model including core concepts about social networks, stressful events, and personality factors, with perceived social support, stress appraisal, and support behaviors ultimately affecting the development of a disorder. Basing his conclusion on several studies, Cohen indicated that one personality feature that seems particularly important to include in addition to social support is the sense of internalized control or self-efficacy. Coping styles and genetic predispositions are other psychological variables that need to be included in an integrated theory of the relation between stress and disorder surrounding the buffering hypothesis.

On a larger than individual scale, community settings and institutions, such as churches, schools, and senior centers, can provide buffers for stress (Maton, 1989; Hettler & Cohen, 1998). Group interventions, such as workshops on stress inoculation for people in dangerous occupations or students facing examinations, may provide social support as well as increase self-efficacy.

REFERENCES

Cohen, L. H., Hettler, T. R., & Park, C. L. (1997). Social support, personality, and life stress adjustment. In G. R. Pierce & B. Lakey (Eds.), *Sourcebook of social support and personality* (pp. 215–228). New York: Plenum.

Cohen, S. (1991). Social supports and physical health: Symptoms, health behaviors, and infectious disease. In E. M. Cummings, A. L. Greene, & K. H. Harraker (Eds.), *Life-span developmental psychology: Perspectives on stress and coping* (pp. 213–234). Hillsdale, NJ.: Erlbaum.

Cohen, S. (1992). Stress, social support and disorder. In H. O. F. Veiel & U. Baumann (Eds.), *The meaning and measurement of social support* (pp. 109–124). New York: Hemisphere.

Cohen, S. (1996). Psychological stress, immunity, and upper respiratory infections. *Current Directions in Psychological Science, 5,* 86–90.

Cohen, S., Kessler, R. C., & Gordon, L. U. (Eds.). (1997). *Measuring stress: A guide for health and social scientists.* New York: Oxford University Press.

Hettler, T. R., & Cohen, L. H. (1998). Intrinsic religiousness as a stress-moderator for adult Protestant churchgoers. *Journal of Community Psychology, 26,* 597–609.

Holmes, T. H., & Rahe, R. H. (1967). The Social Readjustment Rating Scale. *Journal of Psychosomatic Research, 11,* 213–218.

Lazarus, R. S., DeLongis, A., Folkman, S., & Gruen, R. (1985). Stress and adaptational outcomes: The problem of confounded measures. *American Psychologist, 40,* 770–779.

Maton, K. I. (1989). Community settings as buffers of life stress? Highly supportive churches, mutual help groups, and senior centers. *American Journal of Community Psychology, 17,* 203–232.

Monroe, S. M., & Simons, A. D. (1991). Diathesis-stress theories in the context of life stress research: Implications for depressive disorders. *Psychological Bulletin, 110,* 406–425.

Sarason, I. G., Johnson, J. H., & Siegel, J. M. (1978). Assessing the impact of life changes: Development of the Life Experiences Survey. *Journal of Consulting and Clinical Psychology, 46,* 932–946.

Smith, T. E., McGreer-Whitworth, B., & French, J. A. (1998). Close proximity to the heterosexual partner reduces the physiological and behavioral consequences of novel-cage housing in black tufted-ear marmosets. *Hormones & Behavior, 34,* 211–222.

N. D. SUNDBERG
University of Oregon

COPING
GENERAL ADAPTION SYNDROME
HEALTH PSYCHOLOGY
HYPERTENSION
LOCUS OF CONTROL
STRESS

BURT, CYRIL L. (1883–1971)

Cyril L. Burt was a leading British psychologist, especially in the areas of child development and statistics. Born the son of a doctor, he soon showed his talents in mathematics and classics. At Oxford University he was influenced by William McDougall to take up psychology. After studying under Külpe at Würzburg, he became a lecturer at Liverpool University in Charles Sherrington's Department of Physiology in 1909. In 1913 he was appointed by the London County Council as educational psychologist—probably the first psychologist anywhere to be so employed. In 1919 he joined Charles Myers's National Institute of Industrial Psychology, and in 1924 became professor of education at the University of London. In 1931 he succeeded Charles Spearman as professor and head of the Psychology Department at University College, London, where he remained until his retirement in 1950.

At Oxford and Liverpool he developed his interests in child

guidance and delinquency, and also in mental tests and their statistical properties. The years with the London County Council were extremely prolific. He devised a large battery of achievement tests for 5- to 15-year-olds, as well as group intelligence tests, and compared the ability levels of various London boroughs with their vital statistics and delinquency rates (*Mental and Scholastic Tests,* 1921). He translated and standardized the Binet-Simon intelligence scale, and later adapted the Stanford–Binet scale for use in the United Kingdom. In statistics he developed techniques of factor analysis, including the formula for centroid analysis later used by Thurstone. While accepting the importance of "g" (the general intelligence factor), he broke away from Spearman by demonstrating the existence of other so-called group factors in particular kinds of tests such as sensory discrimination, verbal, and number.

He pioneered the development of child guidance clinics in England, arguing that these should be led by psychologists rather than psychiatrists, since children's problems are a psychological, not a medical, matter. He tested and amassed information on large numbers of delinquents and on backward or retarded, and emotionally maladjusted children. These culminated in his best known books, *The Young Delinquent* and *The Backward Child.* They involved statistical comparisons of large groups of problem children with normal controls for isolating the main environmental and other factors underlying their symptoms. He combined these with detailed case studies of individuals, based on the application of clinical insight. At the National Institute of Industrial Psychology he developed a system of vocational guidance which is still widely used. This included intelligence tests, educational records supplied by the schools, and interviews with the candidates and their parents. Here too he insisted that the psychologist's expertise is essential, requiring a thorough knowledge of occupations and their requisite qualifications, abilities, and personality characteristics.

Burt's interests ranged widely, including studies of personality, educational and vocational selection, examinations, psychology of aesthetics, mental telepathy, typography of books, and body-mind issues. His very numerous publications were not only fluent and lucid, but remarkable for their scholarship and erudite knowledge of history and culture. During World War II he gave unlimited help to psychologists involved in personnel work for the Armed Forces. He was in constant demand as a book reviewer, committee member, and/or consultant (e.g., to government commissions on educational matters). In 1946 he was knighted for his services to education and psychology—the first psychologist to be so honored.

His major interest, especially after retirement, was the application of Fisher's methods of analysis of variance to analyzing the factors involved in polygenic inheritance of intelligence. He claimed to have tested the intelligence of 53 pairs of identical twins reared apart, thus providing crucial data for demonstrating a large hereditary component. But many psychologists, particularly in the United States, doubted the validity of his work.

Although Burt gave immense amounts of help to students and others seeking advice all around the world, he could not brook any opposition to his views, and often showed paranoiac tendencies in his relations with colleagues and critics. This was especially apparent in the 21 years after his retirement, when he suffered much bad health. Most of his contemporaries had died, and his marriage had broken up. Shortly after his death, critics pointed out that many of his published correlations (e.g., between twins) had to be erroneous. A lengthy investigation undertaken by Hearnshaw was published in 1979. This provided irrefutable evidence that much of this work was fraudulent: Many of the twin pairs never existed; to prove his views right, he had invented them. The tragic aspect is that such faking was unnecessary: Most of his conclusions have been confirmed by other, more scrupulous, psychologists. It is not known how much of his earlier publications may likewise be flawed. Nevertheless, the value of Burt's influence on the development of psychology in Britain cannot be denied.

P. E. Vernon

AUTHOR NOTE
With reference to the final paragraph of this biography that some of Burt's data on twins and other kinships were fraudulent has been brought into question recently by two independent investigations of the Burt scandal (Fletcher, 1991; Joynson, 1989), both summarized by Jensen (1992). The evidence in these two books cannot be ignored in making an assessment of Burt's contributions and his reputation.

Both authors conclude that the charges of fraud cannot be substantiated: Some of the charges asserted by Hearnshaw (1979) are proved to be simply wrong and others are shown to be based only on conjecture and surmise. It remains undeniable that some of Burt's published studies on the inheritance of mental ability are flawed by unsystematic numerical errors in some of his tables (mainly in his articles published between his ages of 75 and 88) and, judged by the editorial standards of present-day journals, by unduly sketchy reporting of methodological and statistical details.

BYSTANDER INVOLVEMENT
In March 1964, Kitty Genovese was brutally murdered in New York while 38 of her neighbors watched from their apartment windows. Even though the attack lasted over half an hour, no one called the police until it was over. As a direct result of this incident, a great deal of empirical and theoretical knowledge has been generated on the topic of bystander involvement.

One of the earliest theoretical models to account for bystander involvement in emergency situations was developed by Latané and Darley (1970). According to this model, the decision to intervene or not actually consists of a series of decisions. First, the bystander must notice that something is happening. Second, the bystander must interpret or label what has been noticed as an emergency. Third, the bystander must decide that he or she has a responsibility to become involved. Fourth, the bystander must decide what form of assistance to render. And fifth, a decision must be made about how to implement the previous decision. Research supporting the model attests to the important role played by social influence factors at two stages of the model—labeling the event as an emergency and feeling responsible for becoming involved. Bystanders may use the actions of others in the situation to help them interpret the event. If the others are unsure themselves about what is happening and hesitate to take action, each may use this seeming passivity of others to label the event as a nonemergency. Even when a bystander is certain that the event is an emergency, the presence of others may diffuse responsibility for taking action. As a result, bystanders are less likely to aid the victim. This "diffusion of responsibility" explanation of bystander involvement is supported by a wide range of empirical findings, which show that the greater the number of bystanders present, the less likely a victim is to receive aid (Latané & Nida, 1981).

Another model of bystander involvement for which there is considerable empirical support is the Arousal: Cost-Reward Model, which was first proposed by I. Piliavin, Rodin, and J. Piliavin (1969), and was more recently expanded to cover nonemergency helping (Dovidio, J. Piliavin, Gaertner, Schroeder, & Clark, 1991, p. 89). The model consists of two components—an arousal component and a cost/reward component. The components are conceptually distinct, but functionally related. The model proposes that bystanders are aversively aroused by the victim's distress, that they are motivated to reduce their arousal, and that helping the victim is one way to accomplish this. According to the model, "arousal is a function of the clarity and severity of the crisis and of the psychological and physical closeness of the bystander to the victim" (Dovidio, Piliavin, Gaertner, Schroeder, & Clark, 1991, p. 89). In their search for ways to reduce their arousal, bystanders are guided by their assessment of the rewards and costs of each option. The model proposes that they will prefer responses that most rapidly and completely reduce arousal and that yield the most favorable costs/benefits ratio. For example, the costs of intervening could include effort and physical harm, whereas the rewards could include feelings of efficacy and expressions of gratitude from the victim. Alternatively, the costs of not assisting the victim could include feelings of guilt and criticism from others, whereas the rewards could include avoiding the risks of harm and injury.

The latter model is sufficiently broad to account for the influence of a wide array of personality and situational variables. A recent review of relevant research indicates strong empirical support for many aspects of the model (Dovidio et al., 1991). While successive versions of the model have added to its breadth, the model has become increasingly complex (the current version has eight boxes and seventeen arrows), making causal understanding more difficult.

Batson and his colleagues have challenged the preceding model, claiming that it assumes bystanders are egoistically motivated (Batson, 1987; Batson & Oleson, 1991). That is, by-standers' primary concern is to reduce their own distress, and that helping the victim is a means for achieving this goal. In contrast, Batson proposes a model of helping based on empathic concern. According to his empathy-altruism hypothesis, witnessing another individual in distress can lead to empathic concern, involving feelings of sympathy, compassion, and tenderness. Such emotions can "evoke motivation with an ultimate goal of benefitting the person for whom the empathy is felt—that is, altruistic motivation" (Batson, 1998, p. 300). In a series of experiments that controlled for alternative egoistic motivation, Batson (1987) demonstrated strong support for altruistically-motivated helping. The research thus suggests that there can be multiple motives for bystanders' reactions and that their helping behavior can best be viewed as a weighted function of egoistic and altruistic motives.

Two important moderators of bystander reactions are attributions and type of relationship. The types of attributions bystanders make about the victim and about themselves (e.g., their arousal) can influence their helping behavior. For example, bystanders have been found to be less likely to aid a victim if they view the victim as being responsible for his/her fate (Lerner, 1980). The type of relationship that the bystander has with the victim can also moderate helping. Bystanders who feel a sense of "we-ness" with the victim, or who are in a communal relationship with the victim (Clark & Mills, 1979), may feel more empathy for the victim and thus experience greater arousal and distress than bystanders who perceive the victim as being different or as being a member of a negatively-perceived groups.

Personality factors have been found to provide a poorer accounting of bystander involvement than have features of the situation. Although there has been some recent success in identifying dispositional predictors of helping, correlations rarely exceed .30 to .40, leaving about 85% to 90% of the variance unaccounted for (Batson, 1998). Previous research suggests that studying personality-by-situations interactions is likely to yield fruitful insights about the role of dispositional variables in predicting bystander responses.

REFERENCES

Batson, C. D. (1987). Prosocial motivation: Is it ever truly altruistic? In L. Berkowitz (Ed.), *Advances in experimental social psychology* (Vol. 20, pp. 65–122). New York: Academic Press.

Batson, C. D. (1998). Altruism and prosocial behavior. In D. T. Gilbert, S. T. Fiske, & G. Lindzey (Eds.), *The handbook of social psychology* (Vol. 2, pp. 282–316). New York: McGraw-Hill.

Batson, C. D., & Oleson, K. C. (1991). Current status of the empathy-altruism hypothesis. In M. S. Clark (Ed.), *Prosocial behavior* (pp. 62–85). Newbury Park, CA: Sage.

Clark, M. S., & Mills, J. (1979). Interpersonal attraction in exchange and communal relationships. *Journal of Personality and Social Psychology, 37,* 12–24.

Dovidio, J. F., Piliavin, J. A., Gaertner, S. L., Schroeder, D. A., & Clark, R. D., III. (1991). The Arousal Cost-Reward Model and the process of intervention: A review of the evidence. In M. S. Clark (Ed.), *Prosocial behavior* (pp. 86–118). Newbury Park, CA: Sage.

Latané, B., & Darley, J. M. (1970). *The unresponsive bystander: Why doesn't he help?* New York: Appleton-Century-Crofts.

Latané, B., & Nida, S. A. (1981). Ten years of group size and helping. *Psychological Bulletin, 89,* 308–324.

Lerner, M. J. (1980). The belief in a just world: A fundamental delusion. New York: Plenum.

Piliavin, J. A., Dovidio, J. F., Gaertner, S. L., & Clark, R. D., III. (1981). *Emergency intervention.* New York: Academic.

Piliavin, I. M., Rodin, J., & Piliavin, J. A. (1969). Good Samaritanism: An underground phenomenon. *Journal of Personality and Social Psychology, 13,* 289–299.

M. S. GREENBERG
University of Pittsburgh

ATTITUDES
CONFORMITY
SOCIAL CLIMATE RESEARCH
VIOLENCE

C

CALKINS, MARY (1863–1930)

Mary Calkins was awarded the PhD in psychology by Harvard University, where she worked under William James. When Hugo Munsterberg came to Harvard she worked for 3 years in his laboratory. At Wellesley College she established a psychological laboratory which she directed for 10 years. During this period she invented the method of paired associates for the study of memory.

As Calkins's interests shifted toward philosophy, she became increasingly dissatisfied with the Wundt-Titchener experimental tradition. She supported a self psychology which recognized the self as an integrating agent in the conscious life. As an introspectionist she appealed to the direct experience of the person. Her revised textbook, *A First Book in Psychology* (1909), presents her mature position. Calkins argued that the various schools of psychology might unite in a personalistic psychology.

Calkins served as president of the American Psychological Association and has been ranked in the second 10 of psychologists starred in the first edition of *American Men of Science*.

P. E. LICHTENSTEIN

CAMPBELL, DONALD T. (1916–1996)

Donald T. Campbell got the BA and PhD at the University of California at Berkeley in 1947. He was a psychology faculty member at Ohio State University (1947–1950), at the University of Chicago, (1950–1953), and at Northwestern University (1953–1979). He was on the social science faculty at the Maxwell School, Syracuse University (1979–1982), and on the social relations faculty at Lehigh University (1982–1996). While defining himself from the beginning as a social psychologist, he retained a persisting interest in a general theory of behavior that was indebted to Tolman's purposive behaviorism; to Egon Brunswik's distal behaviorism and perceptual constancies; to the phenomenological social psychologies of Mustapha Sherif, Solomon Asch, David Kretch & Richard Crutchfield; and to cybernetics, resulting in a "phenomenological behaviorism" in which learned views of the world or tendencies to perceive are translated as equivalent to learned response tendencies. Research on social attitudes and intergroup stereotypes came out of this perspective.

He was best known for his methodological writings, of which "Convergent and discriminant validation by the multitrait-multimethod matrix" (Campbell and Fiske), and *Experimental and Quasi-Experimental Designs for Research* (Campbell and Stanley) are the best known.

These methodological interests combined with his perceptual, learning, and evolutionary interests to produce a naturalistic, evolutionary, and sociological epistemology and theory of science (see Campbell, "Evolutionary epistemology"). A bibliography and brief research autobiography are included in Brewer & Collins, *Scientific Inquiry and the Social Sciences: A Volume in Honor of Donald T. Campbell.*

Among his many honors were presidency of the American Psychological Association (1975) and membership in the National Academy of Sciences (1973).

STAFF

CANADA, PSYCHOLOGY IN

Psychology in Canada is of relatively recent origin in comparison with the European and Asian tradition, and is the product of many diverse influences. The roots are European (primarily British and French) but development at all phases, early and late, for good and for bad, has been strongly influenced by events and developments in the United States.

Psychology, as a part of the discipline of philosophy, has been taught in Canada since universities were first established in the early 1800s. As an experimental science, psychology came first to Canada in 1889 when James Mark Baldwin, a young American who had studied under Wundt in Leipzig, was appointed to the Philosophy Department of the University of Toronto as professor of logic, metaphysics, and ethics, and there established the first Laboratory of Psychology anywhere on British soil. In 1892, Baldwin was one of 26 members who met to form the American Psychological Association. In 1906, James McEachern, a Canadian, returned from Wundt's laboratory to join the faculty of the recently established University of Alberta. In 1910, William Tait, a Canadian trained at Harvard, was appointed as an experimental psychologist to the Philosophy Department of McGill University in Montreal and he established a Psychology Laboratory there.

It is of passing interest to note that Titchener expressed serious interest in a psychology position at both Toronto and McGill. Titchener, who was at Cornell at the time, was anxious to be offered "a chair of psychology with an adequate laboratory on British soil." For some reason, he did not receive an appointment at either Toronto or McGill, leaving open, according to Ferguson of McGill University (Wright & Myers, 1982), "the question of whether Titchener, the displaced Englishman who devoted his life to German Psychology on American soil, could find fulfillment in Canada."

During the early 1900s, experimental psychologists were appointed to virtually all the Canadian universities that had been established up to that time. In each case, however, the appointment was to the Department of Philosophy. Of those appointed, approximately one-quarter were trained in Europe and three-quarters in North America. In the 1920s, independent departments of psychology separate from the departments of philosophy appeared in two major Canadian universities. These were at the University of Toronto under the chairmanship of Bott and at McGill under the chairmanship of Tait.

The liberation of psychology from philosophy occurred more gradually in other English-speaking Canadian universities, and the separation of the departments of philosophy and psychology in all universities was not accomplished until the early 1960s. In universities where arts and science faculties were separate, the psychology departments were associated initially and primarily with the faculties of arts, but, as time went on, an increasing number of psychology departments were located within the faculties of science. Sometimes this movement of psychology into the "hard" sciences took place with what undoubtedly were the highest, most academic, and most rational of reasons, but such was not always the case. Newbigging of McMaster University (Wright & Myers, 1982) recounts in an amusing anecdote that the recognition of psychology as a subject worthy of acceptance by the faculty of science at McMaster University occurred as a result of a close vote of the university faculty. All those in favor of the motion to have psychology taught in the faculty of science were humanists or social scientists and all those who were against the motion came from the science departments. Psychology at McMaster University owes its ultimate placement in the faculty of science to the fact that at a poorly attended faculty meeting, the humanists outnumbered the scientists by a small margin.

In the French-speaking universities, the lead in establishing psychology departments was taken by the University of Ottawa and the University of Montreal. The philosophical orientation of Thomas Aquinas and a Roman Catholic orientation to the study of man prevailed in both universities. In 1941 in Ottawa under Shevennel, and in 1942 in Montreal under Noel Mailloux, separate psychological institutes were established. Most of the research and training in these institutes was concerned with applied and clinical topics. Not until the late 1960s did experimental psychology emerge as an important aspect of psychology—and it did so more rapidly and prominently at the University of Montreal where the psychological research of David Belanger played an important role. However, the overall orientation of the French-speaking universities continues to be primarily in applied research and professional training.

In other parts of Canada, psychology had, from the earlier years, strong applied leanings, especially at the University of Toronto where, during the depression, to supplement meager academic salaries virtually all of the staff conducted research in applied problems such as delinquency, enuresis, or rehabilitation. The first Child Study Institute in Canada was established at the University of Toronto by Blatz in the early 1920s.

In all of Canada, the growth of psychology in universities was slow and conservative until 1960. In 1960, there were less than a dozen departments of psychology that offered the PhD degree: McGill University; the University of Toronto; Queen's University, Kingston; the University of Western Ontario, London; McMaster University, Hamilton; the University of Ottawa; the University of Montreal; the University of Manitoba, Winnipeg; the University of Saskatchewan, Saskatoon; the University of Alberta, Edmonton; and the University of British Columbia, Vancouver.

World War II had an important effect on the development of Canadian psychology. Up until the late 1930s, most of the 40 or so Canadian psychologists were content to be members of the American Psychological Association. However, in 1938, it became apparent that there would be a war and that Canada would be involved. Accordingly, to focus and coordinate their efforts, the Canadian Psychological Association was formed in 1939. Canadian psychologists during the war worked effectively on problems of test construction, personnel selection, and rehabilitation.

So successful were the psychologists in their efforts, and so great were public expectations, that in the immediate postwar era (1945–1949) virtually all students of psychology in Canada were engaged in applied psychology and mission research. This preoccupation with applied psychology was so intense that some psychologists began to fear that pure research would be ignored or neglected. Hebb stated that "academic or ivory tower psychology . . . was the goose that laid the golden egg of applied and clinical methods. In Canada if the goose is not dead it is very skillful at feigning death" (Hebb, 1948). The concern of Hebb and others about the future of scientific psychology was such that at most universities deliberate, powerful, and sustained efforts were made to have psychology become more scientific and less applied. The early 1950s were a time when many departments of psychology in Canada actively recruited hard-nosed scientists. The conflict between pure and applied psychology, between academic and professionals, became intense and labored. It continued throughout the 1950s as most graduate training programs became oriented toward pure scientific psychology and most faculty members became devoted to pure experimental research. Most of Canadian psychology was concerned with scientific training and the Opinicon Conference (Bernhardt, 1961) was devoted to training for research in psychology.

In the late 1960s, loud cries were heard from professional and applied psychologists, who complained about the inappropriateness and sterility of the scientific approach and wanted research and training that would better prepare them for work in applied settings. The Couchiching Conference (Webster, 1967) was intended to lay the ground rules for training in applied psychology. Several models were discussed (e.g., the Scientist's Practitioner) and several novel degree programs (e.g., the D. Psych.) were considered as well. The scientific-applied conflict began to be resolved in the late 1960s and early 1970s.

In addition to being a period of considerable conflict in Canadian psychology, the decade of the 1960s was a period of tremendous growth. Not only in psychology, but in all university departments, enrollments burgeoned and many new universities were created (especially in Ontario and Quebec). At the beginning of the decade, the number of universities offering PhD degree programs was 11. By the end of the decade, this number had more than doubled to 24. When the decade began, psychology was one of the minor disciplines at both the undergraduate and graduate levels. When it ended, enrollment in undergraduate psychology courses was high, and in graduate schools, psychology was rapidly catching up with physics and chemistry as the discipline in which most Ph.D. degrees were awarded.

To fill the faculty positions in psychology that were so rapidly being created, recruitment efforts were necessary. Since Canada was, in the early 1960s, not producing the large numbers of psychology graduates needed, such recruitment efforts were directed primarily south of the border, and most of the newly appointed faculty members to Canadian psychology departments were Americans, or Canadians who had been trained at universities in the United States.

Wright (1969) noted that less than half of academic psychologists in Canada were members of the Canadian Psychological Association and that the nonmembers included some of the most prominent names in Canadian psychology departments. This orientation appears to have changed. During the 1970s, although the number of psychologists in Canada did not increase as dramatically as it had during the 1960s, the membership in the Canadian Psychological Association tripled (from less than 1,000 to almost 3,000). During the 1970s, the major growth in psychology was in applied rather than academic settings. This resulted from the combination of rapidly increasing job opportunities in the former and decreasing opportunities in the latter.

Throughout the history of Canadian psychology, research productivity—both theoretical and applied—has been high, as judged by various quantitative and qualitative measures. First, however, it should be noted that much of the psychological research in Canada is, according to Myers (1976) and others, Canadian only because it is carried out in that country. Such research is indistinguishable from research done in the United States, in Great Britain, or in France. Examples of areas of research in Canadian psychology include cognition and memory, drugs and behavior, developmental psychology (especially within a Piagetian framework), and theoretical and practical aspects of psychological assessment. For a recent review of Canadian research in selected areas, see "A decade review" in *Canadian Psychology* (Janisse, 1981). It includes summaries prepared by invited contributors of research in Canada during the 1970–1980 decade on behavior modification, clinical intervention, feminism, infant development, experimental social psychology, human neuropsychology, visual information processing, college teaching, and second language acquisition.

Many Canadian psychologists have been honored for the excellence of their research by such eminent organizations as the Royal Society (of England), the Royal Society of Canada, and the American Psychological Association. Recently Endler (1979) identified A. Paivio of the University of Western Ontario and E. Tulving of the University of Toronto as among the "superstars" of psychology. Endler's criterion is that the two are among the 50 psychologists whose work is most frequently cited at the top 100 graduate schools in Great Britain and the United States.

Another eminent psychologist, whose major contributions were made during his professional career in Canada was D. E. Berlyne (1924–1976). Born in England and extremely knowledgeable about psychology in both England and the United States (Berlyne, 1968), his longest professional affiliation was for 14 years with the University of Toronto. Here he produced some of his most creative and internationally acclaimed research on the motivating effects of curiosity and the judgment of esthetics.

The most eminent Canadian psychologist is D. O. Hebb of McGill University. A native Canadian, Hebb joined the McGill faculty in 1949. During his career at McGill, he assumed responsibility for the introductory psychology course and the first graduate psychology course.

Three areas of research are distinctively Canadian, inspired by some special conditions of Canadian life (Myers, 1976). These are bilingualism, multiculturalism, and native and isolated northern life.

Canada is, officially, a bilingual country with two "charter" members: the English speaking and the French speaking. Since many Canadians acquire a second language at some point, the country has been described as a natural laboratory for the study of the cognitive and social effects of second language acquisition. In the early 1960s, researchers at McGill University demonstrated that, in contrast to previous theoretical formulations and earlier research findings, when social and economic factors are properly controlled, the acquisition of a second language has beneficial rather than detrimental cognitive effects. The same researchers also developed the "matched guise" technique, which involves one individual presenting the same message in each of two languages, a useful technique for the study of attitudes toward linguistic groups. Research studies in this important area have become more complex and numerous and have spread to other Canadian universities in recent years.

A major part of the Canadian population (now approximately 30%) has neither French nor English as its native language. These Canadians, many relatively new (since World War II), have been encouraged by a policy of cultural pluralism to retain their own values and customs. The result has been a cultural mosaic in contrast to the melting-pot concept in the United States. These ethnic variations have produced a rich area for social and cross-cultural research, which is being explored by many Canadian psychologists.

A small portion of the Canadian population consists of native groups: Indian and Inuit. A relatively small but increasing research emphasis is being directed toward these groups. Canada also has groups of mixed European and native parentage "Métis" and of European settlers who have lived for generations in small and isolated settlements. The effects of such circumstances on the development of intellectual abilities and on personality dynamics are also being studied at several Canadian universities. Research in these areas was recently reviewed by Gardner and Kalin (1981).

Finally, research on subhuman species should not be completely ignored. Major research has been undertaken on the behavior of marine species such as the seal and the whale, and on numerous species of bird life. It is interesting to note that the goal of such research is not only to acquire a scientific and theoretical understanding of animal behavior, but also to obtain the answer to such applied and practical questions as the best methods of keeping whales away from fishing nets.

REFERENCES

Berlyne, D. E. (1968). American and European psychology. *American Psychologist, 23,* 447–452.

Bernhardt, K. S. (Ed.). (1961). *Training for research in psychology.* Toronto: University of Toronto Press.

Gardner, R. C., & Kalin, R. (1981). *A Canadian social psychology of ethnic relations.* Toronto: Methuen.

Hebb, D. O. (1948). Report on experimental, physiological and comparative psychology. In E. A. Bott (Ed.), Research planning in the Canadian Psychological Association. *Canadian Journal of Psychology, 1,* 13–14.

Janisse, M. J. (1981). A decade review. *Canadian Psychology, 22*(1) 3–99; *22*(2), 113–172.

Myers, C. R. (1976). Psychology in Canada. In V. S. Sexton & H. Misak (Eds.), *Psychology around the world.* Monterey, CA: Brooks/Cole.

Webster, E. C. (Ed.). (1967). *The Couchiching Conference on Professional Psychology.* Montreal: Eagle.

Wright, M. J. (1969). Canadian psychology comes of age. *The Canadian Psychologist, 10(3),* 229–253.

Wright, M. J., & Myers, C. R. (Eds.). (1982). *A history of academic psychology in Canada.* Toronto: Hogreffe.

A. M. SULLIVAN
Memorial University, Newfoundland, Canada

CANNON, WALTER B. (1871–1945)

Walter B. Cannon attended Harvard University, and studied medicine. After his graduation in 1900, he took a position there, lecturing, consulting, and doing research. He remained at Harvard 42 years.

In his study of endocrinology and physiology, Cannon made several discoveries that have been significant for psychologists. Cannon's research on emotion and its effect on digestive processes was especially important. Further exploration in this area led him to discoveries of other adaptive changes in the physiology of the body under emotion, stress, and tissue need which he reported in *Bodily Changes in Pain, Hunger, Fear, and Rage.*

A critique of William James's theory of emotion was presented in this book. The *James-Lange theory* held that physical response preceded the appearance of emotion, that if bodily changes such as increased heart rate or muscle tension did not occur, there would be no emotion. Cannon's substitute theory, now known as the *Cannon-Bard Theory of Emotion,* held that emotion was an emergency reaction that caused the body to react with the resources needed to cope with the emergency. Cannon identified the hypothalamus as the control center in emotional behavior, and the adrenal gland as the mobilizer of energy resources of the body under stress.

Cannon studied the effects of traumatic shocks during World War I and published them in "Traumatic shock." He discovered a hormone that stimulates heart activity and named it sympathin. Other discoveries of the autonomic nervous system followed which resulted in Cannon's formulation of the concept of homeostasis: the tendency for the body to maintain a steady internal state, a constancy of bodily environment, and to attempt to restore equilibrium if constancy is disturbed. This concept has strongly influenced psychology as well as other disciplines.

N. A. HAYNIE

CAREER COUNSELING

Career counseling is one of several interventions used to assist clients with career issues and problems. Other interventions include career appraisal and testing, the use of computer-assisted career guidance systems, job simulations, gaming, and a variety of self-directed initiatives designed to help clients clarify their personal strengths and weaknesses, as well as their aptitudes, interests, values, and aspirations. Both self-directed and counselor-directed processes focus on helping the client explore available jobs, occupations, and other career options, evaluate them, and examine their congruence with client preferences and abilities.

Historically, career counseling was treated as separate from psychotherapy or personal counseling. Within the past two decades, however, the content of career counseling has broadened as career counseling has been used throughout the life span with populations who are experiencing an increasingly comprehensive array of career concerns. Thus, while traditional models of career counseling tend to focus on career exploration, job selection, clarifying life and career goals, and improving decision-making skills, more recent applications of career counseling tend to address problems that require a fusion of career and personal counseling. In the latter approaches, career counseling may address the provision of support for persons experiencing job stress, job loss, and major career transitions, often involuntary; helping clients deal with work adjustment issues, such as coping with negative relations with a supervisor or co-workers; learning to deal with anger management; restructuring work dysfunctions; modifying irrational career beliefs; or resolving conflicts between work and family roles.

DEFINITIONS OF CAREER COUNSELING

As the problems clients bring to career counselors have expanded and become more complex, the definitions of career counseling have changed. These definitions have increasingly shifted from viewing career problems as rational, objective, and unaffected by emotional crises outside of the workplace to examining the interaction of work-related problems with those of personal identity, family concerns, mental health, and related issues. Krumboltz (1993), for example, has stated emphatically that "career and personal counseling are inextricably intertwined. Career problems have a strong emotional component" (p. 143). Betz and Corning (1993) have argued that career and personal counseling should not be viewed as different types of counseling:

The holistic philosophy of counseling emphasizes helping whole persons whose lives contain many important and meaningful roles and activities, including among others, work or career and love and friendship . . . recent research on the implications of gender and race for career development further demonstrates the inseparability of our "career" and "personal lives." (p. 137)

Two definitions will serve to summarize current perspectives on career counseling. The first focuses on the counselor-client relationship:

Career counseling is (1) a largely verbal process in which (2) a counselor and counselee(s) are in dynamic interaction and in which (3) the counselor employs a repertoire of diverse behavior (4) to help bring about self-understanding and action in the form of "good" decision-making in the counselee, who has responsibility for his or her own actions. (Herr & Cramer, 1996, p. 592)

The second definition focuses somewhat more on the content of career counseling. It states:

Career counseling is an interpersonal process designed to assist individuals with career development problems. Career development is that process of choosing, entering, adjusting to and advancing in an occupation. It is a life-long psychological process that interacts dynamically with other life roles. Career problems include but are not limited to career indecision and unde-cidedness, work performance, stress and adjustment, incongruence of the person and work environment, and inadequate or unsatisfactory integration of life roles (e.g., parent, friend, citizen). (Brown & Brooks, 1991, p. 5)

These definitions suggest that career counseling is used with individuals and with groups, represents a continuum of approaches tailored to the career concerns and needs of individual clients, and is likely to be part of a program of interventions including career assessments, self-directed activities, assistance with skill development, and related functions.

APPROACHES TO CAREER COUNSELING

Given the wide-range of career and personal concerns to which career counseling can be applied, there are varied approaches to career counseling which emphasize different theoretical perspectives. Whatever the precise theoretical framework used, however, career counseling emphasizes maximum collaborative efforts between the counselor and the client to clarify the current situation of concern (e.g., needs for career planning, choice among possible options, an untenable work environment, work-family issues); clarify the client's personal role within the situation; identify action goals to be pursued in the career counseling process; identify information of relevance to the situation; develop insight about behavioral options available; and engage in problem-solving to develop a plan of action. Within this general outline of a career counseling process, there are variations in what goals are emphasized, depending on individual differences and on theoretical orientations. For example, Brown and Brooks (1991) emphasize that many persons lack *cognitive clarity,* the ability objectively to assess one's own strengths and weaknesses and relate the assessment to environmental situations. In this view, persons who lack cognitive clarity also possess faulty logic systems that may result in what theorists describe as irrational beliefs, negative self-talk, or faulty private rules for decision-making.

These manifestations of a lack of cognitive clarity may require the career counselor to use various cognitive-behavioral techniques to modify inaccurate or maladaptive cognitive sets about self, others, or specific life events; to analyze the client's automatic thoughts and irrational beliefs about their abilities, worth, work opportunities, or performance; and to help clients with cognitive restructuring or reframing of their concerns about career planning, work adjustment, or other career issues.

Beyond helping the client to achieve cognitive clarity or to confront faulty logic and negative cognitions about their career development, career counseling may include other approaches. Perhaps the most venerable is what has historically been called trait and factor, and in more recent perspective, person-environment fit (Chartrand, 1991). Such an approach focuses on helping clients match individual traits to the performance requirements and work culture of particular jobs, occupations, or training. The intent is to increase the congruence between the client's abilities, interests, and values and the technical and psychosocial aspects of the job, occupation, or training option chosen. Embedded in such an approach is the goal of helping the client evaluate the probabilities or odds of gaining access to and being successful in different jobs, occupations, or educational opportunities. Such an approach is typically information and assessment driven. It often involves considerable analysis of the client's self-understanding, abilities, and preferences as an evaluative base to which to relate possible career options. Trait and factor (person-environment fit) approaches also are likely to help the client gain insight into the elasticity of their previous work experience with other jobs or occupations for which there is compatibility and fit.

While there are client-centered, psychodynamic, and behavioral approaches, the final major approach to be discussed is the developmental approach to career counseling. This approach emphasizes the client's coping with developmental tasks in the past and in the current choice situation. Such an analysis may focus on the client's readiness to cope with emerging roles and developmental requirements, relinquishing roles that are no longer appropriate and acquiring the attitudinal and behavioral elements of career adaptability required in one's current life stage: planfulness, exploration, time perspective, assertiveness, flexibility, reality orientation, and so forth.

Each of the approaches cited here may be used either in combination with the others cited or as the primary approach. How these approaches are combined depends on the needs of the client and the goals of the career counseling process. The use of these approaches also depends on the competence of the career counselor to function in an electic, rather than theory-bound, manner.

EVALUATION OF CAREER COUNSELING

A large number of studies have reported effects for career interventions on diverse career outcomes (Sexton, Whiston, Bleuer, & Walz, 1995). Within the positive effects found for career interventions in general, individual counseling has constantly been found to be the most effective intervention per unit of time involved (Oliver & Spokane, 1988; Sexton, Whiston, Bleuer, & Walz, 1997). Specifically, the reviews by Oliver and Spokane (1988) of the research literature on career counseling indicate that, although more costly than other approaches, individual counseling is the most efficient intervention in terms of amount of gain per hour of effort. They have also reported that longer (at least 10 sessions) and more comprehensive sessions, although requiring much more time from the client and from the counselor, yield roughly twice the beneficial effects of briefer career interventions. Swanson (1995) concluded that while both individual and group counseling yield positive outcomes, they may be differentially effective for different types of clients.

REFERENCES

Betz, N. E., & Corning, A. F. (1993). The inseparability of "career" and "personal" counseling. *The Career Development Quarterly, 42*(3), 137–148.

Brown, D., & Brooks, L. (1991). *Career counseling techniques.* Boston: Allyn & Bacon.

Chartrand, J. M. (1991). The evolution of trait and factor career counseling. A person x environment fit approach. *Journal of Counseling and Development, 69,* 518–524.

Herr, E. L., & Cramer, S. H. (1996). *Career guidance and counseling through the lifespan: Systematic approaches* (5th ed.). New York: HarperCollins.

Krumboltz, J. D. (1993). Integrating career and personal counseling. *The Career Development Quarterly, 42*(2), 143–148.

Oliver, L. W., & Spokane, A. R. (1988). Career intervention outcome: What contributes to client gain? *Journal of Counseling Psychology, 35*(4), 447–462.

Sexton, T. L., Whiston, S. C., Bleuer, J. C., & Walz, G. R. (1995). *A critical review of the counseling outcomes research.* Technical report for the Human Development Foundation, American Counseling Association, Alexandria, VA.

Sexton, T. L., Whiston, S. C., Bleuer, J. C., & Walz, G. R. (1997). *Integrating outcome research into counseling practice and training.* Alexandria, VA: American Counseling Association.

Swanson, J. L. (1995). The process and outcome of career counseling. In W. B. Walsh & S. H. Osipow (Eds.), *Handbook of vocational psychology: Theory, research and practice* (pp. 217–259). Mahwak, NJ: Erlbaum.

E. L. HERR
Pennsylvania State University

CAREER DEVELOPMENT
COUNSELING
INDUSTRIAL PSYCHOLOGY
OCCUPATIONAL PSYCHOLOGY

CAREER DEVELOPMENT

Virtually all persons engage in multiple forms of career behavior throughout their life. Examples include preparing for a work role, choosing and entering a job or occupation, dealing with the dynamics of work adjustment, moving from one job to another, becoming unemployed, and making plans for retirement. Although there are similarities in how persons approach such work-related tasks, there also are significant variations between males and females, persons of different educational or socioeconomic levels, persons of different racial and ethnic backgrounds, and persons with physical and mental disabilities. The term *career development* describes the processes and factors that influence how individuals develop a personal identity in regard to work, and how their beliefs,

values, interests, and aptitudes are reflected in the transition, induction, and adjustment to work.

CAREER DEFINED

In order to understand the term career development, it is useful to consider the term *career.* Jobs and occupations are part of one's career but are not synonymous with this concept. Jobs and occupations describe groups of tasks or work performances that occur within a workplace, and that constitute paid positions that can be identified, applied for, and achieved. But the term career means more than work performance. Among the classic definitions of career is that of Raynor and Entin (1982) who contend that:

A career is both a phenomenological concept and a behavioral concept. It is the link between what a person does and how that person sees him or herself. A career consists of time-linked senses of self that are defined by action and its outcomes. A career defines how one sees oneself in the context of one's social environment—in terms of one's future plans, one's past accomplishments or failures, and one's present competencies and attributes. (p. 262)

The important perspectives of Raynor and Entin affirm the earlier language of Super (1976), who indicated that career could be defined as:

The course of events which constitutes a life; the sequence of occupations and other life roles which combine to express one's commitment to work in his or her total pattern of self-development. . . . Careers exist only as people pursue them. (p. 4)

These definitions affirm that careers are unique to each person and created by what one chooses or does not choose. They are dynamic and unfold throughout life. They include not only jobs and occupations but pre-vocational concerns (school courses, job training) and post-vocational concerns (retirement) as well as integration of other roles: family, community, and leisure.

PERSPECTIVES ON CAREER DEVELOPMENT

Career development is a comprehensive process that is of interest to researchers and theorists in many disciplines. It can be understood as one of the many aspects of socialization that combine to create human development; in this case the focus is on occupational or work socialization. As a socialization process, career development is a product of multiple factors: psychological, sociological, cultural, political, and economic. In psychological terms, the individual acquires motivation to act in certain ways related to his or her beliefs about personal self-efficacy in particular work domains, the likelihood that certain valued outcomes will occur—for example, prestige, affiliation, economic well-being, security, purpose, productivity—from some choices and not others, and the salience of work to his or her personal identity. In sociological terms, however, individual career development is also a product of the constraints and barriers to choices that individuals might prefer to make. Such constraints can occur because of limitations on individual choice that arise from political conditions or from economic circumstances. Persons in a generation whose behavior is dramatically affected by a major and enduring economic depression or by transformations in political systems—from communism to a market economy, from apartheid to free mobility and choice—choose differently or have different opportunities than persons living in a different historical period. Sociological effects on choice also can be seen in family and cultural influences. Families with differing educational and socioeconomic backgrounds tend to reinforce different educational and occupational goals and belief systems related to career choice. Nations and cultural groups also differ in how particular types of education, work, or family roles are valued, and these perceptions tend to be internalized by group members and reflected in their choices.

Career development can be thought of in both structural and developmental terms (Herr & Cramer, 1996). The structure of career development refers to the elements that comprise concepts like career maturity, career adaptability, and career planfulness. Career maturity, for example, whether in adolescence or in adulthood tends to include five factors—planfulness or time perspective, exploration, information, decision-making, and reality orientation. These five factors are structural components of career maturity and each factor has its own structural subelements. A structural approach to career development essentially asks, what does it mean to be occupationally socialized, career mature, and an effective career decision-maker? How would I know such persons if I met them?

In addition to a structural approach to career development, there is also a developmental approach. In such an approach, the questions change from what are the factors that comprise career maturity? Does career maturity change over time? Is behavior described as career mature at age 18 the same as career maturity at age 25 or 45? What are the factors that influence career behavior at different life stages: childhood, adolescence, young adult, mid-career adult, older adult?

Another perspective views career development as a life-style concept. In essence, the work roles that one implements throughout the life span are not independent of other life roles; indeed, they may be in conflict with them. Being a workaholic, a spouse, and a parent may be problematic if the amount of energy or time given to the work role is significantly out of balance with that given to these other life roles. Similar role conflicts can occur when the work and leisure roles or the worker and student roles are out of balance, or when the work role and the role of caregiver for elderly parents are in conflict.

THEORIES OF CAREER DEVELOPMENT

The theories that offer explanations of career behavior are multidisciplinary. This is true in part because career identity and the socialization to work are such important aspects of human development in the developed nations of the world, and in part because the factors that influence career development take many forms. In capturing such a perspective, Super (1990) contended that:

The pioneers of career development are people from four disciplines: differential psychologists interested in work and occupations, developmental psychologists interested in the "life course," sociologists focusing on occupational mobility as a function of social class, and personality theorists who view individuals as organizers of experience. (p 197)

To these theorists of different aspects of career development, one can add the growing attention of political scientists, economists, and organizational theorists as persons concerned about career development. As a result of this disciplinary diversity focused on career behavior, some theory and research is primarily applied to job or occupational choice at a specific period in time, to adjustment within a work setting, or to the decision-making process used by different persons. Some research is concerned with the structure of choice, work behavior, or "career maturity" within a particular life stage; other theory is concerned with how such structures change over time, the role of chance in career choice, and the continuities and discontinuities in career patterns throughout the lifespan. Some theories are more focused on the roots of career behavior in childhood and adolescence; other theories give greater attention to career behavior in middle and late adulthood. Growing attention is being given to the unique dimensions of career development in women, in different cultural groups, and as it relates to mental health.

REFERENCES

Herr, E. L., & Cramer, S. H. (1996). *Career guidance and counseling through the lifespan: Systematic approaches.* New York: HarperCollins.

Raynor, J. O., & Entin, E. E. (1982). *Motivation, career striving, and aging.* New York: Hemisphere.

Super, D. E. (1976). *Career education and the meaning of work.* Monographs on career education. Washington, DC: The Office of Career Education, the U.S. Office of Education.

Super, D. E. (1990). A life-span, life-space approach to career development. In D. Brown & L. Brooks (Eds.), *Career choice and development: Applying contemporary theories to practice* (pp. 197–261). San Francisco: Jossey-Bass.

E. L. Herr
Pennsylvania State University

CAREER COUNSELING
INDUSTRIAL PSYCHOLOGY
OCCUPATIONAL COUNSELING

CATHARSIS

Catharsis is a term used in aesthetics and the psychology of art with reference to spectator response, and in psychotherapy with reference to the release of repressed affect or psychic energy.

In ancient Greek, "katharsis" most commonly meant physical or spiritual purgation, ridding one of uncleanliness or guilt. Empedocles used it to speak of religious purification; Plato, to speak of purification of the soul by means of philosophy; and Hippocrates and his followers, to speak of the evacuation of morbid humors. But its most notable use in ancient times occurs in Aristotle's cryptic definition of tragedy as drama which "accomplishes through pity and fear the catharsis of such feelings" (*Poetics* 1449b). Literary critics, philosophers, and psychologists have argued about what Aristotle meant, notably over whether the emotions are aroused in spectators or simply depicted in the drama and, if the former, whether they are purged, sublimated, or in some other way resolved. The term has been applied to a wide range of art forms and emotional responses or representations.

In psychoanalytic literature the term first appeared in *Studies on Hysteria* by Breuer and Freud, although both the naming and the therapeutic method initially associated with it are credited to Breuer. (Perhaps unjustly; Jacob Bernays, uncle of Freud's wife, believed that "catharsis" referred to a medical healing process, and his articulated view may well have influenced both Breuer and Freud.) Breuer had apparently cured patients of hysterical symptoms by inducing them, under hypnosis, to relive or remember forgotten childhood events—often but not always traumatic—and the affects associated with them. Freud hypothesized that in such cases the mental or nervous energy which would have led to the original affect was diverted into hysterical symptoms, and that memories of the experiences were repressed into the unconscious. When, under hypnosis, both the memory and the associated affect were brought into consciousness, the affect was thereby discharged and the symptom eliminated. The process of affective discharge was also called "abreaction."

Although Freud soon replaced hypnosis with free association and enlarged his theory, he stated in "A Short Account of Psychoanalysis" (1961) that the cathartic method was both the precursor and the ongoing nucleus of psychoanalysis. Catharsis thus remains a basic concept, even though the term itself has lost favor among psychoanalysts. In its psychoanalytic context—referring to the release of repressed ideas and affects—it has also been an important and fruitful concept in theorizing about spectator responses to works of art by thinkers within the psychoanalytic tradition (such as Kris) and others outside it (such as Vygotsky).

In contemporary psychotherapy outside the psychoanalytic tradition, "catharsis" is often defined much more loosely as referring in a general way to the therapeutic release of emotions or tensions, including some which might be conscious or related to conscious experiences. A central concept in psychodrama, catharsis is also a major aspect of Gestalt and primal therapies and of most brief and crisis-oriented therapies. Sometimes it is called "talking out," "acting out," or "ventilation." In implosive therapy there is a deliberate attempt to elicit strong emotions in order to bring about cathartic release of tension. Controversy persists concerning the effectiveness of catharsis as merely emotional release rather than its more fundamental role in a psychotherapeutic process of reintegration.

REFERENCES

Freud, S. (1961). A short account of psycho-analysis. In *The standard edition of the complete psychological works of Sigmund Freud.* Vol. 19. London: Hogarth Press. (Original work published 1924)

SUGGESTED READING

Breuer, J., & Freud, S. (1957/1895). *Studies on hysteria.* New York: Basic Books.

Jackson, S. W. (1994). Catharsis and abreaction in the history of psychological healing. *Psychiatric Clinics of North America, 17,* 471–491.

Kellerman, P. F. (1992). *Focus on psychodrama: The therapeutic aspects of psychodrama.* London: Jessica Kingsley.

Kris, E. (1964). *Psychoanalytic explorations in art.* New York: Schocken. (Original work published 1952)

Moreno, J. L. (1940). Mental catharsis and the psychodrama. *Sociometry, 3,* 209–244.

Nichols, M. P., & Zax, M. (1977). *Catharsis in psychotherapy.* New York: Gardner.

Scheff, T. J. (1979). *Catharsis in healing, ritual, and drama.* Berkeley, CA: University of California Press.

Vygotsky, L. S. (1971). Art as a catharsis. In L. S. Vygotsky (Ed.), *The psychology of art.* Cambridge, MA: MIT Press.

F. W. HANSEN
Lake Forest College

BRIEF PSYCHOTHERAPY
CRISIS INTERVENTION
IMPLOSIVE THERAPY

CATTELL, JAMES M. (1860–1944)

James M. Cattell attended Lafayette College for his undergraduate work. He traveled to Europe and studied at Göttingen and then in Leipzig under Wilhelm Wundt. He received a fellowship to return to Johns Hopkins in 1882 and study philosophy. G. Stanley Hall began his lecture there in psychology; Cattell attended the course and began research on mental activities. He returned to Wundt in 1883 to study individual differences, which was characterized as a typically American project by the Germans. Cattell received his degree in 1886 in psychology.

Cattell lectured at Bryn Mawr and at the University of Pennsylvania. He went to England to lecture at Cambridge University, where he met Sir Francis Galton, who shared Cattell's interest in individual differences. From Sir Francis he learned measurement and statistics, and then became the first psychologist to teach and emphasize statistical analysis of experimental results. In 1888 Cattell was appointed professor of psychology at the University of Pennsylvania, the first psychology professorship in the world.

In 1891 Cattell went to Columbia University as professor of psychology and head of the department, where he remained for 26 years. During these years, more doctorates in psychology were awarded by Columbia than by any other graduate school in the

United States. Cattell's students were encouraged and, indeed, required to do independent research and to work on their own. Many of them became prominent in the field.

As the years passed, Cattell's personal and professional independence strained his relationship with the administration at Columbia. During World War I he was dismissed on the grounds of being disloyal to his country. Cattell sued for libel and won, but he was not reinstated in his professorship.

In 1921 Cattell organized the Psychological Corporation to provide applied psychological services to industry, the professional community, and the public. As a spokesman and editor, he was an active supporter of psychological organizations and societies.

The theme of all of Cattell's research was mental tests and individual differences, a feature of American as opposed to German psychology. His mental tests were different from later intelligence tests, for he measured elementary bodily or sensory-motor responses. Correlations between his tests and the students' academic performance was low. Although tests of this kind were not valid predictors of intellectual ability (Alfred Binet developed a test of higher mental abilities that *was* an effective measure of intelligence), Cattell's influence was strong, particularly through his student, E. L. Thorndike. Columbia University was the center of the testing movement; Cattell's work contributed to the practical and applied psychology that was uniquely American, and functional.

N. A. HAYNIE

CATTELL, RAYMOND B. (1905–1998)

Raymond B. Cattell received his education at Kings College, London, where he received the BS in 1924 and the PhD in 1929, and came under the influence of Charles Spearman, the founder of factor analysis. Cattell lectured at University College in Exeter, England, from 1928 to 1931. The following year he undertook the directorship of the City Psychological Clinic in Leicester, England. In 1937 he left for the United States, spending a year at the Teachers College of Columbia University, and three more years at Clark University. The war years were spent at Harvard as a lecturer in psychology. His long tenure at the University of Illinois began in 1944.

Cattell derived his distinction in psychology from multivariate factor analysis. His books are generally based on factor analysis, and his theory of personality is a factor analytic or statistical approach to personality. His work in factor analysis culminated in the voluminous *Handbook of Multivariate Experimental Psychology.* His many books on personality are written from the factor analytic orientation, including *Description and Measurement of Personality; An Introduction to Personality Study; Personality: A Systematic Theoretical and Factual Study; Personality and Motivation: Structure and Measurement; Personality and Social Psychology; The Scientific Analysis of Personality; Personality and Learning Theory: A Systems Theory of Maturation and Structures Learning;* and *Per-*

sonality and Learning Theory: The Structure of Personality in its Environment.

Cattell based his findings on the inductive-hypothetico-deductive method, defining personality as "that which enables us to predict what [the individual] will do in a given situation" (*An Introduction to Personality Study,* p. 21).

STAFF

CELL DEATH

The father of modern pathology, Rudolph Virchow (1821–1902), introduced the term "necrosis" (from the Greek *nécrõs,* or "dead body"). He did not imply a specific mechanism of death, and until the turn of the century, "necrosis" was used interchangeably with "cell death." In the late 19th century, Walter Flemming described ovarian follicle cells that died spontaneously (without obvious toxins). He termed this process chromatolysis, referring to the breakage and disappearance of the nucleus. A few months later, the same phenomenon was reported in lactating mammary glands, creating the concept of spontaneous (or non-pathological) death.

During the first two decades of the 20th century, specific rules distinguished between spontaneous and other forms of cell death. The term "necrosis" was restricted to the latter. A turning point was the introduction of the physiological concepts of programmed cell death and apoptosis. Building on studies of embryological cell death by Saunders and colleagues (finally published as Saunders, 1966), Lockshin and Williams in 1964 (Lockshin and Williams, 1964) introduced the term programmed cell death to describe a developmental situation in which cell death was controlled. In 1972 Kerr, Wyllie, and Currie introduced "apoptosis" to describe morphology common to most spontaneous cell deaths and to emphasize that it was general and widespread (Kerr, Wyllie, and Currie, 1972). In the 1970s Sulston and Horvitz (1977) first identified cell death genes, a topic subsequently followed in extensive detail by Horvitz and his colleagues.

APOPTOSIS VS. NECROSIS

Apoptosis (Greek: "dropping of leaves from a tree") refers to cytologically observable changes associated with active, gene-directed, cellular self-destruction, which differs considerably from necrosis. Necrosis is caused by massive cell damage and is passive and independent of gene activity. Through loss of energy resources or direct damage, the cell membrane fails to maintain ion pumps and regulate osmotic pressure. The cell lyses, and the release of cell contents elicits inflammatory reactions. Necrosis results, for example, from injuries, severe hypoxia, hypothermia, lytic virus infections, or strong toxins.

Cells that have sufficient time to organize a series of intracellular processes culminating in the destruction of the cell undergo apoptosis. Unlike necrosis, apoptosis requires a functional energy-producing system. The earliest indications of apoptotic cell death are morphological: chromatin condensation and margination at the inner surface of the nuclear membrane, disappearance of the nucleolus, and blebs and other alterations of the cell surface. Eventually, activation of specific proteases—caspases—leads indirectly to fragmentation of DNA, generating a so-called DNA ladder on electrophoresis. The cell typically fragments into several large blebs, which are most commonly phagocytosed. Intracellular contents are not released from apoptotic cells and inflammation does not occur.

Control of apoptosis is often linked with the progression of cells through the cell cycle. Apoptosis allows selective elimination and swift clearance by phagocytosis of cells from a proliferating cell population. Apoptosis is observed, for example, during embryonic development, morphogenesis, metamorphosis, cell turnover, and tumor regression, and during disappearance of excess lymphocytes and damaged cells after an infection. Apoptosis also occurs in non-dividing cells such as cardiac muscle and neurons.

Apoptosis involves specific activators, effectors, and negative regulators. Particularly in developmental situations, apoptosis can be inhibited by inhibitors of RNA and protein synthesis (technically programmed cell death), indicating that these regulators must be synthesized. In many other situations, cell death involves the activation of preexisting proteins rather than control of transcription. Whether they pre-exist or are synthesized as the cell dies, the products of many genes control apoptosis. Regulation of the expression of these genes and activation of their products are both very complex.

DISEASE

Disruption of normal apoptosis causes disease. Failed or excess apoptosis leads to inappropriate cell survival and causes developmental abnormalities or cancer development. Apoptosis is the major source of loss of neurons in neurodegenerative diseases such as Parkinson's and Alzheimer's (Senile Dementia of Alzheimer Type). During development of the embryonic central nervous system, in some regions up to one-third of neurons are eliminated by apoptosis; it appears that the pathological loss is similar.

In the lymphatic system, aberrant apoptosis produces many pathologies. In autoimmune diseases, initiated by the generation of anti-self antigens, the interaction of Fas ligand (as a soluble molecule or cell surface protein on one cell) and Fas on the other cell activates the cell death machinery on the Fas-bearing cell. Genetic loss of either of these interactants results in lymphadenopathy or lymphoproliferative disease. Viruses such as HIV can instigate apoptosis even in bystander cells. Alternatively, overactivation (by translocation) of the anti-apoptosis gene bcl-2 results in B-cell lymphoma, which is caused by decrease in the death rate of B cells rather than by increased mitosis; and many cancers become far more aggressive and less subject to control when they mutate the gene p53, which induces apoptosis of damaged cells that have committed to mitosis. The damaged cells continue to divide and produce new mutants of the tumor.

FINAL WORD

When apoptosis was recognized as part of normal physiology and, consequently, as important in disease, interest grew exponentially.

Over the last 15 years, cell death research has been one of the fastest growing biomedical fields. Direct targeting of signals to die to malignant cells may prove to be an effective and less toxic therapy, and specific protection of threatened cells may prove valuable in diseases as diverse as AIDS, myocardial infarct and Alzheimer's. The fields of apoptosis and programmed cell death remain among the most promising for the future.

REFERENCES

Clarke, P. G. H. (1990). Developmental cell death: Morphological diversity and multiple mechanisms. *Anatomy and Embryology* 181, 195–213.

Cotter, T. G., Lennon, S. V., Glynn, J. G., & Martin, S. J. (1990). Cell death *via* apoptosis and its relationship to growth, development and differentiation of both tumour and normal cells. *Anticancer Research,* 10, 1153–1160.

Flemming, W. (1885). Über die Bildung vom Richtungsfiguren in Säugethiereien beim Untergang Graff'scher Follikel. Archiv fur Anatomie und Entwickelungsgeschichte 221–44.

Kerr, J. F. R., Wyllie, A. H., & Currie, A. R. (1972). Apoptosis: a basic biological phenomenon with wide-ranging implications in tissue kinetics. *British Journal of Cancer,* 26. 239–257.

Lockshin, R. A., & Williams, C. M. (1964). Programmed cell death. II. Endocrine potentiation of the breakdown of the intersegmental muscles of silkmoths. *Journal of Insect Physiology,* 10, 643–649.

Saunders, J. W., Jr. (1966). Death in embryonic systems. *Science* 154. 604–612.

Schwartz, L. M. (1991). The role of cell death genes during development. *Bioessays* 13, 389–95.

Sulston, J., & Horvitz, H. R. (1977). Postembryonic cell lineages of the nematode *Caenorhabditis elegans. Developmental Biology* 56, 110–156.

Wyllie, A. H., Kerr, J. F., & Currie, A. R. (1980). Cell death: the significance of apoptosis. International Reviews of Cytology 68, 251–306.

SUGGESTED READING

Ellis, R. E. et al. (1991). Mechanisms and functions of cell death. *Annual Review of Cell Biology, 7,* 663–698.

Cotter, T. G. et al. (1990). Cell death via apoptosis and its relationship to growth, development, and differentiation of both tumor and normal cells. *Advances in Cancer Research, 10,* 1153–1159.

Johnson, E. M. R., & Deckwerth, T. L. (1993). Molecular mechanism of developmental neuronal death. *Annual Review of Neuroscience, 16,* 31–46.

Majno, G., & Norris, I. (1995). Apoptosis, oncosis, and necrosis. *American Journal of Pathology, 146,* 3–15.

Z. ZAKERI
S. KANE
Queen's College, City University of New York

CELL DIFFERENTIATION
Although the tissues of the body differ in many ways, they all have certain basic requirements, which are usually provided by a mixture of cell types. These cell types in a multicellular organism become different from one another or undergo differentiation because they synthesize and accumulate different sets of RNA and protein molecules. Some of these specialized cell types, such as fibroblasts, provide mechanical strength by secreting a supporting framework of extracellular matrix. Others, like macrophages, are usually present to dispose of dying cells. Table 1 describes some of the specialized cell types that are found in most tissues of vertebrates.

Most of these cell types originate outside the tissue and invade it either early in the course of the development of the tissue (endothelial cells, nerve cell axons into target tissues, Schwann cells, germ cells, and melanocytes) or continually during life (macrophages and other white blood cells). This complex supporting apparatus is required to maintain the principal specialized cells of the tissue. These cells enable the tissue to perform its primary duty and efficiently contribute its share to the function of the body. For example, the testes, in addition to the germ cells that have migrated to the region, contain specialized cells called Sertoli cells and Leydig cells. Table 2 lists some of the specialized cells (primary functional cells) of tissues in mammals.

Like the specialized cells common to all tissues (Table 1), the principal specialized cells of a tissue (specific to that tissue) originate during one of two times during the life of the organism:

1. During embryonic development, persisting throughout life without dividing and without being replaced (e.g., neurons, and striated and skeletal muscle). These differentiated cells become specialized early in embryonic life and constitute a large mass, but a small percentage, of cell types in the body.

2. From determined stem cells or already differentiated cells (via cell division) during life after embryological development. These differentiated cells are formed to replace worn-out cells in order to maintain a certain number of cells in a given tissue and proper functioning of that tissue. For instance, sperm are generated throughout mature life, but oocytes, especially in mammals, are all formed during embryonic life or early infancy and do not undergo further mitoses. Recently, new neuron formation in adult mammals has been demonstrated in the hippocampus and cerebral cortex.

CHARACTERISTICS OF DIFFERENTIATION
During early embryogenesis, cells divide and move and become limited in their potential to become different cell types. This process of limiting the developmental potential of cells is called *determination,* which:

1. Is heritable in that a cell and its daughter cells have the same limited potential, except that one or both of the daughter cells may become further restricted in potential.

Table 1. Specialized cell types in vertebrate tissues

Cell Type	Function
Fibroblasts	Excrete extracellular matrix to provide support
Endothelial cells	Line blood vessels and organs and help to extend and remodel the blood vessel network
Erythrocytes	In vertebrates, carry respiratory pigment (hemoglobin)
Macrophages	Dispose of dying cells and unwanted extracellular matrix
Lymphocytes	Responsible for immune responses
Neurons	Allow for fast and efficient communication within the central nervous system and between the CNS and the other parts of the body
Schwann cells	Insulate and support neurons
Melanocytes	Provide a protective or decorative pigmentation

Table 2. Specialized cells of mammalian tissues

Tissue	Specialized Cell(s)	Function
Brain	Neuron	Generation and transmission of electric signals
	Glia	Structural and metabolic functions
Eye	Rods and cones	Photoreceptors, used to detect light
Heart	Cardiac muscle	Contractile element of heart
Stomach	Mucus cells	Secretion of mucus for aid in digestion and protection of stomach lining
	Chief cells	Produce and secrete hydrochloric acid for digestion
Lungs	Alveolar epithelium	Permits gas exchange between gas surface and red blood cells
Kidneys	Tubal epithelium	Several types, which are responsible for controlling active or passive movement of ions and fluids, producing urine from blood plasma
Gonads (testes and ovaries)	Spermatocytes and Oocytes	Spermatocytes differentiate into spermatids and spermatozoa; and oocytes mature into ova or ripe eggs. These generally arise from cells that have migrated from elsewhere into supportive tissue to complete the gonad
	Leydig Cell	Production of male sex hormones
	Sertoli Cell	Nourishment and protection of developing sperm cells
	Follicle cells (various)	Nourishment for egg cells; production of female sex hormones
Skin	Epithelial cells	Protect surfaces of animal from abrasion, loss of fluid, or other damage
Skeletal muscle	Myocytes	Attach to skeletal system and provide mechanism for movement; typically a syncitium formed by the fusion of many immature muscle cells, or myoblasts
Endocrine glands	Endocrine cells	Various; secrete hormones directly into blood stream for effect elsewhere in the body

2. Typically activates or represses specific genes associated with the determination event.

3. Is permanent under normal conditions but, with difficulty, is sometimes possible to reverse experimentally.

Differentiation is a maturing process in which a determined cell (the progeny of a stem cell, usually not the stem cell itself) becomes a recognizable, specialized cell. Differentiated cells:

1. Produce and use cell-specific proteins characteristic of their type (e.g., myosin in muscle cells, hemoglobin in red blood cells).

2. Must be metabolically active in order to produce the specific proteins and carry out the specialized function.

3. Often assume a characteristic shape.

4. Are usually terminally differentiated and non-dividing, although some may be induced to divide because of injury.

5. Are triggered to differentiate by external stimuli.

The types of signals that control the activity of genes in the processes of determination and differentiation are:

1. *Hormones,* such as

a. Steroid hormones, which typically control activity of genes

b. Protein hormones, which often act by binding to the cell membrane and initiating a cascade of events within the cell

c. Catecholamines or peptide hormones, which usually act by binding to the cell membrane and initiating a cascade of events within the cell. These cascades most typically begin with an intracellular intermediate, such as cyclic adenosine monophosphate or cyclic guanosine monophosphate

2. *Protein factors.* These differ from hormones either in being secreted locally or in not having sharply limited or defined target organs. They include molecules such as

a. growth factors, such as BDNF, NGF

b. interleukin

c. interferon

3. *Cell-to-cell signals* transmitted across the surface of the cell. In these situations one cell expresses a signal or ligand on its surface, and the other cell expresses on its surface a molecule that will bind the ligand, causing the cell to differentiate or to move in a specific direction. The ligand may also be secreted into the extracellular matrix, allowing cells to interact with it. Growing neurons find their direction in this manner.

4. *Environmental factors.* Although embryos are well protected against minor or common contaminants or problems, it is possible to escape these protections and generate developmental abnormalities. Common environmental factors known to create problems include

a. Nutrition—too little or too much food

b. Heat shock

c. Toxic substances

SUGGESTED READING

Clark, W. E. L. (1971). *The tissues of the body* (6th ed.). Oxford, UK: Clarendon Press.

Gilbert, S. (1997). *Developmental biology* (5th ed.). Sunderland, MA: Sinauer.

Goss, R. J. (1978). *The physiology of growth.* New York: Academic Press.

Weiss, L. (Ed.). (1988). *Cell and tissue biology: A textbook of histology* (6th ed.). Baltimore: Urban and Scwartenberg.

Z. ZAKERI
S. KANE
Queens College, City University of New York

CENTRAL LIMIT THEOREM

The central limit theorem concerns the distribution of a linear composite. Y is a linear composite of a set of variables (X_1, X_2, X_3, etc.) if $Y = a_1X_1 + a_2X_2 + a_3X_3 + \ldots$, where the as are weights. For example, if Y equals $3X_1 + 4X_2$, then a_1 equals 3 and a_2 equals 4. The central limit theorem states that the shape of the distribution of Y becomes more and more like the normal distribution as the number of variables included in the composite increases. Specifically, the central limit theorem states that Y is asymptotically normal as the number of composited variables approaches infinity. The central limit theorem is one of the principal reasons that psychologists and statisticians make regular use of the normal distribution.

Notice that the theorem does not require that the variables in the composite be normally distributed. Y is asymptotically normal even when the composited variables have very nonnormal distributions. Perhaps this is most easily illustrated by compositing a set of coin tosses. Imagine tossing a fair (unbiased) coin one time, recording 0 for a tail and 1 for a head. This experiment has two possible outcomes, each equally likely. If we call the experiment's outcome X, it can be concluded that P ($X = 0$) = 0.5 and P ($X = 1$) = 0.5. The distribution of X is given in Table 1.

Repeat this simple experiment 10 times, generating values for X_1, X_2, X_3, ... X_{10}. Each of the Xs has the same distribution. It is possible to create a new variable that is a linear composite of the Xs. Let $Y = X_1 + X_2 + X_3 + \ldots + X_{10}$. Y is the number of heads in 10 tosses of a fair coin, and the distribution of Y is given in Table 2. Notice that with only 10 variables in our composite, Y resembles the normal distribution; probabilities are highest in the middle of the distribution and gradually decrease for more extreme scores. If the coin were tossed 1,000 times and the outcomes were summed, the distribution of this sum would almost be indistinguishable from the normal distribution.

The central limit theorem is introduced frequently as a special case, to describe the distribution of the sample mean. The sample mean is a linear composite of the scores in the sample, with each score weighted by $1/N$, where N is the sample size. If N is large enough, the distribution of the sample mean will be normal, so the normal distribution can be used to build confidence interval estimates of the population mean and to test hypotheses concerning the sample mean. Researchers generally assume the sample mean

Table 1

X	Probability
0	.500
1	.500

Table 2

Y	Probability
0	.001
1	.010
2	.044
3	.117
4	.205
5	.246
6	.205
7	.117
8	.044
9	.010
10	.001

has a normal distribution if N is at least 30, but how quickly the distribution assumes the normal shape depends on how normal the Xs are. If the X scores are normally distributed, their mean always will be normally distributed. If the X scores are very nonnormal, N may have to be larger than 30 for the distribution to be normal.

The central limit theorem also can explain why many physical measurements are normally distributed. Human heights and weights are determined by many factors, probably including hundreds of genes and thousands of variables related to nutritional and psychological history. Heights or weights can be thought of as composite of thousands of variables, so they should be normally distributed. Many psychological traits, such as intelligence, also are normally distributed, probably because they are influenced by thousands of genes and by prenatal and postnatal events. Deviations from normality suggest the heavy influence of one event that overrides the linear composite. For example, extremely short people, so extreme that their presence is not consistent with the normal distribution, may have heights determined by a pituitary problem. Their heights are not influenced by the genes and events that under other circumstances would have made them taller. Similarly, people with extremely low intelligence may have a rare genetic defect or may have been subject to some trauma that damaged the central nervous system.

M. J. ALLEN
California State University, Bakersfield

STATISTICS IN PSYCHOLOGY

CENTRAL NERVOUS SYSTEM

The central nervous system (CNS) refers to the portion of the nervous system that lies within the skull and spinal column and receives nervous impulses from sense receptors throughout the organism, regulates bodily processes, and organizes and directs behavior. Anatomically, the CNS is composed of the brain and spinal cord, which float within the cranial cavity of the skull and in the vertebral canal of the spinal column in a liquid matrix called cerebrospinal fluid, which also fills their hollows and serves as a protective cushion against damage. Central nervous system tissue is further protected by three enfolding membranes called the meninges. The outer and toughest, the dura mater, attaches to skull and spine, encasing the spongy arachnoid membrane within which the cerebrospinal fluid circulates. The soft pia mater is contiguous with the outer layer of brain and cord.

The basic structural unit of nervous tissue is the nerve cell or neuron, a specialized body cell of elongated shape (from a few microns to feet in length), whose enhanced reactivity and conductivity permit it to propagate or conduct an electrical impulse along its length, and to chemically stimulate adjacent neurons to do likewise at specialized junctions called synapses. The nervous system is made up of billions of neurons, which interconnect every part of the organism to monitor and regulate it. Receptor neurons lead like the twigs of a tree inward to branches and thence to great trunks, called nerves, which enter the CNS and ascend into the brain. There, effector neurons originate and descend to exit the CNS as nerves branching repeatedly out to regulate all muscle tissue, and therefore, all bodily activity. Twelve bilateral pairs of cranial nerves enter the brain directly. The cord is the origin of 31 bilateral pairs of spinal nerves which exit the CNS through openings between adjacent vertebrae. Each spinal nerve contains both entering receptor fibers and departing effector fibers; these two types of fibers divide on reaching the cord, sensory fibers entering on the back, motor fibers exiting on the front (Steen & Montegu, 1959).

The spinal cord is thus a great pathway for ascending and descending nerve tracts, but connectedness is a property of the CNS, within which a third type of neuron, the interneuron, is found. Interneurons connect effector and receptor neurons, and by repeated branchings of their tips may synapse at either end with many hundreds of other neurons. The functional unit of the nervous system is the reflex arc, which links receptor and effector neurons so that a stimulus at a sense receptor capable of causing its nerve to conduct will automatically trigger an effector neuron to produce a response in a muscle or gland. Some reflexes are extremely simple, but most are not. The CNS is hierarchically organized such that higher centers are stimulated by and act upon lower centers, so that progressively more complex reflexes are organized progressively higher in the CNS. Certain muscle-stretch reflexes operate spinally for the most part. Respiratory reflexes are largely centered in the brain stem, the part of the brain that is contiguous to the spinal cord. Homeostatic reactions depend upon reflexes organized higher still, in the hypothalamus, which may give rise to motivational states such as hunger and thirst. It is thought that by means of progressively more complex reflexes (some inborn, but most acquired through learning), all functions of the CNS are conducted, including the higher mental functions, the seat of which is the brain. The CNS is also symmetrically organized. Midline structures like the cord have two symmetrical halves. Other structures, such as the two cerebral hemispheres, are duplicated. Most fibers cross the midline (e.g., the left brain controls the right hand).

The brain is an organ of unparalleled complexity of parts and functions, a reality that may be obscured by summary description. A great deal has nevertheless been learned about the pathways followed by ascending and descending nerve tracts. Much of the CNS is white matter: the encased processes or extensions of nerve cells, bundles of which indicate pathways called tracts. The nerve bodies are encased and are present as gray matter, clusters of which indicate centers of activity called nuclei. Evolutionary influences have given characteristic shapes to the complex arrangements of neurons in the CNS, permitting sites to be named and located on charts or in living tissue.

The gross anatomy of the brain, in greatly oversimplified summary, may be divided into three regions: (a) the brain stem, the parts of which (medulla, pons, mesencephalon) contain the nuclei of the brain stem reticular formation, which is vital in consciousness and level of arousal of the brain above; (b) the cerebellum, a center for the smooth regulation of motor behavior; and (c) the cerebrum, which is of greatest interest to psychology for its organizing role in the higher mental functions and emotion. Between brain stem and cerebrum are the thalamus and hypothalamus, which some authorities class with the brain stem, some with the cerebrum (Hubbard, 1975). Thalamic nuclei largely integrate and relay sensory impulses upward to the cerebrum. Hypothalamic nuclei, however, are vital in the regulation of homeostatic reactions and in integrating the reflexes of the nuclei of the limbic system (Papez, 1964), structures embedded deep within the cerebrum that give rise to emotional experience and expression.

The cerebrum's deeply fissured gray outer surface, the hemispheres of its cerebral cortex, are the terminus of sensory processes and the origin of motor processes. Much of this area is given over to association areas of interneurons, whose complex interconnections give rise to memory, speech, purposive behavior, and generally, the higher mental functions.

The pathways, relays, and sensory and motor areas of the brain have been mapped by largely physical and physiological methods. But the nature of the higher mental processes of humans remains elusive because they cannot be charted thus. As Minckler (1972) observed, the structure and function of nervous tissue are so intertwined that they must be studied together. At some levels of the CNS, the appropriate units of function are physiological. Other levels are best studied through discrete behaviors. Still more complex functions of brain, however, require the scrutiny of complex patterns or styles of behavior, and the highest levels of brain function shade into issues of intelligence, logic, purpose, and consciousness, themselves as little understood as the brain.

The study of the CNS in humans is thus the study of brain-mind and brain-behavior relationships, a field in which psychology is heavily involved. That there is a relationship between brain and mind is well established (Dimond, 1978) and has been observed for a very long time. Golden (1980) noted that Pythagoras, in 500 BC, linked brain and human reasoning. In the second century AD, Galen of Pergamum observed the effects on consciousness of brain injury in gladiators and described animals rendered senseless by pressure on their brains (Clarke & O'Malley, 1968).

Galen was incorrect in attributing mental processes to the fluid-filled hollows of the brain, a view that nevertheless endured until the Renaissance (Chapman & Wolff, 1959). Modern concepts regarding brain functions did not begin to develop until the 1800s (Golden, 1980). This delay resulted from vitalistic and imprecise views of both brain and mind, and endured until a more scientific and reductionistic view of brain and behavior emerged. Rarnón y Cajal forwarded neuron theory in the late 1800s and received a Nobel Prize in physiology in 1906 (Gardner, 1963/1975), the same year that Sherrington, who developed the concept of the reflex arc, published on integrative mechanisms of the nervous system (1906). Galton's work with the behavioral measurement of individual differences contributed greatly to the emerging science of psychometrics, or mental measurement (Galton, 1883/1907, 1879–1880). Watson moved psychology toward the study of behavior rather than mental states (1913); he and Skinner (1938) both contributed to a science and technology of behavior that has meshed well with biology in permitting brain-behavior studies. But the complexities of mind or behavior and brain are such that the more we learn, the more there remains to be learned. Sommerhoff put it thus: "The peculiar fascination of the brain lies in the fact that there is probably no other object of scientific enquiry about which we know so much and yet understand so little" (1974, p. 3).

At the heart of the problem lies the fact that the nervous system, so simple in basic elements, is so complex in arrangements. As Hubbard (1975) observed, it is easy to imagine neuronal arrangements capable of causing muscles to contract or glands to empty, but difficult to imagine such arrangements permitting the aging Beethoven to compose works he could no longer hear. The sheer complexity of interconnections, which could well permit such complex behaviors, virtually defies understanding. Some five million neurons, for example, may lie beneath a single square centimeter of brain surface (Dimond, 1978), each of which synapses with perhaps 600 other neurons (Smith, 1970). Virtually the entire depth and surface of the brain may be involved in any given behavior: "although very basic skills can be localized, all observable behavior is a complex interaction of numerous basic skills so that the brain as a whole is involved in most actual behavior" (Golden, 1980, p. 225).

To be understood, the brain (and possibly all the CNS) must be understood as a whole. Yet owing to limits in theory, knowledge, and perhaps capacity, we must approach the whole through study of the parts, viewed at many levels and from many perspectives. Full understanding of the CNS thus lies beyond any one discipline. Pschyology, however, contributes in many ways to the expanding interdisciplinary study of the CNS called neuroscience (Miller, 1995). Psychologists have put forward or contributed to models of mind compatible with known facts of brain function (Miller, Galanter, & Pribram, 1960; Carver & Scheier, 1982), and have helped develop new models of neural function drawing on and contributing to computer modeling (Parks, Levine, & Long, 1998). They have also used neuroscientific findings to develop broad models of human behavior (Powell, 1979; Somers, 1999). They commonly contribute directly to knowledge of brain-behavior relationships through experimental and clinical neuropsychology.

Experimental neuropsychologists have long studied such things as the behavioral derangements caused by known lesions and other disturbances of CNS tissue in animals. Clinical neuropsychologists study qualitative and quantitative aspects of behavior on special tasks to deduce or infer the probable locus and nature of brain tissue impairments in humans. The accuracy of such assessment had reached very substantial levels by the 1970s (Filskov & Goldstein, 1974). Behavioral mappings of individual patient strengths and deficits contributed significantly to treatment and rehabilitation efforts (Golden, 1980; Lezak, 1976; Small, 1973), and contributed to clinical neuropsychology's movement into full participation in the treatment process (Nelson & Adams, 1997).

Ongoing developments in knowledge and methodology continue to require new connections among the disciplines comprising the evolving field of neuroscience. Miller described the process by which clinical and laboratory advances interact to stimulate the growth of knowledge in the field and summarized the excitement for psychology of brain research at all levels, saying of the range of functions studied that they " . . . have relevance to all aspects of psychology, and all aspects of psychology have contributions to make to understanding them" (1995, p. 901).

SUGGESTED READING

Carver, C. S., & Scheier, M. F. (1982). Control theory: A useful conceptual framework for personality—social, clinical, and health psychology. *Psychological Bulletin, 92(1)*, 111–135.

Chapman, L. F., & Wolff, H. (1959). The cerebral hemispheres and highest integrative functions of man. *Archives of Neurology, 1*, 357–424.

Clarke, E., & O'Malley, C. D. (1968). *The human brain and spinal cord.* Berkeley, Los Angeles: University of California Press.

Ciba Foundation. *Brain and mind: Ciba Foundation Symposium 69.* Amsterdam, Oxford, New York: Excerpta Medica.

Dimond, S. J. (1978). *Introducing neuropsychology.* Springfield, IL: Thomas.

Filskov, S. B., & Goldstein, S. G. (1974). Diagnostic validity of the Halstead-Reitan neuropsychological battery. *Journal of Consulting and Clinical Psychology, 42(3)*, 382–388.

Gardner, E. (1975/1963). *Fundamentals of neurology.* Philadelphia, London: Saunders.

Galton, F. (1879-1980). Psychometric experiments. *Brain, 2*, 149-162.

Galton, F. (1907/1883). *Inquiries into human faculty and its development.* London: Macmillan.

Gellhorn, E. (Ed.). *Biological foundations of emotion.* Glenview, Ill.: Scott, Foresman.

Golden, C. J. (1980). Organic brain syndromes. In R. H. Woody (Ed.), *Encyclopedia of clinical assessment* (Vol. 1). San Francisco: Jossey-Bass.

Hubbard, J. I. (1975). The biological basis of mental activity. Reading, MA: Addison-Wesley.

Lezack, M. D. (1983/1976). *Neuropsychological assessment.* New York: Oxford University Press.

Luria, A. R. (1973). *The working brain.* New York: Basic Books.

Miller, G. A., Galanter, E., & Pribram, K. (1960). *Plans and the structure of behavior.* New York: Holt.

Miller, N. E. (1995). Clinical-experimental interactions in the development of neuroscience: A primer for nonspecialists and lessons for young scientists. *American Psychologist, 50*(11), 901–911.

Minkler, J. (Ed.). *Introduction to neuroscience.* St. Louis, MO: Mosby.

Nelson, L. D., & Adams, K. M. (1997). Challenges for neuropsychology in the treatment and rehabilitation of brain-injured patients. *Psychological Assessment, 9*(4), 368–373.

Papez, J. W. (1964). Aproposed mechanism of emotion. In R. L. Isaacson (Ed.) *Basic readings in neuropsychology.* New York; Evanston, IL; London: Harper & Row.

Parks, R. W., Levine, D. S., & Long, D. L. (Eds.). (1998). *Fundamentals of neural network modeling: Neuropsychology and cognitive neuroscience.* Cambridge: The MIT Press.

Powell, G. E. (1979). *Brain and Personality.* Westmead, England: Saxon House/Teakfield.

Sherrington, C. S. (1906). *The integrative action of the nervous system.* New Haven, CN: Yale University Press.

Skinner, B. F. (1938) *The behavior of organisms: An experimental analysis.* New York: Appleton-Century.

Small, L. (1973). *Neuropsychodiagnosis in psychotherapy.* New York: Brunner/Mazel.

Smith, C. U. M. (1970). *The brain: towards an understanding.* New York: Putnam's.

Somers, M. J. (1999). Applications of two neural network paradigms to the study of voluntary employee turnover. *Journal of Applied Psychology, 34*(2), 177–185.

Sommerhoff, G. (1974). *Logic of the living brain.* New York: Putnam's.

Steen, E. B., & Montagu, A. (1959). Anatomy and Physiology, Vol. 2. New York: Barnes & Noble.

Watson, J. B. (1913). Psychology as the behaviorist views it. *Psychological Review, 20*, 158–177.

R. E. ENFIELD
Columbus, GA

HOMEOSTASIS
HYPOTHALAMUS
LIMBIC SYSTEM
NEUROSURGERY
RETICULAR ACTIVATING SYSTEM

CENTRAL NERVOUS SYSTEM DISORDERS

The central nervous system (CNS) is composed of the brain and the spinal cord. The spinal cord controls movement and feeling of body regions located below the brain; because the brain and the spinal cord are connected, the brain also plays a role in movement and feeling. However, the brain controls complex psychological processes such as attention, perception, motivation, emotion, language, cognition, and action. When certain parts of the brain are damaged, specific functions may be lost. The type and extent of functional loss depends upon the location of the brain damage and the amount of brain tissue that is compromised. For example, damage to a strip of cortex in the posterior part of the frontal lobes controlling movement of parts of the body will result in paralysis of those body parts. Lesions within relay stations along the visual sensory system—from the optic nerves to the occipital lobes—will result in visual field defects such as scotomas (blind spots). Lesions deep in the hypothalamus may produce hunger, uncontrolled eating, and obesity. A destruction of areas involved in arousal may result in a permanent comatose state.

Damage to specific regions of the brain usually produces behavioral abnormalities that can be measured quantitatively and qualitatively by employing sensitive tests of impaired or lost functions. For example, an analysis of specific sensory functions can reveal basic sensory defects. Cognitive and intellectual defects can be measured through the skillful administration and interpretation of tests specifically designed to elucidate organically-based impairments. Descriptions of many of these tests may be found in books such as those by Lezak (1995) and Spreen and Strauss (1998), and in a chapter by Oscar-Berman and Bardenhagen (1998).

Disorders of the CNS usually are classified according to lesion location (e.g., abnormalities occurring after frontal lobe damage) or according to symptomatology and functional loss (e.g., amnesia and aphasia). The following discussion focuses on specific exemplars of CNS disorders. The first, frontal system disorders, exemplifies some possible consequences of damage to the anterior regions of the frontal lobes. The others exemplify disorders recognized by their presenting symptoms and functional abnormalities: Amnesia refers to disorders of memory, including memory for recent events (anterograde amnesia) and for events long ago (retrograde amnesia); aphasia refers to language disturbances. Keep in mind, however, that the distinction between structure and function is not meant to be a mutually exclusive one. The brain has many highly-interconnected parts, and when one part is damaged, other parts will be affected as well. In addition, the behavioral abnormalities under discussion are complex; they involve a broad spectrum of perceptual and cognitive deficits that may be integral to the presenting symptoms of many disorders of the CNS.

FRONTAL SYSTEM DYSFUNCTION

The frontal lobes are connected with all of the other lobes of the brain, and they receive and send fibers to numerous subcortical structures as well. While control of motor function takes place in the posterior region of the frontal lobes, the anterior region of the frontal lobes (prefrontal cortex) has other functions (Lezak, 1995). For example, one prefrontal area plays a kind of executive regulatory role within the CNS, inhibiting the occurrence of unnecessary or unwanted behaviors. Disruptions of normal inhibitory functions of frontal lobe neuronal networks often will have the interesting effect of releasing previously-inhibited behaviors from frontal control. The resultant aberrant conduct of a frontal patient may be due to the free, unregulated functioning of the released

brain region rather than a direct effect of a lesion within the frontal lobes. This disinhibition phenomenon was described by Lhermitte (1986) as an "environmental dependency syndrome" associated with loss of personal autonomy.

Early evidence for a role of the frontal lobes in supporting the ability to inhibit impulsivity came from the 1868 report of a physician on his patient, Phineas Gage. Gage, a railway workman, survived an explosion that blasted an iron bar (about four feet long and an inch wide) through his frontal lobes. After recovering from the accident, Gage's personality changed. He became irascible, impatient, impulsive, unruly, and inappropriate. The damage had mostly been in the orbital frontal region of Gage's frontal lobes (Damasio, Grabowski, Frank, Galaburda, & Damasio, 1994).

Damage to frontal brain systems occurs in a number of CNS disorders, including stroke, brain tumors, dementing diseases (e.g., Alzheimer's), and head trauma. Patients with bilateral frontal disorders often display a pull to nearby objects (e.g., grabbing at doorknobs) and a remarkable tendency to imitate the actions of people nearby (echopraxia). The behaviors of a frontal patient appear not to be based on rational decisions, but rather to be under the control of salient objects around them—that is, objects that capture the attention. In other words, the patient's behaviors are environmentally driven rather than personally chosen. Such behaviors may extend to otherwise embarrassing gestures such as urinating in public or chewing paper. Environmental dependency and imitation behaviors can also be associated with "utilization behavior" (Lhermitte, Pillon, & Serdaru, 1986); that is, if the examiner places a set of everyday objects in front of the patient with instructions neither to use them nor to pick them up, the patient nonetheless will do just that. If one of the objects were a comb, the patient would likely pick it up and begin combing his or her hair. Utilization behavior may even extend to dangerous objects such as hypodermic needles, with patients' attempting to give themselves injections.

BRAIN MECHANISMS IN MEMORY

Amnesia, especially anterograde amnesia (or memory loss for recent events), is an intriguing but serious disorder. When amnesia occurs as a consequence of long-term alcoholism, it is referred to as alcoholic Korsakoff's syndrome. Patients with Korsakoff's syndrome are permanently unable to remember new information for more than a few seconds. However, old memories that were formed prior to the onset of alcohol-related brain damage are relatively well preserved. Because new events are forgotten a few seconds after they occur, virtually nothing new is learned, and the patient with Korsakoff's syndrome lives in the past.

George Talland, in his classic book, *Deranged Memory* (1965), linked the etiology of Korsakoff's disease most frequently with the polyneuropathy of chronic alcoholism and associated malnutrition. The critical brain lesions are thought to include the mammillary bodies of the hypothalamus and/or medial thalamic nuclei. Damage to these or to other regions of the brain (hippocampus, fornix, anterior thalamus) identified with the classic interconnected circuit described by Papez (1937) has been associated with memory impairments. The impairments include severe anterograde amnesia for recent events, and some retrograde amnesia for events prior to the appearance of obvious symptomatology. Damage to basal forebrain structures (important in the production of neurotransmitters that are needed for normal memory functions) may also be involved.

Although anterograde amnesia is the most obvious presenting symptom in Korsakoff patients, it has been suggested that, in addition to having severe memory problems, these individuals have other cognitive impairments as well. Like patients with bilateral prefrontal cortical lesions, Korsakoff patients are abnormally sensitive to distractions (proactive interference). This sensitivity may be due to prefrontal dysfunction, which impairs the ability to counteract the effects of cognitive interruptions. Memory encoding requires the ability to resist displacement of the to-be-remembered information from ongoing memory processing. Similarly, memory retrieval requires the ability to screen out irrelevant contextual cues in order to focus on relevant cues and thus to select the target memory. In addition to their memory problems and their sensitivity to interference and perseverative responding, Korsakoff patients also have restricted attention, retarded perceptual processing abilities, and decreased sensitivity to reward contingencies (Oscar-Berman & Evert, 1997). These additional abnormalities probably reflect widespread cerebral atrophy accompanying sustained alcohol abuse. Thus, consideration should be given to sensory and cognitive deficits, which may be integral to the disease process caused by chronic alcoholism.

APHASIA

The term "aphasia" literally means "no language." More realistically, the aphasic patient suffers from impairment in his or her previous level of ability to use language expressively or receptively, or both. For that reason, the term "dysphasia" (impairment in language) sometimes is used. There are many different forms of aphasia, and classification schemes can be found in Harold Goodglass' book, *Understanding Aphasia* (1993). Pathology is almost always within the left hemisphere of both right-handers and a majority of left-handers. Frequently, the location of the brain damage is in the frontal lobe (Broca's aphasia) or the temporal lobe (Wernicke's aphasia), and usually is the result of a cerebrovascular accident (stroke), tumor, or trauma.

There are components of aphasia that can be considered as language-specific amnesias (e.g., the anomias; Goodglass & Wingfield, 1997). If a lesion is in the neighborhood of a cortical sensory projection zone, the resulting disorder may involve one or another of the sensory modalities (audition or vision). If a lesion is in a polysensory integration zone, it will cause a disorder of more highly elaborate functions (e.g., spatial recognition, language, and/or voluntary movement). Some have argued that aphasia is a mere loss of certain linguistic abilities, and that the intellect remains intact. Others, however, regard aphasia as either the manifestation of a primary intellectual loss or as the loss of a restricted aspect of intellect. As cautioned earlier, the problem can be oversimplified by regarding either aphasia or intellectual impairment as unitary deficits. Both are known to vary with locus and extent of lesion, and any overlap in symptoms may result from overlapping anatomical representation rather than from the nature of the disorder.

REFERENCES

Damasio, H., Grabowski, T., Frank, R., Galaburda, A. M., & Damasio, A. R. (1994). The return of Phineas Gage: Clues about the brain from the skull of a famous patient. *Science, 264,* 1102–1105.

Goodglass, H. (1993). *Understanding aphasia.* San Diego: Academic Press.

Goodglass, H., & Wingfield, A. (Eds.). (1997). *Anomia.* San Diego: Academic Press.

Lezak, M. D. (1995). *Neuropsychological assessment* (3rd ed.). Oxford: Blackwell Scientific Publications.

Lhermitte, F. (1986). Human autonomy and the frontal lobes: Part II. Patient behavior in complex and social situations: The "environmental dependency syndrome." *Annals of Neurology, 19,* 335–343.

Lhermitte, F., Pillon, B., & Serdaru, M. (1986). Human autonomy and the frontal lobes: Part I. Imitation and utilization behavior: A neuropsychological study of 75 patients. *Annals of Neurology, 19,* 326–334.

Oscar-Berman, M., & Bardenhagen, F. (1998). Nonhuman primate models of memory dysfunction in neurodegenerative disease: Contributions from Comparative Neuropsychology. In A. Tröster (Ed.), *Memory in neurodegenerative disease* (pp. 3–20). New York: Cambridge University Press.

Oscar-Berman, M., & Evert, D. L. (1997). Alcoholic Korsakoff's syndrome. In P. D. Nussbaum (Ed.), *Handbook of neuropsychology and aging* (pp. 201–215). New York: Plenum.

Papez, J. W. (1937). A proposed mechanism of emotion. *Archives of Neurology and Psychiatry, 38,* 725–743.

Spreen, O., & Strauss, E. (1998). *A compendium of neuropsychological tests* (2nd ed.). New York: Oxford University Press.

Talland, G. A. (1965). *Deranged memory: A psychonomic study of the amnesic syndrome.* San Diego: Academic Press.

M. Oscar-Berman
P. McNamara
Boston University School of Medicine and VA New England Healthcare System, Boston Division

APHASIA
BRAIN INJURIES

CENTRAL TENDENCY MEASURES

It is often desirable to provide some summary numbers that best describe a set or distribution of scores. These include measures of location, which indicate a typical or average value for the scores in the distribution; measures of dispersion, which indicate how spread out the scores are; and other measures that describe the shape of the distribution.

A measure of central tendency is a measure of location. The goal of such a measure is to provide a single number that best describes the values of a set or distribution of scores. The terms "measure of central tendency" and "average" are often used interchangeably, although some authors use "average" only to refer to the arithmetic mean. Although there are many measures of central tendency, those most commonly encountered are the mode, median, and mean.

Given a set of scores, the *mode* is simply the score that occurs most often. If scores are grouped into classes, the mode is considered to be the midpoint of the class that contains the largest number of scores. The mode is not a very useful summary measure of a whole set of scores, because it does not take into account scores that do not have the modal value. Also, a distribution of scores may be multimodal, that is, there may be two or more values that occur with high frequency.

The *median* is the middle score of a distribution; that is, if the scores in a distribution are ordered from smallest to largest, the median is the middle score. If there are an even number of scores, the median is considered to be halfway between the two middle scores. So, for example, given sets of scores A (6, 8, 4, 9, 11) and B (6, 8, 4, 9, 11, 14), the median of set A is 8 and of set B is 8 5. For grouped data, the median is taken to be the fiftieth percentile point; that is, the value below which 50 percent of the scores fall. The median is particularly useful for characterizing distributions that are asymmetric or that include outliers, extreme scores that are quite different from the scores in the center of the distribution. This is because the median is insensitive to the values of scores at the extremes of the distribution. The median for (6, 8, 4, 9, 11) is exactly the same as for (6, 8, 4, 9, 11944).

The *arithmetic mean* of a set of scores is the most commonly encountered measure of central tendency. It is obtained by adding up all of the scores in the set and dividing by the number of scores. (It should be noted that there are other kinds of means, such as the geometric mean of *n* scores which is obtained by multiplying all the scores together and taking the *n*th root of the resulting product. However, these other kinds of means are encountered much less frequently and will not be considered further here. In what follows, the term "mean" will refer to the arithmetic mean.) The mean depends on all the scores in the set; as a result, the mean is very sensitive to extreme values. Although the medians for the sets (6, 8, 4, 9, 11) and (6, 8, 4, 9, 11944) are the same, 8, the means are 7.6 and 2394.2, respectively. Here the median does a much better job of characterizing the typical value of the scores than the mean does.

It is useful to think of the mean of a distribution of scores as the "balance point" of the distribution. Imagine that scores are represented by weights placed on a balance beam at locations corresponding to their values. The location of the balance point of the set of scores corresponds to the value of the mean. For example, suppose that equal weights are placed at locations 4, 6, 8, 9, and 11 units from the left edge of a weightless, rigid beam; if the beam is placed on a fulcrum located 7.6 units from the left edge of the beam, it will balance. Another way of thinking about this is that if we find the deviation of each score from the mean, then add up all these deviations, they will sum to zero.

Another useful characteristic of the mean is that it minimizes the *sum of squared deviations*. If we find the deviation of each score from a value *M,* square each deviation, then add all these squared deviations together, the sum is smaller if *M* is the mean than if it is any other value. In contrast, the median is the value that minimizes the sum of the *absolute values* of the deviations.

For a symmetrical, bell-shaped distribution of scores, the mean and median will have similar values. If the distribution of scores is skewed to the right (that is, if the distribution is asymmetrical, with a short tail on the left side of center and a longer tail on the right side), the mean will be larger than the median. If the distribution is skewed to the left, so that it has a longer tail on the left side, the mean will be smaller than the median.

We are very often interested in estimating the mean of a population of scores on the basis of samples of scores selected from the population. We can use a measure of central tendency of the sample, such as the sample mean or median as an estimator of the population mean. If we take a number of samples of the same size, these sample means and medians will vary from sample to sample because of the variability in the scores selected to be in each sample. If the population is bell-shaped (i.e., if the scores are distributed like the "normal distribution" that is often referred to in the literature), it can be shown that the sample mean is a more efficient estimator than the sample median. The mean is more efficient in the sense that the means of samples can be shown to cluster more closely around the population mean than the sample medians, and so tend to be better estimates of the population mean. If on the other hand, the population is asymmetric or heavy-tailed (i.e., it tends to contain extreme scores), the sample mean may not be as good an estimator as the sample median or certain kinds of trimmed means (that is, sample means obtained after discarding some of the smaller and larger scores in the sample).

REFERENCES

Moore, D. S. (1995). *The basic practice of statistics.* New York: Freeman.

Myers, J. L., & Well, A. D. (1995). *Research design and statistical analysis.* Hillsdale, NJ: Erlbaum.

Pollatsek, A., Lima, S. L., & Well, A. D. (1981). Concept or computation: Students' understanding of the mean. *Educational Studies in Mathematics, 12,* 191–204.

A. D. WELL
University of Massachusetts

STATISTICS IN PSYCHOLOGY

CEREBELLUM

The cerebellum is one of two distinct cortical sub-systems in the mammalian brain. From an evolutionary perspective it is subdivided into three parts: (a) the archicerebellum, consisting of the flocculus and nodulus; (b) the palaeocerebellum, consisting of parts of the vermis; and (c) the neocerebellum, made up of the middle part of the vermis and cerebellar hemispheres. Ontogenetically and phylogenetically the archicerebellum develops before the cerebral cortex and is therefore the first functional cortical part of the brain. The neocerebellum develops later, along with the cerebral cortex. The cerebellar cortex has two hemispheres, which are functionally connected mainly to the ipsilateral brain stem and contralateral cerebral hemispheres.

The cerebellum receives a full range of information (sensory and motor) directly from the peripheral sensors. In addition, it receives a full range of information (sensory and motor) from the cerebral cortex. Primarily, the cerebellum is involved in the control and elaboration of reflex homeostatic responses at brain-stem and spinal-cord level. In this respect it may operate in parallel with, but independently of, the cerebral cortex in controlling motor performance. However, the cerebellar system is particularly important for the control of frequently executed or rehearsed movements that become automatized and are performed fluently or quickly and without conscious effort.

At a neuronal level the cerebellum is characterised by in-parallel transmission. Its microstructural and functional characteristics indicate that the cerebellum is essentially a parallel distributed subsystem that represents and processes information in a probabilistic manner. As a result of these characteristics it is able to represent and process both spatial information and temporal information and to do so as undifferentiated space-time representations. On a gross anatomical level, and at a neuronal level, information from the various peripheral sensory receptors appears to be received and represented largely in a polymodal or amodal manner. The cerebellum therefore represents and processes both sensory and motor information in a unified manner and may be regarded as a sensorimotor sub-system. As a consequence of its parallel distributed amodal representation and processing, the cerebellum is considered to be an analog or holistic type of system and to facilitate naturomorphic representation and associative storage (Parkins, 1997). It is capable of rapid information processing and real-time regulation of coordinated sensorimotor activity. However, it lacks potential for highly specialized analysis of specific sensory information and is therefore a relatively low-discrimination system.

Based on parallel distributed representation and processing models of cerebellar function (for example, Fujita's adaptive filter model [1982]), and connectionist theory a number of other processing or computational features have been inferred. Parallel processing allows for the evolution and detection of patterns or features that are determined partly on the basis of the relative frequency with which they occur. Parallel processing facilitates the automatic statistical revelation and statistical evaluation of features that are, to varying extents, common to a number of information inputs or experiences; it can, therefore, generalize from experience. Another important feature of in-parallel processing is that of pattern completion. That is, when a significant part of a frequently occurring pattern is received as an input, the system will tend to respond to that part as if it is the whole pattern. This phenomenon may occur for spatial information and so may be involved in nonverbal analogical reasoning. It may also occur for a temporal pattern; that is, when part of a familiar sequence is received as an input, the system will respond so as to complete that sequence. This temporal induction is, in effect, a predictive mechanism that facilitates anticipatory responses based on the learned response sequences (stored as sensorimotor schemata). The paral-

lel distributed sensorimotor characteristics facilitate associative learning in the form of classical conditioning or operant conditioning. These characteristics would allow for sensory stimuli to act as retrieval cues for stored information concerning the most probably beneficial response based on past experience. The cued or released sensorimotor information would automatically, through its motor component, involve a behavioral response. Such motor patterns or sequences generated by the cerebellum would appear to be released in an all-or-none fashion, that is, as wholes. It is thought that the cerebellum does not allow for the erasure of recorded information; that is, it has a permanent memory. The only way that information can, in effect, be forgotten is by functionally overlaying the information to be forgotten with the information to be remembered in preference (a process similar to the behaviorist notion of extinction).

Over the years there has been a steady accumulation of experimental evidence that the cerebellum is critically involved in the classical conditioning of simple motor responses. Most recently it has been shown that the essential memory traces for a range of classical conditioning responses are formed in, and reside in, the cerebellum (Thompson et al., 1997). It is clear that the cerebellum plays a major role in sensorimotor learning. This form or learning is evident at the earliest stage in human cognitive development, and is typified by the psychological concept of sensorimotor intelligence (Piaget).

With the development of new technology, a range of research (including tomographic regional cerebral blood flow [rCBF], computerised magnetic resonance [rCMR], and positron emission topography [PET] studies) now indicates that in humans the cerebellum contributes not only to motor control but also to affective and cognitive processing. It appears to be involved in verbal processing, including speech, writing, and reading, not only in the direct motor expression of these skills, but also in the mental simulation and rehearsal of these skills, and in related non-motor aspects such as word association. It further appears to be involved in visual processing, including imagined motor expression (tennis movements, writing, speech), visual discrimination, mental rotation of simple drawings, and visuospatial organization tasks. Studies have indicated that the cerebellum contributes to IQ, mainly visual IQ (Performance Scale IQ test ability on the Wechsler Adult Intelligence Scale, in particular, Picture Completion, Picture Arrangement, and Object Assembly). Other higher-order cognitive processes in which the cerebellum has been implicated include the skilled manipulation of symbols, conceptual reasoning, and what are described as complex planning activities. In summary, several publications have suggested that the cerebellum is involved in a range of cognitive processes, including what has been described as pure mental activity and pure cognitive activity.

It appears that there is some lateralization of cognitive function within the cerebellum. Data suggest that for verbal processing, including writing and spoken language (verbal working memory and non-motor processing of words, such as semantic association tasks), it is the right cerebellar hemisphere that is most involved. The lateralization to the right cerebellar hemisphere is consistent with observations that each cerebellar hemisphere is anatomically and functionally related to the contralateral (in this case the left, language-dominant) cerebral hemisphere. In contrast, complex cognitive spatial operations (visual reasoning) are associated with processing in the left cerebellar hemisphere.

Concerning motor function, it is considered that the cerebellum does not operate at the level of normal consciousness but, relative to the cerebrum, at an unconscious level. Similarly, cerebellar sensory processing operates not at a conscious level but rather as what might be described as an unconscious mind's eye. Consequently, it is possible that cerebellar cognitive processing may constitute part of what has been called "the cognitive unconscious," and may be particularly involved with the execution of automatized cognitive processes.

To summarize, the cerebellum is one of two cortical sub-systems capable of the cognitive processing of information from the environment and of controlling the behavior of the organism; in evolutionary terms it is, in part, the earliest to develop and therefore, in part, relates to earlier stages of cognitive development. It is particularly associated with unconscious control and cognition. In information representation and processing terms it may be described as a parallel processing sensorimotor sub-system of a relatively low level of discrimination, and from this perspective, it is complementary to the cerebrum.

REFERENCES

Fujita, M. (1982). Adaptive filter model of the cerebellum. *Biological Cybernetics, 45,* 195–206.

Parkins, E. J. (1997). Cerebellum and cerebrum in adaptive control and cognition: A review. *Biological Cybernetics, 77,* 79–87.

Piaget, J. (1947). The psychology of intelligence. London: Routledge & Kegan Paul.

Thompson, R. F., et al. (1997). Associative learning. *International Review of Neurobiology, 41,* 151–189.

SUGGESTED READING

Parkins, E. J. (1990). *Equilibration, mind and brain: Toward an integrated psychology.* New York: Praeger.

E. J. Parkins
Nottingham University, England

BRAIN
BRAIN LATERALITY
CEREBRUM
INFORMATION PROCESSING
SENSORIMOTOR PROCESSES

CEREBRAL LOCALIZATION

The theory that different parts of the brain subserve different functions is known as localization theory. It is consistent with the basic biological principle that structures that do not look alike should have different functions. Localization of function is the theoretical backbone of modern neuropsychology, neurology, and related disciplines, all of which attempt to correlate specific behaviors with specific brain parts.

In the history of the brain sciences, it is possible to conceive of the theory of localization as being applied first to the whole and then to increasingly smaller parts of the brain (Finger, 1994, 2000). At first the question seemed to be, "Why is the brain special and how is it different from other organs, such as the heart?" This was an important question in Classical and Hellenistic Greece, where opinions were divided. Aristotle (384–322 B.C.), the greatest of the Greek naturalist philosophers, believed that the heart was the seat of sensory and cognitive functions and that the brain simply tempered "the heat and seething" of the heart. In this regard, he was consistent with the archaic Greeks and the Egyptians. In contrast, Plato (c. 429–348 B.C.) believed that intellect belonged not in the heart but in the head, in agreement with the thoughts of the Hippocratic physicians.

During the Roman period, Galen (130–200 A.D.) reasoned that the seat of the highest soul, and hence the seat of intellect, had to be the brain itself. He listed imagination, cognition, and memory as the basic components of intellect. He also believed that the soft front of the brain was likely to be sensory, whereas the harder cerebellar region in the back was likely to be motor.

The church fathers of the 4th and 5th centuries A.D. went one step further when they localized imagination, intellect, and memory in the different ventricles of the brain. One of the earliest advocates of ventricular localization was Nemesius (fl. 390 A.D.), a bishop in Syria. He localized perception in the two lateral ventricles, cognition in the middle ventricle, and memory in the posterior ventricle. This early localization theory was also embraced by St. Augustine, and it was broadly accepted for more than 1,000 years.

During the Renaissance, as scientists returned to dissection and experimentation, observation began to replace conjecture. Leonardo Da Vinci made molds of the ventricles to reveal their shape, and Andreas Vesalius showed that the ventricles vary little across mammals. Consequently, the idea of ventricular localization slowly gave way, while increased attention began to be given to differences in the size and makeup of the brain itself.

The freer thinking and questioning of the Renaissance set the stage for Thomas Willis of Oxford to published his *Cerebri anatome* in 1664. Willis proposed that the corpus striatum, which he defined as all white matter between the basal ganglia and the cerebral cortex, plays a role in sensation and muscle movement, and that the cerebral cortex controls memory and the will. The cerebellum (which was broadly defined to include some pons and midbrain) was thought to regulate involuntary, smooth motor functions. This division of the brain into functional parts, based partly on comparative anatomy, partly on clinical material, and partly on speculative theories, changed existing thinking about the brain.

The opening decades of the 1800s proved to be an especially important time in the history of localization theory (Finger, 2000). First, Julien Jean César Legallois provided the first accepted localization within a region of the brain. In 1812, he pinpointed the area responsible for respiration within the medulla.

In addition, the seeds were planted for modern cortical localization theory when Franz Gall presented his theory of organology (his assistant, Spurzheim, preferred the word "phrenology") at about the same time (Finger, 1994; Young, 1970). Gall maintained that different areas of the cerebral cortex govern different mental faculties and that cranial features reflect the development of the different underlying organs of mind. Among other things, Gall was convinced that humanity's highest functions (e.g., speech) belonged in the front of the cerebral cortex.

The theories of the phrenologists stimulated great debate. Some scientists thought they had merit, others found them absurd, and still others were led to believe that cortical localization made sense but that cranioscopy was a dead end and should be replaced by neurological examinations. The latter position was advocated by Jean-Baptiste Bouillaud, who began to localize speech in the frontal lobes in 1825, then spent years collecting autopsy material in support of this localization.

The debates over cortical localization continued to heat up until 1861, when Paul Broca presented his celebrated case of M. Leborgne (Tan). His sickly patient had lost his capacity for articulate language (among other things), and an autopsy revealed a lesion involving the third frontal convolution of the left hemisphere. Broca's localization of a center for articulate language in the back of the frontal lobes became the first cortical localization to receive broad acceptance.

In 1865, Broca published another landmark paper. As his collection of cases continued to grow, he recognized that the left hemisphere must be special for speech. Cerebral dominance was something that Marc Dax had recognized in 1836. Unfortunately, Dax failed to make his findings public in his lifetime. Thanks to his son Gustave, however, his report on more than 40 cases also appeared in print in 1865 (Joynt & Benton, 1964).

In 1870, Gustav Fritsch and Eduard Hitzig discovered the motor cortex of the dog, first by stimulation and then by ablation. This was a significant accomplishment, because it showed that cortical localization could be studied under controlled conditions in laboratory animals. In the wake of this paper, lesion studies were conducted to localize sensory functions, such as vision and hearing, as well as higher intellectual functions. The leader of the new localization movement was David Ferrier, whose influential book, *The Functions of the Brain,* was first published in 1876 and later updated. Two other important contributors to the localization movement, at least for sensory functions, were Hermann Munk and Edward Schäfer.

The success of localization theory was not based solely on pathological (brain lesion) material; it also received good support from other sources. In 1875, Richard Caton of Liverpool reported that cortical electrical activity varied in accord with Ferrier's maps when his animals were chewing, looking at flashing lights, or doing other things. In addition, Paul Flechsig showed that different cortical areas became myelinated at different times, a finding he correlated with the attainment of different functions. Cytoarchitectonic studies of the cerebral cortex, such as those of Korbinian Brodmann represented another significant source of support for localization theory.

Today, efforts continue to divide the brain into smaller functional units, albeit with positron emission tomography and other tools that could not even have been imagined when Broca or Hitzig were living. In this regard, localization theory is alive and well. Yet,

so is the moderate holistic notion, which holds maintains that we also must not forget about what may be happening simultaneously in other parts of the remarkably unified organ known singularly as the brain.

REFERENCES

Finger, S. (1994). *Origins of neuroscience.* New York: Oxford.

Finger, S. (2000). Minds behind the brain. New York: Oxford.

Joynt, R. A., & Benton, A. L. (1964). The memoir of Marc Dax on aphasia. *Neurology, 14,* 851–854.

Young, R. M. (1970). *Mind, brain and adaptation in the 19th century.* Oxford, U.K.: Clarendon.

S. FINGER
Washington University

BRAIN INJURIES
BRAIN LATERALITY
CENTRAL NERVOUS SYSTEM
ELECTROENCEPHALOGRAPHY
PHRENOLOGY

CEREBRAL PALSY

"Cerebral palsy" is a term for those disorders of impaired brain and motor functioning with onset before or at birth, or during the first year of life. It is the result of a static lesion of the brain that cannot be cured and does not progress. The causes, clinical manifestations, and prognosis are widely variable. Manifestations may include mental retardation, learning disabilities, seizures, sensory and speech deficits, and impaired ability of voluntary muscles. The incidence of cerebral palsy is 1.3 to 5.0 per 1,000 live births (Downey & Low, 1982).

ETIOLOGY

Both genetic and acquired factors may be responsible for these syndromes, though the cause is often obscure or multiple. The acquired causes usually result in damage to the fetal central nervous system during the early gestational period, and may be related to faulty implantation of the ovum or to diseases of the mother. Extreme nutritional deficiencies, infections, injuries, and toxins can interfere with the developing fetal brain and lead to permanent motor defects. During the perinatal period a rapid succession of events occurs that may damage the brain and result in cerebral palsy. Prematurity predisposes the neonate to asphyxia and cerebral bleeding. Full-term neonates small for their age are also prone to cerebral palsy.

CLASSIFICATION

Classification of syndromes is commonly based on the predominant motor deficit and includes the following forms. (A) The *spastic* forms comprise approximately 75% of the cases, are due to involvement of the upper motor neurons, and are characterized by increased tone of the involved musculature, rhythmic muscle contractions, abnormal reflexes, and a tendency to contractures. Types include spastic hemiplegia, implying that both extremities on one side are involved, and spastic tetraplegia, involving spasticity of all four extremities to approximately the same degree. Spastic paraplegia refers to involvement of both legs but complete sparing of the upper extremities. (B) *Dyskinetic* cerebral palsies imply impaired voluntary activity by uncontrolled and purposeless movements that disappear during sleep. Athetosis is the most common type and is characterized by slow, writhing movements usually involving all four extremities, the face, and the neck. (C) *Ataxic* cerebral palsy is related to a static lesion of the cerebellum or its pathways. Involved children have a wide-based walk and experience difficulty in turning rapidly, performing fast repetitive movements poorly. This type has the best prognosis for functional improvement. (D) *Mixed* forms may be present with clinical manifestations of more than one type. The combination of spasticity and athetosis is seen most frequently.

TREATMENT

The management varies with the child's age, the type and severity of involvement, the presence or absence of seizures, and the degree of intellect. The motor aspects can be modified to a certain degree. Spastic children develop contractures, and this can be counteracted by surgical and nonsurgical means. The physical therapist can produce beneficial results through stretching tight tendons by passive and active exercises and by utilizing certain mechanical devices. Medications are frequently unsuccessful in reducing spasticity or influencing the abnormal movements. The management of seizures requires the daily use of anticonvulsants. Psychological counseling and support of the child and family are essential. In severely involved cases, especially those with spasticity with profound retardation and seizures that are difficult to control, death due to infections is not uncommon. Many children with cerebral palsy of average or near-average intelligence lead fairly normal, satisfying, and productive lives.

REFERENCES

Downey, J., & Low, N. (1982). *The child with disabling illness: Principles of rehabilitation.* New York: Raven.

SUGGESTED READING

Franco, S., & Andrews, B. (1977). Reduction of cerebral palsy by neonatal intensive care. *Pediatric Clinics of North America, 24,* 639.

Milner-Brown, H., & Penn, R. (1979). Pathophysiological mechanisms in cerebral palsy. *Journal of Neurological Neurosurgical Psychiatry, 42,* 606.

Nogen, A. (1976). Medical treatment for spasticity in children with cerebral palsy. *Child's Brain, 2,* 304.

R. T. GIUBILATO
Thomas Jefferson University

BRAIN INJURIES
NEUROPSYCHOLOGY

CEREBRUM

The cerebrum is the largest of two cortical subsystems in the mammalian brain, the other smaller subsystem being the cerebellum. Most of the cerebrum is cortex made up of two hemispheres each containing four lobes (frontal, parietal, temporal, and occipital). In evolutionary terms the cerebral cortex is the most recent structure to evolve in phylogeny and ontogeny.

The cerebrum controls and elaborates reflex homeostatic responses at the brain stem and spinal cord levels. It is particularly involved with control of discrete and precisely refined movement. It normally operates as the highest level subsystem within the brain and is associated with conscious control of behavior. This control may be directly from the cerebrum to the brain stem and spinal system, or indirectly through cerebral control of cerebellar output. Motor sequences that are practiced may subsequently be carried out by the cerebellum, and may then be performed more quickly and more automatically, with less conscious effort. The process of conscious practice is one of subprogramming the cerebellum by the cerebrum.

Sensory input direct from the peripheral sensors first reaches the cerebral cortex in the various unimodal primary areas. The most basic cerebrocortical processing is therefore concerned with sensory processing limited to a single modality. These single modality systems contain different specific areas specialized for different aspects, features, or components of information. Within the cerebral cortex as a whole, there is directionality of information flow from primary sensory areas through secondary association areas and tertiary amodal regions that integrate information, and eventually to output areas that control motor function. Anatomic, physiological, and behavioral studies have all emphasized that there is a clear *sequential processing* built into cerebrocortical organization. The unimodal primary reception areas of the cerebral cortex result in a process of information abstraction by sensory modality. In addition, the cerebral cortex can selectively control its own input via the thalamus, and most of this control is inhibitory, that is, of a filtering kind. Fundamentally, therefore, the cerebrum is an *abstract processing subsystem.* Through its ability to abstract and sequentially process information, the cerebral cortex is thought to provide the brain with a system for high level discrimination and for analytical and abstract processing that is characteristic of logical thought or formal operational reasoning (see Piaget). Overall, the evolution of the cerebral cortex, with its cerebrocortical primary sensory and motor areas, may, in itself, be viewed as providing the brain with an additional cortical subsystem with a higher level of discrimination, capable of abstracting detail and of analytical sequential processing, and with the ability for more refined and elaborated control.

It is generally accepted that the cerebrum is involved in the whole range of affective and cognitive processes, including nonverbal communication, recognition and expression of emotion, visuospatial skills, imagination, mathematical processing, language skills (spoken language, reading, and writing), problem solving, planning, analytical and logical reasoning, and aspects of memory and recall. Indeed, until recently the prevailing view in contemporary brain research was that cognitive functions were mediated almost exclusively by the cerebral cortex (Thompson, 1993). However, there is now evidence that the other cortical subsystem, the cerebellum, may also be involved in many of these affective and cognitive processes.

Although the cerebrum as a whole is considered to be involved in a wide range of cognitive processes, these processes appear to be performed by different parts of the cerebrum. In particular, there is evidence that the two cerebral hemispheres represent and process information in different ways and have different roles. The dominant (most often left) cerebral hemisphere is associated with information representation and processing that is in-series or sequential, digital, and abstract. It is characterized by analytical and logical processing that deals with detail. It plays a major role in the processing of verbal information, and in particular "digital" or abstract linguistic representation. Of the two cerebral hemispheres, the dominant one is considered to be involved in consciousness, especially "self-consciousness." The minor (most often right) cerebral hemisphere is associated with information representation and processing that is in-parallel or simultaneous, analog, and holistic. It is characterised by Gestalt, analogical, and integrative processing that deals with more spatial and global information and with novel or unfamiliar information. It plays a major role in the processing of naturomorphic or imagistic representations and in particular the processing of nonverbal and emotional information, spatial and pictorial information, and music and other nonlanguage sounds. The minor hemisphere is often associated with processing that is at a lower level of consciousness than the dominant hemisphere.

One reason given for hemispheric specialization within the cerebral cortex is that it allows for the coexistence of two incompatible but complementary modes of information processing (Zaidel et al., 1990). To some extent this may be true; however, the two cerebral hemispheres have the same fundamental cytoarchitecture, have unimodal primary reception areas, and receive filtered input. In fact, much of the currently available information points to differences between the cerebral hemispheres that are merely relative or quantitative rather than qualitative. Furthermore, there is evidence from various sources that indicates that the cognitive processes attributed to one or the other of the cerebral hemispheres are not exclusive to that hemisphere. Most basically, the two cerebral hemispheres are *both* abstract in-series processors, but they appear to have different patterns of development. As a result of this differential development, the dominant hemisphere appears to represent and process information at a much higher and relatively incompatible level of abstraction compared with that of the minor hemisphere.

Association areas within the minor hemisphere temporal lobe, particularly the infero-temporal region, are thought to be involved in emotional processes, experiential memory, and imagination. There is some evidence that the temporal lobe may not be the location of the experiential memory record, but that this information may be transmitted to the temporal lobe from subcortical areas. Transmission from subcortical regions appears to involve the hip-

pocampus and the brain stem monoamine systems. As noted earlier, the cerebrum projects to the cerebellar cortex and can contribute to cerebellar processing. However, it is also evident that the cerebellum projects to the cerebral cortex, including association areas, and can contribute to cerebral processing in the cognitive domain. Reciprocal interaction between the cerebral neocortex and the cerebellar cortex involves the hippocampus and the brain stem monoamine systems. A range of evidence supports the suggestion that norepinephrine or its precursor dopamine facilitates excitatory output from the cerebellum to the cerebrum, whereas 5-hydroxytryptamine appears to inhibit output from the cerebellar to the cerebrum. Furthermore, there is evidence of lateralization of neurotransmitter activity and lateralization of interaction between the cerebellum and cerebrum. It is therefore possible that some of the subcortical input to association cortex processing is of cerebellar origin, and that some of the cognitive processes attributed to the minor hemisphere cerebral hemispheres are of cerebellar origin.

To summarize: the cerebrum is one of two cortical subsystems capable of cognitive processing of information from the environment and of controlling the behavior of the organism; in evolutionary terms, as a whole, it is the most recent to develop and therefore relates to later stages of cognitive development; it is particularly associated with conscious control and cognition; in information representation and processing terms the cerebrum may be described as a sequential processing abstract subsystem of relatively high discrimination and from this perspective it is complementary to the cerebellum.

REFERENCES

Parkins, E. J. (1997). Cerebellum and cerebrum in adaptive control and cognition: A review. *Biological Cybernetics, 77,* 79–87.

Parkins, E. J. (1990). *Equilibration, mind and brain: Toward an integrated psychology.* New York: Praeger.

Thompson, R. (1993). Centrencephalic theory, the general learning system, and subcortical dementia. *Annals of the New York Academy of Sciences, 702,* 197–223.

Zaidel, E., Clarke, J. M., & Suyenobu, B. (1990). Hemispheric independence: A paradigm case for cognitive neuroscience. In A. B. Scheibel & A. F. Wechsler (Eds.), *Neurobiology of higher cognitive function* (pp. 297-355). New York: Guilford.

E. J. Parkins
Nottingham University, United Kingdom

BRAIN LATERALITY
CEREBELLUM
INFORMATION PROCESSING

CHARACTER DISORDER

The conception of character reflects humanity's understanding of human nature. Plato and Aristotle recognized individual differences; Hippocrates and Galen offered humoral theories of temperament; and Theophrastus described 30 character types, some of which resemble modern personality typologies (Watson & Evans, 1991). By the early 19th century psychopathology became linked to character. For example, Pinel (1801/1962) described *manie sans délire* (insanity without delirium), Rush (1812) wrote about moral depravity, and Prichard (1835) advanced the concept of moral insanity.

According to Pierce's (1924) *The Philosophy of Character,* personality and character are equivalent; both reflect the sum of attributes of the person, the agglomeration of all knowledge, innate and acquired, teleological and non-teleological, which forces action and thus, taken with the environment, determines the conduct of individuals. Similarly, Roback's *The Psychology of Character* (1927) defined character as the disposition to inhibit impulse and narrow self-seeking in light of some value principle. Included in this meaning of character were the concepts of emotional control, affiliation orientation, and emotional investment in distant goals. Thus, an individual with a character disorder demonstrated a deficiency in these three psychological spheres.

From this traditional definition, the concept of character disorders evolved to also include four rather diverse patterns of abnormal behavior. These are alcoholism, drug addiction, sexual deviancy, and psychopathy. Despite their diversity, several characteristics common to individuals so categorized are cited as justification for viewing them within a single conceptual framework. The behavior patterns typically constitute a violation of the codes and conventions of society. The problem behaviors most often result in immediate positive reinforcing consequences, although the delayed or long-term effects are usually negative. Finally, these individuals do not seem to experience guilt over repeated violation of societal conventions and are rarely motivated to change their behavior.

A slightly different meaning of the term *character* can be found within psychoanalytic theory. Early analysts began by investigating neurotic symptoms, phenomena that do not fit within a customary mode of behavior. Realizing the importance of these customary modes of "character" in the analysis of symptoms of therapeutic resistance, analysts began describing the nature of character and the role it played within the ego. The publication of Reich's *Character Analysis* (1933/1949) was an impetus for the serious study of character types. It represented a shift in psychoanalytic theory away from unconscious material and toward the characteristic behavior that is used as a defense against analytic insight and unconscious material. Character became viewed as the habitual mode of bringing into harmony the tasks presented by internal demands and by the external world; it is necessarily a function of the constant, organized, and integrating part of the personality which is called ego. Psychoanalytic theory attributes the formation of character to multiple sources. At its foundation is the maturation of natural growth (the progression through the states of psychosexual development) and learning to overcome frustrations, avoid pain, resolve conflicts, and reduce anxiety. Thus, character is so central to the individual that it determines much of normal and abnormal functioning. In fact, many of the neuroses were believed to have their root in character.

The most common example of character disorder is the condition classically designated as the psychopathic or sociopathic personality. These individuals appear to be virtually without character in the sense Roback describes. The psychopath seems to regard others not as persons, with feelings and rights comparable to his or her own, but as things to be used, exploited, and manipulated. Cleckley in *The Mask of Sanity* (1941) describes the psychopath as having superficial charm, untruthfulness, insincerity, poor judgment, failure to learn from experience, unresponsiveness in interpersonal relationships, and a failure to follow any life plan. Frequent involvement with criminal justice systems is expected for these individuals, along with participation in fraud and swindling activities. Modern assessment, such as Hare's (1991) checklist, preserves a set of core attributes: glib and superficial charm, grandiose sense of self-worth, need for stimulation/proneness to boredom, pathological lying, conning and manipulativeness, lack of remorse or guilt, shallow affect, callousness and lack of empathy, parasitic lifestyle, poor behavior controls, promiscuous sexual behavior, early behavior problems, lack of realistic long-term goals, impulsivity, irresponsibility, failure to accept responsibility for one's own actions, many short-term marital relationships, juvenile delinquency, revocation of conditional release, and criminal versatility.

Current reviews of the experimental literature on the psychopath find children from chaotic, disorganized family environments with maternal deprivation and a sociopathic father at risk for psychopathy. There also appears to be a biological understructure with at least a partly genetic etiology, possible serotonergic dysregulation, brain abnormalities in the frontal and temporal regions, lack of inhibitory anxiety, and diminished responsiveness to aversive consequences. Confusingly, the term psychopath is almost absent from widely accepted modern nomenclature, replaced by the more ubiquitous "Antisocial Personality Disorder" which substituted more reliable behavioral criteria of lawlessness and deviance for richer, albeit less reliable, etiologic and theoretic formulations. The prevalence of Antisocial Personality Disorder in the general population is estimated to be about three percent for males and about one percent for females (American Psychiatric Association, 1994).

Alcoholism and drug abuse have traditionally been included under the heading of character disorders. Individuals with these disorders generally show many dependency-autonomy conflicts and problems in the areas of impulse control, conformity to social expectations, and personal value commitments that are common to disorders of character. Similarly, sexual deviations including exhibitionism, transvestitism, voyeurism, sadomasochism, fetishism, rape, homosexuality, pedophilia and incest have historically been included in this category. Modern classification systems have discarded the notion of character as defining in these disorders and separated substance abuse and sexual paraphilias into discrete diagnostic categories. In some cases, for example, homosexuality, the behavior no longer is considered a disorder.

In psychology's more recent history, *character disorder* is used as a generic term referring to disorders of personality. Such disorders represent any deeply ingrained inflexible, maladaptive patterns of relating to, perceiving, and thinking about the environment and oneself. They may cause either significant impairment in adaptive functioning or subjective distress. Thus, they are pervasive personality traits and are exhibited in a wide range of social and personal contexts. While the classification of character disorders is varied and somewhat subjective, commonly accepted nosological systems of character (personality) disorders exist.

The Diagnostic and Statistical Manual of Mental Disorders–IV (American Psychiatric Association, 1994) provides one system for describing these conditions. The atheoretical orientation of the current diagnostic system allows the elucidation of behavioral criteria necessary to identify a specific character type without reliance on a specific theoretical system. As the etiology and pathophysiological process of mental disorders, and particularly character disorders, are often unknown or not well established by existing research, this approach provides a comprehensive description of the manifestation of personality disorders without an implicit description of their origin and course.

The personality disorders are grouped into three clusters based on similarities among the disorders (American Psychiatric Association, 1994). Cluster A includes Paranoid, Schizoid, and Schizotypal Personality Disorders. These individuals often appear odd or eccentric. The paranoid is described by a pervasive, unwarranted suspicion and mistrust of other people, a hypersensitivity, and restricted affectivity. Schizoid types are seen as having emotional coldness, aloofness, and indifference to the feelings of others; they have few close friendships, but do not exhibit eccentricities of speech, behavior, or thought. The schizotypal, on the other hand, is likely to exhibit magical thinking such as superstition, clairvoyance, and telepathy, and also ideas of reference, recurrent illusions, social isolation, and speech that is digressive, vague, overly elaborate, or circumstantial.

Cluster B includes Histrionic, Narcissistic, Antisocial, and Borderline Personality Disorders. These individuals have a common tendency to be dramatic, emotional, impulsive, and erratic. Histrionics are prone to self-dramatization, overreaction, irrational and angry outbursts, and attention-seeking behavior. They are perceived by others as dependent, shallow, egocentric, vain, and demanding. This disorder has traditionally been labeled the hysterical or psychoinfantile personality, or Briquet's syndrome. Narcissistic individuals often have a grandiose sense of self-importance or uniqueness, a preoccupation with fantasies of unlimited success, power, brilliance, or beauty, and display exhibitionism. Their interpersonal relationships are characterized by exploitation, entitlement (expecting special favors without assuming reciprocal responsibilities), and a lack of empathy. The essential feature of the antisocial type is a history of continuous and chronic behavior in which the rights of others are violated. Frequent involvement with criminal justice authorities is likely. Associated features include early delinquency, truancy, persistent lying, fighting, theft, vandalism, and chronic rule violations. Adulthood may be marked by an inability to sustain consistent work, poor and irresponsible parenting, failure to maintain enduring attachment to sexual partners, irritability, aggressiveness, failure to honor financial obligations, impulsiveness, recklessness, and fraud. This disorder has traditionally been referred to as the psychopathic, sociopathic, asocial, or amoral personality. The borderline type is characterized by instability in a variety of areas. These individuals may be unpredictable, self-harming, and moody; they may display unstable and intense interpersonal relationships, show inappropriate and intense anger at times, and often feel emptiness or boredom.

Cluster C includes Avoidant, Dependent, and Obsessive-Compulsive Personality Disorders. Individuals with these disorders often appear anxious or fearful. The avoidant type is hypersensitive to rejection, often interpreting innocuous events as ridicule, and is unwilling to enter into relationships unless given uncritical acceptance. These individuals are prone to social withdrawal and low self-esteem. The dependent type passively allows others to assume responsibility for major areas of life because of an inability to function independently. These individuals lack self-confidence and subordinate their needs to those of other persons on whom they depend. Obsessive-compulsive types may be characterized by restricted ability to express tender emotions and experience pleasure. They display perfectionism and are preoccupied with trivial details, rules, order, organization, schedules, and lists. They may display an excessive devotion to work and productivity, yet be extremely indecisive, fearing mistakes or ruminating about priorities. These individuals have traditionally been referred to as anal, anankastic, or obsessional personalities.

Finally, it is important to recognize that character disorders need not be exclusively defined by their clinical, symptomatic, or, maladaptive components. Indeed, there are examples of constellations of traits that might be considered maladaptive in one setting, but adaptive, perhaps even richly rewarding, in another setting. Lasch's (1978) The Culture of Narcissism and Smith's (1978) The Psychopath in Society have taken an even broader view by implicating certain character "disorders" as ascendant over aspects of modern culture and commerce.

In summary, character disorders, a slightly archaic term by standards of contemporary nomenclature, have their origin in conceptions of human nature and individual difference. As a class, the character disorders subsumed a number of conditions for which a moral defect was believed responsible, including alcoholism, drug addiction, sexual deviancy, and psychopathy. Modern conceptions of the character disorders are relegated to descriptions of the antisocial personality disorder, personality disorders in general, or substance abuse and sexual disorders.

REFERENCES

American Psychiatric Association (1994). Diagnostic and statistical manual of mental disorders (4th ed.). Washington, DC: Author.

Cleckley, H. (1941). The mask of sanity. St. Louis, MO: Mosby.

Hare, R. D. (1991). The Hare psychopathy checklist—revised. Toronto, Canada: Multi-Health Systems.

Lasch, C. (1978). The culture of narcissism: American life in an age of diminishing expectations. New York: Norton.

Pierce, E. (1924). The philosophy of character. Cambridge, MA: Harvard University Press.

Pinel, P. (1962). A treatise on insanity (D. Davis, Trans.). New York: Hafner. (Original work published 1801)

Prichard, J. C. (1835). *A treatise on insanity and other disorders affecting the mind.* London: Sherwood, Gilbert & Piper.

Reich, W. (1949). *Character analysis* (3rd ed.). New York: Orgone Institute. (Original work published 1933)

Roback, A. A. (1927). *The psychology of character.* New York: Harcourt Brace.

Rush, B. (1812). *Medical inquires and observations upon the diseases of the mind.* Philadelphia, PA: Kimber & Richardson.

Smith, R. J. (1978). *The psychopath in society.* New York: Academic Press.

Watson, R. I., & Evans, R. B. (1991). *The great psychologists: A history of psychological thought* (5th Edition). New York: Harper Collins.

R. M. ASHBROOK
Capital University

PERSONALITY DISORDERS

CHARCOT, JEAN-MARTIN (1825–1893)

Jean-Martin Charcot was appointed professor of pathological anatomy at the University of Paris in 1860. Two years later he was appointed senior physician at Salpêtrière, a hospital for mental patients in Paris.

He is best known for his studies on hypnosis and hysteria. An eminent physician of his time, his theory of hypnosis was in direct conflict with that developed shortly before by A. A. Liébeault and Hippolyte Bernheim at Nancy. They had placed emphasis on the suggestion of sleep to induce the hypnotic state. As the leader of what became known as the Paris School, Charcot believed that hypnosis was a condition peculiar to hysterical patients and a useful method for investigating hysterical predispositions. Further, he believed that there was a neurological predisposition for hysteria, while Liébeault and Bernheim felt that hypnosis was merely a special case of normal suggestibility.

Sigmund Freud had heard of Charcot's work and his use of hypnosis. In 1885 Freud went to Paris to hear Charcot's lectures and witness his hypnotic demonstrations. By this time Charcot had found hypnosis an excellent treatment for hysteria: In treating a patient with a hysterical paralysis, he would utter the phrase "ça passe" (it's going away), and presumably it did.

At one of Charcot's lectures that Freud attended, a member of the audience had asked about a difficulty he did not understand. As the story goes, Charcot replied, "This has to do with the sexual zone—always, always, always!" Whether this incident had any effect on Freud's theory of psychosexuality is debatable.

R. W. LUNDIN
Wheaton, Illinois

CHEN, LI (1902–   )

Born in 1902, Li Chen took his first degree in science at Shanghai University. In the early 1930s, he studied at University College at London and obtained the PhD under the supervision of Charles Spearman. He worked at the National Institute of Industrial Psychology, London, and later at the Institute of Psychology, Berlin. In 1935, Chen returned to China as a senior researcher at the Institute of Psychology, Academia Sinica, and became professor at Qinhua University and later Zhejiang University. He then became the president of Hangzhou University. Chen is a past vice president of the Chinese Psychological Society; for more than 60 years, he has taught and done research in psychology, especially industrial psychology, and has made contributions to the development of modern Chinese psychology. His book *Essentials of Industrial Psychology* was the first industrial psychology book in China. Based on Chen's doctoral dissertation, his article, "Periodicity in oscillation," demonstrated the use of a smoothing curve to eliminate fatigue and adaptation and was considered a new perspective in this area. His study on the differentiation and integration of the g factor, published in the *Journal of Genetic Psychology,* was recognized as a landmark in understanding intellectual development. After the founding of the People's Republic of China, Chen published many books and more than 100 articles, including "Prospectus of industrial psychology" and "Psychology of industrial management." He has worked in such diverse areas as children's physical growth, feedback in technical training, programmed instruction, cognitive development, test theory, and organizational reform. His work on attribution theory, group dynamics, managerial decision-making, human-computer interaction, and macro-ergonomics in the 1980s has affected the development of social, organizational, and engineering psychology in China.

STAFF

CHI-SQUARE TEST

The chi-square (χ^2) test was developed in 1900 by Karl Pearson. This development has been called one of the most important breakthroughs in the history of statistics. The test and the statistical distribution on which it is based have a wide variety of uses and applications in psychological research. Its principal uses are to test the independence of two variables and to assess how well a theoretical model or set of a priori probabilities fits a set of data. In both cases the chi-square test is typically used as a nonparametric procedure involving observed (O) and expected (E) frequencies. The expected frequencies may be determined either theoretically or empirically. The basic formula for calculating the chi-square statistic is:

$$\chi^2 = \sum_{1}^{k} [(O - E)^2 / E].$$

The χ^2 test is commonly applied to a wide variety of designs, including $k \times 1$ groups, $2 \times k$ groups, 2×2 contingency tables, and

$R \times C$ contingency tables. It is most appropriately used with nominal level (categorical) data but is frequently used with ordinal level data as well. The χ^2 statistic is related to several measures of association, including the phi coefficient (ϕ), contingency coefficient (C), and Cramer's phi (ϕ' or ϕ_C). The equation $\phi^2 = \chi^2/N$ is frequently used as a measure of practical significance or effect size for 2×2 tables.

Historically, there has been concern over the use of the chi-square test when any E was small (e.g., < 5–10) because the underlying χ^2 distribution is continuous whereas the distribution of observations is discrete. For 2×2 tables this led to the development of the widely used and recommended Yates' correction for continuity. However, most recent evidence seems to suggest that the use of Yates' correction is unnecessary even with very small E.

The χ^2 distribution is related to the normal distribution, such that the square of a standard normal deviate (z^2) is distributed as a χ^2 with one degree of freedom. The chi-square distribution also describes the sampling distribution of the variance, s^2, such that $\chi^2 = (N-1) s^2/\sigma^2$ with $N-1$ degrees of freedom. These relationships form the basis for many tests of statistical significance. For example, the analysis of variance F statistic may be thought of as the ratio of two χ^2 statistics. The χ^2 statistic is also used in many multivariate statistical tests and in calculating multinomial probabilities, especially for log-linear models. Multivariate statistics that use both generalized least squares and maximum likelihood procedures also rely on the χ^2 statistic. For example, in structural equation modeling, the χ^2 statistic forms the basis for many goodness-of-fit tests. In the 1930s, Fisher developed a procedure using the χ^2 test to combine the results of several independent tests of the same hypothesis, an early version of meta-analysis.

J. S. ROSSI
University of Rhode Island

STATISTICS IN PSYCHOLOGY

CHILD ABUSE

Child abuse is defined as the nonaccidental injury of children by their parent or guardian. Severity of the injury is not included in this definition; however, definitions based upon severity vary across states in legal interpretations, the courts, and their rulings, and even across time with the history of childhood. The history of American approaches to child abuse has followed the shifting history of social values and attitudes toward children. Throughout our history, and across other cultures where social values have fluctuated or the value of children varies, the attitudes toward children and definition of what constitutes abuse vary. At times in our history when children were devalued and seen as the property of their parents, abuse was ignored if not even tolerated or at times encouraged. There have even been times in other countries when infanticide by parent or guardian was tolerated or even encouraged. The record of violence toward children dates back to biblical times, including the occasion when Abraham nearly killed his son as a sacrifice.

From ancient to colonial times, children were seen as the property of their parents, who had the legal right to treat or mistreat the children in any way they saw fit. In some cases children were castrated or physically mistreated under the sanction or direction of a religious leader. In colonial America, religious ideology dictated that children were born with original sin and were therefore to be punished and directed by their parents to obtain salvation. Present-day agencies designed to specifically address the concerns of physical abuse with children trace their origins to a now classic case of a foster child named Mary Ellen in 1874. She had been beaten daily by her stepmother and there appeared to be no legal means to protect her. At the time there were no laws against cruelty to children, although such laws did exist with regard to animals. Mary Ellen's case was brought to the Society for the Prevention of Cruelty to Animals, which referred her to the court as an "animal who is getting mistreated." It was from this case that the Society developed the children's division of the American Humane Association. The American Society for the Prevention of Cruelty to Animals had itself been established in 1866.

In 1974 the Federal Child Abuse, Prevention and Treatment Act was passed by Congress, providing direct assistance to states to help them develop child abuse and neglect programs. The act further provided for research in child abuse and neglect, and established the Center for Child Abuse and Neglect with the Children's Bureau in the Department of Health and Human Services' Office of Child Development. By 1968 protective services for children and reporting laws were provided universally in all 50 states. Renewed interest in child abuse came about as the result of several factors, not the least of which was the concern of physicians during the 1960s for the medical and emotional damage being done to children.

As attitudes toward children and violence itself have changed within our society, the problem has developed in distinguishing between discipline which is necessary and legitimate in its own right, and excessive and inappropriate violence toward children. Definitions vary from individual to individual and judge to judge, and even from state to state. The most seriously injured children are usually referred to as "battered children," whereas the term "abused child" is considered less extreme. The physical and psychological neglect of a child is even more difficult to define and has received significantly less attention in social science literature and legal intervention. The exception to this is where the neglect is so extreme as to produce possible physical harm to the child.

Sexual abuse of children is a separate area which deserves attention in its own right. Sexual abuse can take place with or without other physical abuse or neglect.

It is impossible to know the exact incidence of abuse, neglect, and sexual abuse, since only the more serious cases tend to be reported. All states now have a law which mandates official reporting of all forms of abuse; however, the number of cases officially reported are quite conservative. Individuals of higher socioeconomic status are underrepresented in the statistics, since they are most likely to go to private treatment facilities which are the least likely to report incidents of abuse, except in extreme cases. Gertrude Williams (1980) indicates that, owing to the vagueness of definitions of abuse and neglect and the difficulties in relying on reports, the incident estimates range from 60,000 to 4 million annually. It is a serious problem, whatever the numbers may be. Most investigators agree that child abuse and neglect vary as a function of the social stresses that society is experiencing. Because of increased willingness to report cases, better public awareness of the problem, and less public tolerance of violence toward children, more cases are reported each year.

Even though statistics are highly suspect because of the previously mentioned problems, they do provide some information. The majority of physically abused children require no medical treatment and probably fewer than 1% receive fatal injuries. Studies find boys to be more frequently abused than girls until adolescence, when, with the inclusion of sexual abuse, girls are more frequently abused. With the exclusion of sexual abuse, males are the most frequent victims of physical abuse at all age levels. These statistical investigations suggest that the majority of abused children are 6 years of age or older, with a much smaller percentage under 2; however, children of preschool age are not as likely to be noticed by outside agencies such as schools.

Difficulties with the statistics are further reflected in reviewing the sources of the abuse reports. Friends, neighbors, and relatives are the most frequent source of referrals, while law enforcement agencies, schools, and social agencies report much less frequently. Many studies have found medical agencies to be the least likely to report, possibly because of the desire to avoid the time-consuming legal process.

The statistics overemphasize lower-income families. While male abusers slightly outnumber females, the statistics are nearly equal. Often there is a history of family discord among parents with limited education and employment skills; however, abuse is found among all socioeconomic groups. In this regard, public hospitals and clinics are more frequently sources of abuse reports than private hospitals or private family physicians. Individuals of lower socioeconomic status are less likely to have a relationship with their physician, which would help cover up the abuse.

It appears that most physical abuse of children, excluding sexual abuse, is of an unplanned, unintentional nature, being committed by a parent facing extreme environmental stress. Usually the abuse stems from expectations that the child was unable to meet, and an overly punitive parent who relies on corporal punishment for discipline. In some cases the parents expect behaviors or development considerably beyond the age-specific abilities of the child, or are unrealistic within the situation presented. Many parents were found to actually expect the child to care for them: A child who had been crying for an extended period of time was seen as rejecting the parent and unloving.

By far, the majority of abusive acts stem from attempts at discipline that become exaggerated to the point of abuse. In almost all cases the subsequent injuries—particularly if serious—were not intended. Even in cases of sexual abuse, the parent will often report having meant no harm, and may justify the act as an attempt to educate the child sexually.

Most parents who abuse their child carry no serious psychiatric diagnosis, but they do often have difficulty with social relationships, and with controlling their temper and impulsive reactions which quickly become violent. Frequently they not only experience considerable stress from their environment, but—much more importantly—have difficulty dealing with stress through appropriate nonviolent means.

Most explanations of child abuse revolve around combinations of factors, including an individual who is predisposed to reacting physically when confronted with the need to discipline a child, particularly when that individual is overly stressed. In addition, environmental circumstances often help to stress and disinhibit the individual. Environmentally the situation appears to be exacerbated by various factors: social isolation; the use of alcohol or drugs; lack of support systems or a way to at least periodically, for even a brief period of time, escape from the child through the use of sitters or day-care facilities; and frustration from lack of social and economic power.

Certain predisposing characteristics of children can enhance the likelihood of abuse as well. Children resulting from an unwanted or particularly stressful pregnancy or delivery are more likely to be abused, as are children who have had low birth weights or are hyperactive or have any types of learning or behavioral difficulties. Even where there was an extended separation between the parents and the child—particularly within the first year of life—such circumstances seem to increase the potential for abuse.

A number of methods for treating and preventing abuse have been attempted. The treatment and prevention of physical abuse tends to be more successful than that of sexual abuse or neglect. Certainly the first and most immediate concern is to remove children who are in serious physical danger. In the majority of such cases, children removed from the home because of physical abuse eventually are returned.

Most approaches to abuse revolve around two general areas. The most direct approach is working with the parents themselves to help them cope with stress, modify their behavior, and come to understand the dynamics of the abuse. The second, more general, approach tries to improve the parents' contacts with the larger society. Attempts are made to reduce the amount of stress that the family is experiencing, while increasing the amount of support and facilitative services. Day-care services, babysitting, foster care, and homemaker services, as well as organizations such as Parents Anonymous, are designed to diminish the environmental circumstances which can result in abuse. In all cases, and particularly in cases of sexual abuse, at least initial outside supervision appears to be extremely important.

With a combination of the intensive individual and broader social interventions, the likelihood of being able to successfully intervene and diminish the chances of severe damage to the child is greatly enhanced.

REFERENCES

Williams, G. (1980). Child abuse and neglect: Problems of definition and incidence. In G. Williams & J. Money (Eds.), *Traumatic abuse and neglect of children at home.* Baltimore: John Hopkins University Press.

SUGGESTED READING

Cook, J., & Bowles, R. (Eds.). (1980). *Child abuse: Commission and ommission.* Scarborough, Canada: Butterworth.

Finkelhor, D. (1979). *Sexually victimized children.* New York: Free Press.

Frude, N. (1981). *Psychological approaches to child abuse.* Toloma, NJ: Rowman & Littlefield.

Kadushin, A., & Martin, J. (1981). *Child abuse: An interactional event.* New York: Columbia University Press.

S. D. Sherrets
Maine Head Trauma Center

AGGRESSION
BATTERED PEOPLE
BYSTANDER INVOLVEMENT
STRESS
VIOLENCE

CHILD GUIDANCE CLINICS

The child guidance clinic movement, which spanned the decades of the 1920s to the 1940s, was marshaled by the National Committee for Mental Hygiene. Child guidance clinics were established for the psychiatric study, treatment, and prevention of juvenile delinquency, other social ills, and conduct and personality disorders in 3- to 17-year-old non-mentally retarded children. The child guidance clinic approach to children's mental health represented a shift from traditional treatment models of the era—which were largely individual, psychoanalytically-oriented play therapy sessions conducted by a psychiatrist or psychologist—to more innovative modes of intervention. Child guidance clinics' comprehensive, community-based approach to children's mental health service was carried out by multidisciplinary teams of psychologists, psychiatrists, psychiatric social workers, speech therapists, and psychiatric occupational therapists. In the 1940s the mental health focus shifted from the child guidance clinic movement to World War II–related mental health issues.

The next large impact on children's mental health services was the Community Mental Health Centers (CMHC) Act of 1963. Like child guidance clinics, CMHCs sought to address both the treatment and prevention of mental illness within communities. However, unlike child guidance clinics, CMHCs were not solely child-focused, but rather addressed mental health issues across development from prenatal health to coordination of services for the elderly at individual, family, and community levels. Community mental health centers were responsible for a comprehensive menu of services including outpatient treatment, primary and secondary prevention efforts, 24-hr crisis response, and community mental health education. The CMHCs fulfilled their community education responsibility through consultation with schools in the area of early child-risk evaluation.

Partly in response to changes in insurance reimbursement systems, such as Health Maintenance Organizations, mental health services for children have continued to evolve. Currently they include varied theoretical orientations and treatment approaches. Current work with children emphasizes child-centered, family-focused, community-based efforts in the planning and implementation of treatment. Mental health services strive to be both culturally competent and responsive to the cultural, racial, and ethnic differences of varied service populations. Services available to children within the mental health system include inpatient and outpatient psychiatric and psychological treatment facilities, partial programs, mobile therapy, crisis teams, foster care, juvenile justice, education, social welfare, primary health care, emergency shelter, and home-based interventions. In addition, wraparound services that meet a child's mental and physical health needs across his or her varied environments have been added to the children's mental health services menu. Case managers, whose job it is to coordinate children's mental health services within this complex system, have emerged to ensure that services are not fragmented, but rather work in an interactive therapeutic manner to meet children's mental health needs. Undoubtedly, the mental health service system will continue to evolve in an effort to meet children's ever-changing physical, emotional, social, and educational needs.

SUGGESTED READING

Horn, M. (1989). *Before it's too late: The child guidance movement in the United States, 1922–1945.* Philadelphia: Temple University Press.

E. K. Lanphier
Pennsylvania State University

COMMUNITY PSYCHOLOGY

CHILD, IRVIN L. (1915–   )

Irvin L. Child was born March 11, 1915, in Deming, New Mexico, a small town near the Mexican border. Features of his family background were consonant with his development as a psychologist. His father, the rebellious son of a Connecticut minister, led a frequently-moving business life in Mexico and the border regions. His mother was the daughter of a Pennsylvania businessman of German background who made a fortune in Mexico while never becoming Mexicanized. From both sides Child received an interesting cultural variation and a rejection of established convention. From majors in psychology and philosophy at UCLA (BA, 1935), he formed a respect for the use of scientific procedures to arrive at the truth, and a readiness to doubt whatever was generally accepted as truth without substantial scientific background. Graduate study at Yale (PhD, 1939) strengthened his devotion to empirical testing, and added an anthropological perspective to his reasons for doubting anything too-readily accepted as valid by his fellow psychologists. Child's research career during long tenure on the faculty of the Yale Department of Psychology (1942–1985; Emeritus since 1985), has been characterized throughout by collaboration, profiting from interaction with the diverse talents and backgrounds of others and sharing credit with them for achievements—the spirit on which Yale's Institute of Human Relations was founded. At Yale, Child completed major work with his wife, Alice Child, and with Joseph Slate, Rosaline Schwartz, and Edward Kelly. Child was a fellow at the Center for Advanced Studies in 1958 and 1959. In 1999, he received the Arnheim Award for Contributions to Science and the Arts for Division 10 of the American Psychological Association.

Beginning his research career in psychology when the spirit of the time stressed the process of learning, Child tried to show that process to be relevant in unexpected ways. His theoretical analysis, followed by a new experiment, showed that an emphasis on learning could clarify the effects of frustration, especially the effects on level of aspiration. Viewing persistence as a product of learning suggested that it might result from experiences of initial frustration followed by success—an effect that could be demonstrated experimentally. Analysis of college students' memories of their daily life experiences confirmed the relevance of both these points. In a carefully planned test of Sheldon's claims of correlations between physique and temperament, Child showed that Sheldon's claims had at least some limited merit, and then went on to show how profitable the concept of learning could be in posing questions not even asked in a simple constitutional approach (a problem that arises with any attempt to interpret behavior as an exclusive product of nature or nurture alone). These diverse studies, each focusing on the individual's changing through a process of learning, had common threads that led to a more humanistic approach to psychology, an approach that characterized Child's work in the three fields in which he then principally worked.

In the first of these fields, cross-cultural research, Child came to graduate work already oriented toward psychological comparison between one cultural setting and another. In his doctoral dissertation he approached such a comparison in studying the meaning of growing up in a cultural minority in the United States—specifically, the meaning of being second-generation Italian-American (a much more distinct category then than it is 60 years later). Collaboration with anthropologist John Whiting later offered the opportunity to pursue this topic further, but in a very different way: a psychologically relevant study of varying cultures. Child and Whiting began with the established culture patterns of mostly non-literate peoples all over the world as reported by anthropological field workers, and considered the relation between child training practices and various aspects of adult culture, using group projective tests of characteristics that should result from the child's training. There was sufficient confirmation of the predictions to support the view that some important aspects of psychological theory have universal validity (in disagreement with the hypothesis then entertained by some anthropologists—that of practically universal and unpredictable freedom of intercultural variation). With other collaborators, Child then looked at other aspects of the same cultures that seemed likely to reflect, in part, the general tendencies of members of each society, aspects including the themes of folktales, antisocial behavior, and the use of alcohol. Each of these could be considered a group projective test. Relation of each to a pertinent aspect of child training practices could be predicted from psychological theory, and these predictions were strikingly confirmed.

In the field of psychological esthetics, Child asked: What are the sources of agreement about which artistic works are better or poorer? Psychologists' explanations had mostly fallen in two simple, mechanistic categories: (a) inborn tendencies to prefer certain colors, shapes, and so on, to others; and (b) simple acceptance of evaluations by others. Child, while recognizing the importance of both these sources of agreement, offered in addition a more humanistic alternative, and tested some of its implications. He began with the supposition that people devoting themselves wholeheartedly to an art—as creators or critics—have evaluation standards that merit special attention. He used reproductions of paired works of art similar in subject and style but differing greatly in esthetic merit according to experts. Research subjects were asked to express their preferences or judgments within each such pair, and scored on the tendency to make the choices made by experts. Taking this score as a measure of esthetic orientation, Child then asked how it was related to age and to other personal characteristics. Most notably, it was related to various indicators of independence of judgment—just the opposite of what would be expected if acceptance of others' opinions were the major influence. Research in several cultural settings confirmed the generality of this finding that esthetic sensitivity is, in important part, an outcome of the individual's own discovery of characteristics that offer special opportunity for enjoyment.

Finally, in the field of parapsychology, Child believed that a humanistic approach might increase the chances of psychologists' taking seriously those aspects of possibly paranormal phenomena for which objective evidence is apparently available. This led Child to an active visit to J. B. Rhine's laboratories and to participation as both subject and discussant in Charles Honorton's research. These experiences confirmed his feelings that there is substantial knowledge to be developed here, but that its integration into general psychology will remain slow.

STAFF

CHILD PSYCHOLOGY

Child psychology deals with the personality and behavior of children, typically from conception to puberty. While some authors and researchers include adolescence in their definition of child psychology, most current writers see adolescence as a separate field. In the past, child psychology has referred to both normal and abnormal behavior, and has historically included both theory and research concerning the development, rearing, and education of children, as well as psychotherapy or counseling of disturbed children. Current usage, however, appears to limit the term more to a branch of the *science* of developmental psychology, its theory, and its research while also specifying "child clinical" when referring to the practice of child psychology as a profession.

Among the research interests of child psychologists are social and emotional development, physical growth and motor behavior, learning and intellectual growth, language development, and personality development. Some researchers restrict their work to a particular age period such as the prenatal period, the newborn era, infancy, the preschool years, or the school years. Others emphasize the changes across the years in psychological constructs such as cognition, socialization, aggression, dependency, morality, learning, or achievement. Some topics such as language development have been studied in terms of specific behaviors (e.g., number of words at a given age, the use of given parts of speech, and so on) as well as psychological constructs (e.g., language socialization, language and cognition).

The period of childhood is generally divided for didactic purposes into substages. The prenatal period can be further divided into the periods of the zygote (0 to 2 weeks), embryo (2 weeks to 2 months), and fetus (2 months to birth). Similarly the postnatal period can be divided into infancy, toddlerhood, preschool, middle childhood, and later childhood.

There has been a growing tendency, however, to avoid segmenting developmental psychology into its components of infancy and childhood, adolescence, adulthood, and senescence. Some researchers have argued that the processes of development are best understood in the context of the total span of life. Thus a good deal of research and theory in child psychology comes under the heading of "life-span developmental psychology." Additionally, the most current research has focused on the contexts influencing development, including the family, school, peers, and others. In fact, Bronfenbrenner (1989, 1993) has developed a theory of human development that addresses the significant contexts, both direct and indirect, in human development.

HISTORY OF CHILD PSYCHOLOGY

At least four sorts of history can be considered with respect to child psychology. Ontogenetic history, the history of the organism from conception to death, is the basic material of human development. Phylogenetic history refers to the evolutionary development of the species. According to one theory—proposed by Hall in his treatise on *Adolescence* (1904), but now largely discounted—the ontogenetic history of individuals represented a "recapitulation" or repeating of the species' phylogenetic history. A third sort of history refers to the changes over time of the concept of childhood. Such a notion is related to the sociocultural history of the family. In his work on *The Tasks of Childhood,* Müller (1969) identified four periods in the cultural history of the family which corresponded to changing conceptions of the child.

1. First stage, before 1750. Birth and death were "natural." There was no prevention of birth, nor was medicine very effective in delaying death. Since the infant mortality rate was high, children were fragile yet easily replaceable, and therefore not especially important. Under such harsh circumstances children were expected to grow up quickly, and were for the most part treated like miniature adults.

2. Second stage, 1750–1880. For some reason the mortality rate fell and the population increased. This demographic change, perhaps attributable to the development of the microscope and the resulting screening of water for bacteria, led to a change in the family structure and in the conception of "the child." After

tolerating harsh conditions of child labor at the beginning of the Industrial Revolution, the attitude of many, especially the privileged, began to change. Childhood came to be seen as a period of innocence, and children began to be protected from the harsh realities of the adult world and to be considered, as Rousseau suggested in *Emile* (1762), as individuals with their own needs relative to their own stage of development.

3. Third stage, 1880–1930. By the end of the nineteenth century the birth rate began to drop dramatically. Once again a change in demographic structure coincided with a change in family structure and in the concept of childhood. With the emergence of the nuclear family as the unit of recreational, social, and cultural significance, parents took a more direct role in the education of their children. Rewards and punishments were meted out in the hopes of instilling a firm conscience.

4. Fourth stage, from 1930 until the present. Finally, according to Müller, the family had reached a stage in its development in which the child had been accorded a position of privilege. The child was no longer seen as an easily replaceable or fragile commodity, nor was he or she exploited as a member of the workforce. Rather the child assumed the importance of a little prince, around whom revolve several professions, considerable marketing efforts, and a certain amount of legislation. As the demographic structure of the human race has changed, so have family characteristics and our resulting concept of what it means to be a child.

A fourth kind of history in child psychology is the history of the field itself. Most research on the processes of development has been concerned with variables or logical constructs, the intellectual origins of which can be traced to ancient philosophy. The antecedents of psychology lie in philosophy and physiology; child psychology is no exception. Early Greek writers were concerned with the stages of development and with the socialization process, as well as with such practical issues as the proper education of children. The origins of child psychology as a science, however, can be traced to the careful observations recorded in early "baby biographies," often by parent observers. The works of Tiedemann (1787), Darwin (1877), and Preyer (1882) are among the most often-cited examples. Despite their shortcomings as scientific data, these biographies paved the way for more careful observations, for attention to child psychological processes, and finally for experiments dealing with the behavior of children.

More recent influences on child psychology have been the testing movement and the development of child guidance clinics and major university centers for research on child behavior. The most current literature emphasizes the optimal ways to work with parents and children, or developmentally appropriate guidance.

THEORIES IN CHILD PSYCHOLOGY

Early theories of child psychology were largely implicit. Children were thought of as miniature adults, and as such, no special logical constructs were necessary to explain their behavior. Not until the late nineteenth century and the emergence of a formal discipline of psychology did theories about child behavior become prominent.

One early child psychologist was Hall, who proposed a biogenetic theory which posited that behavior was influenced mainly by biological growth and genetic predispositions.

Freud, the father of psychoanalysis, emphasized environmental and especially social factors in the development of child behavior and personality. Freud was one of the first to stress the influence of early experiences on later behavior, and to assign a major role to the unconscious in explaining behavior. He postulated that individuals pass through a series of psychosexual stages which are defined by the characteristic way in which libido, or mental sexual energy, gets expressed. For example, the first is the oral stage, during which the child is stimulated mainly by feeding.

Piaget developed a major theory explaining cognitive development. The cognitive-developmental position of Piaget is a stage theory, with stages referring to the increasingly complex way in which the individual can incorporate and process information and assimilate it into his or her own previously developed mental structures. Piaget's first stage is called the perceptual-motor or sensorimotor stage. This is followed by a brief preoperational stage (i.e., before the use of logical operations). The period of concrete operations begins at about six years of age, and is followed by the final stages, formal operations, which begins during early adolescence.

Learning theorists have viewed children's behavior as based on environmental rather than organism factors and, like Freud, see the organism as passive rather than active in its own development. The emergence of social learning theory is in some respects a combination of psychoanalytic and learning theory concepts.

RESEARCH METHODS IN CHILD PSYCHOLOGY

Since the days of the baby biographies, child psychology has progressed in both theory and methods. When the issue of concern has been age changes in some trait or behavior, two procedures have been used. With the longitudinal approach, investigators follow the same subjects over the years of interest and observe age changes. With the cross-sectional approach, the researcher tests subjects of different ages. Each of these procedures has advantages and limitations. A combination of the two procedures has been suggested by some authors (Schaie, 1970) as a more powerful approach with fewer disadvantages.

A variety of research methods have been used, including questionnaires, ratings and rankings by teachers, peers, parents, and oneself; interviews; observation; projective tests; personality and intelligence tests; and direct experimentation. A good source for understanding the basic information on research methods in child psychology is *Research Methods in Human Development* (Brown, Cozby, Kee, & Worden, 1999).

ISSUES IN DEVELOPMENTAL PSYCHOLOGY

The contrasting views of the child as an active agent or a recipient in his or her own development remains a salient issue in child psychology, and one on which theorists and researchers remain divided. The relative influence of environmental factors, contrasted with genetic predispositions in child behavior, is also a dimension of importance to child psychologists. Finally, child psychologists differ with respect to the importance they place on stages in development: While some theorists perceive development as proceeding by discrete stages, other assume a more continuous unfolding of personality and behavior.

REFERENCES

Bronfenbrenner, U. (1989). Ecological systems theory. In R. Vasta (Ed.), *Six theories of child development. Annals of Child Development, 6,* 187–249. Greenwich, CT: JAI.

Bronfenbrenner, U. (1993). The ecology of cognitive development: Research models and fuguitive findings. In R. H. Wozniak & K. W. Fisher (Eds.), *Development in context: Acting and thinking in specific environments* (pp. 3–44). Hillsdale, NJ: Erlbaum.

Brown, K. W., Cozby, P. C., Kee, D. W., & Worden, P. E. (1999). *Research methods in human development* (2nd ed.). Mountain View, CA: Mayfield.

Darwin, C. A. (1877). A biographical sketch of an infant. *Merid, 2,* 285–294.

Hall, G. S. (1904). *Adolescence: Its psychology and its relations to physiology, anthropology, sociology, sex, crime, religion, and education.* Vol. I. Englewood Cliffs: NJ: Prentice-Hall.

Müller, P. (1969). *The tasks of childhood.* New York: McGraw-Hill.

Preyer, W. (1888/1882). *The mind of the child.* New York: Appleton-Century.

Rousseau, J. J. (1762/1738). *Emile, or concerning education.* New York: Dutton.

Schaie, K. W. (1970). A reinterpretation of age-related changes in cognitive structure and functioning. In L. R. Goulet & P. B. Baltes (Eds.), *Life-span developmental psychology: Research and theory.* New York: Academic.

Tiedemann, D. (1787). *Beobachtungen über die Entwicklung der Seelenfähigkeiten bei Kindern.* Altenburg: Bonde.

J. P. McKinney
Michigan State University

K. McKinney
University of Wisconsin, Stevens Point

EARLY CHILDHOOD DEVELOPMENT
INFANT DEVELOPMENT

CHILD SEXUAL ABUSE

DEFINITION

In the United States, child protective services in each state individually define child sexual abuse. Generally, any sexual activity with a child by an adult constitutes sexual abuse. However, sexual activity with a child by a teenager can be defined as abuse if the teen is significantly older (e.g., five years) in age and development. Sexual abuse can be physical, verbal, or emotional and may include the following: sexual touching and fondling; exposing children to adult sexual activity or pornography; having children pose, undress, or perform in a sexual fashion on film or in person; "peeping" into bathrooms or bedrooms to spy on a child; and/or rape or attempted rape.

PREVALENCE OF SEXUAL ABUSE

Prevalence rates for child sexual abuse are difficult to determine because child sexual abuse is a crime that is underreported. According to the National Women's Study completed by the National Crime Victims Research and Treatment Center in Charleston, South Carolina, the majority of women who were sexually abused as children did not disclose that abuse. Victims of sexual abuse may not disclose their experiences for a variety of reasons. For example, disclosure may be embarrassing, or in some cases victims may not disclose due to threats of harm to them or their family members. When national surveys are conducted, victims are often able anonymously to disclose abuse that they could not disclose earlier. Such surveys, in which a random sample of individuals is interviewed about any experiences of sexual abuse, indicate that between 32% and 38% of females and between 13% and 16% of males report being sexually abused prior to age 18. Some studies have found that rates of sexual abuse are higher when noncontact offenses are included.

EFFECTS OF CHILD SEXUAL ABUSE

A wide range of social and emotional difficulties has been associated with child sexual abuse. However, the current literature does not point to any specific difficulty that all sexually abused children experience. As a result, there is no set of symptoms that one can observe to conclude that a child has experienced sexual abuse. In fact, one fourth to one half of children with sexual abuse histories report no mental health problems. Whether these children experience difficulties as they continue to develop, however, is currently unclear. Furthermore, although physical injury and/or evidence (e.g., vaginal tears, sexually transmitted diseases) may be conclusive evidence of abuse, such injury occurs in only about 15% of child sexual abuse cases.

Whether children experience social and emotional effects of sexual abuse will likely be related to the severity and duration of the abuse, the relationship between the child and the offender, the age of onset of the abuse, the child's current developmental level, and the presence of life threat during the abuse. Younger children may display symptoms of anxiety and depression, sleep disturbances, difficulties separating from their parents, copying of adult sexual activity, and a general regression in behavior. School-aged children may also display symptoms of anxiety, depression, and posttraumatic stress. However, they are also likely to exhibit problems in school and may have physical complaints (e.g., headaches, stomach aches) and discipline problems. In adolescents, the emergence of delinquent behavior may occur, including drug and alcohol problems and running away. Adolescents may also evince school problems, in addition to symptoms of depression and anxiety, and may make suicide attempts. Many of these symptoms frequently persist into adulthood. In fact, women who report a history of childhood sexual abuse have higher levels of sexual disturbance, anxiety and fear, depression, substance abuse, and suicide attempts than their non-abused counterparts.

TREATMENT APPROACHES

Recent research on treatment of sexually abused children and nonoffending parents indicates that cognitive behavioral treatment shows promise for reducing the effects of sexual abuse. Of course, treatment should focus directly on the problems that children and families are experiencing rather than exercising a "one size fits all" program. Components of treatment that appear particularly promising include the following:

Psychoeducation

Information is provided to the child and parent about child sexual abuse, including who is responsible for the abuse (the offender), common mental health effects on children who have been sexually abused, potential course of symptoms, and general knowledge regarding sexuality. Further, the child and family are given information regarding steps they can take to reduce risk for future abuse.

Cognitive Restructuring

Cognitive restructuring may be used with children to correct any misinterpretations they have (e.g., "only bad children are abused, therefore I must be bad"; "the sexual abuse was my fault"). Similar strategies are often used with parents to correct any misconceptions they may have about their child and the abuse (e.g., "the child is damaged goods").

Relaxation

Relaxation strategies (i.e., deep breathing, progressive muscle relaxation) are often employed for children and parents who have elevated levels of anxiety.

Exposure

Exposure techniques may be used to help break the link between anxiety and reminders of the abuse and include recapitulation of the abuse along with use of anxiety management. Telling about the abuse can be conducted through a variety of means, such as direct talk or telling through drawing or puppets.

In addition to providing treatment related to child symptoms of abuse, current approaches in the child sexual abuse field also target the other family members and the offender. Stopping future sexual abuse will require effort from the whole family.

REFERENCES

Berliner, L., & Elliott, M. D. (1996). Sexual abuse of children. In J. Briere, L. Berliner, J. A. Bulkley, C. Jenny, & T. Reid (Eds.), *The APSAC handbook on child maltreatment* (pp. 51–71). Thousand Oaks, CA: Sage.

Kendall-Tackett, K. A., Williams, L. M., & Finkelhor, D. (1993). Impact of sexual abuse on children: A review and synthesis of recent empirical studies. *Psychological Bulletin, 113,* 164–180.

Lutzker, J. R., Bigelow, K. M., Swenson, C. C., Doctor, R. M., & Kessler, M. L. (1999). Problems related to child abuse and neglect. In S. Netherton, D. Holmes, & C. E. Walker (Eds.), *Comprehensive textbook of child and adolescent disorders: A guide to DSM-IV* (pp. 520–548). New York: Oxford University Press.

Swenson, C. C., & Hanson, R. F. (1998). Sexual abuse of children: Assessment, research, and treatment. In J. R. Lutzker (Ed.), *Handbook on research and treatment in child abuse and neglect* (pp. 475–499). New York: Plenum.

Swenson, C. C., Henggeler, S. W., Kaufman, K. L., Schoenwald, S. K., & Randall, J. (1998). Changing the social ecologies of adolescent sexual offenders: Implications of the success of multisystemic therapy in treating serious antisocial behavior in adolescents. *Child Maltreatment, 3,* 330–338.

C. E. Ezzell
C. C. Swenson
Medical University of South Carolina

CHILD ABUSE

CHILDHOOD DEPRESSION

DEFINITIONS AND COMMON SUBTYPES

Depression is a disorder that has as its defining symptom a disturbance in mood (either dysphoria, anger, or anhedonia) and a cluster of emotional, cognitive, behavioral, and vegetative symptoms that occur for an extended duration and result in functional impairment. Depressive disorders are episodic. In other words, the symptoms tend to remit after a period of time and then return again in the future. However, some individuals may experience a chronic depressive disorder in which there are no symptom-free periods or in which symptom-free periods are short in duration. The *Diagnostic and Statistical Manual of Mental Disorders*–fourth edition (*DSM-IV;* American Psychiatric Association, 1994) identifies three diagnostic categories of unipolar depressive disorders: major depression, dysthymic disorder, and depressive disorder not otherwise specified. The diagnostic categories differ in the number, severity, and duration of symptoms. Major depression is the most severe expression of depression in terms of the number of symptoms and functional impairment of the disorder. Dysthymic disorder is less severe both in terms of number and experience of symptoms, but it is a long-lasting disturbance. Depressive disorder not otherwise specified is a category for children who exhibit depressive symptoms but do not meet the diagnostic criteria for either of the other two disorders. The diagnostic categories are not exclusive. A child may experience more than one depressive disorder at a time. For example, a child may experience an episode of major depression which is superimposed on a preexisting dysthymic disorder. Criteria for a diagnosis of depression are generally the same (with some difference in duration) for youths and adults.

PREVALENCE OF CHILDHOOD DEPRESSION

Prevalence rates of depression differ across ages, subgroups, and diagnostic categories. Depressive disorders are rare among preschool-aged children and tend to be associated with extreme abuse, chaos, or neglect in this age group. Among elementary school-aged children, investigators commonly report rates of just under 2% for major depressive disorder and between 2% to 3% for dysthymic disorder. Prevalence rates increase with age and are higher for adolescents, with investigators reporting rates of 3% for major depression and even higher rates for dysthymic disorder. Prior to adolescence there does not appear to be a difference in the prevalence rates of depressive disorders for boys and girls. Following puberty, more females report depressive disorders than males. Children of color, especially females, tend to be at greater risk relative to Anglo males. Higher prevalence rates also are reported for children with a medical condition, learning disability, or other type of exceptionality.

PROGNOSIS

Depressive disorders during childhood tend to be of longer duration and are more severe than those experienced by adults. Although most children naturally recover from an episode of depression, depression leaves children impaired socially, cognitively, and academically. The average duration of an episode of major depressive disorder is reported to be between 32 and 36 weeks. The rate of recovery tends to be slow, with the greatest improvement starting between the 24th and 36th week. Within six months of the onset of an episode of major depressive disorder, the episode has remitted for 40% of the children. At one year, 80% of the children are no longer experiencing a depressive episode. The natural course of dysthymic disorder is more protracted, with the average length of an episode being three years. A chronic course is reported for a significant percentage of depressed children, although it is not clear whether these figures vary between the diagnostic groups (major depression and dysthymic disorder).

A few variables have been identified that appear to predict the duration of a depressive episode. Age of onset may be a predictor, but results of this research have been contradictory. Several investigators reported that an earlier age of onset was associated with a more protracted course, and others have reported that a more problematic course was found for youngsters who reported a first depressive episode following puberty. Severity is a definite predictor of duration, with more severe episodes having a more protracted course. Family dysfunction is associated with a more protracted course. Finally, gender has been associated with the overall severity and course of a depressive disorder, with females experiencing more severe and protracted episodes.

Depressive disorders are recurrent. Within three years of the first depressive episode, over half the children will experience another episode. Within five years, about 75% will have experienced another episode. Thus, evidence suggests that depressed youths are at risk for experiencing additional depressive episodes. In addition, a substantial percentage of youngsters who are depressed will later develop bipolar (manic-depressive) disorder. It appears as though an episode of psychotic depression or comorbid attention-deficit/hyperactivity disorder (ADHD) may be risk factors for the later occurrence of bipolar disorder.

COMORBIDITY

Most depressed youths are experiencing at least one other psychological disorder, a phenomenon referred to as comorbidity. Approximately one-half to 75% of depressed youths are experiencing another psychological disorder. Anxiety disorders are the most common co-occurring disorders; however, conduct disorder, oppositional defiant disorder, and ADHD are other common co-occurring disorders. During adolescence some additional comorbid conditions may be present, including substance abuse and eating disorders.

ETIOLOGY OF DEPRESSIVE DISORDERS

There does not appear to be a single cause of depressive disorders during childhood. Rather, there appear to be a number of possible biological and psychosocial causes, and these vary across youngsters. The most widely accepted causal theories of depressive disorders are stress diathesis models in which stress within the youngster's life interacts with a vulnerability within the child (the daithesis) to produce a depressive episode. The nature of the stress varies across children from chronic to acute, and from daily hassles (day-to-day frustrations) to chronic strains (e.g., living in a conflict-ridden environment, having a chronically ill family member) or major life events (e.g., divorce of parents, death of a family member). The theories of depression are defined by the nature of the diathesis and include both biological and psychosocial variables. The diathesis may have a genetic or psychosocial basis. Data from family studies have consistently shown higher concordance rates of mood disorders in monozygotic twins than dizygotic twins, siblings, or other first-degree relatives, suggesting an inherited biological predisposition.

Most biological theories of depression assume that the diathesis is a dysfunction of one or more neurochemical systems in the brain. The "classic" biogenic amine theory suggests that depression is caused by depletion of monoamines at critical synapses in the brain (Schildkraut, 1965). The monoamine system includes the neurotransmitters norepinephrine, serotonin, and dopamine. In individuals with depression, the levels of these neurotransmitters are hypothesized to be below a critical level. The biogenic amine theory, in its original form, was too simplistic. Subsequent modifications of this model have emphasized long-term changes in receptor function. Additionally, there is an increasing appreciation of the synergistic action of multiple neurotransmitter systems. These theories have been buttressed by the effectiveness of medications that prevent the reuptake of serotonin and norepinephrine. Hormonal and neuroendocrine systems also may be involved in depression. Hormonal changes during puberty, especially in estrogen levels in girls, may be linked with depression. Girls appear to release more growth hormone (GH) than boys, and GH release was found to be greater during sleep of prepubertal children with depression. The hypothalamic-thyroid system may contribute to depression as well. Some patients with clinical depression have exhibited mild hypothyroidism, with thyroid replacement therapy decreasing depressive symptoms.

A number of psychosocial models of depression during childhood have received empirical support. Cognitive models have received much attention in the adult and child depression literature. The basic premise of these models is that a depressive disorder stems from a disturbance in the child's thinking. The specific disturbance varies across theories. According to Beck's (1967) cognitive theory, depression stems from a disturbance in the memory structures that form the rules that guide an individual's attention, perceptions of experiences, and other thought processes. Due to distortions in thinking, the depressed individual views him- or herself, day-to-day experiences, and the future, and the impact of these events on the self, in an unrealistically negative way. The thinking of the depressed youngster is characterized by thoughts of worthlessness, unlovability, and loss. In some instances, due to stressful life situations, the negative thoughts of these children accurately reflect reality. Since the memory structures are being formed through learning experiences within this environment, they reflect the environment. The problem for the youngster is that these memory structures guide the child's thinking, especially perceptions about the self, when he or she is not in the stressful environment. Thus, the youngster misperceives the actions and intentions of others as well as their meaning for the self. These negative thoughts are believed to cause the mood disturbance and other symptoms of depression. The primary target of intervention is the individual's distortions in thinking and the behaviors and environmental events that support them.

Another theory that has received a great deal of empirical attention is the learned helplessness model of depression (Abramson, Metalsky, & Alloy, 1989). Once again, it is hypothesized that a disturbance in the child's thinking interacts with stress to cause a depressive disorder. When a negative or stressful event occurs, the individual asks him- or herself why it happened. The answer to this question is referred to as an attribution and each affects the youngster's emotional adjustment. Depressed individuals tend to attribute the causes of undesirable events to something inside themselves; they see these causes as affecting various things, and as recurring over time. Thus, they think they are helpless in the face of a negative event that they cannot stop. When desirable things occur, they attribute the cause to something outside of themselves, accepting that the benefit is specific to the situation and that it is not likely to occur again.

Other psychosocial theories of the etiology of depressive disorders among children include a deficit in the youngster's ability to form and maintain interpersonal relationships, deficits in emotion regulation skills, deficits in social skills, deficits in social problem solving, and a lack of personal competence. As noted above, no single theory seems to account for all cases of depression. Thus, it is likely that any of the aforementioned variables may be one of a complex set of variables including stress that causes depression. Furthermore, a disturbance in one area is likely to impact other areas of functioning. For example, within a stressful environment, a biological disturbance could cause a cognitive disturbance, which could lead to behaviors that undermine the child's happiness. Similarly, a child who learns to see him or herself as unlovable is likely, in a stressful environment, to experience a change in brain chemistry that supports the negative way of thinking and maladaptive social interactions that confirm the belief that he or she is unlovable.

ASSESSMENT OF DEPRESSION DURING CHILDHOOD

Assessment of childhood depression utilizes a multi-trait, multi-informant, and multi-method approach. Typically, a combination of paper-and-pencil measures along with a diagnostic interview are completed by the child and his or her parents. The questionnaires and interview are designed to assess the presence and severity of symptoms associated with depressive disorders. Because depression is such a subjectively experienced disturbance and many of the symptoms are not visible to others, the youngster is the primary source of information about his or her phenomenological experience. Parents are a good source of information about more observable symptoms and time-related information about the date of onset and the duration of the episode. Measures of symptom severity, including self-report questionnaires, interviews, and parent report measures serve as a means of assessing the presence and initial severity of a depressive disorder. Following best practices guidelines, we assess for the presence and severity of a depressive disorder using a semistructured interview with the child and his or her caregivers. In addition, we use a self-report measure as a means of further quantifying the subjective severity of depressive symptoms. A variety of tools may be used to assess cognitive, interpersonal, and family variables that inform treatment. Ongoing assessment is necessary to determine whether an intervention is effective.

TREATMENT OF DEPRESSIVE DISORDERS DURING CHILDHOOD

Similar interventions are used for treating depressed children, adolescents, and adults. Both medical and psychological treatments have been successfully employed with children. The "advent of antidepressants, and their effectiveness in the treatment of depression of adult patients, can be considered the greatest success in psychiatric treatment in the past four decades" (Campbell & Cueva, 1995, p. 1266). Historically, the same could not be said about antidepressants and the treatment of depressive disorders during childhood and adolescence. In fact, as recently as 1995, Vitiello and Jensen stated that there "is still no proven superiority of antidepressant drugs over placebo in children or adolescents" (p. 75). However, research is beginning to appear that suggests that the selective serotonin reuptake inhibitors (SSRIs) may be effective treatments for depressed adolescents. Despite the lack of a substantial body of empirical evidence for the efficacy of antidepressants, they are so commonly used with depressed youngsters that many consider them to be the standard of care (Dillon, Tsai, & Alessi, 1996).

Pharmacological Treatments

Currently, there are four main classes of antidepressants that may be prescribed to youths: tricyclics, monoamine oxidase inhibitors, SSRIs, and second-generation antidepressants. The specific mechanisms of action of the antidepressants is on the monoamine neurotransmitter system, or more specifically, on the neurotransmitters, including acetylcholine, norepinephrine, serotonin, and (to a lesser extent) dopamine. Antidepressant medications influence the metabolism or reuptake of the neurotransmitters, which results in increased levels of functionally available neurotransmitters. Most of the antidepressants have a broad spectrum effect. In other words, they affect the metabolism or reuptake of acetylcholine,

norepinephrine, serotonin, and dopamine. A few of them are more focused and influence specific brain monoamine systems. Desipramine, for example, mainly affects norepinephrine reuptake, fluoxetine affects serotonin, and buproprion affects dopamine.

Conclusions regarding the effectiveness of the tricyclic antidepressants is mixed for children. Initial controlled studies indicated no difference between imipramine and placebos. When the plasma level of imipramine is controlled for, treatment success rates have been high. There is no evidence that the tricyclics are effective with adolescents. This outcome does not appear to vary depending on whether the youngsters are treated as inpatients or outpatients, nor does it appear to be affected based on whether the youngsters are experiencing an endogenously- or exogenously-based disorder. In contrast, there is room for optimism concerning the effects of the SSRIs. Investigators are using more sophisticated and methodologically elegant experimental designs, and they are reporting that the SSRIs are superior to a placebo in double-blind studies with depressed adolescents.

There are two basic approaches to pharmacotherapy. The more conservative approach involves using a single medication, and another approach involves poly-medicating. Proponents of the latter approach believe that one medication may potentiate the effectiveness of the other medication. There is some literature that suggests that adolescents who are nonresponsive to an antidepressant may respond favorably to augmentation of the antidepressant with lithium. Other augmentation strategies include the use of thyroid supplements and stimulants.

In a recent article, five preeminent psychiatrists were interviewed regarding their approach to treating depressed children and adolescents (Ambrosini, Emslie, Greenhill, Kutcher, & Weller, 1995). All five stated that they would first try an SSRI due to its efficacy, safety profile, and because they produce fewer side effects. Another rule that seemed to guide their choice of treatment was the presence and types of comorbid conditions. If the youngster was experiencing a comorbid ADHD, then buproprion would be the first choice or a tricyclic may be used. If the youngster was experiencing comorbid obsessive-compulsive disorder, then fluoxetine would be the preferred choice. If the youngster was experiencing a comorbid anxiety disorder, then doxipin or amitriptyline was the preferred medication. Since there is no way to know with complete confidence whether a youngster is going to respond to an antidepressant, recommendations were offered regarding the duration that a medication would be tried before moving to an alternative. The recommended length of a trial was six to ten weeks. If the medication did not result in improvement during this time period, then an augmentation strategy would be initiated. If the medication regimen is successful, the recommended duration of treatment ranges from two months to two years.

Psychological Treatments

A number of studies have been published that document the effectiveness of psychological interventions for depressed youths. Almost all of these investigations have compared the effectiveness of cognitive-behavioral treatments to control conditions. Results indicate that cognitive-behavioral treatments are effective. Cognitive-behavioral interventions are time-limited, relatively short-term, structured interventions that are designed to change the depressed youngster's maladaptive style of thinking, behaving, and managing emotions. The child and therapist form a collaborative team in which the child is responsible for describing his or her symptoms, stressors, thoughts, behaviors, and strategies for managing unpleasant emotions. The therapist is responsible for teaching the child to independently employ a variety of coping, cognitive, and interpersonal skills. More specifically, children are taught a variety of skills for emotion management, coping with stress, interacting with peers and adults, and problem solving. They are also taught how to identify and change negatively distorted thoughts about the self, world, and future. Within the treatment literature, the interventions typically consist of 12 to 16 one-hour group sessions over a period of 5 to 12 weeks. The sessions are highly structured and usually involve a blending of the child's experiences with the acquisition of coping skills. The coping skills are taught in a sequential fashion in which they build upon one another. At the end of each session, the youngsters are assigned therapeutic home-work to monitor the application of the skill that was taught during the session. The treatment approach is directive and involves much more than playing with the child or discussing how the child is feeling.

To produce some initial enhancement in mood, activity scheduling and mastery experiences are employed. The youngsters are asked to do fun things and to engage in behaviors that enable them to feel successful. In addition, engagement in pleasant activities provides them with a skill for controlling their emotions and some distance from their depressogenic thinking. The overall goal of treatment is change at the level of the memory structures that serve as the central rules for deriving meaning from daily interactions. Cognitive restructuring procedures are used to change the child's automatic thoughts and the rules that underlie them. In addition, cognitive modeling, behavioral assignments, problem solving, and self-instructional training may be used to help the youngster change his or her maladaptive thoughts. The most powerful way to produce a change in thinking is through behavioral assignments. Thus, children are given enactive assignments that require action and provide the youngsters with concrete evidence that is contrary to a dysfunctional rule or thought.

Parents may be included in the treatment program in a number of different capacities. They receive education about depressive disorders during childhood and are asked to recognize and reinforce their child's use of the coping strategies that he or she is learning during treatment. They may be taught a variety of parenting skills, and also may be instructed to change any of their own behaviors that contribute to their child's depressive disorder. Since depressed children are more likely to have a depressed parent, the parent may be encouraged to seek treatment. In other instances, the entire family may be encouraged to participate in therapy.

REFERENCES

Abramson, L. Y., Metalsky, G. I., & Alloy, L. B. (1989). Hopelessness depression: A theory-based subtype of depression. *Psychological Review, 96,* 358–372.

Ambrosini, P. J., Emslie, G. J., Greenhill, L. L., Kutcher, S., & Weller, E. B. (1995). Selecting a sequence of antidepressants for treating depression in youth. *Journal of Child and Adolescent Psychopharmacology, 5,* 233–240.

American Psychiatric Association. (1994). *Diagnostic and statistical manual of mental disorders* (4th ed.). Washington, DC: Author.

Beck, A. T. (1967). *Depression: Clinical, experimental, and theoretical aspects.* New York: Harper & Row.

Campbell, M., & Cueva, J. E. (1995). Psychopharmacology in child and adolescent psychiatry: A review of the past seven years. Part II. *Journal of the American Academy of Child and Adolescent Psychiatry, 34,* 1262–1272.

Dillon, J. E., Tsai, L., & Alessi, N. E. (1996). Child and adolescent psychopharmacology: A decade of progress. In F. L. Mak & C. C. Nadelson (Eds.), *International Review of Psychiatry* (pp. 379–423).

Schildkraut, J. (1965). The catecholamine hypothesis of affective disorders: A review of supporting evidence. *American Journal of Psychiatry, 122,* 508–522.

Vitiello, B., & Jensen, P. S. (1995). Developing clinical trials in children and adolescents. *Psychopharmacology Bulletin, 31,* 75–81.

K. D. STARK
S. SWEARER
D. SOMMER
L. GULI
University of Texas, Austin

ADHD
CHILD PSYCHOLOGY
COGNITIVE BEHAVIOR THERAPY
DEPRESSION
MAJOR DEPRESSIVE DISORDER
PSCHOSTIMULANT TREATMENT FOR CHILDREN
SSRI
SUICIDE BEHAVIOR AMONG YOUTHS

CHINA, PSYCHOLOGY IN

EARLY HISTORY

Chinese psychological thought may be traced as far back as 500 B.C. in diverse philosophical, political, and other writings. A distinctive feature of ancient Chinese philosophy was its emphasis on education in cultivating human personality. The great Chinese philosopher-educator Confucius (551–479 B.C.), who had profound influence on the development of China's cultural history, was one of the first scholars to discuss the essence of human nature and how it can be modified through education. The Confucian principle of education was the imitation of the model behavior of sages and scholars, a principle that still influences China's current educational system. Later, Xun Zi (313–328 B.C.) developed a systematic theory of knowledge stressing that the mind, as a function of the body, is capable of knowing the external world, and human nature can be modified by external influences. He proposed the trinity of human nature, feeling, and desire. These examples indicate the richness of psychological thought embodied in ancient Chinese philosophy. Problems such as the mind-body relationship, the origin and acquisition of knowledge, and the nature-nurture controversy were discussed together with other general philosophical and epistemological issues.

Modern Chinese scientific psychology came into existence after China had more contact with the West. During the first decades of the 20th century the first group of Chinese students went to Europe and the United States to study psychology, returned to China, and established psychology as an independent scientific discipline. Psychology was first taught in some pedagogical institutions during the late Qing dynasty (c. 1900). The earliest psychology laboratory was established at Peking University in 1917. In 1921 the Chinese Psychological Society was founded, and the first psychology journal appeared in 1922. With the introduction of the Western educational system into China, psychology expanded rapidly, so that in the 1930s there were about 10 departments of psychology in various universities. Around this period more psychological organizations were established, including the Society of Psychological Testing, the Society of Psychoanalysis, and the Society of Mental Health. The main influences in the 1930s were Functionalism and Behaviorism, although Gestalt psychology and psychoanalysis were also introduced into China.

The outbreak of the Sino-Japanese War in 1937, which resulted in the military occupation of a large part of China by Japan, caused serious setbacks in the progress of psychology. Major universities were moved to temporary quarters in the mountainous regions in western China, and with shortages of books and equipment, the development of psychology was halted. This lasted until the end of World War II.

PSYCHOLOGY AFTER THE FOUNDING OF THE PEOPLE'S REPUBLIC OF CHINA

The People's Republic of China was founded in 1949. Although psychology in China before 1949 had been mainly Western-oriented, after the founding of the People's Republic, Chinese psychologists started a movement for reform and independence from Western influences. The new psychology took Marxist dialectical materialism as its guiding principle; psychology in the then–Soviet Union was looked upon as the model for Chinese psychology and the Pavlovian theory of conditioned reflexes was seen as the physiological basis of human behavior. Marxism stressed that human beings are social beings, constantly under the influences of society, and that consciousness is a mental reflection of the material and social world in which one lives. As to the origin of knowledge, according to the Chinese leader Mao Tzedong, sensory knowledge is the first level of knowledge, while rational knowledge formed by a process of abstraction and generalization is a higher level of knowledge.

During the first three decades of the People's Republic, Western social psychology and psychological testing were abolished on the grounds that the former ignored the class struggle of social groups, which is a basic principle of Marxist social theory, and the latter placed too much emphasis on individual differences, laying the groundwork for the selection of children of the elite class into schools. Following the educational system in the Soviet Union, there were no independent departments of psychology in Chinese universities. Psychology was a secondary discipline in the departments of philosophy or education.

After 1949, as psychology was being reformed based on the Soviet model, it was frequently attacked by leftist political ideologists. It was argued that in basic psychological research, many experiments without practical significance were conducted in the laboratory; such controlled variables were simply nonexistent in real-life situations. Was this kind of research really necessary? Hence, the role of basic research in psychology was challenged. Critics often asked, "Is psychology a necessary discipline or is it simply a luxury science? In a developing country like China, with a vast population and modest resources, should such a luxury science be developed at all?"

These attacks on psychology set the stage for the liquidation of psychology between 1966 and 1976, the period of the well-known Chinese Cultural Revolution. Psychology was attacked as a so-called bourgeois pseudoscience, a mouthpiece of Western capitalism. During the Cultural Revolution, psychology was uprooted completely as a scientific discipline. Leading psychologists were labelled as "reactionary academic authorities," scientific research and teaching institutions in psychology were dissolved, and psychologists were dispatched to remote areas of the country to work on the farms. The turmoil ended with the termination of the Cultural Revolution in 1976.

RECENT DEVELOPMENTS

Soon after the end of the Cultural Revolution, from 1978 on, the Chinese government launched a policy of reform and opening-up to the outside world. The change has pushed Chinese psychology into a new era of development. New departments of psychology opened in many universities; there are now more than 20 such departments, and the Chinese Psychological Society now has about 5,000 members.

Chinese psychology has since moved into the international community. The Chinese Psychological Society joined the International Union of Psychological Science (IUPsyS) in 1980; many Chinese psychologists have visited other countries; and psychologists from abroad have lectured in China's universities. In 1983, Nobel laureate Herbert Simon visited Beijing and lectured for three months on cognitive psychology. Exchanges were established between foreign and Chinese universities.

As experimental psychology has become less affected by ideology, cognitive theory has penetrated into many fields of psychology. Basic research in cognitive processes has increased, and studies of perception, memory, and learning have attracted consistent interest. Not only has the acquisition of knowledge been studied through a cognitive perspective, even the cultivation of moral qualities of students has been viewed in terms of moral cognition and moral beliefs.

The Chinese language, as an ideographic language with a unique writing and structural system, has attracted much attention in attempts to understand its acquisition and learning processes. Studies have included the ideographic and sound characteristics of Chinese characters, their reading and comprehension, the relationship between the Chinese language and Western languages, and the hemispheric laterality of information processing of the Chinese language. Exciting findings have been reported in this field.

Neuropsychology is also a field of interest; studies have included neural mechanisms of memory, memory changes in aging, the effects of drugs on behavior, and psychoimmunology. Recently, studies have been made using PET and fMRI on basic cognitive functioning.

The areas of developmental and educational psychology have always been lively fields of research in China. There are 300 million children in China, and any new knowledge in this field would have implications for the cultivation of an entire generation. About half of the 5,000 Chinese psychologists now work in normal (teacher training) universities or pedagogical institutes.

Since the early 1980s, Piaget's genetic theory of development has had great impact on Chinese developmental psychology. Collaborative research teams have been organized from various universities and institutes to study the mental characteristics of children at different age levels. A series of papers was published on the development of children's concepts of number, class, color, shape, direction, and cause and effect. Another area of research has been the study of supernormal (talented) and mentally retarded children. Yet an additional area of study has stemmed from China's family planning policy advocating the "one-child" family program (only one child per family). The cognitive and social development of these only children has been studied by Chinese psychologists.

Since China has a large population and only a limited number of colleges and universities, college enrollment is extremely competitive. Thus, most schools concentrate on teaching essential school subjects, and try to make students acquire high examination scores in preparation for application to universities. The children are usually overloaded by homework and have no time to devote to their own interests or to develop potential talents. This kind of educational model is now called Examination-Oriented Education and is to be abolished. In its place, the Ministry of Education is advocating the Quality-Oriented Education model to give children a rounded education—morally, intellectually, physically, and aesthetically. Such an education is achieved by improving teaching methods, revising curriculum arrangement, stressing moral education, and requiring students to participate in social activities.

Psychologists work in practical fields in which psychology can make effective contributions to society. Health psychology and psychological counseling are becoming popular in China, the latter mainly serving the younger generation. A large number of counseling centers have been established in schools and social institutions. Personnel selection and human resource evaluation centers have been set up to aid in the selection of government employees and workers in industrial and commercial enterprises. Other newly developed applied fields are industrial psychology and managerial psychology. The economic reform of China calls for the introduction of new methods of management in industrial enterprises. Incentive and motivational studies have been carried out to promote efficiency. Managerial assessment methods are being introduced from Western countries and adapted for domestic use. Psychology in China, after having undergone full-fledged development for only 20 years after the Cultural Revolution, has developed into a mature scientific discipline able to serve society in both its basic and its applied fields.

REFERENCES

Jing, Q. C. (1994). Development of psychology in China. *International Journal of Psychology, 29,* 667–675.

Zhang, H. C. (1987). People's Republic of China. In A. R. Gilgen & C. K. Gilgen (Eds.), *International handbook of psychology.* New York: Greenwood Press.

Q. C. JING
Institute of Psychology, Chinese Academy of Sciences

CHOI, DENNIS

Dennis Choi has contributed importantly to current understanding of mechanisms responsible for neuronal cell death after acute central nervous system (CNS) insults, including NMDA receptor-mediated excitotoxicity, excessive calcium or zinc influx, and programmed cell death. Choi was born in Ann Arbor, Michigan, and grew up in Watertown, Massachusetts. He graduated from Harvard College in 1974, and in 1978 received both the MD and PhD degrees (the latter in pharmacology) from Harvard University and the Harvard-MIT Program in Health Sciences and Technology. After completing residency and fellowship training in neurology at Harvard, he joined the neurology faculty at Stanford University in 1983.

In 1991, Choi went to St. Louis to be the Jones Professor and Head of Neurology at Washington University Medical School, and neurologist-in-chief at Barnes-Jewish Hospital. At Washington University he also currently directs the Center for the Study of Nervous System Injury and the McDonnell Center for Cellular and Molecular Neurobiology, and is a co-master of a medical-student academic society, the Lowry-Moore Society. He is the current president of the Society for Neuroscience, chairman of the U.S. National Committee to the International Brain Research Organization, and past vice-president of the American Neurological Association. He has served on the councils of the National Institute of Neurological Disorders and Stroke, the Society for Neuroscience, the Winter Conference for Brain Research, and the Neurotrauma Society. He is a member of the editorial boards of more than a dozen journals, including *Science,* and is a founding co-editor of *Neurobiology of Disease,* a new journal positioned at the interface of basic and clinical neuroscience.

Choi is an associate of the Neurosciences Institute in San Diego, a trustee of the Grass Foundation, a member of the Dana Alliance for Brain Research, and a member of the board on Neuroscience and Behavioral Health at the Institute of Medicine. He also is a member of the scientific advisory boards of several foundations and companies, the former including the American Paralysis Foundation, the Hereditary Disease Foundation, the Max-Planck Institute in Heidelberg, and the Korea Institute for Advanced Study (KIAS). He is a past member of advisory committees to the Food and Drug Agency and the National Institute on Aging. His research has been recognized by the 1992 Wakeman Award, the 1994 Silvio Conte Decade of the Brain Award from the National Foundation for Brain Research, a Bristol-Myers Squibb Unrestricted Neurosciences Grant Award, the 1997 Ho-Am Prize in Medical Science from the Samsung Foundation, and the 1998 Reeve Irvine Medal for work relevant to spinal cord injury.

STAFF

CHOMSKY, A. NOAM (1928–   )

A. Noam Chomsky is a controversial figure in psycholinguistics and probably the foremost theorist in the field. For his achievements he has received numerous honorary doctorates. Chomsky was educated at the University of Pennsylvania, where he received the BA, MA, and PhD (1955). From the time he received the PhD, he has been on the faculty of Massachusetts Institute of Technology, although he has offered courses and lectured throughout the world, including Oxford and Berkeley.

Chomsky's books include *Syntactic Structures, Current Issues in Linguistic Theory, Aspects of the Theory of Syntax, Cartesian Linguistics, Topics in the Theory of Generative Grammar, The Sound Pattern of English* (with Morris Halle), *Language and the Mind, Studies on Semantics in Generative Grammar, Reflections on Language,* and *Language and Responsibility.*

Chomsky views the understanding of language as genetically determined and developing comparably to other bodily organs. Because the human brain is preprogrammed by a "language acquisition device," humans generate sentences the grammar of which is universal. Chomsky argues that humans have an innate capacity for grasping language. Learning a language is both species-specific and species-uniform: only humans have the capacity for language acquisition, and all languages share a common underlying logical structure. Thus the logic (or logical syntax) of all languages is the same. Terming the logical structure *deep structure,* Chomsky holds that it is not learned. The language that human beings must learn is a *surface structure*—phonetic sounds or the sentence as uttered. Chomsky's psycholinguistics is labeled *generative transformational grammar,* a system that integrates both surface and deep structure.

Chomsky's psycholinguistics is diametrically opposed to B. F. Skinner's verbal learning theory.

STAFF

CHROMOSOME DISORDERS

In 1962, after textbooks had proclaimed for 30 years that there were 48 chromosomes in human cells, Joe Hin Tjio and Albert Levan, by growing human cells in their laboratory, discovered that they contained only 23 pairs, or 46 chromosomes. This is important in understanding a chromosomal disorder such as Down syndrome, where 47 chromosomes exist in each cell.

Most knowledge of chromosomal changes that cause phenotypic or bodily alterations or abnormalities comes from the study of the genotype (gene arrangements) of the salivary gland chromosomes of the common fruit fly, *Drosophila melanogaster,* although the same changes apparently occur also in humans and other organisms. While many human diseases are inherited, in only a few are the exact chromosomal distortions known. One can only infer from the phenotypic results that chromosome and gene changes have occurred.

Chromosomes are double-spiraled molecules of deoxyribonucleic acid (DNA), the chemical basis of inheritance. Chromosomal disorders are believed to result from rearrangements in the order or number of genes in the chromosomes. These genes are atom clusters within the DNA molecules that determine the nature of ribonucleic acid or RNA molecules, which serve as messengers to determine the structure and function of organic tissues. This primary genetic substance, DNA, acts on and through the cytoplasm as a catalyst for changing the characteristics of cells to form skin and muscles, nerves and blood vessels, bones and connective tissue, and other specialized cells, without the genes themselves being changed in this process. Multiple genes are often involved in the same physical construction in the body: Not every physical trait is the result of the action of a single gene.

Various chromosome changes have genetic consequences:

1. *Chromosome breakage.* Rearrangement of chromosomes can result from X rays, ionizing radiation, perhaps cosmic rays, and many other still unknown biochemical or other environmental influences. In 1926 Herman J. Muller discovered that X rays produced mutations (phenotypic changes) in fruit flies and other forms, and thereafter cautioned the public to forego X-ray exams that were not absolutely necessary, suggesting also careful lead shielding of the breasts, ovaries, testes, and other vital areas. Muller's discovery of the effect of X rays led to the creation of the Thomas Hunt Morgan laboratory at Columbia University, which was later transferred to the California Institute of Technology, where Morgan, with such other pioneers as Calvin B. Bridges, Alfred Henry Sturtevant, Theodore Dobzhansky, and George Beadle, developed a cold storage museum of live mutants of *Drosophila melanogaster* and other fruit fly species grown in agar bottles, which are shared with genetic centers all over the world. The method of X-raying the fruit fly was utterly simple: Salivary gland larvae (which have enormous chromosomes, easily seen under ordinary microscopes) were put in medicine capsules, taped to a small piece of wood, and exposed to X rays not strong enough to kill the larvae, but sufficiently powerful and prolonged to develop mutations (gene changes) like curly or shortened wings, or bifurcated setae (bristles ending in a Y-shaped division). By examining the chromosomes of the altered offspring, one could tell where the mutated gene or genes were located from the break or breaks in the chromosomes created by the irradiation.

X rays can break a chromosome into one or more pieces, and in the rearrangement process a segment of one chromosome may be lost causing a mutation or phenotypic change. Thus a defective or abnormal recessive gene may now express itself, because the normal allele (corresponding gene on the sister chromosome) is lost and therefore cannot neutralize the impact of the defective gene. When chromosomal deficiencies in the human embryo have a lethal effect, the baby would not be born, so that lethal genes have no bearing on the evolution of a species.

2. *Crossover.* Chromosome pairs are twisted in a spiral around each other like mating earthworms, and may break at any homologous point—that is, on the same level in the two chromosomes of a pair. Meiosis (the reduction division that occurs in developing the gametes or sex cells, ova, and sperm) causes a separation of each pair of chromosomes, so that only one chromosome of each pair enters the egg or sperm. When a break occurs, one end of one chromosome may now connect to a broken end of the second chromosome, with the remaining two pieces also joining together, so as to form two entirely new and different chromosomes. This is called crossing over. Any two genes on the original chromosomes may now be separated by these breaks. It was found that the crossover frequency of chromosomes can aid in mapping the chromosomes (in which Bridges pioneered), because the crossover frequency varies in direct proportion to the distance between two genes.

3. *Duplication or loss of genes.* A piece breaks off one chromosome and attaches to its partner, duplicating in the second chromosome genes already present. The extra group of genes is usually less harmful than the loss of genes in the first chromosome, and if benign, may even create new inherited combinations. The chromosome with the deficiency (loss or change of genes) may result in a mutation or phenotypic change. Thus one amino acid missing in the DNA, among the 574 necessary amino acids that make up the normal code sequence for the hemoglobin molecule, can cause sickle-cell anemia (SCA). Protein chains in the DNA are called polypeptides. There are, in all, 20 amino acids that form the necessary body proteins for tissue building and energy. Only 10 of these are essential, since from them the body can create the remaining 10. The protein hemoglobin, which gives a red color to the blood corpuscles and the blood, is composed of four polypeptide chains, two alpha chains of 141 amino acids in length, and two betas, each of 146 amino acids, in sequence: Hemoglobin S individuals with SCA have glutamic acid missing in the sixth position of the beta chain, this protein factor being replaced by valine. SCA is found mostly in blacks, but also occasionally in Italians, Turks, and East Indians; it is caused by an autosomal recessive gene so that two carriers, each with one of the defective recessives, will have children with a 25% chance of inheriting the anemia. The resultant densely compressed sickle-shaped red cells clog the capillaries and do not survive for the normal length of time, so that the body cannot manufacture red cells fast enough to replenish the failing supply of disintegrating sickle cells. With less hemoglobin bringing oxygen to the cells, the latter are starved, hence the anemic condition. Adults, though they can work in a mildly strenuous job, have a shortened life span.

4. *Translocations.* Chromosome segments are transferred from one chromosome to a nonhomologous one, causing sterility.

Thus any negative phenotypic expression at least cannot be passed on to the succeeding generations.

5. *Inversion.* A chromosome is broken in two or more places and a segment becomes inverted (turned end to end) before being reincorporated in the reconstructed chromosome. This is very common, and is the chief natural method for gene rearrangement in species evolution. However, the new hybrid may be isolated in its new form, since it is sterile in reproductive attempts with the original form (Pauli, 1949).

6. *Position effect.* A gene changed to a new chromosomal position on the same chromosome may display a changed phenotypic appearance in the organism.

7. *Polyploidy.* Failure of meiosis (the chromosomal reduction division in preparation for reproduction) to occur in a germ cell may double the normal chromosomal number in a gamete (sperm or egg). Triploids have three complete sets of chromosomes in the gametes instead of the two just mentioned. Or there is a duplication without separation of the chromosomes in mitosis (ordinary cell division), creating a tetraploid cell with four instead of two homologous chromosomes of each kind. We all normally possess polyploid cells in our livers and elsewhere, without their doing any noticeable harm (Pauli, 1949). Where polyploidy occurs in only one chromosome, an extra chromosome appears in the genotype that may cause a serious phenotypic change as in Down syndrome (DS, or mongolism), in which there is an extra #21 chromosome in each cell. A small percentage of abnormal births occurs in DS offspring, in which this extra autosome (non–sex-determining chromosome) causes the affected infant to be smaller, and its mental and physical development to be slower. Down syndrome victims have 47 chromosomes and function in a way opposite to PKU victims — in PKU, or phenylketonuria, an enzyme is lacking, so that the amino acid, phenylalanine, cannot be properly used by the body cells, causing abnormal brain development and nervous system function, resulting in mental retardation and other negative consequences. The disorder is caused by an autosomal recessive. In Down syndrome the extra chromosome causes the sufferer to produce too much of an enzyme that breaks down the necessary protein tryptophan, which occurs in milk and assists sleep, and is essential to normal brain function. Only a small percentage of DS births are definitely hereditary, but prebirth detection is possible by amniocentesis (examination of the mother's intrauterine fluid for the extra #21 chromosome).

REFERENCES

Pauli, W. F. (1949). *The world of life.* New York: Houghton Mifflin.

H. K. FINK
Honolulu, Hawaii

GENETIC DOMINANCE AND RECESSIVENESS HERITABILITY OF PERSONALITY

CIRCADIAN RHYTHM

A circadian rhythm (from *circa* = approximately, and *dies* = 24 hours) is a regular variation in a biological or behavioral characteristic, with period or cycle length of about 24 hr. For example, body temperature in a healthy human usually fluctuates a degree or two during the 24 hr, typically reaching its maximum a few hours before sleep onset and its low point an hour or two before waking, in a pattern fairly consistent for a given individual.

It has been known for hundreds of years that daily cycles of leaf and petal movements occur in some plants, and over the past few decades the ubiquity of circadian rhythmicity in animals has been demonstrated. Illustrations can be chosen from a broad range of functions from single-celled organisms to humans, as for instance spontaneous activity, hormone production, rate of cell division, urine volume and constituents, sensory acuity, digit span, reaction time, learning efficiency, drive intensity and reinforcement effects, muscular strength, response to noxious stimulation, spontaneous electrical discharge, and rate of drug uptake. Particularly striking is temporal variation in the organism's response to physiological challenges. The dose of amphetamine that will kill 78% of a group of rats at 0300 hours is lethal for only 7% if injected at 0600; several times as many mice will survive a given exposure to X-ray irradiation at 0800 as at 2000 hours; identical injections of lidocaine hydrochloride precipitate convulsions in 6% and 83% of rodents at 1500 and 2100 hours, respectively; inescapable shock is much more likely to induce stomach ulceration in rats during the dark 12 hr than during the light; allergic reactions to certain antigens tend to be more severe in the evening than during the morning hours. Time-related variations in therapeutic effectiveness and toxic side effects have been demonstrated for a number of medicinal substances routinely used with human patients.

Early observers assumed that daily rhythms are simply direct responses to such environmental signals as the natural sequence of day and night. This interpretation has been challenged by the discovery that, in the absence of such obvious time cues (Zeitgebers) as regularly alternating light and dark, many of the organism's cycles persist or "free run," but with a period deviating significantly from 24 hr and differing from individual to individual. The most widely accepted interpretation is that the organism possesses an intrinsic and innate quality of circadian rhythmicity, as if under the influence of an internal system of self-sustaining oscillators, ordinarily synchronized to exactly 24 hr by recurring external stimuli but not necessarily dependent upon them. The ability of many species to use the sun's position as a cue for maintaining directional orientation, constantly correcting for its relative movement during the day (the so-called time-compensated sun compass), seems to imply some sort of internal cycling or time sense.

The search for the postulated biological clock(s) has involved the examination of changes in the rhythms subsequent to surgical or chemical intervention. Among the sites thus implicated are the pineal gland (in birds) and the suprachiasmatic nucleus of the hypothalamus (in rodents). It must be noted, however, that free-running circadian rhythms have been recorded in tissue cultures and organs maintained in vitro and it is therefore likely that the concept of control by one or a few central pacemakers is an oversimplification.

Most investigators believe that the ontogenetic development of rhythms does not depend on exposure to time-giving cues in the immediate environment—in other words, that learning is not required. This is not to say, however, that the rhythms are immutable. It has clearly been demonstrated in some species that early experience with light/dark cycles a few hours longer or shorter than 24 hr can have a long-lasting effect on the free-running period of an individual's circadian rhythms.

It is hypothesized that loss of the normal temporal relations among the various circadian rhythms (internal desynchronization) interferes with the bodily economy and impairs psychological functioning. This may account in part for the perturbations experienced following rapid transmedidial travel and during irregular living schedules imposed by industrial shift work.

According to the standard terminology of chronobiology, the limits of a free-running circadian cycle are defined as 20 and 28 hr. Rhythms of slower frequency are designated "infradian," and those of faster frequency "ultradian."

SUGGESTED READING

Aschoff, J. (Ed.). (1981). *Handbook of behavioral neurobiology* (Vol. 4). New York: Plenum.

Finger, F. W. (1982). Circadian rhythms: Implications for psychology. *New Zealand Psychologist, 11,* 1–12.

Luce, G. G. (1978/1970). *Biological rhythms in psychiatry and medicine* [DHEW Publication No. (ADM)78–247]. Washington, DC: U.S. Government Printing Office.

Rusak, B., & Zucker, I. (1975). Biological rhythms and animal behavior. *Annual Review of Psychology, 26,* 137–171.

Rusak, B., & Zucker, I. (1979). Neural regulation of circadian rhythms. *Physiological Reviews, 59,* 449–526.

Suda, M., Hayaishi, O., & Nakagawa, H. (Eds.). (1979). *Biological rhythms and their central mechanism.* Amsterdam: Elsevier North Holland.

F. W. FINGER
University of Virginia

CLARK, KENNETH B. (1914–   )

Kenneth B. Clark was brought to New York City by his mother when he was four. He attended schools in Harlem and graduated from George Washington High School in 1931. He received the BS and MA from Howard University, and the PhD in psychology from Columbia University in 1940.

As a social psychologist, Clark worked with the lawyers in the series of cases on equality of educational opportunity which led to the historic 1964 *Brown v. Board of Education of Topeka, Kansas* decision. His studies on the effect of segregation on the personality development of children were cited by the U.S. Supreme Court in footnote 11 of the decision.

In 1946 Clark and his wife, Dr. Mamie Phipps Clark, founded

the interracial Northside Center for Child Development for the treatment of children with personality and learning problems. In 1964 he became founder and director of Harlem Youth Opportunities Unlimited (HARYOU), a prototype community development program which sought to increase the participation of low-income groups in decisions on education, housing, employment and training, and economic development.

A member of the faculty at City College of the City University of New York from 1942 to 1975, he was named Distinguished Professor of Psychology in 1971. He has been a member of the New York Board of Regents since 1966.

A member of Phi Beta Kappa and Sigma Xi, Clark has been president of the American Psychological Association (1970), of the Society for Psychological Studies of Social Issues (1959), and of the Metropolitan Applied Research Center (1967–1975). Since 1975 he has been president of Clark, Phipps, Clark & Harris, Inc., a human relations consulting firm.

STAFF

CLASSICAL CONDITIONING*

Classical conditioning is also called conditioned response, conditioned reflex, conditional response, and conditional reflex. Ivan Pavlov, the Russian physiologist and Nobel prize winner in physiology (1904), was not the first to discover the conditioned response—such a ubiquitous behavioral phenomenon had not gone unnoticed—but, beginning at the turn of the century, he was the first to explore its characteristics extensively. The great volume of work done in Pavlov's laboratory showed conditioning to have many unsuspected facets that led to the development of integrated conditioning theory and eventually to the application of conditioning explanations to behavior in general.

Conditioning, a form of learning, consists of the pairing of two stimuli, each of which originally produces a response different from the other. Typically, the response to one consists of little more than attending to it (technically called the orienting response). This is termed the conditioned stimulus (CS). The response to the other, the unconditioned stimulus (UCS), is the response that is measured directly, or occasionally indirectly, and is called the unconditioned response (UCR). The UCS evokes this response consistently and shows little or no adaptation; its occurrence is determined by the experimenter and not by the subject's actions. Conditioned stimuli that are often used include food-producing salivation, a shock that generates a defense or emotional reaction, a puff of air to the eye. Conditioning occurs if the other stimulus (the CS) acquires the capacity to produce a response like the one given to the UCS. This is called the conditioned response (CR). In other words, the original response to the CS has been modified and learning has occurred. The conditioned response is seldom if ever a replica of the UCR and may differ very markedly from it. This is a fact of importance with regard to the theoretical interpretation and meaning of conditioning; recognized early by American researchers, it led to the

*David S. Tuber contributed to the development of this article.

substitution of "response" for "reflex," since the concept of reflex implies a fixed and stereotyped movement.

EMPIRICAL CHARACTERISTICS OF THE CONDITIONED RESPONSE

Temporal Relationships of CS and UCS

An important variable in conditionability is the temporal relationship between the onset of the two stimuli—the potential CS and the UCS. The CS precedes the UCS in *forward conditioning;* the onset of CS and UCS coincide in *simultaneous conditioning;* the CS follows the UCS in *backward conditioning.* The bulk of the evidence suggests that conditioning does not occur in the backward or simultaneous situations. Occasionally, an experiment reports some minimal data interpreted as backward or simultaneous conditioning, but such responding may not really represent a conditioned response in the usual meaning of that term. Forward conditioning obviously occurs, but not as a simple relationship between the difference in onset times of the CS and the UCS. Figure 1 shows this relationship much as reported in a number of experiments that have used different responses as well as different species as subjects. Conditioning does not occur until the CS onset precedes the UCS onset by about 0.15 sec, and then the efficiency of conditioning rises quite steeply to reach a maximum at about 0.5 sec, from which point it begins a gradual decline. Although experiments differ somewhat in their temporal values, a curve such as that of Figure 1 with a maximum at about 0.5 sec or slightly less, has been obtained sufficiently often to lead one to conclude that it describes general and basic characteristics of conditioning that must be considered in any theoretical interpretation of the conditioned response.

In forward conditioning the CS may continue until the UCS occurs, then terminate with it. This is called *delayed conditioning.* In *trace conditioning* the CS continues for a short time, then terminates, and sometime later the UCS occurs. Conditioning develops in this case even though the CS was not physically present with the UCS. This phenomenon led Pavlov to state that the actual CS must be the neural trace left by the now departed physical stimulus. Trace conditioning develops more slowly than does delayed conditioning, but otherwise differs little from it.

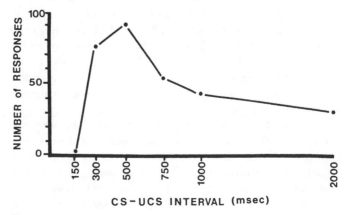

Figure 1.   The relationship between time of onset of the CS and the UCS.

Conditionable Stimuli and Conditionable Responses

There has been a great deal of research investigating the types of stimulation that can become conditioned stimuli and the types of responses that can be conditioned. It seems that any stimulus that can be properly controlled may serve as a conditioned stimulus. Lights and tones are used most frequently, but even a shock to one part of the body can serve as a CS for a response produced by a shock to another part of the body. A temperature change produced in the stomach can serve as a CS and is an example of a class of conditioning called *interoceptive-extroceptive*. Direct stimulation of the sensory areas of the brain can become conditioned stimuli. Words can also be CSs.

The range of conditionable responses is as wide as that of conditioned stimuli, and a variety of unconditioned stimuli have been used successfully to produce varying responses. Electric shock as a UCS can bring about specific motor responses at various locations, as well as more general emotional responses activating many components such as breathing, heart rate, or pupillary change. A sudden loud sound that produces a fear response may serve as a UCS. Attitudes and meanings of words can be conditioned as well. Just as stimulation of a visceral organ can be a CS, so also it may be a UCS. If this class of stimulation becomes both CS and UCS, it is termed *interoceptive-interoceptive* conditioning. This is an area of much research by Russian experimenters, and of course is directed toward the clinical problem of psychosomatic illness.

Conditioning can also occur even though no response was made to the UCS during pairing. Curare-type drugs, which block the neural impulses to the muscles, are administered during the pairing session, yet on recovery from the drug effect, conditioned responses are given.

What Is Conditioned?

In the laboratory, the CS is a specific stimulus and the UCS another specific stimulus producing a particular response. Actually, on both stimulus and response side what is learned is broad and general in nature as well as specific. On the stimulus side, this is demonstrated in the concept of *stimulus generalization.* If the CS for an acquired conditioned response is a tone of middle value, tests will show that the response is given to tones both higher and lower than the original tone, and that the strength of the response decreases as the tones depart farther and farther from the actual conditioning tone. The principle holds true for other sensory fields, and for language as well. If typical college students are visually presented with the word "won" as a CS, they will not only give a CR to the word "won" but also to "beat," "loss," and the homophone "one" in decreasing order. What is learned on the stimulus side is to respond to a class of stimuli, even though the experience is limited to a single member of that class.

The term of *response generalization* refers to a similar process with regard to the response that is conditioned. Two examples suffice. First, a standing sheep is conditioned to lift its leg with shock as the UCS; when turned on its back, the animal struggles to right itself. Second, a human subject with palm down and fingers on an electrode is conditioned to make an upward-moving extension response to a buzzer; when the arm is turned over so that the palm of

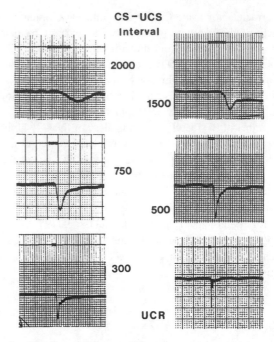

Figure 2. The form of the conditioned paw movement in a cat as a function of the CS–UCS onset differential. The thickened line at the top of each panel indicates the onset and offset of the CS, beginning at the left; the middle line is the response. The darker vertical lines are one second apart.

the hand is up, the subject responds to the CS alone with a flexion response that leads to an upward movement, although a downward movement can still be made. Clearly, more than a specific muscular movement has been learned. One can assume that what is conditioned represents a schema from which specific responses functionally appropriate to the realities of the current situation can be generated. The CR seems to be an intelligently adaptive process capable of being molded to the requirements of a new situation.

The conditioned response is no mere replica of the unconditioned response—no simple substitution of one stimulus for another in producing the same response. This fact is demonstrated by the nature of the response created in forward conditioning to different onset times between the CS and the UCS. The results of such an experiment are shown in Figure 2. The response being conditioned is the leg jerk to a very brief shock on the paw of a cat that is suspended and supported in a sling. The conditioned response given at CS–UCS intervals of 0.3, 0.5, 1.0, 1.5, and 2.0 seconds, as well as the response to the UCS alone, appear in the figure. It is clear that all responses differ from each other, and none of the conditioned responses is like the shock response. This is true not only for the form of the response but also for its latency—that is, the time between onset of the CS and the beginning of the response. In all cases, the conditioned responses begin before the shock would normally occur and anticipate it, but the latencies become longer and longer as the CS–UCS interval increases. Just as the sensitively sculpted wood figure is adapted to the varying grains and knots of the wood, so too the form of the CR is adapted to the temporal differences of the CS–UCS interval.

Extinction

If, after a conditioned response has been acquired by the pairing of conditioned and unconditioned stimuli, the CS is presented alone a number of times, responding to it will decline until, with enough presentations, the CR will no longer occur to the CS. This operation is called *experimental extinction,* or simply extinction. Pavlov concluded that the maintenance of the conditioned response was *conditional* upon the occasional occurrence of, or reinforcement by, the unconditioned stimulus, and he called such learned reflexes *conditional reflexes* to distinguish them from the innate reflexes. In the early translation of Pavlov's work from the Russian, the term "conditioned" rather than "conditional" was used, even though "conditional" is more appropriate to the phenomena.

The rate at which a response will extinguish is determined by various factors such as the number of training or reinforced trials that have been given, and the intensity of the unconditioned stimulus. These factors seem obvious, but there is another very potent factor in extinction that is not so obvious, called *partial reinforcement.* If, during the conditioning process, reinforced trials are not given steadily but are randomly mixed with nonreinforced presentations of the CS, the resulting conditioned response will require more trials before extinction occurs than it would have if all trials had been reinforced. The rate of extinction will depend upon the ratio of reinforced to nonreinforced trials during the training; up to a certain limit, resistance to extinction increases as the proportion of nonreinforced trials increases. This same characteristic is found in many other types of learning; the partial reinforcement effect is a basic characteristic of behavior in general, as is also inconsistency of reinforcement in the world.

If the response is extinguished and some extended period of time passes without interpolated pairing of the CS and the UCS, the conditioned response will again appear. Called *spontaneous recovery,* this is a very pervasive and robust effect. The term "spontaneous recovery" is of course not explanatory; it simply describes the fact that an extinguished response will be revived with the passage of time despite lack of further training. The overall behavioral significance of the phenomenon is great. Because of repeated experience with the conditioned stimulus alone, an individual may seem to have eliminated some undesirable response such as fear of an object not inherently harmful. There may be no contact with that object for a long period of time, yet once it is again encountered, the fear of it revives.

Discrimination

The principle of stimulus generalization indicates that, even though only one CS of a particular value is used, conditioning develops to other stimuli that are along that same psychological dimension. *Differential conditioning* between one stimulus, called the positive, and any other stimulus, the negative, can be obtained by continuing to reinforce the original stimulus while frequently presenting the other without the UCS, thus extinguishing its response. After this response has been extinguished, one can present another stimulus with a value between it and the positive stimulus but closer to the negative one. Some responsiveness will be found to it, but if it is never reinforced, it too will be extinguished. By progres-

sively moving closer and closer to the ever reinforced stimulus, a finer and finer discrimination can be achieved. In some instances, however, not only does the differentiation break down, but the subject may develop an *experimental neurosis.* Pavlov reported an instance in which marked changes occurred in a dog's behavior during differential conditioning. Instead of going willingly to the laboratory as it had done before, the animal hung back; on some days it responded to neither CS, and on others to both. After a long period of rest, the dog returned to the laboratory regimen, reacquiring the conditioned response and the easy discrimination. Once again, the negative CS was brought closer and closer to the positive stimulus, and once again the animal developed neurotic behavior. In this instance the break occurred at a physical difference between stimuli that had been mastered before. A differentiation that earlier had seemed to present no great difficulty could no longer be tolerated. This result suggests that the experimental neurosis is not exclusively dependent on a sensory inability to make the necessary discrimination.

Extensions of Conditioning

In the examples of conditioning presented so far, the unconditioned stimulus has always been one for which the unconditioned response is innately determined. The conditioned stimulus, by virtue of its pairing with the unconditioned stimulus, itself acquires the ability to elicit a response of that general class. A logical extension is to investigate the possibility that the conditioned stimulus may now be used as an unconditioned stimulus for a new conditioned response. This procedure, termed *higher order conditioning,* was undertaken in Pavlov's laboratory and was followed by more extensive work by others. The process has been generally successful. Since the first conditioned stimulus—now the unconditioned stimulus—may itself be extinguished, there are some failures, but all in all there have been enough positive instances to demonstrate the potentialities of higher order conditioning. There have even been demonstrations of extension beyond a single step, wherein the second or new conditioned stimulus has been used to develop a third conditioned response. Conditioning, therefore, is not limited to the use of inborn unconditioned stimuli.

The phenomenon known as *sensory preconditioning* is a further extension of conditioning. In this situation two stimuli, neither of which produces a clearly defined unconditioned stimulus—for example, a light and a tone—are first paired together; then one of them is used as a conditioned stimulus for a response such as leg withdrawal to a shock unconditioned stimulus. After this conditioning has been established, the response of leg withdrawal will be given to the other of the two originally paired stimuli of the preconditioning session. The work completed to date suggests that the principles or rules for this process are the same as those that hold for ordinary conditioning. As with higher order conditioning, sensory preconditioning considerably broadens the potential range of conditioning as a determinant of behavior.

Retention of the Conditioned Response

One of the empirical characteristics of the laboratory-produced CR is that, once acquired, it seems to be—in contrast with many other learning activities—quite immune to the forgetting process. It seems likely that the extreme resistance to forgetting that has been noted in the conditioned response may be an artificial consequence of the experimental programs. Research in the verbal field, in which memory has been investigated most extensively, has clearly indicated that retention is very markedly influenced by the learning of other materials of the same class both before and after the acquisition of the information to be tested. In most conditioning research only a single CR is learned, hence interference from other conditioned responses is not present. When, however, more than one CR is learned in the same experimental context, forgetting of the conditioned response can be quite marked.

CLINICAL APPLICATIONS OF CONDITIONING

Since conditioning essentially consists of changing a response to some stimulus event, its value as a therapeutic tool for eliminating undesirable reactions was recognized very early. Jones (1924) was able to eliminate a child's fear reaction to a white rabbit by what is called a *counter conditioning* process. The feared animal was introduced into the room at some distance from the seated child, who was simultaneously given favored food to eat, this serving as a UCS to produce a positive response. The procedure is called counter-conditioning rather than simple extinction because the UCS produces a response that is counter to a fear reaction. On successive days the experimenter brought the animal closer and closer to the child, who was eating chocolate, until eventually the child's reaction to the animal changed from one of fear to liking.

A modification of this method called systematic desensitization uses the gradual introduction of the feared stimulus without an unconditioned stimulus. Conceptually, this is simple extinction. The procedure begins by teaching the patient to relax completely; then, after this state is readily adopted, some representation of the feared object is introduced. The patient may be asked to try to have an image of it when it is far away, but also to remain relaxed. Next, the patient is asked to summon an image of the object at a closer distance, and so on until the actual object—perhaps a snake—is physically present and handled. At all times the procedure is stopped if fear occurs, and is moved backward before progression resumes. Another method, called implosive therapy, also uses the extinction procedure, but forces contact with the feared stimulus itself after the therapist is assured that it in itself is not harmful. This is exactly comparable to the usual extinction procedure wherein the conditioned response occurs but is never reinforced.

Conditioning has also been used to eliminate undesired habits such as smoking, or drinking alcohol. Thus a bottle of vodka may be shown to the patient followed by a strong electric shock or some other painful stimulus. The method has been successful, but recidivism is always likely if the smoking or drinking is only a symptom of some deeper psychological problem, and the conditioning may be effective only to produce a change of brands.

THE IMPACT OF CLASSICAL CONDITIONING ON PSYCHOLOGICAL THEORY

The growth of conditioning as a broad and important concept in general psychological theory was originally stimulated by a controversy that occurred during the second and third decades of this century. During this span of time the structuralists, represented by E. B. Titchener, and the behaviorists, represented by J. B. Watson, were arguing about what constituted the proper raw data of psychology. To the structuralists, psychology's aim was the study of consciousness, and psychology's raw data were provided by the method of introspection from reports of highly trained students of this method. For the behaviorist, the raw data consisted of behavioral observations and measurements, objectively obtained. The battle was more or less officially joined in Watson's 1913 paper, which challenged the need for introspective data and even questioned the need for verbal reports. However, there were already in existence data that could not be excluded from the realm of any psychology—data based upon personal, experiential reports. One such body of information dealt with sensory discrimination, the determination of whether one tone is higher than another, or one light brighter than another. A psychology that could not address such questions would be a trivial and narrow one. Watson introduced the conditioned response, and the use of differential conditioning in particular, as a method for handling the discrimination area, and suggested that the tradition-hallowed field of psychophysics could then be entered by nonverbal behavioral measurements. So in the beginning the conditioned response served only as a tool, but later, as behaviorism sought a more general theoretical basis, it became an essential part of its theory and was used to a great extent as the basic unit from which most, if not all, complicated behavior could be built.

In this theoretical application, the conditioned response was represented as being a fairly stereotyped and fixed stimulus-response connection, unlike the picture of its true characteristics presented earlier in this article. There were at least two reasons why it was considered in this fashion then. First, there was little first-hand understanding of conditioning until the varied conditioning research began to burgeon in the American laboratories of the 1930s. Second, the behaviorists were fighting the "mentalism" that abounded in earlier psychology, and it suited their purposes to consider conditioning processes as the building blocks of more complex behavior, very mechanical and stereotyped in nature: a stimulus directly produced a response without mediation of mentalistic processes. This position readily came from Pavlov's concepts of inhibition and excitation interacting at a cortical level.

An inevitable consequence of the use of the conditioned response was to shift the explanatory emphasis of behavior away from an instinctive one to an environmental one. The lesson to be learned from the conditioning laboratory seemed to be that the response to any stimulus may be modified and a new one substituted for the old by the appropriate pairing of CS and UCS. Watson used this concept to attack the then current extensive usage of instinct as an explanation of much behavior. Certainly psychological thinking puts a heavier emphasis on environment today than it did before 1920, and the phenomena of conditioning undoubtedly played an important role in producing this shift.

Pavlov was a physiologist rather than a psychologist, and his interpretation of the conditioning process used the behavior obtained as an analog of neural processes in the cortex of the brain. His theory paralleled, for these so-called psychic reflexes, the theory of I. M. Sechenov, a mid-19th-century Russian physiologist, for the physical or bodily reflexes. Conditioning behavior was a function of two opposing processes, *excitation* and *inhibition,* with excitation resulting primarily from the pairing of CS and UCS, and inhibition from presenting the CS alone, with the magnitude of the conditioned response being the result of the summation of these two independent neural processes. These concepts have been perpetuated and they reoccur in one form or another in modern theoretical psychology. Excitation and inhibition formed the basis of Hull's influential 1943 behavior theory, which generated a great deal of research.

A basic characteristic of the Pavlovian situation is that the occurrence of the UCS, or reinforcement, is independent of the organism's response. Its scheduling is controlled by external forces, and there is no contingency between reinforcement (the UCS) and the organism's actions. This differs from the instance in which the organism's actions determine whether or not reinforcement will be received, as in the operant chamber introduced by B. F. Skinner. The term "classical conditioning" thus has come to refer exclusively to the Pavlovian conditioning situation.

ASSOCIATION, PERFORMANCE, AND THE CONDITIONED RESPONSE

In forward conditioning one stimulus, the CS, occurs and is followed by the UCS with regularity. The subject learns that the two events are associated at some probability level. If this were all there was to conditioning—simply the fact that the subject now knows that, when the first stimulus occurs, the other is likely to follow—then, since dogs do not talk, Pavlov would never have reported the discovery of the CR. Few persons anywhere would be impressed with the finding, since associations between two closely occurring events have certainly been noted since Aristotle's day. What makes the conditioned response of great interest is the fact that the first stimulus produces an overt response highly similar to the response given to the second stimulus. In conditioning, then, the subject acquires not only an association but a way of acting. This is reminiscent of the distinction made by E. C. Tolman between *learning* and *performance.* As he pointed out, a rat may know the correct pathway through a maze, but it will not perform and demonstrate its knowledge unless it is hungry and there is food at the end of the maze. In other words, in many situations an incentive must be added independently to produce the performance that demonstrates knowledge. Just being in the maze is not enough to elicit the running response of threading its alleys without error. In conditioning, the CS evokes both knowledge and action. Inherent in the CS is not only information, but also a command to respond overtly and appropriately. It is this fact that sets conditioning apart from simple associative learning, which requires some additional operation or operations to demonstrate the learning.

By indirection, the above statements raise the question of whether the CR is voluntary or involuntary, whether the execution of the response is intentional or automatic. One way of approaching the voluntary-involuntary question is to give subjects complete knowledge of what is to happen in a conditioning situation, then ask them to facilitate or inhibit their responding. The outcome of various researches does not offer unequivocal support for the ex-

clusion of either position. But it does lead to an interaction position, namely, that the two processes contribute jointly to the behavioral outcome, and that the behavior is not a consequence of the environmental pairing alone or of a subject-produced attitude alone.

CONDITIONING AS AN ADAPTIVE AND FUNCTIONAL PROCESS

Pavlov commented upon the potential adaptive value of the conditioned response, and many of its characteristics can be so interpreted. It is a mechanism that permits the organism to prepare for an oncoming event by making an appropriate anticipatory response. The failure to obtain backward or even simultaneous conditioning can be understood in this light, for in neither case does the CS *predict* the UCS and thereby permit some action to be taken prior to its presentation. The fact that conditioning does not occur for these temporal relationships does not preclude the formation of associations between the two stimulus events in both forward and backward order. Certainly a person experiencing simultaneous conditioning can readily report the concurrence of both of the two physical events, the potential CS and UCS. Also, in the backward arrangement the subject, presented with a properly phrased question, can state which event preceded the other (forward) and which event was preceded by the other (backward). Nevertheless, the research on backward conditioning indicates that the second of the two stimuli would not produce the UCR of the first, that is, a conditioned response. This result is perfectly consistent with the differentiation between learning and performance, and with the conclusion that in conditioning two processes occur: Cognitive associations are formed, and motivational tendencies to react in a certain way are acquired. In the simultaneous and backward arrangements, the motivational component is lacking because the "conditioned stimulus" cannot serve to predict the other stimulus. The time relationships to do so are simply not there, since a subsequent event cannot predict an earlier one, nor can simultaneous events predict each other.

A contradiction to the general predictability explanation is introduced by the fact that conditioning also does not develop at very short forward intervals (from simultaneity to about 0.15 sec). From a logical point of view, predictability of the UCS is possible, so the simple prediction interpretation needs modification. The difficulty can be met by assuming that time must be added to permit the initiation of the response mechanism prior to the occurrence of the UCS. Figure 3 shows the mean latency of conditioned paw responses in the cat, and the mean latency for human eyelid conditioning for forward CS–UCS intervals ranging from 0.15 to 2.00 sec. The dotted diagonal line shows the curve that would be obtained, if the CR commenced at the same time as the onset of the UCS. The solid line connects the data points of the actual latencies of the CRs. It can be seen that the CR is concurrent with or anticipates the UCS from about 0.30 sec out, but its latency is clearly greater than the CS–UCS interval for the 0.15 interval, a value of null conditioning. The latency of the CR cannot be accounted for by the slowness of the response mechanism as a whole, since the latency of the response to the UCS is much less than the 0.15 CS–UCS interval at which conditioning fails to occur.

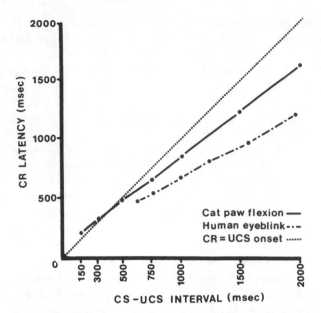

Figure 3.   The relationship between CS–UCS interval and latency of the CR. The dotted 45° line indicates what would occur if the response exactly equaled the CS–UCS interval.

If one accepts the view that the generality of conditioning across many species and many responses has evolved because of its functional value as an adaptive mechanism, then the lack of conditioning at the short, forward interval leads to a further stipulation concerning the predictability interpretation. It is simply that prediction of the UCS alone is not sufficient, but that also there must be available, with a moderate degree of consistency, additional time to activate the program that produces the adaptive response prior to the onset of the UCS. Viewed in this light, the conditioned response is seen as a finely tuned and intelligent process, a component of the behavior of the entire organism.

REFERENCES

Hull, C. L. (1943). *Principles of behavior.* New York: Appleton-Century-Crofts.

Jones, M. C. (1924). Elimination of children's fears. *Journal of Experimental Psychology, 7,* 325–341.

Watson, J. B. (1913). Psychology as the behaviorist views it. *Psychological Review, 20,* 158–177.

D. WICKENS
Ohio State University

OPERANT CONDITIONING

CLIENT-CENTERED THERAPY

Client-centered therapy is an approach to psychotherapy based on trust in the self-directive capacities of the individual. In this re-

spect, it contrasts with other therapeutic orientations where the therapist characteristically acts as an expert. Rogers first described this new approach in a talk in 1940, not realizing the impact it was going to have. This was followed by a full-length book on psychotherapy containing a clearly stated theory of therapy together with a verbatim account of an eight-interview case. This made up approximately two-fifths of the book and was a pioneering method of case presentation at the time. As client-centered theory and practice developed in the 1940s and 1950s at Ohio State University and the University of Chicago, a far-reaching body of research on a new hypothesis grew up: If the therapist offered, and the client experienced, a particular kind of relationship characterized by genuineness, unconditional positive regard, and empathy, a self-directed process of growth would follow. Moving to the University of Wisconsin from 1957 to 1963, Rogers and his associates undertook a major research project which tested the client-centered hypothesis with schizophrenic patients. In 1964, he moved to La Jolla, California, using the approach in the United States and abroad, in small and large groups, school systems, workshops, and conflict resolution. The broader application of the principles of client-centered therapy became known as the person-centered approach. Rogers died in February, 1987. The movement he fathered (but did not wish to dominate) is carried on by a diverse and dedicated international community.

BASIC THERAPEUTIC CONCEPTS

- An actualizing tendency, which is present in every living organism, expressed in human beings as movement toward the realization of an individual's full potential.

- A formative tendency of movement toward greater order, complexity, and interrelatedness can be observed in stars, crystals, and microorganisms, as well as human beings.

- Trust that individuals and groups can set their own goals and monitor their progress toward these goals. Individuals are seen as capable of choosing their therapists and deciding on the frequency and length of therapy. Groups are trusted to develop processes that are right for them and to resolve conflicts within the group.

- Trust in the therapist's inner, intuitive self.

- The therapist-offered conditions of congruence, unconditional positive regard, and empathy:
  —Congruence has to do with the correspondence between the thoughts and behavior of the therapist, who is genuine and does not put up a professional front.
  —Unconditional positive regard, also identified as "caring," "prizing," and "nonpossessive warmth," is not dependent on specific attributes or behaviors of the client.
  —Empathy reflects an attitude of profound interest in the client's world of feelings and meanings, conveying appreciation and understanding of whatever the client wishes to share with the therapist.

- Self-concept, locus-of-evaluation, and experiencing, basic constructs which emerge from the client's own interaction with the world:

—The self-concept is made up of the person's perceptions and feelings about self. Self-regard or self-esteem is a major component of the self-concept.

—Locus-of-evaluation refers to the roots or wellspring of the person's values and standards for self or others.

—Experiencing has to do with whether the person, in interacting with the world, is open and flexible or rigid and guarded.

THEORY OF PERSONALITY

In his approach to therapy, Rogers initially was very pragmatic, exhibiting a disinterest in psychological theory. He was interested in what worked. By the time he published his second book on therapy in 1951, he felt it was desirable or even necessary to construct a theory to explain the observed facts in therapy, and he put forward a set of nineteen propositions which he described as basically phenomenological in character, relying heavily on the concept of self as an explanatory construct. He saw the culmination of personality development as a congruence between the phenomenal field of experience and the conceptual structure of the self. This resulted in freedom from internal strain and anxiety, and the establishment of an individualized value system which would still have much in common with that of other well-adjusted people. Some of the concepts included in Rogers' personality theory are:

- The internal frame of reference, the perceptual field of the individual, the way the world appears, and the meanings attached to experience and feeling. It is the belief that it provides the fullest understanding of why people behave as they do, superior to external judgments of behavior, attitudes, and personality.

- *Symbolization,* the process by which the individual becomes aware or conscious of an experience. Symbolization tends to be denied to experiences at variance with the self-concept.

- The *organismic valuing process,* which exists when individuals rely on the evidence of their own senses for making value judgments, as distinct from a system based on a concern with what others may think of them or regard as right or wrong.

- The *fully functioning person* lives with an openness to all experiences, with no need to edit or censor. Such people tend to have a positive self-concept, make better use of the environment, and even possess greater physiological responsiveness.

APPLICATIONS

Many of the concepts and principles of client-centered therapy which have been defined lend themselves to applications beyond the one-on-one therapy situation. These concepts embrace an actualizing tendency; trust; the therapist-offered conditions of congruence, unconditional positive regard, and empathy; the internal frame of reference; and the fully functioning person. The applications include the classroom, the workplace, administration, group therapy, play therapy, conflict resolution, and the development of community. The concept of community is used in a number of ways in the client-centered movement.

- A workshop or conference may begin with a variety of activities which might include individual presentations, panels, small group meetings, and meetings of the entire group. During the course of the meeting, which may take place over a weekend or several days, the group as a whole may develop a sense of community.

- Daily meetings of all the participants which involve no designated leaders and no agenda might be employed. Often extremely frustrating in the initial stages, they offer the opportunity to create an experience or community of the members' own design.

- At least one person-centered organization has functioned successfully for many years with no officers or elections. Tasks such as the scheduling of presentations at the annual meetings, membership issues, the responsibility for newsletters and journals, and the planning of future conferences are carried out by individuals who volunteer. Any conflicts are negotiated. There is a general assumption that the conference's schedule may be changed, that someone may volunteer a presentation that is not listed in the program, or that a new interest group may spring up.

- There is a growing international person-centered community, which has developed out of individuals getting to know one another in different conferences and training programs held in many countries around the world. One aspect of the community is an international e-mail network with daily messages of a personal and professional nature.

- Peace and conflict resolution is a particular aspect of the international person-centered community. Since the 1980s, there has been person-centered facilitation of groups in conflict from Northern Ireland, South Africa, Central America, and other parts of the world. A central dynamic in such meetings is the movement from negative stereotyping and the blaming of particular individuals and groups to the sharing of (often deeply moving) personal experiences. One person taking this risk can propel the whole group to a level of common experiences and emotions, where conflicts dissolve. Genuine, empathetic, respectful responsiveness by a group facilitator or participant may promote such a process.

N. J. RASKIN
Northwestern University Medical School

PSYCHOTHERAPY
PSYCHOTHERAPY TECHNIQUES
REFLECTIVE LISTENING

CLINICAL ASSESSMENT

Clinical assessment is the process by which clinicians gain understanding of a patient necessary for making informed decisions. The type of knowledge gained from this process depends on the approach of the assessor and the type of instruments used. Usually the intent is description and prediction in order to plan, execute, and evaluate therapeutic interventions and predict future behavior. Assessment may be used to provide an understanding of a particular area of a person's functioning (such as cognitive processes, social skills, emotions), to catalog the type and circumstances of certain behaviors (for example, symptomatic ones), to form a complex description or model of the person, or to assign the client to a particular diagnostic category.

Any number of assessment techniques may be used, singly or in combination, depending on the orientation of the clinician and the specific questions for which answers are sought. Interviews, observations, and tests are commonly used. A typical test battery might include an objective test of cognitive functioning such as the Wechsler Adult Intelligence Scale (WAIS-R) or Wechsler Intelligence Scale for Children (WISC-R), an objective personality inventory such as the Minnesota Multiphasic Personality Inventory (MMPI), projective tests such as the Rorschach Inkblot Test or Thematic Apperception Test (TAT), and a test which involves psychomotor functioning such as the Bender Gestalt or Draw-a-Person test. When the subject is a child, various play situations may be used.

It is useful to think of these assessment techniques as varying in *structure*, both that of the stimulus situation and that of the subject's options for responding. A person looking at an ambiguous picture in a projective test is faced with a relatively unstructured situation, whereas an information question on an intelligence test presents a more structured stimulus. Similarly, the subject may be allowed to respond freely in his or her own words, or be required to mark "true" or "false" in more structured procedures. Each of these situations poses particular problems for the subject and calls for the demonstration of different skills and personal styles; each also requires different sorts of operations by the clinician interpreting the subject's responses.

THREE MODELS OF CLINICAL ASSESSMENT

Psychodiagnosis

This, the dominant model of clinical assessment since the postwar era, might better be termed psychodynamic or personological assessment. Psychodiagnosis uses a number of assessment procedures, including both projective techniques and more objective and standardized tests, in order to tap a number of areas of psychological functioning on both conscious and unconscious levels. The goal is to describe individuals in personological rather than normative terms. Although it may involve applying a psychiatric diagnosis, the primary purpose is to describe the particular individual in as full, multifaceted, and multilevel a way as possible. The psychodiagnostic model emphasizes the role of the clinician's judgment and inference in organizing and conceptualizing the questions to be answered and the techniques to be used, and integrating diverse findings into a coherent whole.

Supporters of the psychometric model are critical of the subjectivism and lack of demonstrated reliability and validity of the tests favored by psychodiagnosticians, especially projective tests. They have also questioned the abilities of clinicians to synthesize assessment data. Others have accused the psychodiagnostic model of putting undue emphasis on intrapsychic processes.

The Psychometric Model

An alternate model of assessment might be termed the psychometric orientation. Although clinicians of varying orientations use standardized tests, in the psychometric tradition they are particularly valued as objective measurement instruments allowing individuals to be compared along empirically defined trait dimensions. Clear, structured items are preferred to the less structured stimuli of the projective techniques, and the reliability and validity of the tests are of central importance. The role of judgment and inference on the part of the examiner is minimized.

In principle, adherents of this model believe that test scores should be able to stand on their own without requiring interpretation by an experienced clinician. The psychometric and psychodiagnostic traditions have clashed on this point. The controversy over "clinical versus statistical prediction" debates whether behavior can be better predicted by combining objective test data in empirically derived prediction equations, or whether a clinician can better combine the data and make predictions by more subjective methods.

The recent dramatic rise of automated systems for administering and interpreting tests reflects a desire for standardized testing procedures and for "cookbook" or statistical approaches to interpreting the subject's responses.

The Behavioral Model

Behavioral assessment concentrates on measuring overt behaviors, particularly problem behaviors, as well as the contexts in which they occur. The intent is to discover *what* people do, *when, where,* and *under what circumstances.* This is in contrast to searching for the underlying reasons *why* people behave as they do, or seeking to classify people in traditional diagnostic groups. Dispositional constructs, such as traits or personality dynamics, are considered either nonexistent or irrelevant to the prediction and modification of behavior. The emphasis is on data immediately useful for planning and evaluating treatment.

Today behavioral assessment makes use of observations in naturalistic, contrived, and role-playing situations, while also assessing the subject's self-reported behavior by means of inventories and clinical interviews. With the rise of *cognitive-behavioral* approaches to assessment there is increasing concern not only with what clients do and say they do, but also with such phenomena as their feelings, thoughts, goals, internal images and conversations, and the personal meanings of stimuli.

CRITICISMS OF CLINICAL TESTING

In the past, assessment and in particular testing were closely identified with the professional role of clinical psychologists and accounted for a large proportion of their work. More recently there has been a decided decline of commitment to this role among psychologists and growing criticism of testing. Although many of these criticisms are aimed primarily at the psychodiagnostic model, the entire assessment endeavor has come on hard times.

Criticisms of testing from within the psychometric and behavioral models have already been mentioned. Humanistic psychologists have also criticized testing, saying that nothing discovered about a client makes any difference in psychotherapy until it becomes evident to the client in the course of the therapeutic encounter. Community psychologists have emphasized the role of external social factors in causing psychological problems.

Diagnostic testing was also seen as exemplifying the concepts and role relations of the medical model. Assessment has become identified with psychiatric labeling and has been criticized as useless, if not harmful. The poor reliability and meager validity of such diagnostic categories as schizophrenia reflected on the usefulness of tests and interviews as well.

Others have charged that tests invade privacy and enforce conformity, and deny opportunity to nonmainstream citizens. Minority psychologists have criticized tests developed and standardized on white, largely middle class populations—and often interpreted by clinicians of like background—as unfairly judging minority individuals in work, educational, and clinical situations. Thus clients differing in race—as well as in class, sex, and lifestyle—may be seen as sicker and also less apt to gain from verbal, insight-oriented therapy. This criticism has resulted in a growing tendency to assess strengths as well as weaknesses and to develop culturally appropriate norms and instruments.

Finally, clinical testing is expensive. The classic model of psychodiagnostic testing arose in the context of long-term psychotherapy, within which the proportionately small amount of time involved could be justified. The time spent on assessment becomes harder to justify with brief therapies.

TRENDS IN ASSESSMENT

Despite these criticisms, testing appears to be alive and well. In general, the field is changing in a number of ways. Some trends are the development of techniques which focus more directly on *particular* specific questions of relevance to treatment; refinement of the measurement properties of assessment devices of all kinds; more reliance on lower level interpretations of test findings which remain close to the data; greater concern with the situational, interpersonal, and environmental factors relevant to determining behavior; and at the same time, more respectful attention to the person's own views of his or her character, problems, or situation.

Such developments include the introduction of structured procedures intended to improve the reliability of the interview. A good example is the Schedule of Affective Disorders and Schizophrenia, an interview designed to gather the information for making a diagnosis according to the third edition of the *Diagnostic and Statistical Manual* (3rd ed., rev.) of the American Psychiatric Association (DSM-III-R).

Another area of interest is the assessment of particular psychological processes relevant to medicine. Neuropsychological assessment is used for evaluating intellectual and emotional functioning of patients suffering from traumatic brain injury, disease processes, reactions to drugs and toxins, and the like. Commonly used tests include the Wechsler scales, the Halstead–Reitan battery, the Wide Range Achievement Test, the Bender Gestalt, and the Luria–Nebraska test. Psychological assessment is also finding use in predicting the response of certain medical conditions (e.g., chronic pain) to somatic or behavioral treatment.

As techniques of psychological treatment continue to multiply, assessment techniques are likely to see increasing use in matching clients with the most appropriate form of treatment. They are also valuable for evaluating the effectiveness of therapy. With a greater and more diverse segment of the population needing and seeking psychological help, and with third-party payments and accounta-

bility an increasing reality, clinicians must be prepared to evaluate the usefulness of interventions both in general and for specific individuals.

Assessment procedures continue to make contributions to research. They can provide measures of both independent and dependent variables, and are useful for establishing criterion groups (e.g., of subjects with bipolar affective disorders) in studies, for example, of biochemical, psychophysiological, or cognitive processes.

Finally, assessment procedures are valuable in the training of psychologists. They remain one of the best ways to learn about the structure and functioning of humans for research and personality study, and to sharpen the understanding of clinicians.

D. SCHULDBERG
University of Montana

CRITICAL INCIDENT TECHNIQUE
CULTURAL BIAS IN TESTS
MEASUREMENT
QUESTIONNAIRES

CLINICAL GRADUATE TRAINING IN PSYCHOLOGY

Clinical graduate training in psychology has undergone many changes during the past 50 years. After World War II, there was an increased need for qualified psychologists to meet the emotional, psychiatric, and medical needs of military personnel returning from overseas. The American Psychological Association (APA) responded by developing a core curriculum for the training of psychologists and, in 1948, granted accreditation to 35 doctoral programs. In 1949, the Boulder Conference promulgated a scientist-practitioner model as the goal of instruction. Although the majority of institutions continue to adhere to the Boulder model, the 1973 Vail Conference proffered a scholar-practitioner model and called for the establishment of free-standing professional schools and the granting of the Doctor of Psychology (PsyD) degree. Applied psychologists may have the PhD, PsyD, or EdD degree.

Graduate training continued to develop, and recently the American Psychological Association (APA) published new guidelines for doctoral programs in professional psychology (APA, 1996). The guidelines focused on the competency of students, thereby requiring doctoral programs and internship centers to determine the skills they wanted their trainees to demonstrate prior to graduation. This necessitated the development of evaluative methodologies to ensure compliance with accepted guidelines.

COMPETENCIES

To meet APA standards, graduate programs declare the competencies they wish their students to demonstrate. These are observable, measurable, practical, and flexible (Stratford, 1994). To be practical, a competency must consist of a manageable number of sub-skills. To be flexible, it must allow students a variety of approaches (e.g., psychotherapy: psychodynamic or behavioral; research: quantitative or qualitative) so that they can follow through with a task in a manner that best suits the client or most effectively addresses the research topic.

Relevant skills are determined by training faculty, after which a method of measuring designated target behaviors is developed. This approach recognizes that a minimal standard must be set, below which one is not considered competent (Fantuzzo, 1984). Pretraining behavior may be assessed and then followed by a variety of educational and training activities. The use of video/audio tape presentations, oral feedback regarding specific skill deficiencies, and suggestions for remediation may constitute effective means for improving skill levels. For example, competency in the administration of the Wechsler Scale may be verified by use of the Administrative Checklist for the WAIS-III (Sattler & Ryan, 1999). Once students demonstrate competence in a given area, they must show an appreciation of the legal and ethical issues relevant to the practice of the proficiency.

DEVELOPMENTAL ISSUES IN COMPETENCY ASSESSMENT

Many educators (e.g., Stoltenberg, 1981) consider the acquisition of psychotherapeutic skills and their evaluation from a developmental perspective. Novices need information concerning their knowledge and comprehension of fundamental principles. Thus, entry level skills are best evaluated by the use of tests (Chambers & Glassman, 1997).

Students who are more advanced can be assessed through simulation. This may entail an evaluation of the individual's breadth of knowledge as well as hands-on performance in scenarios that closely emulate actual practice. Training methods might include problem-based learning, close supervision in practica, and the writing of research proposals.

When students' competency levels will soon allow them to function autonomously, direct evaluation is required. This may involve research studies, record reviews, and/or case presentations and should include detailed coverage of relevant ethical issues (Chambers & Glassman, 1997). Supervisors may assess how the student integrates individual components such as test scores with overall treatment, and evaluate the adequacy of the student's practice management skills. The latter competency may be evaluated through case selection, preparation, and timeliness of reports. In the portfolio approach, faculty identify competencies, provide students with definitions of target behaviors, and give examples of how skills might be demonstrated. Students are required to collect material that demonstrates competence and present this to the faculty.

CORE BODY OF KNOWLEDGE

An essential body of knowledge has been identified and graduate programs attempt to teach it (Fox & Barclay, 1989). The APA (1996) criteria concerning the elements of psychological knowledge that should be acquired by students include the biological, cognitive, affective, and social aspects of behavior. Additional important domains of study include the history of the field, psycho-

logical assessment, research methods, individual differences, ethics, human development, psychopathology, psychodiagnosis, intervention, cultural differences, and the attitudes that facilitate problem-solving, scholarly investigation, and lifelong learning. Without this core background, it is unlikely that competency in clinical practice can be achieved.

Building on a strong psychological knowledge base, the National Council of Schools and Programs in Professional Psychology (Peterson et al., 1991) proposed the following competency areas, presented here in modified form (Sumerall, Lopez, & Ochlert, 2000):

Relationship

Relationship refers to the capacity to develop and maintain a constructive working alliance with clients.

Assessment

Assessment is an ongoing, interactive, and inclusive process that serves to describe, conceptualize, characterize, and predict relevant aspects of a client.

Intervention

Intervention includes activities that promote, restore, sustain, or enhance positive functioning and a sense of well-being in clients through preventive, developmental, or remedial services. The concept of empirically validated treatments is gaining acceptance and a task force within Division 12 (Clinical) of APA has published a listing of such interventions (Task Force, 1993). Knowledge and skill related to these specific treatments may be considered as elements of the intervention competencies. Educational techniques such as the "Structured, Clinical, Objective-Referenced, Problem-based, Integrated, and Organized (SCORPIO)" approach recommended by Hill, Stalley, Pennington, Besser, and McCarthy (1997) may be an alternative means to present new information and assess the student's ability to utilize it.

Intervention competencies may be divided into those for individual, couples, families, and groups, as well as infants, children, adolescents, adults, and the elderly. They may be classified according to the complexity or acuteness of the presenting problem. At one level are patients with simple phobias or social anxiety disorder. At another level of complexity are those with dual diagnoses, chronic psychosis, or severe personality disorders.

Research

Research involves a systematic inquiry that focuses on problem identification and the acquisition, organization, and interpretation of information pertaining to psychological phenomenon. In addition to traditional research, instruction might be given to clarify how experimenter expectancy confounds the results of an investigation and how the use of volunteers, though randomly assigned, may restrict the generalizability of findings (Cook & Campbell, 1979). Other potentially important topics include qualitative studies, base rates, actuarial versus clinical prediction, and testing clinical hypotheses. Each student is involved in research early in the educational process and assists with ongoing studies prior to initiating a thesis project.

Education

Education refers to the enhancement of knowledge, skills, and attitudes in the learner, whether a student, client, allied professional, or family caregiver.

Management

Management includes activities that direct, organize, or control the services that psychologists and other professionals offer or render to the public.

Advanced Clinical Skills

These skills are areas of expertise represented by specialties such as neuropsychology and forensic practice.

Ethics

Ethics involves the acquisition of strategies for addressing conflicts in principle ethics (e.g., how one should act in specific situations; Meara, Schmidt, & Day, 1996) and virtue ethics (educating professionals toward being a certain type of person—competent, honest, etc.), as opposed to training them how to perform under given situations.

Attitudes

Attitudes refers to the appreciation and understanding of individual differences, cultural diversity, and professional development.

The core areas can be addressed via practicum and internship training, whereas supervision sessions and case conferences may be used to highlight the relevant ethical issues. Seminar settings may address the APA guidelines, state laws, and court rulings. Regardless of the methods utilized to teach and/or assess students, the establishment of competency requirements is a landmark development in the history of psychological training.

REFERENCES

American Psychological Association Office of Program Consultation and Accreditation. (1996). *Book 1: Guidelines and principles for accreditation of programs in professional psychology.* Washington D.C.: Author.

Chambers, D. W., & Glassman, P. (1997). A primer on competency-based evaluation. *Journal of Dental Education, 61,* 651–666.

Cook, T. D., & Campbell, D. T. (1979). *Quasi-experimentation: Design and analysis issues for field settings.* Boston: Houghton Mifflin.

Fantuzzo, J. W. (1984, Winter). Mastery: A competency-based training model for clinical psychologists. *The Clinical Psychologist,* 29–30.

Fox, R., & Barclay, A. G. (1989). Let a thousand flowers bloom: Or, weed the garden? *American Psychologist, 44,* 55–59.

Hill, D., Stalley, P., Pennington, D., Besser, M., & McCarthy, W. (1997). Competency-based learning in traumatology. *The American Journal of Surgery, 173,* 136–140.

Meara, N. M., Schmidt, L. D., & Day, J. D. (1996). Principles and virtues: A foundation for ethical decisions, policies, and character. *The Counseling Psychologist, 24,* 4–77.

Peterson, R. L., McHolland, J. D., Bent, R. J., Davis-Russell, E., Edwall, G. E., Polite, K., Singer, D. L., & Stricker, G. (Eds.). (1991). *The core curriculum in professional psychology.* Washington, DC: American Psychological Association.

Sattler, J. M., & Ryan, J. J. (1999). *Assessment of children: Revised and updated third edition, WAIS-III supplement.* San Diego: Jerome M. Sattler.

Stoltenberg, C. (1981). Approaching supervision from a developmental perspective: The counselor complexity model. *Journal of Counseling Psychology, 28,* 59–65.

Stratford, R. (1994). A competency approach to educational psychology practice: The implications for quality. *Educational and Child Psychology, 11,* 21–28.

Sumerall, S. W., Lopez, S. J., & Ochlert, M. E. (2000). Competency-Based Education and Training in Psychology: A primer. Springfield, IL.: Charles C. Thomas

Task Force on Promotion and Dissemination of Psychological Procedures. (1993). *A report adopted by Division 12 Board,* 1–17.

S. W. SUMERALL
William Jewell College

J. J. RYAN
Central Missouri State University

CLINICAL PSYCHOLOGY, HISTORY

Clinical psychology is probably the most common specialty within psychology around the world today (Lunt & Poortinga, 1996). Its principal aims include the study of psychopathology and its assessment and treatment. This same territory is shared by a number of other professional disciplines, including psychiatry, social work, mental health nursing, and various types of counseling. Compared to professionals in these neighboring fields, present day clinical psychologists are distinctive in the quality of their training in research, psychometric testing, and behavior therapy.

Although concepts of psychopathology keep on changing, it is a reasonable presumption that some of the basic phenomena involved are characteristic of human beings throughout their history, in all cultures. Classical writings, whether Chinese, Egyptian, Greek, Hebrew, or Indian, all refer in their own terminologies to instances of "madness," often interpreted within a religious framework—for example, as an experience that could be visited on a person by divine forces. When formal legal systems developed, they contained regulations for the management of insane persons, such as the appointment of conservators or guardians to help manage their affairs. An early example is the Greek law labeled "dike paranoia." Shamans and physicians were generally considered responsible for diagnosing and treating such mental health problems.

Within the western tradition, the earliest influential concepts of psychopathology are those found in the writings attributed to the

Greek physician Hippocrates (c. 460–377 B.C.E.), who viewed madness as an illness like any other (Routh, 1998). For example, Hippocrates identified the condition called melancholia as being due to an excess of black bile produced by the pancreas (the very word "melancholia" means "black bile"). Such an imbalance of the internal fluids, or "humors," was treated by administering purgatives, while a furious manic state was more likely to be treated by bleeding the patient. Madness accompanied by fever (called phrenitis), on the other hand, was considered to have a good prognosis and was dealt with simply by waiting for the fever to abate.

The most influential ancient physician was no doubt Galen (c. 130–200 C.E.), a Greek whose travels took him to Alexandria and Rome. He generally followed Hippocratic concepts of madness. Although the term is anachronistic, Galen could be considered a "scientist-practioner" in that he was an expert anatomist and physiologist as well as a physician. In fact, he was of the opinion that the best physician must also be a philosopher. Galen elaborated the concept of humors into an early personality typology, describing persons as melancholic (with a supposed excess of black bile, as mentioned earlier), phlegmatic (excess of phlegm), choleric (excess of yellow bile), or sanguine (excess of blood). He also did true physiological experiments, as in his demonstration that one could eliminate a pig's squeal by severing a certain nerve.

The specialty of psychiatry did not develop until the 18th century, and it did so simultaneously in a number of different countries, including England, Italy, France, and the new United States of America. The most famous figure of this era was the physician Philippe Pinel (1745–1826), who was in Paris at the time of the French Revolution. He elaborated the principles of moral treatment of mental patients. The basic idea was that it was not necessary to chain a mental patient to the wall. Instead, one should treat the individual in a kind and considerate way, minimizing coercion. Patients would often respond well to this kind of management. It was during this time that asylums began to be considered as a means of treating the insane and not simply a way of confining them to protect society. In 1838 a French law was passed creating a national system of such asylums. The same kinds of legislation were passed in England and in the United States at about this time. Soon afterward, formal organizations of "alienists," or psychiatrists, developed and began to publish scholarly journals. For example, the organization that became the American Psychiatric Association was founded in 1844.

The founding of modern psychology is usually dated from the establishment of the first psychology laboratory by Wilhelm Wundt (1832–1920) at the University of Leipzig in 1879. Practitioners in this new field, modeled upon experimental physiology, typically studied topics such as sensory processes, reaction time, and later, memory. It is not so widely realized that the permissable topics of the day also included psychopathology. The eminent German psychiatrist Emil Kraepelin (1856–1926) tells us in his memoirs (published posthumously, Kraepelin, 1987) that from his youth he was interested in psychological questions, admired Wundt's work, and "decided to become a psychiatrist, as it seemed that this was the only possibility to combine psychological work with an earning profession." Indeed, Kraepelin studied in Wundt's

laboratory between 1882 and 1885 and later set up his own psychology laboratories as part of his psychiatric clinics in Heidelberg and Munich. In this context it might be recalled that many of the early psychologists, including Wundt, William James (1842–1910), and Morton Prince (1854–1929), were originally trained as physicians. In France, one of the earliest students of this kind of medico-psychology was Theodule Ribot (1839–1916), who wrote books on disorders of memory and disorders of personality. Another was Pierre Janet (1859–1947), who wrote about anxiety and obsessional disorders and elaborated the concept of dissociation. Prince, a Boston neurologist, continued to believe that the study of abnormal psychology was more a liberal arts subject than a medical one. He founded the *Journal of Abnormal Psychology* in 1906 and later donated it to the American Psychological Association. In 1926, Prince founded the Harvard Psychological Clinic, a facility devoted to research rather than to the treatment of psychopathology.

In 1896, a psychological clinic was founded at the University of Pennsylvania by Lightner Witmer (1867–1956), a professor there. This event is generally regarded as the origin of the field of clinical psychology. Witmer, who had obtained his doctorate under Wundt, was especially interested in children with learning problems, including those in reading and spelling as well as general academic retardation. What was especially new was his suggestion that psychologists not only study people but also attempt to help them. He used the techniques being developed by experimental psychologists to study children and worked with teachers, physicians, and others to try to remediate such problems. Witmer trained doctoral students in these activities, and in 1907 founded a journal, *The Psychological Clinic*, in which he outlined his ideas concerning the new field (Witmer, 1907).

Psychology was hardly the only new mental health field that was founded at about this time. The year 1898 brought the first formal instruction in the new field of social work. Simultaneously, in Vienna, Sigmund Freud (1856–1939), originally trained in neurology, began developing the field of psychoanalysis. Breuer and Freud's book *Studies in Hysteria,* was published in 1895 (Breuer & Freud, 1986), and Freud's book on the interpretation of dreams in 1900. Psychoanalysis had profound effects on all mental health disciplines, effects that have reverberated throughout the 20th century. At the most practical level, Freud and his disciples certainly demonstrated that it was possible to make a living doing outpatient psychotherapy. The first international congress of psychoanalysis met in Salzburg in 1908, and in 1909 Freud made his only trip to America.

In France in 1905, the first successful intelligence test was developed by the experimental psychologist Alfred Binet (1857–1911) and a physician, Theodore Simon (1873–1961). This test was quickly translated into English and imported by the United States, where it soon underwent various technical refinements by Lewis M. Terman (1877–1956) and became the Stanford-Binet (Terman, 1916). Administering Binet tests became the most characteristic activity of the first generation of clinical psychologists in the United States. For example, psychologists were incorporated into the clinical team of the first child guidance clinics primarily as mental testers. The first child guidance clinic was founded by physician William Healy in Chicago in 1907. In 1908, psychologist Henry Goddard founded the first psychology internship program at the Vineland School in New Jersey; the program mainly provided extensive experience in such mental testing. The first organization of clinical psychologists, the American Association of Clinical Psychologists, founded in Pittsburgh in 1917, had as one of its main purposes the staking-out of individual mental testing as the professional domain of clinical psychologists (Routh, 1994). A cofounder of this organization, Leta Hollingworth (1886–1939), first suggested the need for a special professional degree, the doctor of psychology (PsyD), as opposed to the PhD, for persons working in applied psychology.

Before World War II, clinical psychology was a small field. However, even before 1945, the repertoire of clinical psychologists in the area of mental testing expanded greatly, establishing its pattern for the remainder of the century. The Personal Data Sheet, developed in 1917 by Robert S. Woodworth (1869–1962) as a screening procedure to identify psychoneurosis in military recruits, was the forerunner of self-report measures of psychopathology that subsequently proliferated greatly. Various other projective tests were also developed. The Rorschach inkblot test was developed by Herman Rorschach (1884–1922), a Swiss psychiatrist (Rorschach, 1921). The Thematic Apperception Test was developed in 1935 by Henry A. Murray (1893–1988), a physician and psychologist. In 1935 the Vineland Social Maturity Scale, important in the practical assessment of mental retardation, was developed by psychologist Edgar A. Doll (1889–1969). In 1939, the Wechsler-Bellevue Intelligence Test was published by psychologist David Wechsler (1896–1981). This was but the first of the intelligence tests that have dominated the field ever since. In 1943, the first edition of the Minnesota Multiphasic Personality Inventory was published by psychologist Starke R. Hathaway (1903–1984) and psychiatrist J. C. McKinley. The *Journal of Consulting Psychology*, now one of the premier journals in clinical psychology, was established in 1937; during its first decade, it was devoted largely to professional issues and to advances in mental testing.

After World War II, clinical psychology was newly supported by government funds and expanded enormously. In the United States, the Veterans Administration and the National Institute of Mental Health requested information about which universities provided adequate training in clinical psychology. The American Psychological Association responded by setting up an official system for accrediting training in clinical psychology. In 1949, the Boulder Conference set the pattern for such programs, which sought to train "scientist-practitioners." Accredited programs then received large government training grants on a continuing basis. In Britain and on the European continent, clinical psychologists began to be incorporated into the national health systems of many countries, requiring a similar elaboration of accredited training programs. In the United States, state licensing laws legitimating psychological practice developed over the years from 1945 to 1977.

In this era, clinical psychologists have generally expanded their scope of practice beyond mental testing to include various intervention activities. Although the American Psychoanalytic Association tried to permit only psychiatrists to practice psychoanalysis,

Freud himself was willing to encourage psychologists' interest in this domain, and in 1926 explicitly defended psychologist Theodore Reik's right to be a psychoanalyst (Freud, 1927). In the postwar United States, the most influential clinical psychologist involved in psychotherapy was no doubt Carl R. Rogers (1902–1987), who had been influenced by Freud's work via Otto Rank and Jessie Taft. Rogers developed his own brand of psychotherapy and demonstrated that it was actually possible to carry out empirical research on the effects of therapy. He tape-recorded therapy sessions, developed innovative measures of therapy outcome, and introduced research designs such as the use of waiting-list control subjects.

Other psychologists, such as Hans Eysenck (1916–1997) in Britain, critically reviewed the meager evidence concerning the efficacy of traditional psychotherapy (Eysenck, 1952) and argued that psychologists should devise their own therapies, using the principles they had discovered in their own laboratories. Thus, the behavior therapy movement was launched. In 1962, an important conference on the behavior therapies was launched in Charlottesville, Virginia, by psychiatrist Joseph Wolpe and his psychologist colleagues. Soon, controlled treatment studies of behavioral methods such as desensitization began to appear (Lang & Lazovik, 1963). Such experimental studies of therapy not only focused on adult psychopathology but also included parent training for dealing with children's behavior problems (e.g., Wierson & Forehand, 1994). Behavior therapists and their Skinnerian cousins, applied behavior analysts, organized themselves and began to publish scientific journals. Eventually, full-scale clinical trials, supported by government agencies, suggested comparable efficacy of behavior therapy, interpersonal psychotherapy, and medication for the outpatient treatment of depression.

Clinical psychologists also continued to carry out basic research concerning psychopathology. This domain is too vast to be covered in any detail here. Perhaps psychological research on the complex set of phenomena encompassed by the term "schizophrenia" could be taken as representative. David Shakow (1901–1981) carried out a systematic series of studies on attentional processes in schizophrenia as manifested by difficulty maintaining "set" in reaction time experiments. Paul Meehl (1962) presented an influential model of how genetic factors might be involved in schizophrenia. The work of Sarnoff A. Mednick and his colleagues capitalizes on the excellent public records kept in countries such as Denmark to carry out longitudinal epidemiological studies of family risk factors for schizophrenia (e.g., Mednick, Parnas, & Shulsinger, 1987). In 1973, psychologist Philip Holzman and his colleagues identified a specific problem characterizing schizophrenics and their first-degree relatives in smooth pursuit eye movement (Holzman, Proctor, & Hughes, 1973). This is a trait marker that does not change as the person decompensates into a schizophrenic episode or recovers from one.

In conclusion, clinical psychology has emerged from its first century of existence as the largest psychological specialty. It has taken its place beside psychiatry, social work, nursing, counseling, and related fields as an essential component in the group of sciences and professions concerned with mental health problems.

REFERENCES

Breuer, J., & Freud, S. (1986). *Studies in hysteria.* In *The standard edition of the complete psychological works of Sigmund Freud.* (Vol. 2). London: Hogarth Press. (Original work published 1895).

Eysenck, H. J. (1952). The effects of psychotherapy: An evaluation. *Journal of Consulting Psychology, 16,* 319–324.

Freud, S. (1927). *The problem of lay analysis.* New York: Brentano's.

Holzman, P. S., Proctor, L. R., & Hughes, D. W. (1973). Eye tracking patterns in schizophrenia. *Science, 181,* 179–181.

Kraepelin, E. (1987). *Memoirs.* (Translated by C. Wooding-Deane). Berlin: Springer-Verlag.

Lang, P. J., & Lazovik, A. D. (1963). Experimental desensitization of a phobia. *Journal of Abnormal and Social Psychology, 66,* 519–525.

Lunt, I., & Poortinga, Y. H. (1996). Internationalizing psychology. *American Psychologist, 51,* 504–508.

Mednick, S. A., Parnas, J., & Shulsinger, F. (1987). The Copenhagen High Risk Project. *Schizophrenia Bulletin, 13,* 485–495.

Meehl, P. E. (1962). Schizotaxia, schizotypy, and schizophrenia. *American Psychologist, 17,* 827–838.

Rorschach, H. (1921). *Psychodiagnostic.* Bern: Huber.

Routh, D. K. (1994). Clinical psychology since 1917: Science, practice, and organization. New York: Plenum.

Routh, D. K. (1998). Hippocrates meets Democritus: A history of psychiatry and clinical psychology. In A. S. Bellack & M. Hersen (Eds.), *Comprehensive clinical psychology* (Vol. 1, pp. 1–48). New York: Pergamon.

Terman, L. M. (1916). *The measurement of intelligence.* Boston: Houghton Mifflin.

Wierson, M., & Forehand, R. (1994). Parent behavioral training for child noncompliance: Rationale, concepts, and effectiveness. *Current Directions in Psychological Science, 3,* 146–150.

Witmer, L. (1907). Clinical psychology. *Psychological Clinic, 1,* 1–9.

D. K. ROUTH
University of Miami

CLUSTER ANALYSIS

Cluster analysis is a general term applied to any of a wide variety of methods used to classify objects, events, or individuals into groups (clusters) on the basis of similarity of salient attributes (Sokal, 1974). Although there is no single definition of a cluster, all definitions stress terms such as similarity, likeness, and proximity. In more technical terms, clusters are homogeneous subgroups formed by a method that minimizes variance within groups (clusters) and maximizes variance between groups.

Clustering techniques are used to identify similar subgroups of objects or individuals and to develop taxonomies. Thus they allow the investigator to describe the structure and relationship of objects to each other and to develop laws and statements about classes of objects. Cluster analysis can be used for such purposes as finding typologies, fitting models, making predictions from groups, testing hypotheses, exploring data, generating hypothesis, and reducing data.

All clustering methods involve four basic steps: (a) obtaining measures of the attributes of the objects or individuals to be classified; (b) deciding on a measure of similarity; (c) developing rules and procedures for forming clusters; and (d) applying these rules to the data to form clusters. Because a number of alternative procedures can be used at each step, a wide variety of clustering methods have been developed.

A first decision involves what attributes or properties to use as the basis of classification. This of course will vary with the problem and nature of the objects being classified. And while each attribute is usually weighted equally, differential weighting can be used. The second decision is the appropriate measure of similarity. This can be the number of common attributes, the correlation between attributes, a distance function, or some other measure.

A third decision involves the method of classification. Agglomerative methods start with individuals and combine them into groups; divisive methods start with a broad group and subdivide it into subgroups. Monothetic classifications involve classes in which all members have at least one attribute in common; polythetic classification groups share a number of properties but do not necessarily have a single common attribute.

A fourth decision is how many groups to form. This can be determined by internal criteria (e.g., natural breaks between groups) or by external criteria (e.g., what classification scheme results in the most useful laws). Finally, one must determine whether to use a hierarchical or nonhierarchical classification scheme. In the former, groups are at different levels of generality (as in biological taxonomies); in the latter, groups are at the same level of generality (as in Q factor analysis). The results of these decisions will determine the appropriate method of analysis to use and the nature of the clusters formed.

SUGGESTED READING

Everitt, B. (1974). *Cluster analysis.* London: Heinemann.

Mezzich, J. E., & Solomon, H. (1980). *Taxonomy and behavioral science.* New York: Academic Press.

Sneath, P. H. A., & Sokal, R. R. (1973). *Numerical taxonomy: The principles and practice of numerical classification.* San Francisco: Freeman.

Tryon, R. C., & Bailey, D. E. (1970). *Cluster analysis.* New York: McGraw-Hill.

F. G. BROWN
Iowa State University

MEASUREMENT

STATISTICS IN PSYCHOLOGY

COCKTAIL PARTY PHENOMENON

The cocktail party phenomenon is an important, yet everyday example of selective attention. Under some circumstances, we are capable of focusing our attention so intently on an event or task that we fail to attend to other events occurring simultaneously (Cherry, 1953). On the other hand, there are occasions where we are faced with many conflicting inputs and are compelled to shift our attention. A prime example is a large, crowded party with many loud conversations occurring at the same time. To understand the person we are talking to, we have to focus most of our attention to the discussion at hand. All other conversations are shut out or ignored. However, if someone "drops" our name or if a topic of particular interest is discussed in a nearby conversation, we immediately shift our attention to that conversation. The switch from our intense dialogue with our partner to consciously monitoring the other discussion is an example of the *cocktail party phenomenon* (Moray, 1959).

Early explanations of the cocktail party phenomenon were based on filter theory. Broadbent (1958) believed that the amount of information that we can attend to at any moment is limited. If the amount of available information exceeds the capacity of the filter at any point in time, some information is selected for further, higher-order processing, whereas the processing of the remainder is blocked. It was assumed further that the selection of relevant information occurs early and is chosen based on simple perceptual features. Thus, due to limitations of the filter, only the speech of our partner receives full semantic processing.

The ability to readily switch our attention to another conversation creates a serious problem for early selection filter theories like Broadbent's. If the limited filter or channel is set to allow full processing of our partner's monologue, it would be impossible to hear our name since the processing of others' conversations are blocked. According to filter theory, the only way that your name could reach conscious awareness is if, for some reason, the limited filter "accidentally" switched to the unattended conversation.

Treisman (1969) offered a modified filter theory and suggested that rather than completely filtering out other conversations, or rapidly switching among them (as Broadbent's theory would have to predict) we *attenuate* or give those other conversations a low level of attention. Treisman argued that incoming messages are subjected to three types of analyses. First, the message's physical properties, like pitch and loudness are processed. Second, the message is parsed into syllables and words. Finally, semantic processing occurs where the meaning of words and phrases comprising the message is extracted. Due to past experience, certain words and phrases are high in subjective importance (such as your name and phrases like "look out!"). Because of their importance, these words and phrases have a permanent and relatively low threshold (i.e., they require little mental effort to be recognized relative to words or phrases having little subjective importance). Consequently, when these important words and phrases occur in attenuated conversations, they can immediately capture our attention.

Deutsch and Deutsch (1963) and Norman (1968) proposed what have been termed late selection theories to account for selective attention, including exemplars like the cocktail party phenomenon. These theories hold that all messages are routinely processed for at least some aspect of meaning and that information deemed most important is "elaborated" more completely. Elaborated material is more likely to reach consciousness and be retained than unelaborated material. Like attenuation theory, late selection theories hold that a message's importance depends on numerous factors, including its context and its subjective or personal importance (such as your name in the context of a cocktail party). Thus, what occurs late in the process is not semantic processing (since some of it already has occurred) but the selection of which message to elaborate more fully.

A theory that appears to combine the best features of filter, attenuation, and late selection theories is a model by Johnson and Heinz (1978). For them, attention is a flexible system which allows the selection of one message over others at three different points or stages of processing depending on the task. During stage one, sensory representations of stimuli are constructed (Broadbent's early selection theory). In stage two, semantic representations of the message are constructed (similar in part to Triesman's attenuation theory). Stage three is where sensory and semantic processing reach consciousness (similar to the late selection theories of Deutsch and Deutsch, 1963 and Norman, 1968). Messages that are selected based on stage one processing require less cognitive effort or capacity than selection based on stage three.

According to Galotti (1998), multimodal theories like that proposed by Johnson and Heinz (1978) have generated many new metaphors used to describe attentional processes like the cocktail party phenomenon. The most popular is a "spotlight" metaphor, which assumes that attention can vary from a narrow focus on one message or stimulus to a more widespread focus, which can include more than one task, time, or in our case, conversations. Currently, many psychologists are more concerned with what and how much information people decide to focus on than on what is not processed by them (the main emphasis of early and many late selection models of attention).

Recent research in the neurosciences using PET scans and features extracted from the brain's electrical activity strongly indicate that many systems distributed throughout the brain contribute to attention and attentional control (see Gazzaniga, Ivry, & Mangun, 1999, for a detailed review). Some of these brain areas are specific for a given sensory modality, and these cortical areas are the sites of early attentional. processes leading to perception. Specific areas for visual processing, for example, reside in the extrastriate cortex. Higher-order systems that control or switch attention appear to involve the interaction of subcortical structures, primarily the thalamus and the partietal lobe of the cortex. Like multimodal theories, the results from the neurosciences lead us to no longer wonder whether attentional selection is early or late, since it can be both depending on the context a person is in, the task he or she is asked to perform, and his or her intentions.

REFERENCES

Broadbent, D. E. (1958). *Perception and communication.* London: Pergamon.

Cherry, C. (1953). Some experiments on the recognition of speech with one and two ears. *Journal of the Acoustical Society of America, 25,* 975–979.

Deutsch, J. A., & Deutsch, D. (1963). Attention: Some theoretical considerations. *Psychological Review, 70,* 80–90.

Galotti, K. M. (1999). *Cognitive psychology in and out of the laboratory* (2nd ed.). Belmont, CA: Brooks/Cole.

Gazzaniga, M. S., Ivry, R. B., & Mangun, G. R. (1998). *Cognitive neuroscience.* New York: W. W. Norton & Co.

Johnston, W. A. & Heinz, S. P. (1978). Flexibility and capacity demands of attention. *Journal of Experimental Psychology: General, 107*(4), 420–435.

Moray, N. (1959). Attention in dichotic listening: Affective cues and the influence of instructions. *Quarterly Journal of Experimental Psychology, 11,* 56–60.

Norman, D. A. (1968). Toward a theory of memory and attention. *Psychological Review, 75,* 522–536.

Treisman, A. M. (1969). Strategies and models of selective attention. *Psychological Review, 76*(3), 282–299.

B. R. Dunn
University of West Florida

ATTENTION
SELECTIVE ATTENTION

COGNITIVE BEHAVIOR THERAPY

Cognitive behavior therapy is an approach designed to change mental images, thoughts, and thought patterns so as to help patients overcome emotional and behavioral problems. It is based on the theory that behaviors and emotions are caused in part by cognitions and cognitive processes which one can learn to change. Traditional psychotherapies have always recognized that cognitions play an important role in behavior and emotions; however, cognitive behavior therapy is distinct from previous insight therapies in that it deals only with here-and-now cognitions. It also deals with these cognitions in a more systematic way than other therapies. It uses principles of behavior modification to find out what cognitions a patient has and which ones may be causing trouble. Behavioral techniques are then used to reduce the undesired cognitions, to suggest new cognitions and ways of thinking about a problem, and to reinforce these new cognitions. These techniques include: (a) keeping records of desired and undesired cognitions and noting the conditions in which they occur; (b) modeling new cognitions; (c) using the imagination to visualize how new cognitions can be related to desired behaviors and emotional well-being; and (d) practicing in the real world with these new cognitions so that they become the patient's habitual way of thinking.

Cognitions that may need changing include beliefs and belief systems as well as thoughts and images. A person organizes and uses cognitions through cognitive processes. These processes include: (a) ways of evaluating and organizing information about the environment and oneself; (b) ways of processing information for coping with life and solving problems; and (c) ways of predicting and evaluating future events.

HISTORY

Cognitive behavior therapy is an outgrowth of behavior modification and therapy. Behavior therapy of the 1960s attempted to explain and treat emotional and behavioral disorders using the same laws of operant and respondent conditioning that had been used successfully on lower organisms, infants, and retarded persons. However, in dealing with humans, researchers found that even very powerful external manipulations often failed to change behaviors in a consistent way. For example, to treat depressive behaviors one could reward happy behaviors and punish depressive behaviors. However, if a patient's cognitive processes involved a tendency to self-blame or to label himself or herself a failure, the external manipulations would be ineffective.

Interest in self-control, or the ability to be unaffected by immediate rewards and punishments in order to achieve a goal, helped shift many behaviorists' belief in external control of behavior to theories that postulate that a person can use cognitive skills to solve problems presented by the environment. Thought processes were seen to have an important role in determining behaviors and feelings. Cautela's study (1971) of private thought processes, and his technique of using aversive imagery to alter behavior patterns, further stimulated interest in this area.

The publication in 1969 of Bandura's *Principles of Behavior Modification* was a significant event for many behavior therapists searching for more integrative models, in that he presented theoretical interpretations of both operant and classical conditioning while emphasizing the importance of cognitive processes in the regulation of behavior. With the publication of Bandura's book, interest in thoughts and feelings increased. Conditioning models of human behavior began to give way to models emphasizing cognitive mediational processes.

A number of influential books have followed Bandura's. One of his students, Michael Mahoney, has been a major force in the cognitive behavior therapy movement. Several of his works, including *Cognition and Behavior Modification,* have helped define the field. He was also editor of the movement's journal, *Cognitive Therapy and Research,* first published in March 1977.

THEORY

Cognitions are never considered in research with lower animals. It is assumed that rats can learn relationships between cues and events through conditioning, but that they do not make interpretations or judgments, or develop distorted thinking about their environments. Hence a rat's behavior is easy to predict, if one knows what has happened to the rat. Human life is so complex, and so much of the information we receive comes through language, that it is possible for cognitions and cognitive processes to develop which do not reflect accurately the reality of a person's environment; these cognitions can cause inappropriate and undesirable behaviors and/or emotions. In rats, certain conditions usually produce the same behaviors for all rats. In humans, similar conditions might produce fear or depression in some, and no reaction in others.

According to Bandura's social learning theory, outlined in his *Principles of Behavior Modification,* humans learn to satisfy their needs by observing the outcomes of events and behaviors. From these observations they develop expectations about what will happen and about their ability to perform. They also learn to have certain emotions as the result of certain outcomes or events. They compare themselves with others, and make value judgments about their own and others' behaviors. Thus it is not the external conditions alone which determine our behaviors, but the decisions we make based on our cognitions about the conditions. Thus cognitions can result in undesirable behavior or emotions, depending upon what cognitions a person has learned to use in various life situations. If people learn to think of themselves as failures, they may become depressed. If they come to believe they cannot cope with a situation, they will attempt to avoid it. The goal of cognitive therapy is to change patients' faulty ways of thinking about themselves and to teach them the skills needed to cope with problem situations. The therapy involves learning experiences designed to change cognitions so that the latter become more appropriate and do not hamper social or emotional development.

OVERVIEW OF COGNITIVE THERAPIES

Rational-Emotive Therapy

In *The Intelligent Woman's Guide to Dating and Mating,* Albert Ellis recognized that his patients held irrational beliefs such as "I must be perfect" and "Everyone must love me." These beliefs go hand in hand with a preoccupation about what others think of a person. Whenever reality deviates from these beliefs, the patient interprets the deviation as a terrible thing. Since reality seldom meets the irrational expectations, depression can occur. Therapy involves persuading the patient to adopt more rational cognitions through modeling of appropriate thoughts. Patients are urged to monitor the quality of their thoughts, to become aware of their frequency of occurrence and their effect on emotions.

Cognitive Therapy

Aaron Beck, in *Cognitive Therapy and the Emotional Disorders,* described how persons can become depressed by using distorted thinking. Examples of such thinking include focusing on failure more than success, thinking that one failure means total failure, and other cognitive tendencies to think of oneself in a negative light. Therapy consists of recognizing these tendencies and performing homework exercises designed to give success experiences. Examples of more adaptive, positive thinking are given to the patient, who practices them until they replace the old thinking style.

Self-Instructional Training

Meichenbaum, in *Cognitive-Behavior Modification: An Integrative Approach* (1977), viewed cognitions as self-instructions used in the development of behavioral skills. These instructions were at a conscious level when the behavior was first being learned. After it was learned, the instructions faded from awareness, and the behavior was performed automatically. Abnormal instructions may be learned, leading to undesirable behaviors. If the instructions were faulty or incomplete, the patient will later have anxiety about performing the behaviors adequately. Patterns of aggressive behavior may not go away because they are based on a set of instructions that may have been useful at a younger age, but that are now

maladaptive. Therapy consists of learning new self-instructions through modeling. The patient imagines using a new set of instructions for a new set of behaviors. If the behavior is associated with anxiety, the patient is helped to relax in order to imagine following the new instructions. This therapy has been used mainly with aggressive children and for test anxiety.

Covert Modeling Therapy

Cautela has researched ways to help people learn to deal with stressful or anxiety-producing situations by having them mentally rehearse the required behaviors. In his chapter on "Covert conditioning" (1971), he outlined how patients can try out ways of dealing with situations by using their imagination. They learn to imagine what will happen as a result of their behavior and what actions they can take to cope with the situation. This therapy is similar to self-instructional training, since the result is a mental plan of action made up of self-instructions. The patient also practices relaxation techniques, so that anxiety and stress do not interfere with performance of the plan. This therapy has been used with phobias and unassertiveness.

Coping Skills Training

This therapy, described by Goldfried (1971), is similar to covert modeling. The patient imagines a stressful situation and then imagines coping with the anxiety. However, in coping skills training the visualizing is done in a sequence of images of increasing anxiety. At each stage more anxiety is tolerated through the use of relaxation techniques. In this way the patient never becomes too anxious to persevere with coping responses. The patient may also role-play the problem situation as practice. This therapy has been used for test anxiety and to help persons cope with the indecisiveness caused by having to choose between two or more anxiety-producing courses of action.

Anxiety Management Training

This therapy, described by Suinn and Richardson (1971), is similar to other therapies in that the imagination of anxiety-arousing events is used. The therapist trains the patient to recognize and use symptoms of anxiety as a signal to utilize coping strategies such as relaxation or thinking success-oriented thoughts. This therapy emphasizes using a variety of imagined situations so that the patient will be better able to cope with an array of real situations. It is generally used with persons who cannot perform in certain situations owing to excessive anxiety.

Stress Inoculation Training

Meichenbaum (1977) has described how, in this therapy, fear and anxiety are seen as caused by awareness of heightened physiological arousal and by anxiety-causing thoughts. The training involves learning to relax and changing the anxious thoughts and feelings. These techniques are rehearsed mentally and then used in actual stressful situations set up by the therapist, such as unpredictable electric shock. Experience with these stressful activities allows the patient to develop skill in using relaxation and anxiety-reducing thoughts. The stressful activities are carefully controlled, so that the patient gains self-confidence without being overwhelmed by the stressors.

Problem-Solving Therapies

These therapies assume that problems of life require a set of cognitive skills such as being able to see means-ends relationships, to come up with alternative solutions, and to predict the results of these solutions. Behavioral and emotional problems can occur if a person is lacking in these abilities. In behavioral problem-solving therapy, described by D'Zurilla and Goldfried (1971), patients are trained to specify the problems in their life, to generate possible solutions, and to try out the best ones. Patients self-monitor their means-end thinking processes and their abilities to evaluate their behaviors. This therapy has been used with disturbed children and adults who seem to be deficient in problem-solving skills.

Mahoney (1977) suggested that people could adapt better to life if they systematically used a sequence of procedures to arrive at a solution, much the way a scientist or an engineer would. These procedures are: (a) Specify the problem; (b) collect information; (c) identify causes or patterns; (d) examine options; (e) narrow the options and try them out; (f) compare the outcomes; and (g) extend and revise them based on the outcomes.

METHODOLOGY

The methodology of cognitive behavior therapy involves identifying and changing specific cognitive processes as they relate to problems of emotions and behavior. The emphasis in therapy is to deal with here-and-now, goal-oriented cognitions in a systematic fashion, using the social learning principles of modeling and rehearsal along with self-awareness and relaxation training.

The first goal of any therapy is to develop an expectation that help is available and that treatment will be effective. In cognitive behavior therapy this is achieved by helping the patient develop an awareness of maladaptive cognition-behavior-emotion patterns. This can be done by having the patient self-monitor the thoughts, feelings, and behaviors that occur before, during, and after particular problem situations or emotions. A self-monitoring recording sheet is provided to the patient for this purpose. Through therapist interpretation and the patient's own analysis, an agreement is then reached regarding the patient's problems in terms of the inappropriate cognitions associated with them. This mutual understanding provides the patient with a tangible reason for the problems. Rather than thinking he or she is going crazy, the patient now can identify the problems and see what needs to be changed. Together with a feeling of confidence in the therapist, this leads to an expectation that a successful outcome is possible. This in turn provides the motivation to continue treatment.

There are many ways to bring out cognitive information. Direct and indirect questions, correct or purposefully incorrect paraphrasing, or repeating the last words of a sentence may help the patient talk about cognitions. If these methods seem inadequate, additional anxiety-reducing, rapport-establishing techniques may be needed. The patient's cognitive self-awareness can be enhanced, if the therapist can recognize recurring themes and point these out frequently.

If the patient fails to report a self-awareness of the kinds of mal-adaptive cognitions the therapist is looking for, then an alternative strategy is to tell the patient that the cognitions associated with the problems have become automatic. It is explained that the thinking that led to present patterns has faded from consciousness, in the same way that thinking associated with tying a shoe no longer occurs past childhood. Thus the patient is viewed as behaving as if still guided by cognitions. Some therapists may be more forceful in imposing their ideas about which kinds of cognitions need to be treated in therapy, as do rational-emotive therapists, while others allow the patient to take an active role in selecting critical cognitive patterns and directions for change, as do cognitive therapists such as Beck.

Once the patient and the therapist agree upon a set of maladaptive cognitions as explaining the problem feelings or behaviors, a new set of cognitions needs to be developed. It is assumed that the patient is rational enough to distinguish, with the therapist's help, between healthful and unhealthful patterns in cognition, emotion, and behavior. The therapist can provide examples of healthful patterns and reinforce constructive suggestions made by the patient. The goal is to develop a new set of cognitions that the patient can perceive as leading to more adaptive patterns.

The next step is the development of the skills needed to overcome the patient's limitations. In cognitive behavior therapy this involves practice in using the new set of cognitions. This practice is done through either make-believe or real-life experiences. In some therapies (e.g., anxiety management training), the new adaptive cognitive patterns are developed and tested during imagination of situations. Since heightened anxiety may interfere with cognitive processes, practice usually occurs under conditions of relaxation. The goal is for the patient to report cognitive control through a sequence of behaviors and feelings associated with problem situations. This means that at each stage patients tell themselves how to cope, what to do, and how to evaluate behavior and its consequences.

It may be necessary for the patient to get actual experience in using these new cognitive skills. Research in cognitive behavior therapies tends to support Bandura's theory of self-efficacy, which states that treatment using direct behavioral experience should be more effective in increasing the patients' belief that they can perform in problem situations than methods using purely cognitive techniques. In self-instructional training, rehearsal of self-instructions alone was found to be less effective than rehearsal with an opportunity to use the practice cognitions in an actual stress situation. The treatment may thus need to include direct behavior experience, with an emphasis on using new cognitions as a guide for therapeutic change. Patients must realize not only that they know *how* to perform (cognitively), but that they actually *can* perform (behaviorally). The therapist can help patients interpret their performance as evidence of increased ability to deal with problems.

These general methodological principles have been applied to a number of therapeutic techniques. These techniques can be roughly categorized in terms of the types of target problems they address. Cognitive behavior therapies deal with three broad areas: anxiety-stress reactions, depression, and social skills. The methodologies for stress inoculation and cognitive therapy are given here as examples.

Stress Inoculation

The procedures used in stress inoculation training have been described by Meichenbaum (1977), who divides the training into three phases: in the educational phase the therapist and client come to a mutual understanding of the client's stress problem; in the second phase the client is trained in coping skills; and in the third phase the client practices these skills during exposure to actual stress.

In the educational phase the therapist must explain to the client, in lay terms, how the stressful reaction is the result of easily understood processes. A behavioral assessment is taken to discover the extent to which behavior is restricted by stress reactions, such as a particular phobia. The client describes thoughts and feelings when placed in a stressful situation; to help in this the client, eyes closed, can imagine going through a typical stressful episode. The therapist then explains that the anxiety reaction to stress is caused both by perceived increases in physical fear reactions such as rapid heart rate, sweaty palms, and bodily tension, and by a set of anxiety-causing thoughts of helplessness, panic, embarrassment, or fears of becoming insane.

In the last part of the educational phase, the therapist instructs the client to view the stress problem as a series of manageable phases rather than a single overpowering situation. This series includes preparation for stress, confrontation with the stressor, the possibility of being overwhelmed, and self-reinforcement after coping successfully. The possibility of being overwhelmed is included so that it is an expected possibility—a battle lost, but not the war.

In the rehearsal phase the therapist trains the client to become knowledgeable about stressful situations or feared objects, to plan alternative escapes, and to relax. Increased knowledge should minimize any misconceptions and reduce the overwhelming perception of the stressor. Knowing that escape routes are available should make confronting the stressor less frightening. Relaxation helps reduce fear through control of physiological responses.

In the beginning of therapy, maladaptive cognitions are pointed out to the client. These thoughts now become the signals for the use of coping skills. Cognitive coping involves learning self-talk that helps the patient realistically assess the situation, control negative thoughts and images, and recognize physiological arousal. Self-talk also includes convincing oneself to confront the stressor, cope with fear, and self-evaluate performance.

In the third phase of stress inoculation training, the cognitive coping skills are applied in actual stress situations. The therapist exposes the client to ego- or pain-threatening stressors. These stressors do not include the problem situation but may include unpredictable electric shock, imagined stress sequences, or stress-inducing films. During these stress situations, the client is urged to try out a variety of coping skills learned during the rehearsal phase. Clients will eventually develop a variety of coping skills suited to their needs and abilities.

Cognitive Therapy of Depression

One of the founders of cognitive behavior therapy, Beck, has described his approach to the treatment of depression in *Cognitive Therapy and the Emotional Disorders*. Depressed patients see themselves as losers; therapy is designed to make them feel like winners. The therapist will first select several of the patient's problems, which may be emotional, motivational, cognitive, behavioral, or physiological. Each problem is explored at three levels: in terms of abnormal behavior, such as inactivity or social isolation; in terms of emotional disturbances, such as wanting to escape; and in terms of cognitions of hopelessness and defeat.

Patients are told that keeping busy will make them feel better. The therapist and patient can design a daily activity schedule to fill up each day. These behaviors are graded, so that the patient is motivated to perform a series of tasks of increasing difficulty which are related to the alleviation of a target problem. If difficulty is increased slowly, the patient should meet with a series of successes. The therapist can provide feedback about success so that the patient will feel like a winner, thus reversing the depressive cycle of failure and negative self-evaluation.

The patient keeps an account of all daily activities, and puts an "M" by the ones mastered and a "P" by the ones that give some pleasure. Beck feels that self-monitoring and self-evaluation of activities are useful in helping depressed persons to realize their success potential, and to focus on the pleasurable aspects of their lives rather than the negative aspects.

For cognitive reappraisal, the patient and therapist look at the relations between depressive cognitions and symptoms. The patient self-monitors thoughts, feelings, and behaviors that occur before, during, and after problem situations. To change cognitive processes, the therapist can have the patient consider alternative explanations of experiences, showing that there are other ways to interpret events besides those that reflect negatively on the self. The therapist gently explores the patient's closed belief system involving negativism toward the world and the self; the therapist questions the reasons for such beliefs and debates the patient, bringing out evidence to the contrary. Cognitive rehearsal involves having the patient imagine a sequence of events related to a problem area. Perceived obstacles and conflicts are brought up for discussion, and cognitive reappraisal and problem-solving techniques are used to work through them.

SUMMARY

Psychotherapeutic approaches have, from the beginning, considered thought processes as important as causes of problem emotions and behaviors. However, the relation among thoughts, emotions and behaviors was often explained by abstract theories, which made therapy difficult for the patient to understand, and difficult for the researcher to evaluate. As a reaction to this emphasis on unseen and mysterious processes, behavior therapy limited itself only to observable, external events. Then cognitive behavior therapy focused on thoughts as behaviors.

However, cognitive behavior therapy was not a return to the traditional insight therapies. Unlike previous therapies, cognitive behavior therapy is systematic in dealing with internal events, in that it categorizes thought processes and ties them to external events through careful observation over time of thoughts, feelings, and behaviors.

Cognitive behavior therapy is directed toward the learning through practice of specific skills which have direct relevance to the presenting problem. Earlier therapies spent time in an effort to find out what past events caused problem thoughts, emotions, and behaviors. In cognitive behavior therapy the emphasis on learning skills, and on self-responsibility in the application of these skills, may give the patient a greater sense of self-mastery and coping ability. If cognitive behavior therapy proves ultimately to be an effective treatment method, it will mark the successful application of the scientific method to the analysis and change of our unseen thought processes.

REFERENCES

Bandura, A. (1969). *Principles of behavior modification.* New York: Holt, Rinehart & Winston.

Cautela, J. R. (1971). Covert extinction. *Behavior Therapy, 2,* 192–200.

D'Zurilla, T., & Goldfried, M. (1971). Problem solving and behavior modification. *Journal of Abnormal Psychology, 78,* 107–126.

Goldfried, M. (1971). Systematic desensitization as training in self-control. *Journal of Consulting and Clinical Psychology, 37,* 228–234.

Mahoney, M. J. (1977). Personal science: A cognitive learning therapy. In A. Ellis & R. Grieger (Eds.), *Handbook of rational-emotive therapy.* New York: Springer.

Meichenbaum, D. (1977). *Cognitive behavior modification: An integrative approach.* New York: Plenum.

Suinn, R., & Richardson, F. (1971). Anxiety management training: A nonspecific behavior therapy program for anxiety control. *Behavior Therapy, 2,* 498–510.

SUGGESTED READING

Emery, G., Hollon, S. D., & Bedrosian, R. C. (Eds.). (1981). *New directions in cognitive therapy: A casebook.* New York: Guilford.

Eysenck, H. J. (1979). Behavior therapy and the philosophers. *Behaviour Research and Therapy, 17,* 511–514.

Kendall, P. C., & Hollon, S. D. (Eds.). (1979). *Cognitive behavioral interventions: Theory, research, and procedures.* New York: Academic Press.

Mahoney, M. J. (1977). Reflections on the cognitive-learning trend in psychotherapy. *American Psychologist, 32,* 5–13.

Mahoney, M. J., & Arnkoff, D. B. (1978). Cognitive and self-control therapies. In S. L. Garfield & A. E. Bergin (Eds.), *Handbook of psychotherapy and behavior change: An empirical analysis* (2nd ed.). New York: Wiley.

McMullin, P. E., & Giles, T. R. (1981). *Cognitive-behavior therapy: A restructuring approach.* New York: Grune & Stratton.

Meichenbaum, D. (1976). Toward a cognitive theory of self-control. In G. E. Schwartz & D. Shapiro (Eds.), *Consciousness and self-regulation: Advances in research* (Vol. 1). New York: Plenum.

Murray, E. J., & Jacobson, L. I. (1978). Cognition and learning in traditional and behavioral therapy. In S. L. Garfield & A. E. Bergin (Eds.), *Handbook of psychotherapy and behavior change: An empirical analysis* (2nd ed.). New York: Wiley.

Rush, A. J., Beck, A. T., Kovacs, M., & Hollon, S. (1977). Comparative efficacy of cognitive therapy and pharmacotherapy in the treatment of depressed outpatients. *Cognitive Therapy and Research, 1,* 17–37.

Spivack, G., Platt, J. J., & Shure, M. D. (1976). *The problem-solving approach to adjustment.* San Francisco: Jossey-Bass.

Wolpe, J. (1978). Cognition and causation in human behavior and its therapy. *American Psychologist, 33,* 437–446.

J. P. Foreyt
Baylor College of Medicine

G. K. Goodrick
University of Houston

COGNITIVE BEHAVIOR THERAPY
PSYCHOTHERAPY

COGNITIVE DISSONANCE

The theory of cognitive dissonance was proposed by Festinger in *A Theory of Cognitive Dissonance* (1957). Festinger predicated the theory on the assumption that a person is motivated to maintain consistency or consonance among pairs of relevant cognitions, where a cognition refers to any knowledge or belief about self, behavior, or the environment. Cognitions X and Y are regarded as dissonant "if not-X follows from Y" (p. 13); such dissonance is postulated to be "psychologically uncomfortable" (p. 3) and to produce pressure both to reduce the dissonance and to avoid situations or information that would increase the dissonance.

Festinger indicated that the amount of pressure to reduce the dissonance would be a function of the magnitude of the dissonance, where the magnitude of dissonance produced by a given cognition depends both on the importance ascribed to it and other relevant cognitions, and on the proportion of the relevant cognitions that are dissonant. Dissonance may be reduced by altering one of the dissonant cognitions, by reducing the importance of the dissonance, or by adding new information which is consonant with one of the discrepant cognitions or which somehow reconciles the two dissonant elements. For example, one might reduce the dissonance produced by the cognitions "I smoke" and "Smoking causes cancer" by stopping the smoking; by denying or denigrating the evidence linking smoking with cancer; by concluding that the risk associated with smoking is less than the risk produced by the stress with which smoking helps one to deal; or by seeking the company of militant smokers and avoiding nonsmokers. Thus dissonance is postulated to produce cognitive activity designed to reduce the dissonance.

Several points must be made at this juncture. First, Festinger postulated a pressure or tendency to reduce dissonance; this effort may not be successful. Therefore Festinger stated that "in the presence of a dissonance, one will be able to observe the *attempts* to reduce it. If attempts to reduce dissonance fail, one should be able to observe the symptoms of psychological discomfort" (1957, p. 24). Second, attempts to reduce dissonance may fail because the cognitions are resistant to change; for example, changing a cognition might contradict reality or change other consonances into dissonances, change might be painful or impossible, or a behavior may be highly satisfying in other respects. Finally, as subsequent researchers have indicated, Festinger's position concerns psychological inconsistency, not formal logical inconsistency; that is, "I smoke" and "Smoking causes cancer" will produce dissonance only with the assumption that the smoker does not want cancer. As Aronson (1980) indicated, this ambiguity both increases the scope of dissonance theory and makes it difficult to specify when in fact dissonance will occur.

Festinger identified four varieties of dissonance. Post-decision dissonance occurs when one must choose between two alternatives, both of which have positive and negative features. Forced compliance dissonance results when one is induced to behave in a manner that contradicts beliefs, but the external inducement is not substantial enough to justify the counterattitudinal act. Since the belief is less resistant to change than the cognition that the behavior occurred, dissonance typically will be reduced by changing the belief to be more consonant with the behavior. The dissonance and consequent attitude change are maximized when the inducement is barely sufficient to elicit the behavior (or barely insufficient, which produces a strengthening of the attitude). Voluntary or involuntary exposure to new information may threaten or alter existing cognitions, or produce new cognitions, thereby generating dissonance. Finally, social support systems may generate dissonance, as when group members disagree, or membership entails adoption of new cognitions, or when an external event invalidates a belief central to the group. Since 1957, dissonance effects have been demonstrated in other situations as well. For example, justification of cruelty involves denigrating innocent victims. Furthermore, various researchers have provided data indicating that dissonance can alter such fundamental motive states as pain and thirst.

In the final chapter of *A Theory of Cognitive Dissonance*, Festinger noted the certain existence of individual differences in how and how much people respond to dissonance, and proposed a quantifiable "tolerance for dissonance" continuum. Several studies have demonstrated that existing personality scales can serve as moderators of reactions to dissonance. Thus Norman and Watson (1976) proposed that extraverts are more tolerant of inconsistency than introverts, and reported less attitude change for extraverts than introverts after writing a counterattitudinal essay under conditions of high perceived freedom of choice. Similarly, Olson and Zanna (1979) provided evidence of postdecisional selective exposure effects consistent with dissonance theory for repressors but not for sensitizers.

In a 1967 article Bem argued that dissonance phenomena could be accounted for more parsimoniously, without reliance on motive states, by assuming that actors infer their beliefs from observations of their own behavior, just as observers would. Thus if one observes oneself performing an action in the absence of a strong external inducement, the logical inference is that one believes in the act. Bem has provided simulation data consistent with this interpretation. However, Piliavin and colleagues (1969) argued that observers do not have access to the actor's knowledge of original attitudes and consequent dissonance; consistent with this, their simulation subjects did not reproduce the dissonance effects. Furthermore, Zanna and Cooper (1974) reported that subjects led to believe that a pill had aroused them showed no dissonance effects, while subjects told the pill had no side effects exhibited dissonance, and subjects told the pill would relax them demonstrated enhanced dissonance. This and other misattribution studies implicate arousal states as necessary for dissonance to occur, thus placing the phenomenon outside the domain of self-perception theory. Fazio, Zanna, and Cooper (1977) have argued that the two theories are complementary, so that self-perception accounts for attitude change toward an attitude-congruent behavior, while dissonance produces change toward an attitude-discrepant behavior.

In summary, the strength of cognitive dissonance theory has also been its weakness; that is, the postulation of cognitive mechanisms has had a substantial heuristic impact, but the resulting intricate experimental procedures have been subject to alternative interpretations. Attempts to explicate the role of arousal states and the implication of the self-concept (see Aronson, "Persuasion via self-justification," 1980) promise both to clarify the theory and to enhance its contribution.

REFERENCES

Fazio, R. H., Zanna, M. P., & Cooper, J. (1977). Dissonance and self-perception: An integrative view of each theory's proper domain of application. *Journal of Experimental Social Psychology, 13,* 464–479.

Festinger, L. (1957). *A theory of cognitive dissonance.* Stanford, CA: Stanford University Press.

Norman, R. M. G., & Watson, L. D. (1976). Extraversion and reactions to cognitive inconsistency. *Journal of Research in Personality, 10,* 446–456.

Olson, J. M., & Zanna, M. P. (1979). A new look at selective exposure. *Journal of Experimental Social Psychology, 15,* 1–15.

Piliavin, J. A., Piliavin, I. M., Loewenton, E. P., McCauley, C., & Hammond, P. (1969). On observers' reproductions of dissonance effects: The right answers for the wrong reasons? *Journal of Personality and Social Psychology, 13,* 98–106.

Zanna, M. P., & Cooper, J. (1974). Dissonance and the pill: An attribution approach to studying the arousal properties of dissonance. *Journal of Personality and Social Psychology, 29,* 703–709.

SUGGESTED READING

Festinger, L., & Carlsmith, J. M. (1959). Cognitive consequences of forced compliance. *Journal of Abnormal and Social Psychology, 58,* 203–210.

Wicklund, R. A., & Brehm, J. W. (1976). *Perspectives on cognitive dissonance.* Hillsdale, NJ: Erlbaum.

Zimbardo, P. G. (Ed.). (1969). *The cognitive control of motivation.* Glenview, IL: Scott, Foresman.

J. B. CAMPBELL
Franklin & Marshall College

SELF-FULFILLING PROPHECY

SURPRISE

COGNITIVE NEUROSCIENCE

The study of the neural basis of cognition, or cognitive neuroscience, has evolved rapidly in the last ten years. In large part this has resulted from the parallel advances in brain imaging technology and raw computing power. Indeed, the exponential growth and concomitant movement of extraordinarily powerful computers to the desktop has made routine the analysis of large complex datasets. Cognitive neuroscience is an enterprise that depends heavily on the use of modern imaging technologies like positron emission tomography (PET) and functional magnetic resonance imaging (fMRI), and because of this reliance on technology, the ability to look noninvasively at the functionings of the human brain has only very recently become possible.

The fundamental goal of the cognitive neuroscientist is to understand the neural basis of the human mind. Historically, the mind had been thought to be separate from the body. Descartes, the eighteenth century French philosopher/mathematician, was perhaps the most vociferous advocate of mind-body dualism. The locations of the human mind and the soul have plagued humanity for at least as long as written records exist. Until recently, there was no reason to suspect that the mind might have components that were tied to the body. After all, this notion might be discordant with the belief of the immortality of the soul—if the body dies, then so does the mind. Descartes circumvented the problem by separating the mind from the body, and therefore from the brain.

Mind-body dualism did not last long. Neurologists of the nineteenth century began to notice that patients with specific brain injuries, either from stroke or trauma, displayed consistent behavioral deficits. Broca, a French neurologist, systematically described the effect of lesions in the left frontal cortex on language. Insightfully, he was the first to state that language was localized to the left cerebral hemisphere. This opened the door for an explosion of cognitive localization in the brain. In its extreme form, phrenology, every function of the human mind could be localized to some bump or valley in the brain (and skull). The use of brain lesions to deduce brain function subsequently became the predominate method for exploring the mind/brain for the next hundred years.

The lesion method truly was the first cognitive neuroscience technique. Its growth paralleled the recognition of other types of deficiency syndromes in medicine. The lesion method relied solely on the power of observation and a ready supply of patients with various types of brain injury. The history of the field is full of references to famous patients whose unfortunate circumstances led to some insight about the functioning of some particular brain region. Phineas Gage, perhaps the first famous patient, was a nineteenth century railroad worker who had an iron rod accidentally driven upwards from just below his left eye out through the top of his skull. Remarkably, he lived for another decade, and his subsequent change in personality from a reliable steady worker to a profane, erratic, irascible man was aptly characterized by his physician at the time: "Gage was no longer Gage."

James, the father of modern psychology, was attuned to these advancements in understanding the brain in the late nineteenth century. Further evidence linking brain function to cognitive processing continued to accumulate. The observation that regional changes in cerebral blood flow were tied to mental function can be traced to a fortuitous discovery in a patient with an arteriovenous malformation in his frontal lobe. This patient (and his physician) noticed an increase in audible blood pulsation when performing mental calculation. This observation, that local changes in cerebral blood flow are linked to neural activity, underlies all modern functional imaging techniques.

The parallel development of new imaging technologies with increased computational power in the late twentieth century resulted in the development of two new methods to study human brain function. PET developed as an outgrowth of autoradiography. Unlike its predecessor, PET can be performed without the requirement of sacrificing the animal. PET takes advantage of the fact that when a positron (a positively charged electron) encounters an electron, the two particles annihilate each other, and two high-energy gamma rays are emitted in exactly opposite directions. By arranging a series of gamma-ray detectors in a ring, the origin of the particle can be computed. Positron emitters can be synthesized into common molecules, like water or 2-deoxyglucose, and when injected into a subject can be used to map cerebral blood flow or metabolism. Similarly, fMRI relies on the coupling of neural activity to local cerebral blood flow. Current thinking suggests that transient increases in neural activity result in a hyperremic blood flow response. Oxygenated hemoglobin and deoxygenated hemoglobin have different magnetic properties, and because the increase in blood flow results in a transient increase in the oxy- to deoxy- ratio, this can be detected with MRI. By rapidly acquiring MRIs while a subject is performing a cognitive task in the scanner, the changes in blood flow can be correlated to what the subject is doing.

Although PET and fMRI typically measure only relative changes in brain activity, through careful experimental design it is possible to isolate the neural circuits associated with specific cognitive processes. The basis for this is called subtractive design. By designing an experiment with at least two cognitive conditions, one of which is a control state, the brain activity maps obtained during the control state can be subtracted from the brain activity during the condition of interest. In actual practice, a statistical test is usually performed instead of a simple subtraction, but the assumption is that whatever brain regions show different activity between the two conditions represent the circuit associated with processing the extra information. It is critical that the control state be chosen appropriately. Otherwise, one might be subtracting cognitive states that are so different from one another that the assumptions of this method are violated. In particular, subtraction assumes that cognitive process behave linearly, that processes can be added and sub-tracted without interacting with each other. This may be true under some circumstances, but not all.

In general, the subtractive approach to imaging has confirmed what was known from the lesion method, but recent advances in fMRI have allowed the description of more subtle processes. By presenting subjects with very brief stimuli, the cerebral blood flow response can be measured and correlated with individual events. This goes beyond the subtractive approach, which often requires the subject to maintain a cognitive state for tens of seconds to minutes. Event-related fMRI measures the brain response on a scale less than a second, which is much closer to the timescale at which the brain operates. New computational algorithms are also revealing the complex correlations that occur between different brain regions, which begins to reveal the choreography of brain activity that must be the hallmark of cognition. With the combination of rapid imaging and new algorithms, perhaps the elusive goal of identifying the neural basis of the mind will be achieved.

REFERENCES

Damasio, A. R. (1994). *Descartes' error: Emotion, reason, and the human brain.* New York: G. P. Putnam.

Frackowiak, R. S. J., Friston, K. J., Frith, C. D., Dolan, R. J., & Mazziotta, J. C. (1997). *Human Brain Function.* San Diego: Academic Press.

Kwong, K. K., Belliveau, J. W., Chesler, D. A., Goldberg, I. E., Weisskoff, R. M., Poncelet, B. P., Kennedy, D. N., Hoppel, B. E., Cohen, M. S., Turner, R., Cheng, H. M., Brady, T. J., & Rosen, B. R. (1992). Dynamic magnetic resonance imaging of human brain activity during primary sensory stimulation. *Proc. Natl. Acad. Sci. USA, 89,* 5675–5679.

Ogawa, S., Tank, D. W., Menon, R., Ellerman, J. M., Kim, S.-G., Merkle, H., & Ugurbil, K. (1992). Intrinsic signal changes accompanying sensory stimulation: functional brain mapping with magnetic resonance imaging. *Proc. Natl. Acad. Sci. USA, 89,* 5951–5955.

G. S. BERNS
Emory University

GAGE, PHINEAS
NEUROIMAGING
NEURAL MECHANISMS OF LEARNING

COGNITIVE NEUROSCIENCE OF LEARNING AND MEMORY

Cognitive neuroscience approaches, with their focus on relating neural substrates to cognitive functions, have advanced our understanding of the neural basis of learning and memory. In turn, our understanding of the neural basis has informed the way we think about the functional organization of memory systems. One of the most prominent themes in cognitive neuroscience has been trying

to understand which kinds of learning and memory are spared, and which are impaired, with damage to the *hippocampus* (a specialized brain structure in the medial temporal lobe).

We have known for many decades that the hippocampus plays a disproportionately important role in learning and memory, since Scoville and Milner (1957) presented the famous patient HM. HM had severe memory impairments following bilateral medial temporal lobe lesions that included the hippocampus. Despite these severe impairments, including the inability to learn all kinds of factual information (names, places, facts, etc.), HM was nevertheless able to learn to perform new tasks (e.g., tracing while looking into a mirror). Many attempts have been made to characterize precisely what distinguishes these preserved learning abilities from those that are impaired (e.g., Squire, 1992; Schacter, 1987; Sutherland & Rudy, 1989; Cohen & Eichenbaum, 1993; Rolls, 1990). Many of these ideas emphasize a procedural (e.g., sensorimotor task-learning) or implicit (i.e., not explicitly verbalizable) aspect of preserved learning abilities, which is consistent with the data from HM.

Computational neural network models, which simulate cognitive functions using networks of neuron-like processing units constrained according to known properties of different brain areas (O'Reilly & Munakata, 2000), have provided a more precise language for understanding the unique contribution of the hippocampus in learning and memory (McClelland, McNaughton, & O'Reilly, 1995). These models show that there is a basic computational conflict between two essential kinds of learning: the ability to rapidly learn specific, novel information without interfering with previous knowledge, and the ability to learn about the generalities or regularities of the environment. Therefore, it makes sense that two different brain areas should each separately achieve these learning objectives. Biological and behavioral evidence coincide with this computational argument in suggesting that the hippocampus is specialized for the rapid learning of specific information, while the cortex is better suited for learning generalities (O'Reilly & McClelland, 1994; McClelland et al., 1995).

The computationally-motivated division of labor between the cortex and hippocampus is consistent with recent data from individuals who suffered selective hippocampal damage early in life. These people were able to learn several kinds of general information (e.g., language skills, semantic knowledge about the world) and had IQ scores in the normal range, yet suffered from the inability to rapidly encode novel information as measured by \i *episodic* memory tests (Vargha-Khadem et al., 1997). Note that these data violate earlier notions that hippocampal damage spares only procedural or implicit learning, whereas the computational notions based on underlying neural mechanisms provide a more general framework that encompasses these data.

The cognitive neuroscience-based theories can inform our understanding of performance on the kinds of basic memory tasks that psychologists have been studying for many years. For example, many are now arguing that recognition memory (the ability to recognize whether an item has been recently studied) can be subserved by two different neural systems having different functional properties (e.g., Aggleton & Brown, 1999; O'Reilly, Norman, & McClelland, 1998; Yonelinas, 1997). One of these systems is the hippocampus, which can provide an explicit recollection signal (i.e., recalling specific aspects of the study episode), while the other is subserved by cortical areas surrounding the hippocampus, which can provide an indistinct sense of familiarity.

Recent studies on a patient with selective hippocampal damage have confirmed a somewhat counterintuitive prediction that the computational models make regarding the different properties of these two memory systems (Holdstock et al., in press). This patient showed intact recognition memory for studied items compared with similar lures when tested in a two-alternative forced-choice procedure (2AFC), but was significantly impaired relative to controls for the same kinds of stimuli using a single item yes-no (YN) procedure. Because the cortex encodes generalities by representing similar items using similar neural substrates, it is likely that the strong similarity of the lures to the studied items produces a strong familiarity signal for these lures (as a function of this overlap). When tested in a YN procedure, this strong familiarity of the lures produces a large number of false alarms, as was observed in the patient. However, because the studied item has a small but reliably stronger familiarity signal than the similar lure, this strength difference can be detected in the 2AFC version, resulting in normal recognition performance in this condition. The normal controls, in contrast, have an intact hippocampus which keeps the items separate, enabling control subjects to rapidly encode them with minimal interference; they are therefore able to distinguish the studied items from the similar lures, regardless of the testing format.

This example illustrates that more precise understanding of the neural substrates of memory can lead to sophisticated and counterintuitive behavioral predictions. As recent brain imaging techniques (functional MRI, PET, and ERP) improve their ability to resolve active representations in various memory tasks (e.g., Henson, Rugg, & Dolan, 1999; Buckner & Koutstaal, 1998), we should be able to test even more sophisticated and nuanced theories of the cognitive neuroscience of learning and memory.

REFERENCES

Aggleton, J. P., & Brown, M. W. (1999). Episodic memory, amnesia, and the hippocampal-anterior thalamic axis. *Behavioral and Brain Sciences, 22,* 425–490.

Buckner, R. L., & Koutstaal, W. (1998). Functional neuroimaging studies of encoding, priming, and explicit memory retrieval. *Proceedings of the National Academy of Sciences, 95,* 891.

Cohen, N. J., & Eichenbaum, H. (1993). *Memory, amnesia, and the hippocampal system.* Cambridge, MA: MIT Press.

Henson, R. N. A., Rugg, M. D., & Dolan, R. J. (1999). Recollection and familiarity in recognition memory: An event-related functional magnetic resonance imaging study. *Journal of Neuroscience, 19,* 39–62.

Holdstock, J. S., Mayes, A. R., Roberts, N., Cezayirli, E., Isaac, C. L., O'Reilly, R. C., & Norman, K. A. (in press). Memory dissociations following human hippocampal damage. *Hippocampus.*

McClelland, J. L., McNaughton, B. L., & O'Reilly, R. C. (1995). Why there are complementary learning systems in the hippocampus and neocortex: Insights from the successes and failures of connectionist models of learning and memory. *Psychological Review, 102,* 419–457.

O'Reilly, R. C., & McClelland, J. L. (1994). Hippocampal conjunctive encoding, storage, and recall: Avoiding a tradeoff. *Hippocampus, 4*(6), 661–682.

O'Reilly, R. C., & Munakata, Y. (2000). *Computational explorations in cognitive neuroscience: Understanding the mind by simulating the brain.* Cambridge, MA: MIT Press.

O'Reilly, R. C., Norman, K. A., & McClelland, J. L. (1998). A hippocampal model of recognition memory. In M. I. Jordan, M. J. Kearns, & S. A. Solla (Eds.), *Advances in neural information processing systems* (pp. 73–79). Cambridge, MA: MIT Press.

Rolls, E. T. (1990). Principles underlying the representation and storage of information in neuronal networks in the primate hippocampus and cerebral cortex. In S. F. Zornetzer, J. L. Davis, & C. Lau (Eds.), *An introduction to neural and electronic networks.* San Diego, CA: Academic Press.

Schacter, D. L. (1987). Implicit memory: History and current status. *Journal of Experimental Psychology: Learning, Memory, and Cognition, 13*(3), 501–518.

Scoville, W. B., & Milner, B. (1957). Loss of recent memory after bilateral hippocampal lesions. *Journal of Neurology, Neurosurgery, and Psychiatry, 20,* 11–21.

Squire, L. R. (1992). Memory and the hippocampus: A synthesis from findings with rats, monkeys, and humans. *Psychological Review, 99,* 195–231.

Sutherland, R. J., & Rudy, J. W. (1989). Configural association theory: The role of the hippocampal formation in learning, memory, and amnesia. *Psychobiology, 17*(2), 129–144.

Vargha-Khadem, F., Gadian, D. G., Watkins, K. E., Connelly, A., Van Paesschen, W., & Mishkin, M. (1997). Differential effects of early hippocampal pathology on episodic and semantic memory. *Science, 277,* 376.

Yonelinas, A. P. (1997). Recognition memory ROCs for item and associative information: The contribution of recollection and familiarity. *Memory and Cognition, 25,* 747–763.

R. O'REILLY
University of Colorado, Boulder

LEARNING THEORIES
MEMORY
NEURAL MECHANISMS OF LEARNING

COGNITIVE THERAPY

DEFINITION

Cognitive therapy is a psychotherapeutic approach that teaches individuals that their interpretations of situations influence their emotions, physiological reactions, behaviors, and motivations.

Cognitive therapy is a time-effective, structured, psychoeducational form of treatment employing a collaborative process between therapist and patient. This working collaboration is comprised of Socratic questions and answers, mutual reflections and feedback, the employment of hypothesis testing, cognitive reevaluation, behavioral experiments, and experiential exercises. Through these methods, patients recognize thematic biases in their thinking; generate alternative, adaptive viewpoints; and use these new cognitive strategies to improve their mood and problem-solving skills.

HISTORY

Aaron T. Beck, MD developed cognitive therapy starting in the early 1960s. While empirically testing Freud's "anger turned inward" theory of depression, Beck instead found that depression involved a negative bias in thinking that often led clients to feel despondent and hopeless. Through a synergistic cycle of clinical observations and research, Dr. Beck refined his cognitive theory of depression and developed techniques to treat patients by modifying their biased thought processes. Beck's developing theory was influenced by ego-oriented psychodynamic psychotherapy, developmental cognitive psychology, personal construct therapy, social learning theory, behavior therapy, and the phenomenological school of psychology.

Although originally developed as a treatment for unipolar depression (Beck, Rush, Shaw, & Emery, 1979), cognitive therapy subsequently has been applied to a wider range of psychological disorders and clinical populations, such as bipolar disorder (Lam, Jones, Hayward, & Bright, 1999); anxiety disorders (Clark, Salkovskis, Hackmann, Middleton, & Gelder, 1992); eating disorders (Agras, 1999); substance abuse (Beck, Wright, Newman, & Liese, 1993); couples' problems (Baucom, Sayers, & Sher, 1990); personality disorders (Beck, Freeman, & Associates, 1990); and schizophrenia (Kingdon & Turkington, 1994), among others. Cognitive therapy can be used in an individual, couples, family, and group format.

THEORY

According to the cognitive model, biased perceptions adversely affect mood and behavior. For example, an individual suffering from depression may experience automatic thoughts centering on self-criticisms or hopelessness about the self, the world, and the future ("cognitive triad" [Beck et al., 1979]). In addition to being identifiable by their *content,* cognitive distortions can be addressed and studied in terms of their *process.* An example is *fortune telling,* in which individuals assume they know that the outcome of an event necessarily will be negative. This may lead the person not only to be pessimistic, but also prematurely to give up attaining the goal. This unfavorable outcome reinforces the negative belief, thus causing a vicious cycle that solidifies the emotional distress. Beck and colleagues (1979) have elucidated a number of other cognitive errors similar to fortune telling.

Automatic thoughts are theorized to be produced by more basic, fundamental, all-encompassing beliefs called "negative schemas" (Young, 1999). For example, individuals with an *incompetency* schema, upon being presented with a difficult task, may overreact and become despondent. Their "incompetency schema"

exaggerates the meaning of the event for such people, leading them to feel bad about themselves, defeated, and hopeless. In order to cope with this core schema, individuals develop conditional assumptions as well as concomitant, compensatory behaviors. In this case, the conditional assumptions may be, "If I make a mistake there's no point in trying anymore," and "If I receive any corrections at all it means I'm doing a bad job." The compensatory strategies may take the form of setting unrealistic standards for oneself, trying to do everything perfectly, or avoiding opportunities to master important tasks. Sometimes these compensatory strategies can shield an individual from distress, but more commonly they grow to cause their own set of difficulties. It is at this point that people typically decide to seek therapy. A specific treatment plan is then developed from a conceptualization of the patient's automatic thoughts, underlying schemas, and compensatory strategies (Beck, 1995). Subsequently, realistic goals are set and pursued via the use of individually tailored interventions.

CLINICAL APPLICATIONS

Clients are taught to examine and modify distorted thinking to gain a more objective and manageable view of their problems, which they then solve systematically. Therapists conduct a comprehensive diagnostic evaluation and formulate a cognitive conceptualization (Beck, 1995) that is shaped by new data throughout treatment. From this foundation, the treatment plan and goals are set, pursued, and evaluated periodically.

An agenda is set each session, including mood check, summaries of events, the application of new cognitive skills to ongoing issues and goals, and homework. The therapist and patient collaborate to understand the patient's world view, and empirically evaluate specific target areas (e.g., social avoidance, procrastination, impulsivity). Cognitive therapists use a variety of cognitive, behavioral, and experiential interventions to monitor, test, and modify problematic beliefs and their concomitant emotions, strengthen problem-solving skills, replace compensatory behaviors with adaptive strategies, and develop an adaptive coping repertoire. Homework is assigned to reinforce work done in session, apply therapy lessons to the outside world, and design behavioral experiments for examination in the next session. Cognitive therapy clients learn important skills that maximize long-term maintenance of therapeutic gains.

REFERENCES

Agras, W. S. (1999). Cognitive-behavioral therapy for the eating disorders. In D. S. Janowsky (Ed.), *Psychotherapy indications and outcomes* (pp. 197–210). Washington, DC: American Psychiatric Press.

Baucom, D., Sayers, S., & Sher, T. (1990). Supplementary behavioral marital therapy with cognitive restructuring and emotional expressiveness training: An outcome investigation. *Journal of Consulting and Clinical Psychology, 58,* 636–645.

Beck, A. T., Freeman, A., & Associates. (1990). *Cognitive therapy of personality disorders.* New York: Guilford.

Beck, A. T., Rush, A. J., Shaw, B. F., & Emery, G. (1979). *Cognitive therapy of depression.* New York: Guilford.

Beck, A. T., Wright, F. D., Newman, C. F., & Liese, B. S. (1993). *Cognitive therapy of substance abuse.* New York: Guilford.

Beck, J. S. (1995). *Cognitive therapy: Basics and beyond.* New York: Guilford.

Clark, D. M., Salkovskis, P. M., Hackman, A., Middletown, H., & Gelder, M. (1992). A comparison of cognitive therapy, applied relaxation, and imipramine in the treatment of panic disorder. *British Journal of Psychiatry, 164,* 759–769.

Kingdon, D. G., & Turkington, D. (1994). *Cognitive-behavioral therapy of schizophrenia.* New York: Guilford.

Lam, D. H., Jones, S. H., Hayward, P., & Bright, J. A. (1999). *Cognitive therapy for bipolar disorde: A therapist's guide to concepts, methods and practice.* New York: Wiley.

Young J. E. (1999). *Cognitive therapy for personality disorders: A schema-focused approach* (3rd ed.). Sarasota, FL: Professional Resource Press/Professional Resource Exchange, Inc.

M. G. Fox
Beck Institute for Cognitive Therapy and Research

C. F. Newman
University of Pennsylvania

COGNITIVE BEHAVIOR THERAPY
PSYCHOTHERAPY

THE COGNITIVE TRIAD

According to cognitive theory, many of the disturbances associated with depression result from the activation of a set of cognitive patterns that forces the individual to view his or her situation in an idiosyncratic, negative, and pessimistic way (Beck, 1967, 1976; Clark, Beck, & Alford, 1999). This set of negative cognitions is referred to as the *cognitive triad,* as it consists of thought patterns about the world, the self, and the future. The cognitive triad remains active in depressed individuals because such individuals selectively and inappropriately interpret experiences as being negative in some substantive way. Typical cognitions of depressed individuals show a variety of deviations from logical thinking, including making arbitrary inferences of negative meaning, selectively focusing on negative events, overgeneralizing from one negative experience, employing dichotomous thinking, and catastrophizing. As a consequence of these errors in information processing, the patient automatically makes negative interpretations of situations even though more plausible explanations are readily apparent. The continued activation and dominance of the negative cognitive triad leads to other phenomena associated with the depressive state, such as sad affect and the lack of motivation.

NEGATIVE VIEW OF THE PERSONAL WORLD

The first component of the cognitive triad is the tendency of the depressed individual to interpret ongoing experiences in a negative way. Interactions with the environment are often misinterpreted as

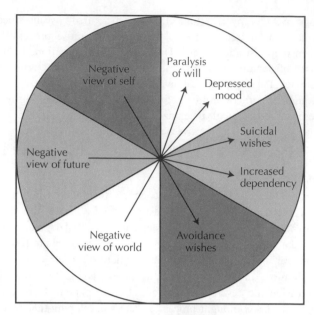

Figure 1.   Cognitive Triad

representing some form of defeat or deprivation. Automatic reactions to problems or difficulties are likely to be thoughts such as "I'm beaten," "I'll never be able to do this," or "I'm blocked no matter what I do." Any problem seems insoluble, and any delay in reaching a goal seems indefinite. For example, a depressed woman had some difficulty finding a pencil in her purse and immediately had the thought, "I'll never be able to find it." She experienced a strong sense of frustration even though she was able to find it in a few seconds.

Many patients with depression are particularly prone to react to achievement-oriented situations with a sense of failure or to make negative attributions whenever they are in a competitive situation. One patient had the highest standing in class, but whenever the teacher called on another student to answer a question, the patient thought, "He doesn't really think I'm smart or he would have called on me." If the professor complimented other students, he would have the thought that the professor had a low opinion of him.

Events seen as relatively trivial to the outside observer are often interpreted by the depressed patient as constituting substantial loss. A patient on his way to see his psychiatrist had to wait about 30 seconds for the elevator and thought, "I'm losing valuable time." As he rode up alone on the elevator, he regretted having no one to ride with and thought, "I'm missing out on the companionship of other people." When he discovered that another patient had an earlier appointment, he regretted that he was not the first patient the psychiatrist would see that day. When he had to wait a few minutes in the waiting room, he had the thought that the psychiatrist did not care for him.

Making comparisons with other people is especially likely to activate feelings of dissatisfaction and deprivation. Many depressed patients have thoughts such as, "I don't have anything" when a friend acquires something new. A well-to-do businessman was prone to regard himself as poor when he heard that someone made more money than he did. A wealthy woman regarded herself as deprived when one of her friends made a new acquisition, whether it was a hat, a dress, or a house. In addition to feeling deprived, the depressed patient is prone to interpreting comments from others as devaluing and is likely to read insults, ridicule, or disparagement into what other people say. In summary, the world of the depressed individual is filled with themes of defeat, deprivation, and devaluation.

NEGATIVE VIEW OF THE SELF

Depressed patients not only interpret their experiences as negative, they devalue themselves as well. If a depressed individual does not do as well as expected on a test or a business venture, a likely immediate reaction is to think of oneself as ineffective and undesirable. A striking feature of the depressed patient is the tendency to overgeneralize from a particular incident. A student who had difficulty getting a date on a single occasion thought, "I must be repulsive to girls." A highly successful businessman who made one transaction that lost money became obsessed by the idea that he was stupid. A mother whose child was untidy on one occasion thought, "I'm a terrible parent."

Depressed patients often see themselves solely in terms of their deficiencies. Further, these negative self-evaluations are usually associated with self-rejection. Patients often will not only see themselves as inferior, but will criticize, reproach, and castigate themselves for being so inferior. Thoughts of ineffectiveness, inferiority, and inadequacy abound in individuals with depression.

NEGATIVE VIEW OF THE FUTURE

Depressed patients often show considerable preoccupation with thoughts about the future, and these ideations may occur in the form of pictorial fantasies or obsessive ruminations. Such thoughts have a negative cast and are usually an extension of the patient's view of the present state, often to the point where the patient sees no possibility for improvement. If patients regard themselves as currently deprived, immobilized, or rejected, then they will likely visualize a future in which they are continually deprived, immobilized, or rejected. Not only are long-range forecasts pessimistic, but short-term predictions are similarly negative. Upon awakening in the morning, many patients anticipate how every experience during the day will pose great difficulties. When contemplating whether or not to perform a task, they predict that they will make a mess of it. When a suggestion is made to engage in an ordinarily enjoyable activity, they assume that they will not have a good time. One patient, for example, frequently had elaborate fantasies of failure before engaging in any activity. When driving to the psychiatrist's office for an appointment, she pictured herself making a wrong turn and getting lost. When she considered calling a friend on the phone, she had a daydream of getting no answer or a busy signal. If she decided to go shopping, she imagined herself losing her purse or making the wrong purchases. Like the present, the future is seen as containing one failure and defeat after another.

IMPLICATIONS

Identifying the automatic negative evaluations that depressed individuals make about their world, self, and future has significant implications for the diagnosis, assessment, and treatment of the condition. Cognitive therapists help patients identify such thoughts and then work to develop ways of challenging these faulty, overly negative evaluations. Such therapy has been demonstrated to be quite effective at alleviating symptoms of depression (Clark et al., 1999).

REFERENCES

Beck, A. T. (1967). *Depression: Clinical, experimental, and theoretical aspects.* New York: Harper & Row.

Beck, A. T. (1976). *Cognitive therapy and the emotional disorders.* New York: International Universities Press.

Clark, D. A., Beck, A. T., & Alford, B. A. (1999). *Scientific foundations of cognitive theory and therapy of depression.* New York: Wiley.

G. HENRIQUES
University of Pennsylvania

**COGNITIVE THERAPY
DEPRESSION**

COIE, JOHN D.

John D. Coie is a professor of psychology at Duke University, where he has been on the faculty since 1968. He received his PhD in psychology from the University of California at Berkeley in 1968, after having completed an MA in mathematics at the University of Illinois at Urbana and a BS in mathematics from Wheaton College. He received an honorary degree, Docteur Honoris Causa, from the University of Montreal in 1998. He was the recipient of a National Institute of Mental Health (NIMH) Career Research Scientist award from 1990 to 2000. He has served on a number of national panels and task forces on violence and its prevention, and chaired an NIMH review panel on child and adolescent risk and prevention issues.

The primary focus of Coie's research has been the development and prevention of serious antisocial behavior. Following a developmental model in which early child, family, and community risk factors place some children at high risk for long-term antisocial outcomes, he proposed that poor peer relations in childhood contribute to the development of conduct problems. He theorized that person-based effects on the social environment mediate the overall development of psychopathology and violence. By this he meant that child characteristics, such as impulsiveness, aggression, and low social competence, may cause peers and adults to reject the child. This rejection, in turn, may reduce the child's opportunities for social, emotional, and cognitive development, increase his or her hostility toward other people, and put him or her at greater risk for disorder. Coie developed widely used methods for assessing children's peer relations and demonstrated the stability of peer rejection across time and new peer circumstances. He introduced experimental methods for observing the process of peer rejection and identifying its causes. In his longitudinal studies of urban youth, he documented the contribution of childhood peer relations to subsequent adjustment or disorder in adolescence and the early adult years.

Building on his early efforts at intervention with high-risk children, Coie and colleagues from three other universities conducted a large-scale prevention research trial at four sites across the United States. By intervening at school entry and providing competence-building programs to very high-risk children, their families, and their schools across the formative years of childhood and early adolescence, the Fast Track project is testing developmental theory regarding chronic and early-starting antisocial behavior.

The early results of the Fast Track project suggest it may provide a model for community-based efforts at preventing serious violence. This balance between studying basic processes in human development and applying this knowledge in real world settings has been the underlying characteristic of Coie's professional career.

STAFF

COLOR VISION

The visual experience of most vertebrates features sensitivity to the intensity of electromagnetic radiation within their range of visible wavelengths, from about 380 to 760 nm. Beyond this achromatic or colorless sensitivity some fish, birds, reptiles, and mammals (mainly human and non-human primates) are additionally sensitive to a wavelength's color (hue) and apparent purity or strength (saturation). Most human beings see the shorter spectral wavelengths as bluish (near 480 nm), medium wavelengths as greenish (near 510 nm) and yellowish (near 580 nm), and longer wavelengths as reddish (near 700 nm). Along with these differences in hue, a color may be seen as ranging from highly saturated (e.g., dark red) to desaturated (e.g., pink).

TYPES OF COLOR VISION

By definition, color vision permits discrimination between at least one frequency of visible monochromatic light versus white light of a comparable brightness. Beyond this minimal ability, considerable inter- and intraspecies differences exist in the extent of color vision capabilities. For those with normal or trichromatic color vision, every wavelength is discriminable from white. Further, for trichromats a combination of three other monochromatic lights (usually a short, medium, and long wavelength) is required to subjectively match all the visible wavelengths.

Not all those with trichromatic color vision necessarily have comparable color vision, however. As depicted in Table 1, various types of color vision anomalies exist for trichromats. While anomalous trichromats are able to see the entire range of colors perceived by those with normal trichromatic vision, they may require supranormal intensities to recognize colors within their range of decreased sensitivity. In addition, within this anomalous range, colors are often seen as faded or less saturated, and a reduced ability to discriminate between adjacent colors is sometimes found.

Differentiation of the various types of anomalous trichromats—for example, in terms of protanomalous or deuteranomalous—can be made with the Rayleigh match or anomaloscope test. With normal trichromatic vision, there is a unique mixture of green light (535 nm, yellowish green) plus red light (670 nm, yellowish red) that cannot be distinguished from a yellow light (589 nm, reddish yellow). For anomalous trichromats, the combination of red and green that matches yellow differs from that for normal trichromats. Protanomalous viewers need additional red in the mixture to match yellow; similarly, deuteranomalous trichromats require a mixture containing a greater amount of green.

Dichromats evidence a more severe limitation of color vision than do anomalous trichromats; for dichromats, not all the visible wavelengths can be distinguished from white, and all the wavelengths can be matched by a mixture of only two other wavelengths. The classification of dichromatic versus trichromatic vision is based upon the neutral point test that examines the ability to discriminate between numerous individual monochromatic wavelengths and white light. While trichromats can discriminate between each individual wavelength and white light when brightnesses are equated, for dichromats there is a narrow range of wavelengths that cannot be so discriminated from white light.

This narrow band of wavelengths indiscriminable from white light is referred to as the neutral point, and its spectral location determines the particular type of dichromatism. As indicated in Table 1, protanopia and deuteranopia are associated with seeing blue and yellow but not red or green. Conversely, tritanopia and tetartanopia are accompanied by perception of red and green but not blue or yellow.

Monochromats can match any visible wavelength by merely adjusting the intensity of a single other wavelength. With the possible exception of some limited color vision associated with blue-cone monochromatism, monochromats do not see color.

SPECTRAL SATURATION

Subjective saturation can be estimated by determining the extent to which a monochromatic light can be diluted by the addition of white light, before this mixture becomes indiscriminable from a white light of equivalent brightness. The greater the amount of white light that can be added in the mixture, before the combination cannot be discriminated from white, the greater the subjective saturation of the hue. With normal trichromatic vision, human beings see the spectrum as being minimally saturated at a narrow region in the yellowish portion of the spectrum (near 567 nm). The perceived saturation of the remaining portions of the spectrum is substantially greater, and the short wavelengths (bluish) are seen as the most saturated of all. Table 1 lists the particular exceptions to this for the anomalous trichromats.

SPECTRAL DISCRIMINABILITY

The richness of color vision is partially indicated by the number of distinct colors that can be seen. The extent of such uniqueness is estimated by the ability to discriminate between adjacent colors

Table 1.   Categories of Color Vision

| Classification | Percentage Incidence in Human Beings | | Appearance of Spectrum |
	Males	Females	
Trichromatism			
Normal			normal
Anomalous			
protanomalous	1	0.02	reduced brightness, saturation, and hue discriminability at long wavelengths
deuteranomalous	4.9	0.38	reduced brightness, saturation, and hue discriminability at medium wavelengths
tritanomalous		rare	reduced brightness, saturation, and hue discriminability at short wavelengths
Dichromatism			
protanopia	1	0.02	gray at 494 nm neutral point; blue below, yellow above
deuteranopia	1.1	0.01	gray at 499 nm neutral point; blue below, yellow above
tritanopia	0.002	0.001	gray at 570 nm neutral point; green below, red above
tetartanopia		rare	gray at 470 and 580 nm neutral points; green between, red above and below
Monochromatism			
rod	0.003	0.002	gray
neural			gray
blue-cone			gray; some blue and yellow possibly seen

Data are from G. Wyszecki & W. S. Stiles, Color science: *Concepts and methods, quantitative data and formulas,* and F. A. Geldard, *The human senses.* A complete description of each deficiency is complex and disputed in some cases. Briefly, a classification may include brightness sensitivity, a neutral point test, a Rayleigh match test, color discrimination ability, and perceived saturation.

measured in Weber fractions ($\Delta\lambda/\lambda$) for color discriminations. Normal trichromatic vision results in detectable changes in color wavelength as small as 0.2% near 480 and 600 nm. Below, between, and above these two points, larger differences between wavelengths are necessary to be seen as noticeably different. However, changes of less than 1% can be detected across most of the visible spectrum.

THEORIES OF COLOR VISION

Recent conceptualizations of the underlying mechanism mediating color vision feature a merger of two accounts initially considered to be in conflict. One approach, trichromatic theory, was advanced by Thomas Young and Hermann von Helmholtz, who stressed the relative activity of cones maximally sensitive to red, green, or blue. The other account, opponent-process theory, was developed by Ewald Hering, Leo Hurvich, and Dorothea Jameson. Their approach considered red-green as well as blue-yellow to be antagonistic processes. These two emphases have now been reconciled so that trichromatic theory describes receptor activity and opponent-process theory applies to higher-order neural integration.

At the receptor level, cone photopigments, while broadly tuned, are maximally sensitive to either a short (440 nm), medium (540 nm), or long (570 nm) wavelength. Thus while some medium wavelength may affect all three types of cones, the greatest relative amount of activity ensues from those cones maximally sensitive to medium wavelengths. This trichromatic component is then integrated at the lateral geniculate nucleus (LGN) level in an opponent-process manner. While precise details have yet to be described, such integration in general may be due to alterations in the baseline activity of LGN opponent cells.

These opponent cells are sensitive to differences in cone inputs and include those mediating red *or* green (R-G) as well as blue *or* yellow (B-Y). For the R-G type, the input from cones maximally sensitive to long wavelengths could decrease the baseline activity in R-G opponent cells, while that from medium wavelength cones increases such neural firing rates. The other group of opponent cells, those integrating B-Y, could have their spontaneous activity increased in response to short wavelength cones and decreased in response to long wavelength cones. For example, the perception of orange could accompany comparable strengths of output from the R-G system signaling red, along with the B-Y system signaling yellow. Such modulated output of opponent LGN cells is somehow ultimately interpreted by cortical neurons (Boynton, 1971).

REFERENCES

Boynton, R. M. (1971). Color vision. In J. Kling & L. Riggs (Eds.), *Woodworth and Schlosberg's experimental psychology* (3rd ed.). New York: Holt, Rinehart & Winston.

Wyszecki, G., & Stiles, W. S. (1967). *Color science: Concepts and methods, quantitative data and formulas.* New York: Wiley.

SUGGESTED READING

DeValois, R. L., & DeValois, K. K. (1975). Neural coding of color. In E. Carterette & M. Friedman (Eds.), *Handbook of perception* (Vol. V). New York: Academic Press.

Fobes, J. L., & King, J. E. Vision: The dominant primate modality. In J. Fobes & J. King (Eds.), *Primate behavior.* New York: Academic Press.

Hurvich, L. M. (1972). Color vision deficiencies. In D. Jameson & L. Hurvich (Eds.), *Handbook of sensory physiology* (Vol. 7/4). Berlin, Germany: Springer-Verlag.

J. L. FOBES
Army Research Institute for the Behavioral Sciences

DEPTH PERCEPTION
NEUROCHEMISTRY

COLUMBIA MENTAL MATURITY SCALE (CMMS)

The Columbia Mental Maturity Scale (CMMS), developed at Columbia University, is designed for ages 3½ through 10 years, consists of 92 items, each printed on a 6- by 19-in. card (15.24 cm X 22.86 cm). Each item measures pictorial or geometric classification skills. Items use the multimental format which requires the child to point to the picture or geometric shape that does not belong with the other elements on the card. Items are grouped into eight overlapping levels, each consisting of 56 to 65 items. Examinees are routed to one of these levels based on their chronological age. Administration is individual and requires 15 to 20 min.

The CMMS was originally developed for testing cerebral-palsied children, but it has proved useful with children having a variety of handicapping conditions as well as with normal children. Popular features are: (a) the minimal dependence on language, both in administering and responding; (b) the large size of the item cards; and (c) the brevity and ease of administering and scoring.

National norms for the 1972 edition (Burgemeister, Blum, & Lorge, 1971) were based on a carefully selected sample of 2,600 children stratified by geographic region, age, sex, race, and socioeconomic status. Total number right converts to an age-based standard score (age deviation score), percentile rank, and stanine (M = 100, SD = 16). A type of age equivalent (maturity index) provides a developmental score. Median split-half reliability ranges from 0.85 to 0.91 with a median of 0.90. Median test-retest reliability is reported as 0.85 for three age groups (Burgemeister et al., 1971). Although significant correlations have been found between CMMS and individually administered intelligence measures, the CMMS cannot be routinely substituted for these, because it measures only one aspect of intellectual functioning.

REFERENCE

Burgemeister, B. B., Blum, L. H., & Lorge, I. (1971). *Manual for the Columbia mental maturity scale.* New York: Psychological Corp.

G. J. ROBERTSON
Wide Range, Inc.

INTELLIGENCE MEASURES
NONVERBAL INTELLIGENCE TESTS

COMMON FACTORS

Common factors refer to effective aspects of psychotherapy that are shared by diverse forms of treatment. These common factors are held to underlie the effectiveness of these treatments. Factors unique to particular treatments are of secondary importance, at best, if this conception is correct. That is, what treatments have in common is more important than what sets them apart. In fact, what they have in common is more important than the factors the various forms of therapy themselves implicate as the effective ingredients of their treatments. The common factors are the actual ameliorative aspects of psychotherapy.

HISTORY

The first theorist to posit common factors was probably Rosenzweig (1936). He argued that psychotherapy, of whatever stripe, worked because of certain ameliorative properties. These included provision of a therapeutic relationship and a systematic ideology or rationale to explain the problem as well as the means for resolving it. Additionally, some therapists are simply good at this kind of thing regardless of their orientation. Therapist personality is therefore a key factor.

The most systematic exposition of the common factors point of view was offered by Frank (1982). According to Frank, people come for psychotherapeutic treatment because they are demoralized. Therapy works by instilling hope in the patient. To do so, all successful forms of therapy, from psychoanalysis to behavior therapy to demonology, provide a meaningful relationship, a healing setting, a rationale that explains the origin of problems, and a set of rituals that will ameliorate the problems. Other seminal works have been reprinted by Goldfried (1982). Weinberger (1993) provide a history and overview of the common factors movement.

At first, most theorists and clinicians did not take the notion of common factors seriously. Instead, rival schools proliferated. Starting in the 1980s, however, common factors became a major aspect of thinking about therapeutic action (Beitman, Goldfried, & Norcross, 1989), and the movement has been mushrooming ever since. There is a positive relationship between year of publication and number of common factor proposals offered (Grencavage & Norcross, 1990). Common factors in one form or another now represent a mainstream view.

Weinberger (1993) suggested that the change in the field's view of common factors was triggered by two events. First was the repeated finding that outcomes for diverse forms of psychotherapy are roughly equivalent (e.g., Lambert & Bergin, 1994; Smith, Glass, & Miller, 1980). There seemed to be no way that the unique actions of individual treatments can account for this finding. Many treatment modalities offer apparently contradictory change mechanisms and techniques, and even have philosophies that seem to contradict one another. Yet, in the end, they all seem to work equally well. Common factors can account quite nicely for these findings. Treatments are equally effective because they share common factors. Despite differences in trappings and ways of conceptualizing change, what is done has enough in common to account for equivalence of effect.

A second impetus for the change in view was the psychotherapy integration movement (Stricker & Gold, 1993). Thinkers began writing about ways to combine heretofore opposing treatment modalities in order to make them more effective. Probably the most influential work of this sort was Wachtel's (1977) effort to integrate psychodynamic and behavioral therapy. Since the two treatments seem so different, at least on the surface, there was an effort to discover underlying similarities. Integration of two modalities is only possible if one can discover some common or complementary aspects or goals. Common factors provided these commonalities or complementary aspects.

WHAT ARE THE COMMON FACTORS?

Many sets of common factors have been proposed over the years. Those offered by Rosenzweig (1936) and by Frank (1982) were listed above. Many others have been offered since then. For the most part, there is agreement on what these factors are. The most frequently proposed common factors, in order of their popularity, have been the development of a therapeutic alliance, the opportunity to vent, the acquisition and practice of new behaviors, positive therapeutic expectations, positive qualities possessed by the therapist, and the provision of plausible explanations for problems and plausible means for resolving those problems (Grencavage & Norcross, 1990). Jensen and Bergin (1988) have added the notion of a shared value system that cuts across the different therapeutic modalities. Kelly (1990) showed that patients come to share values as treatment progresses, so it appears that this factor has some validity.

Weinberger (1993, 1995) reviewed the empirical data and concluded that the extant research most strongly supported five common factors. These are the therapeutic relationship, patient expectancies concerning treatment, exposing patients to problematic issues, mastery of problem areas, and attribution of therapeutic success or failure to internal or external causes. This does not mean that the research has invalidated other proposed common factors. They have, for the most part, not been adequately tested as yet. Much work is still needed to determine what the common factors are and which are of greater and lesser importance.

HOW COMMON FACTORS WORK

Most common factor views see all therapies as employing the relevant factors to roughly equal degrees (e.g., Frank, 1973, 1982). Thus, despite their differences, they all provide a therapeutic relationship, a rationale, mastery experiences, etc. This equivalence of use of the relevant common factors then accounts for equivalence of outcome. In contrast, Weinberger (1995) has argued that different treatments emphasize different common factors. That is, each type of treatment relies on some common factors but neglects others. For example, dynamic treatments emphasize the therapeutic relationship but pay relatively little heed to fostering mastery experiences. Cognitive treatments, on the other hand, strongly emphasize the provision of mastery experiences but show a relative neglect of the therapeutic relationship. All treatment modalities neglect expectancies (Weinberger & Eig, 1999). In this formulation, outcome equivalence is due to the fact that therapies are all in-

complete or unbalanced and do not make maximal use of common factors.

No one has yet offered a viable theory of why common factors work. Frank (1982) has written of provision of hope, but there is no a priori reason why the particular factors thus far identified should be most effective in eliciting hope. Additionally, no one yet understands how the same common factors seem to work in such different therapeutic contexts. All we know as of today is that common factors seem to underlie much of therapeutic success; we do not yet know why. The study of these factors is still in its infancy. Much remains to be done.

REFERENCES

Beitman, B. D., Goldfried, M. R., & Norcross, J. C. (1989). The movement toward integrating the psychotherapies: An overview. *American Journal of Psychiatry, 146,* 138–147.

Frank, J. D. (1982). Therapeutic components shared by all psychotherapies. In J. H. Harvey & M. M. Parks (Eds.), *The Master Lecture Series (vol I): Psychotherapy research and behavior change* (pp. 9–37). Washington, DC: American Psychological Association.

Goldfried, M. R. (Ed.). (1982). *Converging themes in psychotherapy.* New York: Springer.

Grencavage, L. M., & Norcross, J. C. (1990). What are the commonalities among the therapeutic factors? *Professional Psychology: Research and Practice, 21,* 372–378.

Jensen, J. P., & Bergin, A. E. (1988). Mental health values of professional therapists: A national interdisciplinary survey. *Professional Psychology, 19,* 290–297.

Kelly, T. A. (1990). The role of values in psychotherapy: A critical review of process and outcome effects. *Clinical Psychology Review, 10,* 171–186.

Lambert, M. J., & Bergin, A. E. (1994). The effectiveness of psychotherapy. In A. E. Bergin & S. L. Garfield (Eds.), *Handbook of psychotherapy and behavior change* (4th ed., pp. 143–189). New York: Wiley.

Rosenzweig, S. (1936). Some implicit common factors in diverse methods of psychotherapy. *American Journal of Orthopsychiatry, 6,* 412–415.

Smith, M. L., Glass, G. V., & Miller, F. I. (1980). *The benefits of psychotherapy.* Baltimore, MD: John Hopkins University Press.

Stricker, G., & Gold, J. R. (Eds). (1993). *Comprehensive handbook of psychotherapy integration.* New York: Plenum.

Wachtel, P. L. (1977). *Psychoanalysis and behavior therapy: Toward an integration.* New York: Basic Books.

Weinberger, J. (1993). Common factors in psychotherapy. In G. Stricker & J. R. Gold (Eds.), *Comprehensive handbook of psychotherapy integration* (pp. 43–58). New York: Plenum.

Weinberger, J. (1995). Common factors aren't so common: The common factors dilemma. *Clinical Psychology: Science and Practice, 2,* 45–69.

Weinberger, J., & Eig A. (1999). Expectancies: The ignored common factor in psychotherapy. In I. Kirsch (Ed.), *How expectancies shape experience* (pp. 357–382). Washington, DC: American Psychologist Association.

J. L. WEINBERGER
Adelphi University

BEHAVIOR THERAPY
PSYCHOTHERAPY

COMMUNICATION PROCESSES

Communication is essentially a process by which the state of affairs at one place is transmitted to another place by symbolic means. The study of the process has engaged the collaboration of many different disciplines, from electrical engineering to philosophy, from biology to political science. The serious study of communication processes as a separate field of inquiry derived from the realization that different phenomena in each field have something in common, and that application of a unified communications model would be beneficial for each field.

The accepted general form for analysis of the process is due to the need for measuring transmission of information by communications engineers (Shannon & Weaver, 1949) and consists of five steps: (a) the source (the original state of affairs); (b) the transmitter; (c) the channel; (d) the source of noise; and (e) the receiver, leading to the reconstructed state of affairs. The channel has a capacity to vary a certain kind and amount of data; the translation of the data into the form acceptable to the channel (coding), and reverse process for the use by the receiver (decoding), become central problems in analysis and design of communication systems. Noise is defined as the origin of errors in transmission; the signal received by the receiver is a function of the original signal and noise.

The scheme proposed by Shannon and Weaver lends itself nicely to mathematical analysis, giving quantitative measures of information, channel capacity, error reduction, redundancy, and efficiency of coding systems. Beyond this technical use, however, the model allows the discussion of different approaches to communication processes on a common base. Distinctions among similar processes in different fields become mainly differences in emphasis on the links in the process. Thus molecular genetics can be understood as a coding process and research will be directed at deciphering the code, stating the mechanisms which control noise (here called "mutation"), and investigating the mechanisms of decoding—the translation of DNA into protein structures. In literary criticism, the structure of meaning and form in poetry can be analyzed as a choice of coding system.

The study of communication is divided into interpersonal and mass communication. The main difference is that in the first, the receiver can respond immediately, creating a network of several communication chains. Mass communication is not so responsive and each transmission link is separated; however, some technical advances blur this distinction, making mass communication responsive.

The study of interpersonal communication is the more complex of the two, because the units of communication are not easily differentiated. Theoretical approaches and aim of research in this field are heavily dependent on methods of research, observation, experiments, or field study.

Procedures for observation of the communications process define broad categories, which correspond to types of the message. Two of the earliest ones are presented in Bales's *Interaction Process Analysis* and Chapple's "Interaction chronograph." Bales took as a model the case study conference or general problem-solving seminar, and selected emotional reaction, positive and negative, and instrumental categories such as asking for and giving facts or interpretation. Chapple's system is even more abstract, measuring only the amount of talking, overlap, and lengths of contradiction. Both methods seem very simplified and avoid any mention of communication content. Bales's consists of 12 formal categories, and Chapple's essentially of an off-on dichotomy for each participant, but both methods have stood the test of time, and most other observation systems have been elaborations of these systems for specific purposes.

The experimental approach to measuring communication, by contrast, inferred the actual communication processes from measurement of the conditions and the effect of the process. One tradition, stemming from Bavelas (1951) and Leavitt (1951), has been to control the channels of communication of a group (conventionally of five members), determining, for instance, who can talk to whom, and to measure outcomes such as task efficiency or satisfaction with the procedure. The outcomes of the experiments can contrast different patterns such as the most centralized and most egalitarian one, and show that the importance of communication for status inequality, group process, leadership, and morale was concerned with integration of the communicating group (group cohesion), influence, consensus, and deviance. In many experiments an informal social communication process was controlled by experimental instruction and inputs by the experimenter, and outcomes were measured through questionnaires or joint actions by the members of the group. This tradition was started by Leon Festinger and his collaborators (1950). The place of communication in these studies was determined by the condition that nothing else but communication happened during the life of the group, and thus the relationship between the experimenter-controlled conditions and the outcomes, such as change of attitude or consensus, could be seen as a function of the communication process.

The controls exerted on experimental groups have avoided the need for measuring the content of communication, because the conditions themselves restricted and defined the categories of possible content. This procedure is also justified by the potentially infinite variety of topics and measures of ordinary conversation which occurs in controlled conditioning. Another approach has been field observation of actual communication sequences. A large detailed analysis of these communication processes has been conducted by ethnomethodologists and other social psychologists who try to devise a system which can connect individual utterances. Their work has been summarized by Grimshaw (1981). The meagerness of results compared to the large technical apparatus expended to collect the data would indicate that field observation and analysis of interpersonal communication is still in a very weak position, without a good theory to guide data collection.

The study of mass communication has been guided mainly by interest in content. Mass media—books, newspapers, broadcasting, plays, movies, and so on—come naturally in large units; the production is little amenable to experimental control or detailed analysis of communication structure. Thus conditions and consequences are mainly macrosocial; large units of content are the natural targets. The basic method of communication research in mass media is content analysis, but no generally useful systems have emerged, as they have in interaction analysis. Systems of content analysis are specifically designed to fit the problem under consideration.

While some work in content analysis has been directed toward microunits of communication, especially in studies applying the mathematical theory of information to measuring style, most techniques of content analysis use large units, either directly or by inference, such as values expressed or conflicts shown. This analysis may select the demographic traits of characters, the kind of plot in a novel or play, the length in column inches or printing of news articles, or the type of heroes in magazine biographies. Mass communication analysis is concerned primarily with the meanings, with what is in the channel, where the record is generally variable. Correspondingly, there has been less concern with the conditions under which the communication process occurred, which are harder to determine. The direction of research is therefore opposite to that of interpersonal communication, and frequently evidence from content analysis is taken as proof of effects on the audience.

Theoretical work has tried to bridge this gap. Katz and Lazarsfeld (1955) prepared a two-step theory of communication which goes from mass media to designated individuals, the opinion of leaders on different topics, who then transmit this information to a circle of acquaintances. Other theories have concerned themselves with the type of medium—that is, the characteristics of the channel—as providing the link between content and conditions of communication. Lerner (1958) developed a theory of progress of society that ranges from those depending only on interpersonal communication through those with mass literacy to those having electronic communication that develops empathy with a variety of situations and leads to an enlarged personal world. A comprehensive and for some time very popular theory was proposed by McLuhan, who, in such books as *Gutenberg Galaxy* and *The Medium is the Massage* classified media by the number of sensory channels they stimulated and the intensity or clarity of that stimulation, thus including both interpersonal communication and mass media. He identified "cool" media which stimulate many channels vaguely, and "hot" media which stimulate one channel intensively. "Cool" channels are interpersonal or electronic media; "hot" channels are printed media. Thus we have a transition from interpersonal to hot media (the Gutenberg revolution) and from printed to electronic media—mainly television—which is the current change. McLuhan developed a general theory of culture and society on this basis. More recently Klapp (1978) developed a more specifically sociological theory based on an originally more mathematical theory, using a cyclic oscillation of entropy and information. This theory returns to the original problem of efficiency of in-

formation transmission, which depends on a balance of concern for novelty and fidelity. Klapp ties in these concerns with different social mechanisms.

REFERENCES

Bales, R. F. (1950). *Interaction process analysis: A method for the study of small groups.* Reading, MA: Addison-Wesley.

Bavelas, A. (1951). Communication patterns in task-oriented groups. In D. Lerner & H. D. Laswell (Eds.), *The policy sciences.* Stanford, CA: Stanford University Press.

Chapple, E. (1949). The interaction chronograph: Its evolution and present application. *Personnel, 25,* 295–307.

Festinger, L., et al. (1950). *Theory and experiment in social communications.* Ann Arbor, MI: Institute of Social Research.

Grimshaw, A. (1981). Talk and social control. In M. Rosenberg & R. Turner (Eds.), *Social psychology.* New York: Basic Books.

Katz, E., & Lazarsfeld, P. F. (1955). *Personal influence: The part played by people in the flow of mass communications.* Glencoe, IL: Free Press.

Klapp, O. (1978). *Opening and closing.* Cambridge, England: Cambridge University Press.

Leavitt, H. (1951). Some effects of certain communication patterns on group performance. *Journal of Abnormal and Social Psychology, 46,* 38–50.

Lerner, D. (1958). *The passing of traditional society.* Glencoe, IL: Free Press.

McLuhan, M. (1962). *The Gutenberg galaxy.* Toronto: University of Toronto Press.

McLuhan, M., & Flore, Q. (1967). *The medium is the massage.* New York: Random House.

Shannon, C., & Weaver, W. (1949). *The mathematical theory of communication.* Urbana, IL: University of Illinois Press.

K. W. BACK
Duke University

BILINGUALISM

COMMUNICATION SKILLS TRAINING

Therapists of diverse theoretical positions have long realized that numerous clients with a variety of psychopathological complaints are deficient in interpersonal or communication skills. Persons diagnosed as schizophrenic, neurotic, or mildly mentally retarded, as well as alcoholics, those having marital difficulties, and parents with child management problems, have all been seen as having difficulties in interpersonal communication. In the period from 1970 to 1980 three major trends led to the increased emphasis upon communication skills training as an important therapeutic and preventive tool. The first and perhaps most important trend was the disenchantment of many psychologists and other therapists with the medical model of therapeutic intervention. As Goldstein has noted in *Psychological Skills Training,* an increasing number of therapists turned to a different set of assumptions. Basic to this approach is the assumption that the client is suffering from a skill performance deficit, and that the role of the therapist is to teach or train the client to perform the requisite set of skills.

The second trend was the increasing application of behavioral strategies to the treatment of a diversity of behavioral problems. It was quickly recognized that, before psychiatric clients could be deinstitutionalized or normalized they would have to learn an extensive array of communication skills, such as conversational skills and job acquisition and maintenance skills. Those behaviorists working with neurotic clients quickly learned that many of their clients required assertiveness training.

The third trend involved the developing use of the specific procedures delineated in Ivey and Authier's *Microcounseling* to train counselors and psychotherapists. To those using this method of training and to those trained by it, it quickly became obvious that similar methods could be used to train clients in interpersonal communication skills. Thus the microcounseling technology has been used to train institutionalized psychiatric clients, parents, marital partners, and families in communication skills.

Communication skills training usually is focused upon two broad sets of interpersonal skills: skills in simply interacting with one or more persons, and skills involving interpersonal or shared problem solving. (The majority of early communication skill-training programs focused on specific deficits and/or populations.) Conversational skill training is directed toward the enhancement of an individual's ability to initiate and maintain conversations with other people. This form of training has been employed with institutionalized and formerly institutionalized persons and with individuals experiencing social anxiety. Date initiation and heterosexual interaction skills are another set of communication skills training procedures developed for those having difficulty with these spheres of life. Communication skills training is a central component of most assertiveness-training procedures, since effective communication is seen as an important precursor to assertive behavior.

Another specific form of communication skills training is job interview training directed toward chronically unemployed persons and students about to enter, and others reentering, the job market. Most premarital, marital, and parenting programs, whether developed for therapeutic or preventive/educative purposes, include communication skills training in both interactional and shared problem-solving skills. Many organizational development programs directed toward incrementing the quality of working life include communication skills training as a critical component. Programs concerned to facilitate interpersonal communication and/or shared problem solving have been developed for managers, supervisors, and coworkers. With the increasing realization that primary prevention programs are best directed at the younger members of our society, social skills training programs have been developed for use from prekindergarten to high school. Kelly, in *Social-Skills Training,* has presented an excellent review of many of these varied communication skills training programs.

As the various communication skills training programs developed, it became increasingly obvious that there are perhaps a common set of communication skills that pervade the many and varied interpersonal activities in which people engage. Thus the same communication skills are important in interactions with a person's spouse, children, family, friends, and coworkers. Five basic sets of communication skills apply in most situations: (a) visually and physically responsive behavior, listener sensitivity to the communication of another, and congruent expression; (b) skills designed to encourage others to give information, including the use of silence, minimal encouragements, and questioning; (c) information-giving skills such as self-disclosure, feedback, and inferences; (d) skills providing communications designed to change the behavior of others, such as evaluation, requests, and advice; and (e) skills involved in shared problem solving, and in communication, and problem-solving skills that are used to arrive at mutually satisfactory solutions to problems.

With the shift from the assumptions of the medical model of intervention to the assumptions of an education or training model, has come greater reliance on the principles of instructional psychology. Most communication skills training programs are based on a very similar model of training involving an instructional sequence, a practice sequence, and a generalization sequence. Gagné and Briggs in *Principles of Instructional Design* summarize many of the important characteristics of instruction included in various communication skills training programs.

Initial research in this area involved the demonstration that communication skills training methods produced significant increments in performance during training. A second wave of research involved the demonstration that increments in communication skills performance led to changes in other behaviors such as decreased delinquency, improved marital and parent-child relations, and increased academic performance. A subsequent concern of researchers was the demonstration that educationally based methods of communication skills training are superior to methods based upon other assumptions, such as sensitivity training. Yet another focus of research has been the specification of the skills that should be included in communication skills training programs and the best methods of training the constituent skills. It can be concluded that communication skills training programs are effective; however, considerable research is required to develop programs that enhance the generalization of the skills to different situations and over time.

REFERENCES

Gagné, R. M, & Briggs, L. J. (1979). *Principles of instructional design.* New York: Holt, Rinehart & Winston. (Original work published 1974)

Goldstein, A. P. (1981). *Psychological skills training.* New York: Pergamon.

Ivey, A. E., & Authier, J. (1978). *Microcounseling: Innovations in interviewing, counseling, psychotherapy, and psychoeducation.* Springfield, IL: Thomas.

Kelly, J. A. (1982). *Social-skills training.* New York: Springer.

SUGGESTED READING

Evans, D. R., Gemeinhardt, M., Austin, G., Shatford, L., & Bolla, P. *Human adjustment: Skills.* Monterey, CA: Brooks/Cole. (in press).

Gazda, G. M. (1981). Multiple impact training. In R. J. Corsini (Ed.), *Handbook of innovative psychotherapies.* New York: Wiley.

Keane, S. P., & Conger, J. C. (1981). The implications of communication development for social skills training. *Journal of Pediatric Psychology, 6,* 369–381.

O'Leary, K. D., & Turkewitz, H. (1981). A comparative outcome study of behavioral marital therapy and communication therapy. *Journal of Marital and Family Therapy, 7,* 159–169.

Spivack, G., Platt, J. J., & Shure, M. D. (1976). *The problem-solving approach to adjustment.* San Francisco: Jossey-Bass.

D. R. EVANS
Cambridge, England

ASSERTIVENESS TRAINING
CROSS-CULTURAL COUNSELING
GROUP PSYCHOTHERAPY

COMMUNITY PSYCHOLOGY

Community Psychology entered the lexicon of most psychologists in 1965, following a conference designed to establish a role for psychology in the United States's community mental health movement. The report of the conference called for psychologists to become active in the problems of society by assuming the role of social change agent and "participant-conceptualizer" (Bennett et al., 1966). The term "community mental health" refers to a broad array of mental health service delivery programs loosely thought of as a national social policy designed to reduce the incidence and prevalence of mental illness. This public health goal requires an epidemological rather than a clinical view of mental illness.

The roots of the community mental health movement may be found in many of the early traditions of American Psychology (Caplan, 1969), and in the first half of the 20th century as the "mental hygiene movement." The formal onset of the modern community mental health movement, however, did not take hold until well after mid-century, in the form of legislation. The Mental Health Study Act, passed by the U.S. Congress in 1955, established a Joint Commission on Mental Health and Illness and led to the publication of 10 monographs and a final report, *Action for Mental Health* (1961). These reports were the stimulus for the 1963 Community Mental Health Centers Act, mandating centers for comprehensive mental health service delivery throughout the United States.

In 1966 a Division of Community Psychology was established within the American Psychological Association, and Robert Reiff was elected as its first president. In 1973 the *Annual Review of Psy-chology* began to include separate chapters on "Social and community intervention," with Emory L. Cowen as the first contributor. In 1973 Charles D. Spielberger founded the *American Journal of Community Psychology* under the sponsorship of the Division of Community Psychology. In 1975 a national conference on training for community psychology resulted in publication of a volume detailing a variety of approaches (Iscoe, Bloom, & Spielberger, 1977). By 1977 the Council of Directors of Community Psychology Training Programs was organized, under the guidance of Richard Price and later Edward Seidman, to facilitate regular communication among the now large number of training programs throughout the nation.

The community mental health and community psychology movement was originally driven by a desire to deinstitutionalize the mental hospital population and to extend the reach of services to underserved populations. Since then it has taken a more preventive stance—to keep people out of hospitals altogether, by strengthening their social environment (President's Commission on Mental Health, *Report,* 1978); to reduce the negative impact of social institutions on individuals; and to encourage and develop the strengths and competencies of individuals and communities.

PREVENTION, EMPOWERMENT, AND THE PSYCHOLOGICAL SENSE OF COMMUNITY

The basic approach to community mental health has implied a critique of traditional clinical services, which often wait passively for individual clients to seek out a mental health professional who will provide individual psychotherapy, and which isolate people in mental hospitals away from family, friends, jobs, and other community resources. The community mental health concept questions the effectiveness of such services or society's ability to reach large numbers of citizens in need. The concept suggests, instead, a social policy that emphasizes prevention of emotional distress.

The idea of prevention was introduced into the modern mental health movement by Gerald Caplan's *Principles of Preventive Psychiatry.* Caplan described three different ways in which mental health professionals can help communities to reduce the probability of serious mental illness. Tertiary prevention—more properly called rehabilitation—involves providing community supports for those who have already experienced serious maladjustment. Here the aim is to reduce the duration of an identified mental patient's illness or need for continuous or "revolving door" custodial care in mental hospitals. Secondary prevention, by early diagnosis and treatment, attempts to reduce the length and severity of emotional problems by providing services early in the course of the disorder. It entails attempts not only to treat psychopathology at the early stages of its appearance, but also to discover high-risk clients during childhood so as to change the course of their psychological development.

Finally, Caplan (1964, p. 26) introduced the notion of primary prevention:

Primary prevention is a community concept. It involves lowering the rate of new cases of mental disorder in a population over a certain period by counteracting harmful circumstances before they have had a chance to produce illness. It does not seek to prevent a specific person from becoming sick. Instead, it seeks to reduce the risk for a whole population, so that, although some may become ill, their number will be reduced.

The idea of primary prevention has served as a bridge for psychological research on the social conditions of life and how they affect the well-being of individuals. Originally, primary prevention research focused on populations with a high risk for mental illness, and on a search for predisposing factors. Later, it included high-risk situations and events such as school transitions, alienating organizations, unemployment, racism, neighborhood resources, and social networks.

Two key aspects of primary prevention are its "mass orientation and before-the-fact qualities" (Cowen, 1980). Also stressed as areas of research are promotion of health, a search for the strengths rather than the deficits of people, the processes which foster "empowerment" of individuals and communities (Rappaport, 1981), and the "psychological sense of community" (Sarason, 1974).

As community psychology developed in these later directions, a central theme emphasized looking toward psychological knowledge which may be useful for social and public policy in fields as diverse as child rearing, law, education, geriatrics, social welfare, and a variety of other "social dilemmas." Community psychologists in general may be described as concerned with how larger units of social organization affect individual people. Many of the conceptions of community psychology are consistent with and influenced by behavioral, environmental, organizational, ecological, and general systems theory (Trickett, Kelly, & Todd, 1972), as well as with the methods and modes of community organization and self-help.

Influenced by William Ryan's book, *Blaming the Victim,* community psychology has often been concerned with the ways in which social institutions have tended to create and foster a large number of "out groups." Community psychologists are also frequently involved in human services program development, evaluation, implementation, and dissemination (Fairweather, Sanders, & Tornatzky, 1974).

CONCEPTIONS OF SOCIETY

Community mental health professionals have assumed that the major social issues confronting people with problems in living involve learning how to adjust, how to acquire new skills, and how to adapt to the demands of society. This classical view of mental health services suggests that society is and should be relatively stable. An alternative to the stability-oriented viewpoint has been put forth by community psychologists. Despite the reality of individual problems in adjustment, it is suggested that social and community interventions should take place in a context which assumes change. First, it is assumed that society is not as stable as it appears to be in the time-bound present—hence the need for a historical perspective (Gergen, 1973; Sarason, 1981). Second, it is assumed that the direction of social change can be influenced so as to make it more likely that the people of concern to the interventionist will be more, rather than less, able to obtain necessary individual resources. The "people of concern" are most often a variety of "marginal" groups ranging from chronic mental patients to those who find themselves in legal difficulties, the poor, the unemployed, and members of minority groups. This view presumes that changes in

social policy are a necessary part of any comprehensive plan for mental health and human welfare, and conceives of the mental health worker as an advocate as much as a therapist.

STYLE OF SERVICE DELIVERY

Mental health professionals have generally assumed that the proper mode of intervention is defined by the "doctor-patient relationship." Even those who reject a disease conception of human behavior tend to accept the medical style of intervention in which the "expert" or authority, who usually holds some sort of advanced degree, is responsible for diagnosis and prescription. Diagnosis and treatment usually take place in the expert's office, hospital, or clinic. The expert passively waits for the client to find her or his office.

An alternative style of intervention, the *seeking mode,* has been developed by community psychologists to offer services or intervention somewhere other than in a mental health setting. Such services may be delivered by a variety of people, both professional and nonprofessional. This seeking mode permits staff to step out of traditional places, niches, and roles so as to engage people in their own settings. It allows professionals to take on a variety of new roles, as for instance consultants to others who deliver direct service such as college students, volunteers, teachers, or policemen. It lets the professionals help create new settings such as neighborhood drop-in centers for adolescents or the elderly, and also encourages the formation of self-help groups, and helps create alternative educational experiences, community betterment, and economic development and housing programs.

LEVELS OF ANALYSIS

A social/community perspective suggests that the "social order" may be thought of as a series of increasingly complex levels of organization. Each level serves as a point both for understanding and for intervention. Each level can operate according to variables and conceptions which are self-contained, although each level influences the other. Principles and techniques for change at one level (i.e., the individual) are not necessarily operative at other levels (i.e., the organizational). To comprehend the social order community, psychology uses conceptions and principles for understanding individuals, groups, organizations, institutions, communities, and societies, as well as the relationships within and among levels of analysis, and how they influence one another. However, far more than in other areas of psychology, there is emphasis on a broad social critique which may be thought of as the institutional, community, or social policy level.

The social policy level of analysis has generally but not necessarily been consistent with a social change, as opposed to a social stability orientation. It suggests that many social problems are created by our underlying institutions and policies *per se,* rather than by individual persons, groups, or specific organizations. Although many problems in an organization may benefit from specific changes, the key to sensible, efficient improvement of problems in living for entire populations is seen to require change at the level of social policy. Frequently used strategies are advocacy and the creation of new settings. This often involves cultural, value-based, political, and economic decisions. Power relationships, diversity of values, strengths of target populations, cultural relativity, and the need for resources are frequently confronted issues. The very intentions (implicit as well as explicit) of our social institutions, as well as the research questions asked, may come into question (Seidman, 1978).

THE AGENT OF TRANSMISSION

Beginning with the pioneering work of people such as Margaret Rioch (1966), Ernest Poser (1966), Robert Reiff and Frank Reissman (1965), Jules Holzberg (1963), Mort Bard (1970), and Emory Cowen and others (1975), the 1960s and 1970s brought recognition of the value of nonprofessionals in the mental health delivery system. A widespread acceptance evolved regarding the reality that many people who are earning their living in areas other than the mental health professions (such as students, housewives, or retired workers) can be helpful to others with problems in living.

A second consideration bringing recognition to nonprofessional mental health workers has been the observation that certain occupations place people in role relationships which allow them to influence the course of coping with crisis for large numbers of people. For example teachers, librarians, policemen, bartenders, divorce lawyers, ministers, nurses, hairdressers, and plant foremen frequently listen to and perhaps influence people with problems in living (Cowen, "Help is where you find it"). Such helpers are not hired by the mental health system, nor are they volunteering their services as mental health workers. In fact, they probably do not even think of themselves as having anything to do with mental health. Acknowledging that most people do not seek out professional mental health workers, and that help is often wherever one finds it, provides the social/community interventionist with an almost endless set of possibilities for extending influence. Some interventionists may engage in consultation to people in key social roles, so as to help them think more systematically about what they are already doing, or enlist their aid as people to whom others in need might be referred for advice, friendship, and assistance. Other interventionists may conduct research to learn how such people are effective, in order to add to our knowledge base.

A third way in which other than professionally trained helpers have been encouraged is through the development of self-help groups (Lieberman & Glidewell, 1978; Lieberman & Borman, 1979). The ideology of the community mental health and community psychology movements has been quite consistent with the rise in legitimacy of self-help groups. In many ways, people coming together out of mutual concern—not for pay or as volunteers, but rather as peers mutually sharing their lives without professional intervention—is the ideal of a strength-based, preventively oriented mental health system.

A further extension of the agent of transmission of help involves the natural support systems (Gottlieb, 1981). These are the less formal, less intentional helping relationships which exist among significant others. The obvious but heretofore largely ignored reality is that family, friends, church and neighborhood groups, clubs, and organizations make up a human fabric in people's lives through which problems in living are often filtered, solved, made more complicated, or altered. Those who take a public health, preventive, or policy-oriented view stress that most people never seek out professional or formal nonprofessional mental health service, but work out their problems living in their own natural support settings. Some of these settings will be effective, helpful ones, and others less so. Recognition of natural support systems has lead to a realization that by studying such settings it may be possible for helping professionals to learn important information about how the process of help proceeds.

The social/community interventionist is interested in studying as well as using all possible agents of transmission and all possible settings. This perspective is particularly salient to those with an interest in prevention of problems in living, since learning how already existing settings work when they are helpful, and encouraging their use, may be a more realistic way to extend help than expecting everyone to seek out clinical services.

REFERENCES

Bard, M. (1970). Training police as specialists in family crisis intervention. Washington, DC: National Institute of Law Enforcement and Criminal Justice, U.S. Government Printing Office.

Bennett, C. C., Anderson, L. S., Cooper, S., Hassol, L., Klein, D. C., & Rosenblum, G. (Eds.). (1966). Community psychology: A report of the Boston conference on the education of psychologists for community mental health. Boston: Boston University Press.

Caplan, G. (1974/1964). Principles of preventative psychiatry. New York: Basic Books.

Caplan, R. B. (1969). Psychiatry and the community in nineteenth century America. New York: Basic Books.

Cowen, E. (1980). The wooing of primary prevention. American Journal of Community Psychology, 8(3), 258–284.

Cowen, E. L. (in press). Help is where you find it: Four informal helping groups. American Psychologist.

Cowen, E. L., Trost, M. A., Lorion, R. P., Dorr, D., Izzo, L. D., & Isaacson, R. V. (1975). New ways in school mental health: Early detection and prevention of school maladaption. New York: Human Sciences Press.

Fairweather, G. W., Sanders, D. H., & Tornatzky, L. G. (1974). Creating change in mental health organizations. New York: Pergamon Press.

Gergen, K. J. (1973). Social psychology as history. Journal of Personality and Social Psychology, 26, 309–320.

Gottlieb, B. (1981). Social networks and social support. Beverly Hills, CA: Sage Publications.

Holzberg, J. D. (1963). The companion program: Implementing the manpower recommendations of the Joint Commission on Mental Illness and Health. American Psychologist, 18, 224–226.

Iscoe, I., Bloom, B., & Spielberger, C. D. (Eds.). (1977). Community psychology in transition. Washington, DC: Hemisphere.

Joint Commission on Mental Health and Illness. (1961). Action for mental health. New York: Basic Books.

Lieberman, M. A., & Borman, L. D. (1979). *Self-help groups for coping with crisis: Origins, members, processes, and impact.* San Francisco: Jossey-Bass.

Lieberman, M. A., & Glidewell, J. C. (Eds.). (1978). The helping process [Special issue]. *American Journal of Community Psychology, 6*(5).

Poser, E. (1966). The effect of therapist training on group therapeutic outcomes. *Journal of Consulting Psychology, 30,* 283–289.

President's Commission on Mental Health. (1978). *Report to the President from the President's Commission on Mental Health* (Vols. 1–4). Washington, DC: U.S. Government Printing Office.

Rappaport, J. (1981). In praise of paradox: A social policy of empowerment over prevention. *American Journal of Community Psychology, 9,* 1–25.

Reiff, R. R., & Reissman, F. (1965). The indigenous nonprofessional: A strategy of change in community action and community mental health programs. *Community Mental Health Journal,* Monograph no. 1.

Rioch, M. (1966). Changing concepts in the training of therapists. *Journal of Consulting Psychology, 30,* 290–292.

Sarason, S. B. (1974). *The psychological sense of community: Prospects for the community psychology.* San Francisco: Jossey-Bass.

Sarason, S. B. (1981). *Psychology misdirected.* New York: Free Press.

Seidman, E. (1978). Justice, values and social science: Unexamined premises. In J. R. Simon (Ed.), *Research in law and sociology* (Vol. 1). Greenwich, CT: JAI Press.

Trickett, E. J., Kelly J. G., & Todd, D. M. (1972). The social environment of the high school: Guidelines for individual change and organizational redevelopment. In S. E. Golann & C. Eisdorfer (Eds.), *Handbook of community mental health.* New York: Appleton-Century-Crofts.

SUGGESTED READING

Bloom, B. L. (1975). *Community mental health: A general introduction.* Belmont, CA: Wadsworth.

Cowen, E. L. (1973). Social and community interventions. *Annual Review of Psychology, 24,* 423–472.

Heller, K., & Monahart, J. (1977). *Psychology and community change.* Homewood, IL: Dorsey Press.

Muñoz, R. F., Snowden, L. R., & Kelley, J. G. (Eds.). (1979). *Social and psychological research in community settings.* San Francisco: Jossey-Bass.

Rappaport, J. (1977). *Community psychology: Values, research and action.* New York: Holt, Rinehart & Winston.

J. RAPPAPORT
University of Illinois

CRISIS INTERVENTION
MENTAL ILLNESS: EARLY HISTORY

COMPARATIVE NEUROPSYCHOLOGY

Results of nonhuman animal research can provide new information that human experimentation does not permit, usually for ethical considerations, or because of limited control over complex environmental influences. The new knowledge can then be used to help understand human disorders. One approach to understanding interspecies brain functions, comparative neuropsychology, involves the direct evaluation of human clinical populations by employing experimental paradigms originally developed for nonhuman animals (Oscar-Berman & Bardenhagen, 1998; Roberts & Sahakian, 1993). Over many decades of animal research, the paradigms were perfected to study the effects of well-defined brain lesions on specific behaviors, and later the tasks were modified for human use. Generally the modifications involve changing the reward from food to money, but standard administration of the tasks in humans still involves minimal instructions, thus necessitating a degree of procedural learning in humans as in nonhuman animals alike. Currently, comparative neuropsychological paradigms are used with neurological patients to link specific deficits with localized areas of neuropathology (for comprehensive reviews, see Fuster, 1997; Meador, Rumbaugh, Pate, & Bard, 1987; Oscar-Berman & Bardenhagen, 1998).

The comparative neuropsychological approach employs simple tasks that can be mastered without relying upon language skills. Precisely because these simple paradigms do not require linguistic strategies for solution, they are especially useful for working with patients whose language skills are compromised or whose cognitive skills may be minimal. Comparative neuropsychology contrasts with the traditional approach of using tasks that rely upon linguistic skills, and that were designed to study human cognition (e.g., Lezak, 1995; Spreen & Strauss, 1998). Because important ambiguities about its heuristic value had not been addressed empirically, only recently has comparative neuropsychology become popular for implementation with brain-damaged patients (e.g., see reviews by Oscar-Berman & Bardenhagen, 1998; Squire, 1992). Within the past decade, it has had prevalent use as a framework for comparing and contrasting the performances of disparate neurobehavioral populations on similar tasks.

Among the paradigms that have been employed are classical delayed reaction tasks such as delayed response (DR) and delayed alternation (DA). Both tasks measure a subject's ability to bridge a time gap (see Fuster, 1997). This ability has been termed "working memory," which is a transient form of memory. Working memory is multimodal in nature, and it serves to keep newly-incoming information available online; it acts much like a mental clipboard for use in problem solving, planning, and so on. In the classical DR task, the experimenter places a small reward into a reinforcement—well under one of two identical stimuli. The subject is able to see the experimenter put a reward there, but cannot reach it. After the experimenter covers the reinforcement-wells with the stimuli, he or she lowers a screen, obscuring the stimulus tray. After a delay period, usually between 0 and 60 seconds, the experimenter raises the screen to allow the subject to make a choice. The subject then pushes one of the stimuli away and, with a correct choice, takes the reward; attentional and spatial memory skills are needed to do this.

DA shares important features in common with DR. Both are spatial tasks, and both have a delay between the stimulus presentation and the opportunity to make a response. In DA, however, subjects must learn to alternate responding from left to right. On each trial, the side not previously chosen is rewarded, and a brief delay (usually 5 seconds) is interposed between trials. Instead of having to notice and remember the location of a reward placed there by the experimenter (in DR), subjects must remember the side last chosen, and whether or not a reward had been available. Subjects must also learn to inhibit, on each trial, the previously rewarded response (i.e., they must not perseverate with consecutive responses to one side only). Rankings of the performance levels of a wide range of mammals, including children, on delayed reaction tasks have been reported to parallel the phylogenetic scale.

Comparative neuropsychological tasks such as DR and DA are simple to administer and do not rely on intact language abilities. Both tasks also are sensitive to abnormalities after damage to frontal brain systems. Furthermore, successful performance on DR and DA tasks is known to rely upon different underlying neuroanatomical and neuropsychological mechanisms. Thus, prefrontal cortex is host to at least two subsystems: the dorsolateral and the orbitofrontal (on the ventral surface). While the dorsolateral system contains intimate connections with other neocortical sites, its connections with limbic sites are less striking than the orbitofrontal system's connections. The dorsolateral system, although important for successful performance on both DR and DA, is especially important for DR performance, in which visuospatial, mnemonic, and attentional functions are considered critical. By contrast, functions involved in response inhibition have been linked to the orbitofrontal system. With an inability to inhibit unintended responses comes abnormal perseverative responding, a salient characteristic of orbitofrontal damage (e.g., Freedman, Block, Ebert, & Binns, 1998). The orbitofrontal system is intimately connected with basal forebrain and limbic structures; its connections with other neocortical regions are not as extensive as the dorsolateral system's connections. The orbitofrontal system, like the dorsolateral system, supports successful performance on both DA and DR, but it is especially important for DA performance.

Comparative neuropsychological research has provided a framework that is helpful for understanding memory dysfunction in neurodegenerative disorders. In some neurodegenerative diseases (e.g., Parkinson's disease and progressive supranuclear palsy), patients may have working-memory and attentional impairments resulting from prefrontal system damage. In other disorders (e.g., Korsakoff's syndrome and herpes encephalopathy), there may be new learning impairments suggestive of limbic system damage (Oscar-Berman & Bardenhagen, 1998).

Implicit in nonhuman research models of human brain functioning is the assumption of homologous structural-functional relationships among the species (e.g., Riley & Langley, 1993; Wasserman, 1993). Research on brain mechanisms underlying behaviors across species, contributes to the discovery of common and divergent principles of brain-behavior relationships. Ultimately this helps neuroscientists to understand how the brain functions. With understanding, comes the potential for assessment and treatment of human neurobehavioral disorders.

REFERENCES

Freedman, M., Black, S., Ebert, P., & Binns, M. (1998). Orbitofrontal function, object alternation and perseveration. *Cerebral Cortex, 8,* 18–27.

Fuster, J. M. (1997). *The prefrontal cortex* (3rd ed.). New York: Lippincott-Raven.

Lezak, M. D. (1995). *Neuropsychological assessment* (3rd ed.). Oxford: Blackwell Scientific Publications.

Meador, D. M., Rumbaugh, D. M., Pate, J. L., & Bard, K. A. (1987). Learning, problem solving, cognition, and intelligence. In G. Mitchell & J. Erwin (Eds.), *Comparative primate biology* (Vol. 2. Part B. Behavior, cognition, and motivation; pp. 17–83). New York: Alan R. Liss.

Oscar-Berman, M., & Bardenhagen, F. (1998). Nonhuman primate models of memory dysfunction in neurodegenerative disease: Contributions from Comparative Neuropsychology. In A. Tröster (Ed.), *Memory in neurodegenerative disease* (pp. 3–20). New York: Cambridge University Press.

Riley, D. A., & Langley, C. M. (1993). The logic of species comparisons. *Psychological Science, 4,* 185–189.

Roberts, A. C., & Sahakian, B. J. (1993). Comparable tests of cognitive function in monkey and man. In A. Sahgal (Ed.), *Neurobehavioral neuroscience: A practical approach* (Vol. 1, pp. 165–184). New York: Oxford University Press.

Spreen, O., & Strauss, E. (1998). *A compendium of neuropsychological tests* (2nd ed.). New York: Oxford University Press.

Squire, L. R. (1992). Memory and the hippocampus: A synthesis from findings with rats, monkeys, and humans. *Psychological Review, 99*(2), 195–231.

Wasserman, E. A. (1993). Comparative cognition: Beginning the second century of the study of animal intelligence. *Psychological Bulletin, 113,* 211–228.

M. Oscar-Berman
Boston University School of Medicine, and
Boston VA Medical Center

COMPARATIVE PSYCHOLOGY
ETHOLOGY

COMPARATIVE PSYCHOLOGY

Animal behavior is the subject matter of comparative psychology. Animal behavior research has two basic goals. The first is to find principles and theories that govern animal behavior. These may be specific to one or a few closely related species or they may have universality and include humans. The second goal is to understand how an animal's behavior in the laboratory or its natural habitat contributes to its total evolutionary fitness. Historically, comparative psychology has focused on generalizations across species and ethology has focused on detailed descriptions of particular species.

HISTORY

Behaviors and antics of animals have evoked curiosity and amusement in people since antiquity. Perhaps the mixture of the familiar with the unfamiliar makes animal behavior fascinating for humans. Aristotle (384–322 BC) wrote extensively on animal habits, as did Pliny (AD 23–79). Those reports, based extensively on hearsay, were often infused with anthropomorphism. Until the late 19th century, no one attempted any systematic, scientific study of animal behavior. Instead, pre-19th-century literature and natural history are punctuated with assorted stories, anecdotes, and nonscientific speculations about animal behavior. The scientific neglect of animal psychology, and by extension the animal mind, was consistent with the well-known dictum of René Descartes (1596–1650) that animals were automata, creatures driven only by mechanical reflexes and instincts, without minds, souls, or free will.

The strict separation of animal and human behavior was ended by Darwin's theory of evolution, which was the starting point for present-day comparative psychology. Evolutionary development had two important implications: first, that elements of human mentality would be found in animals; and second, that elements of animal mentality would be found in humans. Charles Darwin, well aware of these implications, addressed the first in *The Descent of Man* (1871) and the second in *The Expression of Emotions in Man and Animals* (1872). However, in Darwin's notebooks, he stated a subtler implication: that the human mind and behavior were as subject to natural law and were as much a product of natural selection and evolution as animal behavior.

The late 19th and early 20th centuries saw the publication of many stories about amazing animal accomplishments, along with speculations about the presumed accompanying mental gyrations of gifted animals. The underlying assumption was that if an animal's behavior was similar to one's own behavior in some particular setting, then one only need examine one's own mental events to find a good approximation of the animal's thinking. Evolutionary continuity was the justification for this assumption. This strategy may appear naive, but even today it is sometimes applied.

The extravagant and often colorful interpretations of animal behavior inevitably provoked a counterreaction. The British comparative psychologist C. Lloyd Morgan argued in 1894 that only directly observable behavior should be used to develop theories about animal behavior, particularly behavior that involved animal intellectual capabilities. A central tenet of comparative psychology is Morgan's canon: "In no case may we interpret an action as the outcome of the exercise of a higher psychical faculty if it can be interpreted as the outcome of the exercise of one which stands lower in the psychological scale." In other words, we should apply to animal behavior the simplest possible explanation consistent with the

observations. It was a short step from the objective comparative psychology of Morgan to John B. Watson's behaviorism, which eliminated all reference to unobservable mental events and processes in animals. Morgan's rigorous version of comparative psychology and Watson's behaviorism were responses to overzealous attribution of human intellectual abilities to animals. The case of Clever Hans is the most celebrated illustration of the problem.

CLEVER HANS: A HORSE'S WARNING TO PSYCHOLOGY

In 1904, a retired Berlin mathematics teacher, Wilhelm von Osten, captured public attention with claims that his horse, Clever Hans, could read, spell, and answer an astounding variety of arithmetic problems, including multiplication of fractions (Candland, 1993). Von Osten's technique was to assign each letter of the alphabet a number that was then presented to Hans on a blackboard. Thus instructed, Hans could respond to questions by tapping out answers with his right foot on a board. This case was different from many other similarly performing animals of the time because von Osten was not deliberately prompting Hans about when to start and stop tapping. Hans' act puzzled many experts who viewed it, and the mystery was not solved until a young psychologist, Oskar Pfungst, subjected Hans and von Osten to a series of systematic observations which indicated that von Osten was unintentionally cuing his horse. Specifically, subtle changes in von Osten's breathing, facial movements such as flaring of the nostrils, and head movements were being used by Hans as signals to start or stop the tapping. Pfungst calculated that movements as small as 1 mm at the edge of von Osten's wide-brimmed hat were detected by the attentive horse. Von Osten was shattered by this revelation, but never could admit that Hans lacked remarkable linguistic and calculating talents.

The Clever Hans episode illustrates the wisdom of Morgan's canon in interpretation of animal behavior. Unintentional manipulation of human as well as nonhuman subjects by experimenters should be a serious concern in psychological research.

PHYLOGENETIC TREES AND PHYLOGENETIC SCALES

Darwin recognized that the evolutionary process was one of constant divergence and diversification. Therefore, evolution can be likened to an enormously elaborated branching tree, with living species represented by the tips of the branches, while the remainder of the tree represents extinct species. One implication of this branching is that in most cases it is meaningless to place different species in an ordinal sequence from lower to higher. For example, birds evolved from a line of reptiles different from those that evolved into mammals. Similarly, carnivores evolved along a different branch of mammals than did primates. Consequently, pigeons, cats, monkeys, and humans do not form an evolution-based continuum—they are four distinct types of animals. In no sense has evolution been an orderly process producing organisms of consistently increasing subtlety and complexity culminating in humans. The line of organisms leading to humans is only one branch among multitudes of other branches. Thus, interesting as humans with their peculiar behaviors and impressive minds may be, this species does not actually deserve the immense evolutionary importance given to it. Comparative psychology, therefore, has the virtue of illuminating human behavior as only a small part of a much wider context involving enormous interspecies variation.

Similarities in behavioral characteristics of two species with a common ancestor may arise in either of two different ways. The characteristics may have been present in the common ancestor and persisted down to the present descendents, in which case the behavioral similarities are homologous. Alternatively, the characteristics may have been absent in the common ancestor but have evolved independently in the lines leading to the present species, in which case the behaviors are analogous.

Common ancestors of different living species are usually extinct, and usually little can be inferred about an animal's behavior from its fossil remains. Therefore, indirect techniques must be used to infer the phylogenetic development of a behavioral characteristic.

Occasionally, a group of closely related species display continuous, simple variation in some behavior, with most species displaying behavior at one end of the continuum. This strongly suggests that the behavior expressed by most species is phylogenetically older, or more primitive, than the behavior displayed by the remaining species. Empiid or balloon flies provide an amazing example of this type of variation (Kessel, 1955). In most species of these flies, mating includes no particular ritual. However, females sometimes attempt to eat the male before or during copulation. In other species, males capture a small insect and present it to the female before copulation, thereby diverting her cannibalistic appetites. Males of two other species wrap their prey in a balloonlike ball constructed of secreted silk thread before giving it to the female, thus preoccupying her even longer. Males of yet another species wrap the prey quite loosely, so that the prey will fall out. The female nevertheless unwraps the empty thread ball with apparent relish. Small inanimate objects such as leaves are wrapped by another species. The most recently evolved form in the development of these appeasement offerings is shown by one species in which males simply present females with a wrapped silk ball containing neither prey nor object.

When a convenient behavioral gradient such as that in balloon fly species does not occur, inferences about evolution are necessarily more tentative. For example, if several species with a common ancestor all show a behavioral trait, then the shared trait was probably present in the common ancestor (Alcock, 1998).

Evolutionary considerations can also lead to questions about how a behavior affected a species' adaptation to its environment and about the role of the behavior in the evolutionary history of the species. Alcock (1998) describes techniques for empirically testing hypotheses about the evolutionary adaptiveness of particular behaviors. Evolutionary-based questions, however, are not the only ones that can be addressed to animal behavior.

THE HOW AND WHY OF ANIMAL BEHAVIOR

Suppose we observe a group of recently hatched goslings eagerly following their mother in single file. The most obvious and basic question that could be asked is why the goslings are following. Some psychologists would say that the behavior, a result of imprinting, is obviously adaptive. It occurs in birds that have well-developed locomotor and sensory capabilities at or shortly after

hatching. Furthermore, the mother typically perambulates on the ground or water during the day instead of flying. In the past, those goslings with genes predisposing them to follow their mothers closely were more likely to survive than goslings with weaker following tendencies. Furthermore, goslings that were highly precocial (well-developed at hatching) were better equipped to follow their mothers than those that were more immature and weaker. Thus, through natural selection, some avian species became precocial and developed tendencies to follow moving objects presented shortly after hatching. Some water birds, such as mallard ducks, typically inhabit areas where tall vegetation often obscures a view of the mother. It is therefore no surprise that mallards evolved a following response elicited by repetitive vocalizations of the mother.

An experimental psychologist might be somewhat dissatisfied with this evolutionary explanation of imprinting and therefore offer an alternative account. Laboratory experiments have demonstrated that precocial birds' imprinting is formed within a few hours or even minutes after hatching. Therefore, a rapid conditioning probably underlies imprinting.

These two accounts are examples of ultimate and proximate explanations. Ultimate explanations emphasize how the behavior contributes to the total evolutionary fitness of a species. Thus, these explanations are closely associated with the function of the behavior in solving a species' problems in its natural habitat.

Proximate explanations address the question of how a behavior occurs. These explanations answer questions about a behavior's ontogenetic development, how it was affected by learning, physiological variables, and environmental stimulation. Proximate explanations incorporate mechanisms that exert effects within an animal's lifetime. In contrast, ultimate explanations incorporate mechanisms that have been affecting natural selection long into the phylogenetic past of the species.

Ultimate and proximate explanations are both clearly legitimate scientific approaches to understanding animal behavior and in no way conflict with each other. There has been considerable recent interest in finding ultimate or evolutionary explanations for basic learning phenomena that had previously been viewed only in terms of proximate causes (Shettleworth, 1998).

Taste aversion learning is a good example of a phenomenon that can be usefully examined from both ultimate and proximate perspectives (Garcia, Rusiniak, & Brett, 1977). It has long been known that rats and many other species, including humans, will often avoid a particular food after eating some of it and becoming ill. This phenomenon interests comparative psychologists because the taste aversion is usually learned in one trial and occurs despite long intervals (six hours or more) between the consummatory response and the onset of illness. Furthermore, in many species the illness is associated with taste but not with visual or auditory stimuli. This high aptitude for acquiring taste aversions obviously increases an animal's fitness, if it eats a meal and then waits several hours before starting another meal. Most carnivores, rodents, and primates conform to this pattern. In contrast, aptitude for taste aversion learning would have reduced value for grazing animals that spend many hours each day contentedly eating a variety of plants. It is therefore not surprising that grazing animals do not show the rapid taste aversion learning characteristic of many other animals.

Ultimate reasons for some properties of taste aversion learning are evident. Natural selection no doubt favored one-trial learning: An animal's genes can ill afford the luxury of many learning trials when toxic food is nearby. Furthermore, since toxic substances usually do not make an animal sick immediately, taste aversion learning should occur with long delays between eating and consequent illness. In contrast, most other environmental contingencies that are learned occur quickly. Therefore, learning with long-delayed unconditioned stimuli is not required.

Several important proximate variables that affect taste aversion learning have been identified. For example, familiar tastes become conditioned to toxic substances far less readily than do novel tastes. A "learned safety" theory states that rats are reluctant to consume novel foods. However, with repeated exposures the reluctance to accept the food dissipates. The animal has learned that the now familiar food is safe, and this consequently impedes later formation of an association between food and illness. Young organisms are more prone to acquire taste aversions than older ones, an effect consistent with the learned safety hypothesis, since the young typically lack experience with a variety of tastes.

MINDS AND LANGUAGE

The possibilities and manifestations of mind and consciousness in animals were topics of active speculation in the early post-Darwinian period of comparative psychology. *The Animal Mind* by Margaret Floy Washburn, published in four editions from 1908 to 1936, was a popular, widely used textbook in comparative psychology. But then the increased influence of behaviorism and the warnings of Morgan's canon relegated mind, consciousness, and similar anthropomorphic attributes to the dustbin of comparative psychology. Within the last 25 years, these and similar terms have reemerged as a result of research on nonhuman primates.

The feat of communicating with animals through language has fascinated humans throughout history. The period from 1932 to 1950 saw one Russian and five American attempts to teach apes to speak; all were largely unsuccessful (Rumbaugh & Savage-Rumbaugh, 1994). Since chimpanzees are avid imitators of human actions, sign language seems to be an obvious alternative to speaking. Although Yerkes (1927) speculated about the possibility of apes learning a gestured language, it was not until 39 years later that a determined effort was made to teach sign language to a chimpanzee.

In 1966 Gardner and Gardner (1971) began tutoring a young chimpanzee, Washoe, in American Sign Language. The project was far more successful than the earlier attempts with vocalization. Within the first three years of the project, Washoe learned a naming vocabulary of over 85 signs.

In the more than 30 years since the original Washoe study, several other ape language projects have been reported, some with manual signing and others in which the ape directed manual responses toward abstract symbols (Rumbaugh & Savage-Rumbaugh, 1994). The projects evoked considerable criticism from many psychologists who were quick to point out that although the apes were displaying formidable learning, their performance nevertheless lacked one or more fundamental properties of true (human) language. Many properties of human language were indeed lacking in the early studies of ape language.

Generativity was probably the most important of these language properties. Generativity in language production is the ability of a person to speak or write novel sentences containing particular combinations of words that the person has never before produced. Generativity in comprehension is a corresponding ability to comprehend sentences never before heard or seen as long as the words and grammar are familiar. In 1993 Savage-Rumbaugh described a remarkable experiment with the bonobo Kanzi. Under well-controlled laboratory conditions, Kanzi could respond appropriately to a large number of spoken English sentences that he had never previously heard. His comprehension of spoken language was about equal to that of a two-and-a-half-year-old human child who was tested under equivalent conditions.

Kanzi's ability to understand novel spoken sentences is the most impressive evidence to date that the language capabilities of bonobos (and probably chimpanzees) can closely approximate that of humans who are first learning language. Since humans and chimpanzees shared a common ancestor as recently as five million years ago, this finding adds weight to the evidence that evolution of cognitive abilities underlying language extends far back into hominid evolution.

A second important issue in recent comparative psychology is whether apes and possibly monkeys have a theory of mind. An animal with a theory of mind can understand the intentions, mental states, personalities, and perceptions of other animals. Although the existence of theories of minds in nonhumans is still a contentious question, considerable evidence of several types of animal behavior consistent with a theory of mind have been reported (Whiten & Byrne, 1997).

Tactical deception is one expression of a theory of mind that has received considerable observational support. Tactical deception is more than simply misleading or deceiving another animal. The deception must be based on deliberately presenting incorrect, deceptive information with an understanding that the other animal will be misinformed by it. Of course, observation of a behavior consistent with tactical deception is not proof that tactical deception played a part. An analysis of reports about tactical deception by behavioral primatologists (Whiten & Byrne, 1997) showed that chimpanzees and baboons were more likely than other primate species to display possible tactical deception.

A third important issue in recent comparative psychology is whether social interactions of primates reveal evidence of rudimentary forms of ethical or moral behavior, or even a sense of justice. Frans de Waal (1996) has amassed impressive supporting evidence from observation of apes as well as monkeys. Chimpanzees, as well as many monkey species, show strong tendencies to reconcile following a fight and the immediate emotional aftermath. Male chimpanzees are more likely to reconcile than female chimpanzees. Negative reciprocity (in which an aggressive, unfriendly act toward an animal is reciprocated at a later time) as well as positive reciprocity of friendly acts has been observed in chimpanzees. Interestingly, monkeys apparently only reciprocate negative reciprocity.

REFERENCES

Alcock, J. (1998). *Animal behavior* (6th ed.). Sunderland, MA: Sinauer Associates.

Candland, D. K. (1993). *Feral children and clever animals.* New York: Cambridge University Press.

Desmond, A. J. (1979). *The ape's reflection.* New York: Dial Press.

Garcia, J., Rusiniak, K. W., & Brett, L. P. (1977). Conditioned food illness aversion in wild animals: *Cavaent canonici.* In H. Davis & H. M. B. Huritz (Eds.), *Operant-Pavlovian interactions.* Hillsdale, NJ: Erlbaum.

Gardner, B. T., & Gardner, R. A. (1971). Two-way communications with an infant chimpanzee. In A. M. Schrier & F. Stollnitz (Eds.), *Behavior of nonhuman primates* (Vol. 4). New York: Academic Press.

Kessel, E. L. (1955). The mating activities of balloon flies. *Systematic Zoology, 4,* 97–104.

Rumbaugh, D. M., & Savage-Rumbaugh, E. S. (1994). Language in comparative perspective. In N. J. Mackintosh (Ed.), *Animal learning and cognition.* San Diego, CA: Academic Press.

Shettleworth, S. J. (1998). *Cognition, evolution and behavior.* New York: Oxford University Press.

de Waal, F. B. M. (1996). *Good natured: The origins of right and wrong in humans and other animals.* Cambridge, MA: Harvard University Press.

Whiten, A., & Byrne, R. W. (1997). *Machiavellian intelligence II: Extensions and Evaluations.* Cambridge, UK: Cambridge University Press.

Yerkes, R. M. (1927). *Almost human.* New York: Century.

SUGGESTED READING

Greenberg, G., & Haraway, M. M. *Comparative psychology: A handbook.*

Dewsbury, D. A. *Comparative psychology in the twentieth century.*

J. E. King
University of Arizona

ANIMAL COMMUNICATION
ETHOLOGY
EVOLUTION
IMPRINTING
LANGUAGE IN GREAT APES

COMPETENCY TO STAND TRIAL

A defendant can be found incompetent to stand trial, under provisions in criminal law, if he or she is unable to understand or participate adequately in his or her defense. If found incompetent, further judicial proceedings are suspended until his or her competency is restored. The purposes behind this procedure are to ensure that a defendant receives a fair trial and to preserve the dignity of the adversarial process (Melton, Petrila, Poythress, & Slogobin, 1997).

The competency standard that is currently recognized by the courts was established in *Dusky v. United States* (362 U.S. 402, 1960). It held:

> It is not enough for the district judge to find that "the defendant is oriented to time and place and has some recollection of events," but that the test must be whether he has sufficient present ability to consult with his lawyer with a reasonable degree of rational understanding—and whether he has a rationale as well as factual understanding of the proceedings against him. (p. 402)

Competency and criminal responsibility are often confused. However, while competency is concerned with a defendant's present ability to participate in the defense, criminal responsibility refers to a defendant's mental state at the time of the alleged crime. It is quite possible that a defendant could be found to be competent to stand trial and then later successfully raise the insanity defense. Indeed, if the competency issue had been raised, a defendant would have to be considered competent before being allowed to proceed with an insanity defense.

Based on a thorough review of case law, the legal scholar Bonnie (1993) outlines two types of competence, *competence to proceed* and *decisional competence.* Competency to proceed refers to the minimum capacities a defendant would need to assist in his or her defense, such as the capacity to understand the criminal charges and the role of defense counsel. These capacities are different from those capacities that may be needed to make decisions that arise in a particular case. Decisional competency refers to the ability to "understand and choose among alternative courses of action" (p. 556). In Bonnie's view, (Bonnie, 1993), it is possible that some defendants could be considered competent to assist their attorney but incompetent to make certain decisions that arise during the course of the defense, such as whether to enter a guilty plea, to waive constitutional rights, or to employ an insanity defense.

Decisional competence appears to be recognized in recent American court decisions, such as *Cooper v. Oklahoma* (116 S.Ct. 1373, 1996) and *Godinez v. Moran* (113 S.Ct. 2680, 1993). Canadian courts, on the other hand, seem to endorse a lower level of competency, which is tantamount to Bonnie's competence to proceed (Roesch, Hart, & Zapf, 1996).

COMPETENCY ASSESSMENTS

Both defense and prosecution can raise the issue of competence. The court will then order an evaluation if doubt exists about the defendant's competence. Since a conviction can be overturned on appeal if a defendant's competency was questionable and an evaluation was not ordered, it is very rare that a court will refuse a request for evaluation.

The courts have historically used mental health professionals, including psychologists and psychiatrists, to evaluate competency. Since competency is a legal issue, a judge makes the final determination. However, in the most cases the judge concurs with the opinion offered by the evaluator (Roesch & Golding, 1980).

Until quite recently, evaluations were conducted in inpatient facilities and were completed in one to three months (Roesch & Golding, 1980). This practice, however, was criticized as costly and inefficient, as well as unnecessarily restrictive. In addition, concern was expressed regarding defendants' constitutional rights to a speedy trial. Results from a comprehensive 50-state survey, conducted in 1994 by Grisso and his colleagues, indicate a clear shift toward outpatient evaluations. Although 10 states continue to rely on inpatient evaluations, the majority of states report increased use of community mental health centers, private practitioners, and courts clinics.

Only a small proportion of defendants referred for fitness evaluations is found incompetent. In a review of 10 studies, Roesch and Golding (1980) found that an average of 30% of referred defendants were incompetent. Recent research has found similar or lower rates (Roesch, Ogloff, & Golding, 1993). As a result of the low rates of incompetency among defendants referred for evaluations, the legitimacy of some competency referrals has been questioned.

Research has, for example, found that attorneys have a poor understanding of the competency standard, and that both attorneys and mental health professionals often equate mental illness with incompetence although the two are not synonymous (Roesch & Golding, 1980). In addition, research has suggested that above and beyond confusion regarding the standard, competency evaluations may be intentionally misused by attorneys to delay the trial, investigate the feasibility of an insanity plea, or discover new information about the defendant (Roesch & Golding, 1980). Finally, another line of research has investigated the hypothesis that competency evaluations may be used as a "back door" to the hospital when a mentally ill individual does not meet the "dangerousness criteria" for civil commitment (Cooper & Grisso, 1997; Zapf & Roesch, 1997). Furthermore, several studies suggest that although lawyers have doubts about the competency of their clients in 10% of cases, they refer less than half of these defendants for evaluation (Hoge, Bonnie, Poythress, & Monahan, 1992; Poythress, Bonnie, Hoge, Monahan, & Oberlander, 1994). It is possible that inappropriate use of competency evaluations has decreased due to recently enacted limits on the lengths of competency commitments, as Slovenko (1995) asserts, and perhaps also as a result of improvements in evaluation procedures.

ASSESSMENT INSTRUMENTS

Robey's competency checklist, developed in 1965, is considered to be the first formalized measure of competency. Following this, the National Institute of Mental Health funded a research project that enabled the development of both the Competency Screening Test (CST; Laboratory of Community Psychiatry, 1973), a 22-item screening test, and the Competency Assessment Instrument (CAI; Laboratory of Community Psychiatry, 1973), a more thorough semistructured interview. Other structured and semistructured interviews include the Georgia Court Competency Test-R (GCCT-R; Johnson & Mullett, 1987), the Interdisciplinary Fitness Inter-

view (IFI; Golding, Roesch, & Schreiber, 1984), and the Fitness Interview Test (FIT; Roesch, Zapf, Eaves, & Webster, 1998). As an alternative format to interviews, the Computer-Assisted Competence Assessment Tool (CADCOMP; Barnard et al., 1991), is a series of 272 questions completed at a computer terminal. Most of these instruments take from 30 to 45 minutes to administer.

The newest competency assessment instrument, released in 1998, is the MacArthur Competency Assessment Tool—Criminal Adjudication (MacCAT-CA; Hoge et al., 1996). The MacCAT-CA differs in significant ways from previous instruments. It is grounded in Bonnie's theoretical model of competency. In addition, it assesses not only a defendant's ability to stand trial but also his or her ability to plead guilty, because in 90% of all cases defendants plead guilty rather than proceed to trial (Melton et al., 1997).

Research generally indicates that competency assessment instruments have strong reliability and validity (Melton et al., 1997). In addition, judges appear to value reference to competency assessment instruments in evaluator's reports (Terhune, 1990). Despite this, only one-third of psychologists who conduct competency evaluations report regular use of competency assessment instruments (Borum & Grisso, 1995).

TREATMENT OF INCOMPETENT DEFENDANTS

Defendants who are found incompetent to stand trial are remanded for mental health treatment. A large proportion of defendants who are found incompetent is diagnosed with a psychotic disorder (Nicholson & Kugler, 1991). In the United States, another sizable proportion of incompetent defendants, perhaps as much as 15% is mentally retarded (Grisso, 1992). In other countries, such as Canada, mental retardation does not appear to be commonly recognized as a basis for incompetence (Roesch et al., 1998).

Prior to *Jackson v. Indiana* (405 U.S. 715, 1972), incompetent defendants could be treated for an indeterminate length of time. Research in North Carolina found that incompetent defendants were held for an average of nearly three years, and some defendants were held for 10 years or more (Roesch & Golding, 1980) without ever having gone to trial *Jackson v. Indiana,* however, held that an incompetent defendant "cannot be held more than the reasonable period of time necessary to determine whether there is a substantial probability that he will attain that capacity in the forseeable future" (p. 738). In response to this decision, most states established limits on the length of time a defendant could be held incompetent, and defendants now are held for considerably shorter periods of time, and are typically returned to court as competent to stand trial within about six months (Roesch et al., 1993).

Treatment of competency is, in general, successful (Nicholson, 1999). Nicholson and McNulty (1992) found that competency could not be restored for only 10% of defendants. In such cases alternative dispositions, including dismissal of charges or civil commitment, are considered. The most common form of treatment is psychotropic medication (Roesch et al., 1996). However, while psychotropic medication addresses a defendant's mental disorder, it does not address his or her psycholegal impairments (Siegel & Elwork, 1992). In contrast, psycholegal education programs do address psycholegal impairments, focusing on topics such as the roles of key players and courtroom procedures (Heilbrun & Griffin, 1999).

In the past decade, significant breakthroughs have been made in the assessment of competency (Nicholson, 1999). The development and empirical evaluation of assessment instruments and the trend towards outpatient assessments have helped to preserve defendants' constitutional rights to a fair and speedy trial. Although research on the treatment of incompetent defendants is, at present, a largely undeveloped area, developments in treatment might do well to mirror those in assessment. Experts, for example, have argued that incompetent defendants can be treated on an outpatient basis (Roesch et al., 1993). Similarly, the empirical evaluation of treatment programs might enable significant improvements in the treatment of incompetent defendants.

REFERENCES

Barnard, G. W., Thompson, J. W., Freeman, W. C., Robbins, L., Gies, D., & Hankins, G. C. (1991). Competency to stand trial: Description and initial evaluation of a new computer-assisted assessment tool (CADCOMP). *Bulletin of the American Academy of Psychiatry and Law, 19,* 367–381.

Bonnie, R. J. (1993). The competence of criminal defendants: Beyond Dusky and Drope. *Miami Law Review, 47,* 539–601.

Borum, R., & Grisso, T. (1995). Psychological test use in criminal forensic evaluations. *Professional Psychology: Research and Practice, 26,* 465–473.

Cooper, D., & Grisso, T. (1997). Five year research update (1991–1995): Evaluations for competence to stand trial. *Behavioral Sciences and the Law, 15,* 347–364.

Golding, S. L., Roesch, R., & Screiber, J. (1984). Assessment and conceptualization of competency to stand trial: Preliminary data on the Interdisciplinary Fitness Interview. *Law and Human Behavior, 8,* 321–334.

Grisso, T. (1992). Five-year research update (1986–1990): Evaluations for competence to stand trial. *Behavioral Sciences and the Law, 10,* 353–369.

Grisso, T., Cocozza, J., Steadman, H., Fisher, W., & Greer, A. (1994). The organization of pretrial forensic evaluation services. *Law and Human Behavior, 18,* 377–393.

Heilbrun, K., & Griffin, P. (1999). Forensic treatment: A review of programs and research. In R. Roesch, S. Hart, & J. Ogloff (Eds.), *Psychology and law: The state of the discipline* (pp. 242–274). New York: Kluwer/Plenum Publishers.

Hoge, S., Bonnie, R., Poythress, N., & Monahan, J. (1992). Attorney-client decisionmaking in criminal cases: Client competence and participation as perceived by their attorneys. *Behavioral Sciences and the Law, 10,* 385–394.

Johnson, W. G., & Mullett, N. (1987). Georgia Court Competency Test-R. In M. Hersen & A. S. Bellack (Eds.), *Dictionary of behavioral assessment techniques.* New York: Pergamon.

Laboratory of Community Psychiatry, Harvard Medical School. (1973). *Competency to stand trial and mental illness.* Rockville, MD: Department of Health, Education and Welfare.

Melton, G. B., Petrila, J., Poythress, N. G., & Slogobin, C. (1997). *Psychological evaluations for the courts: A handbook for mental health professionals and lawyers* (2nd ed.). New York: Guilford.

Nicholson, R. A. (1999). Forensic treatment: A review of programs and research. In R. Roesch, S. Hart, & J. Ogloff (Eds.), *Psychology and law: The state of the discipline* (pp. 122–173). New York: Kluwer/Plenum Publishers.

Nicholson, R. A., & Kugler, K. E. (1991). Competent and incompetent criminal defendants: A quantitative review of comparative research. *Psychological Bulletin, 109*(3), 355–370.

Nicholson, R. A., & McNulty, J. L. (1992). Outcome of hospitalization for defendants found incompetent to stand trial. *Behavioral Sciences and the Law, 10,* 371–383.

Poythress, N., Bonnie, R., Hoge, S., Monahan, J., & Oberlander, L. (1994). Client abilities to assist counsel and make decisions in criminal cases: Findings from three studies. *Law and Human Behavior, 18,* 437–452.

Robey, A. (1965). Criteria for competency to stand trial: A checklist for psychiatrists. *American Journal of Psychiatry, 122,* 616–623.

Roesch, R., & Golding, S. L. (1980). *Competency to stand trial.* Urbana, IL: University of Illinois Press.

Roesch, R., Hart, S. D., & Zapf, P. A. (1996). Conceptualizing and assessing competency to stand trial. Implications and applications of the MacArthur Treatment Competence Model. *Psychology, Public Policy, and Law, 2,* 96–113.

Roesch, R., Ogloff, J. R., & Golding, S. L. (1993). Competency to stand trial: Legal and clinical issues. *Applied and Preventive Psychology, 2,* 43–51.

Roesch, R., Zapf, P. A., Eaves, D., & Webster, C. D. (1998). *Fitness Interview Test* (Rev. ed.). Burnaby, BC: Mental Health, Law and Policy Institute.

Siegel, A., & Elwork, A. (1990). Treating incompetence to stand trial. *Law and Human Behavior, 14,* 57–65.

Slovenko, R. (1995). Assessing competency to stand trial. *Psychiatric Annals, 25,* 392–393, 397.

Terhune, S. (1990). Forensic vs. standard assessment instruments: Preference of judges in a competency to stand trial case. *Dissertation Abstracts International, 51*(2-B), 1007.

Zapf, P. A., & Roesch, R. (1997). Assessing fitness to stand trial: A comparison of institution-based evaluations and a brief screening interview. *Canadian Journal of Community Mental Health, 16,* 53–66.

R. ROESCH
J. L. BODDY
Simon Fraser University

EXPERT TESTIMONY
FORENSIC PSYCHOLOGY
PSYCHOLOGY AND THE COURTS
PSYCHOLOGY AND THE LAW

COMPULSIONS

Compulsions, along with obsessions, are a hallmark feature of obsessive-compulsive disorder (OCD). According to the *Diagnostic and Statistical Manual of Mental Disorders* (*DSM-IV*) (APA, 1994), compulsions are "repetitive behaviors . . . or mental acts . . . the goal of which is to prevent or reduce anxiety or distress" (p. 418). While behaviors resembling compulsions occur at a range of frequencies in the normal population, in order to be considered pathological the compulsions must be associated with either intense distress or functional impairment. Impairment from compulsions can be quite severe, with some individuals spending several hours per day performing rituals, feeling unable to stop and attend to their daily responsibilities. While the label "compulsion" has been applied to a broad range of repetitive behaviors, including excessive drinking, gambling, shopping, and so on, these behaviors are differentiated from true compulsions by the function they serve.

TYPES OF COMPULSIONS

While many different classifications of compulsive behavior have been proposed, two of the most common compulsions are cleaning and checking. Hodgson and Rachman (1977) reported that 52% of OCD patients reported checking compulsions, and 48% reported cleaning compulsions. Although cleaning and checking appear to be the most common forms of compulsion, other forms of compulsive behavior are also reported frequently. These include collecting or hoarding useless objects, ordering and arranging objects, repeating actions, and seeking reassurance from others (Foa & Kozak, 1995).

Early definitions of OCD maintained that obsessions were mental events, and compulsions were overt behaviors. Under this definition, some OCD patients without overt rituals were labeled "pure obsessives." However, current theories recognize that compulsions can be either actions or thoughts; nearly 80% of OCD patients describe mental compulsions (Foa & Kozak, 1995). Mental compulsions are differentiated from obsessions according to their function, for example, whether they elicit distress or reduce it (Foa & Kozak, 1995). Whereas obsessions elicit anxiety or distress, compulsions are defined as overt (behavioral) or covert (mental) actions that reduce or prevent distress elicited by obsessions. Examples of mental compulsions include attempting to think "good thoughts," counting objects or counting up to a certain number, saying certain prayers in a rigid or repetitive manner, and mentally reviewing past actions or conversations to hunt for mistakes or other infractions. Thus, it appears that nearly all OCD patients have some form of compulsion, either overt or covert.

ASSOCIATION BETWEEN OBSESSIONS AND COMPULSIONS

For most patients with OCD, obsessions are followed by compulsions. Usually, the compulsions are thematically related to the obsessions; however, there is a broad range of logical coherence of this connection. Washing rituals, for example, are usually motivated by fears of contamination or illness. Checking rituals are usually prompted by worries that an action (e.g., turning off the stove) was performed incorrectly and that some catastrophic event (e.g., fire) will occur as a result. Other connections are less logical; for example, turning a light switch off and on several times in order to prevent one's family from dying in a car accident.

FUNCTIONAL SIGNIFICANCE OF COMPULSIONS

Given their often bizarre appearance, compulsions are often difficult to understand. Why would an individual choose to engage in such behavior, and why does the behavior persist despite marked functional impairment and distress? Compulsions are best understood within the context of the function they serve. Learning theory models of OCD (e.g., Kozak & Foa, 1997) have traditionally been based to some extent on Mowrer's (1960) two-factor theory of fear. Briefly, two-factor theory posits that classically conditioned fear motivates avoidance behavior. When the organism avoids the feared stimulus successfully, anxiety is reduced and the avoidance is therefore negatively reinforced. The avoidance also prevents extinction of fear by limiting exposure to the feared stimulus; therefore, the fear is maintained. OCD theorists have suggested that compulsions are a form of active avoidance, which are cued by obsessive fears. When the individual performs a compulsion, fear is reduced. Thus, compulsions are negatively reinforced, and obsessive fear is increased. While there is little evidence for the role of classical conditioning in OCD, studies have supported the anxiety-reduction hypothesis of compulsions: Exposure to feared stimuli increased participants' anxiety, while performing compulsions led to decreased anxiety (Hodgson & Rachman, 1972). One problem with a two-factor model of compulsions is the fact that some individuals with OCD report that compulsions are associated with increased, rather than decreased, fear. For example, Röper, Rachman, and Hodgson (1973) found that a subsample of compulsive checkers reported higher levels of fear after checking. Cases such as these might be better explained by Herrnstein's (1969) learning theory, which suggests that mildly anxiety-evoking behaviors might be considered avoidant if they serve to prevent the occurrence of strong anxiety. Thus, while checking may elicit anxiety in some patients, refraining from checking is perceived as even more aversive. In summary, the specific function of compulsions may vary, but the general function appears to be one of anxiety or prevention. In this manner, compulsive behavior is negatively reinforced, and extinction of fear is blocked.

Attention to the function of compulsion may help with the differential diagnosis of OCD. Many *DSM-IV* impulse control disorders have been classified as part of an "OCD spectrum." These disorders include "compulsive" overeating, gambling, and sexual behaviors. However, these problems tend to be functionally distinct from compulsions because they are not triggered by obsessions or fears, and are not negatively reinforced by fear reduction. On the contrary, disinhibited behaviors are more likely to be triggered by feelings of tension or boredom, and because the behaviors are satisfying, they are positively, rather than negatively, reinforced (Steketee, 1993). Although this distinction does not apply to every patient, until more convincing data are produced, the term "compulsion" is best reserved to indicate a specific functional relationship between behavior and fear.

REFERENCES

American Psychiatric Association (1994). *Diagnostic and statistical manual of mental disorders* (4th Ed.). Washington, DC: Author.

Foa, E. B., & Kozak, M. J. (1995). *DSM-IV* field trial: Obsessive-compulsive disorder. *American Journal of Psychiatry, 152,* 90–96.

Hodgson, R. J., & Rachman, S. (1972). The effects of contamination and washing in obsessional patients. *Behaviour Research and Therapy, 10,* 111–117.

Hodgson, R. J., & Rachman, S. (1977). Obsessional-compulsive complaints. *Behaviour Research and Therapy, 15,* 389–395.

Kozak, M. J., & Foa, E. B. (1997). *Mastery of obsessive-compulsive disorder: A cognitive-behavioral approach.* Albany, NY: Graywind.

Mowrer, O. H. (1960). *Learning theory and behavior.* New York: Wiley.

Röper, G., Rachman, S., & Hodgson, R. (1973). An experiment on obsessional checking. *Behaviour Research and Therapy, 11,* 271–277.

Steketee, G. S. (1993). *Treatment of obsessive compulsive disorder.* New York: Guilford.

SUGGESTED READING

Foa, E. B., Franklin, M. E., & Kozak, M. J. (1998). Psychosocial treatments for obsessive-compulsive disorder. In R. P. Swinson, M. M. Antony, S. Rachman, & M. A. Richter (Eds.), *Obsessive-compulsive disorder: Theory, research, and treatment* (pp. 258–276). New York: Guilford.

Herrnstein, R. J. (1969). Method and theory in the study of avoidance. *Psychological Review, 76,* 49–69.

D. F. TOLIN
University of Pennsylvania

E. B. FOA
University of Pennsylvania

ANXIETY
OBSESSIVE-COMPULSIVE DISORDER
OBSESSIONS

COMPUTERIZED PSYCHOLOGICAL ASSESSMENT

Computerized psychological assessment refers to the use of the computer to collect, analyze, and report data concerning a client's psychological functioning. The role of the computer in psychological assessment has increased commensurately with software and hardware advances and the affordability of the technology (Richard & Mayo, 1997). Increasingly, psychologists are using computers to interview clients, manage client self-monitoring, aid in diagnostic decision-making, conduct psychophysiological assessment, produce automated test interpretations, and facilitate a broad array of other assessment activities.

These practices continue to be scrutinized by researchers, especially with regard to: (a) the equivalence of data collected by the computer to data collected through traditional means; and (b) the reliability, validity, and utility of inferential and interpretive statements printed in automated test reports.

TYPES OF COMPUTER APPLICATIONS

Computerized interviewing involves having a client respond to a series of queries (e.g., a structured interview) presented by a computer. Software programs written for this purpose usually present items on the screen followed by several response options. Once the client has entered his or her response, the computer algorithm stores the data and branches to a subsequent query. Eventually, the program compiles the data, applies a set of programmed diagnostic decision-making rules, and prints an interpretive report. The potential advantages of assessing client symptoms using a computer include increased reliability of data collection, complex algorithmic branching between content domains, and potentially more candid client responses, especially when items may include embarrassing content or involve assessment of illicit activity (see, e.g., Turner et al., 1998, for results regarding computerized assessment of adolescent sexual behavior, drug use, and violence).

Computer-based test interpretations (CBTIs) often summarize results from a computerized interview, but also are used as stand-alone applications to analyze the results of traditional test administrations (e.g., a CBTI for the MMPI-2). While CBTIs have become increasingly popular in the last few years, many scholars are concerned that test reports produced by a computer are not sensitive to important idiosyncratic client variables (for a seminal discussion, see Matarazzo, 1986). However, recent reviews have suggested that CBTIs can be useful sources of information for clinicians when used responsibly (Butcher, Perry, & Atlis, 2000).

Computer applications in psychological assessment, however, are not limited to automated interviews and computerized test interpretations. While space does not permit a full discussion of all applications, clinical researchers have been working on computerizing self-monitoring protocols; therapeutic interventions (e.g., treatment of arachnophobia; see Whitby, 1996); diagnostic decision-making process (Garb, 2000; Price et al., 2000); treatment recommendations (e.g., Hile, Ghobary, & Campbell, 1995); and increasingly rely on computer technology when conducting psychophysiological assessments.

ISSUES SURROUNDING COMPUTERIZED PSYCHOLOGICAL ASSESSMENT

Equivalence

Several research studies have shown that client data that have been collected by a computer are not significantly different from client data that have been collected using other traditional techniques (e.g., questionnaires, structured interviews). For example, Richard

(1999) found that the total severity score from a computerized version of the Clinician Administered PTSD Scale correlated .91 with its human-administered counterpart. No significant differences were found between the two instruments at the scale or total score level.

In addition, the results from computerized interviews are often consistent with clinician judgments. For example, Meszaros, Engelsmann, Meterissan, and Kusalic (1999) recently found that a computerized version of the Zung Depression Status Inventory, Beck Depression Inventory, and Hamilton Depression Rating Scale correlated significantly (r = .69) with clinician ratings of depressive symptoms. Although, the correlation was high, patient self-ratings of depressive symptoms to the computer were significantly greater than clinician ratings of depressive symptoms. Clearly, establishing equivalence is a multimodal and complex task. For example, many clinician-administered screening instruments yield quantitative indices of behavior, but they also provide a mechanism by which a clinician can establish rapport, derive qualitative observations of behavior, and provide a starting point for investigating relevant functional and causal variables. Researchers have not examined how a computerized interview or screening instrument affects these ancillary variables.

The equivalence of data and inferences from computer and traditional assessment methods has not been shown in all studies. Equivalence of derived scores may be affected by the following factors: (a) sensitivity of item content; (b) sample characteristics; and (c) degree of computer anxiety. With regard to sensitivity of item content, Turner and colleagues (1998) found that male teenagers reported greater incidences of homosexual activity, marijuana use, cocaine use, and street drug use of any kind to a computer than to a human interviewer. A negative view of computers may also affect self-report of unrelated psychological symptoms to a computer. For instance, Schulenberg and Yutrzenka (1999) recently showed that individuals who react negatively to computers report greater global negative affect during a computer interview than a human interview.

To summarize, equivalence is a multimodal and complex concept that is affected by the types of questions being asked, the sample being used, the comparison standard (i.e., questionnaire, human interview), and a client's computer experience or computer attitudes. To date, researchers have largely treated equivalence as a unidimensional construct without systematically examining its parameters. A programmatic exploration of which variables exert the greatest impact on data equivalence has not been done.

Client Reactions

A common objection to direct computerized assessment is that clients will react negatively to the procedure. However, a consistent finding in the literature has been that patients are either neutral or actually prefer computerized assessment procedures to face-to-face interviews. For example, Richard (1999) had 128 college students with a trauma history complete a computerized version of the Clinician-Administered PTSD Scale. He then asked the students whether they would have preferred a human interviewer for the questions that were asked of them. Forty-two percent strongly disagreed, 17% mildly disagreed, and 27% were neutral. Only 13% either mildly or strongly agreed that they would have preferred a human interviewer.

Validity of Computer-Based Test Interpretations (CBTIs)

As noted above, computers have also been used to facilitate and speed interpretation of popular psychological tests. Ball, Archer, and Imhoff reported in 1994 that approximately two-thirds of clinical psychologists used computers to facilitate scoring of assessment instruments. That proportion is probably higher today. However, these efforts have not been without criticism. While Meehl (1956) provided an early rationale for a quantitative-based approach to test interpretation, it is difficult to provide individually meaningful interpretations using a canned software algorithm.

Critics like Matarazzo (1986) have pointed out that computerized test interpretations do not possess inherent validity and ignore important idiosyncratic variables. Despite Matarazzo's objections, Butcher (1995) contended that computer-based test interpretation systems: (a) provide a more "comprehensive and objective" summary of test results than a clinical practioner; (b) minimize subjectivity and clinical bias in interpreting results; (c) produce results rapidly and cost-effectively; (d) reliably produce interpretive remarks from score profiles; and (e) reflect the testing industry's high standards; clinicians can thus be confident in the quality of the interpretations (Butcher, 1995, pp. 78–79).

Graham (1999) recently reviewed the literature surrounding computer-based test interpretations of the MMPI. He concluded that the accuracy and validity of computerized scoring programs and services are variable, should not be assumed, and that computerized reports should not supplant a comprehensive psychological evaluation. A significant problem in evaluating the accuracy of computer-based test interpretations involves operationalizing report narratives. Most CBTIs include vague statements that are context-independent and not testable. Graham (1999) provided a copy of a computer-generated MMPI interpretation. One report paragraph reads as follows: "He avoids deep emotional attachments and tends to be quite vulnerable to being hurt. He tends to blame himself for interpersonal problems. The intense problems may diminish over time or with treatment" (Graham, 1999, p. 298). The problem with the interpretation is twofold. First, the terms are vague, general, and not context-specific. Second, the narrative implies specificity but, in reality, ignores behavioral base rates and makes general statements that broadly apply to most individuals (e.g., most behavioral problems diminish with time or treatment).

EVALUATION OF COMPUTER APPLICATIONS IN PSYCHOLOGICAL ASSESSMENT

Computers will continue to play an increasingly large role in the practice of clinical psychology. However, numerous issues remain. First, the facets of equivalence should be identified and explored more comprehensively. Additionally, equivalence must be demonstrated for each computerized measure, since equivalence does not generalize across computerized assessment instruments. Second, interpretations of popular test instruments need to demonstrate more than just reliability—they must also be accurate, valid, and useful. While few researchers would disagree with the conclusion that a computer can score a profile more reliably than a clinician, the validity and utility of inferences and interpretive remarks generated by automated reports remains controversial. Successfully addressing these issues has implications not only for computerized assessment, but for the future of psychological assessment.

REFERENCES

Ball, J. D., Archer, R. P., & Imhof, E. A. (1994). Time requirements of psychological testing: A survey of practitioners. *Journal of Clinical Psychology, 16,* 304–307.

Butcher, J. N. (1995). How to use computer-based reports. In J. N. Butcher (Ed.), *Clinical personality assessment* (pp. 78–94). New York: Oxford University Press.

Butcher, J. N., Perry, J. N., & Atlis, M. M. (2000). Validity and utility of computer-based test interpretation. *Psychological Assessment.*

Garb, H. N. (2000). Introduction to the special section on the use of computers for making judgments and decisions. *Psychological Assessment.*

Graham, J. R. (1999). *MMPI-2: Assessing personality and psychopathology* (3rd ed.). New York: Oxford University Press.

Hile, M. G., Ghobary, B. B., & Campbell, D. M. (1995). Sources of expert advice: A comparison of peer-reviewed advice from the literature with that from an automated performance support system. *Behavior Research Methods, Instruments, and Computers, 27,* 272–276.

Matarazzo, J. D. (1986). Computeried clinical psychological test interpretations: Unvalidated plus all mean and no sigma. *American Psychologist, 41,* 14–24.

Meehl, P. E. (1956). Wanted—A good cookbook. *American Psychologist, 11,* 263–272.

Meszaros, A., Englesmann, F., Meterissian, G., & Kusalic, M. (1995). Computerized assessment of depression and suicidal ideation. *Journal of Nervous and Mental Disease, 183,* 487–488.

Price, R. K., Spitznagel, E. L., Downey, T. J., Meyer, D. J., Risk, N. K., & El-Ghazzawy, O. G. (2000). Applying artificial neural network models to clinical decision making. *Psychological Assessment.*

Richard, D. C. S. (1999). Development and psychometric evaluation of the Computerized PTSD Scale. Unpublished dissertation manuscript, University of Hawaii at Manoa.

Richard, D. C. S., & Mayo, S. (1997). Computers in the twenty-first century: The challenge to behavioral assessment and behavior therapy. *Behavior Therapist, 20,* 186–190.

Schulenberg, S. S., & Yutrzenka, B. A. (1999). The equivalence of computerized and paper-and-pencil psychological instruments: Implications for measures of negative affect. *Behavior Research, Methods, Instruments, and Computers, 31,* 315–321.

Turner, C. F., Ku, L., Rogers, S. M., Lindberg, J. H., Pleck, J. H., & Sonenstein, F. L. (1998). Adolescent sexual beahvior, drug use, and violence: Increased reporting with computer survey technology. *Science, 280,* 886–873.

Whitby, P. (1996). Spider phobia control (SpiderPC). *Behavior Research Methods, Instruments, and Computers, 28,* 131–133.

D. C. S. Richard
Southwest Missouri State University

S. N. Haynes
University of Hawaii

CLINICAL ASSESSMENT
DIAGNOSIS

CONDITIONED FOOD AVERSION

A conditioned food aversion is a learned dislike for and rejection of particular flavors that have been associated with illness. The strength of such learning depends on the procedure used to pair the food with the illness in time, the characteristics of the food, and the nature of the illness.

CONDITIONING PROCEDURE

The procedure used to produce conditioned food aversions resembles classical conditioning. The conditioned stimulus (CS) is usually a novel flavor and the unconditioned stimulus (US) is often an emetic agent. The unconditioned response (UR) is not well defined, and is assumed to be related to the nausea, malaise, or other internal disruptions induced by the US. After one or more pairings with the US, the CS then comes to elicit a conditioned response (CR) that presumably resembles the illness of the UR, and the subject acts as if the CS is aversive and avoids further contact with it. An important control procedure is an unpaired group that receives equivalent experience with both the CS and US, but at sufficiently different times that conditioning to the CS does not occur.

Two types of tests commonly used to evaluate the effects of conditioning are the preference test and the taste reactivity test. In the preference test, animals are given a choice between the CS and another neutral substance, such as their normal diet or water. After conditioning, intake of the CS is selectively reduced. In the taste reactivity test (Grill & Norgren, 1978), the CS is infused directly into the mouth of the subject, and species-typical ingestive or rejection reactions are quantified. After aversion conditioning with emetic agents, subjects increase their rejection reactions and decrease their ingestive reactions.

In sharp contrast to the traditional classical conditioning procedure, the interval from the CS to US in food aversion conditioning can be as long as a few hours and still produce robust conditioning in a single trial (Garcia, Hankins, & Rusiniak, 1974). These features of aversion conditioning help an animal to learn to avoid poisonous foods without multiple experiences with the poison, even if the poison does not immediately make the animal sick.

CHARACTERISTICS OF THE FOOD

The phenomenon of conditioned food aversion is also known as conditioned taste or flavor aversion, poison-based avoidance conditioning, bait shyness, or aversion therapy, depending on the interests of the investigator. A taste aversion implies that the aversion is limited to a gustatory CS, that is, one that is sensed by the tongue. A flavor aversion implies that both taste and odor cues compose the CS and that both contribute to the conditioning.

Substances having a bitter, sour, or putrid flavor may evoke an unconditioned aversion, but investigators in food aversion studies typically use flavors that produce positive ingestive responses, such as a dilute solution of saccharin. After administration of an emetic agent such as lithium chloride (LiCl), a decrease in ingestion rapidly emerges in animals that received the CS and US paired closely in time. Any distinctive taste or flavor can be the target of a conditioned aversion, but some types of flavors seem to be particularly prone to the development of aversions. For example, proteins such as eggs, cheese, and meat are more likely to become targets of conditioned food aversions than carbohydrates, and novel foods are more likely to become targets than familiar foods (Bernstein, 1999).

NATURE OF THE ILLNESS

Unconditioned stimuli that are known to induce food aversions usually produce some type of gastric distress, including nausea, vomiting, or malaise. LiCl is commonly used for experimental treatments in rats. Emetic agents used for conditioned aversion therapy in humans with alcohol dependency include apomorphine, emetidine, Syrup of Ipecac, disulfiram, ethanol, and others (Howard & Jenson, 1990). Non-drug experimental procedures that produce conditioned aversions include rotational dizziness and some abdominal surgical procedures such as a subdiaphragmatic vagotomy or a bile duct ligation (Lane, Starbuck, & Fitts, 1997). Accidental pairings of harmless novel foods with subsequent gastrointestinal illness probably account for many food aversions in humans, including persons who experience nausea as a result of cancer or cancer chemotherapy.

Other types of treatments that may induce avoidance when they are paired with certain foods or tastes include drugs such as amphetamine, cocaine, morphine, and phencyclidine. Curiously, and in great contrast to the emetic drugs, rats will self-administer these drugs under certain experimental circumstances. The avoidance of a food after its pairing with a rewarding drug may be fundamentally different from the avoidance induced by emetic drugs: after conditioning with a rewarding drug, rats still drink less of a CS in preference tests, but they fail to show large increases in rejection reactions in the taste reactivity test (Parker, 1995).

NEUROBIOLOGY OF CONDITIONED FOOD AVERSIONS

Certain parts of the brain related to autonomic activity and emesis become active following administration of an emetic US, and an analysis of such brain activity is improving our understanding of what constitutes the US, UR, and CR in food aversion studies (Bernstein, 1999). The nucleus of the solitary tract (NTS) in the hindbrain receives much afferent input from both the abdominal viscera and the gustatory system, and an injection of LiCl, the US, in rats produces a characteristic pattern of neural activation in NTS as measured by expression of the immediate early gene c-Fos. Intraoral infusions of a preferred solution such as saccharin or of a noxious tastant such as quinine do not by themselves induce c-Fos expression in the NTS. However, once saccharin has been paired with LiCl, an intraoral infusion of saccharin alone, the CS, thereafter evokes activity in the NTS as if LiCl had been given instead (Swank & Bernstein, 1994). Thus, the CR as measured by c-Fos expression in the brain resembles the UR. This activation of the NTS results from descending information from the forebrain, suggesting a learning interpretation, and does not result simply from conditioned fear or autonomic arousal (Bernstein 1999; Schafe, Fitts, Thiele, LeDoux, & Bernstein, 2000).

The neural substrates of conditioned food aversions differ considerably depending on the procedures used to elicit them. Lesions in the amygdala abolish aversions conditioned by intraoral infusion of a CS but do not disrupt those conditioned by drinking the CS from a bottle (Bernstein, 1999); lesions of the inferior olive disrupt aversions conditioned by a concurrent acquisition procedure but not by a sequential procedure (Mediavilla, Molina, & Puerto, 1999); and lesions of the area postrema eliminate aversions conditioned by emetic agents such as LiCl (Ritter, McGlone, & Kelley, 1980) but not those conditioned by amphetamine or apomorphine (Berger, Wise, & Stein, 1973; Van der Kooy, Swerdlow, & Koob, 1983). Clearly, conditioned food aversions are not a unitary phenomenon, but represent several different neural processes that may reflect different kinds of learning (i.e., classical and instrumental conditioning).

REFERENCES

Berger, B. D., Wise, C. D., & Stein, L. (1973). Area postrema damage and bait shyness. *Journal of Comparative and Physiological Psychology, 82,* 475–479.

Bernstein, I. L. (1999). Taste aversion learning: A contemporary perspective. *Nutrition, 15,* 229–234.

Garcia, J., Hankins, W. G., & Rusiniak, K. W. (1974). Regulation of the milieu interne in man and rat. *Science, 185,* 823–831.

Grill, H. J., & Norgren, R. (1978). The taste reactivity test. I: Mimetic responses to gustatory stimuli in neurologically normal rats. *Brain Research, 143,* 263–279.

Howard, M. O., & Jenson, J. M. (1990). Chemical aversion treatment of alcohol dependence. II. Future Research Directions for the '90s. *International Journal of the Addictions, 25,* 1403–1414.

Lane, J. R., Starbuck, E. M., & Fitts, D. A. (1997). Ethanol preference, metabolism, blood pressure, and conditioned taste aversion in experimental cholestasis. *Pharmacology Biochemistry and Behavior, 57,* 755–766.

Mediavilla, C., Molina, F., & Puerto, A. (1999). Inferior olive lesions impair concurrent taste aversion learning in rats. *Neurobiology of Learning and Memory, 72,* 13–27.

Parker, L. A. (1995). Rewarding drugs produce taste avoidance, but not taste aversion. *Neuroscience and Biobehavioral Reviews, 19,* 143–151.

Ritter, R. C., McGlone, J. J., & Kelley, K. W. (1980). Absence of lithium-induced taste aversion after area postrema lesion. *Brain Research, 201,* 501–506.

Swank, M. W., & Bernstein, I. L. (1994). C-Fos induction in response to a conditioned stimulus after single trial taste aversion learning. *Brain Research, 636,* 202–208.

Schafe, G. E., Fitts, D. A., Thiele, T. E., LeDoux, J. E., & Bernstein, I. L. (2000). The induction of c-Fos in NTS following taste aversion learning is not correlated with measures of conditioned fear. *Behavioral Neuroscience, 114,* 99–106.

Van der Kooy, D., Swerdlow, N. R., & Koob, G. F. (1983). Paradoxical reinforcing properties of apomorphine: Effects of nucleus accumbens and area postrema lesions. *Brain Research, 259,* 111–118.

D. A. FITTS
University of Washington, Seattle

CONDUCT DISORDER

Within the framework of the *Diagnostic and Statistical Manual of Mental Disorders,* conduct disorder (CD) is one of the disruptive behavior disorders which are usually first diagnosed in childhood or adolescence. Conduct disorder is a repetitive and persistent pattern of behavior which violates societal norms or the basic rights of others. The symptoms cover four behavioral areas, and consist of: aggressive behavior that threatens or causes physical harm to other people or animals (bullies, threatens, or intimidates others; often initiates physical fights; uses a weapon); nonaggressive conduct that causes property loss or damage (fire-setting; property destruction); deceitfulness or theft (stealing; breaking into someone's house or car); and serious violation of rules (truancy from school; running away from home). The two subtypes of conduct disorder identified in *DSM-IV* are childhood-onset (in which at least one of the behavioral characteristics are evident before age ten) and adolescent-onset. The diagnosis of conduct disorder is made if the child or adolescent has displayed at least three of the 15 symptoms during the past twelve months.

Although some forms of aggressive behaviors are relatively common in mild forms during early childhood years, aggressive and antisocial behavior become more clinically significant if the instances are highly intense, if they occur with high frequency, or if they are characterized by notably violent elements in later childhood and adolescent years. Rates of conduct disorder are estimated to be in the range of 6% to 16% for boys and 2% to 9% for girls (American Psychiatric Association, 1994), and to be more prevalent in boys than girls at a rate of about 3:1 (Lochman & Szczepanski, 1999). Loeber (1990) hypothesized that aggressive behavior in elementary school years is part of a developmental trajectory that can lead to adolescent delinquency and conduct disorder. In a similar manner, the *DSM-IV* taxonomic system (American Psychiatric Association, 1994) indicates that oppositional defiant disorder in early childhood can evolve into childhood-onset conduct disorder and then into antisocial personality disorder in adults. Childhood-onset conduct disorder is expected to be preceded by physical aggression and poor peer relationships in the elementary school years. Longitudinal research has documented this

evolution of disorders by noting that aggressive behavior and rejection by children's peers can be additive risk markers for subsequent maladjusted behavior in the middle school years (Coie, Lochman, Terry, & Hyman, 1992), and that aggressive behavior is a risk marker for early substance use, overt delinquency, and police arrests in the later adolescent years (Coie, Terry, Zakriski, & Lochman, 1995). Children are more at risk for continued aggressive and antisocial behavior if they display aggressive behavior in multiple settings within their home, school, and neighborhood, and if they develop "versatile" forms of antisocial behavior, including both overt (assaults, direct threats) and covert (theft) behaviors by early to mid-adolescence (Lochman & Szczepanski, 1999).

For adolescents with childhood-onset conduct disorder, the developmental trajectory leading to the disorder may start very early among infants with irritable, difficult-to-soothe temperaments (Loeber, 1990), who are less adaptable to change. These temperamentally difficult children are at risk for failing to develop positive attachments with caretakers, for displaying high rates of hyperactive behavior, for poor attentional control in the preschool years, and for becoming involved in increasingly coercive interchanges with parents and significant adults, such as teachers. Moffitt (1993) has suggested that life-course-persistent delinquents, or "early starters," are at early risk because of combined biological and family factors. In some children, family dysfunction may be sufficient to initiate this sequence of escalating aggressive behavior. Living in poor, crime-ridden neighborhoods also adds to the environmental risk factors leading to seriously aggressive, problematic behavior (Frick, 1998). Loeber (1990) hypothesized that children then begin to generalize their use of coercive behaviors to other social interactions, leading to increasingly aggressive behavior with peers and adults by early elementary school and to dysfunctional social-cognitive processes. Because of their aggressive behavior, these children are often socially rejected by their peer group and can become more withdrawn and isolated. Partially as a result of these worsening relationships with teachers and peers, their academic progress deteriorates. Poor verbal fluency and poor abstract reasoning abilities both contribute to and are affected by the children's increasing behavior problems. By early to middle adolescence, they are then prone to meeting their affiliation needs by gravitating toward deviant peer groups, and these deviant peer groups can become an additional proximal cause for delinquent behavior (Coie et al., 1995; Patterson, Reid, & Dishion, 1992).

Children and adolescents with conduct disorders often have a number of co-occurring conditions which can affect the course of the disorder and complicate treatment. Attention-deficit/hyperactivity disorder (ADHD) is the most common comorbid diagnosis in children with conduct disorders, with rates ranging from 65% to 90% in clinic-referred children (Abikoff & Klein, 1992). Children with comorbid ADHD and conduct disorder have more conduct problem symptoms, an earlier onset of severe conduct problems, more aggressive conduct problems, and earlier and greater substance use than non-ADHD children with conduct disorders (Frick, 1998). Other common comorbid conditions are anxiety disorders, which occur in 60% to 75% of clinic-referred CD children (Zoccolillo, 1992), depressive disorders, which occur in

15% to 31% of CD children (Zoccolillo, 1992), and substance use. Children and adolescents with both CD and substance use have an earlier onset of substance use and are more likely to abuse multiple substances (Lynskey & Fergusson, 1995).

PARENTAL AND SOCIAL-COGNITIVE CORRELATES

The developmental trajectory leading to conduct disorder often includes deficient parenting practices and distorted and deficient social-cognitive processes in the children. These particular correlates are potentially mutable, and thus can become an important focus for intervention. Parents of aggressive conduct problem children have been found to generally display high rates of harsh or inconsistent discipline, have unclear rules and expectations, and have low rates of positive involvement, adaptive discipline strategies, and problem-solving skills (Lochman & Wells, 1996). As children enter the adolescent years, the parents' poor abilities to monitor and supervise their children provides a double risk factor, because with the lack of effective monitoring, the young adolescents are even more likely to gravitate to deviant peer groups.

Partially as a result of growing up with rigidly controlling, authoritarian parents, aggressive children develop dysfunctional social-cognitive processes, which in turn serve to maintain problem behavior sequences. Aggressive children have characteristic problems with their social information-processing (Crick & Dodge, 1994), including tendencies to overly encode hostile social cues, to have hostile attributional biases, to have problem-solving strategies that rely on forceful direct action rather than verbal negotiation strategies, and to expect that aggressive solutions will work in resolving their interpersonal problems. These information processing difficulties are made worse for aggressive children because of their dominance-oriented social goals, their pervasive schema-based expectations for others' behavior, and their strong physiological reactivity in response to provocation, especially for reactive aggressive youth (Dodge, Lochman, Harnish, Bates, & Pettit, 1997; Lochman & Dodge, 1998; Lochman & Szczepanski, 1999).

TREATMENT AND PREVENTION

Historically, psychosocial treatment of antisocial, conduct-disordered youth has been perceived to be difficult and not very productive. However, in recent years randomized clinical research trials have begun to identify empirically-supported treatments for oppositional defiant disorder and conduct disorder. Brestan and Eyberg (1998) have carefully reviewed the treatment research literature for conduct disorder and have identified two parent training intervention programs as having well-established positive effects (Patterson, Reid, & Dishion, 1992; Webster-Stratton, 1994) and have identified ten other programs as being probably efficacious. Kazdin and Weisz (1998) have similarly identified several sets of positive treatment approaches for conduct disorder, including cognitive problem-solving skills training, parent management training, functional family therapy, and multisystemic therapy. Parent management training and functional family therapy are directed at the dysfunctional parenting processes that have been identified in prior research, and these approaches have produced significant improvements in parenting practices and reductions in children's

aggressive conduct problem behavior (Eyberg, Boggs, & Algina, 1995; Webster-Stratton, 1994). Cognitive-behavioral treatments designed to assist children's anger management, perspective-taking, and problem-solving skills have produced improvements in children's abilities to accurately perceive others' intentions, to generate more competent problem solutions, and to show reductions in problem behaviors at posttreatment and at followup (Kazdin, Siegel, & Bass, 1992; Lochman, Burch, Curry, & Lampron, 1984). Multisystemic treatment relies on individualized assessments of antisocial youth and the impaired systems around them, and uses intense, individualized treatment plans to impact the youths' social skills, parenting skills, peer group involvement, school bonding, and academic functioning, and has produced significant reductions in antisocial behavior among seriously delinquent youth (Henggeler, Melton, & Smith, 1992). In recent years there has been an increasing focus on developing and evaluating effective multi-component interventions which target both the social-cognitive and parenting skill deficits evident in conduct disordered youth and their families (Kazdin, Siegel, & Bass, 1992; Webster-Stratton & Hammond, 1997). Treatment research has also begun to refocus existing intervention programs in new ways, such as with foster parents who care for conduct disordered youth (Chamberlain & Reid, 1998). Intensive, comprehensive prevention programs have also been developed and evaluated with high-risk children starting as early as first grade, and the results of these programs indicate that aggressive behavior and conduct disorder can be reduced through early intervention (Conduct Problems Prevention Research Group, 1999; Vitaro, Brengden, Pagani, Tremblay, & McDuff, 1999).

REFERENCES

Abikoff, H., & Klein, R. G. (1992). Attention-deficit hyperactivity and conduct disorder: Co-morbidity and implications for treatment. *Journal of Consulting and Clinical Psychology, 60,* 881–892.

American Psychiatric Association (1994). *Diagnostic and statistical manual of mental disorders* (4th ed.). Washington, DC: Author.

Brestan, E. V., & Eyberg, S. M. (1998). Effective psychosocial treatments of conduct-disordered children and adolescents: 29 years, 82 studies, and 5,272 kids. *Journal of Clinical Child Psychology, 27,* 180–189.

Chamberlain, P., & Reid, J. B. (1998). Comparison of two community alternatives to incarceration for chronic juvenile offenders. *Journal of Consulting and Clinical Psychology, 66,* 624–633.

Coie, J. D., Lochman, J. E., Terry, R., & Hyman, C. (1992). Predicting early adolescent disorder from childhood aggression and peer rejection. *Journal of Consulting and Clinical Psychology, 60,* 783–792.

Coie, J. D., Terry, R., Zakriski, A., & Lochman, J. E. (1995). Early adolescent social influences on delinquent behavior. In J. McCord (Ed.), *Coercion and punishment in long-term perspectives* (pp. 229–244). Cambridge, England: Cambridge University Press.

Conduct Problems Prevention Research Group (1999). Initial impact of the Fast Track prevention trial for conduct problems: I. The high-risk sample. *Journal of Consulting and Clinical Psychology, 67,* 631–647.

Crick, N. R., & Dodge, K. A. (1994). A review and reformulation of social information-processing mechanisms in children's social adjustment. *Psychological Bulletin, 115,* 74–101.

Dodge, K. A., Lochman, J. E., Harnish, J. D., Bates, J. E., & Pettit, G. S. (1997). Reactive and proactive aggression in school children and psychiatrically impaired chronically assaultive youth. *Journal of Abnormal Psychology, 106,* 37–51.

Eyberg, S. M., Boggs, S., & Algina, J. (1995). Parent-child interaction therapy: A psychosocial model for the treatment of young children with conduct problem behavior and their families. *Psychopharmacology Bulletin, 31,* 83–91.

Frick, P. J. (1998). *Conduct disorders and severe antisocial behavior.* New York: Plenum.

Henggeler, S. W., Melton, G. B., & Smith, L. A. (1992). Family preservation using multisystemic therapy: An effective alternative to incarcerating serious juvenile offenders. *Journal of Consulting and Clinical Psychology, 60,* 953–961.

Kazdin, A. E., Siegel, T. C., & Bass, D. (1992). Cognitive problem-solving skills training and parent management training in the treatment of antisocial behavior in children. *Journal of Consulting and Clinical Psychology, 60,* 733–747.

Kazdin, A. E., & Weisz, J. R. (1998). Identifying and developing empirically supported child and adolescent treatments. *Journal of Consulting and Clinical Psychology, 66,* 19–36.

Lochman, J. E., Burch, P. R., Curry, J. F., & Lampron, L. B. (1984). Treatment and generalization effects of cognitive-behaviorial and goal-setting interventions with aggresive boys. *Journal of Consulting and Clinical Psychology, 52,* 915–916.

Lochman, J. E., & Dodge, K. A. (1998). Distorted perceptions in dyadic interactions of aggressive and nonaggressive boys: Effects of prior expectations, context, and boys' age. *Development and Psychopathology, 10,* 495–512.

Lochman, J. E., & Szczepanski, R. G. (1999). Externalizing conditions. In V. L. Schwean & D. H. Saklofske (Eds.), *Psychosocial correlates of exceptionality* (pp. 219–246). New York: Plenum.

Lochman, J. E., & Wells, K. C. (1996). A social-cognitive intervention with aggressive children: Prevention effects and contextual implementation issues. In R. D. Peters & R. J. McMahon (Eds.), *Prevention childhood disorders, substance abuse, and delinquency* (pp. 111–143). Thousand Oaks, CA: Sage.

Loeber, R. (1990). Development and risk factors of juvenile antisocial behavior and delinquency. *Clinical Psychology Review, 10,* 1–42.

Lynskey, M. T., & Fergusson, D. M. (1995). Childhood conduct problems, attention deficit behaviors, and adolescent alcohol, tobacco, and illicit drug use. *Journal of Abnormal Child Psychology, 23,* 281–302.

Moffitt, T. E. (1993). Adolescence-limited and life-course persistent antisocial behavior: A developmental taxonomy. *Psychology Review, 100,* 674–701.

Patterson, G. R., Reid, J. B., & Dishion, T. J. (1992). *Antisocial boys.* Eugene, OR: Castalia.

Vitaro, F., Brendgen, M., Pagani, L., Tremblay, R. E., & McDuff, P. (1999). Disruptive behavior, peer association, and conduct disorder: Testing the developmental links through early intervention. *Development and Psychopathology, 11,* 287–304.

Webster-Stratton, C. (1994). Advancing videotape parent training: A comparison study. *Journal of Consulting and Clinical Psychology, 62,* 583–593.

Webster-Stratton, C., & Hammond, M. (1997). Treating children with early-onset conduct problems: A comparison of child and parent training interventions. *Journal of Consulting and Clinical Psychology, 65,* 93–109.

Zoccolillo, M. (1992). Co-occurrence of conduct disorder and its adult outcomes with depressive and anxiety disorders: A review. *Journal of the American Academy of Child and Adolescent Psychiatry, 31,* 547–556.

J. E. LOCHMAN
University of Alabama

AGGRESSION
CHILDHOOD PSYCHOLOGY
TEMPERAMENT

CONDUCTION APHASIA

Conduction aphasia is a specific language deficit that consists of impaired repetition that is disproportionate to any defects in fluency or comprehension. Literal paraphasias—errors in which incorrect syllables are substituted within words for correct ones—are frequent and are exacerbated by attempts at repetition. In contrast to Wernicke's aphasia, patients are aware of their deficit and have no difficulty in comprehension. Ideomotor apraxia—inability to perform a manual task despite comprehending its goal—can also be present. To neurologists, conduction aphasia is an important clinical finding because it reliably indicates a brain lesion involving the dominant posterior perisylvian region. To cognitive neuroscientests, conduction aphasia is at the center of a long-standing debate on whether complex behaviors are created from joinings of simple cortical regions or are mediated by more specialized cortex.

LOCALIZATION

Classically, conduction aphasia results from lesions of the arcuate fasciculus that disconnect receptive from expressive language regions. The arcuate fasciculus is a white-matter tract that runs from Wernicke's area in the posterior superior temporal gyrus, arches around the sylvian fissure, and runs anteriorly from the inferior parietal lobe to the inferior frontal lobe of Broca's region (Damasio & Damasio, 1980). Many lesions that cause conduction apha-sia not only involve the arcuate fasciculus but include the supra-marginal gyrus; and sometimes, the posterior superior temporal gyrus, left auditory complex; and portions of the insula.

Most cases of conduction aphasia follow cerebral infarcts of the dominant hemisphere involving thromboembolic occlusion of a posterior branch of the middle cerebral artery. It is relatively rare in comparison to other major aphasias (global, expressive, and re-ceptive) because thromboemboli usually lodge more proximally, causing more anterior or widespread infarcts.

Wernicke postulated that a lesion of the arcuate fasciculus that disconnected receptive from expressive centers would produce a deficit in repetition, or conduction aphasia. Others proposed that a single cortical center was responsible for integration of receptive and expressive regions yet was independent of them (Goldstein, 1948). This hypothesis lead to adoption of the alternative term "central aphasia" because the specific cortical region mediated central, or inner, speech.

EVIDENCE SUPPORTING DISCONNECTION

Evidence from subjects with conduction aphasia usually supports the concept of disconnection. In these studies (usually of patients with strokes examined at autopsy or by neuroimaging), disruption of the arcuate fasciculus is obligate with variable involvement of adjacent regions of supra- or subsylvian cortex (Benson et al., 1973; Damasio & Damasio, 1980). Studies of cortical strokes, how-ever, in determinations of cortical versus subcortical mechanisms, can be misleading because regions of destruction involve both the cortex and the arcuate fasciculus.

Circumscribed lesions of the arcuate fasciculus that spare the overlying cortex also support disconnection (Aihara et al., 1995; Arnett, Rao, Hussian, Swanson, & Hammeke, 1996; Tanabe et al., 1987), but with white-matter lesions (caused by multiple sclerosis, for example) it is not possible to differentiate between the relative importance of disruption of the arcuate fasciculus versus discon-nections of overlying neurons along its course.

Physiological findings have also supported disconnection as the mechanism of conduction aphasia. Regional blood flow deter-mined by xenon CT-scan was absent in Broca's region in stroke pa-tients with conduction aphasia, suggesting functional disconnec-tion (Demeurisse & Capon, 1991).

Electrical stimulation, unlike clinical-pathological correlations in stroke, can more selectively separate cortical from white-matter dysfunction. Electrical stimulation of eloquent cortex produced both Broca's and Wernicke's aphasias but not conduction aphasia (Schäffler, Lüders, & Beck, 1996), suggesting that conduction aphasia is not cortically mediated. Notably, in this series of patients with implanted subdural electrodes, the testing paradigm involved mainly reading aloud, and repetition may not have been tested (Schäffler et al., 1996).

EVIDENCE SUPPORTING CORTICAL SPECIALIZATION

Other studies suggest that disconnection may not be the only mechanism of conduction aphasia. Some cases of conduction aphasia were caused by lesions that clearly spared the arcuate fas-

ciculus (Marshall, Lazar, Mohr, Van Heertum, & Mast, 1996; Mendez & Benson, 1985). Similarly, lesions confined to the arcuate fasciculus have not always resulted in conduction aphasia (Shuren et al., 1995).

Physiologic data provided by positron emission tomography (PET) imaging does not clearly support the disconnection theory. In one study of stroke and conduction aphasia, cerebral metabolic patterns had no clear correlation to clinical findings (Kempler et al., 1988), suggesting that functional disconnection is not neces-sary to produce conduction aphasia.

PET studies are correlated by a report of cortical mapping us-ing electrical stimulation of implanted electrodes. In this case, im-paired repetition, sparing naming and command-following, was transiently elicited by stimulation of the posterior superior tempo-ral gyrus (Quigg & Fountain, 1999). The selective and reversible impairment of a specific region of the cortex suggests that conduc-tion aphasia may be induced by means other than disconnection.

Although the classic Wernicke model cannot account for all cases of conduction aphasia, it remains a clinically useful means by which to organize deficits in language.

REFERENCES

Aihara, M., Oba, H., Ohtomo, K., Uchiyama, G., Hayashibe, H., & Nakazawa, S. (1995). MRI of white matter changes in the Sjö-gren-Larsson syndrome. *Neuroradiology, 37,* 576–577.

Arnett, P. A., Rao, S. M., Hussian, M., Swanson, S. J., & Ham-meke, T. A. (1996). Conduction aphasia in multiple sclerosis: A case report with MRI findings. *Neurology, 47,* 576–578.

Benson, D., Sheremata, W., Bouchard, R., Segarra, J., Price, D., & Geschwind, N. (1973). Conduction aphasia. *Archives of Neurol-ogy, 28,* 339–346.

Damasio, H., & Damasio, A. (1980). The anatomic basis of con-duction aphasia. *Brain, 103,* 337–350.

Demeurisse, G., & Capon, A. (1991). Brain activation during a lin-guistic task in conduction aphasia. *Cortex, 27,* 285–294.

Goldstein, K. (1948). *Language and language disturbances.* New York: Grune & Stratton.

Kempler, D., Metter, E., Jackson, C., Hanson, W., Riege, W., Mazziotta, J., & Phelps, M. (1988). Disconnection and cerebral metabolism: The case of conduction aphasia. *Archives of Neu-rology, 45,* 275–279.

Marshall, R., Lazar, R., Mohr, J., Van Heertum, R., & Mast, H. (1996). "Semantic" conduction aphasia from a posterior insu-lar cortex infarction. *Journal of Neuroimaging, 6,* 189–191.

Mendez, M., & Benson, D. (1985). Atypical conduction aphasia: a disconnection syndrome. *Archives of Neurology, 42,* 886–891.

Quigg, M., & Fountain, N. (1999). Conduction aphasia elicited by cortical stimulation of the posterior superior temporal gyrus. *Journal of Neurology, Neurosurgery & Pyschiatry, 66,* 393–396.

Schäffler, L., Lüders, H., & Beck, G. (1996). Quantitative compar-ison of language deficits produced by extraoperative electrical stimulation of Broca's, Wernicke's, and basal temporal lan-guage areas. *Epilepsia, 37,* 463–475.

Shuren, J., Schefft, B., Yeh, H., Privitera, M., Cahill, W., & Houston, W. (1995). Repetition and the arcuate fasciculus. *Journal of Neurology, 242,* 596–598.

Tanabe, H., Sawada, T., Inoue, N., Ogawa, M., Kuriyama, Y., & Shiraishi, J. (1987). Conduction aphasia and arcuate fasciculus. *Acta Neurologica Scandinavica, 76,* 422–427.

M. QUIGG
University of Virginia

APHASIA

CONFIDENCE INTERVAL

The concept of the confidence interval was introduced and developed theoretically by Neyman in the 1930s. The confidence interval represents the range of values around a parameter estimate that indicates the degree of certainty that the range contains the true value of the population parameter. The upper and lower boundaries of the range are the confidence limits. The width of the confidence interval indicates the degree of precision associated with the parameter estimate. Wider intervals indicate less precision, and narrower intervals indicate greater precision. The width of the interval can never be zero, because there will always be some sampling error associated with estimating a population parameter from sample data. Sampling error may be due to measurement unreliability or other chance factors causing fluctuations from sample to sample. The result is that no matter how carefully a sample is drawn or how large it is, there can be no certainty that the sample estimate is exactly equal to the parameter (population) value.

The calculation of the confidence interval for any parameter is based on the standard error of the relevant sampling distribution. For a simple observation, X, assuming an underlying normal distribution with mean μ and standard deviation σ, the confidence limits on the observation can be stated simply as: $X = \mu \pm z\sigma$, where z represents the standard normal deviate associated with any particular level of confidence. Any confidence level may be specified, but in practice the most commonly used intervals are the 95%, 99%, and 99.9% levels:

$$95\% \quad \text{confidence limits: } -1.96\sigma \leq X - \mu \leq +1.96\sigma$$
$$99\% \quad \text{confidence limits: } -2.58\sigma \leq X - \mu \leq +2.58\sigma$$
$$99.9\% \text{ confidence limits: } -3.29\sigma \leq X - \mu \leq +3.29\sigma$$

Confidence limits can be computed for any sample statistic for which the sampling distribution is known. For example, for the mean (M), the standard error of the mean (σ_m) is used so that $M = \mu \pm z\sigma_m$. When sampling distributions are unknown, various techniques can be employed to estimate the standard error, such as bootstrapping, jackknifing, and computer simulation. Confidence intervals are most commonly determined for well-known statistics such as sample means, correlation and regression coefficients, proportions, and predicted scores, but should also be reported for less commonly used statistics, such as measures of effect size and goodness-of-fit indexes.

As an example of the use of confidence intervals, consider an incoming class of 750 college freshman with an average recorded S.A.T. score of 550. Assuming an underlying normal distribution with $\mu = 500$ and $\sigma = 100$, then $\sigma_m = 3.65$. The resulting 95% confidence interval is 543–557. This interval is typically interpreted as meaning that there is a 95% chance that the interval 543–557 contains the true value of the freshman class S.A.T. score. However, since any specific interval either does or does not contain the true score, it is probably fairer to say that if a very large number–in principle, an infinite number–of such group means were sampled, 95% of the resulting confidence intervals would contain the true score.

The use of confidence intervals is increasingly being recommended as a substitute for statistical significance testing. This position received its first major explication by Rozeboom in 1960 and has been elaborated by others since, especially Cohen. This position holds that null hypothesis significance testing is a barrier to progress in behavioral science, especially with respect to the accumulation of knowledge across studies. The use of confidence intervals, in conjunction with other techniques such as meta-analysis, is proposed to replace traditional significance testing. The idea here is that confidence intervals can provide all of the information present in a significance test while yielding important additional information as well.

J. S. ROSSI
University of Rhode Island

STATISTICS IN PSYCHOLOGY

CONFLICT MEDIATION

Conflict mediation is defined as the efforts of a neutral third party who, at the request of the conflicting parties, assists them in establishing an acceptable resolution of their conflicts. Mediation differs from arbitration in that arbitration imposes a settlement on the parties after they have requested the intervention of the neutral judge. It differs from litigation in that in litigation the parties are represented by opposing council, each of whom seeks to establish a victory for his or her client. Mediation returns the opportunity and the responsibility for conflict resolution to the people directly involved in the conflict. The mediator assists the parties in finding their own way out of a dispute.

Mediation was first widely known during the period of the Italian city-states in the 14th and 15th centuries. Since then it has been expanding into interpersonal, interorganizational, and international affairs. The use of mediation ranges from marital dispute resolution to negotiations of out-of-court settlements. The Federal Mediation and Conciliation Service, the Community Relations Service of the Department of Justice, the American Arbitration Association, and private mediators as well provide mediation services for thousands of citizens.

The first public mediation centers in the United States emerged in the late 1960s. In 1968 the Institute for Mediation and Conflict Resolution in New York City began its operations. The Federal Disputes Resolution Act of 1980 established nationwide Neighborhood Justice Centers through which minor disputes can be handled without legal intervention. Cases referred to mediation centers include domestic relations, commercial relations, interpersonal affairs, and divorce mediation.

The mediation process seeks to do the following:

1. Reduce the expense of litigation

2. Ease the load on courts

3. Lessen the degree of stress and tension experienced by the disputants

4. Provide the possibility of a win/win outcome

5. Provide a setting where the disputants can be authors of the settlement rather than victims of an imposed judgment

THE MEDIATOR'S ROLE

The mediator is primarily a facilitator providing the parties with a joint examination of issues, a recognition of common objectives, and insights into opposing perspectives. The mediator performs as courier, interpreter, catalyst, and gentle persuader, making no judgments as to the merit of positions and rendering no decision as to who shall prevail. Roles played include educator, translator, agent of reality, and idea generator.

The mediator helps the parties to do the following:

1. Communicate with each other. When necessary, the mediator puts each party's terms into language that the other party can understand.

2. Identify substantive issues and separate them from emotional issues.

3. Identify and clarify the issues causing the dispute.

4. Reassess their own positions.

5. Recognize superordinate goals.

The mediator should:

1. Probe and ask direct questions to provide information and clarify misunderstanding.

2. Listen objectively to what the parties are really saying.

3. Observe what the disputants say and do. Body language and nonverbal behavior become an important source of information.

4. Maintain control of the hearing.

The mediator must remain objective and impartial, be reassuring and calm, maintain steadiness and warmth, be attentive and empathetic, and be supportive and willing to reach out to both parties. The mediator must also be patient and allow the parties time to work through problems. Even though solutions may not always be evident, the mediator must hold out the realistic hope that solutions are possible.

Upon first encountering the parties involved, the mediator must make an immediate assessment of the parties' level of hostility, anxiety, willingness to be involved in the process, need to withdraw, and any other signs transmitted. Based on an assessment of the parties, a planned seating arrangement is established to convey the mediator's neutrality and ensure the safety of those involved.

THE OPENING STATEMENT

The mediator's opening statement sets the basic procedural ground rules. These preliminaries are critical to successful negotiations. The presentation should put the disputants at ease and introduce a win/win problem-solving approach to the conflict. Points that should be covered include:

1. A welcoming statement

2. An introduction of the mediator panel and participants

3. An explanation of the process

4. An explanation of the basic premises of confidentiality and impartiality

5. An explanation of ground rules concerning:

   (a) Initial statements by complainant/respondent

   (b) Interruptions

   (c) Caucusing

   (d) Name calling

   (e) Written agreements

THE STAGES OF MEDIATION

The stages of mediation comprise of ventilation, information gathering, problem solving, and bargaining.

If the parties have not developed the issues of the conflict in the initial joint exchange, the mediator must find a means to secure this information without either party's losing face. The disputants frequently bring with them feelings of anger, frustration, disappointment, and revenge. During the ventilation period mediators need to be aware that people ventilate on different levels. Thus the mediator must be flexible and able to cope with uncertainty and changing conditions. Essentially, during ventilation the mediator must listen actively to the disputants' issues and show concern for their feelings. This allows the mediator to gather as much information about the problem as possible, including those feelings that are central to the issues. Ventilation is often handled in private caucus.

After a hearing has reached the point where the disputants have drained at least a portion of their respective emotions, the parties can move toward problem solving and bargaining. It is important that the disputants now take an active role and directly communicate their needs and demands. This will create the psychological ownership that will make the final agreement work. The amount of commitment to resolving the dispute is proportional to their commitment to the outcome. During this phase the mediator channels the disputants toward the following:

1. Developing tradeoffs.

2. Establishing superordinate goals. If the disputants realize that only through a combined effort can the goals of both parties be achieved, then resolution becomes of utmost importance.

3. Creating a synthesis. The mediator may determine that the values in conflict are total opposites, and so may help foster a third view. This is not necessarily a compromise.

4. Allowing graceful retreat. The mediator must help parties in retreating without loss of face.

5. Identifying and suggesting possibilities not apparent to the disputants.

6. Narrowing the gap by pointing out similarities and minimizing differences.

When a hearing has reached an impasse, the mediator must take the time to work it through. This requires patience and skill. If the parties are not willing to negotiate, the mediator must look for motivating factors that can break the impasse. These factors have usually appeared during the initial stage, when needs and feelings were expressed. The mediator must refer back to this information and use it to reopen the negotiation.

To reach the agreement stage, the mediator must:

1. Be positive

2. Take control of the hearing

3. Remain neutral

4. Help the disputants see alternatives and options

5. Be concrete

6. Emphasize areas of agreement

7. Narrow the impasse area

8. Describe, not evaluate

9. Check perceptions

10. Test hypothetical alternatives

11. Differentiate between needs and wants

12. Be sensitive to feelings

If the mediator does the above, most disputants will be able to reach the agreement stage.

S. Leviton
J. L. Greenstone
Southwestern Academy of Crisis Interveners

CONFORMITY

Conformity is agreement on some trait, attitude, or behavior, based on common group membership. The empirical as well as conceptual problem involves the establishment of this agreement (which does not need to be perfect), and showing that it would not have occurred in the absence of the group. Conformity can be distinguished from other concepts by the absence of one of these conditions: If there is agreement on traits, but it is independent of group membership (e.g., if it is due to common circumstances), one speaks of *uniformity* of attitude or behavior. If agreement is obtained through force, promise of reward, or threat of punishment, one speaks of *compliance.* If uniformity has become so much a part of a person's self that it would persist in the absence of group membership, one speaks of *internalization;* the process by which this is accomplished during the life course is *socialization.* Conformity can be seen as an intermediate stage between superficial compliance and permanent internalization—as a conflict between what a person basically is and what group membership induces. The existence of common attitudes and action patterns within social groups is a principal precondition of society.

The identification of conformity as a separate topic coincided with methodological advances in creating and measuring conformity. These achievements in turn led to a number of detailed investigations of conforming behavior, but eventually this increased understanding became again subsumed under the general problems of the relation of individual and society. This article will discuss the particular study of conformity before returning to the general problem.

The interest in conformity as a topic in its own right is partly due to the social concerns of the second quarter of this century. Events in totalitarian countries, including extreme and virtually inhuman behavior on the one hand, and systematic enforcing of conformity on the other (e.g., "brainwashing"), prompted a need to distinguish between personal- and group-induced beliefs. In part, this was motivated by the hope that people's individual beliefs are good, and the fear that people's views could be swamped by a social juggernaut. Techniques to reproduce some of these influences in an isolated laboratory setting led to a detailed analysis of conformity and group influences and to a better understanding of the social process.

One of the earliest empirical studies of conformity was done by Allport (1934). He proposed that conforming behavior can be recognized by its distribution, which follows an inverted J; few people overconform (are to the left of the peak); the overwhelming majority are positioned exactly at the peak, accounting for the spike of the J; and a minority deviate from the norm, accounting for an elongated but low-level tail. He validated this hypothesis primarily by observation in field situations such as reporting to work, stopping at a stop sign, or using holy water in a Catholic church.

The classical experiments on conformity are those by Sherif (1935) and Asch (1951). Sherif's experiment was based on the phi phenomenon, an optical illusion in which a light point in a dark room seems to move in a straight line. Sherif showed that if a subject was paired with a confederate who judged the movement as larger than the subject did, the subject would increase his or her distance judgments gradually, and correspondingly with a decrease of distance. Sherif thus established a common "frame of reference" for judging the size. Asch's study had the naive subjects give perceptual judgments in a group of confederates who agreed on the wrong answer; a considerable proportion of subjects gave the clearly wrong answer.

Although these studies showed that individuals change under social conditions, one must note that the connection with group membership is tenuous at best. Allport's data refer mainly to situations where adherence to standards is enforced (compliant behavior). The other experimental situations reported do not represent any importance of group membership. In Sherif's situation the frame of reference was not even established by agreement with the other person in the group, but only reflected in the next trial, which would go in the direction of the confederate's previous choice. In the Asch situation, there was no pressure to agree with the other members of the group; in fact, the situation might be even slightly competitive in arriving at the correct answer. In both cases there is a question whether the agreement represents any kind of conformity, or simply using other people's answers to obtain a better score—a kind of cribbing. But one counterargument might ask: if conformity can be produced in such a weak situation, how much more might it be produced in an actual, long-lasting situation?

Critical analysis of the classical conformity experiments has shown that ostensibly conforming behavior can be derived from many different sources, not all of which have anything to do with social conformity. Staying on a simplified empirical level, research needs to identify the instances which would confirm the presence of conformity in the sense of the definition.

The presence of social conformity can be established only by looking both at agreements and at their social basis—the nature of groups—in which agreement occurs. An early study in which both aspects were taken into consideration was Festinger, Schachter, and Back's *Social Pressures in Informal Groups.* Here, several aspects of strength of group membership could be related to agreement on attitudes as well as on action. Among them were the ratio of friendship choices within and outside of a specific group, the strength and nature of the network within the group, and the reaction toward deviants, leading to possible exclusion from the group. In the presence of several groups, thus, one criterion of conformity is the concentration of traits within the groups and differences among the groups. However, the second criterion of conformity requires that the extent of this agreement be in some way related to the criterion of a measure of group cohesion. Further experiments varied the measures to be used, conditions of conformity, and the processes through which conformity was achieved, controlling communication processes and structural differentiation in groups.

Most of these studies relate the desire to belong to a group to several expressions of conformity. These different processes define different conditions under which conformity occurs. One situation is that of extreme subjectivity of the issue, where only consent of a relevant group can assure belief of the individual; this is called the establishment of social reality through conformity. On the other hand, conforming may be individually advantageous, as mentioned above in the reference to "cribbing." It might also be one way of obtaining some goal through cooperation, or might be an assertion of group membership, such as a uniform or sign. In each case a different set of issues will be a field for conformity, and different mechanisms will be used to achieve it, such as appeals to self-interest, reasoning based on social reality, or the threat of rejection for nonconformity. This combination of the need for some conformity for organizational functioning, and the danger of establishing a purely arbitrary social framework, has been explored by Janis (1972).

Because of the different meanings, it is not surprising that experimental studies have not been able to consistently relate conforming with personality traits or with kind or strength of pressure. In fact, although conformity is a recognizable social event, its structure is too complex to be a very meaningful concept in contemporary social psychology. Thus conformity is deemphasized in current treatises on social psychology, though theories dealing with a variety of topics, including some conditions of conformity, are discussed in detail. Examples would be social learning or modeling.

The main contribution of the detailed experimental study of conformity consists in explicating the different conditions under which conformity occurs. This gives a better understanding of the social concerns from which this research originated. The fact that individuals can succumb to social pressure and act and even feel in a way which they would deny is their own, is undoubted; it can be reproduced under controlled conditions as well as observed under realistic conditions.

The original question was ethical, political, and epistemological: to what extent can individual attitudes and actions be changed through social conformity, so that the resulting actions are not one's own? In other words, are there individual values without society, and are individuals responsible for their actions without putting the blame on socialization? The many ways in which conformity can be achieved have shown that one cannot easily distinguish between a person's own and group-induced actions. A person without group membership—without roles and place in society—is a complete abstraction; all actual behaviors are varying mixtures of individual tendencies and social influence. Conformity research has shown, however, that some of the mechanisms lead to intense conformity, which then becomes a part of the person himself. If effective, it is more properly called socialization; in fact, the development of a person is frequently seen as conformity behavior. On the other hand, historical experience has shown how outward conformity can be maintained for a long time, then dissolved when the pressure is removed.

However, some new tendencies in philosophy and social theory would regard the distinction between individual and socially induced traits as altogether spurious. Adherents of social reality construction (Berger & Luckman, 1967) insist that all attitudes and actions are constructed among individuals through negotiation. Division between personal and social aspects are conventions which in turn reflect the social arrangements of what is to be considered either. In fact, as the philosopher Stephen Toulmin (1982) has pointed out, when the term consciousness means something known with others (con-scious), the notion of individual actions, attitudes, or traits in the absence of others becomes an untenable abstraction, and assignment of acts to conformity a matter of social ethos.

REFERENCES

Allport, F. H. (1934). The J-curve hypothesis of conforming behavior. *Journal of Social Psychology, 5,* 141–183.

Asch, S. E. (1951). Effects of group pressure upon the modification and distortion of judgment. In H. Guetzkow (Ed.), *Groups, leadership, and men*. Pittsburgh, PA: Carnegie.

Berger, P., & Luckman, T. (1967). *The social construction of reality*. New York: Doubleday/Anchor.

Festinger, L., Schachter, S., & Back, K. (1950). *Social pressures in informal groups: A study of human factors in housing*. New York: Harper.

Sherif, M. (1935). A study of some social factors in perception. *Archives of Psychology, 27* (entire no. 187).

Toulmin, S. (1982). The genealogy of "consciousness:" In P. F. Secord (Ed.), *Explaining human behavior: Consciousness, human action and social structure*. Beverly Hills, CA: Sage Publications.

K. W. BACK
Duke University

BYSTANDER INVOLVEMENT
SCAPEGOATING

CONJOINT THERAPY

Conjoint therapy describes a treatment method simultaneously involving two or more members from a family or marital unit in a treatment session. The exact number of individuals present from the relational unit will vary, depending upon the therapist's orientation. Some therapists, such as Carl Whitaker, defer initial treatment of a family until all living immediate relatives can be organized for a conjoint session. Other therapists advocate the use of networks of supportive individuals involved in assessing the patient/client adjustment. These individuals may come from a variety of settings in the patient's neighborhood, family kinship, or work environments. Fullmer and Bernard (1968) suggest that families come together in groups of two or three to discuss their problems under the direction of one or more therapists. Others, such as Salvador Minuchin, often favor reducing the number present in an effort to focus more strongly on detriangularizing family members who have joined together in an unhealthy alliance. Indeed, some psychotherapists such as Hoffman (1976) believe that when a child is brought to the therapist's office as the identified, the child's symptoms result from marital discord of the parents which the parents are unable to resolve between themselves and which they refocus upon the child. Within this theoretical framework, all family therapy would seem to titrate eventually to marital therapy.

Conjoint therapy is the treatment of choice of most marital and family therapists. The methods used in conjoint therapy are essentially the same in form and rationale for both family and marital therapy. Probably the most publicized marital therapy model using a conjoint approach is that of Masters and Johnson (1966, 1970), who advocate the involvement of the partner as critical to treatment success in sexual dysfunction.

Conjoint therapy did not evolve from a particular school of therapy, but rather was the somewhat simultaneous occurrence in the 1950s of a number of individuals across the United States. According to Jay Haley, in his article, "Family therapy," all persons who ventured into conjoint treatment methods had their original training in individually oriented psychotherapy. Many of the well-known therapists in this area acknowledge the influence of systems theory upon their thinking. Essentially, systems theory emphasizes the interactive and interrelated nature of behavior. A person's behavior in this theory does not occur in a vacuum but rather is influenced by, and in turn influences, the environment in which it occurs. To fully understand a person's behavior, therefore, it is important to observe it within the context in which it occurs. The context of behavior in conjoint therapy is typically the relational unit—the marital partners or the family.

While it is important to observe the natural unit as a way of understanding behavior, access to the natural unit for treatment is often critical if behavior change is to occur. The marital or family balance (homeostasis) is threatened when one of its member's behavior changes. When change occurs, the unit members will typically mobilize to bring the deviant member back into his/her previous behavior pattern. This mobilization often occurs regardless of whether the behavior in question is perceived as positive or negative by the other unit members. Consequently, any treatment that changes a person's behavior yet does not change the environment is likely to fail, because of the environmental pressure upon the person to return to prior behavior patterns.

Frequently, conjoint treatment avoids the stigmatizing of one or more unit members as the patient or the person who is psychologically dysfunctional. The focus of both the therapy itself and the individuals involved in treatment is turned toward the interrelated actions and reactions which cause the marital or family problems.

Currently, conjoint treatment approaches are used by professionals with a variety of theoretical backgrounds. The most common backgrounds include the psychodynamic approach, the behavioral model, and the communication and systems theory.

REFERENCES

Fullmer, D., & Bernard, H. (1968). *Family consultation*. Boston: Houghton Mifflin.

Hoffman, L. (1976). Breaking the homeostatic cycle. In P. Guerin (Ed.), *Family therapy*. New York: Gardner.

Masters, W. H., & Johnson, V. E. (1966). *Human sexual response*. Boston: Little, Brown.

Masters, W. H., & Johnson, V. E. (1970). *Human sexual inadequacy*. Boston: Little, Brown.

R. P. KAPPENBERG
Hawaii Professional Psychology Group

MARRIAGE COUNSELING

CONNECTIONISM

The term "connectionism" refers to any more or less systematic attempt to develop the basic principles of associationism into an explanation of behavior or, for that matter, of any problem area.

ASSOCIATIONISM: HISTORICAL ROOTS

The basis of Thorndikian connectionism and, to a lesser extent perhaps, contemporary forms of connectionism can be found in the writings of early philosophers. It is customary to point to Aristotle as the originator of associationistic principles, but credit for establishing connectionistic ideas as fertile explanatory concepts belongs more properly to the British empiricists of the 17th and 18th centuries. Thomas Hobbes, often regarded as a founder of the British tradition of empiricism, held that lawfulness in thought and action was produced by the connections of ideas through their occurrence in temporal proximity. An independent and more complete contiguity position was developed by John Locke, who also accepted similarity of ideas as a basis for their association. Further refinements on this general theme were subsequently made by other British philosophers writing in the empiricist tradition (George Berkeley, David Hume, and David Hartley). Although none of these philosophers were empiricists in a contemporary, scientific sense (i.e., their empiricism was preached but not practiced), their work and that of their successors helped lay the groundwork for the connectionism that developed over the following two centuries.

Although associationistic principles were subjected to rigorous scientific testing by the Russian physiologists I. P. Pavlov and V. M. Bekhterev, their theoretical efforts were sharply restricted to the problem of conditioning. It remained for Edward Lee Thorndike to develop a more comprehensive account of experience and behavior on the connectionistic principle.

Some idea of the thoroughness with which Thorndike adopted the connectionistic principle may be seen in these excerpts from his *Selected Writings from a Connectionist's Psychology* (1949).

Connections lead from states of affairs within the brain as well as from external situations. They often occur in long series wherein the response to one situation becomes the situation producing the next response and so on. They may be from parts or elements or features of a situation as well as from the situation as a whole. . . . They lead to responses of readiness and unreadiness, awareness, attention, interest, welcoming and rejecting, emphasizing and restraining, differentiating and relating, directing and coordinating. The things connected may be subtle relations or elusive attitudes and intentions. (p. 81)

The major theoretical gun in Thorndike's associationistic arsenal was the law of effect. In brief, this proposition held that it was the positive or negative consequences of responses that determined the degree to which they would be strengthened or weakened. As a result of extensive research using human subjects and relatively mild positive reinforcements (e.g., saying "right" after a subject made a correct response) or negative reinforcements (e.g., saying "wrong" after an error), Thorndike concluded that positive responses were more effective than negative, and he emphasized them in his theoretical writings. Thorndike (1933) later reported what he apparently regarded as an independent proof of the law of effect. The so-called spread of effect referred to the empirical strengthening of responses made in close contiguity to a reinforced (rewarded) response, even if they themselves were not directly rewarded. Although Thorndike's early postulation of a physiological

confirming reaction as a basis of the law of effect was subsequently justified by the independent discovery of the reinforcing potency of intracranial self-stimulation (Olds, 1958), no such confirmation occurred for his spread-of-effect hypothesis (Marx, 1956). The law of effect and the spread of effect were vigorously criticized on both theoretical (Meehl, 1950) and methodological grounds. Nevertheless, they represent a kind of culmination of the early philosophical ideas within a strictly scientific (empirical) framework and so stand as one exemplification of the potential inherent in connectionistic thinking.

Other salient characteristics of Thorndikian connectionism were its elementarism, illustrated by his identical-elements theory of transfer of training (Thorndike & Woodworth, 1901), and its stress on the automaticity of fundamental behavioral functions (e.g., regarding animal learning, in which field Thorndike was himself a pioneer researcher, as essentially mechanical as trial and error, in contrast to the Gestalt emphasis on insightful learning).

The learning theory of Guthrie (1935) also was based on strictly connectionistic, stimulus-response assumptions. Contiguity alone, without effect, was assumed to be responsible for learning. A similar but more sophisticated statistical learning theory was produced by Estes (1950, 1959); it can be considered to be a kind of springboard to the more recent surge of connectionistic theorizing.

CONTEMPORARY CONNECTIONISM

Given the fervor with which the so-called cognitive revolution of the 1960s strove to break with traditional, stimulus-response types of theoretical frameworks, it is all the more surprising to find connectionism playing a central role (and arguably *the* central role) in so much cognitive theorizing of the 1990s. As suggested by the rather unusual heading "Where Next? Connectionism Rides Again!" in Baddeley's (1990) book on memory, there has been a veritable explosion of connectionistic, network-type theorizing applied to cognitive problems. The ready availability of such concepts as weighted nodes and the like in such network patterns as the increasingly popular parallel distributed processing proposal have made this kind of theoretical model attractive to researchers and theorists in a wide spectrum of problem areas. Indeed, the common amenability to a network type of theoretical framing has probably been the factor most responsible for the synthesis of such seemingly diverse topics and functions as learning, language comprehension, artificial intelligence, computational science, and neuroscience. From neural networks in biology to knowledge representations in artificial intelligence, connections are now playing a key role in tying together many loose strands of data.

Serial processing, in which activation occurs in successive nodes along a chain of connections in a network, was initially a theoretically preferred concept. More recently, however, parallel processing, in which two or more independent lines of activation are assumed to occur, has become a more attractive alternative. A major advantage of this type of processing concept is that it more readily accommodates the simultaneous functioning of both conscious and nonconscious activations, thus taking into account the recently accelerated interest in nonconscious processes, such as those occurring in implicit learning and procedural tests of memory.

There have been some critics of this headlong rush to the bandwagon of connectionistic theorizing. McCloskey (1991), for example, has argued that in spite of their "explosion" into cognitive science with "conferences and symposia too numerous to count" (p. 580), connectionistic networks should be regarded more as theoretical tools than as theories themselves. McCloskey pointed to the need to understand how the networks operate before appropriate theoretical accounts can be developed from them. He analyzed the influential, much-cited connectionistic network, which Seidenberg and McClelland (1989) applied to the problems of word identification and lexical decision (deciding whether a presented string of letters is a word). His conclusion was that in spite of the multiple, detailed weighing and such used in the network to account for experimental results, there was still a fundamental need for more verbal explanations before an adequate theoretical explanation could be achieved.

These cautions notwithstanding, the fact remains that connectionism has made a remarkable comeback within the past decade and that its scientific future seems to be well assured, as both a theoretical tool and a theoretical framework.

For balanced presentations of the details of this renaissance of connectionism the books by Baddeley (1990), Bechtel and Abrahamsen (1991), and Morris (1989) may be consulted.

REFERENCES

Baddeley, A. D. (1990). *Human memory: Theory and practice.* Hillsdale, NJ Hove: Erlbaum.

Bechtel, W., & Abrahamsen, A. (1991). *Connectionism and the mind.* Cambridge, MA: Basil Blackwell.

Estes, W. K. (1950). Toward a statistical theory of learning. *Psychological Review, 57,* 94–107.

Estes, W. K. (1959). Component and pattern models with Markovian interpretations. In R. R. Bush & W. K. Estes (Eds.), *Studies in mathematical learning theory.* Stanford, CA: Stanford University Press.

Guthrie, E. R. (1935). *The psychology of learning.* New York: Harper & Row.

Marx, M. H. (1956). Spread of effect: A critical review. *General Psychology Monographs, 53,* 119–186.

Meehl, P. E. (1950). On the circularity of the law of effect. *Psychological Bulletin, 47,* 52–57.

Morris, R. G. M. (Ed.). (1989). *Parallel distributed processing: Implications for psychology and neurobiology.* Oxford, UK: Clarendon Press.

Olds, J. (1958). Self-stimulation of the brain: Its use to study local effects of hunger, sex, and drugs. *Science, 127,* 315–324.

Thorndike, E. L. (1933). An experimental study of rewards. *Teachers College Contributions to Education, 580.*

Thorndike, E. L. (1949). *Selected writings from a connectionist's psychology.* New York: Appleton-Century-Crofts.

Thorndike, E. L., & Woodworth, R. S. (1901). The influence of improvement in one mental function upon the efficiency of other functions. *Psychological Review, 8,* 247–261, 384–395, 553–564.

M. H. Marx
N. Hutchinson Island, Florida

EMPIRICISM
LEARNING THEORIES
OPERANT CONDITIONING

CONSCIOUSNESS

Although consciousness is the most obvious and intimate feature of our being, philosophical as well as psychological discourse on it is replete with conceptual confusions and conflicting characterizations. Perry (1904) remarked, "How can a term mean anything when it is employed to connote anything and everything, including its own negation?" (p. 282). Contemporary transdisciplinary interest in the study of consciousness, which goes beyond the traditional boundaries of philosophy and psychology to include physics, neuroscience, information theory, and artificial intelligence, further exacerbates the problem of communication among scientists and scholars concerned with consciousness studies. Pribram (1976) referred to 12 different meanings of consciousness given in *Webster's* dictionary. Natsoulas (1978) pointed out seven distinct senses of consciousness in everyday thought and commonsense usage as revealed by the seven entries in the *Oxford English Dictionary.* He suggested that in all its seven meanings consciousness refers to awareness. In addition to awareness, consciousness also is used frequently to refer to wakefulness—alertness and knowledge.

Most psychologists regard consciousness as awareness. Unfortunately, the concept of awareness is no less ambiguous. Awareness is used in almost every sense in which consciousness is employed. For example, awareness signifies perceptual awareness, introspective awareness, reflective awareness, subliminal awareness, self-awareness, awareness of awareness, and so on. Awareness is sometimes used to denote a process or a state of the brain; at other times, it is referred to as a quality bestowed on the contents of one's experience.

CONSCIOUSNESS AND THE UNCONSCIOUS

According to John Locke (1894), consciousness is reflection, included in different mental acts such as perception, thinking, doubting, believing, willing, and so on. Consciousness is the essential transparent aspect of mind; nothing is hidden from it. The Lockian view of consciousness had such a pervasive influence that until the advent of Freudian psychoanalysis the notion of unconscious thought or perception was considered self-contradictory. Freud (1915) showed how complex thought processes can occur without awareness and how one's unconscious may contain beliefs, desires, and feelings of which one is unaware.

Freud saw meaning and purpose in unconscious material.

Seemingly innocuous and unintentional acts such as slips of the tongue, forgetting, and misplacing of objects may be motivated at the unconscious level. That being so, the earlier characterization of consciousness as intentional, purposeful mental activity must be taken to apply to the unconscious as well.

Jung went further to blunt the distinction between consciousness and the unconscious. The unconscious, according to Jung, is the consummate source of our collectivity and creativity. The collective unconscious is "an image of the world which has taken aeons to form. . . . [It] consists of the sum of instincts and their correlates, the archetypes. Just as everybody possesses instincts, so he also possesses a stock of archetypal images" (Jung, 1919/1954, p. 138). In his later years, Jung was led beyond archetypal images to the concept of the archetype-as-such and the psychoid level of the unconscious. The archetype-as-such, a transpsychic concept, is an a priori ordering principle by virtue of which we experience synchronistic events that suggest an "acausal orderedness." This advance in Jung's thinking from subjectively experienced archetypal image to archetype as an a priori ordering principle obscured his earlier distinction between consciousness and the unconscious (Frey-Rohn, 1974/1990). Consciousness was originally associated with a certain degree of brightness and luminosity. Jung increasingly saw that this luminosity also was to be found in some of the unconscious contents. Jung (1919/1954) thus came to the "paradoxical conclusion that there is no conscious content which is not in some other aspect unconscious" (p. 185).

Recent advances in cognitive psychology suggest that complex mental activity, including our ability to acquire, store, and retrieve information, is carried out by operations that are primarily unconscious and inaccessible to introspection. Velmans (1991) has reviewed evidence suggesting that consciousness does not enter into the processing of information at any level, including the organization of complex activity that requires planning, reflection, or creativity. Thus, much mental activity seems to go on without awareness, traditionally regarded as an essential aspect of mind.

The studies of blindsight and memory without awareness also show the contradictions involved in the conscious-unconscious dichotomy. Blindsight is the capacity among those with a damaged visual cortex to discriminate and respond to visual stimuli without being aware of them. Weiskrantz (1986) carried out a series of tests with a subject whose right visual cortex had been removed. As one would expect, the subject reported that he saw nothing when the stimuli were presented to his left hemifield. However, when he was asked to guess whether the stimulus was x or o, the subject guessed correctly in 27 of 30 trials, thus suggesting that he perceived the stimuli at some level. It is known that damage to certain midline structures in the brain can lead to serious amnesia in humans so that they are unable to remember their experience beyond a few seconds. An amnesia patient who just solved a jigsaw puzzle is typically unable to remember how he or she did it, but if he or she is asked to solve the same puzzle the next day, the patient will solve it faster, which suggests that though unaware of it, the patient was able to retain some of his or her previous learning of the puzzle.

The realization that thought processes such as perceiving, believing, willing, remembering, and so forth are also found at the unconscious level, though inaccessible to introspection, and that the line between consciousness and unconsciousness is not as sharp as it was once believed to be, renders the discussion of consciousness immediately complicated. The commonsense simplicity of conceiving consciousness as awareness becomes deceptive and sterile. If we can meaningfully refer to conscious as well as nonconscious awareness, the usefulness of awareness as a descriptor of consciousness becomes problematic. Consciousness as simple introspective awareness becomes a mere quality imposed on certain contents of experience. That quality may indeed be no more than certain cortical processes, because their destruction leads to loss of introspective awareness. Consciousness as a defining characteristic of mental phenomena is generally taken, however, to imply more than introspective awareness.

MANY SHADES OF CONSCIOUSNESS

If awareness in the sense of introspective awareness is an inadequate description of consciousness, what else is consciousness? The answer seems to depend largely on one's theoretical orientation and metaphysical presuppositions. The relationship of being to consciousness has been a perennial problem for philosophers. At the level of common sense, it is generally taken for granted that human beings are endowed with a body and a mind and that they interact to form functioning persons. In an attempt to provide a clear analysis of the mind and the body and their interaction, philosophers have arrived at a variety of views, which give us the various perspectives we have of consciousness in scholarly discourse. These speculations fall broadly into two categories: those that assert the reality of both the mind and the body and those that deny the reality of one in favor of the other. The dualist theories build on the commonsense notion that the mind and the body are two different independent and interacting things. According to Descartes, for example, consciousness is the essence of mind and the mind is different from the body. There are in existence two radically different substances—the extended physical substance and the thinking, unextended mental substance. The latter in principle is irreducible to the former.

The main problem with such dualism is the problem of interaction. How does the unextended mind interact with the extended body? Any kind of causal interaction between them, which is presumed by most dualist theories, comes into conflict with the physical theory that the universe is a closed system and that every physical event is linked with an antecedent physical event. This assumption preempts any possibility that a mental act can cause a physical event, unless the mental act itself is presumed in some sense to be physical. Parallelist theories attempt to circumvent this problem by assuming that physical and mental processes run parallel without influencing each other.

In contrast to dualistic theories, monistic theories postulate only one kind of substance: mind or matter. The subjective idealism of George Berkeley eliminated matter in favor of mind, and materialism denied mind in favor of matter.

Materialistic denial of mind-consciousness takes on several forms. Among these are: (a) outright denial of anything mental, including consciousness, that does not translate itself into objective behavior and performance; (b) acceptance of mental phenomena and denial that they have any causal efficacy because they are by-products of physical processes in the brain; and (c) identification of mental phenomena with brain states. Similar views are found in psychological theory. Materialist accounts of consciousness that are currently fashionable fall into two main categories: the peripheralist and the central-state materialism. The peripheralist view is akin to behaviorism that eliminates consciousness altogether. Watson (1928) declared that there can be no such thing as consciousness. Contemporary resonance of such a radical view may be seen in the assertion of the futility of consciousness as a psychological concept. Stanovich (1991), for example, writes: "Every issue in psychology that has touched 'consciousness' has become confused; and every bit of theoretical progress that has been attained has been utterly independent of any concept of 'consciousness'" (p. 647). Skinner (1974) and those who followed him subscribe to the view that consciousness is an epiphenomenon of brain activity and has no causal efficacy; therefore, it can be denied any explanatory role in understanding behavior. The central-state materialism identifies consciousness with purely physical processes in the brain. Identity theorists like Feigl (1967) argue that consciousness is identifiable with the referents of neurophysiological concepts.

The newer materialism, unlike behaviorism, accepts the possibility of inner experience and its influence on the body and at the same time sees nothing in conscious experience that cannot be accounted for in strictly physical terms. The experience of consciousness, according to Armstrong (1968, 1980), is no more than one part of the brain scanning another. "In perception," he says, "the brain scans the environment. In awareness of the perception another process in the brain scans that scanning" (1968, p. 94). The inner sense that gives us introspective awareness is simply another brain process, and therefore, according to this view, there is no reason to hypostatize the existence of a process that can function independently of the brain.

There are well-known objections to all the above renderings of consciousness entirely into behavioral, neural, or information-processing terms. As a fact of immediate experience, consciousness cannot be denied. The phenomenological experience of pain, for instance, is qualitatively different from neural excitations in the brain. The pain experience is homogeneous and continuous whereas the neural events accompanying pain are heterogeneous, discontinuous, and spatially discrete events. In other words, unlike felt experience, brain activity is "grainy" (Sellars, 1963; Meehl, 1966). Again, we know that our mental states may have profound effects on our bodily state. Placebos are known to have tangible effects. Psychosomatic illness is not delusional.

Phenomenologists like Husserl (1964) advance powerful arguments in support of consciousness as an essential aspect of our experience, without espousing a dualistic interactionism. Like Descartes, Husserl believed in the self-revealing character of consciousness, that consciousness cannot be denied without contradiction and that its nonbeing is utterly unimaginable. Consciousness is seen by Husserl as a function rather than an entity. Like Brentano (1874/1973) before him, he emphasized the intentional nature of consciousness. The external object, the content of consciousness, and our awareness of it are directly related by the intentionality of consciousness. Our knowledge of the world is not via sensations we receive, but is a consequence of the logical process of intention. The common world we share with each other is not made possible by the sensations that tend to be discrete and private and cannot, therefore, reveal the universal and unitary character of their objects but by a constitutive function of consciousness that intuitively grasps their essence. The constitutive function of consciousness lies in the intuiting of the essence of objects so that we may understand their significance and meaningfulness to us. The unitary character that objects have as phenomena of our experience can only be understood in terms of their essences and not as a summation of their shifting qualities.

The centrality of consciousness in the human condition also is emphasized by Sartre (1956) in his existential philosophy. The very nature of consciousness, according to Sartre, is intentional and is always directed at something. Consciousness is not a container and not a stage on which objects are played. Its characteristic is the relevation of the thing to which it is directed. Its uniqueness consists in that it reveals itself while revealing the object. Thus for both Husserl and Sartre, consciousness is the principle of subjectivity that accounts for the manifest unity and significance of the phenomena of our experience.

CONSCIOUS PERSON VERSUS MACHINE

Clearly, consciousness is something that seems to bind us to the world and at the same time give us a sense of identity. There is nothing mysterious in asserting that consciousness enables us to interweave the immediately given sensory input and our reflection on it. We may differ, however, in our belief about whether it is a mode of being that is autonomous and utterly independent of the brain. On this point it may be instructive to see the respects in which a conscious person differs from a machine. It is suggested that the advances in neuroscience, computer simulation, artificial intelligence, and cognitive psychology increasingly threaten the notion that consciousness involves processes beyond the brain. Recent attempts to design representational schemes by which computers may be able to generate global understandings have left many with the belief that the human mind may be no more than an information-processing machine and that all information is completely diffused in the brain. The distinction between conscious experience and the brain may be the same as the logical-structural distinction in the Turing machine (Turing, 1950).

We can all agree that discriminatory and purposive behavior is involved in most conscious activities. Our ability to react, reflect, possess images, and use them as representational; control and plan programs of action; project into the future; use language; process information; and perceive our own state are some of the general functions of our consciousness. It is suggested that all these functions also can be performed by a cleverly designed computer and that the so-called conscious activities are but a manifestation of complex computations carried out by the brain (Minsky, 1986). Penrose (1989) points out, however, that the outward manifestations of conscious activity cannot in principle be simulated by a computer because conscious thinking is not an algorithmic activity.

The idea that computers have subjective and personal experiences as we do has little intuitive appeal. The subjectivity involved in our conscious experience does not appear to be the same as the ability of the machine to perceive the state that it is in at a given time. More importantly, conscious functions have the capacity for intentional action, while a machine is entirely constrained to operate in a predictive pattern. Regardless of whether machines can simulate brain functions, the intentionality and the volitional freedom it implies seem to be the characteristics that distinguish conscious activity from machine operations. The ability to exercise volitional freedom implies that consciousness is self-manifesting and that it cannot be reduced to brain states. Whether subjectivity itself is a construction of the brain or is something that we must presuppose as a necessary condition of experience can be a matter of contention even among those who believe in the causal efficacy of consciousness.

Whether a person is any more than a machine is a recent issue prompted by the remarkable progress in physical sciences. In the past, natural scientists did not hesitate to relegate everything and anything that they could not deal with to the realm of the mind. Both physics and psychology originally commanded exclusive domains, and it did not seem necessary to integrate them. Thoughtful physicists throughout history have wondered at the basic relationship between consciousness and the physical processes without assuming the primacy of one over the other. It was psychology's concern to become a science that led psychologists to look to physics for solutions to their problems.

Burns (1990) points out that contemporary attempts to explore the relationship of consciousness to physical laws fall broadly into four categories: (a) those that consider consciousness as emerging from the physical and therefore, not in principle different from it; (b) those that regard consciousness as belonging to a realm different from and independent of the physical and yet capable of interacting with it; (c) those who consider them independent and see no causal but only a synchronistic relationship between them; and (d) those who make no assumption about independence or dependence of consciousness on the physical. Clearly, most physicists today belong to the first category, even though few of them make any systematic attempts to account for consciousness in strictly physical terms.

CONSCIOUSNESS AND THE BRAIN

A. R. Luria, following Lev S. Vygotskii, held that consciousness is a complex structural system with semantic function. He rejected the dualistic postulation that consciousness-mind is fundamentally different in principle from material objects. At the same time, he viewed attempts to locate the mechanisms of consciousness inside the brain as misguided. Consciousness, according to Luria (1978), is the ability "to assess sensory information, to respond to it with critical thoughts and actions, and to retain memory traces in order that past traces or actions may be used in the future" (pp. 5–6). This ability is not a function of any one part of the brain. Rather, it "must be sought in the combined activity of discrete brain systems, each of which makes its own special contribution to the work of the functional system as a whole" (p. 31). Among the brain systems that are involved in conscious mental activity are: (a) the brain

stem reticular formation, which controls the levels of wakefulness; (b) secondary zones of the posterior (afferent) cortical areas, which are involved in the recording of incoming information; and more importantly, (c) the medial zones of frontal lobes, which intimately participate in the formation of intentions and of action programs and play an essential role in the conscious regulation of goal-directed behavior.

Searle (1983) asserts that mental states are real and have properties of their own. At the same time, these states are not dissociated from the brain. On the contrary, they are biologically based. Searle believes mental phenomena "are both caused by the operations of the brain and realized in the structure of the brain. On this view, consciousness and intentionality are as much a part of human biology as digestion or circulation of the blood. It is an objective fact about the world that it contains certain systems, viz., brains, with subjective mental states, and it is a physical fact about such systems that they have mental features" (p. ix).

Sperry (1969) regards consciousness as a primary source of causal influence. Consciousness is autonomous in its own right. It is not reducible to electrochemical processes. It is an "integral working component" in the brain. Sperry considers consciousness as a dynamic, emergent property resulting from the higher level functional organization of the cerebral cortex. As an emergent property, consciousness is in a sense determined by the neural infrastructures of the brain at the highest levels of its organizational hierarchy. But at the same time, consciousness not only manifests characteristics not attributable to any of the constituent brain systems but also exerts regulatory control influence in brain processes. Thus mental phenomena are "causes rather than correlates" of neural events. "The brain physiology determines the mental effects and the mental phenomena in turn have causal influence on the neurophysiology" (Sperry, 1976, p. 168). As emergent properties of cortical activity, conscious phenomena could functionally interact at their own level while at the same time exerting downward control over their constituent neural processes. Thus, according to Sperry, conscious states supervene rather than intervene in the physiological processes.

The attempts to grant reality and causal efficacy to conscious phenomena and yet regard them as manifestations of brain activity are criticized on the grounds that they are based on false analogies. It is difficult to conceive how a complex organization of neural processes gives us mental phenomena that are considered to be qualitatively different from physical phenomena (Globus, Maxwell, & Savodnik, 1976).

Eccles (Popper & Eccles, 1977) rejected the notion that consciousness is a function of complex neural organization. He found it difficult to account for the unity of conscious experience in terms of heterogeneous, discontinuous, and spatially discrete neural events. Similarly, self-consciousness and volition require for their explanation an agency independent of brain processes. Phenomena such as antedating, by which conscious experience does not immediately follow stimulation but is referred backward in time, do not fit with the hypothesis of psychoneural identity. We do not know the precise physiological processes involved in the synthesis of perceptual experience. Eccles pointed out that the surface-negative potential in the cerebral cortex preceding simple voluntary moments, called readiness potential, takes considerable time to develop and is distributed widely over the cortex. This phenomenon, according to Eccles, suggests the action of the self-conscious mind on the specialized modules in the cortex that are critically poised at a special level of activity to produce consciously willed actions.

CONSCIOUSNESS AND PSYCHOLOGY

When psychology began as a separate discipline a little more than a century ago, it was defined as the science of consciousness. William James (1890/1990), for example, regarded psychology "as the description and explanation of states of consciousness-as-such" (p. 1). James's *The Principles of Psychology* (1890) profoundly influenced subsequent developments in Western psychology. Of the many different psychological doctrines of James contained in the *Principles,* none is more influential than his conception of the stream of consciousness. Affirming that consciousness is the "first and foremost concrete fact" of one's inner experience, he characterizes consciousness as an activity that is personal, selective, changing, and yet sensibly continuous. It has the function of choosing which objects to welcome and which to reject.

The changing, yet continuous, character of consciousness does not consist in any kind of linking discrete psychological events. One's mental life is not a chain or train of jointed bits of consciousness. Consciousness feels continuous because it flows like a river or a stream. Therefore, James (1900) calls it "the stream of thought, of consciousness, or of subjective life" (p. 159). The stream metaphor reflects the twin aspects of the continuous character of consciousness. First, when there is a time gap, the consciousness that follows relates itself to the one before it as if they belonged to one and the same self. Second, when there are shifts in the quality of consciousness from one moment to another they are never absolutely abrupt because no current psychological event takes place in a vacuum without some reference to the preceding events.

The stream of consciousness contains substantive and transitive states. The former are relative resting places in the flow of consciousness. James speaks of a fringe as well as a focus of consciousness, reminding us of the preconscious and focal-attentive processing distinction in cognitive psychology. While one's attention is focused on a center and around a theme, there also is a vast surround of impressions and sensations at the periphery. The fringe in a sense is the transitive, floating backdrop of substantive states that are the focus of attention.

There are three distinctive strands in James's conception of consciousness, reflected in current discussions. The preceding account of consciousness contained in the *Principles* is generally accepted by cognitive psychologists concerned primarily with human information processing. In *The Varieties of Religious Experience* (1902/1914), James expanded consciousness to include nonrational forms. He wrote, "It is that our normal waking consciousness, rational consciousness as we call it, is but one special type of consciousness, whilst all about it, parted from it by the filmiest of screens, there lie potential forms of consciousness entirely differ-

ent" (p. 298). In his *Essays in Radical Empiricism* (1912/1947), however, we find: "For twenty years past I have mistrusted 'consciousness' as an entity; for seven or eight years past I have suggested its nonexistence to my students and tried to give them its pragmatic equivalent in realities of experience. It seems to me that the hour is ripe for it to be openly and universally discarded" (p. 3).

James was of the view that religious experience, an outcome of mystical states, may reveal some other forms of consciousness. He argued that if a mystical truth comes to an individual with such a force that he or she cannot help but live by it, no one has any legitimate right to interfere with his or her way of living, for mystics have the same kind of evidence in favor of their convictions as any of us in ours. "Mystical experiences are as direct perceptions of fact for those who have them as any sensations ever were for us" (James, 1902/1914, pp. 423–424).

In the *Varieties* and the *Essays,* James abhorred intellectualism and defended experience against transempirical agencies, whether matter or mind. James's rejection of consciousness is methodologically akin to George Berkeley's rejection of matter. In rejecting dualism and its interactionist mode, James locates both mind and matter, the knower and the known in experience-as-such. What that experience is, however, remains as elusive as the interaction of mind and matter in dualistic postulations.

If there is any inconsistency in James, it is due to the two different senses in which he used consciousness, first in the sense of phenomenal awareness in the *Principles* and then in the sense of consciousness-as-such in the *Varieties.* The phenomenal and transcendental connotations continue to color much of the controversy surrounding the consciousness debate today. Some consider consciousness as a fact of its own, that it is autonomous and irreducible. It is the principle of subjectivity, whose reality is intuitively evident. Descartes' noncorporeal mind, Kant's noumenal self, Bergson's pure memory, Husserl's transcendental ego, and Sartre's nothingness seem to imply the existence of consciousness-as-such that, to use a term from quantum physics, seems to signify a nonlocal aspect of reality and the subjectivity in our being. Among contemporary schools of psychology, the transpersonal school holds such a view of consciousness. If we accept the reality of psi phenomena (Rao & Palmer, 1987), it would be all the more compelling to consider the nonlocal aspects of consciousness.

The main stream of psychologists, however, limits consciousness to its restricted sense of phenomenal awareness. In that sense, consciousness is obviously localized and subject to space-time formulations. It is likely that the brain has much to contribute to our awareness of the world. Consequently, various sorts of mental phenomena may correlate with physiological processes in the brain and nervous system, and they could be investigated from a neurophysiological perspective. It does not follow, however, that all mental phenomena are ultimately reducible to brain states or that consciousness does not exist apart from these states. Some systems of Indian philosophy, notably the Sankhya school, consider mind to be essentially material while at the same time holding that consciousness-as-such is nonmaterial. Bergson (1913) also has insights as to the nature of the transition from the nonmaterial, pure memory to the material perceptions, that is, consciousness-as-such to conscious phenomena.

Although those who believe in consciousness-as-such, like the transpersonal psychologists, have little common ground with those who restrict consciousness to phenomenal awareness, as in cognitive psychology, one process of the mind is emphasized by all those who regard consciousness as legitimate subject matter for psychology. This is attention. In information-processing models (Neisser, 1967) as well as in the transpersonal psychologies (Tart, 1975), attention occupies a central role. Several of the so-called psychic development techniques believed to produce higher order conscious phenomena seem essentially to involve manipulation of attention.

There is already an impressive scientific literature on meditation, even though much of it has suffered from conceptual confusion, methodological weaknesses, and some overgeneralizations (Rao, 1989). At any rate, future developments in the study of attention may hold the key for a more comprehensive understanding of consciousness.

REFERENCES

Armstrong, D. M. (1968). *A materialist theory of the mind.* London: Routledge.

Armstrong, D. M. (1980). *The nature of mind and other essays.* Ithaca, NY: Cornell University Press.

Bergson, H. (1913). *Matter and memory* (N. M. Paul & W. S. Palmer, Trans.). New York: Macmillan.

Brentano, F. (1973/1874). *Psychology from an empirical standpoint.* New York: Humanities Press.

Burns, J. E. (1990). Contemporary models of consciousness: Part I. *Journal of Mind and Behavior, 11,* 153–172.

Freud, S. (1915). The unconscious. In J. Strachey (Ed.), *Standard edition of the complete psychological works of Sigmund Freud* (Vol. 14). London: Hogarth.

Frey-Rohn, L. (1990). *From Freud to Jung: Comparative study of the psychology of the unconscious.* Boston: Shambhala. (Original work published 1974).

Globus, G. G., Maxwell, G., & Savodnik, I. (Eds.). (1976). *Consciousness and the brain: A scientific and philosophical inquiry.* New York: Plenum.

Husserl, E. (1964). *The idea of phenomenology.* The Hague: Martinis Nijhoff.

James, W. (1990). *The principles of psychology.* New York: Henry Holt. (Original work published 1890)

James, W. (1900). *Psychology: Briefer course.* New York: Henry Holt. (Original work published 1892)

James, W. (1914). *The varieties of religious experience: A study in human nature.* New York: Longmans, Green. (Original work published 1902)

James, W. (1947). *Essays in radical empiricism.* New York: Longmans, Green. (Original work published 1912)

Jung, C. G. (1954). On the nature of psyche. In H. Read et al. (Eds.), *Collected works of C. G. Jung* (Vol. 8, R. F. C. Hull, Trans.). Princeton, NJ: Princeton University Press. (Original work published 1919)

Luria, A. R. (1978). The human brain and conscious activity. In G. E. Schwartz & D. Shapiro (Eds.), *Consciousness and self-regulation: Advances in research and theory* (Vol. 2). New York: Plenum.

Meehl, P. (1966). The complete autocerebroscopist: A thought experiment on Professor Feigl's mind/body identity thesis. In P. K. Feyerabend & G. Maxwell (Ed.), *Mind, matter, and method.* Minneapolis: University of Minnesota Press.

Minsky, M. (1986). *Society of mind.* New York: Simon & Schuster.

Natsoulas, T. (1978). Consciousness. *American Psychologist, 10,* 906–914.

Neisser, U. (1967). *Cognitive psychology.* New York: Appleton-Century-Crofts.

Penrose, R. (1989). *The emperor's new mind: Concerning computers, minds and the laws of physics.* Oxford, UK: Oxford University Press.

Perry, R. B. (1904). Conceptions and misconceptions of consciousness. *Psychological review, 11,* 282–296.

Popper, K. R., & Eccles, J. C. (1977). *The self and its brain: An argument for interactionism.* Berlin: Springer-Verlag.

Pribram, K. H. (1976). Self-consciousness and intentionality: A model based on an experimental analysis of the brain mechanisms involved in the Jamesian theory of motivation and evolution. In G. E. Schwartz & D. Shapiro (Eds.), *Consciousness and self-regulation* (Vol. 1, pp. 51–100). New York: Plenum.

Rao, K. R. (1989). Meditation: Secular and sacred: Review and assessment of some recent research. *Journal of the Indian Academy of Applied Psychology, 15,* 51–74.

Rao, K. R., & Palmer, J. (1987). The anomaly called psi: Recent research and criticism. *Behavioral and Brain Sciences, 10,* 539–555.

Sartre, J. P. (1956). *Being and nothingness* (H. E. Barnes, Trans.). New York: Philosophical Library.

Searle, J. R. (1983). *Intentionality: An essay in the philosophy of mind.* New York: Cambridge University Press.

Sellars, W. (1963). *Science, perception, and reality.* London: Routledge & Kegan Paul.

Skinner, B. F. (1974). *About behaviorism.* New York: Knopf.

Sperry, R. (1969). A modified concept or consciousness. *Psychological Review, 76,* 532–536.

Sperry, R. W. (1976). Mental phenomena as causal determinants in brain function. In G. G. Globus, G. Maxwell, & I. Savodnik (Eds.), *Consciousness and the brain* (pp. 163–177). New York: Plenum.

Tart, C. T. (1975). *States of consciousness.* New York: Dutton.

Turing, A. M. (1950). Computing machinery and intelligence. *Mind, 59,* 433–460.

Velmans, M. (1991). Is human information processing conscious? *Behavioral and Brain Sciences, 14,* 651–726.

Watson, J. B. (1928). The unconscious of the behaviorist. In C. M. Child, K. Koffka, & J. E. Anderson (Eds.), *The unconscious: A symposium* (pp. 91–113). New York: Knopf.

Weiskrantz, L. (1986). *Blindsight: A case study and implications.* Oxford, UK: Oxford University Press.

SUGGESTED READING

Baars, B. J. (1988). *A cognitive theory of consciousness.* New York: Cambridge University Press.

Globus, G. G., Maxwell, G., & Savodnik, I. (Eds.). (1976). *Consciousness and the brain: A scientific and philosophical inquiry.* New York: Plenum.

Ornstein, R. E. (1977). *The psychology of consciousness* (2nd ed.). New York: Harcourt Brace Jovanovich. (Original work published 1972)

Smythies, J. R., & Beloff, J. (Eds.). (1989). *The case for dualism.* Charlottesville, VA: University Press of Virginia.

Tart, C. T. (1975). *States of consciousness.* New York: Dutton.

K. R. RAO
Duke University

ATTENTION
INTROSPECTION
SPLIT BRAIN RESEARCH
STRUCTURALISM

CONSUMER RESEARCH

Each one of us is a consumer. We eat, sleep, bathe, dress, exercise, gather, read, travel, and have a host of other daily and weekly activities. In an earlier era it was a major challenge to find any product or service to meet a given need. If a product or service was available and affordable, it was readily accessed and used. This reality continues to be true in underdeveloped, third-world countries; but industrialized nations—those that commonly comprise the world's "G-7"—provide a very different picture and challenge. In these countries, every item and service comes in a vast array of brands representing an equally vast array of companies. The challenge is no longer simply to get a specific product or service to market and consumers. Now the challenge becomes one of assuring that the consumer will prefer and will purchase a specific brand of product or service . . . to be the chosen one among the available many. To meet this challenge, companies invest heavily in research to learn about their prospective consumers, their habits, their personalities, and their preferences. To misread the consumer can spell millions of dollars in company losses and, in some instances, bankruptcy. Because the stakes are high, methodical information-gathering becomes essential and critical.

DEFINITION AND EVOLUTION

Consumer research systematically studies the many aspects of human behavior related to the purchase and use of economic goods and services. The product-related focus includes research in advertising effectiveness, product features, and marketing techniques. Focus upon the consumer has included the study of attitudes, feelings, preferences, and the many group influences upon the decision-making process of the individual consumer. The field also studies the consumer as citizen and as a central figure in social/environmental problem solving. This scope and range make consumer research highly interdisciplinary. It integrates theoretical concepts and research approaches from social psychology, sociology, and economics.

While in one sense consumer research is as old as the dawn of recorded human history, in still another sense it is as young as the last few decades. Not until the 1920s did consumer research begin to focus on two-way communication—gathering information from consumers to prepare more effective advertisements. Still later, attention was given to consumer attitudes and opinions prior to product design. As this consumer focus steadily grew, it marked the appearance of a newly independent member of the advertising family—consumer psychology. Official recognition came in 1960 when the Division of Consumer Psychology was formed within the American Psychological Association.

The early-era, primitive question was one of "What do people need?" Economic growth and increased personal income spawned the more probing questions of "What do people want?" and "What can people be enticed to want?" These questions form the basis of consumer research today.

Consumer research takes many forms and spans many different settings. Prevalent forms include a variety of survey and polling methods, in-depth projective techniques, and behavioral studies.

RESEARCH METHODS

Survey and Polling Techniques

Most research utilizes some form or variation of survey or polling. It has the advantage of gathering input from large groups of consumers quickly and relatively inexpensively. This research approach assumes that consumers know their likes, dislikes, and preferences and will be forthright in expressing them.

The method is premised on random selection of consumers within a target market. Where this market is the US population at large, the survey or polling typically focuses on carefully selected communities that, taken collectively, proportionally represent the various constituencies within the broader community. Where the market is more product line-specific, a select group of consumers in a given demographic or socioeconomic group becomes the focus.

The survey and polling methods themselves are wide-ranging. Selected consumers may receive a survey by mail, may be visited at home by an interviewer, or may be telephoned. Other consumers may be surveyed within a grocery store or a shopping mall. They may be asked about a specific product, about sizes, colors, textures, and shapes. They may be asked to come into a mall-based test room where they express actual preferences of products or features. Or, in the case of food items or personal hygiene products, they may be asked to try different samples and register preferences. Logical consumers of a given product (e.g., mothers with infants, where the product is baby care-related) may be gathered in focus groups to determine product features and preferences.

Rapid technological advances have brought prominent growth in surveying by internet and the prospect of virtually instant response via integrated systems combining cable, computer, and television. While the technologies will rapidly change, the basic principles underlying surveying and polling will remain constant—principles of random sampling within representative general or target-market populations.

In notable instances, polling or surveying will target those consumers who have purchased a given product or brand. What attracted them to the product, why they selected it, how satisfied they are with its features and performance, and related questions hold central interest for the company whose product was selected or, in some instances, a competing company who seeks to win the consumer in the future. The questionnaire may come in the just-purchased box of shoes, radio alarm clock, or computer. In the broad, total-market context, Japan uses purchaser surveying exclusively. It is their belief that random surveying within the broader consumer population is too capricious and subject to change.

Depth/Projective Techniques

Projective techniques probe below the surface of a consumer's cognizant behaviors, preferences, and motivations. These techniques are premised on the belief that consumers in the marketplace are motivated by desires they do not know and cannot consciously express. To access these motivations, the technique, in effect, removes the question from the person through interpretation of abstract stimuli or pictures, sentence or story completion, questions about what their neighbor would consider most important in selecting a given product, describing the personality of a consumer who would select a given product or grouping of products, and so on. Through techniques such as these the consumer unwittingly expresses her or his own underlying motivations while responding on the basis of stimuli, sentences, or other individuals.

Historically, projective techniques have been very meaningful in designing advertising campaigns to effectively move beyond a marketing problem or roadblock. When Duncan Hines introduced a cake mix which required only adding water, it sat quietly on supermarket shelves. Projective techniques revealed the homemaker felt guilt in baking a cake so easily, and the product was reformulated to require adding an egg. Similar projective techniques have been useful in revealing and overcoming resistances in a wide variety of product areas including microwave dinners and instant coffee, to name but a few.

Behavioral Techniques

Behavioral techniques examine the actions of the prospective consumer in several facets of the purchasing arena. Children and their parents may be invited to shop in a mock grocery or toy store. Consumers and their actions in store aisles may be observed first-hand or through one-way-mirror windows. Selected consumers may be given scanner cards which register all their purchases at designated/scanner-cable-equipped supermarkets. These scanner-cable-

panels of consumers provide important data to major food manufacturers.

CONCLUSION

Though this discussion has focused upon the commercial marketplace, the techniques of consumer research are used extensively in broader nonprofit and societal orientations as well. Questions of consumer welfare, product safety, and "truth-in-packaging" legislation have been central among these broader concerns. Equally central have been issues relating to quality of life and the reciprocal nature of consumer behavior: (1) the responsibility of society toward the individual consumer, and (2) the responsibility of the individual consumer toward society. Society's responsibility encompasses areas such as health care delivery systems, education, cultural, and recreational facilities. The individual consumer's responsibility encompasses respect for the environment, for communities, and for natural resources.

SUGGESTED READING

Anastasi, A. (1966). *Psychological testing.* New York: Prentice Hall.

Foxall, G. (1998). *Consumer psychology for marketing.* London: International Thomson Business.

Schultz, D. P., & Schultz, S. E. (1997). *Psychology and work today.* New York: Prentice Hall.

E. L. PALMER
Davidson College

APPLIED RESEARCH

CONTROL GROUPS

A control group is a group of subjects not subjected to the experimental treatment but like the experimental group or groups in every other way. The purpose of the control group is to provide a base against which to determine whether a change in the experimental group occurred, and to eliminate all explanations other than the treatment that differentiates the groups. For example, consider a study of the effects of caffeine on improving the behavior of hyperactive children. One would need an experimental group for caffeine, and a control group with which the experimental group would be compared to determine if caffeine had the expected effect. To form the groups, each child in a sample of hyperactive children might be randomly assigned by a flip of a coin: if heads, to one group, and if tails, to the other; when one group is filled, assign the remainder to the other. Which group is experimental and which control would similarly be determined by a coin flip, to avoid unconsciously giving the treatment to the group appearing more favorable. Since with random assignment every person has as much chance of being assigned to one group as another, over enough cases differences between groups will cancel out; on the average, one group will be like the other. If the groups are alike in every way except that only one receives the treatment, caffeine, then behavioral differences between the children in the experimental and control groups may presumably be traced to caffeine. That is the logic of the method of differences expounded by Mill in *A System of Logic* (1843/1973, pp. 452ff.)—a cornerstone of scientific method.

But even with large groups, where chance presumably evens things out, are the groups *exactly* alike? No, not really, they cannot be, for each person is unique; it has been said no two persons have the same number of hairs on their heads. It is essential only that the groups be alike with respect to aspects related to that which is being studied. The problem, of course, is whether we know all those aspects. This is why random assignment is important; on the average, it evens out all characteristics—even the average number of hairs on the head—but also, and more significantly, unsuspected important variables. Indeed, Campbell and Stanley (1966) distinguish true experimental designs from quasi-experimental ones on the basis of whether subjects were randomly assigned to groups.

The effect of randomization on known important variables can be uneven, however. To assure equivalent groups, we may block or stratify on such variables. If having groups with equivalent basal metabolic rates (BMR) is important in a study of hyperactive children, one might divide the subjects into those with high, middle, and low BMRs (blocks), and then randomly assign equal numbers from each block to the groups.

For some time, it was thought that initial differences—even those between control and experimental groups occurring after random assignment—could be corrected by use of analysis of covariance. This is no longer believed to be the case. As Cronbach states, "No statistical adjustment . . . of supposedly equivalent groups leads to a dependable estimate. . . ." (1980, p. 302).

Differences between the groups which leave open alternative explanations of the results may result from (a) initial differences, (b) events occurring during treatment but unrelated to it, and (c) aspects of the treatment itself.

Initial group differences often appear where random assignment is not feasible—for instance, when one must use intact classrooms, or when characteristics of the experimental variable—length, complexity, unpleasantness—may require the use of volunteers. Rosenthal and Rosnow (1969) concluded that volunteers are usually better educated, higher in occupational status, higher in need of approval, and brighter, and have lower authoritarianism than nonvolunteers. Thus if volunteers must be used, the control group should also consist of volunteers; to use nonvolunteers as a control may risk an unfair comparison.

Rival explanations may also result from events that occur during a study. For the control group to serve to eliminate such explanations, it must be exposed to the events as well. For example, a teacher might learn to more effectively prevent hyperactive outbursts, so that caffeine-treated students would appear less hyperactive. Unless *both* experimental *and* control group children were assigned to his or her class, or measures were taken to equate the way teachers of both groups learned to handle such incidents, this could become a rival explanation.

Finally, aspects of the intervention that are not part of the treatment being tested (caffeine) may produce differences. For example, the fact that one group knows they are being treated because they are given pills, may itself produce an expectation of improved behavior in parents, teachers, and the children. To eliminate this rival explanation, the control group must also be given a treatment indistinguishable by subjects, teachers, and researchers from the real treatment. In this instance a placebo—an inert pill that looks just like the caffeine pill—might be administered, with knowledge of who received it kept by a neutral party until after the results are in. This is known as a double-blind study.

REFERENCES

Campbell, D. T., & Stanley, J. C. (1966). *Experimental and quasi-experimental designs for research.* Chicago: Rand McNally.

Cronbach, L. J., et al. (1980). *Toward reform of program evaluation.* San Francisco: Jossey-Bass.

Mill, J. S. (1973). A system of logic ratiocinative and inductive. In J. M. Robson (Ed.), *Collected works of John Stuart Mill* (Vol. 7). Toronto: University of Toronto Press. (Original work published 1843)

Rosenthal, R., & Rosnow, R. L. (1969). The volunteer subject. In R. Rosenthal & R. L. Rosnow (Eds.), *Artifact in behavioral research.* New York: Academic Press.

SUGGESTED READING

Cook, T. D., & Campbell, D. T. (1979). *Quasi-experimentation: Design and analysis issues for field settings.* Boston: Houghton Mifflin.

D. R. KRATHWOHL
Syracuse University

DOUBLE-BLIND RESEARCH
RESEARCH METHODOLOGY
SAMPLING

CONTROL THERAPY

Control therapy is an integrated approach to psychotherapy and health care that combines theory, research, and practice. It is based on the premise that issues of control (e.g., fear of loss of control, desire for control, power struggles) underlie most concerns brought to therapy (Frank, 1982; Strupp, 1970; Shapiro, Schwartz, & Astin, 1996). A reliable and valid standardized psychological assessment inventory (the SCI, or Shapiro Control Inventory) was developed to both measure the theory and provide an individual client "control profile" (Shapiro, 1994). Finally, control-based therapeutic techniques, including an assertive change mode of control, and an accepting/yielding mode of control, are "matched" to the client's control profile and taught as interventions. The theory, test construction, and interventions have been developed and empirically tested over a period of twenty-five years involving research and clinical work with thousands of individuals in over a dozen countries.

A UNIFYING THEORY OF CONTROL
The theoretical basis of control therapy builds upon and integrates several literatures, including self-efficacy (Bandura, 1977), learned helplessness and optimism (Seligman, 1975, 1991); competence (White, 1959); dyscontrol (Menninger, Mayman, & Pruyser, 1963); reactance (Brehm, 1966); will to meaning (Frankl, 1980); will to superiority (Adler, 1964); cybernetic feedback models and dysregulation (Schwartz, 1983); internal and external locus of control (Rotter, 1966; Wallston, Wallston, & DeVellis, 1978); self-determination (Deci & Ryan, 1985); and self-control/delay of gratification (Mischel, 1974; Mahoney & Thoresen, 1984).

Control theory is based on an unifying biopsychosocial theory of human control and self-control and has three postulates that can be summarized as follows: (a) all individuals want a sense of control in their lives; (b) there are healthy and unhealthy ways by which they attempt to gain or regain that sense of control; and (c) there are individual differences in control profiles of individuals and in how they face this central issue of maintaining a healthy sense of control in their lives (Shapiro & Astin, 1998).

DEVELOPING A CLIENT "CONTROL PROFILE": ASSESSING THE THEORY
A client "control profile" is based on clinical assessment with the SCI, which has undergone extensive reliability and validity testing (including an investigation of neurobiological correlates of control using Positron Emission Tomography; Shapiro, 1994; Shapiro et al., 1995). The 187-item, nine-scale SCI inventory is a clinically reliable and valid multidimensional instrument that measures four primary and interrelated components of clients' control profiles: (a) desire for control (i.e., where they want control, why they want it); (b) current sense of control in both general and specific domains; (c) the modes by which they seek control (assertive/changing and yielding/accepting); and (d) and use of both self and other agency in gaining control. Research shows that this method of assessing client control profiles is the most sensitive inventory yet devised to differentiate among clinical disorders, and between clinical and normative populations (Shapiro, Potkin, Jin, Brown, & Carreon, 1993).

Assessment also includes methods for listening to client speech, including the client narrative (their "control story"), control-related beliefs and assumptions, and assaults to the client's sense of control which brought them into the therapy session. Assessment also includes having clients identify and monitor their area of concern (e.g., domains where they feel a lack of control).

In goal-setting, clients examine their preferred style or mode (assertive/changing or yielding/accepting) for regaining control, and are helped to determine whether that mode best "matches" the current situation. In other words, is the issue something best addressed by learning greater self-control, learning to change the situation that exists, or learning to accept a situation outside of one's active control?

Through such precise assessment, the clinician can differentiate between different control profiles of various clinical populations. Further, by measuring a client's individual control profile, the clinician is assisted in matching the most effective intervention to a particular client.

CONTROL-BASED INTERVENTIONS
Control therapy consists of an eight- to twelve-week step-by-step-treatment program involving defining the area of concern, assessment, monitoring, goal-setting, determining the appropriate strategy or strategies, teaching the strategies, and evaluation. Therapeutic interventions involve detailed and well-defined clinical instructions for matching treatment strategy to the client's control profile, thus offering both standardized, replicable techniques, and providing flexibility and sensitivity to each client's individual needs and style.

Based on the goal selected, individually tailored cognitive and behavioral strategies are utilized to help clients regain a sense of control through one or both of the positive modes of control. The assertive/changing mode of control, which has historically been emphasized by Western scientific psychology, involves having individuals learn to identify, monitor, and gain active control of those aspects of their lives which are or should be amenable to change.

The yielding/accepting mode, which has historically been emphasized by non-Western philosophical and psychological traditions, helps clients learn the value of surrendering, accepting, and letting go with serenity (i.e., without feelings of helplessness or resignation) of those aspects of their lives that are not under personal control, or of inappropriate active control efforts. Practical instructions in each mode are explained, as well as ways to integrate and achieve balance between the two positive modes.

A CONTROL-BASED VIEW OF PSYCHOLOGICAL HEALTH: SUBOPTIMAL, NORMAL, AND OPTIMAL
Traditional Western psychology argues that loss of control and learned helplessness are unhealthy and suboptimal. Normal control is defined as gaining control (even including an illusion of control) and is equated with mental health. This traditional view argues that instrumental control is good, and that "the more control the better" (Thompson, 1981). "Healthy normals" often maintain control through illusory, overinflated perceptions of control (Taylor & Brown, 1994), and they use defense mechanisms such as making external attributions for failure (Seligman, 1991).

The theory, research, and practice of control therapy agree that "normal" control is better than suboptimal. However, it maintains that "normal" control strategies can also be problematic. For example, they can keep individuals from being aware of the unconscious, reflexive, and reactive nature of many of their control desires and efforts; are often insular and self-serving; and can keep people from learning about their mistakes.

Therefore, a concept of optimal control is needed. Optimal control, according to control therapy, involves:

- Increased conscious awareness of one's control dynamics, including affective, cognitive, and somatic experiences, to learn when and how the desires and efforts for control are expressed; when control beliefs, goals, desires, and strategies are reflexive, limiting, and potentially destructive; and when they should be increased, decreased, or channeled.

- A balanced and integrated use of assertive/changing and yielding/accepting modes of control matched to situation and goals, desires, and temperament.

- The ability to gain a sense of control from both self (self-regulation of cognitions, affect, and behavior) and from others (gaining a sense of control from a "powerful benevolent other," whether from a doctor [see Taylor, 1983] or from one's view of the nature of the universe, including religious and spiritual beliefs).

BENEFITS OF CONTROL THERAPY

Control therapy has been shown to be effective in both assessment (sensitivity and specificity) and treatment (clinical outcome), with a wide range of *DSM* diagnoses and health-related concerns (Shapiro & Astin, 1998). Clinical areas investigated include generalized anxiety disorder, panic attack, depression, borderline personality, eating disorders, and adult children of alcoholics. Control issues have also been investigated in "Type A" individuals with myocardial infarction, women with breast cancer, and individuals at high cardiovascular risk (see Shapiro, 1994 for summary; Astin et al., in press).

There are several advantages to control therapy and to the unifying theory upon which it is based. First, a unifying theory helps clinicians understand control as a central component underlying all schools of therapy: the analytic view that humans are governed by "unknown and uncontrolled forces"; the cognitive/behavioral schools' emphasis on self-control; and the humanistic/existential focus on personal choice, individual freedom, and self-determination.

Secondly, in addition to the theory's universality and parsimony, it also can be operationalized, thereby providing an empirical foundation for assessing a client's control profile. Based on individual variations in control profiles, specific techniques can be matched to client needs and clinical problems (Evans et al., 1993).

Third, based on a systems approach to clinical issues, control therapy provides for systematic feedback at each step of the clinical process. Such feedback allows specific common client difficulties in gaining or regaining a sense of control to be pinpointed, and explicit guidelines are provided for helping clients deal with problems such as resistances, lack of motivation, unclear goals, and poor self-efficacy beliefs.

Finally, control therapy examines the importance of therapists becoming aware of their own control dynamics because of the potential effect those dynamics may have on the therapeutic encounter. It also examines matching the therapists' method of "teaching" interventions to the client's control style: e.g., teaching control strategies in a "self-directed way" to those clients with a higher "desire for control" profile; increased therapist-directed teaching for those clients with a lower desire for personal control and more willing to gain a sense of control from an "other."

SUMMARY

To recap, Control Therapy is based on a unifying theory of control, and provides a multi-dimensional psychological inventory to both measure the theory and assess a client's "control profile." Further, drawing from both Eastern and Western psychological traditions, Control Therapy involves specific assertive/change and yielding/accepting modes of control intervention techniques; and the matching of these techniques to a client's control profile, goals, and clinical problem. Finally, Control Therapy articulates a control-based vision of mental, physical, and interpersonal health involving suboptimal, normal, and optimal control profiles. Thus, although Control Therapy was designed to specifically address individual mental and physical health problems, it can also be used as a means to help promote "growth," including intrapersonal, interpersonal and even societal health, healing, and well-being.

REFERENCES

Adler, A. (1964). *Superiority and social interest: A collection of later writings.* In H. L. Ansbacher & R. Ansbacher (Eds.). New York: Viking.

Astin, J. A., Anton-Culver, H., Schwartz, C. E., Shapiro, D. H., McQuade, J., Breuer, A. M., Taylor, T., Lee, H., & Kurosaki, T. (in press). Sense of control and adjustment to breast cancer: The importance of balancing control coping styles. *Behavioral Medicine.*

Bandura, A. (1977). Self-efficacy: Toward a unifying theory of behavioral change. *Psychological Review, 84,* 191–215.

Brehm, J. (1966). *A theory of psychological reactance.* New York: Academic.

Deci, E., & Ryan, R. (1985). *Intrinsic motivation and self-determination in human behavior.* New York: Plenum.

Evans, G. E., Shapiro, D. H., & Lewis, M. (1993). Specifying dysfunctional mismatches between different control dimensions. *British Journal of Psychology, 84,* 255–273.

Frank, J. (1982). Therapeutic components shared by all psychotherapies. In J. J. Harvey & M. M. Parks (Eds.), *Psychotherapy research and behavior change. Master lecture series* (Vol. 1, pp. 9–37). Washington, DC: American Psychological Association.

Frankl, V. (1980). *Man's search for meaning: An introduction to logotherapy.* New York: Simon and Schuster.

Mahoney, M., & Thoresen, C. (1974). *Self-control.* Monterey, CA: Brooks-Cole.

Menninger, K., Mayman, M., & Pruyser, P. (1963). *The vital balance: The life process in mental health and illness.* New York: Viking.

Mischel, W. (1974). Processes in the delay of gratification. In L. Berkowitz (Ed.), *Advances in experimental social psychology* (Vol. 7). New York: Academic.

Rotter, J. (1966). Generalized expectancies for internal versus external control of reinforcement. *Psychological Monographs, 80* (Whole No. 609).

Schwartz, G. E. (1983). Disregulation theory and disease: Applications to the repression/cerebral disconnection/cardiovascular disorder hypothesis. In J. Matarazzo, N. Miller, & S. Weiss (Eds.), *Revue Internationale de Psychologie Appliquee* [special issue], *32,* 95–118.

Seligman, M. E. P. (1975). *Helplessness.* San Francisco: Freeman.

Seligman, M. E. P. (1991). *Learned optimism.* New York: Knopf.

Shapiro, D. H., & Astin, J. A. (1998). *Control therapy: An integrated approach to psychotherapy, health, and healing.* New York: Wiley.

Shapiro, D. H., Potkin, S., Jin, Y., Brown, B., & Carreon, D. (1993). Measuring the psychological construct of control: Discriminant, divergent, and incremental validity of the Shapiro Control Inventory and Rotter's and Wallston's Locus of Control Scales. *International Journal of Psychosomatics, 40*(1–4), 35–46.

Shapiro, D. H., Schwartz, C. E., & Astin, J. A. (1996). Controlling ourselves, controlling our world: Psychology's role in understanding positive and negative consequences of seeking and gaining control. *American Psychologist, 51*(12), 1213–1230.

Shapiro, D. H., Wu, J., Buchsbaum, M., Hong, C., Elderkin-Thompson, V., & Hillard, D. (1995). Exploring the relationship between having control and losing control to functional neuroanatomy within the sleeping state. *Psychologia, 38*(3), 133–145.

Shapiro, D. H. (1994). *Manual for the Shapiro Control Inventory (SCI).* San Jose, CA: Behaviordata.

Strupp, H. (1970). Specific versus non-specific factors in psychotherapy and the problem of control. *Archives of General Psychiatry, 23,* 393–401.

Taylor, S. (1983). Adjustment to threatening events: A theory of cognitive adaptation. *American Psychologist, 38,* 1161–1173.

Taylor, S., & Brown, J. D. (1994). Illusion and well-being revisited: Separating fact from fiction. *Psychological Bulletin, 116,* 21–27.

Thompson, S. (1981). Will it hurt less if I can control it? A complex answer to a simple question. *Psychological Bulletin, 90,* 89–101.

Wallston, K. A., Wallston, B. S., & DeVellis, R. (1978). Development of the multidimensional health locus of control scales. *Health Education Monographs, 6*(2), 160–170.

White, R. W. (1959). Motivation reconsidered: The concept of competence. *Psychological Review, 66*(5), 297–331.

D. H. SHAPIRO, JR.
University of California, Irvine

J. A. ASTIN
University of Maryland School of Medicine

S. L. SHAPIRO
C. SANTERRE
University of Arizona

PSYCHOTHERAPY TECHNIQUES

CONVERSION DISORDER

The term *conversion* derives from the Freudian concept of conversion hysteria, in which a psychosexual conflict was seen as being *converted* into a bodily disturbance. Today conversion disorders represent a rather specific and rare clinical entity within the more general family of somatoform disorders. As such, one of the essential features is the presence of a physical complaint without demonstrable physiological or disease mechanisms to account for it. Specifically, according to the American Psychiatric Association's *Diagnostic and Statistical Manual of Mental Disorders (DSM-III),* conversion disorders present a "clinical picture in which the predominant disturbance is a loss of or alteration in physical functioning that suggests physical disorder but which instead is apparently an expression of a psychological conflict or need" (p. 244). Furthermore, the symptoms are not under the person's voluntary control, and they cannot be explained by pathophysiological processes. Under this definition, disorders in which there is: (a) no actual loss or alteration of physical function (e.g., hypocondriasis); (b) a psychophysiological relationship between the symptoms and an organic pathology (e.g., ulcer and bronchial asthma); or (c) evidence that the symptoms are actually under voluntary control (e.g., malingering and factitious disorder with physical symptoms), are not diagnosed as conversion disorders. Similarly, symptoms restricted to pain or sexual functioning, or that are part of a more pervasive somatization disorder, are not classified as conversion.

CLINICAL PRESENTATION

Conversion symptoms tend to be fairly discrete and singular, with an abrupt onset during times of extreme psychological stress. In the most obvious or classic cases, the conversion symptoms involve pathological changes in sensory and motor functions, mimicking those found in neurological diseases. The most common symptoms cited in *DSM-III* include paralysis, aphonia (disturbance of speech volume), blindness or tunnel vision, seizures, anesthesia (loss of sensation) or paresthesia (abnormal spontaneous sensation), and dyskinesia (disturbance of coordinated movements). In less common cases the conversion disorder may involve the endocrine or autonomic system, and result in such symptoms as false pregnancy (pseudocyesis) or vomiting. Among medically sophisticated patients, the conversion disorder may mimic fairly exotic diseases; thus E. McDaniel, in her chapter "Hysterical neurosis," cites an example of a man who developed the symptoms of myasthenia gravis, a neuromuscular disease.

DSM-III notes that the level of functional impairment resulting from a conversion disorder is "usually marked and frequently prevents normal life activities" (p. 245). It is easy to see how tunnel vision might affect a radar operator, or how aphonia or mutism could disrupt the life of a teacher. However, prolonged conversion reactions can also produce serious organically-based complications such as muscular atrophy and contractures from disuse in conversion paralysis. In dependent personality types, the attention and sympathy given to the person with a conversion disorder can also reinforce or enhance the development of a chronic sick role.

ETIOLOGY

McDaniel identifies five groups of etiological factors in the development of conversion disorders: sociocultural, intrapsychic, secondary gain, iatrogenic, and situational. The prevailing social and cultural norms greatly influence the direct or indirect expression of various psychological impulses and needs, and determine the types of sick roles sanctioned or prohibited. The culture's exposure to various disease entities also affects the patient's choice of symptoms. Intrapsychic and secondary gain factors have long been cited in the etiology of conversion disorders, and are the two most stressed in the current *DSM-III* criteria. Intrapsychic mechanisms involving *primary gain* are thought to be operating when the appearance of the conversion symptom allows the person to temporarily avoid or exclude awareness of an unpleasant emotion conflict. *Secondary gain* mechanisms, on the other hand, are believed to be operating when the conversion symptom prevents the individual from having to engage in an aversive activity and/or elicits others' attention and support that might not otherwise be forthcoming. According to McDaniel, iatrogenic factors may contribute to the refinement and elaboration of the conversion symptoms, if the health care professional inadvertently communicates approval and additional information about the simulated illness. Finally, situational factors can trigger unresolved interpersonal and intrapersonal conflicts, as in the case of "anniversary reactions."

EPIDEMIOLOGY

Although once fairly common in both civilian and military life, conversion disorders—particularly the classical loss-of-function type—are now relatively rare, and occur primarily among rural and medically unsophisticated subgroups. Also undoubtedly adding to this decrease are the more stringent diagnostic criteria of *DSM-III* and the separate categorization of such symptoms as psychogenic pain, psychosexual dysfunctions, and physical symptoms that are part of a more pervasive somatization disorder. Still, conversion disorders comprise about 5% of all neuroses treated, according to Coleman, Butcher, and Carson in *Abnormal Psychology and Modern Life*. The age of onset is quite variable, although McDaniel states that the mean age of people diagnosed as having a conversion disorder is roughly 40 and that women are more frequently given the diagnosis than men. Intelligence and genetic factors do not seem to be predisposing variables.

REFERENCES

American Psychiatric Association. (1980). *Diagnostic and statistical manual of mental disorders (DSM-III)*. Washington, DC: Author.

Coleman, J. C., Butcher, J. N., & Carson, R. C. (1980). *Abnormal psychology and modern life*. Oakland, NJ: Scott, Foresman.

G. J. CHELUNE
Cleveland Clinic Foundation

ANXIETY
HISTRIONIC PERSONALITIES
OPTIMAL FUNCTIONING
PERSONALITY DISORDERS

CONVULSANTS

Convulsants are substances that induce seizure-like paroxysmal behaviors by producing patterns of electrical activity in the brain resembling those seen in human epilepsy. Epilepsy is characterized by recurring episodes in which the electrical activity of many thousands of neurons becomes abnormally elevated and pathologically synchronized. This discharge interrupts normal brain function and leads, in some forms of epilepsy, to alterations in behavior ("seizures"). Seizures occur in many varieties, ranging from brief, barely detectable losses of consciousness in the "absence" or "petit mal" epilepsies, to uncontrollable tonic-clonic contractions of large muscle groups in the so-called "grand mal" epilepsies. The behavioral manifestations and severity of the seizure reflect primarily the size and localization of the abnormal electrical discharge.

One remarkable aspect of the human epilepsies is the diversity of underlying etiological factors, including perinatal trauma, brain infection, drug and alcohol withdrawal, tumors, and stroke. Our current understanding of epilepsy is that epileptiform brain activity, and the behavioral seizures produced by that activity, arise as the symptom of some underlying brain pathology. Perhaps it not surprising, therefore, that an incredibly diverse group of chemical substances can produce convulsions when given centrally or applied directly to brain tissue.

The study of the mechanism of action of convulsants has led to the formulation of one of the more enduring hypotheses of the generation of epilepsy (Traub & Miles, 1991). It would appear that there is a delicate balance between the strength of inhibitory and excitatory synaptic transmission in the brain. Any disturbance in this balance that favors excitation will lead to the uncontrolled spread of excitation between cells, so that their discharge becomes rapidly synchronous. In this sense, epilepsy is a disease of populations of cells, rather than individual cells. In fact, not all brain regions are equally likely to be identified as sites of epileptiform discharge in patients, and not all brain regions are equally sensitive to convulsants. It is thought that the ability of a convulsant to trigger seizures in a given brain region depends on a number of factors. First, the convulsant's appropriate target must be present. The convulsant strychnine, for example, will be inactive in nuclei lacking glycinergic inhibition. Second, the necessary neuronal circuitry must be present. In particular, there must be local excitatory axon collaterals so that excitation is able to spread between cells. These connections are particularly prominent between pyramidal cells in the hippocampal formation and neocortex, two regions that are highly sensitive to most convulsants and in which epileptic discharge is typically initiated in human epilepsy patients. Finally, some output connections capable of influencing behavior and/or consciousness must be present.

Several of the most widely used and better understood convulsants are listed in Table 1 (for reviews see Fisher, 1989; Löscher &

Table 1.   Widely Used Convulsants and Their Mechanism of Action

CLASS OF ACTION	TARGET SYSTEM	MECHANISM OF ACTION	EXAMPLES
Decreased inhibition:	1. γ-aminobutyric acid	a. Receptor antagonists	penicillin, bicuculline, picrotoxin
		b. Synthesis inhibitors	methoxypyridoxine, isoniazid, 3-mecaptoproprionic acid
		c. Benzodiazepine receptor	inverse agonists
		d. Release inhibitors	opioid peptides
	2. Glycine	a. Receptor antagonists	strychnine
Enhance excitation:	1. Excitatory amino acids (e.g., glutamate)	a. NMDA receptors	magnesium-free saline
		b. non-NMDA receptors	kainic acid
		c. Potassium channel blockers	tetraethylammonium, 4-aminopyridine, various peptide toxins
	2. Acetylcholine	a. Receptor agonists	pilocarpine
		b. Cholinesterase inhibitors	soman
Unknown		a. Neurotoxins	cholera toxin, tetanus toxin
		b. Injury/Trauma	alumina hydroxide, cobalt
		c. CNS Stimulant	pentylenetetrazol

Schmidt, 1988), and they have been classified by their actions on the balance of excitatory and inhibitory synaptic transmission, when known. It should be noted that the patterns of seizures and electrical abnormalities are not the same for all convulsants, and may vary for any one convulsant depending on where and how the substance is applied.

CONVULSANTS THAT DECREASE INHIBITION
Much of our understanding of the cellular basis of epilepsy comes from the application of convulsants to the brain in whole animal experiments and, more recently, to isolated slices of brain tissue maintained *ex vivo.* Penicillin was the first widely used convulsant. After many years of use, it was found that penicillin is a weak antagonist of the receptors for the predominant brain inhibitory neurotransmitter, γ-aminobutyric acid (GABA). More potent antagonists, such as bicuculline and the ion channel blocker picrotoxin, have since replaced penicillin. Seizures and epileptiform discharge can also be elicited by blocking the synthesis or release of GABA. In addition, substances active at modulatory sites on GABA receptors, such as inverse agonists of the benzodiazepine receptor, can also exert convulsant activity.

CONVULSANTS THAT INCREASE EXCITATION
Substances that directly or indirectly increase excitation are also powerful convulsants. For example, application of saline containing a lower-than-physiological concentration of Mg^{2+} relieves the normal block of the ion channels gated by N-methyl-D-aspartate (NMDA)-preferring excitatory amino acid receptors, and thus considerably enhances the synaptic excitation of cells. Application of kainic acid, an agonist of non-NMDA excitatory amino acid receptors, is also widely used to trigger seizures in whole animals, by injection either into the cerebral ventricles or directly into the tissue. The release of endogenous excitatory amino acids can also be triggered by increasing the excitability of neurons with substances that block repolarizing K^+ conductances. Neurons have perhaps hundreds of such K^+ conductances, and numerous antagonists of these channels are effective convulsants, including tetraethylammonium, 4-aminopyridine, and various naturally occurring peptide toxins. Finally, modulators of central cholinergic synaptic function are also employed as convulsants, including direct agonists such as pilocarpine as well as acetylcholinesterase inhibitors, and are believed to act by increasing neuronal excitability.

OTHER CONVULSANTS
While the mechanism of action of these convulsants fits well with the hypothesized balance of synaptic excitation and inhibition in epilepsy-prone brain regions, it is less well understood how other important convulsants exert their effects. Cholera toxin is an activator of adenylate cyclase, and may therefore trigger seizures by mimicking any of the many cellular actions of cAMP and cAMP-dependent protein kinase, including reduction of K^+ conductance and facilitation of transmitter release. Tetanus toxin inhibits the release of both excitatory and inhibitory neurotransmitters. Epileptiform activity elicited by focal application of alumina hydroxide or cobalt has been used as a model for posttraumatic epilepsy, although the mechanisms underlying seizure generation remain unclear. Pentylenetetrazol is a powerful and widely used convulsant whose mechanism of action is also unknown.

REFERENCES
Fischer, R. S. (1989). Animal models of the epilepsies. *Brain Research Reviews, 14,* 245–278.

Löscher, W., & Schmidt, D. (1988). Which animal models should be used in the search for new antiepileptic drugs? A proposal based on experimental and clinical observations. *Epilepsy Research, 2,* 145–181.

Traub, R. D., & Miles, R. (1991). *Neuronal networks of the hippocampus.* New York: Cambridge University Press.

S. M. THOMPSON
University of Maryland

EPILEPSY
EXCITATORY & INHIBITORY SYNAPSES

COOPERATION/COMPETITION

Although philosophers and theologians have long been interested in factors which foster cooperation or competition, usually viewing the former as a social virtue and the latter as selfishness and/or antisocial behavior, social scientists began to show serious interest in the empirical study of these concepts only in the late 1940s and early 1950s. This came about as conflict theorists came to view differences of interest, rather than anger or prejudice, as basic to the more serious forms of conflict. In a related development, researchers in social interaction turned toward theories based on the importance of the rewards and punishments that each person in an interaction can deliver to others, and away from viewpoints stressing the central importance of the attitudes and beliefs of individuals involved in an interaction (Pruitt & Kimmel, 1977).

The terms "cooperation" and "competition" refer essentially to collaborative effort and rivalry respectively, with respect to either mutually desired goals or the means of achieving individual or mutual goals. For example two individuals, one skilled in carpentry and the other an expert painter, may cooperate to build a mutually desired boathouse; or two individuals, each building separate structures, may cooperate in the sharing of tools.

If the cooperation is pure, in the technical sense described by Deutsch (1950), the goal of one individual can be reached only if the other participants also attain their goals. In the case of pure competition, an individual's goals can be attained only if the others do not attain theirs, as for example in a game of poker. However, the extremes of pure cooperation and pure competition are rarely encountered; most situations are a blend of both. For example, although there would appear to be no room for cooperation in a poker game, at a higher level of analysis it becomes evident that the participants must indeed cooperate in order to come together to play the game and abide by its rules. Even in war, which approaches pure competition, elements of cooperation are found in agreements about how to treat prisoners of war and agreements not to use certain types of weaponry such as poison gas or dumdum bullets.

A considerable amount of empirical psychological inquiry into factors which foster cooperation or competition was stimulated by theoretical developments in mathematics and economics, beginning with von Neumann and Morgenstern's work, *Theory of Games and Economic Behavior* (1947). This mathematical game approach generated models which described the behavior of "rational" individuals in certain restricted situations of interdependence. A "rational" individual was taken to be fully knowledgeable about the nature of the interdependence and to be motivated by self-interest, seeking to maximize personal gain and minimize personal loss without regard for the gains and losses of the other parties. Psychologists developed laboratory analogies of these game situations in order to examine the extent to which "real" behavior approached "rational" behavior, and to study the influence of various situational variables (the nature of the interdependence, the presence or absence of communication, etc.) and predispositional variables (the age, sex, cultural background, and motivational predispositions of the participants) on the course of the interaction.

Other approaches to the study of cooperation and competition also were developed, such as: (a) laboratory interactions which mimicked real-life bargaining situations, and which can be traced to the seminal work of economists Siegel and Fouraker (1960); and (b) "locomotion games." The best-known example of the latter is the trucking game devised by Deutsch and Krauss (1960), in which each of two players attempt to move their imaginary trucks from their own factories to their own markets. Cooperative action is necessary for each person to earn a profit in the game, since the two routes from factory to market share a common stretch of narrow road where the two trucks, each going in opposite directions, cannot pass each other. This game led to the realization that the ability to threaten one another makes cooperation very difficult, and that the presence of a communication channel is of little help in bringing about cooperation, once threats have been used.

While the use of such games produced many conclusions about factors affecting cooperative and competitive behavior, the popularity of these games declined in the 1970s. This was in large part due to growing concern about the apparent triviality of many of the game situations, and about the generalizability of the conclusions drawn from such studies to situations in real life. Another concern was the lack of a comprehensive theory to encompass the findings of the myriad studies.

Psychologists interested in social interaction and the effects of group membership have also carried out empirical studies of cooperation and competition, but have generally avoided the laboratory game approach. The classic study in this domain is the Robber's Cave field experiment carried out by Sherif and his colleagues (1961), in which boys at a summer camp were divided into two groups which were then separated. In the first phase of the study, each group was put into situations designed to develop group solidarity and group identity. In the second phase, the two groups participated in a series of contests aimed at producing competitiveness and increased group solidarity. This led to considerable rivalry and even hostility between the groups. The last phase of the study addressed the question of how two hostile groups can be brought into harmony. Simply bringing the groups together for social events only increased hostility. However, when the experimenters created a series of "urgent" problems which required the collaborative efforts of the two groups to overcome—such as a breakdown in the camp water supply—intergroup hostility gradually decreased, new friendships developed across group lines, and a spirit of cooperativeness ensued.

In general, psychological research has shown that cooperative activity is most likely to emerge when the interacting parties share both a common goal and a common means of attaining that goal, while competition is most likely to occur when either the individual goals of the parties involved or the means of obtaining them are incompatible (Raven & Rubin, 1976). Diverse peoples rally together to defeat a common enemy or to overcome a common problem. All too often, unfortunately, once the common threat is vanquished, cooperation declines as well.

REFERENCES

Deutsch, M. (1950). A theory of cooperation and competition. *Human Relations, 2,* 129–152.

Deutsch, M., & Krauss, R. M. (1960). The effect of threat upon interpersonal bargaining. *Journal of Abnormal and Social Psychology, 61,* 181–189.

Pruitt, D. G., & Kimmel, M. J. (1977). Twenty years of experimental gaming: Critique, synthesis, and suggestions for the future. *Annual Review of Psychology, 28,* 363–392.

Raven, B. H., & Rubin, J. Z. (1976). *Social psychology.* New York: Wiley.

Sherif, M., Harvey, O. J., White, B. J., Hood, W. R., & Sherif, C. W. (1961). *Intergroup conflict and cooperation: The Robber's Cave experiment.* Norman: University of Oklahoma Press.

Siegel, S., & Fouraker, L. E. (1960). *Bargaining and group decision making: Experiments in bilateral monopoly.* New York: McGraw-Hill.

von Neumann, J., & Morgenstern, O. (1947). *Theory of games and economic behavior.* Princeton, NJ: Princeton University Press.

SUGGESTED READING

Apfelbaum, E. (1974). On conflicts and bargaining. *Advances in Experimental Social Psychology, 7,* 103–156.

Deutsch, M. (1973). *The resolution of conflict.* New Haven, CT: Yale University Press.

Kidder, L. H., & Stewart, V. M. (1975). *The psychology of intergroup relations.* New York: McGraw-Hill.

Wrightsman, L. S., O'Connor, J., & Baker, N. J. (1972). *Cooperation and competition: Readings on mixed-motive games.* Belmont, CA: Wadsworth.

J. E. ALCOCK
The Australian National University

ALTRUISM
BYSTANDER INVOLVEMENT
SOCIAL CLIMATE RESEARCH

COPING

Coping has been long and widely regarded as having a central role in adaptation, yet it has defied universal agreement on definition and has been the object of little systematic research. Because coping has always been linked to the concept of stress, its recent popularization has been occasioned by a marked growth of interest in the stress concept. The links between stress, impaired functioning, and human misery on the negative side, and health, morale, and accomplishment on the positive side, have gradually led to the recognition that while stress is an inevitable feature of the human condition, how people cope with stress is crucial in whether the adaptational outcome will be negative or positive (Lazarus, 1966). The 1960s and 1970s produced an outpouring of works devoted to coping, including books by Menninger (1963), Horowitz (1976), Moos (1977), Murphy and Moriarty (1976), Haan (1977), Janis and Mann (1977), Monat and Lazarus (1977), and Antonovsky (1979), as well as chapters in books on behavioral medicine and health psychology, and a proliferation of popular self-help treatments of stress management.

Three approaches to coping can be distinguished. The first is a model derived from drive-reinforcement learning theory and is largely centered on animal experimentation (e.g., Levine & Ursin, 1980; Miller, 1980). From this perspective, coping consists of acts such as escape and avoidance, that successfully control aversive environmental conditions, thereby lowering the psychophysiological disturbance or degree of disequilibrium created by the aversive conditions. Among those using this model, primary theoretical and research interest is centered on a set of variables relevant to stress reduction—namely, the predictability and controllability of the environment, and feedback from the environment about the effects of coping. Research focus is on the objective environmental display, observable coping actions, and the psychophysiological response, which includes both autonomic nervous system reactions and adrenal medullary and adrenal cortical hormonal secretions. These physiological changes are commonly assimilated into a unidimensional concept of degree of disequilibrium or arousal.

The preeminent outlook of this approach is Darwinian. Organisms are considered to have evolved through the principle of natural selection, whereby species and individual survival depends on the capacity to learn regularities in the environment and apply this learning in overcoming threats to survival. Coping processes operate to master dangers and satisfy vital needs, thus reducing tension and promoting physiological equilibrium. The principles of coping are regarded as applying to all mammals and perhaps all animals.

The second model of coping is centered on psychoanalytic ego psychology concepts. Coping is understood as a set of ego processes which develop from infancy and are centered on ways of thinking about relationships between the self and the environment. The essential tasks of living are to survive and flourish in the human social environment, and this requires that instinctual drives be gratified while at the same time socially based dangers and constraints are managed realistically.

This model of coping is hierarchical. Coping is regarded as the most advanced or mature set of ego processes; events are handled realistically and flexibly in such a way as to maintain and promote mental and physical health. Defense mechanisms represent more primitive, neurotic processes characterized by greater rigidity and poorer reality testing. Ego failure represents severely disorganized and ineffectual management of the person's relationship with the environment. Prominent exponents of this view are Menninger and others (1963), Haan (1977), and Vaillant (1977). This is the most widely used model among social scientists and is represented empirically in the research of Janis (1958).

Three shortcomings of these traditional models have been suggested. First and foremost, coping has been almost universally equated with adaptational success, as in the expressions "I can cope with it" or "I learned how to cope." In the animal model, coping is defined as behavioral control over the environment through actions that prevent or turn off aversive conditions. Since, in the psychoanalytic ego psychology model, the most successful forms of coping are defined by a realistic or flexible rather than neurotic cognitive or ego process, the process of coping and its outcomes are confounded. That is, regardless of whether the person feels or functions better, coping adequacy is judged by the nature of the thought process itself. One could argue, however, that even so-called neurotic processes such as denial, cognitive avoidance, or intellectualized detachment can have optimal or at least favorable consequences under some conditions, as for example those in which nothing can be done to alter the situation. Indeed, this argument is supported by some research. By prejudging some ego processes as neurotic and others as mature or healthy, one can make a pejorative evaluation about many modes of coping that are both common and functional under certain conditions.

A second shortcoming of certain traditional approaches is that coping success is regarded exclusively in terms of the reduction of bodily disturbance. By definition, coping involves mobilization and effort. An interesting case in point is the Type A syndrome, which has as its cost the increased risk of heart attack. In tune with the physiological insights of Cannon (1935) and Selye (1976), the animal model especially tends to treat stress and emotion solely in terms of increases or decreases of affective or bodily disturbances, thus omitting from concern diverse emotional qualities such as anger, fear, anxiety, guilt, relief, and happiness.

A third shortcoming is that research approaches arising from the above models—especially psychoanalytic ego psychology— have almost exclusively treated coping in research as a static trait or style when, in reality, coping is an active, complex process that changes with the phases of a stressful encounter, and from one context to another. Field studies and clinical observation (Folkman & Lazarus, 1980; Pearlin & Schooler, 1978; Pearlin, Lieberman, Menaghan, & Mullan, 1981) show that the thoughts, actions, and feelings involved in coping depend on the type of stressful encounter being experienced—for example, a work encounter versus a health encounter. The pattern of coping also depends on how the person appraises the situation, as for example whether it is judged as uncontrollable or as open to ameliorative action. In the former instance, coping becomes more heavily oriented toward the regulation of emotion by avoidance, wishful thinking, or detachment, whereas in the latter, problem-focused modes predominate. Drive reinforcement and animal-centered views of stress and coping, in particular, are characterized by very limited versions of the cognitive and emotional richness and complexity characteristic of human adaptation.

With these issues in mind, the Berkeley Stress and Coping Project (Folkman & Lazarus, 1980; Lazarus, 1981; Lazarus & Launier, 1978) offers a third model of coping that emphasizes cognitive appraisal processes and a fluid, transactional, and process-centered approach to coping and its assessment. Coping is viewed as responsive to contextual variables, temporal factors, and feedback from the flow of events which affect adaptational outcomes. It is defined as efforts to manage demands that tax or exceed the person's resources. The word "manage" in this definition means that coping can include toleration of harm or threat, redefinition of past events, acceptance, and putting a positive light on the situation—a set of ways for managing oneself and one's thoughts and feelings—as well as mastery of the environment. By referring to demands that tax or exceed resources, coping is limited to conditions of stress in which one must mobilize to deal with new situations and draw on resources not typically used, and is distinguished from automatized adaptational behaviors that draw upon readily available habits of response involving minimal effort. Two major functions of coping are delineated—problem-focused and emotion-focused—the latter representing cognitive forms of coping that include the traditional defenses. Other writers (Cohen & Lazarus, 1979) have included functions such as maintaining self-esteem, supportive relations with others, and a positive outlook on living.

EVIDENCE FOR THE IMPORTANCE OF COPING

Has research supported the assumption that coping affects long-term morale, social and work functioning, and somatic health, as well as short-term affects or moods, actions to manage stress, and functioning? The answer is a qualified "yes", the qualification being that the evidence is spotty, and the rules and mechanisms underlying such effects far from clear. In fact, when coping is examined in field studies it is either diversely defined and assessed, or it is present only implicitly. For example, Aldrich and Mendkoff (1973) studied aged people who were relocated from one custodial institution to another. As shown in other research of this kind, relocation was highly stressful and produced a marked increment in mortality. However, patients who reacted to the relocation philosophically showed the lowest mortality, followed closely by those who reacted with marked anger. Those who did most poorly were the confused, senile patients and those who reacted with depression.

Studies involving coping more directly have been performed with patients facing surgery, including a classic study by Janis (1958) in which patients with low preoperative fear, presumably because they denied the danger and potential discomfort and failed to do the "work of worrying," reacted postoperatively with great disturbance, as compared with vigilant patients. On the other hand, both Cohen and Lazarus (1973) and George and colleagues (1980) have shown that avoidant/denial modes of coping with surgery facilitated early discharge from the hospital and, in the case of denial, even faster healing of dental surgery wounds. The juxtaposition of these types of findings, and others with conflicting results, leaves the issue of the role of denial and avoidance in adaptational outcome unsettled.

Similar uncertainty is generated by research on the stress of coronary heart disease and other illnesses in which denial-like forms of coping sometimes produce favorable and sometimes unfavorable outcomes. Hackett and Cassem (1975) presented some evidence that attempts to deny that a heart attack is occurring may lead its victims greatly to endanger their lives: With seeming irrationality, they did push-ups or ran up and down stairs to convince themselves that the symptoms experienced were not serious. On the other hand Hackett, Cassem, and Wishnie (1968) found that those who engaged in denial in the immediate postcoronary period had a lower rate of mortality, and returned to work and sexual functioning sooner and more fully, than those who engaged in more vigilant modes of coping. Katz and his colleagues (1970) have observed that denial-like coping is very common in women who have noticed a breast lump; this mode of coping, as with the coronary patients during heart attack, leads them to delay seeking medical attention and hence adds to the danger of metastasis. In a similar vein, Staudenmayer and colleagues (1979) found that asthmatics who deny the implications of early warnings of an asthmatic attack are hospitalized far more often than those who cope vigilantly, presumably because the latter medicate themselves at the first signs of trouble.

It seems clear that denial/avoidant modes of coping have sometimes favorable and sometimes unfavorable outcomes. It is quite possible that what is most adaptive depends on when in the course of a threat such coping modes are activated; early denial and numbing may be useful, if ultimately abandoned for more realistic modes of coping. Also, the content and context of the threat itself—for example, the type of illness as a source of stress—may determine which mode of coping is more adaptive. The actual cognitive processes involved in a given form of coping could also be important. Perhaps denial of fact—for example, a diagnosis of cancer—puts the person at greater risk for damaging outcomes than denial of the implications of the fact. The latter process seems more refractory to being demolished by subsequent evidence, and may indeed be analogous to the illusions we all live by (Lazarus, 1983).

HOW COPING MAY AFFECT HEALTH

There are a number of possible psychophysiological and psychosocial routes by which coping can affect health and well-being, and these have seldom been outlined or thought through systematically. Since the mechanisms underlying divergent adaptational outcomes are probably not exactly the same, it is best to restrict discussion to somatic health.

To examine how coping might affect somatic health, one must first distinguish between short-term effects evident throughout a specific stressful encounter, and long-term effects. Consider the example of an argument between husband and wife. At the end of such a stressful encounter the person being observed may or may not believe that the argument has ended. The fundamental issue dividing the couple may seem to have been resolved; may simply have been suppressed only to emerge again later; may have failed to produce essential communication, although the argument has ended in embrace and temporarily cooled tempers; may leave the person with the feeling of either having won the other over or having had to submerge key personal agendas; or, in the most positive outcome, may have brought a new and satisfying level of understanding, whether or not the couple's appraisal is realistic. Short-term affective consequences and associated physiological response patterns will reflect the nature of the ending or resolution, as experienced by the person whose coping is being explored.

These short-term effects have long-term analogues, as for example the person's overall morale, somatic health or illness, and the overall quality of social and work functioning. To still restrict ourselves to the health consequences, with rare exception these cannot depend on the handling of a single encounter, but rather on the extent to which coping has been effective over the long run in many stressful encounters and arenas of living. To contribute to disease, coping ineptitude must occur repeatedly or chronically, as it were, and probably over a long period of time. Such a generalization flows readily, for example, from the formulations of stress physiologists, for whom many ailments are best regarded as disorders in the tissues produced by excessive or prolonged mobilization to manage stress (Selye and the "diseases of adaptation").

In light of the above, there are three main routes through which the coping process might adversely affect somatic health. First, it can influence the frequency, intensity, duration, and patterning of neurochemical stress reactions in one of three ways: (a) by failing to prevent or ameliorate environmentally noxious or damaging conditions; (b) by failing to regulate emotional distress in the face of uncontrollable harms or threats; or (c) by expressing a set of values and a corresponding life-style that are constantly mobilizing in a harmful way. However, we must recognize that diseases attendant on a specific coping pattern (for example, Type A and the increased risk of heart disease) may be the price paid for other, more salutary psychological outcomes, such as a high level of commitment and satisfaction in sustained effort or competition. Any mode of coping can have mixed outcomes, positive in some respects and negative in others; it is important for researchers to view the problem in its larger frame and to evaluate coping outcomes from the standpoint of multiple consequences and values and in diverse contexts.

Second, coping can affect health negatively, increasing the risk of mortality and morbidity, when it involves excessive use of injurious substances such as alcohol, other drugs, and tobacco, or when it involves the person in activities of high risk to life and limb.

Third, emotion-focused modes of coping can impair health by adversely affecting the management of stress. This principle was illustrated concretely in some of the studies cited earlier. For example, denial or avoidance of thinking about a harm or threat can succeed in lowering emotional distress but simultaneously prevent the person from realistically addressing a problem that is responsive to suitable action. Farberow's observations (1980) on indirect self-destructive behavior in diabetics, and Goldstein's (1980) on hemodialysis patients, are illustrative. The patient fails to do what is prescribed because the serious implications of the disease are terrifying, creating emotion-focused efforts to deny them. To survive and live well, the diabetic and kidney failure patient, among others, must remain actively responsible for a multitude of self-managed activities such as diet, exercise, medication, and treatment, while retaining a positive outlook toward living and refusing to be demoralized by the vulnerabilities created by the disease. Yet the converse coping strategy, vigilant concern for control over the environment, may be counterproductive and distress-producing in a setting such as a hospital that elicits passivity and dependency and leaves the patient little or nothing constructive to do.

Research and theory on the psychology of coping seems to be coming of age in the 1980s. Along with the widespread public and professional intuition that coping is an essential ingredient of life, there is substantial evidence that the coping process does indeed affect adaptational outcomes for better or worse. What is lacking is specific information on which forms of coping have favorable and unfavorable consequences, in given types of persons and under specifiable conditions; also, there is little clarity about how coping produces the adaptational outcomes of interest.

In seeking the answers to these issues, there is a natural convergence between two professional enterprises: the scientific search for valid principles, and the clinical effort to facilitate stress management by interventions designed to help people cope successfully with life stress, including related efforts at education and prevention. This convergence gives the concept of coping its importance to social and biological scientists and to mental health practitioners alike.

REFERENCES

Aldrich, C. K., & Mendkoff, E. (1973). Relocation in the aged and disabled: A mortality study. In B. L. Neugarten (Ed.), *Middle age and aging: A reader in social psychology.* Chicago: University of Chicago Press.

Antonovsky, A. (1979). *Health, stress and coping.* San Francisco: Jossey-Bass.

Cannon, W. B. (1935). Stresses and strains of homeostasis. *American Journal of Medical Science, 189,* 1–14.

Cohen, F., & Lazarus, R. S. (1973). Active coping processes, coping dispositions, and recovery from surgery. *Psychosomatic Medicine, 35,* 375–389.

Cohen, F., & Lazarus, R. S. (1979). Coping with the stresses of illness. In G. C. Stone, F. Cohen, & N. E. Adler (Eds.), *Health psychology: A handbook.* San Francisco: Jossey-Bass.

Farberow, N. L. (Ed.). (1980). *The many faces of suicide.* New York: McGraw-Hill.

Folkman, S., & Lazarus, R. S. (1980). An analysis of coping in a middle-aged community sample. *Journal of Health and Social Behavior, 21,* 219–239.

George, J. M., Scott, D. S., Turner, S. P., & Gregg, J. M. (1980). The effects of psychological factors and physical trauma on recovery from oral surgery. *Journal of Behavioral Medicine, 3,* 291–310.

Goldstein, A. M. (1980). The "uncooperative" patient: Self-destructive behavior in hemodialysis patients. In N. L. Farberow (Ed.), *The many faces of suicide: Indirect self-destructive behavior.* New York: McGraw-Hill.

Haan, N. (1977). *Coping and defending.* New York: Academic Press.

Hackett, T. P., Cassem, N. H., & Wishnie, H. A. (1968). The coronary-care unit: An appraisal of its psychologic hazards. *New England Journal of Medicine, 279,* 1365–1370.

Hackett, T. P., & Cassem, N. H. (1975). Psychological management of the myocardial infarction patient. *Journal of Human Stress, 1,* 25–38.

Horowitz, M. (1976). *Stress response syndromes.* New York: Aronson.

Janis, I. L. (1958). *Psychological stress: Psychoanalytic and behavioral studies of surgical patients.* New York: Wiley.

Janis, I., & Mann, L. (1977). *Decision making: A psychological analysis of conflict, choice and commitment.* New York: Free Press.

Katz, J. L., Weiner, H., Gallagher, T. G., & Hellman, L. (1970). Stress, distress, and ego defenses. *Archives of General Psychiatry, 23,* 131–142.

Lazarus, R. S. (1966). *Psychological stress and the coping process.* New York: McGraw-Hill.

Lazarus, R. S. (1981). The stress and coping paradigm. In C. Eisdorfer, D. Cohen, A. Kleinman, & P. Maxim (Eds.), *Theoretical bases for psychopathology.* New York: Spectrum.

Lazarus, R. S. (1983). The costs and benefits of denial. In S. Breznitz (Ed.), *The denial of stress.* New York: International Universities Press.

Lazarus, R. S., & Launier, R. (1978). Stress-related transactions between person and environment. In L. A. Pervin & M. Lewis (Eds.), *Perspectives in interactional psychology.* New York: Plenum.

Levine, S., & Ursin, H. (1980). *Coping and health.* New York: Plenum.

Menninger, K., Mayman, M., & Pruyser, P. (1963). *The vital balance.* New York: Viking.

Miller, J. R. (1980). Problems of single parent families. *Journal of New York State Nurses Association, 11,* 5–8.

Monat, A., & Lazarus, R. S. (1977). *Stress and coping: An anthology.* New York: Columbia University Press.

Moos, R. H. (1977). *Coping with physical illness.* New York: Plenum.

Murphy, L. B., & Moriarty, A. E. (1976). *Vulnerability, coping, and growth.* New Haven, CT: Yale University Press.

Pearlin, L. I., Lieberman, M. A., Menaghan, E. G., & Mullan, J. T. (1981). The stress process. *Journal of Health and Social Behavior, 22,* 337–356.

Pearlin, L. I., & Schooler, C. (1978). The structure of coping. *Journal of Health and Social Behavior, 19,* 2–21.

Selye, H. (1976). *Stress in health and disease.* Toronto: Butterworth.

Staudenmayer, H., Kinsman, R. A., Dirks, J. F., Spector, S. L., & Wangaard, C. (1979). Medical outcome in asthmatic patients: Effects of airways hyperactivity and symptom-focused anxiety. *Psychosomatic Medicine, 41,* 109–118.

Vaillant, G. D. (1977). *Adaptation to life.* Boston: Little, Brown.

R. S. Lazarus
University of California, Berkeley

CORRELATION METHODS

The topics of correlation and regression are related to the questions of how closely variables are related, and how well the value on one variable, say *Y*, can be predicted, given that the corresponding values on one or more another variables are known. If we are dealing with *bivariate* (i.e., concerned with two variables) linear correlation and regression, a measure of correlation assesses the degree to which the variables X and Y have a linear relationship, and regression refers to the prediction of one variable, say Y, from another, say X, using a linear equation of the form

$$\hat{Y} = b_0 + b_1 X$$

The theoretical developments underlying correlation and regression were published in 1885, and the most commonly encountered measure of correlation was published by Pearson a decade later.

THE CORRELATION COEFFICIENT

The Pearson product-moment correlation coefficient for X and Y is most easily thought of as the mean of the summed cross-products of the z-scores of X and Y; that is,

$$r_{XY} = \frac{1}{N}\sum_i z_{X_i} z_{Y_i} \quad \text{where} \quad z_{X_i} = \frac{X_i - \text{mean of } X}{\text{standard deviation of } X}$$

although it can be written in many other forms. This coefficient takes on a value of +1 if all of the data points (X, Y) fall exactly on a straight line with a positive slope, so that Y increases as X increases, and -1 if they all fall on a straight line with a negative slope. If there is no linear component to the relationship between Y and X, the correlation coefficient will have a value of close to 0.

The size of the correlation coefficient stays the same if either or both of X and Y undergo linear transformations in which each value is multiplied by a constant and another constant is then added to or subtracted from the product. This means that the correlation coefficient stays the same if units are changed; so that the correlation between height and weight would be the same if height was measured in inches or meters.

Even though the correlation coefficient is very commonly used, it is often misinterpreted. Among the many issues to consider are the following:

1. The correlation coefficient is an index of linear relationship, not relationship in general. So a correlation of 0 does not rule out the existence of a systematic nonlinear relationship between the variables.

2. If X and Y are correlated, it does not necessarily follow that there is a direct causal relationship between them; the correlation could occur because of the influence of other variables. For example, among elementary school students, vocabulary size is strongly correlated with height because both are related to chronological age.

3. Although the correlation coefficient is an index of linear relationship, unless the variances of X and Y are equal, r doesn't directly provide information about the nature of the best-fitting linear function. In particular, the slope, or rate of change of Y with X, is given by

$$b_{YX} = r_{XY} s_Y / s_X.$$

that is, the correlation coefficient multiplied by the ratio of the standard deviations. So if in two groups, the rates of change of Y with changes in X are the same, the correlations may well be different if there is more variability in the values of X and Y in one group than in the other. For this reason, r is often referred to as a sample-specific measure. Given a particular linear relationship in a population, the correlation of the scores in a sample will depend on the variability in the sample.

CORRELATIONAL VERSUS EXPERIMENTAL RESEARCH

A distinction is often made between experimental and correlational research. In true experiments, independent variables are manipulated; that is, the assignment of subjects to the level of the independent variable is under control of the experimenter. If the experiment is conducted properly, it is possible to make causal statements about the effect of the independent variable on the dependent variable. In correlational studies, values are simply observed, and no attempt is made to manipulate the independent variables; therefore, it is not possible to make causal statements. For example, suppose we were interested in comparing the effectiveness of two methods of teaching reading. If we were simply to measure the reading ability of students taught by the two methods, we could not be sure any differences that we found were due to the teaching methods themselves, or to other factors "correlated" with the use of the methods. It could be that one of the methods tended to be used more in neighborhoods that had schools with smaller class sizes and families who provided more support to students.

SOME OTHER CORRELATION COEFFICIENTS

A number of other correlation coefficients are also encountered. Some of these are simply the Pearson coefficient applied to specific classes of data. Examples are the *Spearman rank-order correlation coefficient,* which is just the Pearson coefficient applied to ranked data, and the *point-biserial correlation coefficient,* which can be thought of as the regular Pearson coefficient applied to data in which Y is continuous and X is dichotomous (i.e., X takes on only two possible values, such as 0 and 1). The so called "*phi coefficient*" is merely the Pearson coefficient applied to data in which both X and Y are dichotomous.

Several other measures make assumptions of underlying normality to estimate what the correlation would have been if one or both variables had not been artificially dichotomized. For example, suppose we wish to correlate math and verbal ability in a sample. Assume we have scores on a verbal ability test which are reasonably normally distributed but all we know about math ability is whether or not each member of the sample passed a math ability test. If we assume that the underlying dimension of math ability is normally distributed, we can generate the *biserial correlation coefficient,* which we can consider to be an estimate of what the correlation coefficient would be if we had continuous scores on both dimensions. The *tetrachoric correlation coefficient* results if we apply the same logic to two dichotomous variables.

MULTIPLE CORRELATION

Suppose we wish to predict a criterion variable Y from a number of predictor variables $X_1, X_2, \ldots X_p$. For example, we may wish to predict a measure of success in graduate school on the basis of undergraduate grades and verbal and quantitative GRE scores. Using the procedures of multiple regression, we can find the equation of the form

$$\hat{Y} = b_0 + b_1 X_1 + b_2 X_2 + \ldots + b_p X_p$$

that optimally predicts Y. The multiple correlation coefficient, $R_{Y.12..p}$, is simply the Pearson product-moment correlation coefficient between the predicted and actual Y scores. The multiple correlation can take on values between 0 and +1.

PARTIAL CORRELATION

The partial correlation $r_{XY.W}$ is an index of the strength of linear relationship between X and Y with the effects of the variable W "partialed out." It was mentioned earlier that in elementary schools, vocabulary size and height are positively correlated. Obviously, this correlation occurs because both vocabulary size and height are correlated with age for elementary school students. Suppose we wish to statistically control for age and test whether there still is a correlation between height and vocabulary size. To do so, we can calculate the partial correlation, $r_{\text{Vocabulary, Height. Age}}$, which, in effect, removes from both vocabulary size and height the component predictable from age and then correlates the two residuals. It is possible to partial out the effect of more than one variable.

SUGGESTED READING

Cohen, J., & Cohen, P. (1983). *Applied multiple regression/correlation analysis for the behavioral sciences.* Hillsdale, NJ: Erlbaum.

Myers, J. L., & Well, A. D. (1995). *Research design and statistical analysis.* Hillsdale, NJ: Erlbaum.

A. D. WELL
University of Massachusetts

STATISTICS IN PSYCHOLOGY

CORSINI, RAYMOND J. (1914–   )

Raymond J. Corsini, the original editor of *The Corsini Encyclopedia of Psychology and Behavioral Science,* has been declared one of the 500 most significant psychologists in the world since 1850 in the 1997 *Biographical Dictionary of Psychology.* He is the subject of *On the Edge,* a book that demonstrates Corsini's unique style of dealing with problems in counseling and psychotherapy (Dumont, 2000). Corsini was born in 1914. He began as a psychology trainee at the Riker's Island penitentiary in 1935, and by 1953 had quit penology after having been the supervising psychologist of the Department of Correction of Wisconsin, the most prestigious position in the field at that time.

Corsini received a PhD in 1955 at the age of 41. Since then, he has written or edited 35 books, including *Current Psychotherapies,* the foremost text in the field, now in its sixth edition, and the *Dictionary of Psychology,* which contains three times the quantity of material as the next-largest dictionary on the subject. He has written over 100 articles in the literature of psychology. He was a successful industrial organizational psychologist in Chicago and later in counseling and psychotherapy practice in Honolulu, Hawaii. He held professorships at the University of Chicago, the Illinois Institute of Technology, and the University of California. He has been on the board of several journals and has edited one as well. He has also received awards from the James McKeen Cattell Foundation, the Sertoma Educational Award, and the Hawaii Psychological Association's Significant Professional Contribution Award.

STAFF

COUNSELING

The term "counseling" has a generic and a more specific meaning. Generally speaking, counseling represents a set of problem-solving actions—developing a working relationship, assessing the problem, initiating behavior change, maintaining change, and evaluating the outcomes. These generic actions are used by counselors working in a variety of professions including business, law, education, health, and so on. Thus, we have financial counselors, legal counsel, academic advisors, and nutritional consultants—all identified as performing counseling. From a more specific stance, counseling also represents a professional identity and tradition with ethical codes, licensure procedures, scholarly journals, professional organizations, and academic requirements. Counseling in the professional sense, the topic of this narrative, has been associated with education and medicine, providing the historical traditions through which counseling has evolved. Counseling as an educational intervention has been associated with schools and guidance programs, whereas counseling as a more medically oriented intervention has become interchangeable with psychotherapy practiced in clinical settings. While such diversity is viewed as a strength by some, others note the lack of consensus reflected in professional identity problems.

COUNSELING AS EDUCATION

Counseling as education—or guidance, as it is often called—is related to the historical use of the term "counseling." Dictionary definitions of counseling emphasize giving advice and exchanging information. Since the earliest times, people have sought advice and counsel—from Greek philosophers, Old Testament prophets, and medicine men.

Although such earlier antecedents can be identified, guidance developed in the industrialized Middle West and East. The merger of vocational guidance and psychological testing established it as an important foundation of counseling. Before the development of testing, vocational guidance relied on vocational education that stressed occupational information and advice. With the development of testing in the areas of ability, interests, occupations, and personality, vocational guidance obtained a scientific means to realize its commonsense notion of improving the worker-occupation relationship. As articulated by the leaders of vocational guidance, perhaps most persuasively by Parsons in *Choosing a Vocation,* (1909), worker-occupation relationships depended on a suitable match between the worker and the job. This match was predicated on the ability to gather accurate information about the individual, his or her abilities and interests, and the job itself. Scientific methods helped transform guidance workers into professionals, and established the respectability of vocational counseling and facilitated its acceptance by public institutions such as school systems and later the Veterans Administration. Such a transformation was largely carried out at the University of Minnesota through the pioneering work of Patterson and his colleagues and students, especially Williamson.

In the 1950s and 1960s, counseling as guidance—while less popular than psychotherapy—was stimulated by the development of professional organizations (e.g., American Personnel and Guidance Association and now the American Counseling Association) and the reemergence of the importance of schooling (Russian Sputnik I) and work (the Vocational Rehabilitation Act of 1954). As a result, there was a great demand for school counselors (the National Defense Act of 1958) and rehabilitation counselors. In response, professional organizations lobbied for funds, and later established accreditation programs (for example, Council for the Accreditation of Counseling and Related Programs) for the preparation of counselors. Through their respective journals, concerns of counselors were given a voice.

On the other hand, another organization with members representing the guidance tradition—originally the Division of Counseling and Guidance, and renamed in 1952 as the Division of Counseling Psychology (American Psychological Association)—competed for psychological services (e.g., the Veterans Administration). These activities contributed to the further decline of the guidance tradition, and to a separation of counseling psychologists with doctoral-level training from school and rehabilitation counselors with subdoctoral-level training.

During this same time period, advances in social sciences brought significant conceptual developments (self-concept theory, stage theory) that transformed vocational guidance into career development. Today the emphasis is on addressing the theoretical and empirical inadequacies of this tradition that neglected the role of gender, race, class, sexual orientation, and disability. New programs are being developed to address these deficiencies such as the school-to-work transition movement.

COUNSELING AS THERAPY

Around 1940, the dominance of the guidance model began to erode; by the end of the decade it was replaced by psychotherapy, an intervention often associated with a more medically oriented setting. A number of factors contributed to the decline. Part of the downfall coincided with social changes brought on by the end of the Depression and the beginning of World War II. People were confronted with rapid social change that affected their lives broadly.

Effects went beyond educational or occupational problems as people sought help with all types of personal adjustment issues. In this "Age of Psychotherapy" the publication of *Counseling and Psychotherapy* (1942) by Rogers was important. Rogers, trained as a clinical psychologist, brought psychotherapy from the medical clinic to nonmedical practitioners. He transformed therapy as a medical intervention by framing therapy in terms of a humanistic philosophy, an approach more congenial to counselors.

This psychotherapy tradition represented by Rogers had multiple sources. Perhaps the most central experience for Rogers was his work with clients. From these experiences, Rogers formulated and reformulated his approach to counseling and psychotherapy. Although there have been changes and shifts of emphasis, the basic outlook has been a person-centered approach in which the self-determination capacities of the client are the focus of attention, concern, activity, and acceptance conveyed through a therapeutic relationship. Like Parsons' conceptual contribution to the guidance tradition, Rogers focused on individual assets. Both of these traditions, guidance and therapy, highlight the worldview of counseling, a focus on strengths rather than pathology.

Since Rogers, there have been numerous counseling and psychotherapy approaches advanced, from psychoanalysis to behavioral counseling and psychotherapy. As the twenty-first century begins, there is renewed emphasis on counseling that mainly focuses on cognitive-behavioral treatment. For psychotherapy, the challenge in a rapidly changing health care market is to document the effectiveness of counseling practices, especially the external validity of our treatments (e.g., racial/ethnic minorities).

CHALLENGES

Up to this point, counseling has been evolving as a field through education, vocational guidance, and psychotherapy. Although counseling often has multiple meanings, it continues to represent a disciplined mode of action of working with people. Counseling faces numerous future challenges, but diversity and managed health care appear to have the largest potential for influencing the nature of counseling in the new millennium. The growing diversity of our population and the inadequacy of our traditional counseling worldview has stimulated a multicultural revolution. Beginning with the unmet need for counseling women, counselors have struggled to develop approaches that are effective with various oppressed groups in our society (racial and ethnic minorities; gay, lesbian, bisexual, and transgender identified individuals; and persons with disabilities). The traditional counseling competencies—relationship, assessment, interviewing, intervention, and research skills—need a cultural transformation from a set of competencies reflecting a universal cultural myth to a set of cultural practices appropriate to a worldview of multiple perspectives. The other challenge, managed care, has focused attention on examining the effectiveness of counseling practices. In putting these challenges together, the big question is not if counseling works, but if counseling works for the neglected groups of our society.

REFERENCES

Parsons, F. (1909). *Choosing a vocation.* Boston: Houghton Miflin.

Rogers, C. R. (1942). *Counseling and psychotherapy.* Boston: Houghton Miflin.

Super, D. E. (1955). Transition from vocational guidance to counseling psychology. *Journal of Counseling Psychology, 2,* 3–9.

SUGGESTED READING

Brown, S. D., & Lent, R. W. (2000). *Handbook of counseling psychology.* New York: Wiley.

Nathan, P. D., & Gorman, J. M. (1998). *A guide to treatments that work.* New York: Oxford University Press.

Sue, D. W., & Sue, D. (1998). *Counseling the culturally different: Therapy and practice* (3rd ed.). New York: Wiley.

G. L. STONE
University of Iowa

OCCUPATIONAL COUNSELING PSYCHOTHERAPY

COUNSELING PSYCHOLOGY: HISTORY

Counseling Psychology is Division 17 of the American Psychological Association (APA), in recognition of that division's members' special interests and competence. Within the APA, counseling psychology is also identified as one of the major areas of applied psychology, along with clinical, industrial/organizational, and school psychology. These labels accord with those of the American Board of Professional Psychology, an affiliated but independently incorporated body, whose award of diplomate status certifies that the recipients are professionally qualified to practice in one of the four specialties. Periodically, information of this kind is published by the APA in its *Directory.* In 1981, for example, Counseling Psychology had 2,595 members, ranking seventh in membership among 38 APA divisions. Divisional and specialty interests are served by two periodicals: the *Journal of Counseling Psychology,* published by APA, and *The Counseling Psychologist,* subsidized by the dues of Division 17's members.

The APA was reorganized into a prototype of its current divisional structure during and immediately following World War II. Records of these events are cited in Winfield Scott's "The History of Counseling Psychology, 1945–1963," published in 1980 as the adaptation of a report in 1963 to the division's Executive Committee. Prior to the reorganization, a merger had been effected between the American Association for Applied Psychology and the APA. Under two other names, Counseling Psychology became a charter division.

First identified unofficially as the Division of Personnel Psychologists in 1945, a charter Division of Counseling and Guidance held its initial public business meeting as part of the APA's annual convention at the University of Pennsylvania in 1946. Edmund Williamson acted as the division's first president; John Darley, as its secretary-treasurer. By-laws of the new division, drafted by Darley, had been adopted by mail ballot of its charter members in May 1946.

The origins of Counseling Psychology are implied in these earlier titles. Most of the division's early leaders were university teachers and administrators, training and supervising others for activities that had become generally known as student personnel work in colleges and universities and as guidance in elementary and secondary schools. By 1946, the counseling of students in face-to-face interviews had come to be regarded as an essential part of both guidance and student personnel services.

By 1946, moreover, counseling and guidance psychology had achieved additional synthesis. During the Great Depression of the 1930s, research as part of the Minnesota Employment Stabilization Research Institute and the Maryland youth study had demonstrated how psychometric methods might be applied in the matching of people and jobs. During World War II many of the division's early leaders had served with the U.S. armed forces, either in or out of uniform, helping to develop and implement programs of personnel classification, selection, and training. Toward the end of the war the Veterans Administration (VA) was assigned the mission of assisting millions of veterans to return to civilian life. Lack of adequately trained personnel for this work forced the VA to seek outside help. The VA's Division of Vocational Rehabilitation and Education supplemented its internal counseling services by contracting with colleges and universities to provide for the vocational-educational advisement of veterans, so as to guide them into appropriate programs of education or training. As Dreese pointed out in 1949, numerous community and college counseling centers, recently established, owed their existence to an initial VA subsidy.

Under a second mandate, to assist returning veterans with emotional problems, the VA's Division of Medicine and Neurology also had established within its hospitals and outpatient clinics the post of clinical psychologist, a move accompanied by the creation in 1946 of the Division of Clinical Psychology (Division 12), another part of the reorganized APA. A number of doctoral training programs for clinical psychologists were established within university departments of psychology. In 1950, Raimy's *Training in Clinical Psychology,* reporting an APA-sponsored conference, was published; it recommended the content, standards, and modes of doctoral training for that specialty.

By 1950, negotiations were underway among representatives from the APA's Divisions 12 and 17 and the VA's Central Office staff in Clinical Psychology to create in the medical setting yet another position for psychologists. That could happen if the Division of Counseling and Guidance were to explicate and upgrade its standards for training and practice to the level that Clinical Psychology had set for itself. The staff person would help emotionally disturbed veterans to obtain and maintain suitable gainful employment outside the hospital. Since the proposed activities ostensibly required something other than knowledge of neurological impairment and psychopathology, the new position would serve as a lever to move all psychology out from under psychiatry's control.

The plan was set in motion under the divisional presidencies of Hugh Bell, John Darley, and Gilbert Wrenn. The work of Division 17's Committee on Counselor Training headed by Francis Robinson was partitioned into assignments for two subcommittees: one on PhD training programs chaired by Edward Bordin, and the other on practicum training under Donald Super. Draft reports by the two subcommittees then were reviewed by a larger task force, which also decided upon Division 17's current title of Counseling Psychology. All this took place during an invitational conference at Northwestern University in September 1951, convened by President Wrenn and attended by some 60 leading psychologists interested in vocational guidance and in counseling.

Super's article "Transition: From Vocational Guidance to Counseling Psychology" attached considerable importance to the conference, calling attention to the creation of "a new job title . . . of *counseling psychologist* . . . and a new field . . . of *counseling psychology.*" Super's paper, the lead article for Volume 2 of the *Journal of Counseling Psychology,* chronicled the occasion and provided useful historical sketches of events prior to and immediately following it.

Public announcement of the change in title at the APA's annual convention in 1951 brought quick results. A brief chronology of subsequent events may be found in the preface of an article on "Counseling Psychology as a Specialty" written by the division's Committee on Definition, accepted by the Executive Committee, and published with their approval in the *American Psychologist* in 1956. As reported there, "the term was adopted by the Division in 1951 and was given currency in 1952, with the publication of the two [subcommittee] reports. In 1952, also, the Division changed its official title from that of Counseling and Guidance to Counseling Psychology." Both subcommittees' reports, each containing the words "counseling psychologists" in its title, were published in the *American Psychologist.*

"Almost simultaneously," the 1956 article continued, the VA announced—also in a 1952 issue of the *American Psychologist*—its creation of "two major positions": counseling psychologist (vocational) and counseling psychologist (VR&E). As implied by its new title, the latter position remained within the VA's Division of Vocational Rehabilitation and Education. Significantly, the position retained its minimal requirement of subdoctoral training. The former position was a distinctly new one, however, established as anticipated under medical auspices to provide for the vocational counseling and rehabilitation of veterans with emotional problems. Moreover, training requirements for the new post were to be on a par with those of the clinical psychologist.

The *Journal of Counseling Psychology* began publication in 1954, with Wrenn as editor and Frank M. Fletcher, Jr., as managing editor. In 1955 the American Board of Examiners in Professional Psychology, as it was then known, obligingly changed the title of its diploma in "counseling and guidance" to "counseling psychology." Super's 1955 article also mentioned a report in 1954 by the APA's Education and Training Board on "(APA-approved) doctoral training programs in clinical and counseling psychology." This too appeared in the *American Psychologist.*

The division's ad hoc Committee on Definition, created in 1954 by President Francis Robinson, included ex-presidents Wrenn, Super, and Milton Hahn, and president-elect Edward Bordin. Harold Pepinsky, who chaired the committee, was to become president-elect in the following year. In addition to sketching the historical development of counseling psychology, the committee's report described the specialty's current status and discussed its future. Counseling psychologists were reported to be at work in a variety of organizational settings, helping individuals by varied means to achieve harmonious relations with their environments. Though special kinds of competence were identified for this work—notably in distinguishing between the activities of clinical and counseling psychologists—"no distinct cleavage" was reported. Here and elsewhere, in discussing the present and future status of counseling psychology, the committee—reflecting its members' own diverse viewpoints—took a conciliatory stance.

Looking back on the "Landmark years and the growing edge" of counseling psychology, Wrenn described those events of 1951 through 1956 as "bearing directly on the identity of the counseling psychologist" (1980). As he indicated, however, the idea of counseling psychology's collective unity and vitality that the early documents conveyed was soon to be tested: "One of the spasms of alarm aroused by Sputnik resulted in Congressional action in 1958 to establish the National Defense Education Act . . . that permitted thousands to select university training in counseling at both the master and doctoral levels . . . and many counselors were born at the doctoral level who were not psychologists" (1980). Curiously, that source of competition for counseling psychologists' services was not voiced as a major concern by Division 17's early leaders. More evidently at issue were counseling psychology's "legitimate areas and methods of practice" vis-à-vis those of psychiatry, social work, and especially clinical psychology. This definition of the situation was explicit in Hahn's presidential address, "Counseling psychology" (1955).

Graduate Education in Psychology (1959), the report of a conference edited by Roe and others, made the dominant view of the conferees quite clear on the level of training for psychologists to be endorsed by the APA. Minimally, the doctoral level was to be required. Through their benign neglect in failing to sponsor the training of psychologists at subdoctoral levels, both the APA and the Division of Counseling Psychology ceded control of training for rehabilitation counselors to organized social work and education, and control of training for elementary and secondary school counselors to education. In consequence, most graduate departments of psychology and their students were denied access to training funds in these specialties, as for instance provided under the Vocational Rehabilitation Act of 1954 and the National Defense Act of 1958.

To complicate matters, toward the end of the 1950s jurisdictional disputes arose over the entitlements of clinical and counseling psychology. Despite the youth of both groups as visible specialties under APA sponsorship, counseling psychology was the newer arrival and less well entrenched politically; hence its legitimacy could be the more expediently questioned. In 1959 the APA's Education and Training Board commissioned such an investigation. Its special task force consisted of Irwin Berg, chair, Harold Pepinsky, and Joseph Shoben. Pepinsky and Shoben were ex-presidents of Division 17; Berg was soon to become president-elect. Their report, "The status of counseling psychology," was given in 1969 to the Education and Training Board, which recommended publication of the document in the *American Psychologist.* The report remained unpublished until 1980, however, when it was included in John Whiteley's compendium of published and hitherto unpublished documents comprising *The History of Counseling Psychology.*

Though its public distribution was suppressed, the report did elicit an immediate flurry of responses. The division's Executive Committee in 1960 appointed immediate ex-president Leona Tyler as chair of an ad hoc investigative committee that included ex-president Wrenn and future president David Tiedeman, "to write . . . a positive statement deducing conclusions from documented evidence." Whereas Berg's task force had claimed to have "clear evidence that counseling psychology is declining," Tyler's committee found the specialty in good health and enjoying a distinctive identity, a normal rate of growth, a considerable demand for well-prepared counseling psychologists, and "a deep professional obligation" to meet the evident social need for their services. Again, whereas Berg's group had recommended counseling psychology's assimilation into other seemingly more viable areas—notably as part of a broader clinical psychology—Tyler and colleagues recommended a number of means to enhance its current strength and distinctiveness.

Submitted in 1961, the Tyler report on "The Current Status of Counseling Psychology" was approved by successive executive committees of the division during the presidencies of Harold Seashore and Robert Waldrop. This statement was first published in 1964 as an appendix to *The Professional Preparation of Counseling Psychologists' Report of the 1964 Greyston Conference,* edited by Thompson and Super. It and three other papers on the topic also were reissued in *The History of Counseling Psychology* in 1980.

Berg's document does seem to have been a catalyst for constructive soul searching on the part of Division 17's leadership in the early 1960s, an inference supported by Thompson and Super's edited *Report* on the conference at Greyston Center held in 1964. Sixty invited persons attended, representing training and service programs in counseling psychology, government agencies in a position to fund and monitor such programs, and the APA and American Personnel and Guidance Association as concerned professional organizations.

Super and Thompson's prefatory chapters summarizing the conference, its planning, and the recommendations that grew out of it, attest to counseling psychologists' expanding mission yet prevailing "unity in diversity." The invited addresses also reaffirm counseling psychology's distinctive contributions, in particular those based on counseling psychologists' training and experience in vocational psychology. The conference was planned over the course of the years 1960 to 1963 under the presidencies of Seashore, Waldrop, and Thompson. Although it was actually held during Irwin Berg's presidency, he is not listed among the participants.

A well-organized and more complete account of these events is contained in Whiteley's *History,* appearing originally in the *Counseling Psychologist* and published as a book in 1980. Editor White-

ley's introductory chapter helpfully outlined, summarized, and commented upon source materials originally contributed by other authors between 1952 and 1978. Whiteley also mentioned the launching in 1968 of *The Counseling Psychologist,* designed as a house organ of the division and issued periodically "for critical analysis and commentary on major professional problems" and as "a forum for . . . matters of professional concern."

The last two chapters in the *History* were reports from the Professional Affairs Committees of Division 17, representing divergent views of counseling psychology as a specialty and originally written at different times following the Greyston conference. The first of these chapters, by Jean-Pierre Jourdaan, future president Roger Myers, Wilbur Layton, and Henry Morgan, was excerpted from their edited booklet *The Counseling Psychologist* and published under APA copyright in 1968. It opened with a definition of "psychologist, counseling" adapted from the 1965 description provided in the *Dictionary of Occupational Titles.* Contents of the document were consistent with those contained in the Greyston Conference *Report.* The booklet, emphasizing the preparation and work of the counseling psychologist, was accepted by the division's Executive Committee.

The last chapter, "Counseling Psychology, the Psychoeducational Model, and the Future," was written by Allen E. Ivey as the chair of a later Committee on Professional Affairs and was "intended to integrate the several papers of the Committee's long report." The document was originally published in 1976. In reprinting the paper, Whiteley described it as controversial and reported that the division's Executive Committee had refused to endorse it. Apparently, if counseling psychologists were not to be confused with clinicians, they were also not to be identified as a kind of professional educator.

In the latter 1970s, issues of *The Counseling Psychologist* also were devoted to the specialty's present and projected identities. Reedited and reprinted in 1980 as *The Present and Future of Counseling Psychology* and coedited by Whiteley and Fretz, this collection of statements usefully extended Whiteley's edited *History* of 1980. In the opening chapter of the second volume, Fretz presented a succinct account of events conspicuously impinging on counseling psychology as a specialty in the 1970s.

First was "a tightening employment market" for psychologists with an accompanying demand for "higher credentials," in which counseling psychologists "often find themselves categorically excluded from a variety of internships and positions regardless of skills because they graduated from counseling, rather than clinical psychology, programs." Second, counseling psychologists had been grossly underrepresented on the APA's governing boards and committees, hence unfairly discriminated against in such matters as accreditation and governmental funding. Fretz could "note optimistically" that constructive changes in these matters were occurring. Third, however, the public image of counseling psychology was still clouded by "stereotypes and misperceptions."

As ex-president of Division 17, Samuel Osipow was invited to comment on the discussions of professional identity in *The Present and Future of Counseling Psychology.* His chapter "Will the real counseling psychologist please stand up?" pinpoints a continuing source of invidious comparison between counseling and clinical psychology. The latter term, "clinical," is conventionally used as an adjective. Hence, the phrase "clinical psychology" connotes a set of diverse scientific and professional activities. In the phrase "counseling psychology," however, the word "counseling" becomes a noun, such that the entire phrase connotes "counseling" only as a specific activity in which that kind of psychologist engages.

Three prominent actions by leaders in Division 17 were taken to remedy the problems to which Fretz and Osipow had alluded. One, described in "A brief history of the Council of Counseling Psychology training programs," was written by Fretz and is to be found in the *Manual of Policies and Procedures* for the Council (1982). As reported there, the Council for Counseling Psychology began its work in 1975 and has since developed a set of by-laws, active liaison with a variety of other pertinent groups, and such other activities as an annual survey of counseling psychology programs. Successive chairs of the council have included Fretz, Lyle Schmidt, Naomi Meara, and David Dixon.

From 1979 to 1981 another pivotal activity was conducted with Division 17's sponsorship, under presidents Carl Thoresen, Allen Ivey, Donald Blochor, and Henry Borow. Directed and coordinated throughout by ex-president Norman Kagan, the activity culminated in an impressive document, "Counseling Psychology—The Next Decade," published in 1980 as a whole issue of the *Counseling Psychologist* and coedited by Kagan and the chairs of four committees: Bruce Fretz, Mary Tanney, Lenore Harmon, and Roger Myers. Principal sections of the document include reports on "Perspective and Definition" (Fretz), "The Marketplace" (Tanney), "Scientific Affairs" (Harmon), and "Education and Training" (Myers). Kagan's introductory chapter describes the lengthy and painstaking process by which the document was produced. An invited address by John Holland on "Planning for Alternative Futures" set the stage for the committees' chapters.

"Counseling Psychology—The Next Decade" takes account of major societal changes and their implications for counseling psychology. For example, a disproportionately large number of elderly persons in the United States creates new demands for services. Because governmental funding for these and other services has dropped off sharply, counseling psychologists have had to look elsewhere for financial support. A third important activity along these lines is well underway. In a 1983 issue of *The Counseling Psychologist,* articles by Osipow, Toomer, and Lacey attest to new challenges for counseling psychologists in business and industrial settings. *The Handbook of Vocational Psychology* (1983), edited by counseling psychologists Bruce Walsh and Osipow, has described a revitalized vocational psychology and its import for the training and services of counseling psychologists. In this context, counseling psychologist Donald Super's chapter, "The History and Development of Vocational Psychology: A Personal Perspective," provides an illuminating postscript to his 1955 article.

REFERENCES

American Psychological Association. (1956). Counseling psychology as a specialty: Report of the committee on definition, division of counseling psychology. *American Psychologist, 11,* 282–285.

Dreese, M. (1949). Present and future plans of college guidance centers operating under VA contracts as related to pre-VA status of center. *American Psychologist, 7,* 297.

Hahn, M. E. (1955). Counseling psychology. *American Psychologist, 10,* 279–282.

Raimy, V. C. (Ed.). (1970). *Training in clinical psychology.* New York: Prentice-Hall. (Original work published 1950)

Roe, A., Gustad, J. W., Moore, B. V., Ross, S., & Skodak, M. (Eds.). (1959). *Graduate education in psychology.* Washington, DC: American Psychological Association.

Scott, C. W. (1980). The history of counseling psychology: 1945–1963. In J. M. Whiteley (Ed.), *The history of counseling psychology.* Monterey, CA: Brooks/Cole.

Super, D. E. (1980). Transition: From vocational guidance to counseling psychology. In J. M. Whiteley (Ed.), *The history of counseling psychology.* Monterey, CA: Brooks/Cole. (Reprinted from *Journal of Counseling Psychology, 2,* 3–9. 1955)

Thompson, A. S., & Super, D. E. (Eds.). (1964). *The professional preparation of counseling psychologists. Report of the 1964 Greyston Conference.* New York: Bureau of Publications, Teachers College, Columbia University.

Tyler, L. E. (1969/1961). *The work of the counselor.* New York: Appleton-Century-Crofts; Prentice-Hall. (Original work published 1953)

Walsh, W. B., & Osipow, S. H. (1983). *Handbook of vocational psychology.* Hillsdale, NJ: Erlbaum.

Wrenn, C. G. (1980). Landmark years and the growing edge. In J. M. Whiteley & B. R. Fretz (Eds.), *The present and future of counseling psychology.* Monterey, CA: Brooks/Cole.

SUGGESTED READING

American Psychological Association. (1980). Division of Counseling Psychology, Committee on Counselor Training. Recommended standards for training counseling psychologists at the doctorate level. In J. M. Whiteley (Ed.), *The history of counseling psychology.* Monterey, CA: Brooks/Cole. (Reprinted from *American Psychologist, 7,* 175–181, 1952)

American Psychological Association. (1980). Division of Counseling Psychology, Committee on Counselor Training. The practicum training of counseling psychologists. In J. M. Whiteley (Ed.), *The history of counseling psychology.* Monterey, CA: Brooks/Cole. (Reprinted from *American Psychologist, 7,* 182–188, 1952)

Bell, H. M. (1940). *Matching youth and jobs.* Washington, DC: American Council on Education.

Brewer, J. M. (1942). *History of vocational guidance.* New York: Harper & Row.

Darley, J. G., Paterson, D. G., & Peterson, I. E. (1933). *Occupational testing and the public employment service.* Bulletin of the Employment Stabilization Research Institute, Additional Publication no. 19. Minneapolis, MN: University of Minnesota Press.

Ganikos, M. L. (Ed.). (1979). *Counseling the aged: A training syllabus for educators.* Washington, DC: American Personnel and Guidance Association.

Harmon, L. W., Birk, J. M., Fitzgerald, L. E., & Tanney, M. F. (Eds.). (1978). *Counseling women.* Monterey, CA: Brooks/Cole.

Lacey, D. E. (in press). Industrial counseling psychologists—The professional road not taken. *The Counseling Psychologist.*

Osipow, S. H. (in press). Counseling psychology: Applications in the world of work. *The Counseling Psychologist.* (Original work published 1982)

Pedersen, P. B., Lonner, W. J., & Draguns, J. G. (Eds.). (1976). *Counseling across cultures.* Honolulu: University of Hawaii.

Pepinsky, H. B., Hill-Frederick, K., & Epperson, D. L. (1980). The *Journal of Counseling Psychology* as a matter of policies. In J. M. Whiteley (Ed.), *The history of counseling psychology.* Monterey, CA: Brooks/Cole, 1980. (Reprinted from *Journal of Counseling Psychology, 25,* 483–498, 1978)

Rogers, C. R. (1942). *Counseling and Psychotherapy.* Boston: Houghton Mifflin.

Toomer, J. E. (in press). Counseling psychologists in business and industry. *The Counseling Psychologist.* (Original work published 1982)

Williamson, E. G. (1939). *How to counsel students.* New York: McGraw-Hill.

Williamson, E. G., & Darley, J. G. (1937). *Student personnel work.* New York: McGraw-Hill.

Wrenn, C. G. (1980). Birth and early childhood of a journal. In J. M. Whiteley (Ed.), *The history of counseling psychology.* Monterey, CA: Brooks/Cole. (Reprinted from *Journal of Counseling Psychology, 13,* 485–488)

H. B. PEPINSKY
Ohio State University

COUNSELING
COUNSELING PSYCHOLOGY
PSYCHOTHERAPY, HISTORICAL ROOTS OF
PSYCHOLOGY, HISTORY OF

COUNSELING PSYCHOLOGY: PAST AND PRESENT

Counseling Psychology has been defined as "a general practice and health service-provider specialty in professional psychology" (APA, 1999, p. 589). Counseling psychology blends science and practice such that science informs and strengthens the practice of counseling psychology, and practice in turn informs science. Counseling psychology focuses on normal as well as atypical or disordered developmental issues pertaining to individuals, couples, families, groups, and organizations. Thus, counseling psychologists focus on a wide range of problems across the life span including, but not limited to, vocational choice and career planning, personal/social adjustment, physical health and disabilities, relationship and marital/family difficulties, learning and skill deficits, stress management and coping, multicultural and cross-cultural issues, substance abuse, personality dysfunction, and systemic or organizational problems. Counseling psychology focuses on people's strengths to help resolve problems, alleviate physical/psychological distress and maladjustment, and improve coping and psychological well-being. Counseling psychologists use a broad array of therapeutic procedures, including individual, family, group, and systemic counseling; psychodiagnostic assessment; psychoeducational and preventive programming; crisis intervention; and organizational consulting. In addition, counseling psychologists use quantitative and qualitative methodologies to evaluate the efficacy of therapeutic interventions as well as to continually develop scientific knowledge bases to empirically support and extend the practice of counseling psychology (APA, 1999).

Counseling psychology has a long and distinguished history (e.g., Heppner, Casas, Carter, & Stone, 2000; Whiteley, 1980). Discussions of the origins of the profession often include the work of Parsons and the vocational guidance movement in the early 1900s; vocational psychology has evolved over the century and today represents a central and active focus of counseling psychology (see Heppner, 2000). A second root of the profession was what was referred to as the mental hygiene movement of the early 1900s, which also has grown to be a core component of counseling psychology's focus on promoting psychological health. Closely related is a third historical root, a focus on nonmedical perspectives within counseling, as illustrated by the work of Rogers. Again, this perspective continues today as counseling psychologists focus on the strengths of individuals as well as on restoring and promoting physical and psychological well-being. A fourth historical root is the psychometric movement and study of individual differences, which grew considerably during both World Wars, and ultimately led to a wide range of opportunities for counseling psychologists in assessment and training. In the last 20 years, counseling psychology has expanded the study of individual differences into a significant focus on diversity issues, including issues pertaining to racial/ethnic minorities, gender, sexual orientation, persons with disabilities, and the elderly.

Counseling psychologists engage in a wide range of research which traditionally has emphasized quantitative methods, but more recently also includes qualitative methods, both of which are increasingly seen as "essential for important advances in the field of counseling" (Heppner, Kivlighan, & Wampold, 1999, p. 11). Periodic reviews of the counseling psychology literature reveal a vast and ever-changing knowledge base (e.g., Borgen, 1984; Brown & Lent, 1992; Gelso & Fassinger, 1990; Heppner et al., 2000). Significant areas of research within the last 20 years pertain to counseling interventions, process, and outcomes; career development and counseling; multicultural counseling; issues of gender and sexual orientation; and supervision. Methodological diversity and sophistication are increasing with each decade, resulting in important new knowledge that is furthering the development and refinement of counseling psychology theory and practice (Heppner et al., 2000). Clearly, the discipline has an active and successful research agenda, and cutting-edge research regularly appears in rigorous, mature, and stable journals. For example, the *Journal of Counseling Psychology* started 45 years ago, has an excellent reputation for rigorous empirical research, and is one of the most widely circulated APA journals. *The Counseling Psychologist* celebrated its 30th birthday in 1999, and is widely cited not only in counseling psychology but also in psychology and other disciplines, both in the United States and internationally (Flores, Rooney, Heppner, Browne, & Wei, 1999). The *Journal of Vocational Behavior* is almost 30 years old and continues to publish some of the best research in vocational psychology.

Professional organizations serve an important function not only in the changing roles in the practice and training of counseling psychologists, but also in the management and direction of the profession within the broader disciplines of psychology and education as well as in light of changing societal needs. Perhaps the most central organization within counseling psychology is the Division of Counseling Psychology of the APA (Division 17), which celebrated its 50th anniversary in 1996. Division 17, consisting of around 3,000 members, represents a vital core of counseling psychology. Its central mission is to promote the specialty of counseling psychology. The Division is governed by an elected executive board and fosters grassroots participation and governance within six sections: The Society for Vocational Psychology; the Section for the Advancement of Women; the Section for Lesbian, Gay, and Bisexual Awareness; the Section of Ethnic and Racial Diversity; the Counseling Health Psychology Section; and the Section on Independent Practice.

In the mid 1970s, the Council of Counseling Psychology Training Programs (CCPTP) was established to promote the doctoral training of counseling psychologists. Initially CCPTP focused on providing information about setting up a training program; it later became more active within the national domain of professional psychology as well. Today CCPTP provides the best vehicle to address day-to-day concerns as well as larger training issues within counseling psychology. The Association of Counseling Center Training Agencies (ACCTA) was established in 1978 to provide a forum to discuss common education and training issues in university counseling centers. Starting with 20 members, ACCTA now has over 120 members and has become a strong force within organized psychology with regard to pre- and postdoctoral internship training. In essence, within the last 10 years counseling psychology has evolved beyond any one organization, although Division 17 formally represents the specialty of counseling psychology. In 1999, Jean Carter spearheaded the development of a Council of the Specialty of Counseling Psychology to further enhance the collaboration among the various organizations in counseling psychology.

In essence, counseling psychology represents an applied health service provider specialty that blends practice and science to further both science and practice. Counseling psychologists address a wide range of problems across the life span within individuals, groups, and organizations, primarily with a developmental focus. The specialty of counseling psychology is further enhanced by (a) scholarly research that advances the knowledge base of the profession, and (b) several national organizations which not only promote practice and training in the discipline, but also the management and direction of the profession. In short, counseling psychology is a strong and vibrant specialty, which promotes the well-being of a wide range of people across the life span.

REFERENCES

American Psychological Association. (1999). Archival description of counseling psychology. *The Counseling Psychologist, 27,* 589–592.

Borgen, F.H. (1984). Counseling psychology. *Annual Review of Psychology, 35,* 579–604.

Brown, S.D., & Lent, R.W. (1992). *Handbook of counseling psychology (2nd ed.).* New York: Wiley.

Flores, L.Y., Rooney, S.G., Heppner, P.P., Browne, L.D., & Wei, M. (1999). Trend analysis of major contributions in *The Counseling Psychologist* cited from 1986–1996: Impact and implications. *The Counseling Psychologist, 27,* 73–95.

Gelso, C.J., & Fassinger, R.E. (1990). Counseling psychology: Theory and research of interventions. *Annual Review of Psychology, 41,* 355–386.

Heppner, M.J. (2000). Career counseling. *Encyclopedia psychology.* New York: Oxford University Press.

Heppner, P.P., Casas, J.M., Carter, J., & Stone, G.L. (2000). The maturation of counseling psychology: Multifaceted perspectives, 1978–1998. In S.D. Brown, & R.W. Lent, *Handbook of counseling psychology (3rd ed.)* (pp. 3–49). New York: Wiley.

Heppner, P.P., Kivlighan, D.M., Jr., & Wampold, B.E. (1999). *Research design in counseling (2nd ed.).* Pacific Grove, CA: Brooks/Cole.

Whiteley, J.M. (1980). *The history of counseling psychology.* Monterey, CA: Brooks/Cole.

P. P. HEPPNER
University of Missouri, Columbia

CAREER COUNSELING
COUNSELING
COUNSELING PSYCHOLOGY: HISTORY
OCCUPATIONAL COUNSELING

COUNTERTRANSFERENCE

Countertransference refers to feelings that arise in the therapist in response to the patient during the course of the patient's treatment. In its narrowest sense, the term countertransference is defined as the therapist's transferential reactions to the patient. Like all transferential reactions, countertransference involves a displacement onto the patient of feelings, beliefs, or impulses that were experienced previously by the therapist toward another person or persons.

The term "counter-transference" was first articulated by Freud to describe the therapist's affective reactions to the patient: "We have begun to consider the 'counter-transference', which arises in the physician as a result of the patient's influence on his unconscious feelings, and have nearly come to the point of requiring the physician to recognize and overcome this counter-transference in himself" (1961, pp. 144–145). Although Freud never explicitly defined the scope and nature of countertransference feelings, his work has largely been interpreted to mean that countertransference interferes with the progress of therapy. Accordingly, the neutrality required of the therapist in the therapeutic setting cannot be achieved unless countertransference feelings are contained or eliminated. This interpretation of Freudian theory conforms with the classical definition of countertransference feelings as deriving solely from the therapist's unresolved conflicts, without regard for the patient's contribution to the therapist's affective response.

The classical definition of countertransference went largely unchallenged until the middle of the twentieth century, when relational models of psychoanalytic thought began to reconceptualize the meaning of emotional experience as a reflection of self in relation to other. This shift from intrapsychic drive to interpersonal interaction was accompanied by a shift in the theory of therapy that recast the therapist in the role of "participant-observer" in the therapeutic process (Sullivan, 1953). The relational model of psychotherapy viewed the therapist's countertransference feelings as both relevant and inevitable. In contrast to classical theory, the feelings aroused in the therapist provided a critical source of information about both the patient and the therapeutic process. Furthermore, the distinction between real and distorted countertransference responses was rejected as a false one. A new definition, variously termed "totalist" or "objective" countertransference, broadened countertransference to include the therapist's total response to the patient, conscious and unconscious, real and distorted.

The role of countertransference in therapy varies depending on whether countertransference is defined from a classical or totalist perspective. According to the classical approach, countertransference derives solely from the therapist's own, unresolved conflicts, and must be avoided or controlled if the therapist is to work effectively with the patient. The task of the classical therapist is to become a tabula rasa, free of subjective distortions. This means that the therapist strives to banish emotional reactions to the patient in order more effectively to attend to the patient's unconscious communications. Only by maintaining neutrality can the therapist accurately interpret the patient's transference distortions. For example, a therapist who finds the patient to be flirtatious will strive to banish from the therapist's own affective responses and actions any reciprocal response. In this way, the material remains untarnished by the therapist's countertransference reactions.

By contrast, the totalist approach includes in its definition of countertransference both "real" and distorted reactions to the patient and considers these reactions to be unavoidable. Far from impeding the interpretation of the patient's unconscious communications, the totalist view regards countertransference as a mechanism by which the patient's unconscious communications may be understood. The relational therapist, therefore, attends carefully to countertransference feelings to expand his or her awareness of the relational patterns that manifest themselves in the therapeutic setting. The therapist who becomes aware of a patient's flirtation, for example, might then use his or her awareness of the flirtation as a source of data with regard to the patient's relational experience.

The neutrality of the classical therapist removes countertransference feelings from the realm of therapeutic inquiry. Because the therapist disregards emotional reactions to the patient, the patient's experience of the therapist is necessarily transferential. In other words, the patient's primary experience of the therapist has nothing to do with the therapist's actual behavior, thoughts, or feelings, but instead reflects some aspect of the patient's past that has been transferred into the therapeutic relationship. The manifestation of countertransference feelings, if it does occur, is a mistake that must be rectified. The classical approach avoids discussion of countertransference feelings by interpreting the patient's experience of the therapist as a manifestation of transference. For example, the therapist might interpret the patient's experience of irritation on the part of the therapist to be a transferential reaction stemming from the patient's aggressive wishes.

Because the totalist view considers countertransference reactions to be an inevitable component of the therapeutic process, the patient's observations of the therapist always reflect some mixing of objective reality and transferential distortions. Rather than assuming the patient's reactions to be transferential, the therapist examines the nature of the transference-countertransference interactions to see how they reflect the patient's relational history and experience. While the classical approach is to keep countertransference feelings out of the room, the totalist sees the inevitable unfolding of the transference-countertransference enactment as a potential roadmap to the patient's intrapsychic experience. In the example of the patient who experiences the therapist as irritated, the therapist might consider whether the therapeutic interaction comprises an unconscious enactment of aggressive behavior. Rather than viewing the patient's experience as a reflection of transferential material, the therapist might interpret the intrapsychic function of the enactment to the patient. In this way the totalist approach steers clear of the "reality" versus "distortion" dichotomy, and focuses instead on the meaning of inevitable affective exchanges in the therapeutic relationship.

How do the differences between classical and totalist approaches to countertransference manifest themselves in the current practice of psychodynamic psychotherapy? This question was addressed in a survey of attitudes toward countertransference among experienced analysts whose theoretical orientations, classical and interpersonal, were believed to correspond, respectively, with the classical and totalist approaches to countertransference (Mendelsohn, Bucci, & Chouhy, 1992). Classical analysts continued to understand countertransference as a distorted and inappropriate response to the patient, and therefore viewed countertransference as an obstacle to the therapeutic work. Interpersonalist analysts defined countertransference as the total emotional reaction to the patient and viewed it as an important treatment tool. However, with respect to therapeutic technique, classical and interpersonalist analysts were in agreement that the analyst's emotional responses, including dreams, unconscious associations, and fantasies should be used as sources of information about the patient's dynamics and transferences. Classical analysts differed from interpersonalist analysts in reporting both significantly less frequent use of their emotional reactions to the patient and significantly less frequent communication to the patient of their emotions and associations. Although this survey suggests that the debate between classical and totalist camps regarding the role of countertransference reflects in part a semantic difference regarding the term countertransference, it also demonstrates that the different understandings of countertransference conform to different uses of countertransference in current analytic practice (Mendelsohn et al., 1992).

REFERENCES

Freud, S. (1961). The future prospects of psycho-analytic therapy. In J. Strachey (Ed. and Trans.), *The standard edition of the complete psychological works of Sigmund Freud* (Vol. 11, pp. 144–151). London: Hogarth Press. (Original work published 1910.)

Mendelsohn, R., Bucci, W., & Chouhy, R. (1992). Transference and countertransference: A survey of attitudes. *Contemporary Psychoanalysis, 28,* 364–390.

Sullivan, H. S. (1953). *The interpersonal theory of psychiatry.* New York: W. W. Norton.

S. Keller
G. Stricker
Adelphi University

DISPLACEMENT
PSYCHOANALYSIS

COVERT CONDITIONING

Covert conditioning is a process through which behavior changes occur, and is a set of behavior therapy procedures based on the covert conditioning model. This process involves the interaction of covert events such as imagery, thinking, and feeling. When covert conditioning is employed, the client is asked to imagine the target behavior and then to imagine a consequence that can change that target behavior; thus if the target behavior is to reduce smoking, the client is asked to imagine himself or herself smoking, and then an aversive consequence such as vomiting. If the target behavior is to be increased, then the client first imagines performing the target behavior, and then a reinforcing consequence such as listening to pleasant music.

Three basic assumptions underlie covert conditioning: (a) the homogeneity assumption; (b) the interaction assumption; and (c) the learning assumption. The *homogeneity assumption* states that all categories of behavior, including overt and covert behaviors obey the same laws. According to the *interaction assumption,* the various categories of behavior such as covert psychological behavior, physiological behavior, and overt behavior interact and influence one another in predictable ways. The *learning assumption* simply states that all behaviors are subject to the same laws of learning.

The behavior therapy procedures based on the covert conditioning process were developed by Cautela in the 1960s and 1970s. These six covert conditioning procedures correspond to their overt, operant conditioning counterparts. In covert conditioning, however, both the behavior to be changed and its consequence—which is responsible for changing the behavior—occur in imagination according to the therapist's instructions. The first procedure developed was covert sensitization. Because Wolpe (1958) had shown that imagery could be used to desensitize clients to stimuli which once elicited a phobic reaction, Cautela reasoned that the opposite should also be true. That is, by pairing a stimulus that the client would like to avoid with an aversive stimulus, and by presenting both stimuli to the client via imagery, the client would learn to avoid the appetitive stimulus and reduce the rate of the maladaptive approach behavior.

Cautela published the first report of the use of covert sensitization in 1966. In using covert sensitization or any covert conditioning procedure, the therapist should not assume that, just because a scene of a particular consequence would be aversive (or pleasurable) to most people, every client will find it aversive. The aversiveness of scenes must be verified with the client before attempting to employ them therapeutically.

Covert sensitization has been used successfully with many behavior problems, including obesity, drug abuse, self-injurious behavior, alcoholism, sexual disorders, smoking, and compulsive stealing. Several studies conducted by Barlow and colleagues (Barlow, Leitenberg, & Agras, 1969; Barlow, Agras, Leitenberg, Callahan, & Moore, 1972; Barlow, Reynolds, & Agras, 1973; Brownell, Hayes, & Barlow, 1977; Hayes, Brownell, & Barlow, 1978) have empirically demonstrated that covert sensitization is an effective treatment procedure with relatively long-lasting effects.

In 1970 Cautela described the development of covert positive reinforcement (CPR). While covert sensitization was designed to decrease the frequency of inappropriate, unwanted target behaviors, CPR was intended to increase the likelihood of appropriate, wanted behaviors. The client employing CPR tries to experience, in imagination, situations involving the target behavior. In CPR the image of the desired target behavior is immediately followed by the client's experiencing an image of a pleasant, hopefully reinforcing scene. Covert positive reinforcement is therefore analogous to its operant counterpart, positive reinforcement. Covert positive reinforcement has been used to modify troublesome behaviors such as heroin addiction, phobias, and pain perception. In range of application, CPR may be the most useful of all the covert conditioning procedures.

There are some similarities between CPR and Wolpe's systematic desensitization (1958): reliance on imagery, frequent use of relaxation training, and effectiveness in dealing with phobias. Because of these similarities, some psychologists mistakenly consider CPR to be a variant of desensitization. The applicability of CPR to a wider range of behaviors, including those without an affective component, and the results of experimental investigations into the mechanics of CPR, have provided very strong evidence in support of the operant theoretical bases of CPR.

Soon after CPR, four more covert conditioning procedures were developed: covert modeling (CM), covert negative reinforcement (CNR), covert extinction (CE), and covert response cost (CRC). In all cases, the covert conditioning procedure was based on its operant counterpart.

Covert modeling has been the most thoroughly investigated and widely used of these additional procedures. Kazdin (1978) wrote a summary of CM research in Singer and Pope's book, *The Power of Human Imagination.* Covert modeling has been used in cases involving social skills training and motor behaviors, and is particularly helpful with clients who have difficulty imagining themselves in appropriate situations or performing certain behaviors. In CM the client imagines seeing a model—usually similar to the client in several characteristics—performing the target behavior. This example, and the consequences which the model experiences, influence the future likelihood of the client's performing the target behavior.

Covert negative reinforcement, CRC, and CE are useful in specific situations. CNR can be an alternative to CPR with clients who have difficulty imagining something pleasurable happening to them. In CNR the client begins by visualizing an aversive scene, then switches to a scene of the behavior to be increased. Covert response cost is a useful adjunct to covert sensitization in which the client imagines the loss of a reinforcing stimulus contingent upon the performance of a maladaptive behavior. Covert extinction is especially effective in modifying consummatory behaviors such as drug abuse and eating disorders: The client simply imagines performing the target behavior without the expected result (e.g., taking drugs without getting high, or eating apple pie that is tasteless).

Covert conditioning procedures are applicable to persons of all ages, including children and the elderly. They have been demonstrated to be effective with individuals diagnosed as schizophrenic and autistic, and as having Down syndrome.

Although covert conditioning procedures are usually first taught to clients by behavior therapists, the procedures are readily adaptable to self-control, thereby allowing the client to become more independent of the therapist. One such application, which exemplifies the way individual procedures can be combined, is the self-control triad (SCT). The SCT combines thought stopping, relaxation training, and CPR. The client is taught to covertly shout "Stop!" in the presence of a stressful stimulus. This serves to distract the client, who then quickly relaxes and follows the relaxation response with a reinforcing scene. Cleveland (1981) found the SCT to be significantly more effective than biofeedback in reducing myofacial pain dysfunction syndrome.

Other self-control uses of covert conditioning are tailor-made to meet the needs of individual clients and the behaviors they wish to modify. Self-control should be seen as a logical goal of counseling with covert conditioning. In this way, the client is helped to become as independent as possible of the therapist with greater responsibility for, and control over, his or her own behavior.

REFERENCES

Barlow, D. H., Agras, W. S., Leitenberg, H., Callahan, E. J., & Moore, R. C. (1972). The contribution of therapeutic instructions to covert sensitization. *Behavior Research and Therapy, 10,* 411–415.

Barlow, D. H., Leitenberg, H., & Agras, W. S. (1969). Experimental control of sexual deviation through manipulation of the noxious scene in covert sensitization. *Journal of Abnormal Psychology, 74,* 596–601.

Barlow, D. H., Reynolds, E. J., & Agras, W. S. (1973). Gender identity change in a transsexual. *Archives of General Psychiatry, 28,* 569–576.

Brownell, K. D., Hayes, S. C., & Barlow, D. H. (1977). Patterns of appropriate and deviant sexual arousal: The behavioral treatment of multiple sexual deviation. *Journal of Consulting and Clinical Psychology, 45,* 1144–1155.

Cautela, J. R. (1970). Covert reinforcement. *Behavior Therapy, 1,* 33–50.

Hayes, S. C., Brownell, K. D., & Barlow, D. H. (1978). The use of self-administered covert sensitization in the treatment of exhibitionism and sadism. *Behavior Therapy, 9,* 283–289.

Wolpe, J. (1958). *Psychotherapy by reciprocal inhibition.* Stanford, CA: Stanford University Press.

SUGGESTED READING

Ascher, L. M., & Cautela, J. R. (1972). Covert negative reinforcement: An experimental test. *Journal of Behavior Therapy and Experimental Psychiatry, 3,* 1–5.

Ascher, L. M., & Cautela, J. R. (1974). An experimental study of covert extinction. *Journal of Behavior Therapy and Experimental Psychiatry, 5,* 233–238.

Bistline, J. L., Jaremko, M. E., & Sobleman, S. (1980). The relative contributions of covert reinforcement and cognitive restructuring to test anxiety reduction. *Journal of Clinical Psychology, 36,* 723–728.

Cautela, J. R. (1967). Covert sensitization. *Psychological Record, 20,* 459–468.

Cautela, J. R. (1976a). Covert response cost. *Psychotherapy: Therapy, Research and Practice, 13,* 397–404.

Cautela, J. R. (1976b). The present status of covert modeling. *Journal of Behavior Therapy and Experimental Psychiatry, 7,* 323–326.

Cautela, J. R. (1977). Covert conditioning: Assumptions and procedures. *Journal of Mental Imagery, 1,* 53–64.

Cautela, J. R., & Baron, M. G. (1977). Covert conditioning: A theoretical analysis. *Behavior Modification, 1,* 351–368.

Cautela, J. R., Flannery, R. B., Jr., & Hanley, S. (1974). Covert modeling: An experimental test. *Behavior Therapy, 5,* 494–502.

Gotestam, K., & Melin, L. (1974). Covert extinction of amphetamine addiction. *Behavior Therapy, 5,* 90–92.

Kazdin, A. E. (1978). Covert modeling: The therapeutic application of imagined rehearsal. In J. L. Singer & K. S. Pope (Eds.), *The power of human imagination.* New York: Plenum.

Kazdin, A. E., & Smith, G. A. (1979). Covert conditioning: A review and evaluation. *Advances in Behavior Research and Therapy, 2,* 57–98.

Olson, R. P., Ganley, R., Devine, V. T., & Dorsey, G. C., Jr. (1981). Long-term effects of behavioral versus insight-oriented therapy with inpatient alcoholics. *Journal of Consulting and Clinical Psychology, 49,* 866–877.

Reynolds, G. S. (1968). *A primer of operant conditioning.* Glenview, IL: Scott, Foresman.

Skinner, B. F. (1953). *Science and human behavior.* New York: Macmillan.

Upper, D., & Cantela, J. R. (1977). *Covert conditioning.* New York: Pergamon.

Wish, P. A., Cautela, J. R., & Steffan, J. J. (1970). Covert reinforcement: An experimental test. *Proceedings of the Annual Convention of the American Psychological Association, 5,* 513–514.

Wisocki, P. A. (1973). The successful treatment of heroin addiction by covert conditioning techniques. *Journal of Behavior Therapy and Experimental Psychiatry, 4,* 55–61.

J. R. Cautela
Boston College

A. J. Kearney
Behavior Therapy Institute

BEHAVIOR THERAPY
PSYCHOTHERAPY
PSYCHOTHERAPY TECHNIQUES

COYLE, JOSEPH T.

Joseph T. Coyle was the third and last child born to his physician father and nurse mother in Chicago, Illinois. During his youth, he was particularly fascinated by natural sciences. At the College of the Holy Cross in Worcester, Massachusetts, he pursued a combined major in French and philosophy, spending his junior year in Paris, France. He was accepted into the Johns Hopkins School of Medicine in Baltimore, Maryland, in 1965. During the sophomore year course in pharmacology, he was particularly intrigued with the lectures of Solomon Snyder on the emerging field in neuropsychopharmacology, and asked to work in Snyder's research laboratory during elective time. Coyle's early research focused on the pharmacologic distinctions among catecholamine transporters in isolated nerve terminals, demonstrating for the first time that dopaminergic neurons express a unique transporter for dopamine.

After completing an internship in pediatrics at Johns Hopkins Hospital, Coyle joined the laboratory of Julius Axelrod (Nobel Prize winner, 1971) at the National Institute of Mental Health (NIMH) in 1970. As a post-doctoral fellow, he focused on characterizing the development of brain neurotransmitter systems in the rat. He developed highly sensitive methods for measuring presynaptic markers for catecholaminergic, GABAergic, and cholinergic neuronal systems required to study their development in the rat brain. His research provided the first evidence that catecholamin-

ergic systems emerge quite early in fetal brain development and thus may play a role in regulating fetal brain maturation.

In 1973, he returned to Johns Hopkins to pursue his residency training in psychiatry at the Phipps Clinic (1973–1976) and was concurrently named to the faculty in the Department of Pharmacology in 1974. He was promoted to the rank of associate professor in 1978 and to professor in 1980. Research in his laboratory demonstrated that intrastriatal injection of the conformationally restricted analogue of glutamate, kainic acid, in the rat reproduced the neurochemical and histologic pathology of Huntington's disease, leading to the proposal that dysfunction of glutamatergic neurotransmission might account for the pathophysiology of neurodegenerative disorders. Subsequent studies demonstrated that the persistent activation of all three of the glutamate receptor subtypes—NMDA, KA, and AMPA receptors—produced selective patterns of neuronal degeneration. Excitotoxic lesion of the basal forebrain reproduced the cortical cholinergic deficits associated with Alzheimer's disease and led to the proposal that degeneration of this pathway might account for the cognitive deficits in the disorder.

In 1982, Coyle was appointed the director of the Division of Child and Adolescent Psychiatry at the Johns Hopkins School of Medicine and was designated the Distinguished Service Professor of Child and Adolescent Psychiatry in 1985. These clinical responsibilities led to several studies on the pharmacologic management of serious psychiatric disorders in children. In 1991, he was recruited to Harvard Medical School, where he was appointed chairman of the Consolidated Department of Psychiatry and Eben S. Draper Professor of Psychiatry in Neuroscience: The Consolidated Department of Psychiatry consists of 10 psychiatry programs in hospitals affiliated with Harvard Medical School, more than 1,600 faculty members, and more than 300 trainees including psychology interns, adult and child psychiatry residents, and research fellows.

Coyle's current research continues to address the role of glutamate in brain pathology. He pioneered studies demonstrating that oxidative stress is an important intermediary in delayed neuronal degeneration caused by glutamate and that this delayed death occurs by apoptosis. In addition, he has clarified the role N-acetylaspartyl glutamate, a neuropeptide co-localized to many glutamatergic neuronal systems, in modulating glutamatergic neurotransmission via inhibition of NMDA receptors or through generation of extrasynaptic glutamate by hydrolysis of the peptide by glutamate carboxypeptidase II. Postmortem studies indicate that the disposition of N-acetyl-aspartyl glutamate is altered in neuropsychiatric disorders, including schizophrenia, epilepsy, and amyotrophic lateral sclerosis.

Coyle's research contributions have been recognized by numerous awards, including Foundations' Fund Research Award of the American Psychiatric Association, the John Jacob Abel Award from the American Society for Pharmacology and Experimental Therapeutics, the A. E. Bennett Award and the Gold Medal Award from the Society of Biological Psychiatry, the Daniel Efron Award from the American College of Neuropsychopharmacology, the Thomas W. Salmon Medal from the New York Academy of Medicine, and the Pasarow Foundation Award. He was elected president of the Society for Neuroscience (1991) and served as a member of the National Advisory Council for NIMH (1990–1994). He was elected to the Institute of Medicine of the National Academy of Sciences in 1990 and was named fellow of the National Academy of Arts and Sciences in 1994.

STAFF

CRAIGHEAD, W. EDWARD (1942–   )

W. Edward Craighead was born in the small Appalachian town of Gainesboro, Tennessee, in 1942. His early career aspirations were toward the ministry, but several college professors and friends encouraged him to pursue a career in clinical psychology, which he chose to do. He enjoyed a balanced college life, lettering in volleyball and tennis and participating in intercollegiate debate, after changing majors several times. He subsequently graduated magna cum laude from Abilene Christian College in 1965.

Craighead received his PhD in psychology from the University of Illinois at Champaign-Urbana in 1970. From 1970 to 1985 he was a member of the faculty of the Department of Psychology at Pennsylvania State University, where he was professor and director of clinical training. He became professor and director of the Cognitive-Behavior Therapy Program in the Department of Psychiatry at Duke University Medical Center in 1985. In 1990, he also became professor and director of the clinical program in the Department of Psychology: Social and Health Sciences at Duke University. In 1995, he moved to the Department of Psychology at the University of Colorado, Boulder, where he is currently professor and director of the clinical program. He is married to Linda Wilcoxon Craighead, who is also a professor of psychology at the University of Colorado, Boulder, where they work together; they have four children.

He has written/edited six books, including *The Corsini Encyclopedia of Psychology and Behavioral Science.* One of those books is a widely used text on cognitive and behavior therapies. He has published extensively on the psychosocial aspects and treatments of depression and manic-depression. His early work focused on identifying cognitive distortions that distinguish depression from anxiety. More recently, his work has focused on the recurrence of depression and how recurrence of the disorder may be prevented. He has been editor of *Behavior Therapy* and has served on the editorial boards of numerous scientific journals, including the *Journal of Consulting and Clinical Psychology; Journal of Abnormal Psychology; Cognitive Therapy and Research; Behavior Therapy;* and *Depression.*

Craighead is a past president of the Association for the Advancement of Behavior Therapy and of the Society for a Scientific Clinical Psychology. He is a Fellow, a member of the board of directors, and President (2000) of the Society of Clinical Psychology, a large division of the American Psychological Association. He is a Distinguished Practitioner of the National Academies of Practice, has served on several scientific review committees at the National Institute of Mental Health, and is a diplomate of the American Board of Professional Psychology.

Craighead has trained over 40 doctoral students, about one-half of whom have gone on to establish clinical research careers of their own. He has also worked with an equal number of undergraduates in his laboratory who have gone on to obtain doctoral degrees in psychology and related disciplines.

Craighead and his wife have always maintained a small private practice in clinical psychology. They subscribe to the "Boulder Model" in that their research informs their practice and their practice informs their research.

STAFF

CREATIVITY

J. P. Guilford (1950) devoted his American Psychological Association presidential address to the topic of creativity, pointing out that only 186 out of some 121,000 entries in *Psychological Abstracts* had dealt with the topic. Since Guilford's remarks in 1950, the situation has changed dramatically; an average of 250 dissertations, articles, or books have appeared each year since 1970; since 1960, over 10,000 research articles about creativity have been published and more than 600 books about creativity were published in the 1990s. Several journals attest to the vigor of the field, such as *Creative Research Journal, Empirical Studies of the Arts, Gifted Child Quarterly, Imagination, Cognition and Personality, Journal of Creative Behavior,* and *Journal of Mental Imagery.* Even so, the term *creativity* lacks a precise definition in psychology, and attempts to measure creativity have encountered controversy.

DEFINITIONS AND DESCRIPTIONS

It may be helpful to recall that the terms in which the world is understood are social artifacts, products of historically situated interchanges among people. Societies have constructed an assortment of terms to describe activities that resemble what Western psychologists refer to as "creativity." The first hexagram (or *kuan*) of the Chinese "Book of Changes," *I Jing,* is *Ch'ien,* "the Creative Principle." This hexagram expresses both the creative action of the "Source of All," which causes "objects to flow into their respective form," and the "Superior Person," who interacts with these forms when the time is ripe. This "Creative Principle" functions when "Superior Persons" harmonize their way of life with the universal flow. Confucius added, "Great indeed is the generating power of the Creative; all beings owe their beginnings to it; this power permeates all heaven."

Most Asian, African, and Native American traditions used creative imagination to enrich and enhance everyday life; novel, original contributions were typically seen as gifts from deities or spirits who used humans as "channels" (a formulation not unlike Skinner's [1972] notion that the creator adds nothing to creation but is merely the "locus" through which environmental variables act). These insights would often come in nighttime dreams or daytime visions (Krippner, 1999), and they were thought to recreate divine truth rather than to innovate. Yet, in some of these societies an individual who conceived or produced something unprecedented (e.g., a mask) would have been censured for breaking with tradition. In these societies, talented craftspeople were valued, but individuals with a flair for novelty were chastised. In Western civilization, not all individuals had equal opportunities for creative expression; for example, women's creativity was not valued or encouraged, and women were given few occasions to develop the skills (e.g., critical thinking) or life circumstances (e.g., solitude) on which creative productivity often depends.

The English word "creativity" is linked, historically and etymologically (from the Latin *creare,* to make, and the ecclesiastical Latin, *creator,* Creator), with the concept of origin itself (consider the related term "originality"). Some psychologists require *products* to be of social value or to have attained some other type of consensual agreement if they are to be called "creative," while other psychologists focus on the *process* by which these products come into being. Other attempts at definition conceptualize creativity as a unique *achievement, ability,* and/or *attitude* of a person or consortium of people. In each of these outlooks, there can be levels of accomplishment, utility, or originality, implying that some persons, groups, processes, or objects can be more or less creative than others. The concept of "everyday creativity" directs attention to creative outcomes in office management, raising children, home repairs, food preparation, or community service, as well as the "dark side of creativity" characterizing innovative but destructive acts (Richards, 1999).

Thus, from the Western psychological perspective, "creativity" is a term that can be used to describe the process of bringing something new into being (e.g., May, 1975) by becoming sensitive to gaps in human knowledge, identifying these deficiencies, searching for their solutions, making guesses as to a potential solution, testing one's hypotheses (sometimes modifying and refining the results of these examinations), and communicating the final product (Torrance, 1962). However, the creative process is imperfectly understood; these steps may be linear or overlap, may occur in a planned sequence or spontaneously, and/or may be intentional or largely unconscious. It could also be said that people, groups, or cultures are "creative" during those periods of time when they exhibit activities that are innovative for a given group; that is, that yield concepts, items, or behaviors that address human needs (e.g., for survival, for enhanced work performance, for enjoyment, for esthetic satisfaction, for enriched quality of life) in ways considered valuable by a society. These novel and effective concepts, objects, and behaviors (e.g., a scientific discovery, a mathematical theorem, a philosophical insight, an artistic masterpiece, a technological product, a military victory, a diplomatic accomplishment) can also be termed "creative," although one social group might arrive at a different consensus than another group. In other words, the term "creativity" is a social construct used to describe various outcomes in a number of domains, such as linguistic, musical, logical, spatial, kinesthetic, interpersonal, and intrapersonal (Gardner, 1983).

ASSESSING AND ENHANCING CREATIVITY

Attempts to measure the "process of creativity" have led to the development of various tests and rating scales of "divergent thinking," "problem solving," "creative activities," "creative attitudes," "creative problem-solving," and "creative thinking." Biographical inventories and personality measures have been devised in an attempt to identify the "creative person." The "creative environment" has been assessed by various scales and questionnaires focusing on the classroom or the workplace, and "creative products" have been rated (Runco, 1999). Some of these attempts at assessment have been used to identify highly creative individuals in order to offer them special instruction; entire programs in the United States—some of them statewide—have been based on these or similar assessments. However, these measures have been criticized on the basis of content validity, construct validity, reliability, clarity of instructions, relevance to different populations, and comprehensiveness, as well as the proclivity for their results to be influenced by situational or contextual factors (e.g., Cooper, 1991). A number of promising outcomes have resulted from assessing level and/or type of creativity through the use of such naturalistic assignments as writing poetry or short stories, assembling collages, or engaging in spontaneous problem-solving (e.g., Amabile, 1983).

Despite their shortcomings, creativity tests have been utilized in many important research projects. Barron and Harrington (1981) collated 70 studies in which positive and statistically significant relationships were observed "between various divergent thinking test scores and reasonably acceptable nontest indices of creative behavior or achievement" (p. 447). Even so, in some studies creativity test scores failed to correlate significantly with creative behavior or achievement, suggesting the importance of identifying field-relevant thinking abilities in each professional area, and selecting the test accordingly (p. 448). Cognitive research has identified such qualities of creative thinking as the importance of extended work sessions, "playing" with ideas in various ways, using counterintuitive strategies, analyzing paradoxical elements of a problem, and shifting back and forth between the general and the specific.

Creativity training programs assume that creative behavior can be enhanced, an assumption that has not gained universal acceptance among psychologists who emphasize the importance of biological determinants and early learning. The authors of some approaches admit that important creativity-relevant skills cannot be influenced within a short span of time, since these components include such elements as knowledge of the topic, technical skills, working and cognitive styles, and so forth. As a result, these programs emphasize task motivation (through modeling, fantasy, emphasizing choice, and de-emphasizing evaluation) so that one's abilities are allowed expression rather than undermined (Amabile, 1983). Other programs take a more optimistic view regarding creativity enhancement, focusing on cognitive rather than social-psychological methods. For instance, programs in "brainstorming" accentuate deferment of judgment; "synectics" attempts to stimulate creativity through instruction in developing analogies; "creative problem-solving" teaches people how to generate unusual ideas, using such techniques as combining two or more disparate notions. Some programs for school children, such as the Purdue Creativity Training Program and the Productive Training Program, have been found effective in improving scores on standard creativity tests (Amabile, 1983).

RESEARCH FRONTIERS

When personality characteristics of people identified as "creative" are identified, a common set of characteristics emerges, such as high valuation of esthetic qualities in experience, broad interests, high "energy," attraction to complexity, independence of judgment, autonomy, intuition, self-confidence, ability to resolve paradoxes or to accommodate apparently opposite or conflicting aspects of one's self-concept, and a firm sense of one's self as "creative" (Barron & Harrington, 1981). In addition, firstborn and laterborns appear to manifest more creativity than middleborns, but achieve eminence in different ways. Firstborns gravitate toward conservative, clearly defined problems and win more Nobel Prizes in science, whereas laterborns tend to endorse new points of view and win more Nobel Prizes in literature and peace (Sulloway, 1999). There are important differences among groups of creative people. For example, artists have been described as more "emotionally sensitive, tense, and impractical" than scientists (Helson, 1999); many research scientists grew up as "intellectual rebels" who tended to break their intimate family ties at adolescence. Musicians have suffered more problems with substance abuse, poets more mania and psychosis, and "artistic" (as opposed to "objective") writers more bipolar disorders (Ludwig, 1995). However, there are data indicating that creative people are not driven so much by conflict as by intense and constructive states of consciousness (Ayers, Beaton, & Hunt, 1999).

Future research studies need to identify the genetic markers for creative behavior, reconcile personality and cognitive research data in creativity, evaluate the part played by altered states of consciousness in creative ideation, determine the role of mental illness in blocking or facilitating creative expression, and specify what home and school variables are key factors in the development of highly creative individuals. The need for creative solutions to the world's many social, economic, and environmental problems reflects the importance of this field, and of the psychologists who dedicate themselves to understanding the *I Jing*'s "Creative Principle" as it manifests itself in human life.

REFERENCES

Amabile, T. M. (1983). *The social psychology of creativity.* New York: Springer-Verlag.

Ayers, A., Beaton, S., & Hunt, H. (1999). The significance of transpersonal experiences, emotional conflict, and cognitive abilities in creativity. *Empirical Studies of the Arts, 17,* 73–82.

Barron, F., & Harrington, D. M. (1981). Creativity, intelligence, and personality. *Annual Reviews of Psychology, 32,* 439–476.

Cooper, E. (1991). A critique of six measures for assessing creativity. *Journal of Creative Behavior, 25,* 194–205.

Gardner, H. (1983). *Frames of mind: The theory of multiple intelligences.* New York: Basic Books.

Guilford, J. P. (1950). Creativity. *American Psychologist, 14,* 469–479.

Helson, R. (1999). Personality. In M. A. Runco & S. R. Pritzker (Eds.), *Encyclopedia of creativity* (vol. 2, pp. 361–371). San Diego: Academic Press.

Krippner, S. (1999). Dreams and creativity. In M. A. Runco & S. R. Pritzker (Eds.), *Encyclopedia of creativity* (vol. 1, pp. 597–606). San Diego: Academic Press.

Ludwig, A. M. (1995). *The price of greatness.* New York: Guilford.

May, R. (1975). *The courage to create.* New York: Norton.

Richards, R. (1999). Everyday creativity. In M. A. Runco & S. R. Pritzker (Eds.), *Encyclopedia of creativity* (vol. 1, pp. 683–687). San Diego: Academic Press.

Runco, M. A. (1999). Tests of creativity. In M. A. Runco & S. R. Pritzker (Eds.), *Encyclopedia of creativity* (vol. 2, pp. 755–760). San Diego: Academic Press.

Skinner, B. F. (1972). *Cumulative record* (3rd ed.). New York: Appleton-Century-Crofts.

Sulloway, F. J. (1999). Birth order. In M. A. Runco & S. R. Pritzker (Eds.), *Encyclopedia of creativity* (vol. 1, pp. 189–202). San Diego: Academic Press.

Torrance, E. P. (1962). *Guiding creative talent.* Englewood Cliffs, NJ: Prentice-Hall.

S. KRIPPNER
Saybrook Graduate School, San Francisco, California

HUMAN INTELLIGENCE
SOFT DETERMINISM

CRISIS INTERVENTION

Crisis intervention is an emerging discipline the major concern of which is providing immediate temporary emotional first aid to victims of psychological and physical trauma. Rape, child abuse, attempted suicide, spouse abuse, family disputes, assault, robbery, and burglary all have the potential for creating severe and unusual stress in a person's life. When such stresses occur, and tax the coping skills of the individual to the point that effective and adaptive living is not possible, crisis occurs and the need for effective intervention is paramount. Without it, severe emotional disorganization often results, and the physical as well as psychological well-being of the individual is threatened. With sensitive intervention, the likelihood of further injury is decreased, the possibility of resuming precrisis functioning is maximized, and the need for subsequent psychotherapy, counseling, or hospitalization is markedly reduced. Time is always a critical element. Because the ineffective or maladaptive behavior of the crisis victim must be interrupted, reduced, and redirected at the earliest possible moment after crisis onset, the intervener—unlike in other forms of individual care—must act with the greatest dispatch.

The crisis intervener is to the victim of severe and devastating emotional trauma what the emergency room physician is to the victim of life-threatening physical injury. Individuals be said to bleed to death from emotional wounds just as they do from physical violation of the body. At least one difference, however, is that emotional wounds are less easy to see or to deal with in relatively short periods of time than their physical counterparts. Little is known, and less is understood, about the effects of emotional stress on body and mind. For many relevant reasons, the study of crisis intervention is critical, regardless of academic or nonacademic background. Crisis intervention skills must be adapted to personal styles. Though based on current psychological and psychotherapeutic thought, they must be developed specifically in relationship to the problems for which they will be called into play. (For a comparison with psychoanalysis and short-term psychotherapy, see Table 1.) Being a psychologist, psychiatrist, social worker, counselor, or other helping professional does not in itself ensure proper knowledge and skill training. Lack of professional training in no way precludes the potential for skillful and effective functioning during crisis situations. The necessary skills can be developed, refined, and utilized by any professional, paraprofessional, volunteer, lay person, law enforcement officer, attorney, minister, hotline worker, teacher or friend who cares about the mental well-being of those with whom they come into contact.

HISTORY OF THE CRISIS INTERVENTION MOVEMENT

The concept of "crisis" has been with us since the ancient Greeks. Since that time, it has come to mean everything from its original medical definition to how to deal with economic adversities and even to how to pick up dates.

The term "crisis intervention" has been equally overused and randomly applied, and has come to mean many different things. To the psychologist it may mean psychotherapy; to the counselor, short-term counselling; to the psychiatrist, perhaps hospitalization. Until recently, crisis intervention was unrecognized as a distinct discipline, referred to a wide variety of concepts, and remained the bastard child of other entities.

Crisis intervention theory is usually credited to Gerald Caplan and Erich Lindemann. Their studies of persons in actual crisis situations provided basic information in this area. While their work was done subsequent to World War II, what would now be considered crisis intervention can be traced at least to the beginning of this century, to the help centers and settlement houses of the Northeast. Probably the earliest of these was the Save-A-Life League in New York and the Suicide Centers in Chicago. Since that time agencies, hot lines, help houses, and the like have proliferated. The Samaritans in England; the Benjamin Rush Center in Los Angeles; the Medical College–Metropolitan Hospital Center Walk-In Clinic in New York; the Suicide Prevention Center in Los Angeles; Rescue, Inc., in Boston; Friends, Inc. in Miami; and We Care, Inc., in Orlando, Florida—all attempt to assist people in crisis.

In 1969 the National Conference of Christians and Jews (N.C.C.J.) established a major project in Louisville, Kentucky, to provide training in community relations and crisis intervention primarily for police officers. As the program grew, not only was it clearly important to the law enforcement community, but it was also requested by and experienced enrollment of many profession-

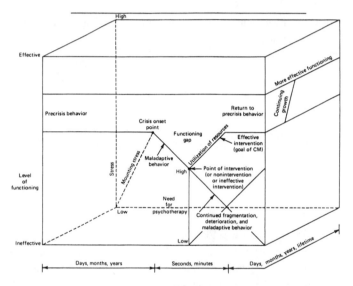

Figure 1.   Crisis cube. (Copyright J. L. Greenstone, 1977. All rights reserved.) From *The Crisis Intervener's Handbook* (Vol 1), by J. L. Greenstone and S. C. Leviton, 1979. Reprinted by permission.

Table 1.   Comparison of Psychoanalysis and Short-term Psychotherapy with Crisis Intervention

Areas	Psychoanalysis	Short Therapy	Crisis Management
Focus	Past and the unconscious	Past as related to current situation, unconscious	Present. Restore precrisis levels of functioning
Role of therapist	Exploratory; nondirective, passive observer	Indirect, passive observer	Direct, active participant
Control	Shared	Shared	Intervener
Awareness	Unconscious	Mixed	Conscious
Goals	Restructuring the personality	Removal of specific symptoms	Management of immediate crisis situation
Range	Limited	Varied	Limited
Indications	Neurotic personality patterns	Acute emotional pain and disruptive circumstances	Sudden loss of ability to handle life situations in way usually handled
Average length of treatment	Indefinite	One to 20 sessions	Usually only a few sessions, may be no longer than one

Note: From *Handbook of Innovative Therapies,* R. J. Corsini (Ed.), 1994, New York: John Wiley & Sons. Reprinted with permission.

als, paraprofessionals, and lay volunteers who found themselves working in crisis situations with crisis victims, but whose skills in this area were vastly lacking. While most reputable counselor training programs in this country were turning out highly trained counselors, they were not receiving specialized instruction in crisis intervention. Such training was difficult to find and prohibitively expensive, and often one program of instruction was inconsistent with another. The Louisville N.C.C.J. programs began to change the approach to this critical need.

From these early beginnings and awarenesses came the National Institute for Training in Crisis Intervention. Conferences held by this body brought together academics, professionals, paraprofessionals, lay volunteers, police officers, and others under one roof. Not only did crisis intervention theory begin to be further developed and standardized, but many of the traditional barriers—especially between law enforcement officers and helping agency personnel—began to fall away. The end result was better emotional first-aid care for crisis victims.

In 1976, the American Academy of Crisis Interveners was formed, followed in 1978 by the Southwestern Academy of Crisis Interveners, and in 1980 by a Southeastern Academy. At the same time the National Conference for Training in Crisis Intervention has continued to meet, with a basic format similar to that used at the National Institute. Subsequently, various levels of training were developed, and a plan proposed for the certification of interveners. In 1980 the American Board of Examiners in Crisis Intervention was founded, which certifies individual interveners from agencies and professions. The common denominator in all these groups is the consistent adoption of an interdisciplinary approach to the teaching and procedures of crisis intervention. All training is open to all levels of individuals working with crisis victims. The publishing of *Emotional First Aid: A Journal of Crisis Intervention* and *The Crisis Intervener's Newsletter* by the American and Southwestern academies further serves to establish the discipline. Crisis interveners now have their own academies, their own programs, their own heritage and future.

CRISIS INTERVENTION PROCEDURES

Crisis intervention is an immediate response to immediate problems. The often disorganized, confused, and dangerous behavior of the crisis victim must be dealt with as quickly as possible by an intervener who can react immediately and skillfully. Such a response is designed to help the victim use personal and social supports and help him or her return to precrisis functioning levels.

To that end, a standard set of procedures is advocated. These instructions are not intended to concretize a pat set of rules, or to obviate the need for personal style or creativity on the part of the intervener; to the contrary, they are designed to allow the maximum of both. Such a simplified format may be helpful, however, because of the many and varied behaviors and concerns with which an intervener must be concerned during high-stress encounters. More often than not, some stress and anxiety will also be present in the intervener as intervention is attempted. With simplified guidelines, the intervener can be sure that all areas are being covered regardless of his or her own emotional state or that of the victim.

Immediacy

The crisis intervener must act to reduce the crisis level as soon as the victim is encountered. Act *now!* Crises may develop over time, and the results of intervention may be felt for a long time to come. However, the intervention itself may take only seconds or minutes and can have profound effects on the victim.

Control

Persons in crisis are often not in control of themselves or of their situation. For this reason and for reasons of safety, the crisis intervener must assume control of the situation and of the crisis victims. This is done quickly and maintained only as long as the victims are not able to maintain control themselves. This may involve only seconds or minutes, or at times somewhat longer periods. A crutch is valuable when it is needed; a disability, when it is not. Ways of gaining and maintaining control vary with the situation and with the creativity of the intervener. The physical presence of the intervener, having the victims seated, making unusual requests, lowering or raising the voice, a whistle or other loud noise, intervening with a partner, even the mannerisms of the intervener—all may contribute to the control exercised in a given situation. Without control, little else is possible that will help the victim, and the intervener may be in great danger.

Assessment

Why did the victim go into crisis at this particular time? What precipitating events led up to the crisis? What was tried by the victim or others to reduce the stressful situation? The crisis intervener must perform a quick and accurate assessment of the total situation and persons involved to determine how the crisis may be effectively handled. Time determines how much information can be gathered. What is obtained must be accurate and usable. Concentrate on recent history only.

Disposition

Everything done will affect a crisis victim in some way. The old maxim, "If you don't help them, at least don't hurt them," is nonsense in crisis intervention. What the intervener does will either help or hurt the victim. Therefore very careful consideration must be given to the intervention "game plan." The more the victim or victims can be helped to work out by themselves, with the intervener's assistance, the more substantial the results will be. The intervener's job is only to help the victim to return to a level of precrisis functioning. This is probably the major difference between crisis intervention and psychotherapy: Intervention concerns itself with problem management, not problem resolution. If the intervention is done effectively, the probability of eventual problem resolution is greatly enhanced.

Referral

Critical, and yet often overlooked, in many crisis interventions is the referral of the victim, as needed, for additional or ongoing professional or community assistance. Many otherwise skillful interventions have failed because a referral was either not made or made ineffectively by the intervener. Successful referrals are the result of careful planning and source investigation. Such information must be gathered by the intervener prior to intervention, so that referral can be done easily and provide the victim with all necessary information. Looking through the yellow pages during an intervention generates lack of confidence and invites problems for all concerned.

Follow-up

A luxury item in intervention is follow-up. Time schedules, other appointments, case loads, long hours, and other pressing problems often keep the intervener from checking to see if referrals were actually utilized. Such a final step is necessary to ensure the viability of the intervention. A call to a former victim may reveal new problems, such as a lack of transportation to the referred-to agency or a myriad of other occurrences that the intervener may correct, thereby saving an endangered but otherwise sound intervention.

Crisis intervention can be effective at various times of crisis in a person's life. It can be used in conjunction with ongoing psychotherapy or prior to treatment. Intervention may be effective in isolated reactive crisis situations, when additional therapy is either not warranted or not accepted. These skills can be utilized in the field, in the office, in private practice, in agency work, in the church, in the home, or at any time when the emotional health of an individual is acutely threatened.

REFERENCES

Corsini, R. J. (Ed.). (1981). *Handbook of innovative psychotherapies.* New York: Wiley.

Greenstone, J. L., & Leviton, S. C. (1979). *The crisis intervener's handbook* (Vol. 1). Dallas, TX: Crisis Management Workshops.

SUGGESTED READING

Greenstone, J. L., & Leviton, S. C. (1980). *The crisis intervener's handbook* (Vol. 2). Dallas, TX: Rothschild.

Rosenbluh, E. S. (1974). *Techniques of crisis intervention.* New York: Behavioral Science Services.

J. L. GREENSTONE
S. LEVITON
Southwestern Academy of Crisis Interveners

COUNSELING
SOCIAL CASEWORK

CRITICAL INCIDENT TECHNIQUE

The critical incident technique is a job analysis method first described by John Flanagan in 1954. The method involves the collection of hundreds of anecdotal descriptions of effective and ineffective job behaviors which job incumbents, supervisors, and others have actually observed in the work setting. These anecdotes, called critical incidents, must be specific behaviors which exemplify success or failure in some aspect of the job being analyzed. For ex-

ample, a critical ineffective incident for a truck driver would be: "The driver failed to look in his rear-view mirror when backing up the truck and consequently hit a parked car." The observer reporting the critical incident is typically asked to describe: (a) what led up to the incident and the context in which it occurred; (b) exactly what the individual did that was effective or ineffective; (c) the apparent consequences of this behavior; and (d) whether or not the consequences were under the individual's control.

After several hundred critical incidents are collected, they are content-analyzed and sorted by one or more judges into categories or dimensions of critical job behavior. These dimensions then serve as the basis for the identification or construction of job-related tests and other selection devices. They can also be used as a basis for the development of training programs.

In *Applied Psychology in Personnel Management,* Cascio noted that a major advantage of the critical incident technique as a job analysis method is that it focuses on observable, measurable job behaviors. Disadvantages of the method include the considerable amount of time and effort required to implement it, as well as its neglect of average job performance.

The critical incident technique has been employed for several purposes other than job analysis. In 1959 Herzberg and his coworkers used the method to research work motivation and satisfaction. Flanagan and Burns (1955) showed how the critical incident technique could be adapted for use as a work performance appraisal and development tool. The application of Thurstone scaling to critical incidents, suggested most notably by Smith and Kendall (1963), has led to the development of several work performance appraisal techniques, including behaviorally anchored rating scales, mixed standard rating scales, and weighted checklists. In "Spin-offs from behavior expectation scale procedures," Blood showed how critical incidents could be used to investigate organizational policy. The critical incident technique has also been used to improve workplace and product safety and efficiency.

REFERENCES

Blood, M. R. (1974). Spin-offs from behavior expectation scale procedures. *Journal of Applied Psychology, 59,* 513–515.

Cascio, W. F. (1982). *Applied psychology in personnel management* (2nd ed.). Reston, VA: Reston.

Flanagan, J. C., & Burns, R. K. (1955). The employee performance record: A new appraisal and development tool. *Harvard Business Review, 33*(5), 95–102.

Herzberg, F., Mausner, B., & Snyderman, B. (1959). *The motivation to work.* New York: Wiley.

Smith, P. C., & Kendall, L. M. (1963). Retranslation of expectations: An approach to the construction of unambiguous anchors for rating scales. *Journal of Applied Psychology, 47,* 149–155.

SUGGESTED READING

Dunnette, M. D. (1976). Aptitudes, abilities, and skills. In M. D. Dunnette (Ed.), *Handbook of industrial and organizational psychology.* Chicago: Rand McNally.

McCormick, E. J. (1979). *Job analysis: Methods and applications.* New York: Amacom.

Smith, P. C. (1976). Behaviors, results, and organizational effectiveness: The problem of criteria. In M. D. Dunnette (Ed.), *Handbook of industrial and organizational psychology.* Chicago: Rand McNally.

W. I. SAUSER, JR.
Auburn University

APPLIED RESEARCH
FIELD RESEARCH
INDUSTRIAL PSYCHOLOGY
JOB ANALYSIS
JOB EVALUATION

CRONBACH, LEE J. (1916–   )

Lee J. Cronbach received the BA from Fresno State College and the PhD at the University of Chicago in 1940. He has taught at the universities of Chicago, Illinois, and Stanford. In 1957, he served as president of the American Psychological Association and, in 1974, received the Distinguished Scientific Contribution Award.

His most important books are *Essentials of Psychological Testing* and *Educational Psychology.* In his research, he has been concerned with new approaches to the validation of psychological tests. His book on psychological testing emphasized general critical principles for test development and use. He chaired the 1951–1955 Committee on Test Standards of the American Psychological Association, to develop the original code for maintaining quality in tests of ability and personality.

In educational psychology Cronbach has stressed the relationship between classroom practices and basic psychological principles, particularly those of generalization and the transfer of training.

STAFF

CROSS-CULTURAL COUNSELING

Cross-cultural counseling is any broadly defined psychological helping relationship in formal or informal settings where the provider assesses, understands, and/or evaluates a client's behavior in the client's cultural context where those behaviors were learned and displayed. Since all behavior is learned and displayed in a cultural context, accurate assessment, meaningful understanding, and appropriate counseling intervention need to take the perspective of the client's cultural context.

SOURCES OF CROSS-CULTURAL COUNSELING

The interface between culture and counseling has become popular and has been recognized as important to counseling in the last two decades. Initially, the fields of psychoanalysis and anthropology were the focus of interest in studying cultures and mental health. The focus has since shifted from the anthropological study of remote and exotic cultures to cultural variations in modern pluralistic and complex societies. Psychology has conventionally assumed that there is a fixed, absolutist perspective of mental functioning and that culture distorts that universal definition of normal behavior. The contrasting perspective of anthropology assumed that cultural differences illuminate attitudes, values, and perspectives that differ across cultures in a relativist perspective. Cross-cultural counseling attempts to reconcile these two extreme positions.

The cultural context can be narrowly defined to include only ethnic or national aspects, but culture may also be broadly defined to include ethnographic, demographic, status, and affiliational identifiers. Cross-cultural counseling has generally been used to describe the national and international applications of counseling across all cultural boundaries (Pedersen, Draguns, Lonner, & Trimble, 1996). In recent years the term "multicultural" has been preferred over "cross-cultural" to emphasize the multiplicity of cultural groups and contexts in which counseling occurs. Another weakness of the cross-cultural counseling term is that it promotes the comparison of cultures with an implicit judgment that some cultures are better than others. The notion of culture-centered counseling has been introduced as a means of addressing the weaknesses of cross-cultural and multicultural descriptors (Pedersen, 1997).

There is general agreement that the cultures of both providers and consumers of counseling services pervasively and profoundly influence the counseling process (Ponterotto, Casas, Suzuki, & Alexander, 1995). As countries and cultures have modernized on a world-wide scale, sources of traditional village, religious, and family authority have been weakened. As a result, outside professionals offer counseling services to manage personal problems in the urbanized and modernized context. The applications of counseling outside the Euro-American envelope has revealed cultural biases in the conventional descriptions of counseling and therapy. Alternative and complementary therapies are more popular on an international level than are talk therapies.

CULTURAL BIAS

The presence of cultural bias in counseling has been well documented. Wrenn (1962) defined the "culturally encapsulated counselor" as one who had substituted symbiotic modal stereotypes for the real world, disregarded cultural variations among clients, and dogmatized technique-oriented definitions of counseling and therapy. Counselors are likely to promote the individualistic assumptions of a dominant culture intentionally or unintentionally as they impose the dominant culture's perspective on minorities. The culturally different client approaches counseling with a majority counselor asking, "What makes you, a counselor/therapist, any different from all the others out there who have oppressed and discriminated against me?" (Sue & Sue, 1990, p. 6). The Behavioral Science Task Force of the National Advisory Mental Health Council (1996) has identified specific examples of how social and cultural beliefs influence diagnosis and treatment, how diagnostic categories reflect majority culture values, how diagnosis differs across cultures, how symptoms are expressed differently across cultures, and the effect of most providers' being from a majority culture background while most clients come from minority cultural groups.

CULTURAL BARRIERS TO COUNSELING

Evidence came to light in the 1970s that mental health services were being underutilized by minority groups and that behavior described as pathological in a minority culture, such as individualistic assertiveness, may be viewed as adaptive in a majority culture client. Asian-Americans, Blacks, Chicanos, American Indians, and other minority groups terminate counseling significantly earlier than do Anglo clients (Sue & Sue, 1990). In most of the psychological literature these examples of differentiation are credited to cultural barriers that hinder the formation of good counseling relationships, and to language barriers, class-bound values, and culture-bound attitudes. To some extent these conditions do exist and do result in a minority group's disillusionment with the professional field of mental health as a resource for social and individual coping. A contrasting view, not frequently mentioned but which may also account for underutilization, is based on cultural boundary maintenance functions. This viewpoint suggests that mental health services perceived as alien by the minority group may be avoided in a desire to avoid the erosion of personal identity–sustaining forces in the minority culture. From this point of view, more attractive and effective mental health services might actually result in increased acculturative stress among those being served.

THE DEVELOPMENT OF CROSS-CULTURAL COMPETENCIES

Cross-cultural practitioners have failed to develop grounded theory based on empirical data for several reasons. First, the emphasis has been on abnormal rather than normal behavior across cultures. Second, only in the 1970s did a pancultural core emerge for the more serious categories of disturbance such as schizophrenia and affective psychoses, so that they are recognizable according to uniform symptoms across cultures, even though tremendous cultural variations continue to exist. Third, the complexity of research on therapy across cultural lines is difficult to manage beyond quantified stages. Fourth, the research has lacked an applied emphasis related to practical concerns of program development, service delivery, and techniques of treatment. Fifth, there has been insufficient interdisciplinary collaboration across psychology, psychiatry, and anthropology, each approaching culture and mental health from different perspectives. Sixth, the emphasis of research has been on the symptom as a basic variable, to the neglect of the interaction of personal, professional, institutional, and community needs. Cultural differences introduce barriers to understanding in those very areas of interaction most crucial to the outcome of therapy, through discrepancies between counselor and client experiences, beliefs, values, expectations, and goals.

Culturally sensitive competencies were developed from the mid-1980s describing a three-stage developmental sequence beginning with multicultural awareness, then moving to multicultural knowledge, and finally to multicultural skill competencies (Sue, Bernier, et al., 1982). This framework has been elaborated by Sue, Carter, and colleagues (1998), and others have described those competencies of cross-cultural counseling. These competencies have been adopted by Division 17 (Division of Counseling Psychology) of the American Psychological Association as well as by the American Counseling Association as standards for professional conduct.

THE FUTURE OF CROSS-CULTURAL COUNSELING

The future of cross-cultural counseling will depend on advances in four areas. First, conceptual and theoretical approaches need to be developed beyond the diffuse and incomplete theoretical alternatives now available (Sue, Ivey, & Pedersen, 1996). Second, a sharpening of research efforts is needed to identify those primary variables that will explain what has happened, interpret what is happening, and perhaps predict what is going to happen in the migration of persons and ideas across cultures. Third, criteria of expertise for the education and training of professionals to work across cultures need to be defined to adequately equip providers to deal with the troubles of a pluralistic society. Finally, revolutionary modes of providing services need to be developed based on new theory, research, and training so that mental health care is equitably and appropriately provided to all members of our pluralistic society.

REFERENCES

Basic Behavioral Science Task Force of the National Advisory Mental Health Council (1996). Basic behavioral science research for mental health: Sociocultural and environmental processes. *American Psychologist, 51,* 722–731.

Pedersen, P. (1997). *Culture-centered counseling interventions.* Thousand Oaks, CA: SAGE.

Pedersen, P., Draguns, J., Lonner, W., & Trimble, J. (1996). *Counseling across cultures: Fourth edition.* Thousand Oaks, CA: SAGE.

Ponterotto, J. G., Casas, J. M., Suzuki, L. A., & Alexander, C. M. (1995). *Handbook of Multicultural Counseling.* Thousand Oaks, CA: SAGE.

Sue, D. W., Bernier, J. E., Durran, A., Fineberg, L., Pedersen, P., Smith, C. J., & Vasquez-Nuttall, G. (1982). Cross-cultural counseling competencies. *The Counseling Psychologist 19*(2), 45–52.

Sue, D. W., Carter, R. T., Casas, J. M., Fouad, N. A., Ivey, A. E., Jensen, M., LaFromboise, T., Manese, J. E., Ponterotto, J. G., & Vasquez-Nuttall, E. (1998). *Multicultural counseling competencies.* Thousand Oaks, CA: SAGE.

Sue, D. W., Ivey, A. E., & Pedersen, P. B. (1996). *Multicultural counseling theory.* Pacific Grove, CA: Brooks/Cole.

Sue, D. W., & Sue, D. (1990). *Counseling the culturally different: Theory and practice.* New York: Wiley Interscience.

Wrenn, G. (1962). The culturally encapsulated counselor. *Harvard Educational Review, 32,* 444–449.

P. PEDERSEN
University of Alabama at Birmingham

ACCULTURATION
COUNSELING
COUNSELING PSYCHOLOGY: PAST AND PRESENT
CROSS-CULTURAL PSYCHOLOGY: INTRODUCTION AND
    OVERVIEW
CULTURE AND PSYCHOTHERAPY

CROSS-CULTURAL PSYCHOLOGY: CULTURE-UNIVERSAL AND CULTURE-SPECIFIC FRAMEWORKS

EMICS AND ETICS

The jargon of cross-cultural specialists includes the terms *emics* and *etics* which summarize important central concepts and analytical tools (Berry, 1969; Poortinga, 1997). To best explain these concepts, a problem which can be analyzed with their help will first be posed. Emics and etics will then be introduced in their abstract form and subsequently applied to the problem.

The problem involves drought and starvation in East Africa (Talbot, 1972). A group of European consultants recommended that development projects be established to increase water availability and grasslands for the Masai, an East African culture long involved in raising cattle. Instead of leading to healthier herds and better grazing areas, however, the development projects led to starvation for the cattle and eventually for some of the Masai. How can this be explained? The cross-cultural concepts of emics and etics provide useful explanatory tools.

Emics and etics refer to the two goals of cross-cultural research. One is to document valid principles in all cultures and to establish theoretical frameworks useful in comparing human behavior in various cultures. This is the "etic" goal—a term that comes from phonetic analysis. In linguistics, a phonetic system is one that documents and analyzes all meaningful sounds present in all languages and integrates them into a general framework. The other goal of cross-cultural research is to document valid principles of behavior within any one culture, with attention to what the people themselves value as important as well as what is familiar to them. Such an analysis has to reject the importation and imposition of frameworks from outside a culture since, by definition, a researcher cannot gain insight into emics by using foreign tools; the tools must be indigenous (Kim & Berry, 1993). This latter type is an "emic" analysis—a term from phonemics. In linguistics, a phonemic analysis documents sounds meaningful in a specific language.

An example from linguistics may be helpful. A phonetic system will have an initial *ng* sound, an initial *l* sound, and an initial *r* sound, since these are important in at least one of the world's languages. In addition, these sounds can be integrated into a general framework based on such concepts as activation of vocal cords and parts of the mouth used in making the sounds. An English phonemic system will have the *l* and *r* sounds, but not the initial *ng* sound, since the latter is not part of the English language. Japanese does not have the initial *l* and the initial *r* sounds, since the language does not make a distinction between them. English speakers thus have to put special effort into learning the initial *ng* sound—a task faced by many Peace Corps volunteers assigned to Pacific Island cultures. Japanese speakers have to work hard on the *l-r* distinction, as most teachers of English as a second language will testify. The "metaphor" of emics and etics for cross-cultural research contains the elements referred to above: what is present and absent, what is meaningful, what has to be given special attention since it is common in one system but not another, and what can be systematized into integrative frameworks.

Cross-cultural researchers have attempted to deal with both etics and emics in their research. A system proposed by Brislin (1976; 2000), drawing upon earlier work by Przeworski and Teune (1966, 1970), represents such an attempt. The researcher starts by examining concepts that may have cross-cultural validity, but keeps in mind that not all aspects of those concepts will be the same in all cultures under study. Aspects may be different for cultures across nations as well as for various cultures or subcultures within a country.

In discussing the effects of range development on the Masai culture of East Africa, Talbot (1972) analyzed the concept "uses and care of cattle" from the perspective of the Masai, and from the perspective of people from Europe and North America in charge of the development. Members of both cultures have similar conceptualizations about several core connotations, and these are the proposed etics: provision of milk, fertilizer, and demands placed on humans for caring of cattle. But in addition to this etic core, there are differences which can be called the emics within each group.

North America, Europe Emics	Masai Emics
Cattle used for meat	Cattle not primarily used for meat
Cattle raised for sale	Cattle not generally raised for sale
Grazing over a large area	Grazing in small areas (to protect from predators)
Emphasis on quality as much as quantity	Emphasis on quantity
Other signs of wealth and prestige available besides cattle	Cattle are a major sign of wealth and prestige
Experience with conservation	Always a struggle to maintain limited herds, hence no opportunity to think about conservation when large numbers of cattle are present

The emphasis on quantity was a major problem in the range development projects. Prior to European contact, natural conditions such as droughts and fires effectively limited the size of herds, so the intelligent practice was always to have as many cattle as possible. But when water and grasslands became more common after development, the Masai norm of "desirability of quantity," without a self-imposed norm of "desirability of limitations for the purpose of conservation," led to herds of unreasonable size. The cattle then overgrazed and destroyed the available range. In turn, cattle then died for lack of food, and the Masai themselves faced starvation. This case is frequently cited as an example of failure of technology (range development) due to ignorance of a human variable (norm of quantity).

EMICS AND ETICS IN PRACTICE: RESEARCH ON PERSONALITY

Considerable evidence exists that there are etic aspects of people's personalities. Research has been carried out in a variety of countries (reviewed by McCrae & Costa, 1997; Brislin, 2000) including the United States, Canada, Israel, Finland, Poland, Germany, Russia, Korea, Hong Kong, Japan, and the Philippines. Five aspects of personality (also called "traits") seem to be universal, or "etic" in the language of this article. Sometimes called the "Big Five," these aspects are:

1. *Extraversion.* People with this trait are sociable, expressive, and look forward to spending time with others. In contrast, introverts are more likely to be shy and to withdraw from social encounters, often viewing them as burdensome rather than stimulating.

2. *Conscientiousness.* This trait label describes people who are dependable, careful about work assignments, and who have reputations as responsible citizens in their communities. This contrasts with careless people who lack self-discipline.

3. *Agreeableness.* People who are easy to get along with and who have the reputation of "good natured" are said to be agreeable, in contrast to others who are uncooperative and irritable.

4. *Emotional stability.* Some people have the reputation of having good control over their emotions. They do not become easily excited and remain calm in stressful situations. This contrasts with people who are insecure, become upset easily, and who break social norms by expressing more emotion than is considered acceptable in many social situations.

5. *Openness to experience.* Some people enjoy participating in new activities and actively seek out challenges. Other people prefer participating in activities with which they are already very familiar.

In addition to these etic or universal aspects of personality, there are at least two types of emic aspects. A combination of etics and emics is necessary for a complete analysis of personality traits within any one culture. One type of emic involves adding in details summarizing how the etic personality traits are expressed and how they manifest themselves given a culture's norms. This is sometimes called the emic coloring of etic concepts. In some cultures

(e.g., Japan), there is a value placed on the control of emotional displays, such as the amount of enthusiasm and excitement a person expresses on their face and in their body language. Extraverts, then, would not display as much expressiveness in various social situations as would people in cultures where norms against open displays of emotions are weaker (e.g., the United States). Put another way, it is harder to differentiate extraverts from introverts in Japan than in the United States. In the case of conscientiousness, details include what people are expected to be conscientiousness about. In Korea, conscientious schoolchildren would work extremely hard toward getting the best grades possible. In other cultures (i.e., United States, Canada) conscientiousness involves developing a "well-rounded" personality, so that time in extracurricular activities is combined with formal classroom education.

A second type of emic focuses on aspects of personality that are unique to certain cultures. Such aspects deal with traits that are valued in a culture but that are not captured by the universal or etic aspects. In China, for instance, Zhang and Bond (1998) accepted the descriptive value of the Big Five factors but also documented the importance of uniquely Chinese factors. One factor, called "Chinese tradition," includes behaviors long valued among the Chinese, such as filial piety. The importance of filial piety can be seen when adults take care of their aging parents and do not avail themselves of nursing homes except in the most extreme medical circumstances. Another Chinese emic factor is that behaviors should be directed toward maintaining social harmony. Such behaviors include knowing and participating in a variety of social rituals, being deferent to older people and people with status and authority, being careful about reciprocating favors, and nurturing and utilizing a collection of people who can be helpful in obtaining goals in society (people with whom one has "guanxi").

It is no accident that the emic items demand long labels and explanations. These are the characteristics of a general concept somewhat unfamiliar to people from one country who are trying to understand another. Since Zhang and Bond (1998) wanted to communicate their results to audiences all over the world, the emics had to be interpreted. The core aspects of personality (e.g., the Big Five) are relatively easy to describe, since by definition they are aspects of the general concept in both countries. But since one country's emics are less familiar to people from other countries, long explanations are sometimes necessary.

Use of the emic-etic framework also has practical purposes; for instance, it is useful in preparing people who are about to live in a country other than their own (Gudykunst, Hammer, & Wiseman, 1977; Brislin & Yoshida, 1994; Brislin, 2000). The etic aspects of a concept can be used to introduce material about life in another culture, since these aspects represent the shared meaning. The emic aspects can subsequently be introduced and receive special attention, since another country's emics will be unfamiliar and sometimes seem bizarre. Using the example of personality again, the emic aspects of the concept are indeed startling to sojourners from various countries adjusting to life in China. Sojourners are frequently very surprised at the amount of time and energy that has to be invested in developing relationships with people so that favors can be asked later of these people. Many times, these "favors" are tasks that would be considered everyday job expectations in some countries, such as the efforts of a government bureaucrat to process a simple request. Similarly, Chinese people living in highly industrialized nations such as the United States are struck by the number of older people living in nursing homes, separate from their children. Chinese sojourners are pleasantly surprised by the attentiveness of government bureaucrats who do not feel the need to develop relationships with people prior to giving them the services called for in their job descriptions.

REFERENCES

Berry, J. (1969). On cross-cultural comparability. *International Journal of Psychology, 4,* 119–128.

Berry, J., Poortinga, Y., & Pandey, J. (Eds.). (1997). *Handbook of cross-cultural psychology: Vol. 1. Theory and method* (2nd ed.). Boston: Allyn and Bacon.

Brislin, R. (1976). Comparative research methodology: Cross-cultural studies. *International Journal of Psychology, 1,* 215–229.

Brislin, R. (2000). *Understanding culture's influence on behavior* (2nd ed.). Fort Worth, TX: Harcourt Brace.

Brislin, R., & Yoshida, T. (1994). *Intercultural communication training: An introduction.* Thousand Oaks, CA: Sage.

Gudykunst, W., Hammer, M., & Wiseman, R. (1977). An analysis of an integrated approach to cross-cultural training. *International Journal of Intercultural Relations, 1*(2), 99–110.

Kagitcibasi, C. (1997). Individualism and collectivism. In J. Berry, M. Segall, & C. Kagitcibasi (Eds.), *Handbook of cross-cultural psychology: Vol. 3. Behavior and applications* (2nd ed., pp. 1–49). Boston: Allyn and Bacon.

Kim, U., & Berry, J. (Eds.). (1993). *Indigenous psychologies.* Newbury Park, CA: Sage.

Kogan, N., & Wallach, M. (1964). *Risk taking: A study in cognition and personality.* New York: Holt.

Kroeber, A., & Kluckhohn, C. (1952). Culture. *Papers of the Peabody Museum, 47*(1).

Labov, W. (1970). The logic of non-standard English. In F. Williams (Ed.), *Language and poverty.* Chicago: Markham.

LaFromboise, T., Coleman, H., & Gerton, J. (1993). Psychological impact of biculturalism: Evidence and theory. *Psychological Bulletin, 114,* 395–412.

Landis, D., & Bhagat, R. (Eds.). (1996). *Handbook of intercultural training* (2nd ed.). Thousand Oaks, CA: Sage.

Levine, R. (1997). *A geography of time.* New York: HarperCollins.

Levine, R., & Norenzayan, A. (1999). The pace of life in 31 countries. *Journal of Cross-Cultural Psychology, 30,* 178–205.

Malinowski, B. (1927). *Sex and repression in savage society.* New York: Harcourt, Brace, & Co.

Markus, H., & Kitiyama, S. (1998). The cultural psychology of personality. *Journal of Cross-Cultural Psychology, 29,* 63–87.

Maslow, A. H. (1943). A theory of human motivation. *Psychological Review, 50,* 370–396.

McClelland, D. C. (1961). *The achieving society.* Princeton, NJ: Van Nostrand.

McCrae, R., & Costa, P. (1997). Personality trait structure as a human universal. *American Psychologist, 52,* 509–516.

Poortinga, Y. (1997). Towards convergence? In J. Berry, Y. Poortinga, & J. Pandey (Eds.), *Handbook of cross-cultural psychology: Vol. 1. Theory and method* (2nd ed., pp. 347–387). Boston: Allyn and Bacon.

Przeworski, A., & Teune, H. (1966). Equivalence in cross-national research. *Public Opinion Quarterly, 30,* 33–43.

Przeworski, A., & Teune, H. (1970). *The logic of comparative social inquiry.* New York: Wiley.

Talbot, L. (1972). Ecological consequences of rangeland development in Masailand, East Africa. In M. Farvar & J. Milton (Eds.), *The careless technology: Ecology and international development.* Garden City, NY: Natural History Press.

Zhang, J., & Bond, M. (1998). Personality and filial piety among college students in two Chinese societies: The added value of indigenous constructs. *Journal of Cross-Cultural Psychology, 29,* 402–417.

SUGGESTED READING

Butcher, J., Lim, J., & Nezami, E. (1998). Objective study of abnormal personality in cross-cultural settings: The Minnesota Multiphasic Personality Inventory (MMPI-2). *Journal of Cross-Cultural Psychology, 29,* 189–211.

Cheung, F., & Leung, K. (1998). Indigenous personality measures: Chinese examples. *Journal of Cross-Cultural Psychology, 29,* 233–248.

Church, A., & Lonner, W. (Eds.). (1998). Personality and its measurement in cross-cultural perspective. *Journal of Cross-Cultural Psychology, 29,* 5–270.

Ho, D. (1998). Indigenous psychologies: Asian perspectives. *Journal of Cross-Cultural Psychology, 29,* 88–103.

LaFromboise, T., Coleman, H., & Gerton, J. (1993). Psychological impact of biculturalism: Evidence and theory. *Psychological Bulletin, 114,* 395–412.

R. W. BRISLIN
University of Hawaii

ETHNOCENTRISM

CROSS-CULTURAL PSYCHOLOGY: INTRODUCTION AND OVERVIEW

The study of human behavior must include observations made all around the world, not just in the few highly industrialized nations where most research has historically been done. The concept of *culture* summarizes many of the major influences on human behavior and the bases for concepts of self and group identity that people hold. Further, aspects of culture have major effects on the formulation, dissemination, and acceptance of programs designed to deliver psychological services or to use psychological principles. Cross-cultural research is also central to theory development and programs aimed at applying the lessons learned from research (Brislin, 2000; Berry, Poortinga, & Pandey, 1997).

DEFINITIONS OF CULTURE

As with many complex concepts in psychology, no one definition of "culture" is widely accepted. Psychologists have not expended much effort developing definitions of culture, but have benefited from the efforts of their colleagues in anthropology. Alfred Kroeber and Clyde Kluckhohn, in "Culture: A Critical Review of Concepts and Definitions," concluded by suggesting that many definitions contained "patterns, explicit and implicit, of or for behavior transmitted by symbols, constituting the distinctive achievements of human groups . . . [and] ideas and their attached values" (Kroeber & Kluckhohn, 1952, p. 181). Melville Herskovits, in *Man and His Works* (1948, p. 17), proposed the equally influential generalization that culture is "the man-made part of the human environment." In *The Analysis of Subjective Culture,* Harry Triandis benefited from Herskovits' contribution and made a distinction between physical and subjective culture. The former would include humanly constructed objects such as houses and tools, while the latter comprises people's responses to those objects in the form of values, roles, and attitudes.

It is important to delimit the concept of culture, lest it be so all-encompassing as to explain little or nothing in particular. Violent storms are not best conceptualized as part of a culture, even though a certain society may inhabit an area in a hurricane belt. However, people's reactions to storms in the form of preparations, or collective action following a disaster, are indeed part of their culture.

Since much cross-cultural research has the goal of understanding concepts as seen by people in the culture under study, the influence of cognitive psychology has been strong. Much research has focused on people's knowledge about their world, their communication with one another given this shared knowledge, and the transmission of this knowledge to the next generation. Given this emphasis, a third definition of culture suggested by Clifford Geertz (1973) captures the flavor of much cross-cultural research: "Culture denotes an historically transmitted pattern of meanings embodied in symbols, a system of inherited conceptions expressed in symbolic forms by means of which men communicate, perpetuate, and develop their knowledge about and attitudes toward life" (Geertz, 1973, p. 89).

In research programs, many psychologists use aspects of all three definitions. In studies of ethnocentrism, for instance, the fact that ideas have "attached value"—suggested by Kroeber and Kluckhohn (1952)—should be added to the concept of "symbolic forms" which Geertz formulated. The fact that people's symbols are valued leads to ethnocentric thinking, especially concerning subjective elements such as ideology, religion, morality, or law. Ethnocentrism refers to the deeply held belief that one's own culture is the best (defined by that culture's own standards), and that others are inferior in many ways. People almost uniformly believe that what they do is good or right, and that members of other cultures are somewhat backward and/or illogical with regard to their customs, rituals, food, interpersonal relationships, and other aspects of everyday behavior.

DEFINITION OF CROSS-CULTURAL PSYCHOLOGY

Cross-cultural psychology is the study of culture's effects on human behavior. More formally, cross-cultural psychology is the empirical study of members of various culture groups with identifiable experiences which lead to predictable and significant similarities and differences in behavior.

A term related to culture that has received a great deal of attention from psychologists is *subculture.* This term is frequently used when referring to groups of people who have had experiences (which can and do affect behavior) different from those of most people in a given country or society. People from the subculture live in the same country or society as another larger group, the latter group often being called the *majority culture.* Examples of subcultures in the United States include Italian Americans and Japanese Americans; other examples are religious groups such as the Amish or the Latter-Day Saints. Subculture is a flexible term, and has been used to refer to deviant groups such as the drug subculture or the motorcycle gang subculture. Whenever a group of people develop their own norms, jargon, and means of communication, their actions become similar to that of various subcultures. Negative consequences, such as distrust of outsiders, also usually develop. Examples are the advisors who surround a head of state, scientists within a specialized interest area, and amateur musicians interested in a certain kind of music.

A person can belong to several subcultures as well as to a majority culture. For instance, individuals who grow up in an Italian American neighborhood can accept the values of the Roman Catholic religion and guide parts of their lives according to its tenets. These people can also subscribe to the values of the middle-class majority culture, such as believing in hard work and the accumulation of individual wealth. Such people can be said to belong to an ethnic (Italian American) and a religious (Roman Catholic) subculture, as well as to the American middle-class culture.

Some people might be considered members of a given culture, but explicitly reject certain of the values and prescribed behaviors of that culture. An example would be young, well-educated people who reject the work ethic and the accumulation of individual wealth, and instead prefer collective ownership of property. Several important points can be made in such cases, which are found in virtually all large and complex cultures. First, even though the people may reject the culture's values and behaviors, they are familiar with what they are rejecting, since the values and desirable behaviors were communicated to them, and they had observed others who did accept the cultural norms. Many people who reject the American work ethic have relatives who went through the behavioral steps (e.g., specialized schooling) so as to benefit from the fruits of the ethic. Thus the nonaccepters are quite familiar with this major aspect of their culture. Such nonaccepters are sometimes supported financially by friends and relatives who are centrally involved in the majority culture.

A second point worth noting is that the entire span of individuals must be considered. People may rebel against convention in their youth, but as they become older, acceptance of their culture's norms and values often proves functional. The responsibilities of parenthood often seem to conventionalize the most fiery radicals. Since they already know the accepted values and norms, it is easy to make the transition from nonaccepter to accepter. This example is consistent with the observations of Hermans and Kempen (1998), who discuss the functional nature of people's identities in cross-cultural situations. People have a number of possible identities because of ethnic background (which often allows claims of *multiple* ethnic group membership), religious affiliations, extensive travel to other cultures, education, job experiences, and so forth. People can then draw from this "smorgasbord" to meet the demands of various situations. If scholarships for advanced study become available to members of a certain ethnic group, then people may rediscover their link to that group through some long-forgotten relative. If entry into the workplace is desired, then the intercession of a friend (who has long accepted the work ethic) may be tapped.

WIDESPREAD USE OF "CULTURE" AS A THEORETICALLY IMPORTANT VARIABLE

Any definition is helpful insofar as it assists researchers to gather better data. The concept of "culture" may run the danger of being so broad as to limit its usefulness. Reviewing research in developmental psychology, Harkness (1980, p. 11) pointed to the "invisibility of the culture in psychological theory," arguing that the historical neglect of the concept led to an overemphasis on nativist theories of child development. Since so many aspects of culture are not assessed in the typical study *within* any one country, results are too often attributed to genetic factors or to the presence or absence of some supposed universal process. Similarly, Touhey pointed to the importance of culture in analyzing failures to replicate studies in social psychology: "A rapidly expanding body of research in cross-cultural psychology has alerted investigators to the possibility that many basic findings on personality and micro social processes will not generalize across cultures" (Touhey, 1981, p. 594). Expanding on this point, Touhey argues that it is necessary to gather data on the sorts of variables that Geertz (1973) specifies when researchers make attempts to generalize across subpopulations or subcultures within a country. The lack of information on such critical aspects of culture as preferences, knowledge about a topic, and salient symbols (which may be present but unanalyzed in the research situation) makes failures to replicate almost impossible to explicate.

THE USES AND BENEFITS OF CROSS-CULTURAL RESEARCH

While benefiting from the contributions of anthropologists in conceptualizing "culture," psychologists themselves have analyzed the uses and benefits that cross-cultural research can add to theory development. The following benefits also begin to answer the question: "Why should one do cross-cultural research, given the additional problems caused by work in unfamiliar settings with people who speak a different language and are often unfamiliar with empirical inquiry, and the bothersome regulations required by the government of the country hosting the research?"

Increasing Range of Variables

The most frequently cited use of cross-cultural research (e.g., Berry, Poortinga, & Pandey, 1997) is to increase the range of independent variables, or a wider range of conceivable responses to dependent variables, in other cultures or in comparisons across cultures. The clearest example (Whiting 1954, 1968) is undoubtedly the age at which babies are weaned. If researchers are interested in the relationship between the age of weaning and other parental decisions about child-rearing behavior, or between age of weaning and personality when the children reach adulthood, there is a restricted range within any one culture. In the United States and most countries in Western Europe, for instance, the age of weaning is six months to one year. But since the accepted age is different in other cultures, ranging up to five years, researchers can relate the age-of-weaning variable to others if they compare samples across cultures. Information concerning many everyday behaviors of people around the world have been conveniently collected in the Human Relations Area Files (Barry, 1980), a well-organized compilation of information about hundreds of cultures. The data contained there has been gathered largely by anthropologists, therefore topics of interest to them (e.g., kinship, land tenure, ritual) are emphasized. The data also center on directly observable behaviors such as age of weaning, parental disciplinary practices, and number of caretakers for children. More abstract questions of interest to psychologists, which could be gathered only by extensive questioning (e.g., people's connotations of intelligence, desirable personality traits in children to help them meet future uncertainties) are only occasionally found in HRAF.

Another example of increased range can be found in the research of Segall, Campbell, and Herskovits (1966), who studied the origin of basic perceptual processes. Are these processes present at birth, given people's genetic endowment, or are they learned? In one of the first large-scale research programs to investigate native versus learned theories, Segall and his colleagues attempted to relate features of the environment in which people are raised to independently assessed perceptual mechanisms. However, they could not do this research effectively within any one country, since in any particular country the range of environmental features is relatively narrow. Instead, they studied a number of cultures with widely ranging features, especially the presence or absence of buildings built with tools, the number of 90° angles in the arrangement of the building materials, and the number of open vistas extending to the horizon. Data were gathered from 17 different samples in the United States, Africa, and the Philippines on people's reactions to a number of visual illusions that constituted the research project's test of perceptual tendencies. Since wide differences in susceptibility to visual illusions across cultures were found to be systematically related to environmental features, the existence of learned perceptual mechanisms was demonstrated. An important methodological feature of this study is worthy of note, as it is of potential usefulness in large numbers of cross-cultural studies (Brislin, Lonner, & Thorndike, 1973). Segall and his colleagues found that people from cultures with many buildings constructed with 90°

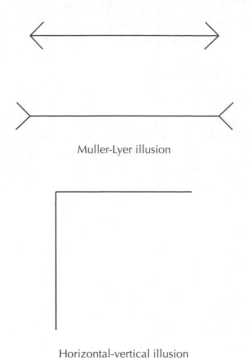

Muller-Lyer illusion

Horizontal-vertical illusion

Figure 1.   Two visual illusions: is one line longer than the other?

angles (called "carpentered environments") were more susceptible to the Muller-Lyer illusion, while people from cultures with many open vistas were more susceptible to the horizontal-vertical illusion. For instance, United States subjects were more susceptible to the former, but less susceptible to the latter, than subjects in rural African villages.

The interaction between sample and stimuli rules out many plausible alternative explanations, such as lack of familiarity with the task among one or more of the samples.

Unconfounding Variables

An intriguing possibility is that variables that occur together in one culture and hence are confounded in any statistical analysis can be studied separately in other cultures or when comparisons across cultures are made (Brown & Sechrest, 1980). The classic example is Branislaw Malinowski's analysis (1927) of the behaviors Sigmund Freud called the Oedipal complex (an example also analyzed by Jahoda & Krewer, 1997). Freud, observing tension and a certain amount of hostility in boys' relations to their fathers, proposed that the boy is jealous of the father because the father is the lover of the boy's mother. In cross-cultural analyses of the Oedipal complex, it appeared that Freud's observations were based on a limited set of conditions found in Vienna in the late 1800s.

In the Trobriand Islands, Malinowski observed that the father was not necessarily the object of a boy's hostility. Rather, ill feelings were directed toward his mother's brother, who is the family disciplinarian in that culture. A boy's tense relations with his uncle, then, could be predicted from knowledge that it is the source of discipline who is disliked. Malinowski suggested that the boy may indeed dislike his father, but because of the father's role as disciplinarian rather than as his mother's lover. Cross-cultural obser-

vations, then, unconfounded a situation found in Euro-American nations.

After World War II, schools based on those in the United States were introduced into many Pacific societies (see Colletta, 1980, for a review). Because there were not enough Pacific Islanders trained to work as teachers in such schools, educators from the United States were imported on a contract basis. Naturally, these teachers attempted to form support structures with which they were familiar. One was the formation of a Parent-Teachers Association (PTA), but the educators were surprised to learn that there was little PTA support from the Pacific Islanders. After discussions with community leaders, the educators discovered that these parents do not take responsibility for seeing that their children do well in the schools. That task was the responsibility of the mother's brother! The joke made the rounds that educators should have started a UTA: an Uncle-Teachers Association. But there *was* more community support of the schools once the mothers' brothers were involved.

In many studies, the "cross-cultural" or "culture" variables are simply labels for a package of confounded concepts. In analyzing intercultural marriages, Fontaine and Dorch (1980) worked with different categories of married couples so as to break down the overly general label of "cross-cultural." They gathered data from couples whose marriage was interethnic, involving different skin color; intercountry in origin, but not involving a skin color difference; and interreligious. They also gathered data from intracultural marriages so as to differentiate the issues faced by all married couples from those arising from the intercultural aspect. The researchers found that there were different dynamics in the marriages of interethnic couples, compared to intercountry couples. Interethnic couples reported more problems as being due, in their perceptions, to external factors in their communities, while the intercountry couples traced more problems to factors internal to the marriage partners or to the marriage itself. The authors interpreted these results as showing that differences in country of origin do not produce the same level of negative community response as do differences in skin color. Thus, interethnic couples indeed have external factors to which they have to react, and which, understandably, are used as the explanation for many marriage problems. The intercountry differences are less visible to the community but are no less real to the partners, so intercountry couples attribute more problems to internal factors than do interethnic couples. The important procedural point is that Fontaine and Dorch could not have made the distinction in locus of attribution (internal versus external) if they had worked only with the broad category of "cross-cultural marriages." Instead, they unconfounded this packaged variable into the important component parts of interethnicity and intercountry of origin.

Study of the Context in Which Behavior Occurs

The social environment in which people find themselves has been notoriously difficult to operationalize (Markus & Kitayama, 1998). The study of social context has been an active research focus for cross-cultural psychologists (Bilmes & Boggs, 1979; Harkness, 1980; Cole & Means, 1981; Kagitcibasi, 1997). In their own culture, investigators are so close to the same social contexts as the participants in their research projects that separation of person from context is difficult. In other cultures, since visiting investigators have not had so much experience with various everyday social contexts, they can more easily separate themselves from social situations and formulate hypotheses about the relative contributions of individual and contextual factors (Hall, 1977; Brislin, 1981, 2000).

At times, psychologists interested in the applications of research knowledge can take advantage of knowledge about social context. Jordan and Tharp (1979) developed programs to teach Hawaiian and part-Hawaiian children to read. They had little success after importing methods found to be effective in the United States or Western Europe. They did research, however, on children's everyday behavior in their homes and in their communities, and found that the children spent large amounts of time sitting around telling stories to one another and listening to adults tell such stories. The researchers then used knowledge of this practice, called "talk story" in Hawaii, in the classroom. They found that if children read their books as members of small groups, and then discussed what they had just read, reading skills improved dramatically.

So-called standardized tests are usually normed on children from the middle-class in the United States. The question arises: Are these tests fair for children from quite different cultures (Greenfield, 1997)? This difficult question has been examined by some of the foremost scholars in test theory (Glaser & Bond, 1981). The answer depends on the social context in which test scores are to be used. If used to make inferences about children's underlying competencies, how they think, or their native ability compared to some other group, the tests would be used unfairly and would be inappropriate. However, if the purpose of testing is to assess the classroom progress of children from one cultural group in schools that are more familiar to children from another group, then the tests can be used fairly.

There are alternatives to the use of tests, however. One is to devise entire curricula and even school structures around ideas and materials with which children from various cultural groups are familiar, eliminating the imposition of a system from one culture on children from another. This approach, however, is impractical. There is not a well-developed body of knowledge concerning the transfer of learning methods from one context (children's everyday lives in their culture) to another (any kind of formal schooling). The expense and even political give-and-take of such efforts are also drawbacks, as exemplified by experience in bilingual education (Gersten & Woodward, 1995). The culture-sensitive methods of assessing cognitive skills (e.g., Cole & Scribner, 1974) demand large amounts of one-on-one interaction between highly trained professionals and children. The massive number of students whose progress must be assessed in American schools prevents the luxury of such testing sessions. With all of its imperfections, then, the use of standardized tests together with careful interpretation of students' scores remains a reasonable approach.

Maximization of Differences in Respondents' Attributes

If research hypotheses are supported in studies with different populations, the findings can be taken more seriously than hypotheses supported only by studies of homogeneous populations within one country. In cross-cultural studies, variances of respondents' attributes not directly related to the hypotheses are maximized, and these variances are often extremely difficult to obtain within any one research site. If research findings are supported despite the variance added from other cultures, then the hypotheses must be robust.

Robert Levine (1997; Levine & Norenzayan, 1999) was interested in examining the hypothesis that a fast pace of life can lead to stress-related health problems such as coronary heart disease (Taylor, Repette, & Seeman, 1997). He chose the cross-cultural approach because, based on his observations during his travels and on the experiences of others, people in some cultures have a much faster pace of life than people in other cultures. Three types of information were collected in 31 countries. These were (a) the amount of time it takes pedestrians to walk 60 feet in cities; (b) the amount of time it takes postal clerks to take a banknote, sell a stamp, and return change to the customer; and, (c) the accuracy of public clocks compared against the standard within any one country. Results showed large differences, with industrialized, economically successful countries in Europe having a fast pace of life, and countries in Latin and South America having a slower pace. With the exception of Japan, Levine found the hypothesized relationship between pace of life and coronary heart disease. Reasons for the exception in Japan may be due to the social support that can be expected in a collectivist culture, a low fat diet, or other currently unknown factors. Another important finding, perhaps conflicting with "common sense," is that a fast pace of life was related to an independent measure of people's happiness. One explanation is that a fast pace of life contributes to economic success ("time is money") and that economic success contributes to people's happiness.

The importance of the cultural context in which behavior occurs was discussed previously and was examined by Levine in this study. The pace of life in Japan, which measured fourth fastest out of 31 countries, would have been even faster if postal clerks had not carefully wrapped each customer's stamp order in nice paper. In India, the study could not be carried out since Indian postal clerks did not view making change as part of their jobs. These findings allow the analysis of behavior in context and allow such research questions as, "What are differing views of customer service and clerk responsibilities?" At times, the study of context can be amusing. In cities in California, it was difficult to find a place where people walk 60 feet, given the ubiquity of automobile travel. Parking lots were not always a possible research site, since people driving their cars would circle lots until they found a spot less than 60 feet from their destinations. Levine (1997) admitted the temptation of following people as they drive to health spas and then timing their pace on Stairmaster exercise machines.

In addition to understanding the benefits of gathering data in other cultures, two other ways of introducing cross-cultural psychology are: (a) examining one of the major conceptual tools for the analysis of equivalence across cultures, as well as the analysis of culture-specific meaning; and (b) examining some specific cross-cultural studies to determine what contributions to more general theoretical developments can be made.

CONCLUSION

Any definition of psychology must take into account observations made in various parts of the world, not just those few countries in which most psychological research has historically been done. Cross-cultural studies, then, are central to the development of psychology. Cross-cultural contributions should increase in the future, as more and more psychologists in various countries free themselves from the shackles of imposed theories from Euro-American sources. Psychologists in various countries can develop their own theories to explain research findings that differ from predictions based on Euro-American theories.

REFERENCES

Barry, H. (1980). Description and uses of the Human Relations Area Files. In H. Triandis & J. Berry (Eds.), *Handbook of cross-cultural psychology* (Vol. 2., pp. 445–478). Boston: Allyn & Bacon.

Berry, J., Poortinga, Y., & Pandey, J. (Eds.). (1997). *Handbook of cross-cultural psychology: Vol. 1. Theory and method* (2nd ed.). Boston: Allyn and Bacon.

Bilmes, J., & Boggs, S. (1979). Language and communication: The foundations of culture. In A. Marsella, R. Tharp, & T. Ciborowski (Eds.), *Perspectives on cross-cultural psychology.* New York: Academic Press.

Brislin, R. (1981). *Cross-cultural encounters: Face-to-face interaction.* Elmsford, NY: Pergamon Press.

Brislin, R. (2000). *Understanding culture's influence on behavior* (2nd ed.). Fort Worth, TX: Harcourt Brace.

Brislin, R., Lonner, W., & Thorndike, R. (1973). *Cross-cultural research methods.* New York: Wiley.

Brown, E., & Sechrest, L. (1980). Experiments in cross-cultural research. In H. Triandis & J. Berry (Eds.), *Handbook of cross-cultural psychology* (Vol. 2., pp. 297–318). Boston: Allyn & Bacon.

Cole, M., & Means, B. (1981). *Comparative studies of how people think.* Cambridge, MA: Harvard University Press.

Cole, M., & Scribner, S. (1974). *Culture and thought: A psychological introduction.* New York: Wiley.

Colletta, N. (1980). Ponape: Cross-cultural contact, formal schooling, and foreign dominance. In M. Hamnett & R. Brislin (Eds.), *Research in culture learning: Language and conceptual studies* (pp. 61–69). Honolulu: University Press of Hawaii.

Dorfman, P. (1996). International and cross-cultural leadership. In B. Punnett & O. Shenkar (Eds.), *Handbook for international management research* (pp. 267–349). Cambridge, MA: Blackwell.

Fontaine, G., & Dorch, E. (1980). Problems and benefits of close inter-cultural relationships. *International Journal of Intercultural Relations, 4,* 329–337.

Francesco, A., & Gold, B. (1998). *International organizational behavior.* Upper Saddle River, NJ: Prentice Hall.

Gersten, R., & Woodward, J. (1995). A longitudinal study of transitional and immersion bilingual education programs in one district. *Elementary School Journal, 95,* 223–239.

Glaser, R., & Bond, L. (Eds.). (1981). Testing: Concepts, policy, practice, and research. *American Psychologist* [special issue], *36,* 995–1189.

Geertz, C. (1973). Thick description: Toward an interpretive theory of culture. In *The interpretation of cultures.* New York: Basic Books.

Greenfield, P. (1997). You can't take it with you: Why ability assessments don't cross cultures. *American Psychologist, 52,* 1115–1124.

Hall, E. (1977). *Beyond culture.* Garden City, NY: Anchor Books.

Harkness, S. (1980). The cultural context of child development. *New Directions for Child Development, 8,* 7–13.

Hermans, H., & Kempen, H. (1998). Moving cultures: Perilous problems of cultural dichotomies in a globalizing society. *American Psychologist, 53,* 1111–1120.

Herskovits, M. (1948). *Man and his work.* New York: Knopf.

Jahoda, G., & Krewer, B. (1997). History of cross-cultural and cultural psychology. In J. Berry, Y. Poortinga, & J. Pandey (Eds.), *Handbook of cross-cultural psychology Vol. 1. Theory and method* (2nd ed., pp. 1–42). Boston: Allyn and Bacon.

Jordan, C., & Tharp, R. (1979). Culture and education. In A. Marsella, R. Tharp, & T. Ciborowski (Eds.), *Perspectives on cross-cultural psychology.* New York: Academic.

Kagitcibasi, C. (1997). Individualism and collectivism. In J. Berry, M. Segall, & C. Kagitcibasi (Eds.), *Handbook of cross-cultural psychology, 2nd ed., vol. 3: Behavior and applications* (pp. 1–49). Boston: Allyn and Bacon.

Kroeber, A., & Kluckhohn, C. (1952). Culture. *Papers of the Peabody Museum, 47,* (1).

Levine, R. (1997). *A geography of time.* New York: HarperCollins.

Levine, R., & Norenzayan, A. (1999). The pace of life in 31 countries. *Journal of Cross-Cultural Psychology, 30,* 178–205.

Malinowski, B. (1927). *Sex and repression in savage society.* New York: Harcourt, Brace, & Co.

Markus, H., & Kitayama, S. (1998). The cultural psychology of personality. *Journal of Cross-Cultural Psychology, 29,* 63–87.

Segall, M. H., Campbell, D. T., & Herskovits, M. J. (1966). *The influence of culture on visual perception.* New York: Bobbs-Merrill.

Taylor, S., Repette, R., & Seeman, T. (1997). Health psychology: What is an unhealthy environment and how does it get under the skin? *Annual Review of Psychology, 48,* 411–447.

Touhey, J. (1981). Replication failures in personality and social psychology. Negative findings or mistaken assumptions. *Personality and Social Psychology Bulletin, 7,* 593–595.

Whiting, J. (1954). The cross-cultural method. In G. Lindzey (Ed.), *Handbook of social psychology* (Vol. 1). Reading, MA: Addison-Wesley.

Whiting, J. (1968). Methods and problems in cross-cultural research. In G. Lindzey & E. Aronson (Eds.), *Handbook of social psychology* (2nd ed., Vol. 2). Reading, MA: Addison-Wesley.

SUGGESTED READING

Adler, N. A. (1997). *International dimensions of organizational behavior* (3rd ed.). Boston: PWS-Kent.

Berry, J., Poortinga, Y., & Pandey, J. (Eds.). (1997). *Handbook of cross-cultural psychology* (2nd ed., 3 vols.).

Bond, M. (1995). Doing social psychology cross-culturally: Into another heart of darkness. In G. Brannigan and M. Merrens (Eds.), *The social psychologists: Research adventures* (pp. 187–205). New York: McGraw-Hill.

Cushner, K., & Brislin, R. (1996). *Intercultural interactions: A practical guide* (2nd ed.). Thousand Oaks, CA: Sage.

Dorfman, P. (1996). International and cross-cultural leadership. In B. Punnett, & O. Shenkar (Eds.), *Handbook for international management research* (pp. 267–349). Cambridge, MA: Blackwell.

Francesco, A., & Gold, B. (1998). *International organizational behavior.* Upper Saddle River, NJ: Prentice Hall.

Goldstein, S. (1995). Cross-cultural psychology as a curriculum transformation resource. *Teaching of Psychology, 22,* 228–232.

Landis, D., & Bhagat, R. (Eds.). (1996). *Handbook of intercultural training* (2nd ed.). Thousand Oaks, CA: Sage.

Segall, M., Lonner, W., & Berry, J. (1998). Cross-cultural psychology as a scholarly discipline: On the flowering of culture in behavioral research. *American Psychologist, 53,* 1101–1110.

Singelis, T. (Ed.). (1998). *Teaching about culture, ethnicity, and diversity. Exercises and planned activities.* Thousand Oaks, CA: Sage.

Triandis, H., Berry, J., Lonner, W., Heron, A., Brislin, R., & Draguns, J. (Eds.). (1980). *Handbook of cross-cultural psychology* (6 vols.). Boston: Allyn & Bacon.

Triandis, H., Kurowski, L., & Gelfand, M. (1994). Workplace diversity. In H. Triandis, M. Dunnette, & L. Hough (Eds.), *Handbook of industrial and organizational psychology* (2nd ed., Vol. 4, pp. 769–827). Palo Alto, CA: Consulting Psychologists Press.

R. W. BRISLIN
University of Hawaii

ACCULTURATION

CROSS-CULTURAL RESEARCH EXAMPLES

THE GROUP POLARIZATION PHENOMENON

One way to explain the benefits of cross-cultural research is to examine a number of specific research examples. A good example is the polarization of an individual's decisions after discussions with other people. An intriguing finding from social psychological research in the 1960s (Kogan & Wallach, 1964) was that groups seemed to make more risky decisions than individuals. People given choice dilemma situations would be asked to decide on their recommended course of action. One dilemma concerned a well-paid engineer in a secure job who was offered a new position in a small, newly formed, innovative company. If successful, the engineer would become a part owner of the company. Should the engineer take the new job? The major result of research using this paradigm was that people in the United States made riskier decisions after discussions with other people. The difference between individual recommendations and those same individuals' recommendations after discussion with others came to be known as the "risky shift" phenomenon.

Two major cross-cultural studies shed a great deal of light on this phenomenon. One explanation of the risky shift effect (e.g., Aronson, Wilson, & Akert, 1999) is that innovative, daring decisions are valued in the American culture. Since people were reminded of this value and reinforced for expressing it in group discussions, they would be more likely to adopt riskier decisions after the interaction with others. If this explanation is true, then the risky shift would not be found in cultures that have strong norms about the values of caution, respect for tradition, and conservatism. Carlson and Davis (1971) carried out an experiment involving individual and group decisions in both the United States and Uganda, choosing the latter because of its strong conservative values. As predicted, there were more risky shifts in the United States and more cautious shifts in Uganda. For a time, the phenomenon was called the "value shift" effect, to incorporate this and similar data.

Gologor (1977), working in Liberia (likewise chosen for its greater respect for tradition than the United States), hypothesized that all the previous data were correct but that there was a better explanation. In the United States research there was too little variety in the choice dilemmas to which people were asked to respond. Researchers continued using the same ones over and over, so that the results became method-bound to those few dilemmas. There are undoubtedly decisions about which individuals in the United States are very cautious (e.g., flying an airplane in poor weather).

Realizing the possibility of a shift toward caution as well as a shift toward risk, Gologor proposed that the best label for the observed phenomena is "group polarization." For choice dilemmas about which individuals tend to make conservative decisions, group discussions lead to more conservative decisions. For choice dilemmas about which individuals tend to make risky decisions, group discussions lead to decisions recommending more risk. In addition to expanding the scope of the hypotheses, Gologor also created new choice dilemmas meaningful to the research participants in Liberia. Such a procedure has at least two benefits. First, choice dilemmas are meaningful to respondents. If they do not take into account choice dilemmas relevant to a culture, researchers can easily gather reactions to unfamiliar, imposed dilemmas from another culture—hardly a worthwhile procedure. The other benefit is that any results and theoretical explanation can be generalized beyond the original set of choice dilemmas used in too many studies in the United States.

Two possible explanations for the group polarization phenomenon (McGrath & Kravitz, 1982; Aronson et al., 1999), both of which undoubtedly are present in many group discussion situations, are "social comparison" and "persuasive arguments." The former refers to the reinforcement an individual finds for his or her preconceived view about a dilemma after hearing that others in the group share similar opinions. Persuasive arguments are among the verbalizations the individual will undoubtedly hear from like-minded people in the group, giving the individual new information to bolster the preconceived view.

WORKER MOTIVATION

The need hierarchy theory of motivation (Maslow, 1943) hypothesizes that various levels of motives have an influence on people's behavior. The needs at lower levels must be satisfied before people become concerned about higher level motives. From lowest to highest, the needs are: (a) physiological needs which reflect people's basic demands for food, water, shelter, and sleep; (b) safety, satisfied by a secure environment; (c) love, or the desire to be accepted by others; (d) esteem, especially satisfaction with one's own work and respect from others; and (e) self-actualization, or the striving toward the fulfillment of one's unique interests and abilities.

The intriguing idea that lower level needs (the first two levels, also called "maintenance needs" in the collective) have to be satisfied before higher level needs (called "growth needs" in the collective) are considered may be better supported in cross-cultural research than in research carried out within any one country (Aram & Piraino, 1978), because of the increase in variance obtained when working across cultures. Looking at behavior across different countries, one finds a greater range in the satisfaction of people's basic maintenance needs than within the countries (e.g., the United States, Australia, Great Britain) where most empirical research has been done.

Another important aspect of need hierarchy theory is that there is more cross-cultural variability in the specific higher level motives that workers find important. Basic level motives, closely tied to the satisfaction of bodily demands such as food and protection from the elements, are not different from country to country, though workers in some countries are more likely to have these motives satisfied than are workers in other countries. Higher level motives, on the other hand, are much more likely to be influenced by cultural factors. The definitions of culture reviewed previously, such as "ideas and their attached values" (Kroeber & Kluckhohn, 1952), include phenomena frequently observed in anecdotal accounts of work in various countries.

Hofstede (1980, 1991) combined work-related anecdotes with extensive data from surveys of worker behavior in over 50 countries. Using questionnaires completed by workers, he identified four higher level motivational concepts which vary greatly from one country to another. An understanding of these four motives is helpful in answering questions about why workers' values in various countries appear to be so different once basic needs have been met. Similarly, the motives are helpful for an understanding of multinational organizations, since managers accustomed to one pattern of the four motive hierarchies might be confronted with another pattern when assigned to another country.

The first motive discussed by Hofstede is *power distance.* This refers to the preferred amount of psychological distance between workers and managers. Questions used to measure the motive's strength ask how often employees are afraid to express disagreement with their managers; what workers prefer in the decision-making style of their boss (autocratic, paternalistic, consultative, democratic); and what bosses actually do, independent of employee preference. Countries with a high power-distance index are those where authority is concentrated among a relatively small number of managers, as in the Philippines, Mexico, Venezuela, and India. Countries low on this dimension include New Zealand, Denmark, Israel, and Austria. With respect to understanding worker behavior, differences in the motive involve what workers want from their jobs: participation in decision making versus clear-cut guidelines from authorities. Differences also indicate that young managers from countries high on this index may work to advance themselves so as to eventually have power over others.

The second motive is *uncertainty avoidance.* "Uncertainty about the future is a basic fact of human life with which we try to cope through the domains of technology, law and religion. In organizations these take the form of technology, rules, and rituals" (Hofstede, 1980, p. 153). Questions measuring this motive ask about the wisdom of breaking company rules even if an employee is convinced that such action is best; perceived length of an employee's stay with a given company; and frequency of stress experienced at work. Countries combining a high degree of rule orientation and employment stability with a high accompanying stress level are said to be high on uncertainty avoidance. The interrelation among the three uncertainty factors is not intuitively obvious. Hofstede writes: "The conceptual link among the stress question and the other two questions is the mean level of anxiety in a country. When this is higher, people feel more stressed; but at the same time they try to cope with the anxiety by a greater need for security, which is visible in both rule orientation and employment stability" (p. 164). Countries high on this index include Japan, Portugal, Greece, and Peru. Countries low on the index include Singapore, Denmark, Sweden, and the United States. Probably the best-known correlate of this index is managers' willingness to take risks in various countries (McClelland, 1961). The higher the uncertainty avoidance level, the lower the willingness to take risks. Note that the frequently made observation of Japanese as risk avoiders and Americans as risk takers fits with this conception.

Analysis of the third motive, *individualism* contrasted with *collectivism* (see also Triandis, 1995), follows directly from the discussion of self-growth motives. Workers in the 50 countries were surveyed to discover what they found important in their jobs. The individualism index was composed of work goals such as sufficient time for personal and family life, considerable freedom to design one's own approach to the job, and challenging work from which an individual can obtain a personal sense of accomplishment. Countries high on this index include the United States, Australia, Great Britain, and Canada. The lowest are Peru, Pakistan, Columbia, and Venezuela. These countries are referred to as collectivistic, and people in such countries are much more likely to define themselves in relation to other people rather than in terms of individual traits and goals (Markus & Kitayama, 1998; Triandis, 1995). Again, these data shed insights on old anecdotes. Most multinational organizations have staff from "high individualism" countries who have worked in one of the collectivistic countries. When such people try to manage by encouraging individualistic motives rather than contributions to a group effort, there is almost inevitably a failure. Individualism and collectivism were the most well-researched concepts in cross-cultural psychology during the 1990s (Triandis, 1995; Kagitcibasi, 1997). Important work has conceptualized individualism and collectivism as orthogonal dimensions rather than as polar opposites. Consequently, people can have both individualistic and collectivist tendencies and can call upon either or both depending on the social context in which they find themselves.

The fourth motive, derived from the same survey about aspects of work considered important, is called *masculinity-femininity* (Hofstede, 1998). This label was chosen because it best summarizes two sets of work goals, one traditionally preferred by males and one traditionally preferred by females in highly industrialized countries. Masculine goals include advancement, earnings, training, and being up-to-date; feminine goals include a friendly atmosphere, position security, good physical conditions, good relations with one's manager, and cooperation with coworkers. Countries high on the masculinity index include Japan, Austria, Venezuela, and Italy. Countries low on the index—that is, where the feminine goals are more important—are Chile, Portugal, and the Scandinavian countries including Finland.

These motivational factors should not be overinterpreted. The finding that Scandinavian countries are low on masculinity goals does not mean that promotions and advancement are totally unimportant there; rather, they are less important relative to the feminine goals for a significant number of workers in those countries. At times, motivational patterns will be the starting point for much more thought. It is surprising that the Japanese are not high on such feminine goals as "cooperation," since the popular view posits a close and cordial relationship between management and labor. It is possible that "cooperation" is so prevalent that it is taken for granted by workers filling out the questionnaire, so that they emphasize the relatively less fulfilled masculine goals. Alternatively, given that Japan is highly collective, the cooperation they expect may stem from this cultural value.

LEARNING AND COGNITION

In much early cross-cultural research on learning and cognition, investigators compared responses of cultural groups in various parts of the world with responses from Euro-American groups. Inevitably, the researchers were struck by how slowly learning seemed to progress in the other cultures, how inefficient the people were in organizing material to be learned; how unsophisticated the explanations for their responses seemed to be, or how quiet and unresponsive people seemed to be in what—to the experimenters—was an interesting opportunity to learn new material and/or demonstrate learning prowess. Reacting against these interpretations, several more sophisticated cross-cultural researchers took a careful look at the results of such studies and recommended much more caution and sensitivity in interpreting results. One of the major thrusts of this more recent research is the demonstration that learning is strongly affected by the social context in which people live and work (Miller, 1997).

For example, Labov (1970) analyzed the puzzling problem that young black children in the United States are often termed "noncommunicative" and "nonfluent" by their white teachers in school. However, when these same children are among their peers outside of school, communication and fluency are striking; indeed, verbal repartee is a desirable, status-giving characteristic. In a similar analysis, a group led by Cole (Cole, Gay, Glick, and Sharp, 1971) analyzed the difficulties encountered by the Kpelle of Liberia in schools, contrasting this with their skills at tasks outside of school. The verdict of "inadequacy in school" was often made by teachers, yet the skills that Cole tested outside of school (such as the estimation of volume) sometimes surpassed those of comparison groups in the United States (see also Kim & Berry, 1993).

Close examination of these and other learning situations prompted Cole to summarize a great deal of work in a short statement: "Culture differences in cognition reside more in the situation to which particular cognitive processes are applied than in the existence of a process in one cultural group and its absence in another" (Cole et al., 1971, p. 233). This summarizing principle has many implications. It means that people in all cultures have skills, but situational characteristics are important in allowing the skill to be easily used. The black children in the example studied by Labov have verbal skills, but the school situation, most often administered by people from another (white majority) culture, does not elicit such skills. Similarly with the Kpelle studied by Cole: Skills useful in their farming community do not transfer directly to the school. The challenge for educational institutions is to take advantage of the skills already possessed by children so as to find ways to use the use the old in learning new material.

Another implication is that competence cannot necessarily be judged from performance. If a person cannot perform a task or do well on a test, this does not mean there is a deficiency in ability. This implication contrasts with the normal inference that if a person does not perform well, then *ipso facto* there is no competence or ability. The preferred interpretation, supported vigorously by Cole, is that the task itself or the situational nature of the testing situation may well be causing the poor performance. These situational elements include uncommon materials involved in the task; unfamiliar time pressures to complete the task; the presence of a nervousness-producing, high-status "outsider" doing the testing; and so forth. Cole has used the research technique of redesigning the testing situation until the person performs well on the task, taking the original poorer performance only as a starting point. Sometimes this is a very difficult research procedure to implement, but when successful, it gives infinitely more information about the exact reasons and exact cues for good performance than if one stops immediately after the first testing. The cues that brought out good performance—such as those that encourage effective organization of information rather than rote memorization—can then be used in other learning situations.

The competence-performance distinction contributes to the basis of various research studies. Hudson (1981, p. 336), in compiling a collection of principles on which virtually all linguists agree, based one of them on the competence-performance distinction: "A child's poor performance in formal, threatening, or unfamiliar situations cannot be taken as evidence of impoverished linguistic competence, but may be due to other factors such as low motivation for speaking in that situation, or unfamiliarity with the conventions for use of language in such situations."

This important work has led to the following conclusion among sophisticated researchers who review the work of their colleagues. If a study's investigators conclude that people from one culture perform better on a task that people from another culture, there has to be evidence that such a result is not a failure on the part of the investigators to elicit good performance from members of the latter culture.

CROSS-CULTURAL RESEARCH METHODS: COMMUNICATING WITH SUBJECTS

Cross-cultural research methods have become a specialized study area and have been the focus of entire texts (Brislin, Lonner, & Thorndike, 1973; Triandis, Lonner, Heron, Brislin, & Draguns, 1980; Berry et al., 1997). A basic aspect of good methodology is communicating with subjects. Without clear understanding of instructions directed from the researcher to the participants, and without clear understanding of what responses mean, a research study may not only be misleading but may also possibly be damaging.

Various techniques have been devised to ensure good communication between researchers and participants. Irvine and Carroll (1980) suggest a number of steps in testing, such as separation of individual subtests to avoid confusion, oral instructions with visual aids, translation of instructions carried out by typical members of the respondent group, supervised practice on sample items, beginning any test session with items already familiar to respondents, and creation of an enjoyable atmosphere for testing. If the subject matter under study is a complex concept, such as the stage reached according to Piagetian theories of mental development, training studies can be introduced (Dasen, Lavallee, & Retschitzki, 1979). The acquisition of Piagetian stages is influenced by people's previous experiences; people in various cultures do not have the same everyday experiences which might lead (at least at the same rate) to the various stages. Realizing this, Dasen and his colleagues (working among the Baoule in West Africa) created training studies in which the same sorts of experiences, theoretically posited as triggering a given stage, were emulated. Compared to a control group which did not have the training experience, experimental subjects scored higher on independently assessed Piagetian tasks. Without the training study—one example of researchers' attempts to empathize with respondents, so that competencies and not just atypical performances are assessed—conclusions about "slower development" might have been made.

A little creativity may ensure researcher-participant communication. De Lacey (1970) made sure that Australian aboriginal children understood such terms as "red," "circle," and "round" by showing them wooden replicas and inviting them to handle the different shapes painted different colors. They were also asked to in-

dicate examples of the terms before the actual experiment on classification ability began. In another study, Price-Williams (1961) tested the acquisition of various Piagetian concepts among the Tiv of Central Africa. In his experiment on the conservation of discontinuous qualities, the normal Piagetian method is to use beads in containers. Price-Williams tried his method but found communication difficulties were prevalent, so he changed the materials to nuts, far more familiar in the Tiv culture. Results showed a degree of conservation similar to acculturated European groups of children. In many cross-cultural studies of theoretical ideas where Euro-American children might be compared with children from other cultures, there is a factor which can be called "explicit attention to communication with subjects." When this factor is clearly present in a study, there is a much greater probability of similar Euro-American and other-culture results (e.g., Dasen & Heron, 1981; Bickersteth & Das, 1981).

In cross-cultural studies, research instruments have to be prepared in languages other than the researchers' own. One of the most important recommendations in such studies is to "decenter" instruments (Brislin, 2000). Instruments should not be prepared in one language with the expectation that they be translated into other languages. Such a procedure often forces the use of stilted, unfamiliar phrases in other languages that leads to poor communication. In decentering, materials are prepared at the earliest stages so that the wordings chosen will lead to clear and familiar wordings in all the languages that are part of the research study. There is no "center" to the research (e.g., instruments from the United States that must be translated verbatim) in this recommended procedure.

Cross-cultural data can edit findings drawn from only a few countries, pointing to the specific limitations of theories. Further, cross-cultural data can provide a stimulus to new thinking, which in turn leads to new and more powerful theories. As more and more psychologists accept the necessity of taking a worldwide view of human behavior, the necessity for a special section on cross-cultural studies will vanish.

REFERENCES

Aram, J., & Piraino, T. (1978). The hierarchy of needs theory: An evaluation in Chile. *Interamerican Journal of Psychology, 12*, 179–188.

Aronson, E., Wilson, T., & Akert, R. (1999). *Social psychology: The heart and the mind* (3rd ed.). New York: Addison-Wesley.

Berry, J., Poortinga, Y., & Pandey, J. (Eds.). (1997). *Handbook of cross-cultural psychology: Vol. 1. Theory and method* (2nd ed.). Boston: Allyn and Bacon.

Bickersteth, P., & Das, J. (1981). Syllogistic reasoning among school children from Canada and Sierra Leone. *International Journal of Psychology, 16*, 1–11.

Brislin, R. (2000). *Understanding culture's influence on behavior* (2nd ed.). Fort Worth, TX: Harcourt Brace.

Brislin, R., Lonner, W., & Thorndike, R. (1973). *Cross-cultural research methods*. New York: Wiley.

Carlson, J., & Davis, D. (1971). Cultural values and the risky shift: A cross-cultural test in Uganda and the United States. *Journal of Personality and Social Psychology, 20,* 392–399.

Cole, M., Gay, J., Glick, J., & Sharp, D. (1971). *The cultural context of learning and thinking.* New York: Basic Books.

Dasen, P., & Heron, A. (1981). Cross-cultural tests of Piaget's theory. In H. Triandis & A. Heron (Eds.), *Handbook of cross-cultural psychology* (Vol. 4). Boston: Allyn & Bacon.

Dasen, P., Lavallee, M., & Retschitzki, J. (1979). Training conservation of quantity (liquids) in West African (Baoule) children. *International Journal of Psychology, 14,* 57–68.

De Lacey, P. (1970). A cross-cultural study of classificatory ability in Australia. *Journal of Cross-Cultural Psychology, 1,* 293–304.

Gologor, E. (1977). Group polarization in a non-risk taking culture. *Journal of Cross-Cultural Psychology, 8,* 331–346.

Hofstede, G. (1980). *Culture's consequences: International differences in work-related values.* Beverly Hills, CA: Sage.

Hofstede, G. (1991). *Cultures and organizations: Software of the mind.* London & New York: McGraw-Hill.

Hofstede, G. (1998). *Masculinity and femininity: The taboo dimension of national cultures.* Thousand Oaks, CA: Sage.

Hudson, R. (1981). Some issues on which linguists can agree. *Journal of Linguistics, 17,* 333–343.

Irvine, S., & Carroll, W. (1980). Testing and assessment across cultures: Issues in methodology and theory. In H. Triandis & J. Berry (Eds.), *Handbook of cross-cultural psychology* (Vol. 2). Boston: Allyn & Bacon.

Kagitcibasi, C. (1997). Individualism and collectivism. In J. Berry, M. Segall, & C. Kagitcibasi (Eds.), *Handbook of cross-cultural psychology: Vol. 3. Behavior and applications* (2nd ed., pp. 1–49). Boston: Allyn and Bacon.

Kim, U., & Berry, J. (Eds.). (1993). *Indigenous psychologies.* Newbury Park, CA: Sage.

Kogan, N., & Wallach, M. (1964). *Risk taking: A study in cognition and personality.* New York: Holt.

Kroeber, A., & Kluckhohn, C. (1952). Culture. *Papers of the Peabody Museum, 47*(1).

Labov, W. (1970). The logic of non-standard English. In F. Williams (Ed.), *Language and poverty.* Chicago: Markham.

Markus, H., & Kitayama, S. (1998). The cultural psychology of personality. *Journal of Cross-Cultural Psychology, 29,* 63–87.

Maslow, A. H. (1943). A theory of human motivation. *Psychological Review, 50,* 370–396.

McClelland, D. C. (1961). *The achieving society.* Princeton, NJ: Van Nostrand.

McGrath, J. E., & Kravitz, D. (1982). Group research. *Annual Review of Psychology, 33,* 195–230.

Miller, J. (1997). Theoretical issues in cultural psychology. In J. Berry, Y. Poortinga, & J. Pandey (Eds.), *Handbook of cross-cultural psychology: Vol. 1. Theory and method* (2nd ed., pp. 85–128). Boston: Allyn and Bacon.

Price-Williams, D. R. (1961). A study concerning concepts of conservation of quantities among primitive children. *Acta Psychologica, 18,* 297–305.

Triandis, H. (1995). *Individualism & collectivism.* Boulder, CO: Westview.

Triandis, H., Berry, J., Lonner, W., Heron, A., Brislin, R., & Draguns, J. (Eds.). (1980). *Handbook of cross-cultural psychology* (6 vols.). Boston: Allyn & Bacon.

Whiting, J. (1954). The cross-cultural method. In G. Lindzey (Ed.), *Handbook of social psychology* (Vol. 1). Reading, MA: Addison-Wesley.

Whiting, J. (1968). Methods and problems in cross-cultural research. In G. Lindzey & E. Aronson (Eds.), *Handbook of social psychology* (2nd ed., Vol. 2). Reading, MA: Addison-Wesley.

Zhang, J., & Bond, M. (1998). Personality and filial piety among college students in two Chinese societies: The added value of indigenous constructs. *Journal of Cross-Cultural Psychology, 29,* 402–417.

SUGGESTED READING

O'Nell, T., & Mitchell, C. (1996). Alcohol use among American Indian adolescents: The role of culture in pathological drinking. *Social Science and Medicine, 42,* 565–578.

Pedersen, P. (1997). Culture-centered counseling interventions: Striving for accuracy. Thousand Oaks, CA: Sage.

Williams, J., & Best, D. (1990). Sex and psyche: Gender and self viewed cross-culturally. Newbury Park, CA: Sage.

R. W. Brislin
University of Hawaii

RESEARCH METHODOLOGY

CROSS-CULTURAL TRAINING PROGRAMS

Cross-cultural training programs refer to formal efforts designed to prepare people to live and work in cultures other than their own (Bhawuk, 1990; Brislin & Yoshida, 1994; Landis & Bhagat, 1996; Paige, 1992). Ideally, such programs are structured, staffed by professionals with relevant training and experience, designed with an adequate budget, and held in a setting designed to create an atmosphere conducive to learning. The nature of cross-cultural training is made clearer when its opposite is considered. Before going overseas on a business assignment, good training can prepare people for the stresses of adjusting to another culture, differing ways of carrying out business negotiations in other cultures, and advice on accomplishing one's goals. The opposite is simply to send people abroad with no preparation and to let them sink or swim on their own.

The vast majority of research and careful thinking about cross-cultural training has taken place since World War II. Reasons include the greater movement of students who take advantage of educational opportunities in countries other than their own, increases in technical assistance programs, the increased availability of jet travel, the development of global marketplaces, increases in the number of programs aimed at person-to-person contact across cultural boundaries (e.g., the Peace Corps and youth exchange programs), and increases in the number of independent countries, necessitating greater amounts of diplomatic contact. In addition to preparing people to live in countries other than their own, cross-cultural training programs also are designed to help people work effectively with culturally different individuals within their own country. For example, programs have been designed for Anglo social workers who are preparing to work with refugees from Southeast Asia and for Japanese-American teachers in Hawaii who have large numbers of students of Hawaiian ancestry. People skillful in designing and implementing cross-cultural training programs can be found in colleges and universities, the personnel departments of large businesses, government service, public school systems, churches, social welfare agencies, counseling centers, and private consulting firms.

GOALS OF TRAINING

Training programs are commonly designed with four goals in mind (Bhawuk, 1990; Brislin, 2000; Hammer, 1989, 1992). For convenience only programs to prepare people for overseas assignments will be addressed here, although very similar arguments can be made about programs to increase effective intercultural contact *within* any one large country. Training programs (a) should prepare people to enjoy and to benefit from their overseas assignment, not simply to tolerate an unpleasant interruption in their lives. Because few people can enjoy their assignments without cordial and effective interactions with others, programs should give guidance on developing good interpersonal relations with host country nationals, both in the workplace and during leisure time. One way of measuring progress toward this goal is that people on overseas assignments should be able to list people with whom they work well, with whom they interact during their leisure time, and whom they can call on in times of need. At the same time, the (b) host country point of view needs to be given attention. Good training increases the probability that host country nationals will have positive attitudes about the sojourners in their country. By examining goals a and b, trainers can avoid the mistake of making conclusions based on people's *reports* of positive relations with hosts. In some cases, people can make a list of friends, but those "friends" might report that the people are insensitive, ethnocentric, and condescending.

Another goal is (c) to provide guidance on how participants in training programs can accomplish their goals. Virtually all sojourners have concrete goals in addition to enjoying and personally benefiting from their assignments. Overseas students want to obtain university degrees within a reasonable amount of time; overseas businesspeople want to enter into trade agreements; diplomats want to develop treaties acceptable to all sides in a conflict; technical assistance advisers want to construct sanitation facilities, irrigation systems, or medical centers; cross-cultural researchers

want to establish collegial relations so that information can be gathered and shared; and so forth. Training can give people guidance on such topics as working through bureaucracies, negotiating with counterparts, keeping legal requirements in mind, identifying the resources needed for project completion, and so forth. Many times, training must be culturally specific, depending on the types of participants in programs. Foreign students working in the United States need to be prepared for the independence in scholarly inquiry that professors expect. American businesspeople working in Asia need to be more sensitive to the effects of their actions on the collective identity of their hosts (Triandis, Brislin, & Hui, 1988; Triandis, 1995). Diplomats need to be aware of the long history of animosities that various ethnic groups within a country may bring to the bargaining table.

The final goal is (d) to assist program participants in dealing with the stress that overseas assignments can bring. The most commonly used term associated with such stress is *culture shock,* or the set of strong emotions that results from having the familiar structures of one's own culture taken away (Bochner, 1994). *People do not interact with each other in familiar ways! How they make decisions is a mystery! They are never clear when they try to communicate! They seem to talk about me all the time!* All of these feelings are very common, and cross-cultural trainers have adopted such stress-reduction methods as relaxation, cognitive restructuring, development and maintenance of valued leisure time activities, exercise, and the avoidance of health-threatening behaviors (e.g., increased alcohol use). Trainers frequently introduce the concept that program participants should not feel singled out for negative self-judgments. The feeling that "*I am the only one*" who is having difficulties adjusting to the other culture is common. If participants learn that most sojourners experience adjustment difficulties and feel the temptation to engage in negative self-thoughts, then the resulting stress is decreased.

APPROACHES TO CROSS-CULTURAL TRAINING

The various approaches to cross-cultural training can be examined by imagining a 3×3 matrix. The three columns have labels that refer to people's cognitions, emotions, and actual behavior. The three rows have labels that refer to low, moderate, and high amounts of trainee activity and involvement in the actual program. Such a matrix was examined by Brislin (1989) and Bhawuk (1990), with the latter adding a dimension that referred to the amount of trainer involvement. For the present discussion, the differences between low and high trainee involvement on people's cognitions, emotions, and behavior will be examined to highlight some key distinctions among choices of the content to be covered in various programs.

In low trainee involvement aimed at cognitions, program participants are placed in the role of audience members for various lectures, films, or carefully prepared demonstrations, or they are given assigned readings. The content of such presentations and readings can include host customs, climate, day-to-day living arrangements, cultural differences that affect behavior in the workplace, advice on visas, and so forth. There are a number of risks in this approach to training. Trainees can become bored because of a lack of activity on their part, or the many facts presented can be overwhelming and may fail to find a place in their long-term memories. However, given the time constraints that most program developers face, there will always be a place for impactful and carefully prepared presentations about key facts that will affect people's adjustment to another culture. Furthermore, many of the more active training methods demand that people have a knowledge base that they can use in their group discussions, role-plays, simulations, and analyses of critical incidents. This knowledge base is often most efficiently presented in lectures, films, and assigned readings.

In high trainee involvement aimed at cognitions, program participants are challenged to think hard about their upcoming overseas assignments and to analyze their probable experiences using sophisticated concepts from research in the behavioral and social sciences. If trainees report that they are tired (as distinguished from bored) at the end of sessions that cover such concepts, trainers have evidence that the program is forcing people to think deeply and carefully. Some concepts have already been mentioned: stress and stress reduction, cognitive restructuring away from viewing oneself as the only one having problems, distinguishing self-reports about success from the reports of hosts, and so forth. Some of the most difficult concepts relate to behaviors that are perfectly appropriate and acceptable in one culture but that are boorish or even illegal in another. For example, teasing and mild sexual innuendo are acceptable behaviors for male-female workplace interactions in many countries. The same behaviors are considered examples of sexual harassment in other countries. One prediction for the future is that virtually all good cross-cultural trainers must cover male-female interactions in the workplace and keep current in research on gender issues in various countries.

In low involvement aimed at people's emotions, trainers move from coverage of the facts about another culture to engaging participants' affective reactions to their upcoming experiences. One method is for participants to hear presentations from either hosts or from "old hands" who have made successful adjustments. The advantage of employing such people is that they can answer questions from the point of view of people who have actually lived in the other culture, either as members or as long-term visitors. The major disadvantage of this approach is that the hosts and old hands may tell a collection of interesting stories that add up to no clear set of conclusions. Program coordinators can avoid this problem through careful preparation and by guiding the guest presenters in what they will discuss. There are a number of topics hosts and old hands can cover that are almost sure to engage people's emotions. For example, the emotions of Americans are almost always aroused when they hear presentations about arranged marriages, suggested reasons for trade disputes with Asian nations, the quality of schools in Europe and Asia compared with the United States, differing views of what constitutes a bribe, and the need to modify familiar behaviors to demonstrate cultural sensitivity as judged by hosts rather than by fellow sojourners.

In high trainee involvement aimed at emotions, participants may engage in role-playing exercises that force them to confront cultural differences (McCafferey, 1995). Often, members of the training staff role-play culturally different others, and program participants must achieve a goal (a visa extension or approval of a plan) by working with the staff. Role-plays can be emotional for participants because they must deal with ambiguity, unfamiliarity, and frustration in their attempts to achieve their goals. Given the strong possibility of intense emotional reactions, role-playing is not recommended as a training approach unless program developers have had a great deal of firsthand experience in its application. One approach has been developed that addresses people's emotions but decreases the chances of reactions being so intense that they bring the training program to a halt. This approach has trainees role-play a set of critical incidents (there are 110 in the collection by Cushner & Brislin, 1996) that provide the outline of the script that trainees follow. Critical incidents are written to communicate a point about intercultural interaction, and they are written with characters, a plot line, and an end to the plot based on a misunderstanding between people from different cultures. For example, several of the 110 incidents describe people who confront behaviors that do not agree with their previous stereotype of how members of the other culture behave. This is a common experience that causes emotional reactions as people learn that their well-formed stereotypes simply do not give any guidance to effective behaviors. Trainees can read the incident, decide how it is to be role-played, and then perform it. Given that almost all the material in the incident will be familiar (at a cognitive level) before its presentation, trainees will be less likely to have emotional reactions to the surprises that totally unscripted role-plays can cause. It is these surprises (e.g., a comment or gesture that reminds a trainee of a stressful event in his or her past) that lead to the risks associated with the use of role-playing as a training approach.

In low involvement aimed at behavior, trainees are introduced to the fact that behaviors different from the ones to which they are accustomed will lead to adjustment and goal achievement. This can be done through the use of modeling, in which members of the training staff demonstrate appropriate behaviors in important areas such as meeting others for the first time, ways of moving from small talk to discussions about important matters, ways of disagreeing without causing offense, and so forth (Brislin, 2000). One way to approach the topic of behavior change is to list a set of social situations with which trainees are familiar in their own culture. Then, given their knowledge of other cultures, trainers can discuss or demonstrate behaviors that are appropriate for similar situations in the culture in which trainees will be living. For example, overseas students accustomed to taking lecture notes in a highly deferential manner will be exposed to behaviors that show how students in the United States can argue with their professors and put forward their own original thinking. Businesspeople accustomed to getting down to business within five minutes of an initial meeting will be exposed to the importance of small talk and the need for behaviors that build trust between sojourners and hosts if the business dealings are in Asia or Latin America. Technical assistance advisers accustomed to hiring employees on the basis of merit will learn, when working in some countries, that there will be pressure to consider the relatives of influential officials.

In high involvement aimed at behavior, trainees are put into social settings in which they have to change familiar behaviors to meet their goals. The difference between this approach and role-playing involves the extent and number of new behaviors that trainees are called on to perform. In this high involvement approach, the culture in which trainees are to live is simulated with as much fidelity as possible. When the training is "in country," this is relatively easy. Peace Corps training in Nepal, for example, calls for trainees to live with hosts for a significant period of time and later to attend sessions where their behaviors can be discussed and evaluated. In one of the most intense training programs that has been documented (Trifonovitch, 1977), participants about to live on remote Pacific Islands lived in a simulated village set up in Hawaii. There they learned to behave in ways that contributed to adjustment and job effectiveness. They learned to gather their own food, because there were few or no grocery stores. They learned to entertain themselves, because there were no televisions or movie houses. They learned to perform their jobs in the absence of technological aides to which they had become accustomed. They learned to deal with a lack of privacy, as many of the islands are simply too small for people to engage in behaviors of which others are unaware. There were many dropouts from this program; these people decided not to continue with preparations for their overseas assignments and left the training site to return to their homes. One defense of this type of program, however, is that it is better to drop out during training in the presence of a supportive and sensitive staff. These supportive individuals will not be present if people decide to return home after beginning their overseas assignments.

BENEFITS OF TRAINING

Evaluation studies have demonstrated that well-designed training programs provide benefits to people's thinking, attitudes, and actual behaviors (Bhawuk, 1998; Cui & Van Den Berg, 1991; Cushner, 1989; Landis & Bhagat, 1996). People who have undergone training use fewer negative stereotypes, develop complex views about other cultures, and become more global in their thinking. They enjoy interacting with hosts and develop methods to cope with the inevitable stresses that even the most successful sojourn will bring. They have better interpersonal relations in multicultural work groups, interact effectively with others as reported by the hosts themselves, and can modify familiar behaviors to better meet the demands of the other culture. They can engage in more effective problem solving in other cultures, especially when there are cultural differences involved in the identification of problems and ways of dealing with them. Given increases in the same factors that lead to the need for effective intercultural communication, such as immigration, global business, and the demands of various ethnic groups to be heard in the political arena, the future will undoubtedly see even more attention to cross-cultural training programs.

REFERENCES

Bhawuk, D. P. S. (1990). Cross-cultural orientation programs. In R. Brislin. (Ed.), *Applied cross-cultural psychology* (pp. 325–346). Newbury Park, CA: Sage.

Bhawuk, D. (1998). The role of culture theory in cross-cultural training: A multidimensional study of culture-specific, culture-general, and culture theory-based assimilators. *Journal of Cross-Cultural Psychology, 29,* 630–655.

Bochner, S. (1994). Culture shock. In W. Lonner & R. Malpass (Eds.), *Psychology and culture* (pp. 245–251). Needham Heights, MA: Allyn and Bacon.

Brislin, R. (1989). Intercultural communication training. In M. Asante & W. Gudykunst (Eds.), *Handbook of international and intercultural communication* (pp. 441–457). Newbury Park, CA: Sage.

Brislin, R. (2000). *Understanding culture's influence on behavior* (2nd ed.) Fort Worth, TX: Harcourt.

Brislin, R., & Yoshida, T. (1994). *Intercultural communication training: An introduction.* Thousand Oaks, CA: Sage.

Cui, G., & Van Den Berg, S. (1991). Testing the construct validity of intercultural effectiveness. *International Journal of Intercultural Relations, 15,* 227–241.

Cushner, K. (1989). Assessing the impact of a culture-general assimilator. *International Journal of Intercultural Relations, 13,* 125–146.

Cushner, K., & Brislin, R. (1996). *Intercultural interactions: A practical guide* (2nd ed.). Thousand Oaks, CA: Sage.

Hammer, M. (1989). Intercultural communication competence. In M. Asante & W. Gudykunst (Eds.), *Handbook of international and intercultural communication* (pp. 247–260). Newbury Park, CA: Sage.

Hammer, M. (1992). Intercultural communication skills. *Communique, 21*(1), 6–15.

Landis, D. & Bhagat, R. (Eds.) (1996). *Handbook of intercultural training,* (2nd ed.). Thousand Oaks, CA: Sage.

McCafferey, J. (1995). Role plays: A powerful but difficult training tool. In S. Fowler & M. Mumford (Eds.), *Intercultural sourcebook: Cross-cultural training methodologies* (pp. 17–25). Yarmouth, ME: Intercultural Press.

Paige, M. (Ed.). (1992). *Education for the intercultural experience.* Yarmouth, ME: Intercultural Press.

Triandis, H. (1995). *Individualism & collectivism.* Boulder, CO: Westview.

Triandis, H., Brislin, R., & Hui, C. H. (1988). Cross-cultural training across the individualism-collectivism divide. *International Journal of Intercultural Relations, 12,* 269–289.

Trifonovitch, G. (1977). On cross-cultural orientation techniques. In R. Brislin (Ed.), *Culture learning: Concepts, applications, and research* (pp. 213–222). Honolulu: University Press of Hawaii.

R. W. Brislin
University of Hawaii

CAREER COUNSELING
CROSS-CULTURAL PSYCHOLOGY
INDUSTRIAL CONSULTANTS

CROWDING

Crowding is a syndrome of stress associated with high-density settings. It is a subjective, psychological state, usually negative in tone, based on appraisal of the impact of density. To say that one is crowded means that one is made uncomfortable by, or is disturbed by, the number of people present in the available space.

Density and crowding are different, and their relationship has been the subject of much debate. Freedman (*Crowding and Behavior*) has argued that crowding and density are equivalent and there is no need to propose an intervening, subjective state. This is similar to the views guiding most animal and sociological/epidemiological research on the topic. However, data obtained in human field and laboratory studies are inconsistent with this notion, and Stokols (1978) has established the necessity of viewing density and crowding as different phenomena. Density is a physical variable, a ratio of group size (the number of people present) to spatial extent (the amount of space available). As either or both of these terms changes, density changes, and as density increases, the likelihood that people will feel crowded also increases. Crowding, then, is an experiential state based on appraisal of density and other factors that may make the effects of density more or less negative. Density is a necessary but insufficient condition for the experience of crowding.

The logic underlying such a statement is simple. First, people do not feel crowded unless there are other people around and space is somewhat limited. Thus density is necessary for the judgment of crowding to be made. However, people do not always feel crowded when density increases. High density at a sporting event, concert, or political rally is necessary to generate desired levels of excitement. In such cases, although density is fairly high, most people do not feel crowded. However, the same density can become aversive and be experienced as crowding under other circumstances such as trying to get to one's car and leave the parking lot after the event is over.

Crowding, then, is a psychological variable that reflects the ways in which people expect or believe density will affect them. Research has indicated that several different kinds of other variables can affect this judgment. Men appear to be more negatively affected by small spaces than are women. In several studies, men in small groups who must interact in a very small room became aggressive and negative about the experience. Women, placed in exactly the same situation, did not feel crowded, become aggressive, or feel negatively. Something inherent in the socialization of men and women seems to predispose men to experience more stress than women under spatially limited conditions. Interestingly, men and women do not differ in their response to high density characterized by large numbers of people in less limited space.

Cultural heritage can also influence judgments of crowding: What is crowding in one culture may not be experienced as crowding in another. The nature of the situation is also important. If high density facilitates the goals of a situation, it is unlikely that crowding will be experienced. If density is high enough to disrupt or interfere with these purposes, crowding is more likely. Thus high density at a party is less likely to be experienced as crowding than is high density in a grocery store.

Research with animals has suggested that high density can have serious consequences. For example, Calhoun (1962) observed reproductive failure, social withdrawal, and other forms of organic and social pathology in high-density rodent colonies. It is tempting to speculate that these effects generalize to human populations, but research indicates that they are milder for people. Because of the complexity of the processes by which people experience their environment, and the greater adaptive capabilities that people possess, these effects are somewhat different in human populations.

Crowding has consistently been linked to negative emotional tone. People feel worse when crowded than when not. This appears to be true whether crowding is experienced or only expected; people who anticipate crowding also report more negative affect. Furthermore, research indicates that crowding results in physiological arousal: Several measures of sympathetic arousal, including heart rate, blood pressure, and skin conductance, have shown increases.

The complexity of these effects was demonstrated in a study of crowded commuter trains in Sweden. Singer, Lundberg, and Frankenhaeuser (1978) found that crowding was associated with negative feelings and physiological arousal. However, this was cross-cut by the finding that people who boarded in when it was empty felt better and were less aroused than people who boarded when the train was half full. Because early boarders could choose their seats and exercise some control over the situation, they experienced less distress when the train became crowded.

Some evidence of density-related health effects has also been reported. Most of this evidence reflects changes in the way people feel. Thus crowding is associated with more health complaints, visits to a clinic or dispensary, and so on. Additional research indicates higher blood pressures in crowded settings. One study reported a rather large correlation between density and death rate in a prison (Paulus, McCain, & Cox, 1978).

Crowding also affects a number of social behaviors. People tend to like other people less under crowded circumstances than under non-crowded circumstances. In addition, people sometimes avoid others when they themselves are crowded. Baum and Valins (1977) reported a series of studies in college dormitories indicating that withdrawal was a primary response to crowding. Other studies have shown that people are less likely to initiate interactions with other people when crowded.

If crowding causes people to avoid one another, it should also reduce their mutual willingness to help. Indeed, research shows that people do offer help to others less often when crowded than when not. In addition, crowding has been associated with aggression. However, the measures of aggression used may be better explained as measures of emotional tone and interpersonal attraction. These measures include play in a bargaining game and judgments in a jury simulation. Few studies have demonstrated overt aggression as a result of crowding.

Crowding also appears to affect task performance. Complex task performance is more affected, with crowding causing poorer performance. This may be related to the arousal also associated with crowding, since arousal often causes decrements in complex task performance. Motivational problems may also influence performance. Several studies have found that prolonged crowding (e.g., in one's home) is associated with learned helplessness or helplessness-like decreases in apparent motivation. As a result, people may not try as hard to solve a problem or complete a task when experiencing crowding.

There are a number of ways to explain how these effects are caused, and several models have evolved around these explanations. One is the *overload* model, which borrows from computer systems concepts in describing how overstimulation can cause crowding. When the number of people in a setting becomes so large that people become overloaded with social inputs, they feel crowded. This model focuses on the frequency of social interaction and on withdrawal as a primary coping response. Another model, concerned with *control,* is a modification of the overload concept. It argues that social interaction during crowding is not only frequent but often unwanted and unpredictable as well. When people can no longer regulate social experience and determine when, where, and with whom they will interact, crowding is experienced.

Another model is based on *behavioral constraint,* or the degree to which one is free to behave as one wishes. Crowding occurs when density is sufficiently high that people get in one another's way and limit what each can do. Other models focus on resource availability and potential for involvement in the setting.

Given the present state of knowledge, it is best to view crowding as a combination of these different views. Crowding may be caused by any of these mechanisms. As a general rule, crowding may be thought of as a state brought about when density is high enough to deprive people of what they desire. If the denied goal is privacy or control over social experience, crowding will be experienced in one way. If the denied goal is behavioral freedom or greater personal space, crowding will be experienced in another and different way.

REFERENCES

Baum, A., & Valins, S. (1977). *Architecture and social behavior: Psychological studies in social density.* Hillsdale, NJ: Erlbaum.

Calhoun, J. B. (1962). Population density and social pathology. *Scientific American, 206,* 139–148.

Freedman, J. L. (1975). *Crowding and behavior.* San Francisco: Freeman.

Paulus, P. B., McCain, G., & Cox, V. C. (1978). Death rates, psychiatric commitments, blood pressure, and perceived crowding as a function of institutional crowding. *Environmental Psychology and Nonverbal Behavior, 3,* 107–116.

Singer, J. E., Lundberg, U., & Frankenhaeuser, M. (1978). Stress on the train: A study of urban commuting. In A. Baum, J. E. Singer, & S. Valins (Eds.), *Advances in environmental psychology* (Vol. 1). Hillsdale, NJ: Erlbaum.

Stokols, D. (1978). A typology of crowding experiences. In A. Baum & Y. Epstein (Eds.), *Human response to crowding.* Hillsdale, NJ: Erlbaum.

A. S. BAUM
University of Pittsburgh Cancer Institute

BYSTANDER INVOLVEMENT
ENVIRONMENTAL PSYCHOLOGY
MOB PSYCHOLOGY
TERRITORIALITY

CULTURE AND HEALTH

Culture is both a product of human behavior and a regulator of behavior. It refers to the particular beliefs, customs, norms, and values of a set of people, usually defined by a special history, geography, and dialect or language. Almost all countries have different cultural groups, often called ethnic groups, within their borders. The United States is multicultural or multiethnic, while Japan is relatively monocultural.

Health is not just the absence of disease or infirmity but is a state of physical, psychological, and social well-being. Health psychology is an applied discipline closely related to public health. It aims to improve human functioning, especially by better health care and prevention programs. Each culture has its own definition of health and health service. The Western industrialized countries tend to use a biomedical model for their services, emphasizing individual physical health. Developing countries, especially Asian ones, have a more collectivist, family-oriented, and holistic view of health and health service. Separation between mind and body is less distinct. Although Western ideas have penetrated deeply into many areas of the rest of the world, there remain strong influences from widespread folk beliefs about health. For instance, most Chinese believe that healthy nutrition requires a balance between hot and cold foods, and they accept and expect traditional Chinese medical practices such as herbal remedies, massage, and acupuncture. Within the United States the many ethnic subcultures vary in their willingness to accept Western medicine and in their faith in traditional helpers such as Latino curanderos.

How much do peoples around the world share regarding health? Obviously, in physical matters (as epidemics and organ transplants demonstrate) there is much in common, but what about psychological and sociocultural characteristics? One major debate in cross-cultural theorizing is between universalists and relativists (the etic-emic distinction). Psychologists tend to try to find categories and principles that apply to all cultures in varying amounts and intensity; anthropologists point out the unique patterns of each particular culture. Attempting to create a universal system, the World Health Organization (1992, 1993) has put forth an international classification system for diseases and indicators of health. The measurable indicators cover health status, policies, social and economic factors, and primary care services. Reports from over 150 WHO member states are useful, but questions remain about the consistency of diagnoses and practices across countries and cultures. Particularly problematic are misdiagnoses because of poor cross-cultural understanding.

Despite the difficulty in transferring Western health practices, Beardsey & Pedersen (1997) describe not only some of the remarkable successes of international public health projects, such as the near eradication of river blindness (in west Africa) and Guinea worm disease, but also the difficulties in controlling malaria and

HIV infection/AIDS because of cultural differences in compliance and education. They discuss how research by Cohen (1988) and others has shown that social support (which varies across cultures) is important for a healthy immune system. Some health-related practices are dramatically culture-bound, such as infanticide and malnutrition with girl children because of boy preference in several Asian countries. Certain mental illnesses, such as amok (sudden frenzy), koro (fear of penis constriction), and taijin-kyofusho (fear of being looked at) are thought to be culture-specific rather than universal. Anorexia nervosa (self-starvation and distorted body image) is mainly confined to Western countries, but more recently has been showing up in Asian locations (Tanaka-Matsumi & Draguns, 1997).

Beliefs about causation of mental illness differ among cultures. For instance, Bedouin-Arabs in Israel believe that symptoms occur because of supernatural powers, such as God's will or sorcery (Al-Krenawi, 1999). The degree of acculturation is another aspect of understanding meanings in cross-cultural work. One American study showed a difference between normative beliefs of adolescents with Middle Eastern backgrounds who were born in the United States versus those who immigrated. The American-born adolescents were more accepting of aggression (Souweidane & Huesmann, 1999). On the positive end of health, that is, life satisfaction, there are strong differences between poorer and wealthier nations, with poor people valuing financial success and people from wealthier countries valuing home life and self-esteem (Oishi, Diener, Lucas, & Suh, 1999). The research questions about health and ethnicity are numerous and intriguingly complex, especially when they overlap with economic and educational factors.

One example of health and cultural issues from Indonesia is the overuse of injections not related to diagnosis. Such injections, especially with reuse of needles, increase the risk of communicable diseases such as hepatitis B and HIV. It is important to understand that Indonesians like ceremonies. From birth to death, Indonesians are accustomed to rituals. The practice of injection by a medical worker is like a ritual. The provider has to go through a certain sequence in the injection preparation and process. The patients feel the pain as the soluble preparation is inserted in their bodies. This ritual seems to give both parties satisfaction. The providers have done something, and the patients have received something directly into their bodies. Such a ritual might seem strange to people from developed countries, who are accustomed to being informed and giving consent before medical intervention takes place yet; for laypeople in Indonesia who are not well educated, the health service provider is the authority for the treatment, and the patients do not have to know anything (Hadiyono, 1997). To overcome this problem, Hadiyono and colleagues (1996) used a behavioral intervention: both providers and consumers discussed the proper use of injections in a small group led by a clinical pharmacologist and a behavioral scientist. This approach, using culturally sensitive behavioral methods and involving the recognition of in-group norms and the development of consensus, has successfully reduced the unnecessary use of injections in public health centers.

Since health is multidimensional world-wide, using only the biomedical model for explaining health issues is limiting and inadequate. Many different disciplines need to take part. Specifically,

social sciences, such as anthropology, demography, economics, education, ethics, political science, psychology, and sociology, have been involved in health-related studies and policy making for decades. To accomplish communication and cooperation among so many disciplines covering many cultures and countries is not an easy task. What names to use? How to bring these different disciplines and traditions together? The involvement of social sciences in health is reflected in names, with specialties such as medical anthropology, medical ethics, medical geography, and medical psychology. The approach is still mostly within the given discipline. Medical psychology, for example, has applied different psychological theories, research, assessment instruments, and therapies to physical diseases. The needed approach for many projects, nonetheless, is more interdisciplinary so that social scientists and health scientists are contributing together to research teams.

When a group has worked together for some time its approach becomes transdisciplinary by nature. The name Health Social Science (HSS) has been used within the International Clinical Epidemiology Network (INCLEN) since June 1987 (Higginbotham, 1994). In his paper, Higginbotham concluded that the INCLEN model aims to inspire a transdisciplinary approach into international health by promoting a common language among social scientists working with clinical epidemiologists, and by sensitizing clinicians to the contribution of social sciences in health research and policy health.

One of the greatest challenges for social scientists is learning how to collaborate successfully as equal partners with health scientists, especially medical doctors. To collaborate on an equal footing demands self-confidence, secure knowledge, and a willingness to learn and communicate across disciplinary boundaries on the part of all team members. This collaboration leads to a multidisciplinary approach in the beginning, an interdisciplinary approach in the process, and ideally, a transdisciplinary approach in the long run as suggested by Rosenfield (1992) and Albrecht, Freeman, and Higginbotham (1997). The area of culture and health requires a broad perspective for working together to meet the challenges of globalization and the rapid growth of medical and social science information.

REFERENCES

Albrecht, G., Freeman, S., & Higginbotham, N. (1997). Complexity and human health: The case for a transdisciplinary paradigm. *Culture, Medicine, and Psychiatry, 00:* 1–38.

Al-Krenawi, A. (1999). Explanations of mental health symptoms by the Bedouin-Arabs. *International Journal of Social Psychiatry, 45,* 56–64.

Beardsley, L. M., & Pedersen, P. (1997). Health and culture-centered intervention. In J. W. Berry, M. H. Segall, & C. Kagitcibasi (Eds.) *Handbook of cross-cultural psychology: Vol. 3. Social behavior and applications* (2nd ed., pp. 413–448). Boston: Allyn & Bacon.

Cohen, S. I. (1988). Voodoo death, the stress response and AIDS. In T. P. Bridge & A. F. Mirsky (Eds.) *Psychological, neuropsychiatric, and substance abuse aspects of AIDS: Advances in bio-*

chemical psychopharmacology (Vol. 44, pp. 95–110). New York: Raven.

Hadiyono, J. E. P. (1997). Overgebruik injecties in Indonesie (in the Dutch Language), *WemosScoop, 3,* 7–8

Hadiyono, J. E. P., Suryawati, S., Danu, S., Sunartono, & Santoso, B. (1996). Interactional Group Discussion: Results of a controlled trial using a behavioral intervention to reduce the use of injections in public health facilities. *Social Science & Medicine: An international journal, 42*(8), 1177–1184.

Higginbotham, N. (1994). Capacity building for health social science: The International Clinical Epidemiology Network (INCLEN) social science program and the International Forum for Social Science in Health (IFSSH). *Acta Tropica, 57,* 123–137.

Oishi, S., Diener, E. F., Lucas, R. E., & Suh, E. M. (1999). Cross-cultural variations in predictors of life satisfaction: Perspectives from needs and values. *Personality and Social Psychology Bulletin, 25,* 980–990.

Rosenfield, P. (1992). The potential of transdisciplinary research for sustaining and extending linkages between the health and social sciences. *Social Science & Medicine, 35*(11), 1342–1357.

Souweidane, V., & Huesmann, L. R. (1999). The influence of American Urban culture on the development of normative beliefs about aggression in Middle-Eastern immigrants. *American Journal of Community Psychology, 27,* 239–254.

Tanaka-Matsumi, J., & Draguns, J. (1997). Culture and psychopathology. In J. W. Berry, M. H. Segall, & C. Kagitcibasi (Eds.) *Handbook of cross-cultural psychology: Vol. 3. Social behavior and applications* (2nd ed., pp. 449–491). Boston: Allyn & Bacon.

World Health Organization (1992). *The international classification of disease and related health problems* (10th revision). Geneva: WHO.

World Health Organization (1993). *World health statistics annual, 1993.* Geneva: WHO.

J. E. P. HADIYONO
Gadjah Mada University, Yogyakarta, Indonesia

CROSS-CULTURAL COUNSELING
CULTURE AND PSYCHOTHERAPY
MULTICULTURAL COUNSELING

CULTURE AND PSYCHOTHERAPY

Several formulations converge in recognizing the importance of the relevance of cultural factors to psychotherapy. Prince (1980) identified the relief of human suffering as the basic objective of psychotherapy and pointed out that the mode of symptom presentation, the interpretation of its meaning, and the methods for eliminating suffering are subject to cultural shaping. Draguns (1975) conceived of psychotherapy as a series of reinitiation and reintegration techniques for enabling a person to function more effectively in his or her social milieu. In this view, psychotherapy is invariably embedded in the context of culturally shared symbols and meanings. Nathan (1994) and Pfeiffer (1995) highlighted the importance of culturally mediated assumptions, expectations, and values for the successful conduct of psychotherapy. Pedersen (1991) described the multicultural perspective as the fourth force in therapeutic psychology, on par with the psychodynamic, behavioral, and humanistic approaches. Toukmanian and Brouwers (1998) focused on the readiness for self-disclosure as a crucial source of cultural variation in psychotherapy.

These statements are for the most part based on clinical observation and are germane both to ethnic differences in culturally pluralistic environments and to variations among geographically and historically distinct cultures. Reports on the procedures of indigenous healers in other cultures, such as shamans in Arctic regions, witch doctors in Africa, and modern therapists applying locally-developed techniques in Japan, have been important sources of information. In North America, awareness of cultural influences was sparked by the documentation of the underuse of mental health services by members of the major sociocultural minority groups (Sue, 1977). A major practical challenge has been the influx of refugees, immigrants, sojourners, and some of whom arrive in their countries of destination in the wake of traumatic experiences. They urgently require therapeutic services but are not able to benefit from them unless these techniques are culturally adapted. Reports have also trickled in on the subtle, yet potentially consequential, variations in psychotherapy even between closely interrelated Euramerican cultures. Finally, psychotherapy has increasingly come to be recognized as an avenue for studying the intricate intertwining of personal dynamics and cultural prescriptions and imperatives that constitute subjective culture.

The initial difficulties faced in cross-cultural therapy encounters were described by Pfeiffer (1995). Across the cultural barrier, the client seeks quick and decisive relief in the form of direction, advice, and guidance. Often, he or she concentrates on physical complaints and expects treatment by medicines and drugs. The ethos of modern Western psychotherapists of facilitating the search for the clients' own solutions to their problems is alien to many newcomers from other cultures. Instead, such clients are often inclined to rely on their kinship or family network for support and guidance while the therapist insists upon the client's self-direction.

Culturally sophisticated therapists recommend an attitude of flexibility, adaptability, and improvisation. On the basis of extensive experience of treating African clients in Paris, Nathan (1994) admonished cross-cultural therapists to take seriously their clients' beliefs, even when they may conflict with the prevailing Western scientific views, and to honor their traditional modes of problem solving and decision making. Several contemporary cultural therapists extend this acceptance to the healing practices. In British Columbia, Jilek (1982) has successfully incorporated Salish Indian healing ceremonies into therapy programs and has collaborated with indigenous healers in implementing the ceremonies. Many healing practices in traditional cultures involve the induction of an alternate state of consciousness.

The experience and expression of empathy across culture lines remains a major challenge. Stereotypes often obstruct the therapist's ability to tune in affectively (emotionally) to a person of a different cultural background and to share his or her perspective on the cognitive plane. Reduction of social distance through egalitarian and spontaneous interaction may be useful in counteracting stereotypic attitudes and perceptions. Role playing also holds promise in enhancing empathic experience across cultural barriers.

Modern psychotherapists tend to be more prepared to accommodate their techniques and conceptions to a culturally distinctive clientele than their predecessors were 50 or more years ago. Training and preparing clients for a culturally different therapy experience is less often advocated, but is undoubtedly frequently practiced. It is an approach that is worth trying and cautiously pursuing, especially with partially acculturated individuals and in those cases where the therapy has a high likelihood of being effective and is urgently needed. In both cases, the client is enlisted as an active partner rather than as a passive recipient of therapeutic interventions.

Systematic research into the weight and role of cultural factors in psychotherapy is in its infancy, and many questions remain unanswered. As yet, we do not know what are the common elements or the active ingredients of psychotherapy in all cultures. Hypotheses have been advanced on the relationship of psychotherapy characteristics to such major cultural variables as individualism-collectivism, power distance, uncertainty avoidance, masculinity-femininity, and Confucian dynamism (e.g., Draguns, 1997; Toukmanian & Brouwers, 1998). However, conclusive data are not yet available. Cultural variations in self-experience may be linked to the preferences and expectations about psychotherapy (e.g., Draguns, 1997, Toukmanian & Brouwers, 1998). A few general predictions have received substantial research support. Thus, the principle that the similarity of therapist and client expectations is a powerful predictor of therapy outcome rests on a solid empirical foundation, and the positive role of cultural empathy has also been largely substantiated. A wide range of research approaches has been proposed, from documented and quantified case studies to the comparison of the results of meta-analyses of national accumulations of psychotherapy data in such countries as the United States, Germany, and France. Some observers (e.g., Fish, 1996) emphasize the need for a continued use of the experiential and naturalistic approach in enhancing our knowledge of the therapeutic experience in different cultural contexts.

REFERENCES

Draguns, J. G. (1975). Resocialization into culture: The complexities of taking a worldwide view of psychotherapy. In R. W. Brislin, S. Bochner, & W. J. Lonner (Eds.), *Cross-cultural perspectives on learning* (pp. 273–289). Beverly Hills, CA: Sage Publications.

Draguns, J. G. (1997). Abnormal behavior patterns across cultures: Implications for counseling and psychotherapy. *International Journal of Intercultural Relations, 21,* 213–248.

Fish, J. M. (1996). *Culture and therapy: An integrative approach.* Northvale, NJ: Jason Aronson.

Jilek, W. (1982). *Indian healing: Shamanistic ceremonialism in the Pacific Northwest.* Vancouver, BC: Hancock House.

Nathan, T. (1994). *L'influence qui guérit* [The healing influence]. Paris: Odile Jacob.

Pedersen, P. B. (1991). Multiculturalism as a generic approach to counseling. *Journal of Counseling and Development, 70,* 3–14.

Pfeiffer, W. M. (1995). Kulturpsychiatrische aspekte der migration [Culturally psychiatric aspects of migration]. In E. Koch, M. Özek, & W. M. Pfeiffer (Eds.), *Psychologie und pathologie der migration* (pp. 17–30). Freiburg/Breisgau, Germany: Lambertus.

Prince, R. H. (1980). Variations in psychotherapeutic procedures. In H. C. Triandis & J. G. Draguns (Eds.), *Handbook of cross-cultural psychology: Vol. 6. Psychopathology* (pp. 291–349). Boston: Allyn & Bacon.

Sue, S. (1977). Community mental health services to minority groups: Some optimism, some pessimism. *American Psychologist, 32,* 616–624.

Toukmanian, S. G., & Brouwers, M. C. (1998). Cultural aspects of self-disclosure and psychotherapy. In S. S. Kazarian & D. R. Evans (Eds.), *Cultural clinical psychology: Theory, research, and practice* (pp. 106–127). New York: Oxford University Press.

SUGGESTED READING

Kazarian, S. S., & Evans, D. R. (Eds.). *Cultural clinical psychology: Theory, research, and practice.* New York: Oxford University Press.

Pedersen, P. B., Draguns, J. G., Lonner, W. J., & Trimble, J. E. (Eds.). (1996). *Counseling across cultures.* (4th ed.). Thousand Oaks, CA: Sage Publishers.

J. G. DRAGUNS
Pennsylvania State University

CROSS-CULTURAL COUNSELING
CULTURE AND HEALTH
MULTICULTURAL COUNSELING

CULTURE FAIR TESTS

The term "culture fair test" refers to tests that are not biased toward a particular cultural group. While it is technically impossible to develop a test that is completely free from cultural bias, there are many examples of tests that purport to be culture fair in nature. Cultural bias exists in a test when members from one culture are discriminated against in their ability to answer the questions solely on the basis of the culture in which they grew up. For example, if test items contain words or phrases that are common for middle class white Americans, but are uncommon for lower class black Americans, then the test is biased against the latter. According to

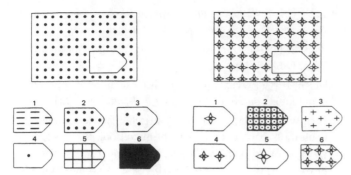

Figure 1.   Examples of items from the Raven Matrices Tests. From *Principles of Educational and Psychological Measurement and Evaluation* (2nd ed.), by G. Sax, 1980, Belmont, CA: Wadsworth. ©1980 by Wadsworth, Inc. Reprinted by permission of Wadsworth Publishing Company.

Popham in *Modern Educational Measurement,* test bias exists whenever members of a subgroup are unfairly penalized, or given an advantage, because of their membership in the subgroup; the bias may appear in (a) qualities of the test such as wording, (b) the way in which the test is administered, or (c) the manner in which the results are interpreted.

A test is considered culturally biased only if it measures something different in two or more subcultures, not because different cultural subgroups attain different scores on the tests. That is, a test is not necessarily culturally biased if minority children score lower as a group than majority children. Such a discrepancy may mean that minority children have not been taught information necessary to answer the item, and hence may be an indication of deficiencies in their instruction. For example, if blacks obtain a higher mean height than whites (or vice versa) for pole vaulting, the measure gives different results for each group, but as long as the vault is measured without regard to whether the vaulter is black or white (i.e., either the bar is cleared or knocked down), it is not culturally biased.

While most test publishers make a conscious effort to reduce cultural bias in the items of a test, instructions, and interpretation of results, there have also been many attempts to develop culture fair tests specially designed to give equal score distributions for different subgroups. Most of these tests measure general nonverbal aptitude skills. One of the first systematic, large-scale attempts to construct a culture fair test was the Davis–Eells Test of General Intelligence (1953). The Davis-Eells test assesses general reasoning ability by using cartoon pictures of persons in familiar situations, rather than relying on highly verbal or abstract content. The test was designed for ages 5 through 12. The examinees look at each picture and choose from three possible explanations of the situation read by the test examiner. However, research has shown that the test possesses questionable reliability and validity, and that it does not reduce the differences among subgroup performance on other intelligence tests.

A different approach to culture fair testing was developed by Penrose and Raven, who published the Raven Matrices Tests (1936). These tests were devised to assess Charles E. Spearman's notion of a single general factor of intelligence common to all cognitive tests. There are three forms of the Raven Matrices Tests: the

Standard Progressive Matrices for ages 6 to adult, the Colored Progressive Matrices for ages 4 to 10, and the Advanced Progressive Matrices for "superior" adolescents and adults. The task of the examinee is to choose which of six alternatives fills the empty cell in a matrix to complete the matrix pattern (see Figure 1). The tests are administered individually or in groups, with no time limit. The instructions are very simple. The Colored Progressive Matrices are easier for young children than the Standard Matrices, and are particularly useful with mentally retarded children. All the tests are completed in one hour or less.

Cattell developed another type of culture fair test, based on his theory of fluid and crystallized intelligence. The Cattell Culture Fair Intelligence Tests (1949/1957) are mostly nonpictorial and nonverbal. The tests are available in three levels that cover ages four through adult. Scale 1, intended for ages 4 to 8, takes about one hour to complete, but depends heavily on verbal directions and includes pictorial and verbal material in some of the items. Scale 2 (ages 8 to 13) and Scale 3 (ages 10 to adult) consist entirely of nonpictorial abstract figural material in four types of items: series, classification, matrices, and conditions (Figure 2). The Cattell test can be given individually or in groups, though the frequent and sometimes lengthy verbal instructions present difficulties for large-group administrations. Research with the Cattell tests shows that different cultural subgroups do not attain the same mean scores. These results, with other studies, indicate that subgroup differences are not attained primarily because of verbal content in the tests.

A different approach to culture fair testing is the *System of Multicultural Pluralistic Assessment* (SOMPA) developed by Mercer. Mercer's approach is to use a battery of instruments and compare the scores attained not only against a national norm group, but also against scores of children from a similar background. The system

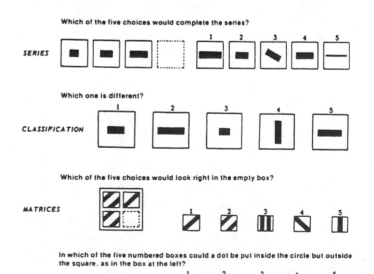

Figure 2.   Types of items in the Cattell Culture Fair Intelligence Tests. Taken from the Culture Fair Intelligence Test, Scale 2, Form A test booklet. © 1949 by the Institute for Personality and Ability Testing, Inc. Reproduced by permission of the copyright owner.

is used with children 5 to 11 years of age. An overall assessment is made after data is gathered from several tests, including the WISC-R, and after an interview with the child's principal caretaker. The WISC-R score is then corrected, based on the results of other tests and the interview. Mercer believes that uncorrected scores are useful in making educational and instructional decisions, but that the corrected scores more accurately reflect the intellectual aptitude of the child.

REFERENCES

Cattell, R. B. (1957). *Culture Fair Intelligence Tests.* Champaign, IL: Institute for Personality and Ability Testing. (Original work published 1949)

Davis-Eells Test of General Intelligence. (1953). New York: Harcourt Brace Jovanovich.

Mercer, J. R. (1977). *SOMPA: System of Multicultural Pluralistic Assessment.* New York: Psychological Corp.

Penrose, L. S., & Raven, J. C. (1936). A new series of perceptual tasks: Preliminary communication. *British Journal of Medical Psychology, 16,* 97–104.

Popham, W. J. (1981). *Modern educational measurement.* Englewood Cliffs, NJ: Prentice-Hall.

Sax, G. (1980). *Principles of educational and psychological measurement and evaluation* (2nd ed.). Belmont, CA: Wadsworth.

J. H. McMILLAN
Virginia Commonwealth University

CULTURAL BIAS IN TESTS
INTELLIGENCE MEASURES
PSYCHOMETRICS

CULTURAL BIAS IN TESTS

Various social class and racial groups show considerable mean differences in scores on a variety of standardized tests of mental ability widely used in schools, college admissions, the armed forces, and personnel selection in hiring. This is especially true of tests of general ability, intelligence or IQ, and scholastic aptitude. One popular explanation for the observed social class and racial differences on such tests is the *cultural bias hypothesis,* which holds that: (a) the typical experiences involving the acquisition of knowledge and skills are different for various subpopulations; and (b) the item contents of the tests are selected much more from the typical experiential background of certain groups (e.g., the white middle class) than from that of other groups (e.g., the poor and racial minorities), thereby favoring certain groups with higher average scores and disfavoring other groups with lower average scores on the test. Psychometrically, the problem is how to determine objectively whether the cultural bias hypothesis is a valid explanation of the observed mean difference between any two specific subpopulations on any specific test. The question cannot be answered in general terms; it is an empirical question referring to a specific subpopulation (e.g., whites and blacks in the present-day United States) and a specific test (e.g., the Scholastic Aptitude Test).

Before listing some of the valid methods for testing the cultural bias hypothesis, the three most common but wholly fallacious criteria of test bias should be discussed at the outset. The *egalitarian fallacy* is the scientifically unwarranted assumption that all subpopulations are equal in whatever ability or trait the test purports to measure, and therefore any mean differences between groups indicates that the test is biased. The *culture-loaded fallacy* is the belief that because the item content of a test involves culturally specific knowledge or skills, it is necessarily biased against any particular group that scores lower than some other groups. The *standardization fallacy* is the notion that because a test was standardized for a particular population, it is necessarily biased against members of any other population. None of these arguments, alone or in combination, is a valid test of the hypothesis that any particular test is biased for any particular group.

The psychometric definition of bias is based on the statistical concept of bias: A measurement is biased if it systematically underestimates or overestimates the true value. A test is biased if an obtained score systematically underestimates or overestimates the true value of the trait it purports to measure in one group as compared with some other groups. More generally, a test is biased with respect to two (or more) groups if the scores for members of one group have a different meaning than they have for members of the other group. That is, the test functions differently for the two groups, and the same interpretation of a given score is not justified for persons from the different groups. Objective statistical tests of bias, therefore, consist of a search for important psychometric features of a particular test that behave differently in the two or more subpopulations in question. The psychometric features of primary importance are those most relevant to the intended use of the test; predictive validity for a particular criterion, construct validity, reliability, and factor structure. Statistically significant differences between groups in any of these psychometric features, or differences large enough to be of consequence for the practical uses of the test scores, are indications of bias. These indicators may be classified as *external* (i.e., they rely on the correlation of the test scores with other variables that are independent of the test) or *internal* (i.e., they rely on internal psychometric characteristics of the test itself). Bias may also result from *situational* factors: the race, sex, dialect, or attitude of the examiner, unequal exposure to previous similar tests, time pressure and anxiety in the test situation, and the like.

External criteria of bias include group differences in: the validity coefficient for predicting a certain criterion; the intercept and slope of the regression of criterion measures on test scores; the standard error of estimate of the predicted criterion measures; and the correlation of test scores with other variables, such as chronological age and various kinship correlations (twins, siblings, etc.), which may be theoretically important for the test's construct validity.

Internal criteria of bias include group differences in: the reliability of the test; the pattern of item intercorrelations; the rank order of item difficulty (i.e., a groups-by-items interaction); the item characteristic curves; the test's factor structure and the relative magnitude of items' or subtests' loadings on each factor; and the relative frequencies of choice of the several distractors (incorrect response alternatives) in multiple-choice items.

Most empirical studies of test bias based on these objective psychometric criteria have addressed the question of bias in the test scores of American blacks, who on average generally score about one standard deviation below the means of the white and Asian populations on most widely used standard tests of cognitive ability and scholastic aptitude. The vast majority of published studies have not supported the culture bias hypothesis with respect to most standard tests; differential validity coefficients for blacks and whites, for example, are a practically nonexistent phenomenon in college and job selection tests (Arvey, 1979; Jensen, 1980; Reynolds & Brown, 1984). The preponderance of present evidence indicates that most current standardized tests of mental ability yield unbiased measures for all native-born English-speaking segments of American society today, regardless of their sex or their racial and social-class background. The observed mean differences in test scores among various groups are generally not an artifact of the tests themselves, but are attributable to factors that are causally independent of the tests.

REFERENCES

Arvey, R. D. (1979). *Fairness in selecting employees.* Reading, MA: Addison-Wesley.

Jensen, A. R. (1980). *Bias in mental testing.* New York: Free Press.

Reynolds, C. R., & Brown, R. T. (1984). *Perspectives on bias in mental testing.* New York: Plenum.

A. R. JENSEN
University of California at Berkeley

BILINGUALISM
CULTURE FAIR TESTS
PSYCHOMETRICS

CYBERNETICS

The concept of cybernetics was originally adapted from biology, computers, communication theory, and mathematics and applied to human social systems. In psychology, it first was adopted by family therapists. Cybernetics and cybernetic systems have not been fully applied to personality theories. "Cybernetics is primarily concerned with understanding and managing the organization of systems" (Keeney & Thomas, 1986, p. 263). Emphasis is placed on discerning and managing specific patterns of the organization of a social system. Cybernetics is concerned with recursive feedback loops or ongoing patterns that connect within a system. The focus is on the relationships between elements within the system. "Cybernetic systems are therefore patterns of organization that

maintain stability through processes of change" (Keeney & Ross, 1983, p. 51).

Cybernetic and cybernetic systems have similarities to and differences with general systems theory, viewing organisms as systems within systems (called suprasystems) (Keeney & Thomas, 1986; Laszlo, 1980). According to a general systems theoretical view, a system is a Gestalt with the whole being more than the sum of its parts, meanwhile maintaining a balanced, homeostatic steady state (Speer, 1970). Keeney (1983) refers to general systems theory as simple cybernetics or a lower level cybernetics.

When using a cybernetic systems perspective, it is necessary to make an epistemological shift, changing the way causality is viewed.

AN EPISTEMOLOGICAL SHIFT

An age-old question among philosophers refers to the causes of human behavior. When using concepts of systems theory, cybernetics, and cybernetic systems, one must shift to an unusual view of causality. A linear view state that A causes B (Keeney, 1983), or one event causes another, for example, as in the stimulus–response concept. Cybernetics and systems theory, on the other hand, are based on circular views of causality, reflected by mutually feeding patterns of behavior (Keeney, 1983): A causes B and B causes A. Keeney (1983) and Keeney and Ross (1983) refer to circular causality as simple cybernetics.

KEY CONCEPTS

Cybernetic systems theory consists of several key dynamics: self-reference, feedback patterns, homeostasis, and self-autonomy.

Self-Reference

Perception can be viewed in terms of relationships, that is, self-reference, or placing the perceiver in the observation. The relationship between the observer–perceiver and perceived reality can be analyzed in terms of patterns of relationships, because the observer is always part of the context by definition.

Feedback Patterns

Any living or mechanical system is organized by patterns connecting each element within the system. These patterns are referred to as feedback loops (Gerson & Barsky, 1976), or recursive (ongoing circularly fed) communicative patterns of behavior. There are positive and negative feedback loops (Gerson & Barsky, 1976; Speer, 1970). Positive feedback loops initiate change by dumping new information into the system. Negative feedback loops are patterns that help maintain the system's status quo, or sameness. Balance or equilibrium can be restored through the calibration of feedback loops. At the highest level of a cybernetic system, equilibrium or homeostasis is continuously maintained through the complementary relationship between patterns of positive and negative feedback loops.

Homeostasis: A Dynamic Balance

Systems maintain a continuous ongoing dynamic balance referred to as homeostasis (Keeney 1983; Speer, 1970). Keeney (1983) emphasized that all living systems maintain a dynamic balance at their highest level, or else they would self-destruct and perish. According to the views postulated by early general systems theorists, change facilitates a state of disequilibrium, and then the organism returns to equilibrium. Change is encompassed by a recursive loop of stability (Keeney, 1983). Change and stability fit together like two sides of a coin; they cannot be separated. Negative and positive feedback loops also are complementary.

Self-Autonomy

The Cybernetic system is self-autonomous and self-maintained at the highest level of observation (Keeney, 1983). It also is a closed system at the highest lever. Self-autonomy is maintained through the processes of morphostasis (patterned processes of change and stability) (Speer, 1970). Paradoxically, a system's structure is maintained through calibrated patterns of change and stability.

REFERENCES

Gerson, M., & Barsky, M. (1976). The new family therapist: A glossary of terms. *American Journal of Family Therapy, 4*(1), 15–30.

Keeney, B. P. (1983). *Aesthetic of change.* New York: Guilford.

Keeney, B. O., & Ross, J. M. (1983). Cybernetics of brief family therapy. *Journal of Marital and Family Therapy, 9*(4), 375–382.

Keeney, B. P., & Thomas, F. (1986). Cybernetic foundations of family therapy, In F. P. Peircy & D. H. Sprenkle (Eds.), *Family therapy sourcebook* (pp.262–287).

Laszlo, E. (1980). *The systems of the world.* New York: Braziller.

Speer, D. (1970). Family systems morphostasis and morphogenesis, or is "homeostasis" enough? *Family Process, 9*(1), 259–278.

M.S. CARICH
Adler School of Professional Psychology

CONNECTIONISM
HOMEOSTASIS
LOGICAL POSITIVISM

CYCLOTHYMIC PERSONALITY

Cyclothymic Personality, or Cyclothymic Disorder as it is called in the *Diagnostic and Statistical Manual of Mental Disorders–Fourth Edition* (*DSM-IV;* American Psychiatric Association, 1994), is characterized by recurrent and intermittent mood episodes in which the individual oscillates or "cycles" between periods of depression and hypomania, with or without normal, euthymic periods in between. Cyclothymic depressed periods include symptoms such as sadness, anhedonia, low energy, pessimism, poor concentration, and sleep and appetite changes resembling those observed in episodes of major depressive disorder, whereas cyclothymic hypomanic periods involve symptoms such as euphoria, high energy/activity, talkativeness, high self-confidence/grandiosity, de-

creased sleep, and impulsive, reckless behaviors typically observed in mania and hypomania. However, unlike major depression and mania, both types of cyclothymic mood episodes are of subsyndromal intensity and duration (2–3 days on average). Cyclothymic Personality can present as predominantly depressed, predominantly hypomanic, or balanced with approximately equal proportions of high and low mood periods (Goodwin & Jamison, 1990).

Historically, controversy has surrounded the issue of whether Cyclothymia is best conceptualized as a personality temperament, a personality disorder, or a subsyndromal mood disorder (Goodwin & Jamison, 1990). Indeed, cyclothymic patients are often perceived as exhibiting features of personality disorder rather than mood disorder at first clinical presentation. Friends and family members often describe them as "moody," "high-strung," "hyperactive," and "explosive" (Akiskal, Djenderedjian, Rosenthal, & Khani, 1977). Moreover, cyclothymics exhibit social role impairment and considerable problems in interpersonal relations (Depue et al., 1981).

Cyclothymia is on a continuum with full-blown Bipolar (Manic-Depressive) Disorder and, indeed, may be a precursor to it. Four lines of evidence strongly support this continuum model and suggest that Cyclothymia is an integral part of the Bipolar Disorder spectrum. First, the behavior of cyclothymics is qualitatively similar to that of patients with full-blown Bipolar Disorder; Cyclothymia merges imperceptibly with Bipolar II (individuals who exhibit major depressive and hypomanic episodes, but not manic episodes), and sometimes Bipolar I (individuals who exhibit both major depressive and manic episodes), disorder at the behavioral level (Akiskal et al., 1977; Akiskal, Khani, & Scott-Strauss, 1979; Depue et al., 1981). Second, equivalent rates of Bipolar Disorder have been reported in the first- and second-degree relatives of cyclothymic and Bipolar I patients (Akiskal et al., 1977; Depue et al., 1981), and increased rates of Cyclothymia are found in the offspring of Bipolar I patients (Klein, Depue, & Slater, 1985). In addition, among monozygotic twin pairs, when one twin was diagnosed with manic depression, the co-twin, if not also manic-depressive, was frequently cyclothymic (Goodwin & Jamison, 1990). These findings suggest that Cyclothymia shares a common genetic diathesis with Bipolar Disorder. Third, cyclothymic patients, like Bipolar I patients, often experience an induction of hypomanic episodes when treated with tricyclic antidepressants (Akiskal et al., 1977). In turn, lithium prophylaxis leads to clinical improvement in a significant proportion of cyclothymics, as it does in bipolar patients (Akiskal et al., 1979). Finally, up to 80% of bipolar patients exhibit cyclothymic premorbid personalities (Goodwin & Jamison, 1990). Moreover, cyclothymics are at increased risk for developing full-blown Bipolar Disorder. Akiskal and colleagues (1977) followed a group of outpatient cyclothymics for 2 to 3 years and found that 35% of them developed syndromal Bipolar Disorder.

The onset of cyclothymic behavioral disturbance usually occurs in early to mid-adolescence (mean age 14 years; Akiskal et al., 1977, 1979), whereas the onset of full-blown Bipolar I or II disorder occurs around age 24 years on average (Goodwin & Jamison, 1990). Thus, there is an approximately 10-year risk period in which cyclothymics could be identified prior to the onset of full-blown

Bipolar Disorder. Depue and colleagues (1981) have developed the General Behavior Inventory (GBI) as a first-stage screening instrument for just this purpose. The GBI has been found to identify cyclothymics in the general population reliably and validly, with high sensitivity and specificity (Depue et al., 1981).

Cyclothymia often presents a problem in differential diagnosis (Goodwin & Jamison, 1990). Symptoms such as hyperactivity and distractability that are often part of the hypomanic periods in Cyclothymia are easily confused with Attention-Deficit/Hyperactivity Disorder (ADHD). The key difference is that when these symptoms are part of Cyclothymia, they are more episodic and are characterized more by rapid swings in attention and activity level than when they are part of ADHD. The impulsive, reckless behaviors (e.g., shoplifting, substance abuse, hostility, difficulties with the law) seen in hypomanic periods of Cyclothymia can also be mistaken for antisocial personality disorder. Here, the association of these behaviors with elevated or irritable mood states is central to the differential diagnosis.

Several personality characteristics and cognitive styles have been associated with Cyclothymia. Beginning with psychoanalytic writers, many investigators have reported that bipolar patients exhibit high levels of obsessional traits (Goodwin & Jamison, 1990). Similarly, among the offspring of bipolar patients, obsessional personality traits also correlated with the presence of Cyclothymia (Klein & Depue, 1985). An association between genetic liability for Bipolar Disorder and creativity has also been reported (Goodwin & Jamison, 1990), with an increased propensity for creative thought and activity being most strongly expressed in individuals with subsyndromal manifestations of the bipolar spectrum (i.e., Cyclothymia). Recent evidence indicates that cyclothymic individuals exhibit stable negative cognitive styles similar to those observed among unipolar depressed people (Alloy, Reilly-Harrington, Fresco, Whitehouse, & Zechmeister, 1999). Alloy and colleagues (1999) reported that cyclothymic individuals exhibited dysfunctional attitudes and attributional styles (styles for explaining the causes of positive and negative life events) as negative as those of dysthymic individuals, and that cyclothymics' dysfunctional attitudes and attributional styles remained stable across large changes in mood and symptomatology over time.

Recent evidence suggests that the extreme mood swings and behavioral variation observed among cyclothymic and bipolar individuals may be attributable to both a behavioral and biological hypersensitivity to stress. Alloy and colleagues (1999) and Reilly-Harrington, Alloy, Fresco, and Whitehouse (1999) found that cyclothymic and bipolar individuals' dysfunctional attitudes and negative attributional styles interacted with the occurrence of stressful life events to predict longitudinally depressive and hypomanic/manic mood swings. Specifically, cyclothymic and bipolar participants with negative cognitive styles were the most likely to experience depressive and hypomanic mood swings in response to stressful events. Similarly, Depue and colleagues (Depue, Kleiman, Davis, Hutchinson, & Krauss, 1985; Depue et al., 1981) found that cyclothymic individuals showed slower behavioral recovery following a stressful life event and slower recovery of cortisol secretion following a laboratory stressor than did normal controls.

REFERENCES

Akiskal, H. S., Djenderedjian, A. H., Rosenthal, R. H., & Khani, M. K. (1977). Cyclothymic disorder: Validating criteria for inclusion in the bipolar affective group. *American Journal of Psychiatry, 134,* 1227–1233.

Akiskal, H. S., Khani, M. K., & Scott-Strauss, A. (1979). Cyclothymic temperamental disorders. *Psychiatric Clinics of North America, 2,* 527–554.

Alloy, L. B., Reilly-Harrington, N., Fresco, D. M., Whitehouse, W. G., & Zechmeister, J. S. (1999). Cognitive styles and life events in subsyndromal unipolar and bipolar disorders: Stability and prospective prediction of depressive and hypomanic mood swings. *Journal of Cognitive Psychotherapy: An International Quarterly, 13,* 21–40.

American Psychiatric Association (1994). *Diagnostic and statistical manual of mental disorders.* (4th ed.). Washington, DC: Author.

Depue, R. A., Kleiman, R. M., Davis, P., Hutchinson, M., & Krauss, S. P. (1985). The behavioral high-risk paradigm and bipolar affective disorder: VIII. Serum free cortisol in nonpatient cyclothymic subjects selected by the General Behavior Inventory. *American Journal of Psychiatry, 142,* 175–181.

Depue, R. A., Slater, J., Wolfstetter-Kausch, H., Klein, D., Goplerud, E., & Farr, D. (1981). A behavioral paradigm for identifying persons at risk for bipolar depressive disorder: A conceptual framework and five validation studies [Monograph]. *Journal of Abnormal Psychology, 90,* 381–437.

Goodwin, F. K., & Jamison, K. R. (1990). *Manic-depressive illness.* New York: Oxford University Press.

Klein, D. N., & Depue, R. A. (1985). Obsessional personality traits and risk for bipolar affective disorder: An offspring study. *Journal of Abnormal Psychology, 94,* 291–297.

Klein, D. N., Depue, R. A., & Slater, J. F. (1985). Cyclothymia in the adolescent offspring of parents with bipolar affective disorder. *Journal of Abnormal Psychology, 94,* 115–127.

Reilly-Harrington, N. A., Alloy, L. B., Fresco, D. M., & Whitehouse, W. G. (1999). Cognitive styles and life events interact to predict bipolar and unipolar symptomatology. *Journal of Abnormal Psychology, 108,* 567–578.

L. B. ALLOY
Temple University

L. Y. ABRAMSON
University of Wisconsin-Madison

DEPRESSION
HYPOMANIA
MANIC-DEPRESSIVE ILLNESS

CZECH REPUBLIC, PSYCHOLOGY IN

Although as a geopolitical reality the Czech Republic did not come into existence until January 1, 1993, as a result of the split of the federated Czechoslovakia into the Czech Republic and Slovakia, the region's history in the field of psychology extends back into the 14th century. A volume of translations into English (Brožek & Hoskovec, 1997a) covers the contributions of former Czech students and teachers associated with the university in Prague since that institution's founding in 1348, with topics in the categories of abnormal, developmental, and educational psychology; mental hygiene and personality; and pastoral, occupational, and social psychology. Another volume of translations (Brožek & Hoskovec, 1995c) deals with articles and book chapters on psychological topics that were written between 1880 and 1900 by Thomas G. Masaryk, professor at the Czech university of Prague (and later, president of Czechoslovakia, 1918–1935).

DEGREES AVAILABLE IN PSYCHOLOGY

Today, the universities offering undergraduate and graduate programs in psychology are located in Prague, Brno, and Olomouc. Standard, five-year undergraduate programs in the Czech Republic include the writing of a diploma paper and ultimately terminate with a master's degree (called a "magister," or Mgr) as a professional degree in psychology. (The PhD is a scientific degree.) It is the bachelor's degree in psychology that has been a bone of contention. In Prague, the bachelor's degree has never been introduced; in Olomouc, after having been offered for a time, the degree was terminated in 1997.

The degree is currently available at the university in Brno, although the situation there is complicated. In January, 1998, a psychology department, currently chaired by I. Plaňava, was established in the new faculty of social sciences. In addition to psychology, the new faculty contains six other fields: political science, sociology, social politics and social work, journalism, mass media, and human environmentalistics. The department offers a bachelor's degree calling for three years of study (a standard 5-yr program is still offered in the Institute of Psychology, in the faculty of philosophy). The field of study for the bachelor's is double-headed, covering both a principal field (such as psychology) and one of the other six fields as a second major. The bachelor's degree may serve both as an undergraduate terminal degree and as a step toward the master's degree—which, unlike the bachelor's, focuses on a single field (applied psychology). Master's students may continue their work toward a PhD.

FIELDS OF STUDY AND ACADEMIC CONTRIBUTIONS

At Prague's Charles University, the department (*katedra*) of psychology, chaired by M. Rymeš, has six sections: general psychology and history of psychology; psychology of work and organization; clinical psychology; social psychology; educational psychology and psychology for teachers; and mathematical psychology and informatics. The department incorporates a psychological guidance center for university students, an extensive library, archives, and a collection of diagnostic aids, together with a historical collection of psychological apparatus and modern research equipment.

Recent publications of the department include a volume on the history of psychology (Hoskovec, Nakonečný, & Sedláková, 1996) and a textbook on the psychology of work and organization (Stikar, Rymeš, Riegel, & Hoskovec, 1996). An international introductory textbook of psychology is available in a second, revised Czech translation (Atkinson, Atkinson, Smith, & Beal, 1998).

In Brno, at the Psychological Institute of the Academy of the Czech Republic, attention has focused on research in psycholexicography (Hřebíčková, 1995, 1997). Factor and cluster analysis of personality are utilized in this research (Osecká, 1999), with V. Smékal in the department being best known for his personality studies. The staff of the Institute (and its Prague branch) cooperate closely with local universities.

M. Svoboda serves as the chairman of the Institute in Brno. He is best known for his *Psychodiagnostic Methods of Adults* (1999), while the department's J. Švancara brought out a volume on terminology and documentation in psychology (1999). Recent volumes of *Annales Psychologici* have appeared in print: volume 45 in 1996, volume 17 in 1998, and volume 47 in 1999. The last-mentioned volume is dedicated to Mihajlo Rostohar (1878–1966), who made significant contributions to the development of general experimental and Gestalt psychology in central Europe.

In northern Moravia, at the University of Ostrava, psychology is studied in the context of an interdisciplinary, 5-year study of social work (with an emphasis on guidance), and leads to the magister's degree (Mgr).

In the Olomouc department of psychology, V. Řehan, chairman of the department, contributed a monograph on alcohol and drug dependency (1994); and the *Acta* series of the University of Olomouc contains also the series *Psychologica*.

REFERENCES

Brožek, J., & Hoskovec, J. (1995b). *Thomas Garrigue Masaryk on psychology: Six facets of the psyche.* Prague: Charles University.

Brožek, J., & Hoskovec, J. (1997a). *Psychological ideas and society: Charles University, 1348–1998.* Prague: Charles University.

Brožek, J., & Hoskovec, J. (1997b). Jan Evangelista Purkyně (Purkinje). In W. G. Bringmann, H. E. Lück, R. Miller, & C. E. Early (Eds.), *A pictorial history of psychology* (pp. 92–96). Chicago: Quintessence.

Hřebíčková, M. (1997). [*Language and personality. Five-factor structure of personality*]. Brno: Masaryk University.

Osecká, L. (1999). [*Application of cluster analysis in psychology of personality*]. Brno: Masaryk University.

SUGGESTED READING

Atkinson, R. L., Atkinson, R. C., Smith, E., & Bem, D. J. (1998). *Psychologie* (2nd ed. of translation from English). Prague: Portál.

Hoskovec, J., Nakonečný, M., & Sedláková, M. (1996). [*Psychology of the XXth century*]. Prague: Karolinum.

Janoušek, J., Hoskovec, J., & Štikar, J. (1993). [*Psychological atlas*]. Prague: Academia.

Řehan, V. (1994). [*Alcohol and drug dependency*]. Olomouc: Palacký University.

Štikar, J., Rymeš, M., Riegel, K., & Hoskovec, J. (2000). [*Methods of psychology of work and organization*]. Prague: Karolinum.

Švancara, J. (1999). [*Terminology and documentation in psychology*]. Brno: Masaryk University.

J. BROZEK
J. HOSKOVEC

D

DAHLSTROM, W. GRANT (1922–   )

Born in 1922 in Minneapolis, MN, Grant Dahlstrom lived in several places before returning to Minneapolis to attend the University of Minnesota. Over a scant few years, he had attended a middle-class school in the Upper Midwest; a small-town, racially-integrated school on an Indian reservation in Montana; and a large Philadelphia high school that was segregated by gender but racially mixed. These experiences made him appreciative of the great diversity of both personality and ability in all class levels and within ethnic groups. Dahlstrom obtained his BA degree in 1944 and his PhD in 1949 at Minnesota; his dissertation mentor was S. R. Hathaway, one of the coauthors of the MMPI. In 1953, after teaching at Ohio Wesleyan University and the University of Iowa, he joined the faculty of the University of North Carolina at Chapel Hill. His original appointment was in the department of psychiatry where he initiated psychological services at the newly established University teaching hospital. In 1957, Dahlstrom moved to the department of psychology at UNC-CH. He was appointed Kenan Professor of Psychology in 1987 and retired in 1993 after 40 years in Chapel Hill, during which time he served a five-year term as chairman of the department and directed over 60 doctoral dissertations.

During the 1950s Dahlstrom had begun a long series of collaborations, first with G. S. Welsh and later with his wife Leona, on reference volumes dealing with the Minnesota Multiphasic Personality Inventory (MMPI). These publications brought together for the first time the growing research literature on the test, as well as providing a readily available source for the clinical interpretation of the inventory. This series of publications began with a collection of *Basic Readings* on the MMPI in 1956 (later revised in 1980) and continued with a *Handbook* (first published in 1960 and later revised in a two-volume format in 1972 and 1975). Together with D. Lachar, Dahlstrom and his wife also published a volume on *MMPI Patterns of American Minorities* in 1986.

In the 1960s, together with E. E. Baughman, Dahlstrom carried out an extensive study of the patterns of ability, personality, and achievement in black and white students in a nearby segregated school system. They published their results in a book (*Negro and White Children: A Psychological Study in the Rural South*) that won the Anisfield-Wolfe Award for 1968 for the Best Contribution of the Year to Race Relations. Also during the 1960s, he served, first as a member and later as the chairman, of a Mental Health Study Section in the National Institutes of Health.

During two academic leaves, Dahlstrom developed new approaches to teaching and research. A year at the Menninger Foundation in Topeka, KS (funded as a senior postdoctoral fellowship from the National Institute of Mental Health) and, later, a year at the Institute for Personality Assessment and Research at Berkeley, CA (sponsored by the James McKeen Cattell Foundation) prompted changes in his teaching of personality assessment and a new formulation of personality systematics.

In the 1980s, Dahlstrom began a long collaboration with colleagues at Duke University and at UNC-CH on a longitudinal study relating personality characteristics of former undergraduates to health outcomes in their later lives. Also during the 1980s, he was a member of the committee charged with the restandardization of the MMPI, leading to the development of the MMPI–2, based on a wider ranging national normative group with more suitable representation of American ethnic groups.

In 1991, Dahlstrom was given the American Psychological Association Award for Distinguished Contribution to Knowledge. In 1994, he received the Bruno Klopfer Award from the Society for Personality Assessment. Other honors include the Significant MMPI Contribution Award (given to Grant and Leona Dahlstrom) in 1986; the Eugene Hargrove Mental Health Research Award from the North Carolina Foundation for Mental Health Research in 1987; the Mary G. Clarke Award from the North Carolina Psychological Association in 1994; the Distinguished Lifetime Contribution to Evaluation, Measurement, and Statistics from Division 5 of the APA in 1997; the Lifetime Career Award from the American Academy of Assessment Psychology in 1998; and the Distinguished Contributions to Science Award from the North Carolina Psychological Association in 1998.

Since retirement, he continues to write and to engage in research. Modernization of the basic scales of the MMPI–2 by means of item response theory (IRT) analysis has been a major focus, as well as the development of a psychometrically-sound shortened version of the inventory to use with physically and emotionally handicapped subjects. In collaboration with two of his students, he developed a measure of Loevinger's concept of emotional immaturity for the MMPI–2 based on the work of Archer, who used the MMPI–A for similar scale development. The longitudinal program based on the data from the undergraduates at UNC–CH in the 1960s has provided information for him to devise a long-range prediction of suicide potential as well as susceptibility to various medical disorders. He is also at work on an expansion of his formulation of personality systematics.

STAFF

DARLEY, JOHN GORDON (1910–1990)

After receiving the bachelor's degree at Wesleyan University in Middletown, Connecticut, John Gordon Darley went to the University of Minnesota, completing the MA and the PhD in 1937; his major adviser was the late Donald G. Paterson. From 1931 through 1934 he served as research assistant, editorial assistant, and psychological examiner in the Employment Stabilization Research Institute. From 1935 through 1938 he was director of the student personnel program of the university's General College. From 1938 through 1947 he was director of Student Counseling Bureau at Minnesota, except for a leave of absence for military service

(1943–1946) with the National Defense Research Committee and the Navy Department. He served as associate dean of Minnesota's Graduate School from 1947 through 1959, when he became the executive officer of the American Psychological Association in Washington, DC Returning to Minnesota in 1962, he was chairman of the psychology department from 1963 to 1975. He retired in 1978, but continued work in psychology as a part-time consultant and editor.

Darley's publications have been in the areas of vocational interest measurement, student performance in higher education, student counseling, individual differences, social psychology, and psychometric theory. He is a member of Phi Beta Kappa and Sigma Xi. He has served on the editorial board of the *Annual Review of Psychology* (1948–1954), *Educational and Psychological Measurement* (1941–1954), and the *Journal of Educational Psychology* (1940–1948). He has been the editor of the *Journal of Applied Psychology* (1955–1960), the *American Psychologist* (1959–1962), and the Journal Supplement Abstract Service's *Catalog of Selected Documents in Psychology,* now entitled *Psychological Documents* (1982 to the present). He is the recipient of the E. K. Strong Memorial Medal (1966), the research award of the American Personnel and Guidance Association (1953), the distinguished contribution award of Division 12 of the American Psychological Association (1958), and the outstanding contribution award of the Minnesota Psychological Association (1982). He was the first secretary-treasurer of the American Board of Examiners in Professional Psychology from 1947 through 1951.

STAFF

DARWIN, CHARLES (1809–1882)

Erasmus Darwin, the grandfather of both Charles Darwin and Sir Francis Galton, anticipated evolutionary theory but did not reveal his beliefs for fear of the effect on his reputation. Charles's father, a wealthy physician, worried lest Charles disgrace the family. He was sent to Edinburgh to study medicine, then to Cambridge for theology, but spent his time with friends and his collections. Finally, one of his instructors got him appointed aboard the *H. M. S. Beagle* for a scientific voyage around the world (1831–1836). The voyage changed Darwin's life; he returned to England a committed and serious scientist whose one ambition was to promote the theory of evolution. However, he was extremely cautious about publicizing his findings. In 1842 a brief summary was begun and expanded into an essay, but Darwin shared his ideas only with Sir Charles Lyell, a geological evolutionist, and Joseph Hooker, a botanist. Finally in 1858, pressured by the creative insight of a young naturalist, Russell Wallace, and his friends, Darwin presented Wallace's paper and portions of his own book to a professional meeting (D. Schultz, 1981). Every copy of *On the Origin of Species by Means of a Natural Selection* was sold on the first day of its publication in 1859.

An exclusive man with an aloof, creative temperament, Darwin avoided the disputes over his theory. While the religionists were arguing that evolution was inconsistent with the Biblical account of creation, Darwin wrote other books for scientists and psychologists. *The Descent of Man and Selection in Relation to Sex* reported evidence for human evolution from lower life forms, for similarities in animal and human mental processes, and for natural selection in evolution. "The importance of mental factors in the evolution of species was apparent in Darwin's theory, and he frequently cited conscious reactions in humans and animals. Because of this role accorded consciousness in evolutionary theory, psychology was compelled to accept an evolutionary point of view" (D. Schultz, 1981, p. 120).

Darwin's work influenced psychology in at least four ways: (a) it stressed the continuity of mental functioning between animals and humans; (b) it changed the subject matter of psychology to functions that consciousness might serve, rather than conscious content (structuralism's subject matter), and changed the goal of psychology to the study of the organism's adaptation to its environment; (c) it provided legitimate support for more eclectic methods of research and study that were not limited to experimental introspection; and (d) it placed increasing emphasis on individual differences with variation among members of the same species.

Darwin's work was an antecedent influence on the development of functionalism as a systematic, though diversified, position in psychology. Functionalists are interested in the applications of psychology to human adaptation and adjustment to the environment.

N. A. HAYNIE

DAVIS, MICHAEL

Michael Davis received his PhD in 1969 at Yale, working with Allan Wagner, a world renowned learning theorist. He spent the next 29 years at Yale in the Department of Psychiatry, and was appointed the Robert W. Woodruff Professor of Psychiatry and Behavioral Sciences at Emory University in 1998.

As a graduate student, Davis recognized that conclusions about the stimulus conditions used to produce different amounts of habituation were confounded with the stimulus conditions used to assess the degree of habituation. When these variables were unconfounded by the use of novel experimental designs, very different conclusions emerged. This early work also led to the idea that repetition of strong stimuli could lead both to habituation and to sensitization. These papers on habituation are considered by many to be classics in the field. A major achievement of Davis's was delineating the neural pathway that mediates the acoustic startle pathway in the rat. This was the first time that an entire neural pathway was proposed to mediate a behavior in any vertebrate used widely in behavioral psychology and psychopharmacology. The detailed map of a primary acoustic startle circuit published in 1982 provided a rationale for determining where various processes such as habituation, sensitization, pre-pulse inhibition, and conditioned fear, as well as various pharmacological treatments, modified neural transmission so as to affect behavior. More recent work has confirmed and simplified the original proposed circuit.

Davis realized the importance of the 1951 discovery of Brown, Kalish, and Farber that the acoustic startle reflex was increased when rats were afraid. He modified their procedure to make it amenable for a pharmacological and physiological analysis and showed it was sensitive to different classes of anti-anxiety medications used in humans. It is now used routinely by many pharmaceutical companies. Davis then went on to systematically delineate brain areas involved in the fear-potentiated startle effect, beginning with the sensory reception of the conditioned stimulus to its eventual modification of the reflex at a particular point along the acoustic startle pathway. This work has singled out the amygdala as a critical part of this neural circuitry, and Davis is now regarded as one of the world's experts on the amygdala as it relates to fear and anxiety. His lab was the first to show that local infusion of N-methyl-D-aspartate (NMDA) antagonists into the amygdala blocks both the acquisition of fear conditioning and the development of extinction. This work continues to provide some of the best experimental evidence that an NMDA-dependent process is critical for learning, and the basic finding now has been replicated in many different laboratories using several different measures of fear conditioning.

In collaboration with Christian Grillon, Davis devised a methodology to measure fear-potentiated startle in humans using either conditioning procedures or verbal instructions. This approach now is being used to explore the neural basis of fear and anxiety in healthy people, and as an objective test to assess levels of fear and anxiety in various types of psychiatric disorders.

More recently, Davis discovered the importance of the bed nucleus of the stria terminalis in facilitation of the startle reflex produced by treatments sensitive to anti-anxiety compounds but not dependent on fear conditioning. This led to the proposal that this structure may be more involved in anxiety than in stimulus-specific fear, which would have major implications for psychiatry. He also has developed procedures to study conditioned inhibition in the fear-potentiated startle paradigm that represent a direct measure of how a safety signal decreases fear. It has experimental advantages over studying the process of extinction to investigate brain areas involved in the inhibition of fear.

STAFF

DAVISON, GERALD C.

Gerald C. Davison is professor of psychology at the University of Southern California, where he was also director of the doctoral program in clinical psychology from 1979 to 1984 and chair of the department of psychology from 1984 to 1990. From 1994 to 1996 he served as interim dean of the Annenberg School for Communication. Previously he was on the psychology faculty at the State University of New York at Stony Brook (1966–1979). In 1969–70 he was visiting associate professor at Stanford University (where he received his PhD in 1965) and in 1975–76, a National Institute of Mental Health Special Fellow at Harvard (where he obtained his BA in 1961, magna cum laude, Phi Beta Kappa). In 1961–62, he was a Fulbright Scholar at the University of Freiburg in Germany.

Davison is a fellow of the American Psychological Association and has served on the Executive Committee of the Division of Clinical Psychology, on the Board of Scientific Affairs, on the Committee on Scientific Awards, and on the Council of Representatives. He is also a charter fellow of the American Psychological Society and the American Association of Applied and Preventive Psychology, on the Advisory Board of the Society for the Exploration of Psychotherapy Integration, a past president of the Association for Advancement of Behavior Therapy, and also served as publications coordinator of that organization. He served two terms on the National Academy of Sciences/National Research Council Committee on Techniques for the Enhancement of Human Performance, funded by the Army Research Institute.

In 1988 Davison received an outstanding achievement award from APA's Board of Social and Ethical Responsibility; in 1989 he was the recipient of the Albert S. Raubenheimer Distinguished Faculty Award from USC's College of Letters, Arts, and Sciences. In 1993 he won the Associates Award for Excellence in Teaching, a university-wide prize, in 1995 he received the Distinguished Psychologist Award from the Los Angeles County Psychological Association, and in 1997 he was given the Outstanding Educator Award of the Association for Advancement of Behavior Therapy.

Among his approximately 120 publications, his book *Clinical Behavior Therapy,* coauthored in 1976 with M. Goldfried and reissued in expanded form in 1994, is one of two publications that have been recognized as Citation Classics by the Social Sciences Citation Index; it appears in German and Spanish translation. This book is widely regarded as one of the definitive texts on how theory and research in cognitive behavior therapy are translated into clinical applications. His textbook *Abnormal Psychology,* coauthored with J. Neale and published (in 2001) in its eighth edition, is a leading abnormal text. Its original publication in 1974 created the mold for most abnormal psychology textbooks with respect to the integration of research with clinical material and in the manner of its engaging the student reader in a process of discovery and critical analysis of the epistemological, theoretical, and empirical aspects of psychopathology, assessment, and intervention. It has been translated into German, Spanish, Italian, and Japanese, and will soon be translated into Turkish; and it is estimated that over 1 million students around the world have read it as part of their undergraduate coursework. Other recently published books are *Case Studies in Abnormal Psychology,* Fifth Ed. (1999) with Oltmanns and Neale and *Exploring Abnormal Psychology* (1996) with Neale and Haaga. Davison is on the editorial board of several professional journals, including *Behavior Therapy, Cognitive Therapy and Research, Journal of Cognitive Psychotherapy, Journal of Psychotherapy Integration,* and *Journal of Clinical Psychology.* His publications over the past thirty-five years have been concerned with experimental analyses of psychopathology, assessment, and therapeutic change; examination of philosophical and theoretical issues in the science and practice of psychotherapy; and conceptual and procedural issues in education and training in clinical psychology. His current research program focuses on the relationships between cognition and a variety of behavioral and emotional problems via his articulated thoughts in simulated situations paradigm.

STAFF

DECLARATIVE MEMORY

Declarative memory involves representations of facts and events that are subject to conscious recollection, verbal reflection, and explicit expression. Sometimes also called explicit memory, declarative memory is contrasted with "procedural," "implicit," or (simply) "nondeclarative" memory. The distinguishing features of declarative memory, as introduced above, involve a combination of two major features. One of these features is its mode of expression, characterized by the ability to bring facts and experiences to mind; that is, the ability to consciously recall items in memory. The second feature involves the ability to express a recalled memory in a variety of ways, most prominently by verbal reflection on a learned fact or past experience, but also by using the memory to answer a variety of questions or solve any of a variety of problems. By contrast, nondeclarative memory is characterized by its inaccessibility to conscious recall and by expression only through implicit measures of performance, typically increases in speed or a shift in choice bias during repetition of a mental procedure (Cohen & Eichenbaum, 1993). Although several dichotomies of human memory have been proposed, most are consensual in these properties that distinguish a conscious, declarative memory from forms of unconscious memory. Finally, declarative memory is sometimes divided into two subtypes—episodic memory for specific autobiographical experiences and semantic memory for general world knowledge.

Conscious and explicit memory can be differentiated from other types of memory expression in normal human subjects (Richardson-Klavehn & Bjork, 1988; Metcalfe, Mencl, & Cottrell, 1994; Schacter, 1987) and in amnesia (e.g., Corkin, 1984; Butters & Delis, 1995; Squire, Knowlton, & Musen, 1993), leading several investigators to propose that declarative memory is a distinct form of memory. Studies on normal subjects have shown that manipulation of memory-testing demands can differentially affect performance on declarative and nondeclarative memory. For example, study instructions that emphasize semantic processing over superficial phonemic processing of verbal material differentially improves success in declarative, but not nondeclarative, memory, even for the same materials. In addition, manipulation of the retention interval and exposure to interfering information can differentially affect declarative memory performance compared to nondeclarative memory performance. Conversely, changes in the modality of learning materials from initial exposure to memory testing (by a change in the typeface of printed words or by a shift from auditory to visual presentation) can affect nondeclarative memory performance, whereas these manipulations have little affect on declarative memory. Other studies have differentiated declarative memory from nondeclarative memory by demonstrating stochastic independence (i.e., lack of statistical correlation) between performance success in typical declarative and implicit expression of memory for the same items.

Studies on human amnesia have also revealed numerous disparities between performance in declarative and nondeclarative memory. In particular, a profound impairment in declarative memory, but not nondeclarative memory, results from damage to the medial temporal lobe region of the brain. For example, following removal of most of the hippocampal formation and its associated medial temporal-lobe structures, the famous patient H. M. suffered a profound impairment in recall and recognition that was remarkable in its severity, pervasiveness, and selectivity. H. M.'s memory was severely impaired regardless of the form of the learning materials or modality of their presentation. Yet even the early observations on H. M. indicated that the hippocampal region was important to only some aspects of memory, and spared other aspects of memory performance. With regard to the distinction between declarative and nondeclarative memory, the range of spared learning capacities in amnesia includes motor, perceptual, and cognitive skills, sensory adaptations, and "priming" of perceptual and lexical stimuli. Even learning involving the identical materials may be either severely impaired or fully spared in H. M. and other amnesic subjects, depending on whether they were asked to use conscious recollection to recall or recognize the study phase, as is typical in most memory tasks, or whether memory was assessed by more subtle measures, such as changes in response bias or speed after exposure to the test materials (for review see Cohen & Eichenbaum, 1993).

We are only beginning to understand the structure of declarative memory and its neurobiological mechanisms. Some success in this understanding has come from the development of animal models of declarative memory, where behavioral, anatomical, and neurophysiological manipulations and measures can be pursued at a level of selectivity and resolution not possible in human subjects. In particular, recent studies in rodents have shown that damage to the hippocampus or its connections results in memory impairments that are severe in degree, pervasive in scope, and selective in the nature of the memory deficit, similar to observations on human amnesia (Eichenbaum, 1997). Furthermore, these studies have offered insights into the nature of the cognitive mechanisms that underlie declarative memory. Thus animals with hippocampal region damage are impaired at a variety of spatial, olfactory, and other learning tasks, but the memory impairment depends on the testing demands and on the type of memory expression, just as it does in humans. Impairments are observed when subjects are required to combine and relate multiple independent experiences obtained across distinct events, and then to express their memory flexibly by inferential use of information acquired in a situation different from that original learning.

For example, rats with hippocampal damage can learn to localize an important place in an environment when they are allowed to navigate directly to a particular complex of spatial cues. Unlike normal rats, however, rats with hippocampal damage are impaired when they must learn to combine and relate spatial information obtained across different experiences viewing the environment from different perspectives, or when they must express their knowledge of the relevant location from a new perspective. Similarly, rats with hippocampal damage can acquire responses to each of a set of particular odors. However, unlike normal rats, rats with hippocampal damage cannot acquire and inferentially express indirect relations among odor memories learned in separate episodes. These qualities of hippocampal-dependent memory in animals bear similarity with James' (1890) characterization of conscious memory as involving numerous diverse connections among individual memories, allowing memories to be retrieved via many routes. Such a characterization suggests that the fundamental basis of declarative memory involves the "networking" of memories acquired across distinct episodes, and the consequent capacity to "surf" such a memory network to retrieve and express memories in a flexible way.

REFERENCES

Butters, N., & Delis, D. C. (1995). Clinical assessment of memory disorders in amnesia and dementia. *Annual Review of Psychology, 46,* 493–523.

Cohen, N. J., & Eichenbaum, H. (1993). *Memory, amnesia, and the hippocampal system.* Cambridge, MA: MIT Press.

Corkin, S. (1984). Lasting consequences of bilateral medial temporal lobectomy: Clinical course and experimental findings in H. M. *Seminars in Neurology, 4,* 249–259.

Eichenbaum, H. (1997). Declarative memory: Insights from cognitive neurobiology. *Annual Review of Psychology, 48,* 547–572.

James, W. (1918). *The principles of psychology.* New York: Holt. (Original work published in 1890).

Metcalfe, J., Mencl, W. E., Cottrell, G. W. (1994). Cognitive binding. In D. L. Schacter & E. Tulving (Eds.), *Memory systems 1994* (pp. 369–394). Cambridge, MA: MIT Press.

Richardson-Klaven, A., & Bjork, R. A. (1988). Measures of memory. *Annual Review of Psychology, 39,* 475–543.

Schacter, D. L. (1987). Implicit memory: History and current status. *Journal of Experimental Psychology: Learning, Memory, Cognition, 13,* 501–518.

Squire, L. R., Knowlton, B., & Musen, G. (1993). The structure and organization of memory. *Annual Review of Psychology, 44,* 453–495.

H. EICHENBAUM
Boston University

MEMORY

DEFENSE MECHANISMS

Defense mechanisms are psychological strategies by which persons reduce or avoid negative states such as conflict, frustration, anxiety, and stress. Because it is assumed that most people are motivated to reduce these negative states, theorists have devoted considerable attention to the identification of defense mechanisms, and a wide variety of mechanisms has been suggested. Most of the theorizing concerning defense mechanisms has been provided by psychodynamically oriented individuals, primarily Sigmund Freud. More recently, however, alternative explanations for some of the behaviors in question have been offered by theorists with different perspectives.

Although the existence and effects of the various defense mechanisms are widely accepted, much of that acceptance is based only on case studies or anecdotal reports rather than on controlled scientific research. Because it is important to be aware of the empirical basis upon which each defense is based, this article, after describing and giving an example of each defense, will provide a brief summary of the experimental research conducted to verify the existence and effect of the defense.

Before the individual defense mechanisms are discussed, three points should be recognized concerning the defenses in general. First, defense mechanisms are used to *avoid or reduce negative emotional states* (e.g., conflict, frustration, anxiety). Second, most defense mechanisms involve *a distortion of reality.* Depending on which defense mechanism is being used, a person might ignore feelings or aspects of the environment (repression, suppression, denial); erroneously attribute traits or characteristics to other persons that those persons do not have (projection); or express a feeling toward one person that really should be expressed toward another (displacement). Third, persons are usually *not consciously aware of their use of most defense mechanisms.* If they were aware of their distortions, those distortions would not be effective for reducing the negative emotional states.

REPRESSION

Repression is the selective forgetting of material associated with conflict and stress. Repression serves as a defense because, if a person is not aware of the conflictive and stressful material, the conflict and stress will not exist for the person. There are three important things to note about repression. First, repression is *motivated selective forgetting:* Rather than being a general loss of memory due to the normal processes of forgetting (i.e., decay, retroactive or proactive inhibition), it is a loss designed to selectively eliminate from consciousness the memories or related associations that cause the individual to experience conflict or stress (S. Freud, *Repression,* 1934). Second, repressed material is not lost but rather *stored in the unconscious.* If for some reason the negative feeling associated with the material is eliminated, the once repressed material can return to consciousness without having to be relearned— an effect referred to as the return of the repressed (S. Freud, *Repression,* 1934). Third, Freud postulated two types of repression. The first type was *primal repression,* which involves a "denial of entry into consciousness" of threatening material. In this type of repression, thoughts are relegated to the unconscious before the individual ever becomes aware of their existence, and thus it appears as if the individual did not even perceive the material. Freud called the second type of repression *repression proper* or *afterexpulsion;* this type involves the assignment of material to the unconscious after the material has been consciously recognized by the individual. Once recognized, however, the material is repressed and the person is no longer aware of the material.

Repression is undoubtedly one of the most important concepts in the areas of personality and psychopathology. Freud (*Repression,* 1934) emphasized its importance when he stated, "The theory of repression is the cornerstone on which the whole structure of psychoanalysis rests." Indeed, the existence of repression is a prerequisite for the development of an unconscious because, apart from Jung's concept (1917–1928/1972) of the collective unconscious, it is through repression that material supposedly enters the unconscious.

Primal repression was studied in the laboratory by flashing slides of stress-provoking and neutral words on a screen for very short periods of time and asking persons to read the words aloud if possible. It was found that the stress-provoking words had to be on the screen for longer periods of time than the neutral words before they could be read; from that it was concluded that the persons were not allowing the stress-provoking words to register in the consciousness. Subsequent research has indicated, however, that the difference in reading/recognition time between the stress-provoking and neutral words was due in large part to the fact that the persons were less familiar with the stress-provoking words and hence were less likely to recognize them when they were presented for only short periods of time. It was also found that persons were embarrassed by the stress-provoking words and therefore waited until they were sure that their reading was correct before saying the words (Eriksen & Pierce, 1968). Empirically based alternative explanations such as these serve to weaken the research support for primal repression.

Research on repression proper mostly used some form of the following approach: Persons were first tested for recall of a series of neutral stimuli (e.g., words); then, for half the persons, stress was experimentally associated with the stimuli (e.g., they were led to believe that they had failed an examination associated with the words), whereas for the other persons stress was not associated with the stimuli. Following that, recall for the stimuli was tested again. Next the stress was eliminated (e.g., the persons passed a test, or they were told that the earlier test was a fake), and finally the persons were tested again for recall of the stimuli. The results of these investigations generally indicated that when stress was associated with the stimuli, the stimuli were less likely to be recalled—an effect attributed to repression. It was also found that when the stress was removed, recall of the stimuli improved—a finding interpreted as evidence of a return of the repressed. Recently, however, it has been suggested that decreases in recall may have been due to interference caused by emotional arousal rather than to repression. In this connection, it was found that associating very *positive* emotions with stimuli can also decrease the recall of the stimuli—an effect that could not be attributed to repression (Holmes, 1974). Selective recall appears to occur, but the process may be somewhat different from what is implied by the term repression (Mischel, Ebbesen, & Zeiss, 1973, 1976).

SUPPRESSION

In suppression, the person avoids stressful thoughts by not thinking about them. Because it is difficult not to think, suppression usually involves thinking about other nonstressful things that can replace the stressful thoughts, causing some writers to refer to this as *avoidant thinking* or *attentional diversion*. Suppression differs from repression in that with suppression, the stress-provoking thought is available but is ignored and blocked by other thoughts, rather than being completely unavailable as is the case with repression. It is important to note that, unlike most other defenses, in some cases persons will consciously initiate suppression: That is, the person will consciously say, "That is very upsetting and I am just not going to think about it any more," and then think or do other things as a distraction. If this is done repeatedly, the avoidance response may become habitual and may be used without awareness. There is a variety of evidence that persons do indeed use suppression and that it is effective in reducing stress (Bloom, Houston, Holmes, & Burish, 1977; Holmes & Houston, 1974; Houston & Holmes, 1974; Lazarus, 1966; Ribordy, Holmes, & Buchsbaum, 1980).

DENIAL

In denial, a person does not attend to the threat-provoking aspects of a situation and changes the interpretation of the situation so as to perceive it as less threatening. For example, a frightened person may ignore the real nature of the arousal and interpret it as excitement, or a person may ignore the negative implications and consequences of a failure and interpret the experience as a valuable learning experience.

Denial differs from repression in that the person selectively attends and reinterprets, rather than obliterates, the experience from consciousness. Insofar as denial involves some selective attention, the process involves some amount of suppression. Because reinterpretation plays a major and unique role in denial, some investigators have used the terms *redefinition* and *reappraisal* as labels for this defensive strategy.

Laboratory research presents rather consistent evidence that persons spontaneously use this defense and that it is effective for reducing both subjective and physiological arousal in the face of threat (e.g., Bennett & Holmes, 1975; Bloom et al., 1977; Houston, 1971, 1973, 1977; Houston & Holmes, 1974; Houston & Hodges, 1970; Lazarus, 1966).

PROJECTION

Projection involves the attribution of personality characteristics or motivations to other persons as a function of one's own personality characteristics and motivations. Three types of projection have been identified (Holmes, 1968). In *attributive projection* a person is aware of possessing a particular trait and then attributes it to another individual. For example, a person who is aware of being afraid may project fear onto others. (It should be noted that the person using this type of projection is aware of the feeling but not of the use of projection.) There is ample research evidence for the existence of attributive projection (Holmes, 1968, 1978, 1981). With regard to the defensive function of attributive projection, it has been theorized that if a person is stressed by the conscious possession of an undesirable personality trait, projecting that trait onto liked or respected individuals would enable the person to reevaluate the traits and thus make possessing it less stressful. Although there is some evidence that persons are more likely to project their traits onto liked or respected persons than onto other persons, there is as yet no consistent evidence that the projection reduces either subjective or physiological stress (Holmes, 1978, 1981). Rather than being defensively motivated, attributive projection may be a case of naive generalization to others who are generally perceived as similar. This latter explanation also accounts for the projection of non–stress-provoking traits.

In *complementary projection* a person is aware of a particular characteristic or feeling and attributes the cause of it to another individual. For example, a person who is afraid might see others as frightening or hostile. There is substantial evidence documenting the existence of complementary projection (Holmes, 1968). It is generally assumed that complementary projection serves a defensive function by enabling the person to see the world as consonant with and justifying his or her own feelings or activities. To this point, however, there is no consistent evidence that complementary projection is effective for reducing subjective or physiological stress (Holmes, 1978).

Finally, in *similarity* or *classical projection,* a person unaware of possessing a particular trait projects that trait onto other persons. Freud (*Repression,* 1934) saw this type of projection as an aid to repression. The person not only repressed awareness of undesirable traits but also projected them outside to others: "I do not have that bad trait—he has it." Although this type of response is probably the response most commonly implied by the use of the word projection, empirical research documenting its existence is wholly lacking (Holmes, 1968, 1978, 1981).

DISPLACEMENT

Two types of displacement have been identified (S. Freud, 1900/1968, *General Introduction,* 1935; A. Freud, 1937/1946). The first, known as *object displacement,* occurs when a person expresses a feeling toward one person or object that in fact should be expressed toward another person or object. For example, a man who is angry at his boss may come home and aggress against his wife, or a man who has lost his loved wife may lavish love on his children. Generally, object displacement is thought to occur when it is not possible to express the feeling toward the primary person or object, and thus it becomes necessary to express the feeling toward a secondary person or object. In the preceding examples, aggression could not be expressed against the boss because that would be dangerous, and love could not be expressed toward the wife because she was gone. There is ample research evidence that object displacement occurs, although in most cases the research is limited to the displacement of aggression (e.g., Frost & Holmes, 1979; Gambaro & Rabin, 1969; Holmes, 1972; Konecni & Doob, 1972).

The defensive function of object displacement can have two components. First, by not expressing the aggression against a dangerous primary target, the person avoids the threat of retaliation. Second, the expression of the feeling or drive is thought to result in a pleasurable cathartic effect. That is, in the case of the object displacement of aggression, danger is avoided and a drive is reduced. Experimental research provides some evidence for the cathartic effect. Specifically, object displacement appears to reduce subsequent aggression (Frost & Holmes, 1979; Konecni & Doob, 1972), but not to reduce physiological arousal (Frost & Holmes, 1979; Gambaro & Rabin, 1969; Hokanson, Burgess, & Cohen, 1963).

In the second type of displacement, *drive displacement,* a person displaces the energy associated with one feeling into another feeling and thus expresses a feeling different from the one originally elicited. In contrast to object displacement, where the feeling remains the same but the target is changed, in drive displacement the target remains the same but the feeling is changed. The most commonly referred to instance of drive displacement occurs with sex and aggression. The energy associated with sexual arousal is often thought to be displaced and expressed as aggression, whereas the energy associated with the arousal of aggression is often thought to be displaced and expressed through sexual activity. From a psychodynamic standpoint, drive displacement occurs because the drive in question cannot be expressed, so the energy associated with that drive is displaced to another drive which can be expressed. The change of feeling enables the person to reduce the underlying drive, and to do so in an acceptable manner. The results of the experimental research on drive displacement are mixed, weak, and subject to alternative explanations, and thus do not provide much evidence for the phenomenon (Barclay, 1969, 1970, 1971; Baron, 1974a, b; Baron & Bell, 1973; Donnerstein, Donnerstein & Evans, 1975; Dutton & Aron, 1974; Jaffe, Malamuth, Feinbold, & Feshbach, 1974; Roviaro & Holmes, 1980; Zillman, 1971).

It should be noted that there are a number of explanations for changes in emotional targets or emotions other than displacement. For example, what appears to be object displacement may be a function of *stimulus generalization.* Specifically, a response that has been associated with a particular stimulus (person) may be elicited by a different but similar stimulus (person). This elicitation of feelings by new stimuli as a consequence of stimulus generalization is independent of any defensive function. With regard to drive displacement it has been suggested, through a Hullian perspective, that any drive energizes all drives and hence arousal is general (Barclay, 1971). It has also been suggested that arousal is nonspecific and becomes associated with specific drives as a function of the environmental cues available to provide labels for the arousal (Schachter & Singer, 1962); thus if the cues change, the arousal will transfer. These explanations do not have the motivated defensive base inherent in the concept of displacement. One must be cautious, then, in ascribing all changes of targets or changes of feelings to defensive displacement.

REGRESSION

The concept of regression suggests that when faced with conflict, stress, and particularly frustration, a person may return to an earlier stage of life in which the person was secure, and in so doing avoid the present conflict or stress. Freud (1935) identified two types of regression. In *object regression* a frustrated individual, attempting to obtain gratification from an object (or person) might go back to obtain gratification from an object (or person) from which gratification had been obtained previously. For example, an abandoned lover might seek attention from an earlier lover or even from his mother. In *drive regression* an individual frustrated in the attempt to satisfy one drive might obtain gratification by working to satisfy another drive. For example, the abandoned lover might obtain gratification by additional eating and drinking. There are obvious similarities between object and drive regression and object and drive displacement. The difference between regression and displacement lies in the fact that, in regression, the selection of alternative objects and drives implies a developmental hierarchy (i.e., the person selects an object or drive that previously provided gratification), whereas displacement does not involve such an assumption.

Experimental psychologists who studied learning introduced another form of regression called *instrumental act regression* (Sears, 1944) or *habit regression* (Mowrer, 1940). This type of regression is said to occur when a recently learned solution to a problem becomes ineffective and the frustrated animal reverts to using a solution learned earlier. Unfortunately, this type of behavior has been studied only in rats; and more important, the behavior in question does not appear to constitute what is usually meant by the term "regression" (i.e., the organism does not return to an earlier stage of life).

Although regression is often cited as the explanation for much of the immature or primitive behavior seen in neurotic and psychotic persons, it does not appear that any empirical research has been published documents the existence of effectiveness of regression. In one frequently cited investigation it was reported that children who were frustrated by not being allowed to play with desirable toys evidenced more primitive forms of play (Barker, Dembo, & Lewin, 1941). It should be recognized, however, that there was no evidence that the observed form of play actually reflected a return to an earlier stage of development, or that the play enabled the children to feel less frustrated and/or more secure. Furthermore, there are alternative explanations for the changed behavior observed in children, as for instance that frustration causes a general deterioration behavior (Child & Waterhouse, 1952; Davis, 1958). In two other experiments, persons were taught first one means of solving a problem, then a second means; then, in a subsequent stressful situation, the persons were asked to solve the problem (Barthol & Ku, 1959; Houston, 1969). The results indicated that in the stressful testing situation the majority of persons used the first-learned method of solving the problem. Although interesting, the changes in response preferences observed in these investigations probably do not embody what is usually meant by the term "regression."

IDENTIFICATION
When using identification, a person takes on the personal characteristics (behaviors, attitudes, etc.) of another person. Defensive identification can serve two purposes. On one hand, if the satisfaction of some need is too threatening for a person to pursue, the person might identify with an individual able to pursue and satisfy the need, and thus can satisfy the need vicariously. On the other hand, by identifying with a feared or threatening individual, the person can take on the strength and threat of the feared individual and thus reduce feelings of vulnerability. The latter use of defensive identification is usually referred to as *identification with the aggressor,* of which the most frequently cited example is the behavior of some of the internees in the Nazi prison camps during World War II. Specifically, some long-term prisoners began to talk, dress, and act like their feared Gestapo captors, and in some cases even ag5gressed against their fellow internees (Bettelheim, 1943). Finally, it might be noted that through *imitation,* which could be considered a superficial version of identification, one could model oneself after a successful person and thus avoid many problems and reduce stress.

COMPENSATION
When a person believes that he or she is inferior in some way, the person may attempt to overcome the feelings of inferiority and related anxiety by devoting additional effort to the area of the inferiority. Such behavior is referred to as *compensation,* and its defensive use was emphasized in the writings of Alfred Adler (1917), who believed that much of a person's lifestyle is determined by attempts to overcome real or imagined weaknesses. In Adler's case, he suggested that he had become a physician in an attempt to overcome his concerns about his physical/medical inferiority. Obviously, in many cases compensation would be an effective and appropriate response. The experimental research on compensation is limited but does support the existence of the phenomenon (Holmes, 1971).

REACTION FORMATION
Freud suggested that if there was a possibility that threatening repressed material might return to consciousness, a person might attempt to reinforce the repression by using behaviors diametrically opposed to the kinds of behaviors that would result from the repressed material. For example, if a person found homosexuality threatening and had repressed homosexual tendencies, to reinforce the repression the person might engage in excessive heterosexual activities. Similarly, generosity is often interpreted as a defense against stinginess, and cleanliness as a defense against messiness (Freud, "Psychoanalytic Notes upon an Autobiographical Account of a Case of Paranoia," 1934). Such countermotive behavior is referred to as *reaction formation.* Although some analogous research on animals has been reported (Mowrer, 1940; Phillips & Hall, 1953), very little experimental research has tested the existence and effects of reaction formation in humans, and what little there is must be interpreted as weak and equivocal (Sarnoff, 1960). Because the behaviors attributed to reaction formation are socially desirable behaviors, their use could simply be seen as attempts to gain reward/approval rather than as defensive attempts to avoid anxiety associated with unconscious material.

OTHER DEFENSE MECHANISMS
In addition to the defenses discussed thus far, others have been identified. Most of these other defenses have considerable overlap with those already discussed, or have not received much attention in the literature. *Rationalization* can be defined as the use of a good reason, but not the real reason, for behaving in a particular way. With this strategy, a person can provide a rational explanation for the behavior, and in so doing conceal from self or others the less appropriate motivation. *Sublimation* occurs when a person converts the energy associated with an unacceptable impulse or drive into a socially acceptable activity (A. Freud, 1937/1946). Such conversions have been suggested as the motivation behind many creative, scientific, and cultural activities. In many respects, sublimination is identical to drive displacement. In *isolation* a person separates the emotion from appropriate c6
ntent and so deals dispassionately with topics that would ordinarily be threatening or emotionally overwhelming. One technique of achieving isolation is to focus attention on the abstract, technical, or logical aspects of a threatening situation, rather than on the

emotional components; this is called *intellectualization. Undoing* occurs when a person acts in an inappropriate way that elicits anxiety, then behaves in the opposite way so as to reverse or balance the original behavior and thus eliminate the anxiety that the first behavior engendered.

REFERENCES

Adler, A. (1917). *Study of organ inferiority and its psychical compensation.* New York: Nervous and Mental Diseases.

Barclay, A. M. (1969). The effect of hostility on physiological and fantasy responses. *Journal of Personality, 37,* 651–667.

Barclay, A. M. (1970). The effect of female aggressiveness on aggressive and sexual fantasies. *Journal of Projective Techniques, 34,* 19–26.

Barclay, A. M. (1971). Linking sexual and aggressive motives: Contributions of "irrelevant" arousals. *Journal of Personality, 39,* 481–492.

Barker, R., Dembo, T., & Lewin, K. (1941). Frustration and regression. In R. G. Barker, J. S. Kounin, & H. F. Wright (Eds.), *Child behavior and development.* New York: McGraw-Hill.

Baron, R. A. (1974a). The aggression-inhibiting influence of heightened sexual arousal. *Journal of Personality and Psychology, 30,* 318–322.

Baron, R. A. (1974b). Sexual arousal and physical aggression: The inhibiting influence of "cheesecake" and nudes. *Bulletin of the Psychonomic Society, 3,* 337–339.

Baron, R. A., & Bell, P. (1973). Effects of heightened sexual arousal on physical aggression. *Proceedings of the 81st Annual Convention of the American Psychological Association, 8,* 171–172.

Barthol, R. P., & Ku, N. D. (1959). Regression under stress to first learned behavior. *Journal of Abnormal and Social Psychology, 59,* 134–136.

Bennett, D., & Holmes, D. S. (1975). Influence of denial (situation redefinition) and projection on anxiety associated with threat to self-esteem. *Journal of Personality and Social Psychology, 32,* 915–921.

Bettelheim, B. (1943). Individual and mass behavior in extreme situations. *Journal of Abnormal and Social Psychology, 38,* 417–452.

Bloom, L., Houston, B. K., Holmes, D. S., & Burish, T. (1977). The effectiveness of attentional diversion and situation redefinition for reducing stress due to a nonambiguous threat. *Journal of Research in Personality, 11,* 83–94.

Child, I., & Waterhouse, I. (1952). Frustration and the quality of performance: I. A critique of the Barker, Dembo, and Lewin experiment. *Psychological Review, 59,* 351–362.

Davis, J. M. (1958). A reinterpretation of the Barker, Dembo, and Lewin study of frustration and regression. *Child Development, 29,* 503–506.

Donnerstein, E., Donnerstein, M., & Evans, R. (1975). Erotic stimuli and aggression: Facilitation or inhibition. *Journal of Personality and Social Psychology, 32,* 237–244.

Dutton, D., & Aron, A. (1974). Some evidence for heightened sexual attraction under conditions of high anxiety. *Journal of Personality and Social Psychology, 30,* 510–517.

Eriksen, C., & Pierce, J. (1968). Defense mechanisms. In E. Borgatta & W. Lambert (Eds.), *Handbook of personality theory and research.* Chicago: Rand McNally.

Freud, A. (1946). *The ego and mechanisms of defense.* New York: International Universities Press. (Original work published 1937)

Freud, S. (1969). *A general introduction to psychoanalysis.* New York: Pocket Books. (Original work published 1920)

Freud, S. (1934). Repression. In *Collected Papers* (Vol. 4). London: Hogarth.

Freud, S. (1934). Psychoanalytic notes upon an autobiographical account of a case of paranoia (dementia paranoides). In *Collected papers* (Vol. 3). London: Hogarth.

Freud, S. (1968). The interpretation of dreams. In *The standard edition of the complete psychological works of Sigmund Freud* (Vols. 4, 5). London: Hogarth. (Original work published 1900)

Frost, R., & Holmes, D. S. (1979). Effects of displacing aggression by annoyed and nonannoyed subjects. *Journal of Research in Personality, 13,* 221–233.

Gambaro, S., & Rabin, A. (1969). Diastolic blood pressure response following direct and displaced aggression after anger arousal in high- and low-guilt subjects. *Journal of Personality and Social Psychology, 12,* 87–94.

Hokanson, J., Burgess, M., & Cohen, M. (1963). Effects of displaced aggression on systolic blood pressure. *Journal of Abnormal and Social Psychology, 67,* 214–218.

Holmes, D. S. (1968). Dimensions of projection. *Psychological Bulletin, 69,* 248–268.

Holmes, D. S. (1971). Compensation for ego threat: Two experiments. *Journal of Personality and Social Psychology, 18,* 217–220.

Holmes, D. S. (1972). Aggression, displacement, and guilt. *Journal of Personality and Social Psychology, 22,* 296–301.

Holmes, D. S. (1974). Investigations of repression: Differential recall of material experimentally or naturally associated with ego threat. *Psychological Bulletin, 81,* 632–653.

Holmes, D. S. (1978). Projection as a defense mechanism. *Psychological Bulletin, 85,* 677–688.

Holmes, D. S. (1981). Existence of classical projection and the stress-reducing function of attributive projection: A reply to Sherwood. *Psychological Bulletin, 90,* 460–466.

Holmes, D. S., & Houston, B. K. (1974). Effectiveness of situational redefinition and affective isolation for reducing stress. *Journal of Personality and Social Psychology, 29,* 212–218.

Houston, B. K. (1969). Regression under stress to early learned behavior. *Proceedings of the 77th Annual Convention of the American Psychological Convention, 459–460.*

Houston, B. K. (1971). Trait and situational denial and performance under stress. *Journal of Personality and Social Psychology, 18,* 289–293.

Houston, B. K. (1973). Viability of coping strategies, denial, and response to stress. *Journal of Personality 41,* 50–58.

Houston, B. K. (1977). Dispositional anxiety and the effectiveness of cognitive coping strategies in stressful laboratory and classroom situations. In C. D. Spielberger & I. G. Sarason (Eds.), *Stress and anxiety* (Vol. 1). Washington, DC: Hemisphere.

Houston, B. K., & Hodges, W. F. (1970). Situational denial and performance under stress. *Journal of Personality and Social Psychology, 16,* 726–730.

Houston, B. K., & Holmes, D. S. (1974). Effectiveness of avoidant thinking and reappraisal in coping with threat involving temporal uncertainty. *Journal of Personality and Social Psychology, 30,* 382–388

Jaffe, Y., Malamuth, N., Feinbold, J., & Feshbach, S. (1974). Sexual arousal and behavioral aggression. *Journal of Personality and Social Psychology, 39,* 759–764.

Jung, C. G. (1972). *Two essays on analytical psychology.* Princeton, NJ: Princeton University Press. (Original work published 1917–1928)

Konecni, V., & Doob, A. (1972). Catharsis through displacement of aggression. *Journal of Personality and Social Psychology, 23,* 379–387.

Lazarus, R. S. (1966). *Psychological stress and the coping process.* New York: McGraw-Hill.

Mischel, W., Ebbesen, E. B., & Zeiss, A. R. (1973). Selective attention to the self: Situational and dispositional determinants. *Journal of Personality and Social Psychology, 27,* 129–142.

Mischel, W., Ebbesen, E. B., & Zeiss, A. R. (1976). Determinants of selective memory about the self. *Journal of Consulting and Clinical Psychology, 44,* 92–103.

Mowrer, O. H. (1940). An experimental analogue of "regression" with incidental observations of "reaction formation." *Journal of Abnormal and Social Psychology, 35,* 56–87.

Phillips, E. L., & Hall, M. (1953). An experimental analogue of reaction formation. *Journal of General Psychology, 49,* 97–123.

Ribordy, S. C., Holmes, D. S., & Buchsbaum, H. K. (1980). Effects of affective and cognitive distractions on anxiety reduction. *Journal of Social Psychology, 112,* 121–127.

Roviaro, S., & Holmes, D. S. (1980). Arousal transfer: The influence of fear arousal on subsequent sexual arousal for subjects with high and low sex guilt. *Journal of Research in Personality, 14,* 307–320.

Sarnoff, I. (1960). Reaction formation and cynicism. *Journal of Personality, 28,* 129–143.

Schachter, S., & Singer, J. E. (1962). Cognitive, social and physiological determinants of emotional state. *Psychological Review, 69,* 379–399.

Sears, R. R. (1944). Experimental analysis of psychoanalytic phenomena. In J. M. Hunt (Ed.), *Personality and the behavior disorders.* New York: Ronald.

Zillmann, D. (1971). Excitation transfer in communication-mediated aggressive behavior. *Journal of Experimental Social Psychology, 7,* 419–434.

D. S. HOLMES
University of Kansas

ANXIETY
PSYCHOANALYSIS

DEFENSIVE PESSIMISM

Defensive pessimists are persons who strategically adopt and benefit from a negative outlook toward upcoming events or performances. Although defensive pessimists acknowledge a past history of success in situations such as academic or social settings, they nevertheless enter those same situations expecting the worst to transpire. Their pessimism is viewed as strategic because it serves at least two major goals. First, it serves a self-protective goal of helping the individual to brace for or be buffered from potential negative outcomes. Second, it serves a motivational goal of inducing increased effort and preparation in order to enhance the prospect of actually doing well. Defensive pessimism is normally measured using a scale called the Defensive Pessimism Questionnaire (DPQ; see Norem & Cantor, 1986b), which has been extended for use in a variety of settings (e.g., Spencer & Norem, 1996).

ANTICIPATORY VS. RETROSPECTIVE STRATEGIES

Defensive pessimists are characterized by their use of anticipatory coping strategies; that is, strategies that are used *before* they enter a performance setting. One hallmark of defensive pessimism is setting low expectations of performance, which serves the self-protective goal: By thinking about how the worst might happen, defensive pessimists attempt to cushion themselves preemptively against possible negative outcomes. If something bad does happen, defensive pessimists are able to think, "I expected it all along," making the negative outcome seem less deleterious. Convincing themselves that they will do poorly also serves a motivational goal by impelling them to redouble their efforts and preparation to better ensure that they actually will do well. This helps to harness the anxiety or negative affect over possible failure (Norem & Cantor, 1986b; Sanna, 1996; Showers & Ruben, 1990).

Defensive pessimists' use of anticipatory coping strategies may appear ironic. First, defensive pessimists are generally very high performers, and in fact they have usually performed well in the past (Norem & Cantor, 1986b). Setting low performance-expectations seems to be at odds with their actual performance histories. Second, convincing themselves that poor performance will happen does not actually make it happen. That is, low performance-expectations are not self-fulfilling because of the buffering and motivational strategies used by defensive pessimists (Norem & Cantor, 1986a).

Defensive pessimism is most often contrasted with the strategy of optimism (e.g., Sanna, 1996; Spencer & Norem, 1996). Rather than using the defensive pessimists' anticipatory strategies, optimists may rely more on retrospective coping strategies; that is, strategies that are used *after* performance outcomes are known. Optimists do not set low expectations before performing as do defensive pessimists, but are more likely instead to engage in cognitive restructuring of performance after the fact (e.g., by using "self-serving attributional biases"; Cantor & Norem, 1989; Showers, 1992), particularly when those outcomes are poor.

Defensive pessimism also differs from true pessimism and depression; true pessimists and depressives do not use their negative outlooks strategically, and their ability to cope does not benefit from their negative world views (Cantor & Norem, 1989; Showers & Ruben, 1990).

MENTAL SIMULATIONS AS STRATEGIES

Particular types of mental simulations appear to be a key part of defensive pessimists' strategies. Mental simulations can differ on the basis of timing (before vs. after performance) and direction (better or worse than expected, vs. actuality).

Defensive pessimists are most likely to use *upward prefactual* thoughts as part of the preferred coping strategy (Sanna, 1996, 1998). Prefactuals are mental simulations of what may be. Upward prefactuals, which occur prior to performance, are alternative pre-outcome mental simulations that are better than what one expects to actually happen (e.g., "If only I had more study time, I could do better on tomorrow's exam.").

By way of comparison, optimists are most likely to use *downward counterfactual* thoughts as part of their own strategies. Counterfactuals are mental simulations of what might have been. Downward counterfactual thoughts, which occur after performance, are alternative post-outcome simulations that are worse than actuality (e.g., "At least I bought the study guide, or my grade might have been worse.").

In the case of defensive pessimists, low performance-expectations function as an anchor from which simulated alternatives are generated. That is, if one expects the worst (to perform poorly), one's *alternative* simulated possible performance outcome is most likely to be upward, or better than expected. Concomitant with these upward simulations is the experience of high anxiety and bad moods. By comparison, optimists use downward counterfactuals after performing to maintain or restore positive moods, which is consistent with notions of cognitive restructuring. In short, defensive pessimists use strategies that lower expectations and increase bad moods before performing, including upward prefactuals, but they do not use many retrospective strategies. Optimists do not use many anticipatory strategies, but employ downward counterfactual simulations retrospectively to maintain or restore good moods.

STRATEGY USAGE AND EFFECTIVE COPING

Defensive pessimists can effectively use their preferred strategies when coping with a variety of life events. However, when use of the preferred strategy is unavailable or is not possible, performance suffers. Research has identified several examples of this. First, defensive pessimists prefer to "think through" (Norem & Illingworth, 1993) possible outcomes, by such tactics as simulating upward prefactuals. When the prospect of thinking through alternative outcomes is interfered with by situational demands, performance suffers for defensive pessimists, but not for optimists, for whom *not* prospectively thinking through alternatives is a preferred strategy (Norem & Illingworth, 1993; see also Spencer & Norem, 1996). Second, defensive pessimists' performance and coping are less effective when they are forced to focus on positive possibilities before performing, such as when they are instructed to think about good things (Sanna, 1996; Showers, 1992), because thinking about bad things is their usual tactic. By way of comparison, thinking about positive alternatives does not adversely affect optimists' coping (Showers, 1992).

One reason that defensive pessimists' strategies can be interfered with is that their mental simulations and affect are strongly linked (Sanna, 1996, 1999). For example, when defensive pessimists are given encouragement and support to do well (Norem & Illingworth, 1993), they ironically seem to perform poorly. This may be because encouragement puts them in a good mood and takes them out of their normal strategy of being in a state of high anxiety and a bad mood before performing. Thus, forcing defensive pessimists to think about good things (Sanna, 1996; Showers, 1992) may analogously put them in good moods and interfere with their usual strategies. However, defensive pessimists who are forced to think about negative possibilities that may put them in bad moods perform best under such conditions. Moreover, directly putting defensive pessimists into bad moods (Sanna, 1998) also seems to improve their performances. In short, defensive pessimists cope most effectively under mood and mental simulation conditions that facilitate their use of preferred anticipatory strategies.

REFERENCES

Cantor, N., & Norem, J. K. (1989). Defensive pessimism and stress and coping. *Social Cognition, 7,* 92–112.

Norem, J. K., & Cantor, N. (1986a). Anticipatory and post hoc cushioning strategies: Optimism and defensive pessimism in "risky" situations. *Cognitive Therapy and Research, 10,* 347–362.

Norem, J. K., & Cantor, N. (1986b). Defensive pessimism: "Harnessing" anxiety as motivation. *Journal of Personality and Social Psychology, 51,* 1208–1217.

Norem, J. K., & Illingworth, K. S. S. (1993). Strategy-dependent effects of reflecting on self and tasks: Some implications of optimism and defensive pessimism. *Journal of Personality and Social Psychology, 65,* 822–835.

Sanna, L. J. (1996). Defensive pessimism, optimism, and simulating alternatives: Some ups and downs of prefactual and counterfactual thinking. *Journal of Personality and Social Psychology, 71,* 1020–1036.

Sanna, L. J. (1998). Defensive pessimism and optimism: The bitter-sweet influence of mood on performance and prefactual and counterfactual thinking. *Cognition and Emotion, 12,* 635–665.

Sanna, L. J. (1999). Mental simulations, affect, and subjective confidence: Timing is everything. *Psychological Science, 10,* 339–345.

Showers, C. (1992). The motivational and emotional consequences of considering positive or negative possibilities for an upcoming event. *Journal of Personality and Social Psychology, 63,* 474–484.

Showers, C., & Ruben, C. (1990). Distinguishing defensive pessimism from depression: Negative expectations and positive coping mechanisms. *Cognitive Therapy and Research, 14,* 385–399.

Spencer, S. M., & Norem, J. K. (1996). Reflection and distraction: Defensive pessimism, strategic optimism, and performance. *Personality and Social Psychology Bulletin, 22,* 354–365.

L. J. SANNA
Washington State University

ANXIETY
COPING
OPTIMISM
STRESS

DEINDIVIDUATION

In his classic book *The Crowd,* French sociologist Gustave La Bon postulated the concept of a group mind. He suggested that in some circumstances persons lose their individuality and merge into the crowd. Such deindividuation was associated with a loss of inhibitions and a tendency to uncharacteristic and antinormative behavior. From a historical perspective, human beings have only slowly escaped from a deindividuated existence immersed in extended kinship relations, bonds, and tribes. In *Escape From Freedom* Eric Fromm examined the emergence of individuality in human history and the sense of uniqueness and freedom that accompanied this development. However, according to Fromm, individuation is accompanied by a feeling of isolation that often motivates people to join various groups.

Festinger, Pepitone, and Newcomb (1952) proposed that the person's focus on the group, which is associated with his or her attraction to the group, lessens the attention given to individuals. The focus on the group deindividuates its members, who are submerged and, in a sense, hidden, within the group. Deindividuation, therefore, lowers the person's inhibitions toward engaging in counternormative actions. Thus, according to this formulation, attraction to a group increases deindividuation, which in turn encourages behavior that is normally inhibited.

In 1964, Ziller suggested that persons learn to associate individuation with rewarding situations and deindividuation with potentially punishing ones. A person learns to expect rewards for performing certain tasks well and wants to appear uniquely responsible for such actions. On the other hand, whenever the person expects punishment, there will be a tendency to hide or diffuse responsibility by submerging the self into a group. Ziller's emphasis was on the rewards and satisfaction that are gained through self-definition and uniqueness.

In still another version of deindividuation theory, Zimbardo (1969) argued that the expression of normally inhibited behavior may include loving and creative behavior as well as counternormative or negative actions. Furthermore, Zimbardo proposed that a large number of factors may lead to deindividuation, in addition to focus on the group or desire to avoid negative evaluation of moral responsibility. Among the deindividuating factors are anonymity (however created), the size of the group, level of emotional arousal, the novelty or ambiguity of the situation, altered time perspectives (such as during drug or alcohol use), degree of involvement in group activities, and so on.

All these factors lead to a loss of identity or self-consciousness, which in turn causes the individual to become unresponsive to inhibiting stimuli and to lose cognitive control over emotions and motivations. As a consequence, the deindividuated person is less compliant to positive or negative sanctions from agents outside the group. Hence, behavior is less apt to conform to external rules and standards.

In 1980 Diener offered a further theoretical modification by associating deindividuation with self-awareness. Deindividuated individuals do not attend to their own behaviors and lack awareness of themselves as distinct entities. The result is a failure to monitor or reflect upon their own behaviors, and a failure to retrieve appropriate norms of conduct from storage in long-term memory. Deindividuated persons also lack foresight, and their behavior lacks premeditation or planning. When there is little self-regulation, individuals are more apt to respond to immediate stimuli, emotions, and motives. Thus, their behaviors tend to be impulsive. In Diener's view the term "deindividuation" is a construct describing a set of relationships among situations, cognitive mechanisms, emotional states, and behavioral reactions.

A rather wide scope of antinormative behaviors has been associated with individuation and deindividuation. For example, drug abuse has been associated with social isolation from friends and family. Riots, lynchings, and other forms of mob violence have been attributed to deindividuation. A loss of inhibitions by members of encounter, marathon, and other non-cognitive therapy groups has frequently been observed, and this may also be attributed to a loss of self-awareness.

REFERENCES

Diener, E. (1980). Deindividuation: The absence of self-awareness and self-regulation in group members. In P. B. Paulus (Ed.), *Psychology of group influence.* Hilldale, NJ: Erlbaum.

Festinger, L., Pepitone, A., & Newcomb, T. (1952). Some consequences of deindividuation in a group. *Journal of Abnormal and Social Psychology, 47,* 382–289.

Fromm, E. (1965). *Escape from freedom*. New York: Avon Books.

LeBon, G. (1960). *The crowd*. New York: Viking. (Original work published 1895)

Ziller, R. C. (1964). Individuation and socialization. *Human Relations, 17,* 341–360.

Zimbardo, P. G. The human choice: Individuation, reason, and order versus deindividuation, impulse, and chaos. In W. J. Arnold & D. Levine (Eds.), *Nebraska Symposium on Motivation.* Lincoln, NB: University of Nebraska Press.

J. T. TEDESCHI
State University of New York at Albany

CONFORMING PERSONALITY
INDIVIDUALISM
NONCONFORMING PERSONALITY

DELTA RHYTHMS

Electrical activity in the brain varies along qualitative and quantitative dimensions. Differences in the frequency of cortical rhythms have long attracted attention because of their correlations with normal and pathological conditions. This entry focuses on delta rhythms, which occupy the lower end of the frequency dimension, and will be divided into three main sections. The biological basis of delta rhythms will be described first, followed by discussions of its roles in normal functioning, and then its involvement in selected psychiatric and neurological conditions.

BIOLOGICAL BASES OF DELTA WAVES

Cortical rhythms, as measured by an electroencephalogram (EEG), largely reflect the algebraic summation of postsynaptic potentials of apical dendrites in cortical neurons. During periods of higher neural activity (e.g., alert wakefulness), waveforms are relatively heterogeneous, or desynchronized from each other. As a result, waves cancel each other out, and appear on the EEG with low amplitudes and high frequencies. In contrast, periods of lower neural activity (e.g., deep sleep) are associated with relatively more homogeneous waveforms, which are somewhat synchronized with each other. This synchrony appears on the EEG with higher amplitudes and lower frequencies. At least three distinct types of delta rhythms have been identified (Amzica & Steriade, 1998), including a slow type (<1 Hz) that is generated cortically in large neuronal networks, a second type that is generated in a clock-like fashion by thalamocortical neurons across a broader frequency (1–4 Hz), and a third type that is generated by cortical neurons with intrinsic bursting properties across a broader frequency (1–4 Hz). These separate rhythms integrate to produce polymorphic delta waves on EEGs in the range of 0.5 to 4 Hz.

Delta rhythms occur with the greatest intensity during deep sleep in humans (stages 3 and 4, which together are also termed "delta sleep"; see Figure 1), and are relatively localized to the prefrontal cortex (Buchsbaum et al., 1982). For this reason, the func-

tions of delta waves are often linked to those of this region of the brain (Horne, 1993). Despite the association, however, it should be stressed that delta waves are not limited either to one part of the brain, or to one state of arousal.

DELTA WAVES IN NORMAL FUNCTIONS

An EEG period, or epoch, is typically classified as stage 3 sleep if delta waves comprise at least 20% of the epoch, and is classified as stage 4 sleep if delta waves comprise at least 50% of the epoch. Thus, because delta waves occur with the greatest intensity and regularity during deep sleep their function has most often been linked to the functions of sleep itself. The latter is a very complex issue that is still unresolved (e.g., Rechtschaffen, 1998), although it is likely that the primary benefits of sleep are to the brain (e.g., Horne, 1988). In particular, the value of deep sleep has been related to the restoration of cerebral function, especially in the prefrontal lobes. Studies of sleep deprivation, for example, provide support for this view.

Among the evidence are findings that sleep deprivation results in neuropsychological deficits similar to those associated with frontal lobe dysfunction, such as diminished verbal fluency and intonation; poor planning; poor organization and encoding of new material (especially in regard to solving novel problems); diminished affect; vulnerability to interference/distraction; perceptual distortions; perseverations and concrete thinking (e.g., Harrison & Horne, 1997; Horne, 1988; Kimberg, D'Esposito, & Farah, 1997). Moreover, when subjects are allowed to sleep freely following periods of deprivation (i.e., recovery sleep), most of the lost sleep is not made up, with the exception of deep sleep (and to a lesser extent, REM sleep), which is then followed by the return of predeprivation levels of cognitive abilities (e.g., Horne, 1988). Although this evidence is intriguing and is consistent with the view that delta waves in particular, and deep sleep in general, may be as-

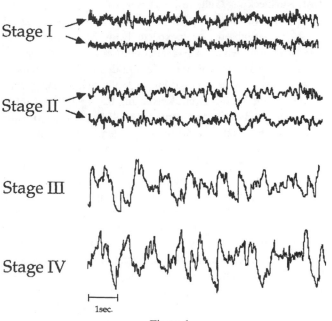

Figure 1

sociated with restorative functions of sleep, it is essentially circumstantial. Descriptions of the specific roles of delta rhythms in these processes await the outcome of additional research.

Relationships among delta waves—usually measured in the context of deep sleep—and other biological processes are even less clear than they are in the restorative aspects of sleep. For example (see also Rechtschaffen, 1998), a variety of substances that stimulate immune responses, such as interferon alpha-2, interleukin-1, and tumor necrosis factor, also stimulate delta sleep (e.g., Krueger, Shoham, & Davenne, 1986). Observations such as these led to the hypotheses that delta sleep–loss impaired host immune responses, while delta sleep itself enhanced it. The effects are far from general, however (they are not present in all species and are not caused by pathogenic challenges), and there is little direct evidence to link delta sleep to immune function (e.g., Benca & Quintans, 1997; Rechtschaffen, 1998). Similarly, hypotheses of a causal relationship between pain thresholds (notably in fibromyalgia syndrome) and delta sleep remain unconfirmed (Older et al., 1998).

DELTA WAVES IN PATHOLOGICAL FUNCTIONS

Delta waves are related to pathological functions in at least two ways. The first of these involves the presence of abnormal delta activity. For example, deafferentation of cortical areas can produce delta waves (which, as noted previously, reflects relatively low levels of cortical arousal/activity), such as might occur in regions contiguous to cortical tumors (Amzica & Steriade, 1998; Gloor, Ball, & Schaul, 1977) or in conditions like Down syndrome (which reflects slow and deficient brain development; Kaneko, Phillips, Riley, & Ehlers, 1996). Such rhythms (during wakefulness) are often localized to the area of dysfunction, and may serve as useful markers of underlying pathophysiological processes. Differential patterns of delta activity have, in fact, been used recently to facilitate the presurgical localization of temporal lobe epilepsies from extratemporal (primarily frontal) lobe epilepsies (Geyer, Bilir, Faught, Kuzniecky, & Gilliam, 1999).

The second way in which delta activity is related to pathological processes is by its absence or unexpectedly low levels during sleep. This occurs prominently in several conditions, including psychiatric disorders such as schizophrenia and depression. Deficits in deep sleep have long been noted in schizophrenia, although with some discrepant findings (cf. Keshavan, Reynolds, & Kupfer, 1990). Recent studies that augmented visual EEG scoring with automated counts of delta activity, however, clearly showed reduced delta waves in schizophrenia (Ganguli, Reynolds, & Kupfer, 1987; Keshavan et al., 1998), especially in the ≥ 1- to 2-Hz range. These findings are particularly interesting in that schizophrenia provides another example of a condition that often involves prominent frontal lobe pathology, related neuropsychological deficits (Seidman et al., 1996), and impaired delta activity reductions. Moreover, deficits in delta activity occur in major depression (Benca, Obermeyer, Thisted, & Gillin, 1992), which may also be associated with frontal lobe dysfunction. Although other, non-delta sleep deficits occur in these disorders as well, these findings raise the possibility that deficits in delta activity during sleep might serve as markers for several psychiatric and neurological disorders.

THE FUTURE

There is still a long way to go before we understand the biological significance of delta waves, in either their normal or pathological expressions. Nevertheless, its putative links, especially to frontal lobe function (at this point), suggest that it may serve as a valuable marker—or risk indicator—of several psychiatric and neurologic conditions. Its importance to normal biological and cognitive functions suggest that potentially, its manipulation may also aid in the amelioration or even prevention of some of these conditions.

REFERENCES

Amzica, F., & Steriade, M. (1998). Electrophysiological correlates of delta waves. *Electroencephalography and Clinical Neurophysiology, 107,* 69–83.

Benca, R. M., Obermeyer, W. H., Thisted, R. A., & Gillin, J. C. (1992). Sleep and psychiatric disorders. *Archives of General Psychiatry, 49,* 661–668.

Benca, R. M., & Quintans, J. (1997). Sleep and host defenses: A review. *Sleep, 20,* 1027–1037.

Buchsbaum, M. S., Mendelson, W. B., Duncan, W. C., Coppola, R., Kelsoe, J., & Gillin, J. C. (1982). Topographical cortical mapping of EEG sleep states during daytime naps in normal subjects. *Sleep, 5,* 248–255.

Ganguli, R., Reynolds, C. F., & Kupfer, D. J. (1987). Electroencephalographic sleep in young, never-medicated schizophrenics. *Archives of General Psychiatry, 44,* 36–44.

Geyer, J. D., Bilir, E., Faught, R. E., Kuzniecky, R., & Gilliam, F. (1999). Significance of interictal temporal lobe delta activity for localization of the primary epileptogenic region. *Neurology, 52,* 202–205.

Gloor, P., Ball, G., & Schaul, N. (1977). Brain lesions that produce delta waves in the EEG. *Neurology, 27,* 326–333.

Harrison, Y., & Horne, J. A. (1997). Sleep deprivation affects speech. *Sleep, 10,* 871–877.

Horne, J. A. (1988). *Why we sleep: The functions of sleep in humans and other mammals.* Oxford, England: Oxford University Press.

Horne, J. A. (1993). Human sleep, sleep loss and behavior: Implications for the prefrontal cortex and psychiatric behavior. *British Journal of Psychiatry, 162,* 413–419.

Kaneko, W. M., Phillips, E. L., Riley, E. P., & Ehlers, C. L. (1996). EEG findings in fetal alcohol syndrome and Down's syndrome children. *Electroencephalography and Clinical Neurophysiology, 98,* 20–28.

Keshavan, M. S., Reynolds, C. F., & Kupfer, D. J. (1990). Electroencephalographic sleep in schizophrenia: A critical review. *Comprehensive Psychiatry, 30,* 34–47.

Keshavan, M. S., Reynolds, C. F., Miewald, J. M., Montrose, D. M., Sweeney, J. A., Vasko, R. C., & Kupfer, D. J. (1998). Delta sleep deficits in schizophrenia. *Archives of General Psychiatry, 55,* 443–448.

Kimberg, D. Y., D'Esposito, M., & Farah, M. J. (1997). Frontal lobes: Cognitive neuropsychological aspects. In T. E. Feinberg

& M. J. Farah (Eds.), *Behavioral neurology and neuropsychology* (pp. 409–418). New York: McGraw-Hill.

Krueger, J. M., Shoham, S., & Davenne, D. (1986). Immune modulators as promoters of slow wave sleep. *Clinical Neuropharmacology, 9* (Suppl. 4), 462–464.

Older, S. A., Battafarano, D. F., Danning, C. L., Ward, J. A., Grady, E. P., Derman, S., & Russell, I. J. (1998). The effects of delta wave sleep interruption on pain thresholds and fibromyalgia-like symptoms in healthy subjects: Correlations with insulin-like growth factor I. *The Journal of Rheumatology, 25,* 1180–1186.

Rechtschaffen, A. (1998). Current perspectives on the function of sleep. *Perspectives in Biology and Medicine, 41,* 359–390.

Seidman, L. J., Oscar-Berman, M., Kalinowski, A. G., Ajilore, O., Kremen, W. S., Faraone, S. V., & Tsuang, M. T. (1996). Neuropsychological measures of prefrontal dysfunction in schizophrenia. *Biological Psychiatry, 39,* 578.

W. S. STONE
Harvard University

BETA AND GAMMA RHYTHMS
BRAIN WAVES

DEMENTIA

Once considered an almost inevitable hallmark of normal aging, it is now recognized that senile dementia is an insidious disease process affecting memory, cognition, orientation, and eventually the ability for self-care. It is clear that normal aging does not necessarily result in senility. However, for individuals 65 and older, an estimated 5–10% of the population will demonstrate the irreversable symptoms of this primary degenerative disease of the brain.

By the year 2000 it is projected that 32 million people will be over 65 years of age, and approximately 12–18 million will be 75 or older. Considering the positive relationship between advancing age and the incidence of dementia, it can be projected that the total number of persons evidencing the symptoms of dementia will increase significantly over the next several decades.

There are many etiological factors associated with dementia. The most frequent include infections of the central nervous systems, brain trauma, various neurological diseases, cerebrovascular disease, and toxic-metabolic disorders. Although the symptoms are most common among the aged population, they can occur in children suffering from neurological disorders associated with dementia (e.g., Huntington's Chorea).

The two most common forms of dementia are related to Alzheimer's disease and cerebrovascular disease. The dementia associated with cerebrovascular disease is sometimes referred to as multiinfarct dementia. Both of these disease processes affect the cerebral cortex. Other dementing illnesses may be related to the degeneration of various subcortical structures. Clinically, the patient with dementia may first present marked behavioral changes which precede the later manifestation of memory and intellectual deterioration. Robert Joynt and Ira Shoulson (1979) suggested three behavioral syndromes. First, normal behavioral traits may be accentuated to the point of eccentricity. Second, resistance may occur in response to novel social situations. Finally, mentally fatiguing operations may become impaired, resulting in more distractable behavior.

Intellectual changes and associated memory deterioration are characteristic of dementia. Memory for recent events or future appointments is generally one of the first areas in which problems are reported. Depression may complicate the difficulty in memory. Also, orientation may quickly become involved—it is not uncommon for the patient to become lost while walking around the block.

While the intellectual deterioration over the typical three-to-eight-year course of the disease can be quite striking, automatic behavior such as walking, eating, and even smoking may not be affected until late in the disease process. In the final stages of the disease the patient may be mute, incapable of self-care, unable to recognize loved ones, and highly distractible. Death typically occurs from intercurrent illness.

Multiinfarct dementia is conceptualized as a distinctly different type of dementia according to the American Psychiatric Association, because its etiology is known to be due to cerebrovascular infarcts. The progression of the focal signs of the dementia is not slow as in Alzheimer's, but manifests itself in a stepwise fashion. The onset of the symptoms may be abrupt, with focal neurological signs evident. Cerebrovascular disease is also present. The pattern of neuropsychological deficits is unique in each case, since the dementia symptoms appear only as a result of each circumscribed infarct. Unlike Alzheimer's or many of the subcortical dementing diseases (e.g., Huntington's, or progressive supranuclear palsy), the course of multiinfarct dementia is erratic, depending on the cerebrovascular pathology.

Morphologically, dementia affecting the cortical structures is characterized by dilation of the ventricles as evidenced on computerized tomographic (CAT) scans. Prominent cortical atrophy is most noticeable in the region of the temporal and frontal cortex. Senile plaques and neurofibrillary tangles are evident in the brain.

Despite the fact that CAT scans, pneumoencephalography, electroencephalography (EEG), and other radiologic techniques can be applied as aids in the diagnosis of dementia, it is often difficult to diagnose because of the insidious onset and relatively long-term course. Multiinfarct dementia is somewhat easier to identify, owing to its unique clinical and cerebrovascular pathology.

The most common and accurate means of clinical diagnosis remains based on data obtained from the neurological and neuropsychological examination. Francis Pirozzolo and Kathryn Lawson-Kerr (1980) suggested that, in addition to the traditional neurological examination incorporating a mental status assessment, the neuropsychological examination should include tests of intelligence, logical memory, paired associate learning, object naming, personality, visual discrimination, spatial reasoning and orientation, perceptual-cognitive speed, measures of right- versus left-sided performance, and language capabilities. Since symptoms associated with agnosia, apraxia, and aphasia will be evident in later stages of the disease, it is important to assess these functions so as to form a baseline against which to measure future performance.

Dementia due to cerebrovascular disease, normal pressure hydrocephalus, and psychogenic (pseudodementia) factors may be treatable. For instance, a reverse or arrest of the cerebrovascular disease associated with multiinfarct dementia will eliminate further deterioration. However, the medical treatment of most other dementias including Alzheimer's, Pick's disease, progressive supranuclear palsy, and Parkinson's disease, has not generally been successful in arresting the course of the disease. Pharmacological intervention has typically aimed at lessening the symptoms associated with progressive decline. Counseling and the development of support networks for the family are probably the most productive forms of intervention from a psychological standpoint.

REFERENCES

Joynt, R. L., & Shoulson, I. (1979). Dementia. In K. M. Heilman & E. Valenstein (Eds.), *Clinical neuropsychology.* New York: Oxford University Press.

Pirozzolo, F. J., & Lawson-Kerr, K. (1980). Neuropsychological assessment of dementia. In G. J. Maletta & F. J. Pirozzolo (Eds.), *The aging nervous system.* New York: Praeger.

SUGGESTED READING

Busse, E. W., & Blazer, D. G. (Eds.). (1980). *Handbook of geriatric psychiatry.* New York: Van Nostrand Reinhold.

Caine, E. D. (1981). Pseudodementia. *Archives of General Psychiatry, 38,* 1359–1364.

Hynd, G. W., Pirozzolo, F. J., & Maletta, G. (1982). Progressive supranuclear palsy. *International Journal of Neuroscience, 6,* 87–98.

Maletta, G., & Pirozzolo, F. J. (1980). *The aging nervous system.* New York: Praeger.

Wang, H. S. (1981). Neuropsychiatric procedures for the assessment of Alzheimer's disease, senile dementia, and related disorders. In N. E. Miller & G. D. Cohen (Eds.), *Clinical aspects of Alzheimer's disease and senile dementia.* New York: Raven Press.

G. W. HYND
University of Georgia

AGING: BEHAVIOR CHANGES
ALZHEIMER'S DISEASE
HUNTINGTON'S CHOREA

DENMARK, FLORENCE L.

Florence L. Denmark is an internationally recognized scholar, administrator, leader, researcher, and policy maker. She received her PhD in 1958 from the University of Pennsylvania in social psychology. Her baccalaureate was also earned at the University of Pennsylvania, where she was the first woman in that school's history to graduate with honors in two majors—in both psychology and history. Denmark, a native of Philadelphia, graduated as valedictorian of her high school class. Although she was trained as a social psychologist and has made many contributions to the psychology of women, her broad interests and distinguished contributions to psychology attest to her being an eminent generalist in an age of specialization.

Denmark is currently the Robert Scott Pace Distinguished Professor of Psychology at Pace University, where she is the chair of the department of psychology. She was previously the Thomas Hunter Professor of Psychology at Hunter College and the Graduate Center of the City University of New York.

Recognition of her impact on the field of psychology is based on her publication of more than 100 articles and 15 books and monographs, her presentation of approximately 100 talks and invited addresses at psychology meetings in the United States, Europe, Canada, and Central and South America, and her appearance on numerous radio and television shows. A pioneer in the field of the psychology of women, Denmark's most significant research has emphasized women's leadership and leadership styles, the interaction of status and gender, women in cross-cultural perspective, and the contributions of women to psychology. One of her recent publications, *The Handbook of the Psychology of Women* (coedited with M. Paludi), was selected by the journal *Choice* in 1995 as an academic book of excellence. Her most recent publication (2000) is a psychology of women textbook entitled *Engendering Psychology,* coauthored with colleagues V. Rabinowitz and J. Sechzer.

Denmark's elections to the following offices are testimonials to her impact on psychology: president, American Psychological Association (APA); president, Psi Chi, the National Honor Society in Psychology; president, Eastern Psychological Association; vice-president, New York Academy of Sciences; president, International Organization for the Study of Group Tensions; member of the Board of Directors, International Council of Psychologists; member of the Executive Committee, Council of Scientific Society Presidents; chair, Board of Directors, Professional Examination Service; and president, APA Division 35, the Psychology of Women and APA Division 1, General Psychology. These are only a few of the many organizations in which she has held membership and elective office. Denmark has been instrumental in the founding of the APA Division of International Psychology, Division 52, which focuses its efforts on the work of psychologists around the world. She served as its president in 1999.

The discretionary money given Denmark as outgoing president of the Eastern Psychological Association was donated to establish an award for faculty advisors who have made outstanding contributions to Psi Chi and the discipline of psychology.

Denmark is a fellow of the American Psychological Association, the American Psychological Society, and the New York Academy of Sciences. She is also a member of the Society for Experimental Social Psychology (SESP) and is currently a member of the editorial board of *Sex Roles.* She served for 14 years as associate editor of the *International Journal of Group Tensions* and was on the editorial board of *Psychology of Women Quarterly.*

Denmark is the recipient of numerous awards, including the American Psychological Association's Distinguished Contributions to Education and Training (1987), APA's Division 35's (Psychology of Women) Carolyn Sherif Award (1991), APA's Centennial Award for Sustained Contribution to the Public Interest Directorate (1992), Distinguished Contribution to Psychology in the Public Interest Award-Senior Career (1992), APA's Distinguished Contributions to the International Advancement of Psychology (1996), and the Interamerican Society of Psychology's (ISP) Interamerican Award in Psychology (1997). Most recently in 1999, APA Division 52 honored Denmark with the Distinguished International Psychologist Award and Psi Chi recognized Denmark as a Distinguished Member.

Other honors and recognition of Denmark's meritorious contributions to scholarship, research, teaching, and policy include: membership in Phi Alpha Theta, Psi Chi, Sigma Xi, and Phi Beta Kappa; Distinguished Lecturer, Hebrew University, Jerusalem, December 1976; Mellon Scholar, St. Olaf College, Northfield, Minnesota, January 1977; Kurt Lewin Award, New York State Psychological Association, 1978; First National Distinguished Service Award, Psi Chi, 1980; Honor Award, Federation of Organizations for Professional Women, 1980, "For contributions to equality for present and future women scholars"; Outstanding Women in Science Award, Association of Women in Science, 1980; Distinguished Contribution Award, International Organization for the Study of Group Tensions, 1981; keynote speaker, First International Interdisciplinary Congress, held in Haifa, Israel, 1981; G. Stanley Hall lecturer, American Psychological Association, 1982; Leadership Citation, Committee on Women in Psychology, American Psychological Association, 1985; Distinguished Career Award, Association for Women in Psychology, 1987, for outstanding contributions in policy and scholarship, and as a mentor in the field of the psychology of women; Wilhelm Wundt Award, Division of Academic Psychology, New York State Psychological Association, 1988; and Allen V. Williams Jr. Award for tireless dedication and outstanding service to the profession of psychology, New York State Psychological Association, 1994. Denmark is the recipient of honorary degrees from the Massachusetts School of Professional Psychology, Cedar Crest College, Illinois School of Professional Psychology, and Allegheny College.

STAFF

DENMARK, PSYCHOLOGY IN

THE FIRST EPOCH: TO WORLD WAR I
Psychology was founded in Denmark as an independent scientific discipline by Alfred Lehmann at the University of Copenhagen in 1886. Thus it is one of the oldest departments of psychology in the world.

Lehmann was a civil engineer who perceived psychology as an experimental science in the psychophysical and psychophysiological spirit of Gustav Fechner and Wilhelm Wundt. He studied for some time with Wundt in Leipzig. He combined these orientations with a more comprehensive understanding of the mind not far from the American functionalism of his age.

Lehmann's interests and scientific works were numerous. Some of his central publications deal with the aesthetics of colors from 1884 and with psychophysiology (translated into German in 1912). He also dealt with cognition, emotions, hypnosis, developmental psychology, industrial psychology, and especially educational psychology. Since then a preoccupation with educational psychology has characterized parts of Danish psychology. Like Wundt, Lehmann was interested in folk psychology, and he published a major work on superstition and witchcraft.

Psychology and philosophy were closely connected in this epoch, a connection that also has characterized parts of Danish psychology since. Lehmann did not hold philosophy in respect; in fact, he rejected it. The consequence, however, was that all kinds of psychology other than his were dealt with by the philosophers of his time. Foremost among these was Harald Høffding whose textbook of psychology from 1882 is the first comprehensive presentation of general psychology in Danish. It investigated the mind within the three classic dimensions of cognition, emotion, and conation and was soon translated into several languages.

THE SECOND EPOCH: WORLD WAR I TO 1960
Lehmann was succeeded by Edgar Rubin. His central publication from 1915 deals with perception of figures, including the exploration of the famous figure-ground relation, probably Rubin's discovery. The work was translated into German and greatly influenced Gestalt psychology.

Together with David Katz, who later became an important figure in Swedish psychology, Rubin studied with G. E. Müller in Göttingen in the years just before World War I and thereby consolidated the experimental orientation inherited from Lehmann. Edmund Husserl taught in Göttingen at the same time and his phenomenological philosophy may have influenced Rubin. That was at least Katz's opinion, although Rubin was most reluctant to admit it. Although a trained philosopher himself, Rubin, like Lehmann, held philosophy in contempt and spoke at best in a sarcastic voice of continental phenomenology. Nevertheless, some influence from Husserl is possible (but definitely not from other phenomenological philosophers).

Furthermore, Rubin was influenced by Gestalt psychology and Kurt Lewin. Internationally, Rubin and Katz are often reckoned among these orientations, although Rubin himself had reservations on the subject, mostly because in his opinion they cherished too many models and theories. Apart from that, the international influence on Danish psychology was modest in this epoch.

Such inspired, a special Danish psychology took shape. With Rubin as the central figure all through the epoch, it can be characterized as an experimental phenomenology concerned with a carefully detailed description of immediate experiences, including everyday psychological phenomena. The focus on immediate experiences distinguish this tradition from continental phenomenological philosophy. The tradition could be called a sort of phenomenalism in its endeavors to analyze a phenomenon into its most simple forms through accurate observations. Yet, the tradition also aimed at a comprehensive understanding of the mind in line with Franz Brentano and the Gestalt school (and the founding fathers Lehmann and Høffding as well).

The tradition became known as the third Copenhagen school along with and sometimes in vivid discussion with the quantum physical school centered around Niels Bohr and the structuralist linguistic school of glossematics centered around Louis Hjelmslev. It is a psychology of consciousness that investigates and classifies immediate experience without any attempt to anchor the content of the mind in either biological or sociological factors outside consciousness. It is, therefore, descriptive and antireductionist with an ideal of high methodological lucidity rather than theoretical explanations. It is almost antitheoretical.

The Copenhagen school exclusively dominated Danish psychology through almost half a century, because there existed only this single center for psychological research, staffed by just a handful of persons, and directed by an incredibly critical Rubin, who allowed few scientific publications by himself and his associates to come forth.

The subject matter studied was the components of cognition. It was Rubin's opinion that cognition had to be examined closely before it would be possible to deal with action, motivation, and emotion. Therefore, his colleagues did not embark on such topics until after the Rubin's death.

The first of the colleagues was Edgar Tranekjær Rasmussen who in 1956 published a phenomenological psychology of understanding or a systematic psychology of the possible contents of consciousness. In 1960, he dealt with needs in the tradition of H. A. Murray. The next was Franz From who in 1957 developed parts of a descriptive social psychology by investigating the purposive aspects of person perception. The work was translated into English after the topic had become known to American psychology through the works of Fritz Heider.

Outside the tradition stood K. B. Madsen, the only person in the epoch to be partly influenced by behaviorism. His comparative analysis of theories of motivation from 1959 has been translated into many languages. Psychoanalysis also was outside the Danish tradition which held psychoanalysis in contempt because of its concept of the unconscious and its alleged propensity toward unscientific speculations.

In 1918, the first formal training in psychology was established. It was exclusively aimed at research, however, and society's need for the services of psychology led to the establishment of a new degree aimed at professional educational psychology in 1944. Interest in educational psychology has remained high and has resulted in considerable research in developmental psychology, intelligence, and skills at the Royal Danish School of Educational Studies.

Rubin was of the opinion that psychology had not yet reached the scientific level necessary to investigate anything but the fundamental cognitive components of consciousness. Because of this position, textbooks in psychology were written by philosophers only. Foremost among these were F. Brandt and especially Jørgen Jørgensen whose *Psychology on a Biological Foundation* (1945) was widely distributed.

THE THIRD EPOCH: 1960 TO TODAY

From 1960 a wealth of new scientific currents poured into Danish psychology and broke the limitations of the relatively narrow research tradition of the Copenhagen school. At the same time the number of students increased dramatically, and in 1960, a thorough reform of education at the University of Copenhagen was instituted. It developed a curriculum that educated students in general and applied psychology. In 1968, a department of psychology was founded at the University of Aarhus with a similar curriculum. In the early 1960s, departments of general psychology and of educational psychology as well as a special degree in educational psychology were established at the Royal Danish School of Educational Studies. Along with the increased number of students, the number of teachers and researchers grew, for the first time covering most of the classic areas of psychology.

In addition, applied research was broadened. Industrial psychology gained ground and clinical psychology developed explosively. Applied psychological research as a whole takes up an important place within the educational, social, and health sectors of the Danish society. Professional psychology developed correspondingly, and Denmark is among the countries of Europe with the highest number of professional psychologists per capita.

The German Influence

The German influence on Danish psychology remained powerful, but it became more diverse, and important parts of it broke with the tradition of the Copenhagen school. Important schools of thought are: psychological thinking grounded in classic continental phenomenology; existentialism; hermeneutics; and especially psychoanalysis in its many forms, including orthodox Freudianism, Freudo-Marxism (Reich), the Frankfurt school (Adorno and Habermas), and theories of socialization (Lorenzer and Ziehe). Jung's psychoanalysis also secured a footing.

Orientations like these make up the foundation for a considerable part of Danish psychological research. Furthermore, influence of the USSR on Danish psychology was in part mediated by German schools (e.g., the so-called critical psychology of Holzkamp).

The Influence of Russia

Russian psychology and its dialectical and historical materialist philosophy has influenced Danish psychology, especially the cultural—historical school and the theory of activity (Vygotsky, Luria, and Leontjev). With it, the relation between the ordinary life of the individual and the economical and political conditions of society has come to be an important subject of research and so has the historicity of the mind in its phylogenetic and sociogenetic development.

These orientations have been fairly easily absorbed. The reason is probably that the Danish appropriation of dialectical and Marxist psychology has emphasized its continuity with German philosophy rather than the aspects that predominated in other countries, for instance, its critique of positivism.

The Anglo-Saxon Influence

A strong Anglo-Saxon orientation also gained considerable influence. It applied to such dissimilar traditions as analytical philosophy and behaviorism, although the latter never really took root in Denmark.

Cognitive psychology, on the other hand, became influential. However, cognitive psychology was not regarded as a break with the tradition of the Copenhagen school but rather as a natural continuation, although of much greater scope in subject matter. The reason is probably because the Gestalt-oriented description of mental phenomena and processes held such a central position in the Copenhagen school.

In connection with the Danish version of the German-Russian accentuation of the relation between the individual and his or her surroundings, it is understandable that the ecologically oriented cognitive psychology (Bruner, Gibson, and Neisser) and developmental psychology (Bronfenbrenner) gained ground in Denmark. The computationally oriented cognitive psychology has not yet had much resonance.

The investigation of the relation between the individual and his or her social surroundings also has influenced Danish psychology from Anglo-Saxon quarters in the shape of interactionism (Mead) and systems theory.

DANISH INTERNATIONAL PSYCHOLOGY

Danish psychology has passed through a rapid development in the last quarter of the century. Its research has considerable breadth inspired by a diversity of international currents.

In some respects it is a drawback to carry out research in a small country with limited economical resources, but it also has advantages. If not locked up in self-satisfaction, this position carries the possibility for true internationality. Although small in size, Denmark, like a number of other small European countries outside the Anglo-Saxon language area, is a melting pot for psychological research from all over the world. Orientations stretch around the international horizon, giving breadth of view and the opportunity to pick out the most promising international tendencies for importation and elaboration.

Among the classic disciplines of general psychology, research in perception, memory, thinking, and knowledge representation is prominent. Considerable research is carried out on high-technological work processes. Research in biological psychology and neuropsychology is also quite comprehensive, especially in connection with clinical problems and rehabilitation. Investigations of the individual in his or her cultural settings and social-biological foundations are numerous. Denmark has pioneered in the development of the study of qualitative research methods. Today, large parts of Danish psychology have no national distinguishing mark but are enrolled into the dominant international currents in regard to both the content and the methods of research.

DANISH NATIONAL PSYCHOLOGY

No single tradition dominates Danish psychological research and professional work, because Danish psychology is open to international trends. Typically, imported international currents inspire each other. That applies not only to research teams but also to the individual research worker. Nevertheless, there is a Danish touch peculiar to parts of Danish psychology. It is, however, more of a perspective or a way of thinking than a demarcated theory or specific method.

The distinguishing Danish national mark is a quest for comprehensiveness, for an integrated view of the human mind in its entirety. The aim is rich in descriptions of mental phenomena together with an understanding of their relations to other phenomena, their mutual familiarity and contrasts, and their individual and historical development. The approaches and instruments are not only empirical in a narrow sense but are in line with the Copenhagen school of self-reflections, elaborations on psychological observations of daily life, general experiences, and relevant philosophical considerations.

It is a comprehensive and, to a high degree, cross-scientific way of thinking, conceiving psychological research as ultimately a contribution to a general anthropology or a view of humanity with the mind conceptualized in terms of the relationship between the biological organism and the cultural horizon. A related characteristic is a tight connection between general and applied psychology, regarding research, courses of study, and institutions. Examples are investigations of psychopathological conditions grounded in general theories of the mind and applied psychological centers within the universities.

And finally the standard question: What influence has Søren Kierkegaard had on Danish psychology? Not much in most researchers' immediate self-understanding. But probably something, after all, because he was a pioneer in the quest for a general view of humankind.

REFERENCES

Koppe, S. (1983). *Psykologiens udvikling og formidling i Denmark i perioden 1850–1980* [The development and dissemination of psychology in Denmark in the period 1850–1980]. Copenhagen.

Madsen, K. B. (1980). Psykologiens historie i Denmark [The history of psychology in Denmark]. In K. B. Madsen (Ed.), *Psykologisk leksikon* (2 udg) [Encyclopedia of psychology (2nd ed., pp. 350–356)]. Copenhagen.

Moustgaard, I. K., & Petersen, A. F. (Eds.). (1986). *Udviklingslinier i dansk psykologi fra Alfred Lehmann til i dag* [Developments in Danish psychology from Alfred Lehman until now]. Copenhagen.

B. KATZENELSON
University of Aarhus, Denmark

DEPENDENT PERSONALITY

Despite the prevalence and well-known features of this personality pattern, only passing reference was made to it in official nosologies published prior to the 1980 *Diagnostic and Statistical Manual of Mental Disorders,* (3rd ed. [*DSM-III*]). Giving the disorder the status of a separate and major disorder, *DSM-III* includes as its central feature behavior such as passively allowing others to take full responsibility for one's significant life activities, a characteristic traceable to the person's lack of self-confidence and to doubts concerning the ability to function independently.

Notable also is a willingness to subordinate one's needs to those of others on whom one is dependent, so as to avoid having to assume independent and self-reliant roles. Self-belittling and lacking in initiative, these patients hesitate to make direct demands of those upon whom they depend, lest they jeopardize the security achieved. Many exhibit a social naiveté that is made tolerable, if not pleasing, by virtue of their genuinely obliging and friendly temperament. Appeasing and conciliatory submission to others is also a common trait, as is a conspicuous and often troublesome clinging to supportive persons. Except where dependency security is at stake, their social and personal difficulties are cognitively denied or neutralized by an uncritical and charitable outlook.

Personality features such as passively allowing others to direct one's life and an unusual willingness to submit to external influence were first noted by Emil Kraepelin in the eighth edition of his *Psychiatrie* (1913). Here he stressed the "irresoluteness of will" of these patients, and the ease with which they could be "seduced" by others. Psychoanalytic formulations of patients such as these were described in accord with psychosexual stage theory: They were identified as "oral" types and, more specifically, as "oral-sucking" or "oral-receptive" characters. They were most clearly presented by Abraham (1927/1924), who noted their typical belief that "there will always be some kind person . . . to care for them and to give them everything they need."

Another parallel to the dependent disorder derived from a psychodynamic perspective was formulated by Horney in *Our Inner Conflicts*. Describing what she terms the "compliant" type, Horney notes their "marked need for affection and approval . . . (the seeking of) a partner . . . who is to fulfill all expectations of life and [to take] responsibility for good and evil." A similar characterization was presented by Erich Fromm in *Man For Himself*. Speaking of those exhibiting what he labeled the "receptive orientation," Fromm notes that "they are dependent not only on authorities, but . . . for any kind of support. They feel lost when alone because they feel they cannot do anything without help."

Utilizing a biosocial-learning theory to deduce personality types, Theodore Millon lists the following diagnostic criteria in *Disorders of Personality* for patients of this character.

1. Pacific temperament (e.g., is characteristically docile and noncompetitive; avoids social tension and interpersonal conflicts).

2. Interpersonal submissiveness (e.g., needs a stronger, nurturing figure, and without one feels anxiously helpless; is often conciliatory, placating, and self-sacrificing).

3. Inadequate self-image (e.g., perceives self as weak, fragile, and ineffectual; exhibits lack of confidence by belittling own aptitudes and competencies).

4. Pollyanna cognitive style (e.g., reveals a naive or benign attitude toward interpersonal difficulties; smooths over troubling events).

5. Initiative deficit (e.g., prefers a subdued, uneventful and passive life-style; avoids self-assertion and refuses autonomous responsibilities).

REFERENCES

Abraham, K. (1927). The influence of oral eroticism on character formation. In *Selected Papers on Psychoanalyses.* London: Hogarth. (Original work published 1924)

Horney, K. (1945). *Our inner conflicts: A constructive theory of neurosis.* New York: Norton.

T. MILLON
University of Miami

AVOIDANT PERSONALITY
LEARNED HELPLESSNESS
PERSONALITY TYPES

DEPENDENT VARIABLES

"Dependent variable" is a term used in research methods and refers to the attribute being measured. In experimental research the dependent variable is what is being assessed to determine the effect of manipulating the independent variable. The dependent variable may involve behavioral, physiological, or social characteristics depending on the nature of the study. It may involve assessment of performance, such as the amount of information a subject might learn as measured by the number of correct responses on a test. A dependent variable is what is being measured to ascertain the effects of some treatment in an investigation or to use as a description of the status of subjects in the study. For example, if two methods of math instruction were being compared, the dependent variable might be the number of correct responses on a math test administered after instruction is completed.

The choice of a dependent measure is often given inadequate attention when researchers are designing studies. However, selection of an appropriate dependent variable is very important to the overall strength, outcome, and interpretation of an investigation. A number of matters should be considered in determining the appropriateness of the dependent variable selected.

One obvious concern is that a dependent measure should reflect the construct being studied. If a researcher is investigating anxiety, the dependent variable should relate to the construct of anxiety. A dependent variable should also be both sensitive and reliable in the context of the phenomenon under study. The measure should be sufficiently sensitive to accurately detect behavioral or performance changes when they occur. The dependent measure should be able to reflect such changes in a reliable fashion. Generally, a researcher will select the most sensitive and reliable dependent variable possible. The only circumstance in which this rule of thumb is not appropriate is when such a measure is obtrusive; that is, when the act of obtaining the measure alters a subject's behavior. If using a particular measure appears to be obtrusive, another dependent variable may be preferred so that the data obtained are not contaminated. Thus, the measure of choice is one that is maximally sensitive, reliable, and unobtrusive.

Another consideration related to selection of a dependent variable involves avoiding ceiling or floor effects in the data. A ceiling effect occurs when the performance range of the task is limited so that subjects "top out." A floor effect reflects a task so difficult that many subjects cannot perform the task at all. Ceiling and floor effects generate inaccurate results or artifactual data. In circumstances in which either ceiling or floor effects exist, the data reflect the limits of the task rather than the subjects' ability to perform.

SUGGESTED READING

Drew, C. J., Hardman, M. L., & Hart, A. W. (1996). *Designing and conducting research: Inquiry in education and social science.* Boston: Allyn and Bacon, Inc.

Schloss, P. J., & Smith, M. A. (1999). *Conducting research.* Columbus, OH: Merrill/Prentice-Hall.

Martella, R. C., Nelson, J. R., & Marchand-Martella, N. E. (1999). *Research Methods: Learning to become a critical research consumer.* Boston: Allyn & Bacon.

C. J. Drew
University of Utah

RESEARCH METHODOLOGY
STATISTICS IN PSYCHOLOGY

DEPRESSION

DESCRIPTION

In the United States, the word "depression" refers to everything from a transient mood state (feeling down) to the clinical disorder known as Major Depressive Disorder (MDD). In order to receive a diagnosis of MDD, a person must experience marked distress and a decrease in level of functioning. In addition, the two weeks preceding the examination must be characterized by the almost daily occurrence of a dysphoric mood (e.g., sadness) or a loss of interest or pleasure (anhedonia) in almost all activities. The individual must also experience at least four (only three if both dysphoric mood and anhedonia are both present) of the following seven symptoms nearly every day for the two week period: (a) significant weight change or change in appetite; (b) insomnia or hypersomnia; (c) psychomotor agitation or retardation; (d) fatigue or loss of energy; (e) feelings of worthlessness or of excessive or inappropriate guilt; (f) decreased concentration or indecisiveness; and (g) suicidal ideation, plan, or attempt (see American Psychiatric Association, 1994). Related disorders (i.e., other mood disorders) include Bipolar I and II (Manic-Depressive Disorder), dysthymia, and cyclothymia.

PREVALENCE AND COSTS

Major Depressive Disorder (MDD) is the most commonly diagnosed psychiatric disorder among adults, with lifetime prevalence rates of 20 to 25% for women and 9 to 12% for men. At any given point in time, the prevalence rates are about 6% for women and 3% for men. MDD is fairly rare among children, but it begins to manifest itself at puberty. Depression has been diagnosed with increased frequency among young people, so that in the current 16-to-25 age group, about 20% have already suffered from MDD. After late adolescence, the prevalence rates and gender differences are fairly constant over the human life span.

Depression tends to be a cyclical disorder. Among those who have had one episode, the probability of a second episode is 50%, and among those who have had two episodes the probability of a third episode is 75 to 80%. After the third episode, the disorder is likely to plague the person on a chronic basis, though episodes of the disorder may come and go even without treatment. The episodes are painful both for the individuals with the disorder and for those around them. As noted, the disorder interferes with functioning in social and work situations. The costs are enormous to both the individual and society; for example, MDD is nearly always rated among the top five most expensive health problems.

TREATMENTS

There are two major approaches to the treatment of MDD: biological interventions and psychotherapies. The major biological intervention is antidepressant medication (see Nemeroff & Schatzberg, 1998). The first major classification of antidepressants was called tricyclic, because of the chemical structure of the medicines. Included in this group were such familiar medicines as amitriptyline (Elavil), imipramine (Tofranil), desipramine (Norpramin), and nortriptyline (Pamelor). These medications work with about 55 to 65% of patients with MDD, but they have fairly severe side effects, including blurred vision, constipation, and orthostatic hypotension. Thus, they are currently used less frequently as a first line of treatment. Another class of antidepressant medications is the monoamine oxidase inhibitors (MAO inhibitors); examples include phenelzine (Nardil) and tranylcypromine (Parnate). These medications are as effective as the tricyclics for MDD and probably slightly more effective for a form of the disorder called Atypical Depression (e.g., symptoms of mood reactivity, extreme sensitivity to rejection, extreme fatigue, increased sleep, and weight gain/appetite increase). However, these medicines necessitate abstinence from several popular foods, so they are not very well tolerated.

By far the currently most popular class of antidepressant medications is the selective serotonion-reuptake inhibitors (SSRIs), which include fluoxetine (Prozac), paroxetine (Paxil), and sertraline (Zoloft). These medications work with 60 to 70% of individuals with the disorder, and the side effects are *relatively* minor. However, one major drawback to the SSRIs is their fairly frequent side effect of inhibiting orgasm.

There are several other, less frequently utilized antidepressants that do not fall into one of the preceding classes. One of these is buproprion (Wellbutrin), which may not be quite as effective as some of the other antidepressants but does have the advantage of facilitating sexual performance in some patients.

For extremely difficult to treat depressions, electric convulsant therapy (ECT) and transcranial magnetic stimulation may be employed. These therapies work very well, but have fairly severe side

---

1. One of the most popular trade names is listed in parenthesis for each of the treatment medications.

effects, and the rates of relapse following these treatments are fairly high.

There are innumerable psychotherapies, but only two have been fairly extensively evaluated as treatments for MDD (see Craighead, Craighead, & Ilardi, 1998). Both of these therapies are short-term, 16–20 sessions conducted over a period of 12 to 16 weeks. Both therapies focus on current life problems and are fairly directive (i.e., the therapist takes an active role in identifying and suggesting possible solutions to problems). The first of these is interpersonal psychotherapy (IPT). This therapy was designed to address interpersonal difficulties associated with MDD, and focuses on one or more interpersonal problems. The topics of therapy include life transitions, losses, lack of social skills, and/or role conflicts.

The second effective psychotherapy for MDD is cognitive behavior therapy (CBT). This therapy focuses on the behavioral deficiencies (e.g., a lack of social skills) and cognitive styles (e.g., the belief that the depressed person causes bad things to happen, has always caused bad things to happen, and causes bad things to happen in many areas of his or her life) associated with MDD.

With outpatients suffering from MDD, IPT and CBT are about equally effective. Each is about as effective as antidepressant medications for mild/moderate depressions. Current studies are underway to determine if these psychotherapies are as effective as the antidepressant medications for more severe depressions. The limited available data suggest that a combination of antidepressant medication and one of these psychotherapies is both the most effective and enduring treatment for MDD.

Pharmacological interventions for children with MDD have been very disappointing; however, recent work has shown that fluoxetine (Prozac) is effective with adolescents over the age of 15. Cognitive behavior therapy has been used in small studies with children; it seems to be reasonably effective, and has been implemented in both the school and family settings.

At least two large research projects have suggested that behavioral marital therapy is an effective treatment for MDD when the depressed person is a partner in an unhappy marriage. It has been found that 50% of married, depressed individuals are in unhappy marriages, and that 50% of individuals in unhappy marriages are depressed. Thus, behavioral marital therapy may be useful to many married patients suffering from MDD.

One of the problems that has plagued the treatment of MDD is that a fairly large percentage of successfully treated individuals suffer from a relapse or recurrence of the disorder. Because the relapse rate is so great when antidepressants are taken for a fairly brief period of time (e.g., 3 months), it is strongly recommended that once an antidepressant medication is begun, it should be continued for at least 9 to 12 months. Combining antidepressant medication and psychotherapy (IPT or CBT) appears to decrease the relapse rate following treatment. It does appear that the most effective treatment for recurrent MDD (three or more episodes) is likely to be continuing the antidepressant medication.

PREVENTION

Because of the increasing rates of MDD among young people, it is becoming more important to prevent first episodes and recur-

rences of the disorder. Prevention programs focused on individuals with some but not all the symptoms of MDD and on individuals with pessimistic cognitive styles, have shown some promise. Small studies also suggest that combined CBT and IPT for individuals who have had an episode of MDD but are not currently depressed may decrease the recurrence rates of MDD.

REFERENCES

American Psychiatric Association. (1994). *Diagnostic and statistical manual of mental disorders* (4th ed.). Washington, DC: Author.

Craighead, W. E., Craighead, L. W., & Ilardi, S. S. (1998). Psychosocial treatments for major depressive disorder. In P. E. Nathan & J. M. Gorman (Eds.), *A guide to treatments that work* (pp. 226–239). New York: Oxford University Press.

Nemeroff, C. B., & Schatzberg, A. F. (1998). Pharmacological treatment of unipolar depression. In P. E. Nathan & J. M. Gorman (Eds.), *A guide to treatments that work* (pp. 212–225). New York: Oxford University Press.

W. E. CRAIGHEAD
University of Colorado

B. H. CRAIGHEAD
Medical College of Virginia

ANTIDEPRESSANT MEDICATIONS
COGNITIVE BEHAVIOR THERAPY
COMMUNICATION
INTERPERSONAL COMMUNICATION
MARRIAGE COUNSELING

DEPRESSION, LEWINSOHN'S MODEL

Lewinsohn's original model of depression (Lewinsohn, Weinstein, & Shaw, 1969) was behavioral and was based on earlier formulations by Skinner (1953) and Ferster (1965). The 1969 model emphasized a "reduced rate of response-contingent reinforcement" as a critical antecedent for depression.

In the 1969 model, reinforcement was defined by the quality of the patient's interactions with his or her environment. Those person-environment interactions with positive outcomes constitute positive reinforcement. Such interactions strengthen the person's behavior. The term "contingent" refers to the temporal relationship between a behavior and its consequences; that is, the reinforcement must follow the behavior. The model assumed that the behavior of depressed persons does not lead to positive reinforcement to a degree sufficient to maintain their behavior. Hence, depressed persons find it difficult to initiate or maintain their behavior, and they become increasingly passive. The low rate of positive reinforcement was also assumed to cause the dysphoric feelings.

Three ways in which a low rate of response-contingent positive reinforcement may occur were suggested. First, events that are contingent on behavior may not be reinforcing. Second, events that are reinforcing may become unavailable; and third, reinforcers may be available but because of a lack of the required skills, the individual is unable to elicit them.

An important supplement to the behavioral position was that often the social environment provides reinforcement in the form of sympathy, interest, and concern, which strengthen and maintain depressive behaviors. These reinforcements are typically provided by a small segment of the depressed person's social environment (e.g., his immediate family). However, since most people in the depressed person's environment (and eventually even the person's family) find these behaviors aversive, they will avoid the person as much as possible, thus decreasing his or her rate of receiving positive reinforcement and further accentuating the depression.

A number of different environmental events (e.g., loss due to a death, separation, rejection, poverty, misfortune) and organismic states and traits (e.g., lack of social skills, ignorance) were presumed to be causally related to a low state of positive reinforcement. Social skills, defined as the emission of behaviors that are positively reinforced by others, was seen as an area of deficit especially important in the development of depressive behaviors.

On the basis of empirical studies (Grosscup & Lewinsohn, 1980; Lewinsohn & Amenson, 1978; Lewinsohn, Lobitz, & Wilson, 1973; Lewinsohn, Mermelstein, MacPhillamy, & Alexander, 1985; Lewinsohn & Talkington, 1979; Lewinsohn, Youngren, & Grosscup, 1979) the theory was expanded to incorporate a relationship between aversive events and depression. Specifically, it was hypothesized that depressed individuals are more sensitive, experience a greater number of aversive events, and are less skillful in terminating aversive events.

An elevated rate of occurrence of aversive events and heightened sensitivity to such events might result in avoidance and withdrawal from aversive situations. The short-term consequence of greater isolation and the long-term consequence of lesser skill acquisition would be expected to increase the probability that the individual would be in a condition of low positive reinforcement. The occurrence of aversive events may also reduce the enjoyment (potential reinforcement value) of behaviors and events that occur in close temporal proximity to aversive events.

In 1985, Lewinsohn, Hoberman, Teri, and Hautzinger broadened the scope of the previously described theoretical efforts and proposed an integrative theory of depression, which is represented in Figure 1. The revision was motivated by the fact that some empirical findings did not support the earlier model. The earlier model also had not incorporated either the cognitive manifestations of depression or individual differences in vulnerability to depression.

The integrative theory views the occurrence of depression as a product of environmental as well as dispositional factors. The chain of events leading to the occurrence of depression is postulated to begin with the occurrence of an evoking event or antecedent (A), which is empirically defined as any event that increases the probability of the future occurrence of depression. The occurrence of antecedents is assumed to initiate the depressogenic process to the extent that they disrupt substantial, important, and relatively automatic behavior patterns of an individual (B). Such disruptions, and the emotional upset they typically engender, are assumed to be related to the occurrence of depression to the extent that they lead to a reduction of positive reinforcement or to an elevated rate of aversive experience (C); that is, they shift the balance of the quality of the patient's interactions with the environment in a negative direction. As the effects of evoking events exert their impact on an individual's obtained level of reinforcement, the individual attempts to reduce that impact. These efforts will be successful to certain degrees, depending on both environmental and dispositional factors (G). The inability to reverse the impact of the stress is hypothesized to lead to a heightened state of self-awareness (D), that is, a state in which attention is focused internally that results in individuals' becoming aware of their thoughts, feelings, values, and standards. Increasing self-awareness is assumed to cause individuals to become more self-critical, to produce an increase in the discrepancy between ideal self and perceived self, and produce dysphoria, which in turn is assumed to lead to some of the cognitive alterations that have been emphasized by cognitive theorists, such as pessimism and attribution of failures to self. The model assumes that feeling increasingly self-aware (D) and dysphoric (E) leads to many of the cognitive, behavioral, and emotional changes (F) that have been shown to be correlated to depression. These changes (F) are presumed to be quite consequential and to play an important role in the maintenance and exacerbation of the depressive state. Numerous studies have shown that in a state of dysphoria negative thoughts and memories become more accessible and that negative information about the self is processed more efficiently. The dysphoria would also be expected to reduce the individual's social and other competence. The lack of competence in important spheres of functioning in turn may make it more likely that a depression-evoking event (A) will occur.

The proposed model allows for the idea that predisposing characteristics of various kinds (G) to either increase (vulnerabilities) or decrease (immunities) the risks for a depressive episode; this idea in turn allows for the fact that individual differences may systematically increase or decrease the probability of an occurrence of depression. These vulnerabilities and immunities are assumed to be relatively stable characteristics of the person or of the person's environment.

As indicated in the figure, predisposing characteristics are assumed to affect all elements of the model. For example, an individual with good coping skills would be more likely to be able to reverse the depressogenic cycle by implementing new behaviors to deal with the disruption (B) or by decreasing self-awareness by finding distractions and thereby staying focused on external events. The behavior of significant others in the person's environment may constitute a vulnerability to the extent that they selectively reinforce the depressed individual's symptoms and complaints.

The model allows for "feedback loops" that are seen as important in determining the level of severity and the duration of an episode of depression. Thus, becoming depressed (F) and thinking and behaving in the depressed mode would be expected to interfere with the individual's problem solving skills (G) and consequently his or her ability to reverse the disruption (B) and the effects of the disruption (C). Feedback loops set the stage for a vicious cycle. By reversing any of the components of the model, the depression will be progressively and increasingly ameliorated.

The model allows for many points of entry into the chain of events leading to depression and thus allows for a multiplicity of causes, each of which is contributory but none of which is essential. The fact that any number of psychological, biological, and eclectic interventions for depression are successful may be explained by the large number of person-initiated, biological, and environmental changes that can affect one or more links of the model.

REFERENCES

Ferster, C. B. (1965). Classification of behavior pathology. In L. Krasner & L. P. Ullman (Eds.), *Research in behavior modification* (pp. 6–26). New York: Holt.

Grosscup, S. J., & Lewinsohn, P. M. (1980). Unpleasant and pleasant events and mood. *Journal of Clinical Psychology, 36,* 252–259.

Lewinsohn, P. M., Weinstein, M., & Shaw, D. (1969). Depression: A clinical research approach. In R. D. Rubin & C. M. Frank (Eds.), *Advances in behavior therapy* (pp. 231–240). New York: Academic Press.

Lewinsohn, P. M., & Amenson, C. (1978). Some relations between pleasant and unpleasant mood-related events and depression. *Journal of Abnormal Psychology, 87,* 644–654.

Lewinsohn, P. M., & Talkington, J. (1979). Studies on the measurement of unpleasant events and relations with depression. *Applied Psychological Measurement, 3,* 83–101.

Lewinsohn, P. M., Youngren, M. A., & Grosscup, S. J. (1979). Reinforcement and depression. In R. A. Depue (Ed.), *The psychobiology of the depressive disorders: Implications for the effects of stress* (pp. 291–316). New York: Academic Press.

Lewinsohn, P. M., Hoberman, H., Teri, L., & Hautzinger, M. (1985). An integrative theory of depression. In S. Reiss & R. Bootzin (Eds.), *Theoretical issues in behavior therapy* (pp. 331–359). New York: Academic Press.

Lewinsohn, P. M., Lobitz, W. C., & Wilson, S. (1973). "Sensitivity" of depressed individuals to average stimuli. *Journal of Abnormal Psychology, 81,* 259–263.

Lewinsohn, P. M., Mermelstein, R. M., Alexander, C., & MacPhillamy, D. J. (1985). The unpleasant events schedule: A scale for the measurement of aversive events. *Journal of Clinical Psychology, 41,* 483–498.

Skinner, B. F. (1953). *Science and human behavior.* New York: Free Press.

P. Lewinsohn
Oregon Research Institute

DEPRESSION
REINFORCEMENT

DEPTH PERCEPTION

Differential distance perception, known generally as depth perception, is primarily a result of the senses of vision and hearing. For vision there are two general classes of depth cues: monocular and binocular. Monocular depth cues are those that indicate distance through the use of one eye, and include texture gradients, size, motion parallax (in which retinal images of close objects move farther across the retina than do far objects when the eye moves laterally), accommodation (changing the focus of the eye for objects at different distances), chromostereopsis (an illusion of depth that results from changing the focus of the eye for coplanar objects of different hues because of chromatic aberration), linear perspective, interposition (in which near objects obscure more distant objects), shadow detail, and visual clarity (atmospheric degradation of more distant objects). Binocular cues are convergence (in which the angle of the visual axes from the left fovea to an object and from the right fovea to that object increases with decreasing distance) and retinal disparity (in which the retinas receive slightly different images of the same object). Several of these cues may operate simultaneously, each one corroborating the others. It is difficult experimentally to identify which cues are operating at a given time.

Visual depth perception is studied in several ways. One approach is to have the subject (under binocular or monocular conditions) adjust a rod or needle such that it is equally distant relative to a standard. The visual cliff (a platform device with a glass floor extending out over an apparently deep side and shallow side) can be used to test depth perception in human and nonhuman subjects by ascertaining the amount of preference for the shallow side. Three-dimensional perception can be provided by the stereoscope, which presents two nearly identical views separately to the two eyes. A later development has been the invention by Julesz (1971) of random-dot stereograms: computer-generated patterns of random dots with pattern pairs that are identical except for a laterally-displaced region. This region, when viewed with a stereoscope, appears to stand above or below the rest of the pattern.

Auditory depth cues are used by blind people who can approach and stop before colliding with a wall. Echolocation in bats and cetaceans represents an elaboration of this capability. Additional auditory cues for depth are the amount of reverberation, spectral characteristics (in which atmospheric absorption is greater for higher frequencies), motion parallax, and relative loudness of known sounds.

Depth cues provided by other senses include proximity detection because of the strength of a familiar odor, thermal detection in pit vipers, and the electric field sensitivity found in some fish.

REFERENCE

Julesz, B. (1971). *Foundations of cyclopean perception.* Chicago: University of Chicago Press.

SUGGESTED READING

Boring, E. G. (1942). *Sensation and perception in the history of experimental psychology.* New York: Appleton-Century-Crofts.

Graham, C. H. (Ed.). (1965). *Vision and visual perception.* New York: Wiley.

Griffin, D. R. (1986). *Listening in the dark: The acoustic orientation of bats and men.* Ithaca, NY: Cornell University Press.

Marr, D. (1982). *Vision.* New York: W. H. Freeman.

Schöne, H. (1984). *Spatial orientation: The spatial control of behavior in animals and man* (C. Strausfeld, Trans.). Princeton, NJ: Princeton University Press. (Original work published 1980)

G. H. ROBINSON
University of North Alabama

EYE

DESCARTES, RENÉ (1596–1650)

René Descartes ran away from his French Jesuit school at La Flèche when he was 16 and joined the army. After several years in military service, he settled in Paris and then in Holland to study mathematics. Descartes is renowned as the father of modern philosophy. He used his training in mathematical methodology to set forth his clear deductions from the analysis of self-evident principles; "out of his attempt grew some of the most persistent problems and basic distinctions of modern philosophy" (Edman & Schneider, 1941, p. 282).

The single feature of Descartes' philosophical writings that distinguishes them sharply from the works of Plato and Aristotle is Descartes's emphasis on the individual thinker: the question of what a particular person may know, rather than what people may know. Descartes, as a rationalist, defined knowledge as judgments or statements that can be said to be certain or indubitable, and denied that sense experience can lead to knowledge in this way. Empiricists, on the other hand, believe that sense experience is the source of knowledge.

Descartes began systematizing his philosophy with radical or absolute doubt and so acquired a new certainty: I cannot doubt that I am doubting. "I think, on this intuitive and certain truth he constructed his system. He gave new proofs for old beliefs, but in claiming to discover certainty for himself by precision of method, by self-examination, and by observation of the Bible, instead of by appeal to faith, schools, and tests, he formulated the principles of a secular philosophy of nature and of an unrestrained confidence in human reason."

Descartes published his *Discourse on Method* in 1637. A few years later *Principia Philosophia* and *Meditationes de Prima Philosophia* came out, but some early works were not published until after his death because he feared the Inquisition.

The Cartesian school of philosophy caught on quickly and influenced the thought of many intellectuals. It was the dominant system of philosophy until Hume and Kant, inspiring the ideas that served the Enlightenment.

N. A. HAYNIE

DEUTSCH, MORTON (1920-   )

Morton Deutsch was born, prematurely, in 1920 into a middle-class family in New York City, the last of four sons. He was always eager to be more advanced than his age, so he skipped through elementary and high school and entered the City College of New York (CCNY) at 15. He started off as a pre-med major with the idea of becoming a psychiatrist. However, after dissecting a pig in biology lab, he switched to psychology. While at college, he was deeply immersed in a student culture that highly valued Marx, Freud, scientific method, and political activism.

After CCNY, he started graduate work in clinical psychology, obtaining a MA in 1940 at the University of Pennsylvania. He then had rich, diverse experiences working with mentally disturbed, retarded, and delinquent individuals in three New York institutions. In January, 1942, he entered the Air Force and served as a lead navigator in a bomber group flying out of England. His war experiences shifted his psychological interests toward social psychology. This shift was reinforced by an interview with K. Lewin in 1945, during which Lewin described his exciting plans for the Research Center for Group Dynamics at the Massachusetts Institute of Technology (MIT).

At MIT, Deutsch was fortunate enough to become a part of a creative, innovative group that would mold the development of social psychology for several decades. The MIT Center was an exhilarating atmosphere in which the new ideas and new methods for research bubbled forth in the constantly occurring discussions of social psychology issues. Under the influence of Lewin's dictum that there is nothing so practical as a good theory, Deutsch turned his concerns about the possibility of a nuclear war arising from international competition into a theoretical and experimental investigation of the effects of cooperation and competition. This classic study, in addition to being the taking-off point for much of Deutsch's subsequent work, has helped to stimulate the development of a movement toward cooperative learning in the schools under the leadership of D. and R. Johnson.

He obtained his PhD from MIT in 1948, and then joined the Research Center for Human Relations headed by S. Cook (at the New School and then at New York University). There, Deutsch worked collaboratively with colleagues on studies of intergroup prejudice and discrimination, on a textbook of research methods, and on a program of theoretical-empirical research on factors affecting the initiation of cooperation. During this period, Deutsch also started training in psychoanalysis, at the Postgraduate Center for Psychotherapy, which he completed in 1958. He has maintained a small practice until recently.

In 1956, C. Hovland persuaded Deutsch to join and help establish a new basic research group in psychology at the Bell Telephone Laboratories. There, he did research on small group processes and interpersonal bargaining, inventing (with R. Krauss) new gaming procedures. He was also the "peacenik" at the Bell Labs, criticizing the strategic thinking current among establishment intellectuals, and coediting a book on *Preventing World War III* (1962).

In 1963, Deutsch accepted an invitation to establish a new social psychology doctoral program at Teachers College. He emphasized social significance as well as basic theory and research, recruiting "tough-minded and tender-hearted" students. With the help of many able students, Deutsch engaged in extensive theorizing and research on conflict resolution and distributive justice. Several basic ideas have emerged from this work, and these ideas have had considerable theoretical and practical import and also have served to integrate much of the research in these areas. This work is summarized in two books: *The Resolution of Conflict* (1973) and *Distributive Justice* (1985). His other books include *Interracial Housing* (1951), *Research Methods in Social Relations* (1951, 1959), *Theories in Social Psychology* (1965), *Applying Social Psychology* (1975), and *The Handbook of Conflict Resolution* (2000).

His work has been widely honored by such awards as the Kurt Lewin Memorial Award, the G. W. Allport Prize, the Carl Hovland Memorial Award, the AAAS Sociopsychological Prize, the Samuel Flowerman Award, APA's Distinguished Scientific Contribution Award, SESP's Distinguished Research Scientist Award, and the Nevitt Sanford Award; and he is a William James Fellow of APS. He has also received lifetime achievement awards for his work on conflict management, cooperative learning, peace psychology, and the applications of psychology to social issues. In addition, he has received the Teachers College Medal for his contributions to education, the Helsinki University Medal for his contributions to psychology, and the Doctorate of Human Letters from the City University of New York. He has been president of the Society for the Psychological Study of Social Issues, the International Society of Political Psychology, the Eastern Psychological Association, the New York State Psychological Association, as well as several divisions of the American Psychological Association.

Deutsch is currently E. L. Thorndike Professor Emeritus and Director Emeritus of the International Center for Cooperation and Conflict Resolution at Teachers College, Columbia University.

STAFF

DEWEY, JOHN (1859–1952)

John Dewey was an American philosopher, psychologist, and educator. He attended the University of Vermont, after which he taught high school and studied philosophy independently. He entered the graduate program at Johns Hopkins University and received his doctorate in philosophy in 1884. He taught at the University of Michigan and the University of Minnesota before going to the University of Chicago in 1894, the same year as James Rowland Angell. Dewey remained at Chicago for 10 years, and his influence and Angell's made the university a center for functional psychology. Dewey started an experimental or laboratory school at Chicago, a new approach to educational methods that made him both famous and controversial. When he left, the leadership of the functionalist school passed to Angell. From 1904 to 1930 Dewey was at Columbia University, working on applications of psychology to educational and philosophical problems.

Dewey's paper "The reflex arc concept in psychology" is usually credited with establishing functionalism as a defined school of psychology, rather than just an orientation or attitude. The paper contained the seeds of all the arguments against the use of the stimulus-response unit as the building block of behavior in psychological theory. In this paper Dewey attacked the molecular reductionism of elements in the reflex arc, with its distinction between stimulus and response. Dewey felt that behavior reduced to this basic sensory-motor description was not meaningful. He taught that behavior is continuous, not disjoined into stimuli and responses, and that sensory-motor behaviors continuously blend into one another.

Dewey understood the organism not as a passive receiver of stimuli but as an active perceiver. He believed that behavior should be studied in terms of its significant adaptation to the environment. The proper subject matter for psychology was the study of the total organism as it *functioned* in its environment. His functionalistic point of view was influenced by the theory of evolution and his own instrumentalistic philosophy, which held that ideas are plans for action arising in response to reality and its problems. The struggle of the human intellect is to activate conscious responses to bring about appropriate behavior that enables the organism to survive, to progress, to function. "Thus, functional psychology is the study of the organism in use" (D. Schultz, *History,* 1981, p. 163).

John Dewey wrote the first American textbook of psychology in 1886, called *Psychology,* which was popular until William James's *The Principles of Psychology* came out in 1890. But Dewey did not spend many years in psychology proper. After the 1896 paper, his interests turned to practical applications. In 1899, after retiring as president of the American Psychological Association, he became the leader of the progressive education movement. It is consistent with his functional psychology and philosophy that he devoted most of his time to American education and its pragmatic development.

N. A. HAYNIE

DIAGNOSIS

Diagnosis is the act of identifying and naming a disorder or disease by using an agreed-upon system of categorization. In North America, mental and emotional syndromes are currently diagnosed according to the *Diagnostic and Statistical Manual of Mental Disorders,* Fourth Edition (*DSM-IV;* American Psychiatric Association, 1994).

ROOTS OF *DSM-IV*

The roots of *DSM-IV* extend back to nineteenth-century German psychiatrist Kraepelin, who believed strongly in detailed medical and psychiatric histories of patients, emphasized thorough observation of signs and symptoms, and considered some disorders, prominently including the psychoses, to be diseases of the brain. In these emphases, Kraepelin both anticipated and influenced future generations of mental health professionals, including our own.

Despite a few earlier unsuccessful efforts, however, it was not until the end of World War II that representatives of the War Department, the Veterans Administration, and civilian psychiatric community in the United States began discussing creation of a national nomenclature that could simultaneously serve their diverse needs. The result was a syndromally-based nomenclature, *DSM-I* (1952).

DSM-I and DSM-II

DSM-I was designed to permit mental health professionals across the United States to use a common diagnostic language for the first time. Notwithstanding, *DSM-I* and its similar successor, *DSM-II* (1968), had serious deficiencies. Because they provided only brief descriptions of each disorder, the reliability of resultant diagnoses was low. Moreover, syndrome descriptions were not empirically based and often failed to correspond to the clinical experience of those working in clinical settings. The low reliability of *DSM-I* and *DSM-II* diagnoses adversely affected validity and clinical utility.

DSM-III

The roots of *DSM-III* lay in: (a) late 1960s research by psychiatrist R. Spitzer at the New York State Psychiatric Institute, which led to the development of a series of structured diagnostic interviews (e.g., Spitzer, Fleiss, Endicott, & Cohen, 1967) designed to gather the data on signs and symptoms on which an empirically based nomenclature could be built; (b) an influential article by Feighner and colleagues (1972) that proposed explicit, empirically-derived diagnostic criteria for 16 major diagnostic categories; and (c) publication of the Research Diagnostic Criteria (RDC; Spitzer, Endicott, & Robins, 1975), designed to allow empirical testing of the reliability of the Feighner criteria.

DSM-III (1980) represented a breakthrough in efforts to heighten the reliability, validity, and utility of syndromal diagnosis. The instrument's diagnostic criteria, and those of its successors, *DSM-III-R* (1987) and *DSM-IV* (1994) represent its major departure from its predecessors. Modeled after the RDC, the diagnostic criteria organized each syndrome's signs and symptoms in a consistent format. Each clinician could approach the diagnosis of a particular syndrome in the same way, defining each sign and symptom consistently, and processing the resultant diagnostic information uniformly. As a result, the reliability of *DSM-III* diagnoses selectively improved.

The clinical utility of the *DSM-III* also improved. The *DSM-III* text, and those of its two successors, contained several times as many pages and words as its predecessors, permitting far greater explication of each of the more than 300 sets of operational criteria (more than three times as many as its predecessors), as well as information on associated features, age of onset, course, nature and extent of impairment, complications, predisposing features, prevalence, sex ratio, familiar pattern, and differential diagnostic issues.

DSM-III also introduced the multiaxial system in a further effort to enhance utility. It assesses each patient along five axes, rather than only one, as in *DSM-I* and *DSM-II*. Not only are patients assessed on psychopathology, on Axes I and II, but also on the physical conditions which might have contributed to their psychopathology (Axis III), the severity of the psychological stressors to which the patient was exposed (Axis IV), and the patient's highest level of adaptive functioning during the preceding year (Axis V).

DSM-IV

A principal goal of the *DSM-IV* process was to create an empirically-based nomenclature; a three-stage process was used. Thirteen Work Groups began their efforts with systematic literature reviews designed to address unresolved diagnostic questions. When literature reviews failed to resolve questions, the Work Groups sought to locate clinical data sets to do so; 40 analyses of existing patient data sets were ultimately carried out. The Work Groups also designed and carried out extensive field trials to generate new clinical data; 12 large-scale field trials at more than 70 sites worldwide, involving more than 7,000 participants, were completed.

RELIABILITY AND VALIDITY OF *DSM-IV* DIAGNOSES

Most data reported to date on the reliability and validity of *DSM-IV* categories have come from the field trials. They suggest modest increments in the reliability of a few diagnostic categories (e.g., oppositional defiant disorder and conduct disorder in children and adolescents, substance abuse and dependence) and in validity (e.g., autistic disorder; oppositional defiant disorder in childhood and adolescence). However, little progress was made in addressing the substantial reliability problems of the personality disorders, the sleep disorders, the disorders of childhood and adolescence, and some of the disorders within the schizophrenic spectrum.

CRITICISMS OF *DSM-IV*

In a response to criticisms that professional issues overshadowed scientific ones in the creation of *DSM-IV* (e.g., Caplan, 1991), Widiger and Trull (1993) admit that issues of utility sometimes preempted issues of validity, as when a valid diagnosis was deemphasized because so few patients meet its criteria. Nonetheless, even though Widiger and Trull (1993) admit that the *DSM-IV* Task Force was sensitive to a variety of professional issues, they nonetheless see it as primarily an empirically-driven instrument.

Psychiatrist S. Guze, a key figure in the development of *DSM-III,* expressed concern in 1995 that many *DSM-IV* diagnostic conditions continue to fail to meet Robins and Guze's (1970) criteria for diagnostic validity; this is a theme others (e.g., Kirk & Kutchins, 1992) have also sounded. To this concern, Pincus, First, Frances, and McQueen (1996) note that while *DSM-IV* contains 13 diagnoses not in *DSM-III-R*, it has eliminated eight *DSM-III-R* diagnoses, for a net gain of only five.

COMORBIDITY OF DIAGNOSES

There is substantial overlap in disorders in *DSM-IV* and its two predecessors. With others, Klein and Riso (1993) have asked whether they are discrete, "natural" classes or artificial categories created by the establishment of arbitrary cutoffs on a continuum, thereby echoing concerns of many others about the substantial comorbidity of *DSM-IV* disorders.

In a report from the National Comorbidity Survey (NCS), Blazer and his colleagues (1994) confirmed the high rates of co-occurrence between major depression and a range of other psychiatric disorders, finding as well that comorbid depression is generally more severe than simple depression. Kessler and colleagues

(1995), in a second NCS article, reported that posttraumatic stress disorder is strongly comorbid with other lifetime *DSM-III-R* disorders in both men and women, especially the affective disorders, the anxiety disorders, and the substance use disorders. Magee and his colleagues (1996) report that lifetime phobias are highly comorbid with each other, with other anxiety disorders, and with affective disorders; lifetime phobias are more weakly comorbid with alcohol and drug dependence. As with major depression, comorbid phobias are generally more severe than pure phobias.

THE CATEGORICAL/DIMENSIONAL DEBATE

Categorical versus dimensional classification first became a matter of concern when *DSM-III* tripled the number of diagnoses described by its predecessors, thereby raising the question of boundaries between old and new diagnostic entities. As diagnoses proliferated, the frequency of comorbidity increased, causing clinicians to ask whether comorbidity represents the co-occurrence of two or more mental disorders or a single disorder that has simply been labeled in different ways. As a consequence, the advantages and disadvantages of dimensional and categorical approaches to personality and diagnosis are now being explored extensively (e.g., Widiger, 1997). The focus of these efforts is on the personality disorders, where symptom overlap is greatest.

Impressive progress has been made in a relatively few years in garnering conceptual and historical support for the advantages of dimensional over syndromal approaches to the personality disorders and other overlapping psychopathological conditions. Nonetheless, the ultimate worth and significance of the trait dimensional approach will not be known until substantially more research data have been gathered that demonstrate empirically the advantages of this approach to these disorders.

REFERENCES

American Psychiatric Association (APA). (1952, 1968, 1980, 1987, 1994). *Diagnostic and statistical manual of mental disorders,* 1st, 2nd, 3rd, 3rd revised, 4th ed. Washington, DC: Author.

Blazer, D. G., Kessler, R. C., McGonagle, K. A., & Swartz, M. S. (1994). The prevalence and distribution of major depression in a national community sample: The National Comorbidity Survey. *American Journal of Psychiatry, 151,* 979–986.

Caplan, P. J. (1991). How do they decide who is normal? The bizarre, but true, tale of the *DSM* process. *Canadian Psychology, 32,* 162–170.

Feighner, J. P., Robins, E., Guze, S. B., Woodruff, R. A., Winokur, G., & Munoz, R. (1972). Diagnostic criteria for use in psychiatric research. *Archives of General Psychiatry, 26,* 57–63.

Guze, S. B. (1995). Review of *American Psychiatric Association Diagnostic and Statistical Manual of Mental Disorders,* 4th ed. *American Journal of Psychiatry, 152,* 1228.

Kessler, R. C., Sonnega, A., Bromet, E., Hughes, M., & Nelson, C. B. (1995). Posttraumatic stress disorder in the National Comorbidity Survey. *Archives of General Psychiatry, 52,* 1048–1060.

Kirk, S. A., & Kutchins, H. (1992). *The selling of DSM: The rhetoric of science in psychiatry.* Hawthorne, NY: Walter deGruyter.

Klein, D. N., & Riso, L. P. (1993). Psychiatric disorders: Problems of boundaries and comorbidity. In C. G. Costello (Ed.), *Basic issues in psychopathology* (pp. 19–66). New York: Guilford.

Magee, W. J., Eaton, W. W., Wittchen, H-U, McGonagle, K. A., & Kessler, R. C. (1996). Agoraphobia, simply phobia, and social phobia in the National Comorbidity Survey. *Archives of General Psychiatry, 53,* 159–168.

Pincus, H. A., First, M., Frances, A. J., & McQueen, L. (1996). Reviewing *DSM-IV. American Journal of Psychiatry, 153,* 850.

Robins, E., & Guze, S. (1970). Establishment of diagnostic validity in psychiatric illnesses: Its application to schizophrenia. *American Journal of Psychiatry, 126,* 983–987.

Spitzer, R. L., Endicott, J., & Robins, E. (1975). *Research Diagnostic Criteria (RDC) for a selected group of functional disorders.* New York: New York State Psychiatric Institute.

Spitzer, R. L., Fleiss, J. L., Endicott, J., & Cohen, J. (1967). *Mental Status Schedule:* Properties of a factor-analytically derived scale. *Archives of General Psychiatry, 16,* 479–493.

Widiger, T. A. (1997). Mental disorders as discrete clinical conditions: Dimensional versus categorical classification. In S. M. Turner & M. Hersen (Eds.), *Adult psychopathology and diagnosis* (pp. 3–23). New York: Wiley.

Widiger, T. A., & Trull, T. J. (1993). The scholarly development of *DSM-IV.* In J. A. C. de Silva & C. C. Nadelson (Eds.), *International review of psychiatry* (pp. 59–78). Washington, DC: American Psychiatric Press.

P. E. NATHAN
University of Iowa

CLINICAL ASSESSMENT
DIAGNOSTIC & STATISTICAL MANUAL OF MENTAL DISORDERS

DIAGNOSTIC INTERVIEW SCHEDULE

The ability to accurately diagnose psychiatric disorders has improved dramatically over the last 20 years. Structured diagnostic interviews have played a major role in this advancement, and the Diagnostic Interview Schedule (DIS) is among the most prominent and popular of these instruments.

OVERVIEW AND HISTORY OF THE DIS

In 1978, development of the original DIS was begun by researchers at the Washington University Department of Psychiatry in St. Louis, at the request of the National Institute of Mental Health (NIMH). At that time, the NIMH Division of Biometry and Epidemiology was planning a set of large-scale, multicenter epidemiological investigations of mental illness in the general adult population in America as part of its Epidemiological Catchment Area Program. Variables to be assessed included incidence and prevalence of many specific psychiatric disorders and utilization profiles of health and mental health services. With this grand purpose in mind, development of a structured interview that could be administered by nonclinicians was imperative due to the prohibitive cost of using professional clinicians for these expansive community studies. As a result, the DIS was designed as a *fully structured* diagnostic interview, which fully specifies all questions and probes and minimizes the amount of clinical judgment and experience required to administer it. In fact, the DIS was explicitly crafted so that it can be administered and scored by lay, nonprofessional interviewers.

Since its early beginnings as a draft version in 1978, there have been six major revisions of the original DIS. For example, the original DIS covered criteria for only 31 *DSM-III* diagnoses, with later versions adding more disorders. Another refinement was the addition of a comprehensive set of training materials including mock interviews, professional training videotapes, and extensive training courses. Perhaps most importantly, DIS questions and diagnostic algorithms were revamped to match new criteria presented in *DSM-III-R* (Version DIS-III-R; Robins, Helzer, Cottler, & Goldring, 1989), and most recently to establish compatibility with *DSM-IV* criteria (Version DIS-IV; Robins, Cottler, Bucholz, & Compton, 1996). Notably, a computerized version of the DIS-IV (C-DIS) is available, as well as DIS-IV data entry, cleaning, and scoring programs. The DIS has been translated into many languages and applied in many countries, and enjoys widespread use in diverse clinical research, especially in large-scale studies.

DESCRIPTION OF THE DIS

As noted previously, the DIS is a fully structured interview which can be administered by nonclinical lay interviewers. The exact wording of all symptom questions and follow-up probes are delineated in an interview book, items are read verbatim to the respondent in a standardized order, and clarification or rephrasing of questions is discouraged, although DIS interviewers can repeat any question as necessary to ensure that it is understood by the respondent. All DIS questions are written to be closed-ended, and replies are coded with a forced choice yes/no format, which eliminates the need for clinical judgment to rate responses. Given the yes/no format, clarification of responses is neither needed nor required. The DIS gathers all necessary information about the subject from the subject, and collateral sources of information are not used, which again obviates the need for advanced clinical skills. The DIS is self-contained and covers all necessary symptoms to make many (but not all) *DSM-IV* diagnoses. Coded responses are entered into a computer, where the diagnosis is made according to the explicit rules of the *DSM-IV* diagnostic system.

Since the DIS was designed for epidemiological research with normative samples, DIS interviewers do not elicit a presenting problem or chief complaint from the subject, as would be typical in unstructured clinical interviews. Rather, DIS interviews begin by asking questions about symptoms in a standardized order. Like other structured interviews, the DIS has sections that cover different disorders. Each diagnostic section is independent, except where one diagnosis preempts another. Once a symptom is reported to be present, further closed-ended questions are pursued to assess additional diagnostically relevant information such as severity, frequency, time frame, and possibility of organic etiology of the symptom. The DIS includes a set of core questions that are asked of each respondent; the core questions are followed by contingent questions that are administered only if the preceding core question is endorsed. DIS interviewers utilize a Probe Flow Chart that indicates which probes to use in which circumstances.

For each symptom, the respondent is asked to state whether it has ever been present and how recently. All data about presence/absence of symptoms and time frames of occurrence are coded and then entered into a computer for scoring. Indeed, consistent with its use of lay interviewers who may not be familiar with the *DSM-IV* or psychiatric diagnosis, diagnostic output of the DIS is generated by a computer which analyzes the coded data from the completed interview. Output of the computer program provides estimates of prevalence for two time periods: current and lifetime.

Due to its highly structured format, full administration of the DIS-IV interview typically requires between 90 and 120 minutes. Administration can even be longer with severely ill or loquacious subjects. To shorten administration time, it is possible to drop evaluation of disorders that are not of interest in a particular study. Another option is to drop further questioning for a particular disorder once it is clear that the threshold number of symptoms needed for diagnosis will not be met. Thus, modules can be dropped, shortened, or asked in full depending on the specific needs of the researchers.

Although designed for use by lay administrators, training for competent administration of the DIS is intensive and includes several components. Trainees typically attend a one-week training program at Washington University, during which they review the DIS manual; listen to didactic presentations about the format, structure, and conventions of the DIS; view videotaped vignettes; and complete workbook exercises. Role-play practice interviews are also conducted with extensive feedback and review to ensure that trainees master the material. Finally, additional supervised practice is also recommended.

The psychometric properties of the original DIS and its revisions have been evaluated in numerous investigations, generally with encouraging results. The interested reader is referred to Segal (1997) for a full discussion of reliability and validity data for the DIS. Overall, the DIS has proven to be a popular and useful diagnostic assessment tool, especially for large-scale epidemiological research. The DIS has been translated into numerous languages; it is used in many countries for epidemiological research and served as the basis for the Composite International Diagnostic Interview (CIDI/DIS) employed by the World Health Organization. Presently, the DIS-IV is the only well-validated case finding strategy that can make *DSM-IV* diagnoses in large-scale epidemiological research. Like earlier versions, the DIS-IV can be expected to enjoy widespread application in psychiatric research, service, and training for many years to come. Given the history of the DIS, its continued evolution will likely make it a popular and effective instrument for psychiatric diagnosis in the 21st century.

REFERENCES

Robins, L. N., Cottler, L., Bucholz, K., & Compton, W. (1996). *The Diagnostic Interview Schedule, Version IV.* St. Louis: Washington University School of Medicine.

Robins, L. N., Helzer, J. E., Cottler, L. B., & Goldring, E. (1989). *The Diagnostic Interview Schedule, Version III-R.* St. Louis: Washington University School of Medicine.

Segal, D. L. (1997). Structured interviewing and *DSM* classification. In S. Turner & M. Hersen (Eds.), *Adult psychopathology and diagnosis* (3rd ed., pp. 24–57). New York: Wiley.

D. L. SEGAL
University of Colorado, Colorado Springs

DIAGNOSIS
STRUCTURED CLINICAL INTERVIEW FOR DIAGNOSIS (*SCID*)

DIAGNOSTIC AND STATISTICAL MANUAL OF MENTAL DISORDERS (*DSM-IV*)

The fourth edition of the *Diagnostic and Statistical Manual of Mental Disorders* was published in 1994 by the American Psychiatric Association, replacing 1952, 1968, and 1980 revisions of the organization's official classification system. Despite misgivings concerning its orientation and scope by other mental health professions, as well as its divergence from the system promulgated by the World Health Organization in the 1977 ninth revision of its *Manual of the International Statistical Classification of Diseases,* the *DSM-IV* is the standard handbook for psychodiagnosis employed by clinicians and researchers in the United States.

Substantially more comprehensive and systematically arranged than its predecessors, the *DSM-III* and *IV* include detailed descriptions of major clinical and personality syndromes. To be exhaustive and inclusionary, information on each syndrome had to be ordered in a standard format. The organizational sequence adopted includes: essential (necessary) features; associated (frequent) features; and where reliable data are available, age of onset, course, impairment, complications, predisposing factors, sex ratio, familial pattern, and differential diagnosis.

A major innovation of the *DSM-III* was the introduction of formal diagnostic criteria—that is, uniform and specific characteristics of behavior which make up the essential elements of each clinical category. The use of precise and standardized criteria was designed not only to facilitate diagnostic decision making, but also to ensure that researchers from diverse settings employ a comparable series of rules and gauges to identify and select their clinical populations.

The decision, in planning the *DSM-III,* to adopt a multiaxial schema signifies a major shift from the more classical approach to diagnosis. The traditional medical task usually consists of making a differential diagnosis, that is, disentangling the web of a patient's complaints and symptoms so as to pinpoint its essence, the underlying disease state. By contrast, the multiaxial approach employed in the *DSM-III* and *IV* asks the clinician to identify the full matrix of symptoms and influences, recording each on a set of five axes, and conceiving all to be integral elements of an interactive complex that, only in its entirety, constitutes the pathologic state. Among the axes that compose an "official" *DSM-IV* diagnosis are "clinical syndrome," "personality disorder," and "physical disorder;" recommended, but not required, are two contextual axes, one cross-sectional in its focus and the other longitudinal—namely, "severity of psychosocial stressors" and "highest level of adaptive functioning."

T. MILLON
University of Miami

PERSONALITY DISORDERS

DINGLEDINE, RAYMOND

Raymond Dingledine attended Michigan State University and received a BS in biochemistry in 1971. He then received his PhD in pharmacology, under Avram Goldstein at Stanford, in 1975. He received postdoctoral training in neuropharmacology and neurophysiology from Leslie Iversen and John Kelly at Cambridge, U.K. (1975–77), then from Per Andersen at Oslo (1977–78). He joined the Department of Pharmacology at the University of North Carolina at Chapel Hill in 1978 and rose to the position of professor. During this time he spent a sabbatical year (1990–1991) in Steve Heinemann's lab at the Salk Institute, where he incorporated molecular biological approaches into his work. Dingledine's honors include being named a Sloan Research Fellow and a Klingenstein Fellow in Neuroscience; receiving the Epilepsy Research Award from the American Society for Pharmacology and Experimental Therapeutics, the Basic Epilepsy Research Award from the American Epilepsy Society, the Bristol-Myers Squibb Neuroscience Award (twice), a Jacob Javits Neuroscience Award (National Institutes of Health [NIH]), the Boezi Distinguished Alumnus Award (Michigan State University), and the PhRMA Career Excellence Award; presenting the Tom Rainbow Lecture (University of Pennsylvania), the Herbert Jasper Lecture (Montreal Neurological Institute), the Koppanyi Lecture (Georgetown University), and keynote addresses at the Western Pharmacological Society, the International Epilepsy Conference (Oslo), the Kiffen Penry Memorial, the Epilepsy and Brain Development Conference (Houston), and the JP Long memorial symposium.

Dingledine's most significant research accomplishments are the discoveries that glycine is a coagonist of NMDA receptors (*Science,* 1988); that the transition between interictal and ictal states in the high potassium model of seizures involves shrinkage of extracellular space (*Journal of Neurophysiology,* 1989; *Science,* 1990); that one amino acid residue controls calcium permeation in glutamate receptor channels (*Science,* 1990; *Journal of Neuroscience,* 1991); that the channel-lining domain of glutamate receptor subunits is a reentrant loop rather than a transmembrane domain (*Neuron,* 1995); and that the potency of certain ifenprodil analogues as NMDA receptor antagonists is enhanced at ischemic pH (*Nature Neuroscience,* 1998). The glycine coagonist report was the fourth most highly-cited paper in the field of neuroscience between 1988 and 1992, and the topology report was deemed a "hotpaper" for 1995 on the basis of citation analysis. His current research focuses on the genetic control of glutamate receptor expression and function, with particular emphasis on the roles of glutamate receptors in neurological disorders. A second research emphasis is the use of microarray and associated technologies to identify novel molecular targets for interrupting epileptogenesis.

Dingledine holds a patent for a cytotoxicity-based reverse two-hybrid system. He has consulted for Nova Pharmaceuticals, Eli Lilly, and Pfizer. He is currently on the scientific advisory boards of Merck Sharp & Dohme Neuroscience Institute, and of Beacon Pharmaceuticals, a start-up.

He has served on a variety of NIH and National Science Foundation (NSF) review panels, including the Integrative and Neural Systems Advisory Panel (NSF), the Neurosciences Special Review Committee (National Institute of Mental Health [NIMH]), and the Neurological Disorders Program Project B Committee (National Institute of Neurological Disorders & Stroke [NINDS]). He currently chairs the Pharmacological Sciences Review Committee National Institute of General Medical Sciences (NIGMS), and serves on the Epilepsy Therapeutics Research Program Advisory Group (NINDS) and the ASPET Board of Publications Trustees. He has served as councilor for the Society for Neuroscience; as president of the North Carolina Chapter of the Society for Neuroscience; and as a member of the ASPET Epilepsy Award Committee and the Program Committee of Society for Neuroscience, and of several international award selection committees. He is currently editor of *Molecular Pharmacology,* the leading primary pharmacology journal, and serves on the editorial boards of seven other journals.

Dingledine moved to Emory University in 1992, where he is professor and chairman of the Department of Pharmacology. He and his wife have been married for 29 years and have two grown sons.

STAFF

DISPLACEMENT

Displacement of aggression refers to a redirection of harm-doing behavior from a primary to a secondary target or victim. An early theory of displacement was proposed by Sigmund Freud in *Beyond the Pleasure Principle* (1950). Freud suggested that persons tend to attack the sources of frustration, but if an individual cannot attack such a source because the target is unavailable or too powerful, a substitute target may become the victim of the pent-up anger. This mechanism explained apparently irrational behavior, such as a person's killing a total stranger for no apparent reason. Frustration causes a buildup of inner tension, which is expended when the individual expresses aggression toward a target. The amount of aggression is postulated to be directly related to the amount of cumulated inner energy. A sudden release of energy through aggressive action is referred to as catharsis.

In *Frustration and Aggression* (1939), Dollard, Doob, Miller, Mowrer, and Sears converted the literary and metaphoric language of Freud into the scientifically more acceptable, positivistic language of laboratory-oriented behavioristic psychologists. According to Dollard and his colleagues, aggressive behavior—like all other kinds of behavior—should be considered subject to the laws of learning. They defined "frustration" as any stimulus that blocked the goal attainment of an organism striving to attain a goal. Frustration causes a buildup of aggressive drive, which presses for behavioral expression in the form of harm-doing. When a person directs an aggressive response at a frustrating agent and the response is successful in removing the barrier to goal attainment, aggression is rewarded. A rewarded response is more likely to recur the next time the individual faces a similar situation. Thus, while harm-doing behavior reduces aggressive drive and additional immediate aggression, it is rewarding and increases the likelihood of harm-doing when the individual is frustrated again in the future.

Rewarding an individual for inhibiting an aggressive response, or punishing harm-doing behavior, may teach self-control. As a result of learned inhibition, the aggressive energy generated by frustration either continues to build up or is expressed in indirect ways. While fear of punishment inhibits aggressive behavior, the cumulated internal energy pushes for its expression. These two conflicting forces were conceptualized by Miller (1948) in terms of a model incorporating approach and avoidance forces, but this conflict model has had little subsequent impact on research. Displacement is essentially a principle of substitution of responses or of targets and may be viewed in terms of response or stimulus generalization.

The concept of displacement has been used to explain a wide variety of behaviors; for example, ethnic prejudice and discrimination may be considered a form of displacement. Thus, researchers have tried to show that historically a decline in cotton prices in the southern United States was associated with an increase in lynchings of African Americans. The reasoning is that bad economic results were frustrating to farmers, who took out their anger on Blacks—a type of scapegoating theory. Similarly, wars have been considered to be a result of the cumulated frustrations of many people manifested in an aggression toward a substitute target: the enemy nation. The importance of understanding displacement effects is certainly underlined by the frequent reference of the concept to ethnic, racial, and religious conflicts, child abuse, lynchings, riots, suicides, revolutions, and many other important social behaviors.

The establishment of the frustration-aggression interpretation is undermined by evidence failing to demonstrate catharsis effects (the reduction of subsequent aggression immediately following aggressive behavior). Furthermore, there is no evidence of a buildup of more intense aggressive behavior over a series of frustrating experiences. The fact of displacement-like effects is indisputable; and alternative theories are being developed that rely on concepts drawn from factors related to interpersonal interactions rather than intrapsychic dynamics. Among these alternative explanations

are active downward comparisons, self-presentation, negative equity, and guilt by association. Active downward comparison refers
to an individual's efforts to lower the performance or identity of
another person or group so as to enhance his or her own identity
(Wills, 1981). For example, acting to block the opportunities of
others (such as providing them with inferior schools) serves to
maintain the relative superiority of the discriminating person or
group. The desire for positive self-esteem is considered the motivating factor.

Tedeschi and Norman (1985), however, argued that putting others down raises the self up, not so much for internal self-esteem reasons, but for the purpose of presenting oneself to others as better
or superior in some way. In this formulation, individuals are highly
motivated to establish and maintain desirable identities in order to
foster positive and rewarding interactions with other people. As a
result, an individual is willing to harm someone else if doing so will
help promote a positive identity for the individual in the eyes of
others. The victims of such harm-doing may have done nothing to
provoke or justify the action. For example, a group of teenage boys,
each one of them motivated by the desire to impress the other boys
with his willingness to use violence, may attack someone at random.

Motivation to restore equity may also produce displacement-
like behavior. Members of most groups expect rewards to be fairly
distributed. The rule of equity prescribes that each member should
receive a share of the rewards proportional to his or her contribution to the group's success in attaining the rewards. It is assumed
that people are motivated to maintain justice and that, when an injustice occurs, something should be done to restore justice. When
rewards are unfairly distributed in a group, disadvantaged members may be motivated to restore equity. If for some reason no action can be taken against the source of the inequity, other means of
restoring equity may be undertaken. For example, if a boss distrib-
utes Christmas bonuses to his or her workers, and a few of the
workers believe they received unfairly low bonuses, they should be
motivated to restore equity. They cannot punish the boss for fear of
losing their jobs, but they might take out their anger by harming
(probably in some nonviolent way) the relatively advantaged workers. Such action restores equity in the sense that the advantaged
workers are made to suffer, detracting from the monetary gain and
thus making outcomes more fair.

Anthropologists and historians have noted that retaliation is often visited upon co-conspirators, blood relatives, or friends of instigators, rather than directly against the instigator. Victims sometimes hold all members of an outgroup equally responsible for
harm done to them and may retaliate against one of the weaker
members of the outgroup. Thus, retaliation may be directed against
any member of a rival gang, or in blood feuds, against any member
of the target family. Hate groups may randomly target any member
of the hated group. The representative target chosen from the category of believed enemies may be completely innocent and unaware
of any harm done to the aggressor. The attack represents a displacement-like effect, since revenge is not taken against a frustrating agent but against an innocent third party—although, such an
attack may serve to punish the frustrating agent by harming a loved
one, or may be motivated to deter future harm-doing by that agent.

REFERENCES

Dollard, J., Doob, N., Miller, N. E., Mowrer, O. H., & Sears, R. R.
(1939). *Frustration and aggression.* New Haven, Ct: Yale University Press.

Freud, S. (1950). *Beyond the pleasure principle* (J. Strachey, Trans.).
New York: Liveright.

Miller, N. E. (1948). Theory and experiment relating psychoanalytic displacement to stimulus-response generalization. *Journal
of Abnormal and Social Psychology, 43,* 155–178.

Tedeschi, J. T., & Norman, N. (1985). Social mechanisms of displaced aggression. In E. J. Lawler (Ed.), *Advances in group processes: Theory and research* (Vol. 2, pp. 29–56). Greenwich, CT:
JAI Press.

Wills, T. A. (1981). Downward comparison principles in social
psychology. *Psychological Bulletin, 90,* 245–271.

J. T. Tedeschi
State University of New York at Albany

PERSONALITY
PSYCHOANALYSIS

DIVORCE

Divorce is the legal dissolution of a marriage. There has been an increase in the incidence of divorce since the 1960s, with a corresponding increase in associated social and psychological problems.

Factors leading to divorce are many and change with time. Traditional reasons for divorce have included drunkenness, desertion,
brutality, or adultery, and these have been legal justification for divorce in most states for many years. More recently, state legislators
have established what are commonly called no-fault divorce laws,
which recognize such grounds as incompatibility and breakdown
of the relationship. These laws allow couples to dissolve marriages
in an equitable, agreed-upon manner without an extended adversarial court proceeding. These laws also make it easier to obtain a
divorce and may explain the increase in incidence. Other possible
contributing factors are the growing financial independence of
women, relaxation of church proscriptions, and alterations in the
purposes of marriage because of technological advances.

Divorce has emotional implications for marital partners, children, and extended family members. Husband and wife often have
feelings of loss of attachment with accompanying grief reactions
and blame of the spouse, coupled with guilt feelings about their
own failures and general feelings of insecurity about social, emotional, and financial issues.

The effect of divorce on children varies with the age of the child,
the process of resolving custody issues, and the parents' ability to
cope with the problems of divorce. Young children are likely to
blame themselves for the divorce, to worry about being abandoned,
and to fantasize about parental reconciliation. Adolescents, despite initial anger and turmoil, have more independent resources
for coping than do younger children (Anthony, 1974). Wallerstein
and Kelly (1974, 1975, 1976; Kelly & Wallerstein, 1976) have de-

scribed the different responses of children of different ages to divorce. Parents have to deal with problems such as raising children without help, maintaining both personal and parental roles, and in the case of noncustodial parents, maintaining parental roles on a part-time basis. All family members face potential financial difficulties, as family income is divided between two residences.

Family members face additional social difficulties following divorce. Relationships with friends often change or end entirely. Divorced adults deal with issues of developing cross-gender relationships, often after years of not dating. Relationships with extended family often become strained as well, as parents of divorced adults deal with concern about their own responsibility for the breakup of the marriage.

The aftermath of divorce is usually quite difficult. Hetherington and colleagues have found that boys from divorced families are often treated more negatively by others than are girls (Hetherington, Cox, & Cox, 1979), that divorced parents are less affectionate with their children (Hetherington, Cox, and Cox, 1977), that adolescent girls of divorced parents are more promiscuous (Hetherington, 1972), and that boys are more "feminized" (Hetherington & Duer, 1972). However, there is also evidence (Rutter, 1979) that children in single-parent families function better than those in families with two parents in frequent conflict.

Growing knowledge about divorce and its effects increases the awareness that members of divorced families face greater risk of a variety of psychological difficulties, which may provide some impetus for developing ways to reduce these potentially damaging effects.

REFERENCES

Anthony, J. (1974). Children at risk from divorce: A review. In J. Anthony & C. Koupernic (Eds.), *The child in his family: Children in psychiatric risk.* New York: Wiley.

Hetherington, B. M. (1972). Effects of father absence on personality development in adolescent daughters. *Developmental Psychology, 7,* 313–386.

Hetherington, B. M., Cox, M., & Cox, R. (1977). The aftermath of divorce. In J. H. Stevens, Jr., & M. Matthews (Eds.), *Mother-child, father-child relations.* Washington, DC: National Association for the Education of Young Children.

Hetherington, E. M., Cox, M., & Cox, R. (1979). Play and social interaction in children following divorce. *Journal of Social Issues, 35,* 26–49.

Hetherington, M., & Duer, J. (1972). The effects of father absence on child development. In W. W. Hartup (Ed.), *The young child: Review of research* (Vol. 2). Washington, DC: National Association for the Education of Young Children.

Kelly, J. B., & Wallerstein, J. S. (1976). The effects of parental divorce: Experiences of the child in early latency. *American Journal of Orthopsychiatry, 46,* 20–32.

Wallerstein, J. S., & Kelly, J. B. (1974). The effects of parental divorce: The adolescent experience. In J. Anthony & C. Koupernic (Eds.), *The child in his family: Children at psychiatric risk.* New York: Wiley.

Wallerstein, J. S., & Kelly, J. B. (1975). The effects of parental divorce: Experiences of the preschool child. *Journal of American Academy of Child Psychiatry, 14,* 600–616.

Wallerstein, J. S., & Kelly, J. B. (1976). The effects of parental divorce: Experiences of the child in later latency. *American Journal of Orthopsychiatry, 46,* 256–269.

T. S. BENNETT
Brain Inquiry Recovery Program

SINGLE PARENTHOOD
SPOUSE SELECTION

DOCTOR OF PSYCHOLOGY DEGREE (PsyD)

The Doctor of Psychology degree (PsyD) is awarded to psychologists whose education and training are designed to prepare them for careers in professional practice. With considerable variation in content and emphasis, the training programs that lead to the degree all include education in basic facts and principles of psychology, extensive supervised experience in application of procedures for the assessment and modification of psychological functioning, and an internship. Early proposals for PsyD programs did not include a doctoral dissertation requirement, but nearly all the programs now in operation do so. Systematic inquiry is regarded as a form of practice rather than an end in itself, and the range of topics is broader than has traditionally characterized PhD dissertations in psychology. Community needs analyses, case studies, and theoretical inquiries, among other kinds of investigations, are all acceptable, so long as each project contributes to improved understanding or constructive change in the way psychologists do their work. A typical program requires five years of graduate study beyond the baccalaureate degree.

The first proposal for use of the Doctor of Psychology degree was advanced by Leta Hollingworth in 1918. Similar proposals were put forward by Loyal Crane in 1925 and A. T. Poffenberger in 1938. All argued that education in the science of psychology was insufficient for the practice of psychology and that the PhD degree, traditionally used as a scholarly credential across all disciplines, was inappropriate as a certificate of knowledge and competence in professional psychology. They urged development of programs expressly designed to prepare people for practice, and awarding a professional doctorate analogous to the MD, DDS, and other professional degrees, upon completion of graduate studies. The proposals were not cordially received in the academic community, however, and only two practitioner programs, both in Canada and both short-lived, were attempted before the 1960s.

A conference on training in clinical psychology at Boulder, Colorado, in 1949 established the scientist-practitioner model as the dominant pattern for the education of professional psychologists, and the PhD as the standard qualifying credential. In the Boulder model, as it came to be called, students were to be prepared as researchers as well as clinicians, in the belief that each form of activity would enhance the other. The Boulder model was widely adopted in American universities, and remains the most common design for the education of professional psychologists.

By the middle of the 1960s, however, expressions of discontent with prevailing PhD programs were often heard. According to critics, most clinical programs in academic departments overemphasized research at the expense of training for practice, and psychologists entering professional careers, as more than half of them were doing by that time, were poorly prepared for the challenges they faced in their work. After lengthy deliberations, an American Psychological Association (APA) committee on the scientific and professional aims of psychology recommended the establishment of practitioner programs leading to the PsyD degree. The proposal was debated at a conference on training in clinical psychology in Chicago in 1965, where it was not generally endorsed, although the majority recognized that programs of this kind might be attempted in some universities and that the results of those efforts would provide a basis for evaluation at a later time. Shortly after the Chicago conference, the faculty of the Urbana-Champaign campus of the University of Illinois voted to inaugurate a PsyD program, and the first program in the United States was established there in 1968.

Five years later, still another conference on training in professional psychology was held in Vail, Colorado. There the concept of direct education for the practice of psychology was endorsed, as was the use of the PsyD degree to certify completion of graduate work in practitioner programs. In the years that followed, additional PsyD programs were developed in universities and professional schools throughout the United States, although the initial program at the University of Illinois was discontinued in 1980.

Beginning in the 1980s and continuing into the 1990s, long-standing educational policies that restricted use of the PhD to mark the highest level of achievement in preparation for careers of creative research and scholarship, and to mandate the use of professional doctoral degrees to recognize completion of academic preparation for professional practice, were actively enforced by agencies responsible for accrediting educational institutions in the United States. During this period, a considerable number of practitioner programs that had previously awarded the PhD were required to employ the PsyD degree to maintain approval. This change, along with continuing development of new programs, led to substantial expansion in the number of PsyD programs in the United States and Canada. Toward the end of the 20th century, some 60 programs were in operation. Approximately half of these were in universities, half were in free-standing professional schools, and two-thirds had been fully or provisionally approved by the APA Committee on Accreditation.

SUGGESTED READING

Peterson, D. R. (1997). *Educating professional psychologists: History and guiding conception.* Washington, DC: APA Books.

D. R. PETERSON
Rutgers University

CLINICAL GRADUATE TRAINING IN PSYCHOLOGY
SCHOOLS OF PROFESSIONAL PSYCHOLOGY

DOLLARD, JOHN (1900–1980)

John Dollard received the PhD in sociology at the University of Chicago in 1931 and then had a year's training in psychoanalysis in Berlin under Hans Sachs. In 1932 he joined the explorations of culture and personality being led by Yale anthropologist Edward Sapir. Dollard spent the rest of his career at Yale; he was a leading member of the Institute of Human Relations during its active years, and subsequently a professor in the Department of Psychology. His work is a notable example of the innovative value of bringing together in one mind central ideas and approaches of the usually separate social sciences.

Dollard's most influential books came during the period of his affiliation with the Institute of Human Relations. In *Criteria for the Life History* he sought to define how life history study could best contribute to a unified understanding of human beings, and applied his analysis to a critique of well-known life histories that had been published by social scientists of diverse theoretical persuasions. In *Caste and Class in a Southern Town,* his master work, he showed the relations between a social system and the psychodynamics of individuals in various positions within the system. He joined with various colleagues in other influential studies, notably *Frustration and Aggression* (with Leonard Doob, Neal Miller, O. Hobart Mowrer, and Robert Sears), *Social Learning and Imitation* (with Neal Miller), and *Personality and Psychotherapy* (also with Neal Miller).

Typifying the work of the Institute of Human Relations, these studies achieve a remarkable synthesis of psychoanalysis, experimental psychology of learning and motivation, sociological analysis of social structure, and anthropological awareness of cultural variation. Though some of their terminology is out of fashion, these books continue to be a direct source of understanding and an inspiration to the further development of psychology in integral relation to the other social sciences. In his later years, Dollard concentrated on teaching psychotherapy and on intensive study of the process of psychotherapy, bringing to this field the integrated viewpoint he had developed.

I. L. CHILD
Yale University

DOPAMINE

Dopamine (DA) is among the most studied of all major neurotransmitters. Dopamine, 3,4-dihydroxy-phenyl-ethyl-amine, is a catecholamine. It possesses a positively charged amino group for electrostatic bonding to the five subtypes of DA receptor and a catechol nucleus in which two hydroxyl groups allow the hydrogen bonding required for receptor activation. Dopamine was initially thought to be merely the precursor of norepinephrine and epinephrine because its synthesis precedes synthesis of the other catecholamine transmitters within adrenergic neurons and adrenal medulla cells. However, the development of sensitive fluorometric assays for DA in the mid-1960s, almost fifty years after the first synthesis of DA, revealed a regional brain distribution different from that of the other major brain catecholamine, norepinephrine. Subsequently, the modern understanding of neurological and psychiatric diseases has been tightly linked with progress in understanding the roles of DA in the brain. Furthermore, DA is widely distributed in the periphery at sites including the pituitary, kidney glomeruli, carotid bodies, and autonomic ganglia, and is present in plasma in high concentrations. Dopamine also has a significant role in neurotransmission in many invertebrate as well as vertebrate species. Together, these observations have propelled DA to the forefront of interest in neuroscience as a major modulator of multiple aspects of physiology, from movement to motivation and cognition. Dopamine is also a major regulator of neuroendocrine functions by inhibiting prolactin. Parkinson's disease is often considered a dopamine deficiency syndrome (of the pathway from substantia nigra to corpus striatum). Schizophrenia was thought for many years to be primarily a syndrome of dopamine imbalance in the limbic forebrain. Today, although changes in dopaminergic function may be a downstream consequence of a primary cortical disturbance, DA is still considered to play a major role in this disorder, the nature of which role is under active investigation.

Dopamine synapses illustrate the key sites of action of many clinically significant compounds. The rate-limiting step in dopamine synthesis is the conversion of dietary tyrosine to L-dopa by tyrosine hydroxylase. The activity of this enzyme is enhanced by administration of classical antipsychotic agents, in part by their blockade of synthesis- and/or release-inhibiting autoreceptors on dopamine nerve terminals. The tyrosine hydroxylation step and the subsequent conversion to dopamine by aromatic amino acid decarboxylase (dopa decarboxylase) occur in the cytoplasm of all catecholamine neurons. Subsequently, dopamine is transported into presynaptic vesicles by a vesicular transport system that is sensitive to inhibition by the drug reserpine, once used to treat hypertension. Vesicular storage protects the catecholamine transmitters from metabolism by monoamine oxidase (MAO), which is contained within the outer wall of mitochondria. Inhibition of one isoform (MAO-B) by the agent selegiline has been suggested to slow progression of some neurodegenerative disorders (including Parkinson's and Alzheimer's diseases). Additionally, inhibition of the other isoform (MAO-A) can effectively reduce depressive symptoms in patients resistant to other antidepressant agents. Catechol-O-methyl-transferase (COMT) is usually considered to be an extra-neuronal enzyme and does not appear to play a major role in catecholamine metabolism. However, inhibitors of COMT are being tested as possible drugs for treating Parkinson's in order to maintain endogenous dopamine transmission for as long as possible in the face of both age-associated and disease-induced dopamine loss. Levels of dopamine metabolites resulting from the actions of MAO and COMT, including homovanilic acid and dihydroxyphenylacetic acid, are often altered in the cerebrospinal fluid of individuals with Parkinson's and schizophrenia.

Dopamine is released by the calcium-dependent process of ex-

ocytosis. In this process the plasma membrane and vesicular membrane fuse to disgorge their contents into the synaptic cleft. Stimulants such as amphetamine can release dopamine by a process that is not calcium-dependent, resulting in a substantial loss of the dopamine content of the neuron. This leads to a marked elevation in synaptic dopamine levels and excess stimulation by dopamine of its receptors. Within dopamine neurons, much of the release occurs from axonal swellings (varicosities) rather than at more typical synaptic buttons (boutons). Once released, dopamine can stimulate axon terminal autoreceptors, thereby inhibiting tyrosine hydroxylase activity to reduce synthesis and release homeostatically. Recent work also suggests that stimulation of these autoreceptors may reduce the size of dopamine quanta released with each axon potential.

Dopamine also diffuses to postsynaptic sites to activate five major types of dopamine receptors (Table 1). All dopamine receptors are G-protein coupled receptors consisting of a single polypeptide chain having seven transmembrane regions, an extracellular amino terminus, an intracellular carboxy terminus, and three each of extracellular and intracellular loops. The size of the human forms of these receptors varies from 387 to 477 amino acid residues. The overall topology provides a clue to the functions of the receptors. D1-like receptors include the D1 and D5 subtypes, which show several similarities to the prototype $\beta2$ adrenergic receptor. These include a long COOH tail and a short third intracellular loop of amino acids. These receptors are positively coupled to the stimulatory G-protein (Gs), which activates adenylate cyclase to increase cellular cAMP levels. The genes encoding the D1-like receptors lack introns within the coding region. Genes for the D2-like receptors contain introns. The receptor subtypes include the D2, D3, and D4, which show several similarities to the prototype $\alpha2$ adrenergic receptor. These include short COOH tails and longer third intracellular loops. These receptors are coupled to the inhibitory G-protein (Gi) and cause inhibition of adenylate cyclase, reducing cellular cAMP levels. Alternatively, D2-like receptors may couple to other G-proteins and additional intracellular signaling systems, such as the GIRK (G protein-regulated, inward rectifying potassium channel). Variant forms of the D2-subfamily exist due to alternative splicing within the G-protein coupling region of the third intracellular loop and to allelic variants associated with the third intracellular loop. The D4 receptor, in particular, exhibits a large number of variants. Identification of genes potentially involved in schizophrenia utilizes genome scanning through association and linkage studies and evaluation of candidate genes such as the various dopamine receptors. This strategy seems to have ruled out D1, D2, and D4. On the other hand, there may be an association between a polymorphism in the extracellular amino terminal domain of the D3 receptor and schizophrenia.

The major means of removing dopamine from the synaptic cleft between adjacent neurons is by uptake back into the nerve terminal. This action is mediated through a non-receptor transport protein (DAT, dopamine transporter). The DAT consists of a single polypeptide chain that, like the vesicular membrane transport protein, has 12 membrane-spanning regions and intracellular amino and carboxy terminals. The DAT is sensitive to blockade by co-

Table 1.   Characteristics and localization of brain dopamine receptors.*

Characteristic	D1	D5	D2	D3	D4
Amino acids (human)	446	477	D2S/D2L: 414/443	400	387
Amino acids (rat)	446	475	D2S/D2L: 415/444	446	368
Introns	NO	NO	YES (SIX)	YES (SIX)	YES (FOUR)
Chromosome	5	4	11	3	11
Neural location	Postsynaptic	Postsynaptic	Presynaptic & postsynaptic	Presynaptic & postsynaptic	Presynaptic & postsynaptic
Transducer	Gs	Gs	Gi/o	Gi/o	Gi/o
Effector	⇑ cAMP	⇑ cAMP	⇓ cAMP, ⇑ K+, ⇓ Ca++, ⇑ AA, ⇑ Na+/K+ ATPase, ⇑ MAP kinase	⇓ cAMP, ⇑ AA[1], ⇑ Na+/K+ ATPase	⇓ cAMP, ⇑ Ca++, ⇑ AA, ⇑ Na+/K+ ATPase
mRNA distribution	Caudate-putamen, nucleus accumbens, olfactory tubercles, anterior lobe of pituitary, intermediate lobe of pituitary	Hippocampus, hypothalamus	Caudate-putamen, nucleus accumbens, olfactory tubercles	Hypothalamus, nucleus accumbens, olfactory tubercles	Frontal neocortex, medulla, midbrain
Effect of gene knockout in mice	Hyper-locomotion, altered response to peptides in striatum, lack of response to agonists		Impaired movements	Hyper-locomotion	Hyper-locomotion & increased sensitivity to ethanol, cocaine, & methamphetamine

*Column 1 (Characteristic) lists features of the subtypes of dopamine (DA) receptors. Columns 2–6 identify those features for each DA receptor subtype. Row 2 (Amino acids) indicates the number of amino acids contained in each receptor protein. Row 3 (Introns) indicates how many non-coding regions (introns) exist in the DNA for the receptor. Row 4 (Chromosome) refers to the number of the chromosome on which the gene for the receptor is found. Row 5 (Neural location) indicates whether the receptor is located on DA neurons (presynaptic) or non-DA neurons which receive DA input (postsynaptic). Row 6 (Transducer) indicates which membrane G-protein is activated by the receptor. Row 7 (Effector) indicates which enzyme or ion channel has its activity changed as a result of activation of the receptor. Row 8 (mRNA) indicates where the RNA for the receptor (and by extension, the receptor protein itself) is found in brain. Row 9 (Effect of gene knockout) indicates the effect of inactivating the receptor gene (which prevents the receptor from being made).
[1]AA = arachidonic acid.

caine, which causes significant elevations of synaptic dopamine content and excess stimulation of dopamine receptors.

Dopamine neurons project throughout the brain, with an especially intense representation in motor, emotional (limbic system), and neuroendocrine areas. These dopamine projections generally match the brain distribution of the dopamine receptors (Table 1). Thus, dopamine is a major modulator of motor and endocrine functions. Dopamine is also strongly implicated in motivational and emotional control mechanisms, reinforcement, and, by extension, the addictive disorders. Within the various forebrain dopamine projection systems there is a marked difference in the regulation of dopamine synthesis and release because of differences in the regional density of axon terminal autoreceptors. The caudate nucleus and putamen of the basal ganglia contain the greatest number of these autoreceptors (and, therefore, shows the tightest regulation of synaptic dopamine content). Frontal and prefrontal cortices, in contrast, contain the fewest number (and, therefore, show the greatest normal fluctuation in synaptic dopamine). These differences in regulation of synaptic dopamine may play a role in the susceptibility of the limbic cortical areas to dysregulation in schizophrenia.

Dopamine receptor densities (estimated by density of the dopamine receptor mRNA) match in a general way the concentration of dopamine nerve terminals. Highest densities of D1 and D2 receptors are found in the corpus striatum. High expression of D2

receptors also occurs within the limbic system. Other D2-like receptors (D3 and D4) appear to be well represented in the limbic system, but less so in motor areas such as the basal ganglia. This brain regional distribution dictates the type of drug used for treating various disorders. To restore deficient dopaminergic tone in the basal ganglia in Parkinson's disease, drugs that fully mimic dopamine (full agonists) at both D1 and D2 dopamine receptors are required. To reduce excess dopaminergic tone in the limbic system of persons who exhibit delusions and auditory hallucinations, blockade of D2-like receptors is sufficient. Core schizophrenia symptoms of flattened emotion and cognitive difficulties have highlighted the need to develop therapeutic agents that may enhance deficient dopaminergic tone in cortical limbic areas while reducing excess dopaminergic tone in subcortical limbic regions.

Drugs that mimic dopamine by binding to one of the dopamine receptor subtypes and activating it are agonists. Some agonists produce only part of the cellular response that dopamine does; these are partial dopamine agonists, whereas dopamine is a full agonist. Other drugs bind equally well to dopamine receptors, but change the receptor conformation in a way that is different from that produced by agonists, thereby producing the opposite cellular response from that of dopamine. Such inverse agonists may be partial or full inverse agonists. Some agents used to treat schizophrenia may be either partial agonists or inverse agonists at dopamine receptors. The future of drug therapy for dopamine-based diseases may be based, in part, on the use of partial or inverse dopamine agonists to restore a normal dopaminergic tone in a dysfunctional brain.

SUGGESTED READING

Avalos, M. N. (1999). *Partial agonist interactions with dopamine in clonal cell lines expressing recombinant receptors: Towards a molecular model of antipsychotic drug action.* Unpublished doctoral dissertation. University of Texas, Austin.

Feldman, R. S., Meyer, J. S., & Quenzer, L. F. (1997). *Principles of Neuropsychopharmacology.* Sunderland, MA: Sinauer.

Hall, D. A., & Strange, P. G. (1997). Evidence that antipsychotic drugs are inverse agonists at D2 dopamine receptors. *British Journal of Pharmacology, 121*(4), 731–736.

Neve, K. A., & Neve, R. L. (1997). *The dopamine receptors.* Totowa, NJ: Humana.

Wilcox, R. E., Gonzales, R. A., & Miller, J. D. (1999). Introduction to neurotransmitters, receptors, signal transduction, and second messengers. In A. M. Schatzberg & C. B. Nemeroff (Eds.), *Textbook of psychopharmacology* (pp. 3–37). Washington, DC: American Psychiatric Press.

R. E. Wilcox
University of Texas at Austin

DOPAMINE SYSTEMS
NEUROTRANSMITTERS

DOPAMINE SYSTEMS

Perhaps more than any other neurotransmitter, dopamine has received attention for its potential involvement in psychiatric disorders ranging from substance abuse to schizophrenia. This focus relies primarily on the capacity of drugs that manipulate dopamine transmission to ameliorate or exacerbate psychiatric conditions. However, our emerging comprehension of brain circuitry and function permits an understanding of dopamine transmission in the brain that is both more integrated and accurate. This short description of dopamine systems will explicate the components of dopamine transmission, such as synthesis, release, and receptor signaling, and using brain circuitry to assemble the dopamine neurons and projections into overall brain functions.

DOPAMINE: THE NEUROTRANSMITTER

Anatomical Organization

Akin to other monoaminergic transmitter systems, the dopamine neurons are located in discrete brain nuclei and are not widely distributed throughout the brain. The largest cluster of dopamine cells is located in the ventral midbrain. The medial portion of cells is located in the ventral tegmental area, while the lateral cluster is in the substantia nigra. In addition, another large group of cells is located in the hypothalamus. This latter group functions primarily to regulate prolactin secretion from the pituitary, while the midbrain neurons project to areas of the forebrain and cortex involved in motor, emotional, and cognitive processing. This includes projections to aspects of the extrapyramidal motor system, prefrontal cortex, and various limbic structures such as the amygdala and hippocampus. These projections are topographically organized, with the more medial neurons providing innervation to the cortex and limbic nuclei, and the more lateral cell group providing innervation primarily to the caudate. Moreover, within certain axon terminal fields there is a medial to lateral topography. For example, in the ventral pallidum or subthalamus, the ventral tegmental area innervates the medial aspect of the nucleus, while the substantia nigra innervates the lateral compartment.

Synthesis, Degradation, and Release

Dopamine synthesis is a multiple enzymatic process involving the hydroxylation and decarboxylation of tyrosine. The rate-limiting enzyme in the synthesis of dopamine is tyrosine hydroxylase, which catabolizes tyrosine into dopa. This is a highly regulated enzyme susceptable to end-product feedback by cytosolic dopamine, as well as by released dopamine via stimulation of dopamine autoreceptors. Following synthesis, dopamine is transported from the cytosol into synaptic vesicles via a proton-dependent vesicular monoamine transporter, and is then sequestered pending release into the synaptic cleft. The physiological release of dopamine is voltage- and calcium-dependent, and is regulated by the frequency and pattern of action potentials, as well as by dopamine autoreceptors. A burst pattern of action potentials is most efficient at releasing dopamine. Dopamine in the synaptic cleft is eliminated by one of three mechanisms: (a) The vast majority of dopamine undergoes re-uptake into the presynaptic terminal via the dopamine transporter; (b) A minor metabolic inactivation in the synaptic cleft involves methylation via catecho-O-methyltransferase to form 3-methoxytyramine; or (c) Dopamine can diffuse into the perisynaptic extracellular space. Following transport into the presynaptic terminal, dopamine is either transported into synaptic vesicles or oxidized by monoamine oxidase. Monoamine oxidase is primarily located in the mitochondria and exists as two isozymes (MAO-A and MAO-B). The two isozymes are differentially distributed in the brain and have different affinities for monoamines. Monoamine oxidase-B is of greater importance in metabolizing dopamine in the nigrostriatal pathway, while MAO-A may be of greater importance elsewhere.

DOPAMINE RECEPTORS

Receptor Subtypes

Dopamine receptors can be localized on neurons post-synaptic to dopamine terminals (post-synaptic receptors), on dopamine axon terminals (autoreceptors), on non-dopaminergic axon terminals (hetero-receptors), or on dopamine cell bodies and dendrites (somatodendritic autoreceptors). Dopamine receptors are synthesized from five different genes, and based upon sequence homology and pharmacological specificity have been divided into two receptor families. The D1 receptor family consists of the D1 and D5 receptor while the D2 family consists of D2, D3, and D4 receptors.

Two splice variants of the D2 receptor subtype have been characterized: D2S and D2L.

Receptor Localization

The various dopamine receptor subtypes are heterogeneously distributed in the nervous system. The D2 receptors are found both post-synaptically and as presynaptic autoreceptors, while the D1 receptors are located post-synaptically and hetero-synaptically on non-dopaminergic axon terminals. Thus D2 receptors, notably the D2 and perhaps D3 subtypes, regulate the release and synthesis of dopamine in response to stimulation by extracellular dopamine. Remarkably, in certain areas where dopamine receptors are in highest density, such as the striatum and substantia nigra, the cells expressing each receptor subtype are distinct. Within each family there also exist distinct distributions of receptors. For example, in the D1 family the D1 subtype is highest in the striatum, olfactory tubercle, amygdala, and parts of the cortex, while the D5 subtype is most dense in the thalamus and hippocampus. Similarly for the D2 family, D2 receptors are dense throughout the basal ganglia, while D3 receptors are localized to the more limbic, ventral portions to the striatum and olfactory tubercle, and D4 receptors are found primarily in the prefrontal cortex and hippocampus.

Receptor Signaling

All of the dopamine receptor subtypes are metabotropic, G protein coupled receptors. The two families of receptors have distinct intracellular signaling mechanisms. The D1 family couples with Gs to activate adenylate cyclase and cAMP production. The ensuing activation of protein kinase A results in the phosphorylation of numerous proteins leading to changes in enzyme activity, signaling in other receptor systems and gene expression. Notably, there is a heterosynaptic inhibition or stimulation of the release of other neurotransmitters, as well as a stimulatory effect on voltage-dependent calcium channels. The transduction pathways for the D2 family of receptors is more complicated, but involves coupling to Gi and Go. The two most well studied signaling pathways are the inhibition of adenylate cyclase and the opening of potassium channels. These actions result in numerous changes in cell functioning. Notably there is a hyperpolarization of membrane potential, due primarily to the opening of potassium channels, which accounts for the inhibition dopamine release by D2 autoreceptors and the inhibition of post-synaptic neurons.

Receptor Pharmacology

The pharmacological stimulation of dopamine receptors can be produced by two types of agonist. Direct agonists have affinity for the dopamine receptors themselves, while the indirect agonists stimulate dopamine receptors by increasing the concentrations of dopamine in the synaptic cleft. Both types of agonist have clinical utility. The indirect agonists produce increases in extracellular dopamine by binding to the dopamine transporter and either preventing dopamine transport or acting as a false substrate. Amphetamine typifies a false substrate that is transported in place of dopamine. Additionally, the false substrates promote the "hetero-exchange" of dopamine, causing reverse transport through the transporter. Therefore drugs like amphetamine not only prevent

the elimination of dopamine from the synaptic cleft but also induce release of cytosolic dopamine via reversal of the transporter. Cocaine and methylphenidate are prototypic drugs that bind to the transporter to prevent the re-uptake of dopamine, but are not themselves transported. Therefore, the increased release of dopamine by these latter drugs relies solely on the accumulation of dopamine released from synaptic vesicles and does not result from hetero-exchange. Direct agonists bind to dopamine receptors and may or may not be selective for the D1 or D2 family of receptors. Given the heterogeneity of receptor localization (discussed previously), the development of highly selective compounds would seem to provide for relatively subtle manipulations of dopamine transmission. While drugs exist to clearly distinguish the D1 and D2 families, no drugs are universally accepted to distinguish between the receptor subtypes within each family. However, progress has been made recently in developing drugs to distinguish the D2 from the D3 receptor. Similarly, dopamine receptor family selective antagonists are well characterized, but the development of antagonists selective for the receptor subtypes within each family is not well evolved. Nonetheless, as outlined in the next section, certain drugs are somewhat preferential for one receptor subtype versus another and the relative clinical utility of these drugs has led to considerable speculation regarding involvement of one versus the other subtype in psychiatric disease processes.

PHYSIOLOGY OF DOPAMINE SYSTEMS

Dopamine neuronal activity is regulated by a variety of neurotransmitters in the ventral midbrain. The neurons themselves are what one might call leaky and will initiate spontaneous action potentials in addition to being driven by various inputs. In general, the activity of dopamine neurons responds to changes in an organism's environment. A novel stimulus activates dopamine cells regardless of whether the stimulus is of positive (e.g., reward) or negative (e.g., stress) valence to the organism. Thus, activation of dopaminergic pathways serves to cue the animal that an important environmental event has occurred in preparation for engaging in an adaptive behavior. Given this function it is rational that the most dense dopaminergic innervation is to the limbic and motor regions of the forebrain. For example, when an animal undergoes a stress or is exposed to a cue, such as the possibility of sex or food, that signals a positive reward there is an increase in dopamine release in the nucleus accumbens (a portion of the ventral striatum thought to be a particularly critical interface for integrating emotions with adaptive motor responses).

PATHOPHYSIOLOGY OF DOPAMINE SYSTEMS

Parkinson's Disease

Parkinson's disease is characterized as a degenerative movement disorder that very clearly results from a loss of dopamine neurons in the substantia nigra and an ensuing loss of dopamine innervation to the basal ganglia. The motor disorder progresses from tremor and slurred speech to akinesia and rigidity. The treatment of Parkinson's disease is initially dopamine replacement in the form of the dopamine precursor l-dopa. However, to be effective, sufficient dopamine synthetic capacity must be available in axon terminals in the basal ganglia. Thus, as the degeneration progresses, 1-dopa becomes a progressively less effective treatment. Based upon understanding of basal ganglia circuitry, manipulating other neurotransmitters such as acetylcholine is also useful in ameliorating the motor symptoms of Parkinson's disease. However, no treatment is available that reverses or inhibits the neurodegeneration.

Substance Abuse

The dopamine projection from the midbrain to the nucleus accumbens is thought to be critical in the development of addiction to most drugs of abuse. Indeed, many drugs such as cocaine, amphetamine, ecstasy, and nicotine have been shown to directly activate dopamine neurons or release dopamine. Even drugs such as alcohol or heroin that do not directly bind to dopamine neurons are thought to produce addiction, at least in part, via indirect stimulation of mesoaccumbens dopamine release. The release of dopamine by these drugs elevates dopamine substantially higher than the level that occurs following physiological response to a stress or a natural reward (mentioned earlier). Such aphysiological elevations precipitate changes in gene expression in dopamine cells and elsewhere in limbic and motor circuits, and ultimately mediate the behavioral changes associated with addiction. Given the apparent role of dopamine in addiction it would be predicted that dopamine antagonists might be useful in treating addiction. However, this has not proven to be the case, presumably because the repeated use of drugs in addiction produces neuroplastic changes beyond dopamine transmission that can mediate the cravings and sensitivity to stress that cause relapse to drug taking.

Schizophrenia

The dopamine hypothesis of schizophrenia remains a well considered postulate of both the etiology and symptomatology of schizophrenia. The primary buttresses of this hypothesis are that certain symptoms of schizophrenia are ameliorated by D2 family dopamine blockers, and that dopamine agonists exacerbate these symptoms. Moreover, there is some evidence to indicate that prophylactic administration of dopamine antagonists inhibits the progressive amplification of psychosis that sometimes occurs in schizophrenia. Although dopamine is no doubt involved in schizophrenia it appears that defects in different pathways mediate different symptoms, and that the primary defect may be in transmitters that regulate the dopamine systems. For example, a deficit in dopamine transmission in the prefrontal cortex may mediate certain cognitive symptoms while enhanced dopamine transmission in the nucleus accumbens likely plays an important role in mediating the positive symptoms of psychosis, such as paranoia. Indeed, a number of current hypotheses regarding the etiology of schizophrenia rely on the primary defect residing in limbic excitatory input to the prefrontal cortex.

CONCLUSIONS

Dopamine is a monoamine transmitter that has been linked to a surprising number of neuropsychiatric disorders. It is among the most well characterized transmitter systems, and drugs manipulating dopamine release and receptor occupation profoundly modify behavior in both a therapeutic and maladaptive manner. Physiologically, dopamine appears to function in linking emotional state with adaptive behavioral responses. Thus, dopamine is perfectly situated to be at least indirectly involved in many psychiatric disorders that are manifested as a maladaptive mismatch between environmental stimulus and behavioral response.

SUGGESTED READING

Cooper, J. R., Bloom, F. E., & Roth, R. H. (1997). *The biochemical basis of neuropharmacology.* New York: Oxford University Press.

Nemeroff, C. B., & Schatzberg, A. F. (1998). *Textbook of psychopharmacology.* Washington, DC: American Psychiatric Press.

Neve, K. A., & Neve, R. L. (1997). *The dopamine receptors.* New Jersey: Humana Press.

Weinberger, D. R. (1995). Neurodevelopment perspectives on schizophrenia. In F. E. Bloom & D. J. Kupper (Eds.), *Psychopharmacology: The fourth generation of progress.* New York: Raven Press.

P. W. KALIVAS
Medical University of South Carolina

DOPAMINE
NEUROTRANSMITTER RELEASE

DOUBLE BIND

Double bind is a concept characterizing an ongoing pattern of communication that imposes painful no-win situations upon its victim through two processes: first, through contradictory demands made at different levels of communication; and second, by preventing the victim from either discriminating and commenting on the bind or withdrawing from it. Originally studied in the relationships between schizophrenic adults and their families, the double bind was viewed as having had causal relevance for their schizophrenia through having impaired their capacities to derive clear meaning from communications and to participate in normal social relationships.

The original clinical studies leading to the double-bind concept were conducted in Palo Alto, California, in the 1950s and 1960s by Gregory Bateson, Don D. Jackson, Jay Haley, and John H. Weakland (1956), a group of clinicians and scholars who collectively introduced a communication theory approach to the mental health field through pioneering contributions to the development of family therapy. Their work emphasized that there are, within families as within the individual's internal environment, homeostatic or stability-making processes that regulate their functioning and contribute to their survival. Within families, communication serves this function.

A single complex human communication can contain many messages of different logical types as defined by Bertrand Russell (Whitehead & Russell, 1910), often involving separate modalities that can contradict or reinforce one another. An aggressive utterance might, for example, be qualified by movements, postures, or voice tones conveying that "this is all in fun." Even the relationship of the message to surrounding events or shared past experience may contribute to its meaning. Put entirely into words, this multilevel message might mean that "I pretend to show aggression in jest because our relationship is such that, under the circumstances, you will find it funny and feel warmly toward me."

In its regulatory role in human interaction, communication carries substantial responsibility for defining the nature and limits of the relationships between or among people and, therefore, the roles appropriately played by each person in a given interaction. The communicational approach holds that each transaction between the parties to a communication involves a relationship message proffering or affirming a relationship of a particular sort, and a response that accepts, modifies, or negates the definition communicated. Thus by the act of scolding a child, a parent affirms the right to scold in the relationship with that child. The angry transactions between adolescents and their parents may well have less to do with the apparent content of the quarrel than with the relationship changes being forged and contested.

Considerable learning, often nonverbal, is involved in the capacity to decode communications, particularly those involving apparent contradictions between levels, as with angry words said laughingly. When meaning is not apparent, people learn to shift to a more abstract level and to communicate about communication, thereby clarifying the meaning of ambiguous messages. Children initially lack this capacity; if they are blocked from learning how to learn about meaning, serious adulthood disorders may result.

The double bind involves a communication style that is pernicious in its reliance upon internal contradictions and blocked learning. As studied in the families of schizophrenics, this style appeared often in mother-child relationships in which the mothers seemed not to want to be understood: They could accept neither their children nor their rejection of those children. The double bind describes their covert pursuit of distant relationships disguised by reciprocal shows of loving behavior. Such parents appeared to invite closeness at one level while negating it at another. A child who responded by approaching was covertly rebuffed, yet efforts to withdraw were also punished. Efforts to shift levels and to question the meaning of the interactions were also punished, impairing the child's capacity to form and trust impressions of reality.

While the double bind as an ongoing pattern cannot be fully represented in a single transaction, the following vignette illustrates many of its features. A young woman hospitalized for schizophrenia improved enough to select and purchase clothing for her first hospital leave. When her parents came for her, however, her mother showed immediate distress over her "juvenile taste" in clothing, and agitatedly undressed her and regarbed her in items of the mother's own choosing. "There," the mother said, "now you look all grown up!" The leave went badly, and the woman was soon back in an acutely psychotic condition. Research with issues beyond schizophrenia is summarized by Sluzki and Ransom (1976).

The mother's emphatic behavioral rejection of her daughter's independence was belied by the verbal message that she urgently must look grown up, indicating to hospital staff a probable conflict regarding the relationship: The patient must be adult and therefore independent, yet a child and therefore dependent. In responding to movement toward independence, the injunction never to be independent was more emphatic than that to be always independent. Enjoined to be a woman and a child, independent and dependent, close and far, the patient responded with disturbed, psychotic behavior. A woman made childlike by an illness, she was incapable of independence, yet too disturbed to be at home: She was neither too close nor too far. Her relationship to her mother was preserved.

REFERENCES

Bateson, G., Jackson, D., Haley, J., & Weakland, J. (1956). Towards a theory of schizophrenia, *Behavioral Science, 1,* 251–264.

Sluzki, C. E., & Ranson, D. C. (1976). *Double bind: The foundation of the communicational approach to the family.* New York: Grune & Stratton.

Whitehead, A. N., & Russell, B. (1910). *Principia mathematica.* Cambridge, England: Cambridge University Press.

SUGGESTED READING

Jackson, D. D. (Ed.). (1968) *Communication, family and marriage* (Vols. 1 & 2). Palo Alto, CA: Science & Behavior Books.

R. E. ENFIELD
Columbus, GA

COMMUNICATION PROCESSES
PARENT/CHILD RELATIONS
SCHIZOPHRENIA

DOUBLE-BLIND RESEARCH

Double-blind research keeps both researchers and subjects "blind" to knowledge of the intervention or treatment. The importance of using double-blind procedures stems from the natural desire of researchers to find positive results for their hypotheses. Researchers or their assistants may inadvertently tip the scales in favor of an experimental treatment by cueing subjects, by deciding in favor of the experimental treatment in situations that are sufficiently ambiguous to be judged either way, or, where errors are made, by inadvertently making errors favoring the experimental treatment. Similarly, subjects aware that they are receiving an experimental treatment expect and accentuate positive changes, even though they are natural variations unrelated to the treatment. Especially if they anticipate further help from the researcher, some subjects try to respond as they think the researcher wants them to, regardless of their actual condition.

Under double-blind conditions researchers, assistants, subjects, and others involved in any way with a study are not allowed to know which subjects received the experimental treatment (experimental group) and which did not (control group). If identical-appearing treatments are used, but are such that some neutral party can tell them apart, subjects in both groups might believe they are receiving the treatment. In a drug study the control group would receive an inert pill called a placebo that looks and tastes just like the drug treatment. Drug studies almost routinely use double-blind procedures, since expectations of efficacy can often be as effective as the drugs themselves. Alternatively, the treatment may be given so subjects are not aware of it. In an experiment involving the effect of food coloring on aberrant behavior, if the food can be made to look the same with and without the small amount of coloring normally involved, neither experimental nor control subjects need be aware that a study is going on.

Double-blind procedures cannot be used when: (a) one's knowledge of treatment is part of the treatment itself; (b) it is obvious which treatment is to be favored from merely observing the treatment or being exposed to it; (c) the treatment can be readily identified from side-effects; or (d) withholding a more favorable treatment would have ethical consequences.

Besides its cumbersomeness, the double-blind technique has the drawback of sacrificing therapeutic knowledge for methodological precision; one's clinical sensitivity is reduced because one is dealing with unknowns. Further, treating subjects with unknowns can be demoralizing to both professional and subject. These objections can often be met, as William Guy and others (1967) suggest, through the use of an independent assessment team who are kept blind even though those who administer the treatment are not.

Research has shown that many steps in an experiment and many kinds of studies are vulnerable to knowledge of the desired result. Rosenthal (1969) found two-thirds of observer errors favored the hypothesis. Rosenthal and Rubin (1980) examined studies ranging from animal research in which experimenters were told they were running especially able mice, to teachers who were told certain children could be expected to show remarkable gains based on test results. In actuality, the mice and children had been randomly chosen. Reaction time studies were least influenced by expectancy effects, 2 out of 9 showing statistically significant results; but surprisingly, 11 out of 15 animal studies also did so. Learning, person perception studies, and laboratory interviews were all subject to expectancy effects. Though interpretation of effect sizes is still open to question, Rosenthal and Rubin's estimate (1980) of the *unintended* impact of expectancy effects suggests it is as large as that of many treatments *intended* to have an effect.

Overly favorable interpretation of data by overzealous researchers can generally be ascertained from the research reports. Blind procedures protect the many hidden parts of a study. They probably should be much more widely used than at present.

REFERENCES

Guy, W., Gross, M., & Dennis, H. (1967). An alternative to double blind procedure. *American Journal of Psychiatry, 123,* 1505–1012.

Rosenthal, R. (1969). Interpersonal expectations: Effects of the experimenters' hypothesis. In R. Rosenthal & R. Rosnow (Eds.), *Artifacts in behavioral research.* New York: Academic Press.

Rosenthal, R., & Rubin, D. B. (1980). Summarizing 345 studies of interpersonal expectancy effects. In R. Rosenthal (Ed.), *Quantitative assessment of research domains. New directions for methodology of social and behavioral science* (No. 5). San Francisco: Jossey-Bass.

D. R. KRATHWOHL
Syracuse University

CONTROL GROUPS
RESEARCH METHODOLOGY

DOWN-REGULATION

Down-regulation refers to any regulatory process in which the amount of a particular substance or a specific activity is decreased. Conversely, up-regulation describes a process in which the amount of a particular substance or activity is increased. Relative to the field of pharmacology and neuroscience, however, the term down-regulation generally refers to the loss of receptors. Receptors are proteins that receive and transmit external signals to the interior of the cell. The signal, once received on the inside of the cell, can then direct various cellular functions. This process of transmitting a signal from the outside of the cell to the inside of the cell is called signal transduction.

Four general classes of receptors exist: G protein-coupled receptors, tyrosine kinase receptors, ion channel receptors, and steroid hormone receptors. G protein-coupled receptors pass through the cell membrane seven times. As their name suggests, these receptors, upon activation by a substance called an agonist (the signal), activate heterotrimeric G proteins on the inside of the cell. G proteins are responsible for directing several cellular functions. Many examples for this type of receptor exist (including rhodopsin, the receptor responsible for receiving light signals for vision; olfactory receptors that receive odor signals; and adrenergic receptors that mediate many functions of the central nervous system, including cardiovascular regulation and mental cognition). Tyrosine kinase receptors pass through the cell membrane only once. Upon activation with an agonist, these receptors undergo auto-phosphorylation of specific tyrosine amino acid residues within the cytoplasmic portion of the receptor. This leads to a series of events that can also regulate cellular functions. Examples include growth factor receptors that receive signals from substances such as growth hormone to stimulate growth, and insulin receptors that receive signals from insulin to stimulate cells to take up glucose from the blood. A third general type of receptor is the ion channel receptor. These receptors consist of several subunits that pass through the cell membrane and collectively form a pore, or channel. Activation of these receptors allows for the passage of ions through this channel. The fourth general class of receptor does not reside within the cell membrane but rather within the cell itself; these are the steroid hormone receptors, and receive signals from hormones that are able to pass freely through the cell membrane. Activation of hormone receptors sends signals to the cell nucleus, where regulation of the expression of various genes can occur.

The process of down-regulation has been most extensively characterized for G protein-coupled receptors and will be explained using this receptor family as an example. Receptor down-regulation occurs when over-activation of a receptor population results in the loss of receptor function. This will occur to prevent over-stimulation of the cell and can happen as two distinct processes, desensitization or down-regulation. Receptor desensitization is a rapid process occurring within minutes of activating a population of receptors. When desensitized, a G protein-coupled receptor is temporarily unable to receive and transmit an external signal to the inside of the cell, and binding of agonist to the receptor no longer results in the activation of G proteins. Desensitization does not result in the actual loss of receptors, and removal of the agonist will allow the receptor population to become active again. Down-regulation, on the other hand, takes much longer to occur, taking place only after hours or days of exposure to agonist. When a population of receptors are down-regulated, an actual destruction of receptors takes place. Removal of agonist will allow the population of receptors to return to normal levels; however, this will take time as new receptors must be synthesized in most cases (Hein & Kobilka, 1995; Toews, Shreve, & Bylund, 1991).

When dealing with human physiology, we are often concerned with the process of receptor down-regulation. Down-regulation can be caused by or associated with many different events, and can be of special concern in the use of therapeutic agents. In the treatment of asthma, over-usage of beta-2 adrenergic receptor agonists can cause down-regulation of these receptors, an undesirable effect (Johnson, 1998). Likewise, treatment of Parkinson's disease with dopamine receptor agonists can down-regulate dopamine receptors (Ahlskog et al., 1991). Treatment of these conditions then becomes difficult, as more of the drug may be needed to maintain the desired level of therapy. Unfortunately, increasing the drug dosage often increases the number and severity of side effects. Down-regulation is not detrimental to all therapies, however. For example, receptor down-regulation is the desired effect of various antidepressants (Feighner, 1999).

Pharmacologists today are studying the mechanisms of receptor down-regulation. Down-regulation of G protein-coupled receptors is not a fully understood process but may involve the structural conformation of the receptor, phosphorylation of specific residues on the cytoplasmic side of the receptor, and binding of other proteins to the cytoplasmic side of the receptor (Hein & Kobilka, 1995; Heck & Bylund, 1998). An understanding of these processes may one day allow for the development of drugs that are better able to produce the desired level of therapy in the treatment of many conditions.

REFERENCES

Ahlskog, J. E., Richelson, E., Nelson, A., Kelly, P. J., Okazaki, H., Tyce, G. M., van Heerden, J. A., Stoddard, S. L., & Carmichael, S. W. (1991). Reduced D2 dopamine and muscarinic cholinergic receptor densities in caudate specimens from fluctuating parkinsonian patients. *Annals of Neurology, 30*(2), 185–191.

Feighner, J. P. (1999). Mechanisms of action of antidepressant medications. *Journal of Clinical Psychiatry, 60* (Suppl. 4), 4–11.

Heck, D. A., & Bylund, D. B. (1998). Role of the third intracellular loop of the alpha-2B adrenergic receptor in regulating receptor density. *Pharmacology Reviews and Communications, 10*(2), 101–110.

Hein, L., & Kobilka, B. K. (1995). Adrenergic receptor signal transduction and regulation. *Neuropharmacology, 34*, 357–366.

Johnson, M. (1998). The beta-adrenoceptor. *American Journal of Respiratory Critical Care and Medicine, 158* (5, part 3), 5146–5153.

Toews, M. L., Shreve, P. E., & Bylund, D. B. (1991). Regulation of adrenergic receptors. In J. R. Martinez, B. S. Edwards, & J. C. Seagrave (Eds.), *Signaling mechanisms in secretory and immune cells* (pp. 1–17). San Francisco: San Francisco Press.

D. A. HECK
Iowa State University

DOWN SYNDROME (MONGOLISM)

Down syndrome is the result of an extra chromosome, number 21. Thus another name for the disorder is trisomy 21. The most common basis for the extra chromosome is called nondisjunction: In the formation of gametes from the parent cell of 46 chromosomes, instead of the two daughter cells each receiving 23 chromosomes, one cell receives 24 chromosomes and the other 22. The egg cell with 24 chromosomes is capable of being fertilized, producing a cell with 47 rather than 46 chromosomes and eventually a child with Down syndrome. The occurrence of nondisjunction increases steadily with the age of the mother. For mothers under 30 one child in 1,500 has Down; for mothers over 45, one in 65.

The main symptom of this chromosomal abnormality is low intelligence. Most people with Down syndrome are in the severely retarded range, with an IQ around 30. A few are only mildly retarded or even borderline, and one such person has even written a book, *The World of Nigel Hunt.*

There are numerous structural characteristics common to Down syndrome, many of which identify the disorder early in life: limpness in infancy; Asian-appearing eyes, from which the name "mongolism" was derived; a small skull flattened in the back; a large, fissured, protruding tongue; short, heavy stature; short, stubby fingers; and the Simian line on the palms of the hands. In addition, many children born with Down syndrome have heart deformities and lowered resistance to respiratory infection (pneumonia), which meant, until the advent of antibiotics, that few Down syndrome children survived to adulthood.

In Down syndrome, development is generally slowed down, and mental age may not level off until an individual is 35 or 40 years of age (Fisher & Zeaman, 1970). Although motor, speech, and sexual development are all slow, people with Down syndrome are often well developed socially, at least in comparison with other categories of mental retardation. They tend to be cheerful, cooperative, friendly, affectionate, and relaxed—just as originally described by Langdon Down in 1866.

Although there is no treatment for Down syndrome, the new technique of amniocentesis permits examination of the fetus's chromosomes. If Down syndrome is detected, the parents can elect to have the fetus aborted.

REFERENCES

Fisher, M. A., & Zeaman, D. (1970). Growth and decline of retardate intelligence. In N. R. Ellis (Ed.), *International review of research in mental retardation* (Vol. 4). New York: Academic Press.

M. R. DENNY
Michigan State University

CHROMOSOME DISORDERS
MENTAL RETARDATION

DREAMS

The study of dreams has moved from a focus on meaning to the underlying neuroscience mechanisms that are involved in their generation. Current research suggests that cortical areas involved in dreaming reflect those areas associated with emotional and sensory processing and lack involvement of higher level logical thinking.

HISTORICAL INTRODUCTION

Since the beginning of recorded history, dreams have played a role in humans' attempts to make meaning of our world and ourselves. Dreams have represented the other, the aspects of ourselves and our world that stood outside of human knowledge or could not be understood within the current paradigm. As illustrated in a variety of religious texts over the last few thousand years, dreams have foretold future events as well as allowed for communication with the gods. Still, during this period, some including the Roman poet Lucretius in 44 BC suggested that dreams are not special but common in all animals. Darwin echoed a similar theme in *The Descent of Man* (1871), in which he suggests that all higher animals including birds have dreams.

Within the last 100 years, the understanding of dreams has been brought into a more theoretical perspective within dynamic and analytic psychology, and more recently within the context of the neurosciences. Although a topic of heated debate, an initial contribution was Freud's perspective that dreams could be understood within the context of instinctual functioning, and the neurology he outlined in the *Project for a Scientific Psychology.* As articulated in this work, dreams offered an understanding of previously established networks of neurons and pointed to the manner in which ideas and events had come to be associated with one another in the brain. In this way, dreams were reflective of an individual's psychology during the waking state. Jung had a more evolutionary perspective, in which he viewed specific processes in our environment as triggers for bringing forth action patterns, or archetypes, in much the same manner as described by the ethologists. Dreams in this context reflect these evoked archetype patterns.

BEGINNINGS OF EMPIRICAL RESEARCH

Many view the scientific study of dreams as beginning in 1953 with the discovery by Aserinsky and Kleitman of an association between dreaming and rapid eye movement (REM) sleep. Sleep generally is characterized by four different stages, as reflected in the electroencephalograph (EEG). In contrast to the higher voltage, more patterned EEG activity found in non-REM sleep, REM sleep appears to have an EEG pattern more like that of the waking state. REM sleep is also referred to as paradoxical sleep and is characterized by low voltage, random appearing EEG activity. Waking an individual during REM sleep is more likely than any other sleep stage to result in a dream report. Following the discovery of the association between REM sleep and dreams, a number of researchers examined the dream state. This work included a variety of foci including the nature of the dream itself, factors involved in dream recall, and the influence of external factors on dreaming. This work used a variety of theoretical perspectives including a more cognitive approach. The main characteristics of dream process include emotionally-laden sensory processes and images without a sense of individual control. Less well understood is the so-called "lucid dream" in which individuals, while dreaming, realize that they are part of a dream and may even experience control of the dream. Lucid dreams are rare and occur in only 1% or 2% of all reported dreams. For an historical overview of psychological dream research, see Foulkes, 1996.

NEUROSCIENCE STUDIES

Recently, dream processes have been examined within the context of current neuroscience work, with the goal of determining brain areas involved in dreaming and the manner in which dreaming and other cognitive processes (e.g., visual imagery) are related. Early speculation suggested that dreams were related to brain stem functioning, and especially to the pons, with its generators for rapid eye movement sleep. However, neuropsychological case studies have shown that damage to the pons does not stop dream reports, whereas damage to the forebrain areas does. Current brain imaging studies suggest that a variety of areas are active during brain states associated with dreaming. These cortical areas include the brain stem, which is responsible for basic arousal; the limbic system, which is highly involved in emotionality; and the forebrain areas involved in sensory processing. Areas involved in higher level cognitive processes, such as planning and logical thinking, show decreased activation during these dream periods. Further explorations suggest that pathways between areas involved in emotional processing and those involved in visual processing are active, whereas those between visual processing and higher level logical thinking are not. This may help to explain the nature of dreams in which emotional and nonlogical sequencing of imagery are accepted without reflective awareness. Implications that can be drawn from the brain imaging work are that a variety of processes are involved in the creation of dreams and that such work helps to characterize the nature of the subjective experience of dreaming. For an overview of dreams from a neuroscience perspective see Braun et al., 1998; Hobson et al., 1998; Jouvet, 1999; and Solms, 1997.

REFERENCES

Braun, A., Balkin, T., Wesensten, N., Gwadry, F., Carson, R., Varga, M., Baldwin, P., Belenky, G., & Herscovitch, P. (1998). Dissociated pattern of activity in visual cortices and their projections during human rapid eye movement sleep. *Science, 279,* 91–95.

Darwin, C. (1871). *The descent of man.* London: J. Murray.

Foulkes, D. (1996). Dream research: 1953–1993. *Sleep, 19,* 609–624.

Hobson, A., Pace-Schott, E., Stickgold, R., & Kahn, D. (1998). To dream or not to dream? Relevant data from new neuroimaging and electrophysiological studies. *Current Opinion in Neurobiology, 8,* 239–244.

Jouvet, M. (1999). *The paradox of sleep: The story of dreaming.* Cambridge, MA: MIT Press.

Solms, M. (1997). *The neuropsychology of dreams.* Mahwah, Erlbaum.

W. J. RAY
Pennsylvania State University

IMAGERY
SLEEP

DRUG REHABILITATION

In the late 1960s narcotic addiction in the United States reached epidemic proportions with an estimated half million active heroin addicts. The federal strategy at that time was to combat the epidemic spread of heroin addiction and to control crime associated with narcotic addiction by prevention and treatment of addicts, while at the same time attempting to control the drug traffic and expand federal law enforcement.

Earlier treatment efforts had included psychiatric hospitals, heroin maintenance provided by physicians or clinics, and civil commitment. These were imperfectly evaluated, but the decision to fund community treatment programs was made under crisis conditions and did not consider evaluative data on earlier approaches. Beginning around 1969, the major modalities of treatment in federally supported, community-based treatment programs were: methadone maintenance (MM) as an outpatient; therapeutic community (TC) with drug free as a resident; drug free (DF) as an outpatient; and detoxification (DT). National evaluation studies of treatment effectiveness (see Gerstein & Harwood, 1990; Hubbard et al., 1982; Tims & Ludford, 1984) have shown that the major

modalities of MM, TC, and DF are effective interventions if delivered as planned, and that first-year posttreatment outcomes improved in direct relation to amount of time spent in treatment. Relapse to drug addiction and readmissions to treatment were common, but follow-up at 12 years after treatment showed that only one-fourth were still addicted (Simpson & Sells, 1990).

Among clients in outpatient treatments for opiate addiction, the most spectacular results were obtained in the MM programs, in which addicts who were stabilized on methadone used virtually no other opiates and engaged in very little criminal behavior. Compared with incarceration, this reflects a preferable and highly cost-effective approach. Whether such results should be attributed directly to specific treatment processes is doubtful. It appears reasonable to conclude, however, that they do represent the interactions of clients motivated to engage in the treatment process and the staffs, environments, and regimens of the respective programs. Clients with negative attitudes toward treatment, such as the hard-core criminal addicts, have for the most part not responded favorably to treatment.

Drug use patterns frequently change over time, however, and additional treatment approaches became popular during the 1980s in an effort to deal with multiple drug use, especially cocaine. Residential chemical dependency (CD) programs—usually lasting 28 days—became widely available, incorporating the 12-step philosophy of the growing Alcoholics Anonymous and Narcotics Anonymous movements during this time. Because CD treatments typically operate as privately supported programs and 12-step community meetings carefully guard confidentiality of its members, wide-scale empirical evaluations of their efficacy have not been carried out.

REFERENCES

Gerstein, D. R., & Harwood, H. J. (Eds.). (1990). *Treating drug problems: Vol 1. A study of the evolution, effectiveness and financing of public and private drug treatment systems* (Committee for the Substance Abuse Coverage Study Division of Health Care Services, Institute of Medicine). Washington, DC: National Academy Press.

Hubbard, R. L., Marsden, M. E., Rachal, J. V., Harwood, H. J., Cavanaugh, E. R., & Ginzburg, H. M. (1989). *Drug abuse treatment. A national study of effectiveness.* Chapel Hill: The University of North Carolina Press.

Simpson, D. D., & Sells, S. B. (Eds.). (1990). *Opioid addiction and treatment: A 12-year follow-up.* Malabar, FL: Krieger.

Tims, F. M., & Ludford, J. P. (Eds.). (1984). *Drug abuse treatment evaluation: Strategies, progress, and prospects.* (DHHS Publication No. 84-1329). Washington, DC: U.S. Government Printing Office.

S. B. SELLS
Texas Christian University

ALCOHOLISM TREATMENT

DYNAMIC ASSESSMENT

Dynamic assessment refers to an approach to conducting assessments that most characteristically involves interacting with the client during the course of the assessment, and using the responsiveness of the client to this interaction as a central source of information about capacity for learning. Dynamic assessment has been developed primarily for use by psychologists or psychoeducational specialists; however, the model has been of considerable interest to speech/language pathologists and reading diagnosticians as well.

Although there are a number of models and developing procedures that vary on dimensions of content and degree of standardization, dynamic assessments often follow a pretest-intervene-retest format. The assessor first determines what the client is able to do without assistance, then proceeds to offer assistance, and finally evaluates the degree and nature of the client's responsiveness to this assistance.

The roots of dynamic assessment extend back into the early 20th century, when many writers expressed their dissatisfaction with the available approaches to the measurement of intelligence (Lidz, 1987b). More specifically, the fatherhood of dynamic assessment is generally assigned to both Vygotsky (1978) and Feuerstein (Feuerstein, Rand, & Hoffman, 1979). Vygotsky's notions of the *zone of actual development* and the *zone of proximal development* are definitive of these dynamic procedures. Feuerstein's descriptions of mediated learning experiences have influenced the development of the interventions offered during the assistance phases of the procedures. It was also Feuerstein who operationalized the notion of dynamic assessment in his Learning Potential Assessment Device, for which there have been a large number of training opportunities. Feuerstein's presentations and publications have served as catalysts for the spurt of activity in the development of dynamic assessment theory and applications. Research and development regarding these procedures had been essentially parallel in the United States, Europe, and Israel. However, more recently, with European publications increasingly available in English, these developments have cross-seminated and current publications tend to present articles and chapters from multiple and diverse sources.

There are essentially four primary models of dynamic assessment. The first, which is characteristic of the Feuerstein et al. approach, is the most loosely structured and diagnostically oriented. The intervention provided to the examinee is tailored to the responses and responsiveness of the examinee, with little preprescription. The second, which characterizes the approach designed by Budoff (1987), offers a standardized intervention to all examinees based on predetermined strategies relevant to the task. The third, exemplified by the Campione and Brown (1987) approach, operationalizes the zone of proximal development as a series of graduated prompts, predetermined on the basis of increasing explicitness in the teaching of the task. The fourth, described by Lidz (1991), is curriculum-based dynamic assessment that utilizes referral-relevant curriculum content, and bases the intervention and interpretation on the degree of match between the process analysis of the demands of the task on the learner and the intactness of the processes the learner applies to the task. Most available specific procedures can be characterized in terms of one of these four models.

While some dynamic assessment procedures remain informal and constructed for application to individual learners (there are group procedures as well), there are an increasing number of packaged procedures. For example, Tzuriel (no date) has designed a number of tests that are relevant for use with children in the early primary grades. Also, Swanson (1995) is the author of the Swanson Conceptual Processing Test, a dynamic assessment of working memory. Guthke (1992) is the author of a number of Learning Tests used throughout Germany. Hamers, Hessels, and Van Luit (1991) have published their Learning Test for Ethnic Minorities in The Netherlands, and Lidz and Jepsen (1999) have developed the Application of Cognitive Functions Scale for use with children functioning from the ages of three through five.

While varying with the model, the information provided by dynamic assessment procedures can include in-depth description of the strengths and weaknesses of the learner's cognitive processing, responsiveness of the learner to intervention, intensity of effort required to facilitate change, and linkage of assessment with intervention.

Several books provide a broad sample of available models and procedures of dynamic assessment from American, Israeli, and European sources, as well as offering discussions regarding their applications. These include Carlson (1995), Gupta and Coxhead (1986), Hamers, Sijtsma, and Ruijssenaars (1993), Haywood and Tzuriel (1992), Lidz (1987a; 1991), and Lidz and Elliott (in press). Reviews of research studies involving this approach are available in Lidz (1991, 1997).

REFERENCES

Budoff, M. (1987). Measures for assessing learning potential. In C. S. Lidz (Ed.), *Dynamic assessment: An interactional approach to evaluating learning potential* (pp. 173–195). New York: Guilford.

Campione, J. C., & Brown, A. L. (1987). Linking dynamic assessment with school achievement. In C. S. Lidz (Ed.), *Dynamic assessment: An interactional approach to evaluating learning potential* (pp. 82–11). New York: Guilford.

Carlson, J. S. (Ed.). (1995). *European contributions to dynamic assessment.* London: JAI Press Ltd.

Feuerstein, R., Rand, Y., & Hoffman, M. (1979). *Dynamic assessment of retarded performers.* Baltimore: University Park Press.

Gupta, R. M., & Coxhead, P. (Eds.). (1986). *Cultural diversity and learning efficiency: Recent developments in assessment.* New York: St. Martin's.

Guthke, J. (1992). Learning tests: The concept, main research findings, problems and trends. *Learning and Individual Differences, 4,* 137–151.

Hamers, J. H. M., Hessels, M. G. P., & Van Luit, J. E. H. (1991). *Leerntest voor etnische minderheden: Test en handleiding* [Learning potential test for ethnic minorities: Test and manual]. Lisse: Swets & Zeitliner.

Hamers, J. H. M., Sijtsma, K., & Ruijssenaars, A. J. J. M. (Eds.). (1993). *Learning potential assessment: Theoretical, methodological, and practical issues.* Amsterdam: Swets & Zeitlinger.

Haywood, H. C., & Tzuriel, D. (Eds.). (1992). *Interactional assessment.* New York: Springer-Verlag.

Lidz, C. S. (Ed.). (1987a). *Dynamic assessment: An interactional approach to evaluating learning potential.* New York: Guilford.

Lidz, C. S. (1987b). Historical perspectives. In C. S. Lidz (Ed.), *Dynamic assessment: An interactional approach to evaluating learning potential* (pp. 3–32). New York: Guilford.

Lidz, C. S. (1991). *Practitioner's guide to dynamic assessment.* New York: Guilford.

Lidz, C. S. (1997). Dynamic assessment approaches. In D. P. Flanagan, J. L. Genshaft, & P. L. Harrison (Eds.), *Contemporary approaches to assessment of intelligence.* New York: Guilford.

Lidz, C. S., & Elliott, J. (Eds.). press (in /) *Dynamic assessment: Prevailing models and applications.* Greenwich, CT: JAI.

Lidz, C. S., & Jepsen, R. H. (1999). *The Application of Cognitive Functions Scale (ACFS).* Unpublished manual, available from C. S. Lidz, Touro College, New York.

Swanson, H. L. (1995). Swanson-Cognitive Processing Test. Austin, TX: Pro-Ed.

Tzuriel, D. (no date). *The Cognitive Modifiability Battery: Assessment and intervention.* Instruction manual. Ramat Gan, Israel: School of Education, Bar Ilan University.

Vygotsky, L. S. (1978). *Mind in society: The development of higher psychological processes* (M. Cole, V. John-Steiner, S. Scribner, & E. Souberman, Eds.). Cambridge, MA: Harvard University Press.

SUGGESTED READING

Campione, J. C. (1989). Assisted assessments: A taxonomy of approaches and an outline of strengths and weaknesses. *Journal of Learning Disabilities, 22,* 151–165.

Grigorenko, E. L., & Sternberg, R. (1998). Dynamic testing. *Psychological Bulletin, 124,* 75–111.

Haywood, H. C., Brown, A. L., & Wingenfeld, S. (1990). Dynamic approaches to psychoeducational assessment. *School Psychology Review, 19,* 411–422.

Missiuna, C., & Samuels, M. (1988). Dynamic assessment: Review and critique. *Special Services in the Schools, 5,* 1–22.

Peña, E. (1996). Dynamic assessment: The model and language applications. In K. Cole, P. Dale, & D. Thal (Eds.), *Assessment of communication and language* (pp. 281–307). Baltimore: Brookes.

C. S. LIDZ
Touro College

CLINICAL ASSESSMENT
MEASUREMENT

DYSPLASIA

The clinical term "dysplasia" has been used to describe a variety of brain development anomalies frequently associated with mild to severe mental retardation. Dysplasias are best defined as microscopic abnormalities in brain cytoarchitecture. These abnormalities can be focal (e.g., ectopias and heterotopias, which appear as islands within an otherwise normal brain) or general (e.g., lissencephaly, micro- or macrogyria, which affect large portions of the brain, if not the entire brain).

With few exceptions, dysplasias have been associated with anomalies in cerebral or cerebellar cortex. This association may reflect, in part, that dysplasias are more easily detected in these two brain structures rather than a paucity of dysplasias in other brain regions. The cerebral cortex and cerebellum share a well-delineated stratified cytoarchitecture that results from a complex developmental history. Classically, neural development is divided into three major stages: neurogenesis (cell proliferation), neuronal migration, and neuronal maturation (including differentiation and synapse formation). In the development of both cerebral and cerebellar cortex, young neurons must migrate through layers of previously generated neurons before they begin differentiating and forming synaptic connections. A number of developmental cues occur between different neuronal populations during this migration phase. After migration, neurons differentiate into cells with distinct shapes and synaptic connections. In both cerebral and cerebellar cortex, the stages of neuronal development are precisely timed and are delicately sensitive to disruption. The dysplasias discussed here result primarily from perturbations in normal neuronal migration and maturation that lead to malformations in the architecture of cerebral and cerebellar cortex (see Figure 1). It is also possible, however, that particular neuronal groups migrate or mature at abnormal times because they were generated aberrantly.

In dysplasias that result from abnormal neuronal migration, small groups of neurons or entire populations may fail to migrate past previously generated neurons. Alternatively, the neurons may move past their normal locations into regions of white matter—for example, into the cortical molecular layer. In the cerebellum, the failure of granule cells to migrate through Purkinje neurons will lead to malformations in cerebellar cytoarchitecture and to abnormal Purkinje cell development. Such dysplasias can affect both motor coordination and some aspects of learning and memory. In cerebral cortex, focal migrational defects appear to disrupt local synaptic circuitry, in particular inhibitory circuitry, and are regarded as a predominant cause of early onset epilepsy. Multiple focal ectopias in cerebral cortex that result from altered neuronal migration are associated with developmental dyslexia. In humans, migrational abnormalities are often compounded by alterations in neuronal generation and/or neuronal maturation, making it impossible to correlate specific behavioral abnormalities with a particular stage of development. In animal studies, however, migrational abnormalities disrupt synaptic connectivity and produce cognitive abnormalities that correlate roughly with the magnitude of the cytoarchitectural abnormalities. Thus, cortical abnormalities that affect larger portions of cortex, or are more general in nature (such as micro- and macrogyria) ordinarily have more profound behavioral consequences than do small focal anomalies.

Alterations in neuronal migration

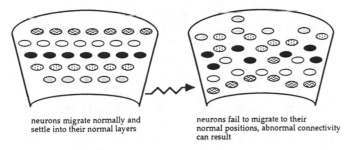

neurons migrate normally and settle into their normal layers

neurons fail to migrate to their normal positions, abnormal connectivity can result

Alterations in neuronal maturation

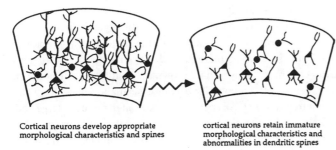

Cortical neurons develop appropriate morphological characteristics and spines

cortical neurons retain immature morphological characteristics and abnormalities in dendritic spines

Figure 1.

Abnormal neuronal maturation, despite normal migration, is frequently the source of dysplasias that can lead to profound developmental disabilities, including mental retardation. Examples include genetic disorders such as Down syndrome and Rett syndrome, as well as many unclassified amentias. In these dysplasias, entire brain regions fail to elaborate normally-shaped dendritic trees and spines, and display altered synaptic densities. Since the early 1970s, alterations in cortical dendritic length and number of spines have been reported in postmortem tissue from individuals with Down syndrome, a developmental disorder that almost invariably is associated with cognitive deficits. In recent years, with the advent of in vivo imaging techniques, dysplasias can be studied in living individuals and correlated more directly with behavioral changes. Increases in the width of cerebral cortex in autism and fragile-X syndrome, as well as decreases in width of cortex in Down syndrome, have been observed. These findings strengthen the hypothesis that abnormal cortical morphology underlies some of the abnormal cognitive behaviors seen in these developmental disabilities. These changes in cortical widths likely reflect alterations in neuropil (dendrites and synapses) and/or glial cell populations, and presumably lead to alterations in synaptic connections within cortex and between cortical and subcortical regions.

The causes for morphogenetic changes leading to dysplasias are only partially understood. Migrational abnormalities may be the consequence of altered cell-cell interactions, but can also result secondarily from radiation exposure. Altered cell-cell interactions can be caused either by mutations in the genes coding for cell surface proteins or by environmental factors that change the expression of cell surface proteins. Neuronal differentiation is controlled by a plethora of factors including cell surface interactions, neurotrophins, cytokines, neurotransmitters/neuromodulators, and

last but not least, synaptic activity. Disruptions of any one or any combination of these factors may induce altered neuronal maturation. The human and rodent literature suggests that alterations in neuromodulators, including serotonin, dopamine, norepinephrine, and acetylcholine, may feature prominently in the generation of cortical dysplasias. Modifications in one or several of these neuromodulators have been documented in developmental and psychiatric disorders that feature dysplasias, including schizophrenia, Tourette syndrome, and Attention-Deficit/Hyperactivity Disorder.

In addition to genetic mutations, causes of aberrant neuronal migration and maturation may be environmental factors such as heavy metals (e.g., lead), ethanol and other psychoactive drugs of abuse, or by gestational and perinatal insults such hypoxia and ischemia.

SUGGESTED READING

Bayer, S. A., Altman, J., Russon, R. J., & Zhang, X. (1993). Timetables of neurogenesis in the human brain based on experimentally determined patterns in rat. *Neurotoxicology, 14,* 83–144.

Berger-Sweeney, J., & Hohmann, C. F. (1997). Behavioral consequences of abnormal cortical development: Insights into developmental disabilities. *Behavioural Brain Research, 86,* 121–142.

Capone, G. T. (1996). Human brain development. In A. J. Capute & P. J. Accardo (Eds.), *Developmental disabilities in infancy and childhood: Vol. 1. Neurodevelopmental diagnosis and treatment* (2nd ed.). pp. 25–75. Baltimore: Paul Brooks.

Jacobson, M. (1978). *Developmental neurobiology.* New York: Plenum.

McKay, R. (1997). Stem cells in the central nervous system. *Science, 276,* 66–71.

J. BERGER-SWEENEY
Wellesley College

C. HOHMANN
Morgan State University

DOWN SYNDROME
MENTAL RETARDATION
RETT SYNDROME

DYSTHYMIA

Dysthymia (or Dysthymic Disorder) is a form of mood disorder characterized by mild, chronic depression. It was introduced into the psychiatric classification system in 1980, in the third edition of the *Diagnostic and Statistical Manual of Mental Disorders* (*DSM-III;* American Psychiatric Association, 1980). Although it is a relatively new construct, it includes a number of features of older diagnostic constructs such as Neurotic Depression and Depressive Personality (Akiskal, 1983).

The current criteria for diagnosing Dysthymia require chronic depressed mood (i.e., depressed most of the day, for more days than not, for at least two years). In addition, the individual must experience at least two of the following six depressive symptoms: low self-esteem, feelings of hopelessness, low energy or fatigue, difficulty concentrating or making decisions, sleep disturbance (insomnia or sleeping too much), and appetite disturbance (poor appetite or overeating). The symptoms must be persistent (i.e., never without depressive symptoms for more than two months at a time during this period), have a gradual (or insidious) onset, and cause significant distress or impairment in social or occupational functioning. Finally, the diagnosis cannot not be made if the individual has a psychotic or Bipolar (Manic-Depressive) Disorder, or if the symptoms are due to drugs, medication, or a general medical condition.

Dysthymia is closely related to the category of Major Depression (or Major Depressive Disorder). Both categories refer to disorders characterized by periods of depressed mood and similar sets of associated depressive symptoms. In addition, neither diagnosis is applied to individuals who have had manic or hypomanic episodes (i.e., persons with Bipolar, or Manic-Depressive, Disorder). However, Dysthymia and Major Depression differ in that episodes of major depression tend to be more severe, have a more rapid (or acute) onset, and are not generally chronic.

Dysthymia is a relatively common condition, with approximately 3% of adults in the community meeting diagnostic criteria during the past 12 months, and 6% meeting the criteria at some point in their lives (Kessler et al., 1997). Like many forms of depression, Dysthymia is approximately twice as common in women than in men. It is evident in all age groups (Kovacs, Akiskal, Gatsonis, & Parrone, 1994). There is some evidence indicating that persons with an onset of Dysthymia in childhood or adolescence are more likely to have other co-occurring psychiatric disorders and a greater family history of mood disorders than individuals with an adult onset. However, the early- and late-onset subtypes of Dysthymia do not differ in response to antidepressant medication (Klein et al., in press).

Persons with Dysthymia frequently meet criteria for other co-occurring (or comorbid) psychiatric disorders. Approximately 75% of persons with Dysthymia experience episodes of Major Depression that are superimposed on the chronic Dysthymic Disorder. This pattern has been referred to as "double depression" (Keller et al., 1983). While this term implies that such individuals suffer from two different kinds of depressive disorders, it is likely that it is a single disorder that waxes and wanes, often in response to stress. Persons with Dysthymia also frequently experience comorbid anxiety disorders, substance abuse disorders, and personality disorders (particularly Borderline Personality Disorder and Avoidant Personality Disorder).

As Dysthymia is, by definition, a chronic condition, it is not surprising that recovery rates are low. In naturalistic follow-up studies (in which there is no attempt to control treatment), approximately 40% of outpatients with Dysthymia recover during the course of the next 24 to 30 months (Keller et al., 1983; Klein et al., 1998). These studies define recovery as no or almost no symptoms for at least two consecutive months. Recovery rates are lower if more stringent criteria are employed. In addition, preliminary data indicate that approximately 40% of patients who recover experience a relapse into another episode of Dysthymia within the next few years.

Persons with Dysthymia appear to be at substantial risk for developing Major Depression (Horwath, Johnson, Klerman, & Weissman, 1992; Kovacs et al., 1994). Some studies have suggested that they may also be at risk for developing Bipolar (Manic-Depressive) Disorder, although the evidence for this is inconsistent.

Dysthymia runs in families, along with Major Depression. Persons with Dysthymia have increased rates of both Dysthymia and Major Depression in their first-degree relatives (Klein et al., 1995). Similarly, some studies have reported an elevated rate of Dysthymia in the relatives of individuals with Major Depression. There also appears to be higher rates of some personality disorders in the families of persons with Dysthymia.

Few studies have been conducted to distinguish the role of genetic from environmental factors in the familial transmission of Dysthymia. However, there is evidence that persons with Dysthymia are more likely to have grown up in adverse early home environments, with increased rates of physical and sexual abuse and poor parenting (Lizardi et al., 1995). Although there is a large body of literature on the biological, psychological, and social variables that may be involved in the etiology and development of Major Depression, much less is known about the role that these variables play in Dysthymia, and more studies are needed in these areas.

A number of studies indicate that Dysthymia is responsive to most types of antidepressant medication (including the cyclic antidepressants, monoamine oxidase inhibitors, and selective serotonin re-uptake inhibitors) (Harrison & Stewart, 1995). In addition, several studies have indicated that maintenance treatment (i.e., continuing on medication after recovery) for Dysthymia and Double Depression can reduce the risk of recurrence (Keller et al., 1998; Kocsis et al., 1996).

Various forms of psychotherapy are also frequently used to treat Dysthymia. While well-controlled trials of the efficacy of psychotherapy are lacking, preliminary evidence suggests that several forms of therapy (e.g., cognitive therapy, interpersonal therapy) may also be effective in treating Dysthymia and Double Depression (Markowitz, 1995). Additional studies are needed to compare the effectiveness of psychotherapy and medication, and to determine whether the combination of medication and psychotherapy confers any benefit over either treatment alone.

REFERENCES

Akiskal, H. S. (1983). Dysthymic disorder. *American Journal of Psychiatry, 140,* 11–20.

American Psychiatric Association (1980). *Diagnostic and statistical manual of mental disorders* (3rd ed.). Washington, DC: Author.

Harrison, W. M., & Stewart, J. W. (1995). Pharmacotherapy of Dysthymic Disorder. In J. H. Kocsis & D. N. Klein (Eds.), *Diagnosis and treatment of chronic depression* (pp. 124–145). New York: Guilford.

Horwath, E., Johnson, J., Klerman, G. L., & Weissman, M. M. (1992). Depressive symptoms as relative and attributable risk factors for first-onset major depression. *Archives of General Psychiatry, 49,* 817–823.

Keller, M. B., Lavori, P. W., Endicott, J., Coryell, W., & Klerman, G. L. (1983). "Double depression": Two-year follow-up. *American Journal of Psychiatry, 140,* 689–694.

Keller, M. B., Kocsis, J. H., Thase, M. E., Gelenberg, A. J., Rush, A. J., Koran, L., Schatzberg, A., Rusell, J., Hirschfeld, R., Klein, D., McCullough, J. P., Fawcett, J. A., Kornstein, S., LaVange, L., & Harrison, W. (1998). Maintenance phase efficacy of sertraline for chronic depression. *Journal of the American Medical Association, 280,* 1665–1672.

Kessler, R. C., McGonagle, K. A., Zhao, S., Nelson, C. B., Hughes, M., Eshleman, S., Wittchen, H-U., & Kendler, K. S. (1994). Lifetime and 12-month prevalence of *DSM-III-R* psychiatric disorders in the United States. *Archives of General Psychiatry, 51,* 8–19.

Klein, D. N., Riso, L. P., Donaldson, S. K., Schwartz, J. E., Anderson, R. L., Ouimette, P. C., Lizardi, H., & Aronson, T. A. (1995). Family study of early-onset dysthymia. *Archives of General Psychiatry, 52,* 487–496.

Klein, D. N., Norden, K. A., Ferro, T., Leader, J. B., Kasch, K. L., Klein, L. M., Schwartz, J. E., & Aronson, T. A. (1998). Thirty-month naturalistic follow-up study of early-onset dysthymic disorder. *Journal of Abnormal Psychology, 107,* 338–348.

Klein, D. N., Schatzberg, A. F., McCullough, J. P., Keller, M. B., Dowling, F., Goodman, D., Howland, R. H., Markowitz, J. C., Smith, C., Miceli, R., & Harrison, W. M. (in press). Early- versus late-onset dysthymic disorder. *Journal of Affective Disorder.*

Kocsis, J. H., Friedman, R. A., Markowitz, J. C., Leon, A. C., Miller, N. L., Gniwesch, L., & Parides, M. (1996). Maintenance therapy for chronic depression. *Archives of General Psychiatry, 53,* 769–774.

Kovacs, M., Akiskal, H. S., Gatsonis, C., & Parrone, P. L. (1994). Childhood-onset dysthymic disorder: Clinical features and prospective naturalistic outcome. *Archives of General Psychiatry, 51,* 365–374.

Lizardi, H., Klein, D. N., Ouimette, P. C., Riso, L. P., Anderson, R. L., & Donaldson, S. K. (1995). Reports of the childhood home environment in early-onset dysthymia and episodic major depression. *Journal of Abnormal Psychology, 104,* 132–139.

Markowitz, J. C. (1995). Psychotherapy of dysthymic disorder. In J. H. Kocsis & D. N. Klein (Eds.), *Diagnosis and treatment of chronic depression* (pp. 146–168). New York: Guilford.

D. N. KLEIN
State University of New York at Stony Brook

ANTIDEPRESSANT MEDICATIONS
DEPRESSION
MAJOR DEPRESSIVE DISORDER: RECOVERY & RECURRENCE
PSYCHOTHERAPY